Location of a Lake

There are several ways of finding out where a lake is located:

A map of the river basin is shown at the beginning of each group of lake chapters. A bar above the lake name tells you what major river basin the lake is in.

The first paragraph in each chapter gives road directions on how to get to the lake from a major population centre.

BEAVER RIVER BASIN

MURIEL LAKE

Muriel Lake is a large lake with lovely beaches and fairly clear water. It is located in the Municipal District of Bonnyville about 13 km south of the town of Bonnyville and 250 km northeast of the city of Edmonton. To reach the lake from Edmonton, take Highways 28 and 28A north and east to Bonnyville. At the junction of Highways 28 and 41 within the town (55 Street), turn south onto a road known locally as the Gurneyville Road. This road joins Secondary Road 657 just south of the locality of Gurneyville, on the western side of the lake (Fig. 1), and provides access to Muriel Lake Provincial Recreation Area. An alternate route, which provides access to the eastern side of the lake and Muriel Lake Park, is to drive east through Bonnyville on Secondary Road 659 and turn south onto Secondary Road 657 at Charlotte Lake. This north-south portion of Secondary Road 657 will be renumbered to 891 in about 1990, when the road is extended south to the hamlet of Lindbergh (Campeau 1989).

The origin of Muriel Lake's name is not known. The first fur-trading post in the area was established in 1781 by the North West Company near the present-day hamlet of Beaver Crossing, about 35 km northeast of Muriel Lake. A second post, Fort Lac d'Original (Shaw House), was established in 1789 on the north shore of nearby Moose Lake. The first settlers came to the Bonnyville area in 1907, and a store, post office and sawmill were established about 10 km east of Bonnyville in 1908. By 1909, two schools were operating in the area (Alta. Mun. Aff. 1978). The local economy in the early 1900s was based on the timber industry, and two sawmills were located at Muriel Lake, one at the northeastern tip and the other on the large island/peninsula on the eastern shore (Fig. 1). In the 1920s, an extensive fire destroyed the timber and the economic base switched to agriculture. The locality of Gurneyville, on the western shore, and the locality of Muriel Lake, northeast of the lake, provided post offices and general stores for local residents. At present, Gurneyville has a gas station, post office and general store, but the post office at Muriel Lake is closed and no one lives there now (Alta. Cult. Multicult. n.d.; Alta. Mun. Aff. 1979). There are several subdivisions around the lakeshore and on the backshore, mostly on the south and

MAP SHEET: 73L/2
LOCATION: Tp59, 60 R5, 6 W4
LAT/LONG: 54° 8'N 110°41'W

Latitude and longitude can be used to find any place on earth. These numbers indicate the approximate centre of the lake.

This is the legal land description. Township (Tp) lines run east-west, 10 km apart; numbers start at the Alberta-US border. Range (R) lines run north-south, 10 km apart. The W4 refers to "west of the fourth meridian", a north-south line. The fourth meridian is the Alberta-Saskatchewan border; the fifth is near the centre of Alberta; the sixth is near the western edge.

The National Topographic Series of maps covers all of Canada. The Alberta sheets are as follows:

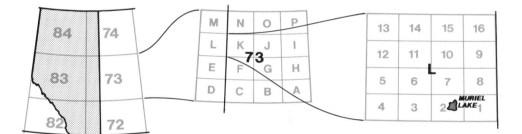

These maps, for example 73L, are at a scale of 1:250 000.

These maps, for example 73L/2, are at a scale of 1:50 000.

Lake Drainage Basin

The land area that contributes runoff to a lake is called its "Drainage Basin."

Figure 1 in each chapter is a map of the drainage basin.
Table 1 summarizes information about the basin.

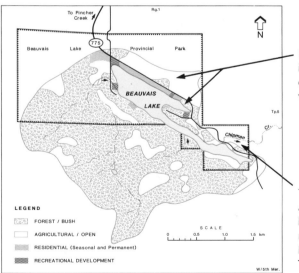

LEGEND

- FOREST / BUSH
- AGRICULTURAL / OPEN
- RESIDENTIAL (Seasonal and Permanent)
- RECREATIONAL DEVELOPMENT

Different types of vegetation and land use are indicated. In some basins, the land has been extensively cleared. Table 1 indicates the dominant vegetation before clearing.

These arrows indicate the direction of flow in creeks and rivers. The volume of runoff that flows into the lake is in Table 1, but that value does not include rain and snow that falls directly on the lake. Information on precipitation and evaporation is in Table 2.

Table 1. Characteristics of Beavais Lake drainage basin.

area (excluding lake) (km²)[a]	7.09
soil[b]	Orthic Dark Gray Chernozemics, Brunisols
bedrock geology[c]	Alberta Group (Upper Cretaceous): shale, sandstone; marine Belly River Formation (Upper Cretaceous): sandstone, siltstone, mudstone, ironstone beds; nonmarine
terrain[d]	rolling foothills
ecoregion[d]	Montane
dominant vegetation[d]	white spruce, trembling aspen, Douglas fir
mean annual inflow (m³)[a, e]	1.02×10^6
mean annual sunshine (h)[f]	2 370

NOTE: [e]excluding groundwater inflow
SOURCES: [a]Alta. Envir. n.d.[c]; [b]Greenlee 1974; [c]Alta. Res. Counc. 1972; [d]Strong and Leggat 1981; [f]Envir. Can. 1982

CONTINUED ON INSIDE BACK COVER

ATLAS OF ALBERTA LAKES

ATLAS OF ALBERTA LAKES

EDITED BY

Patricia Mitchell
Ellie Prepas

Writers J.M. Crosby
M.E. Bradford
P.A. Mitchell
E.E. Prepas
L.G. McIntyre
L. Hart Buckland-Nicks
J.M. Hanson

Contributors W.M. Tonn
P.A. Chambers

THE UNIVERSITY OF ALBERTA PRESS

First published in Canada by
The University of Alberta Press
141 Athabasca Hall
Edmonton, Alberta, Canada T6G 2E8

Copyright © The University of Alberta Press 1990

CANADIAN CATALOGUING IN PUBLICATION DATA

Main entry under title:
    Atlas of Alberta Lakes

ISBN 0-88864-214-8 (bound)
    0-88864-215-6 (pbk.)
    1. Lakes—Alberta—Maps. I. Mitchell, P.
II. Prepas, Ellie, 1947-
G1166.C3A84 1990 551.48'2'097123 C90-091221-9

66165

Typesetting by University of Alberta Printing Services, Edmonton, Alberta, Canada

Printed by Quality Color Press Inc., Edmonton, Alberta, Canada
Bound by North-West Book Co. Ltd., Surrey, British Columbia, Canada

A lake is the landscape's most beautiful and
expressive feature. It is the earth's eye;
looking into which the beholder measures
the depth of his own nature.   *Walden*

Henry David Thoreau

Contents

Foreword

Alberta's many and varied lakes play a special role in the life of this province—they supply water to communities, help promote development and, perhaps most important of all, provide immense pleasure and enjoyment to all who visit them. This *Atlas,* then, will be welcomed throughout the province.

Here, collected in a single volume, is a wealth of interesting and useful information about 100 Alberta lakes, everything from water quality and biological characteristics to the best spots for landing a northern pike. Scientist and student alike will find the *Atlas* valuable and so will any family looking for a recreational site.

At a time when the environment is a major concern for all of us, it is helpful to know as much as possible about Alberta's lakes. The more we know about them, the more we will appreciate them and realize the need to care for them. The *Atlas* serves to remind us that our lakes are part of a priceless natural heritage. It is up to each of us to do our share in protecting that heritage.

On behalf of Alberta Environment, I congratulate and sincerely thank the individuals and agencies responsible for producing this splendid work. They can be deservedly proud of what they have accomplished.

Honourable Ralph Klein,
MINISTER OF ENVIRONMENT

Preface

The *Atlas of Alberta Lakes* was first conceived by University and provincial government scientists in the summer of 1985. We saw it as an opportunity to collect information that was scattered over the province, but largely housed in various offices of Fish and Wildlife Division, Alberta Environment and the University of Alberta. The data were often inaccessible to seasoned workers in the field and to the interested public.

The *Atlas* was a highly ambitious project. It required cooperation from scientists and associates in a diverse group of agencies over a period of five years.The format was developed from the concept used by D.M. Johnson and colleagues in their 1985 edition of the *Atlas of Oregon Lakes* and from lake brochures produced by Alberta Environment. When the project began, we underestimated both the commitment and resources required to complete the task. However, over the last three years of the project we assembled a writing team which included Marie Bradford, Jan Crosby and ourselves. Marie worked to establish a carefully constructed readable format. Jan never lost sight of the ultimate goals and diverse uses for the *Atlas* and the varied background and interests of our potential readers. Each member of the writing team reviewed all of the chapters—some of them several times—and worked out a common style and format. At critical times we were assisted with chapter writing by Leslie Hart Buckland-Nicks, Mark Hanson and Laurie McIntyre. Jan Crosby played a leading role in fitting together the pieces which make up the introductory and other support material (including the Glossary and Species List) which complements and completes the lake descriptions. Her dedication to the project was truly outstanding.

One of the more challenging aspects of the *Atlas* was the selection of 100 lakes and reservoirs. Alberta has thousands of interesting bodies of water, and there was much discussion on how the lakes should be chosen. The availability of recent, well-documented data was a strong selection factor. We also chose lakes that were intensively used for fishing and recreation. Lakes were chosen from across the province, excluding the national parks.

In the end, the *Atlas* reflects state-of-the-art hydrological, water quality, limnological and fisheries data on 100 Alberta lakes. We attempted to include only data that are consistent with the best modern techniques in the field and to reference all sources of baseline data for each of the 100 lakes. Undoubtedly there are errors and omissions for which we accept full responsibility.

We hope you enjoy your sojourn among the interesting features and histories of a group of lakes as diverse as those found anywhere in the world. Lakes in this *Atlas* are large (Lesser Slave Lake and Lake Athabasca), small (Sauer and Eden lakes), deep (Cold and Amisk lakes), shallow (Buffalo and Driedmeat lakes), mainly freshwater, with a few examples of saline lakes (Miquelon and Peninsula lakes); and they extend from the unproductive or oligotrophic (Upper Kananaskis Lake and Spray Lakes Reservoir) to extremely productive or hyper-eutrophic lakes (Nakamun and Winagami lakes). Water residence times are short in the southern onstream reservoirs (Ghost Reservoir has an average water residence time of 22 days), whereas in almost one-third of the lakes in this *Atlas* water residence time is estimated at over 100 years, based on surface water budgets. Some lakes have an extensively documented history of use and development (Wabamun and Chestermere lakes) and others have a colourful history (Moonshine and Pine lakes). Some have an intensively managed sport fishery (Blood Indian Creek Reservoir and Tyrrell

Lake) and a few have no fish at all (Oliva and Peninsula lakes). Many provide a rich habitat for varied wildlife resources (Beaverhill and Moose lakes).

We hope the *Atlas of Alberta Lakes* will extend your appreciation of the tremendous aquatic resources available in our province. We also intend that information presented here will contribute to an improved understanding of prairie lakes, and lakes in general.

For those wishing to use or further explore the information in this volume, the original source material is stored with the Environmental Assessment Division of Alberta Environment.

Ellie Prepas
Zoology Department
University of Alberta

Patricia Mitchell
Environmental Assessment Division
Alberta Environment

Acknowledgements

Compilation of material for the *Atlas of Alberta Lakes* was possible because of the support of many individuals and groups within Alberta. Funding was provided to the University of Alberta by five organizations: the Recreation, Parks and Wildlife Foundation, Alberta Environment (Environmental Assessment, Research Management and Planning divisions), the Water Resources Commission, Alberta Forestry, Lands and Wildlife (Fish and Wildlife Division) and the University of Alberta (Boreal Institute for Northern Studies, Endowment Fund for the Future: University/Community Special Projects Fund and Special Initiatives Fund). Special support was provided through the long and often rocky road to completion by Brian Hammond, Bruce Maclock, Peter Melnychuk, and Fred Schulte (Alberta Environment); Alfred Birch and Bob Cronkhite (Water Resources Commission); Chuck Moser and Glen Semenchuk (Recreation, Parks and Wildlife Foundation); Norma Gutteridge (The University of Alberta Press); Bob Armit, Dick Peter and Don Williams (University of Alberta); and Tom Mill (Alberta Forestry, Lands and Wildlife).

Review of lake chapters was coordinated by the *Atlas* steering committee: Pat Mitchell (chair) and Kim Lalonde (Alberta Environment); Glen Semenchuk; Tom Mill; Alfred Birch; Ken Wilson (Alberta Recreation and Parks); and Ellie Prepas. All chapters were carefully reviewed by Lynne Kemper (Water Resources Commission); Rick Bramm, Geoff Foy, Bill I'Anson and Kim Lalonde (Alberta Environment); Ernie Stenton (Alberta Forestry, Lands and Wildlife); and Larry Nikiforuk (Alberta Research Council). Many others reviewed a variable number of chapters or gave us access to information; these contributors include: Jim Ames, Anne-Marie Anderson, Neil Assmus, Ken Caine, Doug Clark, Tony Epp, Rick Pickering, Al Sosiak, Orest Takarsky, David Trew and Annette Trimbee (Alberta Environment); Dave Barber (Alberta Municipal Affairs); Frank Bishop, Vance Buchwald, Lorne Fitch, Carl Hunt, Mel Kraft, Doug Lowe, Dave Walty, and Darryl Watters (Alberta Forestry, Lands and Wildlife); Stephen Luck, Wayne Nordstrom, Alan Thompson and Ken Wilson (Alberta Recreation and Parks); Bob Riddett (Battle River Regional Planning Commission); Randy Strocki (County of Parkland); Aphrodite Karamitsanis (Alberta Culture and Multiculturalism); Joe Rasmussen (McGill University); Kaz Patalas (Freshwater Institute) and David Boag, Hugh Clifford, Jeff Curtis, Michael Hickman, Bill Mackay, Brenda Miskimmin, Jan Murie, Joe Nelson, Dave Schindler, Dale Vitt and Mark Wilson (University of Alberta). Thanks to the many other reviewers, and in particular the extensive network in Water Resources Management Services of Alberta Environment coordinated by Kim Lalonde.

Photographs were provided by several individuals and government agencies; they are credited with the photographs. Photographs without credit lines were taken by co-editor Patricia Mitchell.

Drafting requirements were provided by Alberta Environment and coordinated by Ian Van Ens, Cas Lukay and Terry Zenith. Long hours were contributed to figure preparation by Gurnam Bhavra. He was assisted by Monica Gavigan, Bridgett Howard, Bruce Sanders, Peter Smith and Inge Wilson. Eva Fekete provided graphics photography. Assistance with reference materials was faithfully provided by the librarians at the Alberta Environment and Alberta Forestry, Lands and Wildlife libraries.

Technical support was coordinated by Laurie McIntyre; Mark Serediak and Leslie Hart Buckland-Nicks provided critical technical assistance; Debbie Webb and Kathy Gibson also assisted with data collection and preparation. Proofreaders for the *Atlas* were Brian Fardoe (Alberta Water Resources Commission), Bernie Jones (Boreal Institute for Northern Studies) and Laurie McIntyre. A substantial portion of the typing was carried out at the University of Alberta by Arlene Cowan, Sandra Fliegel, Elaine Johnston and others in the Zoology Department typing pool.

Most of the phytoplankton data in the *Atlas* were taken from unpublished data prepared by Stewart Anderson when he worked with Alberta Environment; those data enriched an all-too-often sparse information base on small organisms in Alberta lakes. The zooplankton sections were enhanced by unpublished data provided by Kaz Patalas of the Freshwater Institute. Ernie Stenton provided much of the information on fisheries management in the introductory material.

Last but not least we are indebted to the staff at The University of Alberta Press who helped us keep our sights on the final product.

PART I

CHARACTERISTICS OF LAKES
IN THE *ATLAS*

Alberta is graced with a wonderful variety of lakes—perhaps as many different types as in any other region in the country. Within Alberta, clear lakes with sandy beaches decorate the Lakeland Region, warm green shallow lakes dot the prairie and parkland, brown water lakes occur throughout the Boreal forest, and pristine, cold, mountain lakes reflect spectacular scenery. We have added to this variety by creating new lakes, called reservoirs, in the southern half of the province. But particular kinds of lakes are not limited to one area. Lakes that are deep or shallow, green or clear, salty or fresh, may be found in many parts of the province.

Our natural lakes are very young from a geological perspective—most have been in existence no more than 12 000 years. With the retreat of the glaciers, numerous depressions and blocked waterways remained, which filled with water to form the vast array of lakes we see today. Alberta's lakes reflect not only its physical features, but also its climate. Where water is abundant, lakes abound—as in the vast region around Lake Athabasca, and in the Lakeland Region northeast of the city of Edmonton. The arid southeastern part of the province has few natural lakes. There is a surplus of water in the mountains, but much of it runs off to form rivers that flow across the province to the north or east. In the central part of the province between the arid south and the wet north, and in the Peace Country along the west-central edge of Alberta, are parkland and forest dotted with lakes of every size and description. All of these areas, except for the far northwest, are represented by lakes in the *Atlas* (Fig. 1). These lakes are shown on the map as part of the drainage basins of the largest rivers. Within the book, lake descriptions are organized by river basin, because with few exceptions lakes ultimately drain into rivers.

Four major rivers drain most of the province. The Peace and Athabasca rivers drain the northern half of Alberta. Their waters join with water from Lake Athabasca to form Alberta's largest river, the Slave River, which flows into the Northwest Territories and on to the Arctic Ocean. The North Saskatchewan River winds through the foothills and parkland of central Alberta. The South Saskatchewan River, which is fed by three rivers that arise in the mountains, makes its way through dry farmland and prairie. The North and South Saskatchewan rivers join in the province of Saskatchewan and become part of the Nelson-Churchill system, and their waters eventually reach Hudson Bay. There is also the smaller Beaver River, which flows through the heart of the Lakeland Region and then into the Churchill system; and the Milk River, which passes briefly into Alberta from Montana before returning south to flow finally to the Mississippi River and the Gulf of Mexico.

Within these large river basins, water drains into creeks, streams and lakes. The nature of a particular lake depends not only on its physical setting, but also on what enters it from its surroundings. Water enters the lake from its drainage basin, carrying tiny particles of soil and organic matter and dissolved substances, including nutrients such as phosphorus and nitrogen. Water also enters the lake underground. As well, lakes receive dust, precipitation and gases from the atmosphere. Each lake's water quality reflects the contribution of all of these materials, and of sunlight and wind energy.

Within the lake is a complex world of living organisms—the tiny plants called algae that tint the water green, and the large plants that grow in shallow water along the shore. Many animals inhabit or use the lake environment, including fish, waterfowl, muskrats, aquatic insects, snails and tiny crustaceans suspended in the open water.

These plants and animals form an interconnected web. Each is dependent on other organisms for food and shelter. They in turn influence the lake's character and its water quality. People, too, may influence the nature of the lake. They control water levels, divert water, change the land in the lake's drainage basin from forest to farm and urbanize the lakeshore.

All of these characteristics are discussed in the following sections. They are provided to assist readers in understanding the detailed descriptions of the 100 lakes included in the *Atlas*. Table 1 summarizes much of the information provided in each lake description, and allows one to compare various aspects of these lakes. These introductory sections are arranged in the order that they are presented in the individual lake chapters: Drainage Basin Characteristics, Lake Basin Characteristics, Water Quality and Biological Characteristics. These sections are intended to enhance the reader's awareness of a particular lake, or Alberta lakes in general—whether he or she is a cottager, an angler, a student, a scientist or simply a person who appreciates nature, particularly the fascinating world of lakes.

P.A. Mitchell

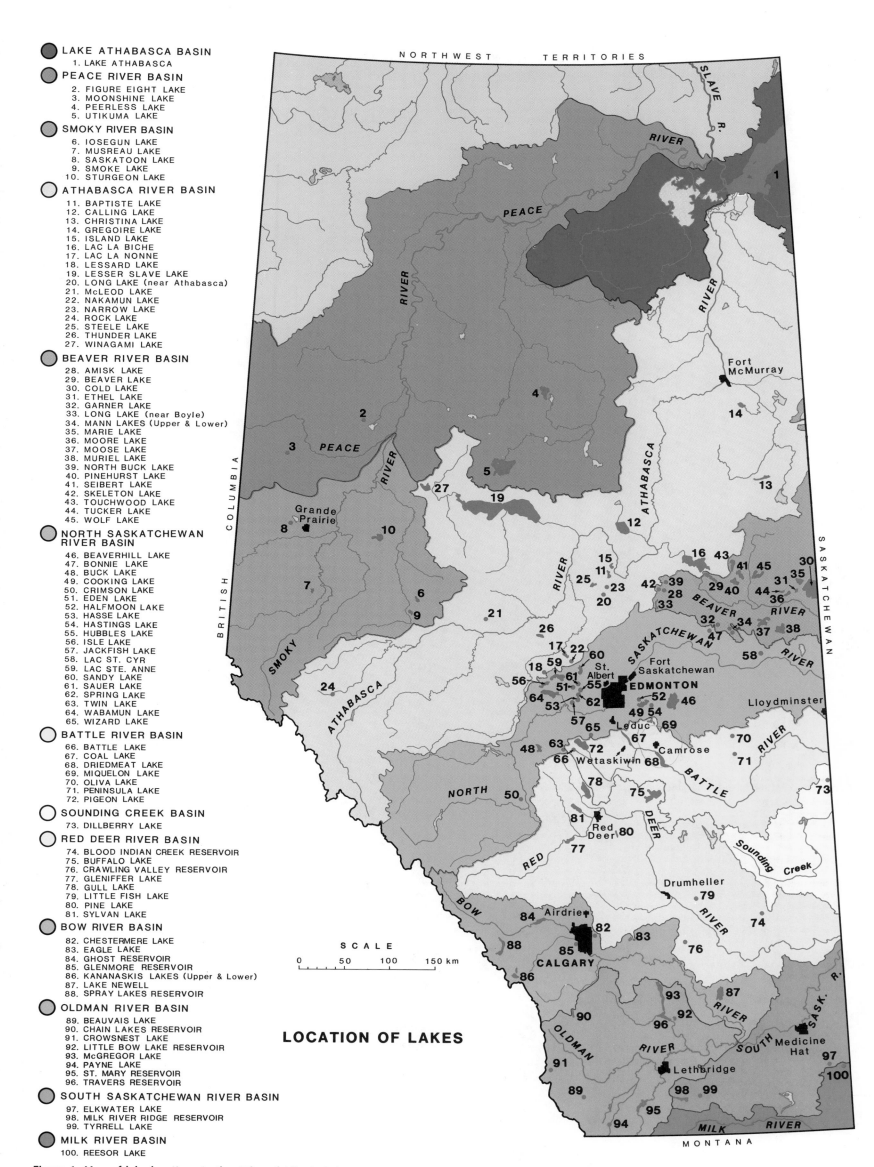

LOCATION OF LAKES

LAKE ATHABASCA BASIN
1. LAKE ATHABASCA

PEACE RIVER BASIN
2. FIGURE EIGHT LAKE
3. MOONSHINE LAKE
4. PEERLESS LAKE
5. UTIKUMA LAKE

SMOKY RIVER BASIN
6. IOSEGUN LAKE
7. MUSREAU LAKE
8. SASKATOON LAKE
9. SMOKE LAKE
10. STURGEON LAKE

ATHABASCA RIVER BASIN
11. BAPTISTE LAKE
12. CALLING LAKE
13. CHRISTINA LAKE
14. GREGOIRE LAKE
15. ISLAND LAKE
16. LAC LA BICHE
17. LAC LA NONNE
18. LESSARD LAKE
19. LESSER SLAVE LAKE
20. LONG LAKE (near Athabasca)
21. McLEOD LAKE
22. NAKAMUN LAKE
23. NARROW LAKE
24. ROCK LAKE
25. STEELE LAKE
26. THUNDER LAKE
27. WINAGAMI LAKE

BEAVER RIVER BASIN
28. AMISK LAKE
29. BEAVER LAKE
30. COLD LAKE
31. ETHEL LAKE
32. GARNER LAKE
33. LONG LAKE (near Boyle)
34. MANN LAKES (Upper & Lower)
35. MARIE LAKE
36. MOORE LAKE
37. MOOSE LAKE
38. MURIEL LAKE
39. NORTH BUCK LAKE
40. PINEHURST LAKE
41. SEIBERT LAKE
42. SKELETON LAKE
43. TOUCHWOOD LAKE
44. TUCKER LAKE
45. WOLF LAKE

NORTH SASKATCHEWAN RIVER BASIN
46. BEAVERHILL LAKE
47. BONNIE LAKE
48. BUCK LAKE
49. COOKING LAKE
50. CRIMSON LAKE
51. EDEN LAKE
52. HALFMOON LAKE
53. HASSE LAKE
54. HASTINGS LAKE
55. HUBBLES LAKE
56. ISLE LAKE
57. JACKFISH LAKE
58. LAC ST. CYR
59. LAC STE. ANNE
60. SANDY LAKE
61. SAUER LAKE
62. SPRING LAKE
63. TWIN LAKE
64. WABAMUN LAKE
65. WIZARD LAKE

BATTLE RIVER BASIN
66. BATTLE LAKE
67. COAL LAKE
68. DRIEDMEAT LAKE
69. MIQUELON LAKE
70. OLIVA LAKE
71. PENINSULA LAKE
72. PIGEON LAKE

SOUNDING CREEK BASIN
73. DILLBERRY LAKE

RED DEER RIVER BASIN
74. BLOOD INDIAN CREEK RESERVOIR
75. BUFFALO LAKE
76. CRAWLING VALLEY RESERVOIR
77. GLENIFFER LAKE
78. GULL LAKE
79. LITTLE FISH LAKE
80. PINE LAKE
81. SYLVAN LAKE

BOW RIVER BASIN
82. CHESTERMERE LAKE
83. EAGLE LAKE
84. GHOST RESERVOIR
85. GLENMORE RESERVOIR
86. KANANASKIS LAKES (Upper & Lower)
87. LAKE NEWELL
88. SPRAY LAKES RESERVOIR

OLDMAN RIVER BASIN
89. BEAUVAIS LAKE
90. CHAIN LAKES RESERVOIR
91. CROWSNEST LAKE
92. LITTLE BOW LAKE RESERVOIR
93. McGREGOR LAKE
94. PAYNE LAKE
95. ST. MARY RESERVOIR
96. TRAVERS RESERVOIR

SOUTH SASKATCHEWAN RIVER BASIN
97. ELKWATER LAKE
98. MILK RIVER RIDGE RESERVOIR
99. TYRRELL LAKE

MILK RIVER BASIN
100. REESOR LAKE

SCALE
0   50   100   150 km

Figure 1. Map of lake locations in the *Atlas of Alberta Lakes*.

Table 1. Summary of information for each lake. Data are compiled from tables and text in lake chapters. Water quality values are averaged where data for more than one year are presented in a chapter.

Lake	PHYSICAL						RECREATIONAL			WATER QUALITY			
	Area km²	Max. Depth m	Mean Depth m	Dr. Basin Area km²	Dam, Weir	Drainage Basin	Camp Ground	Boat Launch	Sport Fish	Trophic Status	TP x µg/L	CHLORO x µg/L	TDS x mg/L
Amisk Lake	5.15	60	15.5	234	W	Beaver	°	√	WE,YP NP,LW	E E	N:38 S:40	N:14.0 S:16.0	N:221 S:220
Lake Athabasca	7770	124	20.0	282 000	W	Athabasca	√	√	LW,WE,YP AG,NP,LT	O-M	M:12	M:1.1	M:50*
Baptiste Lake	9.81	27.5	8.6	288	°	Athabasca		√	NP,WE,YP	H-E H-E	N:54 S:49	N:30.0 S:24.0	S:198* N:194*
Battle Lake	4.56	13.1	6.9	103	°	Battle	√	√	LW,YP,NP	E	31	11.2	200*
Beauvais Lake	0.89	10.7	4.3	7.09	W	Oldman	√	√	RB,BR	M	28	10.9	156*
Beaver Lake	33.1	15.2	7.1	290	°	Beaver	√	√	WE,YP NP,LW	M	33	10.6	239*
Beaverhill Lake	139	2.3	X	1970	°	N. Sask.	°	°	°	H-E	X	54.0	922*
Blood Indian Creek Res.	1.03	13.3	4.6	116	D	Red Deer	√	√	RB	E?	366	19.8	1651*
Bonnie Lake	3.77	6.1	3.1	49.6	°	N. Sask.	√	√	NP,YP	H-E	95	31.5	217*
Buck Lake	25.4	12.2	6.2	233	W	N. Sask.	√	√	WE,YP LW,NP	E	40	18.1	127*
Buffalo Lake	93.5	6.5	2.8	1440	°	Red Deer	√	√	NP	M M	M:59 Se:77	M:5.4 Se:9.4	M:1683* Se:1420*
Calling Lake	138	18.3	X	1090	°	Athabasca	√	√	BR,WE,YP NP,LW	E	50	19.1	99*
Chain Lakes Res.	3.12	10.4	5.4	209	D	Oldman	√	√	RB,CT,BR BK,BU,MW	X	X	X	313*
Chestermere Lake	2.65	7.0	3.47	5.00	D	Bow	°	√	RB,YP,NP	M	32	6.0	175*
Christina Lake	21.3	32.9	17.3	1250	°	Athabasca	√	√	WE,YP NP,LW	X	16	X	123*
Coal Lake	10.9	5.5	3.5	1250	D	Battle	°	√	YP,NP	H-E	176	43.5	288*
Cold Lake	373	99.1	49.9	6140	°	Beaver	√	√	RB,WE,YP LW,NP,LT	O-M	14	3.2	140*
Cooking Lake	36.0	4.6	1.7	158	°	N. Sask.	°	√	°	H-E	251	83.4	1019
Crawling Valley Res.	25.1	16	5.2	802	D	Red Deer	√	√	RB,BK NP,BR	M	57	12.2	238*
Crimson Lake	2.32	9.1	2.2	1.75	°	N. Sask.	√	√	°	M	18	4.8	144*
Crowsnest Lake	1.19	27.4	13.5	85.6	°	Oldman	°	√	LT,RB CT,MW	O	X	X	226*
Dillberry Lake	0.80	10.7	2.8	11.8	°	S. Creek	√	√	RB,YP	O	15	3.4	188*
Driedmeat Lake	16.5	3.7	2.2	7220	D	Battle	√	√	NP	H-E	453	87.0	363*
Eagle Lake	11.8	4.9	2.6	120	W	Bow	√	√	WE,YP,NP	H-E	334	39.5	1299*
Lake Eden	0.161	15.3	6.95	1.5	°	N. Sask.	√	√	RB	M	22	7.6	123
Elkwater Lake	2.31	8.4	3.5	25.7	W	S. Sask.	√	√	YP,NP	M	43	5.9	255*
Ethel Lake	4.90	30	6.6	542	W	Beaver	√	√	WE,YP NP,LW	M	25	8.0	172*
Figure Eight Lake	0.368	6	3.0	4.47	D	Peace	√	√	RB	H-E	182	99.1	X
Garner Lake	6.19	15.2	8.1	25.5	°	Beaver	√	√	NP,WE,YP	M	42	11.0	575*
Ghost Reservoir	11.0	34	14.5	6460	D	Bow	√	√	MW,LW,LT,BR	O	7	2.0	160*
Gleniffer Lake	17.6	33	11.6	5610	D	Red Deer		√	WE,RB,BR MW,CT,NP	O	12	1.2	213*
Glenmore Reservoir	3.84	21.1	6.1	1210	D	Bow	°	√	NP,MW,BR,YP	O-M	8	2	228*
Gregoire Lake	25.8	7.2	3.9	232	W	Athabasca	√	√	NP,LW,WE,YP	E	23	6.2	63*
Gull Lake	80.6	8	5.4	206	°	Red Deer	√	√	LW,WE,NP	M	39	6.6	753
Halfmoon Lake	0.41	8.5	4.7	2.43	°	N. Sask.	√	√	°	H-E	112	57.0	165*
Hasse Lake	0.90	9.5	3.5	7.4	°	N. Sask.	°	H	RB	M	22	5.8	344
Hastings Lake	8.71	7.3	2.4	269	°	N. Sask.	√	H	YP	H-E	136	74.1	605*
Hubbles Lake	0.40	30	10.1	8.33	°	N. Sask.	√	√	YP,NP	M	27	9.0	383
Iosegun Lake	13.4	11.2	4.1	248	W	Smoky	√	√	NP,LW,WE,YP	E	61	26.6	83*
Island Lake	7.81	18	3.7	63.2	°	Athabasca	°	√	LW,YP,NP	M	26	8.3	216*
Isle Lake	23.0	7.5	4.1	246	°	N. Sask.	√	√	NP,WE,YP	H-E	101	39.2	164*
Jackfish Lake	2.39	9	3.4	12.6	W	N. Sask.	°	√	NP,WE,YP	E	39	10.9	600*
Kananaskis Lakes	U:7.80 L:5.25	U:108 L:42.1	U:32.0 L:13.1	U:139 L:307	D	Bow	√	√	RB,BU CT	O O	U:5 L:6	U:2.9 L:1.6	U:95* L:147*
Lac La Biche	234	21.3	8.4	4040	°	Athabasca	√	√	NP,LW,WE,YP	E E	W:117 E:108	W:23.4 E:29.8	W:162* E:161*
Lac la Nonne	11.8	19.8	7.8	277	W	Athabasca	√	√	NP,LW,WE,YP	H-E	168	55.5	186*
Lessard Lake	3.21	6	3.9	9.29	°	Athabasca	√	√	YP,NP	E	30	14.9	166
Lesser Slave Lake	1160	20.5	11.4	12 400	W	Athabasca	√	√	NP,LW,WE,YP	E?	X	X	111*
Little Bow Lake Res.	5.44	11	4.3	37.6	D	Oldman	°	√	RB,YP BR,NP,LW	O-M	14	2.1	215*

Lake	PHYSICAL						RECREATIONAL			WATER QUALITY			
	Area km²	Max. Depth m	Mean Depth m	Dr. Basin Area km²	Dam, Weir	Drainage Basin	Camp Ground	Boat Launch	Sport Fish	Trophic Status	TP x µg/L	CHLORO x µg/L	TDS x mg/L
Little Fish Lake	7.09	3	1.76	157	W	Red Deer	√	√	YP	H-E	876	77.1	1168*
Long Lake (near Athabasca)*	1.62	28	9.4	30.3	°	Athabasca	√	√	YP,NP	M	12	3.3	X
Long Lake (near Boyle)	5.84	9	4.3	82.4	°	Beaver	√	√	NP,WE,YP	E	41	18.8	207*
Mann Lakes	U:4.59 L:5.10	U:9.1 L:6.1	U:5.7 L:4.0	U:116 L:148	°	Beaver	U:° L:√	√	YP,NP	H-E H-E	U:45 L:121	U:22.9 L:103.0	U:239* L:242*
Marie Lake	34.6	26	14.0	386	°	Beaver	°	°	WE,YP NP,LW	M	15	5.6	148*
McGregor Lake	51.4	9.7	6.5	993	D	Oldman	°	√	WE,YP LW,RB,NP	M?	26	8.8	195*
McLeod Lake	3.73	10.7	5.1	45.9	W	Athabasca	√	√	RB	M	26	9.3	165*
Milk River Ridge Res.	15.3	16.5	8.4	168	D	S. Sask.	√	√	LW,WE,NP	O	12	2.6	119*
Miquelon Lake	8.72	6	2.7	35.4	°	Battle	√	√	°	M?	216	5.7	5402
Moonshine Lake	0.28	3.5	1.3	6.84	D	Peace	√	√	RB,NP	E	100	9.8	470*
Moore Lake	9.28	26	8.3	37.1	W	Beaver	√	√	NP,WE,YP	M	26	8.0	422*
Moose Lake	40.8	19.8	5.6	755	W	Beaver	√	√	NP,LW,WE,YP	E	41	16.8	410*
Muriel Lake	64.1	10.7	6.6	384	°	Beaver	√	√	NP,LW,WE,YP	M	36	6.7	753*
Musreau Lake	5.49	13	X	101	°	Smoky	√	√	RB,BU	M	22	4.5	99*
Nakamun Lake	3.54	8	4.5	44.9	°	Athabasca	°	√	YP,NP	H-E	88	44.2	167*
Narrow Lake	1.14	38	14.4	7.17	D	Athabasca	°	√	NP,YP	O-M	11	2.7	162
Lake Newell	66.4	19.8	4.8	84.6	D	Bow	√	√	LW,BU,WE,YP BR,NP,RB	E	29	11.0	196*
North Buck Lake	19.0	6.1	2.5	100	°	Beaver	√	√	NP,LW,WE,YP	E	30	13.3	181*
Oliva Lake	0.52	1.7	1.3	256	°	Battle	°	°	°	M	13 058	4.0	84314
Payne Lake	2.28	7.3	3.8	24.9	D	Oldman	°	√	RB,BU CT,MW,AG	X	25	X	109*
Peerless Lake	82.6	35.4	14.6	338	°	Peace	√	√	LT,NP YP,LW	X	X	X	X
Peninsula Lake	1.39	3.1	2.1	43.9	°	Battle	°	H	°	M	3576	8.9	9600
Pigeon Lake	96.7	9.1	6.2	187	W	Battle	√	√	NP,LW,WE,YP	E	32	12.8	164*
Pine Lake	3.89	12.2	5.3	150	°	Red Deer	√	√	NP,WE,YP	E	56	18.8	475*
Pinehurst Lake	40.7	21.3	12.2	285	°	Beaver	√	√	NP,LW,WE,YP	E	46	14.6	160*
Reesor Lake	0.51	5.5	3.7	5.58	D	Milk	√	√	RB	E	36	14.0	130*
Rock Lake	2.15	27.8	12.1	348	°	Athabasca	√	√	BU,MW,NP,LT	X	X	X	X
Lac St. Cyr	2.46	21	5.1	28.1	°	N. Sask.	°	H	YP,NP	M M	N:29 E:26	N:5.8 E:6.6*	N,E:189*
Lac Ste. Anne	54.5	9	4.8	619	°	N. Sask.	√	√	NP,LW,WE,YP	E	W:44 E:48	W:32.7 E:17.9	W:165* E:174*
St. Mary Reservoir	37.5	56.4	10.4	2250	D	Oldman	√	√	LW,WE,NP RB,CT	O?	X	2.9	114*
Sandy Lake	11.4	4.4	2.6	48.4	°	N. Sask.	√	√	YP,NP	N:H-E S:E	N:221 S:88	N:67.8 S:29.9	N:359* S:373*
Saskatoon Lake	7.47	4	2.6	31.8	°	Smoky	√	√	RB,BR	H-E	728	43.4	591*
Sauer Lake	0.085	14	4.2	0.49	°	N. Sask.	°	°	RB	M	35	5.4	135
Seibert Lake	37.9	11	6.9	67.6	°	Beaver	√	√	NP,LW,WE,YP	X	9	X	318*
Skeleton Lake	7.89	17	6.5	31.7	°	Beaver	√	√	NP,LW,WE,YP	N:M S:E	N:36 S:47	N:10.0 S:20.0	N:181* S:191*
Smoke Lake	9.59	8.3	5.1	127	°	Smoky	√	√	NP,LW,WE,YP	E	53	25.0	96*
Spray Lakes Res.	19.9	65.4	13.5	493	D	Bow	√	√	LT,MW	O	4	2.1	154*
Spring Lake	0.80	9.1	1.9	12.5	°	N. Sask.	√	√	YP,RB	M	21	8.0	360*
Steele Lake	6.61	6.1	3.2	255	W	Athabasca	√	√	YP,NP	H-E	64	25.0	153*
Sturgeon Lake	49.1	9.5	5.4	571	W	Smoky	√	√	WE,YP AG,NP,LW	H-E H-E	M:92 W:103	M:45.2 W:38.8*	M:82*
Sylvan Lake	42.8	18.3	9.6	102	°	Red Deer	√	√	LW,NP,WE,YP	M	20	3.8	357*
Thunder Lake	7.03	6.1	3.0	20.7	W	Athabasca	√	√	YP,NP	E	46	16.6	243*
Touchwood Lake	29.0	40	14.8	111	°	Beaver	√	√	WE,YP LT,NP,LW	M	22	4.6	154*
Travers Reservoir	22.5	39.6	18.3	4230	D	Oldman	√	√	NP,WE,YP LW,RB,BR	O	14	2.2	215*
Tucker Lake	6.65	7.5	2.9	312	W	Beaver	°	√	NP,LW,WE,YP	H-E	64	22.6	210*
Twin Lake	0.24	35	15.7	7.12	°	N. Sask.	√	H	NP,RB,YP	O	14	1.8	188
Tyrrell Lake	3.99	6.1	3.8	122	D	S. Sask.	°	√	RB,NP,LW	X	150	X	7450*
Utikuma Lake	288	5.5	1.7	2170	W	Peace	°	H	NP,LW,WE,YP	X	X	X	331
Wabamun Lake	81.8	11	6.3	259	°	N. Sask.	√	√	NP,LW,WE,YP	E	32	11.5	248*
Winagami Lake	46.7	4.7	1.7	221	W	Athabasca	√	√	LW,YP,NP	H-E	193	61.8	281*
Wizard Lake	2.48	11	6.2	29.8	°	N. Sask.	√	√	YP,NP	E	45	16.3	208
Wolf Lake	31.5	38.3	9.2	693	°	Beaver	√	√	NP,LW,WE,YP	M	25	7.9	165*

LEGEND

√	present
X	no data
°	no,none

Physical

D	dam
W	weir

Recreational

H	hand/small boat
WE	walleye
YP	yellow perch
NP	northern pike
LW	lake whitefish
MW	mountain whitefish
RB	rainbow trout
BU	bull trout
BR	brown trout
BK	brook trout
LT	lake trout
CT	cutthroat trout
AG	arctic grayling

Water Quality

O	oligotrophic
O-M	oligotrophic mesotrophic
M	mesotrophic
E	eutrophic
H	hyper-eutrophic
N	North
S	South
E	East
W	West
M	Main
Se	Secondary
U	Upper
L	Lower
*	calculated TDS values have been modified to be comparable to measured TDS values.

DRAINAGE BASIN CHARACTERISTICS

If each drop of water in a lake could tell its tale of how it got there, we would hear a multitude of stories! Some water falls as rain, snow or hail directly onto the lake; however, in all of Alberta, except for a few small areas in the extreme northwest and the higher elevations of the Rocky Mountains, evaporation exceeds precipitation. Therefore, most lakes in Alberta would recede and eventually dry up if their only source of water was direct rain or snowfall. Most water in a lake comes from rain or snow that falls on land areas around a lake, perhaps many kilometres away. This water may take one of several routes to reach a lake and may be part of the **surface**, **subsurface**, or **groundwater** runoff. A lake **drainage basin** or **watershed** includes all the land that contributes surface or subsurface runoff to that lake (Fig. 2). Groundwater may originate from areas far outside the drainage basin.

Whether the drainage basin is small or large, barren rock or rich soil, heavily forested or recently cleared, it is one of the most important features affecting the nature of a lake. The drainage basin has a very strong influence on the quality of water in a lake, and water quality has a strong influence on the algae, aquatic plants, invertebrates, fish and wildlife that inhabit that lake and affect our use and enjoyment.

Drainage Basin Borders

The border of a drainage basin is the drainage divide—the height of land around the lake. When a map of a drainage basin is drawn, as is shown in Figure 1 of each lake description in the *Atlas*, the border is determined by examining topographic maps. The term **gross drainage area** refers to the largest possible physical area that could potentially contribute surface runoff to the lake. Gross drainage areas include all other water bodies in the basin, areas that are referred to as dead storage, and areas that do not normally contribute water except in years of above-average runoff. The drainage area for each lake in the *Atlas* is presented as the gross drainage area minus the surface area of that lake.

Areas within a lake drainage basin that contribute runoff to that lake during an average runoff year are referred to as **contributing areas**. The size of the contributing area within a drainage basin can vary depending on the amount of runoff produced in a given year. Contributing areas can increase in size during years of above-average runoff when increased runoff volumes exceed the storage capacity within the drainage basin. Similarly, contributing areas can decrease in size during years of below-average runoff, when low-lying areas trap water that would ordinarily pass downstream. In the *Atlas*, the estimated amount of surface runoff is based on the estimated size of the contributing area within the drainage boundary in a year with average precipitation.

Dead storage areas are parts of some drainage basins where surface runoff cannot flow into the lake but becomes trapped in depressions that have no outlet channel to release water downstream, even during years of high runoff. Other low-lying areas that trap runoff and prevent it from contributing to flows downstream during years of average or below-average runoff are called non-contributing areas. Non-contributing areas have the potential to contribute water in above-average runoff years when the limited storage capacity is exceeded by the increased volume of runoff, but runoff generated within non-contributing areas or dead storage

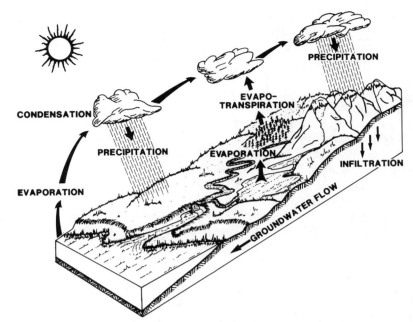

Figure 2. A lake receives water from precipitation, surface runoff, streamflow, subsurface runoff and groundwater.

areas is not included when determining a mean annual (average year) water balance for a lake. However, water lying in dead storage areas may soak down into the ground, become part of the groundwater and so enter a lake. In the *Atlas*, the input of groundwater to a lake is not included in the values in Table 2 of each lake description.

Size of Drainage Basins

In Alberta, the size of lake drainage basins is extremely variable, from Lake Athabasca's enormous 282 000–km² basin which covers more than half of Alberta and parts of British Columbia and Saskatchewan, to the tiny, 0.5–km² drainage basin of Sauer Lake, one of the pothole lakes in the rolling hills west of Edmonton. The size of the drainage basin relative to the area of its lake is also highly variable. In the *Atlas*, drainage basins more than 20 times the area of the lake have been described as relatively large (for example, Crowsnest and Rock lakes), those 10 to 20 times the area of the lake are called medium-sized (for example, Elkwater and Beaverhill lakes) and those less than 10 times the area of the lake are called relatively small (for example, Sylvan and Pigeon lakes). The ratio of the drainage basin area to the lake area is an important factor influencing the water quality of a lake. Lakes with proportionately large drainage basins usually receive more runoff, so the lake level may be more variable. They also receive greater amounts of nutrients and suspended sediment than lakes with small basins.

Many of the water bodies discussed in the *Atlas* are reservoirs whose effective drainage basins may have been changed by the construction of dams and diversion canals. Reservoirs can be either onstream or offstream. **Onstream reservoirs** consist of a structure across a major stream or river that impounds all or part of the flow to store water until it is needed. The water supply for onstream reservoirs is generally provided by the natural drainage area of the river upstream of the structure. For example, the drainage basin for Ghost Reservoir is that of the Bow and Ghost rivers upstream of the Ghost Dam; the drainage basin of Gleniffer Lake is that of the Red Deer River upstream of Dickson Dam. However, in some cases, minor diversions may bring additional water from outside the natural drainage basin. For example, St. Mary Reservoir is an onstream reservoir on the St. Mary River but additional water is diverted to it from the Belly and Waterton rivers.

Offstream reservoirs consist of a structure across a minor stream or coulee and most of its water is diverted from a major source outside the natural drainage basin. The volume of water diverted can be very large and can contribute much more water to the offstream reservoir than is produced from the natural drainage area. Many of the reservoirs in southern Alberta are built in almost-dry coulees and water is brought to them from major rivers via a system of canals. For example, the natural drainage basin of Travers Reservoir provides only 3% of the water in the reservoir; 10% is brought via diversion from the Highwood River, and 87% is brought via diversion from the Bow River. Crawling Valley Reservoir receives less than 1% of its water from its natural watershed; more than 99% is diverted to it by canal from the Bow River. In the *Atlas*, the drainage basin size and the map of the drainage basin in each lake or reservoir description refer only to the natural drainage basin, and therefore exclude areas that may contribute water via canals. However, diversion canals are marked on the maps and their contribution is presented in the tables and discussed in the text.

Runoff: Measured and Estimated

Surface runoff refers to the precipitation that falls on a land area and eventually flows down slopes to gather in streams, lakes and other water bodies. When rainstorms are extreme, precipitation may completely saturate the surface soil layers and water will flow over the land surface, usually in brooks, streams or rivers. If surface runoff reaches a lake, it usually does so in a few hours or days after a rainfall or sudden snowmelt. The predominant nature of surface runoff, however, is not overland flow but rather subsurface flow made up of water that penetrates the upper soil horizons and flows laterally down the slopes before it seeps back to the surface in the lower regions of the slope. The amount of surface runoff can vary significantly, depending on topographic features and the balance between precipitation and evaporation in the drainage basin.

Surface runoff which flows within a watercourse is referred to as **streamflow** and can be measured by hydrometric gauging stations. Water Survey of Canada (WSC) and Alberta Environment have jointly established a network of hydrometric stations on individual streams throughout the province. The hydrometric network has recorded the flow of selected rivers and creeks over many years. The data from these stations were used to estimate the runoff from a monitored watershed and were also used to estimate the surface runoff of ungauged watersheds with similar physical and climatic characteristics.

Surface runoff estimates for the lakes in this *Atlas* are based either on data from a single representative gauging station or on a regional analysis of several stations in the area. Runoff for an average year (mean annual yield) is determined from available data and is usually expressed as a volume of water produced per unit area. The estimated mean annual yield is then multiplied by the contributing drainage area of a lake to estimate the expected inflow for an average year (mean annual inflow).

For example:
mean annual yield = 50 000 m³/km²
contributing drainage area = 100 km²
mean annual inflow = 50 000 m³/km² x 100 km²
= 5 000 000 m³

If there are other lakes in the drainage basin of the lake being discussed, then the runoff to them was estimated, the amount of evaporation from their surface was considered and the balance was considered as outflow which eventually entered the downstream lake.

Subsurface runoff consists of that part of the runoff which infiltrates the surface soils and moves laterally through the upper soil horizons toward the lake. The subsurface flow component moves much more slowly than surface flow and may contribute to the lake for many days or weeks after the surface flow has ceased.

Groundwater is that part of the runoff that has percolated deep into the ground. It may flow laterally to enter a lake under the lake surface. The groundwater component has a very slow response time and may contribute to a lake for many weeks, months or even years after a rainfall or snowmelt event. Groundwater is likely an important source of water for lakes in Alberta, but estimates have been made for only eight lakes in the *Atlas*: Narrow, Spring, Island, Tucker,

Baptiste, Wabamun, Buffalo lakes and Long Lake near Athabasca. For these eight lakes, the groundwater contribution ranged from 4% to 49% (average of 18%) of the total water inputs. The greatest groundwater input was estimated for Spring Lake just west of Edmonton. The quality of groundwater may be quite different from that of surface inflows, partly because the area that contributes groundwater to a lake may be much larger and poorly related to the area contributing surface runoff. Although groundwater inputs (and outputs) may be important, they are difficult to quantify and they have not been included in the mean annual inflow values presented in the lake descriptions.

Biophysical Features of the Drainage Basin

The shape and depth of a lake is largely determined by the underlying bedrock and surficial deposits laid down during the ice age thousands of years ago. These features, plus the climate, soils and vegetation in the drainage basin all affect the quality of water in the lake, which in turn has a strong effect on the plant life, fish and wildlife that inhabit it and determine the water use and recreational potential of that lake.

Bedrock

Bedrock is the continuous layer of rock underlying the soil and unconsolidated surficial deposits on the earth. Some bedrock is sedimentary, formed by the sedimentation of silt and organic matter under seas and lakes; other rock may form as lava from volcanoes or from layers of volcanic ash, or it may form when layers of molten rock harden underground. Bedrock in Alberta is primarily sedimentary and consists of layers of sandstone, siltstone, shale, coal and limestone. In the eastern part of Alberta, bedrock strata are fairly flat, but in the western area it has been greatly shifted, folded, tilted and faulted by the formation of the Rocky Mountains.

The oldest bedrock underlying Alberta was first laid down in Precambrian times, beginning 3 500 million years before the present when most of Alberta was covered by an ocean inundating the land from the west. The repeated inundations and exposures across the ages of the land that is now Alberta are described in Table 2, as are comments regarding conspicuous biological features that occurred in the area. Figure 3 shows a cross-section of Alberta and indicates the present-day position of the bedrock strata. The bedrock formations underlying each lake and reservoir are presented in Table 1 of each lake description.

Surficial Deposits

The present configuration of the bedrock of Alberta was virtually fully established two million years ago. Since then, during the Quaternary Period, there were four ice ages when huge ice caps formed in the Arctic regions and began to flow southward over large areas of Eurasia and North America. The first three advances of ice were located around Hudson Bay and spread outward and southward as far as the confluence of the Ohio and Missouri rivers. The ice flowed westward across Saskatchewan and may have crossed what is now Alberta's boundary; however, until about 35 000 years ago, most of Alberta remained an ice-free corridor.

Finally, in the last great glaciation, called the Wisconsin, sheets of ice up to 1 600 m thick began to grind across Alberta from the east and north. At the same time, another ice sheet massed in the Rocky Mountains and flowed eastward to coalesce with the ice sheet from the north. The two sheets then flowed southward, parallel to the Rocky Mountains, until all of Alberta was under ice except for high mountain peaks, the highest parts of the Cypress Hills and patches of the Porcupine Hills.

As the ice sheets advanced and retreated over Alberta, they sculptured the land, carving and eroding the mountains, moving rocks and depositing gravel and silts until the landscape was virtually as we see it today. The last retreat of the ice, beginning 12 000 years ago, left behind enduring impressions on Alberta. As the ice sheets melted and retreated, they left a blanket of glacial till up to 100 m thick over

most of Alberta east of the mountains. In southern Alberta, the till forms a ground moraine, leaving a gently undulating surface. Water drains into gentle depressions to form shallow lakes like Eagle and Tyrrell lakes. In central Alberta, the terrain is more hummocky and rolling; examples are found around Red Deer, from Elk Island National Park to Cooking Lake and west of Stony Plain. In some areas, large blocks of ice were left by the retreating glacier and till piled up around the ice so when the ice melted, holes, or kettles, were left in the landscape. Small lakes fed and drained by groundwater now fill these kettles; examples are Spring, Eden and Hubbles lakes. In some areas, glacial till blocked preglacial channels, impounding water to form lakes like Crowsnest, Rock and Baptiste.

As the glaciers melted, they produced huge volumes of meltwater, which cut through the till plain and formed long, steep-sided, flat-floored river valleys. Many of these valleys are now dry, or nearly dry. An example on the southern prairie can be seen where Verdigris, Etzikom, Chin and Forty Mile coulees are part of one series of meltwater channels. A number of these channels are now dammed to form offstream storage reservoirs, for example, Milk River Ridge, Crawling Valley, Chin and Forty Mile Coulee reservoirs. Another conspicuous meltwater channel is now followed by the Battle River and includes Driedmeat and Coal lakes. Examples of lakes in smaller meltwater channels in northern Alberta include Long (near Athabasca), Narrow, Long (near Boyle) and Amisk lakes.

Ecoregions

Ecoregions are a classification of the natural zones within Alberta that are defined primarily by geographic and climatic features. The geography and climate subsequently affect the vegetation able to grow in an area, which in turn affects the soils that develop.

An ecoregion was defined in 1969 by Lacate as "an area characterized by a distinct climate as expressed by vegetation." The ecoregions of Alberta were recently mapped by Strong and Leggat (1981) of the provincial government and are shown in Figure 4; their features are summarized in Table 3. Much of the foothills and northern parts of the province have been mapped in detail by the provincial government; reports on these areas were used to describe the drainage basins of several lakes in the *Atlas*, for example, the Kananaskis Lakes, Chain Lakes Reservoir and Gleniffer Lake. Soil surveys done by the Alberta Research Council present detailed mapping of the agricultural areas of the province, and these surveys were used to describe the soils and terrain of the basins of many lakes in the *Atlas*.

In general, the southeast part of the province is warmer, has lower precipitation and higher evaporation rates than the rest of the province. Three grassland ecoregions are found there. The **Short Grass Ecoregion** is the most arid, and the natural vegetation is mostly grama and spear grass. There are few natural lakes in this ecoregion but the naturally rich soil and warm climate have led to high demand for irrigation water. Several offstream reservoirs have been built in this ecoregion, including Crawling Valley, Little Bow Lake and Lake Newell reservoirs. Forming an arc around the Short Grass Ecoregion is the **Mixed Grass Ecoregion**, which supports natural vegetation of spear, grama and wheat grasses. There are also few natural lakes in this area, and most water bodies are offstream reservoirs for storage of irrigation water. Examples include McGregor Lake, Travers Reservoir and Tyrrell Lake (Fig. 5). The **Fescue Grass Ecoregion** curves around the Mixed Grass Ecoregion; rough fescue and Parry oat grass are the dominant natural plants. One of the few natural lakes in this area is Eagle Lake; most water bodies are irrigation reservoirs including tiny Chestermere Lake and large St. Mary Reservoir.

The slightly wetter and cooler area of central Alberta falls within the **Aspen Parkland Ecoregion**. Typified by groves of trembling aspen, it is divided into two subregions. The Groveland Subregion is in the southern and eastern portion where the climate is drier than to the north and west. Fescue grasslands dominate and aspen groves occupy only about 15% of the area, occurring where moisture is available such as in depressions, in coulees and on north-facing slopes. The Aspen Subregion is the northern and western portion where dense forests of trembling aspen are interspersed with small

Table 2. Geological Time Chart

Era	Period	Epoch	Million years before present	Physical conditions now and biological features in region now Alberta
Cenozoic	Quaternary	Recent	0.01	Present Conditions
		Pleistocene		3 ice-ages brought ice from the northeast over eastern Alberta. The 4th (Wisconsin) brought ice from northeast and from the mountains; 35 000 years ago all Alberta except high mountain peaks, the Cypress Hills and parts of Porcupine Hills were covered with ice up to 1 600 m thick. The ice began to retreat 12 000 years ago. Most life was pushed south by ice, then plants and animals returned as the ice retreated.
			1.8	
	Tertiary	Pliocene	6	From the Eocene to the Pliocene, the elevation of the Great Plains resulted in the development of grasslands over southern Alberta. Mammals became the dominant animals, including horses, camels, mammoths and mastodons.
		Miocene	22	
		Oligocene	40	
		Eocene		Rocky Mountains started to uplift. Rock from BC lifted and shifted several miles east over Alberta. Mammals, fish.
			55	
		Paleocene		Central BC rising, debris washed eastward into Alberta and created Paskapoo Formation. Bivalves, gastropods, fish, mammals, amphibians, reptiles, plants. Fish very abundant in ocean.
			65	
Mesozoic	Cretaceous			Late-Cretaceous: Mowry Sea connected to Gulf of Mexico, later also connected to Arctic Ocean, later Alberta rose. Dinosaurs abundant in areas now Drumheller and Dinosaur Provincial Park. Early mammals such as marsupials appeared, also coal-forming plants. Mid-Cretaceous: McKenzie Mountains rose. Alberta flooded by land-locked Mowry Sea. Fish, ammonites, bivalves, plesiosaurs, and mosasaurs (early marine birds), coal-forming plants.

TABLE 2 CONTINUED

Era	Period	Epoch	Million years before present	Physical conditions now and biological features in region now Alberta
				Early-Cretaceous: Alberta rose, end of flooding by Pacific Ocean; later the Coast Range rose, Alberta flooded from Arctic. Most coal-forming plants abundant, McMurray Tar Sands laid down.
	Jurassic		140	Alberta flooded from Pacific, northern area dry. Ichthyosaurs, fish, ammonites, coal-forming plants. Dinosaurs appeared in late Jurassic.
	Triassic		195	Eastern Alberta dry, western edge flooded by ocean. Ammonites, coelocanth fish, ichthyosaurs appeared.
			230	
Paleozoic	Permian			Eastern Alberta dry, western edge flooded by ocean. Fish, few corals, life on ocean bottom diminished.
	Carboniferous		280	Alberta under ocean. Corals, fish. Oil beds formed.
	Devonian		345	Alberta dry, then slowly flooded. Corals, fish appeared. Land plants, early insects, amphibians developed. Major oil beds formed.
	Silurian		395	Alberta under ocean. Corals, trilobites and brachiopods.
	Ordovician		435	Alberta dry then reflooded from ocean. Corals, ostracods and the first primitive vertebrates appeared.
	Cambrian		500	Ocean over most of Alberta. Trilobites, sponges and seaweeds.
			570	
Precambrian	Proterozoic			Most of Alberta under ocean. Sediment eroded from northern and southern land masses was deposited on the sea bottom and formed Precambrian rocks.
	Archeozoic			The only life-forms were some bacteria and blue-green algae. Some multi-cellular organisms developed near the end of Proterozoic Period.
	Azoic		3000	Ocean over Alberta. No life.
			3500	

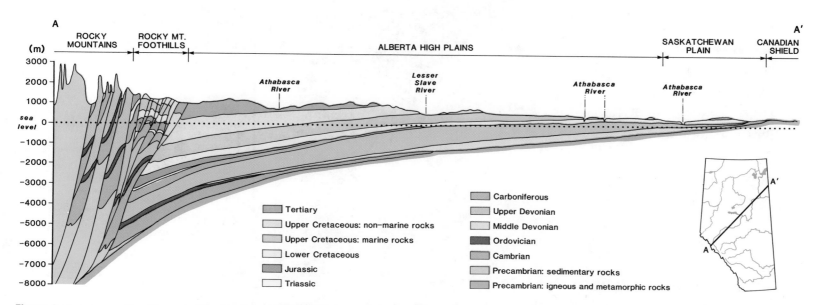

Figure 3. A cross-section through Alberta shows the tilted layers of bedrock under most of the province and the folding and uplifting of bedrock in the Rocky Mountains. SOURCE: adapted from the *Atlas of Alberta* (1969).

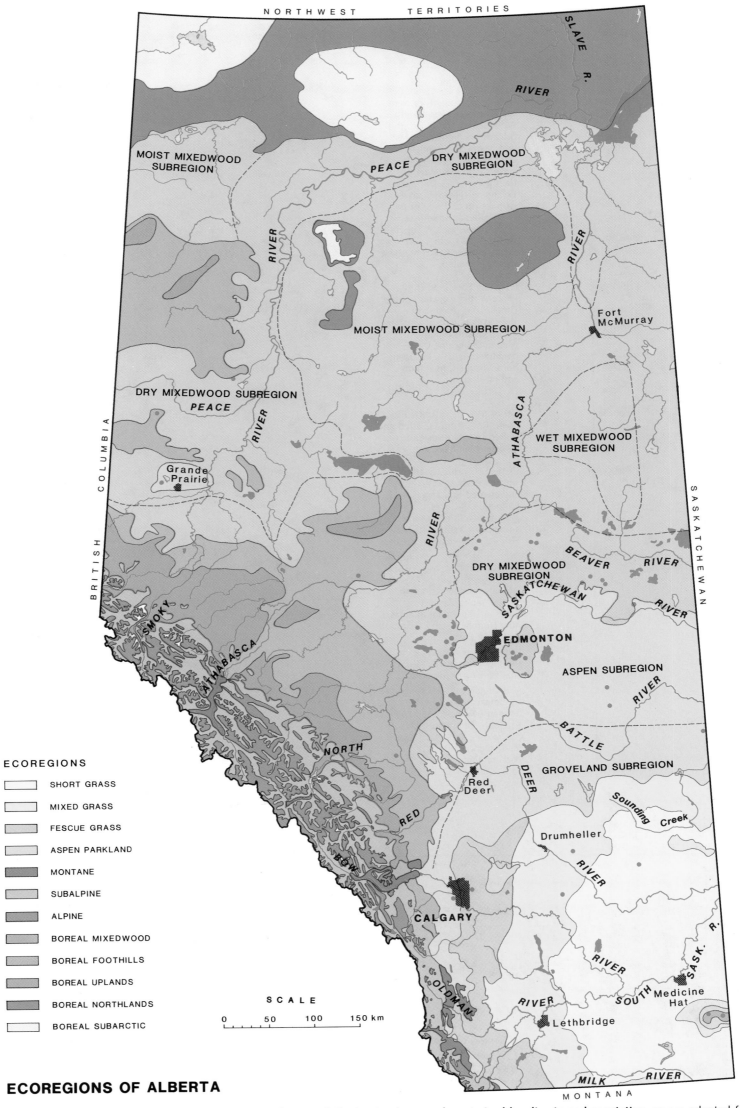

SLAVE R.

RIVER

MOIST MIXEDWOOD
SUBREGION

PEACE

DRY MIXEDWOOD
SUBREGION

RIVER

RIVER

MOIST MIXEDWOOD SUBREGION

Fort
McMurray

DRY MIXEDWOOD SUBREGION

PEACE

RIVER

ATHABASCA

WET MIXEDWOOD
SUBREGION

BRITISH COLUMBIA

Grande
Prairie

SASKATCHEWAN

RIVER

BEAVER

RIVER

DRY MIXEDWOOD
SUBREGION

SASKATCHEWAN

RIVER

SMOKY

EDMONTON

ATHABASCA

ASPEN SUBREGION

RIVER

BATTLE

NORTH

GROVELAND SUBREGION

DEER

Red
Deer

RED

Sounding

Creek

Drumheller

RIVER

BOW

CALGARY

ECOREGIONS

	SHORT GRASS
	MIXED GRASS
	FESCUE GRASS
	ASPEN PARKLAND
	MONTANE
	SUBALPINE
	ALPINE
	BOREAL MIXEDWOOD
	BOREAL FOOTHILLS
	BOREAL UPLANDS
	BOREAL NORTHLANDS
	BOREAL SUBARCTIC

SOUTH

SASK. R.

Medicine
Hat

OLDMAN

RIVER

RIVER

Lethbridge

SCALE

0   50   100   150 km

MILK   RIVER

M O N T A N A

ECOREGIONS OF ALBERTA

Figure 4. Alberta includes portions of twelve ecoregions that are distinct natural zones characterized by climate and vegetation. SOURCE: adapted from Strong and Leggat (1981).

Table 3. Features of Ecoregions in Alberta

Ecoregion	Predominant Natural Vegetation	Predominant Soil	Mean Temp. May-Sept. (°C)	Frost-Free Period (days)	Total Precipitation (mm)
Short Grass	Grama-Spear Grass	Brown Chernozem	15.0	115	330
Mixed Grass	Spear-Grama-Wheat-Grass	Dark Brown Chernozem	14.5	110	400
Fescue Grass	Rough Fescue-Parry Oatgrass	Black Chernozem	12.5	90	420
Aspen Parkland	Aspen and Rough Fescue Grass	Dark gray and Black Chernozem	13.0	95	460
Montane	Douglas Fir	Eutric Brunisol	11.5	75	570
Subalpine	Lodgepole Pine-Engelmann Spruce	Eutric Brunisol	9.5	15	720
Alpine	Heaths-heather	Brunisol	6.5	—	760
Boreal Mixedwood	Aspen-Balsam Poplar	Gray Luvisol	12.0	85	470
Boreal Foothills	Aspen-Balsam Poplar-Lodgepole Pine-White and Black Spruce	Gray Luvisol	11.5	80	610
Boreal Uplands	Lodgepole Pine-White and Black Spruce	Gray Luvisol	10.0	75	600
Boreal Northlands	Aspen White Spruce	Gray Luvisol	11.0	85	410
Boreal Subarctic	Black Spruce-Sphagnum	Organic Cryosol	10.0	—	300+

Figure 5. Tyrrell Lake is situated in the Mixed Grass Ecoregion. Photo by D. Huet.

areas of fescue grassland. The Aspen Parkland is one of the most productive farming areas of Alberta, and much of it has now been cleared and plowed. Natural lakes are fairly numerous in this ecoregion, including Beaverhill, Buffalo and Pine lakes. The location of the Aspen Parkland between the dry grasslands and moist boreal areas results in quite variable amounts of runoff from year to year. This is reflected in lake water levels which exhibit fairly wide natural fluctuations. To combat the variability in water supply, several dams or weirs have been built to stabilize flows in rivers and creeks, including a dam on Chain Lakes Reservoir, and weirs on Coal and Driedmeat lakes. Other lakes have weirs in an attempt to stabilize their water levels, for example, Iosegun Lake. Three others, Gull, McLeod and Lac St. Cyr, have water diverted into them to stabilize their levels.

If one were to travel from the prairie up into the mountains in the southern part of the province, one would encounter several ecoregions. At lower elevations in some southern areas is the **Montane Ecoregion,** which is typified by Douglas fir trees. Examples of lakes in the Montane Ecoregion are Beauvais and Crowsnest lakes and Ghost Reservoir. Higher up in the mountains is the **Subalpine Ecore-**

gion which supports lodgepole pine and Engelmann spruce as the dominant vegetation. Lakes in this ecoregion include the Kananaskis Lakes, Rock Lake and Spray Lakes Reservoir. The highest area is the **Alpine Ecoregion** where the climate is too harsh for tree growth and vegetation is limited to heaths and shrubby willows. Rocky peaks are barren of all vegetation and glaciers top many mountains. No alpine lakes are discussed in detail in the *Atlas*, but runoff and glacial meltwater from the Alpine Ecoregion provide inflow to several lakes and to most of the large onstream reservoirs such as Ghost and St. Mary reservoirs and Gleniffer Lake.

West from Calgary and north and west from Edmonton are the boreal group of ecoregions. The **Boreal Mixedwood Ecoregion** lies north of the Aspen Parkland and covers most of the northern half of the province. This region has higher precipitation and lower evaporation rates than the grasslands or parkland ecoregions. The result is a forest cover of trembling aspen and balsam poplar, and a relative abundance of water. Consequently, the region is dotted with lakes, including large ones like Athabasca, Cold, Utikuma, Peerless and Lesser Slave; medium-sized ones like Wabamun, Pigeon, Cooking,

Figure 6. Beaver Lake is surrounded by trembling aspen, balsam poplar and white spruce typical of the Boreal Mixedwood Ecoregion. Photo by P.A. Mitchell.

Miquelon and Beaver and small ones like Sauer, Eden, Hasse and Twin (Fig. 6).

The **Boreal Foothills Ecoregion** is in the northwest corner of the province and continues southward along the foothills to a point just southwest of Calgary. This region supports a wide variety of tree species; the dominant species in any location varies from trembling aspen and balsam poplar to lodgepole pine, and white and black spruce. Lakes in this area include Buck and Crimson lakes in the south and Moonshine and Musreau lakes to the north near Grande Prairie. There is also a small patch of this ecoregion ringed by Aspen Parkland in the Cypress Hills in southern Alberta. Elkwater and Reesor lakes are in this area. The **Boreal Uplands Ecoregion** lies along the upper foothills north of the Bow River. Trembling aspen and white spruce are the dominant tree species. Lakes in this area tend to be small. There is little information on lakes in the Boreal Uplands Ecoregion and no lakes in this ecoregion are included in the *Atlas*.

The **Boreal Northlands Ecoregion** is found on high plateaus and hills in the northern part of the province. The most abundant trees are trembling aspen and white spruce. There are beautiful lakes in this region, including Gardiner, Namur and Swan, but because the only access to these lakes is by air, little information has been collected on them. In the *Atlas*, only the north shore of Lake Athabasca lies in this ecoregion.

The cold **Boreal Subarctic Ecoregion** supports black spruce and *Sphagnum* moss. Permafrost underlies much of this ecoregion. There are numerous lakes, but little is known about them. No lakes from this ecoregion are included in the *Atlas*.

Soils

The soils around a lake and in its drainage basin have an effect on the lake by contributing nutrients and by influencing the rate of runoff from the land into the lake. Soils that occur in the drainage basin are discussed in each lake description in the *Atlas*. Information regarding soils was usually derived from the soil surveys done by the Alberta Soil Survey (Alberta Research Council and Agriculture Canada Soil Survey Unit) for areas of the province where agriculture is the primary land use. Ecological Land Classification and Evaluation Reports prepared by Alberta Forestry, Lands and Wildlife (formerly Alberta Energy and Natural Resources) provided data on soils in the foothills, mountain and northern portions of the province.

There are seven major groups of soils in Alberta: Chernozemic, Luvisolic, Brunisolic, Regosolic, Gleysolic, Organic and Solonetzic.

Chernozemic soils develop under grasslands on a wide variety of parent materials in well-drained to imperfectly-drained sites. Brown Chernozemic soils are found where there are short grasses and severe moisture deficiency; Black Chernozemic soils occur in less dry areas. Chernozemic soils are usually excellent for agricultural production.

Luvisolic soils develop on a wide variety of parent materials under mixed deciduous-coniferous forests. They are generally found in imperfectly-drained to moderately well-drained sites.

Brunisolic soils develop on imperfectly drained to well-drained sites on various types of parent material. They develop under coniferous or deciduous forests.

Regosolic soils occur in a wide variety of ecological conditions where natural disturbance has inhibited the development of soil horizons. They are common near river beds, on colluvium, on steep and actively eroding slopes and on shallow parent material over bedrock in the mountains.

Gleysolic soils occur in areas of poor drainage where there is prolonged inundation or a high groundwater table.

Organic soils occur in areas of extremely poor drainage. They form by the accumulation of dead organic material such as sedge or moss peat.

Solonetzic soils develop on saline parent material in imperfectly drained to moderately well-drained sites. They form under grassland vegetation, usually in association with Chernozemic soils.

A drainage basin's soils affect a lake by influencing the rate of runoff and the amount and proportion of various nutrients and ions that move from the soils to the lake. However, little research has yet been done in Alberta to directly link the soil types present in the basin to the chemical composition of the receiving lake.

Land Use

The use of the land in a drainage basin has a direct bearing on the quality and quantity of water entering a lake. As discussed in the Water Quality section, the quantities of nutrients such as phosphorus transported from a hectare of urban land are several times that transported from a hectare of cleared or crop land, which in turn are several times greater than nutrient quantities transported from a hectare of forest. The rate that water runs off cleared land is faster than from forested land, so lake level patterns may change as forests are cleared. The distribution of forest/bush and cleared or open areas is marked on the drainage basin map for each lake. Data were taken from National Topographic Series maps, usually at 1:50 000 scale, and air photos taken since 1980 were used to update this information. Alpine areas and glaciers are also marked on the drainage basin maps, as are recreation, residential and urban areas. The major land uses in each drainage basin are discussed in the individual lake descriptions.

The increase in Alberta's population over the last 80 years has had a definite effect on the drainage basins of most Alberta lakes. As settlers came to Alberta, more and more land was cleared for crop production, pasture and intensive agriculture such as feedlots. Increased population also brings increased pressure for recreation, and cottages spring up around lakes. With the cottages comes more cleared land, problems of appropriate waste disposal, and fertilized lawns sloping toward the water—all of which may increase nutrient input to lakes. To protect popular lakes from degradation and inappropriate development, Alberta Environment established the Regulated Lake Shoreland Development Operation Regulations in 1977. These regulations prohibited further development on 15 lakes until a lake management plan and an area structure plan were prepared for each lake and adopted by the local municipalities. Area structure plans suggest ways to minimize environmental impacts and conflicts in lake uses.

Most of the development around lakes is recreational, especially in central Alberta where lakes such as Sylvan, Pigeon, Wabamun, Pine and Chestermere are fairly densely ringed by cottages and resorts. Commercial and industrial uses do not exert a major influence on most of the lakes in Alberta. Some of the lakes in the Cold Lake area, including Ethel, Wolf and Muriel lakes, provide water for heavy oil extraction. McLeod Lake also provides water for the oil industry, and Wabamun Lake supplies cooling water for a coal-fired generating plant. The reservoirs built in the mountains and foothills (Spray Lakes, Minnewanka and Ghost) are managed for hydroelectric power generation, whereas the irrigation reservoirs such as St. Mary, Milk River Ridge and Crawling Valley reservoirs are managed to supply water during the growing season. Logging in the foothills and northern areas of the province has removed forest cover in some drainage basins, as has strip mining for coal, especially in the Wabamun Lake area and in the foothills near Grande Cache and Cadomin.

J.M. Crosby

LAKE BASIN CHARACTERISTICS

A lake basin is a water-filled bowl or depression in the surface of the landscape. With few exceptions, the lakes we now see in Alberta were formed when the last Pleistocene ice sheet retreated from Alberta about 12 000 years ago. As the glacier retreated, large collections of rock debris, called moraines, formed basins or dammed meltwater channels, and new lakes were born. In some areas, large blocks of ice were trapped in the outwash material or in the moraines that were left as the glaciers retreated. These ice blocks may have taken hundreds of years to melt. When they did, they left large holes in the blanket of glacial till. Some of the holes filled with water to form kettle or "pothole" lakes like Dillberry, Sauer and Eden (Fig. 7). Other lakes, such as Rock, Baptiste and Crowsnest, were formed when preglacial river valleys were dammed by moraines. Lake Athabasca was formed when movement of the glacial ice sheet scoured pre-existing valleys.

In areas where there are few natural lakes but a need for water storage, new lakes, called **reservoirs**, were built when dams were constructed across river valleys or coulees (Fig. 8). Reservoirs are similar to lakes in many ways, but their water level usually fluctuates more widely, and often the quantity of water flowing through them in a year is higher.

Lake Basin Morphology

Alberta lakes and reservoirs vary considerably in their size, shape, bottom form and depth, or **morphology**. To a large extent, the origin of the lake basin determined its present-day shape and depth. Many of the depressions left by the retreating glacier are shallow and wide, and therefore lakes formed in them are relatively shallow, such as Buffalo and Beaverhill lakes. Kettle lakes may be deep for their small size, and lakes in preglacial valleys also may be quite deep. Those formed in meltwater channels tend to be long and narrow, such as Battle, Narrow and Amisk lakes. The shape of the lake bottom is also influenced by events that have occurred since the last glacier retreated. For example, a lake with a large watershed, high productivity or a large inflow may have filled in considerably over the past 12 000 years. In contrast, lakes with small watersheds, low productivity and only intermittent inflows, such as Hubbles Lake, are likely to have a thinner layer of bottom sediments. The bottom sediments in Wabamun Lake are nearly 16–m thick in the centre of the basin, and most of this material eroded from the watershed over these years. The lake may not have been much deeper at one time, however. Evidence from core studies suggests the lake has gone through periods of both high and low water levels, depending on the climate at the time. Pollen analysis from other lakes, including Moore, shows that the climate was warmer and lake levels were generally lower between 9 000 and 4 000 years ago than during the last 4 000 years.

The morphology of a lake has a great influence on its ecological characteristics. A description of the lake's size, shape, depth and volume is fundamental information for the lake scientist, and is of interest to anglers and other lake users as well. Such information is best obtained from a map of the depth contours of the lake bottom, or **bathymetric map**. During a bathymetric survey, personnel in a boat or on the ice in winter measure depths along numerous transect lines that stretch across the lake from shore to shore (Fig. 9). For small lakes, depth may be measured simply with a weighted measuring line, but most modern surveys use sonar equipment to record

Figure 7. Lake Eden, a kettle or pothole lake, was formed when water filled a hole left by the melting of a large block of glacial ice. Photo by P.A. Mitchell.

Figure 8. Ghost Reservoir Dam impounds waters of the Ghost and Bow rivers. Photo by P.A. Mitchell.

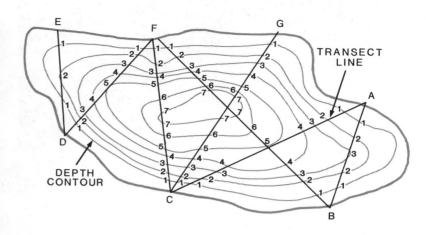

Figure 9. During a bathymetric survey of a lake, depths are measured along transect lines. When the map is constructed, points of equal depth are connected by contour lines.

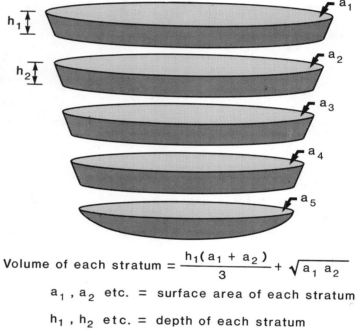

$$\text{Volume of each stratum} = \frac{h_1(a_1 + a_2)}{3} + \sqrt{a_1\, a_2}$$

a_1, a_2 etc. = surface area of each stratum

h_1, h_2 etc. = depth of each stratum

Volume of Lake = sum of volumes of strata

Figure 10. The total volume of a lake is estimated by calculation of the volume of each layer or stratum of water between depth contours, then summing the volumes of each strata.

depth continuously along the transects. No matter how depth is measured, it is essential that the precise location of all depth measurements are known so that they may be accurately plotted on an outline map of the lake. For small lakes, simple survey equipment on shore or in a boat may be used to position depth measurements. However, for large lakes, modern surveys are conducted with shore-based electronic positioning systems that determine the position of the boat at all times, even at varying speed and wind drift. All bathymetric maps have some limitations. Depths are recorded along transects that are usually no closer than 100 m, and may be considerably farther apart on large lakes. Therefore, the point of maximum depth may be missed, or small mounds or other irregularities on the lake bottom may not be recorded. In addition, the depths indicated on the map were recorded at the water level on the date of the survey. If the water level has changed since then, the depth must be adjusted accordingly. For lakes in the *Atlas*, the bathymetric maps constructed since about 1978 most accurately represent their bottom contours.

To construct the bathymetric map, selected depths (for example, 2, 4, 6, 8 and 10 m) are interpolated from field measurements and the interpolations for each depth are connected by continuous lines, which represent depth contours. The area of the lake is determined with a **planimeter**, a device that calculates area or distance as it traces a contour line. **Volume** or **capacity** may then be calculated from the area of each depth contour and the height of the water stratum between successive contours (Fig. 10). The total lake volume is the sum of the volumes of each stratum.

Once the area and capacity are determined, area/capacity curves are drawn. They are used to estimate a new area and volume if the level of the lake should change, or they may be used to estimate the area of a portion of the lake at a certain depth, such as the area of aquatic plant growth. Most of the area/capacity curves for lakes in the *Atlas* are accurate only for elevations below the geodetic or assumed elevation of the water on the date the bathymetric survey was made.

The mean or average depth of a lake is calculated by dividing the lake's volume by its area. The mean depth is one of the best indicators of the morphology of a lake, and it tells a great deal about its limnology or water quality characteristics as well. If the mean depth is shallow, the lake water will mix from the surface to the bottom on windy days. The bottom sediments may be a source of nutrients, which will enhance productivity, potentially reduce dissolved oxygen levels, and thereby contribute to the risk of winterkill or summerkill. For example, the mean depth of Cooking Lake is 1.7 m and that of Driedmeat Lake is 2.2 m; both are highly productive. Cooking Lake cannot sustain game fish populations, and Driedmeat Lake also winterkills frequently. On the other hand, lakes that have a deeper

Figure 11. Sediments cover the lake bottom. Near shore, the lake bottom may be sandy or rocky. Photo by P.A. Mitchell.

the surrounding land or settle from the air. Suspended sediment particles that are carried into the lake by streams quickly settle out once they reach the quiet water of the lake. Thus, the lake acts as a trap for soil particles, nutrients, organic material or pollutants originating in the watershed. The finest sediments are resuspended by wave action near shore, and gradually move toward the deepest areas of the lake. Over time, there is a greater accumulation of bottom sediments in deep water than in shallow water near shore. Even in productive lakes, such as Wabamun, Buck and Pigeon, a firm sand bottom may be present in the shallow water if it is exposed to wave action. But within stands of emergent vegetation or along shorelines protected from wind, the surface of the sediments is loose and yellowish-brown. Below this surface layer, the sediments may be dark greenish-gray and have an unpleasant odour.

In areas of the lake bottom where there is sufficient light penetration and other conditions are suitable, rooted aquatic plants will grow. The **littoral zone** extends from the shoreline to the greatest depth that plants will grow in a particular lake; light penetration is usually the most important factor that determines this depth. The depth of the littoral zone has been measured in several Alberta lakes during plant surveys conducted from 1978 to 1984 by Alberta Environment. For example, the littoral zone extended to 3.5 m in highly productive Baptiste and Nakamun lakes, 4 m in moderately productive Lac St. Cyr and Skeleton Lake, and 5 m in less productive Ethel Lake. The deepest recorded growth of aquatic plants during these surveys was 7 m in Muriel Lake, the lake with the clearest water of the lakes surveyed at the time. The depth of the littoral zone has not been measured for many lakes in the *Atlas*. However, University of Alberta researchers have developed a formula to predict this depth from a measurement of the lake's transparency (see Section 1, "Estimate of depth of the littoral zone in a lake", in the Appendix).

Water Balance

The volume of water in a lake changes in response to the quantity of water that enters and leaves it over a given period of time. An annual **water balance** for a particular lake is calculated by adding all of the inflows over a year, and subtracting the outflows, including evaporation. If the water level in the lake at the end of the year is different from that at the beginning of the year, the change in volume of water that this fluctuation represents must be included in the annual water balance.

Water enters a natural lake through direct precipitation onto the lake surface, runoff from the surrounding land and groundwater inflow. Reservoirs often have an additional input of water, as a diversion from another basin. Water is lost from a lake through evaporation (including **evapotranspiration**, the loss of water from the leaves of aquatic vegetation) and surface or underground outflow (see Fig. 2).

Both precipitation and evaporation were calculated with data obtained from Environment Canada climatological stations closest to the lake. The average annual amount of precipitation that falls in the area (reported as depth in millimetres) may be multiplied by the surface area of the lake to obtain the total volume of water that enters by direct precipitation. The rate of evaporation for a particular location was not measured directly, but was calculated from data on sunshine, temperature and relative humidity with an equation developed by Environment Canada. The loss of water by evapotranspiration has not been estimated for any lake in the *Atlas*, but it is likely to be significant only for small lakes with large areas of emergent vegetation.

Water also enters and leaves a lake over the surface of the surrounding land. Rain or snow falls in the drainage basin and gathers in streams or moves directly toward the lake within soils (subsurface flow). Only a portion of the precipitation that falls in the basin finds its way to the lake. Reservoirs may have additional inflows via canals. The total inflow volume reported in each lake description is based on estimates of annual runoff depth measured at stream gauging stations nearest the lake. Inflow and outflow are measured directly on most reservoirs, and outflow is also measured on some lakes. There is rarely more than one outlet on a lake, except where people have

mean depth may rarely or never winterkill, even though they are eutrophic or productive. Examples are Pinehurst Lake (mean depth of 12 m) and Amisk Lake (mean depth of 15.5 m). Of all the lakes discussed in the *Atlas*, Cold Lake has the greatest mean depth (50 m) and is one of the least productive.

A comparison of mean and maximum depths provides information on the shape of the lake. For example, Crimson and Spring lakes have relatively deep maximum depths (9.1 m for both), but shallow mean depths (2.2 and 1.9 m, respectively). These lakes have very small deep areas, but large areas of shallow water. A large ratio may also result when there is a deep, small basin attached to a large, shallow main basin, as in Island Lake (maximum depth of 18 m, mean depth of 3.7 m). Three-quarters of the lakes and reservoirs in the *Atlas* have maximum depths that are less than 3 times the mean depth. Lake Athabasca has the greatest depth relative to mean depth (ratio of 6).

The shoreline length is also useful for describing the morphology of a lake. It is measured on the map of the lake by tracing the shoreline, or intersection of the land and water, with a map-measuring wheel or an electronic planimeter. Lakes or reservoirs with long shorelines compared to their area would be those with many bays, peninsulas and islands. Reservoirs formed in stream or meltwater channels with many side channels often have very long shorelines relative to their area. Examples include Crawling Valley, Travers and St. Mary reservoirs. Those with the shortest shorelines relative to area are round, with little or no development of bays. The most perfectly round lakes in the *Atlas* are tiny Twin Lake and large Calling Lake.

The Lake Bottom

The lake bottom is covered in a layer of mud called sediments, the soil of the lake (Fig. 11). This material contains organic matter (decomposing plants and animals), mineral matter like clays and carbonates that would be found also in soil, and inorganic material derived from plants and animals, such as the glasslike skeletons of diatoms. These sediment particles may originate within the lake, wash in from

altered outflows or constructed diversions. If a lake originally had more than one outlet, differential erosion and cutting of the sill over hundreds of years would allow one to take precedence over the other. Reservoirs often have two or more outlets—one to maintain flow in the creek or river downstream of the reservoir, and the others to supply water for irrigation, power generation or other needs. Examples are Travers, St. Mary and Spray Lakes reservoirs.

Lakes may be part of groundwater flow systems. Water may enter and leave a lake underground, via bedrock aquifers and porous lenses within surficial materials. But the groundwater exchange with a lake is difficult to quantify, and therefore groundwater-lake interactions have been studied on only a few Alberta lakes. Detailed groundwater studies have been carried out by researchers at the University of Alberta on three lakes in the *Atlas*: Baptiste, Wabamun and Narrow lakes. In these studies, groundwater was estimated to contribute 13%, 5% and 30%, respectively, of the total water input. The first two studies were based on detailed simulation models, the latter was based on several different techniques, which included measurements made in the lake with devices called seepage meters, a detailed water balance and computer models. Within-lake measurements of groundwater input have been made at Buffalo, Spring, Island, Long (near Athabasca) and Tucker lakes by University of Alberta researchers. The average estimate was 19% of total water inflow, with values extending from 4% to 49%. In the two cases where groundwater inflow has been estimated from both detailed models and within-lake measurements, the results were very comparable in Baptiste Lake (13% and 11%), but less similar in Narrow Lake (30% and 16%). For some lakes, the outflow of lake water into groundwater systems may be an important component of the water balance. For example, studies conducted on Wabamun Lake for Alberta Environment suggest that a large volume of water (40% of total annual outflow) must leave the lake underground, otherwise the lake water would be more saline than it is due to concentration of salts by evaporation.

Data on inflows, outflows and volume for a particular lake may be used to calculate a **water residence time**, or the average time required to completely replace the total volume of the lake with inflowing water, less evaporative losses. To calculate water residence time, the average total volume of the lake is divided by the average annual calculated outflow (precipitation plus runoff from contributing areas of the watershed minus evaporation). For most lakes in the *Atlas*, groundwater exchange was not considered in this calculation because information was lacking. No attempt was made to estimate residence times beyond 100 years. Many lakes in Alberta have very long residence times. For example, 40% of the natural lakes described in this *Atlas* have water residence times that exceed 50 years. Compared to most lakes, reservoirs have short water residence times, because their outflows are large relative to their volume. For example, the residence time of Ghost Reservoir averages 22 days over the year, but it can be as little as 10 days at times of high flow in the Bow River. The average residence time for all reservoirs described in the *Atlas* is two years.

Water Levels

Water levels are measured on many lakes in Alberta by the Water Survey of Canada (Environment Canada) or the Survey Branch of Alberta Environment under the terms of the federal-provincial hydrometric cost sharing agreement (1985). The data points chosen for each water level graph in the *Atlas* include the minimum and maximum level for each year, and several additional high and low points to fill out the annual trend. Also, for a few reservoirs, mean monthly water levels were plotted to depict the seasonal variation in these water bodies. If the amount of water leaving a lake by evaporation, the outlet creek and groundwater is equal to the amount of water entering the lake as precipitation, runoff and groundwater, the water level or lake elevation will remain constant. But water levels are never constant in lakes, because they are influenced by numerous natural forces—wind, sun, rain, snow, beaver activity and changes in the water table—so they fluctuate naturally. Short-term water level fluctuations are dependent on whether a particular season is wet, dry,

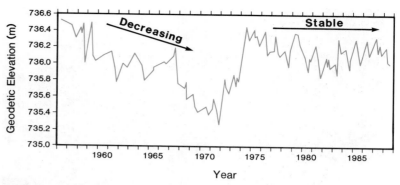

Figure 12. The water level or geodetic elevation in this lake declined in the 1960s, but stabilized after about 1975.

or average. A decline or increase in water level may continue for several consecutive years, depending on the predominant weather patterns. Over the period of record for most lakes, however, the water level shows neither a downward nor an upward trend (Fig. 12).

Some Alberta lakes have no permanent inlet or outlet creeks. Gull, Garner and Dillberry lakes are examples. The water level in these lakes is controlled by a balance between precipitation, diffuse or subsurface runoff, groundwater inflow/outflow and evaporation. Sometimes these closed lakes gradually decline in lake elevation, as have Gull and Miquelon lakes, although the reason for the decline has not been determined.

Lakes attract people, and there is a natural inclination to build houses, cottages and farms near them. But the natural fluctuation of a lake's water level may frustrate lake users—high water may flood property or low water may expose mudflats and inhibit recreation. One approach is to attempt to control the level of the lake with a **weir**, or small dam, on the outlet creek. Such lakes are called **regulated lakes**. But even with a control structure on the outlet, lakes will continue to fluctuate to some extent because the rates of evaporation and precipitation largely control water level in many lakes. During years of low precipitation, there may be insufficient water entering a lake to offset evaporation, and the lake level will decline in spite of a weir. Similarly, during years of excessive precipitation, the level may temporarily rise above the level of the artificial outlet. For large lakes with small outlets, the time required for water to run out of the lake may be several weeks or months, and there is little that can be done to relieve flooding during that time.

For most regulated lakes in Alberta, the new elevation after the weir is built is not greatly different from the natural one, usually less than 1 m higher, and rarely as much as 3 m higher. In some lakes, the sill of the weir may be adjusted by adding or removing stop-logs or by opening gates. Weirs in Alberta are usually made of driven piling and sheet steel, concrete or packed earth and clay (Fig. 13). Twenty-two lakes in the *Atlas* have weirs, including Coal, Driedmeat, Pigeon, Steele, Thunder, Beauvais and Buck. The Kananaskis Lakes are rather a special case as substantial dams were built on both lakes by TransAlta Utilities Corporation to store water and to manage the outflow for electric power generation. The water level of both lakes was raised over 10 m by these structures, but they are regarded as regulated lakes rather than reservoirs because they were naturally large, deep lakes and their size was not greatly changed.

Sometimes the inflow to a lake is modified to further stabilize the water level. Streams from neighbouring drainage basins may be diverted into a lake; for example, Kent Creek is diverted into Lower Kananaskis Lake. Water may be pumped into a lake, such as the diversion from the Blindman River to Gull Lake and from the North Saskatchewan River to Lac St. Cyr.

When a weir is built on the outlet of a lake, even if it is only 1 m high, the outflowing water usually falls in a single cascade, and upstream fish movement is blocked. This is a particular problem in Alberta east of the foothills where the main sport fish is northern pike—a species not renowned for its jumping ability! To overcome this problem, Fish and Wildlife Division, Alberta Environment and the

Figure 13. The weir on Steele Lake is a sheet-pile structure equipped with a step-pool fishway. Photo by J.B. Kemper.

Figure 15. St. Mary Reservoir is an onstream reservoir that was created when a dam was built across the St. Mary River. Photo by P.A. Mitchell.

Figure 14. The Denil II fishway is a long chute with interior baffles to slow the water for fish passage. Photo by J.B. Kemper.

University of Alberta have designed and tested various types of fishways. The most common one is the step-pool fishway: instead of one large cascade, a series of pools are built, each separated by a small cascade that can be negotiated by northern pike. Regulated lakes with weirs and step-pool fishways include Driedmeat, Sturgeon, Steele, and Gregoire lakes. Another fishway, the Denil II, is built as a long, sloping chute with interior baffles to slow the flow of water (Fig. 14). Denil II fishways can be found on Lesser Slave and Iosegun lakes.

Reservoirs

In southern Alberta, where precipitation is abundant in the mountains but scarce on the prairies, reservoirs have been built to store water for various purposes. A reservoir is created when one or more dams are built to block the natural flow of water or to impound water that is imported into a basin. As a general guideline, a weir impounds a proportionally small amount of water compared to natural conditions and the water body it controls is called a regulated lake; a dam is a larger structure that impounds a proportionally large amount of water and the water body it creates is called a reservoir.

The reservoirs in Alberta can be divided into two types based on the source of water: onstream and offstream. **Onstream reservoirs** are those created when a dam is built across a river; most of the water in the reservoir comes from that river. Examples of onstream reservoirs are Gleniffer Lake, which was created by Dickson Dam across the Red Deer River; Ghost Reservoir, which was created by Ghost Dam across the Bow River below its confluence with the Ghost River; St. Mary Reservoir, which was created by St. Mary Dam built across the St. Mary River (Fig. 15); and Glenmore Reservoir, which was created by Glenmore Dam across the Elbow River. Onstream reservoirs are usually long and narrow, and the bottom slopes gently from the shallow inflow end toward the deep end near the dam. A delta often forms at the inflow end. The volume of water flowing through onstream reservoirs is usually large, and therefore the exchange of water is rapid. Reservoirs are designed to be filled to a specific level of water under normal conditions. The **full supply level** or FSL is the maximum level that the reservoir normally attains. Water is released from most onstream reservoirs at all times to maintain flow in the downstream portion of the river. Flow is either passed through turbines in the dam, through a spillway or if flows reach flood proportions, over an emergency spillway.

There are three general functions for onstream reservoirs in Alberta: hydroelectric power generation, irrigation water storage and flow regulation. The power generation reservoirs are in the mountains and foothills where the slope of the river is greatest. The reservoirs are filled to capacity in late fall, and water is released through the turbines to meet daily peak power demand through the winter. These reservoirs begin to fill again with spring runoff, but the water level is usually kept below the full supply level to save some storage capacity for flood protection. Some water is released all summer to meet daily peak power demand and to maintain flow in the river downstream. Examples of reservoirs used primarily for power generation include Spray Lakes and Ghost reservoirs. Onstream reservoirs built for the storage of irrigation water or water for municipal use tend to be in the lower foothills regions. They are filled in spring, then drawn down to meet demand—in summer for irrigation water, and all year for municipal use. Examples of onstream water supply reservoirs in the foothills are St. Mary and Glenmore reservoirs. An example of an onstream water supply reservoir on the prairie is Blood Indian Creek Reservoir southeast of Hanna. Onstream reservoirs built to allow management of downstream flow, such as Gleniffer Lake on the Red Deer River, store water in spring and summer and then release it to augment winter flow to meet downstream demands or to relieve problems of low dissolved oxygen concentrations. Chain Lakes Reservoir is similarly operated to augment late summer and winter flow on Willow Creek.

An **offstream reservoir** is created by building a dam across a natural coulee to block drainage. Water is then diverted from a river and brought to the reservoir by gravity or by pumping. All the offstream reservoirs in Alberta are in the southern half of the province and are primarily used to store water for irrigation. These reservoirs are filled in spring when flow in the rivers is high, then water is withdrawn to irrigate crops in the summer. The reservoirs are partially filled again in the fall if flow in the rivers is adequate. Examples of offstream reservoirs in Alberta include Crawling Valley, Milk River Ridge, Little Bow Lake reservoirs, and Chestermere, McGregor and Payne lakes. Travers Reservoir is an "onstream reservoir" in the sense that it fills the valley of the Little Bow River, but it is also an "offstream reservoir" because 97% of its water is diverted to it from the Bow River.

P.A. Mitchell and J.M. Crosby

WATER QUALITY

Water quality concerns most lake users. How does the water taste and smell? Is it clear or green? Can I swim in it or drink it? Lakes described in the *Atlas* vary from the cool, clear Kananaskis Lakes, to the warm, green Nakamun Lake, to the salty, but clear Oliva Lake. Many aspects of lake water are determined by natural features of the drainage basin, local weather patterns, and shape and size of the lake basin. Changes in the drainage basin, such as forest clearing, construction of dams, diversion of water and disposal of industrial, agricultural and domestic wastes also have a direct impact on water quality. Evaluation of lake water depends on how the water is used. A saline lake such as Miquelon has poor water quality for a town's drinking water supply, but excellent water quality for swimming or boating.

Many of the lakes described in the *Atlas* have algal blooms (or "green scum") in summer and have likely been this productive or fertile for millennia. However, detailed water quality information has only been collected for Alberta lakes since 1980. Thus there is relatively little information on the impacts of human settlement on Alberta's lakes, or on deterioration or change in the quality of their water.

Eight lakes described in the *Atlas* have two basins or are two distinct lakes (Amisk, Baptiste, Kananaskis, La Biche, Mann, Ste. Anne, Sandy and Skeleton) and one lake has three basins (Buffalo). In this section, each lake or basin is considered distinct, but there are few water quality data for about 12 other lakes, therefore the total number of lake basins with good water quality data is about 100. Except where noted, the chemistry described is the average for the euphotic zone in the open-water period. When comparisons are made with lakes on the Canadian Shield, data from the Experimental Lakes Area in northwestern Ontario are used.

Major Ions and Related Characteristics

Lake water contains minute amounts of chemicals, often called **salts**. This general term describes chemicals which, when dissolved in water, separate into positively and negatively charged particles called **ions**. Common **cations** (positively charged ions) include calcium (Ca), magnesium (Mg), sodium (Na) and potassium (K); **anions** (negatively charged ions) include bicarbonate (HCO_3), carbonate (CO_3), sulphate (SO_4) and chloride (Cl). The ions may join in various combinations to form salts such as calcium carbonate. The units used for chemicals reported in each lake description are those familiar to most lake scientists—weight per unit volume (mg/L or μg/L). One milligram per litre (mg/L) is equivalent to one part of chemical per one million parts of water; one microgram per litre (μg/L) is equivalent to one part per one billion. Two other measures of chemicals are also used by lake scientists, **micromoles** and **microequivalents** (conversions between these scales are given in Section 2 of the Appendix). A micromole is a measure of the number of atoms per unit volume. A microequivalent is a measure of the charge contributed by that substance. When the major cations and anions in a water sample are expressed as microequivalents and totalled, the groups will be approximately equal.

Water in lakes described in the *Atlas* contains on average about 50% more dissolved substances than do freshwater lakes around the world. These chemicals come with water that runs over the soils and rocks in the drainage basin and percolates below the surface before entering a lake, or fall directly on the lake in rain or snow or with dust. Water in lakes described in the *Atlas* is generally rich in calcium and magnesium from weathering of carbonates. Carbonates are part of the natural buffering capacity in lake water, and consequently protect lakes from acidification by neutralizing acids. In some cases the water may have a strong flavour; in extreme cases such as some of the saline lakes in southeastern Alberta, the shore may even look crusty or salty.

Salinity

Because anions and cations carry electrical charges, water containing them can conduct electricity, and its ability to do so gives a measure of the total quantity of charged particles (ions) dissolved in it. This is known as the **specific conductivity** of water. Another measure of the total ion content of lake water is **total dissolved solids** (TDS). Specific conductivity (or conductivity) is measured with an instrument that passes an electrical current through a sample of the lake water between two platinum electrodes; units are micro-Siemens per centimetre (μS/cm). Total dissolved solids is the weight of salts remaining after filtered lake water is evaporated at 103°C to 105°C, in units of mg/L. In the *Atlas*'s freshwater lakes, total dissolved solids are consistently less than conductivity (62% on average). In saline lakes such as Oliva Lake, TDS exceeds conductivity.

Throughout the world, lake water ranges from very dilute (conductivity less than 10 μS/cm) to more saline than seawater (which has a conductivity of about 32 000 μS/cm). For example, lakes on the Canadian Shield have an average conductivity of 19 μS/cm; these lakes are in hard rock, granite basins and are as dilute as any group of lakes in the world. Lakes described in the *Atlas* have higher salinity (range from 81 to 60 000 μS/cm conductivity or from 50 to 84 000 mg/L TDS) than water found in hard rock basins such as the Canadian Shield. The salinity of lake water described in the *Atlas* is representative of the waters found throughout most of Alberta and regions extending from southern Manitoba to the interior of British Columbia, excluding some lakes in the Rocky Mountains, small lakes on the western edge of the Canadian Shield in the remote northeast corner of Alberta and lakes situated in northern peatlands, none of which is included in the *Atlas*. Lake Athabasca is the only *Atlas* lake which has part of its drainage basin on the Canadian Shield, and it also has the lowest salinity. The distribution of salinity in lake water described in the *Atlas* is presented as a frequency histogram in Figure 16; most lakes (89) have fresh water (defined for the *Atlas* as having TDS less than 500 mg/L), 7 have **slightly saline** water (between 500 and 1000 mg/L TDS), 5 have **moderately saline** water (between 1000 and 5000 mg/L TDS) and 4 have **saline** water (more than 5000 mg/L TDS).

Water from saline lakes not only tastes different from fresh water, but fewer species of plants and animals are found there. When water reaches the salinity of Oliva Lake (twice the salinity of seawater), a white crust is evident along the water's edge. The saline lakes have higher ionic content as a result of two factors: first, they are in a region where evaporation greatly exceeds precipitation (up to three-fold) and thus there is a trend towards concentration of all ions in surface runoff and precipitation. Second, saline lakes have inputs of saline groundwater.

pH

The **pH** indicates the acidity or alkalinity of water. The term pH refers to the concentration of hydrogen ions on a negative logarithmic scale extending from 1 (acidic) to 14 (basic). A decrease of one unit in pH corresponds to a 10–fold increase in the concentration of hydrogen ions. When the pH is less than 7 the solution is acidic, at pH 7 it is neutral, and above this it is alkaline. All of the lake water described in the *Atlas* has pH between 7 and 10 and is thus alkaline. Water that falls in the drainage basin of these lakes flows over rocks and percolates through glacial deposits and soils that are rich in carbonate salts and thus free hydrogen ions are neutralized. The capacity of soils to neutralize hydrogen ions, called **buffering capacity**, is relatively high over much of Alberta. Also, the pH of precipita-

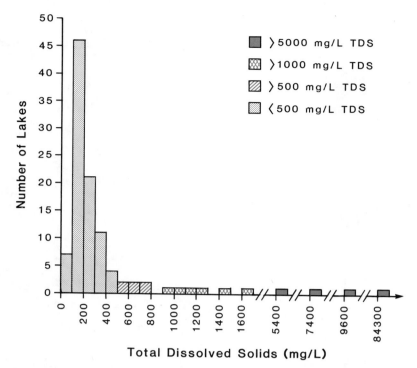

Figure 16. A frequency distribution of average open water, euphotic zone, total dissolved solids (TDS) indicates that the water in most lakes discussed in the *Atlas* have less than 500 mg/L TDS.

tion in this region is relatively high, because the prevailing winds are from the west and the distance from major industrial centres is great. In contrast, lakes in northwestern Ontario, on the Canadian Shield, where rocks and soils are less able to neutralize hydrogen ions, have a pH between 5.6 and 6.7. Similarly, stained or brown water lakes in northern Alberta have a pH as low as 5. Farther east, where lakes are still on the Canadian Shield and near large industrial and urban centres, the pH in lake water can drop to 4 or less due to acidic rain. Many aquatic animals are intolerant of a pH below 5.7, and thus where acidic rain has lowered the pH of lake water below this level, many animal species do not survive. The most devastating impact of acidic rain on aquatic animals has been documented for the lakes in southern Sweden and Norway, which are situated in carbonate-poor, hard rock basins downwind of the polluted air from the rest of Europe. In Alberta, carbonate-rich glacial deposits and soils protect lakewater against such impacts.

Buffering Capacity and Hardness

Total alkalinity is a measure of the capacity of water to neutralize strong acid. It is measured by determining how much strong acid will lower the pH of a water sample to a specific level; units are mg/L equivalent to calcium carbonate ($CaCO_3$). For lakes described in the *Atlas*, this capacity is linked to the amounts of bicarbonate and carbonate ions. In the poorly buffered lakes on the Canadian Shield, total alkalinity is generally less than 15 mg/L $CaCO_3$. In brown water lakes in northern Alberta total alkalinity can be less than 5 mg/L $CaCO_3$. In contrast, the range of total alkalinity for *Atlas* lakes is from 40 mg/L $CaCO_3$ for the dilute Lake Athabasca to 25 000 mg/L $CaCO_3$ for the saline Oliva Lake (Fig. 17); they are all strongly buffered lakes. Most of the *Atlas* lakes (86%) are categorized as **high alkalinity** because alkalinity is greater than 100 mg/L, the remainder are classified as **relatively low alkalinity** for prairie lakes.

Water that is rich in calcium and magnesium is called **hard water**, a term that comes from the amount of soap needed to form a lather—hard water needs more soap to form a lather than soft water. As with alkalinity, water hardness or **total hardness** is expressed as mg/L equivalent calcium carbonate ($CaCO_3$). All lakes described in the *Atlas* have hard water:

Table 4. Mean (X̄) and range concentrations of major ions in the surface waters of the lakes in the *Atlas*.

	Cations (mg/L)				Anions (mg/L)			
	Na X̄ (range)	K X̄ (range)	Mg X̄ (range)	Ca X̄ (range)	Cl X̄ (range)	SO$_4$ X̄ (range)	HCO$_3$ X̄ (range)	CO$_3$ X̄ (range)
Alberta Lakes in the *Atlas*								
Freshwater lakes	20 (0.3–114)	5 (0.2–19)	15 (4–44)	29 (7–59)	3 (0.1–20)	24 (1–209)	178 (49–522)	5 (0–31)
Slightly saline lakes	113 (20–188)	29 (15–60)	59 (41–98)	31 (8–76)	9 (2–17)	209 (15–346)	415 (117–535)	40(0–70)
Moderately saline lakes	379 (239–501)	34 (10–66)	46 (19–55)	21 (9–31)	17 (10–30)	395 (89–817)	647 (356–922)	83 (25–138)
Saline lakes	7172 (1473–21 851)	166 (50–396)	154 (107–206)	21 (14–28)	212 (99–459)	7026 (2413–16 530)	2187 (571–5368)	3291 (107–12 335)
World Average								
Freshwater	8	3	5	30	8	18	105	
Seawater	10 810	390	1300	410	19 440	2710	140	

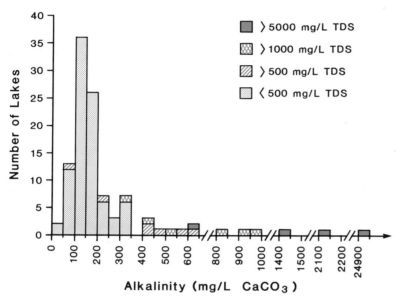

Figure 17. A frequency distribution of total alkalinity indicates that the alkalinity of most lakes in the *Atlas* is between 100 and 200 mg/L CaCO₃.

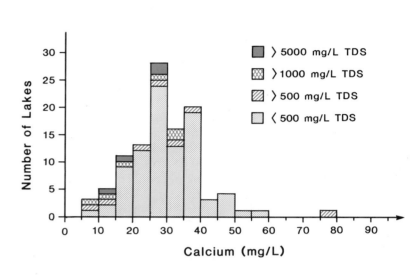

Figure 18. A frequency distribution of calcium shows that calcium concentrations for *Atlas* lakes tend to fall between 20 and 40 mg/L.

Figure 19. Nutrients cycle through various levels of the food chain in a lake.

Definition used for hardness	Range (mg/L CaCO₃)	% lakes in the *Atlas*
relatively low	28 to 120	27
hard	121 to 180	47
very hard	181 to 883	26

In contrast, lakes on the Canadian Shield and some brown water lakes in northern Alberta have soft water; total hardness of these lakes is generally less than 10 mg/L CaCO₃.

Major Ions

The major ions described in the *Atlas* (listed in Table 4), are vital to the health of plants and animals in lakes. For example, **calcium** is a structural component of vertebrate bones, and it forms the shells of many invertebrate animals, especially clams and snails. The use of these major ions by plants and animals does not directly affect the amounts in water because the requirements of these organisms are small compared to concentrations in lake water.

Concentrations of three cations, **magnesium**, **sodium** and **potassium**, are relatively constant over time and at various depths in the water column. In contrast, calcium concentrations are more variable over time and depth within lakes. Calcium concentrations are lowest in the surface waters when large amounts of algae are growing. When carbon dioxide is absorbed from the water for photosynthesis, pH increases and the relatively insoluble salt, calcium carbonate, comes out of solution and precipitates onto the leaves of rooted plants, or on the bottom of the lake, or even forms crystals in the open water. Calcium concentrations in lakes described in the *Atlas* are low for hardwater lakes, and there is no pattern with increasing TDS (Fig. 18). In *Atlas* lakes, relatively low concentrations of calcium are balanced by concentrations of Na, K, and Mg that are 2 to 3 times the world average for freshwater lakes (Table 4).

When people think of salt, they often think of sodium chloride (table salt). Although **sodium** concentrations are high in these 100 lakes, **chloride** concentrations are low as a result of the distance from the ocean and limited use of road salt in this region compared to eastern Canada and northeastern United States. For example, the amount of chloride has tripled in Lake Erie and Lake Ontario over the past half century due to the use of road salt in their drainage basins. The ions in freshwater lakes can come from salts such as calcium carbonate, calcium bicarbonate, sodium sulphate and potassium sulphate. Fresh water contains many salts and has quite a different composition from seawater (Table 4). Similarly, the saline lakes in Alberta have relatively high concentrations of sulphate and bicarbonate and low concentrations of chloride.

Sulphate concentrations are quite variable among lakes in the *Atlas* (over 200–fold in the freshwater lakes) and these concentrations are linked to inputs from atmospheric sources, surface runoff and groundwater, and consumption of sulphide in bottom mud. Oxygen is absent in water in the bottom mud and some bacteria consume sulphates, with hydrogen sulphide as a byproduct. Hydrogen sulphide produces the characteristic rotten egg smell when stagnant muddy water is stirred up. Sulphate is also used in these sediments to produce highly insoluble compounds such as pyrite and ferrous sulphide.

Bicarbonate and **carbonate** (along with a relatively small amount of carbon dioxide) make up inorganic carbon in lake water described in the *Atlas*. Inorganic carbon is used by algae in a process called **photosynthesis**. Water and inorganic carbon are combined by plants in the presence of adequate light, nutrients and the pigment chlorophyll to produce organic carbon or solid plant material. Approximately half the weight of organic material in living cells is carbon. Most plants obtain their carbon through photosynthesis; animals are unable to photosynthesize and therefore must obtain carbon from the carbon-rich bodies of plants and animals (Fig. 19). The amount of carbon fixed in a given time is an important measure of the productivity of a lake; it is often expressed as milligrams of carbon fixed per square metre of lake surface area per unit time (mg C/m² per day) to allow comparisons to be made between lakes of different

depths. Photosynthesis takes place in the **euphotic zone** or **trophogenic zone**, the zone which extends from the lake surface to the depth that 1% of the surface light will penetrate.

Bicarbonate is the highest among the anions in many of the *Atlas* lakes, and these lakes are referred to as *bicarbonate-type*. In summer, inorganic carbon concentrations are generally higher in water over the bottom mud than in the waters near the surface of the lake, as a result of decomposition of organic material by bacteria in the bottom sediment.

Temperature

Temperature, oxygen and pH are often described as the "master variables" structuring aquatic habitats. The temperature of water changes much less rapidly than that of air, so aquatic plants and animals are protected from sudden changes and only have to adjust gradually. As well, the range of temperatures in temperate zone fresh water (0°C to 26°C) is much less than in air. The unique physical properties of water play an important role in structuring the annual temperature patterns in a lake; water at 4°C is heavier than water that is either cooler or warmer. Temperature patterns that develop in water are determined by air temperatures and wind. Water temperature, as with most variables described in this section, is usually measured as a series of measurements from the water surface to the lake bottom, at the deepest part of the lake (Fig. 20).

Studies during the 1980s on 20 lakes located from north of Peace River to south of Kinsella, Alberta, indicate that maximum ice thickness can vary from a minimum of 40 cm to almost 1 m, although the average maximum ice thickness is approximately 60 cm. In Alberta, the duration of ice cover is approximately five months, ranging from more than six months in the mountain lakes and in the northeastern part of the province, to no more than four months in saline lakes and many shallow lakes and reservoirs in southern Alberta. In any individual lake, freeze-up and ice-out will vary from year to year depending on weather patterns. At Narrow Lake, where records of the date of freeze-up and ice-out were kept for six years (1983–1989), the date of first ice-cover extends from 1 to 26 November, and of ice-melt from 19 April to 7 May.

In winter in Alberta, water near the lake bottom is usually near 4°C, whereas water near the surface is colder and approaches 0°C just under the ice. This pattern is illustrated in Figure 21 with data from a shallow lake (Figure Eight) and a relatively deep lake (Narrow). After the ice melts in spring, surface waters in Alberta warm quickly. The thermal patterns observed during the open-water season depend on whether a lake is relatively shallow and the entire depth of water mixes during summer, or whether it is deep enough to be divided into seasonal thermal layers.

In shallow lakes, such as Figure Eight, the entire water column warms during the first few weeks in spring. When the whole water column is the same temperature, all the water in the lake will mix together. In calm weather, the surface water will warm up more rapidly than the deeper water. By May or June the surface layer will approach 15°C to 20°C and the deeper water may be several degrees cooler. The temperature difference between the surface and bottom waters is reduced over the summer, as intermittent periods of cooler air temperatures and strong winds reduce surface water temperatures. By late summer the temperature of the entire water column is uniform or **isothermal**. Occasionally during brief periods of calm, warm weather, the surface waters may be slightly warmer than the waters over the bottom mud. This fairly uniform condition continues through the fall, as water temperatures drop and eventually reach 4°C. Isothermal water is usually well-mixed. When it becomes sufficiently cold, a layer of ice will form and the annual temperature cycle repeats itself.

After ice-out in deeper lakes, such as Narrow, the surface water may warm so rapidly that there is little mixing of this water with the deep water (Fig. 21). Soon, a distinct warm surface layer is separated from the cool bottom waters by a layer where the water temperature changes rapidly. This transition layer is often a repository for small particles and plankton. The three layers have names of Greek origin: **epilimnion**, or "top of the lake", **metalimnion**, or "middle of the lake" and **hypolimnion**, or "bottom of the lake". When these zones

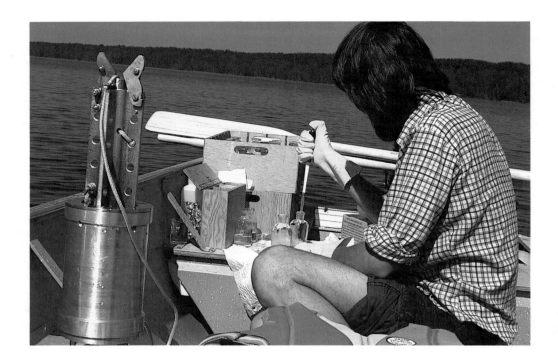

Figure 20. Temperature profiles and water samples for water quality analysis are collected by limnologists, or lake scientists.
Photo by E.E. Prepas.

FIGURE EIGHT LAKE:

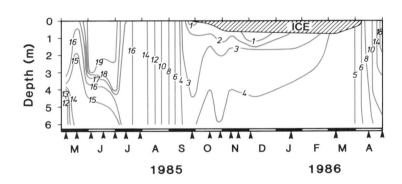

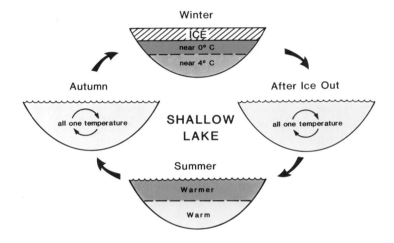

NARROW LAKE:

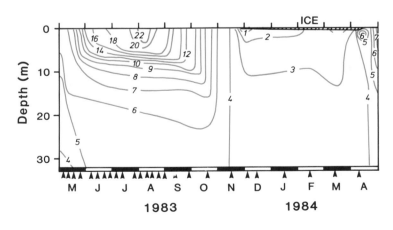

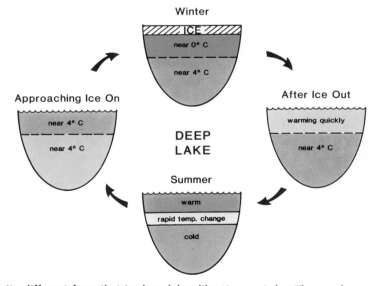

Figure 21. The temperature regime in shallow lakes like Figure Eight Lake is quite different from that in deep lakes like Narrow Lake. The graphs on the left show the temperature (°C) from the top to the bottom of the lakes for a year (note the difference in the depth scale). The cross-sections show typical temperature patterns for each season.

form, a lake is said to be **thermally stratified**. During summer, the depth of the epilimnion increases, as a result of wind mixing and periods of cooler air temperatures. With the onset of cooler air temperatures in fall, the epilimnion deepens faster and the metalimnion becomes less clearly defined until eventually the entire water column reaches 4°C. With sufficient time and wind, the lake may mix for a while before ice forms. But if the onset of ice-cover comes soon after the whole lake is the same temperature, there may be little mixing before the ice forms. In deep lakes, the bottom waters have relatively constant temperatures year-round, but in shallow lakes, bottom water temperatures may range from 2°C to over 20°C.

There are many deviations from this general pattern of annual temperature cycles in lakes. High salt content can change the density of water in any particular layer and alter the patterns described. Very large lakes such as Cold Lake tend to have delayed dates of ice formation, lower temperatures under ice in winter, and delayed dates of ice-off in spring relative to the smaller lakes in the same region. Lakes fed with water from high mountain streams such as the Kananaskis Lakes tend to have cooler water in summer than lakes farther from the mountains. As a consequence of the inputs of warm water from a thermal generating plant, Wabamun Lake has a shorter period of ice-cover than other lakes just west of Edmonton, and one part of that lake remains ice-free most of the winter. The size and shape of the ice-free area at Wabamun Lake can change rapidly, depending on air temperatures, and wind speed and direction.

Oxygen

Just as terrestrial plants and animals require oxygen, so do most aquatic organisms. Aquatic creatures do not breath air, but they can extract dissolved oxygen from their watery medium. Some life stages of animals, such as trout fry, require high concentrations of dissolved oxygen and will not tolerate amounts below about 10 mg/L. Other organisms such as sticklebacks, fathead minnows and many benthic invertebrates are tolerant of lower concentrations and may even survive short periods with no dissolved oxygen. Concentrations of dissolved oxygen in lakes in the *Atlas* range from 0 to above 20 mg/L.

Oxygen enters lake water from three sources: from the air, as a byproduct of photosynthesis and with groundwater. Most oxygen inputs are in the top layers of the lake. Oxygen from the atmosphere enters the lake only at the surface. Under ice-cover, no oxygen can enter the lake from the air. Oxygenated groundwater is more likely in shallow water than in deep water. Photosynthesis, and thus the addition of oxygen by green plants, takes place only in the euphotic zone during daylight hours. Because plants and animals use oxygen for respiration around the clock, oxygen is being continuously taken out of the euphotic zone, although the rate of replenishment during the day often exceeds the rate of uptake. In the deeper, darker water, oxygen is only being taken out. In or near the bottom mud, oxygen demand is often high due to bacterial decomposition. Under very unusual conditions, an algal bloom may die off suddenly in a shallow lake, and oxygen demand for decomposition may be so much higher than the input with photosynthesis that oxygen concentrations will approach zero throughout the water column for a few hours or days. Many animals will perish during the period of uniformly low dissolved oxygen concentrations, and the condition is called **summerkill**.

The amount of oxygen that can dissolve in water depends on water temperature, elevation above sea level and salinity. More oxygen can dissolve in cold water than in warm water; at 4°C, one litre of water can hold (or is **saturated** at) about 12 mg of oxygen, at 20°C it is saturated at 8 mg per litre of oxygen. Similarly, fresh water holds more oxygen than saline water and saturation increases with increased pressure. Water at the surface usually has higher concentrations of dissolved oxygen than water deeper in the lake. This effect may be modified somewhat by the fact that warmer surface water cannot hold as much oxygen as colder, deeper water. An example of highly oxygenated deep water is found in Upper Kananaskis Lake in summer.

The amount of dissolved oxygen in lakes usually decreases under ice-cover primarily due to respiration by all organisms, but mainly bacteria. In shallow lakes, oxygen depletion can proceed rapidly under ice (Fig. 22). If concentrations throughout the water column drop close to zero, as occurred in Figure Eight Lake in February 1986, many fish species (such as yellow perch and walleye) and some invertebrates (such as clams) will not survive and a condition called **winterkill** will develop.

Oxygen loss under ice is often expressed as milligrams of oxygen consumed per square metre of lake surface area per unit time (mg oxygen/m^2 per day). Most of this oxygen loss is due to respiration, primarily by bacteria which break down organic matter in the bottom mud. Oxygen loss from November through February is fairly predictable based on depth of the water column, an estimate of summer algal productivity and water temperature; measured rates of under-ice oxygen depletion for lakes described in the *Atlas* range from 0.2 to 1.0 mg O_2/m^2 per day. In some as yet poorly understood situations, **algal blooms** can develop under ice during midwinter (November through February). These conditions are relatively uncommon, although one spectacular bloom was recorded during the winter of 1985–86 in shallow Driedmeat Lake. Under-ice algal blooms are more common in March and April when light levels are relatively high. These late winter under-ice algal blooms can result in increasing oxygen content, as illustrated in Figure 22; therefore predicting oxygen concentrations in March and April is more difficult than earlier in the winter.

During the ice-free season in shallow lakes, the distribution of dissolved oxygen concentrations is variable, shifting from fairly uniform when the water is well-mixed, to highly stratified when the water column is weakly thermally stratified (Fig. 22).

Compared with shallower lakes, the water in deeper lakes is often not as well-mixed in fall prior to ice cover. Oxygen concentrations are usually higher in the top layer of water than over the bottom sediments during late fall and the early period after ice formation. Under ice, oxygen consumption proceeds as described for shallow lakes, except the larger volume of water protects the lake against winterkill. Oxygen concentrations in the water over the bottom mud often approach zero, particularly in the more productive deep lakes such as Baptiste. After the ice melts, some oxygen is introduced from the atmosphere into the surface layer, but because the surface water usually warms up quickly, there is only limited oxygen transported by mixing into the deeper waters. During summer, oxygen depletion can be rapid in the hypolimnion or deeper water, and most of the deep lakes in regions covered by the *Atlas*, such as Narrow (Fig. 22), Amisk and Ethel, have little or no oxygen in the hypolimnion by late summer. Summer oxygen depletion rates are expressed as milligrams of oxygen per square metre of the area of the top of the hypolimnion per unit time (mg O_2/m^2 per day). For individual lakes, summer oxygen depletion rates are probably slightly higher than winter rates since higher algal production and water temperatures in summer promote increased oxygen consumption by bacteria. In fall, as the epilimnion deepens, the mixed layer increases and the oxygen content of the lake slowly increases until ice forms and the annual cycle repeats itself. The distribution of oxygen in lake water is thus a result of interactions of lake morphometry, wind, air temperatures and biological activities within the lake.

Nutrients

Most users of lakes in Alberta are concerned about water quality for recreation—is the water murky or clear? Is there green scum on the surface? Are there dense masses of plants in the water? These questions refer to the lake's fertility—the quantity of plant nutrients in the water. A nutrient is a chemical that plants need for growth. Phosphorus and nitrogen are familiar nutrients because they are applied to crops or vegetable gardens to help them grow. The same nutrients, plus carbon, are essential for the growth of algae that turn lakes green in summer and for the large water plants called aquatic macrophytes or "weeds".

FIGURE EIGHT LAKE:

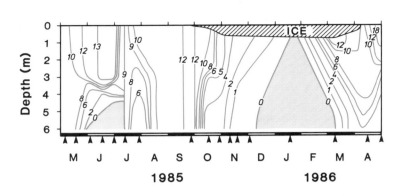

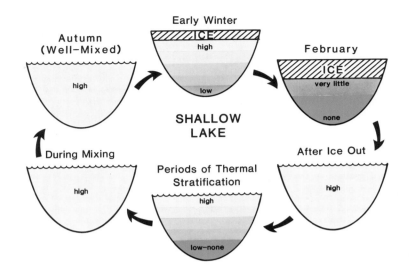

NARROW LAKE:

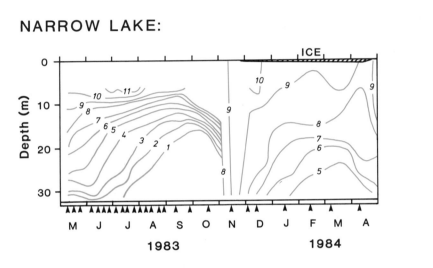

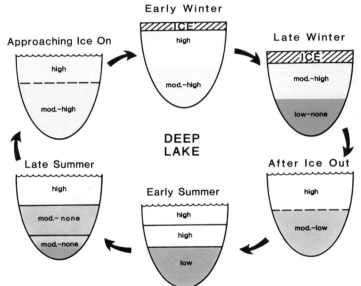

Figure 22. The concentration of dissolved oxygen in a lake changes throughout the year in both shallow lakes like Figure Eight and deep lakes like Narrow. The graph on the left indicates the concentration of dissolved oxygen (mg/L) at all depths for a whole year; the shaded area indicates water with no oxygen. The cross-sections show typical patterns for each season.

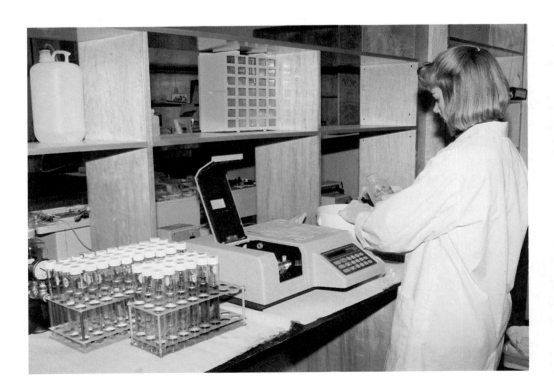

Figure 23. Water samples prepared for phosphorus analysis are analyzed in the laboratory; the darker blue samples indicate higher phosphorus concentrations. Photo by E.E. Prepas.

Phosphorus

Concentrations of **phosphorus** often affect recreational water quality in Alberta lakes. Phosphorus is often present in the surface waters of freshwater lakes (<500 mg/L TDS) in smaller quantities than algae need for maximum growth, thus it is referred to as the **limiting nutrient**. Unlike nitrogen and carbon, phosphorus is not present as a gas in the atmosphere. Once phosphorus in the surface water of a lake is exhausted, algae stop growing and soon die. If more phosphorus is added to a lake where it is the limiting nutrient, larger algal populations will result until their growth is again limited by nutrients or light. Macrophytes, the large shoreline aquatic plants, may not respond as directly to phosphorus in the water as do algae. Many of these large plants take their required nutrients from the bottom sediments through roots, rather than from the open water.

In contrast to the freshwater lakes, algae in saline lakes (> 500 mg/L TDS) in Alberta are limited by chemicals other than phosphorus. In these saline lakes, algal populations (both numbers of algal cells and numbers of species) decline as salinity increases. Some scientists believe that high concentrations of one nutrient (sulphate) may interfere with incorporation by algae of another nutrient (molybdate), thus inhibiting cell growth, which may explain the clear water in phosphorus-rich, saline lakes such as Miquelon, Peninsula and Oliva.

Lake scientists, or *limnologists*, discuss phosphorus as four forms. Two forms (**total dissolved phosphorus (TDP)** and **soluble reactive phosphorus (SRP)**) are dissolved. **Particulate phosphorus** is incorporated into particles suspended in the water—for example, in soil or tiny plants and animals. **Total phosphorus (TP)** is the sum of particulate and dissolved phosphorus. A water sample is analyzed for phosphorus by treating it with specific chemicals. Water for the dissolved fractions is first poured through a fine filter and then treated. For both dissolved and total phosphorus, the treated water sample turns blue (Fig. 23), and the intensity of the blueness is directly proportional to the phosphorus concentration. Particulate phosphorus is estimated from the difference between TP and TDP. SRP is a portion of TDP. Only phosphorus data since 1980 are included in the *Atlas* because earlier data are not reliable.

Total phosphorus concentration has proved to be a powerful predictive tool for lake management, particularly recreational water quality. In the lakes presented in the *Atlas*, total phosphorus concentrations range from 5 to 13 000 μg/L in the euphotic zone during the open-water period. In freshwater lakes described in the *Atlas*, TP concentrations cover a smaller range (5 to 453 μg/L TP, Fig. 24) and are strongly linked to algal abundance or green scum in a lake. For example, total phosphorus concentration in the clear Kananaskis Lakes averages 5 μg/L, whereas in murky Nakamun Lake the average is 88 μg/L. In the freshwater lakes, approximately 60% of the total phosphorus is in the particulate fraction and 40% is in the dissolved fraction at any one time. Soluble reactive phosphorus concentration, which is generally present in very low concentrations (average 7 μg/L for the 27 freshwater lakes which have SRP data), approximates the main form of phosphorus which plants use to grow. In saline lakes, phosphorus concentrations in the euphotic zone, or upper layer, tend to be higher than in freshwater lakes and increase with increasing salinity, from 36 to 13 000 μg/L TP (Fig. 24). Total phosphorus concentration in the moderately saline Cooking Lake averages 251 μg/L, and in saline Oliva Lake 13 058 μg/L. In the saline lakes, total phosphorus is not related to algal growth because growth requirements are easily met by supply; total dissolved phosphorus is a higher proportion of total phosphorus than in freshwater lakes (TDP averages 62% of TP in the moderately saline lakes, 92% of TP in the saline lakes).

Phosphorus sources and cycling have been the focus of many water quality studies in Alberta in the 1980s. Natural sources of phosphorus include **external inputs**—runoff over land, and dust and precipitation directly onto the lake—and **internal inputs**—from sources within the bottom sediments of the lake (Fig. 25). The relative importance of various external sources of phosphorus, such as runoff and the atmosphere (dust and precipitation), is determined by the ratio of the drainage basin area to the lake area, and by the

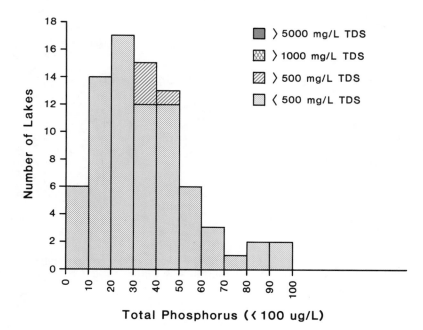

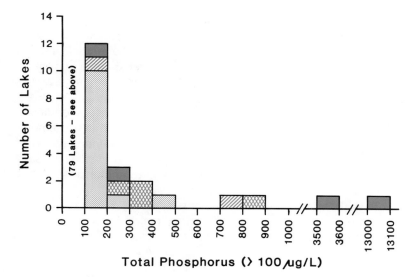

Figure 24. A frequency distribution of average open water, euphotic zone, total phosphorus concentrations for *Atlas* lakes, separated into lakes with lower (<100 μg/L) and higher (>100 μg/L) concentrations of phosphorus, indicates that most of the *Atlas* lakes have a total phosphorus concentration of less than 50 μg/L.

geology and land use in the drainage basin. As rain or snow-melt water runs over or just below the surface of the ground, it picks up dissolved and particulate substances, including phosphorus. In general, more phosphorus is lost per unit time from a square metre of land with soft rock and/or rich soil overlying it (as is common in Alberta) than from hard rock basins, and from cleared as compared to forested land. For example, differences in rocks, soils and vegetation in the drainage basin account for much of the disparity between lakes on the Canadian Shield where total phosphorus concentration in lake water is typically less than 15 μg/L, and freshwater lakes described in the *Atlas* where the amount of phosphorus can be as much as 30 times higher. Further, more phosphorus is lost from areas of intense human usage (cattle feedlots, intense cultivation and urban centres) than from areas with limited cultivation (pastureland or land with only an occasional house or cottage). Atmospheric loading consists of phosphorus which falls directly onto the lake surface in rain, snow or dust. For the 25 lakes described in the *Atlas* where external phosphorus loading has been calculated, the proportion of total phosphorus from the atmosphere ranges from one-twentieth to two-thirds of total external loading. Atmospheric loading is the largest portion of external phosphorus loading for lakes with a small drainage basin relative to the size of the lake basin, and where the natural vegetation is undisturbed.

Internal phosphorus inputs involve transfer from the bottom mud

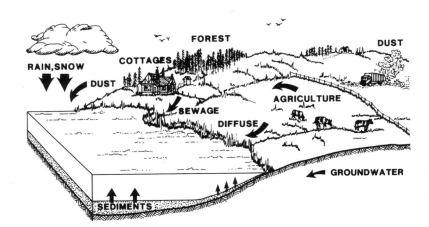

Figure 25. Sources of phosphorus for a prairie lake can be from outside the lake (external sources) or within the lake (internal sources).

or sediments up into the open water. Bottom sediments for most of the 100 lakes in the *Atlas* are made up primarily of organic material produced in the lake, supplemented with material swept in from the drainage basin. Most phosphorus in the bottom sediments is associated with sediment particles; some of this phosphorus is loosely bound, or attached to sediment particles. Under certain conditions, this loosely bound phosphorus can move into the water surrounding the sediment particles, or **porewater**. Once phosphorus is in the porewater, it can be transferred to the water that overlies the sediment. Bottom sediments contain large amounts of phosphorus compared to the open water.

In shallow lakes, bottom sediments gradually warm as the summer progresses. Bacterial activity and chemical reactions consume dissolved oxygen. When this happens, some of the phosphorus stored in the bottom sediments is typically released to the overlying water. The process is illustrated with data from Figure Eight Lake (Fig. 26), where phosphorus accumulation over bottom sediments is evident much of the year. Recent evidence suggests that phosphorus is also transferred fairly rapidly in summer from the bottom sediments into the overlying water, even when dissolved oxygen concentrations are relatively high in the overlying water. This transfer involves chemical diffusion, groundwater flow through the bottom sediments and activity of small organisms such as bacteria and worms which live on the lake bottom. Once phosphorus has moved to the overlying water, wind action mixes this nutrient-rich water into the euphotic zone, and algae respond with a burst of growth. Recycling of phosphorus from the bottom sediments takes place continually during the warm summer months, and may result in the green scums known as algal blooms. This process is important in most lakes in the *Atlas*. Limnologists now believe that for many lakes in Alberta, the bottom sediments annually provide more phosphorus than the total of all the external sources such as runoff and precipitation. Transfer of phosphorus from the bottom sediments to the overlying water also takes place in the deep cool waters of thermally stratified lakes and under ice in winter, although the rate is slower than in shallow warmer water during summer. Coefficients used to estimate phosphorus loading for lakes described in the *Atlas* were developed from studies in central Alberta and are found in Section 3 of the Appendix.

One of the unresolved questions about Alberta lakes is: Why does phosphorus in the bottom sediment in Alberta lakes return so quickly to the water compared to lakes on the Canadian Shield, where relatively little phosphorus is transferred by this route? Two features of lakes described in the *Atlas* which may be related to this condition are the relatively low total iron and calcium concentrations. These two chemicals are thought to regulate phosphorus cycling in lakes. Detailed information on iron cycling is not available for most Alberta lakes. For many lakes, total iron concentrations in the water column

are below the detection level of the method used. For those *Atlas* lakes with reliable iron data, total iron concentrations are often similar to or less than total phosphorus concentrations. In contrast, total iron concentrations are usually several times higher than total phosphorus concentrations in freshwater lakes in other parts of Canada. Total iron concentrations in *Atlas* lakes range from 7 to 285 μg/L in the freshwater lakes (average less than 67 μg/L), which is very similar to the values reported for the Canadian Shield. In contrast, for lakes on the Canadian Shield phosphorus concentrations are much lower than for lakes described in the *Atlas*. Total iron concentration for lakes described in the *Atlas* are only 10% of the world average for fresh water. In saline lakes, total iron concentrations tend to be higher, ranging up to 1 454 μg/L in Peninsula Lake. Many lakes in the *Atlas* have low calcium concentrations (average 28 mg/L Ca) compared to other hardwater lakes. In two lakes and two dozen ponds in Alberta where calcium concentrations have been experimentally increased, phosphorus appears to be more effectively sealed in the bottom mud.

Nitrogen and Carbon

Nitrogen and **carbon** are two essential nutrients for primary producers. Both nutrients are usually present in much higher concentrations than phosphorus in lake water, and in excess of the needs of aquatic plants. The ratio of inorganic carbon to total nitrogen to total phosphorus averages from 3 500 to 20 to 1 in the freshwater lakes described in the *Atlas*. In contrast, the ratios required for growth of freshwater plants average from 80 to 10 to 1. Nitrogen and carbon are present as gases in the atmosphere, and can dissolve in water. Although about half of the total phosphorus in lake water described in the *Atlas* is tied up in living plants and animals, most of the nitrogen is associated with dissolved organic matter in the water and most of the carbon is dissolved inorganic carbon such as bicarbonate.

Some species of blue-green algae can use nitrogen gas directly and incorporate it into organic compounds through a process called nitrogen fixation. Other algae require inorganic forms of nitrogen that are dissolved in the water: **nitrite** and **nitrate** (NO_2 + NO_3–nitrogen) and **ammonium** (NH_4–nitrogen). Ammonium, nitrogen in dissolved organic molecules, and nitrogen contained in the cellular structure of organisms are analyzed together as **total Kjeldahl nitrogen** (TKN). **Total nitrogen** (TN) is the sum of NO_2 + NO_3– and TKN.

In summer, amounts of inorganic nitrogen tend to be very low in the **euphotic zone** of Alberta lakes compared to that in the euphotic zone of lakes throughout much of the rest of the world. The average total inorganic nitrogen concentration for lake water described in the *Atlas* is less than 50 μg/L during the ice-free period, or less than one-twentieth of the world average for fresh water. In the saline

FIGURE EIGHT LAKE:

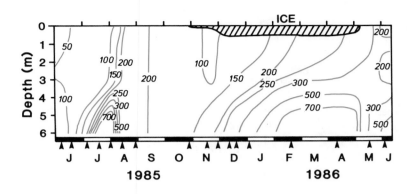

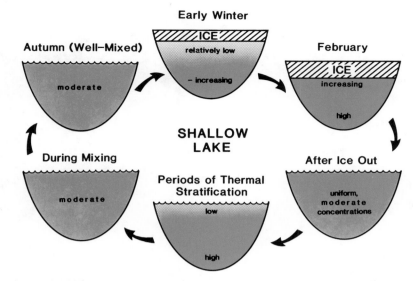

Figure 26. Total phosphorus concentrations in a lake vary with depth and season. The graph on the left shows the concentrations (μg/L) at all depths of a shallow lake for a year. The cross-sections show typical seasonal patterns. Note the accumulation of phosphorus over the bottom sediments when the water is low in dissolved oxygen in summer and winter.

lakes described in the *Atlas*, the average was slightly higher, 136 μg/L inorganic nitrogen. Ammonium averages more than 75% of inorganic nitrogen in the euphotic zone of lakes described in the *Atlas*. The low $NO_2 + NO_3$–nitrogen concentrations given in the *Atlas* reflect low inputs with precipitation and runoff and possibly low rates of nitrogen recycling from the bottom sediments compared to rates of phosphorus recycling. The relative importance of ammonium increases in the more productive lakes and in the saline lakes (Table 5). Because concentrations of nitrogen in samples may change in the transport time from the lake to the laboratory, values for nitrogen presented in the *Atlas* may overestimate the amount of inorganic nitrogen in the lake water.

In contrast to inorganic nitrogen, total nitrogen concentrations for lakes in the *Atlas*, particularly the eutrophic and saline lakes, are relatively high compared to other lakes around the world. The average total nitrogen concentrations in the euphotic zone of freshwater lakes during summer range from 200 to over 10 000 μg/L TN (Fig. 27); the average for freshwater lakes is one-third (1 081 μg/L TN) that of saline lakes (3 336 μg/L TN). The lowest amounts of total nitrogen are recorded in the less productive freshwater lakes (Table 5). Most of the total nitrogen in the water is dissolved organic nitrogen. In the euphotic zone of lakes described in the *Atlas*, organic nitrogen averages more than 95% of the total nitrogen. For example, in the euphotic zone of the north basin of Amisk Lake, on average 82% of organic nitrogen is dissolved. Limnologists know very little about how dissolved organic nitrogen influences and interacts with algal production in Alberta. However, it is known that the amount of nitrogen which can be used directly by algae (inorganic nitrogen and possibly some organic nitrogen) can influence the composition of the algal community. Generally, low concentrations of available nitrogen favour the development of blue-green algae species such as *Anabaena* spp. and *Aphanizomenon* sp., which can fix atmospheric nitrogen.

The rate of carbon fixation is often the unit used to describe production in ecosystems. Carbon is measured in three forms: **dissolved inorganic carbon** (DIC or HCO_3 plus CO_3) (see Major Ions section), **dissolved organic carbon** (DOC) and **total particulate carbon** (TPC). In lakes described in the *Atlas*, DIC is the overwhelming portion of total carbon, followed by DOC and TPC. For the north basin of Baptiste Lake, for example, DIC is 91%, DOC 8% and TPC 1% of total carbon. Although aquatic studies in many regions have focused on carbon, limnologists in Alberta have yet to do any detailed studies on carbon.

Transparency

Transparency, or water clarity, in most lakes is affected mainly by the amount of algae in the water. The clarity of water is measured

Table 5. Examples of average nitrogen concentrations (μg/L), nitrite plus nitrate ($NO_2 + NO_3$), ammonium (NH_4) and total nitrogen (TN), in the euphotic zone of lakes described in the *Atlas*.

Lake	Lake type	$NO_2 + NO_3$	NH_4	TN
Ethel	moderately productive	2	2	722
Nakamun	highly productive	20	67	1629
Miquelon	saline, moderately productive	12	36	5644

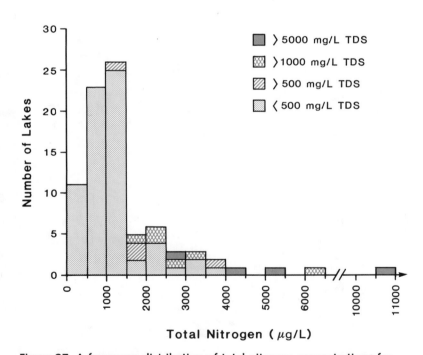

Figure 27. A frequency distribution of total nitrogen concentrations for *Atlas* lakes indicates that the nitrogen concentration of most lakes falls between 500 and 1 500 μg/L.

Table 6. Trophic status of lakes described in the *Atlas*.

Trophic Status	Appearance of water	Maximum Chlorophyll a Concentration (μg/L)	% lakes in the Atlas	Examples
oligotrophic	clear	less than 8	10	Ghost Glennifer Kananaskis
oligo-mesotrophic	usually clear	occasionally over 8	5	Cold Glenmore
mesotrophic	sometimes green	8 to 25	32	Buffalo Crimson Ethel
eutrophic	green most of summer	26 to 75	29	Pigeon Pine Pinehurst
hyper-eutrophic	frequent dense algal blooms	over 75	24	Baptiste la Nonne Winagami

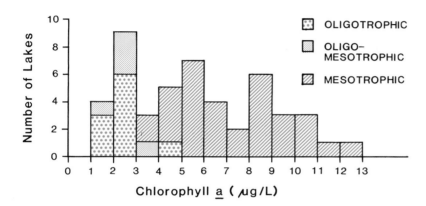

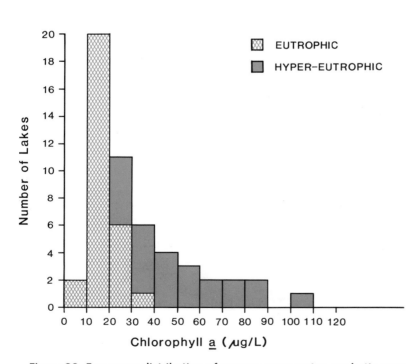

Figure 28. Frequency distribution of average open water, euphotic zone chlorophyll *a* concentrations for *Atlas* lakes, separated into less productive (oligotrophic to mesotrophic) and more productive (eutrophic to hyper-eutrophic) lakes.

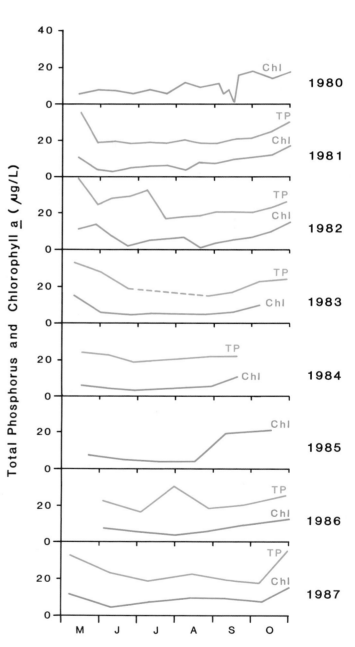

Figure 29. Comparisons of total phosphorus and chlorophyll *a* concentrations over 8 summers in the euphotic zone of Ethel Lake indicates that chlorophyll *a* concentrations are distinctly lower in some years (1982) than other years (1980).

throughout the world by estimating the depth that a black and white plate, called a **Secchi disk**, can be seen. This depth is called the **Secchi depth**. Average Secchi depths for the lakes and reservoirs in the *Atlas* range from over 6 m in Ghost Reservoir (which is very clear), to 0.4 m in some of the most productive lakes such as Little Fish Lake. Secchi depth provides a simple and quick estimate of a lake's fertility. Transparency of water is also measured with a light sensor that is lowered into the water, so that light intensity can be recorded at various chosen depths. Generally the **euphotic zone**, or zone with sufficient light for photosynthesis, is defined as extending from the lake surface to the depth which receives 1% of light recorded just below the surface. If no data were collected with a light meter, the depth of the euphotic zone may be approximated as twice the Secchi disk depth. The extent of light penetration delineates the depth of rooted aquatic plants in lakes and the depth of most algal growth.

Turbidity and colour also affect water transparency. In some reservoirs and shallow lakes, the water may contain suspended silt as well as algae. Turbidity is a measure of particle scattering or the amount of suspended material such as mud, silt and algae and is presented as NTU, the standard international unit. Turbidity ranges from less than 1 to 33 NTU in the euphotic zone of the 41 lakes for which turbidity was measured. All these lakes are considered *not very turbid*. Turbidity for the 32 freshwater lakes averages 3 NTU, and for the nine slightly saline to saline lakes, it averages 12 NTU. Some lake water is highly stained or coloured. **Colour** is a measure of the amount of humic material in the water. It is measured by comparing filtered lake water to a mixture of platinum (Pt)-cobalt compounds, and is presented as units of Pt. Colour is often high in water that flows through muskeg and bogs and picks up humic matter. The scale in the *Atlas* is: *very clear* (colour less than 4 mg/L Pt), *not highly coloured* (from 4 to 55 mg/L Pt), and *highly coloured* (more than 55 mg/L Pt). Colour in the euphotic zone of the 26 lakes in the *Atlas* which have this information, ranges from 2 to 62 mg/L Pt. The 19 freshwater lakes are less coloured (an average of 13 mg/L Pt) than the 7 saline lakes (average colour 35 mg/L Pt). All but two of the lakes, Lessard with 2 mg/L Pt and Little Fish with 62 mg/L Pt, fall in the not highly coloured range. The relatively low colour values for lakes in the *Atlas* reflect a combination of little humic matter in many of the drainage basins and long water residence times. More coloured water is typical of lakes with large bogs or muskeg in their drainage basins; lakes on the Canadian Shield have on average more than twice the colour of the lakes described in the *Atlas*. Similarly, brown water lakes in northern Alberta have more coloured water.

Trophic Status

The information provided in the water quality section in each lake description in the *Atlas* includes an assessment of the lake's level of fertility. Lake scientists call this assessment the **trophic status** of the lake. *Trophic* is a Greek word meaning nourishment. **Eutrophic**, or well-nourished, lakes are very rich in nutrients, so that the water is green with algae during most of the summer. Almost thirty percent of *Atlas* lakes are eutrophic (Table 6). **Oligotrophic**, or poorly nourished, lakes have very low concentrations of nutrients and low algal abundance and hence the water is clear. Ten percent of lakes reported in the *Atlas* are oligotrophic. They include lakes that are fed by nutrient-poor water from the Rocky Mountains. Moderately productive lakes are called **mesotrophic**. Thirty-two percent of lakes described in the *Atlas* are mesotrophic. Five percent of lakes described in the *Atlas* fall between oligotrophic and mesotrophic and are classified as **oligo-mesotrophic**. Twenty-four percent of the lakes reported in the *Atlas* have such large quantities of nutrients that the growth of algae is enormous, and the water resembles pea soup during part of the summer. This condition is termed **hyper-eutrophic**. Because the prairie and parkland soils of Alberta are naturally fertile and phosphorus is poorly bound in bottom sediments, many of the lakes outside of the mountains are eutrophic or hyper-eutrophic. They have likely been this way since the last glaciation ended 12 000 years ago. Some lakes may have become more eutrophic over the past century, largely as a result of land clearing, but very few in Alberta have been studied long enough to confirm this.

Limnologists assess trophic status directly by measuring the concentrations of nutrients in the water of freshwater lakes, or indirectly in all lakes by measuring water transparency or the amount of algae present. Scientists around the world have developed several classification schemes for trophic status. The one used throughout this book was developed during a worldwide study of lake fertility by countries of the Organisation for Economic Co-operation and Development (OECD). It is based on a measurement of **chlorophyll *a***. Chlorophyll *a* is one of the photosynthetic pigments that, under appropriate conditions, converts sunlight to new growth in green plants. To measure chlorophyll, algae from a water sample are collected onto a filter and then the chlorophyll is extracted from the algal cells with a solvent. The colour density of the extract is analyzed and the amount of chlorophyll is calculated. The main type of chlorophyll found in all algal cells is designated with an "a", and the term chlorophyll *a* is used or implied throughout the *Atlas*. The OECD trophic category is based on the maximum chlorophyll *a* concentration measured for a lake (Table 6). Overall average chlorophyll *a* concentration is 20 µg/L for all *Atlas* lakes (Fig. 28); 19 µg/L in the freshwater lakes; 34 µg/L in the slightly and moderately saline lakes, and only 6 µg/L in the saline lakes, despite the excessive nutrient concentrations recorded there. In the freshwater lakes, seasonal patterns of chlorophyll *a* and total phosphorus concentrations are closely related over time (Fig. 29).

The average concentrations of chlorophyll *a*, phosphorus and other constituents reported in the *Atlas* are based on samples collected for one or two years during the period that the lake is free of ice—usually May through October. Typically this is the period that water quality is important to lake users and also when limnologists can best assess some aspects of it. For six Alberta lakes, information has been collected on phosphorus and chlorophyll *a* concentrations almost continuously since 1980. One of these lakes (Narrow Lake), is classified as oligo-mesotrophic, another (Ethel Lake) is mesotrophic, two (Amisk and Wabamun lakes) are eutrophic and two (Baptiste and Nakamun lakes) are hyper-eutrophic. The data collected on these lakes will permit scientists to determine to what extent these important water quality indicators vary naturally from year to year, and what factors are responsible for yearly variation. Limnologists currently believe that year-to-year variation in these trophic indicators is related to variability in nutrient inputs as well as climatic variables such as air temperature. The variation recorded for total phosphorus and chlorophyll *a* concentrations in Ethel Lake over this period is illustrated in Figure 29; chlorophyll *a* was generally lower during years with cool April air temperatures (such as 1982) than for years with warm April air temperatures (such as 1980).

Many users of Alberta lakes are concerned about how to protect or enhance water quality. Once the factors determining a lake's water quality are established, a concerted plan for water quality management can be developed by lake users and agencies responsible for this resource.

E.E. Prepas

BIOLOGICAL CHARACTERISTICS

W̲hen most people think of life in a lake, the first things that come to mind are fish, usually large sport fish like trout, walleye or Northern pike. After a little more thought, many people recall "bugs" and perhaps "green slime" and "weeds". The general wish of most recreationists is "More fish! No bugs! No slime! No weeds!". However, in lakes, as on land, the lives of plants and animals are all delicately entwined, each life form interacting with the others. With no minnows and insects to eat, there would be no trout or pike or walleye. With no insects there would be no minnows, and with no plants there would be no insects. The plants, also called "primary producers", are powered by sunlight to convert carbon and oxygen and trace elements into organic matter. Primary consumers are animals that feed on the plants. Secondary consumers are animals that feed on the animals that eat the plants. In water, the form of the organisms is different than on land because they are adapted to an aquatic environment, but the roles remain essentially the same.

Plants

Plants are primary producers on land and in water. On land the primary producers are plants like grasses, mosses, flowers and trees; in water they are tiny plants like algae (which can float freely in a buoyant world as **phytoplankton**, or grow attached to the lake bottom and other surfaces such as other plants, rocks or even sand grains) or large conspicuous **aquatic macrophytes** which are sometimes called "weeds" but also include cattails and bulrushes that grow along many natural lakeshores.

Phytoplankton

Algae are the most primitive plants, having no roots, no vascular system and no flowers. In lakes they may grow attached to other plants, to rocks or upon the submerged sediments, but usually the most conspicuous algae in Alberta lakes are the phytoplankton. The word "plankton" comes from the Greek word *planktos* which means "wandering" and so the phytoplankton is an assemblage of tiny aquatic plants which are freely suspended in water. Bacteria and fungi are also a component of the plankton, but they are not conspicuous.

Most people become aware of planktonic algae when the population becomes so abundant that the water turns bright green, or a bluish-green scum forms on the surface of the lake and drifts onto shore to die and release distinctly unpleasant odours. Phytoplankton may not be appealing *en masse*, but taken individually and viewed with a microscope, algae are spectacularly beautiful, as lovely as Christmas tree ornaments and as delicate as snowflakes.

TYPES OF PHYTOPLANKTON The incredible beauty and diversity of the algal form has awed lake scientists since it was first discovered that a single drop of lake water could contain more than a hundred algal species. Morphological characteristics such as cell shape, cell walls and the presence or absence of flagella, and biochemical characteristics such as pigment composition as well as physiological traits such as the mode of nutrition, are some of the features used to classify algae into a number of major taxonomic groups. The important ones found in Alberta lakes include the blue-green algae (Cyanophyta or Cyanobacteria), green algae (Chlorophyta), golden-brown algae

(Chrysophyta), diatoms (Bacillariophyta), cryptophytes (Cryptophyta), dinoflagellates (Pyrrhophyta or Dinophyta) and euglenoid flagellates (Euglenophyta).

The **blue-green algae** (Cyanophyta) are the most primitive group of algae, in fact, there is ongoing debate among scientists as to whether this group is more closely allied to bacteria than to plants. Like bacteria, the blue-green algae are single-celled organisms which lack a true nucleus; instead, the chromosomal material is dispersed throughout the cell. However, unlike bacteria, they contain the photosynthetic pigment chlorophyll *a*. In most plant cells the pigments are localized in discrete chloroplasts, but in blue-green algae they are dispersed throughout the cell. There are two groups of blue-green algae (Fig. 30). In one group, cells are solitary or cluster into colonies, for example *Microcystis* and *Synechococcus*. Species in the other group form filaments resembling beaded necklaces with occasional specialized cells including heterocysts, which are capable of fixing nitrogen gas, and akinetes, which appear to be specialized to withstand adverse conditions. Examples of filament-forming blue-greens common in Alberta include species of *Anabaena*, *Aphanizomenon*, *Lyngbya* and *Oscillatoria*.

The **green algae** (Chlorophyta) have a true nucleus and the pigments are localized in one or more discrete chloroplasts in each cell. Pigments are predominantly chlorophylls and food is stored as starch. Some species have two, four, or up to eight flagella and are either solitary (single celled) or colonial (*Volvox* spp.). Some species are nonflagellate and solitary as in the genus *Ankistrodesmus* or colonial as in the genus *Scenedesmus* (Fig. 31). In one group of green algae, the desmids, each cell is constricted into two semi-cells, making each individual look as though it is floating attached to its own mirror image, as in the genus *Staurastrum*. Chlorophytes also grow as long filaments attached to rocks and aquatic plants and form long, hairlike masses, for example, species of *Cladophora* and *Oedogonium*. There is also a species of *Cladophora* that forms matted balls up to the size of tennis balls which roll around in shallow water.

The **golden-brown algae** (Chrysophyta) have a true nucleus and chloroplasts in which the dominant pigments are brown or golden brown (carotenes and xanthophylls) as well as green chlorophylls. Food storage is in the form of oils. Species are unicellular or colonial and some have flagella. Examples are species of *Dinobryon* and *Synura* (Fig. 32).

The **diatoms** (Bacillariophyta) are among the most exquisitely beautiful of the algae. They have a true nucleus and their photosynthetic pigments (carotenes, xanthophylls and chlorophylls) are contained in chloroplasts. Food storage is in the form of oils. Species are unicellular or colonial; they have no flagella. Diatoms usually have thick, ornate cell walls of silica although some planktonic genera have only very lightly silicified cell walls (eg. *Rhizoselenia*). The walls form two distinct halves, like the top and bottom of a box, and they are marked with grooves and holes which form definite, intricate species-specific patterns (Fig. 33). Diatoms are usually of two basic shapes: elongate, as in cigar-shaped *Navicula*, *Pinnularia* and *Nitzschia*, or round, as in species of *Stephanodiscus* and *Cyclotella*. Colonial diatoms include the star-shaped *Asterionella* and ribbonlike *Fragilaria*. The cell walls of the diatoms and the golden-brown algae resist decay and remain in the lake sediment for thousands of years. Therefore, when a core of lake sediments is taken and the age of various strata identified, the kinds of diatoms present thousands of years ago can indicate the predominating conditions of pH, water level, salinity and trophic conditions. Paleolimnological studies of diatoms and pollen grains have been conducted by researchers at the University of Alberta on 18 Alberta lakes, including Baptiste, Buffalo, Cooking, Hastings, Moore, Spring and Wabamun.

The **cryptophytes** (Cryptophyta) are single, biflagellate cells with pigments concentrated into two chloroplasts. Food is stored as starch. Examples are species of *Cryptomonas* and *Rhodomonas* (Fig. 34).

The **dinoflagellates** (Pyrrhophyta) are single biflagellate cells with flagella of different lengths. One flagellum is located in a transverse furrow which encircles the entire cell, and the other is in a longitudinal furrow running backwards along one half of the cell. Of all the algae, the dinoflagellates are the fastest moving. Each cell contains

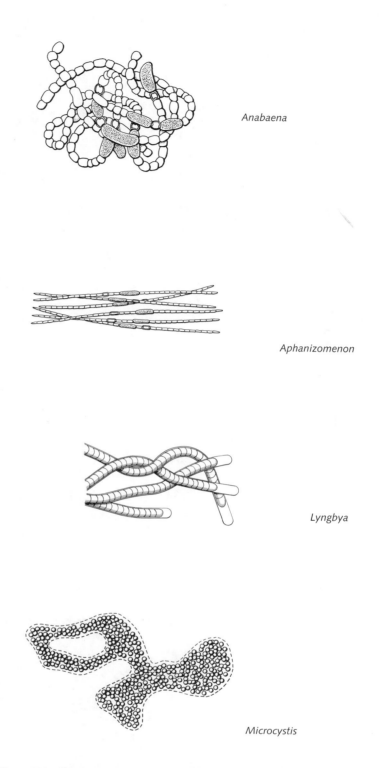

Anabaena

Aphanizomenon

Lyngbya

Microcystis

Figure 30. Blue-green algae (Cyanophyta) are the most common group of algae in many *Atlas* lakes.

numerous chloroplasts; food is stored as starch or oil. Some species of this group can be consumers as well as producers; their main food is other algae. The most common dinoflagellate in Alberta, *Ceratium hirundinella*, looks like a three-legged, scaly Eiffel tower (Fig. 35).

The **euglenoid flagellates** (Euglenophyta) are unicellular flagellate algae. Pigmented and nonpigmented genera occur; the pigmented ones usually have conspicuous green chloroplasts. The common genera include *Euglena*, *Trachelomonas* and *Phacus*. They occur in most Alberta lakes in all habitats and can become particularly abundant in organically polluted water.

MEASUREMENTS OF ALGAL POPULATIONS   The size of planktonic algae is extremely variable, ranging over seven orders of magnitude. If one of the tiniest forms (for example, a blue-green, *Chroococcus* spp.) were the size of a golf ball, then a large colony of *Microcystis aeruginosa* would be as big as a house. Nevertheless, even this "large

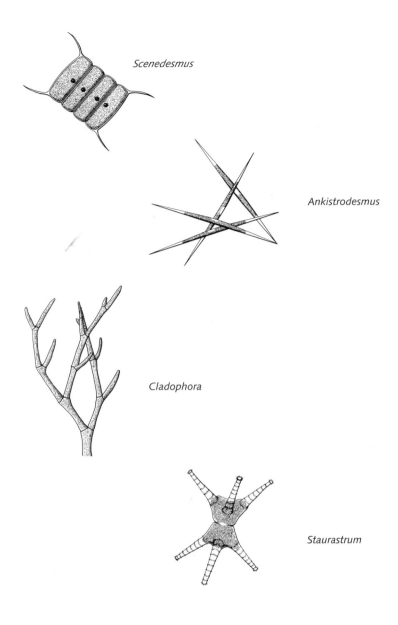

Scenedesmus

Ankistrodesmus

Cladophora

Staurastrum

Figure 31. Green algae (Chlorophyta) include many different shapes and colonial forms.

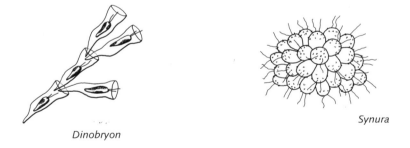

Dinobryon

Synura

Figure 32. Golden-brown algae (Chrysophyta) include colonial forms *Dinobryon* and *Synura*.

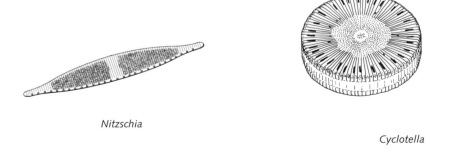

Nitzschia

Cyclotella

Figure 33. The diatoms (Bacillariophyta) have glasslike cell walls that are intricately marked.

Asterionella

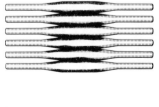

Fragilaria

colony" would actually be smaller than the head of a pin! With individual cells and colonies so small, scientists need efficient ways to assess the crop of algae in a lake. The simplest way to estimate the amount of phytoplankton in a lake is to measure the chlorophyll *a* concentration in a representative sample of water as described in the Water Quality section. Chlorophyll *a*, which is a major photosynthetic pigment and universally distributed among algae, accounts for approximately 0.5% to 2% of the dry weight of algae, depending on the species. Chlorophyll *a* concentrations are not only fairly simple to measure but results are very reproducible. As a rough guideline, lakes with average summer concentrations of chlorophyll *a* less than 5 μg/L are clear and appear algae-free, lakes with average concentrations over 25 μg/L are soupy and not attractive for swimming. A chlorophyll *a* concentration over 30 μg/L at any time is considered to be an "algal bloom".

Although an estimate of the concentration of chlorophyll *a* in a lake is very useful, it tells nothing of the species of algae present which can be indicative of various conditions. Therefore, biologists sometimes undertake a more painstaking way to assess the amount of algae in a lake. The relative abundance of each species of algae present in a representative sample of water is determined, then the biomass of each species is estimated. The sample of water is usually taken from the euphotic zone with a tube that is lowered from the surface to the depth of the bottom of the euphotic zone. The water is trapped in the tube, the sample is brought to the surface, placed in a jar and a preservative is added so the algae cannot reproduce or be eaten before the sample can be analyzed in the laboratory. To measure the weight (biomass) of each algal group and determine its proportion of the total biomass, algae are allowed to settle to the bottom of the water sample in a special cylinder; individual cells, colonies or filaments are then identified and counted under a microscope. The number of individuals for each species is then converted to a volume based on measurements made on representative cells of that species in the sample. The size of cells of different species covers a wide range, for example, one cell of blue-green *Anabaena flos-aquae* has an approximate volume of 50 μm^3; one cell of dinoflagellate *Ceratium hirundinella* has an approximate volume of 65 200 μm^3. Since phytoplankton cells are neutrally buoyant, a volume of phytoplankton weighs the same as a similar volume of water, 1 cubic centimetre weighs 1 gram. Once the weight of each species is determined, the weights are then totalled to give an estimate of the total phytoplankton biomass (wet weight) per unit volume of water. Estimates of algal crop based on chlorophyll *a* measurements and biomass calculation usually follow the same pattern over a season, if samples are taken from the same lake at the same time.

SEASONAL VARIATION   Seasonal variation in phytoplankton biomass and species composition occurs because algae are affected by physical factors such as temperature, currents, lake mixing, light intensity and day length; chemical factors such as dissolved oxygen, nutrient concentrations and salinity; and biological factors such as disease and the density and community composition of their consumers. The abundance of a particular species of algae depends on the balance between factors that cause the population to increase (reproduction, recruitment from lake sediments and immigration via inflowing water) and factors that cause the population to decrease (sinking, death, including grazing by zooplankton or other algae, and loss from the lake through outflowing streams).

In Alberta lakes, as in other north-temperate lakes, phytoplankton biomass is generally lowest from December through February because the cold and darkness under ice and snow result in minimal algal growth. If the ice on a lake is clear and free of snow, under-ice algal blooms may occur occasionally, as in Driedmeat Lake in the winter of 1985/86 when chlorophyll *a* concentrations reached an amazing 459 µg/L. Algal biomass often peaks in the spring when temperature, light levels and nutrient concentrations increase, the latter as a result of lake mixing or a high concentration of nutrients in runoff. A decline in late spring usually occurs as the lake water becomes thermally stratified and nutrient levels in the upper layers of water decrease and algal production slows. At the same time, the abundance of phytoplankton consumers, such as zooplankton, increases. In shallow nutrient-rich lakes such as Nakamun, Baptiste, Tucker, Little Fish, Amisk and Figure Eight lakes, algal blooms occur regularly all summer. In lakes with lower concentrations of nutrients, such as Narrow, Twin and Ethel lakes, algal biomass may remain low until fall. Another peak may occur as the lake water mixes in the fall because nutrients are again recycled into the surface water. In reservoirs with low nutrients and rapid flushing rates, like Spray Lakes, Ghost, Travers and Little Bow Lake reservoirs, algal biomass is low all year.

In spring and fall, the phytoplankton community is dominated by a mixed community of small-celled species from the diatom, green algae, golden-brown algae and cryptophyte groups that have adapted to grow rapidly at low temperatures, relatively low light levels and short day-lengths. These small-celled species are generally very susceptible to grazing by zooplankton. In summer, larger-celled species such as *Ceratium hirundinella,* large diatoms or colonial blue-greens such as *Anabaena flos-aquae* are often dominant. These species grow less rapidly, but are generally resistant to zooplankton grazing. This seasonal succession is clearly seen in freshwater lakes such as North Buck, Buck, Baptiste and Isle, and slightly saline lakes such as Gull. In more saline lakes such as Miquelon, Oliva and Peninsula, this typical seasonal succession is altered and fewer algal species are present because fewer species can thrive in saline water.

Blue-green algal blooms in summer are a concern in many Alberta lakes because these algae tend to accumulate in very thin layers near the lake surface. Wind and wave action concentrate these unattractive scums into bays or along the shore. When the algae in the scum eventually decompose, blue pigments in the cells are released and it looks as if blue paint has been spilled in the water or along the shore (Fig. 36). Strong sewagelike odours are produced. In general, the development of summer blue-green algal blooms in Alberta is triggered by high water temperatures and the onset of low dissolved oxygen concentrations over bottom sediments, which often results in high total phosphorus concentrations.

The most troublesome blooms in Alberta are caused by three species of blue-green algae (*Anabaena flos-aquae, Microcystis aeruginosa* and *Aphanizomenon flos-aquae*) although other species can also cause blooms. Blooms of the first two species can make the lake water look like pea soup. *Aphanizomenon flos-aquae* occurs in flakes that look like tiny grass clippings. Some species of blue-green algae produce toxins which can be fatal to animals. The distribution of these toxins is not well documented in Alberta, although certain lakes such as Hastings, Baptiste and Little Fish have had known occurrences of toxic blooms, and the death of wildlife by algae has been documented in a number of lakes including Steele Lake. In general, avoid drinking water from a bloom-infested lake, and provide alternative water sources for pets and livestock.

J.M. Crosby and A.M. Trimbee

Aquatic Macrophytes

Aquatic macrophytes are also primary producers in fresh water, but unlike individual members of the phytoplankton, they are large and usually conspicuous. Macrophytes are the flowers, bushes and trees of the underwater world. They provide cover and spawning ground for fish, habitat for both the invertebrate community and epiphytic algae, and food and habitat for ducks, moose, muskrats and other animals. In addition, macrophytes release oxygen which can be used

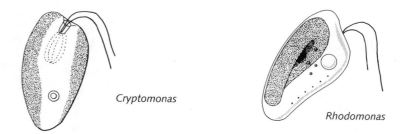

Figure 34. Cryptophytes (Cryptophyta) are single biflagellate cells with two chloroplasts.

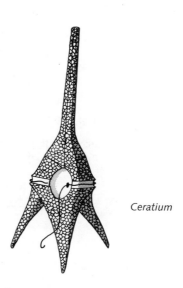

Figure 35. The dinoflagellates (Pyrrhophyta) are single, large, fast-moving cells.

Figure 36. Dense blue-green algal blooms form in nutrient-rich Alberta lakes. Photo courtesy of D. Durand.

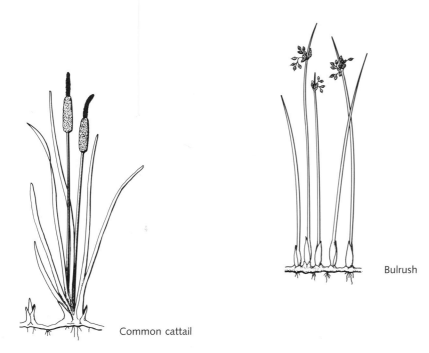

Figure 37. Emergent macrophytes such as cattails and bulrushes are conspicuous along the shore of many Alberta lakes.

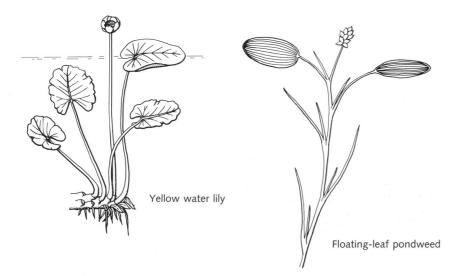

Figure 38. Floating-leaved macrophytes grow in shallow, calm parts of lakes.

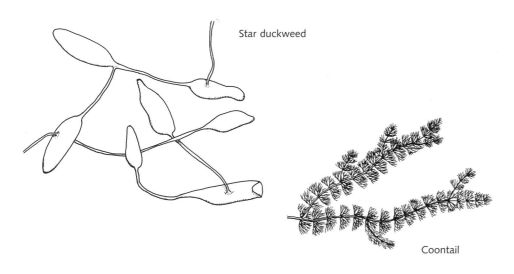

Figure 39. Free-floating macrophytes often have very finely divided leaves.

by freshwater animals. Aquatic macrophytes are vital components of all fresh water and must be preserved in moderate abundance for a healthy, productive lake.

GROWTH HABITS OF AQUATIC MACROPHYTES   Aquatic macrophytes can be classified into four categories based on their growth habits: emergent, floating-leaved, free-floating and submergent. **Emergent macrophytes**, such as cattails (*Typha latifolia*), bulrushes (*Scirpus* spp.) and sedges (*Carex* spp.), are rooted in water-saturated or submerged soils but the shoots emerge above the water surface (Fig. 37). They occur over a depth range from about 0.5 m above the water's edge to a depth of 1.5 m into the water. Emergent plants can take advantage of constituents of both the terrestrial habitat (for example, light and atmospheric carbon dioxide) and aquatic habitat (unlimited water supply), and are one of the most productive plant communities in the world. The **floating-leaved macrophytes**, such as water lily (*Nuphar variegatum*) and some pondweed species (*Potamogeton natans*), are generally rooted in the lake sediments at water depths from about 0.5 to 3 m. These plants are usually restricted to calm waters where their leaves are protected from tearing by strong waves or currents (Fig. 38). **Free-floating macrophytes** are not rooted in the lake bottom, but instead float freely on the water surface or in the water column. They range in form from minute (less than 1 cm in diameter) surface-floating plants with few or no roots, such as duckweed (*Lemna minor*), to large branched forms suspended in the water column, such as bladderwort (*Utricularia vulgaris*) and coontail (*Ceratophyllum demersum*) (Fig. 39). **Submergent macrophytes** such as northern watermilfoil (*Myriophyllum exalbescens*) and many pondweeds (*Potamogeton* spp.), are rooted in the lake bottom and, with the exception of the flowers, do not emerge above the water surface (Fig. 40). They may occur at water depths that receive sufficient light for photosynthesis down to depths as great as 10 m.

CONDITIONS FOR MACROPHYTE GROWTH   In any lake, the extent to which macrophytes colonize an area is determined by the **physical factors** of sediment texture, wave action, water depth, and light (Fig. 41). Water depth restricts emergent vegetation to a maximum depth of about 1.5 m. In addition, wave action abrades emergent, free-floating and floating-leaved foliage, disturbs the bottom sediments and pulls up rooted vegetation; it also increases turbidity and reduces light availability to submerged plants. The scouring of near-shore areas by drifting ice during spring break-up can create a zone relatively free of aquatic plants down to a depth of about 1 m. As a result, aquatic macrophytes grow at shallower depths along protected shorelines than in wave-exposed areas. Good examples of this distribution can be seen in Wabamun, Moose and Muriel lakes.

The maximum depth to which aquatic plants can grow in any lake is largely determined by **light**. As light passes through water it is rapidly reduced in intensity as a result of both scattering and absorption by the water and the particles suspended in it. Aquatic macrophytes generally colonize to depths receiving 1% to 4% of the surface light intensity. The depth to which 1% of the surface light penetrates is determined by the density of planktonic algae, turbidity (concentration of suspended sediment), and water colour (which can range from clear to brown). In eutrophic, turbid or brown-water lakes, aquatic macrophytes are restricted to shallow depths due to the low light penetration, for example, Cooking, Hastings, Isle and Sturgeon lakes. In contrast, plants have been found as deep as 6 to 7 m in Alberta lakes with relatively clear water such as Muriel and Narrow lakes.

Information on the maximum depth of macrophyte colonization is not yet available for many of the lakes discussed in the *Atlas*. However, scientists at the University of Alberta developed a simple formula to predict this depth based on Secchi disc depth and information derived from 23 Alberta lakes. For example, the formula (given in Section 1 of the Appendix) indicates that in a lake with a mean summer Secchi depth of 1.3 m, macrophytes might be expected down to a depth of 3.3 m.

Within the area where plants can live, the variety and abundance of macrophytes is determined by a complex interaction of physical

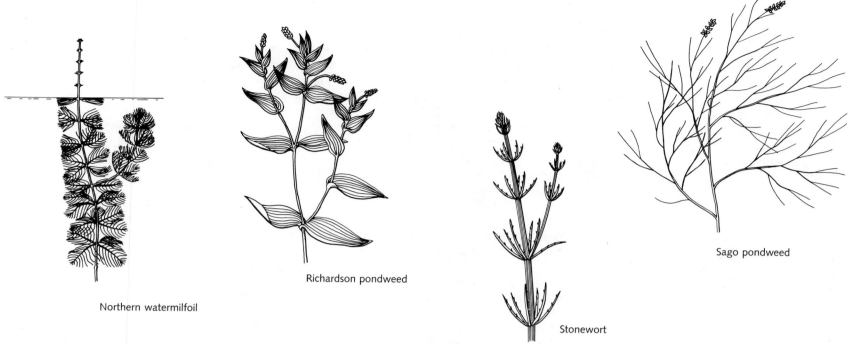

Northern watermilfoil

Richardson pondweed

Stonewort

Sago pondweed

Figure 40. Submergent macrophytes display a wide variety of leaf shapes and sizes.

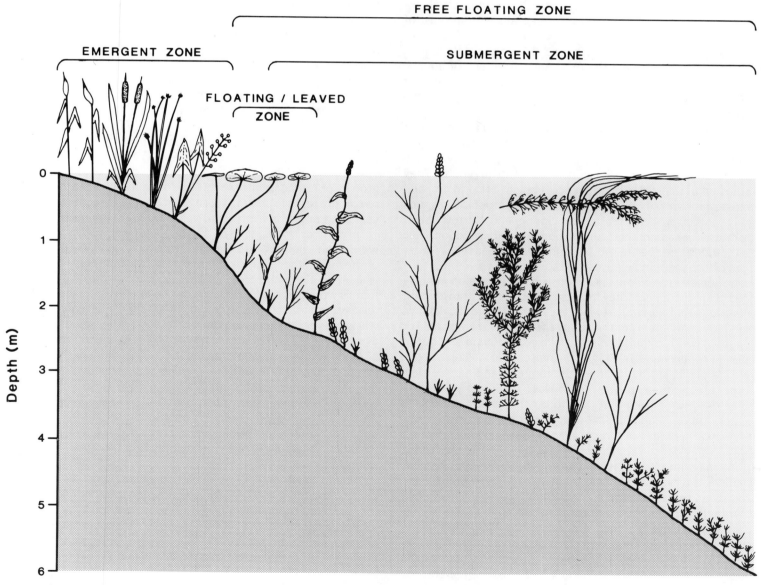

FREE FLOATING ZONE

EMERGENT ZONE

SUBMERGENT ZONE

FLOATING / LEAVED ZONE

Depth (m)

Figure 41. The distribution of different types of macrophytes is largely determined by physical factors such as depth, light, wave action and sediment texture.

and chemical factors, such as light, depth, sediment texture and nutrient availability. In general, aquatic macrophytes are in low abundance in oligotrophic lakes such as Rock and Crowsnest and Chain Lakes Reservoir, presumably due to low nutrient availability. In mesotrophic and eutrophic lakes such as Wabamun, Elkwater, Island, Crimson and Skeleton, macrophytes grow abundantly, probably because of the higher concentrations of nutrients in these lakes. In hyper-eutrophic lakes, such as Cooking Lake, macrophytes are restricted to a fringe along the shoreline because light levels under water are low as a result of high planktonic algal concentrations. In addition to changes in aquatic macrophyte abundance, the forms of plants dominating the community also change with lake trophic status. Thus, nutrient-poor lakes like Narrow, Hubbles and Hasse tend to be dominated by short, slow-growing, often evergreen, species such as stoneworts, whereas nutrient-rich lakes like Pine, Ste. Anne and Pigeon support tall, highly branched species such as northern watermilfoil (*Myriophyllum exalbescens*), coontail (*Ceratophyllum demersum*) and large-sheath pondweed (*Potamogeton vaginatus*).

The growth of macrophytes may be limited by **chemical** factors. Some of Alberta's lakes are moderately saline, such as Miquelon and Buffalo. Here, the only macrophytes to thrive are *Ruppia occidentalis* and *Potamogeton pectinatus*. Other pondweeds, northern watermilfoil, coontails and other macrophytes cannot survive. In extremely saline lakes, such as Oliva Lake, the only macrophyte present is salt-tolerant *Ruppia occidentalis*.

CLASSIFICATION OF AQUATIC MACROPHYTES Aquatic macrophytes encompass the larger aquatic plants as distinct from the microscopic planktonic and benthic algae, and include representatives from most of the major divisions of the Plant Kingdom, specifically macroscopic algae (stoneworts), mosses, horsetails and flowering plants.

Stoneworts and mosses are the most ancient groups of aquatic macrophytes. Stoneworts, also called muskgrasses because of their strong musky odour, are a large form of algae. Like all algae, the stoneworts have no roots; instead they are attached to the lake bottom by rhizoids (rootlike filaments without vascular tissue). These plants consist of an upright jointed stem from which arises a whorl of cylindrical branches. Species of the genus *Chara* are by far the most conspicuous members of the stoneworts found in Alberta. They grow attached to the sediment and reach a height of up to 1 m and occur most abundantly in mesotrophic to mildly eutrophic lakes such as Pigeon, Hasse, Seibert, Wabamun, Spring and Narrow lakes. Aquatic mosses are commonly found in northern soft-water or acidic lakes, although some species can be found in a lake such as Wabamun. They closely resemble terrestrial mosses.

Aquatic horsetails and flowering plants are more developmentally advanced than the algae. They possess a system for transporting nutrients and carbohydrates between the leaves and roots. Aquatic horsetails include members of the genus *Equisetum*, the horsetail or scouring rush, which is found near the lake edge both in and out of the water as, for example, in Gregoire, Crimson and Musreau lakes.

Flowering plants are by far the most common and most widely distributed aquatic macrophytes. Freshwater flowering plants appear to be descended from terrestrial forms that adapted to life in fresh water. Although aquatic flowering plants still possess relics of their terrestrial heritage, including a waxy outer layer and pores (stomata) on the leaf surface to regulate water loss, they have also undergone major modifications to adapt to an underwater habitat. For example, leaves have become thinner, larger and more finely dissected so as to capture more light. The amount of chlorophyll (photosynthetic pigment) on the leaf surface has also increased to enable the plants to use light more efficiently. As well, support tissue, which is no longer necessary in water, has been lost and replaced by air spaces used for storing carbon dioxide to provide buoyancy. Certain species have also gained the ability to use bicarbonate ions as a source of carbon for photosynthesis rather than carbon dioxide. While carbon dioxide is plentiful in air, it is relatively scarce in the hard-water lakes of Alberta. Therefore, plants that can take advantage of the higher levels of bicarbonate in water have an advantage over those that cannot. In addition, freshwater flowering plants have developed a wide variety of ways to reproduce asexually and thus overcome the problem of having to reach the water surface to flower. Many species of submergent macrophytes can reproduce vegetatively—a small cutting can rapidly grow into a new plant.

The largest and most widely distributed group of freshwater flowering plants in Alberta is the genus *Potamogeton*, the pondweeds. They are present in nearly all of the lakes for which plant surveys have been conducted. The pondweeds show great variability in shape: some possess ribbonlike leaves (*P. zosteriformis*) or threadlike leaves (*P. pectinatus*), whereas others have broad, smooth-edged leaves (*P. richardsonii*), and still others have both floating leaves that are broad and submerged leaves that are threadlike (*P. natans*). The pondweeds are a source of food for waterfowl, muskrats, beaver and moose. They also provide cover for fish and for many invertebrates that are a food source for fish.

Other species of flowering plants common in Alberta lakes include coontail (*Ceratophyllum demersum*), northern watermilfoil (*Myriophyllum exalbescens*), common cattail (*Typha latifolia*), common great bulrush (*Scirpus validus*) and sedges (*Carex* spp.). Coontail and northern watermilfoil are found in many Alberta lakes down to a maximum depth of about 6 m. They are eaten by muskrats and waterfowl, shelter young fish and harbour fish food organisms. Cattails, bulrushes and sedges are common in marshy waters and along lakeshores. They are important because they provide food and cover for birds and small animals, and prevent erosion by binding the soil together and by protecting the shoreline from wave action.

STUDIES OF AQUATIC MACROPHYTES IN ALBERTA LAKES The naturally abundant growth of macrophytes in many Alberta lakes can impair recreational activities, lead to summer and winter fish kills, and impede boat traffic. The conflict between plants and recreation prompted many of the studies of aquatic vegetation in Alberta lakes. In particular, Baptiste, Nakamun, Garner, Skeleton, Pine, Crimson, Muriel, Moore, St. Cyr, Ethel, Driedmeat, Coal, Pigeon and Buffalo lakes have been sites of extensive investigation by or for Alberta Environment. Aquatic macrophyte surveys have also been conducted by scientists from the University of Alberta at Figure Eight, Narrow and Long (near Athabasca) lakes. The longest and most intensive macrophyte study in Alberta was started in 1974 at Wabamun Lake by consultants for TransAlta Utilities Corporation in response to abundant growth of Canada waterweed (*Elodea canadensis*), a plant that is rare in the rest of Alberta. Twice-yearly mapping continued for five years and mapping every third year was still ongoing in 1989.

In most of these surveys, transect lines perpendicular to shore were established at 15 to over 100 locations, depending on the size of the lake. Either a large rake was used to obtain samples of plants from sites along the transect line, or plants from within quadrat frames were collected by SCUBA divers. Species were identified and relative abundance was assessed. In addition, the entire shoreline was surveyed to the maximum depth that plants could be seen, to assess plant growth in areas between transect lines. The University of Alberta surveys also determined the fresh and dry weight of plants per unit area of lake bottom. Results of these studies are usually presented as maps of distribution patterns of the dominant species. Most of these maps show plant beds and species composition only for the year surveyed. Emergent beds tend to occur in similar locations year after year, but the long-term Wabamun study showed that submergent beds may vary in abundance, location and composition from year to year.

Alberta Environment has published several manuals on aquatic plants, including a key for identifying the common aquatic macrophytes of Alberta and a guideline for controlling aquatic weed growth in ponds and dugouts. However, it should be noted that aquatic plant control in Alberta lakes requires approval from Alberta Environment and Alberta Forestry, Lands and Wildlife.

P.A. Chambers

Invertebrates

Animals that eat plants are primary consumers. On land, primary consumers include cows, deer, mice, insects and humans. In Alberta lakes, most of the primary consumers are invertebrates, small "bugs and worms", that either drift freely in the water as zooplankton, or live among the aquatic macrophytes or on the sediments as benthic invertebrates. Not all of these small creatures are peaceful plant-eaters, some are voracious predators (secondary consumers) on other invertebrates, whereas others eat organic debris. The zooplankton form a vital link in the chain of productivity in lakes. They transform the algae, the minute producers of the open water, into food for other life forms, including fish.

Zooplankton

Most people who use and enjoy lakes would never realize that there is a multitude of tiny animals suspended in the open water of the lake. These are the zooplankton, a collective word for several types of small invertebrate animals that inhabit the open water. Most range in length from 0.1 to about 3 mm. By peering into the water on the shady side of a boat on a sunny day, one can see the larger zooplankters jerkily swimming past.

TYPES OF ZOOPLANKTON There are three main groups of these organisms in Alberta lakes. The **rotifers** are very small (0.05 to 0.5 mm) and soft-bodied (Fig. 42), but many have a thickened cuticle called a lorica, which may have facets, spines or extensions. They have no swimming legs, but move through the water by beating tiny hairs called cilia, which are arranged in a circle at the forward end of the animal. When the cilia beat, they appear to spin like a wheel, and rotifers are sometimes called "wheel animals". Most rotifers feed on bacteria, small algal cells and organic matter, but a few feed on other tiny animals.

The **copepods** are crustaceans, and are thus related to shrimp. Most adult copepods range between 0.5 and 4 mm in length, and they have swimming and grasping legs and antennae (Fig. 43). Most copepods, like most of the freshwater zooplankton, carry their eggs until they hatch. Newly hatched copepods look quite different from adults. Because their outer skin is hard, as it is in shrimp, copepods must go through a series of 11 to 13 moults before they reach adulthood. There are two main types of copepods in the zooplankton. Calanoid copepods have long antennae and feed mainly on algae. Cyclopoid copepods, with short antennae, are fast-moving little animals; the adults often feed on other animals, but immature stages and some adults eat algae.

Cladocerans, sometimes called water fleas, are also crustaceans (Fig. 44). They have large antennae used for swimming and a thin, bivalved shell that does not cover the head. Their five or six pairs of legs are used for funneling and filtering food particles. Adults of most species range in size between 0.2–mm and 3–mm long. Most of the year, when food is plentiful in the lake water, cladocerans produce female young only, without the benefit of fertilization by males. But when conditions become unfavourable, such as when their food supply dwindles, males are produced and mating occurs. A different kind of egg results; they are enclosed in a heavy-walled case and shed during the next moult. These resting eggs can withstand freezing and drying and allow the population to pass through adverse times in a protected state. Sometimes the lakeshore is strewn with these tiny saddle-shaped egg cases, or they look like large pepper grains on the surface of the water. After a period of time—usually a minimum of three weeks—and in response to little-understood conditions, these eggs hatch, and the young cladocerans renew the population cycle.

ZOOPLANKTON IN ALBERTA LAKES There are a few species of zooplankton in Alberta lakes that are both abundant and widespread. For example, many of the dominant species in deep, unproductive Cold Lake are the same as those in shallow, highly productive Cooking Lake. The ubiquitous cyclopoid copepods *Diacyclops bicuspidatus thomasi* and *Mesocyclops edax* are perhaps the most wide spread

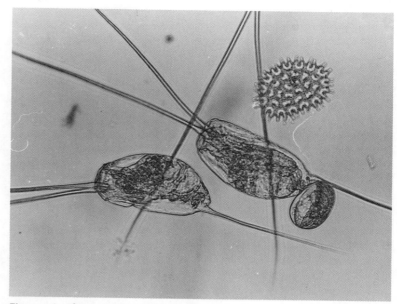

Figure 42. These rotifers (*Filinia* sp.) are from Cooking Lake. One carries an egg. Photo by D. Wighton.

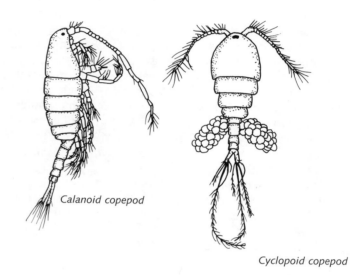

Calanoid copepod

Cyclopoid copepod

Figure 43. Cyclopoid and calanoid copepods are common types of zooplankton in Alberta lakes.

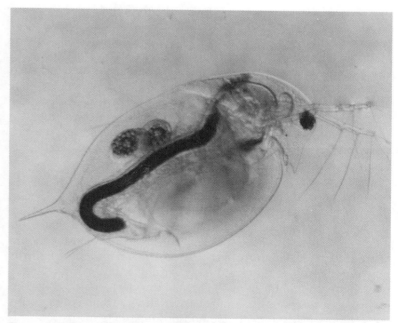

Figure 44. This cladoceran, *Daphnia pulex*, is abundant in many lakes in early summer. The photomicrograph is of a living animal taken from Miquelon Lake. Photo by P.A. Mitchell.

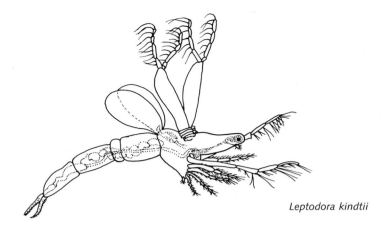

Leptodora kindtii

Figure 45. This large cladoceran, *Leptodora kindtii,* is the only one that feeds on other zooplankton.

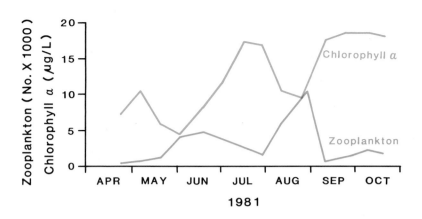

Figure 46. The numbers of large grazing zooplankton and algal biomass (chlorophyll *a*) varied inversely over the summer of 1981 in Wabamun Lake.

and common species of copepod in Alberta lakes. As adults, they feed on other zooplankton. *Diacyclops bicuspidatus thomasi* has some notoriety in Alberta, because it is the intermediate host for *Triaenophorus crassus*, the parasitic worm that infests cisco and lake whitefish. There is usually one or sometimes two dominant calanoid copepod species in each lake as well. In typical freshwater lakes, *Diaptomus oregonensis* is the most common calanoid copepod (as in Baptiste, Tucker, and Lessard lakes), but in more saline lakes *Diaptomus sicilis* is prevalent (as in Gull, Miquelon and Garner lakes), and some lakes have both species (Wabamun, Amisk, Lac La Biche, Hastings). Rotifers are sometimes dominant in some lakes, as in Crowsnest Lake when it was sampled in 1976. The most common species of rotifer in Alberta lakes are *Keratella cochlearis* and *K. quadrata*, but other species may become very abundant at times. The predaceous *Asplanchna priodonta* is one of the largest rotifers in Alberta lakes. Cladocerans, notably *Daphnia pulex*, *Daphnia pulicaria* and *Daphnia galeata mendotae*, may dominate the zooplankton in early summer, to be replaced by other cladocerans such as *Diaphanosoma leuchtenbergianum*, *Chydorus sphaericus* and *Bosmina longirostris* later in the summer and in early autumn.

FOOD AND SEASONAL CYCLES   Most zooplankters eat phytoplankton, the algae of the open water, but filter-feeders like the Cladocera will eat any appropriate-sized organic matter. A few species of rotifers and copepods feed on other zooplankton but the only predaceous cladoceran in Alberta lakes is *Leptodora kindtii*, of fantastic appearance and relatively enormous size — up to 18 mm (Fig. 45).

Populations of the various species of zooplankton change over the seasons in response to changing light conditions, water temperature, dissolved oxygen, food supply and predation, as well as to inherent growth and behavioural factors. In the spring, when zooplankton populations are increasing and small-celled types of algae are present, grazing zooplankton may greatly reduce the quantity of algae in the water. Sometimes the water will become crystal clear, but is teeming with large *Daphnia*, as has been observed in Tucker and Nakamun lakes, for example. As the phytoplankton is grazed, some of the less edible species of algae may increase at the expense of the edible ones, and eventually the water becomes green again.

Population changes of zooplankton over seasons have been little-studied in Alberta lakes, but it is likely there are general similarities among similar types of lakes. One of the few studies in Alberta was conducted in 1981 in Wabamun Lake. The graph in Figure 46 shows how populations of algae and large grazing zooplankton changed over the seasons in this lake. Phytoplankton were already abundant in the water when the ice left the lake in late April, and the cladocerans *Daphnia galeata mendotae* and *Bosmina longirostris* took advantage of this large supply of food. Their populations increased dramatically, so that by June they were very abundant. The June samples indicated an equally dramatic decline in phytoplankton. By July, blue-green algae such as *Anabaena* were becoming abundant,

and the *Daphnia* and *Bosmina* populations declined. In many eutrophic lakes, species of *Daphnia* do not seem to thrive when blue-green algae are abundant, either because the algal colonies are too large for them to eat, or because they may not be able to digest some types of blue-green algae even though the cells are small. In August, blue-green algae declined and there was another pulse of zooplankton, particularly the cladocerans *Chydorus sphaericus* and *Daphnia retrocurva*, and numerous immature copepods. By September, the zooplankton population had declined, and filamentous blue-greens (*Lyngbya birgei*) and diatoms (*Melosira italica, Stephanodiscus niagarae*) were abundant.

Seasonal cycling in zooplankton and phytoplankton is much more complicated than the above description would suggest. Water temperature plays a role, because higher temperatures increase the rate of metabolism in all these organisms. When the water is warm, zooplankton need more food, but they can also reproduce faster. Predation—one animal eating another—also plays a role.

Fish are important predators on the zooplankton. Small crustaceans are the main food of most types of young fish and a few species of adult fish, such as cisco and various minnows. The decline in the *Daphnia* population in Wabamun Lake in July 1981 may have resulted partly from the abundance of young fish, which typically feed in the open water at that time of year.

It is known that the presence or absence of fish can greatly influence the types of zooplankton present in lakes and ponds. Fish tend to eat the largest-sized animals they can find, and therefore will remove large-bodied forms such as *Daphnia* and *Diaptomus*. Smaller-sized zooplankton, such as *Chydorus*, *Bosmina* and some species of cyclopoid copepods, will then become abundant.

Light conditions may also affect the population structure. A copepod or a cladoceran living several metres below the surface of the lake would experience very different light conditions on a day that the water was relatively free of algae, compared to a day when it looked like pea soup. *Chydorus sphaericus* leaves its normal home in the shallow areas among weed beds to move into the open water during the time when blue-green algal blooms develop, perhaps in response to the different light conditions. The types of zooplankton that prefer the open water of lakes will also migrate away from shore if they happen to drift into shallow water.

Copepods and cladocerans also migrate vertically in response to light conditions. During the day, most species tend to stay in deep water, but as darkness approaches they move toward the surface of the lake. The clearer the lake water, the greater the extent of vertical migration. In a murky, green lake, the migration up and down might cover only a metre or so but in a clear lake, such as the Kananaskis Lakes, zooplankton might migrate tens of metres every day. Light—both the colour and intensity—is the cue that stimulates cladocerans and copepods to move up or down. Such migratory behaviour has adaptive significance. It may allow these animals to avoid predators, obtain high quality food, or grow more efficiently at the lower temperatures near the bottom.

ZOOPLANKTON STUDIES   In spite of the importance of zooplankton in transforming algae into food for other life forms including fish, they are often neglected in lake studies, perhaps because their life cycles and population structure are complex and highly variable over the seasons and even from year to year within the same lake. In addition, analysis of zooplankton samples to determine biomass and species composition is very labour intensive.

To sample the zooplankton, a biologist drops a specially-designed net (Wisconsin net) over the side of a boat to the desired depth, and then pulls it up to the surface. The mesh size is usually 64 to 80 μm, which retains all but the smallest animals (a few rotifers will go through mesh of this size range). The animals in the sample are counted and wet or dry biomass may be determined. The volume of lake water that passed through the net is estimated so the number or weight of zooplankton per unit volume of water can be determined. Sometimes a different piece of equipment, called a plankton trap, is used. It is lowered down in an open position, then closed at a particular depth. The water in the trap runs out through a mesh-enclosed "bucket", similar to that used on the end of the Wisconsin net. The sample is reported as number of zooplankton per litre of lake water, or dry or wet weight (biomass) per volume of water for that particular day.

Although there have been few detailed assessments of population dynamics of the zooplankton in Alberta, several inventories of zooplankton species have been conducted as part of limnological or fisheries studies. These include baseline surveys on several lakes in the Beaver River drainage basin (Cold, Tucker, Ethel and Moore lakes). In addition, Alberta Environment has assessed biomass and abundance of zooplankton in Baptiste, Wabamun, Gull, Beaverhill, Cooking, Miquelon and Hastings lakes. The University of Alberta studied the relative importance of zooplankton in 15 central Alberta lakes and conducted intensive studies of plankton dynamics in Narrow and Amisk lakes. The most extensive inventory of zooplankton in Alberta covered mountain lakes, many of which are not included in the *Atlas*.

P.A. Mitchell

Benthic invertebrates

Benthic invertebrates are small animals without backbones that live in or on the bottom mud, on aquatic plants, on or under rocks, on sunken or floating trees, and among the debris on the bottoms of lakes or streams. There are many kinds of benthic invertebrates that inhabit our lakes, but most of them go unnoticed by the casual observer. These animals play a critical role in lakes because, as a group, they eat almost any form of organic material, for example, bacteria, small algae, filamentous algae, large aquatic plants, decaying plant material, microscopic animals, other macroinvertebrates or large dead animals. As well, they are the major food of many fish, waterfowl and shorebirds. Despite their importance in aquatic ecosystems, invertebrate communities have not been intensively studied in Alberta lakes.

Although benthic invertebrates inhabit all lakes in Alberta, the number of animals and the number of types (or species) that occur depends on a large number of factors, including water depth, the amount of nutrients in the water, the presence of oxygen throughout the year, the presence of fish, whether large plants are present, and the connections between water bodies as the last ice sheets retreated. Water depth, lake area and the fertility of the lake are important factors in determining the size of the various depth zones of a lake and the abundance of invertebrates. Lakes can be divided into three depth zones: littoral, sublittoral, and profundal. Each of these zones and the benthic invertebrates that might be found there are discussed separately and summarized in Table 7.

The **littoral zone** can be defined as the area from the water's edge down to the maximum depth at which large aquatic vegetation can grow. The lake bottom in this zone can consist of soft mud, sand or rocks. Typically, there is also a large amount of plant debris, including leaves, stems, twigs and even whole trees, that may fall in the lake. Because there are hiding places and abundant food, the littoral zone

supports a far greater quantity and diversity of invertebrates than the other depth zones. Furthermore, water temperatures and dissolved oxygen concentrations are higher in the littoral zone than in deeper areas, so invertebrates and their food grow more quickly. A sample of plants and sediments from the littoral zone of any Alberta lake could contain an abundance of different species. Scuds (amphipods) (Fig. 47) are usually the most abundant invertebrates in the littoral zone in productive Alberta lakes such as Tucker, Ste. Anne, Gull and Utikuma.

The littoral zone is also home for the invertebrates that are usually among the most conspicuous to recreationists. Water beetles and water boatmen are easily seen dodging among the aquatic plants near shore. Young dragonflies, damselflies and mayflies hatch and feed as nymphs in the littoral zone; when they mature, they emerge as winged insects to dart and hover along the shoreline (Fig. 48, 49). Snails, or at least their shells, are often found along the beach after a windy day. Leeches swim in the littoral zone, or hide in the sediment; some species suck blood and intimidate swimmers, but many species, especially the large ones, feed on other invertebrates and are as harmless to humans as earthworms.

Lakes that naturally contain large fish such as yellow perch, northern pike or suckers, probably also contain large clams, usually *Anodonta grandis*. Large clams are intolerant of low oxygen concentrations, and therefore are usually not found in lakes where summer or winter fish kills occur. Additionally, larval clams require fish as a host for a short time. Most benthic surveys of Alberta lakes either have ignored these large clams or have only sampled deep waters where they do not live. The biomass of clams can be several times greater

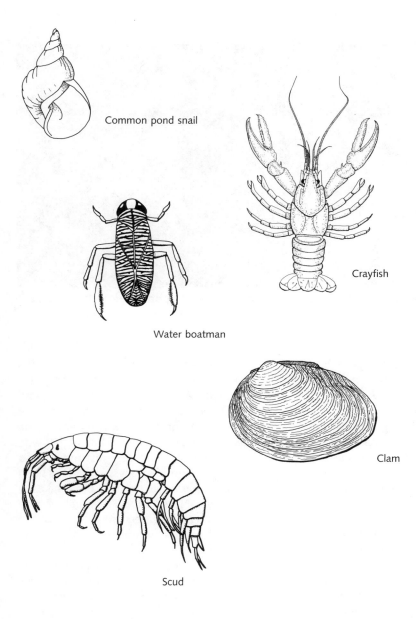

Common pond snail

Crayfish

Water boatman

Clam

Scud

Figure 47. Benthic invertebrates commonly found in the littoral zone are familiar to most lake users.

Table 7. Benthic invertebrate groups commonly found in Alberta Lakes.

Common Name	Phylum	Class	Order/Family	Substrate	Depth Zone
flatworms or planarians	Platyhelminthes	Turbellaria	several	on sediments, under rocks, on plants	littoral
leeches	Annelida	Hirudinea	several	in sediments, under rocks and logs	littoral
aquatic earthworms	Annelida	Oligochaeta	several	mostly in sediments	all depths if oxygen present
scuds or sideswimmers	Arthropoda	Crustacea	Amphipoda	free-swimming, on all surfaces	littoral; 1 profundal sp.
opossum shrimp	Arthropoda	Crustacea	Mysidacea	cold, well-oxygenated water	profundal
crayfish	Arthropoda	Crustacea	Decapoda	under rocks and logs	littoral
midge larvae	Arthropoda	Insecta	Diptera/ Chironomidae	in sediments and occasionally on plants	all depths
phantom midges	Arthropoda	Insecta	Diptera/ Chaoborinae	free-swimming and in sediments	profundal
mayflies	Arthropoda	Insecta	Ephemeroptera	variable habitats	some sublittoral
caddis flies	Arthropoda	Insecta	Trichoptera	mostly on plants, rocks and logs	littoral
water beetles	Arthropoda	Insecta	Coleoptera	free-swimming; on plants, sediments	littoral
water boatmen and back-swimmers	Arthropoda	Insecta	Hemiptera	free-swimming	littoral
dragonflies and damselflies	Arthropoda	Insecta	Odonata	free-swimming; on plants, sediments	littoral
snails	Mollusca	Gastropoda	several	on all surfaces	mostly littoral
fingernail and pea clams	Mollusca	Pelecypoda	Sphaeridae	on and buried in sediments	littoral and sublittoral
unionid clams	Mollusca	Pelecypoda	Unionidae	buried in sediments	littoral and upper sublittoral

Figure 48. Dragonflies live underwater as nymphs before they emerge as beautiful winged adults. Photo by D. Wighton.

Figure 49. In late spring, damselfly nymphs climb out of the littoral zone to take to the air and dart along the shoreline. Photo by A. Lindoe.

than that of all other invertebrates combined. Large clams have been found in Long Lake (near Athabasca) and Narrow Lake but they also occur in Baptiste Lake, Amisk Lake, Lac La Biche, Lac Ste. Anne, and many other lakes. Crayfish (*Orconectes virilis*) are another large type of invertebrate, but they only occur naturally in Alberta in the drainage system of the Beaver River. Crayfish feed at night, hide under rocks and logs during the day, and are very fast moving, so they are seldom seen or collected in benthic surveys. They have been reported only from Amisk Lake but probably occur in other lakes in the Beaver River basin, for example, North Buck, Pinehurst, Moose and Marie lakes. Although crayfish can be eaten, the populations in Alberta lakes are probably too small and slow growing to permit any significant harvest.

The **sublittoral zone** is the most difficult zone in a lake to define. It begins at the point where large plants disappear and continues down to the lower boundary of all plant life. Benthic algae and photosynthetic bacteria often grow on the sediments in the sublittoral zone. The lower boundary is usually not obvious, especially in

shallow, well-mixed lakes. Sublittoral zone sediments are made up of finer particles than littoral sediments, but partly decayed plant material still occurs, particularly near the edge of the weed beds. Lakes that support large numbers of snails and clams often have areas where many empty shells accumulate. There are fewer species of invertebrates present in the sublittoral zone than the littoral zone, largely because food is less abundant and hiding places are fewer. The most common groups of animals are midge larvae, aquatic earthworms and fingernail clams (Fig. 50). Some lakes also have moderate numbers of mayfly nymphs and unionid clams in the area between the lower edge of the weedbeds and the top of the thermocline. As lakes cool in the fall, many scuds and snails migrate down out of the littoral zone and into the upper part of the sublittoral zone, perhaps to avoid being frozen into the ice. In the spring, these animals migrate back up into the littoral zone.

The **profundal zone** is the area below the deepest extent of all plant growth, including algae and photosynthetic bacteria; it is dark and temperatures are characteristically low. Shallow lakes may not have a true profundal zone. However, if some of the bottom area has fine-grained sediments and is free of all conspicuous plants and algae, this area is often considered the profundal zone. The profundal sediments are very fine-grained and vary in consistency from soft muck to a poorly defined, jellylike material. The primary source of food for invertebrates in this zone are organisms or organic particles settling out of the water column. Some of this organic debris originates on land or in the littoral zone; this material decreases with the distance from shore. Very few types of invertebrates live in the profundal zone, because the habitat is fairly uniform (fine sediments), the food supply is sparse and the water is relatively cold. In lakes where oxygen concentrations are very low or nil during all or part of the year, this area may contain few or no organisms. Some species of midge larvae (Fig. 51) can withstand very low dissolved oxygen concentrations and are the dominant invertebrate in the profundal sediments of Alberta lakes. If oxygen concentrations are not greatly depleted, aquatic earthworms can also be found. At certain times of the year, phantom midge larvae also inhabit the profundal zone. Young phantom midge larvae are free-swimming, whereas older larvae rest in the profundal sediments during the day and migrate into the water column at night to feed on small zooplankton. Some of the large, cold, well-oxygenated lakes in Alberta, such as Cold, Athabasca and Lesser Slave lakes, also contain two unusual invertebrates, opossum shrimp (*Mysis relicta*) and deepwater scuds (*Diporeia hoyi*). These two crustaceans usually occur together and are important prey of deepwater fish such as lake trout. Deepwater scuds spend most of their time on the bottom and feed on organic matter in the sediments. Opossum shrimp are found on or near the bottom during the day where they also feed on organic matter in the sediments. Opossum shrimp are strong swimmers, and at night they migrate up into the water column where they actively search for and prey upon all sizes of zooplankton. These shrimp have been stocked into the Upper and Lower Kananaskis Lakes, Spray Lakes Reservoir and Crowsnest Lake to serve as food for young lake trout and rainbow trout. It is too early to determine if the introductions to Crowsnest Lake and Spray Lakes Reservoir have been successful, but rainbow trout in the Kananaskis Lakes make extensive use of opossum shrimp as food. Fisheries managers cannot introduce opossum shrimp into lakes indiscriminately because they are voracious feeders on plankton and have greatly altered the zooplankton community, to the detriment of fish, in some lakes in the western United States and Scandinavia.

STUDIES OF BENTHIC INVERTEBRATES   Benthic invertebrates are very difficult to study. Their abundance varies widely in space and time, therefore many samples must be collected to obtain an adequate estimate of abundance. This is especially true for the littoral zone community. Hence, estimates of invertebrate abundance are only available for a few Alberta lakes, for example, Narrow, Seibert, Sturgeon and Wolf lakes and Lac Ste. Anne. Only for Narrow Lake are there sufficient data to allow examination of the variation in abundance of invertebrates with both space and time. Sampling in most Alberta lakes has been of the survey type, which identifies the most abundant species present in a lake, but does not allow comparison of invertebrate abundance among lakes. Some benthic surveys have only sampled one depth zone of the lake or samples were collected randomly all over the lake and then average abundance was calculated. Whole-lake comparisons require that estimates of abundance in the littoral, sublittoral and profundal zones be multiplied by the area of the respective depth zones. These values are then added together and the resulting number is divided by the total area of the lake. Thus, random sampling can result in highly biased estimates of invertebrate abundance and one could wrongly conclude that one lake is more productive than another, when in fact the opposite is true. Throughout the *Atlas*, efforts have been made to show when and how many samples were collected, which depth zones were sampled and how often samples were collected for any estimates of invertebrate abundance.

J.M. Hanson

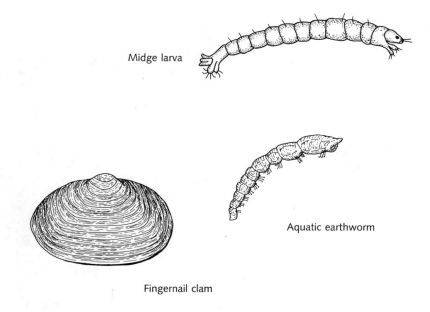

Figure 50. Benthic invertebrates commonly found in the sublittoral zone include many burrowing forms.

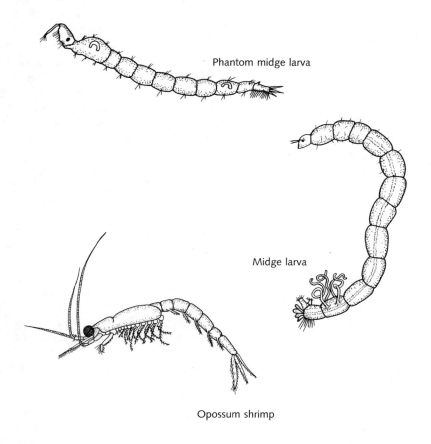

Figure 51. Benthic invertebrates commonly found in the profundal zone include insect larvae and opossum shrimp.

Fish

Fish are among the most important biological components of Alberta lakes. Their ecological importance stems from such activities as their role as predators (of zooplankton, benthic invertebrates, or each other), as occasional consumers of plant material and detritus and as modifiers of habitat and water quality. More obvious are their roles as providers of recreation, food and jobs, directly and indirectly, via the activities of sport, domestic and commercial fisheries. And to a growing number of people, fish populations are used as indicators of the general health of aquatic ecosystems, to be conserved, protected or restored.

Alberta's Fish Fauna

There are 51 species of fish believed to be native to the province, with an additional 8 introduced species that are reproducing and maintaining viable populations. Several other species may also be found occasionally within restricted areas. These numbers can change through time as additional populations immigrate into the province or existing populations are discovered, as rare populations undergo local extinction, and as new introductions are carried out. Among our current 59 species, 45 to 50 can regularly be found in lakes, whereas 10 to 15 species are primarily restricted to rivers and streams. Alberta's fish fauna pales in comparison to more southerly areas (for example, Ohio is much smaller but contains 166 species) and is also smaller than the faunas of our neighboring provinces to the west and east.

It is generally accepted that a combination of historical, geographical, and ecological factors has contributed to our relatively impoverished fish fauna. It is unlikely that many fish were in Alberta at the height of the Wisconsin glaciation, approximately 18 000 years ago, when nearly all of the province was buried under ice. Most, if not all, of the native fishes now present in Alberta must have immigrated from nonglaciated refugia outside of the province, after the glaciers had retreated, 12 000 to 15 000 years ago. To understand the composition of our present-day fauna, we need to know something about the refugia from which they came and the dispersal routes that they used.

The largest areas that could have served as glacial refugia for fishes lay to the south. However, a glance at a map suggests a major difficulty for fish dispersing into Alberta: except for a small area in the southeast drained by the Milk River, the lakes and rivers of the province all drain to the north (Beaufort Sea) or northeast (Hudson Bay), areas that largely remained glaciated until after Alberta was free of ice. Fortunately, however, drainage patterns did not always exist in their present form, or we would probably have far fewer species than we do.

An important feature of the landscape at the end of the ice-age was the formation of postglacial lakes created from the great volumes of water produced by the melting glaciers (Fig. 52). These lakes flooded vast areas and provided major routes for the dispersal of fish, even across what are currently drainage boundaries. Most important for the recolonization of Alberta was Glacial Lake Agassiz, which covered much of Manitoba, as well as parts of Ontario, Saskatchewan, North Dakota and Minnesota. This lake received water from several lakes to the west, and in turn drained to the Mississippi River and the Great Lakes, thus providing a connection from these species-rich areas to Alberta via the North and South Saskatchewan rivers. Movement from the Saskatchewan system into the Peace and Athabasca drainages was possible via Glacial Lake Edmonton. Other dispersal routes included temporary connections between the South Saskatchewan and Milk (and thus Missouri River) drainages and routes across the continental divide, via the Fraser and Peace drainages, from a Columbia River refuge.

It is largely because of the existence and relative importance of these postglacial dispersal routes that we have as many species as we do, and that our fauna is more similar to that of Saskatchewan and Manitoba than to the fishes of British Columbia. Still, because of our headwater position and greater distance from glacial refugia, we have fewer species than our neighbours to the east. Only those

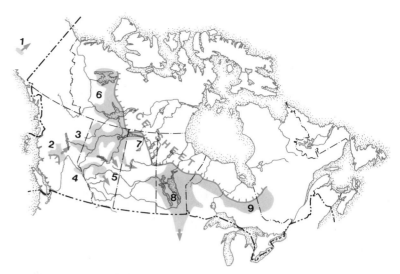

Figure 52. Major postglacial lakes covered large portions of North America as the Wisconsin ice sheet retreated. Although no longer in existence, these lakes provided dispersal routes for fishes recolonizing Alberta from refugia to the south. The lakes were: 1. Dezadeash 2. Prince George 3. Peace 4. Miette 5. Edmonton 6. McConnell 7. Tyrrell 8. Agassiz 9. Barlow-Ojibway. Arrows indicate the direction of flow from postglacial lakes. SOURCE: adapted from Crossman and McAllister 1986.

species capable of dispersing long distances across a variety of habitats were able to reach Alberta and, as a result, many of our fishes are both wide-ranging and able to live in a variety of environments.

Ways of Classifying Fish

Just as anglers, ecologists, and fish biologists may be interested in different aspects of fish, they may also have different systems for classifying them. Indeed, there can be many ways of classifying fishes, depending on which features of fish are chosen as the basis of the classification system.

Fish biologists base their taxonomic classification scheme on the patterns of evolutionary relations among different groups of fishes. The basic unit in this classification is the **species**, a group of similar organisms whose members can breed with one another to produce fertile offspring. Biologists give each species a unique, two-word name, or Latin binomial, that consists of the **genus** to which it belongs (genus is the next larger category above species), and a word that denotes the species. Thus, closely related species, such as brook trout, which is named *Salvelinus fontinalis*, and lake trout, which is named *Salvelinus namaycush* (Fig. 53), are placed together in the same genus, that is, the genus *Salvelinus*. Related genera are placed together into a family, for example, shiners (genus *Notropis*) and dace (genus *Phoxinus*) are placed together into the minnow family (Cyprinidae), which also includes eight other genera in Alberta. Thus, to a fish biologist, a minnow is a member of the family Cyprinidae, a specific group of related species (Fig. 54). In contrast, a common use of the term "minnow" is to describe any small fish, including the juveniles of species in other families. The 51 native fishes in Alberta belong to a total of 13 families, the most diverse being Salmonidae (including trout, charr, and whitefishes), Cyprinidae (minnows), Catostomidae (suckers), and Percidae (perch).

Fishery biologists and anglers often employ a classification system that is based on the use of a particular species. Thus, "sport" or "game" fish include those species pursued by recreational anglers, whereas "commercial" species are the ones sought in commercial fisheries for sale or trade, or to be used as food for other animals (for example, mink) that are sold or traded (Fig. 55). Some species, such as walleye, may fit into both "sport" and "commercial" categories. The use of species in the "bait fish" category should be obvious; a group that overlaps with bait fish is "forage fish", species that are eaten by other fish. Finally, a category variously referred to as "rough fish", "coarse fish", or even "trash fish", includes those

Rainbow trout Black spots on back, sides and tail. Mature fish have a broad pinkish band along sides. Occurs in lakes, ponds and streams throughout Alberta, but mainly in southern half of province.

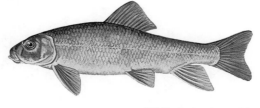

White sucker Snout blunt, mouth slightly subterminal, bottom feeder. Abundant in lakes and rivers throughout Alberta.

Brook trout Sides have many red spots bordering with bluish haloes. Tail is nearly square-cut. Lower fins have pronounced white border, and are often striped with red and black. Occurs mainly in eastern slope streams and ponds.

Longnose sucker Snout projects well beyond upper lip, bottom feeder. Occurs in rivers and deep lakes throughout Alberta.

Cutthroat trout Narrow pinkish band often along sides. Red stripe in crease along inner edge of lower jaw. Large body spots on back and upper sides with more towards tail. Occurs in lakes and streams along southern slopes.

Fathead minnow A blunt-headed yellowish minnow, reaches a maximum length of 9 cm. Widespread in central and southern Alberta, tolerant of extremes of pH and salinity and low dissolved oxygen so it occurs in areas where other fish cannot survive.

Brown trout Golden brown sides sprinkled with pale bordered rusty red or orange spots. Tail is square-cut. Occurs in lakes and streams in the eastern slopes.

Spottail shiner A silvery bluish-green minnow with a distinct black spot at the base of the tail, reaches a maximum length of 10 cm. Common in lakes and streams throughout Alberta.

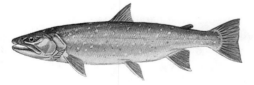

Bull trout Yellow to red spots on back and sides. Pelvic and anal fins often have white leading edge. Mature males often have red belly. Once known as Dolly Varden. Occurs in lakes and streams throughout the eastern slopes.

Lake chub A greenish silver-sided minnow, maximum length of 13 cm. Common in lakes, rivers and creeks throughout Alberta.

Lake trout White spots from head to tail. Tail is deeply forked. Occurs in northern lakes, and in a few lakes in the eastern slopes.

Longnose dace A minnow with a dark back and silvery sides, maximum length of 15 cm. The name comes from the long snout that sticks out in front of the subterminal mouth. Common in lakes, rivers and creeks throughout Alberta.

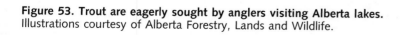

Figure 53. Trout are eagerly sought by anglers visiting Alberta lakes. Illustrations courtesy of Alberta Forestry, Lands and Wildlife.

Figure 54. Minnows (Family Cyprinidae) and suckers (Family Catostomidae) are common in many lakes in Alberta. Illustrations courtesy of Alberta Forestry, Lands and Wildlife.

Walleye Spiny first dorsal fin. Lower tip on tail is white. Glassy eyes. Often found in schools. Occurs in lakes throughout Alberta, except for the eastern slopes.

Northern pike Elongated body, head depressed forward, with ducklike jaws. Occurs throughout Alberta, except in the foothills and mountains.

Yellow perch Sides have broad, dark vertical bars which extend almost to the yellow underside. Fins have sharp spines. Often found in schools. Occurs throughout Alberta, except in the foothills and mountains.

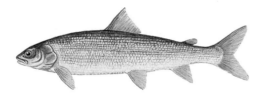

Mountain whitefish Small mouth below a pointed snout. Tail deeply forked. Occurs throughout the eastern slopes.

Lake whitefish Olive-green to bluish on back, and silvery sides. Small mouth below a rounded snout. Tail deeply forked. Occurs in lakes throughout Alberta.

Figure 55. Walleye, northern pike, yellow perch and mountain whitefish are among the favourite sport fishes of Alberta's anglers, and lake whitefish is the main target of the commercial fishery. Burbot are caught by both anglers and in the commercial fishery. Illustrations courtesy of Alberta Forestry, Lands and Wildlife.

Table 8. Temperature requirements for some representative cold-water, cool-water and warm-water fishes.

Group Species	Spawning Temperature[a] (°C)	Optimum Temperature[b] (°C)	Lethal Temperature[c] (°C)
Cold-Water			
Brook trout	2–13	16	20–25
Rainbow trout	3–15	17	21–26
Cisco	1–9	18	20–26
Cool-Water			
Walleye	2–16	23	32
Yellow perch	2–19	25	29–33
Northern pike	7–19	26	28–33
White sucker	8–21	27	29–31
Warm-water			
Largemouth bass[d]	12–27	30	36
Bluegill[d]	22–33	30	37
Carp[d]	12–30	32	35–40

[a]Spawning temperature range observed in the field
[b]Based on growth data
[c]Initial temperature at which prolonged survival is not possible; this will vary with age of fish and acclimation temperature
[d]Established populations do not exist in Alberta, but do occur elsewhere in Canada

species that have no obvious use (at least to those who are doing the classifying!) and *may* compete with more "desirable" fishes. Suckers may be the most abundant fish in Alberta that fall into this category (Fig. 54), as are carp (*Cyprinus carpio*) elsewhere in North America. However, as Dr. J.S. Nelson has stated, they are "no more deserving of this title than is the waxwing or bluejay deserving to be called a 'trash' bird just because they are not hunted and eaten like grouse or ducks".

The fish ecologist also uses a variety of classification systems, which are based on ecological characteristics of the species, for example, what they eat. Piscivores, for example walleye and northern pike (Fig. 55), eat other fish; planktivores, such as cisco and spottail shiners, eat plankton, and so on. Although this system is widely used and quite appropriate in many situations, many fish eat a variety of prey, so categorizing them in this way may not be clear cut. For example, a yellow perch will eat primarily zooplankton during its first year of life, take a mixture of larger invertebrates as it grows, but eventually it will include fish in its diet. Other ecological classifications of fish are based on the habitats in which they live or their mode of reproduction.

Another system is based on temperature requirements for growth, reproduction and other biological processes. These groups consist of "warm-water", "cool-water", or "cold-water" fishes (Table 8), although these names are a bit misleading for north-temperate regions, where even warm-water fishes can survive the winters. Cold-water fishes, such as lake trout, burbot and cisco, prefer temperatures well below 20°C and generally spawn in the fall, winter, or very early spring. Cool-water fishes, including northern pike, yellow perch and white sucker, tend to prefer temperatures in the low 20s (°C) and spawn during the spring. Warm-water species, such as some of our minnows (Cyprinidae) or the sunfish of eastern North America, prefer temperatures near 30°C and spawn during the summer.

Distribution of Fishes within and among Lakes

Many ecological factors interact to influence the distribution and abundance of fishes. Most fishes have physiological mechanisms to deal with relatively small changes in oxygen, pH (acidity) and depth. However, because a fish's body temperature corresponds to the water temperature of its immediate habitat, temperature directly affects rates of metabolism, activity, growth, development, reproduction, and survival and ultimately the distribution and abundance of different species. Therefore, it is no surprise that among all of the physical and chemical factors that may affect fish, temperature is referred to as the "ecological master factor".

The actual temperature experienced by a fish in an Alberta lake, especially during the summer stratification period, depends on where in the lake the fish is located. Because water temperature varies throughout a stratified lake, fish have the potential to select a particular temperature. Anglers know that fish are not randomly distributed in a lake, but that some species are more likely to be found in certain areas, whereas other species will be concentrated in other habitats. Given what we know about fish biology, it is reasonable to believe that each species will select habitat(s) that have temperatures most favourable for growth and reproduction, all other factors being equal. Cold-water fishes, such as lake trout, are generally found in deep, cold waters, whereas warm-water minnows are generally restricted to small, shallow ponds or lake margins that warm up rapidly in spring and remain that way through the summer. A number of studies suggest that fish can even compete for particular areas that possess favourable temperatures.

Of course, all other factors are rarely equal, and other factors present in the environment may prevent fish from occupying the habitat with the most favourable temperature. Low oxygen concentrations may limit use of the hypolimnion by cold-water fishes, forcing them to occupy water warmer than their preferred temperature. This may be common in deeper, stratified lakes in Alberta, such as Baptiste. Detailed sampling in Amisk Lake has shown that by late summer, cisco are restricted to the top 8 m if dissolved oxygen concentrations in deeper water fall under 2 mg/L, but they are found much deeper in lakes where oxygen in the hypolimnion is sufficient, as in Cold Lake. In contrast, high light levels may cause walleye to avoid surface waters and occupy deeper, darker, and cooler zones than would be predicted on the basis of temperature alone. Competition with other fish and the presence of predators may restrict fish distribution; for a particular fish, it may be worth the cost of reduced growth to avoid the greater cost of being eaten by a predator. The distribution of food resources could also influence fish distributions. Even though their effects on distribution can be established for each individual environmental factor, the interactions of several factors can quickly make predictions of habitat use by fishes a rather inexact science, to which most anglers can attest!

One can also use these single-factor relations as the basis for predicting the distribution of fishes among lakes, and for predicting the species composition of a lake's fish community. For example, knowing that lake trout is a cold-water species that is usually restricted to deeper, colder parts of large, deep, oligotrophic lakes (for example, Lake Athabasca), one could predict correctly that this species would be absent from more productive, shallower, and therefore warmer lakes, such as Wabamun. One would similarly predict correctly that other cold-water species, for example, lake whitefish, cisco, burbot, will co-occur with lake trout in other large, deep lakes (for example, Cold and Peerless). Conversely, smaller, shallower lakes and ponds that lack areas of cold water during the summer will likely lack cold-water fishes and are usually dominated by one or another group of cool- or warm-water species, for example, yellow perch, northern pike, or various minnows. These general patterns of fish communities, in which certain species occur together in certain types of lakes, are recognized by fish biologists and anglers alike.

However, just as the prediction of the distribution of a single species within an individual lake is fraught with complexities, so too is trying to understand the composition of a lake's fish community. There are exceptions to even the best single-factor relations, for example, the normally deep-water burbot, a cold-water species, is abundant in shallow Lac Ste. Anne. Furthermore, although some cold-water species may be restricted to larger, deeper lakes, these lakes can also contain cool- or warm-water species, which inhabit surface waters or shallow bays. This latter exception, however, is really an illustration of another general pattern. Larger, deeper lakes contain a greater variety of habitats than small, shallow ponds and, as a result, have a greater number of sites for reproduction, a greater diversity of foraging sites and predator refuges, and as a consequence, are usually able to support a greater number of species. For example, Cold Lake, at 373 km² and 99-m deep, contains 24 species whereas nearby Tucker Lake, at 6.6 km² and 7.5 m, has only 8 species.

Figure 56. Nearly a half-million anglers enjoy fishing in Alberta's waters each year, a dramatic increase over the last 10 years. This increased pressure, however, requires that our fisheries resource be well-managed. Photo courtesy of Alberta Tourism.

Among the biological factors that influence the distribution of species among lakes and the composition of fish communities, predation appears to be most influential. Studies of fish communities in small lakes of southern Ontario and northern Wisconsin, as well as Alberta, have all shown that the presence or absence of a population of piscivorous fish, such as northern pike, yellow perch or largemouth bass, determines what other species will occur in a lake. In small lakes of the Athabasca River drainage basin of central Alberta, only yellow perch and/or white sucker regularly occur with northern pike, whereas brook stickleback, fathead minnow and several other minnows (Cyprinidae) are almost never found in lakes with pike but are common where pike are absent. In spite of the fact that these two kinds of fish communities often occur in environmentally-similar lakes, the presence of northern pike in some lakes can apparently prevent the successful establishment of the small (and easy to eat) species. In larger lakes, the impact is often not so dramatic, but predators and competitors can affect the abundance and sizes of some populations of fish.

Fisheries Management

Albertans are very much interested in the fisheries resource of the province (Fig. 56). An indication of the importance of this resource can be seen in the data on the numbers of people who participate in angling in the province. A survey conducted in 1985 indicated that nearly 450 000 individuals spent an average of 17 days fishing per year, for a total of 7.6 million "fishing days". These numbers represent a substantial increase over the last decade. Because of this high level of interest, and the pressure that this interest places on the fisheries resource, the resource must be well-managed. Although some people involved in sport or commercial fishing are primarily interested in increasing or decreasing the numbers or sizes of fish, depending on whether or not a particular species is considered desirable, the fishery biologist is interested in understanding and quantifying the roles of fishes in the functioning of a lake ecosystem. Of course, greater understanding should lead to an increased ability to manage fish populations and communities in the directions desired by society; achieving these goals via ecologically sound approaches is the major objective of the fishery biologist.

Strategies for fisheries management need to consider and address both the goals of society with respect to fisheries and the major biological and environmental problems that face the resource. Although society's goals for fisheries are varied, H.A. Regier has grouped them into three general categories: *material well-being*, focusing on fish that are caught to be sold commercially as food, *cultural opportunity*, associated with the recreational/cultural experiences of anglers, and *environmental harmony*, involving a nonconsumptive appreciation of the fisheries resource as an indication of ecosystem health. Components of these categories include a healthy

Figure 57. Commercial fishing, a $3 million per year business in Alberta, is most often a part-time, seasonal activity. Gill nets are usually set under the ice, with lake whitefish the primary target species. Photo courtesy of Alberta Forestry, Lands and Wildlife.

Figure 58. The Fish and Wildlife Division of Alberta Forestry, Lands and Wildlife conducts creel censuses on several of the sport-fishing lakes of the province. These surveys provide fisheries managers with important information on fish populations and angler success and satisfaction. Photo courtesy of Alberta Tourism.

environment, an abundant supply of fish for food, employment, income and the maintenance of a way of life, fish that are uncontaminated and therefore suitable for use as food, recreational opportunities and the harmonious use of the fisheries resource so as not to preclude the other elements. Successful fisheries management is thus a complex mixture of natural and social sciences and humanities.

From the elements listed above, it is clear that an important job of a fisheries manager is to determine the quantity and quality of fish available to be allocated to the the three general goals of material well-being, cultural opportunity, and environmental harmony. Managers do not want the quantity that humans take to exceed the maximum **sustainable yield**, which is the proportion of fish that can be harvested during a year without depleting the long-term population level. Within properly set limits (in terms of amount, size, and season of harvest) human-induced fishing mortality in some populations may actually limit population fluctuations and permit a sustainable harvest by removing the portion of the population that would otherwise die from natural factors. The Fish and Wildlife Division of Alberta Forestry, Lands and Wildlife has established management

policies that designate lakes having economically important fish populations for sport, commercial and domestic fishing. It is the job of the fisheries manager to determine the sustainable yield of a population, or an aggregate yield for an entire fish community, and find ways to divide it equitably among the various user groups.

The three major groups involved in the use of fishery resources for material well-being and cultural opportunity are those involved in sport, commercial and domestic fishing. In Alberta, **sport fishing** is the largest of the three. It has both the most participants and the largest harvest. There are 17 species of fish in Alberta that are generally sought after by anglers. Surveys have indicated that walleye is the favorite fish of Alberta anglers that is common in lakes, although they catch more yellow perch and spend more total "recreation days" fishing for northern pike, than any other species. A number of species of "trout" (including lake, rainbow, cutthroat, brook, brown and bull) are also prized in the lakes (and streams) in which they occur, either naturally or through stocking programs. Wabamun Lake is one of the few lakes in the province in which a sport fishery for lake whitefish has developed, although interest in the species, especially for ice fishing, is increasing in other lakes. Anyone may sport fish upon the purchase of a fishing licence, although those under 16 or over 65 do not need a licence. Anglers must become familiar with and abide by the sport fishing regulations, which are updated and published annually by the Fish and Wildlife Division; rules applying to individual lakes are mentioned in each lake chapter of this *Atlas*.

Commercial fishing, which produced $3.15 million in revenues in 1988, is only a part-time occupation for most participants in the province (Fig. 57). Commercial fishing licences have been issued in Alberta since 1910, with catches regulated since 1917. Lake whitefish is the predominant species taken in the commercial fishery; many lakes in Alberta produce large numbers of this cold-water species that would otherwise not be harvested by anglers. In many of the larger lakes, e.g., Athabasca, Lesser Slave, Cold, and Lac La Biche, the commercial fishery also takes northern pike, lake trout and/or walleye incidental to the lake whitefish harvest. Other lakes may have small fisheries for cisco, burbot, and suckers.

Like commercial fishing, the **domestic fishery** is usually conducted with gill nets, set primarily for lake whitefish; however, the purpose of domestic fishing is to provide food directly for the licensee and his/her family and animals, for example, dog teams. Most licences are issued to native people, as the native domestic fishery is guaranteed in treaties and in the Natural Resources Transfer Agreement of 1930. Some non-natives living in remote areas, for example, trappers, also have domestic fishing privileges. As with sport and commercial fishing, domestic fishing requires a licence and is subject to limits and regulations.

SETTING LIMITS   What are the proper limits and how does the fisheries biologist establish them? A key element is the productivity of a lake, in terms of the amount of biomass of fish and other biological elements that is produced during the course of a year. Many factors influence the biological and fisheries production of lakes, some of which were discussed previously in the Water Quality section of this introduction. Although the various individual factors will vary in importance from lake to lake, fisheries biologists wish to establish criteria that can be used in developing a general fisheries strategy. D.S. Rawson, one of the best-known fisheries biologists of an earlier generation, related the trophic nature of a lake, and the quantity and quality of fish production, to four groups of factors: *edaphic/geological*, relating to the chemical fertility of the watershed, *morphometric/topographic*, associated with the physical dimensions of the lake basin, *climatic*, and *biotic/cultural*, including the introduction of materials and non-native species, and the alteration of the habitat.

In the mid-1960s, R.A. Ryder quantified the relationship between two of Rawson's factors (the edaphic and the morphometric) and fish production while developing what he called the "morphoedaphic index". The relationship has subsequently been combined with climatic factors to establish expected regional estimates of fish production; these estimates are, of course, especially useful for regional planning and involves sets of lakes rather than a detailed management plan for any single lake. Other information specific to that lake, for example, from creel censuses and size distributions from test fishing, is then required to determine production estimates, as has been done, for example, with Amisk Lake.

To assess the number, sizes, and species of sport fish that are being harvested from a lake, fisheries managers regularly conduct **creel censuses**, or surveys of anglers (Fig. 58). In its simplest form, a creel census is a survey of anglers regarding the number of fish of each species caught, and the total number of hours fished. These surveys are statistically designed to reduce errors that are inherent in the sampling procedures. It is very important that the anglers participating in these surveys provide honest, accurate information so that fish managers can properly assess total harvests, angler success rates, and angler satisfaction levels. Creel surveys have been used in the management of many Alberta lakes and reservoirs, such as Beauvais, Chain Lakes, Lesser Slave, McLeod, and Payne.

The commercial fishery is now closely monitored to assess its effects on fish populations. Usually, commercial fishing is only allowed in certain parts of a lake and at certain times of the year, to avoid catching species of fish that are allocated to the sport fishery. A sample of the catch is taken from each fishery to determine the age structure of the population. The fisheries manager tries to maintain at least three different year-classes, or fish born in a particular year, of each species in the catch, so that the effects of annual population fluctuations are limited, and the annual quotas are consistent, predictable and attainable. A change in the age structure of the catch is a good indication of over- or under-fishing; if the average age of the population declines, over-fishing is suggested, whereas under-fishing will likely result in an increase in average age. In response to such changes, quotas can be increased or decreased, or permissible mesh sizes of the gill nets can be changed, to exclude more (or fewer) immature fish. The most common mesh size used for lake whitefish is 140 mm (measured on a stretched diagonal). Similar monitoring of the sport fishery can be conducted during creel censuses. Closed seasons, lower catch limits, and increased size limits can be imposed to reduce overfishing effects.

These effects are illustrated by the historical records of the commercial catches from several Alberta lakes. Whitefish fisheries in particular have been subject to large fluctuations, closed seasons, and very slow recovery rates. Although the immediate cause of weak or collapsed fisheries is usually attributed to poor or failed year-classes, the ultimate causes are often not completely understood, although over-fishing is probably a major factor. The Wabamun Lake fishery collapsed in 1961 after reaching levels of nearly 480 000 kg in 1955. Heavy exploitation contributed to the collapse of the lake whitefish and walleye fisheries in Lesser Slave Lake in the mid-1960s; harvests of whitefish alone averaged over 450 000 kg/yr during the five-year period 1958–1962. Other factors that were involved included the use of gill nets with small mesh sizes (set for cisco), which caught many juvenile lake whitefish, and slow growth rates, which reduced replacement rates of catchable lake whitefish. Lower quotas and closure of the small-mesh fishery in 1972 has resulted in more stable year-class structures and increased fishery harvests.

FISH STOCKING   Increased fishing intensity, combined with habitat alteration, are two major pressures on the Alberta sport fishery. One technique used by fishery managers to address these problems is fish stocking. Fish are stocked into lakes for a number of purposes. One is to create angling in fishless lakes or introduce desirable, high-profile species into areas where they did not occur naturally. Many useful introductions have been made into waters that did not previously provide high-quality angling; however, as numerous examples throughout the world can unfortunately demonstrate, prior research and considerable caution must be exercised before an introduction proceeds. Second, fish are stocked to restore populations that have declined severely, for example, due to winterkill. A third purpose of stocking is to augment populations where natural reproduction is unable to provide fish production sufficient to meet the angling demand.

Early efforts in stocking focused on the introductions of salmonid

Figure 59. The culturing and stocking of fish into lakes are important components of fisheries management in Alberta that create or improve fish populations for anglers. Rainbow, brown, brook and cutthroat trout are cultured at the Sam Livingstone hatchery in Calgary. Photo courtesy of Alberta Forestry, Lands and Wildlife.

populations into mountain lakes, and there is a continued emphasis today on salmonid stocking for recreational fishing. Catchable-sized rainbow trout are stocked into many smaller lakes (20 ha) on a seasonal basis to provide a "put-and-take" fishery. Early stocking also included the replenishment of whitefish stocks in commercial waters, or the attempt to establish new whitefish fisheries in other lakes. Lake whitefish populations in McGregor, Muriel, and Newell lakes are the result of the planting of "eyed-eggs" from a hatchery at Lesser Slave Lake that operated from 1928 to 1944. These and other lakes may also have received plantings of fish at later stages in development, such as the fry or fingerling stage. Stocking of yellow perch into Winagami Lake has resulted in an abundant, successfully-reproducing population. Walleye are currently being stocked in a number of lakes, including Gleniffer, Gull, Lac La Biche, North Buck, and Wabamun. These fish are primarily intended for the sport fishery, although some are caught commercially because some of the best walleye waters are large lakes where commercial fishing also takes place. In Upper Kananaskis, an invertebrate animal, the opossum shrimp, *Mysis relicta*, was introduced to provide food for the (stocked) rainbow trout.

As can be appreciated, the ability to conduct a major stocking program requires a full-scale fish culture system, which includes the extraction of eggs and milt from parent stocks (either wild or captive), fertilization, incubation, hatching and the rearing of offspring to a suitable size. Each of these steps requires the proper environment and hygenic conditions, neither of which is always easy to maintain under the high densities required for a large-scale, efficient operation. Fish for Alberta's stocking program are produced at the Sam Livingstone Fish Hatchery in Calgary, the Cold Lake Fish Hatchery in Cold Lake (Fig. 59) and the Sundance Rearing Station near Wabamun Lake. Sam Livingstone produces rainbow, brown, brook, and cutthroat trout; walleye, and rainbow and lake trout are produced at Cold Lake; and the Sundance facility produces rainbows for the "put-and-take" fisheries. Trout eggs are produced at brood stations at Raven, near Caroline, and at Allison, near Coleman,

Figure 60. Common loons feed on small fish in the open water habitat of lakes. Photo courtesy of Alberta Tourism.

Figure 61. Canada Geese and Trumpeter Swans nest and feed in shallow areas of lakes. Photo courtesy of Alberta Tourism.

although cutthroat and lake trout eggs are taken from wild populations. Walleye eggs are taken from populations in Primrose, Lesser Slave and Bistcho lakes.

OTHER PROBLEMS AND MANAGEMENT TECHNIQUES   In addition to overfishing and habitat alteration, other problems that fishery managers face include winterkill, caused by the depletion of dissolved oxygen under the ice, and diseases, including heavy infestations of parasites. Particularly common is the tapeworm *Triaenophorus crassus* that exists as a dormant cyst in coregonid fishes; the cisco in Baptiste Lake and the lake whitefish in Lesser Slave Lake historically have had heavy infestations. This parasite does not affect humans but renders the fish unwholesome as food and therefore limits the sale of infected fish.

Besides closed seasons, catch and size limits, and stocking, fisheries managers may turn to other techniques to achieve their goals. Habitat alteration is used to reclaim or restore fish habitat, or to improve its productivity. For example, shallow lakes can be deepened or their water level raised to reduce the incidence of winterkill. Perhaps the most severe technique is "chemical reclamation", that is, the application of rotenone or another fish poison to eliminate "undesirable" species that may prey upon or compete with more preferred sport fish. Such was the case when McLeod Lake was treated with rotenone in 1976 to eliminate suckers and pike, and subsequently restocked with rainbow trout. McLeod now provides one of the best trout fisheries among the lakes of Alberta.

Fisheries biologists now recognize that they must be concerned with more than just the direct harvesting of fish by the various kinds of anglers, but also with environmental insults that destroy or degrade fish habitat and thus sacrifice productivity of the resource. The three general goals for fisheries, material well-being, recreational opportunity and environmental harmony, are interrelated and must all be integrated as a whole into the fisheries management strategy. However, without protecting the biological productivity of the resource and maintaining the health of the aquatic ecosystems that harbour the resource, few of society's goals for fisheries can be attained. As K.H. Loftus (1978), a former head of Ontario's fisheries, once wrote, "Without the resource there can be no benefits, no alternatives, no strategies, and no need for fisheries management...resource protection must come first and allocation second." Healthy, well-balanced fish communities in Alberta's lakes should not only provide something to be harvested, but serve as an excellent measure of the quality of our aquatic environment and thus as a barometer for our own health and well being.

W.M. Tonn

Wildlife

A specific objective for many visitors to Alberta's lakes, and an added attraction for others, is the opportunity to observe wildlife in its natural habitat. Whether it is the plaintive cry of a loon on a boreal lake, the winnowing of snipe in a marshland, the spectacular dive of an Osprey, the wobbling parade of newly-hatched ducklings, or the silent passage of a muskrat, the sight or sound of wildlife adds immeasurably to an adventure at one of Alberta's lakes.

Alberta stretches from glacier-capped peaks in the west to the boreal forest of the north, through lush rolling farmland to arid flat prairie in the south. The diversity of terrestrial habitats is fascinating; similarly, the diversity of habitats in and around Alberta's lakes is equally impressive. Habitats in or near lakes provide a transition from water to land and there is usually a wide diversity of habitats and wildlife in a relatively small area. Some of the habitat types that develop within or near lakes and reservoirs include expanses of deep open water, shallow marshy wetlands in bays, shoreline mudflats, sand-gravel beaches, and islands of varying size and character. Just back from the shore area, there is often a zone of sedges and willows or bog, then relatively undisturbed bush or forest.

The deep, **open-water habitat** supports various fish species which are an important source of food for Ospreys, Bald Eagles, Common Loons, Common Mergansers, White Pelicans and Double-crested Cormorants (Fig. 60). River otters feed in areas where open water is close to the shore, especially where there are numerous islands or connecting channels between lakes. In the spring and fall, large expanses of open water provide important staging (resting and feeding) areas for migratory ducks and geese. Most of Alberta's large lakes include this kind of habitat; examples can be found at Beaverhill, Gull, Iosegun, and Athabasca lakes, and at St. Mary Reservoir.

Shallow areas in lakes and associated **marshy wetlands** support numerous and diverse species of plants and small organisms which provide shelter and food for many wildlife species. These areas provide habitat for over a dozen species of ducks, Canada Geese, Trumpeter Swans, Franklin's Gulls, several species of grebes, American Bitterns, muskrats and beaver (Fig. 61, 62). Small fish that live in these areas, such as stickleback and fathead minnows, are the prey of Great Blue Herons (Fig. 63), Belted Kingfishers, Black Terns, Western Grebes and mink. Moose come to feed on pondweeds and other aquatic vegetation in many lakes in the foothills and northern Alberta (Fig. 64). The marshy areas of a lake and parts of the littoral zone where aquatic macrophytes grow densely also provide habitat for several species of frogs (Fig. 65). The shallow areas of two lakes in southern Alberta, Tyrrell Lake and Crawling Valley Reservoir, provide habitat for tiger salamanders. The salamander populations in these lakes are thought to be neotenic, a condition in which mature salamanders retain larval characteristics such as external gills. This variant is not common in Alberta. Emergent vegetation such as common cattail and bulrush also provide nesting and feeding habitat

Figure 62. Muskrats are common in the marshy areas of many Alberta lakes. Photo by A. Lindoe.

Figure 63. Great Blue Herons are the largest wading birds in Alberta. Photo by A. Lindoe.

Figure 64. Moose feed on pondweeds in quiet lakes in forested areas of Alberta. Photo by D. Wighton.

Figure 65. Frogs sing in marshy areas soon after the ice melts. Photo by A. Lindoe.

Figure 66. Lesser Yellowlegs feed on insects in exposed areas of mud and gravel along the shore. Photo by P.A. Mitchell.

Figure 67. White Pelicans depend on islands for secure nesting sites. Photo by L. Noton.

for numerous types of small perching birds such as Redwinged and Yellow-headed blackbirds and Long-billed Marsh Wrens. Almost all of Alberta's lakes have examples of this habitat. Notable examples are found in Hastings, Moose, Gull and Driedmeat lakes.

Some lakes have shorelines of exposed **mudflats** or **sand** and **gravel**. These areas provide feeding, resting and, in some cases, nesting habitat for more than two dozen species of shorebirds that are found in Alberta. Some of these species, such as Killdeer, Spotted Sandpipers, Lesser Yellowlegs (Fig. 66) and Willets stay and nest, whereas others, such as Pectoral Sandpipers, Sanderlings, Dunlins, Ruddy Turnstones and American Golden Plovers are spring and fall migrants that rest and feed on their way between their breeding areas in the Arctic and their wintering grounds in the southern United States and Central and South America. A good example of this habitat can be seen on the shores of Beaverhill Lake. Lake Newell, Eagle Lake and Glenmore Reservoir also have some areas of good shorebird habitat.

Some lakes have **islands**, which can be small or large, forested or relatively bare. Islands provide secure nesting sites for White Pelicans (Fig. 67), Canada Geese, Double-crested Cormorants, Common Loons, Common Mergansers, and gulls. Because islands are often free of large predators like coyotes, populations of mice and voles sometimes increase unchecked and reach very high densities. Examples of islands used by wildlife can be found in Lac La Biche and Buffalo, Island, North Buck and Miquelon lakes, and in Milk River Ridge and Little Bow Lake reservoirs. These islands often represent the last nesting refuge for uncommon or rare species. To protect wildlife, islands should not be visited or even approached during the breeding season.

Often an area of **sedges** and **willows** develops a short distance from a lake. Here the soil is usually too wet to support larger trees or agricultural crops, but it is a zone of abundant wildlife. Marsh hawks nest in the tall grass or low shrubs and can be seen flying low over the marsh, seeking voles, frogs and insects. Short-eared Owls nest on the ground in these areas and can also be seen as they prefer to hunt in the day. American Kestrels, commonly called sparrow hawks, are often seen resting on poles or wires near marshes. Common Nighthawks perform their aerial acrobatics in the evening as they pursue insects. As darkness approaches, bats such as the little brown bat and big brown bat flit over the meadow and marshes. If forests grow near the lake, Merlin and Long-eared Owls might also be seen, as well as a wealth of warblers and other songbirds.

Artificially constructed reservoirs, particularly those with deep, open water, can provide areas valuable to some wildlife. Most reservoirs are built to store water when it is available and to release it when demand is high—usually in winter for electric power generation or in midsummer for irrigation. The wide range of water level fluctuations that results from this operation inhibits the establishment of a productive wetland/marsh habitat. Also, low water levels in winter or winter drawdowns cause serious freezing problems for muskrats, beaver, mink and otters. There are, however, two notable examples of reservoirs in southern Alberta in which the operation has been modified to provide excellent wetland habitat in a region where water is very scarce. The Tyrrell-Rush lakes complex is the first completed *Wetlands for Tomorrow* project in Alberta, and the recently built Crawling Valley Reservoir includes sub-impoundments, which promise to provide excellent habitat for muskrats and nesting waterfowl.

Lakes and reservoirs in Alberta are also valuable to terrestrial wildlife because the lake is often a focus for a park where land is preserved in its natural state and wildlife habitat is protected from encroaching agriculture or development. Most of Alberta's provincial parks are near or surround lakes—Crimson, McLeod and Dillberry lakes, to mention only a few. One of the province's largest urban parks, Glenmore, surrounds Glenmore Reservoir in the city of Calgary. The relatively undisturbed area around lakes and reservoirs often provides an oasis for wildlife such as deer, moose, bears, coyotes, badgers and a wide variety of owls, hawks and songbirds.

Readers interested in the wildlife at a specific lake may find more information by consulting the two guides written by the Finlays, or by contacting Fish and Wildlife Division, Alberta Recreation and Parks and local natural history associations. Common names of birds and mammals have been used throughout the *Atlas*; a list of common and specific names is given near the end of the *Atlas*.

J.M. Crosby and H.A. Stelfox

References

For a complete list of abbreviations used in the compilation of this reference list please refer to **Selected References**, on page 661.

Drainage Basin

Atlas of Alberta. 1969. The Univ. Alta. Press, Edmonton in assoc. with Univ. Toronto Press, Toronto.

Hardy, W.G. [ed.-in-chief] 1967. Alberta–A natural history. M.G. Hurtig Publ., Edmonton.

Hausenbuiller, R.L. 1978. Soil Science: Principles and practises. Wm. C. Brown Co., Dubuque, Iowa.

Lacate, D.S. 1969. Guidelines for biophysical land classification. Dept. For. Rural Devel., Ottawa.

Longwell, C.R. and R.F. Flint. 1961. Introduction to physical geology. John Wiley & Sons, New York.

Shaw, R.D. and E.E. Prepas. 1989. Groundwater-lake interactions: II. Nearshore seepage patterns and the contribution of groundwater to lakes in central Alberta. J. Hydrol. [in press]

Shaw, R.D., J.F.H. Shaw, H. Fricker and E.E. Prepas. 1990. An integrated approach to quantify groundwater transport of phosphorus to Narrow Lake, Alberta. Limnol. Oceanogr. [in press]

Strong, W.L. and K.R. Leggatt. 1981. Ecoregions of Alberta. Alta. En. Nat. Resour. Resour Eval. Plan. Div., Edmonton.

Lake Basin

Alberta Environment. n.d.[a]. Envir. Assess. Div., Envir. Qlty. Monit. Br. Unpubl. data, Edmonton.

————. n.d.[b]. Tech. Serv. Div., Hydrol. Br. Unpubl. data, Edmonton.

Bothe, R.A. and C. Abraham. 1987. Evaporation and evapotranspiration in Alberta 1912 to 1985. Alta. Envir., Tech. Serv. Div., Hydrol. Br., Edmonton.

Crowe, A. and F.W. Schwartz. 1982. The groundwater component of the Wabamun Lake eutrophication study. Alta. Envir., Poll. Contr. Div., Water Qlty. Contr. Br., Edmonton.

Hardy, W.G. [ed.-in-chief] 1967. Alberta–A natural history. M.G. Hurtig Publ., Edmonton.

Hickman, M. 1990. Univ. Alta., Dept. Bot., Edmonton. Pers. comm.

————, C. Schweger and T. Habgood. n.d. The paleoenvironmental history of Lake Wabamun, Alberta. Alta. Envir., Poll. Contr. Div., Water Qlty. Contr. Br. Unpubl. rep., Edmonton.

Hutchinson, G.E. 1957. A treatise on limnology, Vol. 1: Geography, physics and chemistry. John Wiley & Sons, New York.

Shaw, R.D. and E.E. Prepas. 1989. Groundwater-lake interactions: II. Nearshore seepage patterns and the contribution of groundwater to lakes in central Alberta. J. Hydrol. [in press]

Shaw, R.D., J.F.H. Shaw, H. Fricker and E.E. Prepas. 1990. An integrated approach to quantify groundwater transport of phosphorus to Narrow Lake, Alberta. Limnol. Oceanogr. [in press]

Trew, D.O., D.J. Beliveau and E.I. Yonge. 1987. The Baptiste Lake study technical report. Alta. Envir., Poll. Contr. Div., Water Qlty. Contr. Br., Edmonton.

Wetzel, R.G. 1983. Limnology. 2nd ed. Saunders College Publ., New York.

Water Quality

Alberta Environment. n.d. Envir. Assess. Div., Envir. Qlty. Monit. Br. Unpubl. data, Edmonton.

Armstrong, F.A.J. and D.W. Schindler. 1971. Preliminary chemical characterization of waters in the Experimental Lakes Area, Northwestern Ontario. J. Fish. Res. Bd. Can. 28:171–187.

Babin, J. and E.E. Prepas. 1985. Modelling winter oxygen depletion rates in ice-covered temperate zone lakes in Canada. Can. J. Fish. Aquat. Sci. 42:239–249.

Barica, J. 1977. Effect of freeze-up on major ion and nutrient content of a prairie winterkill lake. J. Fish. Res. Bd. Can. 34:2210–2215.

Bierhuizen, J.F.H. and E.E. Prepas. 1985. Relationship between nutrients, dominant ions, and phytoplankton standing crop in prairie saline lakes. Can. J. Fish. Aquat. Sci. 42:1588–1594.

Burgis, M.J. and P. Morris. 1987. The natural history of lakes. Cambridge Univ. Press, Cambridge, England.

Chambers, P.A. and E.E. Prepas. 1988. Underwater spectral attenuation and its effect on the maximum depth of angiosperm colonization. Can. J. Fish. Aquat. Sci. 45:1010–1017.

Marino, R., R.W. Howarth, J. Shamess and E.E. Prepas. 1990. Molybdenum and sulfate as controls on the abundance of nitrogen-fixing cyanobacteria in Alberta saline lakes. Limnol. Oceanogr. [in press]

Organisation for Economic Co-operation and Development. 1982. Eutrophication of waters: Monitoring, assessment and control. Organisation Econ. Co-operation Devel. publ., Paris.

Prepas, E.E. 1983. Total dissolved solids as a predictor of lake biomass and productivity. Can. J. Fish. Aquat. Sci. 40:92–95.

———— and D.O. Trew. 1983. Evaluation of the phosphorus-chlorophyll relationship for lakes off the Precambrian Shield in western Canada. Can. J. Fish. Aquat. Sci. 40:27–35.

Prepas, E.E., T.P. Murphy, J.M. Crosby, D.T. Walty, J.T. Lim, J. Babin and P.A. Chambers. 1990. The reduction of phosphorus and chlorophyll *a* concentrations following $CaCO_3$ and $Ca(OH)_2$ additions to hypereutrophic Figure Eight Lake, Alberta. Envir. Sci. Tech. [in press]

Prepas, E.E., J.F.H. Shaw and E.E. Prepas. 1989. Potential significance of phosphorus release from shallow sediments of deep Alberta lakes. ms submitted to Limnol. Oceanogr.

Ruttner, F. 1974. Fundamentals of limnology. 4th ed. (translated from German by D.G. Frey and F.E.J. Fry) Univ. Toronto Press, Toronto.

Shaw, R.D., J.F.H. Shaw, H. Fricker and E.E. Prepas. 1990. An integrated approach to quantify groundwater transport of phosphorus to Narrow Lake, Alberta. Limnol. Oceanogr. [in press]

Shaw, R.D., A.M. Trimbee, A. Minty, H. Fricker and E.E. Prepas. 1989. Atmospheric deposition of phosphorus and nitrogen in central Alberta with emphasis on Narrow Lake, Alberta. Water, Air, and Soil Poll. 43:119–134.

Vallentyne, J.R. 1974. The algal bowl. Dept. Fish. Oceans, Ottawa.

Wetzel, R.G. 1983. Limnology. 2nd ed. Saunders College Publ., New York.

Biological Characteristics

Phytoplankton

Alberta Environment. 1989. Algal blooms. Envir. Assess. Div., Envir. Qlty. Monit. Br., Edmonton.

Hickman, M. and J.M. White. 1989. Late Quaternary paleoenvironment of Spring Lake, Alberta, Canada. J. Paleolimnology 2:305–317.

Prescott, G.W. 1978. How to know the freshwater algae. 3rd ed. Wm. C. Brown Co. Publ., Dubuque, Iowa.

Reynolds, C.S. 1984. The ecology of freshwater phytoplankton. Cambridge Univ. Press, Cambridge, England.

Schweger, C.E. and M. Hickman. 1989. Holocene paleohydrology of central Alberta: Testing the general-circulation-model climate simulations. Can. J. Earth Sci. 26:1826–1833.

Aquatic Macrophytes

Alberta Environment. n.d. Aquatic plant management. Envir. Assess. Div., Pest. Chem. Br., Edmonton.

Beak Consultants Ltd. 1980. The effect of thermal discharges on the aquatic plants and other biota of Wabamun Lake, Alberta. Prep. for Calg. Power Ltd., Calgary.

Burland, R.G. 1981. An identification guide to Alberta aquatic plants. Alta. Envir., Poll. Contr. Div., Pest. Chem. Br., Edmonton.

Chambers, P.A. and E.E. Prepas. 1988. Underwater spectral attenuation and its effect on the maximum depth of angiosperm colonization. Can. J. Fish. Aquat. Sci. 45:1010–1017.

Fassett, N.C. 1975. A manual of aquatic plants. Univ. Wisconsin Press, Madison, Wisconsin.

Moss, E.H. 1983. Flora of Alberta. 2nd ed. Univ. Toronto Press, Toronto.

Sculthorpe, C.D. 1967. The biology of aquatic vascular plants. Edward Arnold Ltd., London, England.

Zooplankton

Alberta Environment. n.d. Envir. Assess. Div., Envir. Qlty. Monit. Br. Unpubl. data, Edmonton.

Anderson, R.S. 1974. Crustacean plankton communities of 340 lakes and ponds in and near the National Parks of the Canadian Rocky Mountains. J. Fish Res. Bd. Can. 31:855–869.

Edmondson, W.T. [ed.] 1959. Fresh-water biology. John Wiley & Sons, New York.

Hutchinson, G.E. 1967. A treatise on Limnology, Vol. II:. Introduction to lake biology and the limnoplankton. John Wiley & Sons, New York.

Patalas, K. n.d. Envir. Can., Freshwater Inst. Unpubl. data, Winnipeg, Manitoba.

Prepas, E.E. and K. Field. n.d. Univ. Alta., Dept. Zool. Unpubl. data, Edmonton.

Prepas, E.E. and J. Vickery. 1984. The contribution of particulate phosphorus (>250 μm) to the total phosphorus pool in lake water. Can. J. Fish. Aquat. Sci. 41:351–363.

Wetzel, R.G. 1983. Limnology. 2nd ed. Saunders College Publ., New York.

Benthic Invertebrates

Clifford, H.F. n.d. The aquatic invertebrates of Alberta: An illustrated guide. Univ. Alta., Dept. Zool. Unpubl. rep., Edmonton.

Wetzel, R.G. 1983. Limnology. 2nd ed. Saunders College Publ., New York.

Fish

Alberta Forestry, Lands and Wildlife. 1984. Status of the fish and wildlife resource in Alberta. Fish Wild. Div., Edmonton.

Crossman, E.J. and D.E. McAllister. 1986. Zoogeography of freshwater fishes of the Hudson Bay drainage, Ungava Bay and the Arctic Archipelago, p. 53–104. *In* C.H. Hocutt and E.O. Wiley [ed.] The zoogeography of North American fishes. John Wiley & Sons, New York.

Hokanson, K.E.F. 1977. Temperature requirements of some percids and adaptations to the seasonal temperature cycle. J. Fish. Res. Bd. Can. 34:1524–1550.

Loftus, K.H., M.G. Johnson and H.A. Regier. 1978. Federal-provincial strategic planning for Ontario fisheries: Management strategy for the 1980s. J. Fish. Res. Bd. Can. 35:916–927.

Nelson, J.S. 1977. The postglacial invasion of fishes into Alberta. Alta. Nat. 7:129–135.

———. 1989. Univ. Alta., Dept. Zool., Edmonton. Pers. comm.

Paetz, M.J. and J.S. Nelson. 1970. The fishes of Alberta. The Queen's Printer, Edmonton.

Paetz, M.J. and K.A. Zelt. 1974. Studies of northern Alberta lakes and their fish populations. J. Fish. Res. Bd. Can. 31:1007–1020.

Rawson, D.S. 1958. Indices to lake productivity and their significance in predicting conditions in reservoirs and lakes with disturbed water levels, p. 27–42. *In* P.A. Larkin [ed.] H.R. MacMillan lectures in fisheries: The investigation of fish-power problems. Univ. BC, Vancouver.

Regier, H.A. 1987. Freshwater fish and fisheries of Canada, p. 295–319. *In* M.C. Healy and R.R. Wallace [ed.] Canadian aquatic resources. Can. Bull. Fish. Aquat. Sci. 215, Ottawa.

Robinson, C.L.K. and W.M. Tonn. 1989. Influence of environmental factors and piscivory in structuring fish assemblages of small Alberta lakes. Can. J. Fish. Aquat. Sci. 46:81–89.

Wildlife

Banfield, W.F. 1974. The mammals of Canada. Natl. Museums Can., Ottawa and Univ. Toronto Press, Toronto.

Finlay, J. [ed.] 1984. A bird-finding guide to Canada. Hurtig Publ., Edmonton.

——— and C. Finlay. 1987. Parks in Alberta: A guide to peaks, ponds, parklands & prairies. Hurtig Publ., Edmonton.

Godfrey, W.E. 1986. The birds of Canada. Natl. Museums Can., Ottawa.

Provincial Museum of Alberta. 1980. A nature guide to Alberta. Hurtig. Publ., Edmonton.

Salt, W.R. and A.L. Wilk. 1966. Birds of Alberta. The Queen's Printer, Edmonton.

Soper, J.D. 1964. Mammals of Alberta. The Queen's Printer, Edmonton.

PART II

LAKE DESCRIPTIONS

PEACE AND ATHABASCA REGION

The vast area included in the Peace-Athabasca Basin stretches from the mountains of central British Columbia and the frozen expanse of the Columbia Icefields and across most of northern Alberta to Lake Athabasca. From rocky peaks through seemingly endless forest to the largest lake in Alberta, this watershed is truly a land of superlatives.

The combined Peace-Athabasca Basin (including the area draining directly into Lake Athabasca) is the largest watershed in Alberta, covering 346 530 km^2 or 52% of the province. The Peace and the Athabasca are two of the three largest rivers in Alberta; the Slave River, formed by their confluence, is the province's largest. On average, 110 billion m^3 of water leaves Alberta via the Slave River every year, approximately 85% of the total annual volume of water flowing out of the province. This basin is also the setting for the three largest lakes in Alberta: Athabasca, Claire and Lesser Slave. The combined area covered by these three lakes is more than 3 times the combined area of all the other lakes and reservoirs discussed in the *Atlas*!

The Athabasca River has its headwaters on Alberta's highest mountain, Mt. Columbia, which soars to 3 750 m in Jasper National Park and is in the centre of the Columbia Icefield, the largest icefield in the Rocky Mountains. The river passes through Alpine, Subalpine and Montane ecoregions before it leaves Jasper National Park, then traverses through the diverse forest of the Boreal Foothills Ecoregion where Smoke and McLeod lakes are located. The Boreal Uplands Ecoregion lies along the foothills to the north and south of the broad Athabasca Valley; Rock Lake is one of the beautiful little lakes in this ecoregion. Before the river reaches the town of Whitecourt, it enters the Boreal Mixedwood Ecoregion and stays in it for the rest of its journey to Lake Athabasca. There are numerous lakes in this part of the Athabasca Basin, including a cluster of four small productive lakes northwest of Edmonton (Lessard, Thunder, Nakamun and Lac la Nonne), and another group north of Edmonton (Baptiste, Island, Narrow, Long (near Athabasca) and Steele). Two other lakes in the *Atlas* lie southeast of Fort McMurray: Gregoire, with a provincial park, and Christina, popular for its fly-in fishery for walleye and pike. The Athabasca River flows north from Fort McMurray then enters Lake Athabasca in the northeast corner of Alberta.

The Peace River starts in the Omineca Mountains in north-central British Columbia, but before it leaves that province it is impounded by the W.A.C. Bennett Dam to create Williston Lake, the largest body of fresh water in British Columbia. The Peace River flows across the Boreal Mixedwood Ecoregion for almost all of its journey across Alberta, cutting briefly into the Boreal Northlands Ecoregion in Wood Buffalo National Park. The region from the town of Peace River south into the Smoky River sub-basin is the most populated portion of the Peace River Basin and is the site of many popular lakes, including Moonshine, Figure Eight, Saskatoon, Sturgeon, Smoke, Musreau and Iosegun. The Peace River flows eastward across northern Alberta until it is 30 km northwest of Lake Athabasca.

The pattern of water flow between Lake Athabasca and the Peace River is unusual and intricate. During most of the year, the elevation of the Peace River is lower than that of Lake Athabasca and water flows out of the lake and northward via Rivière des Rochers and Chenal des Quatre Fourches. These rivers join the Peace River to form the Slave River which flows northwest into Great Slave Lake, which is then drained by the MacKenzie River to the Arctic Ocean.

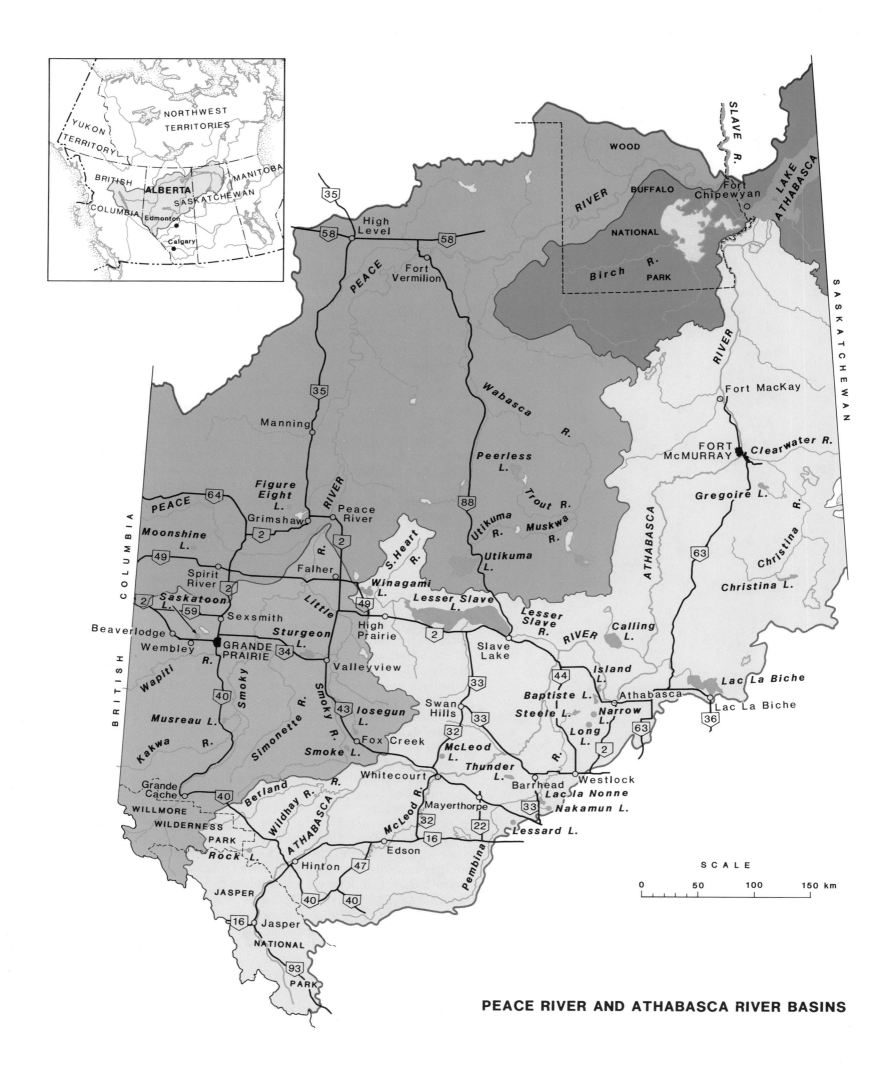

PEACE RIVER AND ATHABASCA RIVER BASINS

McLeod Lake. Photo by P.A. Mitchell

Thunder Lake. Photo by P.A. Mitchell

Musreau Lake. Photo by P.A. Mitchell

Rock Lake. Photo by P.A. Mitchell

However, when water levels are high on the Peace River, usually for about 20 days in early summer, the elevation of the Peace becomes higher than that of Lake Athabasca. When this happens, some of the flow in Rivière des Rochers and Chenal des Quatre Fourches reverses and water from the Peace River flows south. The high water in Rivière des Rochers and in Chenal des Quatre Fourches blocks the outflow of the Athabasca River and leads to the flooding of another outstanding feature of the Peace-Athabasca Basin: the Peace-Athabasca Delta.

The delta is an enormous area of marshes, grasslands and ponds, covering 3 775 km². It is one of the world's most biologically productive areas and is the home of the largest free-ranging herd of buffalo in the world. The delta is of vital importance for waterfowl as a feeding and staging area on all four of the major flyways in North America. The delta was declared a World Heritage Site in 1985 and is the focus of Wood Buffalo National Park, the largest national park in the world and the only remaining nesting area for Whooping Cranes.

Other resources of the basin are also worthy of superlatives. The northern half of Alberta is much wetter than the southern half (precipitation is greater and evaporation is much less), and so trees thrive, mostly trembling aspen, and white and black spruce. Most of the Peace-Athabasca Basin is part of one of the world's largest relatively undisturbed forest areas. South of Lake Athabasca, the Athabasca River flows through the Alberta Oil Sands, a reserve of petroleum estimated to exceed all the other remaining reserves in the world.

The first British explorers came to the Peace-Athabasca area in pursuit of another resource—high quality and abundant furs. When the first fur traders came to what is now Alberta, they followed the Churchill drainage through Manitoba and Saskatchewan, crossing the height of land to the Athabasca drainage in the Clearwater River near present day Fort McMurray. Peter Pond in 1778 built the first white man's house in Alberta 60 km upstream of the mouth of the Athabasca River. The first fur-trade post in Alberta was Fort Chipewyan, built on the shore of Lake Athabasca in 1788—7 years before the start of Edmonton House and almost 90 years before the start of Fort Calgary! Fort Chipewyan is the oldest permanently occupied community in Alberta. The Peace River claims another first—in 1793 Alexander Mackenzie travelled up the Peace River, over the mountains and down to the Pacific Ocean—the first man known to have crossed the continent north of Mexico.

Agriculture is the major land use in the southern portion of the basin and in the area around the town of Peace River and city of Grande Prairie. The Peace River country is the most northerly wheat-growing area in the world; the winters are cold and the growing season is short, but during the summer the day-lengths are long, up to 18 hours. Crops grow fast and the quality is excellent; some of the best-quality wheat and canola in the world comes from this region, as does most of Canada's honey. The population of the basin is concentrated in the farming areas. Approximately 150 000 people live in the Peace-Athabasca Basin, almost half of them in the area bordered by the town of Peace River, Lac La Biche and the southern edge of the Athabasca Basin.

This region not only gives rise to the largest rivers of Alberta; it is also dotted with hundreds of lakes, ponds, wetlands and muskegs. The lakes in these northern basins are numerous and varied in character. Of those discussed in the *Atlas*, they range in size from Lake Athabasca (7 770 km², 124 m maximum depth) to tiny Moonshine Lake (0.3 km², 3.5 m maximum depth). Most of them are nutrient rich and support a lush growth of rooted plants and algae; of the 23 lakes in the *Atlas* in this basin for which there are data, 17 are eutrophic or hyper-eutrophic.

The low population density of the Peace-Athabasca Basin means that recreational development on most of these lakes is little more than small campgrounds and boat launches. Camping, sport fishing and boating are the most popular pursuits, and the sandy beaches of Lesser Slave, Lac La Biche, McLeod, Sturgeon and Gregoire lakes are attractive for swimming and beach activities during the long days of summer. Sport fishing for walleye, pike and perch is popular in most of the lakes, from easily accessible Thunder Lake to the fly-in lodge at Christina Lake. Figure Eight, McLeod, Moonshine, Saskatoon and Musreau lakes are stocked with rainbow trout and provide excellent sport fishing. Lake trout are the target of anglers at Rock and Peerless lakes and some of the clear, cold lakes of the Caribou Mountains.

Over half of the fish taken in Alberta's commercial fishery are taken from the Peace-Athabasca Basin. Lake whitefish constitute most of the catch, but substantial numbers of pike and walleye are also taken. The largest fisheries are on Lake Athabasca, Lesser Slave and Utikuma lakes.

The Peace and Athabasca basins are endowed with an abundance of beautiful lakes but only a few are presented in the *Atlas*. For many lakes the only access is by float plane, thus very little is known about them. Some of these lakes are home to isolated fishing camps, but most are still unchanged wilderness, and a visit to them is a memorable experience.

J.M. Crosby

LAKE ATHABASCA

L. Noton

MAP SHEETS: 74L, M, N, O
LOCATION: Tp115–122 R3–24 W3
           Tp110–118 R1–8 W4
LAT/LONG: 59°11'N 109°22'W

Lake Athabasca is Canada's eighth largest lake. The area near the lake supports a wealth of fur-bearing animals, small and large game, dense flocks of waterfowl, and an abundance of fish. These rich resources drew Indians and, later, fur traders to the area. The lake was very important during the fur-trade era and, for a time, it became the centre of conflict between the Hudson's Bay Company and the North West Company. The Peace-Athabasca Delta, located at the southwest end of the lake, is one of North America's major wetlands, and ranks as one of the most biologically productive areas in the world. It is internationally recognized for its importance as a waterfowl production and staging area.

Approximately 30% of Lake Athabasca lies within Alberta and the remainder is located in Saskatchewan. The southwest tip of the lake is situated about 210 km north of the city of Fort McMurray. Lake Athabasca is not easily accessible by road. From the south, Highway 63 extends from Fort McMurray to the hamlet of Fort McKay, and a winter road extends from Fort McKay to the hamlet of Fort Chipewyan, located on the north shore at the west end of Lake Athabasca (Fig. 1). From the north, an improved road extends from the town of Fort Smith, located just north of the border of Alberta and the Northwest Territories, to the locality of Peace Point, situated on the Peace River north of Lake Claire. From Peace Point southeast to Fort Chipewyan, the road is classed as a winter road. Airports or airstrips are located in Fort Smith, Northwest Territories, in Fort Chipewyan, Alberta, and in Stony Rapids and Uranium City, Saskatchewan. Aircraft can also land on the water at the locations above, as well as at Fond-du-Lac, Saskatchewan.

Lake Athabasca was originally called *Athapiscow* by the Cree. The surveyor Philip Turnor and his assistant, Peter Fidler, visited the lake in 1791 and named the lake *Athapiscow* on Turnor's 1794 map (McCormack 1988). The word describes open areas such as lakes and swamps where willows, reeds and grasses grow (Holmgren and Holmgren 1976). On Peter Pond's 1790 map and Alexander Mackenzie's 1802 map, the lake is named Lake of the Hills (McCormack 1988).

The region's fur trade began in 1778, when Peter Pond established a trading post on the Athabasca River at its junction with the Embarras River (Fig. 2) at a location now known as Old Fort. The location was unsatisfactory and, in 1788, Alexander Mackenzie's cousin, Roderick, established a new post, Fort Chipewyan, for the North West Company. It was located on what is now Indian Reserve 201A, also called Old Fort Point, on the southwest shore of Lake Athabasca west of the Old Fort River (Fig. 2). In 1798, Fort Chipewyan was moved to the north shore to a location about 2 km from its present site. In 1802 and 1815, two Hudson's Bay Company posts were built nearby. Rivalry between the Hudson's Bay and North West companies was intense until the two companies amalgamated in 1821. The Hudson's Bay Company then held a monopoly on trade in the area until 1870, when it sold its holdings to the new Dominion of Canada (McCormack 1988).

Fort Chipewyan is Alberta's oldest permanent settlement, and in 1988, residents celebrated the bicentennial of its establishment. After the explorers and fur traders, missionaries were among the next white people to arrive at the fort. In 1849, Oblate priests established the Nativity of the Blessed Virgin Mission, and in 1874, the Grey Nuns opened Holy Angels Convent, a residential school and orphanage. In 1897, hundreds of prospectors travelled to the Klondike gold

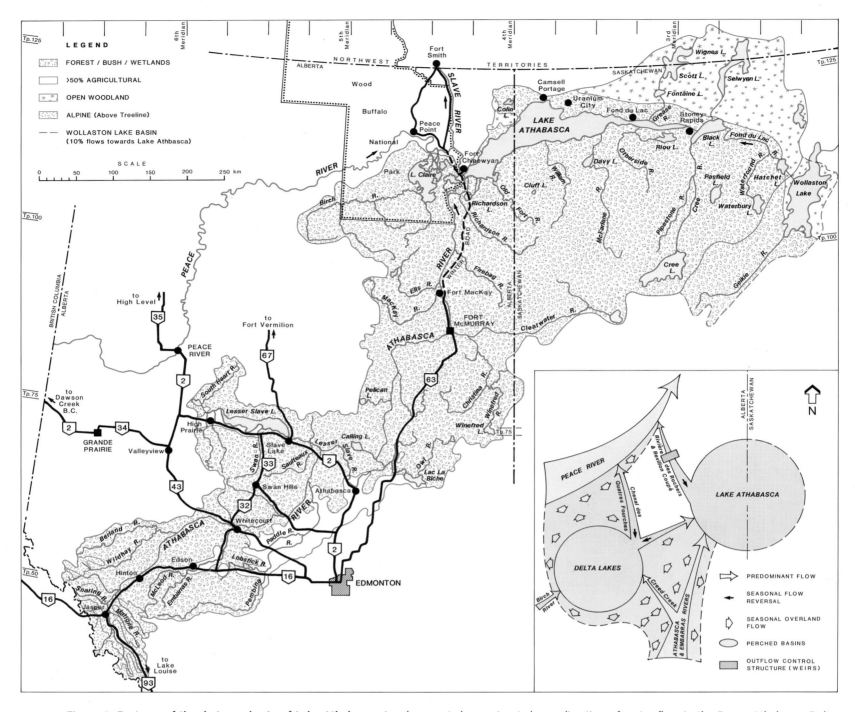

Figure 1. Features of the drainage basin of Lake Athabasca. Land use not shown. Inset shows direction of water flow in the Peace-Athabasca Delta. SOURCES: Atlas Alta. 1969; PADPG 1973; Natl. Atlas Can. 1974; PADIC 1987.

fields through Fort Chipewyan, using the traditional fur trade route down the Athabasca River. This influx of travellers led to the establishment of a North West Mounted Police Post at the fort in 1898 (McCormack 1988).

Beaver, Chipewyan and Cree Indians have inhabited the Athabasca region for the past 2 000 years or more. By the midnineteenth century, the Beaver had moved from the west end of Lake Athabasca and settled farther west, in the Fort Vermilion region. The Chipewyan and Cree then became the two dominant groups trading furs at Fort Chipewyan (McCormack 1988). In 1899, the Canadian government negotiated land cessions with the local Indians and Métis. Chipewyan Indian Reserves 201 and 201A to 201E were assigned. They are located on the delta between Lake Athabasca and Richardson Lake (Fig. 2). Few people live on the reserves; most natives live in Fort Chipewyan, which had a population of 1 767 people in 1986 (Alta. Native Aff. 1986). In 1987, the Cree band signed an agreement with the federal and Alberta governments that will establish a Cree reserve (McCormack 1988).

For many years, the Athabasca-Slave River system served as a

major transportation route. Canoes were the original mode of travel for native people and, subsequently, the fur trade. By 1822, Chipewyan boats, which were similar to York boats, were used on Lake Athabasca and later, steamers plied the waters. By 1937, the Northern Transportation Company operated the first all-steel ships on the Athabasca-Mackenzie River system from the head of navigation in the Fort McMurray area (Brady 1983). Air transport and the opening of the Mackenzie Highway in the 1950s brought competition for cargo transport. Competition increased in 1965, when the railway opened from northern Alberta to Pine Point in the Northwest Territories, and water transport to Pine Point and Hay River via the Athabasca-Slave system was reduced to a trickle (PADPG 1972). In the early 1980s, the mines near Uranium City shut down, reducing the need for barge transport across Lake Athabasca. In 1982, the Northern Transportation Company discontinued its barge service, but some commercial barge service still operates between the Fort McMurray area and Fort Chipewyan. As recently as 1983, a passenger boat service also operated between these two centres (Brady 1983).

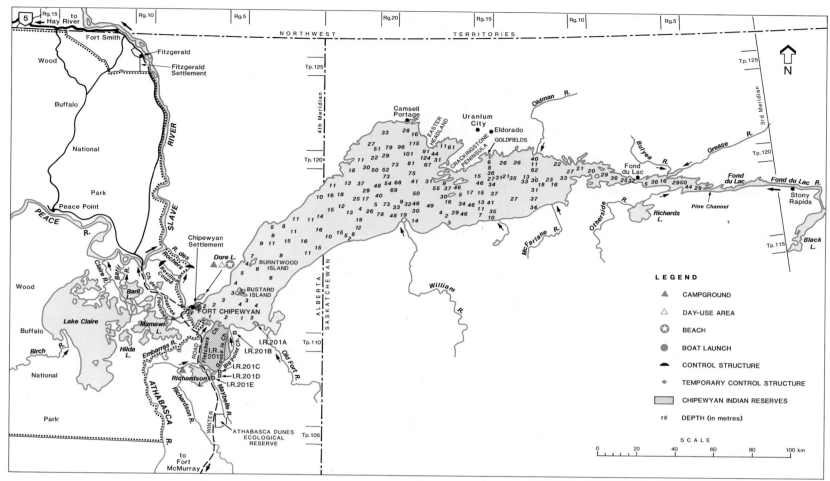

Figure 2. Bathymetry and shoreline features of Lake Athabasca.
BATHYMETRY SOURCE: Can. Dept. Fish. Envir. 1973.

Lake Athabasca does not have a high potential for recreation in comparison to surrounding lakes. The transparency of the water in the main part of the lake is high and algal concentrations are low, but the lake is generally too cold for swimming or water skiing and is often subject to high waves, which are dangerous for pleasure boating (PADPG 1972). There are no provincial boating regulations specific to the lake, but federal regulations apply (Alta. For. Ld. Wild. 1988). Species of sport fish in Lake Athabasca include lake trout, Arctic grayling, lake whitefish, goldeye, northern pike, yellow perch and walleye. There are no sport fishing regulations specific to the lake, but provincial limits and regulations are in effect (Alta. For. Ld. Wild. 1989). Lake Athabasca supports a domestic fishery and a commercial fishery for lake trout, lake whitefish, walleye and northern pike.

There are five recreational facilities on or near the Alberta end of the lake (Fig. 2). Three of them are operated by the Alberta Forest Service. The first facility, Doré Lake Forest Recreation Area, is located 17 km northeast of Fort Chipewyan and about 1.5 km northwest of the shore of Lake Athabasca. It is open from May to September and has ten campsites, pump water, and a day-use area with picnic tables, a beach and a change house. The second and third facilities, Bustard Island and Richardson River Forest Recreation areas, are both boat-in sites that have several random campsites and no services. Fort Chipewyan provides services such as a boat launch, grocery stores, restaurants, hotels, lodges and a gas station.

Wood Buffalo National Park is the fourth recreation area. It was established in 1922 to protect one of the few remaining herds of wood bison and several herds of plains bison (PADPG 1972). It is the second largest national park in the world, and supports the world's largest herd of free-roaming bison. In 1985, it was designated a World Heritage Site. The park includes approximately 80% of the Peace-Athabasca Delta; it is maintained in its natural state and only limited management is permitted (PADIC 1987).

The fifth facility, the Athabasca Dunes Ecological Reserve, is located 160 km north of Fort McMurray and 26 km east of Wood Buffalo National Park (Fig. 2). It is a vast wilderness area where active sand dunes are constantly changing the landscape and stable dunes lie under a cover of grasses. Rare plants grow in the reserve, and its many lakes and wetland areas support waterfowl populations during migration. Ecological reserves are maintained in their natural state and are used for nature appreciation, photography and wildlife viewing (Alta. Rec. Parks n.d.).

Drainage Basin Characteristics

Lake Athabasca drains an enormous area of land (282 000 km², Table 1) that extends southwest across the width of Alberta to the Columbia Icefield in the Rocky Mountains, and east across most of northern Saskatchewan to Wollaston Lake (Fig. 1). The Peace-Athabasca Delta, which is one of the world's largest freshwater deltas, plays an important role in Lake Athabasca's complex drainage system. The delta region consists of three smaller deltas: the Athabasca (1 960 km²), the Peace (1 680 km²) and the Birch (168 km²). Its major lakes—Claire, Baril, Mamawi and Richardson—are all very shallow (PADPG 1973). River channels that meander across the delta join the major lakes to Lake Athabasca and drain upland areas.

The mean annual inflow to Lake Athabasca and the delta system is estimated to be 45 900 x 10⁶ m³ of water (Table 1). A major portion of the inflow enters the lake and delta during the period from April to mid-July. The largest portion of the total inflow (53%) reaches the lake and delta system via the Athabasca River and its tributaries (Fig. 1). The river enters Lake Athabasca through a system of channels that cut through the Athabasca Delta: the Embarras River, Fletcher Channel, Goose Island Channel and Big Point Channel (Fig. 2). Because the Athabasca River flows into Lake Athabasca near the outlet, water from the river tends to flow through the west end of the lake quite directly, without substantial mixing with water in the main part of the lake. Inflowing water from the river usually is restricted to an area that reaches about 8 km offshore of the delta. During periods of high inflow combined with strong westerly winds,

Table 1. Characteristics of Lake Athabasca drainage basin.

area (excluding lake) (km²)[a, b]	282 000
soil[c, d]	Gray Luvisols, Fibrisols, Cumulic Regosols, Humo-Ferric Podzols
bedrock geology[c, e]	Athabasca Formation (Proterozoic): sandstone; conglomerate and shale beds Undivided Granitic Plutonic Rocks (Archean): granite, some metasedimentary rocks
terrain[d]	flat to mountainous
ecoregion[c, f]	north of lake: Boreal Northlands; delta and south of lake: Dry Mixedwood Subregion of Boreal Mixedwood
dominant vegetation[c, f]	trembling aspen, balsam poplar, white spruce
mean annual inflow (m³)[a, g]	45 900 x 10⁶
mean annual sunshine (h)[h]	2 109

NOTES: [c]applies only to area immediately surrounding lake; [g]excluding groundwater inflow
SOURCES: [a]Alta. Envir. n.d.[b]; [b]PADPG 1973; [d]Natl. Atlas Can. 1974; [e]Alta. Res. Counc. 1972; [f]Strong and Leggat 1981; [h]Envir. Can. 1982

Table 2. Characteristics of Lake Athabasca.

surface area (km²)[a]	7 770
volume (m³)[a, b]	155 000 x 10⁶
maximum depth (m)[c]	124
mean depth (m)[b]	20
shoreline length (km)[d]	2 140
mean annual lake evaporation (mm)[e]	541
mean annual precipitation (mm)[e]	363
mean residence time (yr)	not available
control structure[f]	weirs on Revillon Coupé and Rivière des Rochers

SOURCES: [a]PADPG 1973; [b]MRBC 1981; [c]Can. Dept. Fish. Envir. 1973; [d]calculated from shoreline development of Rawson 1947[a]; [e]Alta. Envir. n.d.[b]; [f]PADIC 1987

however, Athabasca River water can flow east as far as Bustard Island (Neill et al. 1981), and has been reported to extend well into Saskatchewan (Rawson 1947[a]).

Lake Athabasca's second largest water source is the Fond du Lac River, which provides approximately 21% of the total inflow to the lake and delta region (Neill et al. 1981). This river drains Wollaston Lake, Saskatchewan and a large area of Precambrian Shield in the eastern part of the drainage basin (Fig. 1). Wollaston Lake has two outlets; about 10% of its outflow enters the Fond du Lac River and the remainder discharges into the Cochrane River (MRBC 1981). The Fond du Lac River flows into Fond du Lac and then into the narrow eastern end of Lake Athabasca (Fig. 2). Along the north and south shores, dozens of other streams flow into the lake. Inflows to the south side of the lake and delta, such as the Richardson, Maybelle, Old Fort, William and McFarlane rivers, provide less than 6% of the total inflow, and the Birch River system, which flows through lakes Claire and Mamawi into the western side of Lake Athabasca, provides less than 3%. Part of the time, flow from the Birch River system bypasses Lake Athabasca and flows north to the Peace River. Miscellaneous inflows and direct runoff from the catchment area provide the final 18% of the total inflow (Neill and Evans 1979).

Lake Athabasca is drained by Rivière des Rochers and its distributary, Revillon Coupé, which carry most of the outflow. Smaller volumes flow from the lake through Chenal des Quatre Fourches (Fig. 2). These three rivers join the Peace River to form the Slave River. Mamawi Lake, to the west of Lake Athabasca, is also drained by Chenal des Quatre Fourches. The volume of water leaving Lake Athabasca via Rivière des Rochers, Revillon Coupé and Chenal des

Quatre Fourches is partly dependent on the water level in the Peace River. The predominant direction of streamflow in the three channels is northward, toward the Peace River (Fig. 1, inset). During spring or summer flooding, however, flow reversals in the channels can occur when the elevation of the Peace River exceeds the elevation of Lake Athabasca. This results in reversed flows in Rivière des Rochers, Revillon Coupé and Chenal des Quatre Fourches. As well, flow reversals can occur between Lake Athabasca and the delta lakes. At these times, strong easterly winds cause water from Lake Athabasca to flow west into the southwestern arm of Chenal des Quatre Fourches and then into the delta lakes rather than north into the Peace River (PADIC 1987). When inflow from the Athabasca River to Lake Athabasca is high during spring and summer, an estimated 80% to 90% of the lake's outflowing water originates from the Athabasca River (Neill et al. 1981). During fall and winter, more of the outflow originates from the main body of the lake.

The drainage network of the delta is made up of open drainage and perched basins. The open drainage network is an interconnected system of lakes and streams. Its extent is related to water levels in the delta. Perched basins, which have surface levels higher than the surrounding water table, are located between the open-water drainages. They are separated from groundwater by impermeable beds, so their existence depends on flooding. The topography of the delta is quite flat, so minor changes in water levels can cause either extensive flooding or drought (PADIC 1987). In the mid–1960s, the Government of British Columbia created Williston Lake by constructing the W.A.C. Bennett Dam on the Peace River. The resulting low water levels downstream threatened the ecological balance in the Peace-Athabasca Delta when annual floods did not occur. In 1971, the governments of Canada, Alberta and Saskatchewan established the Peace-Athabasca Delta Project Group to evaluate methods of raising water levels in Lake Athabasca and the delta lakes (PADPG 1973). In the fall of 1971, a temporary rockfill dam was constructed on the southwestern arm of the Chenal des Quatre Fourches, near Mamawi Lake. On recommendation of the Peace-Athabasca Delta Project Group, the three governments signed the Peace-Athabasca Delta Implementation Agreement. The agreement gave high priority to conservation of the Peace-Athabasca Delta and the governments agreed to jointly construct control structures on Rivière des Rochers and Revillon Coupé.

In 1974, the temporary control structure on Chenal des Quatre Fourches was severely damaged by flooding. It was removed in 1975, and during 1975 and 1976, permanent control structures were built on Revillon Coupé and Rivière des Rochers (PADIC 1987). In order to allow movement of boats past the weir on Rivière des Rochers, a tramway was built in 1976 and upgraded in 1986. The tramway operates during the open-water season and is maintained by Alberta Environment. The success of the two weirs in restoring water levels in the delta and the effect of the weirs on the delta's biological community were evaluated during 1983 and 1984 by the Peace-Athabasca Delta Implementation Committee (1987). It was concluded that, although the weirs did not reproduce natural conditions, they had nearly restored peak summer water levels in the delta and had successfully counteracted many of the hydrological changes in the delta caused by regulation of the Peace River by the Bennett Dam. The weirs did not affect water levels in the Peace River, so the perched basins that relied on flooding from the Peace River were lost.

The Alberta portion of Lake Athabasca's drainage basin covers a range of ecoregions. In the Rocky Mountains, where the headwaters of the Athabasca River are located (Fig. 1), the watershed is part of the Alpine, Subalpine and Montane ecoregions. The dominant vegetation consists of heath (*Phyllodoce* spp.) in the Alpine Ecoregion, lodgepole pine with secondary succession by Engelmann spruce in the Subalpine Ecoregion and Douglas fir in the Montane Ecoregion. North and south of Hinton lie the Boreal Uplands. Lodgepole pine is the dominant tree, with secondary succession by white and black spruce. The area surrounding Hinton and Edson is part of the Boreal Foothills, where trembling aspen, balsam polar and lodgepole pine are the main trees and secondary succession is by white and black spruce. The watershed from Whitecourt northeast to the Peace-

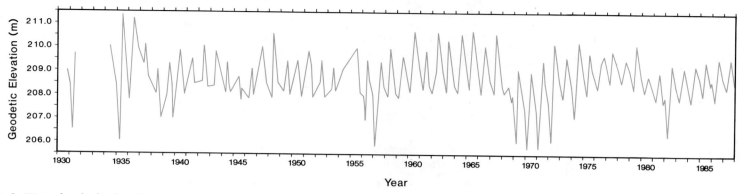

Figure 3. Water level of Lake Athabasca, 1930 to 1987.
SOURCE: Alta. Envir. n.d.[c]; Bennett and Card 1972; Envir. Can. 1973–1987.

Athabasca Delta and the southern shore of Lake Athabasca is mainly Boreal Mixedwood. Trembling aspen and balsam poplar are the major tree species. North of the lake lies the Boreal Northlands, where trembling aspen and white spruce are the dominant trees (Strong and Leggat 1981). The area of open woodland that covers the northeast section of the drainage basin (Fig. 1) is characterized by scattered spruce and tamarack with a lichen understory. South of this area, throughout the Saskatchewan side of the drainage basin, the land is covered by Boreal Forest composed of jack pine and black spruce interspersed with many barren patches (Natl. Atlas Can. 1974).

Except for mountainous areas, soils in the southwest portion of the watershed are mainly Gray Luvisols. Northwest of Lesser Slave Lake, there are large areas of predominantly Gray Luvisols or Organic Fibrisols. In the Peace-Athabasca Delta, Cumulic Regosols are the main soil group, and in the area south of the delta and along the southern shore of Lake Athabasca the soils are mostly Humo-ferric Podzols. The area immediately north of the lake is mainly rockland, and soils in the remainder of the Saskatchewan portion of the drainage basin are excessively stony Humo-ferric Podzols with rock outcroppings (Natl. Atlas Can. 1974).

Generally, most of the drainage basin is covered by forest, bush and wetlands (Fig. 1). Major agricultural areas are located in the southwestern part of the watershed: near Lesser Slave Lake and the town of Edson, along the Paddle and Pembina rivers, around the town of Athabasca, and south of Lac La Biche. Large areas of Precambrian Shield are located north of Lake Athabasca and the Fond du Lac River.

Forestry is a major industry throughout the Alberta side of the drainage basin. In 1988, there were pulp mills operating near the towns of Whitecourt and Hinton, and another pulp mill was scheduled to open in the summer of 1990 near Whitecourt. A pulp mill was also approved on the Lesser Slave River near the town of Slave Lake in August 1989.

The extraction of nonrenewable resources from the drainage area is economically important as well. Minerals present in the Lake Athabasca region include gypsum, granite, gold and uranium. Mining in the region began in the 1930s and was concentrated in the Saskatchewan portion of the drainage basin (PADPG 1972). Uranium is mined at Cluff Lake, Wollaston Lake and at the headwaters of the Geikie River, all in Saskatchewan (Natl. Atlas Can. 1974; Noton 1989). Coal is extracted at several mines in the Hinton area of Alberta and there are two oil sands mining and upgrading plants north of Fort McMurray (Noton 1989).

For the most part, the drainage basin is sparsely populated. The only city is Fort McMurray, and the highest concentration of towns and small communities is in the southwest portion of the watershed. Near Lake Athabasca, the only urban centres are Fort Chipewyan in Alberta, and Uranium City, Eldorado, Camsell Portage, Fond-du-Lac and Stony Rapids in Saskatchewan.

Lake Basin Characteristics

Lake Athabasca covers an area of approximately 7 770 km^2 (Table 2). A bathymetric map is not available, but soundings have been made for navigation routes (Fig. 2). The lake is shallowest on the Alberta side, where the maximum depth is 16 m. The shallow depths and gradual slope of the lake bottom at the western end probably result from sedimentation of the Athabasca River inflow. The central portion of the lake, between Camsell Portage on the north shore and the William River inlet, is the deepest part, with a maximum depth of 124 m near Easter Headland. East of Crackingstone Peninsula, the lake becomes shallower again, with a maximum depth of about 46 m. Lake Athabasca becomes increasingly narrow at its eastern end; soundings east of Fond-du-Lac indicated depths of 29 to 50 m in the centre of the narrow basin. There are dozens of islands throughout the lake. The islands that extend from Fort Chipewyan to the Old Fort River were formed as a result of wave action (MRBC 1981).

The north and south shores of Lake Athabasca are strikingly different. To the north lies rough, rocky Precambrian Shield, whereas to the south lies an extensive area of sand dunes (MRBC 1981). The dunes formed after proglacial lakes drained, when newly exposed sediments were subjected to intense wind storms (Bayrock and Root 1973). This activity formed dunes along the Athabasca River, in the lowlands west of Lake Claire and along the south shore of Lake Athabasca. As well, the William, McFarlane and Archibald rivers deposit large amounts of sand at their mouths, contributing to the beaches along the south shore of the lake.

The elevation of Lake Athabasca has been monitored at Fort Chipewyan for various periods since 1930, at Goldfields from 1942 to 1956, and at Crackingstone Point (on the western tip of Crackingstone Peninsula) since 1956. The water level at the west end of the lake fluctuates because of wind action. During windy periods, water levels at Fort Chipewyan and Crackingstone Point may differ by as much as 1 m for a period of several days (PADIC 1987). Water Survey of Canada reviewed and co-ordinated the records from the three stations for the period from 1930 to 1972 (Bennett and Card 1972). This compilation is presented in Figure 3, along with lake level data recorded at Fort Chipewyan for the period from 1973 to 1987. Over the period of record, the lake level has fluctuated 5.53 m, from a maximum elevation of 211.33 m, recorded in July 1935, to a minimum elevation of 205.80 m, recorded in February 1970. The low levels observed during the period from 1968 to 1971 were due to the filling of Williston Lake on the Peace River. After the temporary control structure was built on Chenal des Quatre Fourches in the fall of 1971, the levels of lakes Athabasca (Fig. 3), Claire and Mamawi increased. Since the permanent control structures on Revillon Coupé and Rivière des Rochers were completed in 1976, the amplitude of annual water level fluctuations in Lake Athabasca appears to be smaller than under natural conditions.

Water levels recorded before and after construction of the weirs do not provide a valid measurement of the effectiveness of the weirs because low precipitation levels during the late 1970s and the 1980s

Table 3. Major ions and related water quality variables for Lake Athabasca, Alberta side. Average concentrations in mg/L; pH in pH units. Composite samples from the euphotic zone collected from the main basin on 06 July 1987 and on 08 Aug. 1988, from near Fort Chipewyan 7 times from 13 May to 19 Oct. 1987, and offshore of the delta 7 times from 25 May to 21 Oct. 1987. S.E. = standard error.

| | Main | | Ft. Chipewyan | | Delta | |
	1987	1988	Mean	S.E.	Mean	S.E.
pH (range)	7.4–7.6	7.2	7.2–8.4	—	7.4–8.2	—
total alkalinity (CaCO₃)	35	40	47	6.9	101	2.6
specific conductivity (μS/cm)	93	81	120	20.0	269	9.1
total dissolved solids (calculated)	47	47	63	9.5	142	5.3
turbidity (NTU)	3	3	57	21.5	38	7.0
colour (Pt)	—	5	11	5.1	31	5.6
total hardness (CaCO₃)	33	28	47	7.5	108	4.0
total particulate carbon	<1	<1	1	0.4	2	0.4
dissolved organic carbon	5	3	4	0.6	7	0.9
HCO₃	43	49	57	8.4	123	3.2
CO₃	0	0	0	0	0	0
Mg	2	3	3	0.5	8	0.4
Na	3	3	4	0.7	11	1.2
K	1	1	<1	—	1	0.05
Cl	4	5	5	0.4	12	1.8
SO₄	6	<5	<7	—	20	1.0
Ca	10	7	13	2.2	30	1.1

SOURCE: Alta. Envir. n.d.[a], Naquadat stations 01AL07MD1150 (main), 01AL07MD1000 (Ft. Chipewyan), 01AT07MA1000 (delta)

Table 4. Nutrient, chlorophyll *a* and Secchi depth data for Lake Athabasca, main basin, near Fort Chipewyan and near the delta. Average concentrations in μg/L. Composite samples from the euphotic zone collected from the main basin on 06 July 1987 and on 08 Aug. 1988, from near Fort Chipewyan 7 times from 13 May to 19 Oct. 1987, and offshore of the delta 7 times from 25 May to 21 Oct. 1987. S.E. = standard error.

| | Main | | Ft. Chipewyan | | Delta | |
	1987	1988	Mean	S.E.	Mean	S.E.
total phosphorus	9	14	60	18.0	63	8.8
total dissolved phosphorus	4	3	6	0.9	9	0.8
total Kjeldahl nitrogen	208	210	250[a]	56.6	384	35.2
NO₃ + NO₂–nitrogen	<1	<1	29	24.7	<3	—
NH₄–nitrogen	18	12	24	10.5	20	6.9
iron	60	70	1 144	416.1	1 009	211.8
chlorophyll *a*	1.1	1.1	2.4	0.46	5.6	0.63
Secchi depth (m)	4.8	3.8	0.6[a]	0.20	0.4	0.10

NOTE: [a]n = 6
SOURCE: Alta. Envir. n.d.[a], Naquadat stations 01AL07MD1150 (main), 01AL07MD1000 (Ft. Chipewyan), 01AT07MA1000 (delta)

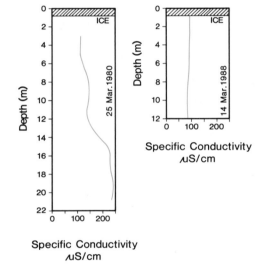

Figure 4. Specific conductance in Lake Athabasca, at Rivière des Rochers near the outlet in 1980 and in the main lake near the Alberta-Saskatchewan border in 1988. SOURCE: Alta. Envir. n.d.[a].

resulted in reduced runoff from the drainage basin. Therefore, a simulation of Lake Athabasca water levels for the period from 1960 to 1984 was conducted to evaluate the effect of the control structures (PADIC 1987). The report concluded that average summer maximum lake levels, simulated with the weirs in place, matched the simulated natural levels (without Bennett Dam or weirs) within 0.1 m. Simulated minimum annual water levels with weirs in place, however, were higher than simulated natural levels by 0.6 m and simulated mean annual levels were higher by 0.4 m. The mean amplitude of annual levels with the weirs in place is about 0.6 m smaller than under natural conditions.

Water Quality

Researchers from the University of Saskatchewan studied the water quality in Lake Athabasca during the late 1940s (Rawson 1947[a]; 1960). More recently, Alberta Environment occasionally sampled water quality from several sites on the Alberta section of the lake in

1979, 1980, 1987 and 1988 (Alta. Envir. n.d.[a]; Neill et al. 1981).

Samples were taken in the main part of the lake at two stations between Burntwood Island and the Alberta/Saskatchewan border in July 1987 and August 1988. These samples indicated that the water was fresh and not very turbid (Table 3). Total hardness and alkalinity values were low for an Alberta lake outside of the mountains. Samples were also taken at the west end of the lake near Fort Chipewyan and offshore of the Peace-Athabasca Delta during the open-water season in 1987. These sites are influenced by inflow from the Athabasca River. This is particularly evident at the delta site, where the water is well-buffered and turbid and the concentrations of most ions are much higher than at the other three sites. As in the late 1940s study, the main ions at all sites in 1987 and 1988 were bicarbonate and calcium.

There is a strong contrast between the specific conductance of Athabasca River water, with a value of 400 μS/cm, and water in the main part of the lake, with a value of about 85 μS/cm. At the lake's outlet, Rivière des Rochers, the two types of water sometimes stratify

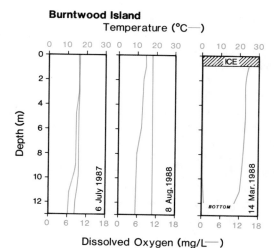

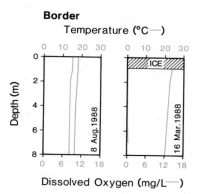

Figure 5. Temperature and dissolved oxygen in Lake Athabasca, near Burntwood Island and the Alberta-Saskatchewan border, 1988.
SOURCE: Alta. Envir. n.d.[a].

and form a distinct conductivity gradient from the surface to the bottom of the water column that is not present in the main part of the lake (Fig. 4). In March 1980, conductivity values in the outlet ranged from about 110 μS/cm at the surface to 233 μS/cm near the bottom, whereas in March 1988 near the provincial border, specific conductivity throughout the water column was more uniform, ranging from 93 μS/cm at the surface to 81 μS/cm at the bottom.

In July 1987 and August 1988, the water column was thermally stratified at the two sampling stations in the main part of the lake (Fig. 5). The temperature gradient was more pronounced at the deeper site (13 m) near the provincial border. The highest surface temperature recorded at the two stations was 17.4°C at the Burntwood Island site in July 1987. Samples were also taken at the two shallower sites, offshore of the delta (2 to 4 m) and near Fort Chipewyan (6 to 8 m). At these two stations the water column was isothermal throughout the open-water season in 1987. The highest surface temperature recorded was 18.9°C near the delta in August 1987.

Dissolved oxygen concentrations were uniform or nearly uniform from surface to bottom at the two stations between Burntwood Island and the border in July 1987 and August 1988 (Fig. 5). During winter, the water column was well oxygenated at these sites. In March 1988, the concentration of dissolved oxygen at a depth of 1 m was 14 to 15 mg/L, and in water near the sediments, the concentration declined only slightly, to 10 to 12 mg/L. At the delta and Fort Chipewyan stations, dissolved oxygen concentrations were uniformly high throughout the water column during the open-water period in 1987 and under ice in March 1988.

It is not possible to properly categorize the trophic status of Lake Athabasca because the lake has not been sampled sufficiently. Low concentrations of total phosphorus (9 to 14 mg/L) and moderately high Secchi transparencies (3.8 to 4.8 m) were recorded in single samples from the main part of the Alberta side of the lake in July 1987 and August 1988 (Table 4). In combination with the low chlorophyll *a* concentration (1.1 μg/L) recorded on both dates, these data indicate that the main part of the lake is quite unproductive, possibly oligotrophic. Near Fort Chipewyan and the delta, however, the lake is more productive. At the delta station, where the influence of Athabasca River water is great, the maximum chlorophyll *a* concentration recorded during the open-water season in 1987 was 7.7 μg/L in mid-June. Near Fort Chipewyan during the same period, the highest chlorophyll *a* concentration was 3.9 μg/L, recorded in mid-May. Average iron concentrations at these two sites are extremely high because of the high concentrations of total suspended solids in the water column. The high turbidity (Table 3) also results in very low Secchi depths (Table 4).

Biological Characteristics

Plants

The phytoplankton and aquatic macrophyte communities in Lake Athabasca have not been studied. The marsh habitat of the Peace-Athabasca Delta was studied by the Canadian Wildlife Service in the late 1960s to examine the effects of regulation of the Peace River by the Bennett Dam on the flooding cycle, plants and animals of the delta (PADPG 1972; 1973). Low water levels in the delta resulted in the exposure of large areas of mud flats that quickly became colonized by spike rush (*Eleocharis acicularis* and *E. palustris*), slough grass (*Beckmannia syzigachne*), common great bulrush (*Scirpus validus*), smartweed (*Polygonum* sp.), sedges (*Carex* spp.), reed grass (*Phragmites communis*) and willows (*Salix* spp.).

Since construction of the Rivière des Rochers weir in 1975 and the Revillon Coupé weir in 1976, water levels in the delta, although higher than during the period from 1968 to 1971, have continued to be relatively low. The low water levels are caused by low precipitation levels that result in reduced runoff from contributory river basins. It is expected that, if runoff increases, vegetation in the parts of the delta affected by the weirs will return to their "natural" condition as it was prior to construction of the Bennett Dam. Perched basins along the Peace River, which are not affected by the weirs, will flood only rarely, and vegetation succession will accelerate toward willow/shrub communities (PADIC 1987).

Invertebrates

The Peace-Athabasca Delta and Lake Athabasca are very different environments, yet they are closely related because the delta and its associated channels and lakes are important spawning and nursery areas for Lake Athabasca fish. Comprehensive surveys of the delta region and Lake Athabasca have not been carried out. In the 1940s, researchers from the University of Saskatchewan examined the zooplankton at 18 stations in the lake but did not examine the species composition (Rawson 1947[a]). As well, 214 bottom samples were taken with an Ekman dredge, primarily in the profundal zone (Larkin 1947). The amphipod *Pontoporeia affinis* was the dominant benthic organism collected and the opossum shrimp *Mysis relicta* was rare. Even in water 0– to 5–m deep, *Pontoporeia* formed as much as 45% of the benthic biomass.

The zooplankton and benthic fauna of the delta were investigated by researchers from the University of Alberta in 1971 (Gallup et al. 1971). The zooplankton was sampled by single horizontal tows at various locations in the delta and was also collected from two sites in the main part of Lake Athabasca. In the lake, the most abundant cladocerans were *Daphnia pulex* and *Bosmina longirostris* and the

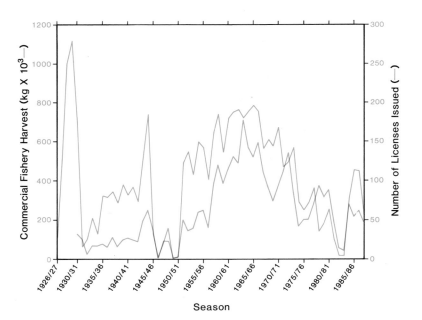

Figure 6. Harvest (kg) of the commercial fishery in Lake Athabasca, 1926 to 1986. The Alberta fishery began in 1943/44. Records for 1945/46 to 1950/51 are incomplete.
SOURCES: Alta. For. Ld. Wild. n.d.; Sask. Parks Rec. Cult. n.d.; Alta. Rec. Parks Wild. 1976.

most abundant copepods were *Epischura nevadensis*, unidentified *Diaptomus* copepodites and unidentified *Cyclops* copepodites. In the lakes and channels of the delta, large daphnids (*Daphnia pulex*, *D. magna* and *D. retrocurva*) were quite abundant, as was the copepod *Epischura nevadensis*. *Diacyclops bicuspidatus thomasi*, which is the intermediate host for the tapeworm *Triaenophorus crassus*, was only locally abundant in the delta. It is likely, however, to be abundant in Lake Athabasca as well, since many lake whitefish and cisco in the lake are infected by *T. crassus* cysts.

In 1971, two replicate samples of bottom sediments were taken with an Ekman dredge at each of a number of locations in the delta and at two locations in Lake Athabasca. Sample depths were not given. The standing stock of benthic invertebrates in many areas of the delta seemed to be low, largely because many areas freeze to the bottom. Fingernail clams (Sphaeriidae: *Sphaerium* and *Pisidium*), midge larvae (Chironomidae) and snails (Gastropoda: *Lymnaea*, *Physa* and *Promonetus*) were collected at almost every station.

Fish

The fish community in Lake Athabasca includes lake trout, lake whitefish, round whitefish, cisco, shortjaw cisco, Arctic grayling, longnose sucker, white sucker, lake chub, flathead chub, emerald shiner, spottail shiner, goldeye, northern pike, ninespine stickleback, trout-perch, yellow perch, walleye, spoonhead sculpin, deepwater sculpin and burbot (Rawson 1947[b]). The Peace-Athabasca Delta is a critical spawning and nursery area for sport and commercial species found in the lake. Walleye tagged in Richardson Lake have been recovered 119 to 138 km away in Lake Athabasca after 94 to 102 days (Bidgood 1961).

Lake Athabasca supports commercial, domestic and sport fisheries. The size of the sport fish harvest is unknown, but is likely to be small because access to the lake is limited and the water often becomes too rough for small boats. The domestic harvest is also unknown, but in 1945, the annual domestic harvest was about 227 000 kg (Rawson 1947[a]). Commercial fishing began in 1926 and the catch has been recorded from 1926 to the present (Alta. For. Ld. Wild. n.d.; Sask. Parks Rec. Cult. n.d.; Rawson 1947[a]; Alta. Rec. Parks Wild. 1976).

From 1926 to 1943, most commercial fishing took place on the Saskatchewan portion of the lake. The main catches were lake trout and lake whitefish. Over this period, the total catch fluctuated widely, from a minimum of about 101 000 kg in 1932/33 to a maximum

of 1 157 270 kg in 1929/30 (Fig. 6). After one fish company stopped operating in 1929, the catch dropped to about 63 000 kg/year in 1931/32 and then continued dropping during the "depression". From 1936 to 1942, the average catch was about 318 000 kg/year.

In 1943, the Alberta fishery near the Peace-Athabasca Delta opened; northern pike and walleye were the principal species caught. In the first two years after the delta fishery began, the average harvest of all species from the whole lake was 625 000 kg/year. The records from 1945/46 to 1950/51 are incomplete, but from 1951/52 to 1959/60, the average total catch was 550 833 kg/year. The catch increased to 747 796 kg/year from 1960/61 to 1965/66. In 1966/67, the lake trout quota was reduced to prevent overexploitation and the average total catch from that year until 1973/74 was 562 114 kg/year. From 1974/75 to 1984/85 the fishery was unstable because of reduced effort, difficulties with processing plant equipment, and limitations imposed by resident fishermen on the issue of licences to nonresidents who traditionally fished for walleye and whitefish. During this period, the total harvest varied between 12 399 and 308 689 kg/year. Before the unstable period, the catch in Saskatchewan waters had been substantially greater than the harvest near the delta. From 1985/86 to 1987/88, however, the Saskatchewan fishery was based only on the south shore and the catch from Alberta was almost twice that from Saskatchewan. The average total catch from 1985/86 to 1987/88 was 377 108 kg/year.

Before the delta fishery opened in 1943/44, lake trout were the primary commercial species in Lake Athabasca. The largest catch of lake trout (1 012 409 kg) was taken in 1929/30. From 1935/36 to 1942/43, the average catch declined to only 258 000 kg/year, representing 81% of the total annual catch. From 1951/52 to 1959/60, the average catch of lake trout rose slightly, to 266 247 kg/year, but represented only 48% of the total catch. This drop in the proportion of lake trout occurred after the opening of the Alberta fishery, which caught other species. From 1960/61 to 1965/66, the average lake trout catch rose again, to 287 000 kg/year, and represented 38% of the total catch. In the early 1960s, a lake trout reported to weigh 47.6 kg was taken in a commercial net in Lake Athabasca (Larkin 1964). In 1966/67, the lake trout quota was greatly reduced, and from 1967/68 to 1973/74 the average catch declined to 110 155 kg/year, or 20% of the total catch. The harvest from 1985/86 to 1987/88 averaged 85 000 kg/year, or 23% of the total catch.

The average whitefish harvest from 1935/36 to 1942/43 was 58 000 kg/year (18% of the total catch). Following development of the delta fishery, the average whitefish catch increased. From 1951/52 to 1959/60 it was 225 375 kg/year (41% of the total catch) and from 1960/61 to 1965/66, it increased again, to 310 112 kg/year (42% of the total catch). From 1967/68 to 1973/74 the catch fell slightly, to 300 639 kg/year (54% of the total catch). Following the problems of the late 1970s and early 1980s, the whitefish harvest declined sharply—from 1985/86 to 1987/88, it was only 63 349 kg/year (17% of the total catch). Lake whitefish from the Alberta side of Lake Athabasca are infested with cysts of the tapeworm *Triaenophorus crassus*. Although fit for human consumption, these whitefish are considered poor quality and are used in commercial products such as fish cakes.

The walleye harvest from 1935/36 to 1942/43 was quite small, only 3 724 kg/year (1% of the total catch). After development of the delta fishery, the harvest increased. From 1951/52 to 1959/60 it was 46 500 kg/year (8% of the total catch) and from 1960/61 to 1965/66, it almost doubled, to 85 400 kg/year (11% of the total catch). From 1967/68 to 1973/74, the walleye harvest declined to 74 000 kg/year (13% of the total catch) and then remained at that level (75 000 kg/year, or 20% of the total catch) for the period from 1985/86 to 1987/88. Almost all walleye are caught in Alberta waters.

The average harvest of northern pike from 1935/36 to 1942/43 was 3 343 kg/year (1% of the total catch). It increased only slightly after development of the delta fishery. From 1951/52 to 1959/60 the harvest was 12 748 kg/year (2% of the total catch), but from 1960/61 to 1973/74, it increased to 65 730 kg/year (10% of the total catch). The average catch from 1985/86 to 1987/88 was

153 600 kg/year (41% of the total catch). Virtually all of the pike are caught in the delta region of the lake.

Wildlife

The Peace-Athabasca Delta region is the part of Lake Athabasca that is most important to wildlife. The delta is one of North America's last relatively undisturbed deltas and is unique because it is situated on all four of the continent's major flyways. Furthermore, the delta is an important breeding, staging and moulting area for waterfowl and is a nesting area for the endangered Peregrine Falcon. It supports the largest area of undisturbed sedge and grass meadows in North America and provides grazing for most of the bison of Wood Buffalo National Park (PADPG 1972). The portion of the delta lying outside Wood Buffalo National Park, with the exception of the Chipewyan Indian Reserves, was proposed as a Wildlife Habitat Management Area by Ducks Unlimited (Canada) and Fish and Wildlife Division in 1986 (Ducks Unltd. (Can.) and Alta. En. Nat. Resour. 1986). The area includes Richardson Lake, which is at present a bird sanctuary.

The effects of changes in the flow of the Peace River on the wildlife and fisheries of the delta after construction of the Bennett Dam were studied by the Peace-Athabasca Delta Project Group (1972; 1973), which was set up by the governments of Canada, Alberta and Saskatchewan. As well, during the 1980s, the effects of the Rivière des Rochers and Revillon Coupé weirs were studied by the Peace-Athabasca Delta Implementation Committee (1987).

More than 200 species of birds have been identified in Wood Buffalo National Park, which includes a large part of the delta region. The delta is a vital stopover for Whooping Cranes, Whistling Swans, Snow, White-fronted, Ross's and Canada geese and a variety of ducks during spring and fall migration. During the spring migration of 1971, about 400 000 ducks, numerous swans, and 145 000 geese used the delta region. As well, 14 species of ducks nest and moult in the delta marshes. In 1971, the ducks that remained after migration produced about 600 000 young. About 500 000 waterfowl used the delta for moulting, and about 1 200 000 ducks and 165 000 geese and swans stopped and fed in the large lakes of the delta during the fall migration that year (PADPG 1972). Other important bird species that inhabit the region include Sandhill Crane, Ring-billed Gull, Common Tern, Greater Yellowlegs, Wilson's Phalarope, Franklin's Gull, Eared Grebe, Western Grebe, Long-billed Marsh Wren, Yellow-headed Blackbird, Osprey, Bald Eagle and Peregrine Falcon (Can. Wild. Serv. 1985; Ducks Unltd. (Can.) and Alta. En. Nat. Resour. 1986).

Statistical analyses of waterfowl populations with data from 1960 to 1980 indicated no significant differences among waterfowl populations for the pre-Bennett dam, post-Bennett dam and postweir periods. A simulation model predicted that long-term production after the weirs were built would approximate production under natural conditions. The available habitat for fall staging, however, would decrease from the amount present under natural conditions because the weirs cause autumn water levels to decline more slowly (PADIC 1987).

The delta region and Wood Buffalo National Park provide important habitat for mammals. Altogether, 45 species of mammals have been recorded in the park (PADPG 1972). Muskrat populations in the delta were estimated to be between 200 000 and 2 000 000 animals prior to construction of the Bennett Dam. Muskrats thrive in the deeper perched basins provided these basins are refilled by floods every four or five years (Can. Wild. Serv. 1985). Muskrat trapping and, to a lesser extent, beaver and mink trapping, are important sources of income to natives in the delta region. In 1974, muskrat numbers peaked in response to higher water levels, which were caused by precipitation levels that were higher than those in previous years. Since 1975, however, muskrat numbers have declined. This decline may have been influenced by trapping, predation and disease, as well as by declining water levels. If overall water levels in the delta increase—for instance, during periods of greater precipitation—the habitat necessary for the muskrat population to recover will be present. Along the Peace River, where less frequent flooding of perched basins since the Bennett Dam was built has not been

influenced by the weirs, a long-term decline in the muskrat population is expected (PADIC 1987).

In 1971, about 10 000 of the 14 000 bison in Wood Buffalo National Park fed in the delta year-round (PADPG 1972). The bison calve and raise their young on the Sweetgrass Meadows north of Lake Claire, then move toward Mamawi Lake in the fall. By midwinter they are dispersed over small sedge meadows near the lake, and in spring they drift back to the Sweetgrass Meadows (Can. Wild. Serv. 1985). Moose inhabit the higher, forested areas of the delta, and in 1971, an estimated 800 moose lived in the area. Timber wolves are the dominant carnivore in the delta and black bears are present as well.

M.E. Bradford and J.M. Hanson

References

Alberta Environment. n.d.[a]. Envir. Assess. Div., Envir. Qlty. Monit. Br. Unpubl. data, Edmonton.
———. n.d.[b]. Tech. Serv. Div., Hydrol. Br. Unpubl. data, Edmonton.
———. n.d.[c]. Tech. Serv. Div., Surv. Br. Unpubl. data, Edmonton.
Alberta Forestry, Lands and Wildlife. n.d. Fish Wild. Div. Unpubl. data, Edmonton.
———. 1988. Boating in Alberta. Fish Wild. Div., Edmonton.
———. 1989. Guide to sportfishing. Fish Wild. Div., Edmonton.
Alberta Native Affairs. 1986. A guide to native communities in Alberta. Native Aff. Secret., Edmonton.
Alberta Recreation and Parks. n.d. Ecological reserves. Now…and forever. Advisory Commit. on Wilderness Areas and Ecol. Reserves, Edmonton.
Alberta Recreation, Parks and Wildlife. 1976. Commercial fisheries catch statistics for Alberta, 1942–1975. Fish Wild. Div., Fish. Mgt. Rep. No. 22, Edmonton.
Alberta Research Council. 1972. Geological map of Alberta. Nat. Resour. Div., Alta. Geol. Surv., Edmonton.
Atlas of Alberta. 1969. Univ. Alta. Press, Edmonton, in assoc. with Univ. Toronto Press, Toronto.
Bayrock, L.S. and J.D. Root. 1973. Geology of the Peace-Athabasca River Delta region, Alberta (Section N). In The Peace-Athabasca Delta Project, technical appendices, Vol. I: Hydrologic investigations. 1973. Prep. by PADPG for Govt. Can., Alta., Sask. Information Can., Ottawa.
Bennett, R.M. and J.R. Card. 1972. History of water levels (Section A). In The Peace-Athabasca Delta project, technical appendices, Vol. I: Hydrologic investigations. 1973. Prep. by PADPG for Govt. Can., Alta., Sask. Information Can., Ottawa.
Bidgood, B.F. 1961. Ecology of walleye in Richardson Lake-Lake Athabasca. Alta. Ld. For., Fish Wild. Div., Res. Rep. No. 1, Edmonton.
Brady, A.J. ca 1983. A history of Fort Chipewyan: Alberta's oldest continuously inhabited settlement. Gregorach Printing Ltd., Athabasca.
Canada, Department of Fisheries and the Environment. 1973. Lake Athabasca. Marine Sci. Directorate, Can. Hydrog. Serv., Ottawa.
Canadian Wildlife Service. 1985. Northern deltas—oases for wildlife: Peace-Athabasca Slave Mackenzie. Supply Serv. Can., Ottawa.
Ducks Unlimited (Canada) and Alberta Energy and Natural Resources. 1986. Waterfowl habitat program. Ducks Unltd. (Can.) Alta. En. Nat. Resour., Fish Wild. Div., Edmonton.
Environment Canada. 1973–1987. Surface water data. Prep. by Inland Waters Directorate. Water Surv. Can., Water Resour. Br., Ottawa.
———. 1982. Canadian climate normals, Vol. 7: Bright sunshine (1951–1980). Prep. by Atm. Envir. Serv. Supply Serv. Can., Ottawa.
Gallup, D.N., P. Van der Giessen and H. Boerger. 1971. A survey of plankton and bottom invertebrates of the Peace-Athabasca Delta region. Prep. for Can. Wild. Serv., Edmonton.
Holmgren, E.J. and P.M. Holmgren. 1976. Over 2000 place names of Alberta. 3rd ed. West. Producer Prairie Books, Saskatoon.
Larkin, P.A. 1947. *Pontoporeia* and *Mysis* in Athabasca, Great Bear, and Great Slave lakes. Fish. Res. Bd. Can. Bull. 73:1–33.
———. 1964. Canadian lakes. Verh. Internat. Verein. Limnol. 15:76–90.
Mackenzie River Basin Committee (MRBC). 1981. Mackenzie River Basin Study report. Govt. Can., Alta., BC, Sask., NWT, YT. Information Can., Ottawa.
McCormack, P.A. 1988. Northwind dreaming, Fort Chipewyan 1788–1988. Prov. Museum Alta. Special Publ. No. 6, Edmonton.
National Atlas of Canada, The. 1974. 4th ed. Macmillan Co. Can. Ltd., in assoc. with Dept. En. Mines Resour. and Information Can., Ottawa.
Neill, C.R. and B.J. Evans. 1979. Synthesis of surface water hydrology. Prep. by Northwest Hydraulic Consult. Ltd. for Alta. Envir., Alta. Oil Sands Envir. Res. Project. AOSERP Rep. 60, Edmonton.
Neill, C.R., G.J. Evans and A.W. Lipsett. 1981. Circulation of water and sediment in the Athabasca Delta area. Prep. by Northwest Hydraulic Consult. Ltd. and Alta. Res. Counc. for Alta. Envir., Alta. Oil Sands Envir. Res. Project. AOSERP Rep. 123, Edmonton.
Noton, L. 1989. Alta. Envir., Envir. Assess. Div., Envir. Qlty. Monit. Br., Edmonton. Pers. comm.

Peace-Athabasca Delta Implementation Committee (PADIC). 1987. Peace-Athabasca delta water management works evaluation. Final report and Appendix A: Hydrological assessment. Prep. for Alta. Envir., Alta. For. Ld. Wild., Sask. Water Corp., Sask. Parks Renewable Resour., Envir. Can., Edmonton.

Peace-Athabasca Delta Project Group (PADPG). 1972. The Peace-Athabasca Delta, a Canadian resource: Summary report, 1972. Govt. Can., Alta., Sask. Information Can., Ottawa; Queen's Printer, Edmonton; Queen's Printer, Regina.

———. 1973. The Peace-Athabasca Delta project: Technical report. Govt. Can., Alta., Sask. Information Can., Ottawa; Queen's Printer, Edmonton; Queen's Printer, Regina.

Rawson, D.S. 1947[a]. Lake Athabasca. Bull. Fish Res. Bd. Can. 72:69–85.

———. 1947[b]. Fishes of Saskatchewan. *In* Report of the Royal Commission on the fisheries of Saskatchewan. King's Printer, Ottawa.

———. 1960. A limnological comparison of twelve large lakes in northern Saskatchewan. Limnol. Oceanogr. 5:195–211.

Saskatchewan Parks, Recreation and Culture. n.d. Renew. Resour. Div., Fish. Br. Unpubl. data, Prince Albert, Sask.

Strong, W.L. and K.R. Leggat. 1981. Ecoregions of Alberta. Alta. En. Nat. Resour., Resour. Eval. Plan. Div., Edmonton.

FIGURE EIGHT LAKE

E.E. Prepas

MAP SHEET: 84C/5
LOCATION: Tp84 R25 W5
LAT/LONG: 56°18′N 117°54′W

Figure Eight Lake is a tiny, naturally productive lake in north-western Alberta. It is located in a treed setting, 45 km northwest of the town of Peace River and 7 km northwest of Lac Cardinal. For over three decades, Figure Eight Lake has received considerable attention from local groups and the provincial government because it is one of the few lakes in the Peace River region that serves as both a sport fishery for trout and a recreational area. To reach Figure Eight Lake, take Highway 2 west from Peace River for 20 km to the junction with Highway 35. Follow the latter north for 9 km and then turn west onto Secondary Road 737 and continue for 16 km. The lake is just northwest of the secondary road (Fig. 1); the turnoff is well marked with a large, carved wooden sign. Alternatively, the lake can be reached by continuing on Highway 2, past Highway 35, to the hamlet of Brownvale. At Brownvale, turn north on Secondary Road 737 and continue to the turnoff for Figure Eight Lake.

Figure Eight Lake is situated between the forested area of the Whitemud Hills to the north and the agricultural lands of the lower Peace River basin to the south and east (Makowecki and Bishop 1978). Although a few settlers had arrived to farm the region before the turn of the century, homesteading began in earnest about 1908 (MacGregor 1972). The number of farms in the area increased rapidly until 1931 (Scheelar and Odynsky 1968).

Figure Eight Lake is a regulated lake that drains south, then southeast to Lac Cardinal. The Peace River area has a shortage of recreational lakes. Consequently, an earthen weir was built on the outflow to raise the lake level for recreational purposes. In 1970, the old weir was replaced with a fixed-crest earthfill dam (Alta. For. Ld. Wild. n.d.). These projects were supported by a number of local and provincial groups, including the Brownvale Community Club, Figure Eight Lake Recreation Club, Alberta Environment, Ducks Unlimited (Canada) and Fish and Wildlife Division, including Buck for Wildlife. In 1975, the first boat launch and pier were constructed at the southwest corner of the lake and fences were erected to protect the shoreline from cattle grazing. In 1981, a site development program was drawn up for the lake (Butler Krebes Assoc. Ltd. 1981). From 1986 through 1988, Alberta Environment and the Lac Cardinal and Figure Eight Lake Recreational Associations coordinated a project to install 42 overnight campsites, a large playground, a concrete boat launch with a dock, a day-use area, a sand beach and two ball diamonds on the southwest corner of the lake (Becker 1988). The group also has plans for ski and nature trails around the lake. The control structure and recreational facilities at the lake are now operated and maintained by Alberta Environment. There are no other developments on the lakeshore.

Figure Eight Lake takes its name from the shape it had before 1970 when the water level was low; in these earlier days the lake had two basins and resembled a figure eight.

Figure Eight Lake has algal blooms in summer, to the extent that it has a tendency to winterkill and occasionally summerkill. Since 1980, Fish and Wildlife Division, Alberta Environment, and recently the University of Alberta, have supported a program to reduce excessive algal blooms and the risk of fish die-offs in the lake. This program has entailed the use of copper sulphate (or "bluestone") from 1980 through 1984, lime (both calcium carbonate and calcium hydroxide) in 1986 and 1987, and the installation of an aerator in 1986. These programs have enhanced the sport fishery (Alta. For. Ld. Wild. n.d.).

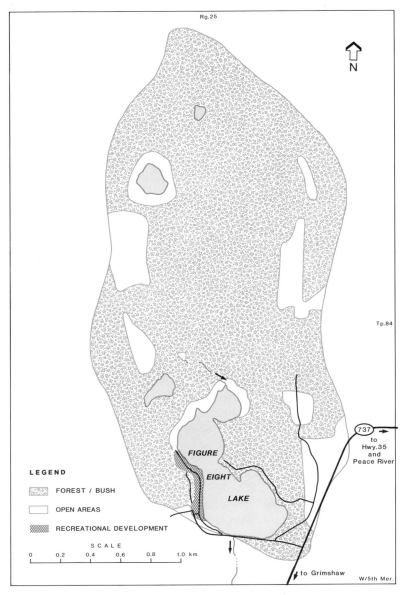

Figure 1. Features of the drainage basin of Figure Eight Lake.
SOURCES: Alta. Envir. n.d.[a]; En. Mines Resour. Can. 1976. Updated with 1984 aerial photos.

The lake is stocked annually with rainbow trout. It is a popular location for family and group recreational fishing and camping, particularly on warm summer weekends. Fishing for bait fish and use of bait fish are not permitted in Figure Eight Lake (Alta. For. Ld. Wild. 1989); only electric motors are permitted on the lake (Alta. For. Ld. Wild. 1988).

Drainage Basin Characteristics

The drainage basin of Figure Eight Lake is gently undulating, with slopes of 0.5 to 2%. Most of the drainage basin is covered by trembling aspen/balsam poplar forest, with 0.37 km², or 8% of the drainage area, cleared for agriculture (Fig. 1). The cleared areas are leased for cattle grazing. The soils are mainly Solonetzic Gray Luvisols (Table 1) and the agricultural capability of the land is rated as fair to fairly good (Scheelar and Odynsky 1968). All of the land in the watershed belongs to the Crown.

One stream flows into the north end of the lake. This stream is dotted with beaver dams and flows through a low area directly north of the western edge of the lake. The stream flows only during spring runoff (Guenther 1983). During a study conducted between 8 April and 27 August 1986, most of the flow (64%) occurred within the first four days of runoff. No measurable flow was recorded past 7 May 1986 (Prepas and Murphy 1987). Outflow is channeled through the control structure at the south end of the lake. Flow is intermittent in the outflow channel, which flows into Lac Cardinal.

Table 1. Characteristics of Figure Eight Lake drainage basin.

area (excluding lake) (km²)[a]	4.47
soil[b]	Solonetzic Gray Luvisols with minor amounts of Humic Luvic Gleysols
bedrock geology[c]	Kaskapau Formation (Upper Cretaceous): shale, thin ironstone beds, sandstone, mudstone; marine
terrain[b]	gently undulating
ecoregion[d]	Dry Mixedwood Subregion of Boreal Mixedwood
dominant vegetation[d]	trembling aspen, balsam poplar
mean annual inflow (m³)[a, e]	0.289 × 10⁶
mean annual sunshine (h)[f]	2 060

NOTE: [e]excluding groundwater inflow
SOURCES: [a]Alta. Envir. n.d.[a]; [b]Scheelar and Odynsky 1968; [c]Alta. Res. Counc. 1972; [d]Strong and Leggat 1981; [f]Envir. Can. 1982

Lake Basin Characteristics

Figure Eight Lake is a tiny lake (Fig. 2, Table 2) with three basins: a shallow southern basin, a shallower and smaller central basin, and a very shallow and small northern basin (maximum depths 6, 5 and 3 m, respectively).

In 1955, the maximum depth of Figure Eight Lake was approximately 3 m. In 1956, local residents constructed a small earthfill dam on the lake's outflow to raise the water level by almost 1 m, to a maximum depth of over 4 m. This dam was washed out and rebuilt at least once before 1968, when the lake was chosen by the Brownvale Community Club and its subsidiary, the Figure Eight Lake Recreation Club, as the site for a lake improvement project (Makowecki and Bishop 1978; Acres Int. Ltd. 1985). In 1970, the club cleared away the old dam and the brush from the flooded and nearshore areas, and rebuilt the dam to a maximum lake depth of 4.6 m. To increase the size of the lake and overcome problems with erosion of the earthfill dam, the dam was upgraded in 1973 by Alberta Environment. The works consist of a drop inlet spillway to accommodate a maximum lake depth of 6 m, an emergency spillway, riprap protection and downstream channel improvement. The increased depth significantly increased both the area and capacity of the lake (Fig. 3) and the new maximum depth was considered adequate to ensure the overwintering of sport fish (Alta. For. Ld. Wild. n.d.).

The elevation of Figure Eight Lake has been monitored since 1982 (Fig. 4). Over the period of record, the water levels have fluctuated by a maximum of 0.32 m. The maximum water level, 683.17 m, was recorded on 21 May 1986, and the minimum level, 682.85 m, was recorded on 5 October 1982.

Water Quality

The water quality of the two larger basins of Figure Eight Lake have been studied since 1971 by Fish and Wildlife Division (Alta. For. Ld. Wild. n.d.; Bishop 1979), in 1980 and 1984 by Alberta Environment (summarized in Acres Int. Ltd. 1985), and from 1985 through 1989 by the University of Alberta and Environment Canada (Prepas et al. n.d.; 1987; 1988; 1990; Prepas and Murphy 1987; Manning et al. 1988). Sediment phosphorus chemistry was examined in August 1986 (Shaw and Prepas 1989).

The water is well-buffered (average total alkalinity 110 mg/L CaCO₃) and slightly coloured. The dominant ions are bicarbonate and calcium (Table 3).

The two deeper basins are weakly thermally stratified during most of the summer, are mixed fairly well during fall and are thermally stratified again under ice cover (illustrated in Figure 5 with data from the deepest basin). The lake is ice-covered for a full six months. When the lake water is thermally stratified, water over the bottom sediments becomes anoxic (Fig. 6). Under ice cover, oxygen depletion is extremely rapid and the lake is often anoxic by January. For

Table 2. Characteristics of Figure Eight Lake.

elevation (m)[a, b]	683.17
surface area (km²)[a, c]	0.368
volume (m³)[a, c]	1.12 x 10⁶
maximum depth (m)[c]	6.0
mean depth (m)[c]	3.0
shoreline length (km)[d]	2.3
mean annual lake evaporation (mm)[e]	581
mean annual precipitation (mm)[e]	447
mean residence time (yr)[e, f]	4.5
control structure[g]	fixed-crest earthfill dam and drop inlet spillway
drop inlet spillway height (m)[g]	unknown

NOTES: [a]on date of sounding: May 1986; [f]excluding groundwater inflow
SOURCES: [b]Alta. Envir. n.d.[b]; [c]Prepas et al. 1987; [d]En. Mines Resour. Can. 1976;
[e]Alta. Envir. n.d.[a]; [g]Alta. Envir. n.d.[c]

Table 3. Major ions and related water quality variables for Figure Eight Lake. Average concentrations in mg/L; pH in pH units. Composite samples from the euphotic zone collected 13 times from 15 May to 27 Aug. 1986. Data are weighted composites from the two largest basins. S.E. = standard error.

	Mean	S.E.
pH (range)	7.8–9.7[a]	—
total alkalinity (CaCO₃)	91[b]	4.9
specific conductivity (μS/cm)	215[c]	3.4
turbidity (NTU)	5[d]	0.7
total hardness (calculated)	106	—
colour (Pt)	28[e]	2.2
total particulate carbon	4[f]	0.6
dissolved organic carbon	18[g]	0.4
HCO₃	94[h]	18.6
CO₃	12[h]	4.1
Mg	10	0.1
Na	2	0.02
K	9	0.1
Cl	1	0.1
SO₄	14	0.2
Ca	26[b]	1.3

NOTES: [a]n = 19; [b]n = 5, 17 July to 27 Aug. 1985; [c]n = 22; [d]n = 10; [e]n = 12; [f]n = 15; [g]n = 9; [h]n = 3
SOURCES: Prepas et al. 1987; Prepas and Murphy 1987

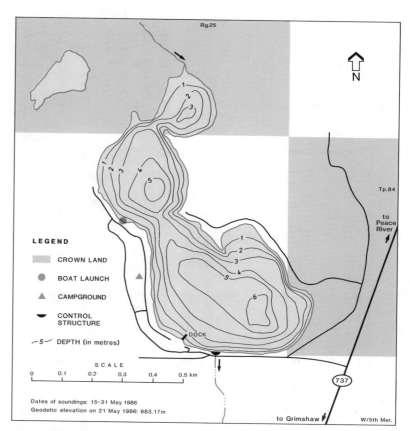

Figure 2. Bathymetry and shoreline features of Figure Eight Lake.
BATHYMETRY SOURCE: Prepas and Murphy 1987.

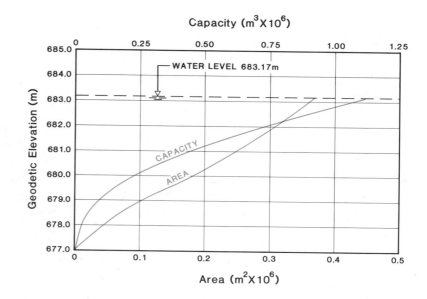

Figure 3. Area/capacity curve for Figure Eight Lake.
SOURCE: Prepas and Murphy 1987.

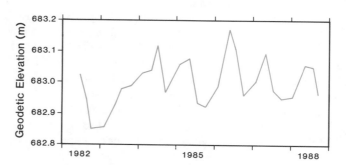

Figure 4. Water level of Figure Eight Lake, 1982 to 1988.
SOURCE: Alta. Envir. n.d.[b].

the first seven weeks of ice cover in 1985, dissolved oxygen consumption rates were 0.610 g/m² per day.

Figure Eight Lake is hyper-eutrophic. Total phosphorus and chlorophyll a concentrations can exceed 200 μg/L in the surface waters (Fig. 7, Table 4). Total phosphorus increases in the surface waters during summer and again under ice in winter. Phosphorus concentrations over the sediments can surpass 700 μg/L. Phosphorus concentrations in the shallow porewater (over 3 600 μg/L soluble reactive phosphorus) and potentially mobile phosphorus in the bottom sediments were the highest measured in nine Alberta lakes. Thus, there is rapid recycling of phosphorus between the open water and the sediments of Figure Eight Lake. Total iron concentrations are relatively high and reflect iron deposits in the region. The possible relationship between iron and phosphorus remains undetermined for this lake; iron can immobilize phosphorus and reduce phosphorus concentrations in the surface waters of some lakes.

The inflowing stream is a major phosphorus source during spring runoff. In April 1986, both total phosphorus and total iron concentrations were high in the stream; total phosphorus averaged

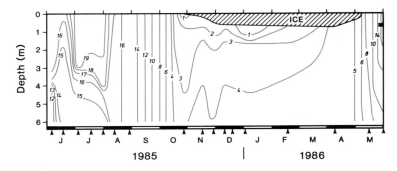

Figure 5. Temperature (°C) of Figure Eight Lake, 1985 and 1986. Arrows indicate sampling dates.
SOURCES: Prepas et al. 1987; Prepas and Murphy 1987.

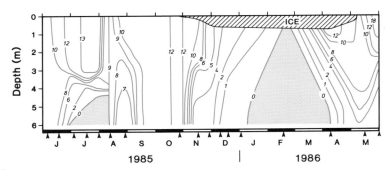

Figure 6. Dissolved oxygen (mg/L) in Figure Eight Lake, 1985 and 1986. Arrows indicate sampling dates.
SOURCES: Prepas et al. 1987; Prepas and Murphy 1987.

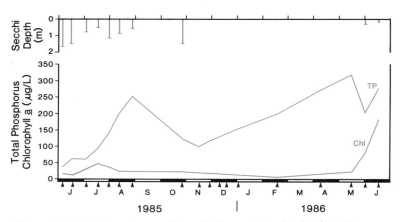

Figure 7. Total phosphorus, chlorophyll a and Secchi depth in Figure Eight Lake, 1985 and 1986.
SOURCES: Prepas et al. 1987; Prepas and Murphy 1987.

671 µg/L and total iron averaged 411 µg/L. During peak flow in late April, total iron concentrations reached a high of 1 560 µg/L.

After the modified reservoir was filled in the early 1970s, the sport fishery blossomed initially, then declined as a result of excessive algal growth, which caused low dissolved oxygen concentrations (Makowecki and Bishop 1978). This algal problem spurred exploration of alternatives to improve the water quality of Figure Eight Lake, which included chemical treatment, aeration, and diversion of water into the lake from the major tributary to Lac Cardinal, which flows to the west of Figure Eight Lake (Guenther 1983). Chemical treatment (Table 5) and winter aeration have been implemented. Water diversion has not been implemented because increased flow would not enhance water quality. Another alternative, increasing lake depth, is not feasible because of the large flat low-lying area at the north end of the lake, thus a very large area would be flooded with a 2–m increase in water levels (Prepas et al. 1987).

Figure Eight Lake has been treated with chemicals to reduce algal biomass in five of the last eight years (Table 5). The data in Tables

3 and 4 and Figures 6 and 7, and the previous discussion on water quality, were selected to represent the natural state of the lake. Following the copper sulphate treatments, algal biomass was reduced, and after some but not all treatments, under-ice dissolved oxygen concentrations improved. However, concern was raised about the accumulation of copper in the sediments of the lake and long-term toxicity problems associated with this treatment. Some of these concerns were confirmed in a 1985 study in which it was documented that copper accumulated in the sediments had suppressed normal bacterial activity for up to one year after treatment and had recycled into the open water for brief periods. In addition, amphipods (a prey popular with trout) disappeared from Figure Eight Lake from June 1980, when the lake was first treated with copper sulphate, until May 1986, after treatment had been discontinued for almost two years, when they returned in high numbers.

In 1986 and 1987, the lake was treated with two forms of lime (Table 5). These treatments had the effect of reducing algal biomass for 1987 and most of 1988. In 1987, both total phosphorus and chlorophyll a concentrations were reduced to less than half of pretreatment levels (246 ± 14 to 75 ± 8 µg/L total phosphorus and 96 ± 14 to 12 ± 7 µg/L chlorophyll a). In addition, under-ice dissolved oxygen depletion rates dropped from a pretreatment rate of 0.610 to 0.363 g O_2/m² per day.

An aerator was installed in Figure Eight Lake in October 1986. In the first winter, two events combined to eliminate any significant improvement in under-ice oxygen conditions. First, it was an unusual fall: it was warm until late October, then it quickly turned cold. Consequently, the lake became ice covered when the water was less than 45% saturated with dissolved oxygen (less than 5.4 mg/L). Dissolved oxygen concentrations at the same time in 1985 were 2.3 times higher (12.4 mg/L). In addition, dissolved oxygen consumption rates were still high in the winter of 1986/87 (0.610 g/m² per day). The aerator could not inject enough air to keep dissolved oxygen levels up that winter. In contrast, in 1987/88, dissolved oxygen concentrations were high (10.9 mg/L) at the onset of ice cover and consumption rates were much lower due to the reduced algal production during the previous summer. Consequently, the aerator was able to ensure that trout could overwinter. The trout overwintered because of the combination of low dissolved oxygen consumption rates following effects of lime treatments, and the extra oxygen injected with the aerator (Walty 1988; Prepas et al. 1990).

Biological Characteristics

Plants

Algal biomass and species composition have been monitored in Figure Eight Lake since the mid-1970s (Alta. For. Ld. Wild. n.d.; Prepas et al. 1987; 1988; Prepas and Murphy 1987). The dominant alga in most summers is the blue-green, *Aphanizomenon flosaquae*.

Aquatic macrophytes in the southwest part of the lake have been monitored annually since 1985 by the University of Alberta (Fig. 8). Plants were most concentrated in areas with shallow slopes and depths of less than 1 m but rooted plants were found to a depth of 2 m. Macrophyte biomass declined slightly after the lime treatments in 1986 and 1987, even though light penetration improved substantially. This unexpected change could be related to decreased phosphorus availablility in the bottom sediments. The following data on fresh weight (g/m²) are averages for all samples collected in July at one depth (±1 S.E.).

Depth	1985	1986	1987
1 m	240 (70)	170 (104)	193 (136)
2 m	199 (77)	250 (82)	56 (20)

Table 4. Nutrient, chlorophyll _a_ and Secchi depth data for Figure Eight Lake. Average concentrations in μg/L. Composite samples from the euphotic zone collected 7 times from 05 June to 27 Aug. 1985 and twice in 1986, on 01 June and 17 June (pretreatment). Data are weighted composites from the two largest basins. S.E. = standard error.

	1985		1986[d]	
	Mean	S.E.	Mean	S.E.
total phosphorus	118	28.9	247	36.3
total dissolved phosphorus	43	14.1	50	22.7
soluble reactive phosphorus	24[a]	14.0	—	—
total Kjeldahl nitrogen	1 697[b]	140.4	2 193	140.6
$NO_3 + NO_2$–nitrogen	5[a]	1.8	3	1.6
NH_4–nitrogen	40[c]	33.1	30	5.0
iron	148[a]	49.1	142	22.0
chlorophyll _a_	26.3	4.64	172.0	62.50
Secchi depth (m)	1.0	0.17	0.2	0.08

NOTES: [a] n = 5; [b] n = .6; [c] n = 3
SOURCES: Prepas et al. 1987; [d] Prepas and Murphy 1987

Table 5. History of chemical treatments of Figure Eight Lake. Copper added as $CuSO_4 \cdot 5H_2O$; Cu additions in kg of Cu; concentration in μg Cu/L. Lime additions in tonnes; concentration in mg Ca/L.

Treatment	Date	Addition	Concentration
$CuSO_4$[a]	11 June 1980	80.4	71.2
$CuSO_4$[a]	11 Aug. 1983	28.0	24.8
$CuSO_4$[a]	25 June 1984	21.6	19.1
$CuSO_4$[a]	14 Aug. 1984	34.4	30.5
$CaCO_3$[b]	18 June 1986	15.8	14.0
$Ca(OH)_2$[b]	30 July 1986	9.4	8.4
$Ca(OH)_2$[b]	08 Aug. 1986	5.4	4.8
$CaCO_3$[c]	14 July 1987	22.5	18.2

SOURCES: [a] Alta. For. Ld. Wild. n.d.; Prepas et al. 1987; [b] Prepas and Murphy 1987; [c] Prepas et al. 1988

Invertebrates

There are no quantitative data on the invertebrates in Figure Eight Lake.

Fish

Two species of fish inhabit Figure Eight Lake: rainbow trout, which are stocked annually, and fathead minnows. Ninespine sticklebacks have been observed below the dam. Rainbow trout production, actual and potential, has been evaluated by Fish and Wildlife Division since 1971 (Alta. For. Ld. Wild. n.d.; Schroeder 1975; Makowecki and Bishop 1978; Bishop 1979; Schwanke and Schroeder 1983; Walty 1988).

The lake was first stocked by Fish and Wildlife Division in 1956 with 750 adult northern pike. They did not become established. Since 1971, the lake has been stocked annually with fingerling rainbow trout (7 to 10 cm), which rapidly grow to catchable size. Larger trout (up to 18 cm in length) are also stocked, to provide some immediate angling opportunities. From 1971 through 1979, an average of 5 600 (range 3 000 to 15 000) rainbow trout were planted yearly. In 1980, stocking increased about 6–fold and an average of 32 300 rainbow trout (range 26 900 to 48 000) were added from 1980 through 1988. In years when Fish and Wildlife Division predicted that the lake would winterkill, salvage netting permits were issued so the trout could be harvested before dissolved oxygen reached critically low concentrations and the fish died.

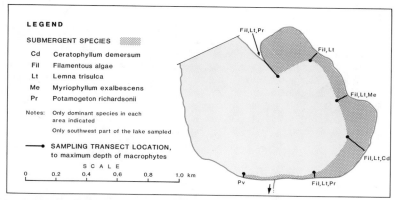

Figure 8. Distribution of submergent aquatic macrophytes in the southwest part of Figure Eight Lake, 1985.
SOURCE: Prepas et al. 1987.

In June 1983, a three-day creel survey was conducted by Fish and Wildlife Division. The catch per unit effort was 0.56 rainbow trout/hour. Growth rates of rainbow trout in Figure Eight Lake are the highest in the region. From 1980 through 1983, fingerlings grew an average of 1.66 g/day and 1.16 mm/day during the open-water period.

Wildlife

Ducks Unlimited (Canada) (1982) report that there is some good upland nesting cover for waterfowl at Figure Eight Lake. However, the generally steep shoreline and poor distribution of emergent and submergent plants restricts the potential for waterfowl production. Nesting species include mainly Lesser Scaup, American Widgeons, teal, Ruddy Ducks, and White-winger Scoters, with production estimated at 4.8 broods per km of shoreline.

E.E. Prepas

References

Acres International Limited. 1985. Figure Eight Lake water quality study. Prep. for Alta. Envir., Plan. Div., Edmonton.

Alberta Environment. n.d.[a]. Tech. Serv. Div., Hydrol. Br. Unpubl. data, Edmonton.

———. n.d.[b]. Tech. Serv. Div., Surv. Br. Unpubl. data, Edmonton.

———. n.d.[c]. Water Resour. Admin. Div., Dam Safety Br. Unpubl. data, Edmonton.

Alberta Forestry, Lands and Wildlife. n.d. Fish Wild. Div. Unpubl. data, Edmonton.

———. 1988. Boating in Alberta. Fish Wild. Div., Edmonton.

———. 1989. Guide to sportfishing. Fish Wild. Div., Edmonton.

Alberta Research Council. 1972. Geological map of Alberta. Nat. Resour. Div., Alta. Geol. Surv., Edmonton.

Becker, T. 1988. Alta. Envir., Water Resour. Admin. Div., Peace River. Pers. comm.

Bishop, F.G. 1979. Limnology and fisheries of seven stocked lakes in the Peace River region. Alta. Rec. Parks Wild., Fish Wild. Div., Peace River.

Butler Krebes Associates Ltd. 1981. Figure Eight Lake site development study. Prep. for Alta. Envir., Plan. Div., Edmonton.

Ducks Unlimited (Canada). 1982. Figure Eight Lake project report. Ducks Unltd. (Can.), Edmonton.

Energy, Mines and Resources Canada. 1976. National topographic series 1:50 000 84C/5 (1976). Surv. Map. Br., Ottawa.

Environment Canada. 1982. Canadian climate normals, Vol. 7: Bright sunshine (1951–1980). Prep. by Atm. Envir. Serv. Supply Serv. Can., Ottawa.

Guenther, G.W. 1983. Figure Eight Lake, Stage II. Alta. Envir.,Tech. Serv. Div., Edmonton.

MacGregor, J.G. 1972. A history of Alberta. Hurtig Publ., Edmonton.

Makowecki, R. and R. Bishop. 1978. Figure Eight Lake development project. Fish. Habitat Devel. Rep. No. 10. Alta. Rec. Parks Wild., Fish Wild. Div., Edmonton.

Manning, P.G., T.P. Murphy, T. Mayer and E.E. Prepas. 1988. Effect of copper sulfate on pyrite formation in reducing sediments. Can. Mineral. 26:965–972.

Prepas, E.E., J. Babin, P.A. Chambers and T.P. Murphy. n.d. Unpubl. data, Univ. Alta., Edmonton and Natl. Water Res. Inst., Burlington, Ontario.

Prepas, E.E. and T.P. Murphy. 1987. Report of the 1986 treatment of Figure Eight Lake. Prep. for Alta. Envir., Plan. Div., Edmonton.

Prepas, E.E., T.P. Murphy and P.G. Manning. 1987. Report on the 1985 evaluation of Figure Eight Lake, Alberta. Prep. for Alta. Envir., Plan. Div., Edmonton.

Prepas, E.E., T.P. Murphy and J. Babin. 1988. Report on the 1987 treatment of Figure Eight Lake, Alberta. Prep. for Alta. Envir., Plan. Div., Edmonton.

Prepas, E.E., T.P. Murphy, J.M. Crosby, D.T. Walty, J.T. Lim, J. Babin and P.A. Chambers. 1990. The reductions of phosphorus and chlorophyll *a* concentrations following $CaCO_3$ and $Ca(OH)_2$ additions to hypereutrophic Figure Eight Lake, Alberta. Envir. Sci. Tech. [in press]

Scheelar, M.D. and W. Odynsky. 1968. Reconnaissance soil survey of the Grimshaw and Notikewin areas. Univ. Alta. Bull. No. SS–8, Res. Counc. Alta. Rep. No. 88. Univ. Alta., Edmonton.

Schroeder, D.G. 1975. Results of the recreational net fishing questionnaire for Figure Eight Lake, 1974–75. Alta. En. Nat. Resour., Fish Wild. Div., Peace River.

Schwanke, T. and D. Schroeder. 1983. Results of the Figure Eight Lake test netting November 1983. Alta. En. Nat. Resour., Fish Wild. Div., Peace River.

Shaw, J.F.H. and E.E. Prepas. 1989. Exchange of phosphorus from shallow sediments at nine Alberta lakes. J. Envir. Qlty. [in press]

Strong, W.L. and K.R. Leggat. 1981. Ecoregions of Alberta. Alta. En. Nat. Resour., Resour. Eval. Plan. Div., Edmonton.

Walty, D. 1988. Alta. For. Ld. Wild., Fish Wild. Div., Peace River. Pers. comm.

MOONSHINE LAKE

Alberta Recreation and Parks

MAP SHEET: 83M/14
LOCATION: Tp79 R8 W6
LAT/LONG: 55°53'N 119°13'W

Moonshine Lake is a very small recreational lake located in improvement District No. 20 about 110 km north of the city of Grande Prairie and 40 km northwest of the town of Spirit River. To reach the lake from Spirit River, take Highway 49 west to Secondary Road 725, then drive north for about 4.5 km to the entrance road to Moonshine Lake Provincial Park (Fig. 1).

The lake's name has a colourful history. Moonshine Lake was situated on a detour from a trail that was known in the 1910s and 1920s as the Moonshine Trail. Sometime during the 1920s, two local residents spilled their illegal brew from a wagon into the lake, and thus christened the lake "Moonshine". At some point after this time, the lake was officially renamed "Mirage", but local residents continued to use the original name. In 1983, the name was changed back to Moonshine Lake (Alta. Cult. Multicult. n.d.).

Cree and Métis lived in the general area before the arrival of the first white settlers in 1891. Cattle grazed near the lake in the early 1900s, but most settlement occurred after the railroad was built as far as Spirit River in 1916 (Finlay and Finlay 1987). Two sawmills were located near the lake, the first in 1928 and the second in 1945, and much of what is now the provincial park was logged. Prior to 1959, the lake was a 0.14 km² slough surrounded by lush grass and trees and local families visited for picnics. The idea for a park was initiated in 1956, and Moonshine Lake Provincial Park was established in 1959 (Big Bend Hist. Commit. 1981). That year, a weir and dyke were built along the east side of the lake, the water level rose and the lake's area was doubled.

Moonshine Lake Provincial Park covers an area of about 8.5 km² and surrounds the entire lake (Fig. 1, 2). It is open year-round and offers 110 campsites, a separate group camping area, sewage disposal facilities, tap water, a concession stand, a hand boat launch, a boat launch for trailers, day-use areas, a change house, a baseball diamond and three playground areas. All boat motors except electric motors are prohibited from the lake. As well, all boats are prohibited from designated swimming areas (Alta. For. Ld. Wild. 1988).

Moonshine Lake supports a very popular year-round rainbow trout fishery. Sport fishing regulations prohibit fishing for bait fish or the use of bait fish in the lake (Alta. For. Ld. Wild. 1989). Winterkill was a problem until aeration equipment was installed in 1983. The lake is quite fertile, and the water turns green by midsummer. Algal concentrations during summer seem to have declined since aeration began, but aquatic vegetation is more abundant. Aquatic plants were cleared mechanically from areas around the beach, boat launch and dam during the mid-1980s.

Drainage Basin Characteristics

Although the drainage basin surrounding the lake is very small, it is 24 times the size of the lake (Tables 1, 2). The natural drainage has been altered by the construction of ditches and an earthfill weir that regulates the lake level (Fig. 1). Moonshine Lake had no defined inlet prior to 1975, when a 2.4–km–long drainage ditch was dug west of the lake. The ditch catches runoff, but water flows only during snowmelt and periods of heavy rainfall (Whitelock 1988). An overflow spillway on the southwest side of the lake flows south intermittently into two sloughs, then east until it joins the main outflow from the dam where the outflow crosses Secondary Road 725.

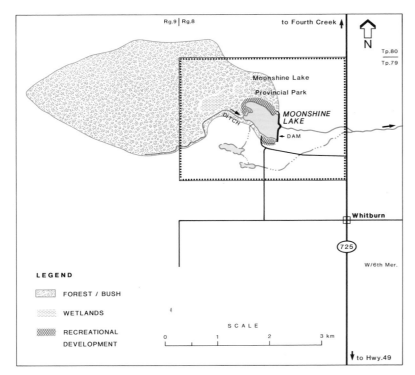

Figure 1. Features of the drainage basin of Moonshine Lake.
SOURCES: Alta. Envir. n.d.[b]; En. Mines Resour. Can. 1975. Updated with 1983 and 1985 aerial photos.

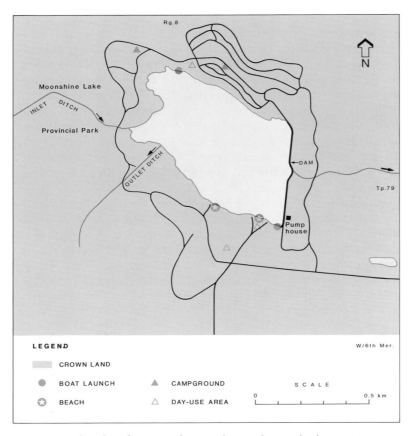

Figure 2. Shoreline features of Moonshine Lake. No bathymetric survey available.

Moonshine Lake's watershed is part of the Boreal Foothills Ecoregion (Strong and Leggat 1981). Most of the soils are moderately well-drained Dark Gray Luvisols and imperfectly drained Gleyed Dark Gray Luvisols. Both soil types have developed on fine-textured glaciolacustrine sediments. They support a forest cover that consists mainly of trembling aspen, white spruce and balsam poplar, with lesser amounts of willow and white birch, and an understory of low-bush cranberry, rose, buffalo-berry and fireweed. Two types of poorly drained soils are present in a large area northwest of the lake.

Table 1. Characteristics of Moonshine Lake drainage basin.

area (excluding lake) (km²)[a]	6.84
soil[b]	Dark Gray and Gleyed Dark Gray Luvisols
bedrock geology[c]	Kaskapau Formation (Upper Cretaceous): shale, thin ironstone beds, sandstone, mudstone; marine
terrain[b]	level to undulating
ecoregion[d]	Boreal Foothills
dominant vegetation[b]	trembling aspen, balsam poplar, white spruce
mean annual inflow (m³)[a, e]	0.404×10^6
mean annual sunshine (h)[f]	2 060

NOTE: [e]excluding groundwater inflow
SOURCES: [a]Alta. Envir. n.d.[b]; [b]MacMillan and Greenlee 1977; [c]Alta. Res. Counc. 1972; [d]Strong and Leggat 1981; [f]Envir. Can. 1982

Table 2. Characteristics of Moonshine Lake.

full supply level (FSL) (m)[a]	718.11
surface area (km²)[b]	0.28
estimated volume at FSL (m³)[a]	0.370×10^6
maximum depth (m)[c]	3.5
estimated mean depth (m)[a, c]	1.3
shoreline length (km)[b]	2.4
control structures[a]	earthfill weir with gatewell and conduit; overflow spillway with fish screen
dam height (m)[a]	3.05
dam crest length (m)[a]	625
dam crest elevation (m)[a]	~719
overflow spillway crest elevation (m)[a]	717.68
mean annual lake evaporation (mm)[d]	581
mean annual precipitation (mm)[d]	536
mean residence time (yr)	not available

SOURCES: [a]Alta. Envir. n.d.[d]; [b]En. Mines Resour. Can. 1975; [c]Alta. Envir. n.d.[a]; [d]Alta. Envir. n.d.[b]

Orthic Gleysols, which developed on fine-textured glaciolacustrine sediments, are located in depressions where runoff frequently collects and water infiltration is slow. The vegetation on these soils is mainly alder, willow, white birch and balsam poplar, with some white spruce and an understory of feathermoss. The other poorly drained soils are undifferentiated Mesisols that developed on sedge and reed peat. Mesisols are located mostly in bogs and fens; they support a cover of black spruce, Labrador tea, *Sphagnum* and feathermoss (MacMillan and Greenlee 1977).

The drainage basin is extensively forested and there is very little agricultural activity and no residential development. Land near the north and south shores of the lake has been developed by Alberta Recreation and Parks for recreational activities such as camping and day use.

Lake Basin Characteristics

The bathymetry of Moonshine Lake has not been surveyed. In 1975, the lake covered an area of 0.28 km² and in 1986 it had a maximum depth of 3.5 m (Table 2). The water level has been monitored since 1978 (Fig. 3). The historic minimum, recorded in August 1980, was 717.70 m, and the historic maximum, recorded in July 1988, was 718.57 m, which is a fluctuation of 0.87 m.

In 1959, a 625–m–long earthfill dam was constructed across the east side of the lake, and an overflow spillway was constructed on the southwest side (Alta. Envir. n.d.[d]). The project was a cooperative effort between the Department of Agriculture (Water Resources Division) and the Department of Lands and Forests, and its purpose

Table 3. Major ions and related water quality variables for Moonshine Lake. Average concentrations in mg/L; pH in pH units. Composite samples from the euphotic zone collected 3 times from 28 May to 22 Sep. 1986. S.E. = standard error.

	Mean	S.E.
pH (range)	7.6–8.4	—
total alkalinity ($CaCO_3$)	155	6.9
specific conductivity (μS/cm)	719	49.9
total dissolved solids (calculated)	446	31.0
total hardness ($CaCO_3$)	279	12.3
HCO_3	184	17.0
CO_3	2	1.4
Mg	36	1.7
Na	48	3.5
K	6	0.4
Cl	<1	—
SO_4	209	16.0
Ca	53	2.5

SOURCE: Alta. Envir. n.d.[a], Naquadat station 01AL07FD1000

Table 4. Nutrient, chlorophyll _a_ and Secchi depth data for Moonshine Lake. Average concentrations in μg/L. Composite samples from the euphotic zone collected 5 times from 31 May to 28 Sep. 1983 and 4 times from 28 May to 22 Sep. 1986. S.E. = standard error.

	1983		1986	
	Mean	S.E.	Mean	S.E.
total phosphorus	147	47.0	54	2.6
chlorophyll _a_	12.7	9.35	6.8	1.62
Secchi depth (m)	2.3	0.79	3.4	0.13

NOTE: [a]n = 3
SOURCE: Alta. Envir. n.d.[a], Naquadat station 01AL07FD1000

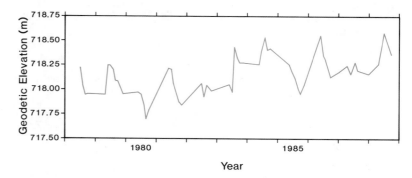

Figure 3. Water level of Moonshine Lake, 1978 to 1988.
SOURCE: Alta. Envir. n.d.[c].

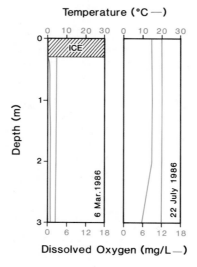

Figure 4. Temperature and dissolved oxygen in Moonshine Lake, 1986.
SOURCE: Alta. Envir. n.d.[a].

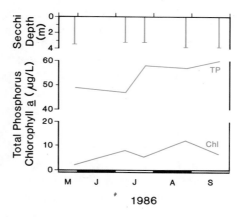

Figure 5. Total phosphorus, chlorophyll _a_ and Secchi depth in Moonshine Lake, 1986.
SOURCE: Alta. Envir. n.d.[a].

was to provide water storage for recreation. The dam is licenced to, and operated by, Alberta Recreation and Parks. A conduit and gatewell are located in the centre of the dam; they allow water to be released from the lake, but releases are made very infrequently. Park staff have allowed beaver dams to remain on the overflow spillway to keep the water level higher in order to enhance the probability that fish will overwinter successfully (Whitelock 1988).

Water Quality

The water quality of Moonshine Lake has been sampled approximately monthly during the open-water season since 1983 as part of a joint monitoring program conducted by Alberta Environment and Alberta Recreation and Parks (Alta. Envir. n.d.[a]). Fish and Wildlife Division has monitored the dissolved oxygen concentration of the water periodically since the 1970s, and frequently since installation of an aerator in October 1983 (Alta. For. Ld. Wild. n.d.; Schroeder 1984; 1988).

Moonshine Lake has fresh water that is very hard and well-buffered (Table 3). The dominant ions are sulphate and bicarbonate.

The lake is typical of very shallow water bodies: the temperature during summer is usually uniform from top to bottom and the water column is usually well oxygenated. A slight depletion in dissolved oxygen concentration was detected near the bottom in August 1983 and July 1986 (Fig. 4). This was because the rate of oxygen consumption by organisms in the surface sediments was higher than the rate of oxygen replenishment from the atmosphere. In some years, as in June 1977, the concentration of dissolved oxygen has fallen to critical levels and a summerkill has occurred. During winter, dissolved oxygen concentrations also have fallen to critically low levels. In the winter of 1981/82, most of the fish population died when oxygen

concentrations at the surface fell to 0.2 mg/L. A few northern pike survived and the lake was restocked with rainbow trout the following summer. During the next winter (1982/83), oxygen concentrations again fell below critical values, and a partial winterkill occurred. An aeration system was installed in the lake in October 1983 and modified in January 1984. After a larger compressor was installed in February 1986, the aerator was able to overcome the high oxygen demand. Although dissolved oxygen levels were only 2.5 mg/L from surface to bottom in March 1986 (Fig. 4), surface concentrations were 6.8 mg/L in February 1987, 9.0 mg/L and 4.4 mg/L at two locations in February 1988, and 4.2 mg/L in February 1989.

Moonshine Lake is eutrophic. The highest chlorophyll _a_ level recorded in the lake was 50 μg/L on 26 July 1983. Over the period of record, phosphorus and chlorophyll _a_ levels were lowest in May and June, increased toward midsummer and reached a maximum in July or August, as in 1986 (Fig. 5). This pattern is typical of many shallow lakes in Alberta. Total phosphorus and chlorophyll _a_ values in Moonshine Lake vary considerably between years. In 1983, the

Table 5. Comparison of growth rates of rainbow trout in Moonshine Lake with growth rates in other stocked lakes in the Peace River region. All trout age 1+.

Lake	Year	Growing Time (d)	Growth Rates Length (mm/d)	Growth Rates Weight (g/d)
Moonshine	1987	428	0.55	0.93
Machesis	1986	331	0.87	1.40
Running	1986	345	0.42	0.50
Spring	1986	351	0.61	1.08
Figure Eight	1982	361	0.42	2.04
Swan	1983	386	0.58	2.40
Hilltop	1987	308	0.53	1.41

SOURCE: Schroeder 1987

Table 6. Angler numbers, effort and harvest of rainbow trout from Moonshine Lake. Data collected on 67 days from Apr. to Sep. 1985, 39 days from Apr. to Oct. 1986 and 25 days from Nov. 1985 to Mar. 1986.

	Summer 1985	Summer 1986	Winter 1985/86
number of anglers	589	229	108
angler-hours	1 654	910	232
total number trout harvested	844	271	73
catch/angler-hour	0.51	0.30	0.32
catch/angler	1.43	1.18	0.68

SOURCE: Alta. For. Ld. Wild. n.d.

average phosphorus and chlorophyll *a* concentrations were much higher than in 1986 (Table 4). It is possible that wintertime aeration affects these variables during the open-water season. Under ice cover, an oxygenated water column could inhibit phosphorus release from sediments so that phosphorus levels would be lower at the start of the growing season in May.

Biological Characteristics

Plants

There are no detailed data available for the phytoplankton in Moonshine Lake. In July 1987, Fish and Wildlife Division noted the dominance of the blue-green genus *Aphanizomenon* (Schroeder 1987).

In July 1985, submergent aquatic macrophytes around the shoreline were surveyed by Fish and Wildlife Division (Schroeder 1985). In order of abundance, the four species identified were small-leaf pondweed (*Potamogeton pusillus*), northern watermilfoil (*Myriophyllum exalbescens*), Richardson pondweed (*P. richardsonii*) and flat-stemmed pondweed (*P. zosteriformis*). The highest density of vegetation was found along the south and southwest shores near the boat launch and beach. Small-leaf pondweed and northern watermilfoil were the main species in these areas. These two species, as well as Richardson pondweed, also grew densely at the northwest corner of the lake near the inlet and outlet. Very little vegetation grew along the north shore, except for a band of Richardson pondweed and flat-stemmed pondweed at the northeast corner near the dam. The only species of emergent vegetation noted was common cattail (*Typha latifolia*). In 1984, 1985 and 1987, mechanical control measures were used to clear vegetation from areas near the boat launch, beach, and along the dam (Schroeder 1985; Whitelock 1988).

Invertebrates

No studies of the zooplankton or benthic invertebrates in Moonshine Lake have been conducted. Rainbow trout are known to feed on scuds (Amphipoda) (Schroeder 1987).

Fish

Four species of fish have been reported in the lake: rainbow trout, northern pike, stickleback and an unspecified minnow. Yellow perch were stocked in 1965, but the population did not survive. Between 1969 and 1988, rainbow trout were stocked in all but two years. The lack of suitable trout-spawning habitat requires that the lake be stocked regularly to maintain the trout population. Since 1984, the average annual stocking rate has been 38 000 trout fingerlings in the 5- to 10-cm-length range, or 1 100 trout/ha (Schroeder 1987). Northern pike were stocked only twice, in 1965 and 1966. They survived a summerkill in 1977 and winterkills in 1981/82 and 1982/83, but now they are the target of a spring trapping program implemented by Fish and Wildlife Divison in 1986 (Schroeder 1984; 1986). Northern pike prey upon small rainbow trout, so they are considered an undesirable species in this lake, where trout are the favoured sport fish.

Test nets in July 1987 caught 269 rainbow trout and only 3 northern pike (Schroeder 1987). The two oldest trout in the sample (age 2+) had a mean weight of 1765 g. Although age 1+ trout in Moonshine Lake gain weight more slowly than trout in most of the other six lakes surveyed in the Peace River region, their gain in length is comparable (Table 5).

Anglers have been surveyed frequently at Moonshine Lake: in 1971, 1976, 1979, and annually from 1981 to 1986 (Alta. For. Ld. Wild. n.d.). Most anglers interviewed live within an 80-km radius of the lake. The fishing intensity varied between years and between seasons (Table 6). Generally, the fishing intensity is high year-round and the catch rate is good (Schroeder 1988).

Wildlife

In a 1977 survey by Alberta Recreation, Parks and Wildlife, 85 species of birds were observed in Moonshine Lake Provincial Park (Wallis 1977; Zurfluh 1982). Swamp Sparrows, Common Snipe, Solitary Sandpipers and Lesser Yellowlegs were among the species sighted in boggy areas of the park, and Mallards, Green-winged Teal, Sora, American Coots, Common Snipe and Red-winged Blackbirds were present at a large marsh in the southwest part of the park. Spotted Sandpipers were observed along the shore of Moonshine Lake and Tree Swallows were observed feeding over the lake. Other species that used the lake were Surf Scoters, Horned Grebes and Common Goldeneye. Barred Owls were heard at the edge of a bog due west of the northeast part of the lake.

Mammals present in the park include moose, mule deer, black bears, coyotes, beavers, muskrats, red squirrels and least chipmunks (Wallis 1977; Zurfluh 1982). Beaver are a problem because they build dams on the inlet to Moonshine Lake.

M.E. Bradford

References

Alberta Culture and Multiculturalism. n.d. Hist. Resour. Div., Hist. Sites Serv. Unpubl. data, Edmonton.
Alberta Environment. n.d.[a]. Envir. Assess. Div., Envir. Qlty. Monit. Br. Unpubl. data, Edmonton.
———. n.d.[b]. Tech. Serv. Div., Hydrol. Br. Unpubl. data, Edmonton.
———. n.d.[c]. Tech. Serv. Div., Surv. Br. Unpubl. data, Edmonton.
———. n.d.[d]. Water Resour. Admin. Div., Records Mgt. Sec. Unpubl. data, Edmonton.
Alberta Forestry, Lands and Wildlife. n.d. Fish Wild. Div. Unpubl. data, Edmonton.
———. 1988. Boating in Alberta. Fish Wild. Div., Edmonton.
———. 1989. Guide to sportfishing. Fish Wild. Div., Edmonton.

Alberta Research Council. 1972. Geological map of Alberta. Nat. Resour. Div., Alta. Geol. Surv., Edmonton.

Big Bend Historical Committee. 1981. The Big Bend. Big Bend Hist. Commit., Blueberry Mountain.

Energy, Mines and Resources Canada. 1975. National topographic series 1:50 000 83M/14 (1975). Surv. Map. Br., Ottawa.

Environment Canada. 1982. Canadian climate normals, Vol. 7: Bright sunshine (1951–1980). Prep. by Atm. Envir. Serv. Supply Serv. Can., Ottawa.

Finlay, J. and C. Finlay. 1987. Parks in Alberta: A guide to peaks, ponds, parklands & prairies. Hurtig Publ., Edmonton.

MacMillan, R.A. and G.M Greenlee. 1977. Soil survey of Moonshine Lake Provincial Park and interpretation for recreational use. Alta. Inst. Pedol. Rep. No. M–77–1. Alta. Res. Counc., Edmonton.

Schroeder, D.G. 1984. Progress report on the aeration system at Moonshine Lake. Alta. En. Nat. Resour., Fish Wild. Div. Unpubl. rep., Peace River.

————. 1985. Test netting and aquatic vegetation survey of Moonshine Lake, July 1985. Alta. En. Nat. Resour., Fish Wild. Div. Unpubl. rep., Peace River.

————. 1986. Pike removal from a tributary of Moonshine Lake May-June, 1986. Alta. For. Ld. Wild., Fish Wild. Div. Unpubl. rep., Peace River.

————. 1987. Moonshine Lake test netting. Alta. For. Ld. Wild., Fish Wild. Div. Unpubl. rep., Peace River.

————. 1988. Alta. For. Ld. Wild., Fish Wild. Div., Peace River. Pers. comm.

Strong, W.L. and K.R. Leggat. 1981. Ecoregions of Alberta. Alta. En. Nat. Resour., Resour. Eval. Plan. Div., Edmonton.

Wallis, C. 1977. Mini-master planning (1977): Resource assessment of Moonshine Lake Provincial Park. Alta. Rec. Parks Wild., Parks Div., Edmonton.

Whitelock, E. 1988. Moonshine L. Prov. Park, Spirit River. Pers. comm.

Zurfluh, K.A. 1982. Moonshine Lake Provincial Park resource management document 1982. Alta. Rec. Parks, Parks Div., Edmonton.

PEERLESS LAKE

Alberta Recreation and Parks

MAP SHEET: 84B
LOCATION: Tp87–89 R4, 5 W5
LAT/LONG: 56°40'N 114°35'W

Peerless Lake, with its beautiful, natural beaches, is a large, deep lake set in the pristine wilderness of north-central Alberta. It is named for the peerless, or unequalled, beauty of its water (Holmgren and Holmgren 1976). The lake is located in Improvement District No. 17, about 450 km north of the city of Edmonton and 220 km north of the town of Slave Lake. To reach the lake from Slave Lake, take Highway 88 (formerly Highway 67) north to the hamlet of Red Earth Creek and continue east on Secondary Road 686 to the settlement of Peerless Lake (Fig. 1). The roads from Slave Lake to Peerless Lake are gravelled, except for the 55 km of Highway 88 north of Slave Lake, which is paved.

The settlement of Peerless Lake, which is situated on the northeastern corner of the lake, is a tiny community that supported a population of only 252 people in 1986. The only other local population centre is the settlement of Trout Lake, located on the south shore of nearby Graham Lake (Fig. 1). In 1986, 290 people inhabited this community (ID No. 17 n.d.). The main occupations of the residents of both centres are commercial fishing in fall, trapping in winter and fighting forest fires in summer (Smith 1970).

Public access to the lake is available at three locations: in the settlement, in East Peerless Lake Forest Recreation Area, and at the channel between Peerless and Graham lakes (Fig. 2). East Peerless Lake Forest Recreation Area is an Alberta Forest Service campground located on the eastern shore, 5 km south of Peerless Lake settlement (Fig. 2). The campground is open from May to the end of September and is used mainly by anglers. Its facilities include 10 campsites, pump water, a boat launch and a beach. Over most of the lake there are no boating restrictions, but in posted areas, power boats are limited to maximum speeds of 12 km/hour (Alta. For. Ld. Wild. 1988).

Peerless Lake is unique because it supports one of the few lake trout populations in Alberta that is readily accessible by road. Trout are the main draw for the sport fishery and lake whitefish are the main harvest for the commercial and domestic fisheries. There are no sport fishing regulations specific to the lake, but general provincial regulations apply (Alta. For. Ld. Wild. 1989). Aquatic vegetation grows densely in shallow areas of the lake, primarily at the south end. Large flocks of ducks, as well as geese and loons, use the lake as a staging area during migration.

Drainage Basin Characteristics

The drainage basin of Peerless Lake is small relative to the surface area of the lake (ratio of 4:1; Tables 1, 2). Water drains into the lake mainly from the north. The main sources of inflow are a creek that flows from Goodfish Lake, several unnamed streams and precipitation. The outlet, at the south end of the lake, is a slow-flowing creek that drains into Graham Lake. From there, water eventually flows to the Peace River via the Trout River, which is a tributary of the Wabasca River.

The watershed consists of hummocky moraine characterized by knob and kettle topography. Small areas of flatter undulating moraine also are present. The surficial deposits are primarily moderately stony, clay loam till, with lesser amounts of glaciolacustrine deposits. The glaciolacustrine materials were deposited when the lake basin was much larger during the last ice age some 12 000 years ago (Alta. Envir. 1978). Extensive areas of organic deposits form the

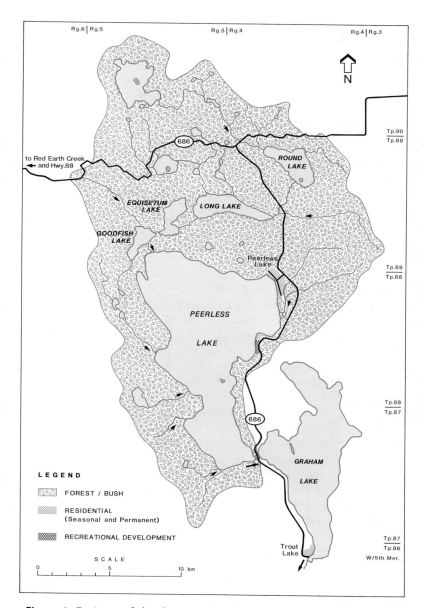

Figure 1. Features of the drainage basin of Peerless Lake.
SOURCES: Alta. Envir. n.d.[a]; En. Mines Resour. Can. 1974. Updated with 1984 aerial photos.

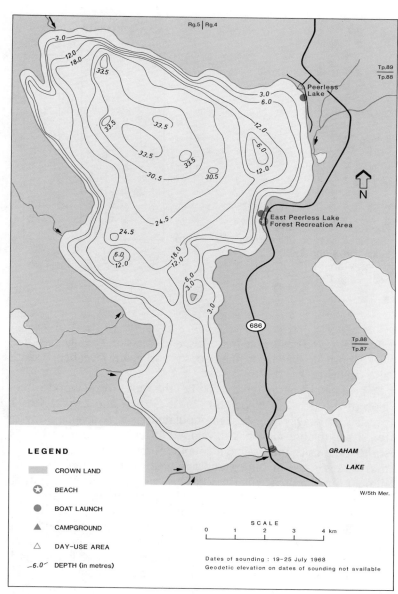

Figure 2. Bathymetry and shoreline features of Peerless Lake.
BATHYMETRY SOURCE: Smith 1970.

Table 1. Characteristics of Peerless Lake drainage basin.

area (excluding lake) (km^2)[a]	338
soil[b]	Orthic Gray Luvisols, Terric Mesisols
bedrock geology[c, d]	Smoky Group (Upper Cretaceous): shale, ironstone; marine La Biche Formation (Upper Cretaceous) shale, ironstone partings and concretions; marine
terrain[b]	undulating to hummocky moraine
ecoregion[e]	Moist Mixedwood Subregion of Boreal Mixedwood
dominant vegetation[f]	trembling aspen, black spruce
mean annual inflow (m^3)[a, g]	23.6 x 10^6
mean annual sunshine (h)[h]	2 160

NOTE: [g]excluding groundwater inflow
SOURCES: [a]Alta. Envir. n.d.[a]; [b]Leskiw 1976; [c]Alta Res. Counc. 1972;
[d]Alta. Envir.1978; [e]Strong and Leggat 1981; [f]Ceroici 1979; [h]Envir. Can. 1982

Table 2. Characteristics of Peerless Lake.

elevation(m)[a, b]	689.2
surface area (km^2)[a, b]	82.6
volume (m^3)[a, b]	1 200 x 10^6
maximum depth (m)[a, b]	35.4
mean depth (m)[a, b]	14.6
shoreline length (km)[a, b]	51.5
mean annual lake evaporation (mm)[c]	582
mean annual precipitation (mm)[c]	478
mean residence time (yr)[c, d]	80
control structure	none

NOTES: [a]on date of sounding: July 1968; [d]excluding groundwater inflow
SOURCES: [b]Smith 1970; [c]Alta. Envir. n.d.[a]

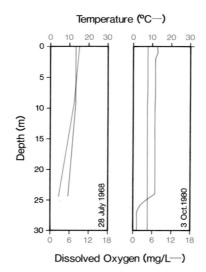

Figure 3. Temperature and dissolved oxygen of Peerless Lake, 1968 and 1980.
SOURCES: Smith 1970; Schroeder 1980.

Table 3. Water quality variables for Peerless Lake. Average concentrations in mg/L; pH in pH units. Data represent averages of samples taken from the surface and 9 m depth at the north end of the lake on 28 July 1968.

	Mean
pH	7.6
total alkalinity (CaCO$_3$)	90
specific conductivity (µS/cm)	149
total hardness (CaCO$_3$)	84

SOURCE: Smith 1970

secondary type of surficial materials, and tracts of gravelly glaciofluvial deposits, clayey lacustrine deposits and nearly level beach sands also occur (Leskiw 1976).

The drainage basin, which is part of the Moist Mixedwood Subregion of the Boreal Mixedwood Forest (Strong and Leggat 1981), consists of heavily forested, unpopulated land. A diverse array of forest-soil relationships has developed in response to variations in surficial deposits and drainage conditions, and the effects of forest fires. Trees grow in pure stands as well as in complex mixtures throughout the area. Their maturity ranges from recent regrowth after burning to overmature. Trembling aspen, which grows on hummocky well-drained sites, is the most abundant tree and is typically underlain by Gray Luvisols, the dominant soil type in the area. White spruce is the climax species on these soils, but its spread has been impeded by forest fires. Other tree species include jack pine, balsam poplar, balsam fir and white birch (Leskiw 1976).

Extensive areas of peat bogs and muskegs occur in low-lying, poorly drained sites. They represent the initial stages of a succession from wet meadow to grassland to a climax vegetation of either black spruce/*Sphagnum* moss or other wooded communities, including tamarack and swamp birch (Ceroici 1979). Terric Mesisols, which are the soils that develop on these organic deposits, cover the second largest area after Gray Luvisols. They are characterized by layers of peat to a depth of 0.5 to 3 m (Leskiw 1976).

All of the land in the Peerless Lake watershed is owned by the Crown. The land is mostly in its natural state, and is used by the local residents for hunting and trapping. The harsh climate, poor soil types, varied topography and insect pests pose severe limitations for commercial crop and livestock operations. Forage for domestic livestock, mainly horses, is supplied by introduced grasses found along roadways, airstrips and seismic lines, and in a few small, dispersed natural sites (Alta. En. Nat. Resour. 1977). Petroleum exploration sites are scattered throughout the area (Ceroici 1979).

Lake Basin Characteristics

Peerless Lake is 16.6–km long and 9.5–km wide at its widest point. The lake is oriented in a northwest-southeast direction that parallels the path of the prevailing summer winds and it is subject to sudden storms and constant wind action. The northern part of the lake basin is much deeper than the shallow southern bay. The slope of the lake basin is steepest in the northwest corner of the lake and most gradual near the outlet (Fig. 2). A small island is located off the central portion of the eastern shore.

Alberta Environment first recorded water levels at Peerless Lake in 1982 (Alta. Envir. n.d.[b]). The water levels are referred to an assumed benchmark rather than geodetic elevation and in 1985, the assumed reference mark was changed (Envir. Can. 1985–1988). Thus, comparisons of annual water levels between the two periods are not possible.

Water Quality

Water quality analyses for Peerless Lake are few; measurements were made by Fish and Wildlife Division biologists in 1968 and 1980 (Smith 1970; Schroeder 1980). As well, in 1974, Alberta Environment measured groundwater quality as part of a water supply study that was conducted to develop potable groundwater sources for residents of the area (Alta. Envir. 1978).

The limited water quality data available (Table 3) suggest that the lake has fresh water (total dissolved solids of 140 mg/L; Smith 1970), that is not as alkaline or as hard as the water in many Alberta lakes. The water supply study determined that the water in shallow wells (maximum depth of 9.1 m) adjacent to the lake was a calcium-bicarbonate type and acceptable for domestic needs. These results may reflect the dominant ionic composition of the water in Peerless Lake.

Peerless Lake is deep and becomes thermally stratified during summer (Fig. 3). The limited data indicate that, in the deepest part of the lake, dissolved oxygen may become depleted during the open-water season and remain at low levels after the water column mixes in fall. For example, on 3 October 1980, after the water column had mixed, the concentration of dissolved oxygen was only 7.8 mg/L at the surface and 1.2 mg/L below a depth of 27 m (Fig. 3). It is possible that the deeper water becomes anoxic during winter. Dissolved oxygen concentrations in the surface layers, however, must be sufficient to support the fish population, as winterkills have never been reported (Alta. For. Ld. Wild. n.d.).

Total phosphorus and chlorophyll *a* data for Peerless Lake have not been collected, so it is not possible to determine the lake's trophic status. In 1968, the Secchi transparency extended to 2.1 m in the north end of the lake and 1.8 m in the south end. It is likely that the lake is fairly low in productivity.

Biological Characteristics

Plants

The phytoplankton community was surveyed briefly by Fish and Wildlife Division biologists in July 1968 (Smith 1970). The dominant species was the green alga *Ulothrix* sp.; the dinoflagellate *Ceratium* sp. was second in abundance. Diatoms and the blue-green alga *Nostoc* sp. were present in low numbers. No recent data are available.

In 1968, rooted macrophytes grew in considerable numbers in shallow areas of the lake, primarily in the south end (Smith 1970). Species composition and depth distribution were not studied in detail.

Invertebrates

No data are available for the zooplankton or benthic communities in Peerless Lake.

Fish

Ten species of fish have been reported in Peerless Lake: lake whitefish, cisco, lake trout, northern pike, white sucker, longnose sucker, burbot, yellow perch, spottail shiner and lake chub (Alta. For. Ld. Wild. n.d.). The lake whitefish are infested with cysts of the tapeworm *Triaenophorus crassus*.

Peerless Lake is known for its lake trout sport fishery. Anglers fish almost exclusively for this species, and northern pike and yellow perch are caught incidentally (Alta. En. Nat. Resour. 1977). The busiest fishing seasons are spring and fall; anglers come to the lake mainly from Edmonton, Slave Lake, High Prairie and Peace River (Walty 1988).

The domestic fishery operates year-round; the target species is lake whitefish (Schroeder 1988). Lake trout are caught as well, mainly in the fall, but sometimes during the summer and winter. The size of the domestic fishery appears to be increasing; the average number of domestic licences issued was 16 for the 1981/82 and 1982/83 seasons, compared to 27 for each season from 1983/84 to 1988/89.

A commercial fishery has operated since at least 1942, when records were first kept (Alta. Rec. Parks Wild. 1976). The primary commercial catch is lake whitefish but there have been incidental catches of lake trout, northern pike and, since the early 1970s, suckers, burbot and cisco. Walleye, which were probably migrants from Graham Lake, were caught until 1962/63 but have not been recorded since. The largest annual commercial harvest (70 836 kg) was taken in 1945/46. It consisted of 43 044 kg of lake whitefish, 26 127 kg of lake trout and 1 665 kg of northern pike. From 1951/52 to 1958/59, the catches of lake trout exceeded those of lake whitefish (Alta. Rec. Parks Wild. 1976). Commercial operations were stopped from 1963/64 to 1967/68 (except for 1965/66) to allow the declining number of lake trout to recover. The commercial fishery resumed in 1968/69, and since that time, the annual commercial limit has been 40 000 kg of lake whitefish, 900 kg of lake trout and 1 200 kg of northern pike (Alta. For. Ld. Wild. n.d.). To ensure that overharvesting of lake trout does not occur again, the fishery is restricted to particular depth zones and times. To increase the harvest of lake whitefish and simultaneously reduce that of lake trout, commercial fishing is allowed only in October when lake whitefish congregate on their spawning grounds (Schroeder 1980). Commercial fishing is restricted to shallow areas, the common habitat of lake whitefish, and is not permitted in deep areas, the preferred habitat of lake trout. During a cold autumn, however, lake trout move from the deep water to the shallows, which have cooled, and are inadvertently caught by the commercial fishery. The control measures on the fisheries have resulted in a stable lake trout population (Schroeder 1988).

Wildlife

Peerless Lake is used primarily as a staging area for migratory waterfowl and is not of major importance as a nesting or breeding ground (Alta. En. Nat. Resour. 1977). Large flocks of migrating ducks, including Bufflehead, Lesser Scaup and White-winged Scoters, and smaller numbers of Mallards and Pintails, have been observed on the lake. Flocks of Canada and Snow geese, as well as small groups of Common Loons, are common visitors in the fall. Summer residents on the lake include Red-necked Grebes and White Pelicans. Bald Eagles have nested on the east side of Graham Lake and the south end of Round Lake (Fig. 1) and a pair of Ospreys may have settled in the vicinity of Round Lake. American Kestrels and Marsh Hawks

are regular residents of the Peerless Lake area, and Golden Eagles, Gyrfalcons and Red-tailed Hawks have been sighted (Alta. En. Nat. Resour. 1977).

The small, narrow island located in the northern portion of Graham Lake (Fig. 1) provides important summer habitat for a large number of terns and gulls. The birds feed offshore of the island and use the island for resting and nesting grounds (Alta. En. Nat. Resour. 1977).

Although the Peerless Lake region provides excellent upland game bird habitat, only two species, Spruce Grouse and Ruffed Grouse, have been found in the area. Hunting pressure on these birds is minimal; the main harvest occurs as hunters pursue moose (Alta. En. Nat. Resour. 1977).

Other wildlife within the Peerless Lake area include moose, black bears, mule deer and wolves. Moose, which are hunted in the region north of the lake, are the most important big game species. They provide the basis for domestic and guided hunting. The black bear population appears to be large; they usually are taken while hunters are in pursuit of moose. Mule deer numbers are low (Alta. En. Nat. Resour. 1977).

Thirteen mammal species are harvested by the trapping industry from the Peerless Lake area: beaver, muskrat, mink, weasel, fox, coyote, wolf, lynx, fisher, otter, red squirrel, pine marten and wolverine. Skunk is also present (Alta. For. Ld. Wild. n.d.).

L.G. McIntyre

References

Alberta Energy and Natural Resources. 1977. Peerless-Graham lakes resource management plan. Alta. En. Nat. Resour. Rep. No. 27. Prep. for Alta. For. Serv. by Resour. Plan. Br., Edmonton.
Alberta Environment. n.d.[a]. Tech. Serv. Div., Hydrol. Br. Unpubl. data, Edmonton.
———. n.d.[b]. Tech. Serv. Div., Surv. Br. Unpubl. data, Edmonton.
———. 1978. Peerless Lake northern water supply program. Prep. by Earth Sci. Div., Groundwater Br., Edmonton.
Alberta Forestry, Lands and Wildlife. n.d. Fish Wild. Div. Unpubl. data, Edmonton.
———. 1988. Boating in Alberta. Fish Wild. Div., Edmonton.
———. 1989. Guide to sportfishing. Fish Wild. Div., Edmonton.
Alberta Recreation, Parks and Wildlife. 1976. Commercial fisheries catch statistics for Alberta, 1942–1975. Fish Wild. Div., Fish. Mgt. Rep. No. 22, Edmonton.
Alberta Research Council. 1972. Geological map of Alberta. Nat. Resour. Div., Alta. Geol. Surv., Edmonton.
Ceroici, W. 1979. Hydrogeology of the Peerless Lake area, Alberta. Earth Sci. Rep. 79–5. Alta. Res. Counc., Edmonton.
Energy, Mines and Resources Canada. 1974. National topographic series 1:250 000 84B (1974). Surv. Map. Br., Ottawa.
Environment Canada. 1982. Canadian climate normals, Vol. 7: Bright sunshine (1951–1980). Prep. by Atm. Envir. Serv. Supply Serv. Can., Ottawa.
———. 1985–1988. Surface water data. Prep. by Inland Waters Directorate. Water Surv. Can., Water Resour. Br., Ottawa.
Holmgren, E.J. and P.M. Holmgren. 1976. Over 2000 place names of Alberta. 3rd ed. West. Producer Prairie Books, Saskatoon.
Improvement District No. 17 (C). n.d. Unpubl. data, High Prairie.
Leskiw, L.A. 1976. Soil survey and interpretations: Peerless-Graham Lakes area. Alta. Inst. Pedol. Rep. No. M–76–2. Alta. Res. Counc., Soils Div., Edmonton.
Schroeder, D.G. 1980. Observations on the lake trout and lake whitefish spawning activity in Peerless Lake, September-October, 1980. Alta. En. Nat. Resour., Fish Wild. Div. Unpubl. rep., Peace River.
———. 1988. Alta. For. Ld. Wild., Fish. Wild. Div., Peace River. Pers. comm.
Smith, A.R. 1970. Preliminary biological survey of waters in the Peerless Lake area: Report No. 1 (1968). Alta. Ld. For., Fish. Wild. Div., Edmonton.
Strong, W.L. and K.R. Leggat. 1981. Ecoregions of Alberta. Alta. En. Nat. Resour., Resour. Eval. Plan. Div., Edmonton.
Walty, D. 1988. Alta. For. Ld. Wild., Fish. Wild. Div., Peace River. Pers. comm.

UTIKUMA LAKE

Alberta Environment

MAP SHEET: 83O
LOCATION: Tp78–80 R8–11 W5
LAT/LONG: 56°52'N 115°27'W

Utikuma Lake is a very large, isolated lake set in the wilderness of Improvement District No. 17 (Central). The hamlets of Gift Lake and Atikameg are the closest population centres (Fig. 1). The nearest towns are Slave Lake, 80 km to the southeast, and High Prairie, 100 km to the southwest. Utikuma Lake has good recreation potential but access is limited and no recreational facilities have been developed. Secondary Road 750, which extends north from Highway 2 at a point 17 km east of High Prairie, skirts the western side of the lake. Access to the lake from Highway 88 (formerly Highway 67), which runs north from Slave Lake and skirts the eastern shore of Utikuma Lake, is possible from a road that branches west from the highway midway along the eastern shore. Although there is no formal boat launch, a small boat can be launched from this side of the lake. Launching can be difficult, however, because boats must be carried to the lakeshore and the water is less than 1–m deep for several hundred metres from shore (Fig. 2).

The lake's name is Cree for "big whitefish" (SATA Systems Inc. 1983). Members of the Whitefish Lake Band live on Utikoomak (Whitefish) Lake Reserves 155, 155A and 155B (Fig. 1). In 1983, the band population was 678 people. Reserves 155 and 155A border the northwest and north shores. Band members are descended from Woodland Cree who lived in the area in the late 1700s. In 1907, after Treaty No. 8 was signed, the three reserves were surveyed and a total of 4 845 ha of land was allocated to the band. The Gift Lake Métis Settlement, which comprises 83 951 ha of land, borders the western shore of Utikuma Lake and extends west past Gift Lake. The settlement was established in 1938 to provide land for descendents of the Métis who had followed the fur trade into the area during the nineteenth century. In 1984, 482 people lived in the settlement (Alta. Native Aff. 1986).

Water quality data are limited, but low transparencies during summer suggest the presence of large quantities of algae. Aquatic macrophytes, which grow densely around the shoreline, can interfere with motorboats in shallow areas during late summer. There are no boating restrictions specific to the lake, but general federal regulations apply (Alta. For. Ld. Wild. 1988). The commercial fishery in the lake was very important until a severe winterkill occurred in March 1989. No licences were issued for the 1989/90 season, and recovery of the fish stocks was expected to take several years. The lake also supported domestic and recreational fisheries. To protect spawning lake whitefish, the portion of Utikuma River that flows from Utikumasis Lake into Utikuma Lake is closed to sport fishing from 15 September to 15 December each year (Alta. For. Ld. Wild. 1989). Utikuma Lake is an important waterfowl production, moulting and fall staging area. The population of Canvasbacks using the lake during summer is particularly large.

Drainage Basin Characteristics

Utikuma Lake has a large drainage basin that includes many rivers and small lakes (Fig. 1). Because of the large size of the lake, however, the area of the drainage basin is only 7.5 times greater than that of the lake (Tables 1, 2). The Mink and Utikuma rivers drain most of the northern and western portions of the watershed and flow into Utikumasis Lake. The outflow from this lake, the Utikuma River, empties into the western side of Utikuma Lake. Several smaller rivers drain the southern and eastern sections of the drainage basin. Utiku-

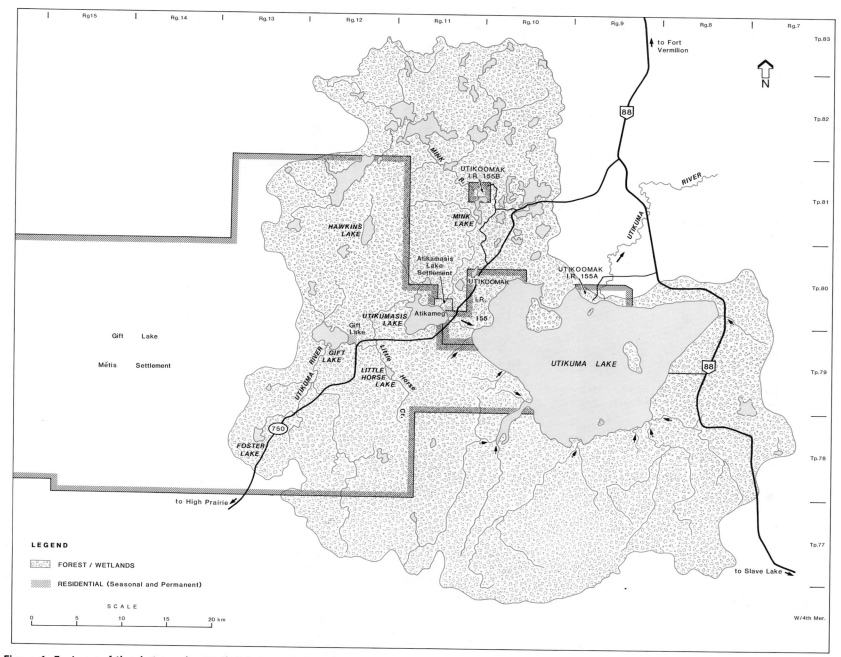

Figure 1. Features of the drainage basin of Utikuma Lake.
SOURCES: Alta. Envir. n.d.[a]; En. Mines Resour. Can. 1966; 1976. Updated with 1983 and 1984 aerial photos.

ma Lake's outlet, the Utikuma River, is located on the north shore in Utikoomak Indian Reserve 155A. It flows into the Peace River via the Muskwa and Wabasca rivers.

Utikuma Lake's drainage basin is situated on the Utikuma Uplands Section of the Northern Alberta Plains Physiographic Region (Pettapiece 1986). The northwestern, western and extreme southern portions of the watershed lie on the Heart River Upland District, an undulating to hummocky morainal (till) upland. The remainder of the watershed is part of the Utikuma Plains District, a hummocky to undulating morainal plain. Elevations range from 762 m along the southern boundary of the watershed to 645 m on the shore of Utikuma Lake.

Soil survey information is not available for the northwestern section of the watershed. West of the lake, the soils are primarily Orthic Gray Luvisols that formed on glacial till, and secondarily, Organic soils that formed on *Sphagnum* moss bog and Orthic Gray or Podzolic Gray Luvisols that formed on shallow outwash materials. The remainder of the watershed is generally poorly drained, with areas of muskeg. Organic soils that formed on *Sphagnum* mosses are predominant in the poorly drained locations, whereas Gray Luvisolic soils are present on till or outwash materials in better drained areas (Wynnyk et al. 1963).

Utikuma Lake is situated in the Moist Mixedwood Subregion of the Boreal Mixedwood Ecoregion (Strong and Leggat 1981). The

Table 1. Characteristics of Utikuma Lake drainage basin.

area (excluding lake) (km²)[a]	2 170
soil[b]	Orthic and Podzolic Gray Luvisols, Organics
bedrock geology[c]	Smoky Group (Upper Cretaceous): shale, ironstone; marine
terrain[b]	flat to rolling
ecoregion[d]	Moist Mixedwood Subregion of Boreal Mixedwood
dominant vegetation[d]	trembling aspen, balsam poplar
mean annual inflow (m³)[a, e]	151 × 10⁶
mean annual sunshine (h)[f]	2 160

NOTE: [e]excluding groundwater inflow
SOURCES: [a]Alta. Envir. n.d.[a]; [b]Wynnyk et al. 1963; [c]Alta. Res. Counc. 1972; [d]Strong and Leggat 1981; [f]Envir. Can. 1982

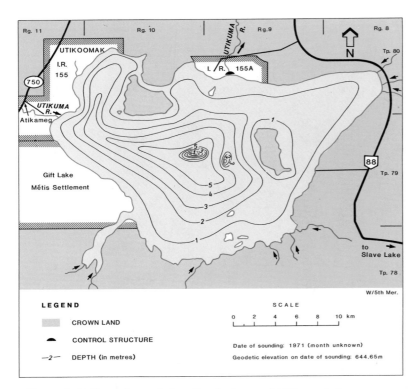

Figure 2. Bathymetry and shoreline features of Utikuma Lake.
BATHYMETRY SOURCE: Alta. Envir. n.d.[b].

Table 2. Characteristics of Utikuma Lake.

elevation (m)[a, b]	644.65
surface area (km^2)[a, b]	288
volume (m^3)[a, b]	492 x 10^6
maximum depth (m)[a, b]	5.5
mean depth (m)[a, b]	1.7
shoreline length (km)[c, d]	145
mean annual lake evaporation (mm)[e]	611
mean annual precipitation (mm)[e]	515
mean residence time (yr)[e, f]	4
control structure[g]	sheet-pile weir with stop-log bay
top of weir height (m)[g]	2.28
crest height (m)[g]	0.82
total length (m)[g]	40.54
crest length (m)[g]	24.38

NOTES: [a]on date of sounding: 1971; [d]includes 30 km for islands; [f]excluding groundwater inflow
SOURCES: [b]Alta. Envir. n.d.[b]; [c]En. Mines Resour. Can. 1966; [e]Alta. Envir. n.d.[a]; [g]Alta. Envir. n.d.[c].

Table 3. Water quality variables for Utikuma Lake. Average concentrations in mg/L; pH in pH units. Samples were collected from 2 sites at 1–m depth on 09 Aug. and 30 Aug. 1976. S.E. = standard error.

	Mean	S.E.
pH (range)	8.4–8.8	—
Secchi depth (m)	0.9	0.10
alkalinity (CaCO$_3$)	110	0
total dissolved solids	344	12.9
total hardness (CaCO$_3$)	101	3.1

SOURCE: Walty 1976

dominant trees on moderately well-drained Gray Luvisols are trembling aspen and balsam poplar. White spruce grows on imperfectly drained Gleysols and Gray Luvisols, black spruce and willows grow on poorly drained Organic soils and Gleysols, and sedges grow on very poorly drained Organic soils.

There is some agricultural activity on the Indian reserves and on the Métis settlement, where about half of the land is capable of producing crops such as oats, barley, canola, perennial forage and vegetables, but the amount of land under cultivation is unknown (Alta. Native Aff. 1986). The forestry and oil and gas industries are active throughout the watershed.

Lake Basin Characteristics

Utikuma Lake is one of Alberta's largest water bodies (Table 2). The single, very shallow basin declines gently to a maximum depth of 5.5 m near the centre of the lake and then inclines rapidly toward a small central island. There were 10 islands in the lake when the 1971 hydrographic survey was conducted (Fig. 2). At least two of the islands are large enough to be permanent, but the number of smaller islands varies with the water level. The total area of the islands is approximately 14 km^2 (En. Mines Resour. Can. 1976).

The elevation of Utikuma Lake has been monitored since 1969 (Fig. 3). The water levels refer to an assumed benchmark rather than geodetic elevation. The range in lake levels over the period of record was 1.14 m. The lowest elevation (29.50 m) was recorded in September 1969, and the highest (30.64 m) in May 1974. Water levels were generally higher during the period from 1971 to 1979 than they were from 1980 to 1987. During the more recent period, the range in lake levels was 0.50 m. Figure 4 illustrates changes in the lake's area and capacity with fluctuations in water level.

The lake level has been controlled since 1948, when Ducks Unlimited (Canada) and the Government of Alberta installed a timber weir at the outlet (Alta. Envir. n.d.[c]; Ducks Unltd. (Can.) n.d.). In 1973, the structure was upgraded to a sheet-pile weir with a stop-log bay; it is maintained by Ducks Unlimited (Canada).

Water Quality

Water quality data for the lake are limited. Fish and Wildlife Division sampled the lake during August 1968 and from June to September

in 1976 (Smith 1969; Walty 1976) and monitored temperature and dissolved oxygen concentrations in March 1979 (Alta. For. Ld. Wild. n.d.).

Utikuma is a well-buffered, freshwater lake (Table 3). During the open-water period in 1976, the temperature of the water column was uniform from surface to bottom except for a short period in early August (Fig. 5). Dissolved oxygen concentrations remained above 5.0 mg/L throughout the open-water period (Fig. 6). In March 1979, dissolved oxygen concentrations declined from 7.0 mg/L at the surface to 3.8 mg/L near the bottom sediments (Fig. 6). In contrast, in March 1989, a severe winterkill occurred when the entire water column went anoxic (Walty 1989).

Detailed chemical data are not available, but the low average Secchi transparency (0.9 m) recorded in Utikuma Lake during the open-water period in 1976 suggests that concentrations of algae are quite high.

Biological Characteristics

Plants

The plant community in Utikuma Lake was studied in August 1968 and from June to September 1976 by Fish and Wildlife Division (Smith 1969; Walty 1976). The relative abundance of phytoplankton species in both studies was determined from net plankton hauls. In 1976, nine species of green algae (Chlorophyta) and five species each of blue-green algae (Cyanophyta) and diatoms (Bacillariophyta) were identified. From July through September in 1976, the blue-green species *Aphanizomenon flos-aquae* was more abundant than the other phytoplankton species.

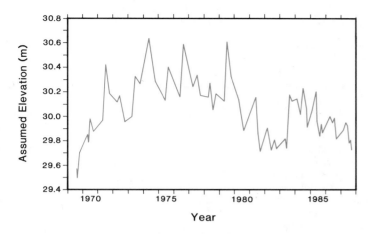

Figure 3. Water level of Utikuma Lake, 1969 to 1987. Water levels refer to an assumed datum.
SOURCE: Envir. Can. 1969–1987.

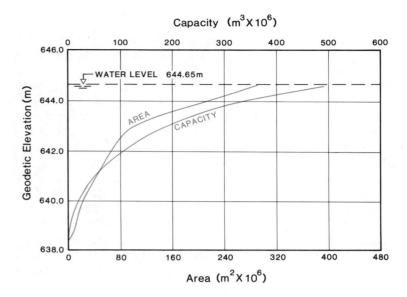

Figure 4. Area/capacity curve for Utikuma Lake.
SOURCE: Alta. Envir. n.d.[b].

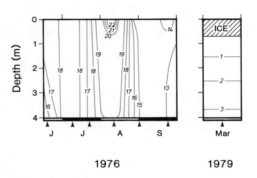

Figure 5. Temperature (°C) of Utikuma Lake, 1976 and 1979. Arrows indicate sampling dates.
SOURCES: Alta. For. Ld. Wild. n.d.; Walty 1976.

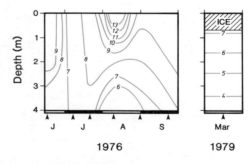

Figure 6. Dissolved oxygen (mg/L) in Utikuma Lake, 1976 and 1979. Arrows indicate sampling dates.
SOURCES: Alta. For. Ld. Wild. n.d.; Walty 1976.

In the 1968 survey, macrophytes were widespread, with dense beds of plants in most of the bays. Most vegetation was submerged, but beds of emergents were also common. Emergent vegetation covered 18% of the surface area. In 1976, macrophytes along a portion of the eastern shore were identified. The single emergent species recorded was bulrush (*Scirpus* sp.). Submergent species included star duckweed (*Lemna trisulca*), stonewort (*Chara* sp.), coontail (*Ceratophyllum demersum*), Richardson pondweed (*Potamogeton richardsonii*) and northern watermilfoil (*Myriophyllum exalbescens*).

Invertebrates

The large zooplankton species in Utikuma Lake were sampled by Fish and Wildlife Division with tow nets both in August 1968 and from June to September in 1976 (Smith 1969; Walty 1976). In both studies, cladocerans, particularly *Daphnia* spp. in 1976, were generally more abundant than calanoid copepods.

In August 1968, benthic invertebrates were sampled once at each of 31 locations, mostly at depths of 2 m or less. The average total density was 3 741 organisms/m², which was considered quite high. Midge larvae (Chironomidae) accounted for 71% of the total numbers and 93% of the total volume (89 mL/m²), and scuds (Amphipoda) accounted for 22% of the total numbers and 2% of the total volume. Leeches (Hirudinea), snails (Gastropoda), aquatic earthworms (Oligochaeta), clams (Pelecypoda) and mites (Acarina) were found in smaller amounts.

Fish

Eight species of fish have been reported in Utikuma Lake: northern pike, yellow perch, lake whitefish, burbot, cisco, walleye, white sucker and spottail shiner (Dietz and Griffiths 1978). Cysts of the tapeworm *Triaenophorus crassus* were reported in Utikuma Lake whitefish during the 1940s and in 1960, but no cysts were found during the 1970s (Alta. For. Ld. Wild. n.d.; Alta. Rec. Parks Wild. 1976). The lake is managed for recreational, commercial and domestic fisheries. The catch by the domestic fishery is not known. Between 1981/82 and 1987/88, an average of 56 domestic licences were issued each year (Alta. For. Ld. Wild. n.d.).

The lake was fished commercially each year from 1942 to 1948 (Alta. Rec. Parks Wild. 1976). Joint records were kept with nearby Utikumasis Lake during this period and until 1966. The total catch from the two lakes declined from an average of 72 112 kg/year for the period from 1942/43 to 1946/47 to 1 400 kg in 1947/48. Following a prolonged summer drought in 1947, there was a partial winterkill in Utikuma Lake in 1948 (Smith 1969). Commercial fishing was discontinued until the 1959/60 season. Catches improved markedly after 1961/62. The largest total catch (390 593 kg) was taken in 1987/88, when a record 896 licences were issued (Alta. For.

Ld. Wild. n.d.). Between 1968/69 and 1987/88, the average annual catch was 273 006 kg. Approximately 50% of this catch was whitefish, 27% was northern pike, 22% was cisco and less than 1% was walleye. In March 1989, a severe fish kill occurred in Utikuma Lake and no licences were issued that year for the commercial or domestic fisheries. Fish from nearby Utikumasis Lake were expected to migrate downstream and supplement the remaining stocks in Utikuma Lake (Walty 1989).

Few data are available for the sport fishery. Winter creel surveys were conducted for one day in February 1983 and for 5 days during February and March 1984 (Alta. For. Ld. Wild. n.d.). In 1984, 80 anglers fished for 294 hours and caught 82 pike, 4 burbot and 5 whitefish. The catch rate for pike was 0.28 fish/hour.

Wildlife

Utikuma Lake is an important area for waterfowl. Three of its islands support colonies of White Pelicans and Double-crested Cormorants (Ducks Unltd. (Can.) n.d.). California Gulls, Common Terns and Western Grebes have also been observed on the lake. A large number of ducks use the lake for moulting and staging. There is, however, a shortage of upland nesting sites and loafing areas. Most duck species that moult at the lake are divers such as Canvasbacks, Lesser Scaup, Common Goldeneye and Bufflehead. Utikuma Lake is particularly important to the continental Canvasback population. In 1975, it was estimated that as many as 40 000 Canvasbacks moulted on the lake during July and August. This was about 20% of the continental population (Alta. For. Ld. Wild. n.d.). Other ducks that nest at the lake in large numbers include dabblers such as Mallards, Gadwalls and Green-winged Teal, and divers such as Ruddy Ducks, Redheads, Canvasbacks and Lesser Scaup. Production of dabblers such as Blue-winged Teal, Shovelers and Pintails is minor (Ducks Unltd. (Can.) n.d.).

M.E. Bradford

References

Alberta Environment. n.d.[a]. Tech. Serv. Div., Hydrol. Br. Unpubl. data, Edmonton.
———. n.d.[b]. Tech. Serv. Div., Surv. Br. Unpubl. data, Edmonton.
———. n.d.[c]. Water Resour. Admin. Div., Records Mgt. Sec. Unpubl. data, Edmonton.
Alberta Forestry, Lands and Wildlife. n.d. Fish Wild. Div. Unpubl. data, Edmonton.
———. 1988. Boating in Alberta. Fish Wild. Div., Edmonton.
———. 1989. Guide to sportfishing. Fish Wild. Div., Edmonton.
Alberta Native Affairs. 1986. A guide to native communities in Alberta. Native Aff. Secret., Edmonton.
Alberta Recreation, Parks and Wildlife. 1976. Commercial fisheries catch statistics for Alberta, 1942–1975. Fish Wild. Div., Fish. Mgt. Rep. No. 22, Edmonton.
Alberta Research Council. 1972. Geological map of Alberta. Nat. Resour. Div., Alta. Geol. Surv., Edmonton.
Dietz, K.G. and W.E. Griffiths. 1978. The growth of young lake whitefish (*Coregonus clupeaformis*) in Lesser Slave and Utikuma Lake. Alta. Rec. Parks Wild., Fish Wild. Div. Unpubl. rep., Edmonton.
Ducks Unlimited (Canada). n.d. Unpubl. data, Edmonton.
Energy, Mines and Resources Canada. 1966, 1976. National topographic series 1:250 000 83O (1966), 84B (1976). Surv. Map. Br., Ottawa.
Environment Canada. 1969–1987. Surface water data. Prep. by Inland Waters Directorate. Water Surv. Can., Water Resour. Br., Ottawa.
———. 1982. Canadian climate normals, Vol. 7: Bright sunshine (1951–1980). Prep. by Atm. Envir. Serv. Supply Serv. Can., Ottawa.
Pettapiece, W.W. 1986. Physiographic subdivisions of Alberta. Agric. Can., Res. Br., Ld. Resour. Res. Centre, Ottawa.
SATA Systems Inc. 1983. Profiles of regions and small communities in northern Alberta: Northeast/central. Prep. for North. Alta. Devel. Counc., Peace River.
Smith, A.R. 1969. Preliminary biological survey of Utikuma and Utikumasis Lakes. Alta. Ld. For., Fish Wild. Div., Surv. Rep. No. 7, Edmonton.
Strong, W.L. and K.R. Leggat. 1981. Ecoregions of Alberta. Alta. En. Nat. Resour., Resour. Eval. Plan. Div., Edmonton.
Walty, D.T. 1976. An investigation of the summerkill phenomena in five lakes in the Peace Region, 1976. Alta. Rec. Parks Wild., Fish Wild. Div. Unpubl. rep., Peace River.
———. 1989. Alta. For. Ld. Wild., Fish Wild. Div., Peace River. Pers. comm.
Wynnyk, A., J.D. Lindsay, P.K. Heringa and W. Odynsky. 1963. Exploratory soil survey of Alberta map sheets 83-O, 83-P and 73-M. Res. Counc. Alta. Prelim. Soil Surv. Rep. 64–1. Res. Counc. Alta., Edmonton.

IOSEGUN LAKE

D. Huet

MAP SHEETS: 83K/7, 10
LOCATION: Tp63, 64 R19, 20 W5
LAT/LONG: 54°28'N 116°50'W

Iosegun Lake is a popular sport fishing lake set in heavily forested, gently rolling land. It is situated in Improvement District No. 16, 260 km northwest of the city of Edmonton, 82 km northwest of the town of Whitecourt and 8 km north of the town of Fox Creek. An industrial road from Fox Creek serves the east side of the lake (Fig. 1) and provides access to Iosegun Lake Forest Recreation Area.

The lake's name originates from a Cree or Stoney word for the Iosegun River that means either "tail" or "hash" (Alta. Cult. Multicult. n.d.). The lake was called Hash Lake by fur traders and natives in the early 1900s.

The native inhabitants in the area northwest of Whitecourt were Woodland Cree, but the Beaver tribe may have lived there at an earlier time (Olecko 1974). The region was close to an aboriginal migration route from Lac Ste. Anne to the Sturgeon Lake area, and sites on Iosegun Lake have traditionally been used as hunting and fishing bases. As well, four sites near the lake have been identified as burial grounds (Alta. For. Ld. Wild. 1988[b]). The first European to arrive in the area was probably David Thompson in 1799; he camped at a site that is now the Whitecourt townsite (Knapik and Lindsay 1983). Missionaries arrived in the region about 40 years later. Industrial development began in 1909 when logging and milling operations were initiated 10 km west of Whitecourt near the Athabasca River. The railroad arrived in Whitecourt in 1921, but was never completed to the Peace River Country, as originally proposed. The area near Iosegun Lake was not developed until oil and gas exploration in the 1950s brought the railroad as far as the Kaybob station, about 15 km south of the lake. Highway 43 opened in 1955, and was paved and completed in 1962 as far as the town of Valleyview, 70 km north of the lake. There have been no residential developments at the lake.

In 1988, a lake management plan for Iosegun Lake was completed by Alberta Forestry, Lands and Wildlife (Alta. For. Ld. Wild. 1988[b]). The plan assesses potential commercial and public recreational development of Iosegun Lake, based on environmental, social and economic constraints. It will be used as the basis for an area structure plan to guide development around the lake, which will be prepared by Improvement District No. 16.

Iosegun Lake Forest Recreation Area was built in 1970 by the Alberta Forest Service and upgraded in 1986. It is located at the southeast end of the lake (Fig. 2), and serves as a staging area for the Alberta Forest Service's Iosegun Lake Snowmobile Trails. Facilities at the recreation area include 50 campsites, a day-use area with 10 picnic tables, a picnic shelter, pump water, a beach and a boat launch. Popular activities on and around the lake are power boating, wind surfing, fishing, picnicking, swimming, cross-country skiing and snowmobiling. There are no boating restrictions specific to Iosegun Lake, but general federal regulations apply (Alta. For. Ld. Wild 1988[a]).

Algal blooms turn the lake water green in late summer, and aquatic vegetation grows in shallow areas at the north end. High concentrations of organic matter reduce water clarity. The main catches of the sport fishery are walleye and northern pike. Iosegun Lake is closed to sport fishing during a designated period in April and May each year. As well, the lake's inlet and outlet streams are closed to fishing from September to mid-June each year (Alta. For. Ld. Wild. 1989). A commercial fishery operates in alternate years.

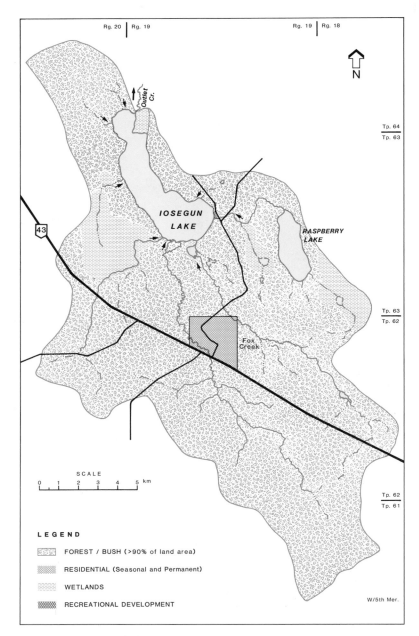

Figure 1. Features of the drainage basin of Iosegun Lake.
SOURCES: Alta. Envir. n.d.[c]; En. Mines Resour. Can. 1976. Updated with
1985 aerial photos.

Table 1. Characteristics of Iosegun Lake drainage basin.

area (excluding lake) (km²)[a]	248
soil[b]	Orthic Gray and Solonetzic Gray Luvisols
bedrock geology[c]	Scollard Member of Paskapoo Formation (Upper Cretaceous): sandstone, mudstone, thick coal beds; nonmarine
terrain[b]	undulating to gently rolling
ecoregion[d]	Moist Mixedwood Subregion of Boreal Mixedwood
dominant vegetation[b, d]	trembling aspen and balsam poplar
mean annual inflow (m³)[a, e]	39.2 x 10⁶
mean annual sunshine (h)[f]	2056

NOTE: [e]excluding groundwater inflow
SOURCES: [a]Alta. Envir. n.d.[c]; [b]Knapik and Lindsay 1983; [c]Alta. Res. Counc. 1972; [d]Strong and Leggat 1981; [f]Envir. Can. 1982

Table 2. Characteristics of Iosegun Lake.

elevation(m)[a, b]	774.92
surface area (km²)[a, b]	13.4
volume (m³)[a, b]	55.5 x 10⁶
maximum depth (m)[a, b]	11.2
mean depth (m)[a, b]	4.1
shoreline length (km)[c]	23.9
mean annual lake evaporation (mm)[d]	612
mean annual precipitation (mm)[d]	536
mean residence time (yr)[d, e]	1.5
control structure[f]	fixed-crest sheet-pile weir with stop-log bays and Denil II fishway
top of side-sheet-piling elevation (m)[f]	775.25
lowest weir crest elevation (m)[f]	773.70

NOTES: [a]on date of sounding: Sep. 1967; [e]excluding groundwater inflow
SOURCES: [b]Alta. Envir. n.d.[d]; [c]En. Mines Resour. Can. 1976; [d]Alta. Envir. n.d.[c]; [f]Alta. Envir. n.d.[a]

Drainage Basin Characteristics

Iosegun Lake has a large, extensively forested drainage basin that is
about 19 times the size of the lake (Tables 1, 2). Raspberry Lake and
several intermittent and permanent streams flow into Iosegun Lake
(Fig. 1). Water leaves the lake at the north end via Outlet Creek,
which flows into the Iosegun River, a major tributary of the Little
Smoky River.

The drainage basin is part of the Iosegun Plain physiographic
division and is underlain by nonmarine sandstones, silty mudstones
and coal beds covered by glacial drift (Knapik and Lindsay 1983).
The land is undulating to gently rolling and the soils are mainly Orthic
Gray Luvisols that developed on clay-loam textured glacial till, and
Gleyed Solonetzic Gray Luvisols that developed on glaciolacustrine
clays. Extensive areas of very poorly drained Mesisols are located
throughout the drainage basin, mainly along inflowing streams.

The watershed is part of the Moist Mixedwood Subregion of the
Boreal Mixedwood Ecoregion. Trembling aspen, which is the dominant vegetation, is replaced by balsam poplar in depressions. White
spruce and balsam fir stands grow in scattered locations that have
escaped recent fires, and willows, sedges and black spruce grow on
poorly drained soils (Strong and Leggat 1981; Knapik and Lindsay
1983).

Only about 1% of the land has been cleared for agricultural use.
Soil limitations for agriculture are severe—soils are imperfectly
drained and dry slowly after becoming wet. There is, however,
forestry and natural gas activity in the area. Iosegun Lake is located
on the Kaybob Oil and Gas Field; many wells are located east of the
lake and the area is criss-crossed by pipelines that carry oil and gas
to processing plants.

Lake Basin Characteristics

Iosegun Lake is a medium-sized lake that is 8–km long and 2–km
wide (Table 2). The slope of the lake basin is relatively gentle at the
north and south ends and steep on the east and west sides. The
deepest spot (11.2 m) is located near the centre of the lake (Fig. 2).
The large bay at the north end is very shallow and supports dense
beds of aquatic plants. A sand and mud beach is located at the
recreation area on the southeast shore. Sections of the east shore are
rocky, and most of the west and north shores are swampy (Hartman
1957).

A water-pumping station owned by Chevron Canada Resources
Limited is located on the eastern shore. Between 1981 and 1988,
Chevron's annual water allocation was 1.480 x 10⁶ m³. Actual with-
drawals, however, were much less: they ranged from a high of
1.056 x 10⁶ m³ in 1982 to a low of 0.5884 x 10⁶ m³ in 1987 (Alta.
Envir. n.d.[e]).

The elevation of Iosegun Lake has been monitored since 1975
(Fig. 3). Over the period of record, the minimum elevation was
773.17 m, recorded in October 1981, and the maximum elevation
was 774.41 m, recorded in June 1985. A fluctuation of this magnitude (1.24 m) would change the surface area of the lake by about
18% (Fig. 4). The maximum lake level occurred the year after Alber-

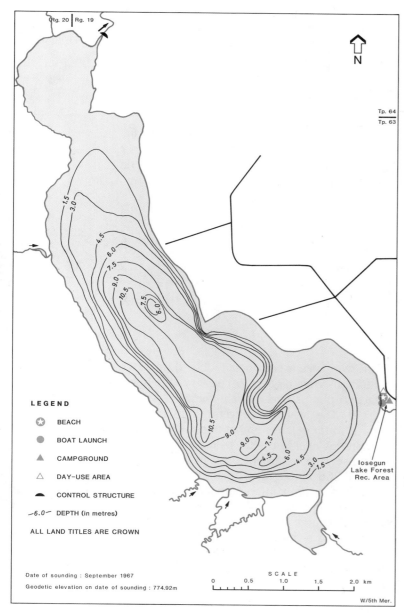

Figure 2. Bathymetry and shoreline features of Iosegun Lake.
BATHYMETRY SOURCE: Alta. Envir. n.d.[d].

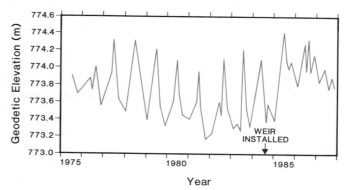

Figure 3. Water level of Iosegun Lake, 1975 to 1985.
SOURCE: Alta. Envir. n.d.[d].

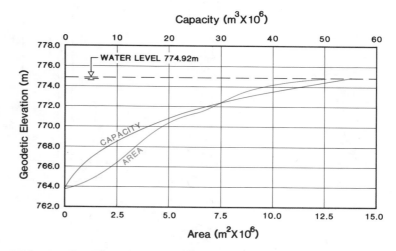

Figure 4. Area/capacity curve for Iosegun Lake.
SOURCE: Alta. Envir. n.d.[d].

ta Environment built a sheet-pile weir across Outlet Creek to stabilize water levels. The minimum crest elevation of the weir is 773.70 m (Table 2), so water will flow out of the lake when the lake level is above this elevation. Since the weir was installed in 1984, the water level has stabilized. The amplitudes of the annual fluctuations have decreased and the minimum elevation has not dropped below 773.75 m. A Denil II fishway at the weir provides access to and from the lake for spawning northern pike, yellow perch and walleye (Alta. Envir. n.d.[a]; Envirocon Ltd. 1983).

Water Quality

The water quality of Iosegun Lake was studied by Alberta Environment during the open-water period in 1983 and 1985, and under ice in February of 1984 and 1986 (Alta. Envir. n.d.[b]).

The lake has fresh water that is not as alkaline or as hard as the water in many Alberta lakes (Table 3). Calcium and bicarbonate are the dominant ions. In 1983, the lake was thermally stratified from June to August (Fig. 5). During summer that year, the dissolved oxygen concentration over the bottom sediments fell to low levels. By late August 1983, the dissolved oxygen concentration over the sediments in the deepest part of the lake had declined to 4 mg/L (Fig. 6). In 1985, the depletion of dissolved oxygen was more pronounced. By July that year, water at depths greater than 10 m was anoxic. Under ice in February 1984, the entire water column remained oxygenated (Fig. 6), but in February 1986, the water below a depth of 10 m was anoxic.

Table 3. Major ions and related water quality variables for Iosegun Lake. Average concentrations in mg/L; pH in pH units. Composite samples from the euphotic zone collected 7 times from 10 May to 18 Oct. 1983. S.E. = standard error.

	Mean	S.E.
pH (range)	7.5–9.8[a]	—
total alkalinity (CaCO$_3$)	59	0.5
specific conductivity (µS/cm)	139	2.2
total dissolved solids (calculated)	79[b]	2.0
total hardness (CaCO$_3$)	55	1.1
total particulate carbon	2[a]	0.6
dissolved organic carbon	19[a]	0.9
HCO$_3$	72	0.9
CO$_3$	0	0
Mg	4	0.3
Na	7	0.5
K	1	0.1
Cl	3	0.2
SO$_4$	<6	—
Ca	16[b]	0.7

NOTES: [a]n = 6; [b]n = 3
SOURCE: Alta. Envir. n.d.[b], Naquadat station 01AL07GG2000

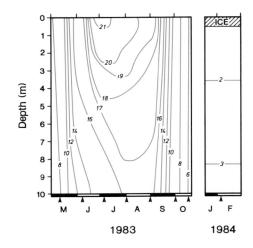

Figure 5. Temperature (°C) of Iosegun Lake, 1983 and 1984. Arrows indicate sampling dates.
SOURCE: Alta. Envir. n.d.[b].

Table 4. Nutrient, chlorophyll *a* and Secchi depth data for Iosegun Lake. Average concentrations in μg/L. Composite samples from the euphotic zone collected 7 times from 10 May to 18 Oct. 1983 and 21 May to 30 Oct. 1985. S.E. = standard error.

	1983		1985	
	Mean	S.E.	Mean	S.E.
total phosphorus	61	8.5	—	—
total dissolved phosphorus	25	4.7	—	—
soluble reactive phosphorus	11	4.2	—	—
total Kjeldahl nitrogen	940[a]	90	970	70
$NO_3 + NO_2$–nitrogen	<10	—	<30	—
NH_4–nitrogen	30	10.0	<20	—
iron	—	—	260[b]	36
chlorophyll *a*	29.2	6.01	23.9	5.95
Secchi depth (m)	1.5	0.25	1.6	0.11

NOTES: [a] n = 6; [b] n = 5
SOURCE: Alta. Envir. n.d.[b], Naquadat station 01AL07GG2000

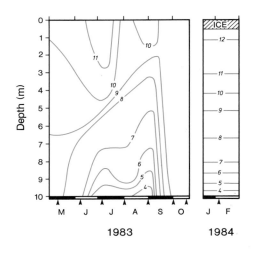

Figure 6. Dissolved oxygen (mg/L) in Iosegun Lake, 1983 and 1984. Arrows indicate sampling dates.
SOURCE: Alta. Envir. n.d.[b].

Iosegun Lake is eutrophic (Table 4). In 1983, chlorophyll *a* concentrations were highest (56 μg/L) at the beginning of August and total phosphorus levels were highest (91 μg/L) at the end of August (Fig. 7). The elevated concentrations of total phosphorus in the surface water in late summer and fall were most likely the result of phosphorus release by the sediments.

The sewage treatment plant in the town of Fox Creek releases about 0.206×10^6 m³ of treated effluent in spring, and a similar amount in autumn, into an unnamed creek that flows into Iosegun Lake (Pentney 1983). A 4–km stretch of winding creek between the lagoon discharge and the lake, which includes several beaver ponds, a marsh and a slough, probably increases retention time and thus reduces nutrient and bacterial levels in the effluent before it reaches the lake. The overall effect of the effluent on the lake, however, is unknown.

Biological Characteristics

Plants

The phytoplankton community in Iosegun Lake was sampled in July 1957 by Fish and Wildlife Division (Hartman 1957) and from May to October in 1983 by Alberta Environment (Table 5). In mid-May 1983, cryptophytes (*Cryptomonas erosa reflexa*, *C. ovata* and *C. rostratiformis*) were the dominant group. From June through August, however, blue-green algae (Cyanophyta) formed most of the biomass. In June and July, the most important blue-greens were *Anabaena flos-aquae* and *A. spiroides crassa*, but by August, another blue-green, *Aphanizomenon flos-aquae*, and a diatom (Bacillariophyta), *Melosira granulata*, were the dominant species. The 1957 study also noted a predominance of blue-green algae in July, primarily *Aphanizomenon* sp. By mid-October in 1983, diatoms (mostly *Stephanodiscus niagarae* and *Melosira italica*) were the major algal group.

Data on the macrophyte community in Iosegun Lake are not available.

Invertebrates

A brief survey of the zooplankton and benthic invertebrate communities was conducted in July 1957 by Fish and Wildlife Division (Hartman 1957). No recent data are available.

Fish

Iosegun Lake supports populations of lake whitefish, cisco, walleye, northern pike, yellow perch, white sucker, burbot and several minnow species (Hawryluk 1982). In addition, trout-perch, longnose

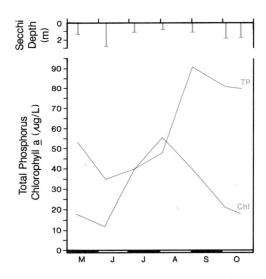

Figure 7. Total phosphorus, chlorophyll *a* and Secchi depth in Iosegun Lake, 1983.
SOURCE: Alta. Envir. n.d.[b].

Table 5. Percentage composition of major algal groups by total biomass in Iosegun Lake, 1983. Composite samples collected from the euphotic zone.

ALGAL GROUP	10 May	07 June	05 July	02 Aug.	31 Aug.	18 Oct.[a]
Total Biomass (mg/L)	5.26	0.66	9.96	8.17	4.11	4.03
Percentage Composition:						
Cyanophyta	0	31	83	79	49	13
		Anabaena ⟶				
			Aphanizomenon ⟶			
Chlorophyta	3	3	0	10	3	0
Chrysophyta	7	0	0	0	0	2
Bacillariophyta	5	31	5	0	42	79
		Asterionella			*Melosira* ⟶	
		Stephanodiscus			*Stephanodiscus* ⟶	
Cryptophyta	85	22	6	7	4	5
	Cryptomonas ⟶					
Pyrrhophyta	0	0	5	2	2	0

NOTE: [a]Euglenophyta = 0.6%
SOURCE: Alta. Envir. n.d.[b].

Table 6. Estimated angler numbers, effort and harvest from Iosegun Lake. Estimates based on creel survey data collected from 15 May to 17 Aug. 1986. A total of 21 weekdays and 14 weekend days were surveyed. WE = walleye; NP = northern pike; YP = yellow perch.

	WE	NP	YP	Total
number of anglers[a]	—	—	—	2918
angler-hours[b]	—	—	—	8224
total number fish caught	2592	2870	12	5474
total number fish harvested[c]	2253	1231	7	3491
catch/angler-hour	0.32	0.35	0.001	0.67
harvest/angler-hour[b, c]	0.27	0.13	0.001	0.40
harvest/angler[a, c]	0.72	0.35	0.003	1.07

NOTES: [a]observed no. anglers = 652; [b]observed hours = 1718; [c]based on observed no. fish kept: WE = 467, NP = 231, YP = 2
SOURCE: Alta. For. Ld. Wild. n.d.

sucker and spottail shiner have been captured near the mouth of Outlet Creek (Envirocon Ltd. 1983). The lake is managed for sport, domestic and commercial fisheries. A few (1 to 3) domestic licences are issued each year, but there are no data for the domestic catch (Alta. For. Ld. Wild. n.d.).

Lake whitefish and cisco are the target species of the commercial fishery. Both species were overexploited during the 1950s and 1960s, and by 1967/68, catches were small. From 1968/69 to 1976/77, the fishery was closed. It reopened for 1977/78, but closed for the following two years, and since 1980/81, it has opened only in alternate years. Initially, in 1980/81, the cisco harvest was high (12 600 kg), but it declined to 2 426 kg in 1984/85 and 4061 kg in 1986/87. Over the same period, the whitefish harvest increased from 2698 kg in 1980/81 to 6355 kg in 1986/87 (Alta. For. Ld. Wild. n.d.). In 1988/89, the quotas for these species were 7000 kg of cisco and 2500 kg of lake whitefish. The quota is usually taken in one lift. Small amounts of walleye and northern pike are also taken in the commercial fishery. From 1980/81 to 1986/87, the annual walleye catch ranged from 7 to 34 kg and the annual northern pike catch ranged from 108 to 431 kg. The 1988/89 quotas for these species were 100 kg of walleye and 400 kg of northern pike.

The lake was test netted in 1968, 1973, 1976 and 1981 (Hawryluk 1973; 1976; 1982). The species composition of the 1981 catch of 496 fish was 66% cisco, 18% lake whitefish, 14% walleye, 2% northern pike and less than 1% burbot and white sucker. The catch of lake whitefish, cisco, walleye and northern pike increased from 1973 to 1981. Lake whitefish made the greatest gains, from 1.7 fish per 91 m of net (various mesh sizes) in 1973, to 17.9 fish per 91 m

of net in 1981. A walleye trapping program in 1985 and 1986 provided a population estimate of 12 908 ± 5 165 mature walleye (Hildebrandt 1986).

Creel surveys were conducted by Fish and Wildlife Division for 8 days from 27 June to 12 August in 1985 and for 35 days from 15 May to 17 August in 1986 (Hawryluk 1986; 1987). In 1986 (Table 6), anglers caught an estimated 2870 northern pike, 2592 walleye and 12 yellow perch and kept 43% of the northern pike, 87% of the walleye and 58% of the yellow perch. The catch rates for northern pike were very similar in 1985 (0.36/angler-hour) and 1986 (0.35/angler-hour), but the catch rate for walleye declined between 1985 (0.55/angler-hour) and 1986 (0.32/angler-hour). No data are available for the winter sport fishery, but ice fishing is a favourite winter activity at the lake and whitefish and cisco form an important part of the winter angler harvest.

Wildlife

A wide range of wildlife species are found near Iosegun Lake. The lake is an important waterfowl staging area and waterfowl are abundant (Alta. For. Ld. Wild. 1988[b]). Species seen at the lake include Common Loons, grebes, Buffleheads and Goldeneye; a Bald Eagle's nest is located nearby. Black bears are common in the area and grizzly bears have been sighted. The land in the drainage basin is excellent moose habitat. Small mammals present include muskrats, beaver and mink.

M.E. Bradford

References

Alberta Culture and Multiculturalism. n.d. Hist. Resour. Div., Hist. Sites Serv. Unpubl. data, Edmonton.

Alberta Environment. n.d.[a]. Devel. Op. Div., Project Mgt. Br. Unpubl. data, Edmonton.

———. n.d.[b]. Envir. Assess. Div., Envir. Qlty. Monit. Br. Unpubl. data, Edmonton.

———. n.d.[c]. Tech. Serv. Div., Hydrol. Br. Unpubl. data, Edmonton.

———. n.d.[d]. Tech. Serv. Div., Surv. Br. Unpubl. data, Edmonton.

———. n.d.[e]. Water Resour. Admin. Div., Sur. Water Rights Br. Unpubl. data, Edmonton.

Alberta Forestry, Lands and Wildlife. n.d. Fish Wild. Div. Unpubl. data, Edmonton.

———. 1988[a]. Boating in Alberta. Fish Wild. Div., Edmonton.

———. 1988[b]. Smoke and Iosegun lake management plan. Alta. For. Serv. Unpubl. rep., Edmonton.

———. 1989. Guide to sportfishing. Fish Wild. Div., Edmonton.

Alberta Research Council. 1972. Geological map of Alberta. Nat. Resour. Div., Alta. Geol. Surv., Edmonton.

Energy, Mines and Resources Canada. 1976. National topographic series 1:50 000 83K/7 (1976), 83K/10 (1976). Surv. Map. Br., Ottawa.

Envirocon Limited. 1983. Iosegun Lake outlet control structure: Fisheries impact. Prep. for Alta. Envir., Plan. Div., Edmonton.

Environment Canada. 1982. Canadian climate normals, Vol. 7: Bright sunshine (1951–1980). Prep. by Atm. Envir. Serv. Supply Serv. Can., Ottawa.

Hartman, G.F. 1957. Report on Iosegun Lake. Alta. Ld. For., Fish Wild. Div. Unpubl. rep., Edmonton.

Hawryluk, R.W. 1973. Test netting of Iosegun Lake, June 1973. Alta. Ld. For., Fish Wild. Div. Unpubl. rep., Edmonton.

———. 1976. Test netting of Iosegun Lake, June 1976. Alta. Rec. Parks Wild., Fish Wild. Div. Unpubl. rep., Edmonton.

———. 1982. An evaluation of the Iosegun Lake fishery, June 1981. Alta. En. Nat. Resour., Fish Wild. Div. Unpubl. rep., Edmonton.

———. 1986. A creel survey and population estimate in Iosegun Lake (May 17–Aug. 15) 1986. Alta. For. Ld. Wild., Fish Wild. Div. Unpubl. rep., Edmonton.

———. 1987. A short term creel survey of Iosegun Lake, 1985. Alta. For. Ld. Wild., Fish Wild. Div. Unpubl. rep., Edmonton.

Hildebrandt, D. 1986. Walleye tagging summary, Iosegun Lake May, 1985 and April-May, 1986. Alta. For. Ld. Wild., Fish Wild. Div. Unpubl. rep., Edmonton.

Knapik, L.J. and J.D. Lindsay. 1983. Reconnaissance soil survey of the Iosegun Lake area, Alberta. Alta. Res. Counc. Bull. No. 43. Alta. Res. Counc., Edmonton.

Olecko, D. 1974. Sagitawah saga—the story of Whitecourt. D. Olecko, Whitecourt.

Pentney, A.E. 1983. Inspection report for Fox Creek, 19 April 1983. Alta. Envir., Poll. Contr. Div., Mun. Eng. Br. Unpubl. rep., Edmonton.

Strong, W.L. and K.R. Leggat. 1981. Ecoregions of Alberta. Alta. En. Nat. Resour., Resour. Eval. Plan. Div., Edmonton.

MUSREAU LAKE

MAP SHEET: 83L/10
LOCATION: Tp64 R5 W6
LAT/LONG: 54°33'N 118°37'W

Musreau Lake is a lovely, popular trout-fishing lake situated in rolling hill country in the County of Grande Prairie. It is located 70 km south of the city of Grande Prairie, 119 km northeast of the town of Grande Cache and 545 km northwest of the city of Edmonton. To reach the lake from Edmonton, take Highway 16 west until you are just past the town of Hinton, then drive northwest and north on Highway 40 for about 250 km. A sign indicates the gravel secondary road that leads to Musreau Lake Forest Recreation Area on the northwest side of the lake (Fig. 1). Prior to the opening of Highway 40 in 1986, Musreau Lake was served by a narrow, local gravel road and was considerably more isolated.

The name of the lake is probably a French translation of a Cree or Stoney word meaning "noisy" or "devil". The name describes the lake in winter, when pockets of gas that form under the ice cause the ice to break and emit loud cracking noises. As a result of these sounds, the Indians feared the lake (Alta. Cult. Multicult. n.d.).

The first fur trader to arrive in the area was Ignace Giasson (Twardy and Corns 1980). In 1820, he and his Iroquois guide, Téte Jaune, began a voyage up the Smoky River to acquire new fur-trapping territory for the Hudson's Bay Company. They travelled south from St. Mary's House, near the present-day town of Peace River, to the location of the present-day town of Grande Cache. Their route brought them very close to the lake, which is located only 15 km east of the Smoky River. There has been no settlement around Musreau Lake. Until the 1960s, the main activities in the region were trapping, some coal mining, and lumbering on a small scale. The area became more accessible in the 1960s, when seismographic crews were active and hunters and anglers made frequent trips to the area. As well, the Alberta Resources Railway was constructed between Grande Cache and Grande Prairie in the late 1960s. It follows a route similar to that taken by Ignace Giasson and Téte Jaune 150 years earlier. In 1973, Procter and Gamble Cellulose Limited opened a pulp mill near Grande Prairie. This accelerated timber harvesting in the region, and construction of forestry roads improved public access to large areas of wilderness that have recreational potential (Twardy and Corns 1980).

Musreau Lake Forest Recreation Area (Fig. 2), operated by Alberta Forest Service, was created in 1978 and upgraded in 1986. It provides 69 campsites, pump water, a day-use area with 13 picnic tables and fireplaces, a small sand beach, 2 boat launches, equestrian trails and all-terrain vehicle trails (Alta. Hotel Assoc. 1989). The main recreational activities enjoyed at the lake and in the vicinity are fishing, canoeing, swimming, hiking, snowmobiling and riding all-terrain vehicles.There are no boating restrictions over most of the lake, but in posted areas such as the designated swimming area, all boats are prohibited, and in other posted areas, motor boats are restricted to a maximum speed of 12 km/hour (Alta. For. Ld. Wild. 1988).

During summer, the concentration of algae in Musreau Lake remains quite low. The water lacks clarity, however, because it acquires a brown tint from muskeg in the drainage basin. Aquatic vegetation is present along most of the southern and western shores, but is less abundant on the windward shores. Rainbow trout are the primary sport fish in the lake. There are no sport fishing regulations specific to Musreau Lake, but general provincial regulations and limits apply (Alta. For. Ld. Wild. 1989).

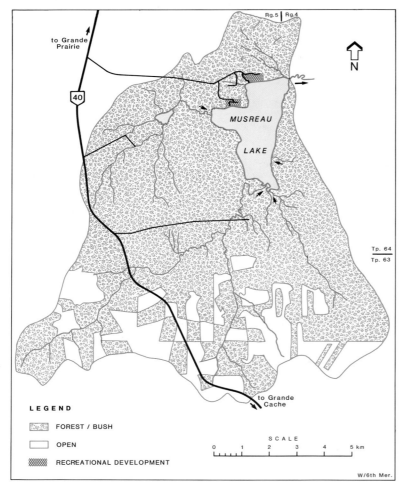

Figure 1. Features of the drainage basin of Musreau Lake.
SOURCES: Alta. Envir. n.d.[b]; En. Mines Resour. Can. 1980. Updated with 1986 aerial photos.

Table 1. Characteristics of Musreau Lake drainage basin.

area (excluding lake) (km²)[a]	101
soil[b]	Orthic Luvic Gleysols, Mesisols, Orthic and Solonetzic Gray Luvisols
bedrock geology[c]	Scollard Member of Paskapoo Formation (Upper Cretaceous): sandstone, mudstone, thick coal beds; nonmarine
terrain[b]	level to gently rolling
ecoregion[d]	Boreal Foothills
dominant vegetation[b]	trembling aspen, white spruce, black spruce, lodgepole pine
mean annual inflow (m³)[a, e]	16.4 x 10⁶
mean annual sunshine (h)[f]	2126

NOTE: [e]excluding groundwater inflow
SOURCES: [a]Alta. Envir. n.d.[b]; [b]Twardy and Corns 1980; [c]Alta. Res. Counc. 1972; [d]Strong and Leggat 1981; [f]Envir. Can. 1982

Table 2. Characteristics of Musreau Lake.

elevation (m)[a, b]	870.63 to 871.91
surface area (km²)[c]	5.49
volume (m³)	unknown
maximum depth (m)[d, e]	13.0
mean depth (m)	unknown
shoreline length (km)[c]	13.4
mean annual lake evaporation (mm)[f]	613
mean annual precipitation (mm)[f]	528
mean residence time (yr)	not available
control structure	none

NOTES: [a]range over period of water level record; [d]on date of sounding: July 1974
SOURCES: [b]Alta. Envir. n.d.[c]; [c]En. Mines Resour. Can. 1980; [e]Smith and Scott 1969; [f]Alta. Envir. n.d.[b].

Drainage Basin Characteristics

Musreau Lake drains a fairly large area that is about 18 times the size of the lake (Tables 1, 2). Most of the watershed lies to the south and west of the lake (Fig. 1). There are six inlet streams, of which the three largest flow into the southern and western shores. The outlet, Musreau Creek, is located at the north end of the lake. It flows in an easterly direction until it enters the Kakwa River, which flows into the Smoky River. Musreau Lake's drainage basin is part of a physiographic division of the Interior Plains called the Alberta Plateau-Benchlands (Twardy and Corns 1980). This division is characterized by isolated, elevated plateaus separated by long, gently sloping benchlands. Most of the land in the drainage basin is level to undulating (0 to 4% slope), although areas near the north shore are gently rolling (5 to 9% slope).

Musreau Lake lies within the Boreal Foothills Ecoregion (Strong and Leggat 1981). The most common soils throughout the watershed are Orthic Luvic Gleysols, Mesisols, Orthic Gray Luvisols and Solonetzic Gray Luvisols (Twardy and Corns 1980). Orthic Luvic Gleysols are poorly drained soils that developed on glaciolacustrine deposits. They have a silty clay to heavy clay texture and lie in depressions or on flat, poorly drained areas near the margins of organic soil areas. The dominant vegetation on these soils is white spruce in areas that have been free of fire for many years, lodgepole pine in areas that are imperfectly drained, and black spruce and willow in areas with poor drainage (Table 1). Mesisols are very poorly drained soils derived from mosses. They are mainly located along inflowing streams and support a plant community characterized by stunted black spruce, tamarack and *Sphagnum* moss. Orthic Gray Luvisols are moderately well-drained soils that developed on glacial till deposits. They characteristically support trembling aspen and lodgepole pine forests. Solonetzic Gray Luvisols are moderately well-drained soils that developed on glaciolacustrine deposits. They are present mostly on the southeast shore of the lake. Trembling aspen

is the main tree on these soils, although white spruce is common on moister sites.

The northern two-thirds of the watershed is completely forested, but much of the southern third has been cleared by the forest industry (Fig. 1). There has been no agricultural development in the area, as agriculture is limited by a short frost-free period, poor soil structure and excessive soil wetness.

Lake Basin Characteristics

Musreau is a shallow, medium-sized lake with a surface area of 5.49 km² (Table 2), a maximum length of 4.2 km and a maximum width of 2.7 km. The lake basin slopes gently to a maximum depth of 13 m in the centre of the basin (Fig. 2). The shallowest areas are located in the large southern and western bays. The lake's elevation has been monitored only since 1986. The maximum water level for the period from 1986 to 1988 was 871.91 m, recorded in August 1987, and the minimum was 870.56 m, recorded in October 1988.

Water Quality

The water quality of Musreau Lake was studied by Fish and Wildlife Division in July 1974, December 1981 and August 1984 (Schroeder 1974; 1984), and jointly by Alberta Environment and Alberta Forestry, Lands and Wildlife during 1986 and 1987 (Alta. Envir. n.d.[a]).

The lake has fresh water; in 1986, the average concentration of total dissolved solids was 94 mg/L (Table 3). The water has lower alkalinity and hardness than the water in many prairie lakes. The major ions are calcium and bicarbonate. In 1974, turbidity was low (25 NTU) and the water was highly coloured (120 mg/L Pt). The brownish colour is typical of lakes in muskeg areas and is reflected

Table 3. Major ions and related water quality variables for Musreau Lake. Average concentrations in mg/L; pH in pH units. Composite samples from the euphotic zone collected 3 times from 11 July to 23 Sep. 1986. S.E. = standard error.

	Mean	S.E.
pH (range)	8.0–8.2	—
total alkalinity (CaCO$_3$)	86	0.3
specific conductivity (µS/cm)	171	2.4
total dissolved solids (calculated)	94	1.3
total hardness (CaCO$_3$)	86	1.3
HCO$_3$	105	0.3
CO$_3$	0	0
Mg	6	0.4
Na	4	0.4
K	1	0.03
Cl	<1	—
SO$_4$	6	1.0
Ca	24	0

SOURCE: Alta. Envir. n.d.[a], Naquadat station 01AL07GB1000

Table 4. Nutrient, chlorophyll *a* and Secchi depth data for Musreau Lake. Average concentrations in µg/L. Composite samples from the euphotic zone collected 5 times from 11 July to 21 Oct. 1986 and 3 times from 18 June to 26 Aug. 1987. S.E. = standard error.

	1986		1987	
	Mean	S.E.	Mean	S.E.
total phosphorus	23	2.0	22	2.6
NO$_3$ + NO$_2$–nitrogen	—	—	<20[b]	—
iron	110[a]	20	60[b]	10
chlorophyll *a*	5.3	1.90	3.7	1.75
Secchi depth (m)	2.1	0.16	2.1	0.20

NOTES: [a]n = 3; [b]n = 2
SOURCE: Alta. Envir. n.d.[a], Naquadat station 01AL07GB1000

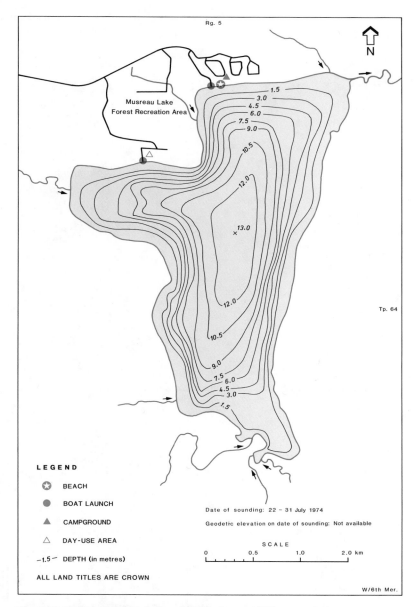

Figure 2. Bathymetry and shoreline features of Musreau Lake.
BATHYMETRY SOURCE: Alta. For. Ld. Wild. n.d.

by the low average transparency measured in 1986 and 1987 (Table 4).

In July 1986, the water column was thermally stratified (Fig. 3) and the concentration of dissolved oxygen declined from 9 mg/L at the surface to 5 mg/L at the bottom. In July 1974, no stratification was detected and dissolved oxygen concentrations were almost uniform (7 to 8 mg/L) throughout the water column. Since the lake is fairly shallow, stratification may be intermittent throughout the summer. In February of 1987, the water column was well-oxygenated to the bottom (Fig. 3).

Musreau Lake is mesotrophic. During 1986, chlorophyll *a* levels were highest in September (10 mg/L), and the Secchi transparency was correspondingly low (Fig. 4). The total phosphorus concentration reached a maximum in late July, possibly because exceptionally heavy rainfall caused an increase in runoff. More than 25% of the total annual precipitation in 1986 fell during July (Envir. Can. 1986).

Biological Characteristics

Plants

No data are available for the phytoplankton community in Musreau Lake.

Fish and Wildlife Division conducted a brief survey of aquatic vegetation in August 1984 (Fig. 5). Emergent plants, particularly water lily (*Nuphar* sp.), bulrush (*Scirpus* spp.) and horsetail (*Equisetum* sp.), were common along most of the southern and western shores. They were less prevalent along the windward northern and eastern shores. The most common submergent species were

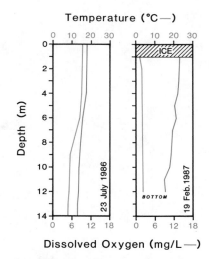

Figure 3. Temperature and dissolved oxygen in Musreau Lake, 1986 and 1987.
SOURCE: Alta. Envir. n.d.[a].

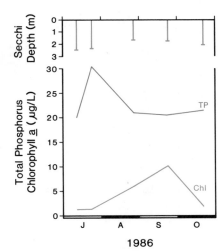

Figure 4. Total phosphorus, chlorophyll *a* and Secchi depth in Musreau Lake, 1986.
SOURCE: Alta. Envir. n.d.[a].

Table 5. Biomass of benthic invertebrates in 9 depth zones of Musreau Lake, July 1974.
Values are wet weight (g/m²).

Taxonomic Group	Depth (m)								
	0–1.5	1.5–3	3–4.5	4.5–6	6–7.6	7.6–9.1	9.1–10.7	10.7–12.2	12.2+
Annelida									
Oligochaeta	0.12	0.03	—	—	0.20	0.04	0.06	0.80	0.42
Hirudinea	0.26	0.10	0.34	0.32	—	—	—	—	—
Amphipoda	0.01	0.10	—	—	—	—	—	—	—
Ephemeroptera	0.34	0.36	—	—	—	—	—	—	—
Trichoptera	0.01	—	—	—	—	—	—	—	—
Diptera									
Culicidae	—	—	—	0.02	0.20	0.18	0.45	0.19	—
Chironomidae	1.13	—	0.25	0.07	0.06	2.88	7.10	6.20	7.50
Gastropoda	0.24	—	0.54	—	—	—	0.83	—	—
Pelecypoda	—	—	0.29	—	—	—	—	0.80	—
TOTAL WEIGHT	2.11	0.59	1.42	0.41	0.46	3.10	8.44	7.99	7.92

NOTE: 100 samples taken with an Ekman dredge at regular intervals along transects
SOURCE: Schroeder 1974

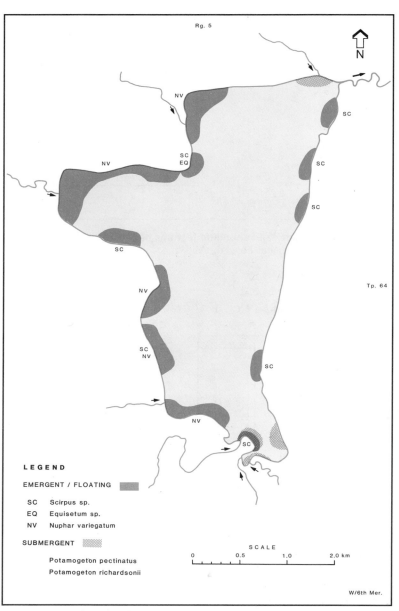

Figure 5. Distribution of aquatic macrophytes in Musreau Lake, August 1984.
SOURCE: Schroeder 1984.

Richardson pondweed (*Potamogeton richardsonii*) and Sago pondweed (*P. pectinatus*).

Invertebrates

No data are available for the zooplankton community in Musreau Lake.

The benthic fauna from nine depth zones was sampled by Fish and Wildlife Division in July 1974 (Table 5). The average standing crop was calculated to be 3.6 g/m² wet weight, or 0.40 g/m² dry weight. Midge larvae (Chironomidae) formed 78% of the biomass; they were most abundant at depths greater than 7.6 m. Aquatic earthworms (Oligochaeta) were found at most depths, but scuds (Amphipoda), mayfly nymphs (Ephemeroptera) and caddis fly larvae (Trichoptera) were found only in water less than 3–m deep.

Fish

Seven species of fish have been reported in Musreau Lake: longnose suckers, white suckers, bull trout, burbot, rainbow trout, pearl dace and brassy minnows (Schroeder 1974). Most anglers using the lake are residents of the County of Grande Prairie, and the recreational fishery is considered important (Nelson 1979; Schroeder 1988).

Rainbow trout were introduced to the lake in 1972. Between 1972 and 1988, the lake was stocked 11 times with an average of 224 000 fish/year (Alta. Ld. For. 1972; 1974; Alta. Rec. Parks Wild. 1975; 1977; 1978; Alta. En. Nat. Resour. 1979; 1980; 1982; 1985; Alta. For. Ld. Wild. 1987; Schroeder 1988). The trout population had not become well established by 1984, probably because of extensive predation by burbot on the newly stocked fingerlings (Schroeder 1984). As well, competition for food between trout fingerlings and suckers probably had an adverse effect on trout growth and survival. Rainbow trout were also lost to the population when they migrated out of the lake via Musreau Creek. In an attempt to increase survival, small yearling trout rather than fingerlings have been stocked since 1985. Anglers have reported greater fishing success since then, but no creel survey to determine catch rates has been conducted (Schroeder 1988).

Wildlife

No data are available for the wildlife at Musreau Lake.

M.E. Bradford

References

Alberta Culture and Multiculturalism. n.d. Hist. Resour. Div., Hist. Sites Serv. Unpubl. data, Edmonton.

Alberta Energy and Natural Resources. 1979, 1980, 1982, 1985. Fish planting list. Fish Wild. Div., Edmonton.

Alberta Environment. n.d.[a]. Envir. Assess. Div., Envir. Qlty. Monit. Br. Unpubl. data, Edmonton.

———. n.d.[b]. Tech. Serv. Div., Hydrol. Br. Unpubl. data, Edmonton.

Alberta Forestry, Lands and Wildlife. n.d. Fish Wild. Div. Unpubl. data, Edmonton.

———. 1987. Fish planting list. Fish Wild. Div., Edmonton.

———. 1988. Boating in Alberta. Fish Wild. Div., Edmonton.

———. 1989. Guide to sportfishing. Fish Wild. Div., Edmonton.

Alberta Hotel Association. 1989. Alberta campground guide 1989. Prep. for Travel Alta., Edmonton.

Alberta Lands and Forests. 1972, 1974. Fish planting list. Fish Wild. Div., Edmonton.

Alberta Recreation, Parks and Wildlife. 1975, 1977, 1978. Fish planting list. Fish Wild. Div., Edmonton.

Alberta Research Council. 1972. Geological map of Alberta. Nat. Resour. Div., Alta. Geol. Surv., Edmonton.

Energy, Mines and Resources Canada. 1980. National topographic series 1:50 000 83L/7 (1980), 83L/10 (1980). Surv. Map. Br., Ottawa.

Environment Canada. 1982. Canadian climate normals, Vol. 7: Bright sunshine (1951–1980). Prep. by Atm. Envir. Serv. Supply Serv. Can., Ottawa.

———. 1986. Climate of Alberta. Prep. by Atm. Envir. Serv. Alta. Envir., Edmonton.

Nelson, L.R. 1979. Summary of creel census at Musreau Lake, June 29–July 2, 1979. Alta. En. Nat. Resour., Fish Wild. Div. Unpubl. rep., Edmonton.

Schroeder, D.G. 1974. Preliminary survey of Musreau Lake, July 1974. Alta. Ld. For., Fish Wild. Div. Unpubl. rep., Edmonton.

———. 1984. Musreau Lake test netting and assessment of potential spawning habitat, Aug. 31–Sept. 2, 1982 and Aug. 22–23, 1984. Alta. En. Nat. Resour., Fish. Wild. Div. Unpubl. rep., Edmonton.

———. 1988. Alta. For. Ld. Wild., Fish Wild. Div., Grande Prairie. Pers. comm.

Smith, L. and B. Scott. 1969. Musreau Lake (7GB–3). Alta. Ld. For., Fish Wild. Div. Unpubl. rep., Edmonton.

Strong, W.L. and K.R. Leggat. 1981. Ecoregions of Alberta. Alta. En. Nat. Resour., Resour. Eval. Plan. Div., Edmonton.

Twardy, A.G. and I.G. Corns. 1980. Soil survey and interpretations of the Wapiti map area, Alberta. Alta. Inst. Pedol. Bull. No. 39. Alta. Res. Counc., Edmonton.

SASKATOON LAKE

MAP SHEET: 83M/3
LOCATION: Tp72 R7, 8 W6
LAT/LONG: 55°13'N 119°05'W

Saskatoon Lake is a medium-sized recreational lake surrounded by agricultural land. It is located in the County of Grande Prairie about 25 km west of the city of Grande Prairie and 4 km north of Highway 2. The population centre closest to the lake is the town of Wembley, about 7 km to the south. A secondary road from Highway 2 leads to Saskatoon Island Provincial Park on the lake's southern shore (Fig. 1).

Saskatoon Lake was originally named by Indians for the saskatoon berry, which grows profusely in the park. Saskatoon means "garden of flowers" (Alta. Cult. Multicult. n.d.). The berries were a staple ingredient of pemmican, and until as recently as 1929, Indians camped each summer on the site of the present-day park to pick the berries (Finlay and Finlay 1987). Historically, Saskatoon Lake and nearby Little Lake were joined and the Indian campground was an island within the larger water body (L. Saskatoon Hist. Book Commit. 1980). Water levels began declining in the 1920s, and by the early 1960s, the island had become part of the mainland (Fairbarns et al. 1981).

The community of Saskatoon Lake was established in 1899 when a trading post was built a short distance west and north of the island (L. Saskatoon Hist. Book Commit. 1980). The location allowed the proprietor to trade with the annual gatherings of Indians. Competition soon arrived in the form of a Hudson's Bay Company post, which was built nearby and operated until 1918. The Lake Saskatoon Mission was established near the lake in 1904 but closed in 1908, when it relocated to the present-day site of Grande Prairie. The Saskatoon Lake area was surveyed between 1909 and 1911 and was opened for homesteading in 1910 (L. Saskatoon Hist. Book Commit. 1980). Local homesteaders held annual picnics on Saskatoon Island. By 1921, the community of Saskatoon Lake had 96 residents (Finlay and Finlay 1987). It was an important centre for the area until 1924, when the railway was built to the south, through Wembley. Within a decade there was little physical evidence left of the community.

Pressure from local residents to protect the berry crop on Saskatoon Island resulted in the establishment of Saskatoon Island Provincial Park in 1932 (Fig. 2). The island was one of Alberta's first six provincial parks. In 1933, the park was designated a game refuge to protect Trumpeter Swans, which nest south of the park at Little Lake (Finlay and Finlay 1987). At present, the park provides day-use services year-round and camping services from 1 May to Thanksgiving Day. There are 96 campsites, a group camping area, sewage disposal facilities, playgrounds, tap water, picnic areas, a boat launch, a beach, a change house and a concession. A hiking trail leads to a viewing platform overlooking Little Lake. In addition to Trumpeter Swans, a major attraction in the park is the abundance of saskatoon berries. Activities at the park and on the lake include fishing year-round; camping, picnicking, motor boating, water skiing, wind surfing and swimming during summer; and cross-country skiing on groomed trails and snowshoeing in winter. There are no boating restrictions over most of the lake, but in posted areas, either all boats are prohibited or power boats are restricted to a maximum speed of 12 km/hour (Alta. For. Ld. Wild. 1988[b]).

Saskatoon Lake is very fertile. Algae turn the water green in mid to late summer and aquatic macrophytes grow abundantly around the shore. The lake has a history of fish kills in winter, and by 1987 no sport fish remained. That year, a rainbow trout and eastern brook trout stocking program began. The growth rates of the fish are

Table 1. Characteristics of Saskatoon Lake drainage basin.

area (excluding lake) (km²)[a]	31.8
soil[b]	Eluviated Black Chernozemic, Orthic Gleysol and Dark Gray Solod
bedrock geology[c]	Wapiti Formation (Upper Cretaceous): sandstone, mudstone, bentonite, scattered coal beds; nonmarine
terrain[b]	level to gently rolling
ecoregion[d]	Aspen Subregion of Aspen Parkland
dominant vegetation[d]	trembling aspen
mean annual inflow (m³)[a, e]	1.17 x 10⁶
mean annual sunshine (h)[f]	2 126

NOTE: [e]excluding groundwater inflow
SOURCES: [a]Alta. Envir. n.d.[b]; [b]Odynsky et al. 1961; [c]Alta. Res. Counc. 1972; [d]Strong and Leggat 1981; [f]Envir. Can. 1982

Table 2. Characteristics of Saskatoon Lake.

elevation (m)[a, b]	711.13
surface area (km²)[a, c]	7.47
volume (m³)[a, c]	19.3 x 10⁶
maximum depth (m)[a, c]	4.0
mean depth (m)[a, c]	2.6
shoreline length (km)[a, c]	16.1
mean annual lake evaporation (mm)[d]	616
mean annual precipitation (mm)[d]	460
mean residence time (yr)[d, e]	>100
control structure	none

NOTES: [a]on date of sounding: 21–22 Aug. 1985; [e]excluding groundwater inflow
SOURCES: [b]Alta. Envir. n.d.[c]; [c]Schroeder 1986; [d]Alta. Envir. n.d.[b]

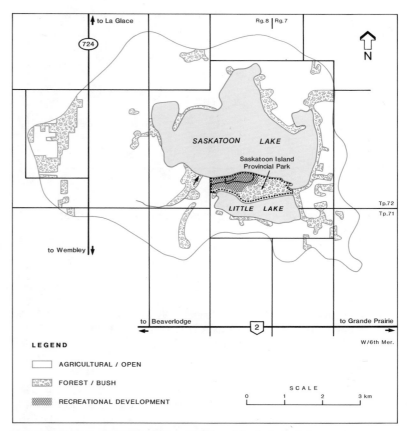

Figure 1. Features of the drainage basin of Saskatoon Lake.
SOURCES: Alta. Envir. n.d.[b]; En. Mines Resour. Can. 1985. Updated with 1985 aerial photos.

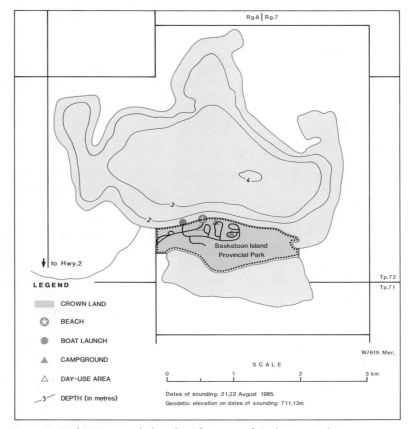

Figure 2. Bathymetry and shoreline features of Saskatoon Lake.
BATHYMETRY SOURCE: Schroeder 1986.

excellent, and the fishery is becoming a popular regional attraction. Fishing for bait fish and the use of bait fish are not allowed in Saskatoon Lake (Alta. For. Ld. Wild. 1989).

Drainage Basin Characteristics

Saskatoon Lake's drainage basin is 4 times the size of the lake (Tables 1, 2). The only defined inflow is a small creek that enters the southwest end of the lake (Fig. 1). Additional inflow is provided by diffuse runoff, precipitation and groundwater.

The drainage basin is part of the Aspen Subregion of the Aspen Parkland Ecoregion (Strong and Leggat 1981). The most extensive soils in the watershed are moderately well-drained Eluviated Black Chernozemics with a sandy loam to silt loam texture (Odynsky et al. 1961). These soils developed on alluvial and aeolian material and are located on undulating slopes over most of the western, northwestern and southern portions of the drainage basin. They support a vegetative cover composed primarily of trembling aspen and secondarily of white spruce, wild rose, saskatoon, buckbrush, wolf willow and rough fescue. Poorly drained Orthic Gleysols are the main soils on level and depressional land along the western shore and in the western part of the provincial park. These soils, which developed on lacustro-till or glaciolacustrine material, have a silt loam to clay loam texture and support a cover of willow. The third major soil is a moderately to imperfectly drained Dark Gray Solod, which is located throughout the eastern and northeastern portion of the drainage basin on undulating to gently rolling land. This soil developed on lacustro-till or glaciolacustrine material and has a loam to clay loam texture. Soils within Saskatoon Island Provincial Park were studied on a smaller scale in 1984 (Greenlee 1984).

Except for a treed buffer around most of the shoreline and along the inflow, most of the land in the watershed has been cleared for agriculture. The main crops grown are wheat, barley, oats, canola, pasture and hay. The provincial park encompasses one of the largest tracts of forested land in the drainage basin. A mature stand of

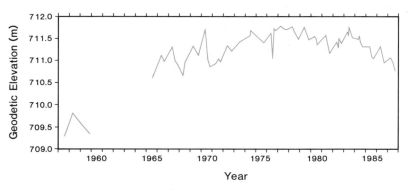

Figure 3. Water level of Saskatoon Lake, 1957 to 1959 and 1965 to 1987.
SOURCE: Alta. Envir. n.d.[c].

trembling aspen and 6 large, 75–year–old white spruce are located in the park, and saskatoon bushes occupy about one-third of the total park area (Van Tighem and Wallis 1973).

Lake Basin Characteristics

Saskatoon Lake is a very shallow, medium-sized water body (Table 2). The maximum depth of 4 m is located in a small hole east of the centre of the basin (Fig. 2). The shoreline substrate is predominantly organic material along the north and west shores, which are protected from the prevailing winds, and predominantly rubble along most of the south and east shores. A sandy beach is located along the south shore at the provincial park (Schroeder 1986).

Water levels were recorded from 1957 to 1959 and have been monitored regularly since 1965 (Fig. 3). The lake's elevation was considerably lower during the late 1950s than it has been since 1965. The minimum elevation (709.27 m), recorded in September 1957, was 2.50 m lower than the maximum elevation (711.77 m), recorded in May 1977. Between 1980 and 1987, the range in water levels was 0.99 m.

Water Quality

Water quality in Saskatoon Lake was monitored by Fish and Wildlife Division in August 1985, and has been monitored jointly by Alberta Environment and Alberta Recreation and Parks since 1986 (Alta. Envir. n.d.[a]; Schroeder 1986). As well, winter dissolved oxygen concentrations were monitored periodically by Fish and Wildlife Division in 1984, 1985 and 1986 (Schroeder 1986).

The lake water is very slightly saline, well buffered and very hard (Table 3). The main ions are sodium and bicarbonate. The lake is so shallow that the water column is well mixed during the open-water season (Fig. 4). Temperature profiles were uniform from top to bottom on 22 July 1986 (18.5°C) and 8 August 1988 (15.8°C). Dissolved oxygen throughout the water column on the 1986 sampling date was lower (6.8 mg/L, Fig. 4) than on the 1988 sampling date (10.1 mg/L). During February 1987 and 1988, dissolved oxygen concentrations were less than 6 mg/L at the surface and less than 3 mg/L on the bottom. A small number of fish died in 1988.

Saskatoon Lake is hyper-eutrophic. The maximum chlorophyll *a* concentrations were 60 μg/L in June and August 1986, and 113 μg/L in September 1988, and the highest total phosphorus concentrations were 766 μg/L in August 1986 and 901 μg/L in July 1988 (Fig. 5). Average total phosphorus concentrations during the open-water season are very high (Table 4). Total iron levels (Table 4) are similar to other lakes in the region, but higher than in most lakes in Alberta.

Table 3. Major ions and related water quality variables for Saskatoon Lake. Average concentrations in mg/L; pH in pH units. Composite samples from the euphotic zone collected 3 times from 26 May to 22 Sep. 1986. S.E. = standard error.

	Mean	S.E.
pH (range)	8.9–9.1	—
total alkalinity ($CaCO_3$)	497	14.4
specific conductivity (μS/cm)	930	30.0
total dissolved solids (calculated)	560	14.3
total hardness ($CaCO_3$)	249	3.7
HCO_3	505	12.2
CO_3	50	7.0
Mg	41	0.9
Na	98	3.8
K	60	0.3
Cl	12	0.7
SO_4	15	2.9
Ca	32	0.3

SOURCE: Alta. Envir. n.d.[a], Naquadat station 01AL07GE1000

Table 4. Nutrient, chlorophyll *a* and Secchi depth data for Saskatoon Lake. Average concentrations in μg/L. Composite samples from the euphotic zone collected 6 times from 26 May to 27 Oct. 1986 and 5 times from 30 May to 27 Sep. 1988. S.E. = standard error.

	1986		1988	
	Mean	S.E.	Mean	S.E.
total phosphorus	654	31.9	802	34.0
NO_3 + NO_2–nitrogen	—	—	<40[b]	—
iron	460[a]	174.7	285[b]	175.0
chlorophyll *a*	37.8	7.93	49.1	23.96
Secchi depth (m)	0.5	0.05	1.2	0.32

NOTES: [a]n = 3; [b]n = 2
SOURCE: Alta. Envir. n.d.[a], Naquadat station 01AL07GE1000

Biological Characteristics

Plants

Two plankton hauls were taken by Fish and Wildlife Division with an unspecified sized net on 23 August 1985 (Schroeder 1986). The blue-green alga *Microcystis* sp. was the most common phytoplankton species observed. An aquatic macrophyte survey, which was part of the same study, noted that an extensive band of vegetation ringed the lake except for a few exposed portions along the south shore and in the northwest bay. The northeast bay was not surveyed (Fig. 6). The two emergent species identified—bulrush (*Scirpus* sp.) and common cattail (*Typha latifolia*)—were both abundant along parts of the shoreline. Water smartweed (*Polygonum amphibium*), the only floating-leaved species present, mainly grew along the east and west shores. Sago pondweed (*Potamogeton pectinatus*), the most common submergent species, grew to a maximum depth of 2.5 m, and isolated areas of northern watermilfoil (*Myriophyllum exalbescens*) were identified along the east and west shores. Other submergent species, noted in a brief survey by Alberta Recreation and Parks in 1981 (Fairbarns et al. 1981), were Richardson pondweed (*P. richardsonii*), large-sheath pondweed (*P. vaginatus*), coontail (*Ceratophyllum demersum*) and star duckweed (*Lemna trisulca*). One floating-leaved species, lesser duckweed (*L. minor*), was also identified.

Invertebrates

There are no data available for the invertebrates in Saskatoon Lake.

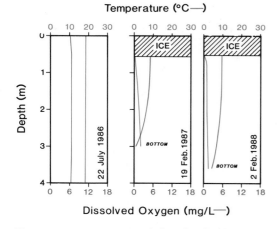

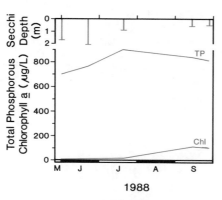

Figure 4. Temperature and dissolved oxygen in Saskatoon Lake, 1986, 1987 and 1988.
SOURCE: Alta. Envir. n.d.[a].

Figure 5. Total phosphorus, chlorophyll *a* and Secchi depth in Saskatoon Lake, 1988.
SOURCE: Alta. Envir. n.d.[a].

Fish

Prior to 1987, only brook stickleback was known to inhabit the lake (Schroeder 1986). Fish and Wildlife Division monitored dissolved oxygen concentrations during 1984, 1985 and 1986 and concluded that the lake was capable of supporting fish year-round during those years. Consequently, the lake was stocked with 143 000 rainbow trout and 258 000 brook trout in 1987, and 91 120 rainbow trout and 184 460 brook trout in 1988 (Alta. For. Ld. Wild. 1987; 1988[a]). Trout are unable to reproduce in Saskatoon Lake because of lack of spawning habitat, so the populations must be maintained by stocking. Survival over the winter of 1986/87 was excellent, but a partial winterkill occurred in 1988 and a severe winterkill occurred in 1989. Stocking was scheduled for the summer of 1989 (Alta. For. Ld. Wild. n.d.; Schroeder 1988; Walty 1989). One-year-old rainbow trout captured in test nets in June 1988 had an average weight of 950 g and a maximum weight of 1 590 g. The growth rate of rainbow trout in Saskatoon Lake is one of the fastest in the region (Alta. For. Ld. Wild. n.d.). The growth of brook trout is not as fast as that of rainbow trout. One-year-old brook trout averaged 276 g, and the largest specimen captured in June 1988 weighed about 450 g (Schroeder 1988).

Wildlife

Saskatoon Island Provincial Park hosts at least 121 species of birds. A minimum of 44 species breed there during June. The area surrounding the park is rated the fourth most important waterfowl habitat in the Aspen Parkland Ecoregion of Alberta by the Canadian Wildlife Service (Finlay and Finlay 1987). The park is one of the few accessible places in Canada where Trumpeter Swans can be regularly sighted during summer. Little Lake, which is quite shallow, contains abundant emergent vegetation that provides ideal conditions for Trumpeter Swans and other waterfowl to raise their young. A platform located on the north shore of the lake is a good spot for viewing the single pair of swans that nest on the lake each year. They arrive in the Grande Prairie area in mid to late April from their wintering grounds in Montana and Idaho, and they migrate south in mid to late October.

The marshes at the southwest and east sides of the park are also productive areas for nesting and foraging birds. Nesting birds include Trumpeter Swans, Eared Grebes, Mallards, Pintails, American Widgeons, Lesser Scaup, Sora, coots, Common Snipe, Black Terns and Yellow-headed and Red-winged blackbirds. Birds that use the marshes extensively for feeding include Green-winged Teal, Blue-winged Teal, Shovellers, Bufflehead and Franklin's Gulls. Muskrats are commonly found throughout the marsh and varying hares, porcupines and coyotes are present throughout the park (Van Tighem and Wallis 1973).

M.E. Bradford

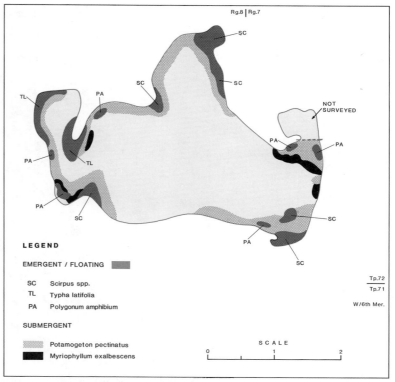

Figure 6. Species composition and distribution of aquatic macrophytes in Saskatoon Lake, August 1985.
SOURCE: Schroeder 1986.
NOTE: Northeast bay not surveyed.

References

Alberta Culture and Multiculturalism. n.d. Hist. Resour. Div., Hist. Sites Serv. Unpubl. data, Edmonton.

Alberta Environment. n.d.[a]. Envir. Assess. Div., Envir. Qlty. Monit. Br. Unpubl. data, Edmonton.

———. n.d.[b]. Tech. Serv. Div., Hydrol. Br. Unpubl. data, Edmonton.

———. n.d.[c]. Tech. Serv. Div., Surv. Br. Unpubl. data, Edmonton.

Alberta Forestry, Lands and Wildlife. n.d. Fish Wild. Div. Unpubl. data, Edmonton.

———. 1987, 1988[a]. Fish planting list. Fish Wild. Div., Edmonton.

———. 1988[b]. Boating in Alberta. Fish Wild. Div., Edmonton.

———. 1989. Guide to sportfishing. Fish Wild. Div., Edmonton.

Alberta Research Council. 1972. Geological map of Alberta. Nat. Resour. Div., Alta. Geol. Surv., Edmonton.

Energy, Mines and Resources Canada. 1985. National topographic series 1:50 000 83M/3 (1985). Surv. Map. Br., Ottawa.

Environment Canada. 1982. Canadian climate normals, Vol. 7: Bright sunshine (1951–1980). Prep. by Atm. Envir. Serv. Supply Serv. Can., Ottawa.

Fairbarns, M., S. Luck and S. Loomis. 1981. Saskatoon Island Provincial Park resource assessment 1981. Alta. Rec. Parks, Prov. Parks Div., Edmonton.

Finlay, J. and C. Finlay. 1987. Parks in Alberta: A guide to peaks, ponds, parklands & prairies. Hurtig Publ., Edmonton.

Greenlee, G.M. 1984. Soil survey of Saskatoon Island Provincial Park and interpretation for recreational use. Alta. Inst. Pedol. No. M–83–10. Alta. Res. Counc., Terrain Sci. Dept., Edmonton.

Lake Saskatoon History Book Committee. 1980. Lake Saskatoon reflections. L. Saskatoon Hist. Book Commit., Sexsmith.

Odynsky, W., J.D. Lindsay, S.W. Reeder and A. Wynnyk. 1961. Reconnaissance soil survey of the Beaverlodge and Blueberry Mountain sheets. Alta. Soil Surv. Rep. No. 20, Univ. Alta. Bull. No. SS–3, Res. Counc. Alta. Rep. No. 81. Univ. Alta., Dept. Extension, Edmonton.

Schroeder, D. 1986. Habitat assessment and fishery potential of Saskatoon Lake. Alta. For. Ld. Wild., Fish Wild. Div., Peace River.

———. 1988. Alta. For. Ld. Wild., Fish Wild. Div., Peace River. Pers. comm.

Strong, W.L. and K.R. Leggat. 1981. Ecoregions of Alberta. Alta. En. Nat. Resour., Resour. Eval. Plan. Div., Edmonton.

Van Tighem, K. and C.A. Wallis. 1973. An ecological survey of Saskatoon Island Provincial Park. Alta. Ld. For., Prov. Parks Plan. Div. Unpubl. rep., Edmonton.

Walty, D. 1989. Alta. For. Ld. Wild., Fish Wild. Div., Peace River. Pers. comm.

SMOKE LAKE

MAP SHEET: 83K/7
LOCATION: Tp62 R20 W5
LAT/LONG: 54°22'N 116°56'W

Smoke Lake is a popular sport fishing lake set in forested hills in Improvement District No. 16. It is located about 245 km northwest of the city of Edmonton, 83 km northeast of the town of Whitecourt and 9 km southwest of the town of Fox Creek. An industrial road that runs south from Highway 43 at Fox Creek branches east and then south and provides access to Smoke Lake Forest Recreation Area on the east side of the lake (Fig. 1).

The lake's name is related to that of the nearby Little Smoky River, which was named for the smouldering beds of coal found along its banks (Holmgren and Holmgren 1976). The lake has also been known as Buck Lake (Alta. Rec. Parks Wild. 1976).

The native inhabitants in the area northwest of Whitecourt were Woodland Cree, but the Beaver tribe may have lived there at an earlier time (Olecko 1974). The region was close to an aboriginal migration route from Lac Ste. Anne to the Sturgeon Lake area, and sites on Smoke Lake have traditionally been used as hunting and fishing bases. One site on the west side of the lake has been identified as a burial ground (Alta. For. Ld. Wild. 1988[b]). The first European to arrive in the area was probably David Thompson in 1799; he camped at a site that is now the Whitecourt townsite. Missionaries arrived in the region about 40 years later. Industrial development began in 1909 when logging and milling operations were initiated 10 km west of Whitecourt near the Athabasca River. The railroad arrived in Whitecourt in 1921, but was never completed to the Peace River Country, as originally proposed. The area near Smoke Lake was not developed until oil and gas exploration in the 1950s brought the railroad as far as the Kaybob station, 4 km south of the lake. Highway 43 opened in 1955, and was paved and completed in 1962 as far as the town of Valleyview, 70 km north of the lake. There has been no residential development at the lake (Knapik and Lindsay 1983).

In 1988, a lake management plan for Smoke Lake was completed by Alberta Forestry, Lands and Wildlife (Alta. For. Ld. Wild. 1988[b]). The plan assesses potential commercial and public recreational development of Smoke Lake based on environmental, social and economic constraints. It will be used as the basis for an area structure plan to guide development around the lake, which will be prepared by Improvement District No. 16.

Access to the lake is provided at the Smoke Lake Forest Recreation Area, an Alberta Forest Service campground that was built in 1968 (Fig. 2). There are 47 campsites, 5 picnic sites, pump water, a small sand beach and a boat launch. Popular activities at the lake are power boating, fishing, windsurfing and swimming. There are no boating restrictions specific to the lake, but general federal regulations apply (Alta. For. Ld. Wild. 1988[a]). The main catches of the popular summer sport fishery are northern pike, walleye and yellow perch. In winter, catches of large lake whitefish in the 2– to 3–kg range attract many anglers (Hunt 1989). Smoke Lake is closed to sport fishing for a designated period during April and May each year. As well, the lake's inlet and outlet streams are closed to fishing from September to mid-June each year (Alta. For. Ld. Wild. 1989). The commercial fishery opens intermittently; its main catch is lake whitefish.

Smoke Lake is quite fertile and the water often turns green with algae during late summer. Water clarity is poor during the rest of the year as well; the lack of clarity may be largely the result of high colour.

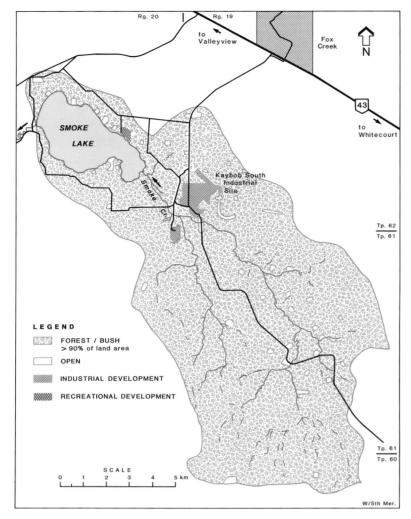

Figure 1. Features of the drainage basin of Smoke Lake.
SOURCE: Alta. Envir. n.d.[b]; En. Mines Resour. Can. 1976. Updated with 1986 and 1987 aerial photos.

Table 1. Characteristics of Smoke Lake drainage basin.

area (excluding lake) (km²)[a]	127
soil[b]	Orthic and Brunisolic Gray Luvisols, Mesisols
bedrock geology[c]	Scollard Member of Paskapoo Formation (Upper Cretaceous): sandstone, mudstone, thick coal beds; nonmarine
terrain[b]	level to rolling
ecoregion[d]	Boreal Foothills
dominant vegetation[d]	trembling aspen, balsam poplar, lodgepole pine
mean annual inflow (m³)[a, e]	20.6 x 10⁶
mean annual sunshine (h)[f]	2056

NOTE: [e]excluding groundwater inflow
SOURCES: [a]Alta. Envir. n.d.[b]; [b]Knapik and Lindsay 1983; [c]Alta. Res. Counc. 1972; [d]Strong and Leggat 1981; [f]Envir. Can. 1982

Drainage Basin Characteristics

Smoke Lake has a fairly extensive drainage basin that is about 13 times the size of the lake (Tables 1, 2). There are no other lakes in the drainage basin. Smoke Creek, the major inflow to the lake, flows into the southeast bay, and the outflow, an unnamed creek, is located on the west side (Fig. 1). The outlet creek joins the Little Smoky River several kilometres to the west, and eventually flows into the Smoky River.

The drainage basin is part of the Fox Creek Benchland physiographic division, and is underlain by nonmarine sandstones, silty mudstones and coal beds covered by glacial drift. Agriculture is

Table 2. Characteristics of Smoke Lake.

elevation (m)[a, b]	837.31
surface area (km²)[a, b]	9.59
volume (m³)[a, b]	49.2 x 10⁶
maximum depth (m)[a, b]	8.3
mean depth (m)[a, b]	5.1
shoreline length (km)[c]	14.7
mean annual lake evaporation (mm)[d]	612
mean annual precipitation (mm)[d]	536
mean residence time (yr)[d, e]	2.5
control structure	none

NOTES: [a]on date of sounding: June 1968; [e]excluding groundwater inflow
SOURCES: [b]Alta. Envir. n.d.[c]; [c]En. Mines Resour. Can. 1976; [d]Alta. Envir. n.d.[b].

Table 3. Major ions and related water quality variables for Smoke Lake. Average concentrations in mg/L; pH in pH units. Composite samples from the euphotic zone collected 6 times from 10 May to 18 Oct. 1983. S.E. = standard error.

	Mean	S.E.
pH (range)	7.4–9.4[a]	—
total alkalinity (CaCO₃)	77[b]	0.5
specific conductivity (μS/cm)	179[b]	1.9
total dissolved solids (calculated)	91[c]	1.2
total hardness (CaCO₃)	71[b]	1.8
total particulate carbon	2	0.4
dissolved organic carbon	15	0.6
HCO₃	93[b]	1.4
CO₃	<2[b]	—
Mg	5[b]	0.4
Na	8[b]	0.3
K	1[b]	0.1
Cl	<1[b]	—
SO₄	11[b]	1.2
Ca	20	0.5

NOTES: [a]n = 7; [b]n = 4; [c]n = 3
SOURCE: Alta. Envir. n.d.[a], Naquadat station 01AL07GG1000

severely limited by a short frost-free period, adverse topography and poor soil structure. The main soils on rolling moraine are Orthic Gray Luvisols that developed on clay-loam textured glacial till. Along the inlet streams, the soils are mostly Mesisols, which developed on very poorly drained moss peat, and in the southern part of the watershed, the soils are mainly poorly drained Gleysols (Knapik and Lindsay 1983).

The watershed is part of the Moist Mixedwood Subregion of the Boreal Mixedwood Ecoregion. The rolling landscape supports a dense cover of trembling aspen and mixed coniferous/deciduous forest. Stands of lodgepole pine grow on well-drained soils at higher elevations, and balsam poplar is a major component of the forest on moderately well-drained soils. Black spruce grows on poorly drained soils and willows and sedges are present in very poorly drained areas (Strong and Leggat 1981; Knapik and Lindsay 1983).

All of the land in the watershed is owned by the Crown and most development is related to the extraction and processing of natural gas from the underlying Kaybob South Oil and Gas Field. Dome Petroleum Limited operates two sour gas processing plants at the Kaybob South industrial site (Fig. 1) and gas wells dot the countryside.

Lake Basin Characteristics

Smoke Lake is a medium-sized lake (Table 2) with a maximum length of 5.4 km and a maximum width of 2.7 km. The lake basin is shallow

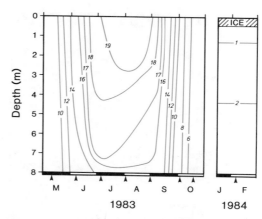

Figure 5. Temperature (°C) of Smoke Lake, 1983 and 1984. Arrows indicate sampling dates.
SOURCE: Alta. Envir. n.d.[a].

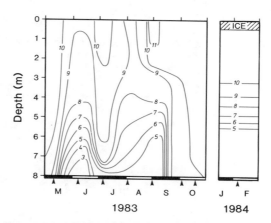

Figure 6. Dissolved oxygen (mg/L) in Smoke Lake, 1983 and 1984. Arrows indicate sampling dates.
SOURCE: Alta. Envir. n.d.[a].

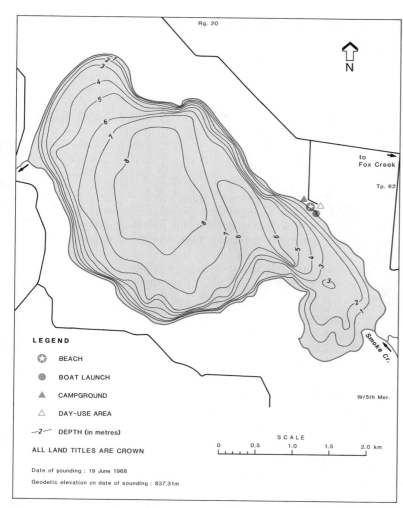

Figure 2. Bathymetry and shoreline features of Smoke Lake.
BATHYMETRY SOURCE: Alta. Envir. n.d.[c].

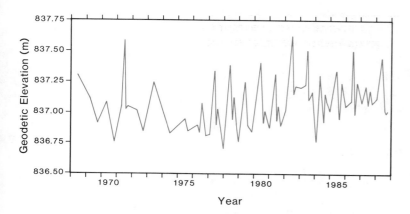

Figure 3. Water level of Smoke Lake, 1970 to 1987.
SOURCE: Alta. Envir. n.d.[c].

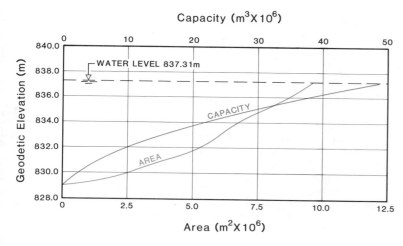

Figure 4. Area/capacity curve for Smoke Lake.
SOURCE: Alta. Envir. n.d.[c].

and slopes gently in the southeast bay, but drops off more abruptly in other areas, particularly along the central parts of the north and south shores (Fig. 2). The maximum depth of 8.3 m is located in the middle of the lake. The banks of the lake drop off sharply in many places, so there is little beach area. The shoreline is sandy at Smoke Lake Forest Recreation Area, but the land is low-lying and poorly drained at the outlet and along the southeast bay and the point of land on the south shore. The remainder of the shoreline is forested down to the water's edge.

The elevation of Smoke Lake has been monitored since 1968 (Fig. 3). The difference between the historic minimum water level (836.71 m), recorded in January 1978, and the maximum level (837.63 m), recorded in July 1982, is 0.92 m. Changes in the lake's area and capacity with fluctuations in water level are shown in Figure 4.

Water Quality

The water quality of Smoke Lake was studied by Alberta Environment during the open-water period in 1983 and under ice in February 1984 (Alta. Envir. n.d.[a]). The lake has fresh water that is not as hard or as alkaline as that of many other prairie lakes (Table 3). The dominant ions are calcium and bicarbonate.

The mixing pattern in Smoke Lake is typical of that in many shallow Alberta lakes: the lake mixes completely in spring and fall and is thermally stratified during summer, as in 1983 (Fig. 5). During the ice-free period in 1983, the upper layers of the water column were saturated with dissolved oxygen, but in the deepest water, the concentration declined to 2.3 to 4.7 mg/L (Fig. 6). Under ice in February 1984, there was an oxygen gradient from surface to bottom, but the concentration of dissolved oxygen was almost 5 mg/L at the greatest depth.

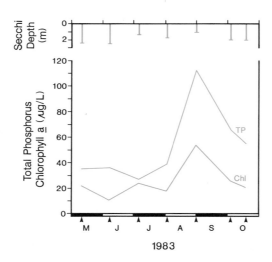

Figure 7. Total phosphorus, chlorophyll *a* and Secchi depth in Smoke Lake, 1983.
SOURCE: Alta. Envir. n.d.[a].

Table 4. Nutrient, chlorophyll *a* and Secchi depth data for Smoke Lake. Average concentrations in µg/L. Composite samples from the euphotic zone collected 7 times from 10 May to 18 Oct. 1983. S.E. = standard error.

	Mean	S.E.
total phosphorus	53	11.1
total dissolved phosphorus	19	4.5
soluble reactive phosphorus	7	1.1
total Kjeldahl nitrogen	783[a]	87.8
$NO_3 + NO_2$–nitrogen	<16[a]	—
NH_4–nitrogen	13	3.0
iron	<285	—
chlorophyll *a*	25.0	5.16
Secchi depth (m)	1.9	0.19

NOTE: [a]n = 6
SOURCE: Alta. Envir. n.d.[a], Naquadat station 01AL07GG1000

Smoke Lake is eutrophic. In 1983, the highest total phosphorus (112 µg/L) and chlorophyll *a* (54 µg/L) levels were detected at the end of August (Fig. 7). This large increase in total phosphorus in late summer is likely associated with the release of phosphorus from the bottom sediments. The clarity of Smoke Lake water is consistently poor. The average Secchi depth was only 1.9 m during 1983 (Table 4). The poor water clarity recorded when chlorophyll *a* levels are low may result from high levels of colour in the water.

Biological Characteristics

Plants

The phytoplankton community in Smoke Lake was studied by Alberta Environment from May to October in 1983 (Table 5). The average biomass recorded was 7.8 mg/L; biomass was highest on 5 July (17 mg/L), 31 August (10.8 mg/L) and 18 October (15.3 mg/L). In spring and early summer, the most important algal species were *Cryptomonas erosa reflexa* and *C. ovata* (Cryptophyta), the colonial golden-brown algae *Synura petersenii* and *Dinobryon divergens* (Chrysophyta), and the diatom *Tabellaria fenestrata* (Bacillariophyta). In midsummer, the phytoplankton community was dominated by single species of blue-green algae: in July, *Gloeotrichia echinulata*, and in August, *Anabaena spiroides crassa*. In early October, the diatom *Stephanodiscus niagarae* accounted for 84% of the total biomass, but by mid-October, this species shared dominance with a green alga, *Coelastrum microsporum* (Chlorophyta), and another diatom, *Melosira italica subarctica*.

There are no specific data on the macrophyte community; aquatic vegetation grows at the northwest and southeast ends of the lake (Alta. For. Ld. Wild. n.d.).

Invertebrates

There are no data available for the invertebrates in Smoke Lake.

Fish

Smoke Lake supports populations of lake whitefish, walleye, yellow perch, northern pike, white sucker, burbot, spottail shiner and Iowa darter (Alta. For. Ld. Wild. n.d.). The lake is managed for commercial, domestic and recreational fisheries. There are no catch data for the domestic fishery. A few domestic licences (3 to 4) are issued each year.

Smoke Lake opened for commercial fishing intermittently from 1944/45 to 1953/54, annually from 1954/55 to 1966/67, and again in 1975/76 (Alta. Rec. Parks Wild. 1976). Low catches during the mid–1960s (less than 875 kg), and a summerkill in 1972 were responsible for the closure from 1968 to 1975 (Hawryluk 1979). The lake next opened for fishing in 1978/79; from 1979/80 to the present, it has been fished in alternate years (Alta. For. Ld. Wild. n.d.). In 1979/80, the gill net mesh size was increased from 140 mm to 152 mm. From 1979/80 to 1987/88, the average catch was 12 274 kg of lake whitefish, 245 kg of northern pike and 48 kg of walleye. Fishing effort has increased steadily over the period, from 28 licences in 1979/80 to 93 licences in 1987/88. Historically, the largest total catch from Smoke Lake was recorded in 1987/88, when 20 600 kg of fish were taken; 99% of this catch was lake whitefish and the remainder was northern pike and walleye.

The sport fishery is popular with local residents and attracts visitors from as far away as Edmonton. Creel surveys were conducted by Fish and Wildlife Division for 6 days from 19 May to 5 July in 1984 and for 35 days from 17 May to 15 August in 1986 (Hawryluk 1984; 1987). In 1986 (Table 6), anglers caught 2 183 northern pike, 935 walleye and 35 yellow perch and kept 60% of the northern pike, 92% of the walleye and all of the yellow perch. The northern pike catch rate in 1986 (0.23/angler-hour) was similar to that calculated for 1984 (0.28/angler-hour), whereas the walleye catch rate for 1986 (0.10/angler-hour) was much lower than the catch rate calculated for 1984 (0.50/angler-hour). The fishing pressure on Smoke Lake is higher than that of nearby Iosegun Lake and concerns have been expressed about excessive fishing pressure on Smoke Lake.

Wildlife

A wide range of wildlife species is found near Smoke Lake. Waterfowl are abundant and the lake is an important staging area (Alta. For. Ld. Wild. 1988[b]). Species sighted at the lake include Common Loons, grebes, Bufflehead and Goldeneye. Black bears are common in the area and grizzly bears have been sighted. The land near the lake is excellent moose habitat and elk are found in the Little Smoky River valley. Small mammals present include beaver, muskrats and mink.

M.E. Bradford

References

Alberta Environment. n.d.[a]. Envir. Assess. Div., Envir. Qlty. Monit. Br. Unpubl. data, Edmonton.
———. n.d.[b]. Tech. Serv. Div., Hydrol. Br. Unpubl. data, Edmonton.
———. n.d.[c]. Tech. Serv. Div., Surv. Br. Unpubl. data, Edmonton.
Alberta Forestry, Lands and Wildlife. n.d. Fish Wild. Div. Unpubl. data, Edmonton.
———. 1988[a]. Boating in Alberta. Fish Wild. Div., Edmonton.
———. 1988[b]. Smoke and Iosegun lake management plan. Alta. For. Serv. Unpubl. rep., Edmonton.
———. 1989. Guide to sportfishing. Fish Wild. Div., Edmonton.
Alberta Recreation, Parks and Wildlife. 1976. Commercial fisheries catch statistics for Alberta, 1942–1975. Fish Wild. Div., Fish. Mgt. Rep. No. 22, Edmonton.
Alberta Research Council. 1972. Geological map of Alberta. Nat. Resour. Div., Alta. Geol. Surv., Edmonton.

Table 5. Percentage composition of major algal groups by total biomass in Smoke Lake, 1983. Composite samples collected from the euphotic zone.

ALGAL GROUP	10 May	07 June	05 July	02 Aug.	31 Aug.	03 Oct.	18 Oct.
Total Biomass (mg/L)	3.11	1.62	17.06	3.32	10.76	3.78	15.31
Percentage Composition:							
Cyanophyta	0	4	88	56	81	1	0
			Gleotrichia	*Anabaena*———→			
Chlorophyta	3	1	1	6	1	2	43
							Coelastrum
Euglenophyta	9	0	0	0	0	0	0
Chrysophyta	30	30	1	7	1	0	0
	Synura	*Dinobryon*					
Bacillariophyta	9	31	10	19	14	96	57
		Tabellaria				*Stephanodiscus*———→	
							Melosira
Cryptophyta	49	34	0	7	2	1	0
	Cryptomonas———→						
Pyrrhophyta	0	0	0	6	0	0	0

SOURCE: Alta. Envir. n.d.[a]

Table 6. Estimated angler numbers, effort and harvest from Smoke Lake. Estimates based on creel survey data collected from 17 May to 15 Aug. 1986. A total of 20 weekdays and 15 weekend days and holidays were surveyed. WE = walleye; NP = northern pike; YP = yellow perch.

	WE	NP	YP	Total
number of anglers[a]	—	—	—	3741
angler-hours[b]	—	—	—	9740
total number fish caught	935	2183	35	3170
total number fish harvested[c]	836	1353	35	2224
catch/angler-hour	0.10	0.23	0.003	0.33
harvest/angler-hour[b, c]	0.09	0.14	0.003	0.23
harvest/angler[a, c]	0.22	0.36	0.01	0.59

NOTES: [a]observed no. anglers = 872; [b]observed hours = 2057; [c]based on observed no. fish kept: WE = 185, NP = 280, YP = 7
SOURCE: Hawryluk 1987

Energy, Mines and Resources Canada. 1976. National topographic series 1:50000 83K/2 (1976), 83K/7 (1976). Surv. Map. Br., Ottawa.

Environment Canada. 1982. Canadian climate normals, Vol. 7: Bright sunshine (1951–1980). Prep. by Atm. Envir. Serv. Supply Serv. Can., Ottawa.

Hawryluk, R. 1979. Evaluation of the Smoke Lake fishery, August, 1978. Alta. En. Nat. Resour., Fish Wild. Div. Unpubl. rep., Edmonton.

———. 1984. An evaluation of the Smoke Lake walleye fishery including a population estimate and assessment of angler success obtained during a creel survey, May 19 to July 5, 1984. Alta. En. Nat. Resour., Fish Wild. Div. Unpubl. rep., Edmonton.

———. 1987. A creel survey of Smoke Lake, May 17 to August 15, 1986. Alta. For. Ld. Wild., Fish Wild. Div. Unpubl. rep., Edmonton.

Holmgren, E.J. and P.M. Holmgren. 1976. Over 2000 place names of Alberta. 3rd ed. West. Producer Prairie Books, Saskatoon.

Hunt, C. 1989. Alta. For. Ld. Wild., Fish Wild. Div., Edson. Pers. comm.

Knapik, L.J. and J.D. Lindsay. 1983. Reconnaissance soil survey of the Iosegun Lake area, Alberta. Alta. Res. Counc. Bull. No. 43. Alta. Res. Counc., Edmonton.

Olecko, D. 1974. Sagitawah saga—the story of Whitecourt. D. Olecko, Whitecourt.

Strong, W.L. and K.R. Leggat. 1981. Ecoregions of Alberta. Alta. En. Nat. Resour., Resour. Eval. Plan. Div., Edmonton.

STURGEON LAKE

MAP SHEETS: 83N/3, 4
LOCATION: Tp70, 71 R23, 24 W5
LAT/LONG: 55°06′N 117°32′W

Sturgeon Lake is a regionally important recreational lake situated in Improvement District No. 16. It is located 90 km east of the city of Grande Prairie and 15 km west of the town of Valleyview. Highway 34, which joins these two population centres, skirts the southern shore (Fig. 1). The lake and the two provincial parks on its shores are destination points for about 50 000 local and regional visitors annually. This is a substantial number in an area with a population of just over 100 000 people. Sturgeon Lake has a reputation for good quality lake whitefish, and is popular for all types of boating and water sports. Development pressures and concerns about water quality have led to a series of intensive studies of the watershed and the effects of various land-use policies on the sediment and nutrient loads entering the lake.

It is unlikely that sturgeon have ever lived in Sturgeon Lake. Speculation on the origin of the name has given rise to two possibilities. One is that a family named Sturgeon once lived nearby; the other is that a visitor who paddled up the outlet creek named the lake for the sturgeon, which also travels upstream (Alta. Cult. Multicult. n.d.).

Indigenous peoples have lived in the area since prehistoric times. Beaver Indians inhabited the area prior to the Cree (Alta. For. Ld. Wild. 1987[b]). The fur trade brought the first Europeans to the Peace Country. Sir Alexander Mackenzie arrived in 1792, but the area was not settled for more than a century. In 1905, St. Francis Xavier Mission was established on the east side of the lake (Mallandaine 1980). The first steady influx of settlers into the area began in 1911, when the Edson Trail was opened; it ran from the present day town of Edson to Grande Prairie via Sturgeon Lake (Odynsky et al. 1956). Sturgeon Lake and Calais settlements, which are located on the southern shore, were surveyed in 1914, and a small settlement was established at Valleyview in the same year (S Peace Reg. Plan. Commis. and ID No. 16 1985). A graded dirt road from Grande Prairie to Calais was completed in 1929, and extended beyond Calais as far as the town of High Prairie in 1933. This road, known as Highway 34 until the new highway was built, still runs close to the south shore of Sturgeon Lake (Fig. 1). The discovery of the Sturgeon Lake Oil Field in 1952 brought about the rapid development of Valleyview, and the completion of Highway 43 to Valleyview in 1962 greatly increased access to the Sturgeon Lake area.

The two provincial parks at the lake are Williamson and Young's Point (Fig. 2). Day-use facilities at both parks are open year-round and camping facilities are open from 1 May to Thanksgiving Day. Williamson Provincial Park occupies 17.4 ha of land on the south shore. It was established in 1960 and named for Alexander Williamson, a former owner of the land. The park is surrounded on three sides by Sturgeon Lake Indian Reserve 154 and bisected by old Highway 34. Access to the park is available via the old highway or via a road built in 1971 from new Highway 34. Park facilities include 61 campsites, tap water, a sewage disposal facility, a concession, a boat launch and pier, picnic shelters, a change house, a playground and a swimming area. The 425–m–long shoreline has a 15–m–wide beach with good quality sand. The lake bottom is firm and slopes gently, so that 90 m offshore the water is only about 2 m deep (Alta. Rec. Parks n.d.). In addition to swimming, popular activities at the park are boating, fishing and picnicking.

Young's Point Provincial Park was named for Frederick Campbell Young, who homesteaded in the area in 1920. It is a large park,

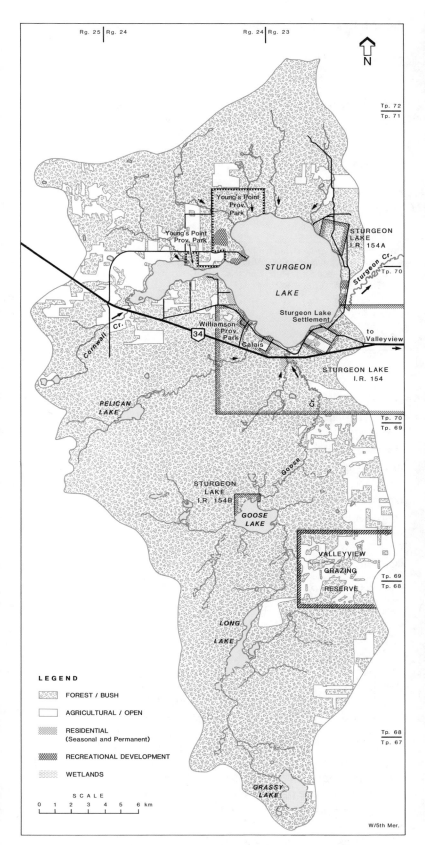

Figure 1. Features of the drainage basin of Sturgeon Lake.
SOURCES: Alta. Envir. n.d.[a]; En. Mines Resour. Can. 1974; 1977; 1979.
Updated with 1985 aerial photos.

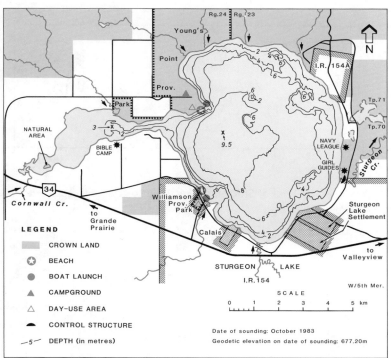

Figure 2. Bathymetry and shoreline features of Sturgeon Lake.
BATHYMETRY SOURCE: Alta. Envir. n.d.[c].

located on 1089 ha of land on the north shore. It can be reached from Highway 34 by a 9–km–long local road at the west end of the lake (Fig. 2). Park facilities include 57 campsites, a sewage disposal facility, a change house, 2 playgrounds, a boat launch, picnic areas, a beach and swimming area, walking trails and a viewpoint. Recreational activities enjoyed by park visitors include swimming, boating, fishing, picnicking, hiking, skating, snowmobiling, tobogganing and cross-country skiing.

Other recreational developments around the lake include the Sturgeon Lake Bible Camp, a commercial campground just north of Williamson Provincial Park in Indian Reserve 154, a commercial

campground and marina on the southern shore of the west bay, a Girl Guide camp and a Navy League of Canada camp on Crown land on the eastern shore, and a commercial resort within Calais (S Peace Reg. Plan. Commis. and ID No. 16 1984). The island in Sturgeon Lake's west basin (Fig. 2) was designated a natural area in 1987. Mature stands of trembling aspen and white spruce and stands of paper birch grow on the island, and the shoreline is surrounded by emergent vegetation (Alta. For. Ld. Wild. 1987[a]).

Sturgeon Lake is rich in nutrients and supports extensive blooms of blue-green algae during summer. In some winters, dissolved oxygen concentrations have become critical for fish; winterkills were recorded in 1976 and 1977. The sport fish in the lake are walleye, northern pike and yellow perch. There are no sport fishing regulations specific to Sturgeon Lake, but provincial limits and regulations apply. Goose Creek, the main inflow to Sturgeon Lake, is closed to sport fishing during April and May to protect spawning walleye (Alta. For. Ld. Wild. 1989). The lake also supports commercial and domestic fisheries, which mainly catch lake whitefish. Aquatic vegetation is abundant along most of the shoreline; it can hamper motor boats at the western end of the west bay, in the cove at Young's Point, and in scattered areas along the north and east shores of the main basin. There are no boating restrictions over most of the lake, but in posted areas such as designated swimming areas, all boats are prohibited, and in other posted areas, power boats are subject to a maximum speed of 12 km/hour (Alta. For. Ld. Wild. 1988).

Drainage Basin Characteristics

Sturgeon Lake has an extensive drainage basin (571 km^2) that is about 12 times the size of the lake (Tables 1, 2). The major inflow is Goose Creek, which drains Goose, Long and Grassy lakes to the south and flows into the south side of Sturgeon Lake (Fig. 1). Several small streams also flow into Sturgeon Lake. The outlet, Sturgeon Creek, is located on the eastern side. It drains into the Little Smoky River, which eventually flows into the Peace River.

Most of the Sturgeon Lake drainage basin is part of the Wapiti Plain physiographic division, which is a broad, generally flat lowland. The northern portion of the drainage basin is influenced by a second landform known as the Puskwaskau Hills (S Peace Reg. Plan. Commis. and ID No. 16 1984). Except for steeper terrain north of the lake, most of the land is gently rolling (Alta. For. Ld. Wild. 1987[b]). Elevations range from 884 m above sea level at the northern tip of the drainage basin to 777 m at the southern tip and 678 m at

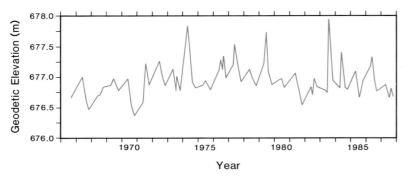

Figure 3. Water level of Sturgeon Lake, 1966 to 1987. Full supply level applicable as of 1970.

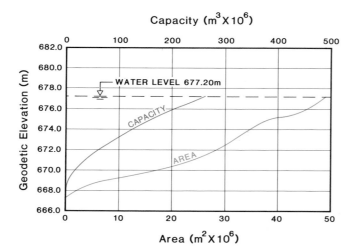

Figure 4. Area/capacity curve for Sturgeon Lake.
SOURCE: Alta. Envir. n.d.[c].

Table 1. Characteristics of Sturgeon Lake drainage basin.

area (excluding lake) (km²)[a]	571
soil[b]	Gleyed, Orthic and Solonetzic Gray Luvisols
bedrock geology[c]	Wapiti Formation (Upper Cretaceous): sandstone, mudstone, bentonite, scattered coal beds; nonmarine
terrain[d]	level and undulating to gently rolling
ecoregion[e]	Dry Mixedwood Subregion of Boreal Mixedwood
dominant vegetation[e]	trembling aspen
mean annual inflow (m³)[a, f]	46.5 x 10⁶
mean annual sunshine (h)[g]	2060

NOTE: [f]excluding groundwater inflow
SOURCES: [a]Alta. Envir. n.d.[b]; [b]Alta. En. Nat. Resour. 1983; [c]Alta. Res. Counc. 1972; [d]S Peace Reg. Plan. Commis. and ID No. 16 1984; [e]Strong and Leggat 1981; [g]Envir. Can. 1982

Table 2. Characteristics of Sturgeon Lake.

elevation (m)[a, b]	677.20
surface area (km²)[a, b]	49.1
volume (m³)[a, b]	266 x 10⁶
maximum depth (m)[a, b]	9.5
mean depth (m)[a, b]	5.4
shoreline length (km)[c, d]	45.2
mean annual lake evaporation (mm)[e]	616
mean annual precipitation (mm)[e]	517
mean residence time (yr)[e, f]	6.5
control structure[g]	fixed-crest weir with step-pool fish ladder
crest elevation (m)[h]	676.87
crest length (m)[g]	21.34

NOTES: [a]on date of sounding: Oct. 1983; [d]includes 1.2 km for islands; [f]excluding groundwater inflow
SOURCES: [b]Alta. Envir. n.d.[c]; [c]En. Mines Resour. Can. 1974; 1979; [e]Alta. Envir. n.d.[b]; [g]Taggart 1982; [h]Lowe and Taggart 1987

Sturgeon Lake. The watershed is underlain by the nonmarine sandstone and shale bedrock of the Wapiti Formation. Underneath this formation lies a sequence of marine shales and sandstones known as the Smoky River Group.

The main soils in the drainage basin are imperfectly drained clay loam to clay textured Gleyed Gray Luvisols and moderately well-drained loam to clay loam textured Orthic and Solonetzic Gray Luvisols. The Gleyed Gray Luvisols have developed on lacustro-till and are found on the lower slopes of the till plain and in basins and valleys adjacent to stream courses. These soils support a forest cover of trembling aspen, balsam poplar, white spruce, willow, alder, birch and shrubs. The Orthic and Solonetzic Gray Luvisols have developed on glacial till, and are found on the upper and midslope positions of the landscape. These soils support a forest cover of trembling aspen, white spruce, lodgepole pine, birch and various shrubs (Odynsky et al. 1956). Over 20% of the surficial deposits in the watershed are Organics (Mallandaine 1980), which support a cover of *Sphagnum* moss, occasional sedges, Labrador tea, cranberry, and stands of black spruce, tamarack, birch and willow (Odynsky et al. 1956).

Most of the drainage basin is forested, but large areas near the west bay of the lake and along the eastern boundary of the watershed have been cleared for agricultural use, including the Valleyview Provincial Grazing Reserve (Fig. 1). The crops are mainly cereal grains and oil seeds, and secondarily, forage crops such as hay (S Peace Reg. Plan. Commis. and ID No. 16 1984).

Since the early 1970s, Sturgeon Lake has been the subject of a number of land-use planning studies (Alta. En. Nat. Resour. 1971; 1983; Peace R. Reg. Plan. Commis. 1975[a]; 1975[b]; 1979; S Peace Reg. Plan. Commis. and ID No. 16 1984; 1985; Alta. For. Ld. Wild. 1987[b]). In 1977, development around Sturgeon Lake was restricted when the provincial government passed the Lake Shoreland Development Operation Regulations, which were administered by Alberta Environment. These regulations required future lakeshore developments to conform to a lake management plan and an area structure plan. Lake management plans determine the extent of future land developments, allocate land use, and determine ways to minimize environmental impacts and conflicts in the use of the lakeshore. In 1979, the lake management plan was completed and adopted by Improvement District No. 16. It was updated in 1985 when the improvement district completed an area structure plan, which guides development around the lake. In 1987, the provincial government prepared the Sturgeon Lake-Puskwaskau East Sub-regional Integrated Resource Plan (Alta. For. Ld. Wild. 1987[b]). This document presents the government's resource management policy for public lands and resources within the area.

The main group of permanent residents living around Sturgeon Lake belong to the Sturgeon Lake Indian Band. Members, who are descended from Woodland Cree, numbered 895 in 1986 (Alta. For. Ld. Wild 1987[b]). The Sturgeon Lake Reserve covers 9091 ha and comprises three areas: 154 and 154A on Sturgeon Lake, and 154B on Goose Lake (Fig. 1). The portion of the band living near Sturgeon Lake, together with the Métis living in the Sturgeon Lake Settlement, made up 88% of the 600 permanent residents living around the lake in 1984 (S Peace Reg. Plan. Commis. and ID No. 16 1984). Local farmers, most of whom live around the west bay, and private landowners account for the remainder of the permanent residents. Residential developments on the lakeshore consist of three cottage subdivisions: Boyd Lakeshore Properties, on the western shore of the main basin; The Narrows, on the southern shore at the entrance to the west basin; and Sandy Bay, immediately west of Reserve 154A. In 1987, these subdivisions had a combined total of 164 approved

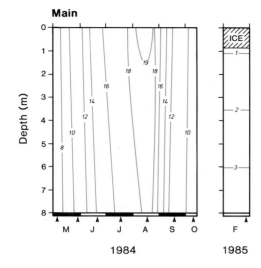

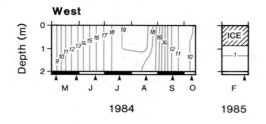

Figure 5. Temperature (°C) of Sturgeon Lake, main and west basins, 1984 and 1985. Arrows indicate sampling dates.
SOURCE: Alta. Envir. n.d.[a].

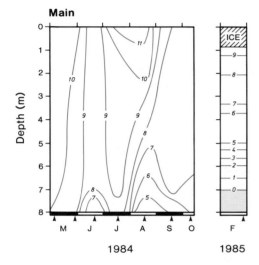

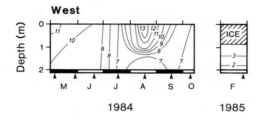

Figure 6. Dissolved oxygen (mg/L) in Sturgeon Lake, main and west basins, 1984 and 1985. Arrows indicate sampling dates.
SOURCE: Alta. Envir. n.d.[a].

and surveyed lots, on which 125 cottages and mobile homes had been built (Alta. For. Ld. Wild. 1987[b]).

Lake Basin Characteristics

Sturgeon Lake has a large surface area (Table 2). It is divided into a main basin, with a maximum depth of 9.5 m, and a long, narrow bay at the western end, which has a maximum depth of 3 m (Fig. 2). Two control structures have been built on the lake's outlet. The first was a rock-filled log crib constructed by Ducks Unlimited (Canada) in 1949. The weir raised the lake's elevation by about 0.76 m, to approximately 677 m. Construction of a new weir began in 1968 and was completed in late 1969 (Taggart 1982). The crest elevation of the new concrete weir was 676.87 m, approximately 0.13 m lower than the original weir (Lowe and Taggart 1987). The new design incorporated a step-pool fish ladder with five steps and four resting areas, and a gate for riparian flow (Bishop 1971). The gate ensured an adequate supply of water to the town of Valleyview, which uses Sturgeon Creek as a water source.

The elevation of Sturgeon Lake has been monitored since 1966 (Fig. 3). Over the period of record, the maximum range in lake levels was 1.58 m. Between 1966 and 1981, the average annual fluctuation was 0.43 m, which is a very narrow band (Taggart 1982). During the mid–1980s, Alberta Environment studied the feasibility of reducing the maximum range of elevations by modifying the control structure, but they concluded that the existing structure provided adequate protection from both the upper and lower extremes of lake level fluctuations (Taggart 1982; Lowe and Taggart 1987). Figure 4 illustrates changes in the lake's area and capacity with fluctuations in water level.

Water Quality

A researcher at the University of Alberta examined Sturgeon Lake's water quality during the summer of 1978 (Mallandaine 1980). During 1983 and since 1986, the lake has been monitored jointly by Alberta Environment and Alberta Recreation and Parks. As well, in 1984 and 1985, it was sampled by Alberta Environment as part of a two-year lake survey program (Alta. Envir. n.d.[a]; Mitchell 1986).

The major ions and related water quality variables in the main and west basins are very similar: the alkalinity, concentration of total dissolved solids, and total hardness are low for a prairie lake and the main ions are calcium and bicarbonate (Table 3). The water is highly coloured and not very turbid (4 to 6 NTU).

Both basins are shallow and well-mixed during summer; thus, temperature profiles in 1984 were uniform from top to bottom (Fig. 5). Despite the mixing, there was a gradual depletion of dissolved oxygen in deeper water over summer (Fig. 6). During some winters, as in February 1985, the bottom water in the main basin becomes anoxic. Although there is usually sufficient oxygen in the upper layers of this basin to sustain fish, winterkills occurred in 1976 and 1977. In the west basin in February 1985, the concentration of dissolved oxygen was very low at all depths (Fig. 6).

Sturgeon Lake is hyper-eutrophic, and is one of the most productive lakes in Alberta. The shallower west basin has a slightly higher average concentration of total phosphorus than the main basin (Table 4). Over a four-year period from 1983 to 1986, the average concentration of chlorophyll *a* was 34 mg/L in the west basin and 27 mg/L in the main basin. Chlorophyll *a* concentrations can vary considerably between years. In 1984 (Table 4), chlorophyll *a* levels were the highest of all years sampled. Variations between years may

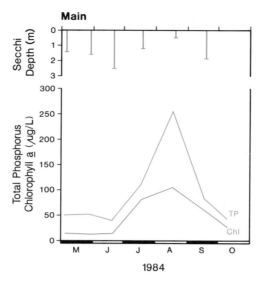
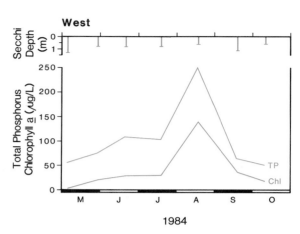

Figure 7. Total phosphorus, chlorophyll *a* and Secchi depth in Sturgeon Lake, main and west basins, 1984.
SOURCE: Alta. Envir. n.d.[a].

Table 3. Major ions and related water quality variables for Sturgeon Lake, main basin. Average concentrations in mg/L; pH in pH units. Composite samples from the euphotic zone collected 7 times from 4 May to 10 Oct. 1984. S.E. = standard error.

	Mean	S.E.
pH (range)	7.2–9.2	—
total alkalinity (CaCO₃)	68	1.1
specific conductivity (μS/cm)	158	1.3
total dissolved solids (calculated)	78	0.8
total hardness (CaCO₃)	54	0.8
total particulate carbon	3	0.9
dissolved organic carbon	17	0.6
HCO₃	80	2.8
CO₃	<2	—
Mg	4	0.2
Na	<6	—
K	3	0.1
Cl	<1	—
SO₄	8	0.4
Ca	15	0.2

SOURCE: Alta. Envir. n.d.[a], Naquadat station 01AL07GH2091

Table 4. Nutrient, chlorophyll *a* and Secchi depth data for Sturgeon Lake, main and west basins. Average concentrations in μg/L. Composite samples from the euphotic zone collected 7 times from 4 May to 10 Oct. 1984. S.E. = standard error.

	Main		West	
	Mean	S.E.	Mean	S.E.
total phosphorus	92	29.2	103	26.0
total dissolved phosphorus	—	—	26[a]	3.2
total Kjeldahl nitrogen	1 404	261.9	1 484	148.6
NO₃ + NO₂–nitrogen	<4	—	6	2.2
NH₄–nitrogen	19	5.2	20	5.1
iron	157	33.1	307	68.2
chlorophyll *a*	45.2	14.12	38.8	8.74
Secchi depth (m)	1.6	0.25	0.8	0.10

NOTE: [a]n = 6
SOURCE: Alta. Envir. n.d.[a], Naquadat stations 01AL07GH2091 (main), 01AL07GH2092 (west)

Table 5. Theoretical total phosphorus loading to Sturgeon Lake from external sources.

Source		Phosphorus (kg/yr)	Percentage of Total
immediate watershed	forested/bush	2 670	40
	agricultural/cleared	2 000	30
	residential/cottage	176	3
sewage[a]		6	<1
precipitation		1 400	21
inflow from other lakes		480	7
	TOTAL	6 732	101

annual areal loading (g/m² of lake surface) 0.14

NOTE: [a]unmeasured: assumes 4% of all sewage effluent from residences and camps enters the lake, as in Mitchell 1982
SOURCE: Mitchell 1988

be caused by year-to-year differences in weather conditions, and the intervals between, and timing of, sample collections.

Over the ice-free period, phosphorus and chlorophyll *a* in Sturgeon Lake are generally lowest in May and June, increase dramatically during July and August, and then decline in September (Fig. 7). Although this pattern is typical of many lakes in Alberta, it is more pronounced in Sturgeon Lake. The seasonal patterns in the two basins are similar, except that the chlorophyll *a* maximum usually occurs earlier in the west basin. This is probably because water in the west basin warms faster than in the main basin. In 1984, chlorophyll *a* levels throughout the lake were highest in August.

The supply of total phosphorus to Sturgeon Lake from various sources has been estimated. External sources such as runoff from the watershed, sewage inputs, atmospheric deposits and inflow from upstream lakes provide about 6 732 kg of total phosphorus to the lake each year (Table 5). The major source of phosphorus, however, is internal. Phosphorus release from the sediments is estimated to be 59 000 kg/year, which is 9 times the estimated load from external sources. Much of the internal loading occurs during July and August. This released phosphorus stimulates the growth of algae and results in intense algal blooms.

The effects of further agricultural development in the watershed on water quality in Sturgeon Lake were studied in 1985 (Stanley Assoc. Eng. Ltd. 1985). The study provided a data base for the Sturgeon Lake-Puskwaskau East Integrated Resource Plan. Nutrient loadings to the lake were estimated under four scenarios that included various amounts and types of agricultural development. It was

Sturgeon Lake 119

Table 6. Percentage composition of major algal groups by total biomass in Sturgeon Lake, main and west basins, 1984. Composite samples collected from the euphotic zone.

ALGAL GROUP	3 May	28 May	28 June	18 July	15 Aug.	18 Sep.	10 Oct.
Main							
Total Biomass (mg/L)	4.22	3.68	1.82	5.47	35.69	10.03	2.86
Percentage Composition:							
Cyanophyta	0	5	43	38	99	94	16
		Anabaena ———→		*Aphanizomenon* ———————→			
Chlorophyta	12	6	10	2	0	0	6
Chrysophyta	5	14	0	0	0	0	0
Bacillariophyta	78	72	17	50	0	3	67
	Stephanodiscus ———————————→			*Melosira*			*Stephanodiscus*
	Melosira ———→						
Cryptophyta	4	2	25	3	0	3	10
			Cryptomonas				
Pyrrhophyta	0	1	5	7	0	0	0
West							
Total Biomass (mg/L)	1.54	11.96	8.12	28.45	13.15	5.02	7.97
Percentage Composition:							
Cyanophyta	12	20	53	79	54	40	31
		Anabaena —————————→		*Microcystis Anabaena*			*Aphanizomenon*
Chlorophyta	28	9	27	11	23	33	16
		Koliella	*Oocystis/Tetraspora* —→		*Staurastrum Scenedesmus/Monoraphidium*		
Euglenophyta	0	5	0	0	0	0	0
Xanthophyta	1	0	0	0	1	2	0
Chrysophyta	23	2	0	0	1	13	30
	Dinobryon						*Chrysochromulina*
Bacillariophyta	35	64	14	7	18	11	14
	Asterionella	*Melosira*					
Cryptophyta	1	0	6	2	2	2	8
Pyrrhophyta	0	0	0	1	1	0	0

SOURCE: Alta. Envir. n.d.[a]

not possible to predict the effect of land-use changes on water quality because internal loading of phosphorus may have an overriding effect.

Biological Characteristics

Plants

The phytoplankton community in Sturgeon Lake was sampled monthly by Alberta Environment during the ice-free period in 1984 and 1985 and in February and July of 1986 (Alta. Envir. n.d.[a]). In 1984 (Table 6), the average biomass in both basins was similar: 9.11 mg/L in the main basin and 10.89 mg/L in the west basin. The highest biomass recorded in the main basin (35.69 mg/L), however, was higher than that recorded in the west basin (28.45 mg/L). In May 1984, the dominant group in both basins was diatoms (Bacillariophyta). The most important diatoms in the main basin during May were *Stephanodiscus hantzschia, S. niagarae* and *Melosira italica subarctica*. In the west bay, the diatom *Asterionella formosa* was dominant in early May and *M. italica subarctica* became dominant later in the month. By June, blue-greens (Cyanophyta) were the largest group. In both basins, the blue-greens *Anabaena flos-aquae, Anabaena spiroides crassa* and *Aphanizomenon flos-aquae* were important at various times throughout the summer and early fall. As well, in the west bay during August, a large part of the biomass was composed of *Microcystis aeruginosa*. By October, the diatom *S. niagarae* had regained its earlier importance in the main basin, and the golden-brown alga (Chrysophyta) *Chrysochromulina breviturri-* ta was codominant with the blue-green *Aphanizomenon flos-aquae* in the west basin.

There are no detailed data available for the aquatic macrophytes in Sturgeon Lake. A band of vegetation with an approximate width of 90 to 250 m completely circles the lake's shoreline. Emergent vegetation grows mainly along the eastern shore of the main basin, the channel into the western bay, and the area east of Williamson Provincial Park. Floating vegetation is most abundant along the western and northern shores of the west bay, and along the western shore of Young's Point. Submergent vegetation is ubiquitous and it is especially abundant in shallow areas and at the mouths of creeks (Peace R. Reg. Plan. Commis. 1975[a]).

Invertebrates

Fish and Wildlife Division determined the relative abundance of zooplankton in the deepest part of Sturgeon Lake between June 1969 and April 1970 (Bishop 1971). The most abundant cladocerans were Chydoridae in October and *Daphnia* spp. throughout the sampling period. Unspecified cyclopoid copepods were present on all but one sampling date and were most abundant from October through April.

Benthic invertebrates were collected in 28 dredge samples taken from 5 depth zones in 1969 and 1970 (Bishop 1971). Midge larvae (Chironomidae), which were the largest group, accounted for 74% of the total number/m². The most important genus was *Tendipes*. Aquatic earthworms (Oligochaeta) were the next largest group (15%). The remaining 11% of the samples comprised phantom

Table 7. Estimated angler numbers, effort, catch and harvest from Sturgeon Lake. Estimates based on creel survey data collected from 01 May to 31 Aug. 1984. WE = walleye; NP = northern pike; YP = yellow perch.

	WE	NP	YP	Combined
number of anglers	—	—	—	35 130
angler-hours	—	—	—	41 953
total number fish caught	17 587	11 969	2 186	31 742
total number fish harvested	15 951	10 073	1 871	27 895
total yield (kg)	10 714	12 930	602	24 246
mean weight (g)	671	1 284	322	2 276
catch/angler-hour	0.42	0.28	0.05	0.76
catch/angler	0.50	0.34	0.06	0.90

SOURCE: Buchwald 1985

midge larvae (Chaoborinae), snails (Gastropoda), scuds (Amphipoda), leeches (Hirudinea), clams (Pelecypoda) and unidentified organisms. The average wet weight (g/m^2) for each 2–m depth zone was determined. The highest biomass (71.7 g/m^2) was present at depths of 2 to 4 m, and the lowest biomass (20.6 g/m^2) at depths of 0 to 2 m. The standing crop was estimated to be 66.8 kg/ha wet weight. This figure is similar to those determined for other northern eutrophic lakes such as Big Peter Pond, Saskatchewan, and Lac La Biche, Alberta (Bishop 1971).

Fish

Sturgeon Lake is one of the most important fishing lakes in the Peace River area. It is managed for commercial, domestic and sport fisheries. Ten species of fish from the lake have been identified: northern pike, walleye, yellow perch, lake whitefish, burbot, Arctic grayling, trout-perch, white sucker, longnose sucker and spottail shiner. The west basin and Goose Creek are important fish spawning areas, primarily for walleye (S Peace Reg. Plan. Commis. and ID No. 16 1984). Whitefish spawning grounds are mainly located along the eastern shore, and secondarily along the northern shore. Whitefish spawning takes place under ice in late December (Walty 1980).

Sturgeon Lake maintains an important commercial lake whitefish fishery. Other species taken are northern pike and walleye, but they account for less than 1% of the total catch. Between 1943/44 and 1984/85, the annual commercial whitefish harvest fluctuated between a low of 7 300 kg in 1945/46 and a high of 39 700 kg in 1962/63 (Alta. For. Ld. Wild. n.d.; Alta. Rec. Parks Wild. 1976). During the 1940s and early 1950s, the whitefish harvest remained quite stable, but during the late 1950s and early 1960s, it increased rapidly to the 1962/63 high. From that season to 1969/70, the annual harvest gradually declined. The whitefish quota was lowered from 22 727 kg to 18 181 kg in 1969, and to 13 600 kg in 1980. By 1988, however, the quota had increased to 28 000 kg (Walty 1988). The lake whitefish catch in 1987/88 was 33 305 kg. During the 1970s and 1980s, the number of licences issued increased sharply, from 12 to 14 during the 1960s, to 91 to 133 during the 1980s.

Studies of the whitefish population conducted during 1977 and 1978 concluded that growth rates had declined since 1969 (Bishop 1971; Walty 1979; 1980). In 1972/73, the mean length, weight and age of maturation of the whitefish population began to change. The mean length of whitefish in the commercial catch declined sharply in 1972 and 1973 and then stabilized after 1973. Mean weight also declined sharply over those two years and then continued to decline gradually until, by 1979, it was almost half the 1969 value. Age of maturation increased from age 3 in 1969 to age 5 in 1978 and catch per unit effort declined. Prior to 1973, age classes 5 to 13 were well represented in commercial catches. In 1974, age classes greater than 10 and fish of lengths greater than 50 cm disappeared from the fishery. Between 1974 and 1978, the commercial catch became increasingly dependent on age classes 8 and 9, but by 1988, the catch was dominated by age classes 9 to 11 (Walty 1979; 1988). As

well, the mean age increased from 6.7 years in 1974 to 9.4 years in 1988 (Schroeder 1989).

A creel survey was conducted on Sturgeon Lake by Fish and Wildlife Division from 1 May to 31 August 1984 (Buchwald 1985). Over this period, an estimated 35 130 anglers spent 41 953 hours fishing (Table 7), which is an increase over the average angling reported in a 1976 survey (Bishop 1977). Most anglers (46%) in 1984 came from Grande Prairie; 40% came from elsewhere in the Peace Country. Walleye were the preferred catch: 55% of the total number of fish caught were walleye, 38% were northern pike and 7% were yellow perch. Only 9% of the walleye, 16% of the northern pike and 14% of the yellow perch caught were released. Fishing success, in terms of both catch rate and total numbers, was greatest for northern pike in May and for walleye and perch in June.

Wildlife

A total of 81 bird species were identified in a 1976 survey of Sturgeon Lake (S Peace Reg. Plan. Commis. and ID No. 16 1984). More recently, 159 species were identified in Young's Point Provincial Park; 73 of these species nest there (Finlay and Finlay 1987). Eighteen species of warblers breed in the park; they include Canada, Palm, Magnolia, Cape May, Black-throated Green and Bay-breasted warblers. Other special birds that have been sighted include Great Gray and Barred Owls, Bald Eagles, Cinnamon Teal, Greater Scaup, Hooded Mergansers, Surf Scoters and Western and Solitary Sandpipers (Finlay and Finlay 1987). As well, Red-necked Grebes nest on floating water lilies, mainly in the west bay (S Peace Reg. Plan. Commis. and ID No. 16 1984).

The west bay and northern shore provide habitat for moose, deer and bears. Beaver, muskrats and mink are the most common small fur bearers in the area. Coyotes, lynx and fishers are present, but less common (S Peace Reg. Plan. Commis. and ID No. 16 1984).

M.E. Bradford

References

Alberta Culture and Multiculturalism. n.d. Hist. Resour. Div., Hist. Sites Serv. Unpubl. data, Edmonton.

Alberta Energy and Natural Resources. 1971. Land use plan Puskwaskau East. Alta. En. Nat. Resour., Edmonton.

———. 1983. Ecological land classification and evaluation, Sturgeon Lake-Puskwaskau East. Resour. Eval. Plan. Div., Resour. Eval. Br., Edmonton.

Alberta Environment. n.d.[a]. Envir. Assess. Div., Envir. Qlty. Monit. Br. Unpubl. data, Edmonton.

———. n.d.[b]. Tech. Serv. Div., Hydrol. Br. Unpubl. data, Edmonton.

———. n.d.[c]. Tech. Serv. Div., Surv. Br. Unpubl. data, Edmonton.

Alberta Forestry, Lands and Wildlife. n.d. Fish Wild. Div. Unpubl. data, Edmonton.

———. 1987[a]. A summary of Alberta's natural areas reserved and established. Pub. Ld. Div., Ld. Mgt. Devel. Br. Unpubl. rep., Edmonton.

———. 1987[b]. Sturgeon Lake-Puskwaskau East sub-regional integrated resource plan. Resour. Eval. Plan. Div., Edmonton.

———. 1988. Boating in Alberta. Fish Wild. Div., Edmonton.

———. 1989. Guide to sportfishing. Fish Wild. Div., Edmonton.

Alberta Recreation and Parks. n.d. Parks Div. Unpubl. data, Edmonton.

Alberta Recreation, Parks and Wildlife. 1976. Commercial fisheries catch statistics for Alberta, 1942–1975. Fish Wild. Div., Fish. Mgt. Rep. No. 22, Edmonton.

Alberta Research Council. 1972. Geological map of Alberta. Nat. Resour. Div., Alta. Geol. Surv., Edmonton.

Bishop, F.G. 1971. Limnology and fisheries of Sturgeon Lake, Alberta 1969–1970. Alta. Ld. For., Fish Wild. Div., Peace River.

———. 1977. Sturgeon Lake creel census and biological survey program—summer, 1976. Alta. Rec. Parks Wild., Fish Wild. Div. Unpubl. rep., Edmonton.

Buchwald, V.G. 1985. Sturgeon Lake—1984 summer creel and boating survey. Alta. En. Nat. Resour., Fish Wild. Div. Unpubl. rep., Slave Lake.

Energy, Mines and Resources Canada. 1974, 1977, 1979. National topographic series 1:50000 83N/3 (1974), 83K/14 (1977), 83K/13 (1979), 83N/4 (1979). Surv. Map. Br., Ottawa.

Environment Canada. 1966–1987. Surface water data. Prep. by Inland Waters Directorate. Water Surv. Can., Water Resour. Br., Ottawa.

———. 1982. Canadian climate normals, Vol. 7: Bright sunshine (1951–1980). Prep. by Atm. Envir. Serv. Supply Serv. Can., Ottawa.

Finlay, J. and C. Finlay. 1987. Parks in Alberta: A guide to peaks, ponds, parklands & prairies. Hurtig Publ., Edmonton.

Lowe, S.A. and J.H. Taggart. 1987. Sturgeon Lake outlet analysis. Alta. Envir., Tech. Serv. Div., Edmonton.

Mallandaine, A.P. 1980. The effect of land uses on lake water quality—Sturgeon Lake, Alberta. MSc thesis. Univ. Alta., Edmonton.

Mitchell, P.A. 1982. Evaluation of the "septic snooper" on Wabamun and Pigeon lakes. Alta. Envir., Poll. Contr. Div., Water Qlty. Contr. Br., Edmonton.

———. 1986. Water quality in Alberta's provincial park lakes: Sturgeon Lake. Alta. Envir., Poll. Contr. Div., Water Qlty. Contr. Br. Unpubl. rep., Edmonton.

———. 1988. Alta. Envir., Envir. Assess. Div., Envir. Qlty. Monit. Br., Edmonton. Pers. comm.

Odynsky, W., A. Wynnyk and J.D. Newton. 1956. Reconnaissance soil survey of the Grande Prairie and Sturgeon Lake sheets. Alta. Soil Surv. Rep. No. 18, Res. Counc. Alta. Rep. No. 74, Univ. Alta. Bull. No. 60. Univ. Alta., Edmonton.

Peace River Regional Planning Commission. 1975[a]. Sturgeon Lake planning study, technical working paper no. 1: Shoreland biophysical field survey, preliminary results. Peace R. Reg. Plan. Commis., Grande Prairie.

———. 1975[b]. Sturgeon Lake planning study: Interim and progress report. Peace R. Reg. Plan. Commis., Grande Prairie.

———. 1979. Sturgeon Lake management Plan. Peace R. Reg. Plan. Commis., Grande Prairie.

Schroeder, D. 1989. Alta. For. Ld. Wild., Fish Wild. Div., Peace River. Pers. comm.

South Peace Regional Planning Commission and Improvement District No. 16. 1984. Sturgeon Lake area structure plan background study. S Peace Reg. Plan. Commis. and ID No. 16, Grande Prairie.

———. 1985. Sturgeon Lake area structure plan. S Peace Reg. Plan. Commis. and ID No. 16, Grande Prairie.

Stanley Associates Engineering Ltd. 1985. Sturgeon Lake water quality study, Vol. 1 and 2. Prep. for Alta. Envir., Plan. Div., Edmonton.

Strong, W.L. and K.R. Leggat. 1981. Ecoregions of Alberta. Alta. En. Nat. Resour., Resour. Eval. Plan. Div., Edmonton.

Taggart, J.H. 1982. Sturgeon Lake hydrologic analysis. Alta. Envir., Tech. Serv. Div., Hydrol. Br., Edmonton.

Walty, D.T. 1979. Population dynamics of the commercial and sportfish populations of Sturgeon Lake 1977–78. Alta. En. Nat. Resour., Fish Wild. Div. Unpubl. rep., Edmonton.

———. 1980. Population dynamics and biology of the Sturgeon Lake whitefish, 1969–1979. Alta. En. Nat. Resour., Fish Wild. Div. Unpubl. rep., Peace River.

———. 1988. Alta. For. Ld. Wild., Fish Wild. Div., Peace River. Pers. comm.

BAPTISTE LAKE

F. Schulte

MAP SHEETS: 83I/12, 13

LOCATION: Tp66, 67 R24 W4

LAT/LONG: 54°45'N 113°33'W

Baptiste Lake is a very productive, moderate-sized lake located within the County of Athabasca in central Alberta. It has two distinct basins joined by a long neck, called the Narrows. The basins are of similar size; the north basin is shallow (16 m), whereas the south basin is deep (28 m). The lake is situated 165 km northwest of the city of Edmonton and 16 km west of the town of Athabasca. To reach the lake, take Highway 2 west from Athabasca and then follow a local access road around the south end of the lake (Fig. 1) to the public boat launch on the southwest corner.

The lake was named after Baptiste Majeau, an early settler in the area (Holmgren and Holmgren 1976). The first permanent native settlement on Baptiste Lake was established in the 1880s by a group of Métis from Saskatchewan. They lived on long, narrow lake-front lots. By 1904 farming had begun in the drainage basin, and by 1909 most of the land that was not already settled was available for homesteaders (Athabasca Hist. Soc. et al. 1986). Much of the present agricultural land was broken first in the period up to 1915 (Stone 1970).

Although most of the drainage basin, particularly the western section, remains undeveloped, much of the land immediately surrounding the lake is cleared. There are three private campgrounds and five summer villages on the lake. The summer villages of Sunset Beach, South Baptiste and West Baptiste can be reached from the gravel road that goes around the south end of the lake (Fig. 2). The summer village of White Gull, located at the north end of the lake, can be reached either from the ring road that goes around the south and west sides of the lake, or from a separate exit directly off Highway 2, at the north end of the lake. The summer village of Whispering Hills, located on the east side of the Narrows, has a separate exit from Highway 2. The road used to reach it is not connected to the ring road. The community centre of Grosmont Hall is located at the north end of the lake (Alta. Mun. Aff. 1979[b]). Three privately owned campgrounds offer cabin accommodation, camp and trailer sites, beach and boat launch facilities. They are all located on the south shore of the lake.

The lake is used extensively for fishing, boating and swimming. The public boat launch on the southwest corner is part of a day-use area operated by the County of Athabasca. The area includes a large dock, washrooms, and a picnic shelter and tables. Popular sport fish in Baptiste Lake include yellow perch, northern pike and walleye. To protect spawning sites, the tributary streams to and the outlet stream from the lake are closed to fishing during a designated period in spring (Alta. For. Ld. Wild. 1989). The water quality reflects the nutrient-rich soils in the drainage basin: very dense algal blooms can develop in summer. The shallower north basin generally has denser blooms than the deeper south basin.

In the early 1970s, concerns were raised about the effects of rapid development on the many users of the lake and on aspects of water quality. These concerns were followed up in 1975 with a cottagers' evaluation of lake conditions (Thomas et al. 1977). In 1977, development around Baptiste Lake was restricted when the lake was placed under the jurisdiction of the Regulated Lake Shoreland Development Operation Regulations which were administered by Alberta Environment. From 1976 through 1979 Alberta Environment carried out an intensive water quality study of the lake. The goals of this project were to develop methods for evaluating the impacts of past, present and future developments, and for managing the water quality of

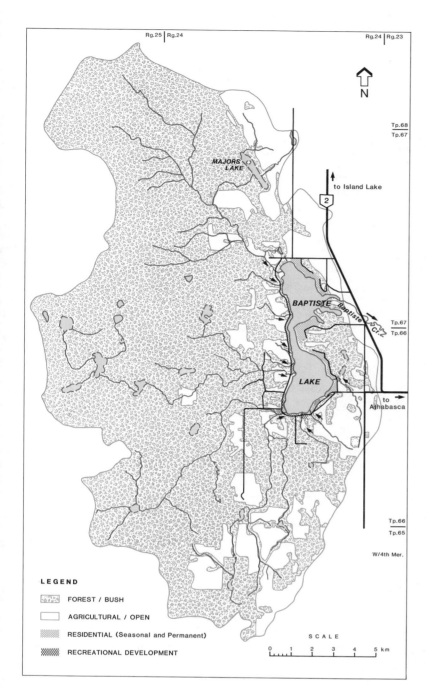

Figure 1. Features of the drainage basin of Baptiste Lake.
SOURCES: Alta. Envir. n.d.[b]; En. Mines Resour. Can. 1973. Updated with 1985 and 1987 aerial photos.

Table 1. Characteristics of Baptiste Lake drainage basin.

area (excluding lake) (km²)[a]	288
soil[b]	Orthic Gray Luvisol with some Organics, Eluviated Black Chernozemics
bedrock geology[c]	La Biche Formation (Upper Cretaceous): shale, ironstone partings and concretions; marine Wapiti Formation (Upper Cretaceous): sandstone, mudstone, bentonite, scattered coal beds; nonmarine
terrain[b]	depressional to moderately rolling
ecoregion[d]	Moist Mixedwood Subregion of Boreal Mixedwood
dominant vegetation[d]	trembling aspen, balsam poplar
mean annual inflow (m³)[a, e]	15.9 x 10⁶
mean annual sunshine (h)[f]	2 160

NOTE: [e]excluding groundwater inflow
SOURCES: [a]Alta. Envir. n.d.[b]; [b]Kjearsgaard 1972; [c]Alta. Res. Counc. 1972; Trew et al. 1987; [d]Strong and Leggat 1981; [f]Envir. Can. 1982

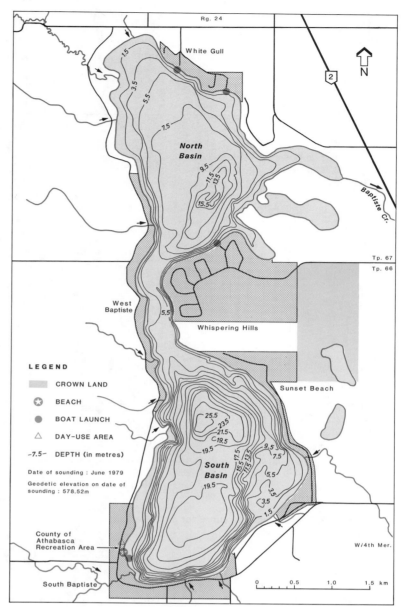

Figure 2. Bathymetry and shoreline features of Baptiste Lake.
BATHYMETRY SOURCE: Alta. Envir. n.d.[c].

Alberta lakes (Trew et al. 1978). In 1977, most lake development was halted while a management plan was developed. In 1979, Alberta Municipal Affairs, in conjunction with the County of Athabasca, developed a plan that would prohibit further subdivision of land for nonfarm-related residential use at Baptiste Lake (Alta. Mun. Aff. 1979[a]). This plan also recommended an approach to deal with concerns about fluctuating water levels and hazardous boating speeds near the lakeshore. As of August 1989, no regulations had been implemented to deal with the concerns on water levels and boating speeds. However, federal boating regulations apply here, as elsewhere in the province (Alta. For. Ld. Wild. 1988).

Drainage Basin Characteristics

The drainage basin is described in detail by Trew et al. (1987); much of the following description is condensed from that report (also see Table 1).

Baptiste Lake is a headwater lake with 12 tributary streams, which flow mainly into the western and southern shores. The outlet stream, Baptiste Creek, flows from the northeast side of the lake into the Athabasca River (Fig. 1). The 12 streams drain 92% of the Baptiste watershed; the remaining 8% drains directly to the lake by way of diffuse runoff. In 1977, 58% of the watershed was forested; the dominant tree species were black spruce, trembling aspen, balsam poplar, willow and birch. Sixteen percent of the watershed was

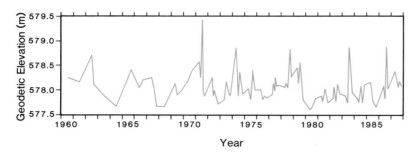

Figure 3. Water level of Baptiste Lake, 1960 to 1987.
SOURCE: Alta. Envir. n.d.[c].

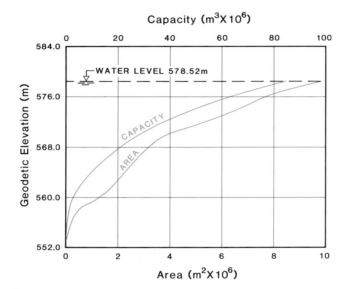

Figure 4. Area/capacity curve for Baptiste Lake.
SOURCE: Alta. Envir. n.d.[c].

Table 2. Characteristics of Baptiste Lake.

	Total	North Basin	South Basin
elevation (m)[a, b]	578.52	—	—
surface area (km²)[a, b]	9.81	5.07[d]	4.74[d]
volume (m³)[a, b]	84.6 x 10⁶	28.1 x 10⁶ᵈ	56.5 x 10⁶ᵈ
maximum depth (m)[c]	27.5	15.5	27.5
mean depth (m)[a, b]	8.6	5.6	11.9
shoreline length (km)[c]	26.4	—	—
mean annual lake evaporation (mm)[d]	638	—	—
mean annual precipitation (mm)[d]	493	—	—
mean residence time (yr)[e]	6	—	—
control structure	none		

NOTES: [a]on date of sounding: June 1979; [e]excluding groundwater inflow
SOURCES: [b]Alta. Envir. n.d.[c]; [c]Trew et al. 1987; [d]Alta. Envir. n.d.[b].

mer. In 1977, there were 310 cottages and 15 permanent residences on the lake, but half of the cottages were used year-round. Over 100 of the cottages were built before 1966 and 20% were locally owned (Thomas et al. 1977). An equal number of registered lots had not yet been developed (Alta. Mun. Aff. 1979[a]). By 1988, there were approximately 420 cottages on the lake, of which 14% were permanent dwellings.

Lake Basin Characteristics

Baptiste Lake has two moderate-sized basins connected by a shallow channel, the Narrows, which has a maximum depth of 5.5 m (Fig. 2). The shallower northern basin is generally less than 8.5–m deep in the western section and has a small, relatively deep hole, maximum depth 15.5 m, in the eastern section. There are three long, shallow bays on the eastern side of the north basin; the most northerly of these forms the channel to the lake outflow. The south basin, with the exception of a small shelf on the most easterly section, has steep sides throughout and three areas near the centre that are more than 20–m deep.

Water levels have been recorded on Baptiste Lake since 1960 (Fig. 3). During this period, long-term average water levels have been relatively constant, although there have been substantial short-term fluctuations. The difference between highest and lowest recorded water levels is almost 2 m; the highest level was recorded in 1971, the lowest in 1980. Changes in the lake's area and capacity, to an elevation of 578.52 m, are shown in Figure 4. There are no permanent structures on the lake outflow, although it is dotted with beaver dams, deadfall trees and aquatic plants (Winhold and DeBoer 1987), as are most streams in the region.

Detailed hydrology budgets were prepared for Baptiste Lake from 1976 through 1978 (Trew et al. 1987). The total annual inflow of water varied 2.5–fold over the three years studied. Total inflow contributions were: streams 67%, direct precipitation 18%, groundwater 10% and diffuse runoff 5%. Over the same period, hydraulic losses were estimated at 67% of the total for the outflow, 18% by lake evaporation and 16% by groundwater. Based on these budgets, the water residence time would be 6 years (Table 2).

Patterns of groundwater flow in Baptiste Lake were estimated a second time in 1986 (R. Shaw and Prepas 1989). The 1986 study focused on an area within 100 m of shore. Groundwater flow in the north basin increased with distance from shore, and in the deeper south basin decreased up to a distance of 35 m from shore, then increased for the remainder of the transect. These patterns are unusual, for in many lakes, groundwater flow decreases rapidly with distance from shore. The reverse pattern, observed in Baptiste Lake, is consistent with the view that there is an offshore hydrological connection between the underlying aquifer and lake bottom sedi-

cleared for agriculture, mainly mixed farming and 25% was covered by lakes, ponds and marshes. Less than 1% was developed for country residential use.

The uppermost bedrock unit underlying Baptiste Lake is the Upper Cretaceous La Biche Formation of marine shales. The hills to the west are formed by exposure of the Upper Cretaceous Wapiti Formation of sandstone, mudstone and coal. The lake is situated in a bedrock depression that is part of a preglacial buried bedrock valley, 15 m below the lake bottom. A tributary buried valley trending northwest to southeast converges with the main channel beneath Baptiste Lake (Crowe 1979; Crowe and Schwartz 1981). Groundwater from deep aquifers discharges into Baptiste Lake through the buried valley.

Glacial till, which is the dominant surficial deposit in the watershed, ranges from 30– to 100–m thick. Overlying the till, near the outlet stream and southeast of the lake, are lacustrine deposits, which are thin layers (0.2– to 3.0–m deep) of dark grey, stone-free silt (Dark Gray Luvisols and Organics). Fluvial deposits, which were formed by deposition from running water, are found at the north end of the lake. Soils that have developed in this area include Dark Gray Luvisols, Humic Eluviated Gleysols, Orthic Gray Luvisols and Organics. Aeolian sands (mostly under Degraded Eutric Brunisols and Orthic Gray Luvisols), which are deposited by the wind, are present at the southwest end of the lake. Soils in the western part of the drainage basin are classified as suitable for pasture only; in the immediate vicinity of the lake, soils are variable and their arability rating ranges from poor to good. The soils are generally medium textured and originate from the La Biche Formation (Kjearsgaard 1972).

Most of the shoreline of Baptiste Lake is privately owned. In 1977, 100 people were estimated to be permanent residents of the watershed. Additional people occupy the cottages near the lake in sum-

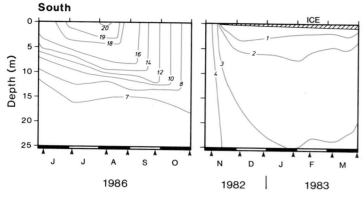

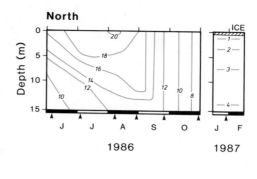

Figure 5. Temperature (°C) of Baptiste Lake, 1986 and 1987 (north basin), and 1982 to 1983 (south basin). Arrows indicate sampling dates.
SOURCES: Prepas et al. n.d.; Alta. Envir. n.d.[a].

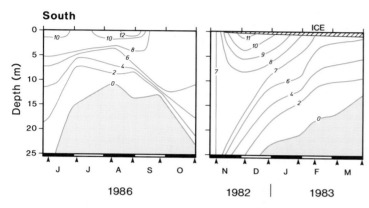

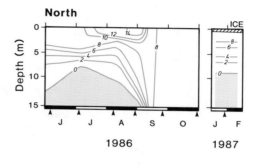

Figure 6. Dissolved oxygen (mg/L) in Baptiste Lake, 1986 and 1987 (north basin), and 1982 to 1983 (south basin). Arrows indicate sampling dates.
SOURCES: Alta. Envir. n.d.[a]; Babin 1984.

ments. In addition, the estimate of groundwater inflow from the 1986 study (11% of the water budget) is remarkably similar to the previous study (Crowe and Schwartz 1981) which used an independent technique.

The sediments of Baptiste Lake were examined with 8–m–long cores collected in 1977 in the deeper part of the south basin (Hickman et al. 1978). Sedimentation rates have averaged 1.8 mm/year over the past 4 600 ^{14}C years (based on dating with the isotope carbon-14). The cores were composed of organic matter for the top 140 cm, laminated clay-organic matter for the next 100 cm, and laminated organic clay plus carbonate bands for the remainder. The diatom and pollen record indicate that Baptiste Lake has undergone little change in the last 4 600 ^{14}C years—it has always been highly productive. There were indications in the record that productivity in the lake increased some 1 500 years ago.

Water Quality

Water quality in Baptiste Lake was studied intensively from 1976 through 1979 by Alberta Environment (Trew et al. 1978; 1987), from 1980 through 1982 by the University of Alberta (Prepas 1983; Prepas and Trew 1983; Babin 1984; Prepas and Vickery 1984; Babin and Prepas 1985), and from 1983 through 1988 by Alberta Environment as part of a long-term monitoring program (Alta. Envir. n.d.[a]; 1989). Sediment chemistry and groundwater patterns were evaluated in 1986 (J. Shaw et al. 1989; J. Shaw and Prepas 1989[a]; 1989[b]; 1989[c]; R. Shaw and Prepas 1989). Baptiste Lake provides an excellent opportunity to follow the long-term dynamics of a naturally hyper-eutrophic lake.

The Alberta Environment study from 1976 to 1979 included a detailed assessment of total phosphorus and nitrogen inputs from streams in the Baptiste watershed. The export coefficients (total input divided by drainage basin area) developed for forested and agricultural lands were 0.14 and 0.27 kg/ha per year, respectively,

for total phosphorus. These figures were similar to coefficients developed from a large study in the United States. In contrast, the export coefficients for total nitrogen for forested and agricultural lands, 2.50 and 2.13 kg/ha per year, respectively, were lower than for other locations. These export coefficients developed by the Baptiste Lake study have been used to estimate phosphorus and nitrogen loading from forested and agricultural areas in many similar regions of Alberta.

Major ions are similar in both basins, and are similar to those in many freshwater lakes in Alberta. The water is well-buffered and calcium and bicarbonate are the dominant ions. The surface water is moderately coloured (Table 3).

Temperature and oxygen dynamics differ between the two basins (Fig. 5, 6). The shallower north basin mixes incompletely in spring, and is weakly thermally stratified during summer. For most of the ice-free period, water in the deep hole is anoxic for as much as 7 m above the bottom sediments. In winter, the bottom waters are anoxic; it is unlikely that the total water column ever is entirely anoxic under ice. In the deeper south basin, thermal mixing is incomplete in spring. In contrast to the north basin, mixing is incomplete in autumn as well. In the south basin, water in the hypolimnion has low (less than 2 mg/L) or no dissolved oxygen throughout most of the summer and autumn. This basin is moderately well-oxygenated at fall turnover (up to 58% in 1982). Under ice cover, dissolved oxygen concentrations are rapidly depleted, as from 1982 to 1983, when the depletion rate was 0.775 g/m^2 per day. Because the south basin is relatively deep, there still is sufficient dissolved oxygen in the top 10 m of water by late winter to overwinter fish.

Baptiste Lake is hyper-eutrophic (Table 4). It has always been productive, although changes in land use in the drainage basin have undoubtedly added to its productivity. In the north basin, total phosphorus concentrations increased threefold from early June through late August over each of the seven years that data were collected (Fig. 7, Table 5). In the south basin, total phosphorus

Table 3. Major ions and related water quality variables for the north and south basins of Baptiste Lake. Average concentrations in mg/L; pH in pH units. Composite samples from the euphotic zone collected 6 times from 05 June to 29 Oct. 1986. S.E. = standard error.

	North		South	
	Mean	S.E.	Mean	S.E.
pH (range)	7.8–8.8	—	7.6–8.8	—
total alkalinity (CaCO₃)	166	2.0	162	4.1
specific conductivity (μS/cm)	331	6.9	343	10.3
total dissolved solids (calculated)	188	2.3	184	3.8
total hardness (CaCO₃)	133	2.3	131	2.7
colour (Pt)	22[a]	—	25[a]	—
turbidity (NTU)	5[a]	—	3[a]	—
total particulate carbon	3[b]	0.8	2[c]	0.4
dissolved organic carbon	17	0.6	17	0.5
HCO₃	199	4.5	191	6.7
CO₃	<2	—	<4	—
Mg	11	0.3	11	0.4
Na	22	0.7	21	0.8
K	4	0.1	3	0.1
Cl	2	0	2	0
SO₄	15	1.0	15	1.6
Ca	35	0.5	35	0.8

NOTES: [b]n = 5; [c]n = 4
SOURCES: Alta. Envir. n.d.[a], Naquadat stations 01AL07BE2090, 01AL07BE2095; [a]Prepas and Trew 1983

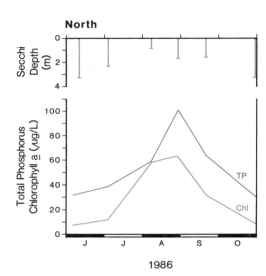

North

South

1986

Figure 7. Total phosphorus, chlorophyll *a* and Secchi depth in Baptiste Lake, north and south basins, 1986.
SOURCE: Alta. Envir. n.d.[a].

Table 4. Nutrient, chlorophyll *a* and Secchi depth data for the north and south basins of Baptiste Lake. Average concentrations in μg/L. Composite samples from the euphotic zone collected 6 times from 05 June to 29 Oct. 1986. S.E. = standard error.

	North		South	
	Mean	S.E.	Mean	S.E.
total phosphorus	54	10.9	49	7.4
total dissolved phosphorus	14	2.2	21	9.3
soluble reactive phosphorus	12[a]	5.1	8[b]	5.9
total Kjeldahl nitrogen	1 142	142.9	1 013	55.6
NO₃ + NO₂–nitrogen	<11	—	<10	—
NH₄–nitrogen	26	5.1	55	31.1
iron	—	—	19[c]	—
chlorophyll *a*	30	10.3	24	8.5
Secchi depth (m)	2.1	0.40	1.9	0.26

NOTES: [a]1984, n = 4; [b]1984, n = 3
SOURCES: Alta. Envir. n.d.[a], Naquadat stations 01AL07BE2090, 01AL07BE2095; [c]Prepas et al. n.d., 08 Aug. 1985, n = 1

concentrations are highest in spring and fall, and oscillate in summer as a function of runoff and transport of phosphorus up from the bottom sediments. In both basins, total phosphorus concentrations near the bottom increase when water over the sediments is anoxic. Thus, total phosphorus concentrations increase under ice in winter. On 30 March 1983 in the south basin they ranged from 87 μg/L at the surface to 170 μ g/L over the bottom sediments. Increases in total phosphorus concentrations in the surface waters during the ice-free season are associated with periods when deep phosphorus-rich water is mixed into the surface water. Also, porewater in the euphotic zone of Baptiste Lake is relatively rich in phosphorus. In 1986, for example, soluble reactive phosphorus concentrations in porewater averaged 456 ± 65 μg/L. Reactive iron (Fe²⁺) concentrations, on the other hand, are relatively low, only 256 ± 36 μg/L in 1986. Over seven summers, average phosphorus release rates from these shallow sediments were estimated to be 11 mg/m² per day. These rates were the highest for the 16 lakes studied in central Alberta. These phosphorus release rates from the shallow sediments

are also much higher (sevenfold) than external inputs estimated for the same time period. Although the open-water patterns of total phosphorus are similar each year in both basins, there are year-to-year differences within each basin (Table 5).

The year-to-year variation in chlorophyll *a* concentrations in Baptiste Lake is greater than for phosphorus (Table 5). In the north basin, chlorophyll concentrations for the ice-free period generally are lowest in June and October and reach their highest peak in July and August (Fig. 7). A similar pattern was found in the south basin. The open-water patterns in the south basin were associated with differences in spring air temperatures; summer chlorophyll *a* concentrations were highest when air temperatures were warmest in April. Chlorophyll *a* concentrations are consistently higher in the north as compared with the south basin, because the north basin is shallower and phosphorus is recycled more rapidly between the open water and sediments. The highest chlorophyll *a* concentration recorded was 840 μg/L from surface scum in the north basin on 30 August 1976. Chlorophyll *a* concentrations were very patchy over the sur-

Table 5. A comparison of average summer chlorophyll *a* and total phosphorus concentrations in Baptiste Lake, 1980 to 1987. Composite samples collected from the euphotic zone from 16 June to 08 Sep. each summer. S.E. = standard error.

Basin and Year	Chl *a* (μg/L)	S.E.	TP (μg/L)	S.E.
North				
1980[a, b]	34.1	4.2	72.5	12.6
1981[a, b]	31.2	9.4	46.2	7.6
1982[a, c]	18.2	4.4	63.8	8.9
1983[b]	41.0	10.7	76.1	22.3
1984[b]	60.6	23.4	76.9	20.0
1985[b]	69.6	27.6	—	—
1986[b]	44.5	16.3	66.3	18.3
1987[b]	55.0	10.2	77.3	24.5
South				
1980[a, b]	50.9	23.7	59.3	13.1
1981[a, b]	25.9	7.0	38.0	5.1
1982[a, c]	13.4	4.0	36.7	4.5
1983[b]	44.4	15.8	58.0	12.9
1984[b]	47.0	16.7	53.7	8.3
1985[b]	37.1	6.2	—	—
1986[b]	36.8	13.9	42.0	5.2
1987[b]	47.5	12.6	67.7	12.4

NOTES: [b]n = 3; [c]n = 4
SOURCES: Alta. Envir. n.d.[a]; [a]Prepas et al. n.d.

face. In 1977, the mean daytime rates of photosynthesis were estimated at 973 and 684 mg C/m^2 of lake surface area per day for the north and south basins, respectively. In the same study, the mean annual rate of carbon fixation was estimated at 302 gm C/m^2 per year.

Biological Characteristics

Plants

The phytoplankton community at Baptiste Lake was examined in detail for an 18–month period in 1976 and 1977 (Trew et al. 1987), in January 1984, and from May through October from 1984 through 1986 (Alta. Envir. n.d.[a]). In spring, the prominent group is diatoms (Bacillariophyta), particularly *Stephanodiscus astraea* and *Asterionella* sp. (Table 6). As well, dinoflagellates (Pyrrhophyta) do well in spring some years, and in August most years. In summer, blue-green algae (Cyanophyta) are the dominant group, particularly *Anabaena flos-aquae*, *Microcystis aeruginosa*, *Aphanizomenon flos-aquae*, *Coelosphaerium* sp. and *Gomphosphaeria* sp. The prominent dinoflagellate is the large *Ceratium hirundinella*. In fall, the diatoms return, including *Stephanodiscus* sp. and *Melosira* sp. Blue-green algae are prominent in summer, likely because of poor oxygen conditions over the bottom sediments and the high total phosphorus concentrations (Trimbee and Prepas 1987; 1988). Baptiste Lake has occasional animal deaths that may be associated with toxic blue-green algae (Alta. For. Ld. Wild. n.d.; Alta. Envir. n.d.[a]; Hoyes 1988). They reportedly include sheep, cattle, fish and dogs.

The macrophyte community in Baptiste Lake was surveyed in 1984 (Stockerl and Kent 1984). Twenty-two species were identified (Fig. 8). Macrophytes were generally restricted to depths of 3 m or less and ringed the entire lake. They were most prominent in the north basin. The most widespread and abundant emergent species were common great bulrush (*Scirpus validus*), common cattail (*Typha latifolia*) and yellow water lily (*Nuphar variegatum*), and the most widespread submergent species were Richardson pondweed (*Potamogeton richardsonii*), large-sheath pondweed (*P. vaginatus*) and northern watermilfoil (*Myriophyllum exalbescens*). The 1984 study noted macrophytes to a maximum depth of 3.5 m, whereas a

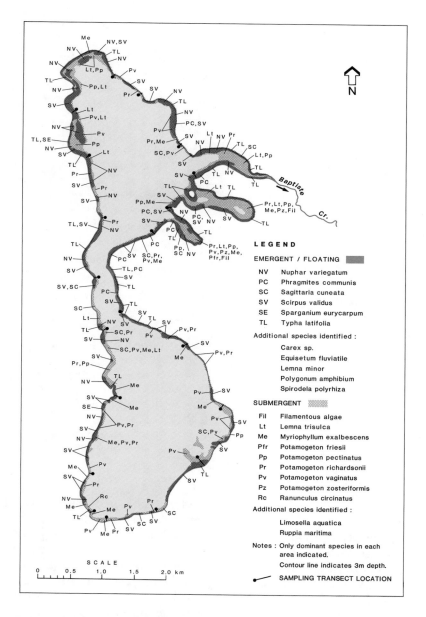

Figure 8. Species composition and distribution of aquatic macrophytes in Baptiste Lake, August 1984.
SOURCE: Stockerl and Kent 1984.

subsequent study found rooted macrophytes to a depth of 4 m (Chambers and Prepas 1988). The littoral zone covers an area of about 3 km^2 (Fig. 4).

Invertebrates

The zooplankton was investigated in 1976 and 1977 (Trew et al. 1987) and data were prepared on relative species abundance. From 1980 to 1982, zooplankton biomass was evaluated and 32 species were identified (Prepas and Vickery 1984). The dominant cyclopoid copepod was *Diacyclops bicuspidatus thomasi*. It was prominent from early spring through mid-July. The dominant calanoid copepod was *Diaptomus oregonensis*, which was found in high numbers throughout most of the ice-free season. The cladoceran *Daphnia galeata mendotae* was common throughout the summer and *Chydorus sphaericus* became numerous in late summer. Populations of *Daphnia* in the north basin peaked in July and August, whereas in the south basin this peak occurred much later. From 1980 to 1982, zooplankton biomass was greatest in July or August.

The benthic invertebrate community in the littoral zone of Baptiste Lake has not been studied intensively but there is an ongoing study of the benthic fauna in the sublittoral and profundal zones of the south basin of the lake (Dinsmore and Prepas n.d.). From 19 June to 15 November 1988, 32 samples were collected with an Ekman dredge from the sublittoral zone and 128 samples were collected from the profundal zone.

Table 6. Percentage composition of major algal groups by total biomass in the north and south basins of Baptiste Lake, 1986. Composite samples collected from the euphotic zone.

ALGAL GROUP	05 June	03 July	07 Aug.	28 Aug.	25 Sep.	29 Oct.
North						
Total Biomass (mg/L)	3.83	3.93	16.81	13.51	5.93	1.30
Cyanophyta	9	76	69	16	22	24
		Anabaena————→		*Coelosphaerium*		*Oscillatoria*
Chlorophyta	1	2	0	1	2	2
Chrysophyta	13	0	0	0	0	8
Bacillariophyta	37	11	3	26	59	17
	Asterionella			*Melosira*————→		
Cryptophyta	23	2	1	2	16	49
	Cryptomonas					*Cryptomonas*
Pyrrhophyta	17	8	26	55	1	0
			Ceratium————→			
South						
Total Biomass (mg/L)	2.16	2.57	8.26	11.88	2.30	0.95
Cyanophyta	0	87	38	7	16	15
		Anabaena————→				
Chlorophyta	3	1	1	0	1	6
Chrysophyta	16	1	0	0	1	11
Bacillariophyta	45	4	1	10	58	20
	Synedra				*Melosira*————→	
Cryptophyta	12	2	1	2	13	46
						Cryptomonas
Pyrrhophyta	25	5	58	80	11	1
	Peridinium		*Ceratium*————→			

SOURCES: Alta. Envir. n.d.[a]

The dominant taxa of the sublittoral zone were midge larvae (Chironomidae), aquatic earthworms (Oligochaeta), fingernail clams (Sphaeriidae) and scuds (Amphipoda). The average biomass (wet weight) was 3.2 g/m², which was very similar to the average biomass measured in the sublittoral zone of the north (3.8 g/m²) and south (3.0 g/m²) basins of nearby Amisk Lake but less than the average biomass (6.2 g/m²) measured in the sublittoral zone of Narrow Lake. The dominant taxa were the same for all three lakes.

The dominant taxa in the profundal zone of Baptiste Lake were phantom midge larvae (Chaoborinae), midge larvae and aquatic earthworms. The average biomass (wet weight) in the profundal zone of Baptiste Lake was 3.7 g/m², which is somewhat higher than the average biomass in the profundal zone of Narrow Lake (2.3 g/m²) and much higher than the average biomass in the profundal zone of the north (0.4 g/m²) and south (0.6 g/m²) basins of Amisk Lake. Baptiste is the only one of the three lakes to have large numbers of phantom midge larvae, which are normally free-swimming, collected in the sediment samples.

Fish

The fish community in Baptiste Lake includes yellow perch, northern pike, walleye, cisco, burbot, white sucker, spottail shiner, Iowa darter, brook stickleback and ninespine stickleback. Arctic grayling are found in the tributary streams. Yellow perch are the most popular sport fish in spring and walleye and northern pike are the most popular in summer.

There was a commercial fishery on Baptiste Lake from 1942 through 1948 and in 1953 and 1964. The lake has not been fished commercially since 1964. The focus of the commercial fishery was to provide cisco for the mink farms near Lesser Slave Lake. A few pike, walleye and perch usually were caught as well. The average annual catches for each species over the nine years of record were: 26 099 kg of cisco, 1 101 kg of pike, 777 kg of walleye and 124 kg of perch. The largest commercial harvest was in 1943, when a total of 85 414 kg of cisco was removed by 20 licensees (Alta Rec. Parks Wild. 1976).

The cisco at Baptiste Lake have been heavily infested with a tapeworm, *Triaenophorus crassus*, since records were kept first

(Miller 1943). For example, in 1945, 130 out of 284 fish were infested (Alta. Rec. Parks Wild. 1976). *Triaenophorus* has a life cycle that involves three distinct hosts: as an adult tapeworm it lives in the intestine of pike and releases its eggs into lake water in early spring; the eggs hatch into larvae which must be swallowed by a copepod, *Diacyclops bicuspidatus thomasi*, to survive. If the host copepod is swallowed by a coregonid fish, such as cisco, the larvae form cysts in the flesh of the fish. When the cisco is eaten by a pike, the cysts develop into adult tapeworms in the pike's intestine and release eggs to the water to start the cycle all over again. A dramatic experiment was carried out in 1945 in an attempt to reduce or eliminate this parasite from the lake (Miller and Watkins 1946; Northcote and Larkin 1963). The objective of Miller's experiment was to lower the pH to 5 in a band of water 1–m deep along 13 km of the Baptiste Lake shoreline where tapeworms released eggs. The acidic conditions would kill the larval *Triaenophorus* before they could be consumed by copepods. On two occasions in May 1945, a total of 18 tonnes of sulphuric acid was applied to the designated areas. Unfortunately, the experiment did not work, mainly due to incomplete information on how lake water circulates and how ions exchange between lake water and bottom sediments.

The fish in Baptiste Lake are managed for the popular sport fishery. Two recent creel surveys have evaluated the spring (Berry 1986) and summer (Sullivan 1985) sport fishery (Table 7). The harvest per-unit-effort for yellow perch was very high in the spring survey (1.09 perch/angler-hour), but was very low (0.01 perch/angler-hour) during summer. In contrast, pike harvest was fairly constant, at 0.13 pike/angler-hour in spring and 0.10 pike/angler-hour in summer. The walleye harvest was relatively low for both time periods. However, these results are somewhat misleading, especially for the summer fishery. Baptiste Lake is not well suited for creel surveys due to the large number of cottages and access points. During winter, anglers could be interviewed on the ice, but after ice-out, surveys were limited to shore contacts at the public boat launches. During the summer survey only 20% of anglers on the lake use the public boat launches. Thus, the harvest rates for perch and walleye during the summer are likely very low because angling success of visitors to the lake is probably much lower than that of cottagers who are familiar with the lake. In addition, the harvest of

Table 7. Estimated angler numbers, effort and harvest from Baptiste Lake. Estimates based on creel survey data collected from 09 Mar. to 20 June 1982 and 15 May to 31 Aug. 1984. In 1982, a total of 32 weekdays and 23 weekend days and holidays were surveyed and information was collected between 10:00 and 16:00. In 1984, a total of 39 weekdays and 31 weekend days and holidays were surveyed and information was collected between 07:00 to 23:00. WE = walleye; NP = northern pike; YP = yellow perch.

	WE		NP		YP		Total	
	1982	1984	1982	1984	1982	1984	1982	1984
number of anglers[a]	—	—	—	—	—	—	8 810	5 229
angler-hours[b]	—	—	—	—	—	—	23 787	15 581
total number fish harvested[c]	2 104	666	3 185	1 493	25 825	471	31 114	2 630
total yield (kg)	2 735	703	4 778	1 465	7 748	93	15 261	2 261
mean weight (g)	1 300	1 055	1 500	981	300	197	—	—
catch/angler-hour	—	0.054	—	0.159	—	0.030	—	0.243
harvest/angler-hour[b, c]	0.088	0.039	0.134	0.102	1.086	0.013	1.308	0.154
harvest/angler[a, c]	0.239	0.127	0.362	0.286	2.931	0.090	3.532	0.503

NOTES: [a]observed no. anglers = 640 (1982) and 830 (1984); [b]observed hours = 1 620 (1982) and 2 472 (1984); [c]based on observed no. fish kept: WE = 36 (1982) and 133 (1984); NP = 139 (1982) and 298 (1984); YP = 1 642 (1982) and 94 (1984).
SOURCES: Sullivan 1985; Berry 1986.

pike is low because most anglers wish to catch perch and walleye and avoid areas where pike occur, despite the fact that pike 90– to 110–cm long have been caught during intensive surveys of the fish community in the littoral zone of the lake (Jansen n.d.).

Two graduate students at the University of Alberta studied the yellow perch at Baptiste Lake from 1985 through 1988 (Abbey n.d.; Jansen n.d.). Young-of-the-year yellow perch grew from an average total length of 5.9 mm when they hatched in May to 60 mm by early October. In comparison to four other deep lakes studied in the County of Athabasca, the growth rate of these young perch was high.

Wildlife

Detailed studies of the wildlife at Baptiste Lake have not been done. Waterfowl known to nest on the lake include American Widgeons, Mallards, teal, Common Loons and Red-necked Grebes. American Bitterns and American Coots can be spotted on the lake from April to October and Great Blue Herons and Ospreys are frequently seen fishing in the lake. Ring-billed Gulls are commonly seen, but it is not known whether they nest on Baptiste Lake. It is not considered a major flyway stop for migratory birds, although they do stop on the unpopulated areas of Baptiste Lake (Alta. Mun. Aff. 1979[b]; Hanson 1989).

E.E. Prepas

References

Abbey, D. n.d. Univ. Alta. Unpubl. data, Edmonton.
Alberta Environment. n.d.[a]. Envir. Assess. Div., Envir. Qlty. Monit. Br. Unpubl. data, Edmonton.
——. n.d.[b]. Tech. Serv. Div., Hydrol. Br. Unpubl. data, Edmonton.
——. n.d.[c]. Tech. Serv. Div., Surv. Br. Unpubl. data, Edmonton.
——. 1989. Baptiste Lake. Envir. Assess. Div., Envir. Qlty. Monit. Br., Edmonton.
Alberta Forestry, Lands and Wildlife. n.d. Fish Wild. Div. Unpubl. data, Edmonton.
——. 1988. Boating in Alberta. Fish Wild. Div., Edmonton.
——. 1989. Guide to sportfishing. Fish Wild. Div., Edmonton.
Alberta Municipal Affairs. 1979[a]. Baptiste Lake area structure plan. Prep. for Co. Athabasca and SV Sunset Beach by Plan. Serv. Div., Reg. Plan. Sec., Edmonton.
——. 1979[b]. Baptiste Lake management study: Summary of evaluation and management alternatives. Prep. for Co. Athabasca and SV Sunset Beach by Plan. Serv. Div., Reg. Plan. Sec., Edmonton.
Alberta Recreation, Parks and Wildlife. 1976. Commercial fisheries catch statistics for Alberta, 1942–1975. Fish Wild. Div., Fish. Mgt. Rep. No. 22, Edmonton.
Alberta Research Council. 1972. Geological map of Alberta. Nat. Resour. Div., Alta. Geol. Surv., Edmonton.

Athabasca Historical Society, D. Gregory and Athabasca University. 1986. Athabasca Landing: An illustrated history. Athabasca Hist. Soc., Athabasca.
Babin, J. 1984. Winter oxygen depletion in temperate zone lakes. MSc thesis. Univ. Alta., Edmonton.
—— and E.E. Prepas. 1985. Modelling winter oxygen depletion rates in ice-covered temperate zone lakes in Canada. Can. J. Fish. Aquat. Sci. 42:239–249.
Berry, D.K. 1986. An assessment of the spring sportfishery at Baptiste Lake, Alberta 1982. Alta. En. Nat. Resour., Fish Wild. Div., Edmonton.
Chambers, P.A. and E.E. Prepas. 1988. Underwater spectral attenuation and its effect on the maximum depth of angiosperm colonization. Can. J. Fish. Aquat. Sci. 45:1010–1017.
Crowe, A.S. 1979. Chemical and hydrological simulation of prairie lake-watershed systems. MSc thesis. Univ. Alta., Edmonton.
—— and F.W. Schwartz. 1981. Simulation of lake-watershed systems, II: Application to Baptiste Lake, Alberta. Can. J. Hydrol. 52:107–125.
Dinsmore, P. and E.E. Prepas. n.d. Univ. Alta. Unpubl. data, Edmonton.
Energy, Mines and Resources Canada. 1973. National topographic series 1:50 000 83I/11 (1973), 83I/12 (1973), 83I/13 (1973), 83I/14 (1973). Surv. Map. Br., Ottawa.
Environment Canada. 1982. Canadian climate normals, Vol. 7: Bright sunshine (1951–1980). Prep. by Atm. Envir. Serv. Supply Serv. Can., Ottawa.
Hanson, J.M. 1989. Univ. Alta., Dept. Zool., Edmonton. Pers. observ.
Hickman, M., D.M. Klarer, C. Schweger and T. Habgood. 1978. The paleoenvironmental history of Baptiste Lake, Alberta. Alta. Envir., Poll. Contr. Div., Water Qlty. Contr. Br. Unpubl. rep., Edmonton.
Holmgren, E.J. and P.M. Holmgren. 1976. Over 2000 place names of Alberta. 3rd ed. West. Producer Prairie Books, Saskatoon.
Hoyes, E. 1988. Alta. Envir., Water Resour. Admin. Div., Edmonton. Pers. comm.
Jansen, W. n.d. Univ. Alta. Unpubl. data, Edmonton.
Kjearsgaard, A.A. 1972. Reconnaissance soil survey of the Tawatinaw map sheet (83–I). Alta. Inst. Pedol. Rep. No. S–72–29. Univ. Alta., Edmonton.
Miller, R.B. 1943. Report of a survey of Baptiste Lake conducted July 1943. Alta. Ld. Mines, Fish Game Admin., Edmonton.
—— and H.B. Watkins. 1946. An experiment in the control of the cestode, Triaenophorus crassus Forel. Can. J. Res. D. 24:175–179.
Northcote, T.G. and P.A. Larkin. 1963. Western Canada, p. 463. In F.G. Frey [ed.] Limnology in North America. Univ. Wisconsin Press, Madison, Wisconsin.
Prepas, E.E. 1983. Orthophosphate turnover time in shallow productive lakes. Can. J. Fish. Aquat. Sci. 40:1412–1418.
——, J. Babin and T.P. Murphy. n.d. Unpubl. data, Univ. Alta., Edmonton and Natl. Water Res. Inst., Burlington, Ontario.
Prepas, E.E. and D.O. Trew. 1983. Evaluation of the phosphorus-chlorophyll relationship for lakes off the Precambrian Shield in western Canada. Can. J. Fish. Aquat. Sci. 40:27–35.
Prepas, E.E. and J. Vickery. 1984. The contribution of particulate phosphorus (>250 μm) to the total phosphorus pool in lake water. Can. J. Fish. Aquat. Sci. 41:351–363.
Shaw, J.F.H. and E.E. Prepas. 1989[a]. Exchange of phosphorus from shallow sediments at nine Alberta lakes. J. Envir. Qlty. [in press]
——. 1989[b]. Relationships between phosphorus in shallow sediments in the trophogenic zone of seven Alberta lakes. Water Res. [in press]
——. 1989[c]. Potential significance of phosphorus release from shallow sediments of deep Alberta lakes. ms submitted to Limnol. Oceanogr.

Shaw, J.F.H., R.D. Shaw and E.E. Prepas. 1989. Advective transport of phosphorus from lake bottom sediments into lakewater. ms to be submitted.

Shaw, R.D. and E.E. Prepas. 1989. Groundwater-lake interactions: II Nearshore seepage patterns and the contribution of groundwater to lakes in central Alberta. J. Hydrol. [in press]

Stockerl, E.C. and R.L. Kent. 1984. Aquatic macrophyte survey of Baptiste and Nakamun Lakes, 1984. Prep. for Alta. Envir., Poll. Contr. Div. by Okanagan Diving Serv. (ODS) Consult., Edmonton.

Stone, D. 1970. The process of rural settlements in the Athabasca area, Alberta. MA thesis. Univ. Alta., Edmonton.

Strong, W.L. and K.R. Leggat. 1981. Ecoregions of Alberta. Alta. En. Nat. Resour., Resour. Eval. Plan. Div., Edmonton.

Sullivan, M.G. 1985. Characteristics and impact of the sports fishery at Baptiste Lake during May-August 1984. Alta. En. Nat. Resour., Fish Wild. Div., St. Paul.

Thomas, J.G., R.R. Erickson, W.W. Warren and C.T. Dack. 1977. Cottage owner survey, Island Lake, Baptiste Lake. Alta. Mun. Aff., Plan. Serv. Div., Edmonton.

Trew, D.O., D.J. Beliveau and E.I. Yonge. 1978. The Baptiste Lake study summary report. Alta. Envir., Poll. Contr. Div., Water Qlty. Contr. Br., Edmonton.

———. 1987. The Baptiste Lake study technical report. Alta. Envir., Poll. Contr. Div., Water Qlty. Contr. Br., Edmonton.

Trimbee, A.M. and E.E. Prepas. 1987. Evaluation of total phosphorus as a predictor of the relative biomass of blue-green algae with emphasis on Alberta lakes. Can. J. Fish. Aquat. Sci. 44:1337–1342.

———. 1988. The effect of oxygen depletion on the timing and magnitude of blue-green algal blooms. Verh. Internat. Verein. Limnol. 23:220–226.

Winhold, T.H. and A. DeBoer. 1987. Investigation into Baptiste Lake outlet control. Alta. Envir., Water Res. Mgt. Serv., Tech. Serv. Div., Edmonton.

CALLING LAKE

Alberta Recreation and Parks

MAP SHEET: 83P
LOCATION: Tp71–73 R21–23 W4
LAT/LONG: 55°15'N 113°19'W

Calling Lake is a large, attractive recreational lake noted for its sandy shoreline. It is located in Improvement District No. 17 (East) about 200 km north of the city of Edmonton. The town of Athabasca, 55 km to the south, is the closest large population centre, and the hamlet of Calling Lake is located on the lake's eastern shore. To drive to the lake from Edmonton, take Highway 2 north to Athabasca, then Secondary Road 813 north to the hamlet and Calling Lake Provincial Park (Fig. 1).

The lake's name is a translation of the Cree name, which refers to the loud noises heard when the lake freezes over and the ice breaks up (Geog. Bd. Can. 1928; Alta. Native Aff. 1986). The Calling Lake area has been inhabited for many thousands of years. Archeological digs near the lake have uncovered the tools and weapons of a band of hunter-gatherers who used the area as a relatively permanent base in about 6 000 B.C. (Athabasca Hist. Soc. et al. 1986). More recent inhabitants of the area were Woodland Cree, and early fur traders who sometimes caught their winter supply of fish in the lake (Finlay and Finlay 1987).

Members of the Bigstone Cree Indian Band live on St. Jean Baptiste Gambler Indian Reserve No. 183, located on the eastern shore of Calling Lake, and in the hamlet of Calling Lake (Alta. Native Aff. 1986). A 1986 census estimated the hamlet's population to be 408 permanent and 720 seasonal residents and the reserve's population to be 93 people (Calling L. Plan. Commit. et al. 1988).

Calling Lake Provincial Park was established in 1971 on 741 ha of land on the southern shore (Fig. 2). The park is open from May to September and has 25 campsites, flush toilets, tap water, a boat launch, a swimming area and a picnic area. Activities enjoyed by park visitors include swimming, fishing, camping, motor boating and canoeing. There is a narrow beach at the park and the lake bottom near shore is sandy. There are no boating restrictions over most of the lake, but in posted areas, either motor boats are restricted to speeds of 12 km/hour or less, or all boats are prohibited (Alta. For. Ld. Wild. 1988).

Recreational facilities within the hamlet of Calling Lake are limited to an undeveloped public beach near the Calling River (Fig. 2). A private sailing club is located between this beach and the provincial park.

The water in Calling Lake is quite transparent for most of the year, but turns green in midsummer. Aquatic vegetation grows sparsely along the northern shore, and the remainder of the shoreline is mostly unvegetated sand or a mixture of rocks and sand. The lake supports a small commercial fishery for lake whitefish. The main sport fish are northern pike, yellow perch and walleye. Brown trout were stocked from 1985 to 1987, but the success of the program was not known as of 1989. All tributary streams to, and the outlet from, Calling Lake are closed to sport fishing for a designated period during April and May each year (Alta. For. Ld. Wild. 1989).

Drainage Basin Characteristics

Calling Lake has a large drainage basin that covers an area of 1 090 km², mostly to the north of the lake (Table 1, Fig. 1). The main inflow is locally known as Rock Island River; it drains Rock Island Lake and the northern portion of the watershed and flows into Calling Lake at the northwest end. Several smaller streams flow into the lake on the east and west sides. The outlet, the Calling River, flows from the

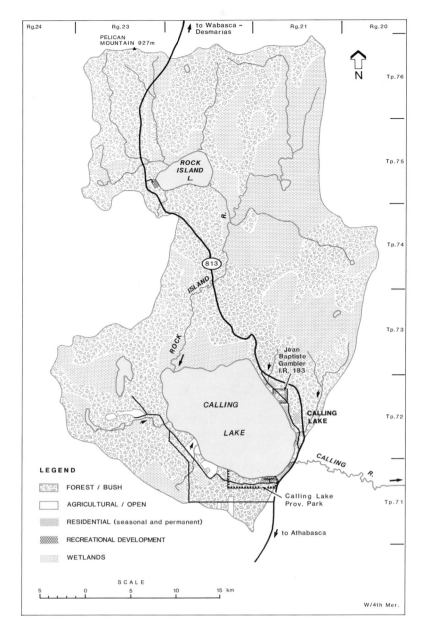

Figure 1. Features of the drainage basin of Calling Lake.
SOURCES: Alta. Envir. n.d.[b]; En. Mines Resour. Can. 1975. Updated with 1983 and 1986 aerial photos.

Table 1. Characteristics of Calling Lake drainage basin.

area (excluding lake) (km²)[a]	1 090
soil[b]	Gray Luvisols, Organics
bedrock geology[c]	La Biche Formation (Upper Cretaceous): shale, ironstone partings and concretions; marine
terrain[b]	depressional to rolling
ecoregions[d]	Moist Mixed Subregion of Boreal Mixedwood (south and northeast), Boreal Foothills (northwest)
dominant vegetation[d]	trembling aspen, balsam poplar, white spruce, lodgepole pine
mean annual inflow (m³)[a, e]	106 x 10⁶
mean annual sunshine (h)[f]	2 160

NOTE: [e]excluding groundwater inflow
SOURCES: [a]Alta. Envir. n.d.[b]; [b]Wynnyk et al. 1963; [c]Alta. Res. Counc. 1972; [d]Strong and Leggat 1981; [f]Envir. Can. 1982

Table 2. Characteristics of Calling Lake.

elevation (m)[a]	593.12 to 595.14
surface area (km²)[b]	138
volume (m³)	not available
maximum depth (m)[c]	18.3
mean depth (m)	not available
shoreline length (km)[d]	48
mean annual lake evaporation (mm)[e]	611
mean annual precipitation (mm)[e]	485
mean residence time (yr)	not available
control structure	none

NOTE: [a]range over period of water level record
SOURCES: [b]En. Mines Resour. Can. 1975; [c]Alta. For. Ld. Wild. n.d.; [d]Calling L. Plan. Commit. et al. 1988; [e]Alta. Envir. n.d.[b].

southeast end to the Athabasca River, which is located about 25 km downstream.

A prominent feature of the watershed is the high land at the northwest corner that forms the southeast face of Pelican Mountain. This hill is part of the divide between the Peace River and the Athabasca River drainage systems. Elevations range from 927 m on the mountain top to 760 m on the adjacent rolling land. Soil parent materials in this northwestern area are gravelly glaciofluvial outwash, till and moss peat bog (Wynnyk et al. 1963). The soils are mainly Podzolic Gray Luvisols or Orthic Gray Luvisols that formed on coarse-textured fluvial material overlying the till. This portion of the watershed is part of the Boreal Foothills Ecoregion (Strong and Leggat 1981). The dominant trees on well-drained to moderately well-drained Gray Luvisols are trembling aspen, balsam poplar and lodgepole pine, with succession by white spruce. Open stands of lodgepole pine are the dominant vegetation on well-drained Brunisols and imperfectly drained Gleysols, and black spruce, willows and sedges grow on poorly drained to very poorly drained Organics and Gleysols.

The remainder of the drainage basin can be divided into two areas, which have some differences in soil parent materials and topography, but similarities in soils and vegetation. In the first area, which is east and northeast of Rock Island Lake, the land is poorly drained and relatively flat, with many depressions and a high proportion of moss and sedge peat bogs (Wynnyk et al. 1963). Elevations

range from 655 m to the east of Rock Island Lake to 760 m at the extreme northeast corner of the drainage basin. Organics and sandy glaciofluvial outwash are the main soil parent materials, with lesser amounts of till. In the second area, which is south of Rock Island Lake, the land is predominantly a gently rolling morainal plain, with occasional small areas of rolling topography (Wynnyk et al. 1963). Elevations range from 610 to 730 m and drainage is poor in many areas. The main soil parent materials are till or sandy glaciofluvial outwash. The most extensive soils in both areas are Organics, Podzols, Podzolic Gray Luvisols and Orthic Gray Luvisols. In both areas, the watershed is part of the Moist Mixedwood Subregion of the Boreal Mixedwood Ecoregion (Strong and Leggat 1981). The forest cover is mainly trembling aspen, balsam poplar and white spruce on moderately well-drained Gray Luvisols, jack pine on well-drained Eutric Brunisols, white spruce on imperfectly drained Gleysols and Gray Luvisols, and black spruce, willows and sedges on poorly drained to very poorly drained Organics and Gleysols.

At the lakeshore, the land on the east and south sides is mainly high and well drained, and slopes gently to moderately toward the water (Alta. For. Ld. Wild. n.d.). The soils within Calling Lake Provincial Park were described and mapped intensively in 1973 (Greenlee 1973). A large area of muskeg is located along the western shore where the more northerly of the two western inflows enters the lake (Fig. 1). The remainder of the western shore is high and well drained, with moderately to steeply sloping banks toward the northwest end. The northern shoreland is low-lying and depressional, and is covered by a large area of muskeg that extends several kilometres north of the lake.

A large portion of Calling Lake's drainage basin is covered by wetlands, and most of the remainder is forested (Fig. 1). Only a few small areas southwest of the lake are being farmed. The oil and gas industry is not significant in the area, and most residents of the

Table 3. Major ions and related water quality variables for Calling Lake. Average concentrations in mg/L; pH in pH units. Composite samples from the euphotic zone collected 6 times from 19 May to 25 Oct. 1988. S.E. = standard error.

	Mean	S.E.
pH (range)	7.4–8.5	—
total alkalinity (CaCO$_3$)	82[a]	0.7
specific conductivity (μS/cm)	168	1.3
total dissolved solids (calculated)	94[b]	2.0
colour (Pt)	<14[c]	—
total hardness (CaCO$_3$)	79	1.0
dissolved organic carbon	10	0.4
HCO$_3$	100	0.8
CO$_3$	<1	—
Mg	6	0.2
Na	5	0.1
K	2	0
Cl	1	0.1
SO$_4$	4	0.3
Ca	22	0.2

NOTES: [a]n = 5; [b]n = 3; [c]n = 4
SOURCE: Alta. Envir. n.d.[a], Naquadat station 01AL07CB1000

hamlet of Calling Lake are employed in the forestry, commercial fishing and trapping industries (Calling L. Plan. Commit. et al. 1988).

The hamlet and St. Jean Baptiste Gambler Indian Reserve are the only residential areas in the drainage basin. Their boundaries encompass almost one-third of Calling Lake's shoreline. The remainder of the shoreline is Crown land. In 1980, a Community Plan was developed for the hamlet (Calling L. Plan. Commit. et al. 1980). This plan served as a general guide for future development, but had no legal status under the Planning Act. In 1988, a Community Development Strategy Area Structure Plan was completed (Calling L. Plan. Commit. et al. 1988). The plan will serve as a decision-making tool for all land use and development matters pertaining to the hamlet. In 1987, there were 270 permanent and 240 seasonal residences within the hamlet and about 100 vacant residential lots (Calling L. Plan. Commit. et al. 1988).

Lake Basin Characteristics

Calling Lake, with a surface area of 138 km^2 (Table 2), is one of Alberta's larger lakes. The lake basin has a simple, regular shape, with three sides that slope gradually to a flat bottom and a western side that slopes somewhat more steeply (Fig. 2). The maximum depth of 18.3 m is located in the centre of the basin.

The lake bottom to depths of 9 to 14 m is composed of sand and small rocks, with very little organic matter. In deeper areas, the bottom is a thick layer of organic matter over sand (Miller and Macdonald 1949). Rocks cover the sand at the water's edge along the west and northeast shores. The lake bottom along south and southeast shores is sandy and has few rocks; the water is shallow for several hundred metres and the sand extends well out into the lake (Alta. For. Ld. Wild. n.d.). Trees grow down to the water's edge along much of the shoreline.

In 1947, Ducks Unlimited (Canada) and the provincial government built a rock-filled weir at the lake's outlet, the Calling River (Ducks Unltd. (Can.) n.d.). Water levels had become undesirably low, and the weir was an effort to reestablish higher levels. By 1952, the lake level had risen, but by 1962, the structure had fallen into disrepair and was removed. The lake's elevation has been monitored since 1957 (Fig. 3). The historic minimum elevation, 593.58 m, was recorded in November 1968 and the maximum, 595.14 m, was recorded in July 1970. This is a maximum fluctuation of 1.56 m. From 1980 to 1987, the maximum fluctuation was 0.87 m. In addition to water level data, Alberta Environment is collecting discharge data for Calling Lake to develop a water balance model.

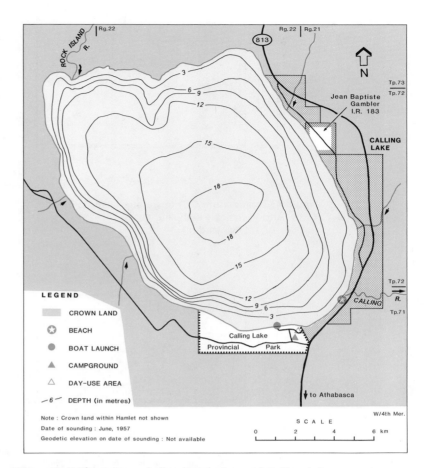

Figure 2. Bathymetry and shoreline features of Calling Lake.
BATHYMETRY SOURCE: modified from Alta. For. Ld. Wild. n.d.

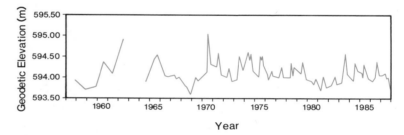

Figure 3. Water level of Calling Lake, 1957 to 1987.
SOURCES: Alta. Envir. n.d.[c]; Envir. Can. 1970–1987.

Water Quality

Water quality in Calling Lake was monitored monthly during the open-water season in 1987 and 1988 by Alberta Environment (Alta. Envir. n.d.[a]). The lake has slightly coloured, fresh water, and alkalinity that is relatively low for an Alberta lake (Table 3). The dominant ions are bicarbonate and calcium.

Although the lake is moderately deep, it was usually well-mixed during the open-water period in 1988. On calm days during summer, weak thermal stratification was evident. The maximum difference in water temperature from the surface to a depth of 17 m was 3°C in July (Fig. 4). Despite some mixing of the water column, dissolved oxygen was depleted in the deeper water during July and August in 1988, with concentrations less than 4 mg/L at depths greater than 14 m (Fig. 5). There was some depletion of dissolved oxygen below the ice during February 1987 and 1988. In 1987, the water was anoxic below 15 m, but there was sufficient dissolved oxygen to sustain the fish population at depths above 12 m. There are no records of fish kills in Calling Lake (Alta. For. Ld. Wild. n.d.).

Calling Lake is eutrophic. In 1988, the mean chlorophyll *a* concentration was 19 μg/L and the mean total phosphorus concentration was 50 μg/L (Table 4). Concentrations of both variables were low in May (Fig. 6); chlorophyll *a* increased to a maximum of

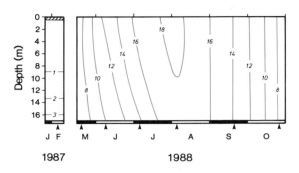

Figure 4. Temperature (°C) of Calling Lake, 1987 and 1988. Arrows indicate sampling dates.
SOURCE: Alta. Envir. n.d.[a].

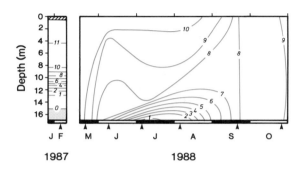

Figure 5. Dissolved oxygen (mg/L) in Calling Lake, 1987 and 1988. Arrows indicate sampling dates.
SOURCE: Alta. Envir. n.d.[a].

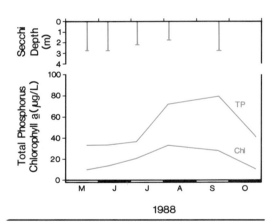

Figure 6. Total phosphorus, chlorophyll *a* and Secchi depth in Calling Lake, 1988.
SOURCE: Alta. Envir. n.d.[a].

33 μg/L in August and total phosphorus reached a maximum of 81 μg/L in September; concentrations of both variables decreased in October. This pattern is typical for mixed lakes in Alberta and probably reflects a release of phosphorus from the sediments as water temperatures increase.

Biological Characteristics

Plants

The phytoplankton in Calling Lake was sampled with nets in August 1949 (Miller and Macdonald 1949). The most abundant species were the blue-green alga *Rivularia* sp., an unidentified filamentous green alga, and the diatom *Stephanodiscus* sp. No recent data are available.

Macrophytes in Calling Lake have not been identified. In a 1957 report, Fish and Wildlife Division noted that there were few macrophytes on the southern and eastern sides of the lake (Alta. For.

Table 4. Nutrient, chlorophyll *a* and Secchi depth data for Calling Lake. Average concentrations in μg/L. Composite samples from the euphotic zone collected 6 times from 19 May to 25 Oct. 1988. S.E. = standard error.

	Mean	S.E.
total phosphorus	50	8.7
total dissolved phosphorus	19	6.0
total Kjeldahl nitrogen	770	79.8
$NO_3 + NO_2$–nitrogen	<7	—
NH_4–nitrogen	33	12.3
iron	75	13.1
chlorophyll *a*	19.1	3.94
Secchi depth (m)	2.7	0.31

SOURCE: Alta. Envir. n.d.[a], Naquadat station 01AL07CB1000

Ld. Wild. n.d.). Plants grew most densely along the north side but, even there, the density was considered light to moderate.

Invertebrates

There is no recent information on the invertebrates in Calling Lake.

Fish

Calling Lake supports populations of northern pike, walleye, yellow perch, lake whitefish, cisco, burbot, white sucker, longnose sucker, spottail shiner and Iowa darter. Brown trout have been stocked since 1985 at a rate of 73 000 fingerlings in 1985, 151 500 juveniles in 1986 and 167 400 juveniles in 1987 (Alta. En. Nat. Resour. 1985; Alta. For. Ld. Wild. 1986; 1987). The success of this stocking program has not been evaluated and it is unknown whether brown trout will spawn in the lake or in its tributaries (Watters 1989). Calling Lake is managed for domestic, commercial and recreational fisheries. There are no data available for the domestic and recreational fisheries.

The commercial fishery has operated at least since records were first kept in 1942 (Alta. For. Ld. Wild. n.d.; Alta. Rec. Parks Wild. 1976). The largest total catch, 325 246 kg, was taken in 1963/64, and the smallest catch, 247 kg, was taken in 1978/79. The fishery was closed for only one year, in 1975/76. In general, catches were highest from 1942/43 until 1970/71—the average total catch during this period was 128 220 kg/year. Between 1971/72 and 1987/88, the average total catch declined to 8 660 kg/year. The number of licences has declined considerably between the two periods, as well. Prior to 1972, 5 to 105 licences were issued annually, with an average issue of 48 licences. Between 1972 and 1988, 0 to 8 licences were issued annually, with an average issue of only 5 licences. Therefore, the lower total catches since 1972 are partly due to the low effort.

The composition of the catch has varied widely. For instance, lake whitefish formed, on average, only 10% of the total catch between 1941/42 and 1970/71, but about 50% of the total catch from 1971/72 to 1987/88. During the earlier period, burbot, cisco and suckers accounted for an average of 88% of the total catch, and walleye, northern pike and yellow perch were a minor proportion. Cisco catches have declined because there is only a very small market for this species since the mink ranching industry declined during the 1970s, and because the minimum mesh size (140 mm) used is too large to retain many cisco. The market for burbot and suckers is also very small. The lake whitefish are infested with cysts of the tapeworm *Triaenophorus crassus* and do not bring the best prices on the commercial market.

Wildlife

There is little information on the wildlife at Calling Lake. Moose, deer, black bears and mink frequent the area, and beaver cut trembling aspen along the shore (Nordstrom and Gregg 1975; Finlay and Finlay 1987). The lake does not support a large waterfowl population because of a shortage of loafing areas, a limited number of upland nesting sites, and sparse emergent aquatic vegetation (Ducks Unltd. (Can.) n.d.). Mallards nest on the lake, and Gadwalls, Common Goldeneye, Common Mergansers and Arctic Loons have been sighted. Bald Eagles have been reported along the shore, and Spruce and Ruffed Grouse are common residents of the area (Nordstrom and Gregg 1975).

M.E. Bradford

References

Alberta Energy and Natural Resources. 1985. Fish planting list. Fish Wild. Div., Edmonton.

Alberta Environment. n.d.[a]. Envir. Assess. Div., Envir. Qlty. Monit. Br. Unpubl. data, Edmonton.

——. n.d.[b]. Tech. Serv. Div., Hydrol. Br. Unpubl. data, Edmonton.

——. n.d.[c]. Tech. Serv. Div., Surv. Br. Unpubl. data, Edmonton.

Alberta Forestry, Lands and Wildlife. n.d. Fish Wild. Div. Unpubl. data, Edmonton.

——. 1986, 1987. Fish planting list. Fish Wild. Div., Edmonton.

——. 1988. Boating in Alberta. Fish Wild. Div., Edmonton.

——. 1989. Guide to sportfishing. Fish Wild. Div., Edmonton.

Alberta Native Affairs. 1986. A guide to native communities in Alberta. Native Aff. Secret., Edmonton.

Alberta Recreation, Parks and Wildlife. 1976. Commercial fisheries catch statistics for Alberta, 1942–1975. Fish Wild. Div., Fish. Mgt. Rep. No. 22, Edmonton.

Alberta Research Council. 1972. Geological map of Alberta. Nat. Resour. Div., Alta. Geol. Surv., Edmonton.

Athabasca Historical Society, D. Gregory and Athabasca University. 1986. Athabasca Landing: An illustrated history. Athabasca Hist. Soc., Athabasca.

Calling Lake Planning Committee, Improvement District No. 17 (East) Advisory Council and Alberta Municipal Affairs. 1980. Calling Lake community plan. ID No. 17 (E), Slave Lake.

——, Improvement District No. 17 (East) Administration and Alberta Municipal Affairs. 1988. Hamlet of Calling Lake community development strategy area structure plan. ID No. 17 (E), Slave Lake.

Ducks Unlimited (Canada). n.d. Unpubl. data, Edmonton.

Energy, Mines and Resources Canada. 1975. National topographic series 1:250 000 83P (1975). Surv. Map. Br., Ottawa.

Environment Canada. 1970–1987. Surface water data. Prep. by Inland Waters Directorate. Water Surv. Can., Water Resour. Br., Ottawa.

——. 1982. Canadian climate normals, Vol. 7: Bright sunshine (1951–1980). Prep. by Atm. Envir. Serv. Supply Serv. Can., Ottawa.

Finlay, J. and C. Finlay. 1987. Parks in Alberta: A guide to peaks, ponds, parklands & prairies. Hurtig Publ., Edmonton.

Geographic Board of Canada. 1928. Place-names of Alberta. Dept. Interior, Ottawa.

Greenlee, G.M. 1973. Soil survey of area adjacent to Calling Lake, Alberta and interpretation for recreational use. Alta. Inst. Pedol. No. M–73–16. Alta. Res. Counc., Edmonton.

Miller, R.B. and W.H. Macdonald. 1950. Preliminary biological surveys of Alberta watersheds, 1947–1949. Alta. Ld. For., Fish Wild. Div., Edmonton.

Nordstrom, W. and A. Gregg. 1975. Beach and backshore assessment of Calling Lake's existing and proposed provincial park areas. Alta. Rec. Parks Wild., Prov. Parks Plan. Div., Edmonton.

Strong, W.L. and K.R. Leggat. 1981. Ecoregions of Alberta. Alta. En. Nat. Resour., Resour. Eval. Plan. Div., Edmonton.

Watters, D. 1989. Alta. For. Ld. Wild., Fish Wild. Div., Edmonton Reg. Office, Edmonton. Pers. comm.

Wynnyk, A., J.D. Lindsay, P.K. Heringa and W. Odynsky. 1963. Exploratory soil survey of Alberta map sheets 83–O, 83–P, and 73–M. Prelim. Soil Surv. Rep. No. 64–1. Res. Counc. Alta., Edmonton.

CHRISTINA LAKE

Christina Lake Lodge

MAP SHEETS: 73M/10, 11
LOCATION: Tp76, 77 R5–7 W4
LAT/LONG: 54°40'N 111°00'W

Christina Lake is a deep, isolated recreational lake located 125 km south of the city of Fort McMurray in Improvement District No. 18 (North). The closest population centre is the hamlet of Conklin, situated immediately west of the lake (Fig. 1). The lake has been accessible by an all-weather road only since 1986. In that year, Secondary Road 881, which ran south from Fort McMurray to the locality of Cheecham, was extended an additional 75 km south to Conklin. In 1989, the road was paved only between Fort McMurray and the hamlet of Anzac, about 90 km north of Christina Lake (Schroder 1988). Christina Lake is not easily accessible from the south. There is a landing strip at Conklin. To drive to the lake from the Lac La Biche area, most visitors take Highway 63 north to Fort McMurray and then Secondary Road 881 south to Conklin. A more rigorous route is along the old Conklin Road, a rough road that begins just north of Lac La Biche (Alta. Native Aff. 1986).

Although spelled incorrectly, the lake was named for Christine Gordon, the first white woman to make her home permanently in Fort McMurray. During the early 1900s, she operated a trading post in competition with the Hudson's Bay Company (Holmgren and Holmgren 1976).

The first settlement at Christina Lake was located at the extreme northwestern end of the lake near the outlet, the Jackfish River. When the Northern Alberta Railway arrived, most of the buildings relocated close to the railroad tracks, in what is now Conklin. Christina Lake is the major domestic water source for residents of the hamlet. From 1940 to 1960, commercial fishing and mink ranching were important industries at the lake. During this period, a fish-processing plant and several mink farms were located at or near the outlet. Another mink farm was located on the large peninsula on the north shore of the eastern basin (Christina L. Mgt. Plan Team 1989).

There are no publicly owned recreational facilities on the lake. Christina Lake Recreation Resort, a commercially operated facility, provides the only access to the water. It is located on the north shore at the west end of the lake (Fig. 2). The resort is open year-round and has 100 campsites, cabins, picnic tables, sewage disposal facilities, pump water, a grocery store, a marina, boat launch, boat rentals, a playground, a beach, and hiking, snowmobiling and cross-country skiing trails. Improvement District No. 18 (North) holds a recreational lease for Crown land at the western end of the lake. The facility, Wassasi Day Use Area, is administered by the Conklin Recreation Society, and access is restricted to local residents.

Camping, picnicking, and fishing for walleye, northern pike and yellow perch are the favoured recreational activities at the lake. Arctic grayling is a popular catch in the Jackfish River. Christina Lake is closed to sport fishing during a designated period in April and May each year (Alta. For. Ld. Wild. 1989). Swimming, wind surfing, water skiing, power boating, row boating, canoeing and hiking are other popular activities (Randall Conrad & Assoc. 1988). There are no boating restrictions specific to the lake, but general federal regulations apply (Alta. For. Ld. Wild. 1988). The water is quite transparent during summer, and the density of aquatic plants is low.

Drainage Basin Characteristics

Christina Lake's extensive drainage basin is almost 60 times larger than the lake (Tables 1, 2). Most of it lies to the south of the lake and much of this portion is drained by Birch and Sunday creeks, which

136

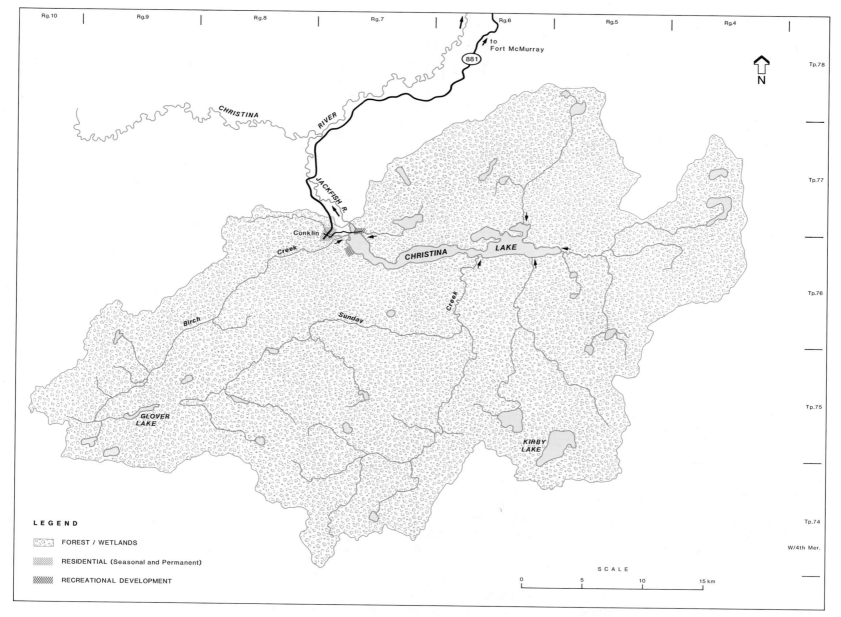

Figure 1. Features of the drainage basin of Christina Lake.
SOURCES: Alta. Envir. n.d.[b]; En. Mines Resour. Can. 1975. Updated with 1983 aerial photos.

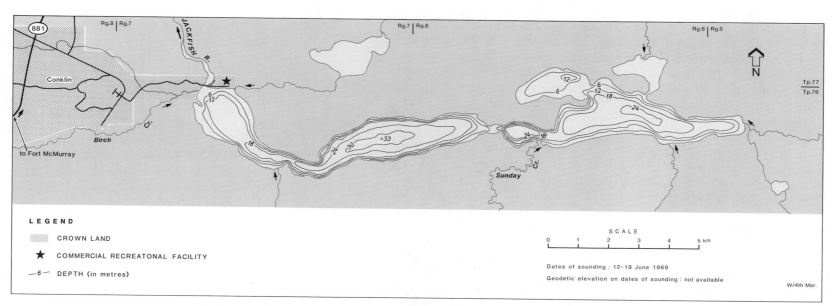

Figure 2. Bathymetry and shoreline features of Christina Lake.
BATHYMETRY SOURCE: modified from Griffiths and Ferster 1974.

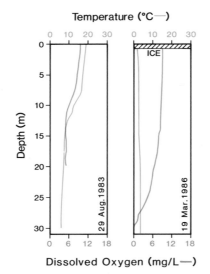

Figure 3. Temperature and dissolved oxygen in Christina Lake, 1983 and 1986.
SOURCE: Alta. Envir. n.d.[a].

are the largest of the six streams that flow into the lake (Fig. 1). The outlet, the Jackfish River, is located at the western tip of the lake. It flows north into the nearby Christina River, which eventually flows into the Athabasca River.

The drainage basin is part of a till plain that slopes gradually downward to the northeast. Land in the northeast portion of the watershed is level to nearly level, and the remainder is gently undulating to gently rolling. The main soil parent material in the drainage basin is sandy or gravelly outwash and the most common soils are Podzolic Gray and Orthic Gray Luvisols (Wynnyk et al. 1963). Generally, the area is poorly drained and muskeg covers up to 80% of the land. The watershed is located in the Wet Mixedwood Subregion of the Boreal Mixedwood Ecoregion (Strong and Leggat 1981). The vegetation consists of black spruce, willows and Labrador tea on Organic soils, trembling aspen, balsam poplar and white spruce on moderately well-drained Gray Luvisols and jack pine on sandy soils. The low hills surrounding the lake are covered with a mixed forest of birch, balsam poplar and white spruce; willows and wet areas are present along the shore.

Although there is no agricultural activity in the drainage basin, there is considerable oil and gas activity. With the exception of Conklin, all land bordering the lake is Crown land. The population of Conklin in 1981 was 116 people. The majority of the residents are Métis, and some of them maintain a traditional hunting and trapping lifestyle (Alta. Native Aff. 1986). Although the eastern boundary of the hamlet touches the lakeshore, there is no residential development along the shore (Randall Conrad & Assoc. 1988). A lake management plan for Christina Lake was drafted by Alberta Forestry, Lands and Wildlife in 1989. The finalized document will be used by Improvement District No. 18 (North) as the basis for an area structure plan that will guide future developments on the lakeshore.

Lake Basin Characteristics

Christina Lake is a long, narrow water body oriented in an east-west direction (Fig. 2). It has three deep basins that drop off abruptly to maximum depths of 33 m, 26 m and 24 m. The east and west basins are long and narrow and, in comparison, the central basin is small and round. In places, the lake is 12- to 15-m deep only 9 m from shore (Bradley n.d.). A shallow constriction joins the west and central basins. In addition to the three deep basins, there are two shallower basins. They branch north from the east basin and reach maximum depths of 12.2 m and 1.5 m. The mean depth of the lake is about 17 m (Table 2). Along the shoreline, extensive areas of sand and gravel form beaches.

Table 1. Characteristics of Christina Lake drainage basin.

area (excluding lake) (km²)[a]	1 250
soil[b]	Podzolic Gray and Orthic Gray Luvisols
bedrock geology[c]	La Biche Formation (Upper Cretaceous): shale, ironstone partings and concretions; marine
terrain[b]	level to gently rolling
ecoregion[d]	Wet Mixedwood Subregion of Boreal Mixedwood
dominant vegetation[b, d]	black spruce, trembling aspen
mean annual inflow (m³)[a, e]	155 x 10⁶
mean annual sunshine (h)[f]	2 109

NOTE: [e]excluding groundwater inflow
SOURCES: [a]Alta. Envir. n.d.[b]; [b]Wynnyk et al. 1963; [c]Alta. Res. Counc. 1972; [d]Strong and Leggat 1981; [f]Envir. Can. 1982

Table 2. Characteristics of Christina Lake.

elevation (m)[a]	approximately 554.1
surface area (km²)[b]	21.3
volume (m³)[b]	369 x 10⁶
maximum depth (m)[b]	32.9
mean depth (m)[b]	17.3
shoreline length (km)[b]	58.4
mean annual lake evaporation (mm)[c]	607
mean annual precipitation (mm)[c]	584
mean residence time (yr)[b, c, d]	2.5
control structure	none

NOTE: [d]excluding groundwater inflow
SOURCES: [a]En. Mines Resour. Can. 1975; [b]Bradley n.d.; [c]Alta. Envir. n.d.[b].

Table 3. Major ions and related water quality variables for Christina Lake. Concentrations in mg/L; pH in pH units. Composite sample from the euphotic zone collected on 29 Aug. 1983.

pH	8.2
total alkalinity (CaCO₃)	115
specific conductivity (μS/cm)	220
total dissolved solids (calculated)	117
total hardness (CaCO₃)	98
HCO₃	140
CO₃	0
Mg	8
Na	7
K	1
Cl	<1
SO₄	<5
Ca	26

SOURCE: Alta. Envir. n.d.[a], Naquadat station 01AL07CE3100

The water level in Christina Lake has been recorded since November 1985 (Alta. Envir. n.d.[c]). Because the elevation of the lake has not been surveyed, the water levels refer to an assumed bench mark rather than geodetic elevation. The maximum observed water level was 29.54 m on 26 July 1986, and the minimum was 28.40 m on 15 October 1987, a fluctuation of 1.14 m.

Water Quality

The water quality of Christina Lake was surveyed by Alberta Environment on 29 August 1983 and 19 March 1986 (Alta. Envir. n.d.[a]).

The limited data suggest that the water is well-buffered and fresh, and not as hard as that of most prairie lakes (Table 3). The main ions are bicarbonate and calcium. Because of its great depth, the lake

Table 4. Nutrient and Secchi depth data for Christina Lake.
Concentrations in µg/L. Composite sample from the euphotic zone collected on 29 Aug. 1983.

total phosphorus	16
total Kjeldahl nitrogen	540
NH$_4$–nitrogen	18
iron	<20
Secchi depth (m)	5.0

SOURCE: Alta. Envir. n.d.[a], Naquadat station 01AL07CE3100

becomes strongly thermally stratified during summer (Fig. 3). By late August 1983, the surface temperature had warmed to 19°C and the dissolved oxygen concentration, which was monitored only to 20 m, declined to about 5 mg/L below a depth of 9 m (Fig. 3). In March 1986, dissolved oxygen concentrations dropped to less than 5 mg/L only at depths below 24 m.

The trophic status of Christina Lake cannot be determined because of insufficient data. However, the relatively low total phosphorus concentration (16 µg/L) and the very clear water on 29 August 1983 (Table 4) suggest that the lake is quite unproductive.

Biological Characteristics

No recent data are available for the plant and invertebrate communities in Christina Lake. A June 1969 survey by Fish and Wildlife Division staff briefly described aquatic macrophyte distribution and the composition of the invertebrate population (Bradley n.d.).

Plants

The density of aquatic macrophytes in June 1969 was low, except in the two shallow northern bays at the east end of the lake and in the western bay. Suitable habitat for macrophytes is limited because of the steeply sloping sides of most of the lake basin.

Invertebrates

The density of benthic invertebrates, calculated from 44 samples taken on 14 and 15 June in 1969, was 1 624 organisms/m^2 for all depths combined. Only the total volume of midge larvae (Chironomidae) and scuds (Amphipoda), the most abundant groups, was calculated (4.66 mL/m^2). Chironomids were most numerous (833/m^2), but accounted for only 26% of the total volume. Amphipods were secondary in abundance (691/m^2), but accounted for 74% of the total volume.

Fish

Seven species of fish have been captured in Christina Lake: walleye, northern pike, yellow perch, lake whitefish, cisco, burbot and white sucker (Bradley n.d.). As well, Arctic grayling are present in the Jackfish and Christina rivers (Sullivan 1988). The lake is managed for domestic, commercial and recreational fisheries. There is no recent information on the domestic fishery, but in 1969 and 1970, nets were set daily and the bulk of the catch was whitefish, white suckers, burbot and pike (Bradley n.d.).

Records for the commercial fishery have been kept since 1942/43 (Alta. For. Ld. Wild. n.d.; Alta. Rec. Parks 1976). Historically, cisco and whitefish were the main catches and burbot, white suckers, northern pike and walleye were of secondary importance. Both whitefish and cisco are infested with cysts of the tapeworm *Triaenophorus crassus*. The largest whitefish catch (12 277 kg) was taken in 1957/58, and the largest cisco catch (33 628 kg) was taken

in 1950/51. The lake was not fished between 1967 and 1970. As well, no licences were issued for six of the nine years from 1979/80 to 1987/88. During the 1970s, the average total catch was 3 951 kg/year. Catch rates declined considerably, however, during the 1980s. From 1980/81 to 1987/88, the average total catch for the three years when the fishery opened was 538 kg/year. The composition of the average catch was 66% whitefish, 20% walleye, 11% northern pike and 3% cisco (Alta. For. Ld. Wild. n.d.). The catch of burbot and white suckers was not recorded for this period.

There is little information available about the sport fishery. Until 1986, when Secondary Road 881 was completed, access to the lake was generally restricted to anglers who arrived by plane or train. District Fisheries Officers have reported that, since 1986, fishing pressure has increased considerably (Sullivan 1988). Walleye is the most valued species in Christina Lake, and Arctic grayling is the prime catch in the Jackfish River (Randall Conrad & Assoc. 1988).

Wildlife

Christina Lake is rated as fair for waterfowl production. Four areas of the lake provide the best waterfowl habitat: the shallowest basin that branches north from the east side of the lake, the Jackfish River at the outlet, the marsh near Sunday Creek and the delta of Sunday Creek. At least 29 species of waterbirds have been observed feeding at the lake or using the lake as a staging area. Bald Eagles and Ospreys have also been sighted (Christina L. Mgt. Plan Team 1989).

Most of the wildlife habitat near the lake is undisturbed, as access is difficult by land, and hunting pressure is not heavy. Caribou are present throughout the area, and the shoreland is classed as fair to good moose habitat. Many beaver lodges are located along the lakeshore, and otters are also present (Christina L. Mgt. Plan Team 1989).

M.E. Bradford

References

Alberta Environment. n.d.[a]. Envir. Assess. Div., Envir. Qlty. Monit. Br. Unpubl. data, Edmonton.
———. n.d.[b]. Tech. Serv. Div., Hydrol. Br. Unpubl. data, Edmonton.
———. n.d.[c]. Tech. Serv. Div., Surv. Br. Unpubl. data, Edmonton.
Alberta Forestry, Lands and Wildlife. n.d. Fish Wild. Div. Unpubl. data, Edmonton.
———. 1988. Boating in Alberta. Fish Wild. Div., Edmonton.
———. 1989. Guide to sportfishing. Fish Wild. Div., Edmonton.
Alberta Native Affairs. 1986. A guide to native communities in Alberta. Native Aff. Secret., Edmonton.
Alberta Recreation, Parks and Wildlife. 1976. Commercial fisheries catch statistics for Alberta, 1942–1975. Fish Wild. Div., Fish. Mgt. Rep. No. 22, Edmonton.
Alberta Research Council. 1972. Geological map of Alberta. Nat. Resour. Div., Alta. Geol. Surv., Edmonton.
Bradley, G.M. n.d. Preliminary biological survey of six lakes in northern Alberta, 1969. Surv. Rep. No. 15. Alta. Ld. For., Fish Wild. Div., Edmonton.
Christina Lake Management Plan Team. 1989. Alternatives document for the Christina Lake management plan: Draft. Alta. For. Ld. Wild., For. Serv. Div. Unpubl. rep., Fort McMurray.
Energy, Mines and Resources Canada. 1975. National topographic series 1:250 000 73M (1975). Surv. Map. Br., Ottawa.
Environment Canada. 1982. Canadian climate normals, Vol. 7: Bright sunshine (1951–1980). Prep. by Atm. Envir. Serv. Supply Serv. Can., Ottawa.
Griffiths, W.E. and D.B. Ferster. 1974. Preliminary fisheries survey of the Winefred-Pelican area. Alta. Ld. For., Fish Wild. Div., Edmonton.
Holmgren, E.J. and P.M. Holmgren. 1976. Over 2000 place names of Alberta. 3rd ed. West. Producer Prairie Books, Saskatoon.
Randall Conrad & Associates. 1988. Athabasca River basin study: Water based recreation component. Prep. for Alta. Envir., Plan. Div. Unpubl. rep., Edmonton.
Schroder, J. 1988. Alta. Transp. Util., Reg. Transp. Div., Lac La Biche. Pers. comm.
Strong, W.L. and K.R. Leggat. 1981. Ecoregions of Alberta. Alta. En. Nat. Resour., Resour. Eval. Plan. Div., Edmonton.
Sullivan, M. 1988. Alta. For. Ld. Wild., Fish Wild. Div., St. Paul. Pers. comm.
Wynnyk, A., J.D. Lindsay, P.K. Heringa and W. Odynsky. 1963. Exploratory soil survey of Alberta map sheets 83–O, 83–P, and 73–M. Prelim. Soil Surv. Rep. 64–1. Res. Counc. Alta., Edmonton.

GREGOIRE LAKE

Alberta Recreation and Parks

MAP SHEETS: 73D/3, 6
LOCATION: Tp86 R7, 8 W4
LAT/LONG: 56°27'N 110°09'W

Gregoire Lake is an important recreational lake for residents of the city of Fort McMurray. The lake is located in Improvement District No. 18 (North), about 30 km southeast of Fort McMurray. To reach the lake from the city, take Highway 63 south and then Secondary Road 881 southeast. Gregoire Lake Provincial Park, situated on the northwestern shore (Fig. 1), is the largest recreational facility at the lake and is the only provincial park in the Fort McMurray area. The hamlet of Anzac is situated on the eastern shore.

Until the 1940s, Gregoire Lake was known as Willow Lake (Alta. Rec. Parks n.d.). It was renamed for its outlet, the Gregoire River, which was named for an early settler (Geog. Bd. Can. 1928).

Woodland Cree and Chipewyan Indians have lived in the area since before the arrival of white explorers. During the early 1900s, there was an Indian settlement on the northwestern shore of the lake. At present, the Fort McMurray Band of Cree and Chipewyan Indians has three treaty reserves on the lake, which cover a total of 1 304 ha. They are Gregoire Lake Reserves 176, 176A and 176B (Alta. Native Aff. 1986). A 1984 census indicated 140 band members, but most of them do not live on the reserves.

The history of the general area involves many of Canada's first explorers. The Athabasca country was opened to the fur trade after 1778, when Peter Pond discovered the Methy Portage to the Clearwater River (Lombard North Group 1974). In 1789, Alexander Mackenzie first travelled the Athabasca River on his journeys to the Arctic and Pacific oceans. In 1799, David Thompson travelled the Athabasca-Clearwater River system, and in 1819, Sir John Franklin passed through the Fort McMurray area on an overland journey to the arctic.

The Gregoire Lake area was surveyed in about 1916 by the Australia-New Zealand Army Corps (ANZAC), which named the hamlet of Anzac. Anzac became a stopover on the Northern Alberta Railway route between Cheecham Siding to the south, and the McInnis fish plant in Waterways Station, near Fort McMurray. The local fishery was centred at Garson Lake, to the east of Anzac on the Saskatchewan border (Alta. Rec. Parks n.d.).

There are several public and private recreational facilities on Gregoire Lake. Gregoire Lake Provincial Park is located on the northwestern shore (Fig. 2). It was officially opened in 1973 (Finlay and Finlay 1987). Day-use services are provided year-round and camping services are provided from 1 May to Thanksgiving Day. Park facilities include 140 campsites (60 with electricity), a group camping area, tap water, a sewage disposal facility, a picnic area, a beach, a boat launch, boat rentals and walking trails. During summer, the main activities of park visitors are swimming, motor boating, picnicking, camping and fishing. During winter, visitors enjoy cross-country skiing and ice fishing. Part of the provincial park, the Anzac Day-use Area, is located on the eastern shore near the hamlet. Facilities include picnic tables, a beach, a dock and an informal boat launch. There are no boating regulations over most of the lake, but in designated swimming areas, boats are prohibited, and in posted areas, power boats are subject to a maximum speed of 12 km/hour (Alta. For. Ld. Wild. 1988).

Improvement District No. 18 (North) maintains Windsurfer Beach on land leased from the province. The area runs east from Reserve 176, past the Gregoire River. Near the river, there are picnic tables, firepits and about 20 primitive campsites; farther west, near the reserve boundary, there is a rocky beach used as a wind surfer

Table 1. Characteristics of Gregoire Lake drainage basin.

area (excluding lake) (km²)[a]	232
soil[b]	Orthic Gray Luvisols and Fibric and Terric Mesisols
bedrock geology[c]	Grand Rapids Formation (Lower Cretaceous): sandstone, siltstone, shale, thin coal beds; shoreline complex Clearwater Formation (Lower Cretaceous): sandstone, siltstone, shale, thin coal beds; shoreline complex Joli Fou Formation (Lower Cretaceous): shale; marine La Biche Formation (Upper Cretaceous): shale, ironstone partings and concretions; marine
terrain[b]	level to hummocky
ecoregion[d]	Moist and Wet Mixedwood Subregions of Boreal Mixedwood
dominant vegetation[b]	trembling aspen, white spruce, black spruce
mean annual inflow (m³)[a, e]	27.3×10^6
mean annual sunshine (h)[f]	2 109

NOTE: [e]excluding groundwater inflow
SOURCES: [a]Alta. Envir. n.d.[c]; [b]Turchenek and Lindsay 1982; [c]Alta. Res. Counc. 1972; [d]Strong and Leggat 1981; [f]Envir. Can. 1982

Table 2. Characteristics of Gregoire Lake.

elevation (m)[a, b]	475.17
surface area (km²)[a, b]	25.8
volume (m³)[a, b]	100×10^6
maximum depth (m)[a, b]	7.2
mean depth (m)[a, b]	3.9
shoreline length (km)[c]	32.2
mean annual lake evaporation (mm)[d]	580
mean annual precipitation (mm)[d]	504
mean residence time (yr)[d, e]	4
control structure[f]	sheet-pile fixed-crest weir and step-pool fish ladder with 6 steps
weir height (m)[f]	3.35
crest length (m)[f]	22.86
target elevation (m)[g]	475.27

NOTES: [a]on date of sounding: 02 Oct. 1982; [e]excluding groundwater inflow
SOURCES: [b]Alta. Envir. n.d.[d]; [c]Bradley n.d.; [d]Alta. Envir. n.d.[c]; [f]Alta. Envir. n.d.[e]; [g]Alta. Envir. n.d.[a].

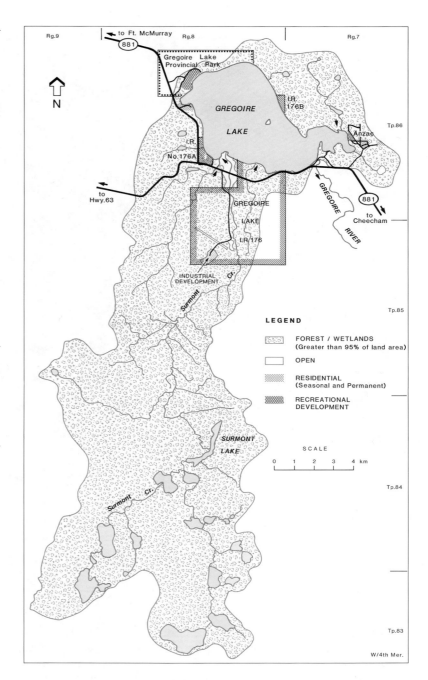

Figure 1. Features of the drainage basin of Gregoire Lake.
SOURCES: Alta. Envir. n.d.[c]; En. Mines Resour. Can. 1979; 1984. Updated with 1985 aerial photos.

staging area, and a few picnic tables. The only commercial campground and day-use area at the lake is operated by the Fort McMurray Band; it is located on Reserve 176A on the eastern shore. Private camps at the lake include Camp Yogi, located north of the Anzac Day-use Area, and Camp Manytrees, located north of Indian Reserve 176A (Fig. 2). Camp Yogi is operated by the nonprofit Camp Yogi Society and is used by community groups for social gatherings, camping and outdoor education. As well, a recreational lease is held by the Fort McMurray Regional Camping Association on 32 ha of Crown land that lies between Reserve 176A and the subdivision on the western shore.

Most of the shoreland around the lake belongs to the Crown or to the Indian reserves. A point of land at the southwest corner of the lake, at the inlet of Surmont Creek (Fig. 2), was reserved as a natural area in 1966, and currently has protected status (Alta. For. Ld. Wild. 1987). Patented land includes a half section of land between Reserves 176 and 176A, subdivided land along the eastern shore south of the provincial park, and land within Anzac.

Aquatic vegetation is abundant around the shoreline of Gregoire Lake and blue-green algae sometimes form blooms during summer.

The lake supports a domestic fishery and a popular sport fishery for walleye, northern pike and yellow perch. The Gregoire River and Gregoire Lake and its tributary streams are closed to fishing for a designated period during April and May each year (Alta. For. Ld. Wild. 1989).

Drainage Basin Characteristics

Gregoire Lake has a large drainage basin that is about 9 times the size of the lake (Tables 1, 2). Most water drains into the lake from the south via Surmont Creek and its tributaries. As well, there are six small streams that enter the lake at various points (Fig. 1). The outflow, the Gregoire River, eventually flows into the Athabasca River via the Clearwater and Christina rivers.

Gregoire Lake's watershed is part of the Boreal Mixedwood Ecoregion and the Interior Plains physiographic division. Turchenek and Lindsay (1982) subdivided the Gregoire Lake drainage basin into three ecodistricts based on relief, geology, geomorphology and vegetation. The ecodistricts are the Garson Plain, the Cheecham Hills Escarpment and the House Plain.

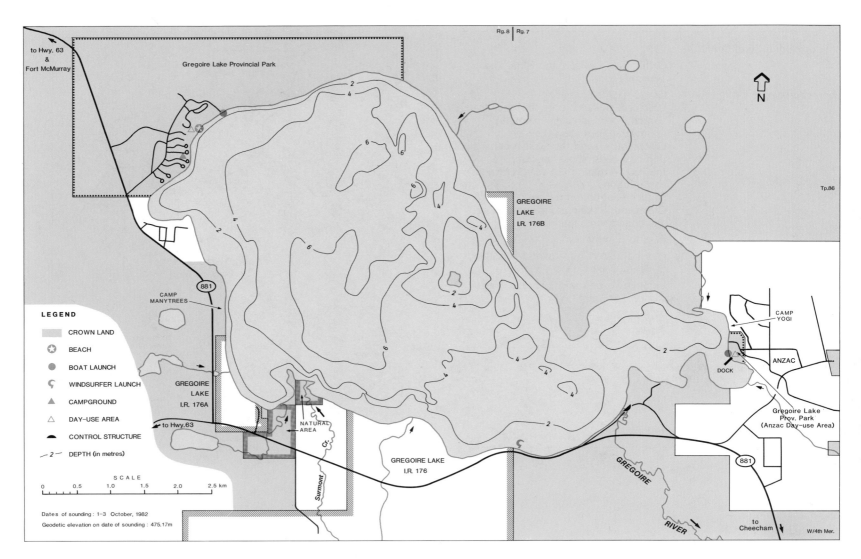

Figure 2. Bathymetry and shoreline features of Gregoire Lake. BATHYMETRY SOURCE: Alta. Envir. n.d.[d].

The Garson Plain is an undulating to hummocky plain that surrounds the lake on the northern, southern and western shores. Surficial material is predominantly glacial till underlain by the Grand Rapids and Clearwater bedrock formations (Table 1). Elevations on the plain range from 450 to 500 m. Soils are mostly moderately well-drained to well-drained Orthic Gray Luvisols and poorly to very poorly drained Fibric and Terric Mesisols. Around the lakeshore, most of the vegetation is deciduous forest composed primarily of trembling aspen, and secondarily of balsam poplar and white birch (Lombard North Group 1974). Occasional areas of deciduous/jack pine forest and deciduous/spruce/feathermoss communities also occur. Several areas of black spruce/tamarack bog are located along the southern shore and to the north of the lake.

The Cheecham Hills Escarpment is the most prominent feature of the drainage basin. It is a highly dissected, north-facing escarpment that lies between Indian Reserve 176 and Surmont Lake. Surficial material is colluvium, and shales of the Joli Fou and La Biche bedrock formations are exposed in the deeper valleys. Elevations range from 550 to 750 m and slopes range from 2 to 30%. Land near the streams on this escarpment is rough and broken, with steep slopes (greater than 15%). The main soils are well-drained Orthic Gray Luvisols and Orthic Regosols, with small deposits of Organics. Vegetation consists mainly of deciduous forest composed of trembling aspen, balsam poplar and white birch, with smaller areas of deciduous/spruce/feathermoss forest and deciduous/spruce/jack pine forest (Lombard North Group 1974).

The House Plain is an undulating to hummocky plain that occupies the most southerly portion of the drainage basin. Kinosis till, the main surficial material, overlies the shales of the La Biche Formation. Elevations range from 650 to 750 m and slopes range from 0 to 15%. Well-drained Orthic Gray Luvisols and poorly to very poorly drained

Fibric, Terric and Typic Mesisols are the dominant soils. Black spruce forest and wetland fen communities are common throughout the area, with mixed coniferous, trembling aspen and jack pine forests on upland sites.

There is no agricultural activity in the drainage basin. Industrial development is centred on resource extraction and most of the land in the drainage basin is held under bituminous sands leases or oil sands leases. The Amoco In-Situ Oil Plant is located on Gregoire Lake Indian Reserve No. 176 (Lombard North Group 1974; Murray V. Jones Assoc. Ltd. 1978).

Lake Basin Characteristics

Gregoire Lake is a large, shallow lake with a surface area of almost 26 km² (Table 2). The deepest water (7.2 m) is located in the western half of the single, large basin, and an island is located near the eastern shore (Fig. 2). The shoreline is composed mainly of rubble and gravel, with the exception of three large, sandy beaches (Bradley n.d.).

The elevation of Gregoire Lake has been monitored since 1975 (Fig. 3). The historic minimum level (475.01 m) was recorded in October 1981 and the maximum level (475.88 m) was recorded in May 1985. This is a range of 0.87 m. Figure 4 illustrates changes in the lake's area and capacity that occur with fluctuations in the water level. In 1973, Alberta Environment built a sheet-pile weir on the outlet to stabilize lake levels (Table 2). The control structure includes a 1.2–m–wide step-pool fish ladder which is operated by Fish and Wildlife Division. The target elevation for the lake was set at 475.27 m at the request of Alberta Recreation and Parks (Alta. Envir. n.d.[a]).

Table 3. Major ions and related water quality variables for Gregoire Lake. Average concentrations in mg/L; pH in pH units. Composite samples collected 9 times from 07 May to 04 Nov. 1980. S.E. = standard error.

	Mean	S.E.
pH (range)	7.1–7.9[a]	—
total alkalinity ($CaCO_3$)	49	1.4
specific conductivity (μS/cm)	117	3.7
total dissolved solids (calculated)	60[a]	0.9
turbidity (NTU)	4[a]	0.5
total hardness ($CaCO_3$)	53[a]	0.9
dissolved organic carbon	12[a]	0.4
HCO_3	59	1.6
CO_3	0	0
Mg	4[a]	0.1
Na	2[a]	0.1
K	0.8[a]	0.06
Cl	0.9[a]	0.04
SO_4	6[a]	0.2
Ca	15	0.3

NOTE: [a] n = 6

SOURCE: Alta. Envir. n.d.[b], Naquadat stations 01AT07CE0020, 01AT07CE0021, 01AT07CE0022

Water Quality

Gregoire Lake's water quality was sampled by Alberta Environment between 1976 and 1983 under the Alberta Oil Sands Environmental Research Program, on 15 August 1988 and during 1989 under a joint sampling program with Alberta Recreation and Parks (Alta. Envir. n.d.[b]).

The lake has fresh water, with alkalinity, hardness and pH values that are very low for an Alberta lake (Table 3). The dominant ions are calcium and bicarbonate.

Gregoire Lake is typical of many shallow Alberta lakes: the water column is well-mixed by wind during the open-water season (Fig. 5), and is thermally stratified on calm days. Dissolved oxygen concentrations during the open-water season are generally high and quite uniform from surface to bottom (Fig. 6). In February 1980, under-ice dissolved oxygen levels throughout the water column declined to less than 3 mg/L.

The limited chlorophyll *a* data available suggest that Gregoire Lake is eutrophic. In 1979, the maximum chlorophyll *a* concentration was 69.9 μg/L, recorded in August (Fig. 7), and the average chlorophyll *a* value for the open-water season was 34.4 μg/L (Table 4). The chlorophyll *a* concentration recorded in August 1988, however, was much lower (13.2 μg/L), as was the average concentration in 1989 (5.3 μg/L). The water was quite murky—the average Secchi transparency was only 1.3 m in 1979 and 2.4 m in 1989. Total phosphorus concentrations are not available for 1979, but the 1989 average was 21 μg/L.

Biological Characteristics

Plants

The phytoplankton in Gregoire Lake was studied by Alberta Environment occasionally from July to October 1977 and intensively from March to November 1980 (Beliveau and Furnell 1980). More than 70 species were identified, but biomass was not calculated for each species. The biomass of the major algal groups was measured as total cell volume per square metre. Blue-greens (Cyanophyta) were the major group measured on 7 of the 11 sampling dates. In late March and from June to September, blue-greens accounted for 44 to 83% of the total cell volume. Cryptophytes were dominant in early March and early May, and diatoms formed 91 to 97% of the total volume in October and early November.

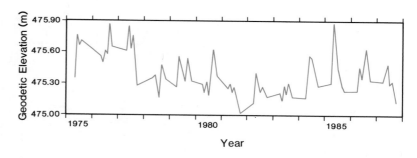

Figure 3. Water level of Gregoire Lake, 1975 to 1987. SOURCE: Envir. Can. 1975–1987.

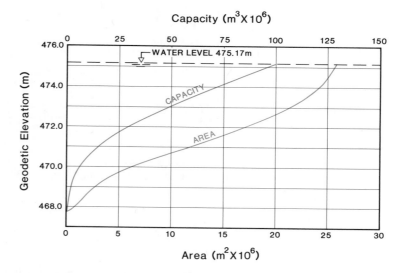

Figure 4. Area/capacity curve for Gregoire Lake. SOURCE: Alta. Envir. n.d.[d].

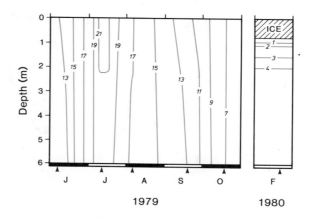

Figure 5. Temperature (°C) of Gregoire Lake, 1979 to 1980. Arrows indicate sampling dates. SOURCE: Alta. Envir. n.d.[b].

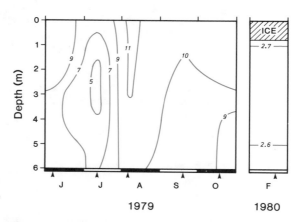

Figure 6. Dissolved oxygen (mg/L) in Gregoire Lake, 1979 to 1980. Arrows indicate sampling dates. SOURCE: Alta. Envir. n.d.[b].

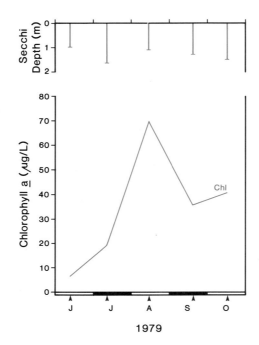

Figure 7. Chlorophyll a and Secchi depth in Gregoire Lake, 1979. Total phosphorus data not available.
SOURCE: Alta. Envir. n.d.[b].

Table 4. Nutrient, chlorophyll *a* and Secchi depth data for Gregoire Lake. Average concentrations in µg/L. Composite sample from the euphotic zone collected 5 times from 12 June to 17 Oct. 1979, once on 18 Aug. 1988, and 4 times from 07 June to 13 Sept. 1989. S.E. = standard error.

	1979		1988	1989	
	Mean	S.E.		Mean	S.E.
total phosphorus	—	—	33	23	2.5
total dissolved phosphorus	—	—	9	—	—
total Kjeldahl nitrogen	—	—	640	—	—
NO$_3$ + NO$_2$–nitrogen	—	—	23	—	—
NH$_4$–nitrogen	—	—	22	—	—
iron	—	—	136	—	—
chlorophyll *a*	34.4	10.58	13.2	6.2	0.96
Secchi depth (m)	1.3	0.12	1.5	2.2	0.13

SOURCE: Alta. Envir. n.d.[b], Naquadat stations 01AT07CE0020, 01AT07CE0021, 01AT07CE0022

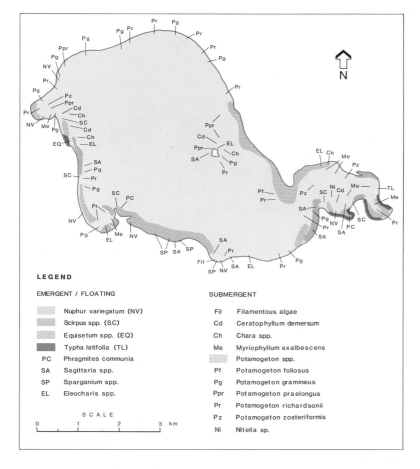

Figure 8. Distribution of aquatic macrophytes in Gregoire Lake, 28 to 30 July 1981.
SOURCE: Alta. Envir. n.d.[b].

Alberta Environment surveyed the macrophyte community in July 1981 (Fig. 8). Dense beds of the emergent species horsetail (*Equisetum* spp.), yellow water lily (*Nuphar variegatum*), bulrush (*Scirpus* spp.) and common cattail (*Typha latifolia*) were observed growing in the eastern bay and along the western shore. The most abundant submergent plants were various species of pondweed (*Potamogeton* spp.). The abundance of aquatic plants was lowest along the northern shore and along a section of the southern shore.

Invertebrates

There are no data available for the zooplankton community.

In May 1969, Fish and Wildlife Division briefly surveyed the benthic invertebrates (Bradley n.d.). Thirty-four samples were taken with a dredge at unspecified depths over the entire lake bottom. Almost 90% of the volume was made up of midge larvae (Chironomidae).

Fish

Eight species of fish are known to inhabit Gregoire Lake: walleye, northern pike, yellow perch, lake whitefish, cisco, burbot, spottail shiner and longnose sucker (Bradley n.d.). Lake whitefish are infested with cysts of the tapeworm *Triaenophorus crassus*. The lake supports a domestic fishery and a popular recreational fishery. A small commercial fishery operated from 1944 to 1966 (Alta. Rec. Parks Wild. 1976). There are no catch data available for the domestic fishery. Between 1985/86 and 1988/89, no domestic licences were issued for the first 2 years, 16 licences were issued in 1987/88 and 9 licences were issued in 1988/89 (Alta. For. Ld. Wild. n.d.).

A creel survey of the sport fishery at Gregoire Lake was conducted during 1984 (Table 5). It was estimated that 5 358 anglers visited the lake and fished for a total of 16 181 hours. Anglers did not actively fish for pike, because the preferred species was walleye. Consequently, 75% of the pike caught were released. The average harvest/angler-hour for 22 lakes in the Northeast Region surveyed between 1984 and 1987 was 0.10 for walleye, 0.22 for northern pike and 0.32 for yellow perch (Alta. For. Ld. Wild. n.d.). In comparison, the harvest per unit effort at Gregoire Lake was more than twice the regional average for walleye (0.21 walleye/angler-hour) and slightly less than average for northern pike (0.17 pike/angler-hour). The yellow perch harvest/angler-hour (0.01) was well below average. Only 32% of the anglers interviewed at Gregoire Lake caught one or more walleye and 28% caught one or more pike. The largest harvests of all species were taken during late June and, for yellow perch, during late July as well (Sullivan 1985). In comparison to six other Northeast Region lakes surveyed during 1984, Gregoire Lake received low to moderate angling pressure (4.8 angler-hours/ha).

Table 5. Estimated angler numbers, effort and harvest from Gregoire Lake. Estimates based on creel survey data collected from 15 May to 31 Aug. 1984. A total of 39 weekdays and 31 weekend days and holidays were surveyed; 36 weekdays were not included. Information was collected from 07:00 to 23:00. WE = walleye; NP = northern pike; YP = yellow perch.

	WE	NP	YP	Total
number of anglers[a]	—	—	—	5 358
angler-hours[b]	—	—	—	16 181
total number fish harvested[c]	3 387	2 810	122	6 319
total yield (kg)	2 683	2 995	18	5 696
mean weight (g)	792	1 066	150	—
catch/angler-hour	0.32	0.68	0.01	1.01
harvest/angler-hour[b, c]	0.21	0.17	0.01	0.38
harvest/angler[a, c]	0.62	0.51	0.02	1.15

NOTES: [a]observed no. anglers = 2 771; [b]observed hours = 8 368; [c]based on observed no. fish kept: WE = 1 729, NP = 1 401, YP = 70
SOURCE: Sullivan 1985

Wildlife

Although Gregoire Lake is used as a staging area for migrating waterfowl, its potential is low compared to other lakes in the area such as Gordon and Garson lakes (Lombard North Group 1974; Finlay and Finlay 1987). Approximately 126 bird species have been sighted in Gregoire Lake Provincial Park; 118 of these were summer residents or were found nesting (Gregg 1976). Spruce Grouse, Gray Jays and Magnolia and Palm warblers are commonly seen in black spruce bogs and waterfowl feed and nest in marsh communities.

Wildlife data specific to Gregoire Lake and its drainage basin are limited. Wildlife species in the Fort McMurray region were summarized in 1974 (Lombard North Group 1974). Fur-bearing animals commonly found in the watershed are beaver, lynx, mink, muskrats, red fox, otters, wolves, coyotes and weasels. The principal ungulates are moose, deer and caribou.

M.E. Bradford

References

Alberta Environment. n.d.[a]. Devel. Op. Div. Unpubl. data, Edmonton.
———. n.d.[b]. Envir. Assess. Div., Envir. Qlty. Monit. Br. Unpubl. data, Edmonton.
———. n.d.[c]. Tech. Serv. Div., Hydrol. Br. Unpubl. data, Edmonton.
———. n.d.[d]. Tech. Serv. Div., Surv. Br. Unpubl. data, Edmonton.
———. n.d.[e]. Water Resour. Admin. Div., Dam Safety Br. Unpubl. data, Edmonton.
Alberta Forestry, Lands and Wildlife. n.d. Fish Wild. Div. Unpubl. data, Edmonton.
———. 1987. A summary of Alberta's natural areas reserved and established. Pub. Ld. Div., Ld. Mgt. Devel. Br. Unpubl. rep., Edmonton.
———. 1988. Boating in Alberta. Fish Wild. Div., Edmonton.
———. 1989. Guide to sportfishing. Fish Wild. Div., Edmonton.
Alberta Native Affairs. 1986. A guide to native communities in Alberta. Native Aff. Secret., Edmonton.
Alberta Recreation and Parks. n.d. Parks Div. Unpubl. data, Edmonton.
Alberta Recreation, Parks and Wildlife. 1976. Commercial fisheries catch statistics for Alberta, 1942–1975. Fish Wild. Div., Fish. Mgt. Rep. No. 22, Edmonton.
Alberta Research Council. 1972. Geological map of Alberta. Nat. Resour. Div., Alta. Geol. Surv., Edmonton.
Beliveau, D. and A. Furnell. 1980. Phytoplankton data summary 1976–1980. Alta. Envir., Poll. Contr. Div., Water Qlty. Contr. Br. Unpubl. rep., Edmonton.
Bradley, G.M. n.d. Preliminary biological survey of six lakes in northern Alberta, 1969. Surv. Rep. No. 15. Alta. Ld. For., Fish Wild. Div., Edmonton.
Energy, Mines and Resources Canada. 1979, 1984. National topographic series 1:50 000 74D/6 (1979), 74D/3 (1984). Surv. Map. Br., Ottawa.
Environment Canada. 1975–1987. Surface water data. Prep. by Inland Waters Directorate. Water Surv. Can., Water Resour. Br., Ottawa.
———. 1982. Canadian climate normals, Vol. 7: Bright sunshine (1951–1980). Prep. by Atm. Envir. Serv. Supply Serv. Can., Ottawa.
Finlay, J. and C. Finlay. 1987. Parks in Alberta: A guide to peaks, ponds, parklands & prairies. Hurtig Publ., Edmonton.
Geographic Board of Canada. 1928. Place-names of Alberta. Dept. Interior, Ottawa.
Gregg, A. 1976. An ecological assessment and development capability of Gregoire Lake. Prep. for Alta. Rec. Parks Wild., Parks Div. Unpubl. rep., Edmonton.
Lombard North Group. 1974. Environmental study, Amoco Canada tar sands lease, Gregoire Lake area, Alberta. Amoco Can. Petroleum Co. Ltd., Calgary.
Murray V. Jones and Associates Limited. 1978. Anzac. NE Alta. Reg. Commis., Edmonton.
Strong, W.L. and K.R. Leggat. 1981. Ecoregions of Alberta. Alta. En. Nat. Resour., Resour. Eval. Plan. Div., Edmonton.
Sullivan, M.G. 1985. Characteristics and impact of the sports fishery at Gregoire Lake during May-August 1984. Alta. En. Nat. Resour., Fish Wild. Div. Unpubl. rep., St. Paul.
Turchenek, L.W. and J.D. Lindsay. 1982. Soils inventory of the Alberta Oil Sands Environmental Research Program study area. Prep. for Alta. Envir., Res. Mgt. Div., AOSERP by Alta. Res. Counc. AOSERP Rep. 122, Edmonton.

ISLAND LAKE

E.E. Prepas

MAP SHEET: 83I/13
LOCATION: Tp67 R24 W4
LAT/LONG: 54°51'N 113°32'W

Island Lake is a picturesque, medium-sized lake that is especially attractive for canoeing. It has several islands and bays, and the water is often fairly clear. The lake is located in the County of Athabasca, about 20 km northwest of the town of Athabasca. The west side is accessible from Highway 2, which passes north through Athabasca from Edmonton then along the west shore of the lake enroute to the town of Slave Lake (Fig. 1). There is no public access by vehicle to the south and east shores.

Homesteads in the region were first established in about 1908 (Alta. Mun. Aff. 1980). Seasonal cottage development on Island Lake began with subdivision of land on the west side in 1956; the summer village of Island Lake was incorporated the following year. In 1983, a second summer village, Island Lake South, was incorporated (Fig. 2). Almost all residential development around the lake is located on the west shore within the two summer villages; in 1988 there were about 265 residences, of which approximately 25% were permanent (Brown 1988; Parsons 1988).

Public access at Island Lake is available at several locations on the west side within the summer villages. Boats may be launched at most of these sites (Fig. 2). An island near the west shore is leased by the Boy Scouts of Canada for camping and pioneering projects and the Young Men's Christian Association (YMCA) operates camping and canoe training programs on its property on the north basin of the lake (Alta. Mun. Aff. 1980). Recreational activities at the lake include swimming, power boating, water skiing, fishing and cross-country skiing. General federal boating regulations apply to Island Lake, but there are no specific restrictions (Alta. For. Ld. Wild. 1988). The nearest population centre is Athabasca, and there is a small store in the summer village of Island Lake.

The main basin of Island Lake is fairly shallow. A smaller, deeper northern basin is connected to the main basin by a narrow channel. The main basin may become green at times, but the water quality is quite good, and water quality in the northern basin is excellent. Shallow areas in the main basin support dense beds of aquatic vegetation. A commercial fishery, mainly for lake whitefish, operates every second year. Sport fishing, particularly for northern pike, is a popular pastime. There are no sport fishing regulations specific to Island Lake, but provincial regulations apply (Alta. For. Ld. Wild. 1989).

Drainage Basin Characteristics

Island Lake's drainage basin is about 8 times the size of the lake (Tables 1, 2). The main inflow drains from Ghost Lake and the northwestern portion of the drainage basin (Fig. 1). The watershed of Ghost Lake accounts for over one-third (22.5 km²) of Island Lake's drainage basin. Several intermittent streams carry runoff to the lake from other portions of the drainage basin. The outflow, Island Creek, flows from the east side of the lake southeast for about 5 km to the Athabasca River.

The land in the drainage basin varies from level to gently undulating areas (0 to 5% slope) west of the lake, to gently rolling (5 to 9% slope) in the southern and eastern regions, to moderately rolling (9 to 15% slope) around the north end of the lake and west of Ghost Lake, where there is rough knob and kettle topography. An area of

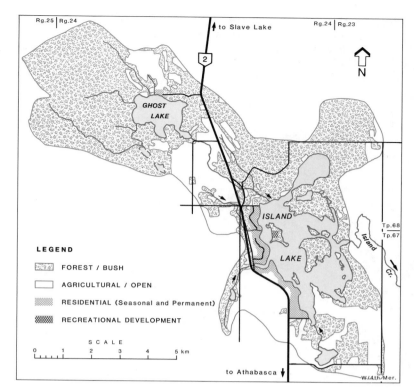

Figure 1. Features of the drainage basin of Island Lake.
SOURCES: Alta. Envir. n.d.[b]; En. Mines Resour. Can. 1973. Updated with 1985 aerial photos.

Table 1. Characteristics of Island Lake drainage basin.

area (excluding lake) (km²)[a]	63.2
soil[b]	Orthic Gray Luvisols
bedrock geology[c]	Lea Park Formation (Upper Cretaceous): shale, ironstone concretions; marine Wapiti Formation (Upper Cretaceous): sandstone, mudstone, bentonite, scattered coal beds; nonmarine
terrain[b]	undulating to moderately rolling
ecoregion[d]	Moist Mixedwood Subregion of Boreal Mixedwood
dominant vegetation[e]	trembling aspen
mean annual inflow (m³)[a, f]	2.96×10^6
mean annual sunshine (h)[g]	2 160

NOTE: [f]excluding groundwater inflow
SOURCES: [a]Alta. Envir. n.d.[b]; [b]Kjearsgaard 1972; [c]Alta. Res. Counc. 1972; [d]Strong and Leggat 1981; [e]Alta. Mun. Aff. 1980; [g]Envir. Can. 1982

Table 2. Characteristics of Island Lake.

elevation (m)[a, b]	±601
surface area (km²)[a, b]	7.81
volume (m³)[a, b]	29.2×10^6
maximum depth (m)[a, b]	18
mean depth (m)[a, b]	3.7
shoreline length (km)[a, b]	28
mean annual lake evaporation (mm)[c]	638
mean annual precipitation (mm)[c]	493
mean residence time (yr)[c, d]	16
control structure	none

NOTES: [a]on date of sounding: Sep. 1967; [d]excluding groundwater inflow
SOURCES: [b]Alta. Envir. n.d.[c]; [c]Alta. Envir. n.d.[b]

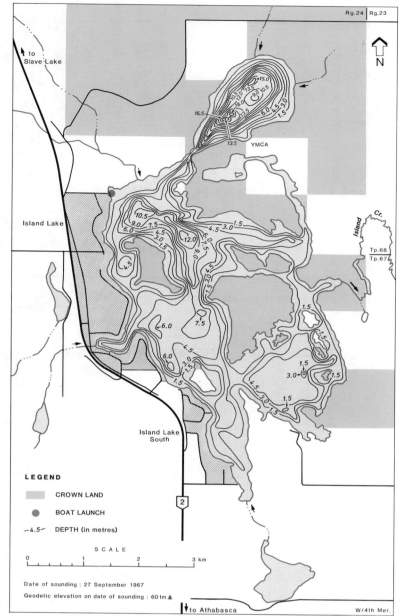

Figure 2. Bathymetry and shoreline features of Island Lake.
BATHYMETRY SOURCE: Alta. Envir. n.d.[c].

strongly rolling hills (15 to 30% slope) is located just northwest of Island Lake (Alta. Mun. Aff. 1980).

The bedrock underlying the lake is part of the Lea Park Formation. Approximately 45 to 60 m of surficial deposits overlie the bedrock. The surficial deposits are predominantly till and glaciofluvial. Landforms are low to high relief hummocks (Alta. Mun. Aff. 1980). The dominant soils throughout the region are moderately well-drained Orthic Gray Luvisols. Pockets of very poorly drained Organic soils are located to the northeast of Island Lake, along the creek to the west of the lake, in the area of the unnamed lake to the south, and south of Ghost Lake (Fig. 1). The soils around Island Lake have severe to very severe limitations for agriculture (Alta. Mun. Aff. 1980).

About 27% of the drainage basin has been cleared, including areas of land around the south and west sides of Island Lake; most of the northern and northwestern regions remain forested (Fig. 1). The most abundant trees are trembling aspen, balsam poplar, white spruce, balsam fir and white birch (Alta. Mun. Aff. 1980). Black spruce grows on poorly drained areas. Mature stands are rare because of past fires and clearing. Mature mixed stands can be found on the large islands and in patches along the north shore of Island Lake (Bird and Hale 1976). Agricultural crops consist primarily of wheat, barley, canola and hay (Alta. Mun. Aff. 1980). Cattle grazing is not intensive in the region (Burger 1988). There are extensive areas of Crown land near the lake, including most of the islands (Fig. 2). Several of these areas have been reserved for recreation.

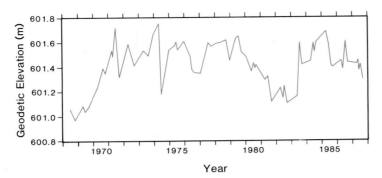

Figure 3. Water level of Island Lake, 1968 to 1987.
SOURCE: Alta. Envir. n.d.[c].

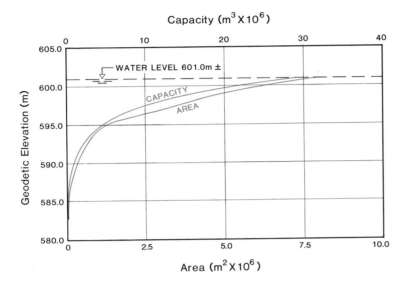

Figure 4. Area/capacity curve for Island Lake.
SOURCE: Alta. Envir. n.d.[c].

Lake Basin Characteristics

Island Lake is a medium-sized water body with a surface area of 7.81/km^2 (Table 2). The main basin is shallow: the maximum depth is about 12 m, but most of the basin is less than 6–m deep (Fig. 2). The deepest part of the lake is in the north basin; it reaches a depth of 18 m.

Extensive low lying and wetland areas are located near the northeast, east, and south shores, and along a section of the northwest shore of Island Lake (Bird and Hale 1976). Steep banks (beach scarp) extend along much of the west shore and parts of the north basin and east side. Recreational development is limited around much of the lakeshore because soils are poorly drained. Several islands are located in the main basin. Most, including the large island near the east side, are low lying and poorly drained, but the large island in the western part of the main basin is relatively well drained.

The lake's outlet, Island Creek, is choked with aquatic plants and has limited flow (Bird and Hale 1976). Between 1968 and 1987 the water level fluctuated between a recorded low of 600.97 m in 1968 and a high of 601.75 m in 1974, a difference of 0.78 m (Fig. 3). Changes in the lake's area and capacity, to an elevation of 601.0 m, are shown in Figure 4. Groundwater inflow was measured by University of Alberta researchers in 1986 (R. Shaw and Prepas 1989). Groundwater inflow was greatest near shore, and decreased with depth of lake water. Rates varied from 0.56 x 10^{-8} to 1.3 x 10^{-8} m/second, which is relatively low among lakes measured. Groundwater was estimated to contribute 4% of total water inflow.

Table 3. Major ions and related water quality variables for Island Lake. Average concentrations in mg/L; pH in pH units. Composite samples from the euphotic zone of the whole lake collected 6 times from 03 May to 19 Sep. 1984. S.E. = standard error.

	Mean	S.E.
pH (range)	8.1–8.6	—
total alkalinity (CaCO$_3$)	199	1.8
specific conductivity (μS/cm)	377	4.6
total dissolved solids (calculated)	205	2.0
total hardness (CaCO$_3$)	133	1.6
total particulate carbon	1	0.2
dissolved organic carbon	16	0.3
HCO$_3$	226	5.5
CO$_3$	8	2.0
Mg	16	0.2
Na	27	0.8
K	8	0.1
Cl	2	0.2
SO$_4$	7	0.7
Ca	26	0.9

SOURCE: Alta. Envir. n.d.[a], Naquadat station 01AL07BE2190

Table 4. Nutrient, chlorophyll *a* and Secchi depth data for Island Lake. Average concentrations in μg/L. Composite samples from the euphotic zone of the whole lake collected 6 times from 03 May to 19 Sep. 1984 and from the north basin collected 7 times from 28 May to 19 Aug. 1986. S.E. = standard error.

	Whole Lake 1984		North 1986	
	Mean	S.E.	Mean	S.E.
total phosphorus	26	1.2	20	1.0
total dissolved phosphorus	12	0.4	—	—
soluble reactive phosphorus	3[a]	1.1	—	—
total Kjeldahl nitrogen	1150	18.8	1105[b]	50.3
NO$_3$ + NO$_2$–nitrogen	11	6.1	13[b]	7.1
NH$_4$–nitrogen	29	10.6	2[b]	0.8
iron	<20	—	30[c]	—
chlorophyll *a*	8.3	2.12	4.8	0.29
Secchi depth (m)	3.4	0.57	4.3	0.52

NOTES: [a]1983, n = 7; [b]n = 3; [c]05 Aug., n = 1
SOURCES: Main Basin—Alta. Envir. n.d.[a], Naquadat station 01AL07BE2190; North Basin—Prepas et al. n.d.

Water Quality

The water quality of Island Lake was studied by Alberta Environment in 1983 and 1984 (Alta. Envir. n.d.[a]; 1989). The north basin was studied by Alberta Environment during 1976 and 1977 as part of an intensive study of Baptiste Lake (Trew et al. 1985), and was sampled by the University of Alberta in 1986 (Prepas et al. n.d.; Prepas and Trimbee 1988; J. Shaw et al. 1989; J. Shaw and Prepas 1989[a]; 1989[b]; 1989[c]).

The lake has well-buffered, fresh water; the dominant ions are bicarbonate, sodium and calcium (Table 3).

The deepest regions of the main basin are weakly thermally stratified during summer (Fig. 5), but it is likely that the shallow areas mix completely much of the time. The north basin is strongly thermally stratified during summer. Hills to the north and west protect the small basin from prevailing winds, and turnover is often incomplete or does not occur in spring, nor sometimes in fall.

Dissolved oxygen concentrations near the bottom decline during summer (Fig. 6). In deeper areas in the main basin and below about 10 m in the north basin, dissolved oxygen concentrations also decline under ice cover.

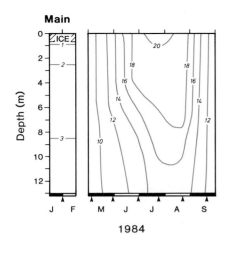

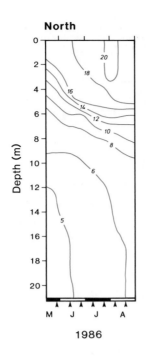

Figure 5. Temperature (°C) of Island Lake, main basin 1984 and north basin 1986. Arrows indicate sampling dates.
SOURCES: Alta. Envir. n.d.[a]; Prepas et al. n.d.

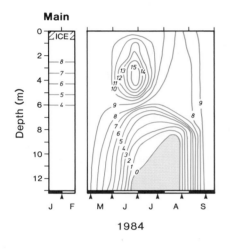

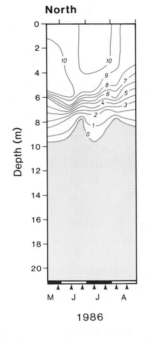

Figure 6. Dissolved oxygen (mg/L) in Island Lake, main basin 1984 and north basin 1986. Arrows indicate sampling dates.
SOURCES: Alta. Envir. n.d.[c]; Prepas et al. n.d.

Table 5. Theoretical total phosphorus loading to Island Lake from external sources.

Source		Phosphorus (kg/yr)	Percentage of Total
immediate watershed	forested/bush	240	29
	agricultural/cleared	298	37
	residential/cottage	67	8
sewage[a]		16	2
precipitation/dustfall		172	21
inflow from other lakes		25	3
	TOTAL	818	100
annual areal loading (g/m² of lake surface) 0.10			

NOTE: [a]unmeasured: assumes 4% of all sewage effluent from residences and camps enters the lake, as in Mitchell 1982
SOURCE: adapted from Alta. Envir. 1989

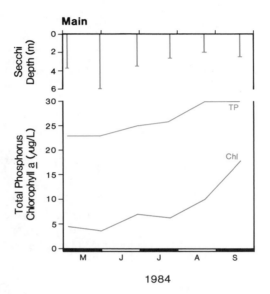

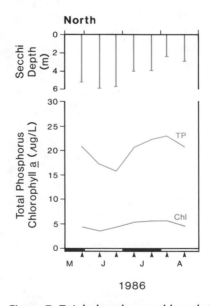

Figure 7. Total phosphorus, chlorophyll a and Secchi depth in Island Lake, main basin 1984 and north basin 1986.
SOURCES: Alta. Envir. n.d.[a]; Prepas et al. n.d.

Island Lake is mesotrophic (Table 4). Total phosphorus in the main basin increases in late summer (Fig. 7), probably as a result of transport of phosphorus from the bottom sediments. In 1986, there was a phosphorus pulse in the surface water due to an unusually heavy rain event. In the north basin, hypolimnetic phosphorus concentrations reached high levels (200 μg/L). However, the strong thermocline in the north basin discourages mixing of phosphorus-rich waters from the hypolimnion to the surface waters. The rate of phosphorus transport across the thermocline was estimated to be very low (0.05 mg/m² per day). In contrast, the release of phosphorus from the bottom sediments in the euphotic zone (to depths of 7.5 m), is estimated to be fairly high (up to 2.5 mg/m² per day). Chlorophyll a concentrations tend to increase in fall (Fig. 7). In 1986, chlorophyll a concentrations generally followed phosphorus concentrations in the north basin; the peak chlorophyll a concentration was 5.7 μg/L. In 1976, in the north basin, chlorophyll a rose from a

summer average of 2.3 μg/L to 8.6 μg/L in the top 3 m in September, and to 12.8 μg/L in November.

An estimate of the total phosphorus loading to Island Lake from external sources indicated that agricultural land in the watershed was the largest single source (Table 5). Phosphorus loading from internal sources may exceed that of all external sources combined.

Table 6. Percentage composition of major algal groups by total biomass in Island Lake, 1983. Composite samples collected from the euphotic zone (whole lake).

ALGAL GROUP	11 May	8 June	6 July	3 Aug.[a]	30 Aug.	28 Sep.	19 Oct.
Total Biomass (mg/L)	1.31	1.08	2.07	1.82	1.85	4.13	2.90
Percentage Composition:							
Cyanophyta	0	2	18	14	42	19	5
					Microcystis		
					Oscillatoria		
Chlorophyta	3	8	3	12	9	4	3
Chrysophyta	61	21	12	16	11	16	16
	Uroglena	*Pseudo.*					
Bacillariophyta	15	21	46	17	27	33	69
		Asterionella	*Fragilaria*		*Fragilaria*	*Melosira*	*Aster.*
			Stephan.				*Synedra*
Cryptophyta	17	48	19	6	4	28	7
		Cryptomonas				*Cryptomonas*	
Pyrrhophyta	4	0	2	36	7	0	0
				Ceratium			

NOTES: *Pseudo.* = *Pseudopedinella*; *Aster.* = *Asterionella*; *Stephan.* = *Stephanodiscus*;
[a]*Euglenophyta* <1%
SOURCE: Alta. Envir. n.d.[a].

Biological Characteristics

Bacteria

Purple sulphur bacteria (Thiorhodaceae) are dense below 10 m in the north basin (Prepas et al. n.d.; Trew et al. 1985). These photosynthetic bacteria live in anaerobic conditions and oxidize hydrogen sulphide and other sulphur compounds to sulphur (Wetzel 1983).

Plants

The phytoplankton community in Island Lake was studied in 1983 by Alberta Environment (Alta. Envir. n.d.[a]) and in 1986 by the University of Alberta (Prepas and Trimbee n.d.). In the main basin in 1983 (Table 6), the common groups were golden-brown algae (Chrysophyta: particularly *Uroglena americana*) in May, cryptomonads (*Cryptomonas erosa reflexa*) in June, diatoms (Bacillariophyta: *Fragilaria crotonensis*) in July and dinoflagellates (Pyrrhophyta: *Ceratium hirundinella*) in early August. Blue-green algae (*Microcystis aeruginosa* and *Oscillatoria agardhii*), which are common in eutrophic lakes, were dominant in late August, but did not develop into a bloom. There is a relationship between sediment phosphorus release and anoxia at the bottom of Island Lake and blue-green algal biomass (Trimbee and Prepas 1987; 1988). The greatest algal biomass was measured in September; diatoms (*Melosira italica subarctica*) and cryptomonads (*Cryptomonas erosa reflexa*) were dominant at that time.

In the north basin in 1976, green algae (*Ankistrodesmus falcatus*) and chrysophytes (*Dinobryon divergens*) were dominant in early spring. Blue-green algae (*Anabaena circinalis* and *Gomphosphaeria naegelianum*) developed by early June and were prominent until fall, when a diatom pulse (*Stephanodiscus astraea* and *F. crotonensis*) developed.

Aquatic macrophytes are abundant in Island Lake; their density is considered excessive by many lake users (Alta. Mun. Aff. 1980). Emergent vegetation grows along most of the lakeshore, particularly in the northeastern region of the main basin, along sections of the north and south shores, around islands and along the north shore of the north basin. Along the west shore, macrophyte growth is patchy. Bulrush (*Scirpus* sp.) and water lilies (*Nuphar* sp.) are the most common emergent plants (Robertson 1968). Other macrophytes include cattail (*Typha* sp.), sedge (*Carex* sp.), pondweeds (*Potamogeton* spp.) and northern watermilfoil (*Myriophyllum exalbescens*).

Invertebrates

The zooplankton in the north basin was studied in 1976 and 1977 by Alberta Environment (Trew et al. 1985). No information is available on benthic invertebrates. In 1976 and 1977, the dominant copepod, particularly in early spring, was the cyclopoid *Diacyclops bicuspidatus thomasi*. The most abundant cladoceran was *Daphnia galeata mendotae*, which was common until late fall. The small cladoceran *Chydorus sphaericus* occurred in low numbers. Rotifers were numerous: *Keratella cochlearis* was the most abundant rotifer in midsummer.

Fish

Species of fish in Island Lake include lake whitefish, northern pike, white suckers, cisco and yellow perch (Alta. Mun. Aff. 1980). Species of forage fish are also present, but they have not been identified. Walleye eggs were stocked in the lake in 1955 but walleye have not been reported in the lake since the 1959/60 commercial catch was taken (Alta. For. Ld. Wild. n.d.). The lake is known for its exceptionally large lake whitefish (Sullivan 1988). Many areas in the main basin support rooted aquatic plants, which provide good spawning and feeding habitat for fish such as northern pike.

Island Lake is managed as a recreational, commercial and domestic fishery. It is moderately popular for sport fishing. Northern pike are the main fish caught although lake whitefish are sought with limited success. The modest commercial fishery concentrates mainly on lake whitefish. In winter, whitefish concentrate in the upper regions of the north basin to avoid the deep layer of anoxic water. Records for the fishery date back to the 1945/46 season (Alta. Rec. Parks Wild. 1976). Since 1976/77, the fishery usually has opened every second year, although it was opened in both 1986/87 and 1987/88 (Alta. For. Ld. Wild n.d.). Between 1980 and 1988, the average harvest of the two commercially important species was 3 235 kg of lake whitefish and 141 kg of northern pike. The largest recorded harvests of fish since 1945/46 were 8 963 kg of lake whitefish in 1958/59, 2 381 kg of northern pike in 1947/48, 816 kg of yellow perch in 1950/51, 816 kg of cisco in 1956/57, and 109 kg of walleye in 1954/55. The record total annual harvest was 9 185 kg in 1958/59.

Wildlife

The islands, sheltered bays and abundant aquatic vegetation in Island Lake provide good waterfowl habitat. Common species observed are Common Loon, Red-necked Grebe, Mallard, American Coot, Bufflehead, Goldeneye and sometimes Canvasback (Alta. Mun. Aff. 1980). An island at the southeast end of the lake supported a Great Blue Heron colony with 43 nests in 1986 (Follinsbee 1988), and Bald Eagles have nested on another island in the lake for several years (Parsons 1988).

L. Hart Buckland-Nicks and P.A. Mitchell

References

Alberta Environment. n.d.[a]. Envir. Assess. Div., Envir. Qlty. Monit. Br. Unpubl. data, Edmonton.
———. n.d.[b]. Tech. Serv. Div., Hydrol. Br. Unpubl. data, Edmonton.
———. n.d.[c]. Tech. Serv. Div., Surv. Br. Unpubl. data, Edmonton.
———. 1989. Island Lake. Envir. Assess. Div., Envir. Qlty. Monit. Br., Edmonton.
Alberta Forestry, Lands and Wildlife. n.d. Fish Wild. Div. Unpubl. data, Edmonton.
———. 1988. Boating in Alberta. Fish Wild. Div., Edmonton.
———. 1989. Guide to sportfishing. Fish Wild. Div., Edmonton.
Alberta Municipal Affairs. 1980. Island Lake management study. Prep. for Co. Athabasca and SV Island L. by Alta. Mun. Aff., Plan. Serv. Div., Reg. Plan. Sec., Edmonton.
Alberta Recreation, Parks and Wildlife. 1976. Commercial fisheries catch statistics for Alberta, 1942–1975. Fish Wild. Div., Fish. Mgt. Rep. No. 22, Edmonton.
Alberta Research Council. 1972. Geological map of Alberta. Nat. Resour. Div., Alta. Geol. Surv., Edmonton.
Bird and Hale Ltd. 1976. Development capability study for Island Lake. Prep. for Alta. Envir., Land Conserv. Reclamation Div., Reg. Land Use Br., Edmonton.
Brown, L. 1988. SV Island L., Edmonton. Pers. comm.
Burger, G. 1988. Alta. Agric., Edmonton. Pers. comm.
Chambers, P.A. and E.E. Prepas. 1988. Underwater spectral attenuation and its effect on the maximum depth of angiosperm colonization. Can. J. Fish. Aquat. Sci. 45:1010–1017.

Energy, Mines and Resources Canada. 1973. National topographic series 1:50 000 83I/13 (1973), 83I/14 (1973). Surv. Map. Br., Ottawa.
Environment Canada. 1982. Canadian climate normals, Vol. 7: Bright sunshine (1951–1980). Prep. by Atm. Envir. Serv. Supply Serv. Can., Ottawa.
Follinsbee, J. 1988. Alta. For. Ld. Wild., Fish Wild. Div., Dist. Office, Edmonton. Pers. comm.
Kjearsgaard, A.A. 1972. Soil survey of the Tawatinaw map sheet (83I). Alta. Inst. Pedol. Rep. No. S–72–29. Univ. Alta., Edmonton.
Mitchell, P.A. 1982. Evaluation of the "septic snooper" on Wabamun and Pigeon lakes. Alta. Envir., Poll. Contr. Div., Water Qlty. Contr. Br., Edmonton.
Parsons, K. 1988. SV Island L. South, Edmonton. Pers. comm.
Prepas, E.E. and A.M. Trimbee. n.d. Univ. Alta., Dept. Zool. Unpubl. data, Edmonton.
———. 1988. Evaluation of indicators of nitrogen limitation in deep prairie lakes with laboratory bioassays and limnocorrals. Hydrobiologia 159: 269–276.
Prepas, E.E. and D. Webb. n.d. Univ. Alta., Dept. Zool. Unpubl. data, Edmonton.
Robertson, M.R. 1968. Vegetation types, distributions and control proposals for Island Lake, Alberta. Alta. For. Ld. Wild., Fish Wild. Div., St. Paul.
Shaw, J.F.H. and E.E. Prepas. 1989[a]. Exchange of phosphorus from shallow sediments at nine Alberta lakes. J. Envir. Qlty. [in press]
———. 1989[b]. Relationships between phosphorus in shallow sediments and surface waters of seven Alberta lakes. Water Res. [in press]
———. 1989[c]. Potential significance of phosphorus release from shallow sediments of deep Alberta lakes. ms submitted to Limnol. Oceanogr.
Shaw, J.F.H., R.D. Shaw and E.E. Prepas. 1989. Advective transport of phosphorus from lake bottom sediments into lakewater. ms to be submitted.
Shaw, R.D. and E.E. Prepas. 1989. Groundwater-lake interactions: II. Nearshore seepage patterns and the contribution of groundwater to lakes in central Alberta. J. Hydrol. [in press]
Strong, W.L. and K.R. Leggat. 1981. Ecoregions of Alberta. Alta. En. Nat. Resour., Resour. Eval. Plan. Div., Edmonton.
Sullivan, M. 1988. Alta. For. Ld. Wild., Fish Wild. Div., St. Paul. Pers. comm.
Trew, D.O., D.J. Beliveau and E.I. Yonge. 1985. The Baptiste Lake study—technical report. Alta. Envir., Poll. Contr. Div., Water Qlty. Contr. Br., Edmonton.
Trimbee, A.M. and E.E. Prepas. 1987. Evaluation of total phosphorus as a predictor of the relative importance of blue-green algae with emphasis on Alberta lakes. Can. J. Fish. Aquat. Sci. 44:1337–1342.
———. 1988. The effect of oxygen depletion on the timing and magnitude of blue-green algal blooms. Verh. Internat. Verein. Limnol. 23:220–226.
Wetzel, R.G. 1983. Limnology. 2nd ed. Saunders College Publ., New York.

LAC LA BICHE

MAP SHEETS: 73L/13, 83I/16
LOCATION: Tp66–69 R12–16 W4
LAT/LONG: 54°52'N 112°05'W

Lac La Biche is a large, scenic lake that is valued for its excellent beaches and well-forested parks and shoreland areas. The lake is located about 220 km northeast of the city of Edmonton in Improvement District No. 18 (South). The closest urban centres are the town of Lac La Biche on the southeast shore and the village of Plamondon, 3 km west of the lake (Fig. 1). To reach the lake from Edmonton, take Highway 28 north to Highway 63. Drive north past the village of Boyle to the junction of Highway 63 with Highway 55, then drive north and east on Highway 55 to the town of Lac La Biche. Secondary Road 868 from Lac La Biche circles the east and northeast sides of the lake and Secondary Road 858 from Plamondon runs along the west and northwest sides of the lake. A local road skirts much of the south shore (Fig. 1).

The Cree name for the lake was *Waskesiu Sakhahegan*, which means Elk Lake. The word *biche* is French for "hind", specifically, the female of the European red deer. French Canadians applied the word to North American elk and brought the term west on their travels. The English translation of Lac La Biche—Red Deer Lake—first appeared on the Mackenzie map of 1793 (Chipeniuk 1975; Alta. Mun. Aff. 1982[a]).

The first recorded voyage into the area was made in 1798 by David Thompson of the North West Company. He established a trading post, Buckingham House, on the southeast shore of the lake (Chipeniuk 1975; McMillan 1977). In 1799, Peter Fidler of the rival Hudson's Bay Company arrived on the south shore of the lake and also established a trading post. This post, Greenwich House, operated until 1821, when the two companies amalgamated. In 1853, the Hudson's Bay Company opened a new trading post at the present townsite of Lac La Biche (Chipeniuk 1975).

The first settlers to arrive in the area were the Oblate Fathers in 1855 (Chipeniuk 1975). They established a mission and farm at Mission Bay, on the south-central shore of the lake. In 1915, the Alberta Great Waterways Railway was built along the eastern shore (Finlay and Finlay 1987). Later that year, the townsite of Lac La Biche was surveyed on land alongside the newly opened railroad. Lac La Biche became a hamlet in 1919, a village in 1922, and a town in 1951 (Chipeniuk 1975). In 1987, the town's population was 2 553 people. Commercial fishing became important with the coming of the railway, and from the 1930s until the late 1940s, mink ranching was a significant industry. The commercial fishery for cisco supported the mink industry until the cisco population collapsed during the 1947/48 fishing season. Subsequently, many mink ranches closed. In 1981, only four ranches were operating (Alta. Mun. Aff. 1982[a]).

In 1925, all of the islands in the lake were established as a bird sanctuary, and in 1952, the largest island became Big Island Provincial Park (Alta. For. Ld. Wild. n.d.[b]) (Fig. 2). In 1965, the park was renamed Sir Winston Churchill Provincial Park, for the British prime minister. In 1968, a 2.5–km–long causeway was built between Big Island, Long Island and the mainland to provide better access to the park. At present, the park provides day-use services year-round and camping services from 1 May to Thanksgiving Day. There are 90 campsites, tap water, outdoor showers, beaches and swimming areas, a change house, a boat launch, playgrounds, viewpoints and a picnic area with a picnic shelter. In 1988, a major upgrading and construction project for park facilities was completed. Except for Big Island, all of the islands in Lac La Biche are reserved for recreation by

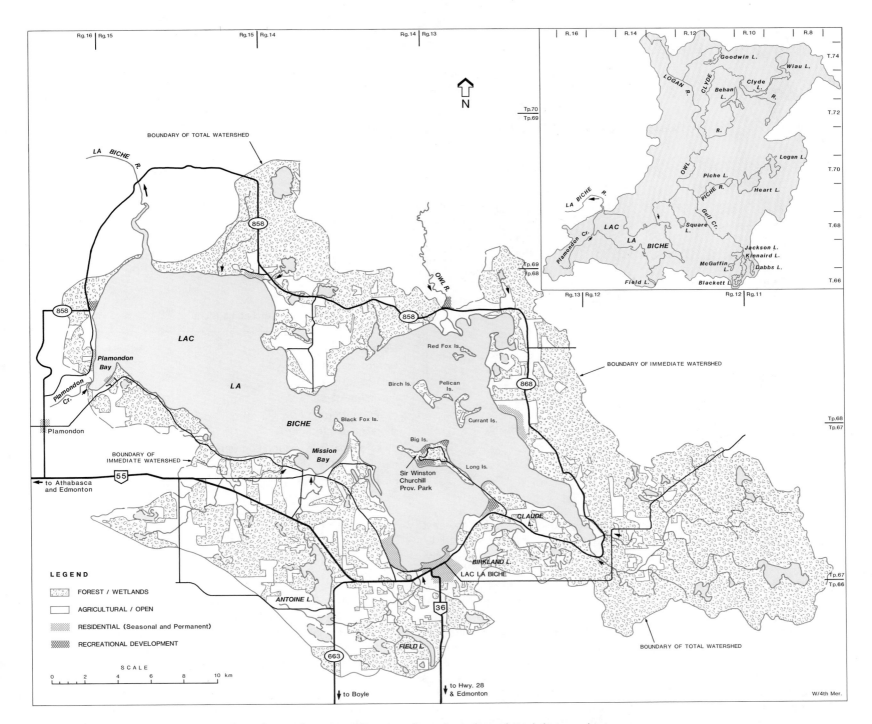

Figure 1. Features of the immediate drainage basin of Lac La Biche. Inset shows boundary of total drainage basin.
SOURCES: Alta. Envir. n.d.[b]; Alta. Mun. Aff. 1982[a]; En. Mines Resour. Can. 1971; 1972; 1975; 1976; 1981. Updated with 1986 aerial photos.

Alberta Forestry, Lands and Wildlife. Since 1984, they have also held the status of protective notation, which means that their potential as a natural area has been recognized but a natural area has not been established (Alta. For. Ld. Wild. 1987).

Plamondon Beach Provincial Recreation Area is located at the west end of the lake (Fig. 2). It is operated by Alberta Recreation and Parks, and is open from Victoria Day to Labour Day. There are 69 campsites, pump water, a beach, a boat launch, picnic tables and a picnic shelter. Within the town of Lac La Biche, there is a public park along the waterfront, a federal wharf and boat launch, and a town dock. There are no boating restrictions over most of the lake, but in posted areas such as designated swimming areas, all boats are prohibited. In other posted areas, power boats are restricted to speeds of 12 km/hour or less (Alta. For. Ld. Wild. 1988).

In a 1976 survey of cottage owners at Lac La Biche, it was noted that many cottagers valued the natural beauty of the lake, good fishing, good water quality, and abundant wildlife (Alta. Mun. Aff. 1977). More than three-quarters of the respondents, however, felt that there were problems with the lake for recreational use. Problems included algal density, aquatic macrophyte growth, fluctuating wa-

ter levels, and water too rough for boating. The two most important summer recreational activities enjoyed by cottagers were swimming and fishing. Sightseeing, power boating, water skiing, picnicking, canoeing, camping, hiking and photography were also important, and nature study, sailing and golfing were of minor importance. During winter, more of the surveyed cottage owners went ice fishing and snowmobiling than they did cross-country skiing and snowshoeing.

Lac La Biche is very fertile. Blue-green algal blooms occur annually in midsummer but the intensity of the blooms varies from year to year. The amount of algae is usually higher in the east basin than in the west basin. Algae often drift in currents onto the provincial park causeway and into the bay on which the town of Lac La Biche is located. Sport fish in the lake include walleye, northern pike, lake whitefish and yellow perch. To protect spawning walleye, sport fishing regulations stipulate that the portion of Lac La Biche within 1 km of the mouth of the Owl River is closed to sport fishing for a period in April and May each year (Alta. For. Ld. Wild. 1989). The lake also supports a commercial fishery for cisco, lake whitefish and northern pike, and a domestic fishery for lake whitefish.

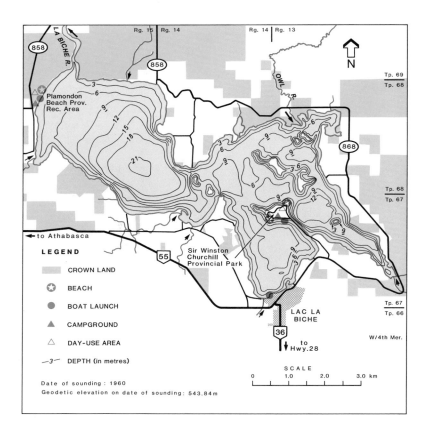

Figure 2. Bathymetry and shoreline features of Lac La Biche.
BATHYMETRY SOURCE: Alta. Envir. n.d.[c].

Drainage Basin Characteristics

Lac La Biche drains an area of 4 040 km², mostly located to the east and north of the lake (Fig. 1, inset). The drainage basin is about 17 times the size of the lake (Tables 1, 2). The major inflow is the Owl River and its tributaries: the Logan, Clyde and Piché rivers and Gull Creek. A small stream, Plamondon Creek, flows into the western side of Lac La Biche and two unnamed creeks flow into the south shore at Mission Bay (Fig. 1). Several unnamed streams also flow into the southeast and north shores and intermittent creeks are located all around the shore. The outflow is the La Biche River, which eventually joins the Athabasca River.

The general physiography, surficial geology and soils of Lac La Biche's drainage basin have been described in several studies (Wynnyk et al. 1963; Kjearsgaard 1972; Kocaoglu 1975). As well, Alberta Environment commissioned two detailed studies, in 1978 and 1979, of the soils and land suitability of most of the land surrounding the lake (Knapik and Brocke 1978; Knapik and Carson 1979).

The drainage basin (Fig. 1, inset) is part of the Eastern Alberta Plains, which is mainly an undulating plain with several isolated areas of rolling and hilly topography. In the northern part of the watershed, the land ranges from mostly level and undulating north of Heart Lake, to gently rolling and rolling northwest of, and surrounding, Heart Lake. The main soil parent material on the level to undulating areas north of Heart Lake is *Sphagnum* moss, and the soils are Luvisolic. In the gently rolling to rolling areas, the main soils are either Podzolic Gray Luvisols formed on sandy outwash material, as in the area northwest of Heart Lake, or Orthic Gray Luvisols formed on sandy clay loam till, as in the area surrounding Heart Lake (Wynnyk et al. 1963). East of Lac La Biche, in the Gull Creek drainage area, the land is a hummocky morainal plain characterized by rough, irregular knob and kettle topography. The soils are mainly Orthic Gray Luvisols formed on glacial till, with Organic and Gleysolic soils in poorly drained depressions (Kocaoglu 1975).

Lac La Biche is underlain by the marine shales of the La Biche Formation. The land close to the lake is level to rolling moraine composed of glacial till that is often blanketed or veneered with glaciolacustrine clays and sands. The lake is at an elevation of approximately 544 m, and the surrounding land generally does not rise higher than 610 m above sea level. Steep escarpments occur along

Table 1. Characteristics of Lac La Biche drainage basin.

area (excluding lake) (km²)[a]	4 040
soil[b]	Gray Luvisols, Brunisols, Organics
bedrock geology[c]	La Biche Formation (Upper and Lower Cretaceous): shale, ironstone partings and concretions; marine
terrain[b]	level to rolling
ecoregion[d]	Dry (in south) and Moist (in north) Mixedwood Subregions of Boreal Mixedwood
dominant vegetation[d]	trembling aspen, balsam poplar
mean annual inflow (m³)[e, f]	316 x 10⁶
mean annual sunshine (h)[g]	2 240

NOTE: [f]excluding groundwater inflow
SOURCES: [a]Alta. Envir. n.d.[b]; [b]Wynnyk et al. 1963; Kjearsgaard 1972; Kocaoglu 1975; [c]Alta. Res. Counc. 1972; [d]Strong and Leggat 1981; [e]Bothe 1989; [g]Envir. Can. 1982

Table 2. Characteristics of Lac La Biche.

elevation (m)[a, b]	543.84
surface area (km²)[a, b]	234
volume (m³)[a, b]	1 960 x 10⁶
maximum depth (m)[a, b]	21.3
mean depth (m)[a, b]	8.4
shoreline length (km)[c]	172
mean annual lake evaporation (mm)[d]	702
mean annual precipitation (mm)[d]	524
mean residence time (yr)[d, e]	7
control structure	none

NOTES: [a]on date of sounding: (month unknown) 1960; [e]excluding groundwater inflow
SOURCES: [b]Alta. Envir. n.d.[c]; [c]Alta. Mun. Aff. 1982[a]; [d]Bothe 1989

many parts of the shoreline, but in other areas the shore has a low profile. Sand and gravel or cobble beaches are present along the shore of the lake and sand dunes are a distinctive feature of the landscape just north of the lake. On the north side of the lake west of Owl River, the soils are mainly Luvisols and Brunisols developed on sandy materials, with Organic soils in depressional areas. The Owl River delta is characterized by a Regosolic-Organic soils association that is often flooded. East of Owl River, the soils are mainly Orthic Gray Luvisols developed on clayey till. At the southeast end of the lake, the soils are mainly Orthic Gray Luvisols that formed on a variety of surficial materials; in this area, Gleyed Gray Luvisols are also common. Organic soils associated with bogs and fens are common in many areas along the south and west sides of the lake (Knapik and Brocke 1978; Knapik and Carson 1979).

The Lac La Biche watershed is part of the Boreal Mixedwood Ecoregion. Land north and east of the lake is part of the Moist Mixedwood Subregion, and land west and south of the lake is part of the Dry Mixedwood Subregion. The main tree in the Dry Mixedwood Subregion is trembling aspen on well-drained to moderately well-drained Gray Luvisols, whereas in the Moist Mixedwood Subregion, the main trees are trembling aspen and balsam poplar on moderately well-drained Gray Luvisols. In both areas, stands of jack pine grow on well-drained Eutric Brunisols, white spruce grows on imperfectly drained Gleysols and Gray Luvisols, black spruce and willows are present on poorly drained Organics and Gleysols, and sedges grow on very poorly drained Organics (Strong and Leggat 1981). At the beginning of the twentieth century, forest fires destroyed the vast spruce forests that grew near Lac La Biche, and few old stands of white spruce remain (Knapik and Carson 1979).

Although a large percentage of the land near the lake is used for agriculture (Fig. 1), less than 5% of the total drainage area (Fig. 1, inset) is used for this purpose. Forest and wetlands cover 90% of the watershed, and lakes other than Lac La Biche cover the remaining

Table 3. Major ions and related water quality variables for Lac La Biche. Average concentrations in mg/L; pH in pH units. Composite samples from the euphotic zone collected 6 times from 18 May to 05 Oct. 1988. S.E. = standard error.

	West Basin		East Basin	
	Mean	S.E.	Mean	S.E.
pH (range)	8.0–8.7	—	7.8–8.9	—
total alkalinity (CaCO₃)	143	0.5	142	1.2
specific conductivity (μS/cm)	288	0.8	286	2.5
total dissolved solids (calculated)	154	1.5	153	1.2
total hardness (CaCO₃)	131	0.9	127	1.3
total particulate carbon	1	0.3	2	0.2
dissolved organic carbon	10	0.5	10	0.6
HCO₃	167	3.0	165	4.0
CO₃	<3	—	4	1.8
Mg	12	0.2	11	0.2
Na	12	0.3	12	0.3
K	2	0.1	2	0
Cl	3	0	3	0.2
SO₄	<7	—	<6	—
Ca	33	0.3	32	0.7

SOURCE: Alta. Envir. n.d.[a], Naquadat stations 01AL07CA2210 (west), 01AL07CA2300 (east)

5.5% of the drainage area. Improved pasture and hay production are the most common types of agriculture, and barley, oats, canola and wheat are also grown (Knapik and Carson 1979). Natural gas is extracted from four fields located near the lake. In 1982, one gas-processing plant was operating northeast of the lake in the Tweedie Field (Alta. Mun. Aff. 1982[a]). A number of oil leases have been issued for land on the east side of the lake, but as of 1982 no wells had been drilled. Forestry is an important industry in the area, and in 1988, construction of a pulp and paper mill west of Highway 63 was proposed. Although the mill site is outside Lac La Biche's drainage basin, some of the trees to supply it may be cut in the watershed (Noton 1989).

Relative to the lake's size and the amount of shoreland present, Lac La Biche is not extensively developed. Land along the south and west shores was subdivided in the early 1900s when 79 Settlement Lots were created, based on the French Canadian system (Alta. Mun. Aff. 1982[a]). In 1977, Alberta Environment prohibited most further development around the lake under the Regulated Lake Shoreland Development Operation Regulations. Subsequently, Alberta Municipal Affairs prepared a lake management plan and an area structure plan, which were adopted by Improvement District No. 18 (South) in 1982 (Alta. Mun. Aff. 1982[a]; 1982[b]; 1982[c]). Lake management plans determine the extent of future land developments, allocate land use and determine ways to minimize environmental impacts and conflicts in uses of the lakeshore. They recommend preferred lake uses and ways to minimize lake-user conflicts. In 1982, 72 of the original 79 lots were privately owned and, between 1945 and 1982, approximately 66 subdivisions around the lake were registered. By 1988, a total of 935 country residential lots had been created within 1.5 km of the lake. Of these lots, 389 were developed and 546 were undeveloped (Alta. Mun. Aff. n.d.).

Lake Basin Characteristics

Lac La Biche comprises two main basins separated by a peninsula and two islands (Fig. 2). The west basin has a simple shape and is relatively deep (maximum depth 21.3 m) compared to the east basin (maximum depth 12.2 m). At the northwest end, the sides of the west basin slope quite gradually, but along the north and south shores the slope of the sides becomes progressively steeper. In comparison to the west basin, the east basin is quite complex, with several sub-basins separated by numerous islands and connecting sand and gravel spits and a causeway between the provincial park and the

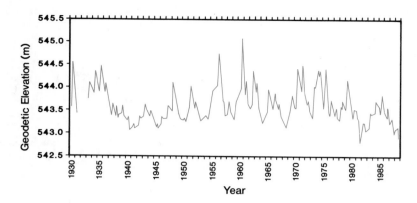

Figure 3. Water level of Lac La Biche, 1930 to 1988.
SOURCE: Envir. Can. 1930–1988.

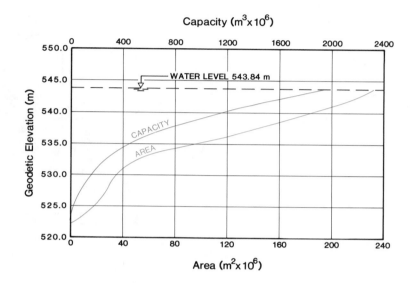

Figure 4. Area/capacity curve for Lac La Biche.
SOURCE: Alta. Envir. n.d.[c].

mainland. Some of the spits are very shallow and create a serious hazard for motor boats.

Sudden storms occur fairly frequently on Lac La Biche. The water level at the east end of the lake can increase by as much as 0.3 m during storms, and rough water creates dangerous conditions for boaters. Because of the many islands and sub-basins in the east basin, large waves are funnelled onto localized areas, such as along the north shore of the provincial park. Areas exposed to heavy wave action in the west basin are the northeast shore of the basin and the east side of Mission Bay (Fig. 1). In spring, ice jams and floods are common along the east shore of the east basin (Alta. Mun. Aff. 1982[a]).

The elevation of Lac La Biche was recorded sporadically in 1930, 1931 and 1932, and has been monitored regularly since 1933 (Fig. 3). The water level has fluctuated over a range of 2.27 m, from a high of 545.08 m in September 1960 to a low of 542.81 m in November 1981. Water level fluctuations have resulted in considerable changes to the lake's area and capacity (Fig. 4) and have caused both flooding and lake access problems. In 1988, Alberta Environment began a feasibility study of water level stabilization.

Water Quality

Water quality in Lac La Biche was studied by the University of Alberta during 1965 and 1966 (Pinsent 1967), by Alberta Environment in 1978, 1979, 1988 and 1989 (Alta. Envir. n.d.[a]; Mitchell 1980; Alta. Envir. 1984).

The ionic composition of the water in the lake's two basins is very similar (Table 3). The water is fresh, hard and well-buffered, and the dominant ions are bicarbonate and calcium.

West

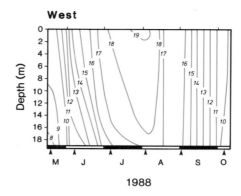

East

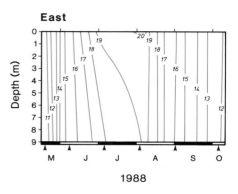

Figure 5. Temperature (°C) of Lac La Biche, east and west basins, 1988. Arrows indicate sampling dates.
SOURCE: Alta. Envir. n.d.[a].

West

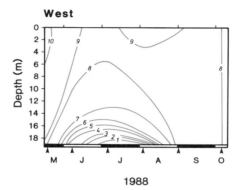

East

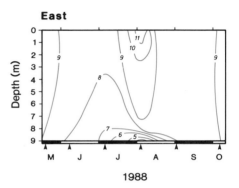

Figure 6. Dissolved oxygen (mg/L) of Lac La Biche, east and west basins, 1988. Arrows indicate sampling dates.
SOURCE: Alta. Envir. n.d.[a].

Both basins are generally well-mixed throughout the open-water period. In early August 1988, the lake was weakly thermally stratified (Fig. 5). During July and August in 1988, dissolved oxygen concentrations declined in the deeper parts of both basins (Fig. 6). In the west basin, dissolved oxygen concentrations declined to less than 5 mg/L below a depth of 16 m, and reached a minimum of 0.2 mg/L at a depth of 20 m. Depletion was not as severe in the east basin, where the concentration of dissolved oxygen in early August fell to 4 mg/L at the bottom in water 9–m deep. During winter, the dissolved oxygen concentration in Lac La Biche sometimes becomes critical for fish survival, and fish kills have been reported in the past. In March 1989, the concentration of dissolved oxygen immediately under the ice in both basins was 12 mg/L. Oxygen depletion was evident, however, at greater depths. In the deeper west basin, the water was anoxic below a depth of 18 m, and in the east basin, the dissolved oxygen concentration declined to 1 mg/L at the bottom depth of 9 m.

Lac La Biche is eutrophic. In 1988, similar patterns of total phosphorus and chlorophyll *a* concentrations were recorded in both basins during the open-water period (Fig. 7). Concentrations of both variables were low during May and June, rose during July and reached maxima in August or September. In 1988, chlorophyll *a* maxima in both basins were about 50 μg/L, but the maximum occurred earlier in the shallower east basin. Total phosphorus levels in both basins rose to almost 180 μg/L by early September, and in the west basin, the level remained that high until early October (Fig. 7). This suggests that phosphorus is released from the bottom sediments during late summer and is then mixed into the surface water when the water column mixes. In 1988, the average concentration of phosphorus was slightly higher, and the average concentration of chlorophyll *a* was slightly lower, in the west basin than in the east basin (Table 4).

The total phosphorus loading to Lac La Biche from sources external to the lake is estimated to be 37 866 kg/year, or 0.16 g/m² of lake surface (Table 5). This loading rate is comparable to rates calcu-

Table 4. Nutrient, chlorophyll *a* and Secchi depth data for Lac La Biche. Average concentrations in μg/L. Composite samples from the euphotic zone collected 6 times from 18 May to 05 Oct. 1988. S.E. = standard error.

	West Basin		East Basin	
	Mean	S.E.	Mean	S.E.
total phosphorus	117	21.0	108	18.5
total dissolved phosphorus	89	17.3	64	16.9
total Kjeldahl nitrogen	766	64.7	824	94.7
NO₃ + NO₂–nitrogen	<5	—	<20	—
NH₄–nitrogen	32	8.6	31	8.7
iron	<22	—	<22	—
chlorophyll *a*	23.4	6.67	29.8	9.02
Secchi depth (m)	2.5	0.21	2.4	0.27

SOURCE: Alta. Envir. n.d.[a], Naquadat stations 01AL07CA2210 (west), 01AL07CA2300 (east)

lated for Sturgeon (0.14 g/m²) and Gull (0.15 g/m²) lakes, but is much higher than the rate calculated for Moore Lake (0.06 g/m²) and much lower than the rate calculated for Lac la Nonne (0.41 g/m²). The largest contributor to the total phosphorus loading to Lac La Biche is runoff from the forested portion of the immediate watershed (59%), followed by runoff from agricultural land and open areas (15%), precipitation and dustfall (13%) and inflow from other lakes (12%). Sewage and runoff from urban and cottage areas contribute minor amounts of phosphorus (less than 2%). Sewage inputs to Lac La Biche were not actually measured; they were calculated from data collected for other Alberta lakes. A gross calculation of phosphorus loading from internal sources during the period from early July to early September in 1988 suggests that internal loading during this period could amount to 4 times the annual external loading (Mitchell 1989).

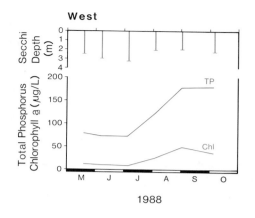

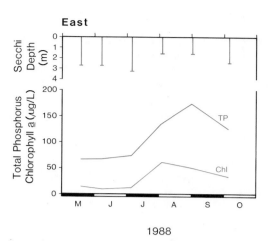

Figure 7. Total phosphorus, chlorophyll *a* and Secchi depth in Lac La Biche, east and west basins, 1988.
SOURCE: Alta. Envir. n.d.[a].

Table 5. Theoretical total phosphorus loading to Lac La Biche from external sources.

Source		Phosphorus (kg/yr)	Percentage of Total
immediate watershed	forested/bush	22 280	59
	agricultural/cleared	5 496	15
	residential/cottage	541	1
sewage[a]		162	<1
precipitation/dustfall	4 750		13
inflow from other lakes		4 637	12
	TOTAL	37 866	100
annual areal loading (g/m² of lake surface) 0.16			

NOTE: [a]unmeasured: assumes 4% of effluent from residences and camps enters the lake, as in Mitchell 1982
SOURCES: Alta. Envir. 1984; Mitchell 1989

Table 6. Species of aquatic macrophytes in Lac La Biche. Survey conducted in 1965 and 1966. Arranged in alphabetical order.

emergent	common great bulrush	*Scirpus validus*
	common cattail	*Typha latifolia*
free-floating	star duckweed	*Lemna trisulca*
submergent	Canada waterweed	*Elodea canadensis*
	northern watermilfoil	*Myriophyllum exalbescens*
	Sago pondweed	*Potamogeton pectinatus*
	small-leaf pondweed	*P. pusillus*
	Richardson pondweed	*P. richardsonii*
	flat-stemmed pondweed	*P. zosteriformis*

SOURCE: Pinsent 1967

Biological Characteristics

Plants

The phytoplankton community in Lac La Biche was sampled monthly from May to September in 1965 and biweekly from May to September in 1966 by a researcher from the University of Alberta (Pinsent 1967). It was also sampled on 19 October 1977, on 20 February in both 1978 and 1979, monthly from May to September in 1978 and 1979 and on 4 July 1983 by Alberta Environment (Alta. Envir. n.d.[a]; Beliveau and Furnell 1980). From October 1977 to February 1978, samples were taken by vertical net (60 micron mesh) hauls, whereas during 1979, samples were taken with a Van Dorn water bottle. The abundance of algal groups was measured by cell counts, and biomass was expressed as total cell volume per m² of surface area. In 1979, blue-greens (Bacillariophyta) were the dominant group at one of the three sampling sites from late June through mid-September, forming 66 to 93% of the volume. At the two other sites, blue-greens were dominant from late July to mid-September (65 to 100% of the volume) and diatoms (Bacillariophyta) and cryptophytes were the most important groups in May and June. Species present on each sampling date were not identified. On 4 July 1983, biomass was measured and species were identified. Blue-greens (particularly *Anabaena flos-aquae*) accounted for 49% of the total biomass of 3.31 mg/L. Of secondary importance (11 to 14% of the biomass) were green algae (Chlorophyta: mostly *Tetraspora lacustris* and *Pediastrum duplex*), Cryptophyta: mostly *Cryptomonas ovata*, dinoflagellates (Pyrrhophyta: entirely *Ceratium hirundinella*) and diatoms (mostly *Fragilaria crotonensis*). The importance of blue-green algae in Lac La Biche in the summer is related to the high total phosphorus concentrations in the surface water and the low dissolved oxygen concentrations that are present over the bottom sediments in midsummer (Trimbee and Prepas 1987; 1988).

The rooted macrophytes in Lac La Biche were surveyed briefly in 1966 (Pinsent 1967). As well, the distribution of emergent vegetation was mapped in 1982 by Alberta Municipal Affairs, but species were not identified (Alta. Mun. Aff. 1982[a]). In 1966, nine species of rooted aquatic plants were identified (Table 6). That year, emergent vegetation, generally common great bulrush (*Scirpus validus*), was most abundant along the north shore and in protected bays. Lac La Biche has extensive areas of sandy and rocky shore where the submergent vegetation was predominantly Richardson (*Potamogeton richardsonii*) and Sago pondweeds (*P. pectinatus*) and the main emergent species was bulrush (*Scirpus* sp.). A large filamentous alga, *Cladophora* sp., was sighted in thick mats on the bottom of several areas in the littoral zone.

Invertebrates

Zooplankton and bottom fauna were sampled during 1965 and 1966 by a researcher from the University of Alberta, but the number of bottom samples was small and collection sites were not separated into depth zones (Pinsent 1967). Zooplankton were collected biweekly at three sites by means of 8–m vertical tows with plankton nets. The dominant cladocerans were *Chydorus sphaericus* and *Daphnia retrocurva* and the dominant copepods were *Diacyclops bicuspidatus thomasi* and *Diaptomus oregonensis*. *Diacyclops* is noteworthy because it serves as the intermediate invertebrate host for *Triaenophorus crassus*. The cysts of this tapeworm heavily infest the lake whitefish and cisco in Lac La Biche; the final host of the tapeworm is northern pike. An August 1978 sample collected by Alberta Environment contained *D. bicuspidatus thomasi*, *Acanthocyclops vernalis*, *Mesocyclops edax*, *Daphnia galeata mendotae*, *Diaptomus sicilis* and *D. oregonensis*.

Fish

The fish species in Lac La Biche are walleye, northern pike, lake whitefish, cisco, yellow perch, burbot, white sucker, longnose sucker, spottail shiner, brook stickleback and Iowa darter. The lake is managed for sport, domestic and commercial fisheries, but catch data are available only for the commercial fishery. Although Lac La Biche has good sport fishing potential, the water can be very rough, so angling from small boats is limited (Chipeniuk 1975; Alta. Mun. Aff. 1982[a]).

Records of the commercial catch have been kept since 1942 (Alta. For. Ld. Wild. n.d.; Alta. Rec. Parks Wild. 1976). The most important commercial species are cisco, lake whitefish and northern pike. The fishery has been fairly erratic due to changes in market demand, overfishing, variable year-class strength, and occasional die-offs. Nevertheless, total harvests in excess of 1 370 000 kg were recorded in 1946/47, 1964/65, 1968/69 and 1969/70; 68 to 89% of the catch in these years was cisco. The total catch from 1980/81 to 1987/88 has varied between only 327 000 and 381 000 kg/year. The average catch for this period, 348 000 kg/year, consisted of 53% cisco, 35% whitefish and 12% pike. The harvest of yellow perch, burbot and suckers was not recorded.

Although cisco are the main catch, they have long been infested with cysts of the tapeworm *Triaenophorus crassus* and are not sold for human consumption. Historically, the cisco catch has been variable, with periods of high catches followed by population crashes. These crashes were caused partly by overfishing and partly by die-offs that coincided with low water levels and reduced oxygen concentrations (Robertson 1969). During the 1920s and 1930s, cisco had little commercial value and were used for fertilizer and hog food. During the 1930s and early 1940s, the mink farming industry in the area grew and developed into the primary market for cisco. The average cisco catch from 1942/43 to 1946/47 was 726 000 kg/year. There was a large die-off of juvenile cisco during June and early July in 1947. Large numbers of juvenile cisco washed ashore, yet shallow-water species apparently were not affected. In 1947/48, the commercial harvest was only about 10 000 kg and in 1948/49, the fishery was closed. Consequently, many mink ranches closed. The cisco population rebuilt slowly during the 1950s, and from 1958/59 to 1975/76, the average catch increased to 594 000 kg/year. The demand for mink food, however, continued to decline as the demand for mink fur declined during the 1960s, 1970s and 1980s. Between 1966 and 1981, mink ranches decreased from 49 to 4 and pelt production declined from 34 000 to less than 10 000 pelts/year (Alta. Mun. Aff. 1982[a]). The reduction in fur ranching led to greatly reduced demand for cisco: the average cisco harvest from 1980/81 to 1987/88 was 184 440 kg/year, or 53% of the total catch.

The commercial harvest of lake whitefish in Lac La Biche has been highly variable. From 1942/43 to 1947/48, the catch varied from 244 to 55 700 kg/year, with an average of 16 400 kg/year. The average catch from 1949/50 to 1978/79 was 87 100 kg/year. The maximum recorded harvest was 353 000 kg in 1960/61. Lake whitefish in Lac La Biche are infested with *Triaenophorus crassus* cysts, which lower the commercial value of the fish. In 1979, a roe fishery for lake whitefish was started. Subsequently, the average catch of whitefish for the period from 1979/80 to 1987/88 increased to 122 000 kg/year.

Burbot and suckers have been a significant part of the commercial catch. Records are available from 1949/50 to 1975/76. The average combined catch for that period was 81 400 kg/year. The maximum catch, 285 000 kg, was taken in 1968/69.

Northern pike have always been an important part of the commercial fishery. Catches averaged 28 000 kg/year from 1942/43 to 1947/48, 28 800 kg/year from 1949/50 to 1975/76, and 40 900 kg/year from 1980/81 to 1987/88. The greatest reported harvest was 84 500 kg in 1949/50 and the second highest harvest was 82 600 kg in 1987/88.

Walleye were abundant in Lac La Biche until the 1960s. Many were caught, both legally and illegally, by the commercial fishery, sometimes in nets set across approaches to the Owl and La Biche rivers during the walleye spawning runs (Chipeniuk 1975). Consequently, the population collapsed. Because of the extent of the illegal harvest, catch records greatly underestimate the total harvest. The maximum reported catch was 58 600 kg in 1946/47. The average reported commercial catch from 1968/69 to 1987/88, however, was only 204 kg/year. A walleye rearing pond was built in 1984 to help rebuild the walleye population. Walleye fingerlings were stocked at a rate of 3 680 in 1985, 522 700 in 1986 and 511 900 in 1987 (Alta. En. Nat. Resour. 1985; Alta. For. Ld. Wild. 1986; 1987[a]). It is too early to assess whether these stockings have helped accelerate the natural, ongoing recovery of the walleye population in Lac La Biche.

Yellow perch have been a small part of the commercial catch since records were first kept. The catch is usually less than 5 000 kg/year. From 1964/65 to 1971/72, however, the perch catch varied between 35 000 and 280 000 kg/year, with an average of 96 500 kg/year. The harvest was only 2 400 kg in 1975/76, the last year for which records are available.

Wildlife

Lac La Biche is an important staging area for migrating birds and is a designated Migratory Bird Sanctuary. Over 200 species of birds in Sir Winston Churchill Provincial Park have been identified (Finlay and Finlay 1987). Almost 41% of the lake's shoreline has only slight limitation to waterfowl production and 53% has some limitation because of steep banks or reduced marsh edge. The lake is an important feeding area for White Pelicans, which occasionally nest on the lake, and for Double-crested Cormorants. The lake provides important nesting areas for Western Grebes, Common Terns and California Gulls. In 1981, one Bald Eagle and three Osprey nests were reported. Frequently observed waterfowl species are Mallard, Lesser Scaup, American Widgeon, White-winged Scoter, American Coot, Franklin's Gull, Blue-winged Teal and Bufflehead. In the backshore areas, Spruce Grouse, Sharp-tailed Grouse and Ruffed Grouse are common (Alta. Mun. Aff. 1982[a]).

White-tailed deer are the most abundant large mammal in the watershed, and timber wolves, coyotes and black bears are often seen. Some mule deer are present and moose roam in areas north of the lake. Red foxes are present throughout the drainage basin and also live on the islands in the lake. Aquatic fur-bearers that use the lake include beaver, mink and muskrats (Alta. Mun. Aff. 1982[a]).

M.E. Bradford and J.M. Hanson

References

Alberta Energy and Natural Resources. 1985. Fish planting list. Fish Wild. Div., Edmonton.
Alberta Environment. n.d.[a]. Envir. Assess. Div., Envir. Qlty. Monit. Br. Unpubl. data, Edmonton.
———. n.d.[b]. Tech. Serv. Div., Hydrol. Br. Unpubl. data, Edmonton.
———. n.d.[c]. Tech. Serv. Div., Surv. Br. Unpubl. data, Edmonton.
———. 1984. Lac La Biche. Alta. Envir., Poll. Contr. Div., Water Qlty. Contr. Br., Edmonton.
Alberta Forestry, Lands and Wildlife. n.d. Fish Wild. Div. Unpubl. data, Edmonton.
———. 1986, 1987[a]. Fish planting list. Fish Wild. Div., Edmonton.
———. 1987[b]. A summary of Alberta's natural areas reserved and established. Pub. Ld. Div., Ld. Mgt. Devel. Br. Unpubl. rep., Edmonton.
———. 1988. Boating in Alberta. Fish Wild. Div., Edmonton.
———. 1989. Guide to sportfishing. Fish Wild. Div., Edmonton.
Alberta Municipal Affairs. n.d. Plan. Serv. Div., Plan. Br. Unpubl. data, Edmonton.
———. 1977. Lac La Biche cottage survey. Plan. Serv. Div., Edmonton.
———. 1982[a]. Lac La Biche lake management plan: Background study. Prep. for ID No. 18 by Plan. Serv. Div., Edmonton.
———. 1982[b]. Lac La Biche lake management plan: Plan alternatives. Prep. for ID No. 18 by Plan. Serv. Div., Edmonton.
———. 1982[c]. Lac La Biche lake management plan: Area structure plan. Prep. for ID No. 18 by Plan. Serv. Div., Edmonton.
Alberta Recreation, Parks and Wildlife. 1976. Commercial fisheries catch statistics for Alberta, 1942–1975. Fish Wild. Div., Fish. Mgt. Rep. No. 22, Edmonton.
Alberta Research Council. 1972. Geological map of Alberta. Nat. Resour. Div., Alta. Geol. Surv., Edmonton.
Beliveau, D. and A. Furnell. 1980. Phytoplankton data summary 1976–1980. Alta. Envir., Poll. Contr. Div., Water Qlty. Contr. Br. Unpubl. rep., Edmonton.
Bothe, R.A. 1989. Lac La Biche historical water balance. Alta. Envir., Tech. Serv. Div., Hydrol. Br. Unpubl. rep., Edmonton.

Chipeniuk, R.C. 1975. Lakes of the Lac La Biche district. R.C. Chipeniuk, Lac La Biche.

Energy, Mines and Resources Canada. 1971, 1972, 1975, 1976, 1981. National topographic series 1:50 000 73L/12 (1971), 73L/13 (1971), 73L/9 (1972), 73L/16 (1972) and 1:250 000 83P (1975), 83I (1976), 73M (1976), 73L (1981). Surv. Map. Br., Ottawa.

Environment Canada. 1930–1988. Surface water data. Prep. by Inland Waters Directorate. Water Surv. Can., Water Resour. Br., Ottawa.

———. 1982. Canadian climate normals, Vol. 7: Bright sunshine (1951–1980). Prep. by Atm. Envir. Serv. Supply Serv. Can., Ottawa.

Finlay, J. and C. Finlay. 1987. Parks in Alberta: A guide to peaks, ponds, parklands & prairies. Hurtig Publ., Edmonton.

Kjearsgaard, A.A. 1972. Reconnaissance soil survey of the Tawatinaw map sheet (83–I). Alta. Soil Surv. Rep. No. 29, Univ. Alta. Bull. No. SS–12, Alta. Inst. Pedol. Rep. No. S–72–29 1972. Univ. Alta., Edmonton.

Knapik, L.J. and L.K. Brocke. 1978. Soil survey and land suitability of the Lac La Biche study areas. Prep. for Alta. Envir., Edmonton by Pedol. Consult., Edmonton.

Knapik, L.J. and B. Carson. 1979. Soil survey and land suitability of the Lac La Biche study areas. Prep. for Alta. Envir., Edmonton by Pedol. Consult., Edmonton.

Kocaoglu, S.S. 1975. Reconnaissance soil survey of the Sand River area (73L). Alta. Soil Surv. Rep. No. 34, Univ. Alta. Rep. No. SS–15, Alta. Inst. Pedol. Rep. No. S–74–34 1975. Univ. Alta., Edmonton.

McMillan, W.J. 1977. An interpretation concept plan for Cold Lake Provincial Park. MSc thesis. Univ. Calg., Calgary.

Mitchell, P.A. 1980. Trophic status of Lac La Biche. Alta. Envir., Poll. Contr. Div., Water Qlty. Contr. Br., Edmonton.

———. 1982. Evaluation of the "septic snooper" on Wabamun and Pigeon lakes. Alta. Envir., Poll. Contr. Div., Water Qlty. Contr. Br., Edmonton.

———. 1989. Alta. Envir., Envir. Assess. Div., Envir. Qlty. Monit. Br., Edmonton. Pers. comm.

Noton, L. 1989. Alta. Envir., Envir. Assess. Div., Envir. Qlty. Monit. Br., Edmonton. Pers. comm.

Pinsent, M.E. 1967. A comparative limnological study of Lac La Biche and Beaver Lake, Alberta. MSc thesis. Univ. Alta., Edmonton.

Robertson, M.R. 1969. The cisco fishery of Lac La Biche, Alberta. Alta. For. Ld. Wild., Fish Wild. Div. Unpubl. rep., St. Paul.

Strong, W.L. and K.R. Leggat. 1981. Ecoregions of Alberta. Alta. En. Nat. Resour., Resour. Eval. Plan. Div., Edmonton.

Trimbee, A.M. and E.E. Prepas. 1987. Evaluation of total phosphorus as a predictor of the relative importance of blue-green algae with emphasis on Alberta lakes. Can. J. Fish. Aquat. Sci. 44:1337–1342.

———. 1988. The effect of oxygen depletion on the timing and magnitude of blue-green algal blooms. Verh. Internat. Verein. Limnol. 23:220–226.

Wynnyk, A., J.D. Lindsay, P.K. Heringa and W. Odynsky. 1963. Exploratory soil survey of Alberta map sheets 83–O, 83–P and 73M. Prelim. Soil Surv. Rep. 64–1. Res. Counc. Alta., Edmonton.

LAC LA NONNE

MAP SHEET: 83G/16
LOCATION: Tp57 R2, 3 W5
LAT/LONG: 53°56′N 114°19′W

Lac la Nonne is a highly developed, popular recreational lake. It is situated about 90 km northwest of the city of Edmonton in the counties of Barrhead and Lac Ste. Anne. To reach the lake from Edmonton, take Highway 16 west, then Highway 43 north and west to the village of Gunn. Highway 33 extends north from Gunn near the west side of the lake, but local roads must be taken to reach the lakeshore (Fig. 1). The east shore can be reached by local roads from Secondary Road 651. The town of Barrhead, 20 km north of the lake, is the closest large population centre.

The lake's name, which means "the nun" in French, has an uncertain origin. The Cree name for the lake, *mi-ka-sioo*, means "eagle". In 1827, Edward Ermatinger recorded the lake's name in his journal as Lac la Nane. The lake may have been named for the White-winged Scoter, a duck that is common on the lake and is similar to an English duck known as "the nun". The bird's colouring, which is black with white wing bars and a white spot on the head, suggests a black-robed nun (Holmgren and Holmgren 1976). Another suggestion is that the lake was named for the nuns at nearby Lac Ste. Anne Mission, though the mission was not founded until 1843.

The Hudson's Bay Company established a trading post at Lac la Nonne in the early 1800s. The post was used to pasture the herds of pack horses needed to portage goods from Edmonton House to Fort Assiniboine on the Athabasca River (Edm. Reg. Plan. Commis. and Alta. Mun. Aff. 1980). By the 1830s, there were considerable numbers of Métis living by the lake. Missionaries arrived in the 1870s, and in 1878, the Oblate Fathers established a mission on the southeast shore at the site of the present-day Catholic Church in Camp Encounter. When the fur trade declined, the Métis moved away and the trading post and mission were closed (Barrhead Dist. Hist. Soc. 1967).

By the 1890s, several white families had settled around the lakeshore, and by 1912, most of the available land had been homesteaded. Horse and cattle raising were important occupations, and sawmills operated periodically near the lake. The first summer cottages were built on the eastern shore in the early 1900s. For many years the local recreation centre was Killdeer Beach Resort on the southwest shore. It began business in about 1928, and held activities such as "amphibious" horse races (Barrhead Dist. Hist. Soc. 1967). At present, it is one of two commercial facilities at the lake, which offer a total of 410 campsites (Alta. Hotel Assoc. 1989). As well, there is a restaurant, a gas station and three small stores in the subdivisions on the lakeshore. There are no provincial or municipal campgrounds at the lake.

There are several public access points with boat launches on Lac la Nonne (Fig. 2). They are maintained by either the County of Barrhead or the County of Lac Ste. Anne. The facilities in Lac la Nonne Subdivision at the southeast tip of the lake consist of three picnic tables, a water pipe and an area where small boats can be hand launched. A picnic area and boat launch are also located at the end of the road allowance near Greendale Subdivision, in the central part of the eastern shore. As well, there is one boat launch in the summer village of Birch Cove on the northwest shore and another in Williams Subdivision on the south shore. There are no boating restrictions over most of the lake, but in posted areas either all boats are prohibited or power boats are restricted to speeds of 12 km/hour (Alta. For.

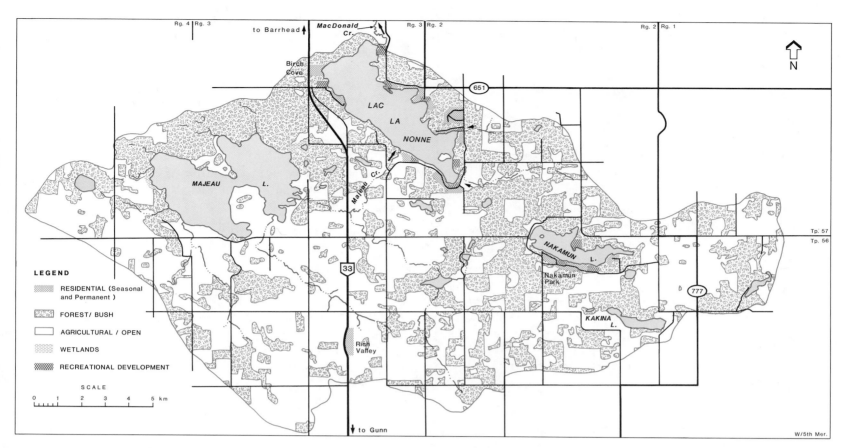

Figure 1. Features of the drainage basin of Lac la Nonne.
SOURCES: Alta. Envir. n.d.[b]; En. Mines Resour. Can. 1975. Updated with 1985 aerial photos.

Ld. Wild. 1988). The County of Lac Ste. Anne maintains a cross-country ski trail, the Yukon trail, on Crown land northwest of the lake.

Lac la Nonne has dense blue-green algal blooms during summer and aquatic plants are abundant around the shoreline. The aquatic vegetation is frequently considered a nuisance by cottage owners, boaters and anglers. Although dissolved oxygen concentrations can become critical for fish survival during both summer and winter, no major fish kills have been reported. Walleye and northern pike are the main catches in the popular summer sport fishery. Walleye may contain concentrations of natural mercury that exceed recommended safe levels (Alta. For. Ld. Wild. 1989). During winter, the most sought-after species are perch and large northern pike. All tributary streams to, and the outlet from, Lac la Nonne are closed to sport fishing for a designated period during April and May each year (Alta. For. Ld. Wild. 1989).

Drainage Basin Characteristics

Lac la Nonne has a very large drainage basin that is about 23 times the size of the lake (Tables 1, 2). The main inflow to the lake is Majeau Creek, which drains the western and central portions of the watershed (Fig. 1). Two smaller creeks flow into the southeast shore. The outflow is MacDonald Creek, which flows into the Pembina River about 3 km north of the lake. The general direction of groundwater movement in the drainage basin is southwest to northeast. The flowing wells located on the east side of the lake indicate a groundwater discharge area there. Groundwater in the area is alkaline and has high concentrations of total dissolved solids (Edm. Reg. Plan. Commis. and Alta. Mun. Aff. 1980).

The land surface throughout the watershed is extremely variable. It ranges from relatively level lacustrine and glacial till plains to moderately and strongly rolling morainal areas (Twardy 1977). Soils have been mapped and described in general for the drainage basin and in detail for an area within 1.6 km of the shoreline (Lindsay et al. 1968; Twardy 1977). In the study area adjacent to the lake, the predominant soils are moderately well-drained to well-drained Gray Luvisols that developed on lacustrine material or glacial till. Regosolic

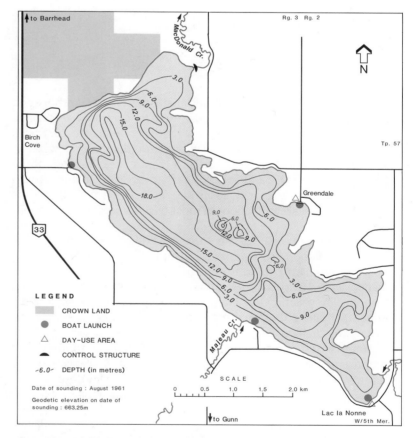

Figure 2. Bathymetry and shoreline features of Lac la Nonne.
BATHYMETRY SOURCE: Alta. Envir. n.d.[c].

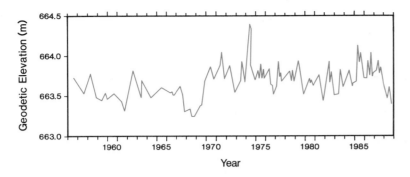

Figure 3. Water level of Lac la Nonne, 1956 to 1988.
SOURCES: Alta. Envir. n.d.[c]; Envir. Can. 1972–1987.

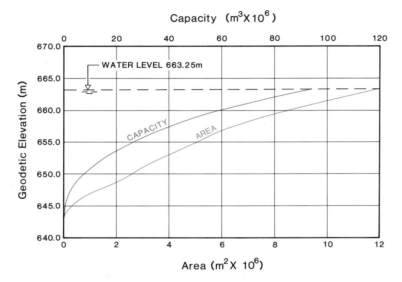

Figure 4. Area/capacity curve for Lac la Nonne.
SOURCE: Alta. Envir. n.d.[c].

Table 1. Characteristics of Lac la Nonne drainage basin.

area (excluding lake) (km²)[a]	277
soil[b]	Gray Luvisols
bedrock geology[c]	Wapiti Formation (Upper Cretaceous): sandstone, mudstone, bentonite, scattered coal beds; nonmarine
terrain[b]	flat to strongly rolling
ecoregion[d]	Moist Mixedwood Subregion of Boreal Mixedwood
dominant vegetation[d]	trembling aspen, balsam poplar
mean annual inflow (m³)[a, e]	6.84 x 10⁶
mean annual sunshine (h)[f]	2 264

NOTE: [e]excluding groundwater inflow
SOURCES: [a]Alta. Envir. n.d.[b]; [b]Lindsay et al. 1968; Twardy 1977; [c]Alta. Res. Counc. 1972; [d]Strong and Leggat 1981; [f]Envir. Can. 1982

Table 2. Characteristics of Lac la Nonne.

elevation (m)[a, b]	663.25
surface area (km²)[a, b]	11.8
volume (m³)[a, b]	92.3 x 10⁶
maximum depth (m)[a, b]	19.8
mean depth (m)[a, b]	7.8
shoreline length (km)[c, d]	25.9
mean annual lake evaporation (mm)[e]	664
mean annual precipitation (mm)[e]	504
mean residence time (yr)[e, f]	18.5
control structure[g]	rock and concrete weir

NOTES: [a]on date of sounding: Aug. 1961; [d]includes 2.9 km for islands; [f]excluding groundwater inflow
SOURCES: [b]Alta. Envir. n.d.[c]; [c]En. Mines Resour. Can. 1975; [e]Alta. Envir. n.d.[b]; [g]Alta. Envir. n.d.[d]

soils are present on the beach sands near parts of the lakeshore and on the floodplains of creeks. Imperfectly to moderately well-drained Solonetzic soils that developed on moderately fine-textured till, weathered bedrock material, and fine-textured lacustrine material, are located northeast of the lake. Throughout the remainder of the drainage basin, Orthic and Solodic Gray Luvisols and Solonetzic soils are common and Organic deposits are significant. The Organics are characterized by accumulations of moss or sedge peat in depressional areas.

The watershed is part of the Moist Mixedwood Subregion of the Boreal Mixedwood Ecoregion (Strong and Leggat 1981). Trembling aspen and balsam poplar are the main trees on moderately well-drained Gray Luvisols. White spruce predominates on imperfectly drained Gleysols and Gray Luvisols, black spruce and willows grow on poorly drained Organics and Gleysols, and sedges are found on very poorly drained Organics.

A large part of the drainage basin, particularly in the southern and central portions, has been cleared of forest (Fig. 1). Soils with the best agricultural rating (fairly good to good arability) are located south of Majeau Lake. Around Nakamun Lake and in the central part of the drainage basin the soil has a poor to fair arability rating. Around Lac la Nonne, large areas that are rated as suitable for pasture and woodland are interspersed with lands that have poor to fair and fair to fairly good ratings (Lindsay et al. 1968). The main agricultural activities in the watershed are cattle and forage production (Mitchell and Hamilton 1982).

Most of shoreline is privately owned. The only Crown land near the lakeshore is located to the northwest (Fig. 2). Grazing leases are held on three of these nine quarter-sections (Edm. Reg. Plan. Commis. and Alta. Mun. Aff. 1980). Subdivision development at Lac la Nonne began in 1947, when 23 lots were created in Lac la Nonne Subdivision. By 1980, 605 resort lots had been registered in 13

subdivisions on or very near the shores of the lake. Between 1982 and 1989, the number of registered lots had increased by 10, and the Birch Cove Subdivision had become a summer village (Yell. Reg. Plan. Commis. n.d.).

Concerns about major developments around the lake increased during the 1970s. The number of applications for subdivisions had increased, more cottages were winterized, and use of the lake by the general public had intensified. In response to these concerns, the provincial government restricted shoreline development in 1977 under the Lake Shoreland Development Operation Regulations, which were administered by Alberta Environment. This allowed preparation of a lake management plan, which was completed in 1980 (Edm. Reg. Plan. Commis. and Alta. Mun. Aff. 1980; Edm. Reg. Plan. Commis. 1981). This plan determined the extent of future land developments, allocated land use and determined ways to minimize environmental impacts and conflicts in uses of the lakeshore. It recommended preferred lake uses and ways to minimize lake-user conflicts. Subsequently, an area structure plan was adopted by the counties of Lac Ste. Anne and Barrhead in 1982 (Edm. Metro. Reg. Plan. Commis. and Yell. Reg. Plan. Commis. 1982). The area structure plan defines land-use and development policies for the area and classifies parcels of land for various uses.

Lake Basin Characteristics

Lac la Nonne is a medium-sized water body with a fairly regular shoreline (Table 2). The lake has a single basin that reaches a maximum depth of almost 20 m at the northwest end (Fig. 2). The sides of the basin slope quite steeply in the northwest half of the lake but more gradually in the southeast half, where the maximum depth is a little over 9 m. A large island is present at the southeast end of the lake.

Table 3. Major ions and related water quality variables for Lac la Nonne. Average concentrations in mg/L; pH in pH units. Composite samples from the euphotic zone collected 5 times from 05 May to 22 Sep. 1988. S.E. = standard error.

	Mean	S.E.
pH (range)	8.1–9.0	—
total alkalinity (CaCO$_3$)	149	0.6
specific conductivity (μS/cm)	314	1.6
total dissolved solids (calculated)	176	0.7
total hardness (CaCO$_3$)	123	0.6
total particulate carbon	7	2.7
dissolved organic carbon	17	0.4
HCO$_3$	164	10.7
CO$_3$	<9	—
Mg	10	0.2
Na	17	0.4
K	10	0.1
Cl	3	0.2
SO$_4$	14	0.6
Ca	33	0.5

NOTE: [a]n = 2
SOURCE: Alta. Envir. n.d.[a], Naquadat station 01AL05EA3302

The provincial government built a rock and timber weir on the outlet, MacDonald Creek, in 1939 (Ducks Unltd. (Can.) n.d.). This structure was funded by a local group of sportsmen and by Ducks Unlimited (Canada). It was replaced by Ducks Unlimited (Canada) in 1948 with another rock and timber structure to help improve waterfowl habitat and create a reservoir that would supply downstream landowners. In 1966, the provincial government replaced the structure with a weir consisting of cement-filled bags and rocks. There has been disagreement among local landowners regarding the preferred level for the lake. Efforts are ongoing to reach a consensus regarding lake levels (Alta. Envir. n.d.[d]).

The elevation of Lac la Nonne has been monitored since 1956 (Fig. 3). The difference between the minimum elevation (663.24 m), recorded in October 1968, and the maximum elevation (664.40 m), recorded in May 1974, is 1.16 m. Precipitation levels in 1974 were very high. Between 1980 and 1988, the range in lake levels was 0.70 m. Figure 4 shows the changes in area and capacity of the lake as the water level fluctuates.

Water Quality

Water quality in Lac la Nonne was studied by Alberta Environment from 1977 to 1979 (Alta. Envir. n.d.[a]; 1985; Hamilton 1980). Phosphorus export from the Majeau Creek watershed to Lac la Nonne was studied in 1981 (Mitchell and Hamilton 1982).

The lake has fresh water that is hard and well buffered (Table 3). The dominant ions are bicarbonate and calcium. The water column becomes thermally stratified during summer (Fig. 5). In some years, as in 1978 (Fig. 6), dissolved oxygen concentrations in the water column become quite severely depleted. From July to September in 1978, water was anoxic below a depth of 15 m. By September, dissolved oxygen concentrations at the surface had declined to 5 mg/L. A similar pattern of dissolved oxygen depletion was observed in 1979. During February 1978, dissolved oxygen concentrations above a depth of 8 m ranged from 6 to 11 mg/L, but were less than 2 mg/L below that depth (Fig. 6). In March 1979, dissolved oxygen levels were only 6 mg/L at the surface and less than 1 mg/L below a depth of 10 m.

Lac la Nonne is hyper-eutrophic. In 1988, chlorophyll *a* concentrations reached a maximum of 140 μg/L in July, and total phosphorus concentrations reached a maximum of 309 μg/L in August (Fig. 7). The water is often fairly clear in early summer, but it becomes turbid with algae by late June or early July. In 1988, the average Secchi depth was only 1.9 m (Table 4).

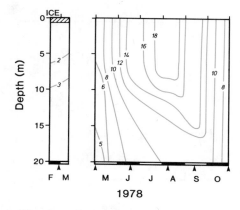

Figure 5. Temperature (°C) of Lac la Nonne, 1978. Arrows indicate sampling dates.
SOURCE: Alta. Envir. n.d.[a].

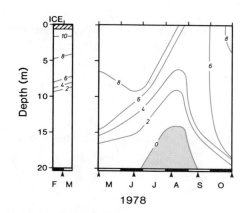

Figure 6. Dissolved oxygen (mg/L) in Lac la Nonne, 1978. Arrows indicate sampling dates.
SOURCE: Alta. Envir. n.d.[a].

The supply of total phosphorus from sources external to the lake has been estimated (Table 5). Runoff from agricultural and cleared land in the immediate watershed accounts for more than half (57%) of the total load of 4 894 kg/year. Inflow from Majeau Lake via Majeau Creek is secondary (20%) in importance. All other sources, such as sewage inputs, are minor in comparison to these two sources. Inputs of phosphorus from the Majeau Creek watershed are high because of the large numbers of cattle produced in the area. In 1981, the average total phosphorus concentration in streams in the entire Majeau watershed was 904 μg/L. In comparison, the concentration of phosphorus in streams draining Lake Wabamun's watershed, where land use is mixed agriculture and forest, is only about 300 μg/L (Mitchell 1985). Phosphorus loading from internal sources has not been estimated, but is likely to be important. The areal loading rate for Lac la Nonne (0.41 g/m^2 of lake surface) is very high. It is similar to the rate calculated for Baptiste Lake (0.35 g/m^2) and much higher than that calculated for Lake Wabamun (0.08 g/m^2).

Biological Characteristics

Plants

The phytoplankton community was sampled at three sites by Alberta Environment 6 times from February to October in both 1978 and 1979 (Beliveau and Furnell 1980). In 1979, blue-green algae (Cyanophyta) were the dominant group at two sites during March, but were replaced by cryptophytes and diatoms (Bacillariophyta) at all three sites during May and June. During July, August and October, however, over 97% of the algal biomass was made up of blue-greens. These blue-greens grow in response to low oxygen conditions over the sediments and high total phosphorus concentrations (Trimbee and Prepas 1987; 1988).

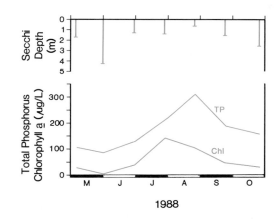

Figure 7. Total phosphorus, chlorophyll *a* and Secchi depth in Lac la Nonne, 1988.
SOURCE: Alta. Envir. n.d.[a].

Table 4. Nutrient, chlorophyll *a* and Secchi depth data for Lac la Nonne. Average concentrations in µg/L. Composite samples from the euphotic zone collected 7 times from 05 May to 25 Oct. 1988. S.E. = standard error.

	Mean	S.E.
total phosphorus	168	28.9
total dissolved phosphorus	104	13.8
total Kjeldahl nitrogen	2 224	337.3
NO$_3$ + NO$_2$–nitrogen	<8	—
NH$_4$–nitrogen	43	17.4
iron	<18[a]	—
chlorophyll *a*	55.5	18.28
Secchi depth (m)	1.9	0.45

NOTE: [a]n = 5
SOURCE: Alta. Envir. n.d.[a], Naquadat station 01AL05EA3302

Invertebrates

There are no data for the zooplankton and benthic invertebrate communities.

Fish

Seven species of fish have been reported in Lac la Nonne: lake whitefish, walleye, northern pike, yellow perch, cisco, burbot and white sucker. Largemouth bass were stocked in 1926, but they are not found in the lake at present (Alta. For. Ld. Wild. n.d.). The lake whitefish and cisco are infested with cysts of the tapeworm *Triaenophorus crassus* (Alta. Rec. Parks Wild. 1976).

Lac la Nonne is managed for recreational and domestic fisheries. There are no data for the domestic fishery. A commercial fishery for lake whitefish and cisco operated in the lake from 1945/46 to 1974/75 (Alta. Rec. Parks Wild. 1976). Walleye were an incidental catch taken under a tolerance quota. The lake whitefish population declined after 1960 and the cisco population increased. The cisco were used for animal food on mink ranches in the Seba Beach and Edmonton areas until the ranches went out of business. In response to the decline in demand for cisco, as well as a conflict between the sport and commercial fisheries over the commercial walleye catch, the commercial fishery was closed after February 1975 (Stenton 1989). Since then, the walleye population has increased considerably (Edm. Reg. Plan. Commis. and Alta. Mun. Aff. 1980).

Lac la Nonne's recreational fishery is quite popular on a local and regional scale. A brief creel survey was conducted in 1988 over three days between 29 May and 7 June (Alta. For. Ld. Wild. n.d.). The 148 anglers interviewed fished for a total of 322 hours and caught 116 walleye and 366 northern pike. Approximately 72% of the northern pike and 12% of the walleye were released. Therefore, although the catch rate was 1.5 fish/angler-hour, the harvest rate was 0.32 fish per angler-hour for both species combined. Most anglers interviewed were fishing for walleye; this accounts for the high release rate for northern pike. The low release rate for walleye indicates that most anglers will keep walleye, regardless of size. In a sample of 100 walleye, the dominant age class was 5 years, the mean fork length was 39.9 cm, and the mean weight was 679 g.

Wildlife

There are few data for the wildlife in the Lac la Nonne area. Water birds that have been observed on the lake include Lesser Scaup, Redheads, White-winged Scoters, Common Goldeneye, Blue-winged Teal, Mallards, Western Grebes, gulls and Common Loons.

There are few data for the macrophyte community. Emergent plants such as bulrush (*Scirpus* spp.), sedges (*Carex* spp.) and cattails (*Typha* spp.), and unspecified submergent plants, grow around the shoreline.

Table 5. Theoretical total phosphorus loading to Lac la Nonne from external sources.

Source		Phosphorus (kg/yr)	Percentage of Total
immediate watershed	forested/bush	537	11
	agricultural/cleared	2 770	57
	residential/cottage	160	3
sewage[a]		20	<1
precipitation/dustfall		260	5
inflow from other lakes	Majeau Lake	957	20
	Nakamun Lake	190	4
	TOTAL	4 894	100
annual areal loading (g/m^2 of lake surface) 0.41			

NOTE: [a]unmeasured: assumes 4% of all sewage effluent from residences and camps enters the lake, as in Mitchell 1982
SOURCES: Mitchell and Hamilton 1982; Alta. Envir. 1985; Mitchell 1989

Waterfowl are limited by lack of nesting sites for upland and overwater nesters, a shortage of loafing areas, the sparseness of emergent aquatic vegetation and increasing recreational use of the lake (Ducks Unltd. (Can.) n.d.).

White-tailed deer are the primary ungulates found in the area, and there is some evidence of mule deer and moose (Edm. Reg. Plan. Commis. and Alta. Mun. Aff. 1980).

M.E. Bradford

References

Alberta Environment. n.d.[a]. Envir. Assess. Div., Envir. Qlty. Monit. Br. Unpubl. data, Edmonton.
———. n.d.[b]. Tech. Serv. Div., Hydrol. Br. Unpubl. data, Edmonton.
———. n.d.[c]. Tech. Serv. Div., Surv. Br. Unpubl. data, Edmonton.
———. n.d.[d]. Water Resour. Admin. Div., Records Mgt. Br. Unpubl. data, Edmonton.
———. 1985. Lac la Nonne. Poll. Contr. Div., Water Qlty. Contr. Br., Edmonton.
Alberta Forestry, Lands and Wildlife. n.d. Fish Wild. Div. Unpubl. data, Edmonton.
———. 1988. Boating in Alberta. Fish Wild. Div., Edmonton.
———. 1989. Guide to sportfishing. Fish Wild. Div., Edmonton.
Alberta Hotel Association. 1989. Alberta campground guide 1989. Prep. for Travel Alta., Edmonton.
Alberta Recreation, Parks and Wildlife. 1976. Commercial fisheries catch statistics for Alberta, 1942–1975. Fish Wild. Div., Fish. Mgt. Rep. No. 22, Edmonton.
Alberta Research Council. 1972. Geological map of Alberta. Nat. Resour. Div., Alta. Geol. Surv., Edmonton.
Barrhead and District Historical Society. 1967. Trails northwest. Barrhead Dist. Hist. Soc., Barrhead.
Beliveau, D. and A. Furnell. 1980. Phytoplankton data summary 1976–1980. Alta. Envir., Poll. Contr. Div., Water Qlty. Contr. Br. Unpubl. rep., Edmonton.
Ducks Unlimited (Canada). n.d. Unpubl. data, Edmonton.

Edmonton Metropolitan Regional Planning Commission and Yellowhead Regional Planning Commission. 1982. Lac la Nonne area structure plan. Prep. for Co. Barrhead, Barrhead and Co. Lac Ste. Anne, Sangudo. Edm. Metro. Reg. Plan. Commis., Edmonton and Yell. Reg. Plan. Commis., Onoway.

Edmonton Regional Planning Commission. 1981. Lac la Nonne management plan alternatives. Edm. Reg. Plan. Commis., Edmonton.

———— and Alberta Municipal Affairs. 1980. Lac la Nonne: Background information and management issues. Edm. Reg. Plan. Commis. and Alta. Mun. Aff., Edmonton.

Energy, Mines and Resources Canada. 1975. National topographic series 1:50 000 83G/15 (1975), 83G/16 (1975). Surv. Map. Br., Ottawa.

Environment Canada. 1972–1988. Surface water data. Prep. by Inland Waters Directorate. Water Surv. Can., Water Resour. Br., Ottawa.

————. 1982. Canadian climate normals, Vol. 7: Bright sunshine (1951–1980). Prep. by Atm. Envir. Serv. Supply Serv. Can., Ottawa.

Hamilton, H.R. 1980. Lac la Nonne water quality report November, 1980. Alta. Envir., Poll. Contr. Div., Water Qlty. Contr. Br., Edmonton.

Holmgren, E.J. and P.M. Holmgren. 1976. Over 2000 place names of Alberta. 3rd ed. West. Producer Prairie Books, Saskatoon.

Lindsay, J.D., W. Odynsky, J.W. Peters and W.E. Bowser. 1968. Soil survey of the Buck Lake (NE 83B) and Wabamun Lake (E1/2 83G) areas. Alta. Soil Surv. Rep. No. 24, Univ. Alta. Bull. No. SS–7, Alta. Res. Counc. Rep. No. 87. Univ. Alta., Edmonton.

Mitchell, P.A. 1982. Evaluation of the "septic snooper" on Wabamun and Pigeon lakes. Alta. Envir., Poll. Contr. Div., Water Qlty. Contr. Br., Edmonton.

————. 1985. Preservation of water quality in Lake Wabamun: Lake Wabamun eutrophication study. Alta. Envir., Poll. Contr. Div., Water Qlty. Contr. Br., Edmonton.

————. 1989. Alta. Envir., Envir. Assess. Div., Envir. Qlty. Monit. Br., Edmonton. Pers. comm.

———— and H.R. Hamilton. 1982. Assessment of phosphorus export from the Majeau Creek watershed Lac la Nonne. Alta. Envir., Poll. Contr. Div., Water Qlty. Contr. Br, Edmonton.

Stenton, E. 1989. Alta. For. Ld. Wild., Fish Wild. Div., Edmonton. Pers. comm.

Strong, W.L. and K.R. Leggat. 1981. Ecoregions of Alberta. Alta. En. Nat. Resour., Resour. Eval. Plan. Div., Edmonton.

Trimbee, A.M. and E.E. Prepas. 1987. Evaluation of total phosphorus as a predictor of the relative importance of blue-green algae with emphasis on Alberta lakes. Can. J. Fish. Aquat. Sci. 44:1337–1342.

————. 1988. The effect of oxygen depletion on the timing and magnitude of blue-green algal blooms. Verh. Internat. Verein. Limnol. 23:220–226.

Twardy, A.G. 1977. Soil survey and land suitability evaluation of the Lac la Nonne study area. Prep. for Alta. Envir. by Pedol. Consult., Edmonton.

Yellowhead Regional Planning Commission. n.d. Unpubl. data, Onoway.

LESSARD LAKE

MAP SHEET: 83G/15
LOCATION: Tp55 R5 W5
LAT/LONG: 53°47'N 114°38'W

Lessard Lake is a quiet, pleasant lake bordered on two sides by extensive wetlands that are home for waterfowl and wildlife. It is located in the County of Lac Ste. Anne between the towns of Onoway and Sangudo. The lake can be reached from the city of Edmonton by driving west on Highway 16 for approximately 26 km, then north on Highway 43 for about 45 km. When you are 7 km past the hamlet of Glenevis, turn south and drive for 2.5 km then turn west and drive for 0.5 km to county-operated Lessard Lake County Park on the southeast side of the lake (Fig. 1). Recreational facilities available at the park include a campground, picnic area, beach, playground and boat launch (Fig. 2). There are no specific provincial boating regulations for Lessard Lake, but federal regulations apply and caution should be taken in the beach area to avoid swimmers (Alta. For. Ld. Wild. 1988).

Lessard Lake was possibly named for Edmond Lessard, first elected to the Alberta legislature in 1909, then called to the senate in 1925 (Alta. Cult. Multicult. n.d.).

Lessard Lake is locally popular for sport fishing for yellow perch and pike. Provincial limits for catch, number and size apply, but there are no special regulations for this lake (Alta. For. Ld. Wild. 1989). The water in Lessard Lake is fairly clear in midsummer, but turns green by late August. The west and north shores support extensive aquatic vegetation, but there are sandy areas along the east shore.

Drainage Basin Characteristics

The Lessard Lake drainage basin is small and less than 3 times the area of the lake (Tables 1, 2). There is no defined inlet to or outlet from the lake; groundwater is likely a major contributor of water.

The land in the watershed is gently rolling (5 to 9% slopes), with extensive flat wetland areas to the west of the lake and pockets of wetlands east of the lake (Fig. 1). The soils in the wetlands are Organics, with extensive accumulations of sedge and *Sphagnum* peat (Lindsay et al. 1968). Farther from the lake on all sides and along the north shore, the soils are Eluviated Eutric Brunisols that formed on moderately well-drained fluvial material. South of the lake, the soils are Orthic Gray Luvisols that formed on glacial till.

The drainage basin is part of the Moist Mixedwood Subregion of the Boreal Mixedwood Ecoregion (Strong and Leggat 1981). Most of the basin is forested with trembling aspen, balsam poplar and some white spruce. The low areas support sedges, willow, black spruce and birch (Clements 1975). A portion of the northern part of the basin has been cleared for agriculture, primarily grazing and some grain production. The southern part of the basin has been subdivided into country residential lots, but only a few had been developed as of 1987.

Lake Basin Characteristics

Lessard Lake is small, and has a single basin shaped like a short-fingered hand with the "fingers" pointing to the east. The lake basin slopes quite steeply along the southeast side of the lake (Fig. 2). Near the park, the slope is about 6% and the bottom drops rapidly to a depth of 5 m (Alta. For. Ld. Wild. n.d.). The slope along the north and west shores is very gradual and shallow water extends well into the lake. The maximum depth of 6 m is located near the center of the lake.

Table 1. Characteristics of Lessard Lake drainage basin.

area (excluding lake) (km²)[a]	9.29
soil[b]	Eluviated Eutric Brunisols, Orthic Gray Luvisols, Organics
bedrock geology[c]	Paskapoo Formation (Tertiary): sandstone, siltstone, mudstone; thin limestone, coal and tuff beds; nonmarine
terrain[b]	gently rolling
ecoregion[d]	Moist Mixedwood Subregion of Boreal Mixedwood
dominant vegetation[d]	trembling aspen, balsam poplar
mean annual inflow (m³)[a, e]	0.455 x 10⁶
mean annual sunshine (h)[f]	2 264

NOTE: [e]excluding groundwater inflow
SOURCES: [a]Alta. Envir. n.d.[a]; [b]Lindsay et al. 1968; [c]Alta. Res. Counc. 1972; [d]Strong and Leggat 1981; [f]Envir. Can. 1982

Table 2. Characteristics of Lessard Lake.

elevation (m)[a, b]	700.06
surface area (km²)[a, b]	3.21
volume (m³)[a, b]	12.5 x 10⁶
maximum depth (m)[a, b]	6
mean depth (m)[a, b]	3.9
shoreline length (km)[c]	9.8
mean annual lake evaporation (mm)[d]	664
mean annual precipitation (mm)[d]	522
mean residence time (yr)[d, e]	>100
control structure	none

NOTES: [a]on date of sounding: 23 Sep. 1982; [e]excluding groundwater inflow
SOURCES: [b]Babin 1984; [c]En. Mines Resour. Can. 1975; [d]Alta. Envir. n.d.[a]

Table 3. Major ions and related water quality variables for Lessard Lake. Average concentrations in mg/L; pH in pH units. Composite samples from the euphotic zone collected 6 times from 25 May to 13 Sep. 1982. S.E. = standard error.

	Mean	S.E.
pH	7.8[a]	—
total alkalinity (CaCO₃)	132[b]	—
specific conductivity (μS/cm)	239	1.4
total dissolved solids	166	5.2
turbidity (NTU)	5[b]	—
colour (Pt)	2[b]	—
total hardness (calculated)	145	—
HCO₃	132[b]	—
CO₃	0[b]	—
Mg	14[a]	—
Na	6[a]	—
K	12[a]	—
Ca	35[a]	—

NOTES: [a]n = 1, 04 Apr. 1989, 75 cm ice, specific conductivity 331 μS/cm; [b]n = 1, 13 Sep. 1982
SOURCE: Prepas and Babin n.d.

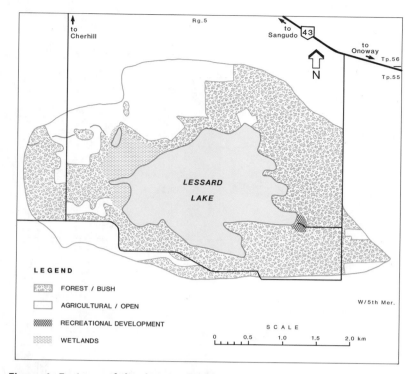

Figure 1. Features of the drainage basin of Lessard Lake.
SOURCES: Alta. Envir. n.d.[a]; En. Mines Resour. Can. 1975. Updated with 1977 and 1987 aerial photos.

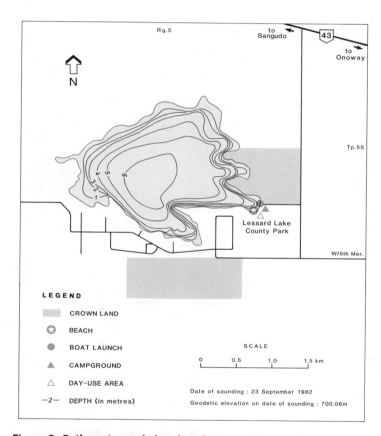

Figure 2. Bathymetry and shoreline features of Lessard Lake.
BATHYMETRY SOURCE: Babin 1984.

of deep snow and heavy spring rains. From 1975 to 1987, the lake level fluctuated over a range of 0.35 m.

Water Quality

The water quality of Lessard Lake was studied from May 1982 through March 1983 by researchers at the University of Alberta (Prepas and Babin n.d.; Prepas 1983; Babin 1984; Prepas and Vickery 1984; Babin and Prepas 1985).

Lessard is a well-buffered, freshwater lake. The water is neither coloured nor turbid. The dominant ions are bicarbonate and calcium (Table 3).

The bottom of most of the lake and along the north and west shores is soft red-brown organic material; the "thumb" and "fingers" are edged by a sandy shoreline with some patches of cobbles just at the points of land separating the "fingers" (Clements 1975). Aquatic vegetation extends to a depth of approximately 3 m (Clements 1975); almost 30% of the lake area is less than this depth (Fig. 3).

The lake elevation has been monitored since 1969 when it was relatively low (Fig. 4). The level reached a maximum in 1974, a year

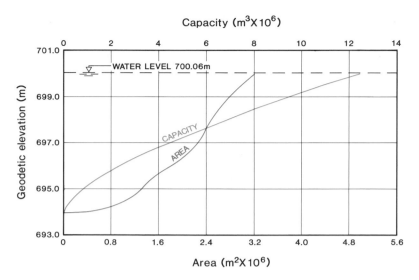

Figure 3. Area/capacity curve for Lessard Lake.
SOURCE: Babin 1984.

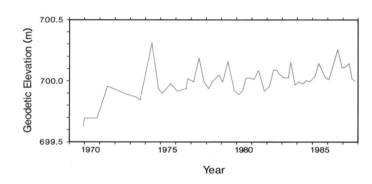

Figure 4. Water level of Lessard Lake, 1969 to 1987.
SOURCE: Alta. Envir. n.d.[b].

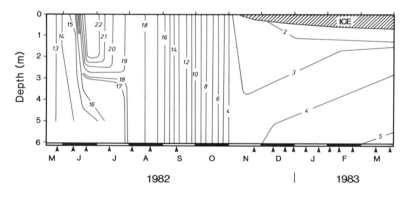

Figure 5. Temperature (°C) of Lessard Lake, May 1982 to March 1983.
Arrows indicate sampling dates.
SOURCES: Prepas and Babin n.d.; Prepas 1983.

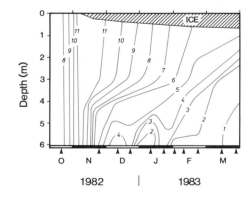

Figure 6. Dissolved oxygen (mg/L) in Lessard Lake, October 1982 to March 1983. Arrows indicate sampling dates.
SOURCE: Babin 1984.

Table 4. Nutrient, chlorophyll *a* and Secchi depth data for Lessard Lake. Average concentrations in μg/L. Composite samples from the euphotic zone collected 7 times from 25 May to 13 Sep. 1982. S.E. = standard error.

	Mean	S.E.
total phosphorus	30	2.5
total Kjeldahl nitrogen	1 414	108.3
NO$_3$ + NO$_2$–nitrogen	15	4.9
chlorophyll *a*	14.9	3.23
Secchi depth (m)	1.9	0.37

SOURCE: Prepas and Babin n.d.

The quality of the water and the patterns of thermal stratification in Lessard Lake are similar to those in many shallow, freshwater lakes in Alberta. During the open-water season of 1982, the lake mixed in spring, and was isothermal except for a six-week period in late June and July when it was thermally stratified. Following this period, the lake was isothermal from early August until freeze-up (Fig. 5). Dissolved oxygen concentrations were monitored beginning in October of 1982 (Fig. 6). Despite the mixing that occurred in late summer and autumn, the water column was still only 77% saturated with dissolved oxygen at freeze-up in early November 1982. Under ice, the depletion of dissolved oxygen proceeded at the relatively slow rate of 0.243 g O$_2$/m^2 per day. By late March 1983, the dissolved oxygen concentration was low throughout the water column, but fish survival was not compromised. In other years, dissolved oxygen concentrations in late winter have dropped to levels below the limit that can support fish. Nearly total fish kills were reported in the winters of 1973/74 and 1975/76 (Alta. For. Ld. Wild. n.d.; Clements 1975).

The trophic status of Lessard Lake is at the low end of the eutrophic range (Table 4). The lake is moderately rich in nutrients and occasionally the chlorophyll *a* concentration rises above 25 μg/L (Fig. 7). Over winter, when dissolved oxygen concentrations are low, total phosphorus is likely transferred from the sediments into the overlying water. This process accounts for the high total phosphorus concentration in the lake in May 1982 (Fig. 7). Following this spring peak, the total phosphorus concentration declined rapidly, then increased slowly over the summer. The major source of phosphorus over the summer was likely the bottom sediments, which release phosphorus to the overlying water. Algal biomass (as measured by chlorophyll *a*) followed the total phosphorus concentration from May through September. Chlorophyll *a* concentrations were very low (less than 1 μg/L) under ice from November 1982 until March 1983, when they began to increase. As algal biomass increased, the rate of oxygen depletion slowed just under the ice.

Biological Characteristics

Plants

The phytoplankton community in Lessard Lake has not been studied. However, in 1982, large filamentous algae (greater than 250 μm in length) were abundant throughout the summer (Prepas and Vickery 1984).

A brief survey of aquatic plants was conducted in 1975 (Clements 1975). All of the shoreline except a small area near the park was edged by bulrush (*Scirpus* sp.) and patches of yellow water lily (*Nuphar variegatum*). Submergent plants (unidentified) were found in patches, particularly along the north, northeast and northwest shores.

Invertebrates

Zooplankton biomass in Lessard Lake was assessed from May through September 1982 (Prepas 1983; Prepas and Vickery 1984). The zooplankton (greater than 250 μm diameter) biomass was very high in May, constituting 14% of the total phosphorus pool in the

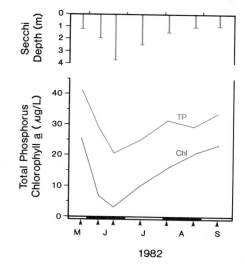

Figure 7. Total phosphorus, chlorophyll _a_ and Secchi depth in Lessard Lake, 1982.
SOURCES: Prepas and Babin n.d.; Prepas 1983.

water; it then dropped to 3% of the total phosphorus pool from June through August. In August, the dominant cladocerans were _Daphnia galeata mendotae_ and _Ceriodaphnia lacustris_; the dominant copepods were _Diaptomus oregonensis_ and _Mesocyclops edax_.

The benthic invertebrate community of Lessard lake has not been surveyed.

Fish

Lessard Lake supports a locally popular sport fishery for northern pike and yellow perch. Pike were stocked in the lake in the early 1950s. Partial winterkills occurred in several years between then and 1973, and a severe winterkill in the winter of 1973/74 eliminated almost all of the sport fish (Clements 1975). This winterkill was followed by another, almost total, fish kill in the winter of 1975/76. In August 1976, 130 000 young yellow perch and 10 adult pike were transplanted from Clear Lake. Both species flourished and the sport fishery was once again popular. In 1986, the perch were so abundant that 3 750 were transplanted from Lessard Lake to Nakamun Lake. There was a partial winterkill of perch in the winter of 1988/89 (Alta. For. Ld. Wild. n.d.).

Wildlife

There are no data on wildlife species or abundance around Lessard Lake.

J.M. Crosby and E.E. Prepas

References

Alberta Culture and Multiculturalism. n.d. Hist. Resour. Div., Hist. Sites Serv. Unpubl. data, Edmonton.

Alberta Environment. n.d.[a]. Tech. Serv. Div., Hydrol. Br. Unpubl. data, Edmonton.
———. n.d.[b]. Tech. Serv. Div., Surv. Br. Unpubl. data, Edmonton.

Alberta Forestry, Lands and Wildlife. n.d. Fish Wild. Div. Unpubl. data, Edmonton.
———. 1988. Boating in Alberta. Fish Wild. Div., Edmonton.
———. 1989. Guide to sportfishing. Fish Wild. Div., Edmonton.

Alberta Research Council. 1972. Geological map of Alberta. Nat. Resour. Div., Alta. Geol. Surv., Edmonton.

Babin, J. 1984. Winter oxygen depletion in temperate zone lakes. MSc thesis. Univ. Alta., Edmonton.
——— and E.E. Prepas. 1985. Modelling winter oxygen depletion rates in ice-covered temperate zone lakes in Canada. Can. J. Fish. Aquat. Sci. 42:239–249.

Clements, G.D. 1975. A preliminary limnological survey of Lessard Lake. Alta. Rec. Parks Wild., Fish Wild. Div., Edmonton.

Energy, Mines and Resources Canada. 1975. National topographic series 1:50 000 83G/15 (1975). Surv. Map. Br., Ottawa.

Environment Canada. 1982. Canadian climate normals, Vol. 7: Bright sunshine (1951–1980). Prep. by Atm. Envir. Serv. Supply Serv. Can., Ottawa.

Lindsay, J.D., W. Odynsky, J.W. Peters and W.E. Bowser. 1968. Soil survey of the Buck Lake (NE 83B) and Wabamun Lake (E1/2 83G) areas. Alta. Soil Surv. Rep. No. 24, Univ. Alta. Bull. No. SS–7, Alta. Res. Counc. Rep. No. 87. Univ. Alta., Edmonton.

Prepas, E.E. 1983. The influence of phosphorus and zooplankton on chlorophyll levels in Alberta lakes. Prep. for Alta. Envir., Res. Mgt. Div. Rep. 83/23, Edmonton.
——— and J. Babin. n.d. Univ. Alta., Dept. Zool. Unpubl. data, Edmonton.
——— and J. Vickery. 1984. The contribution of particulate phosphorus (>250 μm) to the total phosphorus pool in lake water. Can. J. Fish. Aquat. Sci. 41:351–363.

Strong, W.L. and K.R. Leggat. 1981. Ecoregions of Alberta. Alta. En. Nat. Resour., Resour. Eval. Plan. Div., Edmonton.

LESSER SLAVE LAKE

Alberta Tourism

MAP SHEETS: 83N, 83O
LOCATION: Tp73–75 R5–14 W5
LAT/LONG: 55°27′N 115°26′W

Lesser Slave Lake is one of Alberta's largest water bodies. It played an important role in the colourful history of the fur trade during the nineteenth century, and at present, it is the site of several excellent recreational facilities and one of Alberta's largest commercial fisheries. The lake is situated in very diverse countryside in Improvement District No. 17, about 300 km northwest of the city of Edmonton. Highway 2 from Edmonton runs along the southern shore and Highway 88 (formerly Highway 67) skirts the eastern shore (Fig. 1). The drive along the southern shore from east to west is spectacular, as one passes through dense woodland and rolling hills, then flat, open prairie. The towns of High Prairie and Slave Lake are the major urban centres in the area.

The original inhabitants of the Lesser Slave Lake area were either Slave or Beaver Indians. In the mid–1700s, they were displaced by Cree Indians as the Cree moved farther west in search of new sources of fur. The Cree brought with them European weapons and tools, as well as canoes, which were new to western Indians (Alta. Rec. Parks n.d.). The Cree were the first people to use the lake as a transportation corridor.

Sir Alexander Mackenzie learned of Lesser Slave Lake in 1793. He recorded its existence in his journals, but never visited it. In 1799, David Thompson of the North West Company became the first white man to arrive on the shore of the lake (Lombard North Plan. Ltd. 1972). Thompson was responsible for construction of the first trading post in the area, at the junction of the Lesser Slave and Athabasca rivers. By 1802, this post had been relocated to the land that was occupied by the townsite of Slave Lake until 1935, after which the townsite was moved to its present location. The Hudson's Bay Company set up a post nearby in 1815 (Alta. Rec. Parks n.d.) and both companies also established forts on Buffalo Bay at the present townsite of Grouard. The Lesser Slave Lake area was the scene of violent conflict between these rival companies prior to their merger in 1821. Both attempted to gain sole control of the lucrative fur supply, which was considered to be the richest in the whole of Rupert's Land (Lombard North Plan. Ltd. 1972). After the fur resources were depleted, Lesser Slave Lake remained important as a way station for traders and furs travelling to and from the northwest.

A new era began in the early 1900s with the formation of the Northern Transportation Company, which ran steamboats across the lake and provided easy access to the Peace Country. The steamboat *Northern Light* provided service from 1909 to 1915. When the railroad arrived in 1915, steamboats became obsolete. The Edmonton, Dunvegan and British Columbia Railway Company built a line north from Edmonton, west along the southern shore of Lesser Slave Lake, and then west to the Peace Country (Alta. Rec. Parks n.d.).

At present, there are five Indian reserves on the southern and eastern shores of the lake, and on the outlet, the Lesser Slave River. They are, from west to east, the Sucker Creek (150A), Driftpile (150), Swan River (150E), Assineau River (150F) and Sawridge (150G, 150H) reserves (Fig. 1). When Treaty No. 8 was signed in 1899, the five Cree bands that resided around the lake were regarded as one entity and the land was administered jointly. Thirty years later, each band became a separate body with its own chief and council. In 1984, the total membership of the five bands was 1 743 people, and the reserves covered a total area of 18 800 ha (Alta. Native Aff. 1986). Near the hamlet of Grouard on Buffalo Bay, members of the Grouard Indian Band live on three reserves: Freeman (150B), Halcro

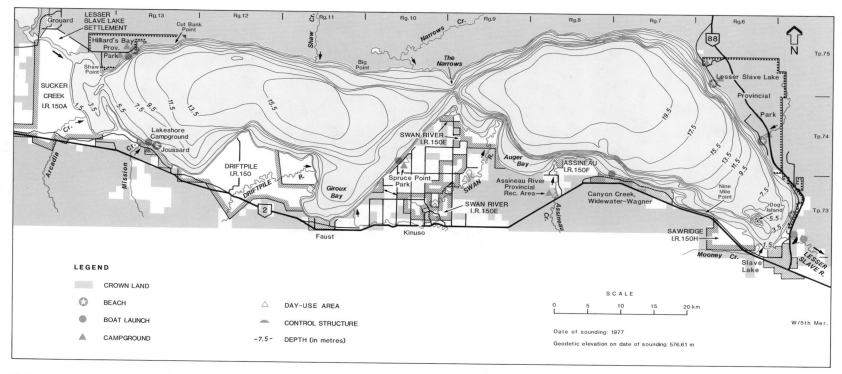

Figure 2. Bathymetry and shoreline features of Lesser Slave Lake. Outlet is Lesser Slave River; all other creeks are inflowing.
BATHYMETRY SOURCE: Alta. Envir. n.d.[c].

(150C) and Pakashan (150D). About 87 people resided on the 444–ha reserves in 1981.

There are four hamlets, one village and one town on or near Lesser Slave Lake and adjoining Buffalo Bay: the town of Slave Lake, the village of Kinuso and the hamlets of Grouard, Joussard, Faust and the hamlet of Canyon Creek, Widewater-Wagner (Fig. 1). Slave Lake was originally named Sawridge and was located downstream along the Lesser Slave River. In 1935, the town moved to its present location because of flooding, and in 1938, the town was renamed Slave Lake (Allen 1989). In 1988, its population was 5 611 people. Kinuso was originally called Swan River, but was renamed Kinuso, which is Cree for fish. In 1981, the population of Kinuso was 282 people (Alta. Native Aff. 1986). The Grouard area was a centre for fur trading during the early nineteenth century. The hamlet was given its present name in 1909, when Lesser Slave Lake Settlement was renamed for Monsignor Grouard, the resident priest. The population of Grouard in 1987 was 545 people. Joussard was originally called Indianna, but was renamed for Bishop Joussard. Historically, the hamlet was an important centre for traders, explorers and settlers, a gathering place for Indians and Métis and the site of a Roman Catholic Mission. In 1987, the population of Joussard was 330 people. Faust was once an important centre for the fishing and trapping industry. The main water and land routes for explorers, traders and settlers were located near the hamlet. In 1987, the population of Faust was 399 people. Canyon Creek, Widewater-Wagner is a single hamlet that had a population of 422 people in 1986. Canyon Creek was established in the 1930s as a major mink ranching area, and commercial fishing to supply mink food soon became an important industry. A fish hatchery operated in the community between 1928 and 1944 (Stenton 1989). It raised lake whitefish, which were stocked in lakes throughout the province.

There are two provincial parks on Lesser Slave Lake (Fig. 2). Both parks provide day-use services year-round and camping services from 1 May to Thanksgiving Day. Hilliard's Bay Provincial Park is located on the northwest shore, 13 km east of Grouard. It has 189 campsites, three group camping areas, sewage disposal facilities, tap water, playgrounds, interpretive programs, a boat launch, a beach and picnic facilities. Swimming, boating, fishing, hiking and cross-country skiing are some of the activities enjoyed at the park. Lesser Slave Lake Provincial Park is located on the northeast shore, 3 km north of the town of Slave Lake, off Highway 88. It has 113 camp-

sites, two group camping areas, sewage disposal facilities, a playground, picnic facilities, a golf course, hiking trails, 5.5 km of sandy beaches and extensive sand dunes. During winter, cross-country skiing on groomed trails and snowshoeing are popular activities. There is no boat launch within the park, but two launches are available just south of the park at an Alberta Environment day-use area at the weir on the Lesser Slave River. Another launch is available in Canyon Creek on the south shore (Fig. 2).

There are several other recreational facilities on or near the lake. Spruce Point Park is administered by the Spruce Point Park Association. It is located on the south side of the lake about 2 km west and 9 km north of Kinuso (Fig. 2). The park is open from May to September, and offers 126 campsites, group camping, pump water, sewage disposal facilities, groceries, a beach, a playground and a boat launch. Swimming, boating, fishing and hiking are popular pastimes there. Assineau River Provincial Recreation Area is located east of Kinuso on Highway 2 where the highway crosses the Assineau River. It is open from the Victoria Day week to Thanksgiving Day, and has 21 campsites, pump water and picnic facilities. Lakeshore Campground is located within the hamlet of Joussard. It is administered by the Joussard Area Development Association, and began operations in 1989. The campground is open from the Victoria Day weekend until the end of September, and offers 16 campsites, flush toilets, tap water, sewage disposal facilities, a boat launch, a sand beach, and a day-use area with picnic tables, a shelter and a playground. As well, there is a commercially operated recreational facility at Shaw Point near Hilliard's Bay Provincial Park.

Police Point Natural Area is located off Secondary Road 750 on the eastern shore of Buffalo Bay (Fig. 1). It was established by Order in Council in 1987. The area is historically important because it contains a section of the Grouard Trail, a major route for traders, missionaries and settlers travelling to the Peace Country. Vegetation in the natural area ranges from extensive wetlands to mature white spruce and trembling aspen forest. The land is rich with wildlife, and there are excellent opportunities for nature observations, birdwatching and outdoor education. The trails that wind through the natural area can be used for hiking in summer and cross-country skiing in winter. There are no facilities on site (Alta. For. Ld. Wild. n.d.[b]).

Lesser Slave Lake is managed for sport, commercial and domestic fisheries. The sport fishery for walleye and northern pike became increasingly popular during the 1980s. The popular Golden Pike

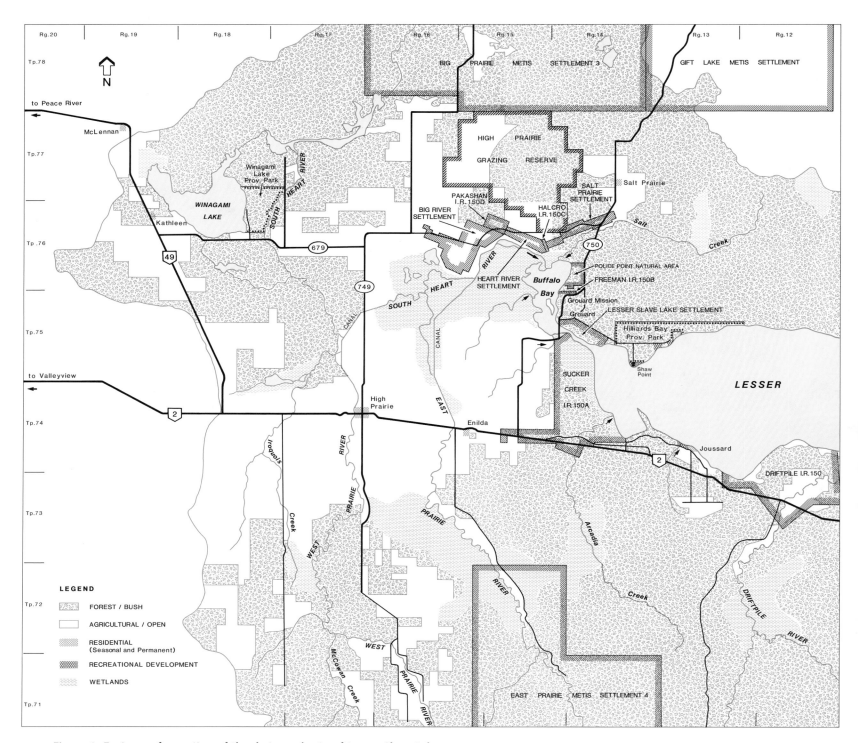

Figure 1. Features of a portion of the drainage basin of Lesser Slave Lake.
SOURCES: Alta. Envir. n.d.[b]; En. Mines Resour. Can. 1964; 1966; 1973; 1976; 1980. Updated with 1983 (east of Hilliard's Bay Provincial Park), 1985 (west of and including Hilliard's Bay Provincial Park) and 1988 (Marten River cottage subdivision) aerial photos.

Fishing Derby has been held each summer since the early 1980s from the town of Slave Lake. Sport fishing is somewhat limited by the large size of the lake and severe wave action, which frequently makes the use of small boats dangerous. Buffalo Bay, Grouard Channel and the portion of Lesser Slave Lake within 4 km of the mouth of the channel are closed to fishing during a specified period in April and May each year (Alta. For. Ld. Wild. 1989). There are no boating restrictions over most of the lake, but in posted areas such as designated swimming areas, all vessels are prohibited. In other posted areas, power boats are restricted to maximum speeds of 12 km/hour (Alta. For. Ld. Wild. 1988).

Moderate blooms of blue-green algae turn the lake water green during late summer. The extent of aquatic vegetation is limited by heavy wave action, except in Buffalo Bay, where there are extensive weed beds. The lake's western basin is shallow and well mixed by wind during the ice-free season, whereas the eastern basin is deeper and does not mix to the bottom. The water in both basins contains sufficient amounts of dissolved oxygen year-round to support the fish population.

Drainage Basin Characteristics

The drainage basin of Lesser Slave Lake is large and covers an area about 11 times greater than the lake (Fig. 3; Tables 1, 2). Much of the inflowing water enters the western end of the lake at Buffalo Bay via the South Heart River, which drains the northwestern part of the watershed. Before the river enters Buffalo Bay, it is joined from the south by the East Prairie and West Prairie rivers. On the southern shore of Lesser Slave Lake, the three largest inflows are the Driftpile, Swan and Assineau rivers, which drain the southeastern part of the watershed. Many small creeks and intermittent streams also flow into the lake. The outflow, the Lesser Slave River, is located at the lake's eastern end. It joins the Athabasca River about 75 km downstream of the outlet.

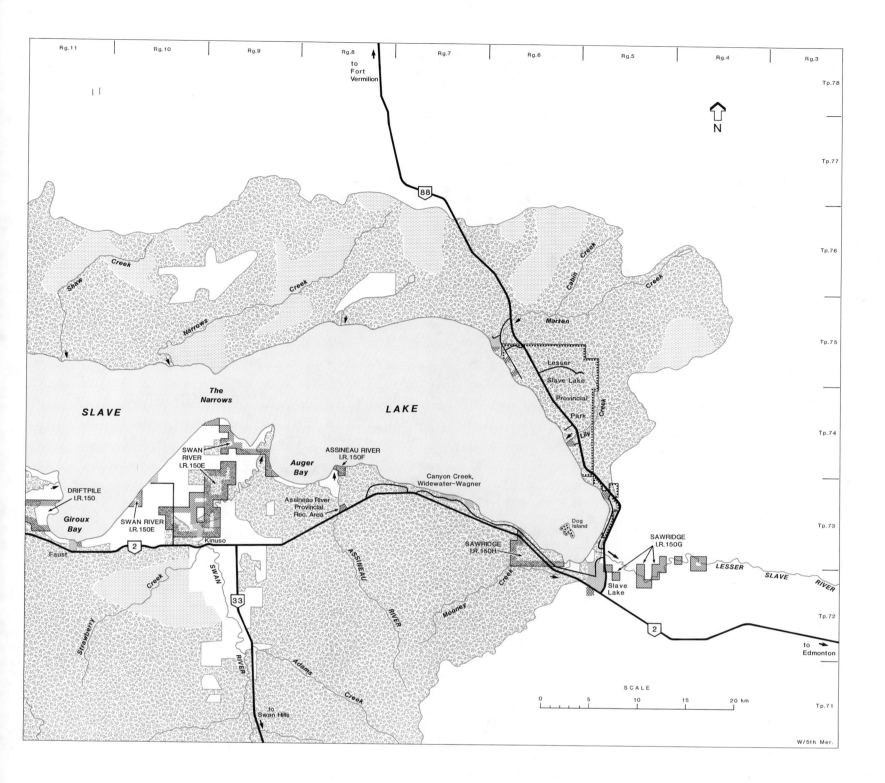

Table 1. Characteristics of Lesser Slave Lake drainage basin.

area (excluding lake) (km²)[a]	12 400
soil[b]	Gray Luvisols and Organics
bedrock geology[c]	Smoky Group (Upper Cretaceous): shale, ironstone; marine
terrain[b]	level to rolling
ecoregion[d]	Boreal Mixedwood, Boreal Foothills, Boreal Uplands
dominant vegetation[d]	trembling aspen, balsam poplar, lodgepole pine
mean annual inflow (m³)[a, e]	1 550 × 10⁶
mean annual sunshine (h)[f]	2 160

NOTE: [e]excluding groundwater inflow
SOURCES: [a]Alta. Envir. n.d.[b]; [b]Odynsky 1952; Wynnyk 1963; [c]Alta. Res. Counc. 1972; [d]Strong and Leggat 1981; [f]Envir. Can. 1982

Table 2. Characteristics of Lesser Slave Lake.

elevation (m)[a, b]	576.61
surface area (km²)[a, b]	1 160
volume (m³)[a, b]	13 200 × 10⁶
maximum depth (m)[a, b]	20.5
mean depth (m)[a, b]	11.4
shoreline length (km)[c]	241
mean annual lake evaporation (mm)[d]	611
mean annual precipitation (mm)[d]	472
mean residence time (yr)[d, e]	9.5
control structure[f]	sheet-pile weir with 1 vertical-slot and 2 Denil II fishways
crest length (m)[f]	30
crest elevation (m)[f]	575.5

NOTES: [a]on date of sounding: July to Aug. 1977; includes Buffalo Bay; [e]excluding groundwater inflow
SOURCES: [b]Alta. Envir. n.d.[c]; [c]Paetz and Zelt 1974; [d]Alta. Envir. n.d.[b]; [f]Alta. Envir. 1988

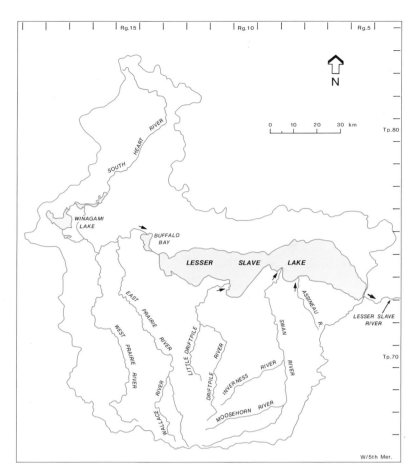

Figure 3. Boundaries of the drainage basin of Lesser Slave Lake.
SOURCE: Alta. Envir. n.d.[b].

Table 3. Major ions and related water quality variables for Lesser Slave Lake. Concentrations in mg/L; pH in pH units. Samples collected from 4 depths on 21 Feb. 1989.

	Depth (m)			
	1	6	12	17
pH	7.7	7.6	7.4	6.5
total alkalinity (CaCO₃)	93	90	88	100
specific conductivity (μS/cm)	211	203	201	221
total dissolved solids (calculated)	110	102	103	112
total hardness (CaCO₃)	90	80	85	90
total particulate carbon	<1	<1	<1	<1
dissolved organic carbon	10	12	10	11
HCO₃	113	110	107	122
CO₃	0	0	0	0
Mg	6	6	7	6
Na	6	6	6	6
K	3	3	3	3
Cl	2	1	2	2
SO₄	12	10	10	9
Ca	26	22	23	26

SOURCE: Alta. Envir. n.d.[a], Naquadat station 01AL07BJ0101

Lesser Slave Lake is a remnant of Lake Peace, a large proglacial lake that formed about 11 500 years ago as the Keewatin glacier retreated (Paetz and Zelt 1974; NW Hydraulic Consult. Ltd. 1983). This extinct proglacial lake was estimated to extend as far west as present-day Winagami Lake, which is now 35 km west of Buffalo Bay. The lake had an elevation of about 687 m above current sea level for a considerable length of time (NW Hydraulic Consult. Ltd. 1983). By about 11 000 years ago, the lake level had dropped to near the present-day level of about 577 m. Much of the area west of Lesser Slave Lake is covered by extensive alluvial and flood-plain deposits. The natural flooding of rivers flowing into Buffalo Bay has often conflicted with agricultural activities in the area. In an effort to reduce flooding, 36 km of the East Prairie, West Prairie and South Heart rivers were channelized between 1953 and 1971. Additional flood control was provided by the South Heart Dam in the early 1950s. Water management projects have continued during the 1980s.

Much of the land north of Lesser Slave Lake and south of Township 76 is level and undulating to gently rolling. The three common soil parent materials are glacial till, organic material and outwash material. Generally, Orthic Gray Luvisols have formed on the till, whereas Podzolic Gray Luvisols have formed on the shallow outwash. Organic soils are mainly the *Sphagnum* moss type. On the southern shore of the lake along the deltas of the Driftpile and Swan rivers, as well as near the town of Slave Lake, the land is undulating and depressional. Gleyed Dark Gray Luvisols that developed on alluvium are common, as are sedge bogs (Wynnyk et al. 1963). Land in the northwestern and southwestern parts of the drainage basin is gently rolling to rolling and soils are frequently Orthic Dark Gray Luvisols that developed on till. They are intermixed with very large areas of Organic soils. In the west-central part of the watershed, particularly in the High Prairie-Buffalo Bay-Winagami Lake area, the land is level to undulating and the soils, which are mostly Gray Luvisols, have developed on glacial till and alluvial and aeolian deposits (Odynsky et al. 1952).

Most of the cultivated land near the lake lies on the Driftpile and Swan River deltas and in the Joussard-High Prairie-Grouard triangle (Fig. 1). The main crops are oilseeds (canola), cereal grains (wheat, oats, barley), small seeds (grasses, legumes) and forage crops (clover, legumes, timothy, fescue, broom grass). Production of field peas became increasingly important during the mid-1980s. Livestock production is a major industry; the land near Lesser Slave Lake is the second largest cow- and calf-producing area in the Peace Country (Dist. Agric. 1988).

With the exception of the southern portion, the drainage basin is part of the Dry and Moist subregions of the Boreal Mixedwood Ecoregion (Strong and Leggat 1981). The dominant trees on moderately well-drained Gray Luvisols are trembling aspen in the Dry Subregion and an association of trembling aspen and balsam poplar in the Moist Subregion. White spruce is the main species on imperfectly drained Gray Luvisols and Gleysols, and black spruce and sedges grow on poorly to very poorly drained Organic soils. Around the shore of Lesser Slave Lake, the mixedwood forest is composed of dense young stands of trembling aspen that are associated with balsam poplar, white birch, green alder and white spruce. A history of fire has modified the forest so that white spruce is present in only a few stands (West. Soil Envir. Serv. 1979). An area of Boreal Foothills vegetation is located south of the lake at the headwaters of the Inverness and Driftpile rivers (Fig. 3). In this area, trembling aspen, balsam poplar and lodgepole pine are the main trees on moderately well-drained Gray Luvisols. In the Swan Hills, which are in the extreme southern portion of the watershed, there is a small area of Boreal Uplands vegetation, where lodgepole pine is the main tree on well to moderately well-drained Luvisols and Brunisols.

Forestry is economically important to the Lesser Slave Lake area. In late 1988, construction of a new pulp mill near the town of Slave Lake was announced. The oil and gas industry is also active, primarily in the Swan Hills, Mitsue Lake and Marten Hills areas and within Lesser Slave Lake Provincial Park (Paetz and Zelt 1974; West. Soil Envir. Serv. 1979).

Lake Basin Characteristics

With a surface area of 1 160 km², Lesser Slave Lake is one of Alberta's largest water bodies (Table 2). The lake is separated into two basins by a stretch of shallow water known as the Narrows (Fig. 2). The maximum depth of the east basin is about 20.5 m and the maximum depth of the west basin is about 15.5 m. Along the north,

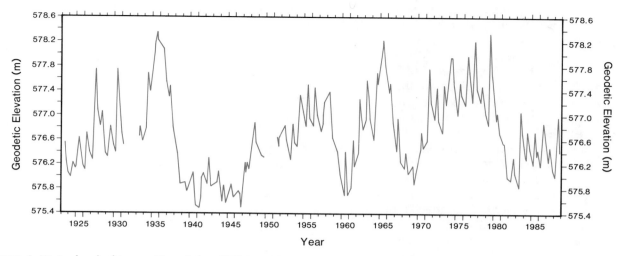

Figure 4. Water level of Lesser Slave Lake, 1923 to 1988.
SOURCE: Envir. Can. 1923–1988.

west and south shores of the east basin, the lake bottom slopes steeply to a depth of about 17.5 m. Along the east side of the basin, slopes are more gradual. The west basin slopes quite gradually except for stretches along the north and south-central sides. Buffalo Bay is a large, shallow body of water that is joined to the west basin by a narrow channel (Fig. 1). The bay's surface area varies considerably when water levels fluctuate.

The elevation of Lesser Slave Lake has been monitored since 1923 (Fig. 4). The lake level has fluctuated over a range of 2.86 m, from a maximum elevation of 578.35 m in 1935 to a minimum elevation of 575.49 m in 1941. Changes in the lake's area and capacity with elevation are shown in Figure 5. At high water levels, flooding occurred along the south and west sides of the lake, where the backshore is shallow and sloping (Alta. Envir. 1988). To resolve the problem, in 1968 the provincial Cabinet decided to purchase all privately owned land adjacent to the lake. Over the following decade, however, residents requested a different solution. In 1978, a ministerial decision to stabilize water levels led to the Lesser Slave Lake Regulation Environmental Impact Assessment study (Alta. Envir. 1979). As a result of this study, the flow capacity of the Lesser Slave River was improved in 1981 and 1982 by construction of eight channel cutoffs. These modifications increased outflow, thereby reducing maximum lake levels. As well, a 30–m–long sheet-pile weir was constructed on the outlet in 1983. It was designed to maintain a minimum lake level of 575.5 m (Table 2).

An experimental fish passage facility was constructed in 1983 as part of the weir. It consists of a vertical-slot fishway and two Denil II fishways of 10% and 20% slope. The effectiveness of the three designs was monitored during May and June 1984 (Schwalme and Mackay 1985). Most large fish swam over the weir and through the spillway rather than through the fishways. Of the fish that ascended the fishways, northern pike preferred the two Denil II fishways, whereas longnose and white suckers preferred the vertical-slot fishway.

Lesser Slave Lake is used as a water supply by municipalities, industries and farming operations. In 1988, 11 user groups were licenced for withdrawal (Alta. Envir. 1988).

Water Quality

Detailed information on water quality in Lesser Slave Lake is not available. The Water Quality Branch of the provincial Department of Health collected three samples in August and September of 1970 (Alta. Envir. n.d.[a]), and Fish and Wildlife Division gathered some limnological data prior to 1974 and during the summer of 1975 (Paetz and Zelt 1974; Weisgerber 1977). In February 1989, Alberta Environment collected a single series of samples from 4 depths in the east basin.

Lesser Slave Lake has fresh water that has relatively low alkalinity for a prairie lake (Table 3). The dominant ions are bicarbonate and

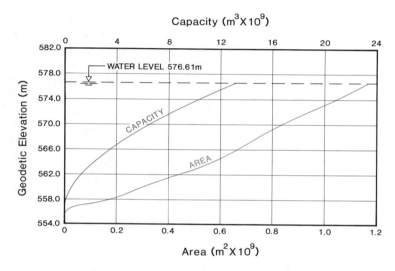

Figure 5. Area/capacity curve for Lesser Slave Lake.
SOURCE: Alta. Envir. n.d.[c].

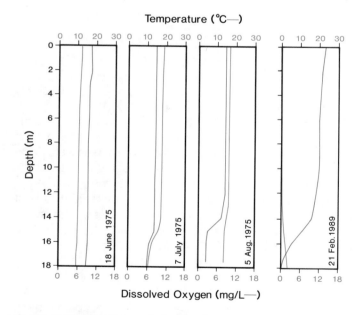

Figure 6. Temperature and dissolved oxygen in the east basin of Lesser Slave Lake, 1975 and 1989. Dissolved oxygen data not available for 24 June.
SOURCES: Alta. Envir. n.d.[a]; Weisgerber 1977.

calcium. Turbidity varies with location. High turbidity occurs near inflows during floods, and also results from shore erosion by wave action at high water levels. During the open-water period in 1975, water transparency, as indicated by Secchi depth, varied from 1.0 to 3.5 m in the east basin and 1.5 to 3.0 m in the west basin.

In spring, the shallower west basin becomes ice free before the east basin, and the whole lake is usually ice free by mid-May. In 1975, the average temperature of the water column from May to early August was higher in the west than in the east basin, partly because of the earlier ice-free conditions. As well, the west basin's shallower depth allows greater mixing than in the deeper east basin, where mixing is greatly inhibited below a depth of about 14 m. The west basin was well mixed throughout the open-water period in 1975. In contrast, the east basin was weakly thermally stratified by 18 June 1975 (Fig. 6). On 7 July, strong winds mixed the water column in the east basin to a depth of almost 15 m, and by 21 July, several windy periods caused the total loss of thermal stratification. The water restratified by 5 August, but was again mixed to the bottom within a week. Ice formation on both basins in 1975 proceeded gradually throughout November, and a solid ice layer had formed by early December.

The two basins have different patterns of dissolved oxygen concentrations throughout the water column. In 1975, the west basin was well mixed for most of the open-water season. Dissolved oxygen concentrations in the east basin, on the other hand, were depleted below a depth of 15 m by 7 July (Fig. 6). By 5 August, the concentration of dissolved oxygen in water near the sediments had declined to less than 3 mg/L. Subsequent mixing of the entire water column raised the concentration of dissolved oxygen to 8 to 9 mg/L from surface to bottom. In the east basin in February 1989, the concentration of dissolved oxygen declined gradually from 13 mg/L at a depth of 1 m to 0 mg/L at a depth of 18 m (Fig. 6).

There are no nutrient data available for Lesser Slave Lake during the open-water season. Winter samples from February 1989 indicated a concentration gradient for total phosphorus, from 11 µg/L at a depth of 1 m to 45 µg/L at a depth of 17 m (Table 4). The presence of moderate blue-green algal blooms in both basins during summer, a high benthic invertebrate standing crop, and low dissolved oxygen concentrations in the deeper water in the east basin during summer suggest that the lake may be eutrophic.

Biological Characteristics

Plants

The phytoplankton community in Lesser Slave Lake has not been studied in detail. Blue-green blooms (*Microcystis* sp., *Aphanizomenon* sp. *and Anabaena* spp.) have been reported, most notably in the west basin (Miller 1941; Weisgerber 1977).

In 1977, Fish and Wildlife Division listed 28 species of aquatic macrophytes in the lake (Table 5). Most of the littoral area is subject to considerable wave action, and submergent weed beds were dominated by large-sheath pondweed (*Potamogeton vaginatus*), Richardson pondweed (*P. richardsonii*) and stonewort (*Chara* spp.). Emergent vegetation was generally sparse and consisted mostly of common great bulrush (*Scirpus validus*) and sedges (*Carex* spp.). Large stands of bulrush and a wide variety of submergent and emergent species were present in Buffalo Bay.

Invertebrates

The zooplankton species in Lesser Slave Lake were studied by Fish and Wildlife Division in 1941 and 1976 (Miller 1941; Chymko 1977). In 1976, the zooplankton was sampled weekly from mid-May to late October. The dominant cladoceran in both studies was *Daphnia* (*pulex* group). *Bosmina* sp. was commonly found in 1941 but rare in 1976. The most common copepods were *Diaptomus ashlandi*, *Acanthocyclops vernalis* and *Diacyclops bicuspidatus thomasi*. *Diacyclops* is important because it is the first intermediate host of the tapeworm *Triaenophorus crassus*. The cysts of this parasite infest the lake whitefish and cisco in Lesser Slave Lake (Miller 1952[a]).

Table 4. Nutrient and chlorophyll *a* data for Lesser Slave Lake. Concentrations in µg/L. Samples collected from 4 depths on 21 Feb. 1989.

	Depth (m)			
	1	6	12	17
total phosphorus	11	11	12	45
total dissolved phosphorus	10	9	10	21
total Kjeldahl nitrogen	480	450	420	530
NO_3 + NO_2–nitrogen	60	60	80	130
NH_4–nitrogen	37	32	45	115
iron	—	37	—	423
chlorophyll *a*	0.6	0.3	0.2	—

SOURCE: Alta. Envir. n.d.[a], Naquadat station 01AL07BJ0101

Only the deep-water benthic invertebrate fauna of Lesser Slave Lake have been sampled (Weisgerber 1977). Based on weekly samples taken by Fish and Wildlife Division from 21 May to 27 October 1975, the mean biomass was 33.9 g/m^2 (wet weight). Midges (Chironomidae) dominated the benthic community and there were small amounts of fingernail clams (*Pisidium*) and aquatic earthworms (Oligochaeta). Higher densities of benthic organisms were found in the west basin than in the east basin. Two unusual species of crustaceans, *Mysis relicta* and *Pontoporeia affinis*, have also been reported in Lesser Slave Lake (Paetz and Zelt 1974). These species are usually restricted to deeper, less productive lakes.

Fish

The fish community of Lesser Slave Lake includes lake whitefish, cisco, mountain whitefish (rare), Arctic grayling (rare), northern pike, burbot, longnose sucker, white sucker, emerald shiner, spottail shiner, trout-perch, brook stickleback (rare), yellow perch, walleye and spoonhead sculpin (rare). Lake trout were abundant in the lake in the early 1900s but were extinct by the early 1940s (Paetz and Zelt 1974).

The commercial, domestic and sport fisheries at Lesser Slave Lake are managed through a quota allocation system. The number of domestic licences issued from 1959 to 1978 varied from a low of one in 1962 to a high of 55 in 1978. Catch statistics for the domestic fishery have not been recorded. The Lesser Slave Lake fishery has also been subject to extensive illegal fishing, either out of season or with illegal gear. Illegal use of gear outnumbered legal use during a period in the mid–1960s when the fisheries collapsed (Ash and Noton 1979). No accurate estimates of the illegal catch are available.

Lesser Slave Lake has a long history of commercial fishing, but records were not kept prior to 1942. Historically, the most important commercially harvested species were lake whitefish, cisco and walleye (Alta. Rec. Parks Wild. 1976). Smaller amounts of northern pike, yellow perch, burbot and suckers were also taken. At present, lake whitefish, suckers and northern pike account for most of the total catch. Between 1981/82 and 1987/88, the average total catch of 510 028 kg/year comprised 57% whitefish, 15% suckers, 12% northern pike, 9% burbot, 6% walleye and 1% cisco (Alta. For. Ld. Wild. n.d.[a]).

Whitefish and walleye catches were highest prior to the mid–1960s, when both fisheries collapsed. The collapse of the whitefish fishery may be attributed partly to overfishing, which was the result of illegal harvest and the harvest of immature fish in the small-sized nets set for cisco (Zelt 1977). It was also partly due to high exploitation during natural periods of low population size (Bell et al. 1977). The growth rate and condition of whitefish declined substantially from the 1940s to the 1970s (Handford et al. 1977). Reduced growth and poor condition may have been caused by increased competition with suckers for food. The heavy exploitation of whitefish and cisco may have allowed an increase in sucker populations when food normally eaten by whitefish and cisco became

Table 5. Species of aquatic macrophytes in Lesser Slave Lake, 1975.
Arranged in alphabetical order.

emergent	sedge	*Carex* spp.
	water hemlock	*Cicuta* sp.
	spike rush	*Eleocharis palustris*
	horsetail	*Equisetum fluviatile*
	wire rush	*Juncus balticus*
	reed canary grass	*Phalaris arundinacea*
	reed grass	*Phragmites communis*
	common great bulrush	*Scirpus validus*
	link	*Scolochloa festucacea*
	giant bur-reed	*Sparganium eurycarpum*
	common cattail	*Typha latifolia*
free-floating	lesser duckweed	*Lemna minor*
	star duckweed	*L. trisulca*
	common bladderwort	*Utricularia vulgaris*
submergent	water-starwort	*Callitriche hermaphroditicum*
	coontail	*Ceratophyllum demersum*
	stonewort	*Chara* sp.
	northern watermilfoil	*Myriophyllum exalbescens*
	pondweed	*Potamogeton friesii*
	pondweed	*P. gramineus*
	whitestem pondweed	*P. praelongus*
	small-leaf pondweed	*P. pusillus*
	Richardson pondweed	*P. richardsonii*
	large-sheath pondweed	*P. vaginatus*
	flat-stemmed pondweed	*P. zosteriformis*
	white water crowfoot	*Ranunculus aquatilis*
floating-leaved	yellow water lily	*Nuphar variegatum*
	water smartweed	*Polygonum amphibium*

SOURCE: Weisgerber 1977

available for consumption by suckers (Dietz and Krujewski 1978). It is not known, however, whether sucker populations actually increased as whitefish and cisco populations declined. In 1978, an increase in the size of the sucker fishery was proposed so that the size of the population could be reduced (Berry 1978), but since the market for suckers has not developed, an increase in sucker catch has not occurred.

Since the 1960s, the whitefish and walleye populations have recovered to a large extent. During the 1980s, both populations sustained good commercial harvests (Walty 1988). In 1972, several years after the collapse of the whitefish fishery, the small-mesh cisco fishery in the lake was closed. Subsequently, the whitefish population showed a strong recovery. The whitefish quota was increased from 68 000 kg/year in 1972, to almost 250 000 kg/year in 1979, and to 500 000 kg in 1988 (Wallace and McCart 1984; Stenton 1989). The walleye population increased because walleye habitat in Buffalo Bay was stabilized, the small-mesh net fishery in Lesser Slave Lake was closed in 1972, and areas in the western region of the lake were closed to commercial fishing. By 1988, the commercial quota for walleye had been raised to 65 000 kg/year from the 1972 quota of 9 070 kg/year (Wallace and McCart 1984).

Cisco were heavily exploited until the early 1970s when the population collapsed. They were primarily used for mink food by area fur ranchers (Bishop 1970). In 1954, 106 300 mink were raised on 220 ranches, mostly along the southern shore of the lake. By 1975, only two ranches, with 1 455 mink, were operating. The mink industry declined because of a decline in demand for fur combined with competition from Scandinavian and Russian furs. The final collapse of this industry was accelerated by the decline in the supply of cisco from Lesser Slave Lake (Stenton 1989). The collapse of the cisco fishery was caused by overfishing and, possibly, by variations in lake water levels and siltation from oil development activities in the Swan Hills (Bishop 1970). Although the cisco population has recovered to some extent since the 1970s, commercial catches have remained low because of lack of demand and because of the larger-sized mesh used in the fishery (Walty 1988; Stenton 1989).

Cisco and lake whitefish are important intermediate hosts of the tapeworm *Triaenophorus crassus*. After the tapeworm releases eggs in the spring, the larvae that hatch must be eaten by the copepod *Diacyclops bicuspidatus thomasi* to survive. If the host copepod is eaten by a whitefish or cisco, the larvae form cysts in the flesh of the fish. If the infested fish are then eaten by a northern pike, the adult tapeworm develops in the pike's intestine. The parasite problem was researched extensively by Miller during the 1940s (Miller 1952[b]). To date, no method of controlling cyst numbers has been found (Walty 1988). Whitefish from Lesser Slave Lake contain more than 80 cysts per 45 kg of fish, and, although edible, are considered to be poor quality and are sold only for commercial products such as fish cakes.

The sport fishery in Lesser Slave Lake is becoming increasingly popular. In 1985, a summer creel survey was conducted at eight access points around Lesser Slave Lake (summarized in Hildebrand and Ash 1986). It was estimated that anglers spent 51 337 hours fishing and caught 12 896 walleye, 15 552 northern pike and 3 861 yellow perch. Almost 78% of the angling pressure occurred at the western end of the lake. In 1986, a more intensive survey was undertaken, but only at the three western access points (Hildebrand and Ash 1986). In 1986, 65% of the anglers interviewed sought walleye, 8% sought northern pike, 0.4% sought yellow perch and 27% had no preference. About 21% of the total number of anglers caught walleye and 33% caught northern pike. Of the fish caught, 6% of the walleye, 44% of the pike and 8% of the suckers were released. Angling success at the western end of the lake was lower in 1986 than in 1985 (Table 6), perhaps because of unseasonably cold, wet, windy weather during July. In 1986, the harvest rate for walleye was 0.26 fish/angler-hour (Table 6), but survey personnel indicated that some anglers under-reported their catch and that there was a substantial illegal harvest as well. The average walleye harvested weighed about 1 kg, and the largest weighed 2.1 kg. The 1978 and 1980 walleye age-classes dominated the fishery. The average catch rate for northern pike in 1986 was 0.21 fish/angler-hour. The mean pike weight was 1 kg and most fish harvested were less than 5 years old. The average catch rate for yellow perch was only 0.04 fish/angler-hour and the average perch harvested weighed 334 g. Perch ages were not recorded in the survey.

Table 6. Estimated angler effort and harvest from the west end of Lesser Slave Lake.
Estimates based on creel survey data collected for two years from 1 May to 31 Aug. in 1985 and 1986. WE = walleye; NP = northern pike; YP = yellow perch.

	WE		NP		YP		Total	
	1985	1986	1985	1986	1985	1986	1985	1986
number of angler interviews	—	—	—	—	—	—	—	3 077
angler-hours	—	—	—	—	—	—	34 195	42 261
total number fish harvested	19 010	13 319	5 416	6 841	3 157	2 104	27 583	22 264
biomass harvested (kg)	16 656	13 387	5 121	6 352	—	702	—	20 441
mean fork length (mm)	—	449	—	508	—	267	—	—
mean weight (g)	—	1 005	—	980	—	334	—	—
dominant age-classes (yr)	5–7	6–8	<5	3–4	—	—	—	—
harvest/angler-hour	—	0.26	—	0.21	—	0.04	—	—

SOURCE: Hildebrand and Ash 1986

Wildlife

Waterfowl surveys were carried out on Lesser Slave Lake in 1976 and 1977 (Alta. Envir. 1978). The best waterfowl habitat is located along the west, north and south shores of the west basin, along the bays on either side of the Swan River delta in the east basin and in Buffalo Bay. In May, more waterfowl use the west end of the lake than the east end. The most abundant ducks sighted were Mallards, Lesser Scaup, White-winged Scoters, Common Goldeneye and Bufflehead. A large gull colony was located on the western shore of the lake and tern and Western Grebe colonies were sighted on the point of land in the Driftpile River Indian Reserve.

Wildlife data are available for the two provincial parks (Lombard North Plan. Ltd. 1972; Smith 1976; Bradley 1980). In Lesser Slave Lake Provincial Park, more than 170 species of birds have been recorded. Colonial nesters in the park include Eared Grebes, Black and Common terns, and Ring-billed and Franklin's gulls. During migratory periods, Yellow-billed Loons have been sighted. Yellow Rails are present in marshy areas and several Bald Eagles nest in the spruce trees on Dog Island. Eighteen mammal species inhabit the park. The main large mammals are moose and white-tailed deer. Mule deer are present in small numbers and woodland caribou are sometimes sighted in the northeast section of the park. The major carnivores are wolves, coyotes, lynx and wolverines and the minor carnivores are fishers, weasels and otters. The park is prime territory for American black bears, and grizzly bears are also sighted occasionally. In Hilliard's Bay Provincial Park, over 100 bird species and 14 mammal species have been sighted.

Buffalo Bay and its surrounding area provides habitat that ranges from extensive wetlands to mature forests. The diverse plant communities at Police Point Natural Area support a wide array of animals and birds, including over 100 species of nesting birds. In the marshes, ducks such as Common Goldeneye and Mallards, shorebirds such as Killdeer and Spotted Sandpipers, and other birds such as Red-necked Grebes, gulls, Sora and Long-billed Marsh Wrens nest and feed (Alta. For. Ld. Wild. n.d.[b]).

M.E. Bradford and J.M. Hanson

References

Alberta Environment. n.d.[a]. Envir. Assess. Div., Envir. Qlty. Monit. Br. Unpubl. data, Edmonton.
———. n.d.[b]. Tech. Serv. Div., Hydrol. Br. Unpubl. data, Edmonton.
———. n.d.[c]. Tech. Serv. Div., Surv. Br. Unpubl. data, Edmonton.
———. 1978. Lesser Slave Lake environmental overview, Vol. 1. Plan. Div. Unpubl. rep., Edmonton.
———. 1979. Lesser Slave Lake regulation environmental impact assessment, Vol. 1: Main report. Plan. Div., Edmonton.
———. 1988. Lesser Slave Lake outlet control works review executive summary. Draft manuscript. Plan. Div., Edmonton.
Alberta Forestry, Lands and Wildlife. n.d.[a]. Fish Wild. Div. Unpubl. data, Edmonton.
———. n.d.[b]. Police Point, an Alberta natural area. Alta. For. Ld. Wild. Publ. No. I/211. Pub. Ld. Div., Edmonton.
———. 1988. Boating in Alberta. Fish Wild. Div., Edmonton.
———. 1989. Guide to sportfishing. Fish Wild. Div., Edmonton.
Alberta Native Affairs. 1986. A guide to native communities in Alberta. Native Aff. Secret., Edmonton.
Alberta Recreation and Parks. n.d. Reflections of Lesser Slave Lake. Alta. Rec. Parks, Edmonton.
Alberta Recreation, Parks and Wildlife. 1976. Commercial fisheries catch statistics for Alberta, 1942–1975. Fish Wild. Div., Fish. Mgt. Rep. No. 22, Edmonton.
Alberta Research Council. 1972. Geological map of Alberta. Nat. Resour. Div., Alta. Geol. Surv., Edmonton.
Allen, E. 1989. Alta. Rec. Parks, Parks Div., Lesser Slave L. Prov. Park. Pers. comm.
Ash, G.R. and L.R. Noton. 1979. Lesser Slave Lake study—fisheries impact assessment final report. Prep. for Alta. Envir., Plan. Div. by R.L. & L. Envir. Serv. Ltd., Edmonton.
Bell, G., P. Handford and C. Dietz. 1977. Dynamics of an exploited population of lake whitefish (*Coregonus clupeaformis*). J. Fish. Res. Bd. Can. 34:942–953.
Berry, D.K. 1978. The feasibility, cost and ecological effects of removing suckers from Lesser Slave Lake, Alberta. Alta. Rec. Parks Wild., Fish Wild. Div. Unpubl. rep., Edmonton.
Bishop, F. 1970. The cisco fishery of Lesser Slave Lake up to 1968. Alta. Ld. For., Fish Wild. Div. Unpubl. rep., Edmonton.
Bradley, C. 1980. Lesser Slave Lake Provincial Park—biophysical inventory and resource assessment. Alta. Rec. Parks, Parks Div., Edmonton.
Chymko, N. 1977. Seasonal patterns and abundance of crustacean zooplankton in Lesser Slave Lake, Alberta, 1976. Alta. Rec. Parks Wild., Fish Wild. Div., Edmonton.
Dietz, K. and A. Krujewski. 1978. Comparative feeding habits of lake whitefish (*Coregonus clupeaformis*) and longnose sucker (*Catostomus catostomus*) in Lesser Slave Lake. Alta. Rec. Parks Wild., Fish Wild. Div. Unpubl. rep., Edmonton.
District Agriculturalist. 1988. Alta. Agric., High Prairie. Pers. comm.
Energy, Mines and Resources Canada. 1964, 1966, 1973, 1976, 1980. National topographic series 1:250 000 83N (1964), 83O (1966), 83J (1973), 84B (1976), 84C (1980), 83K (1980). Surv. Map. Br., Ottawa.
Environment Canada. 1923–1988. Surface water data. Prep. by Inland Waters Directorate. Water Surv. Can., Water Resour. Br., Ottawa.
———. 1982. Canadian climate normals, Vol. 7: Bright sunshine (1951–1980). Prep. by Atm. Envir. Serv. Supply Serv. Can., Ottawa.
Handford, P., G. Bell and T. Reimchen. 1977. A gillnet fishery considered as an experiment in artificial selection. J. Fish. Res. Bd. Can. 34:954–961.
Hildebrand, L. and G. Ash. 1986. A summer creel survey of the west end of Lesser Slave Lake, 1986. Prep. for Alta. For. Ld. Wild., Fish Wild. Div., Slave Lake by R.L. & L. Envir. Serv. Ltd., Edmonton.

Lombard North Planning Ltd. 1972. Lesser Slave Lake Provincial Park—master plan study. Prep. for Alta. Ld. For., Prov. Parks Br., Edmonton.

Miller, R.B. 1941. Lesser Slave Lake investigation. Alta. Ld. Mines, Fish Game Admin. Unpubl. rep., Edmonton.

———. 1952[a]. A review of the *Triaenophorus* problem in Canadian lakes. Fish. Res. Bd. Can. Bull. No. 95.

———. 1952[b]. The status of the Lesser Slave Lake experiment. Alta. Ld. For., Fish Wild. Div. Unpubl. rep., Edmonton.

Northwest Hydraulic Consultants Ltd. 1983. Assessment of hydrotechnical aspects for the proposed Buffalo Bay-Horse Lakes management program, stage 1 study. Prep. for Alta. Envir., Plan. Div., Edmonton.

Odynsky, W., A. Wynnyk and J.D. Newton. 1952. Reconnaissance soil survey of the High Prairie and McLennan sheets. Alta. Soil Surv. Rep. No. 17, Univ. Alta. Bull. No. 59, Res. Counc. Alta. Rep. No. 63. Univ. Alta., Edmonton.

Paetz, M.J. and K.A. Zelt. 1974. Studies of northern Alberta lakes and their fish populations. J. Fish. Res. Bd. Can. 31:1007–1020.

Schwalme, K. and W.C. Mackay. 1985. Preliminary biological evaluation of the Lesser Slave River fishway. Prep. for Alta. Envir., Plan. Div., Edmonton.

Smith, W. 1976. Hilliard's Bay—resource assessment. Alta. Rec. Parks Wild., Parks Div. Unpubl. rep., Edmonton.

Stenton, E. 1989. Alta. For. Ld. Wild., Fish Wild. Div., Edmonton. Pers. comm.

Strong, W.L. and K.R. Leggat. 1981. Ecoregions of Alberta. Alta. En. Nat. Resour., Resour. Eval. Plan. Div., Edmonton.

Wallace, R.R. and P.J. McCart. 1984. The fish and fisheries of the Athabasca River basin: Their status and environmental requirements. Prep. for Alta. Envir., Plan. Div., Edmonton.

Walty, D. 1988. Alta. For. Ld. Wild., Fish Wild. Div., Peace River. Pers. comm.

Weisgerber, J. 1977. A preliminary report on the limnology of Lesser Slave Lake, Alberta. Alta. Rec. Parks Wild., Fish Wild. Div. Unpubl. rep., Edmonton.

Western Soil and Environmental Services. 1979. Land use studies [Part 3]. *In* Lesser Slave Lake regulation environmental impact assessment, Vol. III: Land use impact studies. Alta. Envir., Plan. Div., Edmonton.

Wynnyk, A., J.D. Lindsay, P.K. Heringa and W. Odynsky. 1963. Exploratory soil survey of Alberta map sheets 83–O, 83–P, and 73–M. Prelim. Soil Surv. Rep. No. 64–1. Res. Counc. Alta., Edmonton.

Zelt, K.A. 1977. Potential impact of a small mesh fishery on a lake whitefish population. Alta. Rec. Parks Wild., Fish Wild. Div., Fish. Mgt. Rep. No. 27, Edmonton.

LONG LAKE
(Near Athabasca)

M. Pazlawski

MAP SHEET: 83I/12
LOCATION: Tp64 R25 W4
LAT/LONG: 54°34'N 113°38'W

Long Lake is a deep, peaceful lake set in a little valley among gently rolling, treed hills. It is located in the County of Athabasca southwest of the town of Athabasca. To reach the lake from the city of Edmonton, take Highway 2 north for about 133 km to Secondary Road 663 near the locality of Meanook, the population centre closest to the lake. Follow Secondary Road 663 west for about 16 km, then south for 3 km and west for 1.6 km. Next, take a narrow gravel road north for 1 km then west for 1 km to reach Forfar Park on the east shore of the lake (Fig. 1).

The land around Long Lake is all Crown land and is mostly undeveloped (Fig. 2). The best access is at Forfar Park, which is operated by the county and offers camping and day-use facilities, a concrete boat launch, two sandy swimming areas, tap water, docks and a sewage disposal station. There is also a small day-use area at the north end of the lake. There are three institutional camps on the lake: a Junior Forest Warden's Camp, a Boy Scout Camp and the Athabasca Fish and Game Club Camp. Power boats are restricted to speeds of 12 km/hour or less in posted areas of the lake (Alta. For. Ld. Wild. 1988).

The water of Long Lake is clear most of the summer and algae in the surface water are inconspicuous. Aquatic plants ring most of the lake. The lake provides moderately popular sport fishing for northern pike and yellow perch. Provincial limits for size and catch apply to the sport fishery, but there are no specific regulations in effect (Alta. For. Ld. Wild. 1989).

Drainage Basin Characteristics

The drainage basin of Long Lake is primarily a meltwater channel that was carved in glacial till as the last continental glaciers receded. The valley runs in a north-south direction and includes the basin of Narrow Lake just north of Long Lake (Fig. 1). The land is moderately to strongly rolling (Table 1), with slopes of 9 to 30% (Kjearsgaard 1972). The highest point in the basin is the hill that rises 40 m above the lake to an elevation of 735 m just west of the south end of Long Lake.

The watershed lies in the Dry Mixedwood Subregion of the Boreal Mixedwood Ecoregion (Strong and Leggat 1981). The dominant trees are trembling aspen. Balsam poplar, white spruce and birch are common in slightly wetter areas. Soils under these forests are Orthic Gray Luvisols (Kjearsgaard 1972). Wetlands are common in the drainage basin; the sedges, willows and black spruce in these areas are underlain by Humic Gleysols and Mesisols. The arability of the land is poor and most of the basin is still forested. Some land in the eastern portion, however, has been cleared for pasture and mixed farming. There are no population centres in the drainage basin.

Most of the inflow to Long Lake is unchannelized runoff and groundwater. The few streams that do run into the lake are interrupted by beaver dams. Narrow Lake, 600 m north of Long Lake, overflows into Long Lake only during spring snowmelt and after unusually wet summer storms (Prepas et al. n.d.). Long Lake flows into a creek that enters Bolloque Lake; its outflow, Bolloque Creek, eventually reaches the Pembina River via Dapp Creek.

Lake Basin Characteristics

Long Lake is a small, elongate lake with a surface area of 1.62 km^2 (Table 2), a maximum length of 5.4 km and a maximum width of 0.9

Table 1. Characteristics of Long Lake drainage basin.

area (excluding lake) (km²)[a]	30.3
soil[b]	Orthic Gray Luvisols, Mesisols
bedrock geology[c]	Wapiti Formation (Upper Cretaceous): sandstone, mudstone, bentonite, scattered coal beds; nonmarine
terrain[b]	moderately to strongly rolling
ecoregion[d]	Dry Mixedwood Subregion of Boreal Mixedwood
dominant vegetation[d]	trembling aspen, balsam poplar, white spruce
mean annual inflow (m³)[a, e]	1.45×10^6
mean annual sunshine (h)[f]	2 160

NOTE: [e]excluding groundwater inflow
SOURCES: [a]Alta. Envir. n.d.[a]; [b]Kjearsgaard 1972; [c]Alta. Res. Counc. 1972; [d]Strong and Leggat 1981; [f]Envir. Can. 1982

Table 2. Characteristics of Long Lake.

elevation (m)[a]	approximately 692
surface area (km²)[b, c]	1.62
volume (m³)[b, c]	15.3×10^6
maximum depth (m)[b]	28
mean depth (m)[b]	9.4
shoreline length (km)[a]	16.19
mean annual lake evaporation (mm)[d]	638
mean annual precipitation (mm)[d]	505
mean residence time (yr)[d, e]	12.5
control structure	none

NOTES: [c]on date of sounding: 06 Aug. 1986; [e]excluding groundwater inflow
SOURCES: [a]En. Mines Resour. Can. 1973; [b]Prepas et al. n.d.; [d]Alta. Envir. n.d.[a]

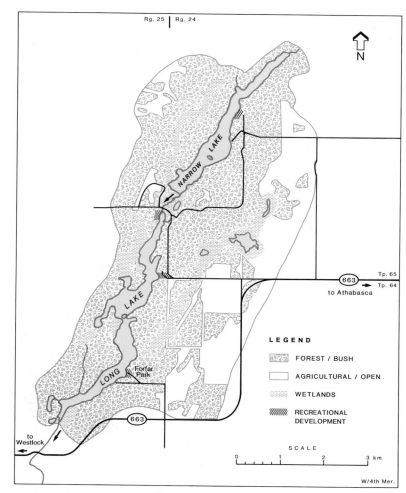

Figure 1. Features of the drainage basin of Long Lake.
SOURCES: Alta. Envir. n.d.[a]; En. Mines Resour. Can. 1973. Updated with 1987 aerial photos.

km. It is surprisingly deep for its small size—the sides of the south basin slope steeply to a maximum depth of 28 m (Fig. 2). The north basin is shallower and has a more gently sloping bottom than the south basin. In years when water levels were low, the lake was separated into two lakes, with the division at the narrows in the centre of the lake.

The maximum depth of macrophyte growth is 3.8 m (Prepas et al. n.d.). Approximately 27% of the lake is less than this depth (Fig. 3). The substrate in the littoral zone is mainly organic material with areas of sand and boulders. The substrate in deeper areas is mostly rich organic material.

The water level was monitored in 1983 and has been monitored every summer since 1985 (Fig. 4). From 1986 to 1987 the level varied almost 1 m. Changes in the level of Long Lake are often linked to changes in the beaver dams on the outflow and to the outflow from Narrow Lake. In May 1986, groundwater flow into the lake averaged 0.9×10^{-8} m/second in the area within 30 m of shore. Groundwater was estimated to be a relatively small fraction (6%) of the total inflow to Long Lake (R. Shaw and Prepas 1989).

Water Quality

The water quality of Long Lake was studied by researchers from the University of Alberta from May through August from 1983 through 1986 in conjunction with long-term studies on Narrow Lake. These studies included detailed evaluation of phosphorus cycling within the open water, between the open water and bottom sediments, and the role of groundwater in transporting phosphorus from the sediments to the open water (Prepas et al. n.d.; 1988; Prepas and Trimbee 1988; J. Shaw and Prepas 1989[a]; 1989[b]; 1989[c]; R. Shaw and Prepas et al. 1989).

Long Lake is well-buffered, moderately alkaline and slightly coloured, but not turbid. Dominant ions are bicarbonate and calcium (Table 3). The lake mixes only partially in spring before it becomes

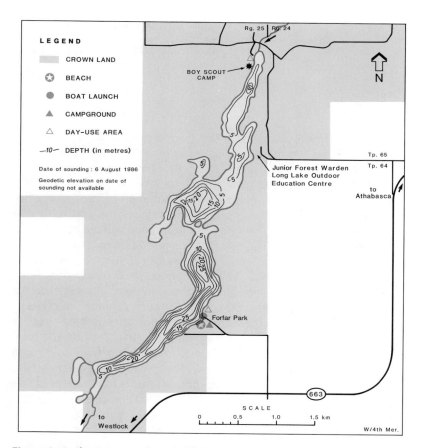

Figure 2. Bathymetry and shoreline features of Long Lake.
BATHYMETRY SOURCE: Prepas et al. n.d.

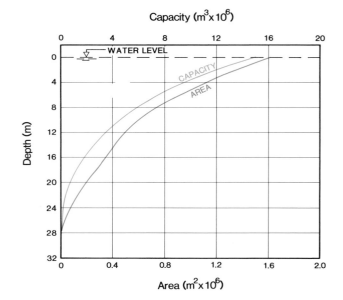

Figure 3. Area/capacity curve for Long Lake.
SOURCE: Prepas et al. n.d.

Table 3. Major ions and related water quality variables for Long Lake. Average concentrations in mg/L; pH in pH units. Composite samples from the euphotic zone collected 1 to 7 times from May to Aug. 1983–86. S.E. = standard error.

	Mean	S.E.
pH (range)	7.9–8.3[a]	—
total alkalinity (CaCO$_3$)	163[b]	3.6
specific conductivity (µS/cm)	287[a]	9.5
turbidity (NTU)	0.6[c]	—
colour (Pt)	15[c]	—
total hardness (calculated)	157	—
HCO$_3$	199[b]	4.4
CO$_3$	0[b]	0
Mg	15[d]	0.6
Na	7[d]	0.4
K	4[d]	0.3
SO$_4$	2[d]	0.1
Ca	38[d]	0.1

NOTES: [a]n = 7; [b]n = 4; [c]n = 1; [d]n = 2
SOURCE: Prepas et al. n.d.

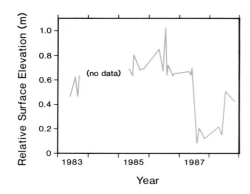

Figure 4. Water level of Long Lake, 1983 to 1987.
SOURCE: Alta. Envir. n.d.[b].

strongly thermally stratified in May. It remains thermally stratified for the rest of the summer (Fig. 5). Water over the bottom sediments becomes anoxic by late summer (Fig. 6). Summer hypolimnetic dissolved oxygen depletion rates are low for lakes in this region; 0.305 g O$_2$/m^2 per day was the average for the summers of 1984 and 1986.

Nutrient concentrations, both total phosphorus and inorganic nitrogen, are relatively low in the euphotic zone and are consistently low from year to year (Table 4). The concentration of total phosphorus in the euphotic zone usually remains low all summer, as typified by 1984 data in Figure 7. The total phosphorus concentration increases in the hypolimnion during the summer from less than 15 µg/L in May to more than 80 µg/L in August. Ammonium concentrations also increase in the water near the bottom sediment over the summer to more than 200 µg/L by late August. Because the total phosphorus concentration in the euphotic zone is fairly low, algal biomass in this zone is also fairly low. Secchi depths are deep and the water is clear. However, because phosphorus is much more abundant below 7 m, and because sufficient light for algal growth can penetrate to 12 m in Long Lake, it is at depths from 7 to 12 m that algal biomass is the greatest. At these depths, biomass can reach to 22 µg/L compared to concentrations of less than 5 µg/L above the thermocline.

An unusual pattern in euphotic zone total phosphorus concentrations occurred in 1986. In this year, the total phosphorus concentration increased sharply in the epilimnion in July. This increase was attributed to an unusually severe storm that resulted in a large amount of phosphorus-rich runoff entering the lake. (Note in Figure 4 the sudden rise in lake level at the same time.) In many lakes it would be expected that the increase in phosphorus would be accompanied by an increase in algal biomass (chlorophyll *a*). However, in this instance, the phytoplankton biomass did not increase and it was found that the algae were nitrogen-limited for a brief period of time (Prepas and Trimbee 1988).

Long Lake is a mesotrophic lake, but as most of the algae are below a depth of 7 m, the surface water is much clearer than in many other mesotrophic lakes in Alberta. When the cycling of phosphorus within the lake was examined, it was found that the lake sediment underlying 2.5 to 5 m of water has a high water content (an average of 87% in the top 10 cm). The porewater (water within the sediment) in these shallow areas in Long Lake has a relatively low phosphorus concentration (an average of 249 µg of soluble reactive phosphorus per litre in the top 10 cm) and a high ferrous iron concentration (942 µg/L). The movement of phosphorus from the sediment under shallow water to the water in the euphotic zone was estimated to be between 0.47 and 1.6 mg total phosphorus/m^2 per day, throughout the summer. In contrast, the movement of total phosphorus from the deep water across the thermocline into the euphotic zone is insignificant, about 0.01 mg/m^2 per day. The external total phosphorus loading is estimated to be 1.03 mg/m^2 per day. Therefore, the return of phosphorus from the sediments under shallow water to the euphotic zone constitutes a substantial proportion (31 to 61%) of the total phosphorus load to the euphotic zone of the lake.

Biological Characteristics

Plants

The phytoplankton in Long Lake has been studied briefly by researchers at the University of Alberta. The densest growth of algae, which occurred at depths of 7 to 12 m, was dominated by the blue-green alga (Cyanophyta) *Aphanizomenon flos-aquae* in 1984. In June 1986, the phytoplankton at depths of 7 to 12 m was dominated by both the diatom (Bacillariophyta) *Asterionella formosa* and the blue-green *Aphanizomenon flos-aquae* (Prepas et al. n.d.).

The aquatic macrophytes in Long Lake were surveyed during 1985 and 1986 during University of Alberta studies (Prepas et al. n.d.; Chambers and Prepas 1988; 1990). Thirteen species of submergent plants and five species of emergent plants were identified (Table 5). The zone from a depth of 1 to 2 m was dominated by coontail and northern watermilfoil. At depths of 2 to 5 m, stonewort was most prevalent with lesser amounts of common bladderwort

Table 4. Nutrient, chlorophyll *a* and Secchi depth data for Long Lake. Average concentrations in μg/L. Composite samples from the euphotic zone collected 6 times from 10 May to 30 Aug. 1983, 8 times from 16 May to 23 Aug. 1984 and 8 times from 16 May to 22 Aug. 1986. S.E. = standard error.

	1983		1984		1986	
	Mean	S.E.	Mean	S.E.	Mean	S.E.
total phosphorus	12	0.9	12	1.0	13[d]	1.0
total dissolved phosphorus	4[a]	0.3	6[b]	1.3	6[b]	0.8
total Kjeldahl nitrogen	787[a]	57.0	—	—	597[c]	38.0
$NO_3 + NO_2$–nitrogen	2[a]	0.5	—	—	6[b]	1.0
NH_4–nitrogen	—	—	10[c]	3.4	4[b]	1.0
iron	—	—	—	—	64[e]	—
chlorophyll *a*	2.9	0.31	3.1[b]	0.48	3.9[d]	0.40
Secchi depth (m)	5.8	0.59	5.4	0.49	4.8	0.42

NOTES: [a]n = 4; [b]n = 7; [c]n = 5; [d]n = 10; [e]n = 1
SOURCE: Prepas et al. n.d.

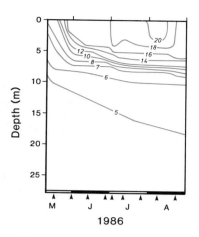

Figure 5. Temperature (°C) of Long Lake, 1986. Arrows indicate sampling dates.
SOURCE: Prepas et al. n.d.

Table 5. Species of aquatic macrophytes in Long Lake. Survey conducted between July and August in 1985 and 1986. Arranged by dominance.

emergent	bulrush	*Scirpus* sp.
	giant bur-reed	*Sparganium eurycarpum*
	bur-reed	*S. angustifolium*
	mare's tail	*Hippuris vulgaris*
	arrowhead	*Sagittaria cuneata*
free-floating	coontail	*Ceratophyllum demersum*
	bladderwort	*Utricularis vulgaris*
	star duckweed	*Lemna trisulca*
submergent	stonewort	*Chara* sp.
	northern watermilfoil	*Myriophyllum exalbescens*
	Richardson pondweed	*Potamogeton richardsonii*
	large-sheath pondweed	*P. vaginatus*
	flat-stemmed pondweed	*P. zosteriformis*
	water buttercup	*Ranunculus aquatilis*
	aquatic moss	*Drepanocladus* sp.
	water naiad	*Najas flexilis*
floating-leaved	yellow water lily	*Nuphar variegatum*
	water smartweed	*Polygonum amphibium*

SOURCE: Prepas et al. n.d.

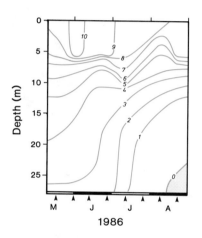

Figure 6. Dissolved oxygen (mg/L) in Long Lake, 1986. Arrows indicate sampling dates.
SOURCE: Prepas et al. n.d.

and Richardson pondweed. Yellow water lilies grew sparsely around the lake and densely in the narrows between the two basins. The dominant emergents were bulrush, especially in the narrows, and bur-reed, both of which occasionally formed large floating mats. In July and August 1985, the average biomass of macrophytes in the 0– to 5–m depth zone was 193 g/m² (geometric mean, linear average 536 g/m²).

Invertebrates

There are no data on the zooplankton or benthic invertebrates in Long Lake.

Fish

Five species of fish are known to occur in Long Lake: northern pike, yellow perch, burbot, Iowa darter and brook stickleback. The lake is locally popular for sport fishing for northern pike; fish over 75 cm are occasionally hooked and one individual of 90 cm was caught and released from a gillnet in 1987 (Prepas et al. n.d.). Pike grow slowly here—fish of age seven were only 50–cm long (fork length). Yellow perch are not sought by anglers, as they grow very slowly in Long Lake. Few perch over 15–cm in length were caught by seining or gill netting from 1985 to 1987. Perch that hatched at a length of 6 mm in May of these years were only 48 mm by mid-August (Abbey and Mackay n.d.).

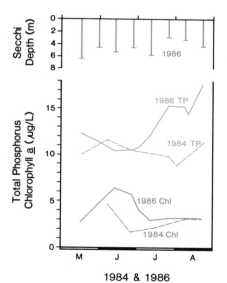

Figure 7. Total phosphorus and chlorophyll *a* in Long Lake, 1984 and 1986 and Secchi depth, 1986.
SOURCE: Prepas et al. n.d.

Kokanee were stocked annually in Long Lake from 1967 through 1969, but they could not successfully reproduce and now there are none in the lake (Watters 1989).

Wildlife

Long Lake is not heavily used by waterfowl. A few Mallards, Common Goldeneye and Red-necked Grebes nest on the lake and two pairs of Common Loons nested on the lake each spring from 1985 through 1988. An Osprey nested near the south end of the lake in 1988 (Prepas et al. n.d.).

Muskrats and beaver are often seen in the south basin and there is a large beaver lodge at each end of the lake. White-tailed and mule deer are seen near the lake and coyotes are common in the area. Black bears are seen occasionally.

J.M. Crosby and E.E. Prepas

References

Abbey, D. and W.C. Mackay. n.d. Univ. Alta., Dept. Zool. Unpubl. data, Edmonton.

Alberta Environment. n.d.[a]. Tech. Serv. Div., Hydrol. Br. Unpubl. data, Edmonton.

——. n.d.[b]. Tech. Serv. Div., Surv. Br. Unpubl. data, Edmonton.

Alberta Forestry, Lands and Wildlife. 1988. Boating in Alberta. Fish Wild. Div., Edmonton.

——. 1989. Guide to sportfishing. Fish Wild. Div., Edmonton.

Alberta Research Council. 1972. Geological map of Alberta. Nat. Resour. Div., Alta. Geol. Surv., Edmonton.

Chambers, P.A. and E.E. Prepas. 1988. Underwater spectral attenuation and its effect on the maximum depth of angiosperm colonization. Can. J. Fish. Aquat. Sci. 45:1010–1017.

——. 1990. Competition and coexistence in submerged aquatic plant communities: The paradox revisited. Freshwater Biol. [in press]

Energy, Mines and Resources Canada. 1973. National topographic series 1:50 000 83I/12 (1973). Surv. Map. Br., Ottawa.

Environment Canada. 1982. Canadian climate normals, Vol. 7: Bright sunshine (1951–1980). Prep. by Atm. Envir. Serv. Supply Serv. Can., Ottawa.

Kjearsgaard, A.A. 1972. Soil survey of the Tawatinaw map sheet (83I). Alta. Inst. Pedol. No. S–72–29, Univ. Alta. Bull. No. SS–12 1972. Univ. Alta., Edmonton.

Prepas, E.E., P.A. Chambers, J.M. Hanson and A.M. Trimbee. n.d. Univ. Alta., Dept. Zool. Unpubl. data, Edmonton.

Prepas, E.E., M.E. Dunnigan and A.M. Trimbee. 1988. Comparison of *in situ* estimates of chlorophyll *a* obtained with Whatman GF/F and GF/C glass-fiber filters in mesotrophic to hypereutrophic lakes. Can. J. Fish. Aquat. Sci. 45:910–914.

Prepas, E.E. and A.M. Trimbee. 1988. Evaluation of indicators of nitrogen limitation in deep prairie lakes with laboratory bioassays and limnocorrals. Hydrobiologia 159:269–276.

Shaw, J.F.H. and E.E. Prepas. 1989[a]. Exchange of phosphorus from shallow sediments at nine Alberta lakes. J. Envir. Qlty. [in press]

——. 1989[b]. Relationships between phosphorus in shallow sediments in the trophogenic zone of seven Alberta lakes. Water Res. [in press]

——. 1989[c]. Potential significance of phosphorus release from shallow sediments of deep Alberta lakes. ms submitted to Limnol. Oceanogr.

Shaw, J.F.H., R.D. Shaw and E.E. Prepas. 1989. Advective transport of phosphorus from lake bottom sediments into lakewater. ms to be submitted.

——. 1989. Groundwater-lake interactions: II. Nearshore seepage patterns and the contribution of groundwater to lakes in central Alberta. J. Hydrol. [in press]

Strong, W.L. and K.R. Leggat. 1981. Ecoregions of Alberta. Alta. En. Nat. Resour., Resour. Eval. Plan. Div., Edmonton.

Watters, D. 1989. Alta. For. Ld. Wild., Fish Wild. Div., Dist. Office, Edmonton. Pers. comm.

McLEOD LAKE

MAP SHEET: 83J/5
LOCATION: Tp61 R11, 12 W5
LAT/LONG: 54°18′N 115°39′W

McLeod Lake is a medium-sized lake set in gently rolling, forested land in Carson-Pegasus Provincial Park. The lake is located 200 km northwest of the city of Edmonton and 24 km north of the town of Whitecourt. It is valued for its excellent rainbow trout fishery, which is the central attraction for visitors to the park. The park itself is one of the more popular parks in Alberta. To reach the lake from Whitecourt, drive west for 9 km on Highway 43 and north for 10 km on Highway 32. Turn east onto the road that leads to the park and drive for about 5 km to the park entrance (Fig. 1).

There is some uncertainty about the origin of the lake's name. The McLeod River, which joins the Athabasca River at Whitecourt, was probably named for Archibald Norman McLeod, a fur trader with the North West Company (MacGregor 1952). In 1790, McLeod was sent by Alexander Mackenzie to build two trading posts near the present-day town of Peace River, 250 km northwest of Whitecourt. In the early days of the fur trade, McLeod Lake was an important stop for travellers who were using an intricate system of rivers and trails to reach northwestern Alberta (Finlay and Finlay 1987). At some point, the lake was renamed Carson Lake, but the name was changed back to McLeod Lake in the mid–1980s. Nearby Little McLeod Lake was formerly known as Pegasus Lake, probably in reference to the Pegasus symbol that was at one time used by Mobil Oil of Canada Limited, which leases much of the land in the drainage basin.

Several significant prehistoric sites are located in the provincial park. Stoney, Woodland Cree, and possibly Beaver Indians lived near the lake until the early part of the twentieth century (Finlay and Finlay 1987). The lake was an important source of fish for these people. The first white settler, Bruce Goodwin, was a timber "cruiser" for the federal government who settled at McLeod Lake in 1904. The lumber industry began in the area in the early 1900s, and most of the park was selectively logged during the 1940s (Olecko 1974; Finlay and Finlay 1987). In 1956, oil was discovered in the region, and since then, many roads and cutlines have been developed.

Carson-Pegasus Provincial Park was established by the provincial government in 1982. Prior to that date, the Alberta Forest Service had operated a campground at the lake. The park was named for Carson (now McLeod) and Pegasus (now Little McLeod) lakes, both of which lie within its boundaries (Fig. 1). It is open year-round and provides 182 campsites, a group camping area, showers, tap water, a concession, sewage disposal facilities, playgrounds, a picnic area, boat launches and rentals and walking trails. All of the facilities are located on the south shore of McLeod Lake and along the peninsula (Fig. 2); a road and hiking trail provide access to Little McLeod Lake.

The water in McLeod Lake is generally transparent, but may turn green in late summer. Bulrushes and sedges ring the lake and two shallow shoals support dense stands of aquatic vegetation. Popular activities at Carson-Pegasus Provincial Park are fishing for rainbow trout, hiking, camping and motor boating in summer, and camping, ice fishing, cross-country skiing, snowshoeing and tobogganing in winter. Little McLeod Lake is good for swimming, but in McLeod Lake, large numbers of leeches are a deterrent to swimmers. All tributary streams to McLeod Lake, and the outlet stream as far downstream as Highway 32, are closed to fishing year-round (Alta. For. Ld. Wild. 1989). As well, fishing for bait and the use of bait fish are not allowed in the lake. Power boats are limited to a maximum

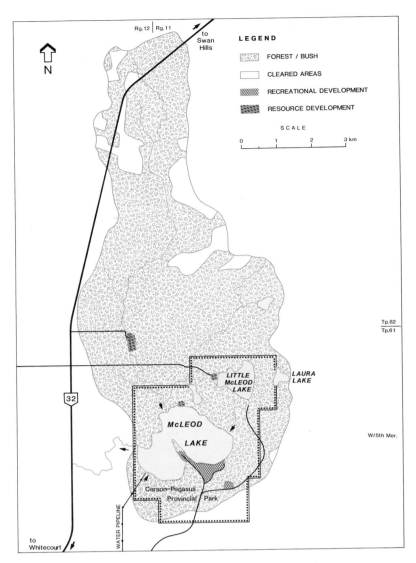

Figure 1. Features of the drainage basin of McLeod Lake.
SOURCES: Alta. Envir. n.d.[b]; En. Mines Resour. Can. 1961; 1981. Updated with 1982 and 1985 aerial photos.

Table 1. Characteristics of McLeod Lake drainage basin.

area (excluding lake) (km²)[a]	45.9
soil[b]	Orthic Gray Luvisols
bedrock geology[c]	Paskapoo Formation (Tertiary): sandstone, siltstone, mudstone; thin limestone, coal and tuff beds; nonmarine
terrain[b]	undulating to rolling
ecoregion[d]	Boreal Foothills
dominant vegetation[d]	trembling aspen, balsam poplar, lodgepole pine
mean annual inflow (m³)[a, e]	3.62 x 10⁶
mean annual sunshine (h)[f]	2 056

NOTE: [e]excluding groundwater inflow
SOURCES: [a]Alta. Envir. n.d.[b]; [b]Wynnyk et al. 1969; [c]Alta. Res. Counc. 1972; [d]Strong and Leggat 1981; [f]Envir. Can. 1982

The major land uses in the watershed are recreational and industrial. There is no residential or agricultural development. Recreational developments are located on the south shore of McLeod Lake within the provincial park (Fig. 1). All of the land in the watershed belongs to the province, and much of it is leased to either Mobil Oil of Canada Limited or, secondarily, to Esso Resources Canada Limited. Mobil Oil is licenced to withdraw water from Little McLeod Lake, whereas Esso Resources is licenced to withdraw water from McLeod Lake.

Lake Basin Characteristics

McLeod Lake is a shallow, medium-sized water body that is divided into two basins by a long peninsula (Fig. 2, Table 2). The east basin, which is deepest, has a maximum depth of 10.7 m, located in the central area. The deepest area in the west basin (6.1 m) is located near the tip of the peninsula. Most of the bottom substrate is highly organic, but there are small areas of sand, clay, rubble, and mixtures of these substrates, as well (Crutchfield and Lane 1971).

The elevation of McLeod Lake was recorded once in 1962 and has been monitored continuously since 1966 (Fig. 3). In September 1962, a water level of 853.06 m was recorded. Similar elevations were recorded in 1966, but after that time, the lake level declined quite steadily to its historic minimum elevation of 851.05 m in May 1971. This decline was attributed to several years of low precipitation levels. Imperial Oil Company (now Esso Resources Canada Limited) was first licenced in September 1962 to withdraw 3.08 x 10⁶ m³/year of water from McLeod Lake (Alta. Envir. n.d.[d]). The licence was increased to 3.58 x 10⁶ m³/year soon after. In November 1968, Imperial Oil built a temporary earthfill weir on the outlet creek.

In 1971, Imperial Oil changed their primary water source from McLeod Lake to the Athabasca River because the water supply from McLeod Lake was not reliable. They constructed a pipeline from the river to the south shore of McLeod Lake to bring water into the lake and raise its elevation. They then pumped water out of the lake from a station on the north shore. In effect, they used the lake as a balancing reservoir. In July 1971, a permanent sheet-pile weir with an elevation of 853.74 m was built on the outlet of McLeod Lake and the company began filling the lake with river water. By mid-July, the lake's elevation had risen by 1.90 m, from the historic minimum of 851.05 m on 17 May to 852.95 m on 14 July (Fig. 3). The company was issued a new withdrawal licence in 1971 for a total of 13.44 x 10⁶ m³ of water per year, to be taken from both the lake and river, and the company was not allowed to draw the lake down below 852.68 m (Alta. Envir. n.d.[d]).

From 1972 to 1979, Imperial Oil withdrew an average of 8.21 x 10⁶ m³/year from the two water sources. Since 1980, the company's water needs have declined and they have not pumped water from the Athabasca River, although they are still licenced to do so. From 1980 to 1988, the company withdrew an average of 2.09 x 10⁶ m³/year, from the lake only (Alta. Envir. n.d.[d]).

speed of 12 km/hour in all areas of the lake, and all boats are prohibited from posted areas of the lake (Alta. For. Ld. Wild. 1988).

Drainage Basin Characteristics

Most of McLeod Lake's drainage basin is situated north of the lake (Fig. 1). The watershed, which covers almost 46 km², is about 12 times larger than the lake (Tables 1, 2). The main inflow is an unnamed creek that flows into the north end of the lake. A small creek flows from nearby Little McLeod Lake into the eastern side of McLeod Lake. McLeod Lake's outlet is located on the western shore. It flows into Carson Creek, which joins the Sakwatamau River on its way to the Athabasca River.

Land in the drainage basin is generally undulating to rolling (Wynnyk et al. 1969). The highest land elevation, 1 067 m, is at the far northern tip of the watershed, where the topography is hilly. Elevations decline to about 854 m near the shore of McLeod Lake.

The drainage basin is part of the Boreal Foothills Ecoregion (Strong and Leggat 1981). Soils are mainly moderately well-drained Orthic Gray Luvisols that developed primarily on glacial till and secondarily on shale. Most of the soils north of the lake are rated as suitable for pasture and woodland. Around the shore the soil arability rating varies from poor to fairly good (Wynnyk et al. 1969). Trembling aspen, balsam poplar and lodgepole pine are the codominant trees on well-drained to moderately well-drained Gray Luvisols. Succession on these soils is by white spruce. Open stands of lodgepole pine grow on well-drained Brunisols and imperfectly drained Gleysols, and black spruce is the main species on poorly drained, depressional areas. Willows and sedges grow in very poorly drained areas.

Table 2. Characteristics of McLeod Lake.

elevation (m)[a]	853.06
surface area (km²)[b, c]	3.73
volume (m³)[b, c]	19.0×10^6
maximum depth (m)[b, c]	10.7
mean depth (m)[b, c]	5.1
shoreline length (km)[d]	9.98
mean annual lake evaporation (mm)[e]	620
mean annual precipitation (mm)[e]	553
mean residence time (yr)[e, f]	5.5
control structure[g]	sheet-pile weir
crest elevation (m)[g]	853.74
crest length (m)[g]	6.4

NOTES: [a]on 17 Sep. 1962; [b]on date of sounding: May 1962; [f]excluding groundwater inflow
SOURCES: [c]Alta. Envir. n.d.[c]; [d]Hildebrandt 1987; [e]Alta. Envir. n.d.[b]; [g]Bucharski 1989

During the 1980s, water levels were quite high in most years (Fig. 3). The historic maximum level, 854.37 m, was recorded in July 1985. These high levels were caused by beaver dams built on and around the control structure. The high water levels caused flooding problems in the provincial park, and Fish and Wildlife Division became concerned that northern pike and white suckers, which had been eliminated from the lake in 1976, might overcome the fish barrier on the outlet, reenter the lake and adversely affect the stocked rainbow trout population. Consequently, a new weir, designed as a fish barrier, was installed in 1987. The project was a joint effort between Esso Resources, Fish and Wildlife Division, Alberta Recreation and Parks and Alberta Environment. The structure is licenced to Esso and is maintained by Fish and Wildlife Division. It is a sheet-pile weir with a crest elevation of 853.74 m, and is located downstream from the old weir, which was removed. To improve outflow, the stream was straightened and excavated, and to discourage beaver dam construction, trees near the channel were removed (Bucharski 1989).

Over the years, the area and capacity of McLeod Lake have fluctuated considerably. The difference between the historic maximum and minimum lake elevation is 3.32 m. This fluctuation would cause large changes in the lake's area and volume (Fig. 4).

Water Quality

The water quality of McLeod Lake was monitored by Alberta Environment in 1976 and 1977, and jointly by Alberta Environment and Alberta Recreation and Parks since 1984 (Alta. Envir. n.d.[a]).

The major ions in the east and west basins of the lake are very similar (Table 3). The water is fresh, relatively hard and well-buffered, and the dominant ions are bicarbonate and calcium. Both basins are quite shallow and generally well mixed throughout the open-water season. The water column is weakly thermally stratified during warm, calm periods, such as on 21 July 1986 (Fig. 5). On this date, dissolved oxygen concentrations declined to less than 5 mg/L below a depth of 9 m in the deeper east basin, and to about 6 mg/L in water near the sediments in the west basin (Fig. 5). Surface concentrations were 9 to 10 mg/L in both basins. In the east basin during August of 1984 and 1985, dissolved oxygen concentrations were less than 1 mg/L at depths greater than 8 m. Data for dissolved oxygen levels in the west basin are not available for these dates.

In late winter, dissolved oxygen concentrations near the bottom sediments become slightly depleted in both basins. In March 1986, they declined to 2 mg/L near the bottom of the east basin and 5 mg/L near the bottom of the west basin (Fig. 5). Although a severe fish kill occurred during the winter of 1970/71, dissolved oxygen levels appear to be adequate for fish survival during most winters. The 1970/71 kill was the result of low water levels and therefore insufficient dissolved oxygen (Hildebrand 1976).

McLeod Lake is mesotrophic. Patterns of total phosphorus and chlorophyll *a* concentrations during the open-water period are sim-

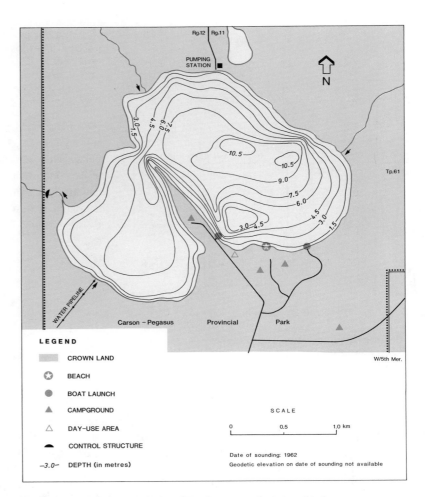

Figure 2. Bathymetry and shoreline features of McLeod Lake.
BATHYMETRY SOURCE: Alta. Envir. n.d.[c].

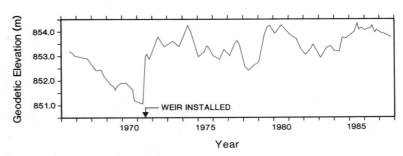

Figure 3. Water level of McLeod Lake, 1966 to 1987.
SOURCE: Alta. Envir. n.d.[c].

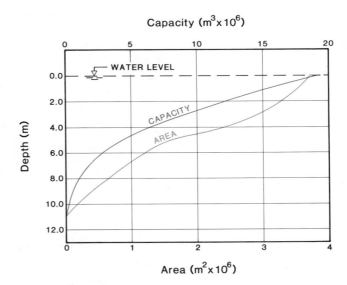

Figure 4. Area/capacity curve for McLeod Lake.
SOURCE: Alta. Envir. n.d.[c].

Table 3. Major ions and related water quality variables for McLeod Lake. Average concentrations in mg/L; pH in pH units. Composite samples from the euphotic zone collected a total of 7 times in the west basin and 8 times in the east basin during the open-water seasons from 1985 to 1987. S.E. = standard error.

	West Basin		East Basin	
	Mean	S.E.	Mean	S.E.
pH (range)	8.1–8.4	—	7.9–8.4	—
total alkalinity (CaCO$_3$)	143	1.1	144	0.7
specific conductivity (µS/cm)	297	2.7	298	1.3
total dissolved solids (calculated)	156	1.2	157	0.8
total hardness (CaCO$_3$)	137	1.3	138	1.2
HCO$_3$	174	0.1	174	0.7
CO$_3$	<1	—	<2	—
Mg	8	0.2	9	0.2
Na	7	0.4	8	0.3
K	2	0	2	0
Cl	5	0.2	5	0.3
SO$_4$	<6	—	<6	—
Ca	41	0.3	41	0.5

SOURCE: Alta. Envir. n.d.[a], Naquadat station 01AL07AE2029 (west), 01AL07AE2040 (east)

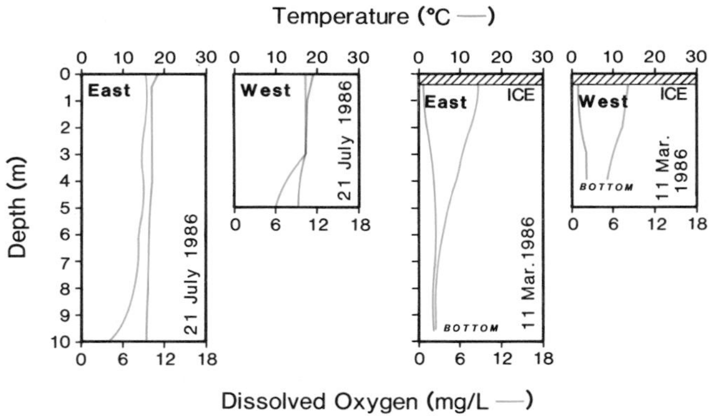

Figure 5. Temperature and dissolved oxygen in McLeod Lake, east and west basins, 1986.
SOURCE: Alta. Envir. n.d.[a].

ilar for both basins and fairly typical of many Alberta lakes: concentrations are lowest in June and July and peak in spring and late summer (Fig. 6). The late summer peak is probably caused by internal loading of total phosphorus from the sediments to the surface water. In 1986, the maximum chlorophyll *a* concentration recorded in late August was 13.1 µg/L in the west basin and 14.5 µg/L in the east basin. The average total phosphorus concentration in 1986 was 26 µg/L in both basins, and the average chlorophyll *a* concentration was 7.7 µg/L in the west basin and 10.9 µg/L in the east basin (Table 4).

Biological Characteristics

Plants

The phytoplankton and macrophyte communities in McLeod Lake have not been studied in detail. Fish and Wildlife Division reported a bloom of blue-green algae, mostly *Aphanizomenon* sp. in June and August 1970 (Crutchfield and Lane 1971). Phytoplankton species and abundance were studied by Alberta Environment in late 1976 and during 1977 but, as this was after the lake was treated with rotenone to remove northern pike and suckers in September 1976, the data could not be considered representative (Alta. Envir. n.d.[a]).

A preliminary survey conducted by Fish and Wildlife Division in 1975 found that emergent vegetation, primarily common great bulrush (*Scirpus validus*) and sedges (*Carex* sp.), ring the lake (Hildebrand 1976). Unidentified submergent species and yellow water lily (*Nuphar variegatum*) were abundant, particularly in the shallow northwest bay.

Invertebrates

The zooplankton and benthic invertebrate communities of McLeod Lake have not been studied, but the lake is known for its large population of leeches.

Fish

McLeod Lake is managed as a recreational fishery. The fishery and its rehabilitation have been studied intensively by Fish and Wildlife Division since 1970 (Crutchfield and Lane 1971; Hildebrand 1976; Makowecki et al. 1978; Hunt 1986; Hildebrandt 1987; Hawryluk 1989). Prior to 1970, the fish fauna consisted of lake whitefish, northern pike, white sucker and burbot. No forage fish were caught in seine netting in 1970, but finescale dace were found in a nearby

slough and in the creek joining the slough to McLeod Lake. In 1970, the lake was stocked with 250 000 walleye fry and 1 180 walleye adults. A severe winterkill in 1970/71 killed all of the walleye and whitefish. From 1971 to 1974, the lake was stocked with 100 000 to 300 000 fingerling rainbow trout each year. From 1972 to 1975, trout fishing was reported to be excellent, and in 1975, a provincial record was set when a trout weighing 7.4 kg was taken. In 1974, test-nets caught a large number of northern pike that apparently had preyed heavily on small rainbow trout. Trout stocking was discontinued that year, and plans were made to rehabilitate the lake by treating it with rotenone to remove all fish and then to restock it with rainbow trout.

In 1976, the chemical treatment of McLeod Lake, a nearby slough, all inlet streams and the outlet stream as far as Highway 32 was carried out. Prior to the treatment, fish barriers were constructed on the outlets of Little McLeod Lake, McLeod Lake and the slough to prevent the movement of northern pike and suckers in and out of McLeod Lake. After the rehabilitation was completed, rainbow trout were stocked at a rate of 1 200 fish/ha in 1977 and 1978 and about 600 fish/ha from 1979 to 1983. In 1984, the stocking rate was increased to about 1 200 fish/ha to compensate for heavy fishing pressure. Test-netting conducted from 1977 to 1986 indicated that northern pike were eliminated from the lake but white suckers were still present. White suckers were also caught by anglers in 1988. The trout fishery in McLeod Lake can be sustained only by stocking because there is no suitable spawning habitat available. Consequently, natural reproduction is very low.

The growth rate of rainbow trout in McLeod Lake is among the fastest of trout planted in 10 other lakes in the Edson region. From 1980 to 1984 in McLeod Lake, the average spring weight of 2–year–old trout was 0.53 kg and the average 3–year–old weighed 0.79 kg (Hildebrandt 1987). In 8 of the other 10 stocked lakes sampled in the region, the weight of the average 2–year–old rainbow trout ranged from 0.14 kg (Mary Gregg Lake, 1976) to 1.48 kg (Grande Cache Lake, 1984). This age-class was not observed in the other two lakes. In 5 of the 10 lakes, the weight of the average 3–year–old trout ranged from 0.25 kg (Middle Pierre Grey Lake, 1981) to a single fish of 1.65 kg (Petite Lake, 1984).

Since 1977, limited creel censuses have been conducted frequently at McLeod Lake. In February and March 1988, a total of 625 anglers were interviewed on 12 census days. The anglers spent 2 436 hours fishing and caught 1 365 rainbow trout. This catch rate (0.56 trout/angler-hour) is above the provincial average of 0.50 trout/angler-hour (Hawryluk 1989).

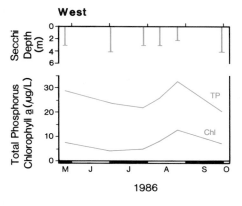 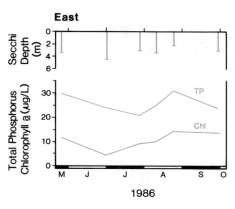

Figure 6. Total phosphorus, chlorophyll _a_ and Secchi depth in McLeod Lake, east and west basins, 1986.
SOURCE: Alta. Envir. n.d.[a].

Table 4. Nutrient, chlorophyll _a_ and Secchi depth data for McLeod Lake. Average concentrations in μg/L. Composite samples from the euphotic zone collected 6 times from 25 May to 29 Sep. 1986. S.E. = standard error.

	West Basin		East Basin	
	Mean	S.E.	Mean	S.E.
total phosphorus	26	1.9	26	1.6
iron	40[a]	5.8	<43[a]	—
chlorophyll _a_	7.7	1.26	10.9	1.47
Secchi depth (m)	3.2	0.30	3.1	0.29

NOTE: [a] n = 3
SOURCE: Alta. Envir. n.d.[a], Naquadat station 01AL07AE2029 (west), 01AL07AE2040 (east)

Wildlife

Carson-Pegasus Provincial Park is located near the Swan Hills and is home to both foothill and boreal bird species. The park is covered by young-mature and over-mature forests, marshes, fens and adjacent thickets. At least 113 species of birds have been reported, with 106 breeding in the park. Each year, the lake is used by waterfowl during spring and fall migration. The mammal population is diverse, with 42 species reported. Moose, deer and black bears are common, and the Swan Hills grizzly, a prairie subspecies, is present in the general area, but not common (Alta. Rec. Parks 1980; Nordstrom 1980).

M.E. Bradford and J.M. Hanson

References

Alberta Environment. n.d.[a]. Envir. Assess. Div., Envir. Qlty. Monit. Br. Unpubl. data, Edmonton.
———. n.d.[b]. Tech. Serv. Div., Hydrol. Br. Unpubl. data, Edmonton.
———. n.d.[c]. Tech. Serv. Div., Surv. Br. Unpubl. data, Edmonton.
———. n.d.[d]. Water Resour. Admin. Div., Sur. Water Rights Br. Unpubl. data, Edmonton.
Alberta Forestry, Lands and Wildlife. 1988. Boating in Alberta. Fish Wild. Div., Edmonton.
———. 1989. Guide to sportfishing. Fish Wild. Div., Edmonton.
Alberta Recreation and Parks. 1980. Master plan: Carson-Pegasus Provincial Park. Parks Div., Edmonton.
Alberta Research Council. 1972. Geological map of Alberta. Nat. Resour. Div., Alta. Geol. Surv., Edmonton.

Bucharski, G. 1989. Alta. Envir., Devel. Op. Div., Edmonton. Pers. comm.
Crutchfield, K. and C.B. Lane. 1971. Walleye introduction—Carson and Gregg Lakes, progress report number 1, 1970. Alta. Ld. For., Fish Wild. Div. Unpubl. rep., Edmonton.
Energy, Mines and Resources Canada. 1961, 1981. National topographic series 1:50 000 83J/5E (1961), 83J/5 (1981). Surv. Map. Br., Ottawa.
Environment Canada. 1982. Canadian climate normals, Vol. 7: Bright sunshine (1951–1980). Prep. by Atm. Envir. Serv. Supply Serv. Can., Ottawa.
Finlay, J. and C. Finlay. 1987. Parks in Alberta: A guide to peaks, ponds, parklands & prairies. Hurtig Publ., Edmonton.
Hawryluk, R. 1989. A short term creel survey of McLeod (Carson) Lake, February and March, 1988. Alta. For. Ld. Wild., Fish Wild. Div. Unpubl. rep., Edmonton.
Hildebrand, L. 1976. Preliminary biological survey of Carson Lake, 1975. Alta. Rec. Parks Wild., Fish Wild. Div. Unpubl. rep., Edmonton.
Hildebrandt, D. 1987. An evaluation of the McLeod (Carson) Lake stocking program, June and October, 1986. Alta. For. Ld. Wild., Fish Wild. Div. Unpubl. rep., Edmonton.
Hunt, C.W. 1986. Fisheries management plan—Carson Lake (1986). Alta. En. Nat. Resour., Fish Wild. Div. Unpubl. rep., Edmonton.
MacGregor, J.G. 1952. The land of Twelve Foot Davis. Inst. App. Art Ltd., Edmonton.
Makowecki, R., C.W. Hunt and L. Hildebrand. 1978. Carson Lake improvement project. Alta. Rec. Parks Wild., Fish Wild. Div., Fish. Habitat Devel. Rep. No. 9, Edmonton.
Nordstrom, W. 1980. Carson-Pegasus Provincial Park resource conservation and management guidelines. Alta. Rec. Parks, Parks Div., Edmonton.
Olecko, D. 1974. Sagitawah saga: The story of Whitecourt. D. Olecko, Whitecourt.
Strong, W.L. and K.R. Leggat. 1981. Ecoregions of Alberta. Alta. En. Nat. Resour., Resour. Eval. Plan. Div., Edmonton.
Wynnyk, A., J.D. Lindsay and W. Odynsky. 1969. Soil survey of the Whitecourt and Barrhead area. Alta. Soil Surv. Rep. No. 27, Univ. Alta. Bull. No. SS–10, Res. Counc. Alta. Rep. No. 90. Univ. Alta., Edmonton.

NAKAMUN LAKE

MAP SHEET: 83G/16
LOCATION: Tp56 R2 W5
LAT/LONG: 53°53′N 114°12′W

Nakamun Lake is an attractive lake set in rolling hills in the counties of Lac Ste. Anne and Barrhead. It is located about 95 km northwest of Edmonton and 28 km south of the town of Barrhead. To reach the lake from Edmonton, take Highway 16 west to its junction with Highway 43. Turn north on Highway 43 and drive north and then west to Highway 33. Turn north and drive 17 km to Secondary Road 650, then drive east along this road to the west end of Nakamun Lake. The north and south sides of the lake can be reached by municipal roads running west from Secondary Road 777 (Fig. 1).

Nakamun is Cree for "song of praise" or "songbird" (Geog. Bd. Can. 1928). Settlers arrived in the area at the end of the nineteenth century and began clearing land for agriculture to the east and northeast of the lake. Most of the land around the lake is privately owned and the south shore is extensively developed. The first subdivision was established in 1960; it was incorporated as the summer village of Nakamun Park in 1966. Four Oakes subdivision was founded in 1962 about 400 m east of Nakamun Park, and Nakamun Court subdivision (also called Losie Glade) was built in 1975 adjacent to the west side of Four Oakes. The north shore is mostly undeveloped except for a Bible camp and a few cottages.

The only public access to Nakamun Lake is on the south shore at several public reserves. Two of these reserves have facilities (Fig. 2). The Nakamun Park reserve has a boat launch, a dock, a day-use area and a small sand beach. The reserve in Nakamun Court has a boat launch, a picnic shelter, a hand water pump and a few campsites. In Four Oakes, the reserve provides only a hand pump and access to the lake. Activities that are popular at Nakamun Lake include boating, fishing, hiking, photography, nature study, picnicking and relaxation. There are no boating restrictions over most of the lake, but in posted areas, power boats are restricted to maximum speeds of 12 km/hour (Alta. For. Ld. Wild. 1988). High nutrient levels in the lake cause excessive algal growth, which impairs water-contact recreation. Sport fishing has been hampered by fish kills in winter, but stocking with yellow perch from 1984 to 1986 has revived the sport fishery. A few northern pike, and many sticklebacks and minnows, also inhabit the lake. There are no sport fishing regulations specific to Nakamun Lake, but provincial limits and regulations apply (Alta. For. Ld. Wild. 1989).

Drainage Basin Characteristics

Nakamun Lake's drainage basin is about 13 times the size of the lake (Tables 1, 2). There are no major inflows to the lake, and the small inflowing creeks tend to dry up after snowmelt in the spring. A small permanent water body, Kakina Lake, is located to the southeast (Fig. 1); it flows intermittently into Nakamun Lake. The outflow, located at the northwest end of the lake, connects Nakamun Lake to Lac la Nonne only during periods when water levels are high. Groundwater inflow to Nakamun Lake has not been estimated, but the direction of flow is from the southeast part of the watershed to the northwest (Edm. Reg. Plan. Commis. 1979).

The topography of the drainage basin is quite varied. To the south and west, the land is gently rolling to rolling, with slopes from 5 to 15%; frequently, sloughs have formed in depressions. To the northwest, the terrain is undulating to gently rolling, with slopes from 1 to 8%, and to the northeast the land is gently rolling to rolling, with

Table 1. Characteristics of Nakamun Lake drainage basin.

area (excluding lake) (km²)[a]	44.9
soil[b]	Orthic and Solodic Gray Luvisols
bedrock geology[c]	Wapiti Formation (Upper Cretaceous): sandstone, mudstone, bentonite, scattered coal beds; nonmarine
terrain[b]	undulating to moderately rolling
ecoregion[d]	Moist Mixedwood Subregion of Boreal Mixedwood
dominant vegetation[d]	trembling aspen, balsam poplar
mean annual inflow (m³)[a, e]	1.32 x 10⁶
mean annual sunshine (h)[f]	2 264

NOTE: [e]excluding groundwater inflow
SOURCES: [a]Alta. Envir. n.d.[b]; [b]Twardy and Brocke 1976; [c]Alta. Res. Counc. 1972; [d]Strong and Leggat 1981; [f]Envir. Can. 1982

Table 2. Characteristics of Nakamun Lake.

elevation (m)[a, b]	682.48
surface area (km²)[a, b]	3.54
volume (m³)[a, b]	15.8 x 10⁶
maximum depth (m)[a, b]	8.0
mean depth (m)[a, b]	4.5
shoreline length (km)[c]	12.5
mean annual lake evaporation (mm)[d]	664
mean annual precipitation (mm)[d]	504
mean residence time[d, e]	21
control structure	none

NOTES: [a]on date of sounding: 12 July 1982; [e]excluding groundwater inflow
SOURCES: [b]Babin and Prepas 1985; [c]En. Mines Resour. Can. 1975; [d]Alta. Envir. n.d.[b]

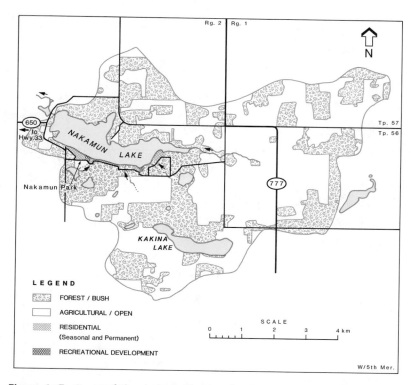

Figure 1. Features of the drainage basin of Nakamun Lake.
SOURCES: Alta. Envir. n.d.[b]; En. Mines Resour. Can. 1975. Updated with 1977 and 1985 aerial photos.

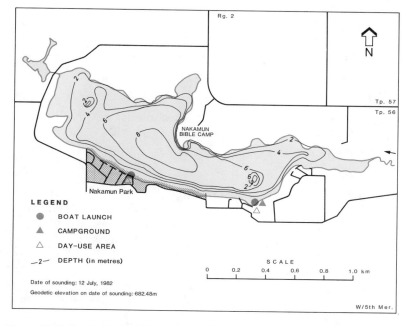

Figure 2. Bathymetry and shoreline features of Nakamun Lake.
BATHYMETRY SOURCE: Riley 1983.

some slopes greater than 15%. The elevation of the land ranges from 732 m at the northeastern and southern edges of the drainage basin to 683 m at the lakeshore.

The watershed is located in the Moist Mixedwood Subregion of the Boreal Mixedwood Ecoregion (Strong and Leggat 1981). The soils are mainly well-drained to moderately well-drained Orthic Gray Luvisols and moderately well-drained to imperfectly drained Solodic Gray Luvisols. Both of these soils developed on moderately fine-textured to medium-textured glacial till. Significant areas of very poorly drained Mesisols are located throughout the watershed, as well. The forest cover is dominated by trembling aspen and balsam poplar on well-drained soils and balsam poplar in moister areas and at the lakeshore. Black spruce grows on poorly drained Organics and Gleysols, most of which are located to the north and east of the lake. There are a number of wet depressions throughout the drainage basin; they generally contain peat, sedges and slough grass and are surrounded by willow, dwarf birch and alder (Twardy and Brocke 1976).

Although undesirable soil structure, adverse topography and, in some areas, excessive moisture, have limited agriculture in the drainage basin, more than half of the land has been cleared for agriculture. The predominant agricultural activity is beef production and most of the cleared land is used for either improved pasture or forage production (Twardy and Brocke 1976; Edm. Reg. Plan. Commis. 1979).

Much of the land near the lake has been developed for seasonal and permanent residences. About 23% of the shoreline is developed, mostly on the south shore, which is extensively subdivided (Fig. 1). There are a few cabins on quarter sections on the northeast shore. Development near Nakamun Lake was restricted in 1977, when the lake became subject to the provincial government's Regulated Lake Shoreland Development Operation Regulations, which were administered by Alberta Environment. The regulations ensured

that additional development did not take place until a lake management plan and an area structure plan were prepared and the area structure plan was adopted by the counties of Lac Ste. Anne and Barrhead as part of their land-use bylaws. This process was completed by 1981 (Edm. Reg. Plan. Commis. 1979; 1980; 1981). Lake management plans determine the extent of future land developments, allocate land use and determine ways to minimize environmental impacts and conflicts in the use of the lakeshore. They also recommend preferred lake uses and ways to minimize lake-user conflicts.

Lake Basin Characteristics

Nakamun Lake is a medium-sized, fairly shallow lake that has a maximum length of 2.2 km and a maximum width of 0.8 km (Fig.

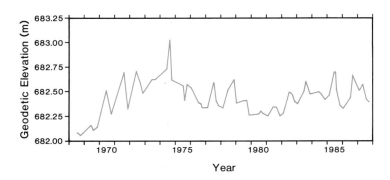

Figure 3. Water level of Nakamun Lake, 1968 to 1986.
SOURCE: Alta. Envir. n.d.[c].

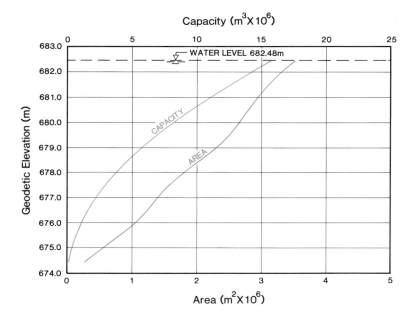

Figure 4. Area/capacity curve for Nakamun Lake.
SOURCE: Riley 1983.

Table 3. Major ions and related water quality variables for Nakamun Lake. Average concentrations in mg/L; pH in pH units. Composite samples from the euphotic zone collected 6 times from 05 May to 21 Sep. 1983. S.E. = standard error.

	Mean	S.E.
pH (range)	7.8–9.5[a]	—
total alkalinity (CaCO₃)	148	2.9
specific conductivity (μS/cm)	294	8.3
total dissolved solids (calculated)	158	3.1
turbidity (NTU)	22[b]	—
colour (Pt)	25[b]	—
total hardness (CaCO₃)	92	3.8
total particulate carbon	3	1.5
dissolved organic carbon	16	0.5
HCO₃	163	12.5
CO₃	9	4.8
Mg	8	0.2
Na	20	0.2
K	8	0.2
Cl	2	0
SO₄	<6	—
Ca	24	1.4

NOTE: [a]n = 5
SOURCES: Alta. Envir. n.d.[a], Naquadat station 01AL07BB2090; [b]Prepas and Trew 1983

2, Table 2). The deepest area (8.0 m) is located in the centre of the basin. There is one small island at the west end of the lake, and an island of reeds at the east end. The lake's elevation has been monitored since 1968 (Fig. 3). The difference between the minimum elevation (682.06 m), recorded in September 1968, and the maximum elevation (683.03 m), recorded in July 1974, is 0.97 m. From 1980 to 1987, the lake level fluctuated by a maximum of 0.46 m. Changes in the lake's surface area and capacity with fluctuations in water level are illustrated in Figure 4.

Water Quality

Nakamun Lake was studied from 1977 to 1979 and since 1983 by Alberta Environment (Alta. Envir. n.d.[a]; 1985), and from 1980 to 1983 by the University of Alberta (Prepas and Babin n.d.; Prepas 1983[b]; Prepas and Trew 1983; Riley 1983; Riley and Prepas 1984; Babin and Prepas 1985). It is one of six lakes in Alberta with extensive long-term water quality data. The lake was chosen for long-term study because it is representative of shallow, eutrophic lakes.

The dominant ions in Nakamun Lake are calcium, sodium and bicarbonate. The water is alkaline and moderately hard (Table 3), and turbidity (25 NTU) and colour (22 mg/L Pt) measurements are moderate (Prepas and Trew 1983).

The water column mixes almost completely after ice-out, and is thermally stratified by early June (Fig. 5). In summer, the lake periodically mixes and restratifies. The water column is well-mixed by late summer, and remains so until ice forms on the surface. Under ice in most years, dissolved oxygen decreases until, between January and March, a large part of the water column is anoxic, as in 1983 (Fig.

6). Surface concentrations of dissolved oxygen, however, are adequate for fish survival in most years.

Nakamun Lake is hyper-eutrophic. The average total phosphorus and chlorophyll *a* concentrations are high and the Secchi transparency is low (Table 4), indicating high concentrations of algae. In one study, the annual external supply of phosphorus to the lake was estimated to be 779 kg/year, or 0.22 g/m² of lake surface area (Table 5). Almost 60% of this phosphorus originates from cleared areas, many of which are agricultural, whereas only 23% comes from forested areas. The remaining 17% originates from urban runoff, precipitation, dustfall, inflow from upstream lakes and sewage from residential areas. The value for sewage was not measured directly; it was calculated from data collected for other Alberta lakes. In another study, the internal loading of phosphorus from the sediments was estimated. Water next to the sediments goes anoxic during stratified periods (Fig. 6) and total phosphorus and total dissolved phosphorus levels in the deeper water increase rapidly. A substantial amount of total phosphorus is released from the sediments: in 1982, it was estimated that 1 468 kg were released during stratified periods from May to November (Riley 1983; Riley and Prepas 1984). In the same study, terrestrial and atmospheric inputs for the period were estimated to be 82 kg (not including spring runoff). The estimated internal load calculated for the six summer months of 1982 is about twice that of the annual external load of 779 kg of phosphorus. In winter, the internal phosphorus load to the surface water is probably equal to that in summer. In March 1986, for example, total phosphorus levels under ice exceeded 100 μg/L (Prepas and Babin n.d.). Therefore, at least 80% of the annual loading of phosphorus to the surface waters originates from the lake sediments.

Total phosphorus concentrations of 100 to 200 μg/L in the euphotic zone are not uncommon in Nakamun Lake in late winter. These concentrations remain high after ice-out, as in May 1982 (Fig. 7). Algal biomass (measured as chlorophyll *a*) was very high in May 1982 as well, but decreased to relatively low levels during June (Fig. 7). Lower concentrations of phosphorus and extensive grazing by zooplankton may limit the algal population at this time. During July and August, recycling of phosphorus from the sediments and subsequent growth of blue-green algae, which may be inedible to zooplankton, turn the lake water to "pea soup". Most of the internal

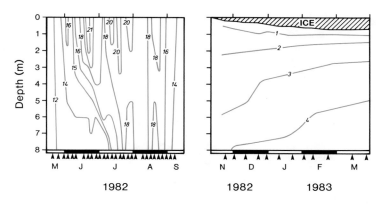

Figure 5. Temperature (°C) of Nakamun Lake, 1982 and 1983. Arrows indicate sampling dates.
SOURCES: Prepas and Babin n.d.; Riley 1983.

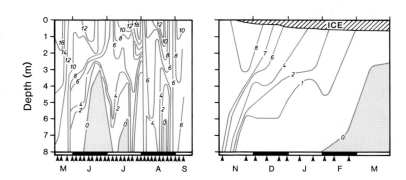

Figure 6. Dissolved oxygen (mg/L) in Nakamun Lake, 1982 and 1983. Arrows indicate sampling dates.
SOURCES: Riley 1983; Babin 1984.

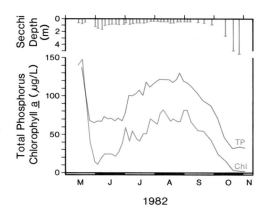

Figure 7. Total phosphorus, chlorophyll a and Secchi depth in Nakamun Lake, 1982.
SOURCE: Riley 1983.

Table 4. Nutrient, chlorophyll a and Secchi depth data for Nakamun Lake. Average concentrations in µg/L. Composite samples from the euphotic zone collected 36 times from 13 May to 12 Oct. 1982 and 7 times from 05 May to 18 Oct. 1983. S.E. = standard error.

	1982		1983[g]	
	Mean	S.E.	Mean	S.E.
total phosphorus	97[a]	4.1	80	11.2
total dissolved phosphorus	22[a, b]	0.7	28	3.1
soluble reactive phosphorus	56[c, d]	19.4	9	2.6
total Kjeldahl nitrogen	2 270[e, f]	106.1	1 609	212.2
$NO_3 + NO_2$–nitrogen	22[e, f]	4.3	20	7.2
NH_4–nitrogen	49[e, f]	10.9	67	20.8
iron	—	—	69	12.0
chlorophyll a	54.7[a]	5.37	33.8	18.20
Secchi depth (m)	0.8[a]	0.07	2.1	0.76

NOTES: [b]n = 30; [c]1980, n = 3; [e]n = 21
SOURCES: [a]Riley 1983; [d]Prepas 1983[b]; [f]Prepas and Babin n.d.; [g]Alta. Envir. n.d.[a], Naquadat station 01AL07BB2090

phosphorus load during stratified periods is total dissolved phosphorus, which is rapidly assimilated by algae when it is mixed into the surface water (Prepas 1983[b]; Riley and Prepas 1984). The amount and timing of phosphorus loading from the sediments varies considerably from year to year. Consequently, average total phosphorus and chlorophyll a levels during summer can vary considerably between years (Table 6). Between 1980 and 1987, average total phosphorus concentrations ranged from a minimum of 59 µg/L in 1987 to a maximum of 163 µg/L in 1981. During the same period, average chlorophyll a concentrations ranged from a minimum of 28 µg/L in 1985 to a maximum of 174 µg/L in 1981. These changes are probably due to weather patterns, but the precise aspects are not yet understood.

Biological Characteristics

Plants

The phytoplankton in Nakamun Lake was surveyed in 1978, 1979 and 1983 by Alberta Environment (Alta. Envir. n.d.[a]) and in 1982 by the University of Alberta (Riley 1983; Riley and Prepas 1984). In 1983, algal biomass averaged about 12 mg/L; the biomass remained

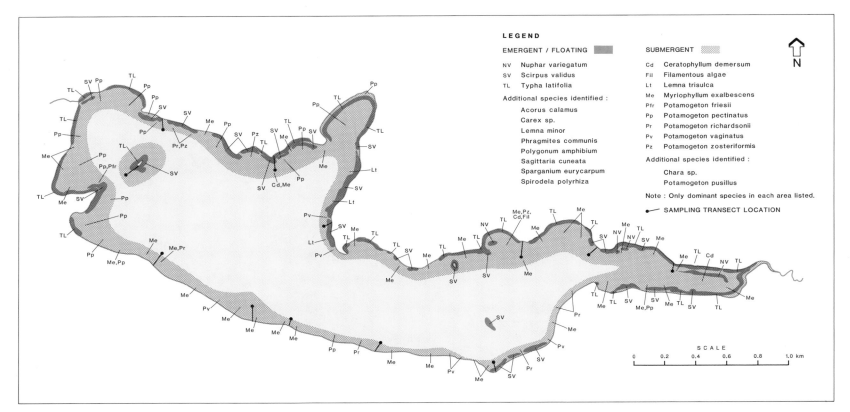

Figure 8. Species composition and distribution of aquatic macrophytes in Nakamun Lake, August 1984.
SOURCE: Stockerl and Kent 1984.

below 5 mg/L until late August, when it increased to almost 65 mg/L (Table 7). The biomass decreased to less than 8 mg/L during September. Cryptomonads (Cryptophyta) were the dominant group from early May to the end of June in 1983. The main species were *Cryptomonas rostratiformis* and *C. erosa reflexa* in May and *C. rostratiformis* and *C. Marsonii* in June. From late July through October, blue-greens (Cyanophyta) were the dominant group. The most important species were *Gloeotrichia echinulata* in late July, *Anabaena spiroides crassa*, *A. circinalis* and *Aphanizomenon flos-aquae* in late August, and *Oscillatoria agardhii* during September and October. High phosphorus concentrations and frequent periods when anoxic water overlies the bottom sediments contribute to the dominance of the algal community by blue-green algae (Trimbee and Prepas 1987; 1988).

Aquatic macrophytes were surveyed in 1979 and 1984 by Alberta Environment (Alta. Envir. n.d.[a]; Stockerl and Kent 1984). In 1984, 22 species were identified (Fig. 8). The dominant emergent species was common great bulrush (*Scirpus validus*) and the most abundant submergent species were northern watermilfoil (*Myriophyllum exalbescens*) and Sago pondweed (*Potamogeton pectinatus*). Three emergent species found in 1984—water smartweed (*Polygonum amphibium*), arrowhead (*Sagittaria cuneata*) and giant duckweed (*Spirodela polyrhiza*)—were not present in the 1979 samples. Similarly, two submergent species—stonewort (*Chara* sp.) and small-leaf pondweed (*Potamogeton pusillus*)—were not identified in 1979.

The distribution of emergent species underwent only minor changes between 1979 and 1984. Along the north shore, the most frequently occurring emergent species was common great bulrush, whereas common cattails (*Typha latifolia*) were dominant at the lake's east and west ends. Along the south shore, wave action and mechanical harvesting by cottage owners had considerably reduced the abundance of these plants. Submergent species grew densely along much of the shoreline, with the exception of the south shore. Between 1979 and 1984, northern watermilfoil replaced Richardson pondweed (*Potamogeton richardsonii*) and large-sheath pondweed (*P. vaginatus*) as the most common submergent species in many areas along the south shore. As well, northern watermilfoil was very abundant along the east half of the north shore in 1984. The

Table 5. Theoretical total phosphorus loading to Nakamun Lake from external sources.

Source		Phosphorus (kg/yr)	Percentage of Total
immediate watershed	forested/bush	182	23
	agricultural/cleared	454	58
	residential/cottage	30	4
sewage[a]		18	2
precipitation/dustfall		68	9
inflow from upstream lakes		27	4
	TOTAL	779	100
annual areal loading (g/m^2 of lake surface) 0.22			

NOTE: [a]unmeasured: assumes 4% of all sewage effluent from residences and camps enters the lake, as in Mitchell 1982
SOURCE: Mitchell 1988.

macrophyte communities of highly eutrophic lakes such as Nakamun are often dominated by only a few species.

Invertebrates

Data on zooplankton numbers are not available. *Bosmina longirostris* and either *Acanthodiaptomus denticornis* or *Diaptomus oregonensis* were very common in samples taken on 22 June 1981 by researchers with the University of Alberta (Prepas 1983[a]). *Mesocyclops edax* and *Acanthocyclops vernalis* were also present, but less abundant. The biomass of large plankton (greater than 250 μm) was more variable within a season and between years in Nakamun Lake than in 12 other central Alberta lakes (Prepas and Vickery 1984).

Benthic invertebrates were sampled by Alberta Environment in 1976 (Table 8). Aquatic earthworms (Oligochaeta) and midge larvae (Chironomidae) were most numerous and molluscs, phantom midges (*Chaoborus* sp.), roundworms (Nematoda) and water mites (Hydracarina) were present in lower numbers.

Table 6. A comparison of average summer chlorophyll *a* and total phosphorus concentrations in Nakamun Lake, 1980 to 1987. Composite samples from the euphotic zone collected from 17 June to 18 Sep. each summer. S.E. = standard error; n = sample size.

Year	n	Chlorophyll *a* (µg/L)	S.E.	Phosphorus (µg/L)	S.E.
1980[a]	4	41.7	8.5	155.4	39.8
1981[a]	3	173.6	43.2	162.6	41.0
1982[b]	23	56.4	3.8	105.2	4.0
1983[c]	3	54.3	43.4	77.9	21.1
1984[c]	3	43.5	15.8	83.0	7.2
1985[c]	3	27.5	2.6	—	—
1986[c]	4	50.8	17.6	95.8	13.8
1987[c]	3	35.5	16.6	58.7	14.3

SOURCES: [a]Prepas and Babin n.d.; [b]Riley 1983; [c]Alta. Envir. n.d.[a]

Table 7. Percentage composition of major algal groups by total biomass in Nakamun Lake, 1983. Composite samples collected from the euphotic zone.

ALGAL GROUP	03 May	31 May	28 June	27 July	24 Aug.	20 Sep.	18 Oct.
Total Biomass (mg/L)	4.89	2.03	1.21	2.77	64.82	7.73	3.04
Percentage Composition:							
Cyanophyta	0	0	7	46	99	94	97
				Gleotrichia	*Anabaena*	*Oscillatoria* ⟶	
Chlorophyta	2	0	0	8	0	5	2
Chrysophyta	2	1	0	10	0	0	1
Bacillariophyta	6	0	4	10	0	0	0
Cryptophyta	90	98	89	12	0	0	0
	Cryptomonas ⟶						
Pyrrhophyta	0	0	0	14	0	0	0

SOURCE: Alta. Envir. n.d.[a]

Fish

Nakamun Lake is managed by Fish and Wildlife Division for recreational fishing. Severe winterkills of fish were recorded in 1955, 1969, 1971 and 1974. In 1969, the owner of a private campground reported that 200 anglers who used the campground that year caught no fish, although fishing success had been moderate the previous year (Alta. For. Ld. Wild. n.d.). The lake was stocked with adult northern pike in 1969 and 1970, but the winterkills in 1971 and 1974 decimated the population. In 1989, yellow perch, large numbers of sticklebacks and minnows, and a few northern pike inhabited the lake and burbot had been reported (Watters 1989). The pike and burbot probably entered Nakamun Lake from Lac la Nonne during years when high water levels provided flow between the two lakes (Edm. Reg. Plan. Commis. 1979; Alta. Envir. 1985). The yellow perch originate from a stocking program implemented by Fish and Wildlife Division in 1984. A total of 13 550 adult and 20 000 subadult yellow perch were stocked between 1984 and 1986 (Berry 1988) and good catches of perch were reported during the winters from 1986/87 to 1988/89 (Watters 1989).

Wildlife

No specific data are available for the wildlife at Nakamun Lake, but shallow bays along the north and east shores are reported to support a variety of waterfowl species (Edm. Reg. Plan. Commis. 1979).

M.E. Bradford

Table 8. Nakamun Lake: Abundance of benthic invertebrates on April 1976. Samples collected with an Ekman dredge.

Invertebrate Group		Number/m²
Diptera:	Chaoborinae[a]	818
	Chironomidae	1 735
Mollusca		733
Oligochaeta		3 730
Nematoda		277
Hydracarina		98

NOTE: [a]*Chaoborus* sp.
SOURCE: Alta. Envir. n.d.[a]

References

Alberta Environment. n.d.[a]. Envir. Assess. Div., Envir. Qlty. Monit. Br. Unpubl. data, Edmonton.
———. n.d.[b]. Tech. Serv. Div., Hydrol. Br. Unpubl. data, Edmonton.
———. n.d.[c]. Tech. Serv. Div., Surv. Br. Unpubl. data, Edmonton.
———. 1985. Nakamun Lake. Poll. Contr. Div., Water Qlty. Contr. Br., Edmonton.
Alberta Forestry, Lands and Wildlife. n.d. Fish Wild. Div. Unpubl. data, Edmonton.
———. 1988. Boating in Alberta. Fish Wild. Div., Edmonton.
———. 1989. Guide to sportfishing. Fish Wild. Div., Edmonton.
Alberta Research Council. 1972. Geological map of Alberta. Nat. Resour. Div., Alta. Geol. Surv., Edmonton.
Babin, J. 1984. Winter oxygen depletion in temperate zone lakes. MSc thesis. Univ. Alta., Edmonton.
——— and E.E. Prepas. 1985. Modelling winter oxygen depletion rates in ice-covered temperate zone lakes in Canada. Can. J. Fish. Aquat. Sci. 42:239–249.
Berry, D. 1988. Alta. For. Ld. Wild., Fish Wild. Div., Edmonton. Pers. comm.
Edmonton Regional Planning Commission. 1979. Nakamun Lake; options for a management direction. Edm. Reg. Plan. Commis., Edmonton.

————. 1980. Nakamun Lake management plan alternatives. Edm. Reg. Plan. Commis., Edmonton.

————. 1981. Nakamun Lake area structure plan. Edm. Reg. Plan. Commis., Edmonton.

Energy, Mines and Resources Canada. 1975. National topographic series 1:50 000 83G/16 (1975). Surv. Map. Br., Ottawa.

Environment Canada. 1982. Canadian climate normals, Vol. 7: Bright sunshine (1951–1980). Prep. by Atm. Envir. Serv. Supply Serv. Can., Ottawa.

Geographic Board of Canada. 1928. Place-names of Alberta. Dept. Interior, Ottawa.

Mitchell, P.A. 1982. Evaluation of the "septic snooper" on Wabamun and Pigeon lakes. Alta. Envir., Poll. Contr. Div., Water Qlty. Contr. Br., Edmonton.

————. 1988. Alta. Envir., Envir. Assess. Div., Envir. Qlty. Monit. Br., Edmonton. Pers. comm.

Prepas, E.E. 1983[a]. The influence of phosphorus and zooplankton on chlorophyll levels in Alberta lakes. Prep. for Alta. Envir., Res. Mgt. Div. Rep. 83/23, Edmonton.

————. 1983[b]. Orthophosphate turnover time in shallow productive lakes. Can. J. Fish. Aquat. Sci. 40:1412–1418.

———— and J. Babin. n.d. Univ. Alta., Dept. Zool. Unpubl. data, Edmonton.

Prepas, E.E. and D.O. Trew. 1983. Evaluation of the phosphorus-chlorophyll relationship for lakes off the Precambrian Shield in western Canada. Can. J. Fish. Aquat. Sci. 40:27–35.

Prepas, E.E. and J. Vickery. 1984. The contribution of particulate phosphorus (>250 μm) to the total phosphorus pool in lake water. Can. J. Fish. Aquat. Sci. 41:351–363.

Riley, E.T. 1983. Internal phosphorus loading from the sediments and the phosphorus-chlorophyll model in shallow lakes. MSc thesis. Univ. Alta., Edmonton.

———— and E.E. Prepas. 1984. Role of internal phosphorus in two shallow, productive lakes in Alberta, Canada. Can. J. Fish. Aquat. Sci. 41:845–855.

Stockerl, E.C. and R.L. Kent. 1984. Aquatic macrophyte survey of Baptiste and Nakamun Lakes, 1984. Prep. for Alta. Envir., Poll. Contr. Div. by Okanagan Diving Serv. (ODS) Consult., Edmonton.

Strong, W.L. and K.R. Leggat. 1981. Ecoregions of Alberta. Alta. En. Nat. Resour., Resour. Eval. Plan. Div., Edmonton.

Trimbee, A.M. and E.E. Prepas. 1987. Evaluation of total phosphorus as a predictor of the relative biomass of blue-green algae with emphasis on Alberta lakes. Can. J. Fish. Aquat. Sci. 44:1337–1342.

————. 1988. The effect of oxygen depletion on the timing and magnitude of blue-green algal blooms. Verh. Internat. Verein. Limnol. 23:220–226.

Twardy, A.G. and L.K. Brocke. 1976. Soil survey and land suitability evaluation of the Sandy Lake-Nakamun Lake study area. Prep. for Alta. Envir. by Pedol. Consult., Edmonton.

Watters, D. 1989. Alta. For. Ld. Wild., Fish Wild. Div., Dist. Office, Edmonton. Pers. comm.

NARROW LAKE

MAP SHEET: 83I/12
LOCATION: Tp65 R24 W4
LAT/LONG: 54°35'N 113°37'W

Narrow Lake is a small, deep, picturesque lake in the County of Athabasca. It is located 25 km southwest of the town of Athabasca and 140 km north of the city of Edmonton. The closest population centre is Meanook, 19 km east of the lake. To reach Narrow Lake from Edmonton, drive north on Highway 2 to its junction with Secondary Road 663, which is just northwest of Meanook. Turn west onto Secondary Road 663 and drive for about 15 km, then turn north onto a municipal road and drive north for 3 km and west for 2 km until you reach the east side of the lake (Fig. 1).

The shoreline of Narrow Lake is owned by the Crown and is undeveloped except for two institutional camps. One camp, a Fish and Wildlife Division hunter-training facility, is located on the central part of the eastern shore, and the other, Camp Wright, an Air Cadet League of Alberta facility, is located at the southwest tip of the lake on land leased from the province (Fig. 2). There are no cottages or permanent residences on the shore. The only public access point is located south of the Fish and Wildlife Division camp. Facilities include a boat launch and picnic shelter. Recreational activities at the lake include swimming, fishing, canoeing and power boating; because of the rapidly sloping lake bottom and high banks, there is no shallow swimming beach. Although there are no specific boating or fishing regulations that apply to Narrow Lake, government regulations apply (Alta. For. Ld. Wild. 1988; 1989).

The water in Narrow Lake is clean and clear and suitable for recreation. The sport fish species in the lake are yellow perch and northern pike. Recreational fishing pressure is moderate. From 1983 through 1987, the lake was the centre of an intense research program on factors controlling water quality and community structure of aquatic plants and animals, based at the University of Alberta's Meanook Biological Station.

Drainage Basin Characteristics

Narrow is a headwater lake that flows into Long Lake, located 0.6 km to the south. Water flows between the two lakes only during spring snowmelt and unusually heavy summer storms (Prepas et al. n.d.). The drainage basin is small relative to the surface area of the lake (Tables 1, 2). Water enters Narrow Lake through runoff, precipitation and groundwater. The inflowing streams and lake outflow (Fig. 1) are dammed by beaver and flow intermittently. During the mid–1980s, researchers with the University of Alberta investigated groundwater seepage conditions at Narrow Lake (R. Shaw and Prepas 1989[a]; 1989[b]; R. Shaw et al. 1990). Data were collected from a drilling program, analyses of water chemistry, studies of environmental isotopes, computer simulations, calculations of a water budget, and measurements by mini-piezometers and seepage meters. Narrow Lake gains water through the nearshore region from a small, shallow groundwater flow system, whereas in deeper offshore regions, water may move from the lake into the groundwater system. Average groundwater seepage into Narrow Lake was estimated to be 0.28×10^6 m³/year, and the net seepage flux about 30% of the annual input of water to the lake. In the University of Alberta study, inflow from surface runoff was estimated to be 0.315×10^6 m³/year from 1983 to 1987 or 80% of the value provided by Alberta Environment in Table 1.

The topography of the land varies from nearly level (0 to 5% slope) to strongly rolling (15 to 30% slope). The drainage basin is

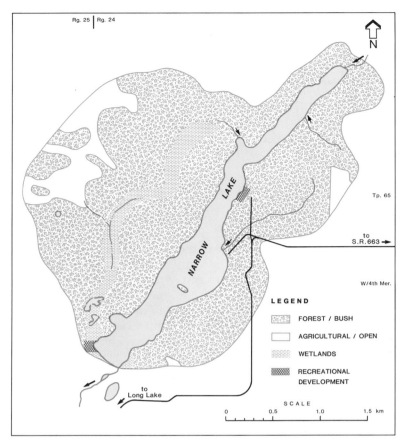

Figure 1. Features of the drainage basin of Narrow Lake.
SOURCES: Prepas et al. n.d.; En. Mines Resour. Can. 1973. Updated with 1987 aerial photos.

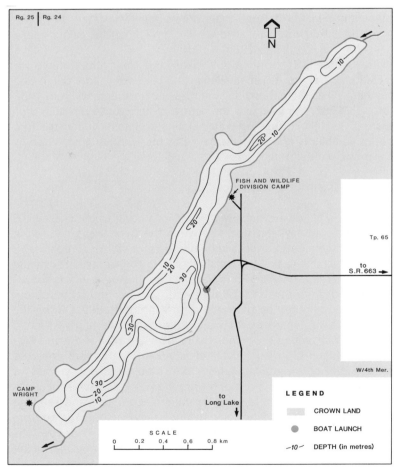

Figure 2. Bathymetry and shoreline features of Narrow Lake.
BATHYMETRY SOURCE: Prepas et al. n.d.

Table 1. Characteristics of Narrow Lake drainage basin.

area (excluding lake) (km²)[a]	7.17
soil[b]	Orthic Gray Luvisols, Fibrisols
bedrock geology[c]	Wapiti Formation (Upper Cretaceous): sandstone, mudstone, bentonite, scattered coal beds; nonmarine
terrain[b]	nearly level to strongly rolling
ecoregion[d]	Dry Mixedwood Subregion of Boreal Mixedwood
dominant vegetation[d]	trembling aspen
mean annual inflow (m³)[e, f]	0.394 x 10⁶
mean annual sunshine (h)[g]	2 160

NOTE: [f]excluding groundwater inflow, which is estimated to be 0.280 x 10⁶ m³/year
SOURCES: [a]Prepas et al. n.d.; [b]Kjearsgaard 1972; [c]Alta. Res. Counc. 1972; [d]Strong and Leggat 1981; [e]Alta. Envir. n.d.[a]; [g]Envir. Can. 1982

Table 2. Characteristics of Narrow Lake.

elevation(m)[a, b]	approximately 685
surface area(km²)[c, d]	1.14
volume(m³)[c, d]	16.4 x 10⁶
maximum depth(m)[c, d]	38
mean depth(m)[c, d]	14.4
shoreline length(km)[b]	9.4
mean annual lake evaporation(mm)[e]	638
mean annual precipitation(mm)[e]	505
mean residence time(yr)[e, f]	21.5
control structure	none

NOTES: [a]elevation on date of sounding not available; [d]on date of sounding: Aug. 1984; [f]excluding groundwater inflow
SOURCES: [b]En. Mines Resour. Can. 1973; [c]Prepas et al. n.d.; [e]Alta. Envir. n.d.[a]

part of the Dry Mixedwood Subregion of the Boreal Mixedwood Ecoregion (Strong and Leggat 1981) and the soils are mainly moderately well-drained Orthic Gray Luvisols that developed on glacial till (Kjearsgaard 1972). Extensive muskeg depressions are located throughout the drainage basin, particularly west of the lake. The soils in the level to depressional areas located throughout much of the western part of the watershed are very poorly drained Organics, primarily Fibrisols. The watershed is almost completely forested and the dominant vegetation on moderately well-drained soils is trembling aspen. White spruce, black spruce and willows grow in wetter areas, and birch are common near the lakeshore. The land is suitable only for pasture because of the topography and the poor quality, stony soil (Kjearsgaard 1972).

Lake Basin Characteristics

Narrow Lake is a small, deep lake (Table 2) that lies in an old glacial meltwater channel that is oriented in a northeast-southwest direction. The lake is situated in glacial drift, and sedimentary bedrock is located 5 to 10 m beneath the deepest part of the basin (Prepas et al. n.d.). Narrow Lake is about 4–km long and 0.6–km wide at its widest point. It is generally bordered by high banks with slopes of 15 to 30% (Alta. Mun. Aff. 1984). Two deep spots are located at the south end where the basin slopes steeply to a depth of more than 30 m (Fig. 2); the north end is shallower, with a maximum depth of about 20 m. The sediments in the littoral zone are mainly organic mud and sand, and fallen trees and shrubs are present in numerous areas around the shore. The lake bottom in deeper areas is composed of rich organic material (Prepas et al. n.d.).

The shoreline at the north end of the lake is dotted with beaver lodges. Since the recolonization of the area by beaver in the 1940s and 1950s, the lake level has risen. Consequently, many trees close to the shoreline have died. Long-term water level data are not

Table 3. Major ions and related water quality variables for Narrow Lake. Average concentrations in mg/L; pH in pH units. Composite samples from the euphotic zone collected 11 times from 17 May to 29 Aug. 1983. S.E. = standard error.

	Mean	S.E.
pH (range)	8.0–8.4	—
total alkalinity (CaCO$_3$)	155	1.0
specific conductivity (μS/cm)	286[a]	6.1
total dissolved solids	162[b]	2.3
turbidity (NTU)	1[c]	0.1
colour (Pt)	8[c]	1.4
total hardness (CaCO$_3$)	153[d]	—
particulate organic carbon	635[e]	27
HCO$_3$	188	0.8
CO$_3$	0.4	0.32
Mg	15[f]	—
Na	7[f]	—
K	3[f]	—
Cl	0.1[g]	0.02
SO$_4$	1[f]	—
Ca	35[f]	—

NOTES: [a] n = 10; [b] 1980, n = 3; [c] 1980, 1981, 1986, n = 3; [d] 1980, n = 1; [e] June to Aug. 1986, n = 6; [f] 1986, n = 1; [g] n = 8
SOURCE: Prepas et al. n.d.

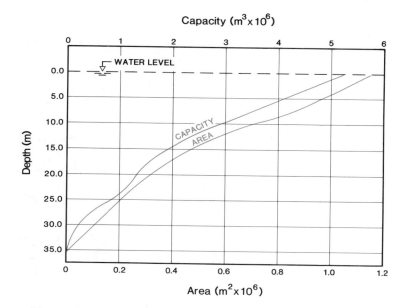

Figure 3. Area/capacity curve for Narrow Lake.
SOURCE: Prepas et al. n.d.

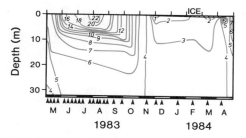

Figure 4. Temperature (°C) of Narrow Lake, 1983 and 1984. Arrows indicate sampling dates.
SOURCE: Prepas et al. n.d.

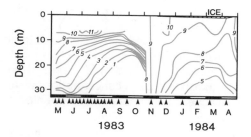

Figure 5. Dissolved oxygen (mg/L) in Narrow Lake, 1983 and 1984. Arrows indicate sampling dates.
SOURCE: Prepas et al. n.d.

available, but over the period of record (1985 to 1988), the lake level fluctuated by 0.55 m, from a minimum on 31 October 1985 to a maximum on 20 July 1986 (Alta Envir. n.d.[b]). Major fluctuations in lake level are controlled by unusually heavy rainstorms and destruction of the beaver dam on the lake outflow. Figure 3 illustrates changes in the lake's area and capacity with fluctuations in water level, based on the limited water level data available.

Water Quality

The water quality of Narrow Lake was monitored in 1980 and 1981, and in 1983, the lake was chosen for intensive, long-term study by researchers with the University of Alberta. It was chosen for study of internal factors controlling productivity in deep prairie-parkland lakes because of its size, relatively small and undisturbed drainage basin, and proximity to the Meanook Biological Station. The lake is unproductive compared to other prairie-parkland lakes in Alberta. Water quality studies have included work on the open water, the littoral zone, the bottom sediments and groundwater-lake interactions (Prepas et al. n.d.; Prepas 1983[a]; 1983[b]; Prepas and Trew 1983; Prepas and Vickery 1984[a]; 1984[b]; Hanson et al. 1988[a]; Prepas et al. 1988; Prepas and Trimbee 1988; Trimbee and Prepas 1988; J. Shaw and Prepas 1989[a]; 1989[b]; 1989[c]; 1989[d]; J. Shaw et al. 1989; R. Shaw and Prepas 1989[a]; R. Shaw et al. 1989; 1990).

Narrow Lake has well-buffered, moderately alkaline water (Table 3) that is often very clear. The dominant ions are calcium and bicarbonate. The water column becomes strongly thermally stratified soon after ice-out, and remains so throughout the summer (Fig. 4). Narrow Lake was only partially saturated with dissolved oxygen when it stratified in the spring of seven of the eight years from 1980 to 1987. The lake was not sampled in the third year, 1982. By August in all seven years, the dissolved oxygen concentrations in water near the deep sediments had decreased to less than 1 mg/L. Dissolved oxygen consumption rates may be a function of the extent of mixing, and thus aeration, during spring and fall turnover. The water column was well mixed in the fall of 1983 (Fig. 5), and the upper layers of water remained well-oxygenated under ice cover during the winter of 1983/84. Dissolved oxygen in the deeper water became depleted over the winter, and by April 1984, the concentration

ranged from 9 mg/L immediately under the ice to less than 5 mg/L near the sediments.

Based on maximum chlorophyll a concentrations, Narrow Lake is considered oligo-mesotrophic. During the open-water period in 1983, the highest concentrations of total phosphorus (16.5 μg/L) and chlorophyll a (5.5 μg/L) were recorded in May, and secondary values were recorded in mid-November (Fig. 6).

Nutrients in the hypolimnion of Narrow Lake increase during the summer and autumn. In 1983, total phosphorus concentrations over the deep sediments increased from 20 μg/L in mid-June to 250 μg/L in October. Total phosphorus concentrations in the surface waters, however, were low compared to other lakes in the region. The average total phosphorus concentration in the euphotic zone of Narrow Lake during the open-water period in 1983 was 12 μg/L (Table 4). From mid-June to mid-September, average total phosphorus and chlorophyll a concentrations in the euphotic zone vary little from year to year (Table 5). Over a seven-year period the average

Table 4. Nutrient, chlorophyll *a* and Secchi depth data for Narrow Lake. Average concentrations in μg/L. Composite samples from the euphotic zone collected 19 times from 05 May to 28 Sep. 1983 and 16 times from 12 May to 24 Aug. 1986. S.E. = standard error.

	1983		1986	
	Mean	S.E.	Mean	S.E.
total phosphorus	12	0.4	10[f]	0.6
total dissolved phosphorus	5[a]	0.3	5[g]	0.2
particulate phosphorus	—	—	5[h]	0.5
soluble reactive phosphorus	1[b]	—	—	—
total Kjeldahl nitrogen	599[c]	18.0	676[i]	42.0
$NO_3 + NO_2$–nitrogen	1[c]	0.2	15	1.3
NH_4–nitrogen	4[d]	1.2	4	0.8
particulate nitrogen	—	—	80[h]	4.9
iron	11[e]	—	45[j]	—
chlorophyll *a*	2.9	0.22	2.5[k]	0.18
Secchi depth (m)	5.1[c]	0.23	6.3[l]	0.33

NOTES: [a]May to Aug. 1984, n = 8; [b]28 July 1980, n = 1; [c]n = 14; [d]May to Aug. 1984, n = 9; [e]1985, n = 1; [f]n = 10; [g]n = 14; [h]n = 6; [i]May to July 1985, n = 5; [j]after a storm, n = 1; [k]n = 11; [l]n = 15
SOURCE: Prepas et al. n.d.

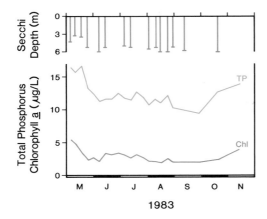

Figure 6. Total phosphorus, chlorophyll *a* and Secchi depth in Narrow Lake, 1983.
SOURCE: Prepas et al. n.d.

Table 5. A comparison of average summer chlorophyll *a* and total phosphorus concentrations in Narrow Lake, 1980, 1981 and 1983 to 1987. Composite samples collected from the euphotic zone from 16 June to 12 Sep. each summer. S.E. = standard error.

Year	n	Chl *a* (μg/L)	S.E.	TP (μg/L)	S.E.
1980	4	2.2	0.1	12.5	0.4
1981	1	3.0	—	11.8	—
1983	11	2.6	0.2	11.7	0.2
1984	7	1.9	0.2	10.9	1.0
1985	4	2.2	0	13.8	0.5
1986	9	2.8	0.1	10.6	0.6
1987	6	2.3	0.3	11.8	0.4

SOURCE: Prepas et al. n.d.

summer chlorophyll *a* concentration fluctuated by 1.1 μg/L and total phosphorus fluctuated by 3.2 μg/L. In 1984, the highest chlorophyll *a* concentrations were found below the epilimnion, at depths from 9 to 12 m. Total phosphorus and total nitrogen concentrations were not elevated at these depths relative to epilimnetic values, but nitrate plus nitrite concentrations were 5 to 10 times higher.

The loading of total phosphorus to Narrow Lake from various sources has been estimated. Groundwater inflow, which may be the single largest source of phosphorus to the lake, is estimated to contribute 43.0 mg/m² of phosphorus per year, whereas precipitation and dustfall contribute 20.3 mg/m² per year and runoff from the watershed contributes 8.0 mg/m² per year. Techniques for evaluating the release of phosphorus from the bottom sediments in Alberta lakes were developed at Narrow Lake. The phosphorus concentration in the porewater in the top 10 cm of the sediment in Narrow Lake were low relative to the eight other Alberta lakes studied. To a lake depth of 10 m, the average porewater soluble reactive phosphorus concentration was 68 μg/L.

Biological Characteristics

Plants

The phytoplankton in Narrow Lake was studied in detail from 1984 to 1986 (Prepas et al. n.d.; 1988). From year to year, variations occurred in the relative contributions of diatoms and blue-green algae to the algal peaks observed below the epilimnion, at depths of 9 to 12 m. In 1984, the greatest biomass at these depths consisted of two layers, an upper layer where the blue-green alga *Aphanizomenon flos-aquae* (Cyanophyta) was dominant, and a lower layer

where another blue-green species, *Oscillatoria limosa*, was dominant. In 1985, diatoms (Bacillariophyta) were more abundant than in 1984. The diatom *Asterionella formosa* was the dominant alga to a depth of 7 m and greatly contributed to the chlorophyll peak, which was observed at depths from 6 to 10 m and was dominated by *A. flos-aquae*. In both years, the production of new algal biomass was not confined to surface waters only, however, the maximum rates of production occurred above the depth of the blue-green algal maxima (9 to 12 m). The dominant species observed in 1986 included the blue-greens *Oscillatoria limnetica*, *Pseudoanabaena* sp. and *Aphanothece* sp., the diatoms *Synedra* sp. and *Navicula* sp., and unidentified flagellates.

The macrophyte community in Narrow Lake was studied in 1985 (Prepas et al. n.d.; Chambers and Prepas 1988). Plants grew to depths of 5 to 5.5 m and the distribution of the various species was very patchy. Overall, the submergent community was dominated by the macroalga stonewort (*Chara* sp.) and a carnivorous species, bladderwort (*Utricularia vulgaris*). Plant beds dominated by the aquatic fern quillwort (*Isoetes* sp.) were found in the north and central parts of the lake, and plant beds dominated by pondweeds (*Potamogeton* spp.), especially Richardson pondweed (*P. richardsonii*), were present throughout the lake. Emergent vegetation consisted of bulrush (*Scirpus* sp.) and several species of bur-reed (*Sparganium* spp.). A small patch of yellow water lily (*Nuphar variegatum*) was located near the public boat launch.

Invertebrates

The zooplankton community in Narrow Lake was sampled in 1981, 1983 and 1984 (Prepas et al. n.d.; Prepas 1983[a]; Prepas and

Table 6. Percentage of total biomass of macroinvertebrates in each depth zone of Narrow Lake, 1986. Samples taken biweekly from 13 May to 02 Sep. 1986. Values are seasonal means. Total samples analysed = 684. Arranged in taxonomic order. Tr = trace.

Taxa	Littoral (0–6.0 m)	Sublittoral (6.1–15.0 m)	Profundal (15.1–37.0 m)
Total Biomass (g/m² fresh wt)	14.06	5.93	2.20
Percentage Composition:			
Platyhelminthes	1.1	0	0
Nematophora	0.2	0.1	Tr
Annelida			
Oligochaeta	1.6	4.1	33.1
Hirudinea	2.1	0.4	0
Amphipoda	30.0	2.8	0
Hydracarina	0.2	0.1	Tr
Ephemeroptera	1.6	Tr	0
Odonata			
Anisoptera	4.6	0	0
Zygoptera	0.1	0	0
Megaloptera (*Sialis*)	0.1	0	0
Trichoptera	3.8	1.0	0
Coleoptera			
Chrysomelidae (*Donacia*)	0.3	0	0
others	0.1	0	0
Diptera			
Culicidae (*Chaoborus*)	0.1	2.8	17.9
Chironomidae	30.4	78.3	49.0
Ceratopogonidae	0.3	0.2	0
Tabanidae	0.1	0	0
Gastropoda	14.8	1.1	0
Pelecypoda			
Sphaeriidae	8.5	9.1	Tr

SOURCE: Hanson et al. n.d.

Vickery 1984[a]). In all years sampled, zooplankton peak biomass (57 mg/m³ dry weight in 1984) occurred at depths from 6 to 12 m. Like the algal peak, this peak was below the epilimnion. The dominant species in July 1981 were the large cladoceran, *Daphnia pulex*, and phantom midge larvae (Culicidae: *Chaoborus* sp.). The copepods *Diaptomus oregonensis*, *Mesocyclops edax*, *Diacyclops bicuspidatus thomasi* and *Acanthocyclops vernalis* were less abundant.

The benthic macroinvertebrate community of Narrow Lake was studied intensively during 1985 and 1986 (Hanson et al. n.d.; 1988[a]; 1988[b]; 1989[a]; 1989[b]). Total biomass was much higher in the littoral zone than in the sublittoral and profundal zones (Table 6). In terms of biomass, scuds (Amphipoda), midge larvae (Chironomidae) and snails (Gastropoda) were dominant in the littoral zone, whereas midge larvae were dominant in the sublittoral zone and midge larvae, phantom midge larvae (Culicidae: *Chaoborus* sp.), and aquatic earthworms (Oligochaeta) were the dominant macroinvertebrates in the profundal zone. Back swimmers (Hemiptera: Notonectidae) and mayflies (Ephemeroptera: *Leptophlebia* sp.) were very abundant near shore at ice-out. Unionid clams (*Anodonta grandis simpsoniana*) were found primarily in the littoral zone and reached a biomass of 124 g/m² (live weight). Field experiments in Narrow Lake suggested that the significantly slower growth rate of clams in Narrow Lake, compared with nearby Long Lake, results from cooler water temperatures in the littoral zone of Narrow Lake. Muskrats prey on unionid clams in Narrow Lake and discard the empty shells along the shoreline in piles called middens. In a one-year period (July 1986 to July 1987) muskrats ate 37 000 clams in the north basin of the lake. This represented 6% of the biomass of clams in the north basin and had a strong effect on the

size-structure of the clam population; muskrats ate the large, fast-growing clams.

Fish

Five species of fish are present in Narrow Lake: yellow perch and northern pike are most abundant, and burbot, Iowa darter and brook stickleback are present in smaller numbers. Fish and Wildlife Division stocked the lake with walleye eggs in 1955 and kokanee fingerlings in 1967, 1968 and 1969, but these introductions were not successful (Alta. For. Ld. Wild. n.d.). Neither species established a population in the lake, probably because of an absence of suitable spawning sites.

The fish community was studied by the University of Alberta from 1983 through 1988 (Abbey and Mackay n.d.; Hanson et al. n.d.). Young-of-the-year perch hatch at a length of 5.9 mm during the third week of May and attain an average length of 46 mm by early October. Growth of young perch in Narrow Lake is very slow compared to growth in three of the four other lakes studied in the Boyle-Athabasca region, and few individuals attain a length of 15 cm. The growth of northern pike has not been studied in detail, but pike greater than 80 cm in total length are rarely caught. Young pike (less than 50 mm in total length) prey on both invertebrates and vertebrates (yellow perch) in Narrow Lake (Chapman et al. 1989).

Wildlife

Narrow Lake does not appear to be extensively used by waterfowl. During the period from 1985 to 1987, two pairs of Common Loons successfully reared young on the lake and one pair of Belted King-fishers nested in the central basin. Common Goldeneye used nest boxes along the shore and several pairs of Mallards nested on float-ing grass mats in the south basin. During 1988, several pairs of Red-necked Grebes raised young in the south basin, and during the period from 1985 to 1988, at least one pair each of Goshawks and Great Horned Owls maintained territories around the northern basin (Hanson et al. n.d.).

Beaver and muskrats are present throughout the lake and mink are seen occasionally along the shore. Mule deer and white-tailed deer have sometimes been seen drinking from the lake. Coyotes are common in the area and black bears have occasionally been ob-served at a nearby land-fill site (Hanson et al. n.d.).

M.E. Bradford, E.E. Prepas and J.M. Hanson

References

Abbey, D. and W.C. Mackay. n.d. Univ. Alta. Unpubl. data, Edmonton.

Alberta Environment. n.d.[a]. Tech. Serv. Div., Hydrol. Br. Unpubl. data, Edmonton.
———. n.d.[b]. Tech. Serv. Div., Surv. Br. Unpubl. data, Edmonton.

Alberta Forestry, Lands and Wildlife. n.d. Fish Wild. Div. Unpubl. data, Edmonton.
———. 1988. Boating in Alberta. Fish Wild. Div., Edmonton.
———. 1989. Guide to sportfishing. Fish Wild. Div., Edmonton.

Alberta Municipal Affairs. 1984. County of Athabasca No. 12: Lake planning frame-work. Plan. Br., Edmonton.

Alberta Research Council. 1972. Geological map of Alberta. Nat. Resour. Div., Alta. Geol. Surv., Edmonton.

Chambers, P.A. and E.E. Prepas. 1988. Underwater spectral attenuation and its effect on the maximum depth of angiosperm colonization. Can. J. Fish. Aquat. Sci. 45:1010–1017.

Chapman, L.J., W.C. Mackay and C.W. Wilkinson. 1989. Feeding flexibility in north-ern pike (*Esox lucius*): Fish versus invertebrate prey. Can. J. Fish. Aquat. Sci. 46:666–669.

Energy, Mines and Resources Canada. 1973. National topographic series 1:50 000 83I/12 (1973). Surv. Map. Br., Ottawa.

Environment Canada. 1982. Canadian climate normals, Vol. 7: Bright sunshine (1951–1980). Prep. by Atm. Envir. Serv. Supply Serv. Can., Ottawa.

Hanson, J.M., W.C. Mackay and E.E. Prepas. n.d. Univ. Alta., Dept. Zool. Unpubl. data., Edmonton.
———. 1988[a]. The effects of water temperature and clam density on the growth of a unionid clam. Freshwater Biol. 19:345–355.
———. 1988[b]. Population size, growth, and production of a unionid clam, *Anodon-ta grandis simpsoniana*, in a small, deep, boreal forest lake in central Alberta. Can. J. Zool. 66:247–253.
———. 1989[a]. Effect of size-selective predation by muskrats (*Ondatra zebithicus*) on a population of unionid clams (*Anodonta grandis simpsoniana*). J. Animal Ecol. 58:15–28.

Hanson, J. M., E.E. Prepas and W.C. Mackay. 1989[b]. Size distribution of the macroinvertebrate community in a freshwater lake. Can. J. Fish. Aquat. Sci. 46:1510–1519.

Kjearsgaard, A.A. 1972. Reconnaissance soil survey of the Tawatinaw map sheet (83–I). Alta. Inst. Pedol. Rep. No. S–72–29 1972, Univ. Alta. Bull. No. SS–12. Univ. Alta., Edmonton.

Prepas, E.E., T.P. Murphy, A.M. Trimbee, R.D. Shaw and J.F.H. Shaw. n.d. Unpubl. data, Univ. Alta., Dept. Zool., Edmonton and Natl. Water Res. Inst., Burlington, Ontario.

Prepas, E.E. 1983[a]. The influence of phosphorus and zooplankton on chlorophyll levels in Alberta lakes. Prep. for Alta. Envir., Res. Mgt. Div. Rep. 83/23, Edmonton.
———. 1983[b]. Orthophosphate turnover time in shallow productive lakes. Can. J. Fish. Aquat. Sci. 40:1412–1418.
——— and D.O. Trew. 1983. Evaluation of the phosphorus-chlorophyll relationship for lakes off the Precambrian Shield in western Canada. Can. J. Fish. Aquat. Sci. 40:27–35.

Prepas, E.E. and J. Vickery. 1984[a]. The contribution of particulate phosphorus (>250 μm) to the total phosphorus pool in lake water. Can. J. Fish. Aquat. Sci. 41:351–363.
———. 1984[b]. Seasonal changes in total phosphorus and the role of internal loading in western Canadian lakes. Verh. Internat. Verein. Limnol. 22:303–308.

Prepas, E.E., M.E. Dunnigan and A.M. Trimbee. 1988. Comparison of *in situ* estimates of chlorophyll *a* obtained with Whatman GF/F and GF/C glass-fiber filters in mesotrophic to hypereutrophic lakes. Can. J. Fish. Aquat. Sci. 45:910–914.

Prepas, E.E. and A.M. Trimbee. 1988. Evaluation of indicators of nitrogen limitation in deep prairie lakes with laboratory bioassays and limnocorrals. Hydrobiologia 159:269–276.

Shaw, J.F.H. and E.E. Prepas. Exchange of phosphorus from shallow sediments at nine Alberta lakes. J. Envir. Qlty. [in press]
———. 1989[b]. Relationships between phosphorus in shallow sediments in the trophogenic zone of seven Alberta lakes. Water Res. [in press]
———. 1989[c]. Potential significance of phosphorus release from shallow sediments of deep Alberta lakes. ms submitted to Limnol. Oceanogr.
———. 1989[d]. Temporal and spatial patterns of porewater phosphorus in shallow sediments, and potential transport in Narrow Lake, Alberta. Can. J. Fish. Aquat. Sci. 46:981–988.

Shaw, J.F.H., R.D. Shaw and E.E. Prepas. 1989. Advective transport of phosphorus from lake bottom sediments into lakewater. ms to be submitted.

Shaw, R.D. and E.E. Prepas. 1989[a]. Groundwater-lake interactions: II. Nearshore seepage patterns and the contribution of groundwater to lakes in central Alberta. J. Hydrol. [in press]
———. 1989[b]. Anomalous short-term influx of water into seepage meters. Limnol. Oceanogr. 34:1343–1351.

Shaw, R.D., J.F.H. Shaw, H. Fricker and E.E. Prepas. 1990. An integrated approach to quantify groundwater transport of phosphorus to Narrow Lake, Alberta. Limnol. Oceanogr. [in press]

Shaw, R.D., A.M. Trimbee, A. Minty, H. Fricker and E.E. Prepas. 1989. Atmospheric deposition of phosphorus and nitrogen in central Alberta with emphasis on Nar-row Lake. Water, Air, and Soil Poll. 43:119–134.

Strong, W.L. and K.R. Leggat. 1981. Ecoregions of Alberta. Alta. En. Nat. Resour., Resour. Eval. Plan. Div., Edmonton.

Trimbee, A.M. and E.E. Prepas. 1988. Dependence of lake oxygen depletion rates on maximum oxygen storage in a partially meromictic lake in Alberta. Can. J. Fish. Aquat. Sci. 45:571–576.

ROCK LAKE

MAP SHEET: 83E/8
LOCATION: Tp52 R2 W6
LAT/LONG: 53°27'N 118°16'W

Rock Lake is a small, deep, very attractive lake situated in the front ranges of the Rocky Mountains. It is located in Improvement District No. 14, 75 km northwest of the town of Hinton, 4 km north of Jasper National Park and 1 km east of Willmore Wilderness Park (Fig. 1). Well-defined trails into these areas begin near Rock Lake, so the lake is an excellent staging area for back-country hiking and horseback trips. To reach the lake from Hinton, take Highway 16 southwest for 8 km to its junction with Highway 40. Travel north for 37 km on Highway 40, then travel west for 32 km on an all-season gravel road that leads directly into Rock Lake Forest Recreation Area. The road usually is not ploughed to the lake in winter.

The lake's name originates from an Indian legend about a banished Stoney Medicine Man who kidnapped a Dog Rib maiden by changing her into a dog. Before he attempted to rejoin his tribe, the Medicine Man returned the maiden to human form but stole her power of speech. His tribe thought him clever when he told them of his "rescue" of the maiden, and they allowed him to stay. Soon after, a Dog Rib warrior—the maiden's betrothed—entered the camp and tricked the Medicine Man into returning the maiden's speech. After she told the true story, the Stoney chief ordered the Medicine Man bound and weighted with a heavy rock, then thrown into the lake (Alta. Cult. Multicult. n.d.).

Rock Lake Forest Recreation Area is an Alberta Forest Service campground located on the northern and eastern shores of the lake. It is open from 15 May to 15 September and offers 86 campsites, 11 remote tenting sites, 18 picnic sites, 2 picnic shelters, pump water, 2 boat launches and a pier. Back-country horseback trips can be staged from the northern end of the recreation area, where there is limited grazing and a place to park vehicles and horse trailers.

The main recreational activities at Rock Lake are camping and sport fishing. The unspoiled surroundings, private campsites and mountain setting make the lake a popular destination, especially for weekend campers from the Edmonton area. No water skiing or towing of surfboards is allowed on the lake (Alta. For. Ld. Wild. 1988). The water is clear and aquatic vegetation is minimal. The main sport fish species are lake trout, mountain whitefish and northern pike; bull trout and rainbow trout are caught less frequently. Fishing for bait fish and the use of bait fish in Rock Lake are not allowed (Alta. For. Ld. Wild. 1989).

Drainage Basin Characteristics

Rock Lake's drainage basin covers a large area that is more than 160 times the size of the lake (Tables 1, 2). It extends far back into the mountains and reaches altitudes greater than 2 700 m (Fig. 1). Except for the land immediately surrounding the lake, the watershed is undeveloped and lies entirely within Jasper National Park and Willmore Wilderness Park. The lake basin was formed during the retreat of the Wisconsin glaciers about 12 000 years ago, and continuous erosion and mountain uplift have contributed to the topography of the area. Three permanent streams enter the lake. Rock Creek, which flows into the western side, provides the majority of the inflow (Lane 1969). The outlet is a fork of the Wildhay River, which eventually drains into the Athabasca River.

The land close to the lake is part of the Subalpine Ecoregion (Strong and Leggat 1981). The topography in this area is characterized by a broad, open meadow west of the lake, a forested mountain

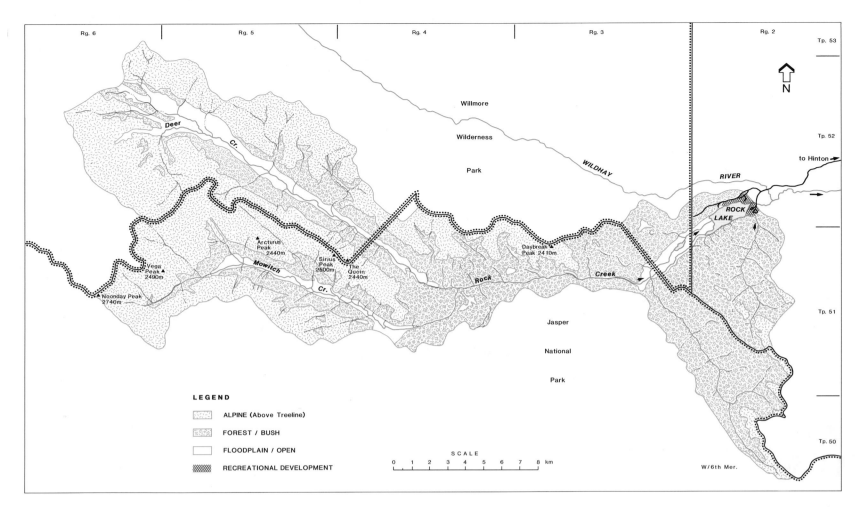

Figure 1. Features of the drainage basin of Rock Lake.
SOURCES: Alta. Envir. n.d.[a]; Govt. Can. 1960; 1962; En. Mines Resour. Can. 1981. Updated with 1985 aerial photos.

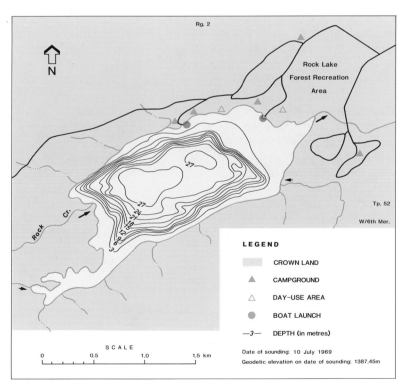

Figure 2. Bathymetry and shoreline features of Rock Lake.
BATHYMETRY SOURCE: Alta. Envir. n.d.[b].

slope near the southern shore and high, open hillsides north of the lake (Miller and Paetz 1952). The main soils in the Subalpine Ecoregion are Eutric Brunisols, and the dominant trees are Engelmann spruce and lodgepole pine. Limber pine, black and white spruce, and Douglas fir are less common and deciduous species such as trembling aspen are present only on the warmest sites.

The Alpine Ecoregion is situated above the forest-line, which is located at elevations of approximately 1 980 to 2 135 m (Strong and Leggat 1981). Above the forest-line, the contiguous forest stops and isolated stands of trees begin. Soils are poorly developed, and vegetation varies with the substrate and amount of protection from the harsh environment. Glaciers are bare of vegetation, whereas rock fields support crustose lichens, most commonly *Rhizocarpon* spp. and *Omphaldiscus* spp. Alpine fir, Engelmann spruce, whitebark pine and alpine larch are the common trees. They are deformed and stunted and grow only on protected sites. Willows grow on Gleysolic or Regosolic soils in wetter areas and heath (*Phyllodoce* spp.), *Kobresia* spp. and fescue communities are present on moderately well-drained Brunisolic soils.

Lake Basin Characteristics

Rock Lake is a small water body that is relatively deep for its size (Table 2, Fig. 2). The lake's maximum depth of 27.8 m is located in the centre of the single basin. The northern and southern shores are rocky and the sides of the basin slope steeply, whereas the eastern and western ends are quite shallow. The bottom substrate in most areas, to a depth of approximately 10 m, is rich in organic matter, with numerous sand and gravel bars. At the eastern end the bottom is sandy (Miller and Paetz 1952; Lane 1969).

The elevation of Rock Lake was recorded once in each of 1968, 1971, 1972 and 1973, and has been monitored regularly since 1974 (Fig. 3). The difference between the historic maximum (1 387.82 m) and minimum (1 386.92 m) observed levels is 0.90 m. This range in

Table 1. Characteristics of Rock Lake drainage basin.

area (excluding lake) (km²)[a]	348
soil[b]	Eutric Brunisols (Subalpine) and Brunisols (Alpine)
bedrock geology[c]	Mississippian Period (Upper Paleozoic): shale, siltstone, limestone, dolomite, anhydrite, sandstone Pennsylvanian-Permian Period (Upper Paleozoic): sandstone, siltstone, dolomite, carbonate
terrain[b]	mountainous
ecoregion[b]	Subalpine; Alpine
dominant vegetation[b]	lodgepole pine, Engelmann spruce; heath
mean annual inflow (m³)[a,d]	70.6 x 10⁶
mean annual sunshine (h)[e]	2 056

NOTE: [d]excluding groundwater inflow
SOURCES: [a]Alta. Envir. n.d.[a]; [b]Strong and Leggat 1981; [c]Alta. Res. Counc. 1972; [e]Envir. Can. 1982

Table 2. Characteristics of Rock Lake.

elevation (m)[a, b]	1 387.48
surface area (km²)[a, b]	2.15
volume (m³)[a, b]	26.1 x 10⁶
maximum depth (m)[a, b]	27.8
mean depth (m)[a, b]	12.1
shoreline length (km)[c]	8.0
mean annual lake evaporation (mm)[d]	621
mean annual precipitation (mm)[d]	513
mean residence time (yr)[d, e]	0.4
control structure	none

NOTES: [a] on date of sounding: 10 July 1968; [e] excluding groundwater inflow
SOURCES: [b] Alta. Envir. n.d.[b]; [c] En. Mines Resour. Can. 1981; [d] Alta. Envir. n.d.[a].

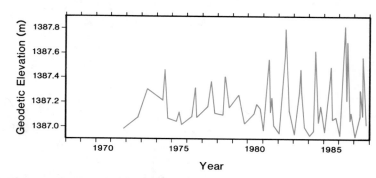

Figure 3. Water level of Rock Lake, 1968 to 1987.
SOURCE: Alta. Envir. n.d.[b].

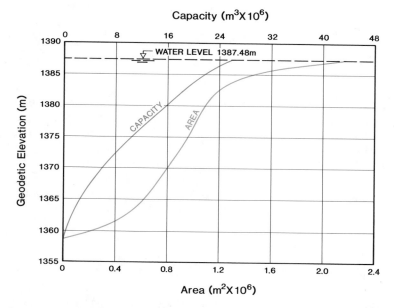

Figure 4. Area/capacity curve for Rock Lake.
SOURCE: Alta Envir. n.d.[b].

lake levels would result in a fluctuation of about 0.3 km² of the lake's area (Fig. 4).

Water Quality

Water quality data for Rock Lake are limited. Fish and Wildlife Division conducted brief surveys in 1952 and 1968 (Miller and Paetz 1952; Lane 1969). Rock Lake has well-buffered, fresh water. In 1968, the ice left the lake on 30 May. By early June, when the water was very turbid because of turnover and spring runoff, the Secchi transparency was only 0.8 m. By August, the Secchi depth had increased to 4.1 m.

Rock Lake is quite deep, but the water column does not become thermally stratified until late in the ice-free period. In 1968, the lake was isothermal in June but a thermocline was present in early August (Fig. 5). After turnover in June, the dissolved oxygen concentration was only 6 mg/L throughout the water column (Fig. 5). By August, the dissolved oxygen concentration in water near the sediments had declined slightly to 5 mg/L.

Data to determine the trophic status of Rock Lake are not available, but it is likely that the lake is relatively unproductive.

Biological Characteristics

Plants

No quantitative data are available for the plant community. Net plankton samples were taken in August 1952 and June and August 1968 (Miller and Paetz 1952; Lane 1969). Both studies reported very low concentrations of algae. In 1968, aquatic macrophytes grew densely at the shallow southwest end of the lake, but density was

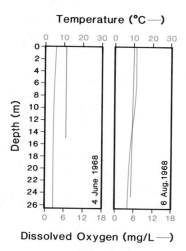

Figure 5. Temperature and dissolved oxygen in Rock Lake, 1968.
SOURCE: Lane 1969.

quite low in other shallow areas. The most common submergent plants were northern watermilfoil (*Myriophyllum exalbescens*) and pondweeds (*Potamogeton* spp.).

Invertebrates

No quantitative data are available for the zooplankton community. Net plankton samples were taken in 1952 and 1968 and relative abundance was determined (Miller and Paetz 1952; Lane 1969).

Table 3. Estimated angler numbers, effort and harvest from Rock Lake.
Estimates based on creel survey data collected from 01 June to 21 Sep.
1979. A total of 66 weekdays and 30 weekend days were surveyed; 26
days were not included. LT = lake trout; MW = mountain whitefish; NP
= northern pike.

	LT	MW	NP	Other[e]	Total
number of anglers	—	—	—	—	1 583
angler-hours	—	—	—		4 538
total number fish harvested[a]	349	281	57	65	750
total yield (kg)	207	254	—		—
mean weight (g)	594[c]	904[d]	—	—	—
catch/angler-hour[b]	0.08	0.06	0.01	0.02	0.17

NOTES: [a]based on observed no. fish caught: LT = 123, MW = 99, NP = 20, bull
trout = 7, rainbow trout = 6, unidentified fish = 10; [b]observed no. anglers =
572, observed hours = 1 565; [c]n = 6; [d]n = 12; [e]includes rainbow trout, bull
trout and unidentified fish
SOURCE: Mentz 1980

Benthic invertebrates were also sampled during these studies. In
1968, the average standing crop of benthos was estimated to be 8.7
kg/ha (dry weight), which is a relatively high biomass for an unproductive lake. Numerically, 37% of the organisms were midge larvae
(Chironomidae), 31% were aquatic earthworms (Oligochaeta) and
27% were molluscs (Sphaeriidae). Most organisms were found at
depths of less than 10 m. Only midges, molluscs and aquatic earthworms were found at greater depths; 72% of the worms were found
between 20 and 27 m.

Fish

Eight species of fish have been caught in Rock Lake: mountain
whitefish, lake trout, bull trout, northern pike, longnose sucker,
burbot, spoonhead sculpin and finescale dace (Miller and Paetz
1952; Lane 1969; Hunt 1989). Other species—white sucker, rainbow trout and yellow perch—have been reported but not confirmed.
In 1983, 1986 and 1987 the lake was stocked with 7 000 lake trout
(Alta. En. Nat. Resour. 1983; Alta. For. Ld. Wild. 1986; 1987). Rock
Lake is managed as a recreational fishery, and there is no commercial
or domestic fishery present.

The most abundant of five species caught in a 1968 test netting
were primarily mountain whitefish (63%) and secondarily lake trout
(27%), whereas in a 1979 creel survey, lake trout accounted for
47% of the catch and mountain whitefish accounted for 37% (Lane
1969; Mentz 1980). The largest whitefish taken in 1968 weighed
almost 1.5 kg and was estimated to be 16 years old. The size-at-age
of 5–year–old Rock Lake mountain whitefish in 1968 (29.5 cm) was
considerably greater than whitefish of the same age from Crowsnest
Lake (21.3 cm), Lake Louise (18.0 cm) and Waterton Lake (22.6 cm).

Most angling at Rock Lake takes place during the summer
months, with peak pressure from 15 August to 15 September (Hunt
1989). Winter angling pressure is low because access is difficult.
During 1979, it was estimated from creel survey data that 1 583
anglers visited the lake from 1 June to 21 September and spent 4 538
hours fishing (Table 3). The preferred catches were mountain white-

fish and lake trout. Approximately 90% of the anglers interviewed
thought that catch rates were poor and the fish were small. Most
anglers (75%) travelled 320–480 km to visit the lake; many of these
people came from the Edmonton area (Mentz 1980). Lake trout
spawning areas in Rock Lake have not been confirmed, but preliminary surveys in 1977 and 1978 found only marginal spawning
habitat. This suggests that suitable spawning habitat could be a
limiting factor to lake trout production. The success of lake trout
stocking in the 1980s had not been evaluated by 1989, but reports
by Fish and Wildlife Division staff suggested that there had been no
improvement in the fishery. In 1989, a lake trout management
proposal for Rock Lake was completed, and the recommendations
were being reviewed (Hunt 1989).

Wildlife

Information about the wildlife at Rock Lake is limited. The lake is not
extensively used by waterfowl because of late ice breakup in spring
and early freeze-up in fall. Waterfowl that have been sighted on the
lake include Mallards, Common Goldeneye and Canada Geese. Elk
are the most numerous ungulate in the area. They use the hills north
of the lake as a winter range, as do moose, mule deer and white-
tailed deer. Bighorn sheep and mountain goats inhabit Willmore
Wilderness Park, and black bears, grizzlies and wolverines are
present in the drainage basin (Smith 1989).

M.E. Bradford

References

Alberta Culture and Multiculturalism. n.d. Hist. Resour. Div., Hist. Sites Serv. Unpubl.
    data, Edmonton.
Alberta Energy and Natural Resources. 1983. Fish planting list. Fish Wild. Div., Ed-
    monton.
Alberta Environment. n.d.[a]. Tech. Serv. Div., Hydrol. Br. Unpubl. data, Edmonton.
———. n.d.[b]. Tech. Serv. Div., Surv. Br. Unpubl. data, Edmonton.
Alberta Forestry, Lands and Wildlife. 1986, 1987. Fish planting list. Fish Wild. Div.,
    Edmonton.
———. 1988. Boating in Alberta. Fish Wild. Div., Edmonton.
———. 1989. Guide to sportfishing. Fish Wild. Div., Edmonton.
Alberta Research Council. 1972. Geological map of Alberta. Nat. Resour. Div., Alta.
    Geol. Surv., Edmonton.
Energy, Mines and Resources Canada. 1981. National topographic series
    1:50 000 83E/8 (1981). Surv. Map. Br., Ottawa.
Environment Canada. 1982. Canadian climate normals, Vol. 7: Bright sunshine
    (1951–1980). Prep. by Atm. Envir. Serv. Supply Serv. Can., Ottawa.
Government of Canada. 1960. National topographic series 1:50 000 83E/7 E & W.
    Army Surv. Establishment, R.C.E., Ottawa.
———. 1962. National topographic series 1:50 000 83E/10 E & W. Dept. Mines
    Tech. Surv., Surv. Map. Br., Ottawa.
Hunt, C. 1989. Lake trout management proposal for Rock Lake. Alta. For. Ld. Wild.,
    Fish Wild. Div. Unpubl. rep., Edson.
Lane, C.B. 1969. The limnology and fishery management of Rock Lake, Alberta. Alta.
    Ld. For., Fish Wild. Div., Surv. Rep. No. 8, Edmonton.
Mentz, E. 1980. Rock Lake creel survey, June 1 to September 21, 1979. Alta. En. Nat.
    Resour., Fish Wild. Div. Unpubl. rep., Edmonton.
Miller, R.B. and M.J. Paetz. 1953. Preliminary biological surveys of Alberta water-
    sheds, Vol. II: 1950–1952. Alta. Ld. For., Fish Wild. Div., Edmonton.
Smith, K. 1989. Alta. For. Ld. Wild., Fish Wild. Div., Edson. Pers. comm.
Strong, W.L. and K.R. Leggat. 1981. Ecoregions of Alberta. Alta. En. Nat. Resour.,
    Resour. Eval. Plan. Div., Edmonton.

STEELE LAKE
(Cross Lake)

MAP SHEET: 83I/12
LOCATION: Tp65 R25, 26 W4
LAT/LONG: 54°39'N 113°46'W

Steele Lake is a very quiet and pretty lake set in one of the best examples of boreal northern forest close to a major population centre. It is located in Improvement District No. 17, about 180 km north of the city of Edmonton. To reach Steele Lake from Edmonton, drive 150 km north on Highways 2, 18 and 44 until you are just beyond the hamlet of Fawcett, turn east on Secondary Road 663 and drive for about 17 km, then turn north and drive for 10 km to reach Cross Lake Provincial Park. The park was established on the west side of the lake in 1955 (Alta. Rec. Parks n.d.). By 1985 it had expanded to its present size of 2 076 ha (Fig. 1). It completely surrounds the lake and offers a 90–site campground, a group camping area, pump water, a day-use area, picnic shelters, sewage disposal facilities, a boat launch, a playground and a beach (Alta. Hotel Assoc. 1989). Although winter camping is permitted, no services are available.

The lake was first named Cross Lake for its shape and it is still called that locally. It was renamed Steele Lake for Ira John Steele DLS, a soldier killed in World War I (Holmgren and Holmgren 1976; Boyd and Cochrane 1981). There was some attempt to farm in the area in the 1940s, but the land and climate were not suitable and few homesteaders remained. Fur farming, trapping and hunting are the most prevalent land uses now (Alta. Rec. Parks n.d.).

The lake is popular for boating in summer and angling for pike and yellow perch year-round. All boats are prohibited in some posted areas of the lake and motor boats are restricted to 12 km/hour in other posted areas (Alta. For. Ld. Wild. 1988). All inlet streams to and all outlet streams from Steele Lake are closed to fishing for a designated period during April and May to protect spawning fish. As well, fishing within 25 m of the fishway is prohibited year-round (Alta. For. Ld. Wild. 1989). The lake water is attractively clear in the early summer, but algal blooms discourage swimmers by early August in most years.

Steele Lake is in an area of northern boreal forest that offers an excellent opportunity for birdwatchers and nature enthusiasts to see species and habitats not seen in more southerly parts of the province. Forty-three plant communities have been identified within the provincial park, as have 212 species of vascular plants, 26 species of mosses, 25 species of lichens, 5 species of amphibians, 139 species of birds and 20 species of mammals (Peters and Nalte 1973; Luck 1981[a]; 1981[b]; Finlay and Finlay 1987).

Drainage Basin Characteristics

The Steele Lake drainage basin is very large compared to that of many Alberta lakes; it is 37 times the area of the lake (Tables 1, 2). The basin lies in the Boreal Mixedwood Ecoregion; the area south of the lake is in the Dry Mixedwood Subregion and the area north of the lake is in the Moist Mixedwood Subregion (Strong and Leggat 1981). Most of the basin is flat to depressional with numerous hummocky peat bogs where the vegetation is typically black spruce, tamarack, Labrador tea and *Sphagnum* moss, with areas of open bog where marsh marigolds are delightful in the spring. Soils here are Mesisols and Fibrisols (Kjearsgaard 1972; Greenlee 1975). Examples of this habitat are found immediately south of Steele Lake and in the low area extending northeast of the lake. The basin also includes areas of higher ground on undulating or gently rolling glacial till where the vegetation is primarily trembling aspen with some willow, balsam poplar, white birch and a few jack pine and white spruce.

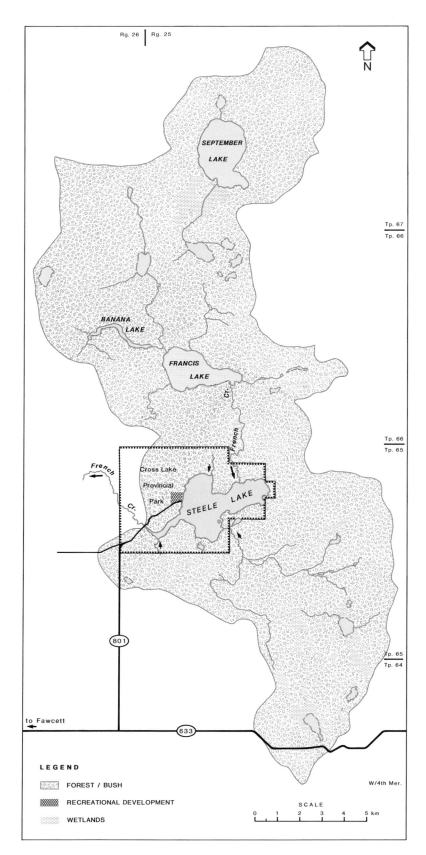

Figure 1. Features of the drainage basin of Steele Lake.
SOURCES: Alta. Envir. n.d.[c]; En. Mines Resour. Can. 1973. Updated with 1985 aerial photos.

Soils on these uplands are Orthic Gray Luvisols with areas of Eluviated Eutric Brunisols (Kjearsgaard 1972; Greenlee 1975). The campground in the provincial park is a good example of this habitat; similar areas interspersed with bogs are found north of Steele Lake. A large area north of the lake was burned in 1968 (Alta. Rec. Parks n.d.).

The basin is almost entirely uncleared and undeveloped except for parts of the provincial park. Less than 1% of the basin has been cleared for buildings, roads or agriculture, 9% is covered by water bodies including Steele Lake, and 90% is forest and bog.

Table 1. Characteristics of Steele Lake drainage basin.

area (excluding lake) (km²)[a]	255
soil[b]	Mesisols, Fibrisols, Orthic Gray Luvisols
bedrock geology[c]	Wapiti Formation (Upper Cretaceous): sandstone, mudstone, bentonite, scattered coal beds; nonmarine
terrain[b]	level to depressional
ecoregion[d]	Boreal Mixedwood: Dry Mixedwood Subregion to south and Moist Mixedwood Subregion to north
dominant vegetation[d]	trembling aspen/white spruce on uplands, blackspruce/tamarack or *Sphagnum* in lowlands
mean annual inflow (m³)[a, e]	12.1 x 10⁶
mean annual sunshine (h)[f]	2 160

NOTE: [e]excluding groundwater inflow
SOURCES: [a]Alta. Envir. n.d.[c]; [b]Kjearsgaard 1972; [c]Alta. Res. Counc. 1972; [d]Strong and Leggat 1981; [f]Envir. Can. 1982

Table 2. Characteristics of Steele Lake.

elevation (m)[a]	656.20 to 657.35
surface area (km²)[b, c]	6.61
volume (m³)[b, c]	20.9 x 10⁶
maximum depth (m)[b, c]	6.1
mean depth (m)[b, c]	3.2
shoreline length (km)[d]	18.2
mean annual lake evaporation (mm)[e]	638
mean annual precipitation (mm)[e]	517
mean residence time (yr)[e, f]	2
control structure[g]	sheet-pile weir with step-pool fishway
weir height (m)[g]	1.6

NOTES: [a]range over period of water level record; elevation on date of sounding is not available; [b]on date of sounding: July 1961; [f]excluding groundwater inflow
SOURCES: [c]Alta. Envir. n.d.[d]; [d]En. Mines Resour. Can. 1973; [e]Alta. Envir. n.d.[c]; [g]Alta. Envir. n.d.[a]

French Creek, the major inlet stream to the lake, enters at the east end of the north shore (Fig. 1). Other smaller streams enter the south and north shores and groundwater probably flows into the lake as well (Borneuf 1973). The outlet, also called French Creek, leaves at the end of the narrow southwest arm of the lake, and flows into the Pembina River, which then joins the Athabasca River.

Lake Basin Characteristics

Steele Lake is a large, cross-shaped lake set in a shallow depression. The lake basin slopes gently to a maximum depth of 6.1 m in the centre and in the northeast arm (Fig. 2). Much of the lakeshore is sandy (Alta. For. Ld. Wild. n.d.) and a beach has been developed near the campground.

The water level of the lake is quite variable (Fig. 3). Between 1975 and 1987 there was a 1.2–m difference between the extreme high level and the extreme low level. Alberta Environment built a sheet-pile weir across the outlet in 1974 to stabilize the lake's elevation, but beaver dams upstream of the weir now also have an influence (Lindner 1988). The weir is equipped with a step-pool fishway that allows the outflowing water to drop in a number of small steps rather than in one large cascade. Small pools (approximately 1 m² in area) between the steps allow fish ascending the fishway to rest between jumps. From 1976 to 1985, the annual average fluctuation in lake levels was about 0.5 m. Figure 4 shows how the area and capacity of Steele Lake would change with a change in lake elevation.

The large drainage basin provides abundant runoff to the lake and the residence time of the water is approximately two years (Table 2),

Table 3. Major ions and related water quality variables for Steele Lake. Average concentrations in mg/L; pH in pH units. Composite samples from the euphotic zone collected 3 times from 05 May to 27 Sep. 1983 and once on each of 27 May and 15 July 1985. S.E. = standard error.

	Mean	S.E.
pH (range)	7.8–8.4	—
total alkalinity ($CaCO_3$)	123	20.7
specific conductivity (µS/cm)	274	5.0
total dissolved solids (calculated)	145	2.4
total hardness ($CaCO_3$)	129	4.6
HCO_3	174	3.3
CO_3	<1	—
Mg	10	0.5
Na	5	0.2
K	2	0.5
Cl	<2	—
SO_4	<5	—
Ca	36	1.1

SOURCE: Alta. Envir. n.d.[b], Naquadat station 01AL07BC1000

which is shorter than the residence time of most lakes in central Alberta (Mitchell 1986).

Water Quality

The water quality of Steele Lake has been monitored jointly since 1983 by Alberta Environment and Alberta Recreation and Parks (Alta. Envir. n.d.[b]).

Steele is a freshwater lake. It is well buffered, and calcium and bicarbonate ions strongly dominate the chemical composition (Table 3). The lake is shallow enough to mix vertically most of the summer. The water temperature in summer is usually uniform from the lake surface to the bottom, and although dissolved oxygen becomes depleted in the lower strata, there was sufficient dissolved oxygen for fish on all summer sampling dates. In March 1985 and in January 1987, the water was anoxic below 4.5 m (Fig. 5). In most winters, the dissolved oxygen concentration remains high enough to over-winter fish; however, severe fish kills have occurred in some years (Alta. For. Ld. Wild. n.d.).

Steele Lake is hyper-eutrophic, as indicated by a mean summer phosphorus concentration of 64 µg/L and a mean summer chlorophyll a concentration of 25 µg/L (Table 4). Phosphorus levels were lowest in May in all years monitored and increased only slightly through June (Fig. 6). Chlorophyll a concentrations were also low at this time and the water was clear. In July and August, when the dissolved oxygen concentration was low and the temperature was high even at the lake bottom, phosphorus was released from the sediment. This stimulated algal production and reduced water clarity. During the summers of 1983 through 1986, the highest chlorophyll a concentration was 105 µg/L on 18 August 1985; the Secchi depth at this time was only 0.75 m (Alta. Envir. n.d.[b]). On 2 August 1985, campers noticed many dead bats and ducks lying on the water, which appeared to have a "blue-green sheen". Over 1 000 bats and 24 Mallards and American Widgeons were found dead. The Provincial Veterinary Laboratory in Edmonton examined specimens and concluded that death was due to poisoning by *Anabaena flos-aquae*, the blue-green alga that made up most of the algal bloom (Pybus et al. 1985).

Biological Characteristics

Plants

There is no information on algae or macrophytes in Steele Lake, except for the presence of a toxic strain of *Anabaena flos-aquae*.

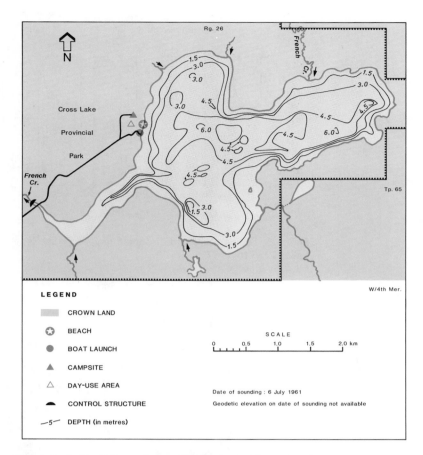

Figure 2. Bathymetry and shoreline features of Steele Lake.
BATHYMETRY SOURCE: Alta. Envir. n.d.[d].

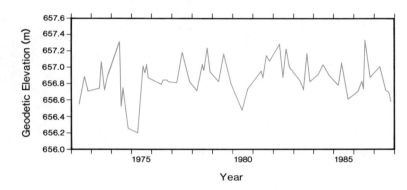

Figure 3. Water level of Steele Lake, 1965 to 1987.
SOURCE: Alta. Envir. n.d.[d].

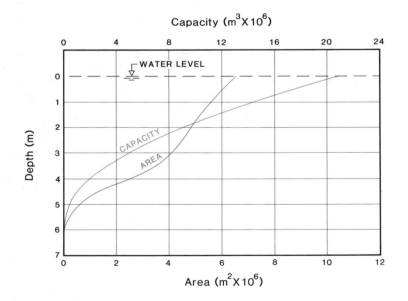

Figure 4. Area/capacity curve for Steele Lake.
SOURCE: Alta. Envir. n.d.[d].

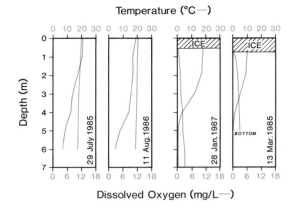

Figure 5. Temperature and dissolved oxygen in Steele Lake, 1985 to 1987.
SOURCE: Alta. Envir. n.d.[b].

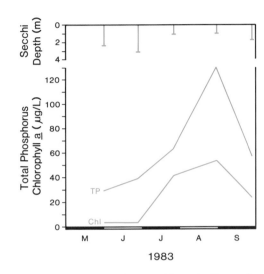

Figure 6. Total phosphorus, chlorophyll *a* and Secchi depth in Steele Lake, 1983.
SOURCE: Alta. Envir. n.d.[b].

Invertebrates

There are no data on invertebrates in Steele Lake.

Fish

Steele Lake supports a popular year-round sport fishery for northern pike and yellow perch; both are native to the lake. A severe winterkill in 1954 almost eliminated the once-abundant perch population (Alta. For. Ld. Wild. n.d.). The lake was stocked with a few perch in 1965, but natural recruitment was likely more effective in replenishing the population (Watters 1989). Perch are now frequently caught by anglers. A partial summerkill of perch occurred in August 1977 and a partial winterkill occurred in 1979/80 (Alta. For. Ld. Wild. n.d.).

There are no commercial or domestic fisheries on Steele Lake.

Wildlife

Cross Lake Provincial Park provides an excellent and easily accessible example of Boreal Mixedwood forest. The 139 species of birds found in the park include Blackburnian Warblers, American Redstarts and

Table 4. Nutrient, chlorophyll *a* and Secchi depth data for Steele Lake. Average concentrations in μg/L. Composite samples from the euphotic zone collected 5 times from 05 May to 27 Sep. 1983. S.E. = standard error.

	Mean	S.E.
total phosphorus	64	17.7
iron	13[a]	1.9
chlorophyll *a*	25.0	10.10
Secchi depth (m)	1.9	0.40

NOTE: [a]n = 3
SOURCE: Alta. Envir. n.d.[b], Naquadat station 01AL07BC1000

Black-and-white Warblers. At the lake and in the marshes are Swamp, Song, LeConte's, White-throated and Savannah sparrows, Common Loons, and grebes. The forest areas harbour Great Grey Owls, White-winged Crossbills, and Bay-breasted, Blackpoll and Palm warblers. Twenty species of mammals live in the area, including moose, deer, snowshoe hares, woodchucks, mink and bog lemmings (Peters and Nalte 1973; Luck 1981[a]; 1981[b]; Finlay and Finlay 1987).

J.M. Crosby

References

Alberta Environment. n.d.[a]. Devel. Op. Div., Design Br. Unpubl. data, Edmonton.
————. n.d.[b]. Envir. Assess. Div., Envir. Qlty. Monit. Br. Unpubl. data, Edmonton.
————. n.d.[c]. Tech. Serv. Div., Hydrol. Br. Unpubl. data, Edmonton.
————. n.d.[d]. Tech. Serv. Div., Surv. Br. Unpubl. data, Edmonton.
Alberta Forestry, Lands and Wildlife. n.d. Fish Wild. Div. Unpubl. data, Edmonton.
————. 1988. Boating in Alberta. Fish Wild. Div., Edmonton.
————. 1989. Guide to sportfishing. Fish Wild. Div., Edmonton.
Alberta Hotel Association. 1988. 1988 Alberta campground guide. Prep. for Travel Alta., Edmonton.
Alberta Recreation and Parks. n.d. Parks Div. Unpubl. data, Edmonton.
Alberta Research Council. 1972. Geological map of Alberta. Nat. Resour. Div., Alta. Geol. Surv., Edmonton.
Borneuf, D. 1973. Hydrology of the Tawatinaw area, Alberta. Alta. Res. Counc., Edmonton.
Boyd, E. and M. Cochrane (ed.). 1981. Hardships and happiness. Fawcett Hist. Book Club, Fawcett.
Energy, Mines and Resources Canada. 1973. National topographic series 1:50 000 83I/12 (1973), 83I/13 (1973). Surv. Map. Br., Ottawa.
Environment Canada. 1982. Canadian climate normals, Vol. 7: Bright sunshine (1951–1980). Prep. by Atm. Envir. Serv. Supply Serv. Can., Ottawa.
Finlay, J. and C. Finlay. 1987. Parks in Alberta: A guide to peaks, ponds, parklands & prairies. Hurtig Publ., Edmonton.
Greenlee, G.M. 1975. Soil survey of Cross Lake Provincial Park and interpretation for recreational use. Alta. Inst. Pedol. Rep. No. M–75–1. Univ. Alta., Edmonton.
Holmgren, E.J. and P.M. Holmgren. 1976. Over 2000 place names of Alberta. 3rd ed. West. Producer Prairie Books, Saskatoon.
Kjearsgaard, A.A. 1972. Soil survey of the Tawatinaw map sheet (83–I). Alta. Inst. Pedol. Rep. No. S–72–29, Univ. Alta. Bull. No. SS–12. Univ. Alta., Edmonton.
Lindner, D. 1988. Alta. Envir., Design Const. Div., Edmonton. Pers. comm.
Luck, S. 1981[a]. Cross Lake study area: Resource assessment (Part I—Resource inventory). Alta. Rec. Parks, Parks Plan. Div., Edmonton.
————. 1981[b]. Cross Lake study area: Resource assessment (Part II—Resource assessment). Alta. Rec. Parks, Parks Plan. Div., Edmonton.
Mitchell, P.A. 1986. An assessment of water quality in Steele (Cross) Lake. Alta. Envir., Poll. Contr. Div., Water Qlty. Contr. Br. Unpubl. rep., Edmonton.
Peters, J. and D. Nalte. 1973. An ecological survey of Cross Lake Provincial Park. Alta. Ld. For., Parks Plan. Div., Edmonton.
Pybus, M.J., D.P. Hobson and D.K. Onderka. 1985. Mass mortality of bats due to probable blue-green toxicity. Alta. En. Nat. Resour., Fish Wild. Div., Edmonton.
Strong, W.L. and K.R. Leggat. 1981. Ecoregions of Alberta. Alta. En. Nat. Resour., Resour. Eval. Plan. Div., Edmonton.
Watters, D. 1989. Alta. For. Ld. Wild., Fish Wild. Div., Edmonton. Pers. comm.

THUNDER LAKE

D. Huet

MAP SHEET: 83J/2
LOCATION: Tp59 R5, 6 W5
LAT/LONG: 54°09'N 114°45'W

Thunder Lake is an attractive recreational lake located in the County of Barrhead. It is situated approximately 22 km west of the town of Barrhead and 130 km northwest of the city of Edmonton. Thunder Lake Provincial Park, on the northeast side of the lake, can be reached by Highway 18 from Barrhead (Fig. 1).

The lake's name is a translation of an Indian word that described the loud thundering sound made by the lake's ice cracking in winter (Holmgren and Holmgren 1976). The first settlement in the area was at Fort Assiniboine, 23 km north of Thunder Lake. The North West Company established a trading post there in 1825, but had abandoned it by 1859. The area between Thunder Lake and Barrhead was settled between 1900 and 1910. In 1912, Barrhead was founded a short distance northeast of its present site. The town relocated in 1927 when the railroad arrived (Wynnyk et al. 1969). The railroad brought a new wave of settlers to the area surrounding Thunder Lake, but rugged topography and poor farmland discouraged much development near the lake (Alta. Rec. Parks n.d.). The first cottage development at the lake was started in 1958, and at present, Lightning Bay village and Thunder Lake community are situated on the southeast shore.

The lake was used for recreational purposes by local residents for many years, and in 1951, they petitioned the provincial government for a park. That same year, the Barrhead Kinsmen cleared a beach at the lake, and in 1958, the province established Thunder Lake Provincial Park (Alta. Rec. Parks n.d.). The park includes the three islands closest to the north shore of the lake. It is open year-round for day use, and from 1 May to Thanksgiving Day for camping. There are three camping loops with a total of 127 sites, a group camping area, a sewage disposal facility, tap water, playgrounds, a change house, a concession, picnic shelters, two swimming areas and beaches, two boat mooring areas, a boat launch and several walking trails. There are no boating restrictions over most of the lake, but in posted areas such as designated swimming areas, all boats are prohibited. In other posted areas, power boats are restricted to a maximum speed of 12 km/hour (Alta. For. Ld. Wild. 1988).

Algae turn the water in Thunder Lake green during summer and aquatic vegetation grows around much of the shoreline. During winter, levels of dissolved oxygen frequently become critical for the fish population, and winterkills have occurred several times since the late 1960s. The lake has been stocked with northern pike and yellow perch, and these species provide a popular sport fishery. A partial winterkill occurred in March 1989. There are no sport fishing regulations specific to the lake, but provincial limits and regulations apply (Alta. For. Ld. Wild. 1989).

Drainage Basin Characteristics

Thunder Lake's drainage basin covers an area of about 21 km^2 and is only 3 times the size of the lake (Tables 1, 2). The land in the watershed is primarily gently rolling (6 to 9% slopes) to moderately rolling (10 to 15% slopes) and soils are mainly moderately well-drained Orthic Gray Luvisols. A large area of Organic soil is located south of the lake. The land is not highly rated for agriculture. Large areas east and southwest of the lake are rated as pasture and woodland, and the land to the south is rated as mainly poor to fair for agriculture. In some areas to the north, however, the agricultural rating is fair to fairly good (Wynnyk et al. 1969).

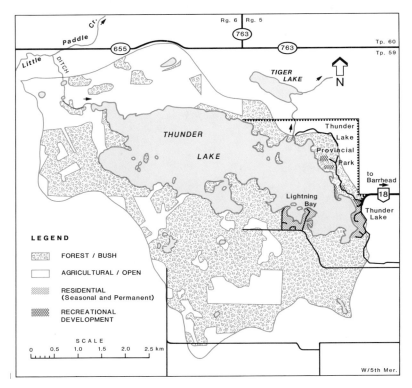

Figure 1. Features of the drainage basin of Thunder Lake.
SOURCES: Alta. Envir. n.d.[c]; En. Mines Resour. Can. 1973. Updated with 1984 aerial photos.

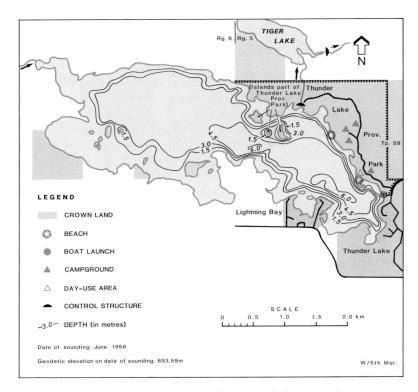

Figure 2. Bathymetry and shoreline features of Thunder Lake.
BATHYMETRY SOURCE: Alta. Envir. n.d.[d].

Much of the land south of the lake is forested, but most of the native vegetation to the north has been destroyed by land clearing and fires (Wynnyk et al. 1969). The watershed is part of the Moist Mixedwood Subregion of the Boreal Mixedwood Ecoregion (Strong and Leggat 1981). The main tree species are trembling aspen and balsam poplar on moderately well-drained Gray Luvisols. Jack pine grows on rapidly drained Brunisols, black spruce and willows grow on poorly drained Organics and Gleysols, and sedges grow on very poorly drained Organics.

Most of the inflow to the lake enters via a diversion ditch that connects the northwestern corner of the lake with what is locally known as Little Paddle Creek, a tributary of the Paddle River. The

Table 1. Characteristics of Thunder Lake drainage basin.

area (excluding lake) (km²)[a]	20.7
soil[b]	Orthic Gray Luvisols
bedrock geology[c]	Wapiti Formation (Upper Cretaceous): sandstone, mudstone, bentonite, scattered coal beds; nonmarine
terrain[b]	gently to moderately rolling
ecoregion[d]	Moist Mixedwood Subregion of Boreal Mixedwood
dominant vegetation[d]	trembling aspen, balsam poplar
mean annual inflow (m³)[a, e]	1.37 x 10⁶
mean annual sunshine (h)[f]	2 056

NOTE: [e]based on natural drainage area—inflow from diversions and groundwater not included
SOURCES: [a]Alta. Envir. n.d.[c]; [b]Wynnyk et al. 1969; [c]Alta. Res. Counc. 1972; [d]Strong and Leggat 1981; [f]Envir. Can. 1982

Table 2. Characteristics of Thunder Lake.

elevation (m)[a, b]	653.59
surface area (km²)[a, b]	7.03
volume (m³)[a, b]	21.2 x 10⁶
maximum depth (m)[a, b]	6.1
mean depth (m)[a, b]	3.0
shoreline length (km)[c, d]	26.8
mean annual lake evaporation (mm)[e]	642
mean annual precipitation (mm)[e]	467
mean residence time (yr)[e, f]	>100
control structures[g]	concrete weir with stop-log bays on outlet and diversion ditch from tributary of the Paddle River
operating full supply level (m)[h]	654.10

NOTES: [a]on date of sounding: June 1959; [d]includes 4.8 km for islands; [f]excluding groundwater inflow
SOURCES: [b]Alta. Envir. n.d.[d]; [c]En. Mines Resour. Can. 1973; [e]Alta. Envir. n.d.[c]; [g]Ducks Unltd. (Can.) 1982; [h]Alta. Envir. n.d.[a].

diversion and associated control structure with stop-log bays, which is situated on Little Paddle Creek, was constructed in 1950 by Ducks Unlimited (Canada) and the provincial government to divert flood water into Thunder Lake (Fig. 1). The purposes of the diversion were to prevent flooding along the Paddle River, raise the water level of the lake and increase waterfowl production areas (Alta. Rec. Parks n.d.). In 1986, Alberta Environment built a second control structure. It is situated on the diversion ditch near the ditch's diversion point from Little Paddle Creek. This structure allows control of the amount of water flowing into Thunder Lake (Alta. Envir. n.d.[a]). Water diversion is controlled by Alberta Environment, which is also responsible for maintenance of the two structures.

Lake Basin Characteristics

Thunder Lake is a medium-sized water body with a maximum length of 6 km and maximum width of 2.4 km. The western half of the lake basin slopes gently to a maximum depth of approximately 4.5 m, whereas the eastern half slopes more steeply to a maximum depth of 6.1 m (Fig. 2). There are several islands in the lake; three of them are part of the provincial park.

Prior to 1963, Thunder Lake had no well-defined outlet, and land near the lake flooded when water levels were high. To control lake levels, Ducks Unlimited (Canada) and the provincial government began construction of a weir and canal on the north shore in 1963, partly within the park boundary (Fig. 2). Water flows north from Thunder Lake to nearby Tiger Lake via this canal, then to the Paddle River via Little Paddle Creek. The control structure consists of two

Table 3. Major ions and related water quality variables for Thunder Lake. Average concentrations in mg/L; pH in pH units. Composite samples from the euphotic zone collected 4 times from 29 May to 14 Oct. 1986. S.E. = standard error.

	Mean	S.E.
pH (range)	8.3–8.7	—
total alkalinity ($CaCO_3$)	216	0.6
specific conductivity (μS/cm)	408	2.0
total dissolved solids (calculated)	230	1.9
total hardness ($CaCO_3$)	135	2.1
HCO_3	249	4.8
CO_3	7	2.5
Mg	18	0.3
Na	38	1.7
K	11	0.1
Cl	<1	—
SO_4	9	1.3
Ca	25	1.0

SOURCE: Alta. Envir. n.d.[b], Naquadat station 01AL07BB2000

1.8–m stop-log bays set in concrete walls. The bays allow variable control and have a range of about 1.65 m above and below the operating full supply level of 654.10 m (Ducks Unltd. (Can.) 1982). The structure is maintained and operated by Alberta Environment. During the spring runoff period, water is diverted into Thunder Lake until the lake's elevation reaches a maximum of 654.10 m. The elevation attained in spring depends on the amount of runoff available. During summer, the water level is gradually drawn down to about 653.83 m (Alta. Envir. n.d.[a]).

Water levels in Thunder Lake were first recorded in 1960 and 1961, and have been monitored regularly since 1964 (Fig. 3). In 1965, the year after the outlet control structure was completed, the lake reached its second highest recorded elevation (654.156 m). During a drought in 1967, the town of Barrhead used Thunder Lake, via the Paddle River, as an emergency water supply (Alta. Rec. Parks n.d.). That year, the water level dropped 0.47 m, and by September of 1968, the lake level had declined to the historic minimum (653.13 m). The elevation rose considerably during 1971, which was a year of high precipitation levels, and continued to rise until May 1972, when the historic maximum elevation (654.162 m) was reached. Since 1972, lake levels have been more stable. From 1980 to 1987 they fluctuated over a range of 0.36 m. This would result in only a small change in lake area (Fig. 4).

Water Quality

Water quality in Thunder Lake has been monitored since 1983 under a joint program between Alberta Environment and Alberta Recreation and Parks (Alta. Envir. n.d.[b]).

The lake has fresh water that is well buffered and hard. The dominant ions are bicarbonate and sodium (Table 3). Because the lake is shallow, it frequently mixes to the bottom during summer. Therefore, temperatures throughout the water column are either uniform or, during calm periods, slightly warmer at the top than on the bottom (Fig. 5). Levels of dissolved oxygen are generally uniform from top to bottom as well (Fig. 5). Thunder Lake often supports a high algal biomass during summer, so sediment oxygen demand from decomposing algae is high during winter and concentrations of dissolved oxygen frequently fall to levels that are critical for fish survival (Fig. 5). In March 1985, the entire water column was anoxic and a partial winterkill was reported.

Thunder Lake is eutrophic. Average total phosphorus and chlorophyll *a* levels vary between years. Over the six years sampled from 1983 to 1988, the levels of these two variables were lowest in 1986 and highest in 1984 (Table 4). In 1984, the maximum chlorophyll *a* concentration recorded was 32 μg/L, whereas in 1986, it was 10

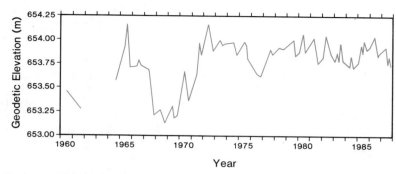

Figure 3. Water level of Thunder Lake, 1960 to 1985.
SOURCE: Alta. Envir. n.d.[d].

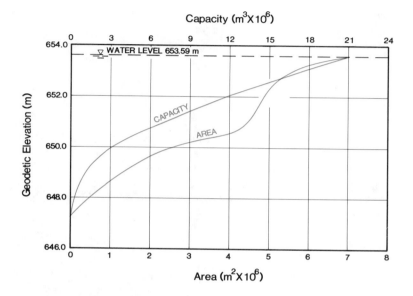

Figure 4. Area/capacity curve for Thunder Lake.
SOURCE: Alta. Envir. n.d.[d].

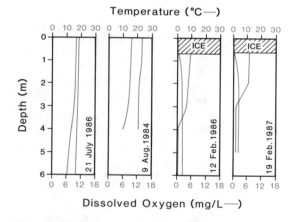

Figure 5. Temperature and dissolved oxygen in Thunder Lake, 1984, 1986 and 1987.
SOURCE: Alta. Envir. n.d.[b].

μg/L (Fig. 6). Despite lower chlorophyll levels during 1986, the Secchi transparency remained low throughout the summer (Fig. 6). Such high turbidity may result from wind disturbance of bottom sediments in this shallow lake.

Biological Characteristics

Plants

There are no recent data about the aquatic plant communities in Thunder Lake. A brief survey by Fish and Wildlife Division in October 1957 noted a heavy growth of blue-green algae at the eastern end

Table 4. Nutrient, chlorophyll *a* and Secchi depth data for Thunder Lake. Average concentrations in μg/L. Composite samples from the euphotic zone collected 5 times from 11 June to 10 Oct. 1984, 6 times from 29 May to 14 Oct. 1986 and 5 times from 29 May to 26 Sep. 1988. S.E. = standard error.

	1984		1986		1988	
	Mean	S.E.	Mean	S.E.	Mean	S.E.
total phosphorus	53	3.7	35	1.8	49	6.7
$NO_3 + NO_2$–nitrogen	—	—	—	—	<20	—
iron	<23[a]	—	<20[b]	—	<40	—
chlorophyll *a*	23.3	4.10	8.2	0.65	18.4	6.00
Secchi depth (m)	1.3	0.18	2.2	0.12	2.6	0.37

NOTES: [a]n = 3; [b]n = 4
SOURCE: Alta. Envir. n.d.[b], Naquadat station 01AL07BB2000

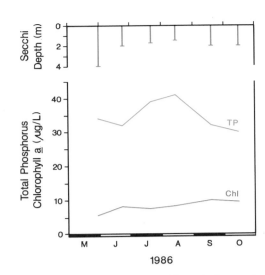

Figure 6. Total phosphorus, chlorophyll *a* and Secchi depth in Thunder Lake, 1986.
SOURCE: Alta. Envir. n.d.[b].

of the lake (Thomas 1957). In a later study, in May 1969, yellow water lily (*Nuphar variegatum*), common great bulrush (*Scirpus validus*) and common cattail (*Typha latifolia*) were present around much of the shoreline except in rocky areas (Erickson and Smith 1969). There were also many weedy bays where large mats of submergent macrophytes grew.

Invertebrates

There are no recent data for the invertebrates in Thunder Lake. A survey by Fish and Wildlife Division in October 1957 reported snails (*Lymnea* sp.), leeches (Hirudinea), clams (Mollusca), midge larvae (*Chironomus* sp.) and phantom midge larvae (*Chaoborus* sp.) in the lake (Thomas 1957).

Fish

The fish fauna in Thunder Lake includes northern pike, yellow perch, suckers and brook stickleback. The lake is managed as a recreational fishery. Yellow perch were introduced in 1959 and subsequently stocked in 1970, 1971, and from 1980 to 1983. Northern pike are indigenous to the lake but were stocked in 1960, 1961, 1966, 1967, 1970 and 1971 (Alta. For. Ld. Wild. n.d.). In 1968, walleye eyed-eggs were planted, but it is unlikely that any walleye survived the almost complete winterkill that occurred during the winter of 1968/69. Partial winterkills were recorded in 1967/68, 1984/85 and 1988/89 (Alta. For. Ld. Wild. n.d.; Alta. Envir. n.d.[a]).

Sport fishing is popular year-round at Thunder Lake. A creel survey conducted for 11 days from February 1983 to March 1984 recorded interviews with 172 anglers (Alta. For. Ld. Wild. n.d.). The anglers fished for 311 hours and caught 1 181 yellow perch and 16 northern pike. This is a very high catch rate for perch (3.8 perch/angler-hour) and a low catch rate for pike (0.05 pike/angler-hour). Since the anglers were fishing for perch, and pike are seldom caught on perch lures and bait, the small catch of pike is not unexpected.

Wildlife

Birdwatching at Thunder Lake is excellent (Finlay and Finlay 1987). In 1982, a survey of the lake by Ducks Unlimited (Canada) staff noted a variety of birds (Ducks Unltd. (Can.) 1982). The more abundant ducks were Mallards, American Widgeons, Lesser Scaup, Blue-winged Teal, Ruddy Ducks, Common Goldeneye and Ring-necked Ducks. Other birds sighted were Common Loons, Belted Kingfishers, Red-necked and Western grebes, Black Terns, Great Blue Herons, Double-crested Cormorants and California, Ring-billed and Bonaparte's gulls. In 1983, Fish and Wildlife Division staff counted 18 Great Blue Heron nests at the lake. By 1984, the herons had departed and Bald Eagles were nesting in the heron colony (Folinsbee 1988).

The population of mammals near the lake is small. Muskrats and beaver have been sighted near stands of emergent vegetation along the shore and red squirrels live in black spruce bogs. Coyotes are present in the park and black bears have been known to pass through the park (Finlay and Finlay 1987).

M.E. Bradford

References

Alberta Environment. n.d.[a]. Devel. Op. Div., Project Mgt. Br. Unpubl. data, Edmonton.
———. n.d.[b]. Envir. Assess. Div., Envir. Qlty. Monit. Br. Unpubl. data, Edmonton.
———. n.d.[c]. Tech. Serv. Div., Hydrol. Br. Unpubl. data, Edmonton.
———. n.d.[d]. Tech. Serv. Div., Surv. Br. Unpubl. data, Edmonton.
Alberta Forestry, Lands and Wildlife. n.d. Fish Wild. Div. Unpubl. data, Edmonton.
———. 1988. Boating in Alberta. Fish Wild. Div., Edmonton.
———. 1989. Guide to sportfishing. Fish Wild. Div., Edmonton.
Alberta Recreation and Parks. n.d. Parks Div. Unpubl. data, Edmonton.
Alberta Research Council. 1972. Geological map of Alberta. Nat. Resour. Div., Alta. Geol. Surv., Edmonton.
Ducks Unlimited (Canada). 1982. Project inspection and biological report, 22/06/82. Alta. Prov. Office, Edmonton.
Energy, Mines and Resources Canada. 1973. National topographic series 1:50 000 83J/2 (1973). Surv. Map. Br., Ottawa.
Environment Canada. 1982. Canadian climate normals, Vol. 7: Bright sunshine (1951–1980). Prep. by Atm. Envir. Serv. Supply Serv. Can., Ottawa.
Erickson, G. and L. Smith. 1969. Thunder Lake. Alta. Ld. For., Fish Wild. Div. Unpubl. rep., Edmonton.
Finlay, J. and C. Finlay. 1987. Parks in Alberta: A guide to peaks, ponds, parklands & prairies. Hurtig Publ., Edmonton.
Folinsbee, J. 1988. Alta. For. Ld. Wild., Fish Wild. Div., Dist. Office, Edmonton. Pers. comm.
Holmgren, E.J. and P.M. Holmgren. 1976. Over 2000 place names of Alberta. 3rd ed. West. Producer Prairie Books, Saskatoon.
Strong, W.L. and K.R. Leggat. 1981. Ecoregions of Alberta. Alta. En. Nat. Resour., Resour. Eval. Plan. Div., Edmonton.
Thomas, R.C. 1957. Report on Thunder Lake. Alta. Ld. For., Fish Wild. Div. Unpubl. rep., Edmonton.
Wynnyk, A., J.D. Lindsay and W. Odynsky. 1969. Soil survey of the Whitecourt and Barrhead area. Alta. Soil Surv. Rep. No. 27, Univ. Alta. Bull. No. 22–10, Res. Counc. Alta. Rep. No. 90. Univ. Alta., Edmonton.

WINAGAMI LAKE

Alberta Tourism

MAP SHEET: 83N/10
LOCATION: Tp76, 77 R18, 19 W5
LAT/LONG: 55°38'N 116°45'W

Winagami Lake is a large, very shallow lake lying in the flat country west of Lesser Slave Lake. It is located in Improvement District No. 17, about 70 km southeast of the town of Peace River. To reach Winagami Lake from Peace River, travel south on Highway 2 for 63 km to the town of Donnelly; take Highway 49 east and then south for 26 km, then turn east onto Secondary Road 679 and drive for approximately 11 km until you reach the short access road to Winagami Lake Provincial Park (Fig. 1). The nearest population centre is the hamlet of Kathleen.

Winagami is the Cree word for "dirty water lake" (Geog. Bd. Can. 1928); the lake was called Stinking Lake at the turn of the century (Sawyer 1981). Homesteaders settled the land near the lake in about 1905 and the town of McLennan on nearby Kimiwan Lake was established in 1915 as a divisional point on the Great Northern Railway (Guiltner 1972). About half of the basin southwest of the lake has been cleared for farming and selected areas north of the lake have been logged for white spruce (O'Leary et al. 1986). Most of the land north and east of the lake is owned by the Crown (Fig. 2).

Before 1950, outflow from Winagami Lake was irregular, the water was stagnant and water levels often dropped and exposed large areas of mudflats (Ducks Unltd. (Can.) n.d.). In 1950, the provincial government built a dam on the South Heart River and a channel from the river into Winagami Lake. The Winagami-Girouxville Canal was built from Winagami Lake to Kimiwan Lake to improve the water supply for the towns of McLennan, Girouxville, Falher and Donnelly.

After water level fluctuations had been reduced by the diverted water, the lake became more attractive for recreation. In 1955, the Winagami Beach Association (mostly cottage owners) cleared a beach area on the east side of the lake (Alta. Rec. Parks n.d.; McLennan Hist. Book Commit. 1981) and in 1956, Winagami Lake Provincial Park was established (Fig. 1). The park covers 12.1 km² and includes a campground with 64 sites, a group camping area, 2 day-use areas with picnic tables, a boat launch and docking area, a playground and sewage disposal station (Fig. 2). Boat traffic is not allowed near the beach and power boats are restricted to 12 km/hour in posted areas near the provincial park (Alta. For. Ld. Wild. 1988). In 1983, at the request of local cottagers, a breakwater was built offshore from the beach and boat launch area. By 1984, aquatic plants had densely colonized the area between the breakwater and shore and as of 1989, modification or possible removal of the control structure was being considered.

Winagami Lake is very nutrient-rich and supports an abundance of algae from midsummer to autumn. The shore is ringed by sedges, cattails and bulrushes, and submergent aquatic plants extend far into the lake. Winterkills of fish are common, but they do not usually affect the entire lake (Alta. For. Ld. Wild. n.d.). The lake is popular for sport fishing for northern pike in winter and summer. General provincial sport fishing regulations apply to Winagami Lake. Fishing or disturbing fish in any way is not permitted within 25 m of the control structure (Alta. For. Ld. Wild. 1989). Lake whitefish were first noticed in the lake in the late 1960s, but they were not abundant until the late 1970s. In 1988, the lake supported a commercial fishery and produced lake whitefish at one of the highest rates of any lake in North America. The lake also provides excellent habitat for waterfowl, including Oldsquaw ducks on the most southerly portion of the inland segment of their migration to the arctic.

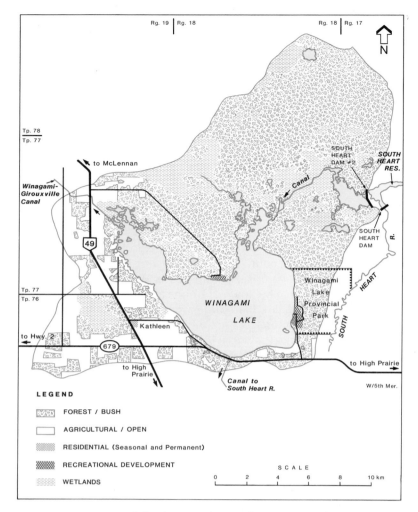

Figure 1. Features of the drainage basin of Winagami Lake.
SOURCES: Alta. Envir. n.d.[b]; En. Mines Resour. Can. 1975. Updated with 1985 aerial photos.

Table 1. Characteristics of Winagami Lake drainage basin.

area (excluding lake) (km^2)[a]	221
soil[b]	Orthic and Solonetzic Gray Luvisols, poorly drained Gleysols
bedrock geology[c]	Puskwaskau Formation (Upper Cretaceous): shale; marine
terrain[d]	level to gently rolling
ecoregion[d]	Dry Mixedwood Subregion of Boreal Mixedwood
dominant vegetation[d]	trembling aspen, white spruce, black spruce, *Sphagnum*
mean annual inflow (m^3)[a, e]	13.3 x 10^6 (natural) and 53.8 x 10^6 (via diversion)
mean annual sunshine (h)[f]	2 060

NOTE: [e]based on 1984 diversion; does not include groundwater inflow
SOURCES: [a]Alta. Envir. n.d.[b]; [b]O'Leary et al. 1986; [c]Alta. Res. Counc. 1972; [d]Strong and Leggat 1981; [f]Envir. Can. 1982

Drainage Basin Characteristics

Winagami Lake lies in a shallow depression in an almost flat (0 to 5% slope), clay-rich glaciolacustrine plain overlying morainal deposits. The relief of the drainage basin varies only 73 m, from a high point of 695 m on a gently sloping hill north of the lake to a low of 621.5 m at the shoreline. The watershed is typified by "humpy doughnut" topography, which is characterized by low-relief mounds with slightly depressed centres interspersed with organic wetlands (O'Leary et al. 1986). The drainage basin is located in the Boreal Mixedwood Ecoregion (Strong and Leggat 1981), and trembling aspen forests with an understory of cranberry and rose predominate. In the area

Table 2. Characteristics of Winagami Lake.

elevation (m)[a]	621.54
surface area (km^2)[b]	46.7
estimated volume (m^3)[b]	80.7 x 10^6
maximum depth (m)[c]	4.7
mean depth (m)[b]	1.7
shoreline length (km)[d]	48.4
mean annual lake evaporation (mm)[b]	598
mean annual precipitation (mm)[b]	474
mean residence time (yr)[b, e]	1.5
control structure	sheet-pile weir and diversion canal from South Heart River

NOTE: [e]after 1984 diversion; natural residence time is 11 years; estimate does not consider groundwater inflow
SOURCES: [a]Alta. Envir. n.d.[c]; [b]Alta. Envir. n.d.[b]; [c]Mitchell 1986; [d]En. Mines Resour. Can. 1975

north of Winagami Lake there is a white spruce and trembling aspen forest that has been selectively logged for spruce. The low-lying areas support either a black spruce/Labrador tea/*Sphagnum* community or willow/sedge community, and open water is a common feature (O'Leary et al. 1986). Much of the area west of Winagami Lake has been cleared for barley or canola production or for grazing.

Soils have been mapped and described in detail for the drainage basin (Table 1) (O'Leary et al. 1986) and for the provincial park (Greenlee 1975). The area north and south of the provincial park lies on coarse glaciolacustrine sediments. Well-drained Orthic and Brunisolic Gray Luvisols and Orthic Eutric Brunisols support trembling aspen and balsam poplar. South of the lake and in the northern portion of the basin, soils are moderately well-drained to well-drained Orthic and Solonetzic Gray Luvisols under aspen or white spruce/aspen forests. The north shore of the lake and the area between Kathleen and McLennan is primarily compact glaciolacustrine veneers (clays) overlying undulating glacial till; soils under white spruce/aspen woodland are well-drained Orthic and Solonetzic Gray Luvisols and poorly drained Orthic Luvic Gleysols.

The hydrogeology of the area was mapped by the Alberta Research Council. Groundwater quantity and quality is variable throughout the area (Borneuf 1980).

Lake Basin Characteristics

Winagami Lake is irregularly shaped; the main body of the lake is approximately 7–km wide and 9–km long and has shallow, marshy arms that extend north and northwest (Fig. 1). The drainage basin is only five times the size of the lake (Tables 1, 2) and does not provide sufficient runoff to maintain a stable water level or reliable outflow. In 1950, a dam was built on the South Heart River northeast of the lake to impound water and divert it via canal to Winagami Lake. A control structure was built on the south shore of Winagami Lake and the outlet stream was channelized as far as a marsh 3 km south of the lake. From there, the water meanders back to the South Heart River. A canal from the northwest corner of Winagami Lake to Kimiwan Lake ensures reliable water supply for McLennan, Girouxville, Falher and Donnelly. This system has decreased the average residence time of Winagami Lake from its natural 11 years to less than 2 years (Table 2).

The lake basin slopes gently to a maximum depth of 4.7 m; no detailed bathymetry is available. The shoreline is mostly soft and dominated by organic deposits. The east shore is sandy. Bulrushes have been cleared at the provincial park and the beach has been augmented with additional sand.

The level of Winagami Lake has been fairly stable since 1962. Annual fluctuations from 1962 to 1986 averaged about 0.5 m and the maximum range of water levels during this period was 1.1 m (Fig. 3).

Table 3. Major ions and related water quality variables for Winagami Lake. Average concentrations in mg/L; pH in pH units. Composite samples from the euphotic zone collected 3 times from 22 May to 09 Oct. 1984. S.E. = standard error.

	Mean	S.E.
pH (range)	8.3–8.9	—
total alkalinity ($CaCO_3$)	161	1.6
specific conductivity (µS/cm)	453	18.4
total dissolved solids (calculated)	266	3.3
total hardness ($CaCO_3$)	203	4.7
HCO_3	185	13.0
CO_3	<5	—
Mg	24	0.3
Na	13	1.2
K	10	0.2
Cl	2	0
SO_4	79	0.9
Ca	42	2.4

SOURCE: Alta. Envir. n.d.[a], Naquadat station 01AL07BF1000

Water Quality

The water quality of Winagami Lake has been monitored several times a year since 1983 in a joint program by Alberta Environment and Alberta Recreation and Parks (Alta. Envir. n.d.[a]).

Winagami Lake is now a well-buffered, freshwater lake; its dominant ions are bicarbonate, sulphate and calcium (Table 3). Before the diversion, Winagami Lake was called a "stagnant salty body of water unfit for any use" (Thomas 1955). The diversion from the South Heart Reservoir brings in water that is much fresher and has quite a different ionic composition than that of the lake. Data collected in 1952 indicate that the water chemistry of Winagami Lake was much more saline 40 years ago. A sample collected in July 1973 had intermediate values, supporting a "freshening trend" (Table 4).

Winagami Lake is shallow and exposed to winds and therefore is well-mixed throughout the open-water season (Fig. 4). In winter, dissolved oxygen rapidly becomes depleted throughout the water column (Fig. 4). By February 1984 and March 1985 dissolved oxygen concentrations were below levels regarded as sufficient for fish survival. Although major winterkills of fish are reported about one year in five, many fish in the lake survive.

Winagami Lake is a hyper-eutrophic lake and produces very dense blooms of blue-green algae from midsummer to fall each year. Mean total phosphorus and chlorophyll *a* concentrations (Table 5) are among the highest of 34 other recreational lakes monitored by Alberta Environment (Mitchell 1986). In 1988, the mean summer chlorophyll *a* concentration (81 µg/L) was extremely high, as was the peak whole-lake concentration of 195 µg/L that was recorded in early September 1988 (Alta. Envir. n.d.[a]). As in many shallow Alberta lakes, phosphorus concentrations increase throughout the summer, mainly due to release from the sediments, and then decline in the fall (Fig. 5). With the release of phosphorus from the sediments, massive blooms of blue-green algae develop. When these blooms die, their decay consumes oxygen and a summerkill of fish may occur.

Biological Characteristics

Plants

The phytoplankton community was sampled briefly in 1974 by Fish and Wildlife Division (Bishop 1976). Blue-green blooms from June to September were almost entirely composed of *Aphanizomenon flosaquae*; the second most abundant species were *Anabaena* sp. in June and *Microcystis* sp. in July and August. A high concentration of the diatom *Stephanodiscus* sp. was found in May and October.

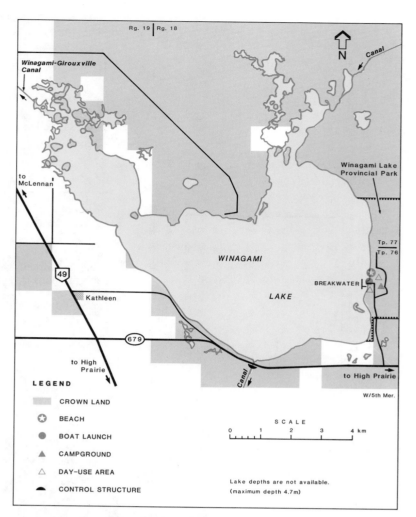

Figure 2. Shoreline features of Winagami Lake. Bathymetry not available.
BATHYMETRY SOURCE: Alta. Envir. n.d.[a].

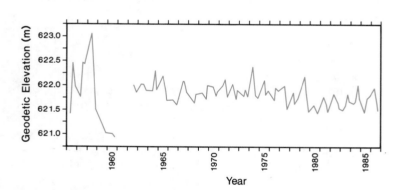

Figure 3. Water level of Winagami Lake, 1956 to 1986.
SOURCE: Envir. Can. 1956–1986.

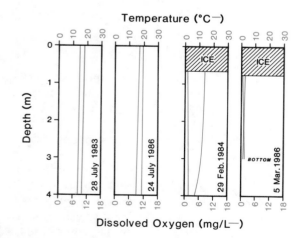

Figure 4. Temperature and dissolved oxygen in Winagami Lake.
SOURCE: Alta. Envir. n.d.[a].

Table 4. Water quality in the South Heart Reservoir in 1988 and in Winagami Lake in 1952, 1973, 1984 and 1988. Concentrations in mg/L.

| | South Heart Reservoir | Winagami Lake | | | |
	1988[a, b]	1952[c, d]	1973[e, f]	1984[a, g]	1988[a, g]
total dissolved solids	165	1 034	—	266	247
hardness	150	600	200	203	200
SO$_4$	25	405	100	79	60
Cl	1	15	5	2	2

NOTES: [b]n = 3, 20 June to 13 Sep.; [d]n = 1, Aug.; [f]n = 1, July; [g]n = 3, 15 May to 15 Oct.
SOURCES: [a]Alta. Envir. n.d.[a]; [c]Thomas 1955; [e]Bishop 1976

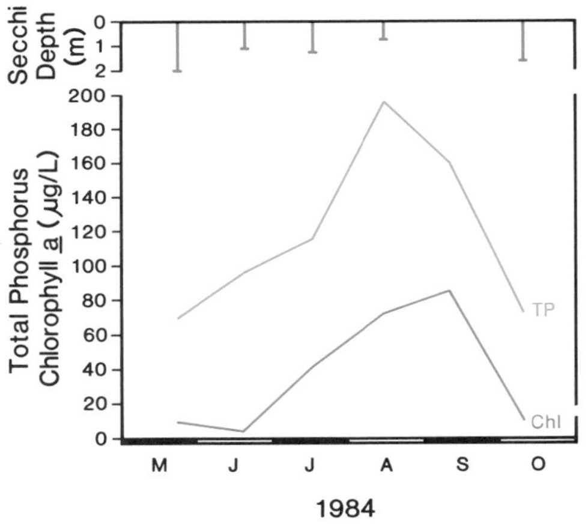

Figure 5. Total phosphorus, chlorophyll *a* and Secchi depth in Winagami Lake, 1984.
SOURCE: Alta. Envir. n.d.[a].

Table 5. Nutrient, chlorophyll *a* and Secchi depth data for Winagami Lake. Average concentrations in µg/L. Composite samples from the euphotic zone collected 6 times from 22 May to 09 Oct. 1984, 5 times from 25 May to 23 Sep. 1986 and 5 times from 10 May to 13 Sep. 1988. S.E. = standard error.

| | 1984 | | 1986 | | 1988 | |
	Mean	S.E.	Mean	S.E.	Mean	S.E.
total phosphorus	119	20.5	223	48.4	237	62.0
iron	10.3	5.0	—	—	—	—
chlorophyll *a*	37.3	14.33	67.0	44.08	81.3	35.22
Secchi depth (m)	1.3	0.21	1.2	0.43	2.4	0.74

SOURCE: Alta. Envir. n.d.[a], Naquadat station 01AL07BF1000

Emergent aquatic plants, including sedges (*Carex* spp.), cattails (*Typha* spp.) and bulrushes (*Scirpus* spp.), ring Winagami Lake and submergent macrophytes are often a nuisance. There are no data on species composition or distribution.

Invertebrates

The zooplankton was sampled monthly in 1974 by Fish and Wildlife Division (Bishop 1976). Cyclopoid copepods and daphnid cladocerans dominated the community most of the year. Chydorid cladocerans were common in the fall.

Benthic organisms in Winagami Lake were sampled at 100 sites in September 1973 (Bishop 1976). Midge larvae (Chironomidae) made up 45% of the wet weight biomass. The remainder of the biomass comprised 17% scuds (Amphipoda), 21% snails (Gastropoda), 13% leeches (Hirudinea) and 4% aquatic earthworms (Oligochaeta). The average wet weight of the benthic organisms was 64.8 g/m^2. Scuds and snails were most dense at sites less than 1.5–m deep whereas all other groups were densest at sites 1.5– to 3–m deep.

Fish

Winagami Lake supports a popular, year-round local sport fishery for northern pike and yellow perch and a commercial fishery for lake whitefish and northern pike. Ninety-eight domestic licences were issued in 1987/88 (Alta. For. Ld. Wild. n.d.). White suckers are abundant; no sampling has been done to determine species of forage fish in the lake (Bishop 1976).

Northern pike are native to the lake. Yellow perch were not found in the lake prior to 1953. They were stocked in 1954, 1963 and 1964 by Fish and Wildlife Division; by 1968 they were abundant, reproducing successfully and growing well (Alta. For. Ld. Wild. n.d.). During a creel census conducted from 1 May to 31 August 1984, anglers fished for a total of 14 000 hours. They caught 13 564 pike (1 pike/hour), with an average weight of 1.2 kg. Six hundred perch were caught over the same period. Most of the fishing was from shore (62%); the breakwater and the outlet canal area were the most popular locations (Buchwald 1985).

The history of the commercial fishery in Winagami Lake is quite dramatic. Until the 1960s there were no lake whitefish in the lake and none have ever been stocked. By the early 1970s a few large lake whitefish were reported in test nettings by Fish and Wildlife Division; it is likely they arrived via the diversion from the South Heart River. The absence of young whitefish indicated poor reproductive success. In 1981, the regional fisheries biologist reported an "alarming increase" in lake whitefish and recommended that a commercial fishery be established (Alta. For. Ld. Wild. n.d.). In 1984/85, the first commercial licences were issued and by 1988 the Winagami Lake lake whitefish production of 70 kg/ha was among the highest in North America (Walty 1988). From the 1985/86 season through the 1987/88 season, an average of 254 000 kg of lake whitefish and 810 kg of pike were harvested annually (Alta. For. Ld. Wild. n.d.). The fish are fast-growing and free of tapeworm (*Triaenophorus crassus*) cysts.

There are several risks to the fish in Winagami Lake. Summerkills occur when algal blooms die off and their decay consumes oxygen and winterkills occur when dissolved oxygen is depleted under ice. Summerkills occurred in four years between 1967 and 1987 (Alta. For. Ld. Wild. n.d.). A winterkill took place in 1983/84 and 1985/86 when a long, warm fall was followed by a rapid freeze-up; lake mixing in the fall was too brief to allow much dissolved oxygen to be incorporated into the water. One risk has been mitigated: before 1984, many fish, both northern pike and lake whitefish, would leave the lake over the outlet structure. Once over the weir, they could not return to the lake and died because of either low water levels, high temperatures, intense angling or vandalism (Bishop 1972). Large numbers of fish were trapped in this way; in 1984, Fish and Wildlife Division lifted 40 000 lake whitefish back over the weir and returned them to the lake (Walty 1988). Since then, screens have been installed on the outlet and the problem has been alleviated.

Wildlife

Winagami Lake provides excellent habitat for waterfowl production, especially for Pintails, Mallards, Gadwall and Shovellers. Canvasbacks and White-winged Scoters are also common. Oldsquaw ducks use the area when migrating; this is likely the southern-most limit of the inland portion of their route (Ducks Unltd. (Can.) n.d.; Finlay and Finlay 1987). The woods of the provincial park provide excellent birdwatching; 150 species have been recorded, including dense populations of Yellow and Canada warblers, plus Cape May, Black-throated Green, Palm and Bay-breasted warblers. The most northwestern nesting colony of Purple Martins in the world was recorded in the park (Finlay and Finlay 1987).

J.M. Crosby

References

Alberta Environment. n.d.[a]. Envir. Assess. Div., Envir. Qlty. Monit. Br. Unpubl. data, Edmonton.

———. n.d.[b]. Tech. Serv. Div., Hydrol. Br. Unpubl. data, Edmonton.

———. n.d.[c]. Tech. Serv. Div., Surv. Br. Unpubl. data, Edmonton.

Alberta Forestry, Lands and Wildlife. n.d. Fish Wild. Div. Unpubl. data, Edmonton.

———. 1988. Boating in Alberta. Fish Wild. Div., Edmonton.

———. 1989. Guide to sportfishing. Fish Wild. Div., Edmonton.

Alberta Recreation and Parks. n.d. Parks Div. Unpubl. data, Edmonton.

Alberta Research Council. 1972. Geological map of Alberta. Nat. Resour. Div., Alta. Geol. Surv., Edmonton.

Bishop, F.G. 1972. Winagami Lake (outlet) survey, 1971. Alta. Ld. For., Fish Wild. Div. Unpubl. rep., Edmonton.

———. 1976. A comparative study of the limnology and fisheries of Snipe and Winagami lakes in northwestern Alberta. Alta. Rec. Parks Wild., Fish Wild. Div., Peace River.

Borneuf, D. 1980. Hydrogeology of the Winagami area, Alberta. Alta. Res. Counc., Earth Sci. Rep. No. 79–3, Edmonton.

Buchwald, V.G. 1985. Winagami Lake summer creel and boating survey, 1984. Alta. En. Nat. Resour., Fish Wild. Div. Unpubl. rep., Edmonton.

Ducks Unlimited (Canada). n.d. Unpubl. data, Edmonton.

Energy, Mines and Resources Canada. 1975. National topographic series 1:50 000 83N/10 (1975), 83N/15 (1975). Surv. Map. Br., Ottawa.

Environment Canada. 1956–1986. Surface water data. Prep. by Inland Waters Directorate. Water Surv. Can., Water Resour. Br., Ottawa.

———. 1982. Canadian climate normals, Vol. 7: Bright sunshine (1951–1980). Prep. by Atm. Envir. Serv. Supply Serv. Can., Ottawa.

Finlay, J. and C. Finlay. 1987. Parks in Alberta: A guide to peaks, ponds, parklands & prairies. Hurtig Publ., Edmonton.

Geographic Board of Canada. 1928. Place-names of Alberta. Dept. Interior, Ottawa.

Greenlee, G.M. 1975. Soil survey of Winagami Lake Provincial Park and interpretation for recreational use. Alta. Inst. Pedol. Rep. No. M–75–2. Alta. Res. Counc., Edmonton.

Guiltner, J.C. 1972. The Peace River Country and McKenzie Highway—Historical and tourist guide. J.C. Guiltner, Peace River.

McLennan History Book Committee. 1981. Trails and rails north—History of McLennan district, Vol. 1. McLennan Hist. Book Commit., McLennan.

Mitchell, P.A. 1986. An assessment of water quality in Winagami Lake. Alta. Envir., Poll. Contr. Div., Water Qlty. Contr. Br. Unpubl. rep., Edmonton.

O'Leary, D., D. Downing, D. Schindeler and L. Boyd. 1986. Integrated resource inventory for the Kimiwan-Winagami study area. Alta. For. Ld. Wild., Resour. Eval. Plan. Br., Edmonton.

Sawyer, G. 1981. A history of Lesser Slave Lake. Alta. Rec. Parks, Parks Div., Visitor Serv. Plan. Br., Edmonton.

Strong, W.L. and K.R. Leggat. 1981. Ecoregions of Alberta. Alta. En. Nat. Resour., Resour. Eval. Plan. Div., Edmonton.

Thomas, R.C. 1955. Report on Winagami Lake. Alta. Ld. For., Fish Wild. Div. Unpubl. rep., Edmonton.

Walty, D. 1988. Alta. For. Ld. Wild., Fish Wild. Div., Peace River. Pers. comm.

BEAVER RIVER REGION

The Beaver River Basin, with its abundance of lakes, sandy beaches, attractive shorelines and extensive fish and wildlife resources, draws visitors from all over the province. The Alberta portion of the Beaver River Basin is located in the east-central part of the province, near the town of Bonnyville. The 15 500 km² basin covers approximately 2% of the province but it includes 19% of the lakes discussed in the *Atlas*—this region is well-deserving of the title "Alberta's Lakeland".

This basin lies entirely within the Boreal Mixedwood Ecoregion. The rainfall is greater and the evaporation less than the southern portion of the province, and the moisture regime is sufficient to support forest growth throughout the basin. The predominant trees are trembling aspen, balsam poplar and white spruce on Gray Luvisolic soils. Numerous pockets of sand were left by the retreat of the Keewatin ice sheet approximately 12 000 years ago. In upland regions, these sandy areas support stands of jack pine. Near water they create beautiful sandy beaches.

The Beaver River starts near the town of Lac La Biche as the outflow from Beaver Lake, a beautiful, clear lake dotted with islands. It is soon joined by the Amisk River, which drains four lakes on the western edge of the basin. Long (near Boyle) and Amisk lakes are two narrow lakes set in dense forest. North Buck Lake is a lovely spot for canoeing with lots of bays and islands, and Skeleton Lake provides an opportunity for lively cottage life. Farther east, the Beaver River meets the Sand River which flows from a northern group of large wilderness lakes including Siebert Lake, renowned for its large northern pike; Wolf Lake, with deep clear water and tiny white beaches; and Pinehurst and Touchwood lakes, both spectacular wilderness lakes prized for fishing.

Farther east and still north of the Beaver River, near the town of Cold Lake, is a group of lakes including Ethel, Marie and Moore lakes—sparkling clear and set in dense forests—and Tucker lake, a shallow, isolated, productive lake with no shoreline development. Straddling the Alberta-Saskatchewan border is Cold Lake. Big, deep (maximum depth 99 m), clear, and with beautiful white sand beaches, it provides excellent opportunities for sailing, motor boating, fishing and beach recreation. Cold Lake has many different habitats; it has the greatest number of fish species and the most diverse invertebrate fauna of any lake surveyed in Alberta. After the Beaver River crosses into the province of Saskatchewan, it continues eastward then flows into the Churchill River at Lac Ile-à-la-Crosse. The Churchill River crosses Saskatchewan and Manitoba then flows into Hudson Bay near the community of Churchill.

All of these lakes lie north of the Beaver River. There are also many lakes south of the river along Highways 28 and 28A. The climate in this area is slightly warmer and drier and the soils are more fertile, and so large areas have been cleared for agriculture, mostly grain and forage crops. Muriel and Moose lakes are two large lakes near Bonnyville. Muriel Lake is popular for boating, and the four arms of Moose Lake provide a wide range of habitats and pelicans are often seen feeding. The Mann lakes are among the most productive in the basin and provide good fishing for yellow perch. Garner Lake has fairly clear water and a groomed beach at the provincial park.

Fur traders with the North West Company were the first white men to come to the basin. Travelling west up the Churchill River system, they reached Lac Ile-à-la-Crosse in what is now Saskatchewan, then branched onto the Beaver River and continued up it, then

BEAVER RIVER BASIN

Skeleton Lake. Photo by P.A. Mitchell

Lower Mann Lake. Photo by P.A. Mitchell

Moore Lake. Photo by P.A. Mitchell

crossed over a low divide to reach Lac La Biche in the Athabasca River Basin. The first building in the basin was Lac d'Orignal Post, built near Moose Lake by Angus Shaw of the North West Company in 1789–six years before the establishment of Fort Edmonton. Agricultural settlement did not begin until the early 1900s; farming is now the major land use in the southern portion of the basin.

The basin is still lightly populated; just over 25 000 people live there. Two-thirds of the population live in the towns of Bonnyville, Grand Centre and Cold Lake or on the Canadian Forces Base at Medley. The major occupations are agriculture, national defence, heavy oil extraction, fishing and trapping.

All 19 lakes listed in the *Atlas* in this basin support sport fishing. Pike are caught in all the lakes; the largest ones (over 10 kg) come from two trophy lakes, May and Siebert, which require a special fishing licence, and from Cold and Muriel lakes. Perch are caught in all 19 lakes, and walleye are sought in most of them, including Moore, Wolf, Touchwood, Cold and Marie lakes. Lake trout over 10 kg have been taken from the deep, cool waters of Cold Lake. Many Alberta lakes are stocked with walleye that come from a provincial government hatchery at Cold Lake. Thirty-three lakes in the Beaver River Basin, including 14 of the lakes in the *Atlas*, support commercial and/or domestic fisheries. Lake whitefish and burbot are the major targets, with lake trout contributing to the harvest from Cold Lake.

Tourism is important to the basin and lake-based recreation is the major attraction. In general, the lakes in this region have clear water. Of the 18 lakes that have been assessed, 10 are mesotrophic or oligo-mesotrophic (meaning that algae are rarely a nuisance) and only 3 are highly productive and develop algal blooms in most years. The sandy beaches on many lakes, for example Cold, Moore, Moose and Muriel, attract visitors for beach activities. Water skiing and

Cold Lake. Photo by P.A. Mitchell

power boating are popular on the large lakes with extensive cottage development, such as at Skeleton and Moose lakes. Canoeing and fishing are peaceful pastimes on North Buck, Amisk and Upper Mann lakes. Whether visitors come to "Alberta's Lakeland" for wilderness camping, water sports or angling, they will not be disappointed.

J.M. Crosby

AMISK LAKE

M. Pazlawski

MAP SHEET: 83I/10
LOCATION: Tp64, 65 R18 W4
LAT/LONG: 54°35'N 112°37'W

Amisk is a beautiful recreational lake, nestled within a mixed forest in the County of Athabasca in central Alberta. It is 175 km northeast of the city of Edmonton and 15 km east of the village of Boyle, south of Secondary Road 663 (Fig. 1). The lake is long and narrow, with a main axis that runs north-south. It has two distinct deep basins: the larger south basin is 60–m deep and the north basin is 34–m deep. The lake derived its name from the local abundance of beaver, or *amisk* in Cree, and the inflow and outflow rivers of the same name (Chipeniuk 1975; Holmgren and Holmgren 1976).

In the early 1940s, a mink farm and a resort were established on the northwest shore of the lake. The mink were fed fish from the lake. The resort had boat and cabin rentals (Chipeniuk 1975; Boyle Dist. Hist. Soc. 1982). Over the years, these developments were replaced by two subdivisions, and a trailer park was also built at the north end of the lake. One of the subdivisions, Pelican Beach, takes its name from the large flocks of pelicans that previously frequented the lake (Boyle Dist. Hist. Soc. 1982). The majority of the shoreline is undeveloped.

Fishing, boating and swimming are popular on Amisk Lake. A public boat launch, Kitty's Landing, and a day-use area on the northwest side are operated by the County of Athabasca (Fig. 2). The sport fishery includes yellow perch, northern pike and walleye. In 1988, a long-term aeration program was begun to enhance sport fish habitat in Amisk Lake. The lake and all inlet streams are closed to fishing for a seven-week period in spring (Alta. For. Ld. Wild. 1989). There are no boating regulations specific to Amisk Lake, but general federal regulations apply (Alta. For. Ld. Wild. 1988). Moderate algal blooms develop in midsummer in Amisk Lake. The lake is surrounded by trembling aspen, willow, and clumps of white spruce and jack pine. Waterfowl and shorebirds are abundant, especially in the shallow bays.

Drainage Basin Characteristics

Amisk Lake lies at the western edge of the Beaver River drainage basin. Skeleton Lake drains into the lake from the west. The Long Lake outflow, which is the headwaters of the Amisk River (Chipeniuk 1975), enters at the south end. Water from Amisk Lake flows over a small control structure at the north end into the Amisk River which flows east to the Beaver River (Fig. 1).

About 88% of the drainage basin of Amisk Lake is forested; the dominant trees are trembling aspen, balsam poplar and jack pine (Table 1). There are two moderate-sized lakes in the drainage basin: Skeleton Lake to the northwest and Long Lake to the southwest. Muskeg areas are scattered throughout the drainage basin along with many temporary ponds and small lakes. The terrain is generally gently rolling to rolling, but the land rises steeply from the banks of the lake in places (Alta. For. Ld. Wild. n.d.).

Agricultural development is limited to only 4% of the drainage basin. There are gas wells on both sides of the lake and a large gravel pit to the northwest. Most of the land surrounding the lake is Crown land and is undeveloped, but there are two moderate-sized cottage subdivisions on the west side of the north basin (Amisk Lake Estates and Pelican Beach), a third subdivision just west of the lake (Baywin Estates) and a large trailer camp (Amisk Lake Trailer Park) at the north end of the lake.

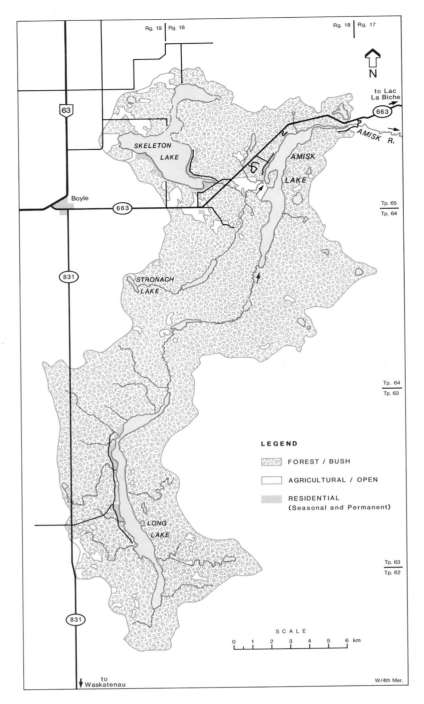

Figure 1. Features of the drainage basin of Amisk Lake.
SOURCES: Alta. Envir. n.d.[a]; En. Mines Resour. Can. 1972; 1973.
Updated with 1985 aerial photos.

LEGEND

FOREST / BUSH

AGRICULTURAL / OPEN

RESIDENTIAL
(Seasonal and Permanent)

SCALE

0 1 2 3 4 5 6 km

Table 1. Characteristics of Amisk Lake drainage basin.

area (excluding lake) (km²)[a]	234°
soil[b]	Orthic Gray Luvisol
bedrock geology[c]	Lea Park Formation (Upper Cretaceous): shale, ironstone concretions; marine bordering on Wapiti Formation (Upper Cretaceous): sandstone, mudstone, bentonite, scattered coal beds; nonmarine
terrain[b]	undulating to gently rolling
ecoregion[d]	Dry Mixedwood Subregion of Boreal Mixedwood
dominant vegetation[d]	trembling aspen, balsam poplar, jack pine
mean annual inflow (m³)[a, e]	10.4 x 10⁶
mean annual sunshine (h)[f]	2264

NOTE: [e]excluding groundwater inflow
SOURCES: [a]Alta. Envir. n.d.[a]; [b]Kjearsgaard 1972; [c]Alta. Res. Counc. 1972; [d]Strong and Leggat 1981; [f]Envir. Can. 1982

Several small streams together with two larger streams—one from Long Lake and the other from Skeleton Lake—flow into Amisk Lake. These streams are dotted with beaver dams, and flow is intermittent.

Lake Basin Characteristics

Amisk Lake is long (8 km) and relatively narrow (on average 0.6 km wide). The depth of the north basin is similar to that of many of the deeper lakes in central Alberta (mean depth of 10.7 m), whereas the depth of the south basin (mean depth of 19.4 m) is greater than most (Table 2). The lake bed drops steeply from the shore, particularly in the central part of the south basin (Fig. 2).

There are extensive beds of rooted macrophytes in the shallow areas at both ends of the lake and in sheltered coves. The near-shore area of the lake has a sandy substrate. The littoral zone extends to a depth of 4 m (Chambers and Prepas 1988) and covers an area of about 1 km² (Fig. 3).

A rock-filled timber weir was built at the Amisk Lake outflow in 1949 by Ducks Unlimited (Canada). The weir is now covered by a gravel pad and is not monitored (Alta. Envir. n.d.[b]). It has deteriorated over time, and has been used as a road. The lake level has been relatively constant over the period of record, which began in 1969 (Fig. 4). The maximum (612.02 m) and minimum (611.50 m) water levels were both recorded in 1986.

Water Quality

The water quality in Amisk Lake was studied intensively by the University of Alberta from 1980 through 1989 (Prepas et al. n.d.; Prepas 1983[a]; 1983[b]; Prepas and Trew 1983; Babin 1984; Prepas and Vickery 1984[a]; 1984[b]; Babin and Prepas 1985; Prepas and Trimbee 1988). Amisk Lake provides an ideal opportunity to evaluate the processes controlling productivity in a deep, naturally eutrophic lake.

Major ions in the surface waters of Amisk Lake are similar in both basins, and to those of many freshwater lakes in Alberta. The water is well buffered, and calcium and bicarbonate are the dominant ions (Table 3). The surface water is slightly coloured—recorded values have varied from 10 to 20 mg/L Pt (Table 3). Colour in Amisk Lake water increases when runoff from the drainage basin increases (Chambers and Prepas 1988).

Both basins are thermally stratified in summer, as illustrated in Figure 5 with data from 1982. The epilimnion extends to 5 m and the thermocline extends to 10 to 15 m. The hypolimnia are cool; the deep water in the south basin is as much as 2°C cooler than in the north basin. Over the eight summers the lake was studied, the maximum surface temperature recorded was 24°C.

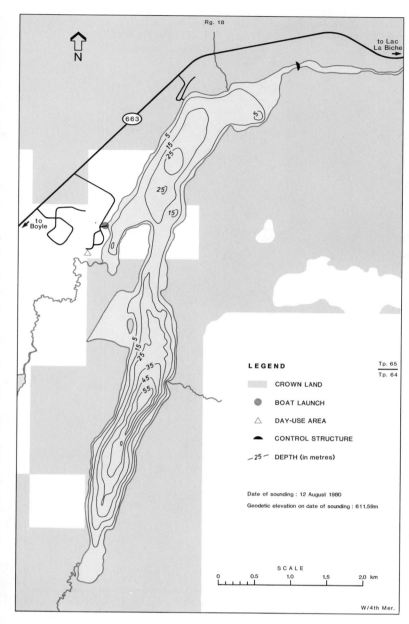

Figure 2. Bathymetry and shoreline features of Amisk Lake.
BATHYMETRY SOURCE: Prepas et al. n.d.

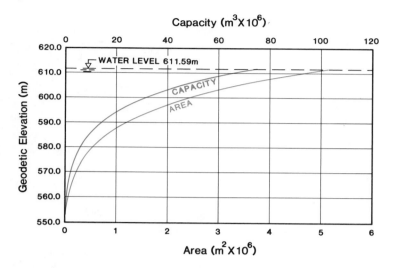

Figure 3. Area/capacity curve for Amisk Lake.
SOURCE: Prepas et al. n.d.

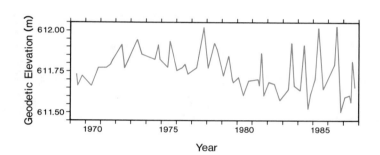

Figure 4. Water level of Amisk Lake, 1969 to 1987.
SOURCE: Alta. Envir. n.d.[b].

Table 2. Characteristics of Amisk Lake.

	Total	North Basin	South Basin
elevation (m)[a, b]	611.70	—	—
surface area (km²)[a, c]	5.15	2.33	2.82
volume (m³)[a, c]	79.7 x 10⁶	25.11 x 10⁶	54.59 x 10⁶
maximum depth (m)[c]	—	34	60
mean depth (m)[c]	15.5	10.8	19.4
shoreline length (km)[d]	24.62	—	—
mean annual lake evaporation (mm)[d]	636	—	—
mean annual precipitation (mm)[d]	517	—	—
mean residence time (yr)[d, e]	8	—	—
control structure	Ducks Unlimited (Canada) rock-filled timber weir		
sill height (m)[f]	611.45	—	—

NOTES: [a]on date of sounding: 12 Aug. 1980; [e]excluding groundwater inflow.
SOURCES: [b]Alta. Envir. n.d.[b]; [c]Prepas et al. n.d.; [d]Alta. Envir. n.d.[a]; [f]Alta. Envir. n.d.[c].

Table 3. Major ions and related water quality variables for the north and south basins of Amisk Lake. Average concentrations in mg/L; pH in pH units. Composite samples from the euphotic zone collected 5 times from 18 May to 21 Sep. 1982. S.E. = standard error.

	North		South	
	Mean	S.E.	Mean	S.E.
pH (range)	8.7–8.9[a]	—	8.4[a]	—
total alkalinity (CaCO₃)	159[b]	—	164[b]	—
specific conductivity (μS/cm)	299	4.6	295	7.6
total dissolved solids	221	10.9	220	8.4
total hardness (CaCO₃)	144[c]	—	140[c]	—
colour (Pt)	10[b]	—	10[b]	—
turbidity (NTU)	2[b]	—	2[b]	—
HCO₃	187[b]	—	185[b]	—
CO₃	4[d]	—	7[b]	—
Mg	14[d]	0.6	14[d]	1.0
Na	18[d]	0.2	18[d]	0.5
K	4[d]	0.2	4[d]	0.3
Cl	2[e]	—	2[e]	—
SO₄	14[f]	0.9	14[e]	—
Ca	30[d]	2.7	31[d]	2.4

NOTES: [a]north—15 May 1984 and 23 July 1986, n = 2, south—14 May 1980, n = 1; [b]21 Sep. 1982; [c]12 Aug. 1980; [d]May to Aug. 1987, n = 4; [e]09 Aug. 1987; [f]22 Oct. 1986 and 09 Aug. 1987
SOURCE: Prepas et al. n.d.

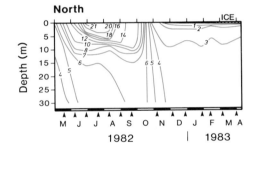

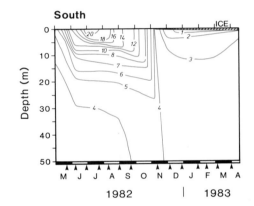

Figure 5. Temperature (°C) in Amisk Lake, north and south basins, May 1982 through March 1983. Arrows indicate sampling dates.
SOURCES: Prepas et al. n.d.; Prepas 1983[a].

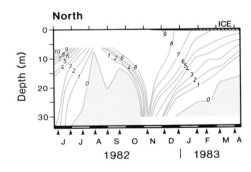

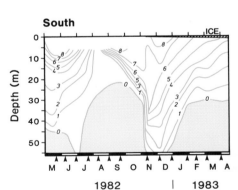

Figure 6. Dissolved oxygen (mg/L) in Amisk Lake, north and south basins, May 1982 through March 1983. Arrows indicate sampling dates.
SOURCES: Prepas et al. n.d.; Babin 1984.

Mixing in spring and fall was incomplete in both basins (Fig. 5, 6). Consequently, dissolved oxygen concentrations were always well below saturation in the deeper waters. In addition, dissolved oxygen consumption rates were very high in the hypolimnia both in summer (in 1980, 0.691 and 0.628 g/m² per day) and under ice in winter (in 1982/83, 0.848 and 0.554 g/m² per day, south and north basins, respectively). Thus, at certain periods such as late summer and late winter, more than half the water in the north basin and three-quarters of the water in the south basin was completely anoxic (Fig. 6). Few macro-organisms can survive extended periods in anoxic water.

In June 1988, a program to aerate the lake with pure oxygen was begun in the north basin of Amisk Lake. The goal of this program is to enhance sport fish habitat by keeping dissolved oxygen concentrations above 2 mg/L throughout the water column year-round. Over the first year, oxygen injection rates varied between 0.3 and

0.9 tonnes per day (Prepas et al. 1989). The project, which has been supported by Alberta Forestry, Lands and Wildlife, Environment Canada and a private company, is intended to continue for a minimum of 10 years. The effect of this treatment on water quality, the plankton, macroinvertebrates and sport fishery is being carefully monitored.

Phosphorus returns from the sediments to the open water at high rates (in 1982, 8.0 and 6.2 mg/m² per day TP, south and north basins, respectively) whenever the dissolved oxygen concentration drops below 3 mg/L. Because these low oxygen conditions exist for long periods, total phosphorus concentrations in the deeper waters often are high; average hypolimnetic and under-ice concentrations frequently reach 150 μg/L. Total phosphorus concentrations are elevated in surface waters during the minimal mixing in spring and thermocline erosion in late summer and fall. Spring total phosphorus

Table 4. Nutrient, chlorophyll _a_ and Secchi depth data for the north and south basins of Amisk Lake. Average concentrations in μg/L. Composite samples from the euphotic zone collected 7 times from May to Sep. 1982 and 13 times from 18 May to 13 Aug. 1987. S.E. = standard error.

| | NORTH | | | | SOUTH | | | |
| | 1982 | | 1987 | | 1982 | | 1987 | |
	Mean	S.E.	Mean	S.E.	Mean	S.E.	Mean	S.E.
total phosphorus	45	6.5	32	2.0	46	7.2	33	2.2
total dissolved phosphorus	10[a, b]	0.6	—	—	11[a, b]	1.0	—	—
soluble reactive phosphorus	2.0[c, d]	—	—	—	1.9[c, d]	—	—	—
total Kjeldahl nitrogen	1 010[e]	53.6	—	—	1 001[e]	56.8	—	—
NO$_3$ + NO$_2$–nitrogen	4.8[e]	1.8	8[g]	1.8	8.4[e]	4.1	9.8	2.5
NH$_4$–nitrogen	10.7[a, b]	6.3	9	2.0	7.1[a, b]	2.7	8.7	1.8
iron	7[d, f]	—	7.4[d,h]	—	—	—	8.7[d, h]	—
chlorophyll _a_	11	1.9	17	1.6	14	1.8	18	1.7
Secchi depth (m)	2.1	0.3	1.5	0.2	2.1[i]	0.2	1.5[g]	0.2

NOTES: [a]1981; [b]n = 3; [c]12 Aug. 1980; [d]n = 1; [e]n = 6; [f]02 Aug. 1985; [g]n = 12; [h]09 Aug. 1987; [i]n = 8
SOURCE: Prepas et al. n.d.

Table 5. A comparison of summer average chlorophyll _a_ and total phosphorus concentrations in Amisk Lake (north basin), 1980 to 1982 and 1984 to 1987. Composite samples collected from the euphotic zone from 15 June to 31 Aug. each summer. S.E. = standard error.

Year	n	Chl _a_ (μg/L)	S.E.	T.P. (μg/L)	S.E.
1980	2	25.4	6.4	40.2	0
1981	3	18.3	1.6	31.6	1.0
1982	4	9.6	1.6	34.5	3.0
1984	9	16.8	1.0	31.0	0.7
1985	4	13.3	1.4	28.4	1.5
1986	3	8.7	0.1	26.2	2.7
1987	10	18.2	1.7	29.6	1.7

SOURCE: Prepas et al. n.d.

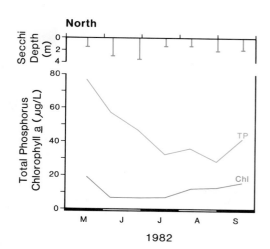

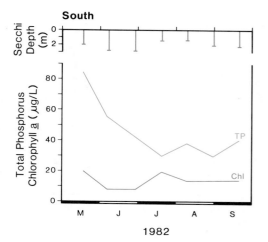

Figure 7. Total phosphorus, chlorophyll _a_ and Secchi depth in Amisk Lake, north and south basins, 1982.
SOURCES: Prepas et al. n.d.; Prepas 1983[a].

concentrations in the surface waters are quite variable. This year-to-year variation probably reflects the extent of winter ice cover and mixing during spring. Higher total phosphorus concentrations in the euphotic zone in 1982 relative to 1987 (Table 4) indicate differences primarily in spring total phosphorus concentrations. Summer total phosphorus concentrations varied between 26 and 40 μg/L over 7 years, from 1980 through 1987 (Table 5). In summer, a small amount (0.05 mg/m^2 per day) of total phosphorus is transported across the thermocline. In contrast, more phosphorus is likely released from the shallower bottom sediments (Shaw and Prepas 1989). Extremely low total iron concentrations in Amisk Lake (Table 4) probably enhance the bioavailability of phosphorus, which first accumulates over the sediments and then is mixed into the surface waters (Nürnberg and Peters 1984).

Phytoplankton biomass (as estimated by chlorophyll _a_) usually follows changes in surface water phosphorus concentrations (Fig. 7). Phytoplankton in Amisk Lake are phosphorus-limited most of the time; that is, biologically available phosphorus concentrations are low relative to concentrations of other essential nutrients. Summer chlorophyll _a_ concentrations are more variable than total phosphorus concentrations in Amisk Lake. Over the 7 years illustrated in Table 5, average summer chlorophyll _a_ concentrations ranged from 9 to 25 μg/L. These annual differences likely reflect yearly variation in spring water temperatures.

Total phosphorus and chlorophyll _a_ concentrations in Amisk Lake are indicative of a eutrophic lake (Table 4). This level of productivity is directly responsible for a substantial portion of the oxygen deple-

tion in deeper water and under ice. High algal biomass is also responsible for a euphotic zone that is relatively shallow (less than 6 m) for such a deep lake. Inorganic nitrogen levels are low, and the ratios of total nitrogen to total phosphorus in summer are high (33 to 54 in 1981, 1982 and 1985). Data collected from Amisk and other lakes indicate that most of the nitrogen does not come from external loading; rather, it is a result of nitrogen fixation by blue-green algae (Prepas et al. n.d.; Prepas and Trimbee 1988).

Biological Characteristics

Plants

The phytoplankton of Amisk Lake was studied during the University of Alberta water quality study (Prepas et al. n.d.). In 1984, the dominant phytoplankton groups in Amisk Lake were diatoms (Bacillariophyta) and cryptomonads (Cryptophyta) in spring, and blue-green algae (Cyanophyta) such as _Aphanizomenon flos-aquae_ and _Anabaena circinalis_ and dinoflagellates (Pyrrhophyta) in summer (Table 6). Blue-green algae are prominent in this lake because of transport of phosphorus-rich water from the hypolimnion (Trimbee and Prepas 1987), particularly during spring and autumn mixing. Macrophytes have not been studied, but Richardson pondweed (_Potamogeton richardsonii_), large-sheath pondweed (_P. vaginatus_) and northern watermilfoil (_Myriophyllum exalbescens_) were widespread during 1988. The macroalga _Chara_ sp. is abundant in a few areas of the lake.

Table 6. Percentage composition of major algal groups by total biomass in the north basin of Amisk Lake. Composite samples from the euphotic zone collected in 1984.

ALGAL GROUP	09 May	15 May	06 June	12 June	10 July	24 July	31 July	21 Aug.
Total Biomass (mg/L)	4.18	0.82	1.10	0.45	6.22	3.85	7.55	10.82
Percentage Composition:								
Cyanophyta	0	0	12	62	60	98	39	30
Chlorophyta	0	0	1	0	0	0	0	0
Chrysophyta	0	0	0	0	0	0	0	2
Bacillariophyta	47	5	0	0	1	0	0	0
Cryptophyta	35	95	87	38	0	1	1	1
Pyrrhophyta	18	0	0	0	39	1	60	67

SOURCE: Prepas et al. n.d.

Invertebrates

Crustacean zooplankton were sampled by University of Alberta researchers in 1981, 1982 and 1984 (Prepas et al. n.d.; Prepas 1983[a]; Prepas and Vickery 1984[a]). In spring 1984, the dominant zooplankton in the top 6 m were copepods such as *Acanthocyclops vernalis* and *Mesocyclops edax*. In May and June, the small cladoceran *Bosmina longirostris* and the larger cladoceran *Daphnia galeata mendota* were prominent, in July *D. galeata mendotae* was the dominant cladoceran, and in August *Diaphanosoma leuchtenbergianum* was most abundant. The large cladoceran, *Daphnia pulex*, was present on most sample dates and the spectacular cladoceran, *Leptodora kindtii* was also present. The dominant cyclopoid copepods were *Acanthocyclops vernalis*, *Mesocyclops edax* and *Diacyclops bicuspidatus thomasi*; the dominant calanoid copepods were *Diaptomus oregonensis* and *D. sicilis*.

The benthic invertebrate community has not been studied in the littoral zone of Amisk Lake but crayfish (*Orconectes virilis*) are known to be present (Chipeniuk 1975). The benthic fauna of the sublittoral and profundal zones in both the north and south basins has been studied by University of Alberta researchers (Dinsmore and Prepas n.d.). From 15 May to 15 November 1988, 120 samples were collected with an Ekman dredge from the sublittoral zone of the north basin and 40 samples from the sublittoral zone of the south basin. For both basins, the dominant taxa were midge larvae (Chironomidae), aquatic earthworms (Oligochaeta), fingernail clams (Sphaeriidae) and scuds (Amphipoda). The average biomass (wet weight) for the north (3.8 g/m²) and south (3.0 g/m²) basins of Amisk Lake compare favourably with the average biomass (3.2 g/m²) measured in the sublittoral zone of Baptiste Lake but is substantially below the average biomass (6.2 g/m²) measured in the sublittoral zone of Narrow Lake.

For the same time period, 440 samples were collected with an Ekman dredge from the profundal zone in the north basin and 200 samples were collected from the profundal zone in the south basin. The dominant taxa were midge larvae and aquatic earthworms. The average biomass (wet weight) of 0.4 g/m² in the north basin and 0.6 g/m² in the south basin was much lower than the average biomass measured in the profundal zones of Baptiste (3.7 g/m²) and Narrow (2.3 g/m²) lakes.

Fish

The fish community includes yellow perch, northern pike, walleye, lake whitefish, cisco, white sucker, burbot, spottail shiner, brook stickleback, ninespine stickleback and Iowa darter (Norris 1987). The most popular sport fish is yellow perch.

There has been a commercial fishery on Amisk Lake since 1944 (Chipeniuk 1975). Initially, its focus was cisco, to provide animal food for local mink ranches. As the mink industry declined, the emphasis of the commercial catch shifted to lake whitefish, but there has been a continuing, though small, market for cisco as mink food (Stenton 1987). Small numbers of pike, perch and walleye are also caught by the commercial fishery. The historical average commercial harvest has dropped from 9 848 kg/year (1944 to 1961) to 4 913 kg/year (1981 to 1986) (Norris 1987).

In 1985 a creel census was conducted at Amisk Lake (Norris 1987). The number of fish caught per hour was high for yellow perch (1.94), low for northern pike (0.21) and poor for walleye (0.02). There were indications that all three species were being harvested at levels exceeding annual production. Both yellow perch and northern pike populations were skewed towards younger, smaller fish (3 to 5 and 2 to 5 year-olds, respectively). The estimated annual rates of production were: 3 120 kg/year for yellow perch, 1 300 kg/year for northern pike, 104 kg/year for walleye, 2 080 kg/year for lake whitefish and 2 600 kg/year for cisco.

Growth of young-of-the-year perch were studied from 1985 through 1987 by the University of Alberta (Abbey n.d.). Young perch grew from an average length of 5.9 mm when they hatched during the third week of May to 62 mm by early October. Growth rates of young perch in Amisk Lake were the highest of those in four deep lakes studied in the Boyle-Athabasca region.

Wildlife

There have been no detailed studies of the waterfowl at Amisk Lake. Ospreys are frequently seen fishing in the lake, and until 1988, had a nest on the island. In 1988, this nest was occupied by a pair of Bald Eagles. Mallards, Common Loons, and Red-necked Grebes nest on the lake and White Pelicans visit the lake to feed in late summer of most years (Prepas et al. n.d.).

E.E. Prepas

References

Abbey, D. n.d. Univ. Alta. Unpubl. data, Edmonton.
Alberta Environment. n.d.[a]. Tech. Serv. Div., Hydrol. Br. Unpubl. data, Edmonton.
———. n.d.[b]. Tech. Serv. Div., Surv. Br. Unpubl. data, Edmonton.
———. n.d.[c]. Water Resour. Admin. Div., Water Resour. Br. Unpubl. data, Edmonton.
Alberta Forestry, Lands and Wildlife. n.d. Fish Wild. Div. Unpubl. data, Edmonton.
———. 1988. Boating in Alberta. Fish Wild. Div., Edmonton.
———. 1989. Guide to sportfishing. Fish Wild. Div., Edmonton.
Alberta Research Council. 1972. Geological map of Alberta. Nat. Resour. Div., Alta. Geol. Surv., Edmonton.
Babin, J. 1984. Winter oxygen depletion in temperate zone lakes. MSc thesis. Univ. Alta., Edmonton.
——— and E.E. Prepas. 1985. Modelling winter oxygen depletion rates in ice-covered temperate zone lakes in Canada. Can. J. Fish. Aquat. Sci. 42:239–249.
Boyle and District Historical Society. 1982. Forests, furrows and faith: A history of Boyle and district. Boyle Dist. Hist. Soc., Boyle.
Chambers, P.A. and E.E. Prepas. 1988. Underwater spectral attenuation and its effect on the maximum depth of angiosperm colonization. Can. J. Fish. Aquat. Sci. 45:1010–1017.
Chipeniuk, R.C. 1975. Lakes of the Lac La Biche district. R.C. Chipeniuk, Lac La Biche.
Dinsmore, P. and E.E. Prepas. n.d. Univ. Alta., Dept. Zool. Unpubl. data, Edmonton.
Energy, Mines and Resources Canada. 1972, 1973. National topographic series 1:50 000 83I/7 (1972), 83I/10 (1973). Surv. Map. Br., Ottawa.

Environment Canada. 1982. Canadian climate normals, Vol. 7: Bright sunshine (1951–1980). Prep. by Atm. Envir. Serv. Supply Serv. Can., Ottawa.

Holmgren, E.J. and P.M. Holmgren. 1976. Over 2000 place names of Alberta. 3rd ed. West. Producer Prairie Books, Saskatoon.

Kjearsgaard, A.A. 1972. Reconnaissance soil survey of the Tawatinaw map sheet (83–I). Alta. Inst. Pedol. Rep. No. S–72–29. Univ. Alta., Edmonton.

Norris, H.J. 1987. Alta. For. Ld. Wild., Fish Wild. Div., St. Paul. Pers. comm.

Nürnberg, G. and R.H. Peters. 1984. Biological availability of soluble reactive phosphorus in anoxic and oxic freshwaters. Can. J. Fish. Aquat. Sci. 41:757–765.

Prepas, E.E. 1983[a]. The influence of phosphorus and zooplankton on chlorophyll levels in Alberta lakes. Alta. Envir., Res. Mgt. Div. Rep. 83/23, Edmonton.

———. 1983[b]. Orthophosphate turnover time in shallow productive lakes. Can. J. Fish. Aquat. Sci. 40:1412–1418.

——— and D.O. Trew. 1983. Evaluation of the phosphorus-chlorophyll relationship for lakes off the Precambrian Shield in western Canada. Can. J. Fish. Aquat. Sci. 40:27–35.

Prepas, E.E. and A.M. Trimbee. 1988. Evaluation of indicators of nitrogen limitation in deep prairie lakes with laboratory bioassays and limnocorrals. Hydrobiologia 159:269–276.

Prepas, E.E. and J. Vickery. 1984[a]. The contribution of particulate phosphorus (>250 µm) to the total phosphorus pool in lake water. Can. J. Fish. Aquat. Sci. 41:351–363.

——— 1984[b]. Seasonal changes in total phosphorus and the role of internal loading in western Canadian lakes. Verh. Internat. Verein. Limnol. 223:303–308.

Prepas, E.E., D.J. Webb and C.L.K. Robinson. 1989. Injection of oxygen into the north basin of Amisk Lake: Final report. Prep. for Alta. Envir., Fish Wild. Div. and Rec. Parks Wild. Foundation, Edmonton.

Prepas, E.E., D.J. Webb, I. Wisheu, A. Trimbee, J.M. Hanson, J. Babin and T.P. Murphy. n.d. Unpubl. data, Univ. Alta., Edmonton and Natl. Water Res. Inst., Burlington, Ontario.

Shaw, J.F.H. and E.E. Prepas. 1989. Potential significance of phosphorus release from shallow sediments of deep Alberta lakes. ms submitted to Limnol. Oceanogr.

Stenton, E. 1987. Alta. For. Ld. Wild., Fish Wild. Div., Edmonton. Pers. comm.

Strong, W.L. and K.R. Leggat. 1981. Ecoregions of Alberta. Alta. En. Nat. Resour., Resour. Eval. Plan. Div., Edmonton.

Trimbee, A.M. and E.E. Prepas. 1987. Evaluation of total phosphorus as a predictor of the relative importance of blue-green algae with emphasis on Alberta lakes. Can. J. Fish. Aquat. Sci. 44:1337–1342.

BEAVER LAKE

MAP SHEET: 73L/12, 13
LOCATION: Tp66 R12, 13 W4
LAT/LONG: 54°43'N 111°37'W

Beaver lake is a large, attractive recreational lake that is popular for boating and fishing. It is situated in the Lakeland Region of Improvement District No. 18 (South), about 170 km northeast of the city of Edmonton. The closest population centre is the town of Lac La Biche, 5 km to the northwest (Fig. 1). To reach Beaver Lake from Edmonton, take Highway 28 north and east to Highway 36, then drive north to the town of Lac La Biche. From there, a secondary road extends east from Highway 36 to the northwest end of the lake, where Beaver Lake community, Beaver Lake Provincial Recreation Area and an Alberta Forest Service ranger station are located.

The name "Beaver" is probably a translation from the Cree name. The lake is the headwater of the Beaver River, which appeared on the Turnor map of 1790, and both lake and river were named on the Harmon map of 1820 (Chipeniuk 1975; Holmgren and Holmgren 1976).

Members of the Beaver Lake Band, who live on Beaver Lake Indian Reserve 131, are descended from the Woodland Cree who traditionally hunted, fished and trapped in the vicinity of Beaver Lake. Chief Peeaysis signed Treaty No. 6 in 1876 and the present reserve was assigned in 1911. In 1984, the band membership was 319 people (Alta. Native Aff. 1986).

Sometime during the 1860s, two Oblate Fathers from the Lac La Biche Mission established Mission du Lac Castor on the south shore of Beaver Lake. Two log churches were built before the present-day church was constructed in about 1907. When Beaver Lake Reserve was created in 1911, title for the mission's land, which is located at the northern boundary of the reserve, was given to the Oblate Fathers (Chipeniuk 1975).

The history of Beaver Lake community dates back to about 1919, when an extensive fire burned the area. Shortly afterward, a settler named Max Huppie acquired land at the northwest corner of Beaver Lake. The area was named Sampietro Beach, and over the years, Huppie sold a number of small parcels of his land to cottagers before his death in 1959 (Chipeniuk 1975).

Access to the lake is available at the Beaver Lake Provincial Recreation Area, which is operated by Alberta Recreation and Parks (Fig. 2). Facilities include 140 campsites, pump water, several docks and boat launches, and a day-use area with a picnic shelter, tables and fireplaces. There is no sandy beach or designated swimming area, but people swim from the sand and stone shore. Two boat launches are available in Beaver Lake community as well.

Although the water in Beaver Lake is green at times, algal blooms rarely occur, and aquatic vegetation grows in shallow areas. Boating and fishing are the most popular activities at the lake. Boats are prohibited in posted areas and the lake is closed to sport fishing for a period during April and May each year (Alta. For. Ld. Wild. 1988; 1989). The main sport fish species are northern pike, yellow perch and walleye. During the August long weekend each year, the town of Lac La Biche holds the Blue Feather Fish Derby on Beaver Lake. The derby attracts about 2 000 anglers, who compete for major prizes. The lake also supports commercial and domestic fisheries for lake whitefish.

Drainage Basin Characteristics

Beaver Lake has a large drainage basin that is about 9 times the size of the lake (Tables 1, 2). Beaver Lake receives water from two other

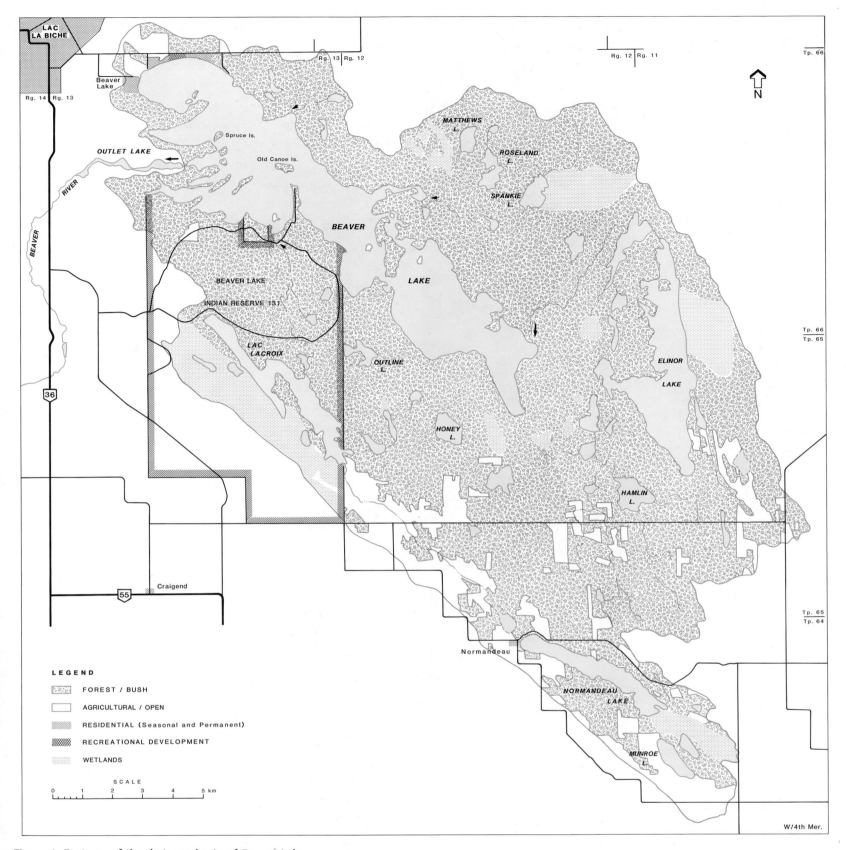

Figure 1. Features of the drainage basin of Beaver Lake.
SOURCES: Alta. Envir. n.d.[b]; En. Mines Resour. Can. 1971. Updated with 1982 and 1986 aerial photos.

lakes in the watershed: a stream from Elinor Lake flows into the southeast basin and a stream from Lac la Croix flows into the northwest basin (Fig. 1). Two large areas, which include Roseland Lake to the east and Normandeau Lake to the southeast, drain into Beaver Lake only during years when water levels are sufficiently high. As well, four small streams enter the lake on the north shore. Beaver Lake is the headwater of the Beaver River. The lake's outlet creek, which is located on the west side of the north basin, flows into Outlet Lake, which drains into the Beaver River and, eventually, into the Churchill River.

In general, the topography of the drainage basin ranges from undulating to strongly rolling, but near the lake, the land is gently to moderately rolling. The main soils throughout the watershed are Orthic Gray Luvisols of a clay loam or loam type. These are moderately well-drained soils that formed on weakly calcareous glacial till. Extensive wetlands are mainly located in four areas: on the Beaver Lake Reserve, east of Spankie and Elinor lakes, west of Matthews Lake and southeast of Normandeau Lake (Fig. 1). Poorly drained Organic soils (Fibrisols and Mesisols) are present in these areas (Kocaoglu 1975).

The Beaver Lake watershed is part of the Dry Mixedwood Subregion of the Boreal Mixedwood Ecoregion (Strong and Leggat 1981). Most of the drainage basin is forested. The dominant tree species on well-drained to moderately well-drained Gray Luvisols is trembling

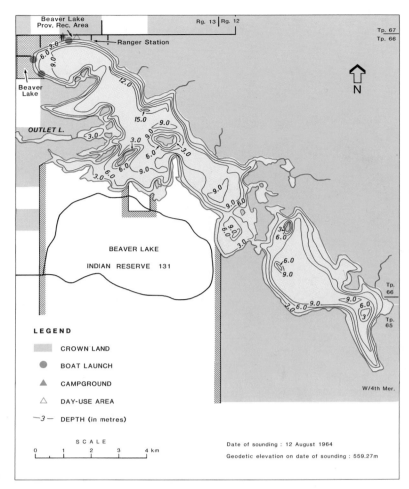

Figure 2. Bathymetry and shoreline features of Beaver Lake.
BATHYMETRY SOURCE: Alta. Envir. n.d.[c].

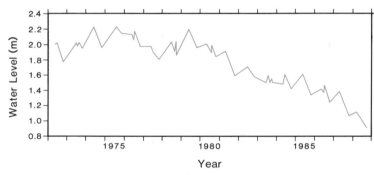

Figure 3. Water level of Beaver Lake, 1972 to 1988. Water levels refer to an assumed datum.
SOURCE: Envir. Can. 1972–1988.

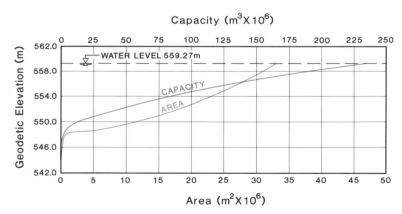

Figure 4. Area/capacity curve for Beaver Lake.
SOURCE: Alta. Envir. n.d.[c].

Table 1. Characteristics of Beaver Lake drainage basin.

area (excluding lake) (km²)[a]	290
soil[b]	Orthic Gray Luvisols
bedrock geology[c]	La Biche Formation (Upper Cretaceous): shale, ironstone partings and concretions; marine
terrain[c]	undulating to strongly rolling
ecoregion[d]	Dry Mixedwood Subregion of Boreal Mixedwood
dominant vegetation[d]	trembling aspen
mean annual inflow (m³)[a, e]	6.92 x 10⁶
mean annual sunshine (h)[f]	2 240

NOTE: [e]excluding groundwater inflow
SOURCES: [a]Alta. Envir. n.d.[b]; [b]Kocaoglu 1975; [c]Alta. Res. Counc. 1972; [d]Strong and Leggat 1981; [f]Envir. Can. 1982

Table 2. Characteristics of Beaver Lake.

elevation (m)[a, b]	559.27
surface area (km²)[a, b]	33.1
volume (m³)[a, b]	234 x 10⁶
maximum depth (m)[a, b]	15.2
mean depth (m)[a, b]	7.1
shoreline length (km)[c]	74.7
mean annual lake evaporation (mm)[d]	640
mean annual precipitation (mm)[d]	528
mean residence time (yr)[d, e]	73
control structure	none

NOTES: [a]on date of sounding: 12 Aug. 1964; [e]excluding groundwater inflow
SOURCES: [b]Alta. Envir. n.d.[c]; [c]En. Mines Resour. Can. 1971; [d]Alta. Envir. n.d.[b]

aspen, whereas in less well-drained areas, trembling aspen may grow in conjunction with balsam poplar. Stands of white spruce occur infrequently, as white spruce is a climax species that succeeds trembling aspen/balsam poplar forests that are past maturity. Jack pine grows on well-drained ridges near wetlands and black spruce and tamarack grow on poorly drained Organic soils (Hay et al. 1985).

Only a small part of the watershed has been cleared for agriculture, mostly in the south and southeast. The main agricultural activities are livestock production and production of pasture and forage crops such as hay, oats and barley. Members of the Beaver Lake Band operate several farms on reserve land. Natural gas is extracted from wells that dot the countryside. Four productive wells and one capped well were located on the Beaver Lake Reserve in 1979 (Esso Resour. Can. Ltd. 1979).

The Beaver Lake shoreline is developed only at the northwest end. In 1988, the hamlet of Beaver Lake comprised two subdivisions with 154 developed lots and a third subdivision that had not been developed (White 1988). Also, in 1988, part of the hamlet obtained its water supply from, and sent its sewage to, the town of Lac La Biche. The rest of the hamlet was scheduled to connect with the Lac La Biche facilities by 1990 (White 1988).

Lake Basin Characteristics

Beaver Lake is a large water body (33 km², Table 2) with an irregular shape. It is divided into two distinct basins that are joined by a narrow channel. The northwest basin, with a maximum depth of 15.2 m, is deepest. It contains several islands, the number of which varies with the water level. The southeast basin, with a maximum depth of 10.7 m, is shallower and contains only one or two islands, depending on water level. Both basins slope quite steeply to their greatest depth; the bottom of each basin is quite flat, except in the vicinity of the islands.

The elevation of Beaver Lake has been monitored since 1972 (Fig. 3) by Environment Canada under the joint federal provincial

Table 3. Major ions and related water quality variables for the northwest basin of Beaver Lake. Average concentrations in mg/L; pH in pH units. Composite samples from the euphotic zone collected 6 times from 28 May to 23 Oct. 1986. S.E. = standard error.

	Mean	S.E.
pH (range)	7.9–8.6	—
total alkalinity ($CaCO_3$)	191	0.6
specific conductivity (μS/cm)	409	2.3
total dissolved solids (calculated)	227	2.0
total hardness ($CaCO_3$)	183	1.1
total particulate carbon	1[a]	0.2
dissolved organic carbon	15	0.2
HCO_3	222	2.7
CO_3	<6	—
Mg	23	0
Na	13	0.9
K	10	0.1
Cl	<1	—
SO_4	29	2.4
Ca	35	0.4

NOTE: [a]n = 5
SOURCE: Alta. Envir. n.d.[a], Naquadat station 01AL06AA1200

Table 4. Nutrient, chlorophyll *a* and Secchi depth data for the northwest basin of Beaver Lake. Average concentrations in μg/L. Composite samples from the euphotic zone collected 6 times from 28 May to 23 Oct. 1986. S.E. = standard error.

	Mean	S.E.
total phosphorus	33	2.3
total dissolved phosphorus	12	2.4
total Kjeldahl nitrogen	1 137	38.0
$NO_3 + NO_2$–nitrogen	<6	—
NH_4–nitrogen	30	5.2
iron	<20	—
chlorophyll *a*	10.6	2.45
Secchi depth (m)	2.9	0.40

SOURCE: Alta. Envir. n.d.[a], Naquadat station 01AL06AA1200

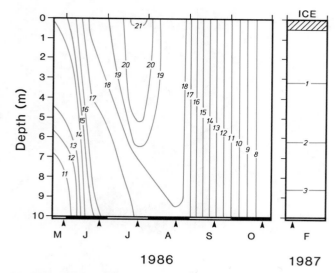

Figure 5. Temperature (°C) of the northwest basin of Beaver Lake, 1986 and 1987.
SOURCE: Alta. Envir. n.d.[a].

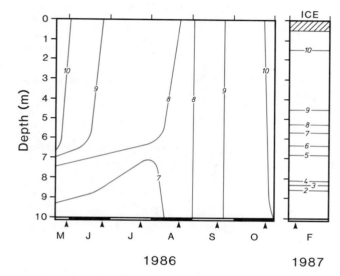

Figure 6. Dissolved oxygen (mg/L) in the northwest basin of Beaver Lake, 1986 and 1987.
SOURCE: Alta. Envir. n.d.[a].

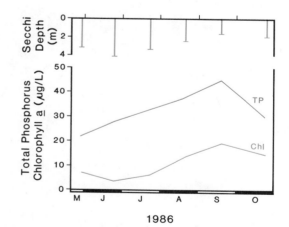

Figure 7. Total phosphorus, chlorophyll *a* and Secchi depth in the northwest basin of Beaver Lake, 1986.
SOURCE: Alta. Envir. n.d.[a].

hydrometric agreement (Alta. Envir. n.d.[c]). The water levels refer to an assumed bench mark rather than geodetic elevation. The water level was quite stable between 1972 and 1980, but declined fairly steadily between 1981 and 1988. The difference between the historic maximum surface elevation, recorded in 1975, and the historic minimum elevation, recorded in 1988, is 1.42 m. Changes in the area and capacity of Beaver Lake with fluctuations in water level are illustrated in Figure 4.

Water Quality

The water quality of Beaver Lake was studied by Alberta Environment from March to October in 1986 and in February of both 1979 and 1987 (Alta. Envir. n.d.[a]). The lake was also studied during 1965 and 1966 by a researcher with the University of Alberta (Pinsent 1967).

Beaver Lake has fresh, hard, well-buffered water. The major ions are bicarbonate, calcium and sulphate (Table 3). During the summer of 1986, the water column in the northwest basin was weakly thermally stratified until mid-August, when it became isothermal (Fig. 5). Throughout the open-water period, the water column was uniformly well-oxygenated at all depths (Fig. 6). In February 1987, the water immediately below the ice was well-oxygenated, but dissolved oxygen concentrations below a depth of 9 m declined to less than 2.0 mg/L.

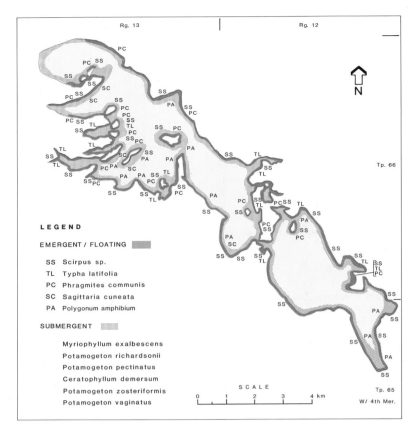

Figure 8. Species composition and distribution of aquatic macrophytes in Beaver Lake, 14 August 1985.
SOURCE: modified from Mills 1987.

Table 5. Average reported domestic catch, average commercial catch and estimated summer/winter sport catch in Beaver Lake. Data in kg/year.

Species	Domestic (1983–1986)	Commercial (1982–1988)	Sport (1983/84)
lake whitefish	29 172	18 037	—
northern pike	2 805	148	11 914
walleye	2 805	114	3 921
yellow perch	—	0	1 608
other	1 883	—	—
TOTAL	36 665	18 199	17 443

SOURCES: Alta. For. Ld. Wild. n.d.; Mills 1987

Beaver Lake is mesotrophic. The average concentration of chlorophyll *a* during the open-water season in 1986 (Table 4) indicates that the lake contains moderate concentrations of algae. The water is green during late summer, but quite clear for the rest of the year. In 1986, the highest concentrations of chlorophyll *a* (19.1 μg/L) and total phosphorus (45 μg/L) were recorded in mid-September (Fig. 7). The reason for the increase in total phosphorus was probably a transfer of phosphorus from the sediments to the euphotic zone. Precipitation levels were low during September 1986. Consequently, phosphorus inputs from runoff and directly from precipitation were low.

Biological Characteristics

Plants

The phytoplankton and macrophyte communities of Beaver Lake were sampled by a researcher at the University of Alberta in 1965 and 1966 (Pinsent 1967). Macrophytes were also surveyed in August 1985 by Fish and Wildlife Division staff (Mills 1987).

During 1966, four blue-green algal species (*Aphanizomenon flos-aquae, Anabaena flos-aquae, Anabaena spiroides* and *Microcystis aeruginosa*) were dominant in summer, and one species of diatom (*Stephanodiscus astraea*) was dominant in spring and fall.

Beaver Lake has many protected backwaters and shallow bays; these areas provide good habitat for aquatic plants. Twelve species were recorded in the 1965 and 1966 studies, and 11 species were recorded in August 1985 (Fig. 8). The most common emergent species were bulrush (*Scirpus* sp.), common cattail (*Typha latifolia*) and reed grass (*Phragmites communis*). Arrowhead (*Sagittaria cuneata*) and water smartweed (*Polygonum natans*) were also recorded. The dominant submergent species were northern water-milfoil (*Myriophyllum exalbescens*), Richardson pondweed (*Potamogeton richardsonii*) and Sago pondweed (*P. pectinatus*). Other submergent species present were coontail (*Ceratophyllum demersum*), flat-stemmed pondweed (*P. zosteriformis*) and large-sheath pondweed (*P. vaginatus*).

Invertebrates

The invertebrate community of Beaver Lake was studied by a researcher at the University of Alberta in 1965 and 1966 (Pinsent 1967). From May to September in 1966, zooplankton were collected by vertical net haul from a depth of 8 m to the surface. Sixteen species of cladocerans and copepods were identified. *Chydorus* sp. and *Cyclops* sp. were most abundant.

Benthic invertebrates were sampled monthly with an Ekman dredge at 14 stations during the open-water period in 1965 and 1966. The standing crop (dry weight) of benthic invertebrates in the littoral and profundal zones was 19.3 kg/ha in 1965 and 9.3 kg/ha in 1966. The lower biomass in 1966 was attributed to a decline in the percentage of total biomass comprising midge larvae (Chironomidae). Midge larvae were more than 90% of the biomass in 1965 but only 50% in 1966. Scuds (Amphipoda) were the second largest component of the biomass in both years. The fauna in the littoral zone was more diverse than in the profundal zone; 32 taxa were identified in the former area, but only 13 in the latter.

Fish

Nine species of fish have been reported in Beaver Lake: northern pike, walleye, yellow perch, lake whitefish, burbot, white sucker, brook stickleback, Iowa darter and spottail shiner (Pinsent 1967; Mills 1987). The lake is managed for domestic, commercial and recreational fisheries.

The Cree living on the Beaver Lake Reserve have traditionally used the lake as a source of fish. The domestic fishery takes the major portion of the annual fish production; the main catch is lake whitefish (Table 5). The fishery has expanded from 1977/78, when 59 licences were issued, to 1986/87, when 202 licences were issued

Table 6. Angler numbers, effort and harvest from Beaver Lake. Creel survey data collected from 20 May to 27 Aug. 1983 and 31 Dec. 1983 to 24 Mar. 1984. WE = walleye; NP = northern pike; YP = yellow perch.

	Summer				Winter			
	WE	NP	YP	Total	WE	NP	YP	Total
number of anglers	—	—	—	6 666	—	—	—	1 739
angler-hours	—	—	—	19 959	—	—	—	11 976
total harvested	5 720	11 319	5 700	22 739	999	2 105	2 664	5 768
total yield (kg)	3 117	10 074	1 083	14 274	804	1 840	525	3 169
mean weight (g)	545	890	190	—	805	874	197	—
harvest/angler	0.86	1.70	0.86	3.42	0.57	1.21	1.53	6.89
harvest/angler-hour	0.26	0.24	0.21	0.71	0.08	0.33	0.73	1.14

SOURCE: Mills 1987

(Mills 1987). Between 1983 and 1986, the average annual domestic catch was reported to be 36 665 kg/year.

The commercial fishery was regulated first in 1926, but records are available only since the 1942/43 season (Alta. For. Ld. Wild. n.d.; Alta. Rec. Parks Wild. 1976). The main catch has been lake whitefish, although in some years between 1942/43 and 1954/55, harvests of northern pike and walleye were almost as large. The largest total catch (91 875 kg) was taken in 1943/44. Since about 1973, harvests were much smaller. From 1973/74 to 1987/88, the average total catch (excluding suckers and burbot), was 16 884 kg/year; 99% of this catch was lake whitefish.

The sport fishery is popular with residents of Lac La Biche and visitors to the area. A large number of anglers use the lake year-round (Table 6). More than 8 400 anglers were interviewed by Fish and Wildlife Division staff during two creel surveys conducted over two three-month periods in the 1983/84 season (Mills 1987). The main sport fish species in Beaver Lake are walleye, northern pike and yellow perch. The sport catch for the 1983/84 season was estimated to be 17 443 kg, mostly northern pike (Table 5).

Wildlife

No data are available for the wildlife community that uses Beaver Lake.

M.E. Bradford

References

Alberta Environment. n.d.[a]. Envir. Assess. Div., Envir. Qlty. Monit. Br. Unpubl. data, Edmonton.
———. n.d.[b]. Tech. Serv. Div., Hydrol. Br. Unpubl. data, Edmonton.
———. n.d.[c]. Tech. Serv. Div., Surv. Br. Unpubl. data, Edmonton.
Alberta Forestry, Lands and Wildlife. n.d. Fish Wild. Div. Unpubl. data, Edmonton.
———. 1988. Boating in Alberta. Fish Wild. Div., Edmonton.
———. 1989. Guide to sportfishing. Fish Wild. Div., Edmonton.
Alberta Native Affairs. 1986. A guide to native communities in Alberta. Native Aff. Secret., Edmonton.
Alberta Recreation, Parks and Wildlife. 1976. Commercial fisheries catch statistics for Alberta, 1942–1975. Fish Wild. Div., Fish. Mgt. Rep. No. 22, Edmonton.
Alberta Research Council. 1972. Geological map of Alberta. Nat. Resour. Div., Alta. Geol. Surv., Edmonton.
Chipeniuk, R.C. 1975. Lakes of the Lac la Biche district. R.C. Chipeniuk, Lac La Biche.
Energy, Mines and Resources Canada. National topographic series 1:50 000 73L/12 (1971), 73L/13 (1971). Surv. Map. Br., Ottawa.
Environment Canada. 1972–1988. Surface water data. Prep. by Inland Waters Directorate. Water Surv. Can., Water Resour. Br., Ottawa.
———. 1982. Canadian climate normals, Vol. 7: Bright sunshine (1951–1980). Prep. by Atm. Envir. Serv. Supply Serv. Canada, Ottawa.
Esso Resources Canada Limited. 1979. Socioeconomic impact assessment of the Cold Lake project on the Beaver Lake Indian Reserve. Esso Resour. Can. Ltd., Calgary.
Hay, W.K., J.M. Veltman and R.W. Haag. 1985. Integrated resource inventory of the east Beaver Lake assessment area: Physical land and forage classifications. Alta. En. Nat. Resour. Tech. Rep. No. T/79, Edmonton.
Holmgren, E.J. and P.M. Holmgren. 1976. Over 2 000 place names of Alberta. 3rd ed. West. Producer Prairie Books, Saskatoon.
Kocaoglu, S.S. 1975. Reconnaissance soil survey of the Sand River area (73L). Alta. Soil Surv. Rep. No. 34, Univ. Alta. Rep. No. SS–15, Alta. Inst. Pedol. Rep. No. S–74–34 1975. Univ. Alta., Edmonton.
Mills, J.B. 1987. Beaver Lake limnological survey, phase 1 and 2. Alta. For. Ld. Wild., Fish Wild. Div. Unpubl. rep., St. Paul.
Pinsent, M.E. 1967. A comparative limnological study of Lac la Biche and Beaver Lake, Alberta. MSc thesis. Univ. Alta., Edmonton.
Strong, W.L. and K.R. Leggat. 1981. Ecoregions of Alberta. Alta. En. Nat. Resour., Resour. Eval. Plan. Div., Edmonton.
White, J.E. 1988. Alta. Mun. Aff., Edmonton. Pers. comm.

COLD LAKE

MAP SHEETS: 73L/8, 9
LOCATION: Tp63–65 R26, 27 W3
Tp63–65 R1, 2 W4
LAT/LONG: 54°33'N 110°06'W

Cold Lake is one of Alberta's largest and deepest lakes, and offers excellent opportunities for fishing, boating and camping. The lake is located on the border between Alberta and Saskatchewan, just south of the Primrose Lake Air Weapons Range (Fig. 1). The Saskatchewan side of the lake is located in Meadow Lake Provincial Park and the Alberta side is part of Improvement District No. 18. To reach the lake from Edmonton, take Highways 28 and 28A northeast for 295 km to the town of Cold Lake on the southwest shore.

The lake was originally named Big Fish Lake by Chipewyan Indians who hunted and trapped in the area (SATA Systems Inc. 1983). Early fur traders and Cree Indians called it Coldwater Lake, and it was named so on the Turnor map of 1790 (Holmgren and Holmgren 1976). The name is indicative of the relatively cool water that persists throughout the year.

The original inhabitants of the Cold Lake region probably were the nomadic Beaver, Blackfoot and Slavey tribes. During the late eighteenth century, these tribes were displaced by the Cree, who arrived in the area in search of furs to supply to traders. Cold Lake was part of a fur trade route into Alberta's northern lake region. The route ran west from Saskatchewan through Waterhen Lake, Lac des Isles and Cold Lake, with a portage from the south end of Cold Lake to the Beaver River (McMillan 1977). The first trading post in the area, Cold Lake House, was established by the North West Company in 1781 near the present day hamlet of Beaver Crossing, about 10 km south of Cold Lake. It was maintained for only a few years, and became a Hudson's Bay post in 1821 when the two companies merged (Alta. Mun. Aff. 1978). Cree and Chipewyan Indians settled in the vicinity of the post, and in 1876 they were assigned Cold Lake Reserve 149, located just south of Beaver Crossing. Two other reserves, 149A and 149B (Fig. 2), were established on the shore of Cold Lake in 1909 and 1911, respectively. In 1984, 1045 band members lived on the three reserves (Alta. Native Aff. 1986).

The first official land survey at Cold Lake was undertaken in 1900 and more detailed surveys were conducted in 1909 and 1914 (McMillan 1977). Settlers arrived soon after, and Cold Lake settlement was established. The settlement became a village in 1953 and a town in 1955 (Acres Consult. Serv. Ltd. 1973). In 1988, the town's population was 3445 people.

Cold Lake is a deep, clear body of water that supports a relatively large number of fish species, including lake trout, which are not present in many Alberta lakes. The provincial size record for lake trout was set in 1929 by a 23.9–kg specimen from Cold Lake (Alta. For. Ld. Wild. 1989). Rainbow trout, yellow perch, walleye, lake whitefish and northern pike are 5 of the 23 other species that inhabit the lake. Algal biomass in Cold Lake is low and aquatic vegetation is restricted to areas sheltered from excessive wave action and ice scour. One of the sheltered areas, in Centre Bay, supports a colony of Western Grebes.

The main recreational activities at Cold Lake are fishing, swimming, motor boating, sailing, canoeing, camping, picnicking, hiking and cross-country and downhill skiing. There are no boating regulations over most of the lake, but in posted areas, boats are either prohibited or subject to maximum speeds of 12 km/hour (Alta. For. Ld. Wild. 1988). Sport fishing regulations prohibit fishing for lake trout from 15 September to 15 November. As well, the entire lake (except that portion lying in Tp62 R2 W4) and all inlet streams are

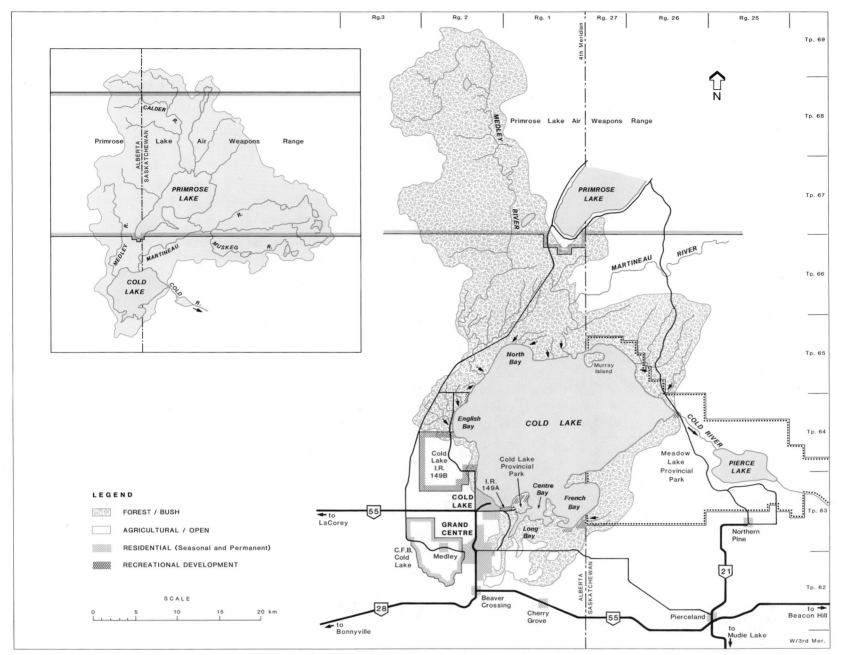

Figure 1. Features of a portion of the drainage basin of Cold Lake. Inset shows boundaries of entire drainage basin. SOURCES: Alta. Envir. n.d.[b]; En. Mines Resour. Can. 1975; 1981; 1987. Updated with 1982 aerial photos.

closed for a designated period during April and May each year (Alta. For. Ld. Wild. 1989).

There are seven areas around the lakeshore that provide recreational facilities for the public (Fig. 2). Three of the areas are operated by Alberta Recreation and Parks: Cold Lake Provincial Park (398 ha), Frenchman's Bay Provincial Recreation Area (449 ha) and English Bay Provincial Recreation Area (18 ha). The provincial park is open year-round and the two recreation areas are open from the Victoria Day weekend to Thanksgiving Day. In total, they provide 154 campsites, pump water, 2 picnic shelters, 3 boat launches, 2 playgrounds and 3 beaches. The provincial park also provides group camping, tap water, a change house, flush toilets, showers, two viewpoints, trails and an amphitheatre.

Three recreational areas are located within the town of Cold Lake (Fig. 2). The first area, Cold Lake Municipal District Park (27 ha), is operated by the Municipal District of Bonnyville. It is open from 15 May to 15 September and provides 40 campsites, flush toilets, tap water, showers, a sewage disposal station, a playground, a sandy beach and swimming area, a boat launch and walking trails. The second area, Kinosoo Park, is operated by the town of Cold Lake. It has washrooms, a playground, a sandy beach and swimming area, a launch for windsurfers and sailboats, picnic tables and a fitness/exercise course. The third area includes a breakwater, marina and boat launch.

On the Saskatchewan side of Cold Lake, Meadow Lake Provincial Park provides Cold Lake campground at the mouth of the Cold River (Fig. 2). This small campground has four random campsites, picnic tables, a small sandy beach and a boat launch for small boats.

Drainage Basin Characteristics

Cold Lake drains an area of approximately 6140 km^2 (Table 1), which is mostly located in Saskatchewan. A large part of the drainage basin is owned by the governments of Canada, Saskatchewan and Alberta. The federal government owns the Primrose Lake Air Weapons Range, a huge tract of land that includes a major portion of the Cold Lake watershed (Fig. 1, inset). Several rivers and streams flow into Cold Lake. The two largest rivers are the Medley, which drains the western part of the watershed, and the Martineau, which drains Primrose Lake and the eastern part of the watershed. Most of the smaller inflows enter the lake on the northern shore. The outlet, the Cold River, flows eastward to the Beaver River in Saskatchewan.

The following discussion of topography and soils applies only to the Alberta portion of the drainage basin south of Primrose Lake Air Weapons Range (Kocaoglu 1975). The land between Cold Lake and the air weapons range is mostly hummocky morainal plain that is characterized by moderately rolling topography (9 to 15% slope) and knobs and ridges interspersed with undrained depressions.

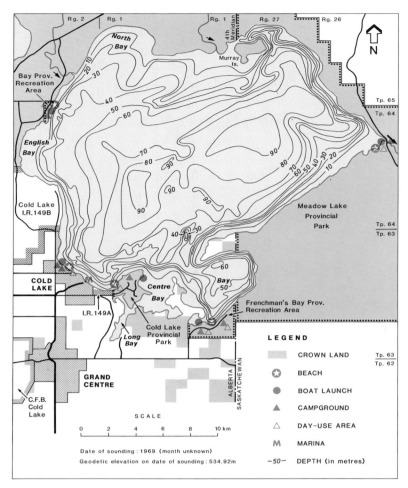

Figure 2. Bathymetry and shoreline features of Cold Lake.
BATHYMETRY SOURCE: Alta. Envir. n.d.[c].

Table 1. Characteristics of Cold Lake drainage basin.

area (excluding lake) (km²)[a]	6140
soil[b, c]	Orthic Gray Luvisols
bedrock geology[b, d]	La Biche Formation (Upper Cretaceous): shale, ironstone partings and concretions; marine
terrain[b, c]	gently undulating to moderately rolling
ecoregion[b, e]	Moist and Dry Mixedwood subregions of Boreal Mixedwood
dominant vegetation[b, e]	trembling aspen, balsam poplar
mean annual inflow (m³)[a, f]	626 x 10⁶
mean annual sunshine (h)[g]	2240

NOTES: [b]Alberta side only; [f]excluding groundwater inflow
SOURCES: [a]Alta. Envir. n.d.[b]; [c]Kocaoglu 1975; [d]Alta. Res. Counc. 1972; [e]Strong and Leggat 1981; [g]Envir. Can. 1982

Table 2. Characteristics of Cold Lake.

elevation (m)[a, b]	534.92
surface area (km²)[a, b]	373
volume (m³)[a, b]	18600 x 10⁶
maximum depth (m)[a, b]	99.1
mean depth (m)[a, b]	49.9
shoreline length (km)[c]	90
mean annual lake evaporation (mm)[d]	634
mean annual precipitation (mm)[d]	460
mean residence time (yr)[d, e]	33
control structure	none

NOTES: [a]on date of sounding: (month unknown) 1969; [e]excluding groundwater inflow
SOURCES: [b]Alta. Envir. n.d.[c]; [c]Alta. Mun. Aff. 1984; [d]Alta. Envir. n.d.[b]

South and east of the lake, the land is rolling morainal plain that is characterized by gently undulating to gently rolling topography (0 to 9% slope). In this area, minor ridges and knobs are interspersed with many wet depressions and small peat bogs. The dominant soils in both land units are moderately well-drained Orthic Gray Luvisols that developed on glacial till. Well-drained to poorly drained alluvial soils are located along the Martineau and Medley river floodplains and large areas of poorly drained Organic soils are located adjacent to English Bay and south of Centre and French bays.

In Alberta, Cold Lake's drainage basin is part of the Moist and Dry Mixedwood subregions of the Boreal Mixedwood Ecoregion (Strong and Leggat 1981). Most of the watershed is covered by forest and muskeg. The dominant trees on Gray Luvisolic and well-drained alluvial soils are trembling aspen, balsam poplar and white spruce. The Gray Luvisols also support white birch, alder and willow. On poorly drained alluvial soils, willows, black spruce, grasses and sedges are common, and Organic soils support black spruce, tamarack, willows, mosses, sedges and coarse grasses (Kocaoglu 1975). The only agricultural activity in the drainage basin takes place south of Cold Lake (Fig. 1). The farms are mixed operations that raise both livestock and grains. The main crops are barley, oats, canola and forage.

Lake Basin Characteristics

Cold Lake is the largest and deepest water body in the Lakeland Region of Alberta. The maximum depth in the central portion of the lake is almost 100 m (Table 2). For the most part, the sides of the basin slope steeply, but there are some relatively shallow areas along the northern and eastern shores and along the southern shore near the provincial park (Fig. 2).

Water levels in Cold Lake have been monitored since 1954 (Fig. 3). The difference between the historic maximum elevation (535.80 m in July 1965) and the historic minimum (534.57 m in December 1967) is 1.24 m. Between 1980 and 1987, the range in water levels was 0.70 m. Changes in the lake's surface area and capacity (up to an elevation of 534.92 m) with fluctuations in water levels are illustrated in Figure 4.

Water is withdrawn from the lake for industrial, municipal and recreational purposes. The two industrial users require water for oil sands plants. Industrial withdrawals from Cold Lake are subject to the Cold Lake-Beaver River Long Term Water Management Plan, which was implemented by Alberta Environment in 1985 (Alta. Envir. 1985). Under this plan, net consumptive withdrawals from Cold Lake are limited to 20.0 x 10⁶ m³/year, but if the lake elevation falls below 534.55 m, industrial withdrawals will be reduced or suspended. In the future, withdrawals by major oil sands plants will be made from the North Saskatchewan River via a water pipeline. Esso Resources Canada has been licenced to withdraw 6.50 x 10⁶ m³/year from Cold Lake since 1983. Between 1984 and 1987, Esso removed an average of 4.23 x 10⁶ m³/year. During the same period, Bow Valley Industries took an average of 0.09 x 10⁶ m³/year from an allocation of 1.40 x 10⁶ m³/year (Alta. Envir. n.d.[d]). The municipal water users are the towns of Cold Lake and Grand Centre, and Canadian Forces Base Cold Lake at Medley. Jointly, they are allocated 7.4 x 10⁶ m³/year of water. From 1984 to 1987, they used an average of 2.40 x 10⁶ m³/year. The only recreational user is a skiing facility, Kinosoo Ridge, which is located within Frenchman's Bay Recreation Area on land leased from Alberta Recreation and Parks. They use about 0.03 x 10⁶ m³ of water each winter to make artificial snow (Alta. Envir. n.d.[d]).

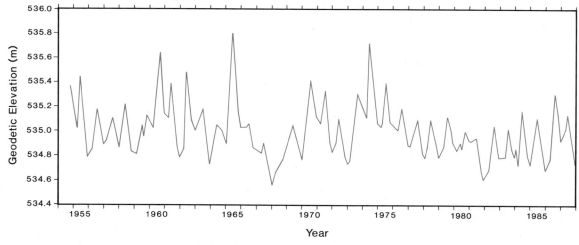

Figure 3. Water level of Cold Lake, 1954 to 1987.
SOURCE: Envir. Can. 1954–1987.

Table 3. Major ions and related water quality variables for Cold Lake.
Average concentrations in mg/L; pH in pH units. Composite samples from the euphotic zone collected 8 times from 05 June to 16 Oct. 1981. S.E. = standard error.

	Mean	S.E.
pH (range)	7.3–8.4	—
total alkalinity (CaCO₃)	129	5.4
specific conductivity (μS/cm)	249	12.4
total dissolved solids (calculated)	133[a]	5.9
total hardness (CaCO₃)	117[a]	4.4
dissolved organic carbon	9[a]	1.3
HCO₃	155[a]	7.2
CO₃	0[a]	0
Mg	10[a]	0.5
Na	8	0.5
K	1.6	0.13
Cl	0.8	0.04
SO₄	3[a]	0.3
Ca	30[a]	1.3

NOTE: [a]$n = 7$
SOURCE: Envir. Can. n.d., Naquadat station 01AL06AF3390

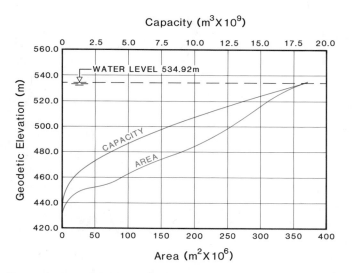

Figure 4. Area/capacity curve for Cold Lake.
SOURCE: Alta. Envir. n.d.[c].

Water Quality

The water quality in Cold Lake has been studied since 1973. Data were collected by the University of Alberta in 1973 and 1974 (Rasmussen and Gallup 1979), by Alberta Environment in 1978 and 1979 and from 1982 to 1986 (Alta. Envir. n.d.[a]), and by the Government of Canada in 1980 and 1981 (Envir. Can. n.d.; Constable 1981).

Cold Lake has fresh water that is well-buffered and moderately alkaline (Table 3); turbidity is low (1.1 NTU) and the water is very transparent (Table 4). The major ions are calcium and bicarbonate.

In spring, ice leaves the lake approximately three weeks later than it does on other lakes in the area, and in autumn, ice forms about six weeks later. The lake becomes strongly thermally stratified by June, but the surface water does not warm to temperatures higher than 19°C even during midsummer (Fig. 5). The concentration of dissolved oxygen throughout the water column is high during the open-water period. During winter, samples have not been taken to the greatest depth, but in February 1986, the dissolved oxygen concentration to 50 m was greater than 10 mg/L.

Cold Lake is oligo-mesotrophic. In 1981, the average concentration of chlorophyll *a* was 3.2 μg/L and the highest concentration (5.5 μg/L) was recorded in early October (Fig. 6). The reasons for the autumn chlorophyll *a* peak are not known. Total phosphorus was highest in early June (19 μg/L) and fell to its lowest level (12 μg/L) in October (Fig. 6).

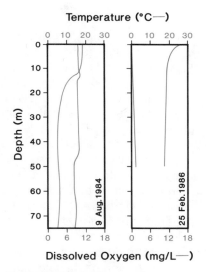

Figure 5. Temperature and dissolved oxygen in Cold Lake, 1984 and 1986.
SOURCE: Alta. Envir. n.d.[a].

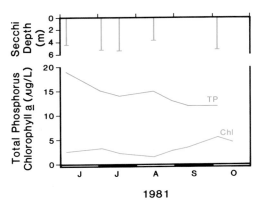

Figure 6. Total phosphorus, chlorophyll *a* and Secchi depth in Cold Lake, 1981.
SOURCE: Envir. Can. n.d.

Table 4. Nutrient, chlorophyll *a* and Secchi depth data for Cold Lake. Average concentrations in μg/L. Composite samples from the euphotic zone collected 8 times from 05 June to 16 Oct. 1981. S.E. = standard error.

	Mean	S.E.
total phosphorus	14[a]	0.9
total Kjeldahl nitrogen	518[b]	53.8
$NO_3 + NO_2$–nitrogen	9	1.7
NH_4–nitrogen	19[a]	4.0
iron	<58	—
chlorophyll *a*	3.2	0.46
Secchi depth (m)	4.9[c]	0.32

NOTES: [a]n = 7; [b]n = 6; [c]n = 5
SOURCE: Envir. Can. n.d., Naquadat station 01AL06AF3390

Table 5. Percentage composition of major algal groups by total biomass in five bays of Cold Lake, 1978. Samples collected from each bay on one day only in May, July and Oct. or Nov. Sampling depth varied from 0.5 to 3.8 m.

ALGAL GROUPS	May					July					Oct./Nov.				
	Cen	Eng	Fre	Nor	Lon	Cen	Eng	Fre	Nor	Lon	Cen	Eng	Fre	Nor	Lon
Total Biomass (mg/L)	3.06	2.17	1.90	2.60	1.22	1.51	0.53	0.57	0.54	2.94	0.52	0.26	0.47	0.56	4.26
Percentage Composition:															
Cyanophyta	1	0	0	0	0	11	28	13	28	43	0	20	45	42	16
Chlorophyta	18	6	1	2	17	24	2	6	4	38	28	10	11	2	33
Chrysophyta	42	2	2	4	55	6	13	15	24	5	47	8	22	12	22
Bacillariophyta	17	38	69	88	20	36	57	59	42	13	0	24	4	33	9
Cryptophyta	22	28	6	7	8	22	0	5	2	1	25	3	10	11	19
Euglenophyta	0	0	0	0	0	0	0	0	0	0	0	0	8	0	0
Pyrrhophyta	0	26	22	0	0	0	0	1	0	0	0	36	0	0	0

NOTES: Total biomass for English Bay is for littoral zone only; Cen = Centre; Eng = English; Fre = French; Nor = North; Lon = Long
SOURCE: modified from Cross 1979

Biological Characteristics

Plants

The phytoplankton community in Centre, Long, French, English and North bays (Fig. 1) was sampled during May, July and October or November in 1978 (Cross 1979). Samples were taken at depths of 0.5 to 3.8 m, except in English Bay, where sample depths ranged from 1 to 6 m. Species were identified and counted, but biomass was calculated only for the various algal groups. The biomass of algae in the littoral zones of all five bays was low throughout 1978 (Table 5). Overall, the greatest biomass was recorded in May, when the dominant groups in all bays were either golden-brown algae (Chrysophyta) or diatoms (Bacillariophyta). During July, diatoms remained important in all bays except Long Bay, and in autumn, they accounted for a large part of the biomass in English and North bays. Blue-green (Cyanophyta) species were also important in English, North and French bays in autumn, whereas golden-brown species dominated Centre Bay samples. Long Bay was the most productive area sampled during summer and autumn. In July, green (Chlorophyta) and blue-green algae were most abundant, and during early November, green algae formed most of the biomass.

The macrophytes in Long Bay were studied briefly in 1981 by Alberta Energy and Natural Resources (McGregor 1983) and the macrophytes between the town of Cold Lake and Cold Lake Provincial Park were studied in 1986 by the University of Alberta (Chambers and Prepas n.d.; 1988). Long Bay is relatively shallow and supports a dense macrophyte population. Emergent or floating-leaved species identified were yellow water lily (*Nuphar variegatum*), arrowhead (*Sagittaria cuneata*), sedge (*Carex aquatilis*) and cattail (*Typha* sp.). Submergent species included flat-stemmed pondweed (*Potamogeton zosteriformis*) and northern watermilfoil

(*Myriophyllum exalbescens*). Species sampled between the town of Cold Lake and the provincial park included white-stem (*P. praelongus*), Richardson (*P. richardsonii*) and Sago (*P. pectinatus*) pondweeds, as well as stonewort (*Chara* sp.). Plants grew to a depth of 6.6 m.

Invertebrates

The zooplankton and benthic communities in Centre, Long, French, English and North bays (Fig. 1) were sampled during February, May, July and October or November in 1978 (Cross 1979). Invertebrates were sampled at 3 depths (one depth per open-water sampling date) in the littoral zone (1 to 3.8 m) in each bay. The profundal zone (5.7–m to 14–m depths) was sampled only in English Bay, at 4 depths. This was also the site of the only February sample.

The zooplankton was sampled with 65–μm mesh net and abundance was reported as number per litre. The dominant species in the littoral zones (less than 4–m deep) of the five bays were very similar. The most abundant copepod in all areas was *Diacyclops bicuspidatus thomasi*. In four of the five bays, the dominant cladoceran was *Bosmina longirostris*, and in the fifth bay (Long Bay), *Chydorus sphaericus* was the main species. The dominant rotifer in Centre and French bays was *Keratella cochlearis*, whereas in Long Bay, this species shared prominence with *K. quadrata*. In English and North bays, *Polyarthra dolichoptera* was most abundant. In the profundal zone (up to 13 m) of English Bay, the most abundant copepod (*D. bicuspidatus thomasi*) and cladoceran (*B. longirostris*) species were the same as in the littoral zone, but the dominant rotifer was *Kellicottia longispina*.

The total volume of benthic invertebrates in the five bays was measured as mL/m^2, but the abundance of individual species was recorded as mean number/m^2. Two species not commonly found in

Table 6. Species of fish reported in Cold Lake.

rainbow trout	spottail shiner	ninespine stickleback
lake trout	fathead minnow	trout-perch
cisco	longnose dace	yellow perch
lake whitefish	pearl dace	walleye
northern pike	longnose sucker	Iowa darter
lake chub	white sucker	logperch
finescale dace	burbot	slimy sculpin
emerald shiner	brook stickleback	spoonhead sculpin

SOURCES: Bidgood and Doonance 1966; Roberts 1975

Table 7. Estimated angler numbers, effort and harvest from Cold Lake. Estimates based on creel survey data collected from 17 May to 26 Aug. 1986. WE = walleye; NP = northern pike; LT = lake trout.

	WE	NP	LT	Total
number of anglers[a]	—	—	—	15 351
angler-hours[b]	—	—	—	46 947
total number fish harvested[c]	662	9 619	214	10 495
total yield (kg)	611	13 601	545	14 757
mean weight (g)	924	1 414	546	—
catch/angler-hour	0.01	0.20	0.01	0.22
harvest/angler-hour[b, c]	0.01	0.19	0.01	0.21
harvest/angler[a, c]	0.04	0.60	0.02	0.66

NOTES: [a]observed no. anglers = 3 849; [b]observed hours = 12 144; [c]based on observed no. fish kept:
   WE = 157, NP = 2 293, LT = 59
SOURCE: Alta. For. Ld. Wild. n.d.

Alberta, the opossum shrimp *Mysis relicta* and the scud *Pontoporeia affinis*, were collected in the littoral area of Cold Lake. The single largest total biomass in the littoral zone (136.5 mL/m²) was recorded in Centre Bay in July at a depth of 1 m. Generally, however, biomass was highest in autumn. The dominant benthic invertebrates collected at most littoral sites during the open-water period were the three scuds (Amphipoda) *Hyalella azteca*, *Gammarus lacustris* and *Pontoporeia affinis*. Several exceptions, however, are notable. In July, midge larvae (Chironomidae: mainly *Microspectra*, *Cladotanytarsus* and *Procladius*) were dominant in North Bay, and in October, aquatic earthworms (Oligochaeta) and midge larvae shared prominence with *Hyalella azteca* in French and North bays. In the profundal zone of English Bay, sphaeriid clams (Pelecypoda) and scuds (*P. affinis*) were the dominant groups in February and chironomids (mainly *Heterotrissocladius marcidus* and *Microspectra* sp.) were the most abundant groups in July. The highest biomass in the profundal zone (84.8 mL/m²) was measured in October at a depth of 13 m; this sample was numerically dominated by two scuds, *Hyalella azteca* and *P. affinis*.

Fish

Cold Lake contains a greater number of fish species than most other lakes in Alberta. The 24 species reported to inhabit the lake are listed in Table 6. Two other species, Arctic grayling and kokanee, were introduced into the Medley River but failed to become established (Roberts 1975). To supplement natural reproduction, lake trout have been stocked in Cold Lake every year since 1974, with the exception of 1984 and 1985. As well, rainbow trout are planted annually in the Medley River just north of Cold Lake. The lake whitefish and cisco in Cold Lake are infested with cysts of the tapeworm *Triaenophorus crassus* (Alta. Rec. Parks Wild. 1976). They are safe to eat, but must be cooked thoroughly.

Most of the lake is deep, cold and relatively unproductive. In general, the fish fauna of the lake proper is dominated by fall-spawning coldwater sport and commercial species such as lake whitefish, cisco and lake trout. Long, Centre and French bays, however,

provide a shallow, warm, productive habitat that supports spring-spawning coolwater species such as northern pike, yellow perch, walleye and a variety of forage species. For northern pike and yellow perch, this complex of bays is probably the most important spawning and rearing area in the lake (Aquat. Envir. Ltd. 1983).

The Cold Lake Fish Hatchery opened on 23 May 1987. It is located on English Bay, 26 km north of the town of Cold Lake. The hatchery produces fish to enhance walleye populations and to sustain or introduce trout populations in provincial lakes. It can produce 16 to 25 million walleye fry, 1.4 million walleye fingerlings (in conjunction with a satellite pond at Lac La Biche), 1.4 million rainbow trout and 550 000 lake trout annually (Alta. For. Ld. Wild. n.d.).

Cold Lake is managed for domestic, commercial and recreational fisheries. Recent data on the domestic fishery at the lake are not available. Between 1970/71 and 1980/81, the number of domestic licences issued in Alberta for Cold Lake ranged from 52 to 102. The main species taken is lake whitefish (Alta. For. Ld. Wild. n.d.).

The commercial fishery on the Alberta portion of Cold Lake has been regulated since 1921, and records have been kept since 1942. Until 1946, the commercial species of primary interest was lake trout. As the commercial fishery for lake whitefish developed during the late 1930s and early 1940s, angling success for lake trout diminished. Lake trout were caught in large numbers by the nets set for lake whitefish. Since the lake trout in Cold Lake grow slowly and mature late, the stock was quickly depleted by the whitefish fishery (Miller 1954). The commercial fishery was closed from 1948 to 1955 to allow the trout stock to recover. When it reopened for the 1955/56 season, a special effort was made to protect the lake trout while whitefish were taken. The commercial trout quota was set at 1 360 kg and the lake was zoned into fishing areas in which trout generally were not found (Allan 1973). The lake trout population received another setback during the 1960s and 1970s when the Canadian Armed Forces sprayed the pesticide DDT in the watershed. Levels of DDT in the natural lake trout population were similar to levels that caused reproductive failure in laboratory populations (Sullivan 1988). By the 1980s, the concentration of DDT in the lake trout had decreased to much lower levels. The trout population, however, has made only a very slow recovery. As of 1988, it still may be reproducing at a low rate (Sullivan 1988). The commercial quota for lake trout was reduced from 1 800 kg in 1987/88 to 900 kg in 1988/89.

The commercial fishery took cisco in large numbers from 1963/64 until the mid–1970s (Alta. Rec. Parks Wild. 1976). Cisco are used for mink food, so the size of the cisco catch depends upon the size of the ranch mink populations. In 1966/67, cisco made up 83% (270 646 kg) of the total catch (326 080 kg), but by 1987/88, they represented only 1% (762 kg) of the total catch (60 862 kg). Whitefish have accounted for the major portion (57%) of the total catch during the 1970s and 1980s.

A creel survey was conducted on Cold Lake from 17 May to 26 August in 1986 (Table 7). Anglers were surveyed in Long Bay at Cold Lake Provincial Park, at the town of Cold Lake dock, in English and Frenchman's bays and at the Meadow Lake Provincial Park campground. The largest catches were northern pike and, secondarily, walleye. Lake trout catches were much smaller and yellow perch were considered incidental. All of the walleye and lake trout caught were kept, but 63% of the northern pike were returned to the water. Harvest rates for walleye (0.01 fish/angler-hour) in Cold Lake were much lower than the average rate for 19 lakes in the Lakeland Region (0.10 fish/angler-hour), but harvest rates for northern pike (0.19 fish/angler-hour) were similar to those for 22 regional lakes (0.22 fish/angler-hour). No other lakes sampled in the region contained lake trout, so comparisons cannot be made for this species. Fishing pressure was quite low (1.3 hours/ha of lake) for Cold Lake as a whole, but was considerably higher for the shoreline area only (44.3 hours/ha of shoreline).

Wildlife

The main basin of Cold Lake does not provide good wildlife habitat in comparison to Long Bay and its associated wetlands. Most of the lake's shoreline is exposed to intensive wave action and ice scour, which eliminate emergent vegetation suitable for wildlife habitat. In addition, the great depth and large volume of water in the lake prevent early spring warming, which is necessary for many wildlife species. The most productive areas in the lake are located at the mouth of the Martineau River and in Long and Centre bays. These areas are relatively shallow and physically protected from waves and ice (Rippon 1983).

Long Bay and the southern half of Centre Bay are separated from the rest of the lake by a submerged sandbar. The bays become ice free and warm before the rest of the lake in spring; this warming allows earlier growth of plants and development of a large invertebrate population. Emergent vegetation such as cattails, sedges, bulrushes, reed grass and water lilies provide abundant wildlife habitat. A colony of 400 to 500 pairs of Western Grebes nests in two locations on Centre Bay and Bald Eagles have nested on the point of land that separates Centre Bay from French Bay (Kristensen and Nordstrom 1979; Rippon 1983).

The area near the mouth of the Martineau River has good wildlife habitat because of shallow water, a complex shoreline, and protection from waves and ice scour provided by Murray Island. Beaver, muskrats, waterfowl and water birds are well represented, but no quantitative wildlife surveys have been made (Rippon 1983).

M.E. Bradford

References

Acres Consulting Services Limited. 1973. A study of the commercial recreational potential of Lund's Point, Cold Lake, Alberta. Prep. for Alta. Ld. For., Edmonton.
Alberta Environment. n.d.[a]. Envir. Assess. Div., Envir. Qlty. Monit. Br. Unpubl. data, Edmonton.
———. n.d.[b]. Tech. Serv. Div., Hydrol. Br. Unpubl. data, Edmonton.
———. n.d.[c]. Tech. Serv. Div., Surv. Br. Unpubl. data, Edmonton.
———. n.d.[d]. Water Resour. Admin. Div., Sur. Water Rights Br. Unpubl. data, Edmonton.
———. 1985. Cold Lake-Beaver River long term water management plan. Plan. Div., Edmonton.
Alberta Forestry, Lands and Wildlife. n.d. Fish Wild. Div. Unpubl. data, Edmonton.
———. 1988. Boating in Alberta. Fish Wild. Div., Edmonton.
———. 1989. Guide to sportfishing. Fish Wild. Div., Edmonton.
Alberta Municipal Affairs. 1978. Cold Lake regional plan, heritage preservation: Heritage resources background paper. Reg. Plan. Sec., Edmonton.
———. 1984. Improvement District No.18 (South) lake planning framework. Plan. Br., Edmonton.
Alberta Native Affairs. 1986. A guide to native communities in Alberta. Native Aff. Secret., Edmonton.
Alberta Recreation, Parks and Wildlife. 1976. Commercial fisheries catch statistics for Alberta, 1942–1975. Fish Wild. Div., Fish. Mgt. Rep. No. 22, Edmonton.
Alberta Research Council. 1972. Geological map of Alberta. Nat. Resour. Div., Alta. Geol. Surv., Edmonton.
Allan, J.H. 1973. The whitefish fishery of Cold Lake. Alta. Ld. For., Fish Wild. Div. Unpubl. rep., Edmonton.
Aquatic Environments Limited. 1983. Fisheries studies; main report and detailed data report [Appendices F and G]. *In* Cold Lake-Beaver River water management study, Vol. 4: Fisheries. Alta. Envir., Plan. Div., Edmonton.
Bidgood, B.F. and J.I. Doonance. 1966. Cold Lake winter commercial fishery. Alta. Ld. For., Fish Wild. Div. Unpubl. rep., Edmonton.
Chambers, P.A. and E.E. Prepas. n.d. Univ. Alta., Dept. Zool. Unpubl. data, Edmonton.
———. 1988. Underwater spectral attenuation and its effect on the maximum depth of angiosperm colonization. Can. J. Fish. Aquat. Sci. 45:1010–1017.
Constable, M. 1981. A baseline limnological survey of Cold and Primrose Lakes, 1980–81. Envir. Can., Envir. Prot. Serv., Sci. Prog. Br., Edmonton.
Cross, P.M. 1979. Limnological and fisheries surveys of the aquatic ecosystems at Esso Resources' Cold Lake base: Data volume. Aquat. Envir. Ltd., Calgary.
Energy, Mines and Resources Canada. 1975, 1981, 1987. National topographic series 1:25 000 73K (1975), 73M (1975), 73L (1981), 73N (1987). Surv. Map. Br., Ottawa.
Environment Canada. n.d. Envir. Prot. Serv., Sci. Prog. Br. Unpubl. data, Edmonton.
———. 1954–1987. Surface water data. Prep. by Inland Waters Directorate. Water Surv. Can., Water Resour. Br., Ottawa.
———. 1982. Canadian climate normals, Vol. 7: Bright sunshine (1951–1980). Prep. by Atm. Envir. Serv. Supply Serv. Can., Ottawa.
Holmgren, E.J. and P.M. Holmgren. 1976. Over 2000 place names of Alberta. 3rd ed. West. Producer Prairie Books, Saskatoon.
Kocaoglu, S.S. 1975. Reconnaissance soil survey of the Sand River area. Alta. Soil Surv. Rep. No. 34, Univ. Alta. Bull. No. SS–15, Alta. Inst. Pedol. Rep. No. S–74–34 1975. Univ. Alta., Edmonton.
Kristensen, J. and W.R. Nordstrom. 1979. Western Grebe colony, Cold Lake. Alta. Rec. Parks Wild., Parks Div. and Esso Resour. Can. Ltd. Unpubl. rep., Edmonton.
McGregor, C.A. 1983. Summary [Appendix K] and Detailed report [Appendix L]. *In* Cold Lake-Beaver River water management study, Vol. 7: Ecological inventory of lake shorelines. Alta. Envir., Plan. Div., Edmonton.
McMillan, W.J. 1977. An interpretation concept plan for Cold Lake Provincial Park. MSc thesis. Univ. Calg., Calgary.
Miller, R.B. 1954. The management of the fish resources at Cold Lake. Alta. Ld. For., Fish Wild. Div. Unpubl. rep., Edmonton.
Rasmussen, J.B. and D.N. Gallup. 1979. A survey of physical, chemical and biological characteristics of a series of lakes of central Alberta. Alta. Envir., Poll. Contr. Div. Unpubl. rep., Edmonton.
Rippon, B. 1983. Water related wildlife resources [Appendix I]. *In* Cold Lake-Beaver River water management study, Vol. 5: Fisheries and wildlife. Alta. Envir., Plan. Div., Edmonton.
Roberts, W.E. 1975. Piscivorous fishes of Cold Lake. MSc thesis. Univ. Alta., Edmonton.
SATA Systems Inc. 1983. Profiles of regions and small communities in northern Alberta: Northeast/central. Prep. for North. Alta. Devel. Counc., Peace River.
Strong, W.L. and K.R. Leggat. 1981. Ecoregions of Alberta. Alta. En. Nat. Resour., Resour. Eval. Plan. Div., Edmonton.
Sullivan, M. 1988. Alta. For. Ld. Wild., Fish Wild. Div., St. Paul. Pers. comm.

ETHEL LAKE

MAP SHEET: 73L/9
LOCATION: Tp64 R3 W4
LAT/LONG: 54°32'N 110°21'W

Ethel Lake is an attractive, peaceful lake set in low, rolling hills. It is located about 18 km northwest of the town of Cold Lake and 295 km northeast of the city of Edmonton near the southern boundary of Improvement District No. 18. It can be reached by two improved roads that branch north from Highway 55. These roads, locally known as Ethel Lake Road and Primrose Lake Road (Fig. 1), are joined by an east-west road at the north end of Ethel Lake that provides access to Ethel Lake Recreation Area on the northeast shore (Fig. 2).

The origin of the name "Ethel" is not known, but in the early part of the twentieth century, Ethel Lake was called Bear Lake (Girard 1984). The original inhabitants of the area probably were the nomadic Beaver, Blackfoot and Slavey tribes. Late in the eighteenth century, these tribes were displaced by Cree who came in search of furs to trade with white traders (McMillan 1977). Nearby Cold Lake was part of a fur trade route into Alberta's northern lake region. The first trading post in the area, Cold Lake House, was established by the North West Company in 1781 near the present-day hamlet of Beaver Crossing, about 28 km southeast of Ethel Lake. It was maintained for only a few years, and became a Hudson's Bay post in 1821 when the two companies merged (Alta. Mun. Aff. 1978).

Ethel Lake Recreation Area is operated by Alberta Recreation and Parks. It is open from Victoria Day to Thanksgiving Day and provides 14 campsites, a picnic shelter, a boat launch and pump water. Favoured recreational activities at the lake include fishing, swimming, canoeing, water skiing and power boating. There are no boating restrictions over most of the lake, but in posted areas, power boats are subject to a maximum speed of 12 km/hour (Alta. For. Ld. Wild. 1988).

Ethel Lake's water is quite clear and the concentration of algae is generally low. The shoreline is ringed by dense beds of aquatic vegetation that restrict boat access to some areas, particularly the southeast bay. Species of sport fish in the lake include lake whitefish, northern pike, yellow perch and walleye. The lake's tributaries and outlet stream are closed to sport fishing during a designated period in April and May each year (Alta. For. Ld. Wild. 1989). A small commercial fishery, which operates every other year, mainly harvests lake whitefish from the lake.

Drainage Basin Characteristics

Ethel Lake's gross drainage basin covers an area of 542 km², which is about 110 times the size of the lake (Tables 1, 2; Fig. 1, inset). Approximately 11% of this area consists of permanent bodies of water. Three-quarters of the water flowing into Ethel Lake comes from the north: from Burnt Lake, through May and Marie lakes, to Ethel Lake via Marie Creek. A smaller amount of water (20%) flows into Ethel Lake from Moore and Hilda lakes to the west (Alta. Mun. Aff. 1980). The remaining inflows originate from the immediate drainage basin (Fig. 1), which is quite small (34 km²). These inflows include precipitation, runoff and water from a small stream that flows into the southeast bay.

Ethel Lake and its drainage basin lie on a rolling morainal plain that is characterized by undulating to gently rolling topography (Kocaoglu 1975). Minor ridges and knobs are intermixed with numerous wet depressions and small peat bogs. The main soils throughout the drainage basin are moderately well drained Orthic Gray Luvisols of

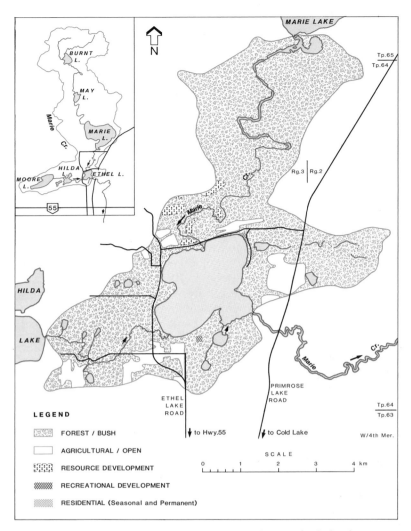

Figure 1. Features of the immediate drainage basin of Ethel Lake. Inset shows the gross drainage area.
SOURCES: Alta. Envir. n.d.[c]; En. Mines Resour. Can. 1971. Updated with 1986 aerial photos.

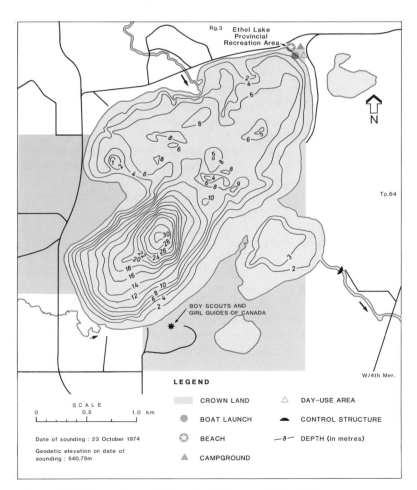

Figure 2. Bathymetry and shoreline features of Ethel Lake.
BATHYMETRY SOURCE: Alta. Envir. n.d.[d].

Table 1. Characteristics of Ethel Lake drainage basin.

area (excluding lake) (km²)[a]	542
immediate area (excluding lake) (km²)[a]	33.8
soil[b, c]	Orthic Gray Luvisols
bedrock geology[d]	La Biche Formation (Upper Cretaceous): shale, ironstone partings and concretions; marine
terrain[b]	undulating to gently rolling
ecoregion[e]	Dry Mixedwood and Moist Mixedwood subregions of Boreal Mixedwood
dominant vegetation[e]	trembling aspen, balsam poplar
mean annual inflow (m³)[a, f]	13.1 x 10⁶
mean annual sunshine (h)[g]	2 240

NOTE: [f]excluding groundwater inflow
SOURCES: [a]Alta. Envir. n.d.[c]; [b]Alta. Mun. Aff. 1980; [c]Kocaoglu 1975; [d]Alta. Res. Counc. 1972; [e]Strong and Leggat 1981; [g]Envir. Can. 1982

Table 2. Characteristics of Ethel Lake.

elevation (m)[a, b]	540.75
surface area (km²)[a, b]	4.90
volume (m³)[a, b]	32.2 x 10⁶
maximum depth (m)[a, b]	30.0
mean depth (m)[a, b]	6.6
shoreline length (km)[c]	11.0
mean annual lake evaporation (mm)[d]	634
mean annual precipitation (mm)[d]	439
mean residence time (yr)[d, e]	2.5
control structure[f]	steel sheet-pile fixed-crest weir with Denil II fishway
main weir elevation (m)[f]	541.25
narrow weir elevation (m)[f]	540.99
fishway sill elevation (m)[f]	540.55

NOTES: [a]on date of sounding: 23 Oct. 1974; [e]excluding groundwater inflow
SOURCES: [b]Alta. Envir. n.d.[d]; [c]En. Mines Resour. Can. 1971; [d]Alta. Envir. n.d.[c]; [f]Alta. Envir. n.d.[a]

either a loam or loamy sand type. These soils formed on fine loamy, moderately to strongly calcareous glacial till. Other common soils include Degraded Eutric and Dystric Brunisols, Brunisolic Gray Luvisols and Mesisols.

Ethel Lake's immediate drainage basin is part of the Dry Mixedwood Subregion of the Boreal Mixedwood Ecoregion, whereas the remainder of the drainage basin is part of the Moist Mixedwood Subregion (Strong and Leggat 1981). The difference between the two subregions is the dominance of balsam poplar. In the dry subregion, trembling aspen is the dominant tree on well-drained to moderately well-drained Gray Luvisols, whereas in the moist subregion, trembling aspen and balsam poplar are dominant on moderately well-drained Gray Luvisols. In both subregions, jack pine grows on rapidly to well-drained Eutric Brunisols and white spruce grows on imperfectly drained Gleysols and Gray Luvisols. Poorly drained Organics and Gleysols support a cover of black spruce and willows, and very poorly drained Organic soils support sedges. Wet, low-lying areas are located along the inflow from Hilda Lake, along Marie Creek at the outlet, and southeast and northeast of Ethel Lake.

Most of the land in the drainage basin is classified as marginal for agriculture, and only a few areas have been cleared (Fig. 1). Agricultural land use includes a few small mixed-farming operations that raise either forage crops and livestock or cash and forage crops. As well, some Crown land is leased for grazing (Alta. Mun. Aff. 1980). Resource extraction is a major industry in the area. Four companies hold leases for oil sands, petroleum and natural gas extraction in the drainage basin, and two Esso Resources Canada heavy oil pilot projects are situated 1.6 km and 6.5 km northwest of the lake. A large gravel deposit is located immediately north of the lake, adjacent to Marie Creek.

About half of the Ethel Lake shoreline is Crown land (Fig. 2). Long-term recreational leases are held by the Girl Guides, the Boy Scouts and the St. Thomas Aquinas Parents and Teachers Association (Alta. Mun. Aff. 1980). Residential development of the shoreline is limited. A small cottage development and several permanent residences are located on the northeast shore. They are accessible from a gravel road that runs south from the recreation area; one cottage on the northwest shore is located near the inlet from Marie Creek.

Lake Basin Characteristics

Ethel Lake consists of four bays: a deep southwest bay with a maximum depth of 30 m, two northern bays with maximum depths of 8 m and 6 m, and a shallow southeast bay with a maximum depth of 3 m (Fig. 2). The southeast bay contains dense beds of aquatic macrophytes. The bottom sediments in the lake consist of organic mud and sand overlying clay. Sandy beaches are located at the recreation area in the northeast bay and on private land near the inlet from Hilda Lake in the southwest bay (McGregor 1983).

In the early 1980s, Alberta Environment initiated studies of the Cold Lake-Beaver River basin to ensure wise management of the basin's water resources and to resolve concerns regarding high demand on local water supplies (Alta. Envir. 1983). A long term plan for water resources management in the Cold Lake region was adopted by the government in October 1985. The long term water management plan applies to the surface and groundwater resources in the Cold Lake and lower Beaver River basins. It is based on long term industrial water supply to oil sands plants in the region by a pipeline from the North Saskatchewan River.

Ethel Lake has been used as a source of water by Esso Resources Canada since 1965, when the company was licenced to withdraw 0.802×10^6 m^3/year for the Leming oil sands pilot plant. The total allocation was increased to 1.54×10^6 m^3/year in 1974, to serve the new May/Ethel plant in addition to the Leming plant (Alta. Envir. n.d.[e]). From 1984 to 1987, Esso withdrew an average of 0.487×10^6 m^3/year, or about 1.5% of the lake's total volume. This volume of water is less than 3% of the lake's mean annual outflow of 17.4×10^6 m^3. In 1985, as part of the long-term water management plan, Alberta Environment set a minimum elevation of 540.72 m for Ethel Lake (Alta. Envir. 1985). If the lake level fell to this elevation, industrial water withdrawals would be suspended. In addition, it was recommended that over the short term, withdrawals should be limited to 0.700×10^6 m^3/year, and the Esso Resources licence was changed accordingly. After the water pipeline to the North Saskatchewan River is completed, Ethel Lake will no longer be used as a major source of water for oil sands plants.

The elevation of Ethel Lake has been monitored since 1973 (Fig. 3). Water levels declined slightly after August 1978, when a property owner removed a beaver dam from Marie Creek (Alta. Envir. n.d.[e]). In March 1980, Esso constructed a weir in Marie Creek to raise the lake level and ensure a constant supply of water for their two pilot plants (Alta. Mun. Aff. 1980). In 1983, Alberta Environment proposed a higher range of lake levels for Ethel Lake. These levels could not be achieved with Esso's old weir, so a new, steel sheet-piling control structure with a higher sill elevation was planned. In May 1986, the new structure was completed and ownership was transferred from Esso to Alberta Environment. The dam has a main weir, a slightly lower narrow weir to maintain downstream flow, and a Denil II fishway to allow fish passage upstream into the lake (Table 2). Water levels reached an historic high in September 1986 (Fig. 3) after the control structure was completed. These levels were due to beaver dams downstream of the lake, not the control structure. The range in lake levels over the period of record is 0.81 m. Changes in the lake's area and capacity with fluctuations in water level are illustrated in Figure 4.

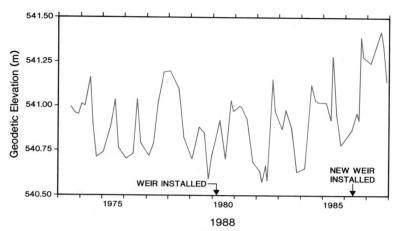

Figure 3. Water level of Ethel Lake, 1973 to 1987.
SOURCE: Envir. Can. 1973–1987.

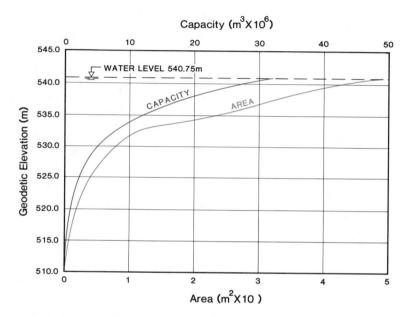

Figure 4. Area/capacity curve for Ethel Lake.
SOURCE: Alta. Envir. n.d.[d].

Water Quality

The water quality of Ethel Lake has been studied intensively by Alberta Environment since 1978 (Alta. Envir. n.d.[b]; Prepas and Trew 1983; Trew et al. 1983) and was studied by the University of Alberta in 1981 (Prepas 1983). Ethel Lake is one of six lakes in Alberta that have an extensive long-term data base for water quality.

The water in Ethel Lake is fresh and well-buffered (Table 3). Bicarbonate and calcium are the dominant ions. The ionic composition of the water reflects the inflow from other lakes in the Marie Creek drainage basin. The concentration of total dissolved solids in Ethel Lake is lower than that in Moore and Hilda lakes, to the west, and higher than that in Marie and May lakes, to the north (Alta. Envir. n.d.[b]).

Ethel Lake is sheltered by trees and has a short fetch. Consequently, winds over the deep basin often are not strong enough to mix the water column in spring. Data for mid- to late May are available for 8 of the 11 years from 1978 to 1988. In five of the eight years, the lake did not mix to the bottom and the deepest water was anoxic. In the other three years, the amount of mixing was variable. In mid-May of 1982, the temperature of the water column was uniform (Fig. 5), but an oxygen gradient was recorded: dissolved oxygen concentrations ranged from 10.6 mg/L at the surface to 8.6 mg/L at the bottom (Fig. 6). The deeper water becomes anoxic every year during summer, when the lake is thermally stratified. The water column usually mixes to the bottom, however, by late October. Exceptions occurred in October of 1979 and 1982, when dissolved oxygen concentrations in the deep basin were less than 1 mg/L at

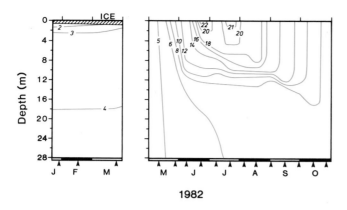

Figure 5. Temperature (°C) of Ethel Lake, 1982. Arrows indicate sampling dates.
SOURCE: Alta. Envir. n.d.[b].

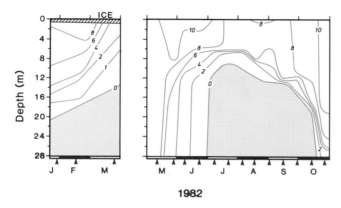

Figure 6. Dissolved oxygen (mg/L) in Ethel Lake, 1982. Arrows indicate sampling dates.
SOURCE: Alta. Envir. n.d.[b].

Table 3. Major ions and related water quality variables for Ethel Lake. Average concentrations in mg/L; pH in pH units. Composite samples from the euphotic zone collected 5 times from 12 May to 27 Oct. 1982. S.E. = standard error.

	Mean	S.E.
pH (range)	8.3–8.4	—
total alkalinity (CaCO₃)	160	1.3
specific conductivity (μS/cm)	300	7.1
total dissolved solids (calculated)	163	2.1
total hardness (CaCO₃)	126	4.9
total particulate carbon	2[a]	0.3
dissolved organic carbon	11[a]	0.3
HCO₃	188	3.3
CO₃	<4	—
Mg	15	0.3
Na	14	0.5
K	3	0.1
Cl	3	0.2
SO₄	4[b]	1.5
Ca	27[b]	1.7

NOTES: [a]n = 12; [b]n = 6
SOURCE: Alta. Envir. n.d.[b], Naquadat station 01AL06AC4690

Table 4. Nutrient, chlorophyll *a* and Secchi depth data for Ethel Lake. Average concentrations in μg/L. Composite samples from the epilimnion collected 13 times from 12 May to 27 Oct. 1982. S.E. = standard error.

	Mean	S.E.
total phosphorus	25	2.0
total dissolved phosphorus	10	0.8
soluble reactive phosphorus	3[a]	0.6
total Kjeldahl nitrogen	720	16.4
NO₃ + NO₂–nitrogen	2[b]	0.2
NH₄–nitrogen	2[b]	0.5
iron	<20[b]	—
chlorophyll *a*	8.0[a]	1.03
Secchi depth (m)	3.1[c]	0.26

NOTES: [a]n = 12; [b]1986 data, n = 6; [c]n = 7
SOURCE: Alta. Envir. n.d.[b], Naquadat station 01AL06AC4690

the bottom. Under ice, the deep water in the southwest bay of Ethel Lake frequently becomes anoxic by February or March, as in 1980, 1981, 1982, 1984 and 1989, or severely depleted in dissolved oxygen, as in 1983, 1986, 1987 and 1988. Surface concentrations, however, have always exceeded 8 mg/L in late winter. The thermal and dissolved oxygen patterns in the deep basin of Ethel Lake are similar to those in many deep lakes in eastern Alberta.

Ethel Lake is mesotrophic. The water is generally clear and attractive for most of the summer because concentrations of algae are low. In 1982, the Secchi depth averaged 3.1 m (Table 4). From 1980 to 1987, year-to-year variations in the average total phosphorus concentration from mid-June to mid-September were less than the variations in chlorophyll *a* concentrations (Table 5). In summer each year, the surface waters are phosphorus-limited (Prepas 1983), and the highest annual phosphorus and chlorophyll concentrations in the euphotic zone (Fig. 7) usually occur after the spring and fall overturn, when phosphorus-rich water from near the sediments is mixed into the surface water.

Phosphorus is released from the bottom sediments of the lake during anoxic periods. In the summer of 1982, the phosphorus concentration at a depth of 30 m increased from about 80 μg/L in mid-June to 220 μg/L in mid-September. Phosphorus levels in the surface water, on the other hand, remained relatively stable during this period. Loading of total phosphorus to Ethel Lake from internal and external sources was calculated for the period from 15 May to 30 October in 1982 (Table 6). The greatest portion of the total phosphorus load (69%) originated from internal sources. Precipitation and dustfall provided 15% of the load, sewage and runoff from residential areas contributed 12% and inflow from other lakes accounted for 5%. In a separate study, the internal loading of total phosphorus from sediments in the euphotic zone (to a depth of 8 m) to the overlying water was calculated to be an average of 4.35 kg/day for the period from 23 May to 26 August 1980 to 1984, and 1986 and 1987 (Shaw and Prepas 1989).

Biological Characteristics

Plants

The phytoplankton in Ethel Lake was studied briefly by Esso Resources Canada in 1978 (Cross 1979). As well, phytoplankton was studied by Alberta Environment bimonthly during the open-water period from 1980 to 1982, monthly under ice in 1980 and monthly during the open-water period from 1983 to 1986 (Alta. Envir. n.d.[b]).

The biomass of algae in Ethel Lake is low. From 1980 to 1986, the mean annual biomass ranged from a low of 1.44 mg/L in 1986 to a high of 3.40 mg/L in 1980 (Table 7). The maximum biomass each year was observed either in spring (May or June) or fall (September or October). These peaks were usually dominated by either blue-green algae (Cyanophyta) or diatoms (Bacillariophyta), except in 1982, when Pyrrhophyta was dominant (Table 7). Low dissolved oxygen conditions over the bottom sediments and moderately high total phosphorus levels enhance the development of blue-green algae in Ethel Lake (Trimbee and Prepas 1987; 1988).

In 1982 (Table 8), diatoms (mostly *Cyclotella compta*, *C. meneghiniana*, *Asterionella formosa* and *Fragilaria crotonensis*) and cryptophytes (mostly *Katablepharis ovalis*, *Cryptomonas erosa*, *C. Marsonii* and *C. rostratiformis*) formed a large part of the biomass from mid-May to early July and from late September to late October.

Table 5. A comparison of summer average chlorophyll *a* and total phosphorus concentrations in Ethel Lake. Composite samples from the euphotic zone collected from 18 June to 18 Sep. 1980 to 1987. S.E. = standard error; n = sample size.

Year	n	Chlorophyll *a* (μg/L)	S.E.	Phosphorus (μg/L)	S.E.
1980	7	8.8	0.9	—	—
1981	6	6.3	0.8	19	0.3
1982	6	4.4	0.7	23	2.3
1983	3	5.7	0.6	17	0.9
1984	3	7.2	2.2	21	1.1
1985	4	6.8	1.0	—	—
1986	3	5.3	0.4	22	4.4
1987	3	9.3	1.0	21	1.2

SOURCE: Alta. Envir. n.d.[b]

Table 6. Theoretical loading of total phosphorus to Ethel Lake from 15 May to 30 October 1982.

Source	Phosphorus (kg/day)	Percentage of Total
sewage and residential	0.56	12
precipitation/dustfall	0.71	15
Marie and Hilda creeks	0.24	5
sediment release (internal loading)[a]	3.31	69
TOTAL	4.82	101
annual areal loading (g/m² of lake surface)[b] 0.10		

NOTES: [a] 21 July to 29 Sep. 1982; [b] for the period 15 May to 30 Oct. 1982
SOURCE: Yonge and Trew 1989

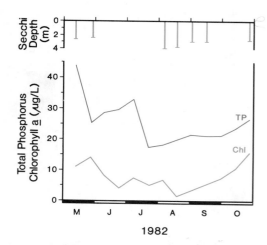

Figure 7. Total phosphorus, chlorophyll *a* and Secchi depth in Ethel Lake, 1982.
SOURCE: Alta. Envir. n.d.[b].

Table 7. Average algal biomass in Ethel Lake, 1980 to 1986. Composite samples from the euphotic zone collected from May to October each summer. S.E. = standard error.

Year	n	Mean Biomass (mg/L)	S.E.	Maximum Biomass (mg/L)	Group Dominating the Maximum
1980	13	3.40	0.379	6.04 (Sep.)	Cyanophyta
1981	12	2.95	0.322	5.86 (Sep.)	Cyanophyta
1982	13	1.94	0.217	3.80 (May)	Pyrrhophyta, Cyanophyta
1983	6	2.16	0.340	3.29 (Oct.)	Bacillariophyta
1984	6	1.80	0.547	4.09 (May)	Bacillariophyta
1985	6	1.48	0.201	2.04 (June)	Bacillariophyta
1986	6	1.44	0.231	2.09 (Oct.)	Bacillariophyta

SOURCE: Alta. Envir. n.d.[b]

Table 8. Percentage composition of major algal groups by total biomass in Ethel Lake, 1982. Composite samples collected from the euphotic zone.

ALGAL GROUP	12 May	27 May	09 June	23 June	07 July	29 July	05 Aug.	18 Aug.	01 Sep.	16 Sep.	29 Sep.	14 Oct.	27 Oct.
Total Biomass (mg/L)	3.80	2.72	2.05	1.14	2.48	1.33	2.02	1.32	1.53	1.04	1.38	1.92	2.49
Percentage Composition:													
Cyanophyta	1	1	2	9	11	27	29	38	49	38	24	19	4
						Lyngbya	*Anab.*	*Lyngbya* →		→	*Aphanizomenon*		
								Aphanothece →					
Chlorophyta	14	11	11	16	8	11	6	7	4	7	8	7	8
Xanthophyta	0	0	0	0	0	3	1	<1	0	0	0	0	
Chrysophyta	6	22	28	11	3	15	9	8	10	16	16	8	11
		Chrysochromulina											
Bacillariophyta	28	33	31	36	31	2	4	4	11	10	19	40	51
	Cyclotella →		*Fragilaria* →								*Asterionella* →		
Cryptophyta	19	27	26	25	33	11	9	5	3	18	28	24	20
	Katablepharis →		*Cryptomonas* →								*Cryptomonas* →		
Pyrrhophyta	32	6	3	3	14	33	40	37	22	11	5	2	6
	Peridinium				*Ceratium* →								

NOTE: *Anab.* = *Anabaena*
SOURCE: Alta. Envir. n.d.[b]

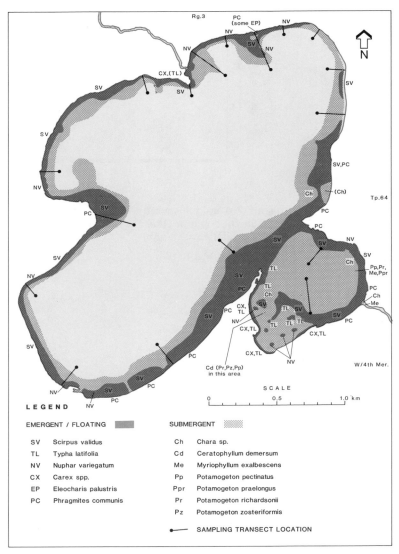

Figure 8. Species composition and distribution of macrophytes in Ethel Lake, 1978.
SOURCE: Alta. Envir. n.d.[b].

Pyrrhophyta were the dominant or codominant group in May (mainly *Peridinium africanum* and *P. palatinum*) and from late July to early September (mainly *Ceratium hirundinella*). Blue-greens (mainly *Lyngbya birgei*, *Anabaena flos-aquae*, *Aphanothece* sp. and *Aphanizomenon flos-aquae*) formed more than 20% of the biomass from late July to late September, and golden-brown species (Chrysophyta: mainly *Chrysochromulina parva*) were important in late May and early June.

The aquatic macrophytes of Ethel Lake were surveyed in 1978 by Alberta Environment (Fig. 8). The lake supports dense growths of aquatic macrophytes, particularly in the shallow southeast bay, which is filled with submergent species. The main submergent species are large-sheath pondweed (*Potamogeton vaginatus*), Richardson pondweed (*P. richardsonii*) and northern watermilfoil (*Myriophyllum exalbescens*). Submergent plants grow to a depth of 4.8 m (Chambers and Prepas 1988). Much of the lake is ringed with emergent species, which often block access to the southeast bay. The dominant emergent species are reed grass (*Phragmites communis*), common cattail (*Typha latifolia*) and common great bulrush (*Scirpus validus*).

Invertebrates

A brief survey of the zooplankton and benthic invertebrate communities in Ethel Lake was conducted for Esso Resources Canada during 1978 (Cross 1979). Based on five samples collected from 2 March to 10 December, the dominant copepod was *Diacyclops bicuspidatus thomasi* (range 12.2 to 291.6/L) throughout most of the year, except in October, when the rotifer *Keratella cochlearis* was extremely

abundant (1 363.7/L). The most abundant cladoceran was *Chydorus sphaericus* (range 14.7 to 230.6/L), particularly in October.

A total of six dredge samples were taken in the littoral zone (2.5–m to 4.8–m deep) on 19 July and 26 October in 1978. The dominant taxonomic group by number on both dates was midge larvae (Chironomidae), with a large number of scuds (Amphipoda: *Hyalella azteca*) recorded in October. A small number of roundworms (Nematoda), mayfly nymphs (Ephemeroptera), caddis fly larvae (Trichoptera), aquatic earthworms (Oligochaeta), snails (Gastropoda: mostly *Physa*) and fingernail clams (Pelecypoda: *Sphaerium*) were also recorded. As well, a total of 18 dredge samples were collected in the profundal zone (7–m to 24–m deep) on five sampling dates from 2 March to 10 December. Snails, which were found in May and October, included round-mouthed snails (Valvatidae) and pouch snails (Physidae). Small numbers of clams (mostly *Pisidium* and *Sphaerium*) were found on all but one sampling date, and aquatic earthworms, leeches (Hirudinea) and mayfly nymphs were found less frequently. The data for both littoral and profundal zones are too few to allow estimation of the total abundance, total biomass or relative abundance of benthic invertebrates.

Fish

Eleven species of fish have been reported in Ethel Lake: northern pike, yellow perch, walleye, lake whitefish, cisco, burbot, longnose sucker, white sucker, spottail shiner, ninespine stickleback and Iowa darter (Aquat. Envir. Ltd. 1983; Longmore and Stenton 1983). The lake whitefish and cisco are infested with cysts of the tapeworm *Triaenophorus crassus* (Alta. Rec. Parks Wild. 1976).

Detailed information on fish spawning habitats is not available, but important areas are probably located at the mouths of inlets. Potentially important areas for pike and perch are the shallow vegetated sections of the southeast bay, the shoreline running south from this bay, and the area near the point of land on the west shore. Spawning areas for walleye and whitefish are probably located in sandy areas off the northwest and northeast shores (Alta. Mun. Aff. 1980).

Ethel Lake's commercial fishery first opened during the 1944/45 season (Alta. For Ld. Wild. n.d.; Alta. Rec. Parks Wild. 1976). The largest total catch (10 945 kg) ever taken in the lake was recorded that year; it was mainly composed of cisco (73%) and lake whitefish (22%). The fishery was closed from 1945/46 to 1951/52. Since 1952/53, the size of the total catch and the proportions of cisco and lake whitefish have fluctuated considerably. Since 1972/73, whitefish have formed the major portion of the catch. During the 1980s, the fishery opened only in alternate years. In 1987/88, the total catch of lake whitefish, walleye, northern pike and cisco was 4 343 kg; 92% of this catch was lake whitefish.

A creel survey was conducted at Ethel Lake from 17 May to 14 August in 1986 (Table 9). Northern pike was the main species caught, with smaller amounts of yellow perch and walleye also taken. Of the total number of each species caught, none of the walleye, 13% of the yellow perch and 55% of the northern pike were released. The harvest rates for walleye (0.02/angler-hour) and yellow perch (0.04/angler-hour) are well below the average rates for 22 lakes in the region (0.10 walleye/angler-hour and 0.32 perch/angler-hour), but the harvest rate for northern pike (0.37/angler-hour) is well above the regional average (0.22 pike/angler-hour).

Wildlife

With the exception of the southeast bay, most of the Ethel Lake shoreline is only moderately productive for waterfowl. Habitat is limited by reduced marsh edge and deep water. The species of birds sighted at the lake include Mallard, American Widgeon, Lesser Scaup, Red-necked Grebe, Western Grebe, American Coot, Common Loon, Common Tern and American Bittern. A colony of Western Grebes is located on the south shore where the southeast bay joins the main part of the lake (Alta. Mun. Aff. 1980; Rippon 1983).

M.E. Bradford

Table 9. Estimated angler numbers, effort and harvest from Ethel Lake. Estimates based on creel survey data collected from 17 May to 14 Aug. 1986. WE = walleye; NP = northern pike; YP = yellow perch.

	WE	NP	YP	Total
number of anglers[a]	—	—	—	1 037
angler-hours[b]	—	—	—	2 183
total number fish harvested[c]	49	802	91	942
total yield (kg)	41	796	38	875
mean weight (g)	834	992	413	—
catch/angler-hour	0.02	0.82	0.04	0.88
harvest/angler-hour[b, c]	0.02	0.37	0.04	0.42
harvest/angler[a, c]	0.06	1.03	0.12	1.21

NOTES: [a]observed no. anglers = 782; [b]observed hours = 1 619; [c]based on observed no. fish kept: WE = 29, NP = 606, YP = 60
SOURCE: Alta. For. Ld. Wild. n.d.

References

Alberta Environment. n.d.[a]. Devel. Op. Div., Sur. Water Rights Br. Unpubl. data, Edmonton.

———. n.d.[b]. Envir. Assess. Div., Envir. Qlty. Monit. Br. Unpubl. data, Edmonton.

———. n.d.[c]. Tech. Serv. Div., Hydrol. Br. Unpubl. data, Edmonton.

———. n.d.[d]. Tech. Serv. Div., Surv. Br. Unpubl. data, Edmonton.

———. n.d.[e]. Water Resour. Admin. Div., Sur. Water Rights Br. Unpubl. data, Edmonton.

———. 1983. Cold Lake-Beaver River water management study, Vol. 1: Main report. Plan. Div., Edmonton.

———.1985. Cold Lake-Beaver River long term water management plan. Plan. Div., Edmonton.

Alberta Forestry, Lands and Wildlife. n.d. Fish Wild. Div. Unpubl. data, Edmonton.

———. 1988. Boating in Alberta. Fish Wild. Div., Edmonton.

———. 1989. Guide to sportfishing. Fish Wild. Div., Edmonton.

Alberta Municipal Affairs. 1978. Cold Lake regional plan, heritage preservation: Heritage resources background paper. Reg. Plan. Sec., Edmonton.

———. 1980. Ethel Lake management study. Reg. Plan. Sec., Plan. Serv. Div., Edmonton.

Alberta Recreation, Parks and Wildlife. 1976. Commercial fisheries catch statistics for Alberta, 1942–1975. Fish Wild. Div., Fish. Mgt. Rep. No. 22, Edmonton.

Alberta Research Council. 1972. Geological map of Alberta. Nat. Resour. Div., Alta. Geol. Surv., Edmonton.

Aquatic Environments Limited. 1983. Fisheries studies; main report and detailed data report [Appendices F and G]. In Cold Lake-Beaver River water management study, Vol. 4: Fisheries. Alta. Envir., Plan. Div., Edmonton.

Chambers, P.A. and E.E. Prepas. 1988. Underwater spectral attenuation and its effect on the maximum depth of angiosperm colonization. Can. J. Fish. Aquat. Sci. 45:1010–1017.

Cross, P.M. 1979. Limnological and fisheries surveys of the aquatic ecosystems at Esso Resources' Cold Lake base: Data volume. Aquat. Envir. Ltd., Calgary.

Energy, Mines and Resources Canada. 1971. National topographic series 1:50 000 73L/9 (1971). Surv. Map. Br., Ottawa.

Environment Canada. 1973–1987. Surface water data. Prep. by Inland Waters Directorate. Water Surv. Can., Water Resour. Br., Ottawa.

———. 1982. Canadian climate normals, Vol. 7: Bright sunshine (1951–1980). Prep. by Atm. Envir. Serv. Supply Serv. Can., Ottawa.

Girard, R. ca 1984. Echoes of the past: History of Bonnyville and district. Hist. Book Commit., Bonnyville.

Kocaoglu, S.S. 1975. Reconnaissance soil survey of the Sand River area. Alta. Soil Surv. Rep. No. 34, Univ. Alta. Bull. No. SS–15, Alta. Inst. Pedol. Rep. No. S–74–34 1975. Univ. Alta., Edmonton.

Longmore, L.A. and C.E. Stenton. 1983. Fish and fisheries; status and utilization [Appendix H]. In Cold Lake-Beaver River water management study, Vol. 5: Fisheries and wildlife. Alta. Envir., Plan. Div., Edmonton.

McGregor, C.A. 1983. Summary [Appendix K] and Detailed report [Appendix L]. In Cold Lake-Beaver River water management study, Vol. 7: Ecological inventory of lake shorelines. Alta. Envir., Plan. Div., Edmonton.

McMillan, W.J. 1977. An interpretation concept plan for Cold Lake Provincial Park. MSc thesis. Univ. Calg., Calgary.

Prepas, E.E. 1983. Orthophosphate turnover time in shallow productive lakes. Can. J. Fish. Aquat. Sci. 40:1412–1418.

——— and D.O. Trew. 1983. Evaluation of the phosphorus-chlorophyll relationship for lakes off the Precambrian Shield in western Canada. Can. J. Fish. Aquat. Sci. 40:27–35.

Rippon, B. 1983. Water related wildlife resources [Appendix I]. In Cold Lake-Beaver River water management study, Vol. 5: Fisheries and wildlife. Alta. Envir., Plan. Div., Edmonton.

Shaw, J.F.H. and E.E. Prepas. 1989. Potential significance of phosphorus release from shallow sediments of deep Alberta lakes. ms submitted to Limnol. Oceanogr.

Strong, W.L. and K.R. Leggat. 1981. Ecoregions of Alberta. Alta. En. Nat. Resour., Resour. Eval. Plan. Div., Edmonton.

Trew, D.O., E.I. Yonge and R.P. Kaminski. 1983. Lake trophic assessment [Appendix M]. In Cold Lake-Beaver River water management study, Vol. 8: Water quality. Alta. Envir., Plan. Div., Edmonton.

Trimbee, A.M. and E.E. Prepas. 1987. Evaluation of total phosphorus as a predictor of the relative biomass of blue-green algae with emphasis on Alberta lakes. Can. J. Fish. Aquat. Sci. 44:1337–1342.

———. 1988. The effect of oxygen depletion on the timing and magnitude of blue-green algal blooms. Verh. Internat. Verein. Limnol. 23:220–226.

Yonge, E.I. and D.O. Trew. 1989. A total phosphorus budget for a stratified, mesotrophic lake: Ethel Lake, Alberta. Alta. Envir., Envir. Assess. Div., Envir. Qlty. Monit. Br. Unpubl. rep., Edmonton.

GARNER LAKE

MAP SHEET: 73L/4
LOCATION: Tp60 R12 W4
LAT/LONG: 54°12'N 111°32'W

Garner Lake is a popular recreational lake located in the counties of Smoky Lake and St. Paul. It is situated 175 km northeast of the city of Edmonton and 5 km north of the hamlet of Spedden. To travel to the lake from Edmonton, take Highway 28 to Spedden, then a paved secondary road north from Spedden to Garner Lake Provincial Park (Fig. 1). A well-oiled gravel road extends north from the park and follows the western shore of the lake, and another gravel road extends east from the park entrance and follows the southeastern shore. The eastern bay can be reached by a gravel road that is connected to Secondary Road 866.

The lake was named for George C. Garner who began homesteading on a parcel of land in 1904 about 2 km to the east. Before the arrival of the Garner family, the lake had been named Hollow Lake by local Indians (Alta. Rec. Parks n.d.).

The first settlers arrived in the area during the early 1900s. The hamlet of Spedden was established around 1912. By 1920, the Canadian National Railway arrived and a railroad station was built at Spedden. Most of the area that is now the provincial park (Fig. 2) was reserved for public recreation by the Alberta government in 1927, but road access from Spedden to the park reserve was not completed until 1949. In 1953, the reserve became Garner Lake Provincial Park (Alta. Mun. Aff. 1982[a]). The park offers 66 campsites, 2 picnic shelters, cold-water showers, sewage dumping facilities, 3 playgrounds, 2 change houses, tap water, picnic areas, a hand boat launch, a boat launch for trailers and a swimming area. Several walking trails are available and one leads to a viewpoint.

The sport fishery at Garner Lake is one of the most popular in the area, and fishing for walleye, northern pike and yellow perch is the preferred recreational activity of lake users. No commercial or domestic fishing is allowed. There are no sport fishing regulations specific to Garner Lake, but provincial limits and regulations apply (Alta. For. Ld. Wild. 1989). Other favourite activities on and around the lake include swimming, sightseeing, general relaxation, water skiing, power boating, rowing, canoeing, snowmobiling, skating and cross-country skiing (Barber 1978). There are no boating restrictions over most of the lake, but in posted areas such as designated swimming areas, all boats are prohibited. In other posted areas, power boats are restricted to a maximum speed of 12 km/hour (Alta. For. Ld. Wild. 1988).

The water in Garner Lake is clear for much of the summer, and although it turns green during the warmest months, it remains quite transparent. Aquatic vegetation is abundant, and mats of filamentous algae float to the surface in most years.

Drainage Basin Characteristics

The watershed around Garner Lake covers an area of almost 26 km² and is about 4 times the size of the lake (Tables 1, 2). There are no major inlet streams to the lake, and the outlet does not flow regularly. The drainage basin is part of a hummocky morainal plain that is characterized by rough, irregular knob and kettle topography where knobs and ridges are interspersed with undrained depressions (Kocaoglu 1975). Land north of the lake is moderately rolling (9 to 15% slope), whereas to the west, it is level to undulating (0 to 5% slope). In the provincial park and on the south side of the lake, the land is gently rolling (5 to 9% slope), and to the east, it varies from level to moderately rolling (0 to 15% slope).

Table 1. Characteristics of Garner Lake drainage basin.

area (excluding lake) (km²)[a]	25.5
soil[b]	Orthic Gray Luvisols
bedrock geology[c]	Belly River Formation (Upper Cretaceous): sandstone, siltstone, mudstone, ironstone beds; nonmarine
terrain[b]	level to moderately rolling
ecoregion[d]	Dry Mixedwood Subregion of Boreal Mixedwood
dominant vegetation[d]	trembling aspen, balsam poplar
mean annual inflow (m³)[a, e]	1.27 x 10⁶
mean annual sunshine (h)[f]	2 168

NOTE: [e]excluding groundwater inflow
SOURCES: [a]Alta. Envir. n.d.[b]; [b]Kocaoglu 1975; [c]Alta. Res. Counc. 1972; [d]Strong and Leggat 1981; [f]Envir. Can. 1982

Table 2. Characteristics of Garner Lake.

elevation (m)[a, b]	603.18
surface area (km²)[a, b]	6.19
volume (m³)[a, b]	50.1 x 10⁶
maximum depth (m)[a, b]	15.2
mean depth (m)[a, b]	8.1
shoreline length (km)[c]	18.5
mean annual lake evaporation (mm)[d]	638
mean annual precipitation (mm)[d]	484
mean residence time (yr)[d, e]	>100
control structure	none

NOTES: [a]on date of sounding: 05 Aug. 1965; [e]excluding groundwater inflow
SOURCES: [b]Alta. Envir. n.d.[c]; [c]Mitchell 1979; [d]Alta. Envir. n.d.[b].

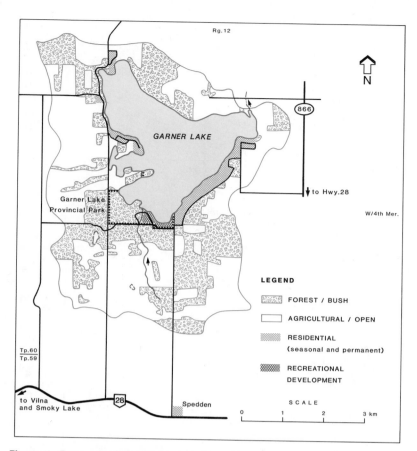

Figure 1. Features of the drainage basin of Garner Lake.
SOURCES: Alta. Envir. n.d.[b]; En. Mines Resour. Can. 1978. Updated with 1986 aerial photos.

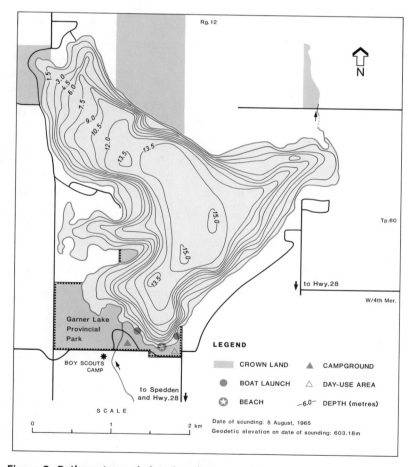

Figure 2. Bathymetry and shoreline features of Garner Lake.
BATHYMETRY SOURCE: Alta. Envir. n.d.[c].

Garner Lake's drainage basin is part of the Dry Mixedwood Sub-region of the Boreal Mixedwood Ecoregion (Strong and Leggat 1981). The soils in the watershed are predominantly moderately well-drained Orthic Gray Luvisols that formed either on fine clayey, weakly calcarious till or on fine loamy, moderately to strongly calcareous till (Kocaoglu 1975). These soils support a native vegetation that consists primarily of trembling aspen and secondarily of balsam poplar, birch, white spruce, alder and willow. Forested areas are located mostly north and south of the lake, where slopes are steeper and less suitable for agriculture. Most of the lake's immediate shoreline is tree covered. In 1982, about half of the watershed had been cleared for agriculture (Fig. 1). Because slopes are steep in some areas, and soils are poor, agriculture is limited to livestock and pasture production (Alta. Mun. Aff. 1982[a]). The soils in the area have low natural fertility, and good yields require applications of fertilizer (Kocaoglu 1975).

A large part of the shoreland has been subdivided. The first subdivision, Sunrise Beach (37 lots), was established north of the provincial park in 1958. Between 1961 and 1979, several subdivisions, comprising a total of 283 country residential lots, were created either on or near the shore (Alta. Mun. Aff. 1982[a]). In response to the increasing development pressures during the 1970s, the provincial government placed Garner Lake under the jurisdiction of the Regulated Lake Shoreland Development Operation Regulations. These regulations restricted lakeshore development until a lake management plan was completed and an area structure plan was adopted by the counties of St. Paul and Smoky Lake in 1982 (Alta. Mun. Aff. 1982[a]; 1982[b]). The lake management plan determines the extent of future land developments, allocates land use and determines ways to minimize environmental impacts and conflicts in uses of the lakeshore. It recommends preferred lake uses and ways to minimize lake-user conflicts. Between 1979 and 1988, shoreland development at Garner Lake was minimal, as no multiple lot subdivisions were approved (Barber 1988).

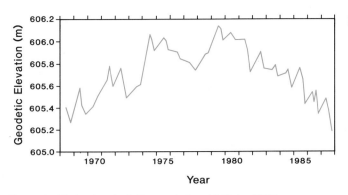

Figure 3. Water level of Garner Lake, 1968 to 1987.
SOURCE: Alta. Envir. n.d.[c].

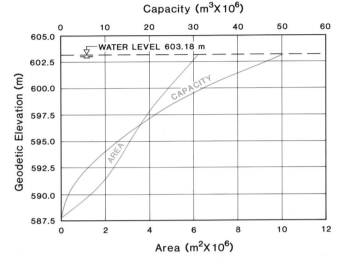

Figure 4. Area/capacity curve for Garner Lake.
SOURCE: Alta. Envir. n.d.[c].

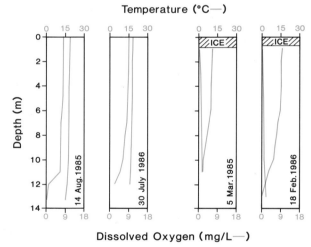

Figure 5. Temperature and dissolved oxygen in Garner Lake, 1985 and 1986.
SOURCE: Alta. Envir. n.d.[a].

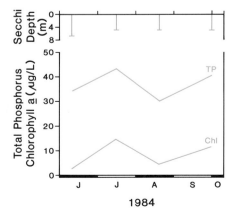

Figure 6. Total phosphorus, chlorophyll *a* and Secchi depth in Garner Lake, 1984.
SOURCE: Alta. Envir. n.d.[a].

Table 3. Major ions and related water quality variables for Garner Lake. Average concentrations in mg/L; pH in pH units. Composite samples from the euphotic zone collected on 15 July and 19 Aug. 1984, 19 June 1985 and 18 June 1986. S.E. = standard error.

	Mean	S.E.
pH (range)	8.9–9.1	—
total alkalinity ($CaCO_3$)	442	2.4
specific conductivity ($\mu S/cm$)	867	11.1
total dissolved solids (calculated)	545	12.9
total hardness ($CaCO_3$)	319[a]	8.4
HCO_3	438	11.8
CO_3	50	6.2
Mg	66[a]	1.8
Na	83[a]	1.2
K	25	0.3
Cl	6	0.3
SO_4	66	1.7
Ca	20	0.5

NOTE: [a]n = 3 (excludes 1985)
SOURCE: Alta. Envir. n.d.[a], Naquadat station 01AL06AA2030

Table 4. Nutrient, chlorophyll *a* and Secchi depth data for Garner Lake. Average concentrations in $\mu g/L$. Composite samples from the euphotic zone collected 4 times from 10 May to 30 Sep. 1984 and 4 times from 01 June to 20 Sep. 1988. S.E. = standard error.

	1984		1988	
	Mean	S.E.	Mean	S.E.
total phosphorus	37	2.9	47	1.8
NO_3 + NO_2–nitrogen	—	—	<15	—
iron	<20[a]	—	<15	—
chlorophyll *a*	8.1	2.88	13.9	3.71
Secchi depth (m)	5.5	0.50	3.7	0.38

NOTE: [a]n = 2
SOURCE: Alta. Envir. n.d.[a], Naquadat station 01AL06AA2030

Table 5. Theoretical total phosphorus loading to Garner Lake.

Source		Phosphorus (kg/yr)	Percentage of Total
watershed	forested/bush	100	11
	agricultural/cleared	679	62
	residential/cottage	159	14
sewage[a]		4	<1
precipitation/dustfall		156	14
	TOTAL	1 098	100
annual areal loading (g/m^2 of lake surface) 0.18			

NOTE: [a]unmeasured: assumes 4% of all sewage effluent from residences and camps enters the lake, as in Mitchell 1982
SOURCE: Mitchell 1989

Lake Basin Characteristics

Garner is a triangular lake of moderate size (6.19 km²). The mean depth is about 8 m and the maximum depth is 15 m (Table 2, Fig. 2). In many areas, the lake basin slopes steeply to depths of 12 m, but a large part of the bottom is quite level. The large northwest bay and part of the southwest shore are the shallowest areas.

The elevation of Garner Lake has been monitored since 1968 (Fig. 3). Between 1968 and 1974, the lake level rose from its second lowest recorded elevation (605.27 m in September 1968) to its second highest recorded elevation (606.05 m in June 1974). The maximum elevation (606.14 m) was recorded in June 1979. From that time, the lake level declined to its minimum level (605.19 m), recorded in October 1987. This range in lake levels (0.95 m) would change the area of the lake by about 0.4 km² (Fig. 4).

Water Quality

The water quality of Garner Lake was studied by Alberta Environment during 1978 and 1979, and has been studied jointly by Alberta Environment and Alberta Recreation and Parks since 1984 (Alta. Envir. n.d.[a]; 1985).

The water chemistry is dominated by sodium, sulphate, magnesium and bicarbonate ions (Table 3). Levels of total dissolved solids are fairly high (545 mg/L) in Garner Lake compared to others in the vicinity, and the lake is considered slightly saline.

Garner Lake mixes periodically throughout the summer, so the temperature and level of dissolved oxygen throughout the water column are usually quite uniform. Weak thermal stratification occurs for short periods only. Slight temperature gradients were noted on 14 August 1985 and 30 July 1986 (Fig. 5). Under these temperature conditions, dissolved oxygen concentrations were low near the lake bottom. In winter, there is a gradual depletion of dissolved oxygen under ice. In some years, as in February 1986 and February 1987, the bottom water becomes anoxic. In other years, as in February 1978 and March 1979 and 1985, dissolved oxygen is present throughout the water column. In all years sampled, dissolved oxygen concentrations in the surface water remained above 6 mg/L.

Garner Lake is mesotrophic. The water is highly transparent, and average chlorophyll a levels (Table 4) are lower in this lake than in lakes with similar total phosphorus concentrations. In 1984, the highest chlorophyll a level recorded in Garner Lake was 14 µg/L (Fig. 6). Although the water appeared green at the time, it was a transparent green, unlike that typically found in other lakes. The difference probably relates to the type of algae found in the lake. Concentrations of chlorophyll a and total phosphorus in 1984 were highest in July and late September. Such peaks during summer are probably the result of the internal loading of phosphorus from the bottom sediments to the overlying water. The supply of total phosphorus from sources external to the lake has been estimated at 1 098 kg/year, or 0.18 g/m² of lake surface area (Table 5). Runoff from agricultural land accounted for 62% of this external loading. Other, smaller sources of supply were runoff from forested land (11%), runoff from residential areas (14%), sewage (less than 1%), and precipitation and dustfall (14%). Sewage inputs were not measured directly at Garner Lake, but were estimated from data collected for other Alberta lakes.

Biological Characteristics

Plants

The phytoplankton community in Garner Lake was studied by Alberta Environment in October 1977 and throughout 1978 (Mitchell 1979). Biomass was determined by cell counts. Blue-green algae (Cyanophyta) dominated the phytoplankton in all samples except those taken in June. In February, the main blue-green species were *Gomphosphaeria* sp. and *Aphanizomenon* sp. By May, blue-greens were dominant as a group, but the single most abundant species was a diatom, *Fragilaria capucina* (Bacillariophyta). In June, several blue-green species as well as the diatom *F. capucina* and the green alga *Actinastrum hantzschii*, formed most of the biomass. The greatest cell numbers were recorded from the end of August throughout October. Blue-greens (*Gomphosphaeria* sp., *Lyngbya* sp., *Aphanizomenon* sp. and *Anabaena* sp.) and secondarily diatoms (*Fragilaria crotonensis* and *Stephanodiscus astrea*) were the major groups during this period. The benthic alga *Cladophora* was also an important species during summer. It grew over macrophytes at the north and west ends of the lake and formed a dense mat near shore in the northern arm.

In November 1969, a large concentration of blue-green algae (including *Microcystis* sp.) was blown into the eastern part of the lake (Alta. For. Ld. Wild. n.d.). Several head of cattle died at the time, but poisoning has not been reported since then.

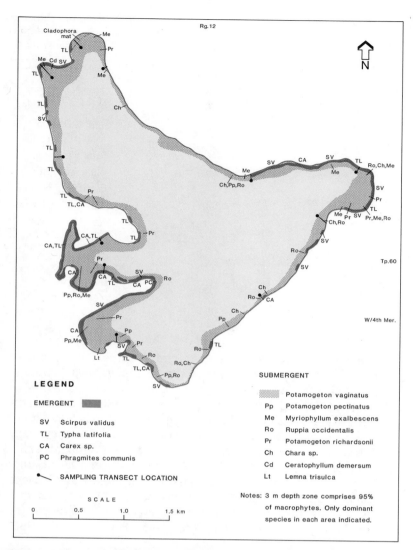

Figure 7. Species composition and distribution of aquatic macrophytes in Garner Lake, August 1978.
SOURCE: Mitchell 1979.

The aquatic vegetation was surveyed by Alberta Environment during August 1978 (Mitchell 1979). Emergent species were most abundant in areas sheltered from wind, as in the northern bay, the eastern bay, and the two small bays on the western side (Fig. 7). Most plants grew at depths of 3 m or less, with the majority of growth in the 1– to 2–m depth zone. The dominant emergent species was common great bulrush (*Scirpus validus*), which grew to a depth of 0.5 m. Common cattail (*Typha latifolia*) grew along the western shore in wind-protected indentations. Sedge (*Carex* sp.), another common emergent, was most abundant on the western shore. Submergent species formed a zone of continuous vegetation around the shoreline. They were particularly dense at the northern end and in the small western bays. Most plants grew at depths less than 3 m. The dominant species were narrow-leaf pondweeds, primarily large-sheath pondweed (*Potamogeton vaginatus*), but also Sago pondweed (*P. pectinatus*) and *P. filiformis*. Northern water-milfoil (*Myriophyllum exalbescens*) was abundant in deeper or more sheltered water and *Ruppia occidentalis*, a plant characteristic of saline waters, was common on the windy southeast shore.

Invertebrates

The zooplankton community was studied during 1978 by Alberta Environment (Mitchell 1979). Species composition and relative abundance were determined, but biomass was not measured. Seventeen species were identified. The dominant species were the copepods *Diaptomus sicilis* and *Diacyclops bicuspidatus thomasi*, and the cladocerans *Daphnia pulicaria*, *D. galeata mendotae*, *Diaphanosoma leuctenbergianum* and *Chydorus sphaericus*.

No data are available for the benthic invertebrate community.

Table 6. Estimated angler numbers, effort and harvest from Garner Lake. Estimates based on creel survey data collected from 17 May to 27 Aug. 1986. WE = walleye; NP = northern pike; YP = yellow perch.

	WE	NP	YP	Total
number of anglers[a]	—	—	—	11 697
angler-hours[b]	—	—	—	18 920
total number fish harvested[c]	189	3 273	6 635	10 097
total yield (kg)	162	3 283	1 473	4 918
mean weight (g)	1 021	1 003	222	—
catch/angler-hour	0.02	0.23	0.87	1.12
harvest/angler-hour[b, c]	0.01	0.17	0.35	0.53
harvest/angler[a, c]	0.01	0.28	0.57	0.86

NOTES: [a]observed no. anglers = 5 694; [b]observed hours = 9 251.5; [c]based on observed no. fish kept: WE = 77, NP = 1 593, YP = 3 269
SOURCE: Alta. For. Ld. Wild. n.d.

Fish

Seven species of fish have been reported in Garner Lake: northern pike, yellow perch, walleye, burbot, spottail shiner, Iowa darter and brook stickleback. Walleye were stocked in 1951 and from 1957 to 1959 (Alta. For. Ld. Wild. n.d.). Despite the presence of potential spawning areas of sand and gravel, the walleye population did not appear to reproduce. The few walleye caught each year in the early 1980s were all large, mature fish that were probably remnants of the original planted stock (Alta. Mun. Aff. 1982[a]). In 1984, Garner Lake became part of a walleye enhancement project and walleye stocking resumed. The lake was stocked with 15 000 half-centimetre walleye in 1984, 31 700 fingerlings in 1986 and 15 000 fingerlings in 1987 (Alta. En. Nat. Resour. 1984; Alta. For. Ld. Wild. 1986; 1987).

Garner Lake is managed for recreational fishing, and the sport fishery is very important to provincial park visitors and nearby residents. In a 1977 survey, cottage owners reported that fishing was their favourite recreational activity year round (Barber 1978). A creel survey at Garner Lake was conducted from 17 May to 27 August in 1986 (Table 6). Northern pike and yellow perch were the main catches, and a few walleye were taken. Of the total number of each species caught, 7% of the walleye, 24% of the northern pike, and 60% of the yellow perch were released. On a regional basis, the average harvest/angler-hour for 22 lakes in the Northeast Region surveyed between 1984 and 1987 was 0.10 for walleye, 0.22 for northern pike and 0.32 for yellow perch (Alta. For. Ld. Wild. n.d.). In comparison, the harvest per unit effort at Garner Lake was lower than average for walleye (0.01 walleye/angler-hour) and northern pike (0.17 pike/angler-hour), and close to average for yellow perch (0.35 perch/angler-hour). The fishing pressure at Garner Lake during the 1986 survey period was 26.7 angler-hours/ha. Most of the angling effort was concentrated along the shoreline.

During the winter of 1948/49, Garner Lake was fished commercially for northern pike and yellow perch. The commercial fishery has not operated since that time.

Wildlife

Although Garner Lake is not as significant for waterfowl production as some of the smaller lakes in the area, it provides habitat for a number of species. Birds identified at the lake include several species of ducks, Common Loons, grebes, American Coots, Common Goldeneye and Great Blue Herons (Alta. Mun. Aff. 1982[a]). Waterfowl habitat generally coincides with areas of abundant emergent plant growth (Fig. 7). Significant nesting areas are located at the east and northwest ends of the lake and in the two large, shallow bays at the southwest end.

M.E. Bradford

References

Alberta Energy and Natural Resources. 1984. Fish planting list. Fish Wild. Div., Edmonton.

Alberta Environment. n.d.[a]. Envir. Assess. Div., Envir. Qlty. Monit. Br. Unpubl. data, Edmonton.

———. n.d.[b]. Tech. Serv. Div., Hydrol. Br. Unpubl. data, Edmonton.

———. n.d.[c]. Tech. Serv. Div., Surv. Br. Unpubl. data, Edmonton.

———. 1985. Garner Lake. Envir. Assess. Div., Envir. Qlty. Monit. Br., Edmonton.

Alberta Forestry, Lands and Wildlife. n.d. Fish Wild. Div. Unpubl. data, Edmonton.

———. 1986, 1987. Fish planting list. Fish Wild. Div., Edmonton.

———. 1988. Boating in Alberta. Fish Wild. Div., Edmonton.

———. 1989. Guide to sportfishing. Fish Wild. Div., Edmonton.

Alberta Municipal Affairs. 1982[a]. Garner Lake management study. Prep. for Co. St. Paul and Co. Smoky Lake by Alta. Mun. Aff., Plan. Serv. Div., Plan. Br., Edmonton.

———. 1982[b]. Garner Lake area structure plan. Prep. for Co. St. Paul and Co. Smoky Lake by Alta. Mun. Aff., Plan. Serv. Div., Plan. Br., Edmonton.

Alberta Recreation and Parks. n.d. Parks Div. Unpubl. data, Edmonton.

Alberta Research Council. 1972. Geological map of Alberta. Nat. Resour. Div., Alta. Geol. Surv., Edmonton.

Barber, W.D. 1978. Garner Lake cottage owner survey. Alta. Mun. Aff., Plan. Serv. Div., Plan. Br., Edmonton.

———. 1988. Alta. Mun. Aff., Plan. Serv. Div., Plan. Br., Edmonton. Pers. comm.

Energy, Mines and Resources Canada. 1978. National topographic series 1:50 000 73L/4 (1978). Surv. Map. Br., Ottawa.

Environment Canada. 1982. Canadian climate normals, Vol. 7: Bright sunshine (1951–1980). Prep. by Atm. Envir. Serv. Supply Serv. Can., Ottawa.

Kocaoglu, S.S. 1975. Reconnaissance soil survey of the Sand River area. Alta. Soil Surv. Rep. No. 34, Univ. Alta. Bull. No. SS–15, Alta. Inst. Pedol. Rep. No. S–74–34 1975. Univ. Alta., Edmonton.

Mitchell, P.A. 1979. Skeleton, Garner, Muriel Lakes water quality studies. Alta. Envir., Poll. Contr. Div., Water Qlty. Contr. Br., Edmonton.

———. 1982. Evaluation of the "septic snooper" on Wabamun and Pigeon lakes. Alta. Envir., Poll. Contr. Div., Water Qlty. Contr. Br., Edmonton.

———. 1989. Alta. Envir., Envir. Assess. Div., Envir. Qlty. Monit. Br., Edmonton. Pers. comm.

Strong, W.L. and K.R. Leggat. 1981. Ecoregions of Alberta. Alta. En. Nat. Resour., Resour. Eval. Plan. Div., Edmonton.

LONG LAKE
(Near Boyle)

MAP SHEET: 83I/7
LOCATION: Tp62 R18 W4
　　　　　　Tp63 R18, 19 W4
LAT/LONG: 54°26′N 112°45′W

Long Lake is a pretty lake set in a steep-sided, heavily wooded valley in the County of Thorhild. It is located about 130 km northeast of the city of Edmonton and 15 km south of the village of Boyle. To reach the lake from Edmonton, take Highway 28 to Highway 63. Drive north on Highway 63 to Newbrook, then east on Secondary Road 661 for 13 km and north on Secondary Road 831 for 7 km; turn east onto the entrance road to Long Lake Provincial Park (Fig. 1).

The name of the lake is descriptive of its shape and has been used locally for many years (Alta. Rec. Parks n.d.). The area around Long Lake was originally fur-trading country, and at one time, many important fur-trade routes passed through the area surrounding Boyle. The land around Long Lake was not settled, because it is steep and wooded, but the lumber industry was important to the area's development. Seven sawmills have operated along the western shore of the lake since the first one was established in 1918 (Alta. Envir. 1985). Frequent forest fires, however, hampered lumbering operations, and timber cutting had ceased by 1940 after most of the white spruce had been logged (Alta. Rec. Parks n.d.).

Long Lake has been locally popular for recreational use since the early part of the twentieth century, and in 1957, Long Lake Provincial Park was established through the efforts of local community organizations. All land around the lake belongs to the Crown. Land within the park was surveyed for a subdivision in 1958, but park policy on subdivisions changed the following year. The park boundary was altered, and the subdivision, which remains on Crown land (Fig. 2), was transferred out of the park (Alta. Rec. Parks n.d.).

At present, Long Lake Provincial Park encompasses 7.68 km² of land on both sides of the lake (Fig. 2), but all recreational development is on the west side. The park provides day-use and camping services year-round. Facilities include a food concession, a boat rental, tap water, several campgrounds with a total of 220 campsites, two day-use areas, two playgrounds, a picnic shelter, two beaches, two docks and two boat launches. Activities that are enjoyed on and around the lake include fishing, swimming, power boating, canoeing, windsurfing, water skiing, hiking and wildlife viewing. There are no boating restrictions over most of the lake, but in posted areas such as designated swimming areas, all vessels are prohibited, and in other posted areas, powerboats are restricted to maximum speeds of 12 km/h (Alta. For. Ld. Wild. 1988).

In 1972, the County of Thorhild developed a ski area one kilometre north of the park boundary on the western shore. Winter facilities include a chalet, five downhill ski runs, toboggan runs, cross-country ski trails and snowmobile trails. In summer, the area offers limited camping facilities and nature trails (Alta. Envir. 1985).

Long Lake turns green with algae in late summer, and aquatic vegetation is abundant in some areas, particularly at the north end near the outflow (Mitchell 1988). The lake supports a year-round sport fishery for walleye, northern pike and yellow perch. Occasional winterkills of fish have been reported (Alta. For. Ld. Wild. n.d.). There are no sport fishing regulations specific to Long Lake, but provincial limits and regulations apply (Alta. For. Ld. Wild. 1989).

Drainage Basin Characteristics

Long Lake's drainage basin is about 14 times larger than the lake (Tables 1, 2). A small spring on the western shore and a dozen small

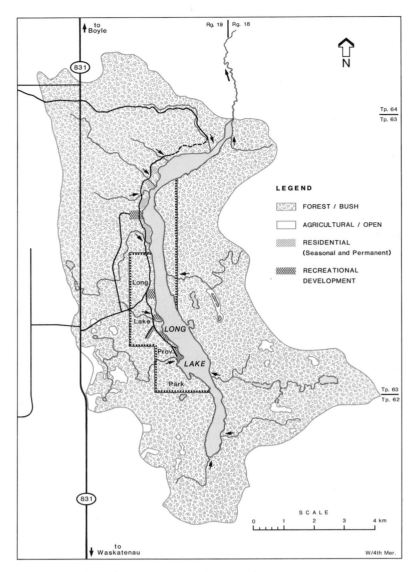

Figure 1. Features of the drainage basin of Long Lake.
SOURCES: Alta. Envir. n.d.[b]; En. Mines Resour. Can. 1972; 1973.
Updated with 1983 aerial photos.

Table 1. Characteristics of Long Lake drainage basin.

area (excluding lake) (km²)[a]	82.4
soil[b]	Orthic Gray Luvisols
bedrock geology[c]	Wapiti Formation (Upper Cretaceous): sandstone, mudstone, bentonite, scattered coal beds; nonmarine
terrain[b]	undulating to strongly rolling
ecoregion[d]	Dry Mixedwood Subregion of Boreal Mixedwood
dominant vegetation[d]	trembling aspen
mean annual inflow (m³)[a, e]	4.60 x 10⁶
mean annual sunshine (h)[f]	2 264

NOTE: [e]excluding groundwater inflow
SOURCES: [a]Alta. Envir. n.d.[b]; [b]Greenlee 1975; [c]Alta. Res. Counc. 1972; [d]Strong and Leggat 1975; [f]Envir. Can. 1982

Table 2. Characteristics of Long Lake.

elevation (m)[a, b]	620.50 to 621.23
surface area (km²)[b, c]	5.84
volume (m³)[b, c]	29.3 x 10⁶
maximum depth (m)[b, c]	9.0
mean depth (m)[b, c]	4.3
shoreline length (km)[d]	29.9
mean annual lake evaporation (mm)[e]	636
mean annual precipitation (mm)[e]	517
mean residence time (yr)[e, f]	7.5
control structure	none

NOTES: [a]range over period of water level record; elevation on date of sounding not available; [c]on date of sounding June 1969; [f]excluding groundwater inflow
SOURCES: [b]Alta. Envir. n.d.[c]; [d]En. Mines Resour. Can. 1972; [e]Alta. Envir. n.d.[b]

streams provide inflow. The lake is located in a large meltwater channel, the Long Lake valley. The valley begins south of Long Lake, where White Earth Creek joins Edwand Creek near the town of Smoky Lake, and extends northward through Long Lake to the northern tip of Amisk Lake. The channel is part of two watersheds, the Beaver River Basin and the North Saskatchewan River Basin, which are divided by a point of land 4.8 km south of Long Lake (Alta. Envir. 1985). Outflow from Long Lake drains north to Amisk Lake and eventually to the Beaver River via the Amisk River. The outlet stream flows intermittently and is dotted with beaver dams along its length.

The drainage basin is an undulating to gently rolling till plain that slopes steeply down to the lake (Greenlee 1975). Surface elevations range from 621 m along the lakeshore to 730 m at the northwest corner of the watershed. Surficial deposits of glacial till mixed with sand and gravel form the east and west slopes of the valley, which are broken by many parallel ridges. On the west side of the lake, the land drops quite steeply to the shore from a height of 40 to 80 m, and the slopes are cut by steep-sided stream channels. On the east side of the lake, the height of the banks is much lower than on the west side (Alta. Envir. 1985). The main soils in the drainage basin are Orthic Gray Luvisols (Greenlee 1975).

Long Lake is part of the Dry Mixedwood Subregion of the Boreal Mixedwood Ecoregion (Strong and Leggat 1981). Most of the drainage basin (98%) is forested. Trembling aspen is the dominant tree, with secondary quantities of balsam poplar. White spruce is the climax community in areas that have escaped fire and harvesting (Alta. Envir. 1985). Jack pine grows in rapidly drained, sandy soil and sedge/grass communities grow on wet margins and in poorly

drained depressions. Black spruce/Labrador tea bogs are located throughout the watershed, and saskatoon/low shrub communities occupy steep, south-facing slopes (Alta. Envir. 1985). Agriculture is severely limited by adverse topography and soil conditions, and only about 1% of the land has been cleared for this purpose. The Thorhild Grazing Reserve is located at the southern end of the watershed.

Lake Basin Characteristics

Long Lake is 13–km long and less than 1–km wide (Fig. 2). The lake has two basins, a larger one at the south end, and a smaller, shallower one at the north end. In the central part of the south basin, the lake bed drops steeply to depths of 6 to 9 m. The lake bottom varies from sand or rocks in shallow areas, to shallow mud at depths of 2.5 to 6.0 m, to a deep layer of organic material and mud in the deepest areas. The shoreline is composed of sandy soil and mud (Thomas and McDonald 1963).

The elevation of Long Lake has been monitored since 1969 (Fig. 3). The difference between the minimum historic lake level (620.50 m), recorded in October 1972, and the maximum level (621.23 m), recorded in July 1986, is 0.73 m. Changes in the lake's surface area and volume with fluctuations in water level are illustrated in Figure 4.

Water Quality

The water quality of Long Lake has been monitored jointly by Alberta Environment and Alberta Recreation and Parks since 1983 (Alta. Envir. n.d.[a]).

Long Lake is a well-buffered, freshwater lake; the dominant ions are calcium, sodium and bicarbonate (Table 3). The lake is shallow, and despite the protection afforded by its high banks, it is frequently mixed by wind during the open-water season. Periodically, very weak thermal stratification occurs, as in July 1985 (Fig. 5), when

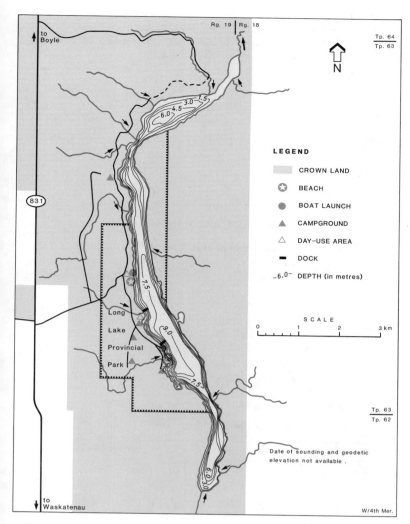

Figure 2. Bathymetry and shoreline features of Long Lake.
SOURCE: Alta. Envir. n.d.[c].

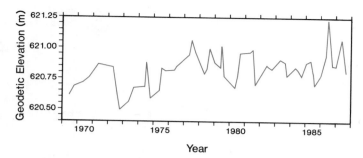

Figure 3. Water level of Long Lake, 1969 to 1987.
SOURCE: Alta. Envir. n.d.[c].

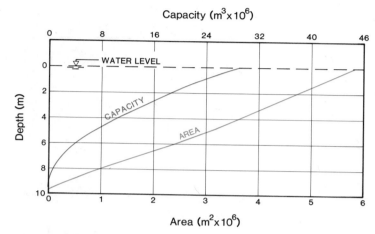

Figure 4. Area/capacity curve for Long Lake.
SOURCE: Alta. Envir. n.d.[c].

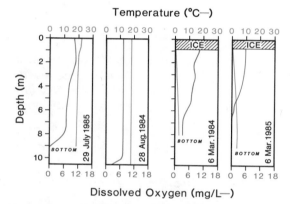

Figure 5. Temperature and dissolved oxygen in Long Lake, 1984 and 1985.
SOURCE: Alta. Envir. n.d.[a].

weak stratification was accompanied by very low dissolved oxygen concentrations (less than 1 mg/L) in water near the bottom sediments. Low concentrations of dissolved oxygen also occur annually under ice cover (Fig. 5). Concentrations over the bottom sediments decline to zero in some winters, as in 1985, 1986 and 1987, but surface concentrations are sufficient to overwinter fish.

During the open-water period, changes in the phosphorus and chlorophyll *a* concentrations in Long Lake (Fig. 6) are similar to those in other shallow, eutrophic, well-mixed lakes in Alberta. Concentrations of phosphorus are highest from mid- to late summer when phosphorus is recycled from the bottom sediments into the upper layers of the water column. Consequently, blue-green algal blooms may occur during these months, as reported in July 1985 (Alta. Envir. n.d.[a]).

Long Lake is eutrophic. Average total phosphorus and chlorophyll *a* concentrations are moderately high (Table 4). The loading of phosphorus to Long Lake from external sources is estimated to be 1 237 kg/year, or 0.21 g/m² of lake surface area (Table 5). Almost three-quarters of the phosphorus load originates from runoff from forested parts of the watershed. The provincial park sewage lagoon and residential septic tank effluents, on the other hand, account for less than 2% of the external load. These sewage inputs were not measured at Long Lake—they were estimated from data collected for other Alberta lakes. Atmospheric deposition and runoff from nonforested parts of the watershed provide the remainder of the input.

Biological Characteristics

Plants

Quantitative information about the phytoplankton and macrophyte communities is not available. In 1963, Fish and Wildlife Division

Table 3. Major ions and related water quality variables for Long Lake.
Average concentrations in mg/L; pH in pH units. Composite samples from the euphotic zone collected 3 times from 18 May to 12 Sep. 1983. S.E. = standard error.

	Mean	S.E.
pH (range)	8.3–8.4	—
total alkalinity (CaCO₃)	179	2.1
specific conductivity (µS/cm)	262	3.7
total dissolved solids (calculated)	196	4.4
total hardness (CaCO₃)	129	4.6
HCO₃	215	3.8
CO₃	<3	—
Mg	15	0.6
Na	24	0.4
K	4	0.1
Cl	<2	—
SO₄	17	1.3
Ca	27	2.5

SOURCE: Alta. Envir. n.d.[a], Naquadat station 01AL05EC1000

Table 4. Nutrient, chlorophyll *a* and Secchi depth data for Long Lake. Average concentrations in μg/L. Composite samples from the euphotic zone collected 5 times from 18 May to 12 Sep. 1983 and 5 times from 07 May to 27 Aug. 1984. S.E. = standard error.

	1983		1984	
	Mean	S.E.	Mean	S.E.
total phosphorus	33	6.2	49[a]	16.8
iron	—	—	<20[b]	—
chlorophyll *a*	14.9	5.15	22.8	8.19
Secchi depth (m)	2.2	0.27	2.8[a]	0.57

NOTES: [a]n = 4; [b]n = 2
SOURCE: Alta. Envir. n.d.[a], Naquadat Station 01AL05EC1000

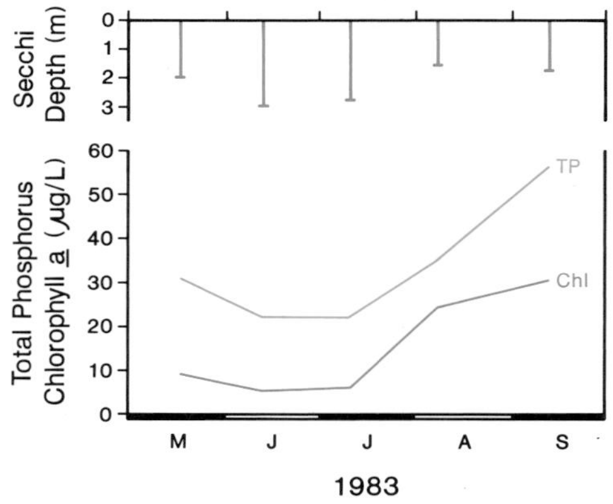

Table 5. Theoretical external phosphorus loading to Long Lake.

	Source	Phosphorus (kg/yr)	Percentage of Total
watershed	forest/bush	889	72
	agricultural/cleared	50	4
	residential/cottage	100	8
sewage[a]	septic systems	16	1
	park lagoon	5	<1
precipitation/dustfall		177	14
	TOTAL	1 237	100

annual areal loading (g/m² of lake surface)   0.21

NOTE: [a]unmeasured: assumes 4% of all sewage effluent from residences and camps enters the lake, as in Mitchell 1982
SOURCE: Mitchell 1988

Figure 6. Total phosphorus, chlorophyll *a* and Secchi depth in Long Lake, 1983. SOURCE: Alta. Envir. n.d.[a].

noted that "heavy plankton blooms are frequent" occurrences in Long Lake (Thomas and McDonald 1963) and in July 1985, Alberta Environment noted a blue-green algal bloom (Alta. Envir. n.d.[a]). Macrophytes are abundant in littoral areas, particularly at the north end of the lake.

Invertebrates

The zooplankton and benthic invertebrates in Long Lake have not been studied in detail.

Fish

The year-round sport fishery for walleye, northern pike and yellow perch is very popular with visitors to Long Lake, although few large pike are caught (Alta. For. Ld. Wild. n.d.). Burbot also inhabit the lake. At present, Long Lake is managed for recreational fishing only, but between 1943 and 1961, the lake supported a commercial fishery for northern pike, yellow perch, walleye and cisco. The largest part of the catch was usually northern pike and cisco (Alta. Rec. Parks Wild. 1976). Cisco harvests fluctuated between 100 and 4 300 kg/ year; the maximum cisco harvest was recorded just prior to the closing of the fishery in 1961. During the mid–1940s, the annual northern pike harvest approached 9 000 kg, but in subsequent decades it declined to less than 2 000 kg.

Wildlife

Approximately 92 bird species have been sighted at Long Lake Provincial Park, including Chestnut-sided Warblers, which are at their northwestern breeding limits, and Nashville Warblers, which are far from their known western breeding limit in Manitoba. An active Osprey nest is located near the southern park boundary (Finlay and Finlay 1987). Birds that use the lake include Red-necked Grebes, Horned Grebes, Blue-winged Teal, Mallards, Lesser Scaup and Lesser Yellowlegs (Friesen and Schaafsma 1973).

Eighteen mammal species, including deer, moose, black bear, coyote, porcupine, varying hare, beaver, muskrat and mink, have been sighted at the park (Friesen and Schaafsma 1973).

M.E. Bradford

References

Alberta Environment. n.d.[a]. Envir. Assess. Div., Envir. Qlty. Monit. Br. Unpubl. data, Edmonton.
———. n.d.[b]. Tech. Serv. Div., Hydrol. Br. Unpubl. data, Edmonton.
———. n.d.[c]. Tech. Serv. Div., Surv. Br. Unpubl. data, Edmonton.
———. 1985. Long Lake background report. Plan. Div., Edmonton.
Alberta Forestry, Lands and Wildlife. n.d. Fish Wild. Div. Unpubl. data, Edmonton.
———. 1988. Boating in Alberta. Fish Wild. Div., Edmonton.
———. 1989. Guide to sportfishing. Fish Wild. Div., Edmonton.
Alberta Recreation and Parks. n.d. Parks Div. Unpubl. data, Edmonton.
Alberta Recreation, Parks and Wildlife. 1976. Commercial fisheries catch statistics for Alberta, 1942–1975. Fish Wild. Div., Fish. Mgt. Rep. No. 22, Edmonton.
Alberta Research Council. 1972. Geological map of Alberta. Nat. Resour. Div., Alta. Geol. Surv., Edmonton.
Energy, Mines and Resources Canada. 1972, 1973. National topographic series 1:50 000 83I/7 (1972), 83I/10 (1973). Surv. Map. Br., Ottawa.
Environment Canada. 1982. Canadian climate normals, Vol. 7: Bright sunshine (1951–1980). Prep. by Atm. Envir. Serv. Supply Serv. Can., Ottawa.
Finlay, J. and C. Finlay. 1987. Parks in Alberta: A guide to peaks, ponds, parklands & prairies. Hurtig Publ., Edmonton.
Friesen, R.D. and S. Schaafsma. 1973. An ecological survey of Long Lake Provincial Park, Vol. 1. Alta. Ld. For., Prov. Parks Plan. Div., Edmonton.
Greenlee, G.M. 1975. Soil survey of Long Lake Provincial Park and interpretation for recreational use. Alta. Inst. Pedol. Rep. No. M–75–5. Alta. Res. Counc., Soils Div., Edmonton.
Mitchell, P.A. 1982. Evaluation of the "septic snooper" on Wabamun and Pigeon lakes. Alta. Envir., Poll. Contr. Div., Water Qlty. Contr. Br., Edmonton.
———. 1988. Alta. Envir., Envir. Assess. Div., Envir. Qlty. Monit. Br., Edmonton. Pers. comm.
Strong, W.L. and K.R. Leggat. 1981. Ecoregions of Alberta. Alta. En. Nat. Resour., Resour. Eval. Plan. Div., Edmonton.
Thomas, R.C. and D. McDonald. 1963. Long Lake survey, St. Paul Region. Alta. Ld. For., Fish Wild. Div. Unpubl. rep., Edmonton.

MANN LAKES
Upper and Lower

MAP SHEETS: 73L/3, 4
LOCATION: Tp59, 60 R10, 11 W4
LAT/LONG: 54°09'N 111°30'W

Upper and Lower Mann lakes are shallow, sparkling lakes set in the rolling, wooded country northwest of the town of St. Paul. To reach the lakes from St. Paul, take Highway 28 west and north for 32 km to the village of Ashmont, then take Highway 28A east for 5 km. Upper Mann Lake is south of the highway, Lower Mann Lake is north (Fig. 1). The lakes are in the County of St. Paul.

The lakes were named after Sir Donald Mann (1853–1934), a vice-president of the Canadian Northern Railway Company, which built a rail line close to Upper Mann Lake in the early 1900s (Holmgren and Holmgren 1976). The rail line is now owned by the Canadian National Railway. Before the advent of the railway, the lakes were collectively called Island Lake because they became one large lake with a central island when the water level was high (Owlseye Hist. Soc. 1984).

The best access to Lower Mann Lake is at Lower Mann Lake Provincial Recreation Area at the south end of the lake, just north of Highway 28A (Fig. 2). This area, which is operated by Alberta Recreation and Parks, provides day-use facilities year-round and camping facilities from the Victoria Day weekend to Thanksgiving Day. Facilities include 70 campsites, pump water, picnic tables and a shelter, a beach, a boat launch and a playground (Alta. Hotel Assoc. 1989). There are no public campgrounds or day-use areas on Upper Mann Lake, but access is available at a boat launch on the northwest shore (Fig. 2).

Both lakes have been moderately to heavily developed for recreation. There are 197 cottage lots in 8 subdivisions on Lower Mann Lake and 211 lots in 6 subdivisions on Upper Mann Lake; in 1989, more than half of the lots had been developed (Alta. Mun. Aff. 1989). About one-third of the shoreline and the islands in Lower Mann Lake are Crown land, as are the islands and most of the east and southeast shores of Upper Mann Lake (Fig. 2). A total of 82 ha bordering Upper Mann Lake, including several of the islands and a disjunct area on the south and southeast shore have protective notation, which means that the areas have been proposed as a natural area. The designated land includes excellent wildlife habitat, a beautiful stand of mature white birch trees and islands where pelicans and cormorants rest and feed (Alta. For. Ld. Wild. 1987).

Both lakes are popular for boating and for sport fishing for northern pike and yellow perch. There are no boating regulations specific to either lake (Alta. For. Ld. Wild. 1988). Provincial limits for sport fish catch and possession apply to both lakes and all tributary streams are closed to sport fishing for a designated period in April and May each year (Alta. For. Ld. Wild. 1989).

The water in both lakes is nutrient-rich and dense algal blooms develop by midsummer. The lower lake is greener and supports more areas of nuisance aquatic plant growth than the upper lake.

Drainage Basin Characteristics

The drainage basin area of the Mann lakes is large compared to the area of the lakes (Tables 1, 2). However, the southern half of the basin is mostly dead storage and does not contribute runoff to the lakes except when precipitation is exceptionally high, possibly only once or twice a century (Alta. Envir. n.d.[b]).

The drainage basin is gently to moderately rolling with slopes of 5% to 15% (Kocaoglu 1975). It lies within the Dry Mixedwood Subregion of the Boreal Mixedwood Ecoregion (Strong and Leggat

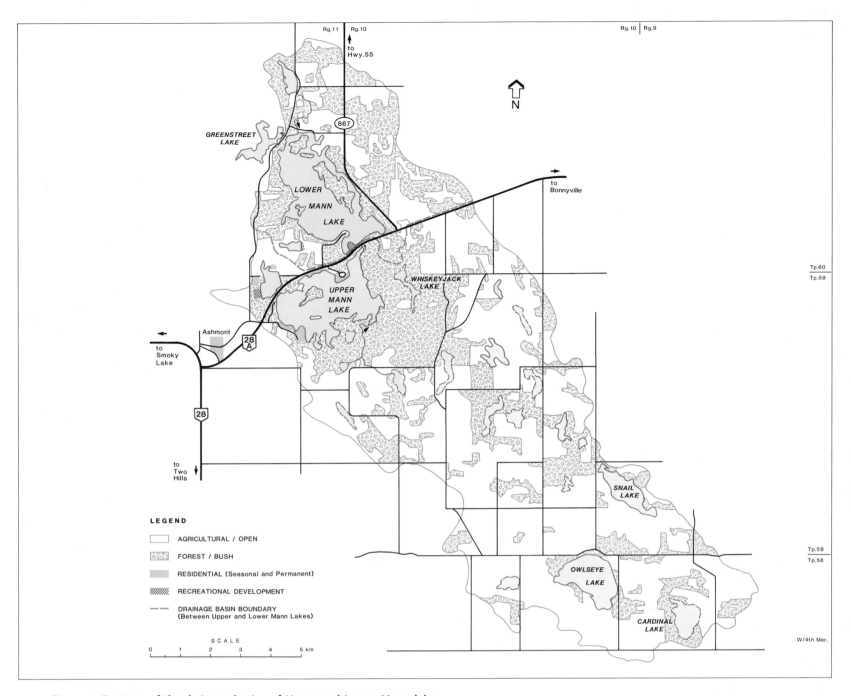

Figure 1. Features of the drainage basins of Upper and Lower Mann lakes.
SOURCES: Alta. Envir. n.d.[b]; En. Mines Resour. Can. 1971; 1978. Updated with 1986 and 1987 aerial photos.

1981). The main soils in the drainage basin are Orthic Gray Luvisols that formed on moderately well-drained, weakly calcareous glacial till (Kocaoglu 1975). The soils in low-lying, poorly drained areas are Orthic Luvic Gleysols. The till in the extended basin area to the southeast of the lakes is more strongly calcareous than in the portion of the basin closer to the lakes and soils are Orthic Gray and Dark Gray Luvisols. The dominant vegetation is trembling aspen with some balsam poplar, white birch and white spruce (Strong and Leggat 1981). Willows are present along the lakeshore and in low-lying areas around reed/grass meadows (Alta. For. Ld. Wild. 1987). Almost two-thirds of the basin has been cleared for agriculture, primarily grazing and forage production (Fig. 1).

Lake Basin Characteristics

Both Upper and Lower Mann lakes are very irregularly shaped and are dotted with numerous islands. Upper Mann is the deeper of the two lakes; its maximum depth is 9.1 m, versus 6.1 m for the lower lake. The basin of the upper lake slopes more steeply than that of the lower lake (Fig. 2).

The water level of Upper Mann Lake has been monitored since 1962 (Fig. 3) and that of Lower Mann has been monitored since 1973 (Fig. 4). The water levels in both lakes were high in 1979 and then steadily dropped to historic low levels in late 1988. Over this period, both lakes declined by 1.3 m. This drop in lake level reduced the area of Upper Mann Lake by only 7% (Fig. 5), but the area of Lower Mann Lake was reduced by approximately 15% (Fig. 6). There is no control structure on either Upper or Lower Mann Lake, but the water level in the two lakes is controlled to some extent by a weir on Greenstreet Lake, which is immediately downstream of Lower Mann Lake. The weir was built in 1983 and is operated by Alberta Forestry, Lands and Wildlife. The weir elevation is 615.85 m. As of 1989, drought conditions since the weir was completed had kept water levels lower than this elevation.

The residence time of water in Lower Mann Lake is much shorter (21 years) than in Upper Mann Lake (69 years, Table 2). These estimates do not consider groundwater inflow or outflow, which is probably significant in maintaining lake levels.

Water Quality

The water quality of Upper and Lower Mann lakes was sampled by Alberta Environment on 6 March 1979 and on 16 August 1983. Upper Mann Lake was also sampled four times in 1984 for nutrients,

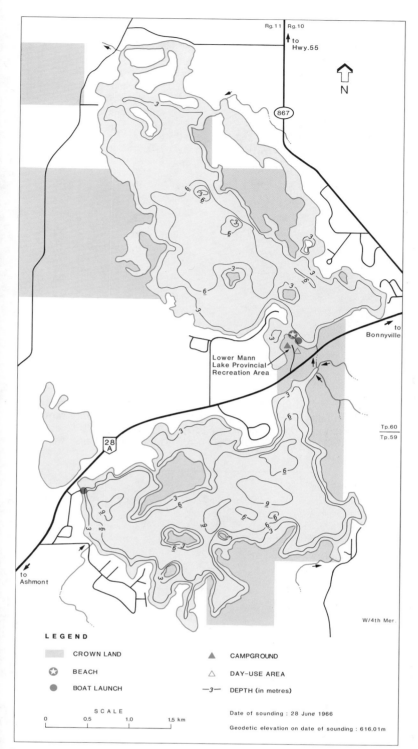

Figure 2. Bathymetry and shoreline features of Upper and Lower Mann lakes.
BATHYMETRY SOURCE: Alta. Envir. n.d.[c].

LEGEND

▨	CROWN LAND	▲	CAMPGROUND
✪	BEACH	△	DAY-USE AREA
●	BOAT LAUNCH	—3—	DEPTH (in metres)

SCALE
0   0.5   1.0   1.5 km

Date of sounding : 28 June 1966

Geodetic elevation on date of sounding : 616.01m

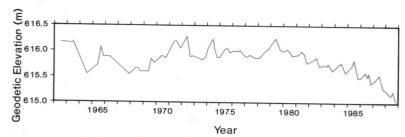

Figure 3. Water level of Upper Mann Lake, 1962 to 1988.
SOURCE: Alta. Envir. n.d.[c].

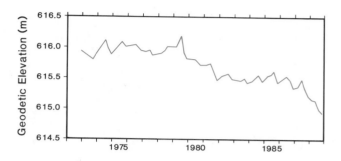

Figure 4. Water level of Lower Mann Lake, 1973 to 1988.
SOURCE: Alta. Envir. n.d.[c].

Table 1. Characteristics of Mann lakes drainage basin.

area (excluding lake) (km^2)[a]	148, of this 116 km^2 to upper lake
soil[b]	Orthic Gray Luvisol
bedrock geology[c]	Belly River Formation (Upper Cretaceous): sandstone, siltstone, mudstone, ironstone beds; nonmarine
terrain[b]	moderately rolling
ecoregion[d]	Dry Mixedwood Subregion of Boreal Mixedwood
dominant vegetation[d]	trembling aspen, balsam poplar
mean annual inflow (m^3)[a, e]	1.08 x 10^6 (upper lake)
	1.76 x 10^6 (lower lake)
mean annual sunshine (h)[f]	2 168

NOTE: [e]excluding groundwater inflow
SOURCES: [a]Alta. Envir. n.d.[b]; [b]Kocaoglu 1975; [c]Alta. Res. Counc. 1972; [d]Strong and Leggat 1981; [f]Envir. Can. 1982

Table 2. Characteristics of Mann Lakes.

	Upper	Lower
elevation (m)[a, b]	616.01	616.01
surface area (km^2)[a, b]	4.59	5.10
volume (m^3)[a, b]	26.1 x 10^6	20.3 x 10^6
maximum depth (m)[a, b]	9.1	6.1
mean depth (m)[a, b]	5.7	4.0
shoreline length (km)[c]	20.0	19.0
mean annual lake evaporation (mm)[d]	638	638
mean annual precipitation (mm)[d]	484	484
mean residence time (yr)[d, e]	69	21
control structure[f]	none	none

NOTES: [a]on date of sounding: 28–30 June 1966; [e]excluding groundwater inflow; [f]a weir on Greenstreet Lake, which has a full supply level of 815.85 m, will affect water levels in both Mann lakes when precipitation raises lake elevations to 815.85 m
SOURCES: [b]Alta. Envir. n.d.[c]; [c]En. Mines Resour. Can. 1971; 1978; [d]Alta. Envir. n.d.[b].

chlorophyll *a*, temperature and dissolved oxygen (Alta. Envir. n.d.[a]).

Both lakes have well-buffered, fresh water (Table 3). The limited sampling has not detected thermal stratification in either lake, except in mid-June 1984, when a 2°C difference in temperature from top to bottom was found in Upper Mann Lake (Fig. 7, 8). In both lakes, dissolved oxygen in the water near the sediment was depleted during summer; in Upper Mann Lake, the water near the bottom was anoxic by mid-August 1983. By October 1983, however, the lake had mixed and the dissolved oxygen concentration near the substrate had increased to 10 mg/L. In the winter of 1978/79, water at the bottom of both lakes was anoxic by 6 March. Severe winterkills of pike and perch are recorded in Lower Mann Lake in most years. In Upper Mann Lake, a severe winterkill occurs occasionally and partial winterkills occur approximately every five years (Sullivan 1989).

The few data collected indicate that both Lower and Upper Mann

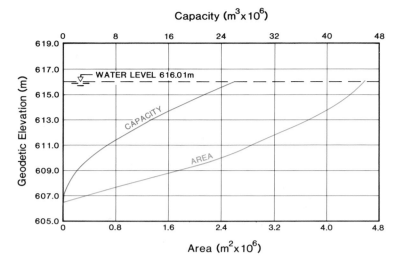

Figure 5. Area/capacity curve for Upper Mann Lake.
SOURCE: Alta. Envir. n.d.[c].

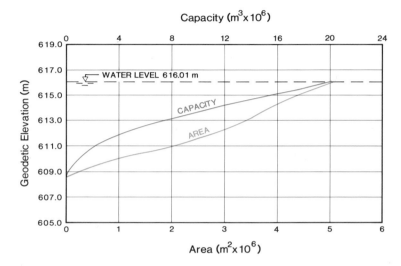

Figure 6. Area/capacity curve for Lower Mann Lake.
SOURCE: Alta. Envir. n.d.[c].

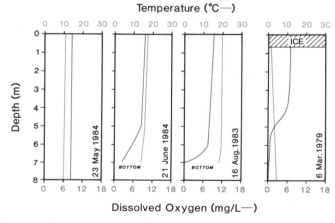

Figure 7. Temperature and dissolved oxygen in Upper Mann Lake, 1983 and 1984.
SOURCE: Alta. Envir. n.d.[a].

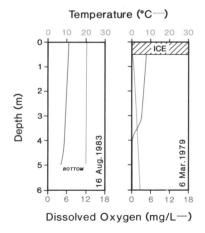

Figure 8. Temperature and dissolved oxygen in Lower Mann Lake, 1983.
SOURCE: Alta. Envir. n.d.[a].

Table 3. Major ions and related water quality variables for Upper and Lower Mann lakes. Average concentrations in mg/L; pH in pH units. Composite samples from the euphotic zone collected once on 16 Aug. 1983.

	Upper Mann	Lower Mann
pH	9.0	9.2
total alkalinity (CaCO$_3$)	203	199
specific conductivity (μS/cm)	411	399
total dissolved solids (calculated)	227	229
total hardness (CaCO$_3$)	146	136
HCO$_3$	202	522
CO$_3$	23	31
Mg	24	24
Na	20	24
K	19	19
Cl	3	3[a]
SO$_4$	20	25
Ca	19	15

NOTE: [a]n=1, 06 Mar. 1979
SOURCE: Alta. Envir. n.d.[a], Naquadat stations 01AL06AA1010 (Upper Mann), 01AL06AA1060 (Lower Mann)

Table 4. Nutrient, chlorophyll *a* and Secchi depth data for Upper and Lower Mann lakes. Average concentrations in μg/L. Composite samples from the euphotic zone collected on 16 Aug. 1983 from both lakes and 4 times from 21 June to 09 Oct. 1984 from Upper Mann Lake. S.E. = standard error.

	UPPER MANN			LOWER MANN
	1983	1984		1983
	Mean	Mean	S.E.	Mean
total phosphorus	112	45	21.2	121
total dissolved phosphorus	24	26[a]	1.0	38
total Kjeldahl nitrogen	2 140	—	—	2 400
NH$_4$–nitrogen	29	—	—	35
iron	—	—	—	40
chlorophyll *a*	68.4	22.9	9.95	103.1
Secchi depth (m)	1.0	3.4[b]	0.80	0.8

NOTES: [a]n = 2; [b]n = 5, 23 May to 09 Oct.
SOURCE: Alta. Envir. n.d.[a], Naquadat stations 01AL06AA1010 (Upper Mann), 01AL06AA1060 (Lower Mann)

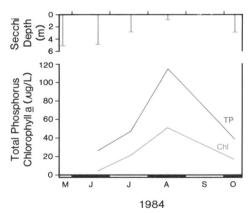

Figure 9. Total phosphorus, chlorophyll *a* and Secchi depth in Upper Mann Lake, 1984.
SOURCE: Alta. Envir. n.d.[a].

lakes are hyper-eutrophic (Table 4, Fig. 9). In Upper Mann Lake, the total phosphorus concentration in the euphotic zone increased to a peak of 113 mg/L on 16 August 1984, likely because phosphorus was released from anoxic sediments. Chlorophyll *a* concentrations followed the total phosphorus concentrations and reached a peak of 51 µg/L (Fig. 9).

Biological Characteristics

Plants

The density of algae in both Upper and Lower Mann lakes is so high that it interferes with recreational use. In summer, blue-green algae cause both visual and odour problems (Alta. Mun. Aff. 1989). The phytoplankton in both lakes was sampled on 16 August 1983 (Alta. Envir. n.d.[a]). In Upper Mann Lake, 85% of the total algal biomass (7.06 mg/L) was blue-green algae (Cyanophyta), mostly *Anabaena flos-aquae* and *Microcystis aeruginosa*. In Lower Mann Lake, 69% of the total biomass (10.91 mg/L) was blue-green algae, mostly *Microcystis aeruginosa*, *Lyngbya Birgei* and *Anabaena flos-aquae*. Upper Mann Lake also supported a small biomass of the dinoflagellate (Pyrrhophyta) *Ceratium hirundinella*, and two species of Cryptophyta, mostly *Cryptomonas erosa reflexa*. Lower Mann Lake differed from Upper Mann Lake in that the algal community in the lower lake included 19% diatoms (Bacillariophyta: mostly *Stephanodiscus niagarae*), compared with less than 1% diatoms in the upper lake. Cryptophytes and pyrrhophytes were similar in abundance in both lakes.

The phytoplankton in Upper Mann Lake was also sampled on 21 June, 14 August and 9 October in 1984. In June, 60% of the total biomass (0.41 mg/L) was cryptophytes and 30% was diatoms. In August, 55% of the total biomass (16.7 mg/L) was blue-greens and 39% was *Ceratium hirundinella*. By October, the biomass had decreased to 9.3 mg/L, and was composed of 67% diatoms and 27% blue-greens.

Macrophytes are a widespread nuisance to boaters in Lower Mann Lake and present problems in shallow, sheltered areas of Upper Mann Lake (Sullivan 1989). In Upper Mann Lake, in August 1986, submergent macrophytes—mostly *Ceratophyllum demersum*, but also some star duckweed (*Lemna trisulca*), white-stem pondweed (*Potamogeton praelongus*) and northern watermilfoil (*Myriophyllum exalbescens*)—were recorded to depths of 2.9 m (Chambers and Prepas n.d.; 1988). In 1988, areas of dense emergent and submergent growth in both lakes were mapped by Alberta Municipal Affairs (Fig. 10). In Upper Mann Lake, the east and south shores supported dense communities of emergent and submergent plants, and the north and west shores were relatively weed-free except in sheltered bays where northern watermilfoil grew abundantly. In Lower Mann Lake, the north and east shores supported dense areas of cattails (*Typha* sp.) and bulrushes (*Scirpus* sp.), and passage along the eastern shore of the large island is often blocked. The entire northern portion of the lower lake supports dense submergent growth.

Invertebrates

There are no data on the invertebrates in either of the Mann lakes.

Fish

The Mann lakes support an erratically popular sport fishery for northern pike and yellow perch. Walleye were stocked by Fish and Wildlife Division in Upper Mann Lake in 1960 and 1984, but there has been only one unconfirmed report of a walleye being caught. Severe winterkills occur in Upper Mann Lake in some years and partial winterkills occur approximately one year in five. Severe winterkills occur in Lower Mann Lake in most years; the lake is repopulated by pike and perch that migrate from Upper Mann Lake through the culverts under Highway 28A. Winterkills keep the size of the perch and pike population low, and high nutrient levels promote abundant food production; therefore, the growth rates of surviving fish are

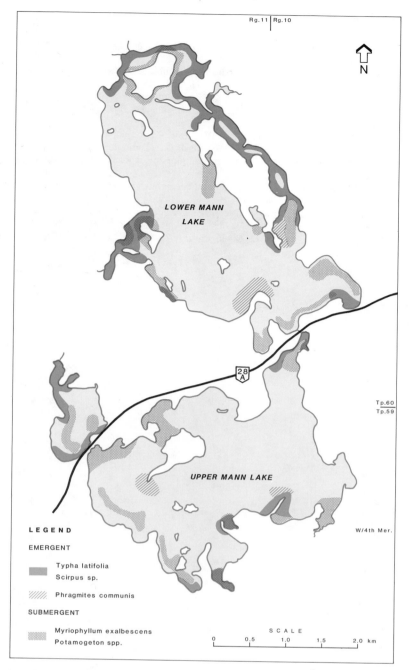

Figure 10. Areas of dense aquatic macrophyte growth in Upper and Lower Mann lakes, 1988.
SOURCE: Alta. Mun. Aff. 1989.

rapid. In winters when the lakes do not winterkill, the pike and perch are large and easily caught, and anglers flock to the lakes. In other years, angling success is negligible (Sullivan 1989).

Both lakes were fished commercially for a few years during the 1940s. A total of three licences were issued for Upper Mann Lake and a total of 18 000 kg of pike were harvested between 1944 and 1947. In Lower Mann Lake, a total of 19 000 kg of pike and 11 500 kg of perch were harvested between 1944 and 1949 (Alta. Rec. Parks Wild. 1976).

Wildlife

Both lakes provide good habitat for waterfowl nesting. Resting and feeding cormorants and pelicans are often seen on or near the islands in Upper Mann Lake.

J.M. Crosby

References

Alberta Environment. n.d.[a]. Envir. Assess. Div., Envir. Qlty. Monit. Br. Unpubl. data, Edmonton.

———. n.d.[b]. Tech. Serv. Div., Hydrol. Br. Unpubl. data, Edmonton.

———. n.d.[c]. Tech. Serv. Div., Surv. Br. Unpubl. data, Edmonton.

Alberta Forestry, Lands and Wildlife. 1987. A summary of Alberta's natural areas reserved and established. Pub. Ld. Div., Ld. Mgt. Devel. Br. Unpubl. rep., Edmonton.

———. 1988. Boating in Alberta. Fish Wild. Div., Edmonton.

———. 1989. Guide to sportfishing. Fish Wild. Div., Edmonton.

Alberta Hotel Association. 1989. Alberta campground guide 1989. Prep. for Travel Alta., Edmonton.

Alberta Municipal Affairs. 1989. Upper and Lower Mann lakes management study. Plan. Div., Plan. Br., Edmonton.

Alberta Recreation, Parks and Wildlife. 1976. Commercial fisheries catch statistics for Alberta, 1942–1975. Fish Wild. Div., Fish. Mgt. Rep. No. 22, Edmonton.

Alberta Research Council. 1972. Geological map of Alberta. Nat. Resour. Div., Alta. Geol. Surv., Edmonton.

Chambers, P.A. and E.E. Prepas. n.d. Univ. Alta., Dept. Zool. Unpubl. data, Edmonton.

———. 1988. Underwater spectral attenuation and its effect on the maximum depth of angiosperm colonization. Can. J. Fish. Aquat. Sci. 45:1010–1017.

Energy, Mines and Resources Canada. 1971, 1978. National topographic series 1:50 000 73L/3 (1971), 73L/4 (1978). Surv. Map. Br., Ottawa.

Environment Canada. 1982. Canadian climate normals, Vol. 7: Bright sunshine (1951–1980). Prep. by Atm. Envir. Serv. Supply Serv. Can., Ottawa.

Holmgren, E.J. and P.M. Holmgren. 1976. Over 2000 place names of Alberta. 3rd ed. West. Producer Prairie Books, Saskatoon.

Kocaoglu, S.S. 1975. Reconnaissance soil survey of the Sand River area. Alta. Soil Surv. Rep. No. 34, Univ. Alta. Bull. No. SS–15, Alta. Inst. Pedol. Rep. No. S–74–34 1975. Univ. Alta., Edmonton.

Owlseye Historical Society. 1984. An era in review—A history of Owlseye—Ashmont, Abilene, Boscombe, Cork, Boyne Lake, Anning and area. Owlseye Hist. Soc., St. Paul.

Strong, W.L. and K.R. Leggat. 1981. Ecoregions of Alberta. Alta. En. Nat. Resour., Resour. Eval. Plan. Div., Edmonton.

Sullivan, M. 1989. Alta. For. Ld. Wild., Fish Wild. Div., St. Paul. Pers. comm.

MARIE LAKE

MAP SHEET: 73L/9

LOCATION: Tp65 R2, 3 W4

LAT/LONG: 54°38'N 110°18'W

Marie Lake is a beautiful lake with excellent beaches and clear water. It is located in Improvement District No. 18 (South), about 300 km northeast of the city of Edmonton and 25 km northwest of the town of Cold Lake. From Highway 55, the lake can be reached by travelling north on a gravel road, locally known as the Primrose Lake Road, which skirts the eastern shore. Local access roads branch west from the Primrose Lake Road to the south and east sides of the lake (Fig. 1). Current development around Marie Lake is very limited, but the lake has good potential for recreational use.

The lake's name is said to be derived from the Cree words *methae* or *merai*, which mean "a fish" (Geog. Bd. Can. 1928). The original inhabitants of the area probably were the nomadic Beaver, Blackfoot and Slavey tribes. Late in the eighteenth century, these tribes were displaced by the Cree, who came in search of furs to trade with white traders (McMillan 1977). Nearby Cold Lake was part of a fur trade route from Waterhen Lake, Saskatchewan, into Alberta's northern lake region via the Beaver River (McMillan 1977; Alta. Mun. Aff. 1978).

Currently, there are no public facilities on Marie Lake. However, demand for public access was such that a lake management study was prepared in 1987 and an area structure plan was completed in 1988 (Alta. Mun. Aff. 1987[a]; 1987[b]; 1988). The lake management plan determines the extent of future land developments, allocates land use and determines ways to minimize environmental impacts and conflicts in uses of the lakeshore. It recommends preferred lake uses and ways to minimize lake-user conflicts.

There are several private recreational developments on the lake, all located on leased Crown land. The Alberta Fish and Game Association has a wilderness camp on the western shore and the Cold Lake Camping Society of Canadian Forces Base (CFB) Cold Lake at Medley leases about 65 ha on the eastern shore (Fig. 2). The CFB recreation area, Marie Lake Campsite, sometimes allows public use of the boat launch and parking area (Lasouski 1989). A commercial campground is slated for development on the peninsula on the northeast corner of the lake. As of 1989, construction of this facility was only in the preliminary stages (Slaght 1989). Other developments on Crown land include a Department of National Defence helicopter landing pad on the western shore and a residential site on the eastern shore just north of Marie Lake Campsite. As well, Alberta Recreation and Parks has reserved an area on the northwest bay with the intent to create a provincial recreation area (Alta. Mun. Aff. 1987[a]).

Only a small portion of the shoreland is privately owned. A registered subdivision is located on private land on the eastern shore (Fig. 2). There are 56 lots, all of which are fully developed, and 4.6 ha of shoreline public reserves. These reserves have no public facilities. Development of the balance of private land includes an abandoned mink farm at the northwest corner of the lake at Marie Creek, and a farm and cottage development along the southern shore near the outflow (Alta. Mun. Aff. 1987[a]).

Surveys of land owners around the lakeshore were conducted in 1977 and 1986 (Alta. Mun. Aff. 1979; 1987[a]). The most popular recreation activities in summer were swimming and fishing, followed by sightseeing, relaxation, power boating, canoeing and water skiing. Sailboats and rowboats are also used by cottagers. Marie Lake is susceptible to sudden windstorms that make the eastern side of the

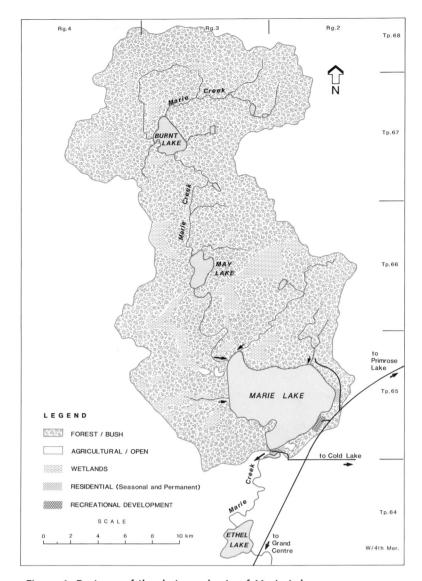

Figure 1. Features of the drainage basin of Marie Lake.
SOURCES: Alta. Envir. n.d.[b]; En. Mines Resour. Can. 1981. Updated with 1982 aerial photos.

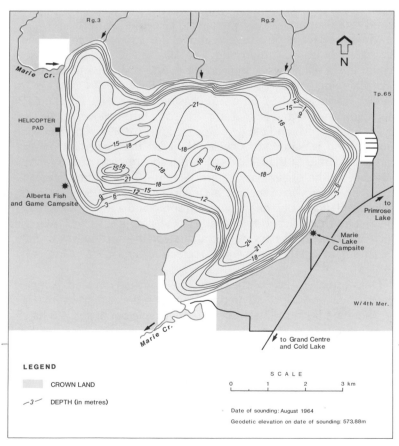

Figure 2. Bathymetry and shoreline features of Marie Lake.
BATHYMETRY SOURCE: Alta. Envir. n.d.[c].

Table 1. Characteristics of Marie Lake drainage basin.

area (excluding lake) (km^2)[a]	386
soil[b]	Orthic Gray Luvisols, Fibrisols, Mesisols
bedrock geology[c]	La Biche Formation (Upper Cretaceous): shale, ironstone partings and concretions; marine
terrain[b]	flat and depressional to undulating
ecoregion[d]	Dry and Moist Mixedwood subregions of Boreal Mixedwood
dominant vegetation[d]	trembling aspen, balsam poplar
mean annual inflow (m^3)[a, e]	17.0 x 10^6
mean annual sunshine (h)[f]	2 240

NOTE: [e]excluding groundwater inflow
SOURCES: [a]Alta. Envir. n.d.[b]; [b]Kocaoglu 1975; [c]Alta. Res. Counc. 1972; [d]Strong and Leggat 1981; [f]Envir. Can. 1982

Table 2. Characteristics of Marie Lake.

elevation (m)[a, b]	573.88
surface area (km^2)[a, b]	34.6
volume (m^3)[a, b]	484 x 10^6
maximum depth (m)[a, b]	26
mean depth (m)[a, b]	14
shoreline length (km)[c]	29
mean annual lake evaporation (mm)[d]	634
mean annual precipitation (mm)[d]	439
mean residence time (yr)[d, e]	47.5
control structure	none

NOTES: [a]on date of sounding: Aug. 1964; [e]excluding groundwater inflow
SOURCES: [b]Alta. Envir. n.d.[c]; [c]Alta. Mun. Aff. 1987[a]; [d]Alta. Envir. n.d.[b].

Table 3. Major ions and related water quality variables for Marie Lake. Average concentrations in mg/L; pH in pH units. Composite samples from the euphotic zone collected 12 times from 14 May to 14 Oct. 1980. S.E. = standard error.

	Mean	S.E.
pH (range)	7.5–8.5	—
total alkalinity (CaCO$_3$)	135	1.2
specific conductivity (μS/cm)	256	2.2
total dissolved solids (calculated)	140[a]	0.3
total hardness (CaCO$_3$)	126	1.0
dissolved organic carbon	10[b]	0.6
HCO$_3$	160[a]	1.1
CO$_3$	<2	—
Mg	12	0.1
Na	6	0.2
K	2	0.04
Cl	<1	—
SO$_4$	<3	—
Ca	30[c]	0.3

NOTES: [a]n = 5; [b]n = 9; [c]n = 7
SOURCE: Alta. Envir. n.d.[a], Naquadat station 01AL06AC5290

lake treacherous for boaters (Alta. Mun. Aff. 1987[b]). In winter, popular activities were general relaxation, ice fishing, cross-country skiing, snowshoeing and hunting. There are no boating restrictions specific to the lake, but general federal regulations apply (Alta. For. Ld. Wild. 1988).

Marie Lake has very clear water with little algal growth. Much of the shoreline is flat and sandy, with only scattered areas of aquatic vegetation. Sport fish species in the lake include northern pike, yellow perch, lake whitefish and walleye. There are no special sport fishing regulations for the lake, but provincial limits apply (Alta. For. Ld. Wild. 1989).

Drainage Basin Characteristics

Marie Lake has an extensive drainage basin that is about 11 times larger than the lake (Tables 1, 2). Most of the water flowing into the lake comes from Marie Creek to the north (Fig. 1). This creek drains Burnt and May lakes before flowing into Marie Lake. Three smaller creeks drain the northeast part of the watershed and flow into Marie Lake's northern shore. As well, a small creek drains the wetland area west of the lake. Marie Creek flows out of the southern bay of Marie Lake into Ethel Lake and then the Beaver River.

The drainage basin is covered by nearly featureless ground moraine and outwash sand islands surrounded by organic materials (Kocaoglu 1975). Soil parent materials are glacial till, glaciofluvial sand and peat. The land is characterized by flat and depressional to gently rolling topography featuring minor ridges and knobs intermixed with numerous wet depressions and small peat bogs. Soils are mostly moderately well-drained Orthic Gray Luvisols on upper and midslopes, and poorly to very poorly drained Fibrisols and Mesisols on depressional to level ground.

Agricultural activity in the watershed is very limited. Most of the land is forested and there are large wetland areas throughout the drainage basin (Fig. 1). The southern half of the lake is part of the Dry Mixedwood Subregion of the Boreal Mixedwood Ecoregion (Strong and Leggat 1981). The dominant trees are trembling aspen on well-drained to moderately well-drained Gray Luvisols, jack pine on rapidly to well-drained Eutric Brunisols, and white spruce on imperfectly drained Gray Luvisols. Black spruce, willows and sedges are the main species on poorly to very poorly drained Organics. The northern half of the lake and the drainage basin north of the lake are part of the Moist Mixedwood Subregion. This subregion differs from the Dry Mixedwood Subregion in that trembling aspen and balsam poplar are codominant.

Marie Lake is underlain by the Muriel Lake aquifer within the Sinclair and Helina Channels (Ozoray and Lytviak 1980). Groundwater is used for stock watering and residential purposes. Regional water needs are met by the aquifers rather than Marie Lake. The largest water user in the region is the oil sands industry, which is also the major industry in the watershed. Activity is centred in the area east of Burnt Lake. These oil sands plants currently use groundwater or water piped from Cold Lake as their water source. As a result of Alberta Environment's studies of the water resources in the Cold Lake-Beaver River basin in the early 1980s (Alta. Envir. 1983), a long-term plan for water resources management in the Cold Lake region was adopted by the government in 1985 (Alta. Envir. 1985). Under this plan, industrial withdrawals from Marie Lake are limited to 0.425×10^6 m³/year while the lake has an unregulated outlet, or 1.2×10^6 m³/year if a weir is built on the outlet.

Lake Basin Characteristics

Marie Lake is a large, deep lake with a fairly regular shoreline (Table 2, Fig. 2). The maximum depth recorded during the 1964 hydrographic survey was 26 m in an area located east of the peninsula.

The lake basin slopes steeply along much of the shoreline, particularly along the north and southeast shores. In those two areas, the backshore is steep, the shoreline banks are steep and jagged, and the water's edge is sharply defined. The basin slopes most gradually near the peninsula on the southwest shore and along the central and northern portions of the east shore. In these areas the backshore has

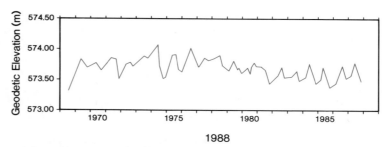

Figure 3. Water level of Marie Lake, 1968 to 1987.
SOURCES: Alta. Envir. n.d.[c]; Envir. Can. 1980–1987.

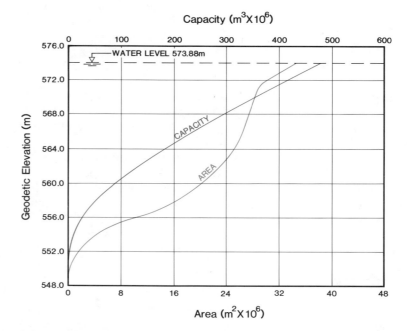

Figure 4. Area/capacity curve for Marie Lake.
SOURCE: Alta. Envir. n.d.[c].

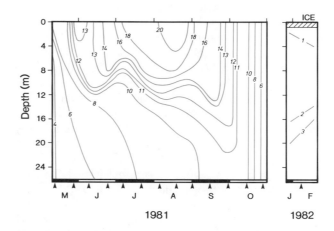

Figure 5. Temperature (°C) of Marie Lake, 1981 and 1982.
Arrows indicate sampling dates.
SOURCE: Alta. Envir. n.d.[a].

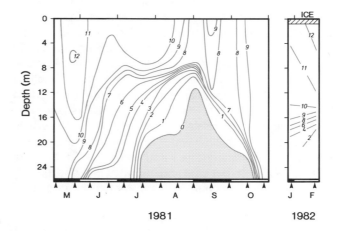

Figure 6. Dissolved oxygen (mg/L) in Marie Lake, 1981 and 1982. Arrows indicate sampling dates.

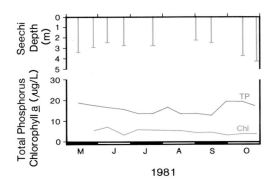

Figure 7. Total phosphorus, chlorophyll *a* and Secchi depth in Marie Lake, 1981.
SOURCE: Alta. Envir. n.d.[a].

Table 4. Nutrient, chlorophyll *a* and Secchi depth data for Marie Lake. Average concentrations in μg/L. Composite samples from the euphotic zone collected 12 times from 14 May to 14 Oct. 1980 and 13 times from 12 May to 27 Oct. 1981. S.E. = standard error.

	1980		1981	
	Mean	S.E.	Mean	S.E.
total phosphorus	—	—	15	0.7
total dissolved phosphorus	—	—	8	0.8
soluble reactive phosphorus	—	—	3[b]	0.6
total Kjeldahl nitrogen	736	43.6	715	49.1
$NO_3 + NO_2$–nitrogen	<1[a]	—	—	—
NH_4–nitrogen	—	—	<22	—
chlorophyll *a*	6.5	1.15	4.6[c]	0.34
Secchi depth (m)	2.5[b]	0.43	3.0[b]	0.22

NOTES: [a]n = 5; [b]n = 9; [c]n = 11
SOURCE: Alta. Envir. n.d.[a], Naquadat station 01AL06AC5290

Table 5. Theoretical total phosphorus loading to Marie Lake from external sources.

Source		Phosphorus (kg/yr)	Percentage of Total
immediate watershed	forested/bush	1 756	60
	agricultural/cleared	3	<1
	residential/cottage	52	2
sewage		104	4
precipitation/dustfall		735	25
inflow from Burnt and May lakes		250	9
	TOTAL	2 900	100
annual areal loading (g/m² of lake surface)	0.08		

SOURCE: Trew 1989

gentle to moderate slopes and the water's edge is flat and sandy. Around the lake, over 95% of the backshore area has a dense tree cover, with trees and shrubs growing down to the water's edge. Areas of organic deposits and marsh, which constitute less than 5% of the backshore, are located along the peninsula and along the Marie Creek inflow and outflow (Alta. Mun. Aff. 1987[a]).

Water levels have been monitored continuously since 1968 (Fig. 3). The historic fluctuation is 0.77 m, from the historic minimum of 573.32 m in July 1968, to the historic maximum of 574.09 m in June 1974. Changes in the area and capacity of Marie Lake with fluctuations in water level are illustrated in Figure 4.

Water Quality

The water quality of Marie Lake was studied by Alberta Environment approximately twice per month during the open-water seasons in 1980 and 1981 and occasionally during the winters of 1980/81 and 1981/82 (Alta. Envir. n.d.[a]; Trew et al. 1983). The water is fresh, well-buffered and moderately hard (Table 3). Bicarbonate and calcium are the dominant ions.

The lake was strongly thermally stratified from June to August in 1980 and June through September in 1981 (Fig. 5). It mixed completely in May of 1981 and in October of both years. In 1981, the bottom water was anoxic by July, and by early September, the water was anoxic at depths greater than 11 m (Fig. 6). Under ice, the surface waters were well oxygenated in January and February of both 1981 and 1982 (Fig. 6), but dissolved oxygen became depleted in the deeper waters in both years. By February of 1982, dissolved oxygen had declined to 1.2 mg/L at a depth of 20 m.

Marie Lake is mesotrophic. Although chlorophyll *a* levels are quite low, there are substantial year-to-year differences. In 1980, chlorophyll *a* levels reached a maximum of 16.1 μg/L in October. In 1981, the maximum value of 7.0 μg/L was recorded in June (Fig. 7). Average chlorophyll *a* values were 6.5 μg/L in 1980 and 4.6 μg/L in 1981 (Table 4). Total phosphorus concentrations are quite low for an Alberta lake; in 1981, they were highest in spring and fall and averaged 15 μg/L. Phosphorus data are not available for 1980.

The phosphorus supply to Marie Lake from external sources has been estimated (Table 5). The largest source of phosphorus is the forested portion of the immediate watershed, which provides 60% of the total input of 2 900 kg/year, or 0.08 g/m² of lake surface. Precipitation and dustfall account for 25% of the total, and inflow from Burnt and May lakes provides another 9%. Contributions from agricultural and cleared land (less than 1%), urban areas (2%) and sewage (4%) are minimal. The release of total phosphorus to Marie Lake from sediments under shallow water (9–m deep or less) during summer has also been estimated (Shaw and Prepas 1989). The rate of release is high (4.9 mg/m² per day) and indicates that phosphorus return from shallow sediments could be a substantial component of the lake's phosphorus budget.

Biological Characteristics

Plants

The composition of the phytoplankton was examined on four dates during 1978 by Esso Resources Ltd. (Cross 1979), once in 1979, approximately twice a month throughout 1980 and 1981, and once in 1983 and 1986 (Alta. Envir. n.d.[a]). In 1980, there were no clear seasonal patterns in phytoplankton biomass (Table 6), but in 1981, biomass clearly decreased from March to October. The average biomass for the period from May to October in the two years was 1.51 mg/L in 1980 and 2.00 mg/L in 1981. During the open-water period in 1980, blue-greens (Cyanophyta), particularly *Oscillatoria agardhii*, *Lyngbya Bergei*, *Anabaena flos-aquae*, *Aphanothece* sp., *Aphanizomenon flos-aquae* and *A. gracile*, were the dominant or codominant group on all sampling dates except for 14 October. Diatoms (Bacillariophyta), particularly *Stephanodiscus niagarae*, were the dominant group on this date. Golden-brown algae (Chrysophyta) such as *Heterochromas globosa* were abundant only in September, and dinoflagellates (Pyrrhophyta) such as *Ceratium hirundinella* were abundant during August and September.

The macrophyte community was surveyed by Alberta Environment in 1978 and 1981 (Alta. Envir. n.d.[a]; McGregor 1983). Five emergent, 3 floating, and 13 submergent species were identified. There were two important macrophyte beds: one stretched north from the central part of the western shore to the centre of the north shore, and the other was located along the western shore of the southern bay (Fig. 8). These areas are essential to fish spawning and production (Alta. Mun. Aff. 1987[b]). The dominant emergent vegetation in the lake was common great bulrush (*Scirpus validus*). The two major macrophyte beds were dominated by pondweeds (*Potamageton richardsonii and P. natans*), stonewort (*Chara* spp.), and northern watermilfoil (*Myriophyllum exalbescens*). Most of the lit-

Table 6. Percentage composition of major algal groups by total biomass in Marie Lake, 1980. Composite samples collected from the euphotic zone.

ALGAL GROUP	14 May	28 May	6 June	25 June	09 July	22 July	06 Aug.	10 Aug.	03 Sep.	16 Sep.	01 Oct.	14 Oct.
Total Biomass (mg/L)	0.90	1.36	0.90	4.73	2.50	1.21	2.03	1.94	2.94	1.03	1.08	3.41
Percentage Composition:												
Cyanophyta	58	37	58	48	70	68	60	61	38	28	43	10
		Oscillatoria	⟶	⟶	*Aphanizomenon*	⟶	⟶		*Anab. Aphano.*	*Oscill.*	*Lyngbya*	
					Lyngbya	⟶	⟶	⟶				
Chlorophyta	6	2	3	2	7	6	7	4	11	17	12	5
Chrysophyta	3	6	9	19	6	7	9	9	36	8	5	3
									Hetero.			
Bacillariophyta	20	30	17	22	7	5	2	0	1	5	13	73
		Steph.		*Asterionella*								*Steph.*
Cryptophyta	8	9	5	7	3	4	4	5	1	13	11	6
Pyrrhophyta	5	15	7	1	6	11	18	20	13	29	16	3
						Ceratium	⟶			*Ceratium*	⟶	

NOTES: *Anab.* = *Anabaena*; *Oscill.* = *Oscillatoria*; *Steph.* = *Stephanodiscus*; *Aphano.* = *Aphanothece*; *Hetero.* = *Heterochromonas*
SOURCE: Alta. Envir. n.d.[a]

toral area outside of the two bays supported a sparse growth of pondweed (either *P. gramineus*, *P. richardsonii* or *P. zosteriformis*) with some stonewort (*Chara* spp.).

Invertebrates

A preliminary survey of the zooplankton and benthic invertebrate communities was made in 1978 for Esso Resources Ltd. (Cross 1979). The number/L of crustacean zooplankton and rotifers varied widely among sample dates and depths. Twelve species of crustacean zooplankton were identified; *Diacyclops bicuspidatus thomasi* and *Diaptomus sicilis* were the dominant copepods and *Chydorus sphaericus* and *Daphnia galeata mendotae* were the dominant cladocerans. *Diacyclops* is important because it is the intermediate invertebrate host for the parasite, *Triaenophorus crassus*, that infests lake whitefish. Seven species of rotifers were identified; *Keratella cochlearis* was the dominant species.

The 12– to 16–m depth zone was the only depth sampled for benthic invertebrates on all five collection dates. Midge larvae (Chironomidae) and aquatic earthworms (Oligochaeta) were consistently present in the samples; fingernail clams (Sphaeriidae) were occasionally present.

Fish

Eleven species of fish have been reported in Marie Lake: lake whitefish, cisco, burbot, northern pike, yellow perch, walleye, white sucker, spottail shiner, lake chub, ninespine stickleback and Iowa darter (Watters 1979; Aquat. Envir. Ltd. 1983). Cysts of the tapeworm *Triaenophorus crassus* have been recorded in the whitefish and cisco (Alta. Rec. Parks Wild. 1976). The lake is managed for domestic, commercial and sport fisheries. There are few data available for the domestic fishery. Four domestic licences were issued from 1982 to 1985, but the only reported catch was 57 kg of burbot (Alta. For. Ld. Wild. n.d.).

Records of the commercial catch have been kept since 1947 (Alta. For. Ld. Wild. n.d.; Alta. Rec. Parks Wild. 1976). The fishery was closed from 1962/63 to 1970/71. As well, in 10 of the 11 years from 1977/78 to 1988/89, either the fishery was closed or there was no catch taken by the single licensee. In the 11th year, 1980/81, the 10 licensees reported a total catch of 4 013 kg: 3 133 kg of burbot, 431 kg of northern pike, 171 kg of walleye, and 273 kg of lake whitefish. Lake whitefish has always been the principal species sought. The highest whitefish catch was 62 800 kg, taken during the 1949/50 season. The whitefish catch averaged 6 200 kg between 1971 and 1976, but only 200 kg were taken in 1976/77 and 273 kg were taken in 1980/81. The catch of cisco averaged 4 800 kg/year from 1953 to 1959, but fell to less than 20 kg/year during the 1970s and 1980s,

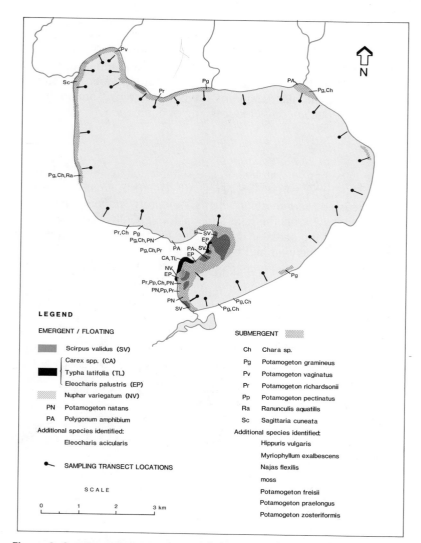

Figure 8. Species composition and distribution of aquatic macrophytes in Marie Lake, 1978.
SOURCE: Alta. Envir. n.d.[a].

probably due to low demand for cisco as mink food. The annual catch of northern pike was about 1 500 kg until 1961/62, but dropped to less than 40 kg/year during the 1970s. The walleye catch varied between 160 and 2 000 kg/year until 1961/62, but was less than 80 kg/year during the 1970s.

Fish and Wildlife Division staff estimated that Marie Lake could sustain a total catch of 14 220 kg/year (Watters 1979). The average commercial catch for the 15 fishing seasons from 1955/56 to 1976/

77 (15 000 kg/yr) exceeded this estimate slightly. Despite the fact that there were only two years of commercial fishing from 1962 to 1971, and the average total catch from 1971/72 to 1976/77 was only 6 000 kg/year, the fishery collapsed. Changes in the age-structure of the whitefish catch from domination by eight-year-old fish in 1969 to domination by four-year-old fish in 1977 supports the hypothesis of overexploitation. A recent model, based on total phosphorus concentration, estimates Marie Lake can only support a total catch of 4 100 kg/year (Hanson and Leggett 1982). In 1980, the commercial quota was set at 2 700 kg/year, of which 2 250 kg was to be whitefish (Longmore and Stenton 1983), but since 1981, no catch has been taken.

There are few data for the sport fishery in Marie Lake and the catch is unknown. Although angling was ranked the second most popular recreation activity in a survey of cottage owners, 42% complained of the poor fishing (Alta. Mun. Aff. 1979). Walleye are the most sought-after species. During the early 1980s, anglers complained of poor walleye catches, so in 1984, 1986 and 1987 about 100 000 walleye fingerlings were stocked. In addition, almost 600 000 walleye fry were stocked in 1987 (Alta. En. Nat. Resour. 1984; Alta. For. Ld. Wild. 1986; 1987). Interestingly, during the summers of 1987 and 1988, anglers reported good catches of 8– to 10–year–old walleye, and test netting in fall 1988 indicated a good walleye population. During the winter of 1988/89, however, anglers again reported a poor walleye catch (Sullivan 1989). In general, fishing intensity at Marie Lake is so low that an attempt to conduct a creel survey failed for lack of anglers. Rough water and sudden storms make the lake dangerous at times for fishing from boats, and the lack of public access reduces angler numbers.

Wildlife

Marie Lake has very little shoreline suitable for use by semiaquatic animals (Rippon 1983; Alta. Mun. Aff. 1987[b]). Small numbers of Red-breasted Mergansers, Mallards, American Widgeons and Common Loons nest on the lake and California Gulls, White Pelicans, Ospreys and the occasional Bald Eagle feed in the lake. Beaver are abundant on the inlet and outlet streams.

M.E. Bradford and J.M. Hanson

References

Alberta Energy and Natural Resources. 1984. Fish planting list. Fish Wild. Div., Edmonton.

Alberta Environment. n.d.[a]. Envir. Assess. Div., Envir. Qlty. Monit. Br. Unpubl. data, Edmonton.

———. n.d.[b]. Tech. Serv. Div., Hydrol. Br. Unpubl. data, Edmonton.

———. n.d.[c]. Tech. Serv. Div., Surv. Br. Unpubl. data, Edmonton.

———. 1983. Cold Lake-Beaver River water management study, Vol. 1: Main report. Plan. Div., Edmonton.

———. 1985. Cold Lake-Beaver River long term water management plan. Plan. Div., Edmonton.

Alberta Forestry, Lands and Wildlife. n.d. Fish Wild. Div. Unpubl. data, Edmonton.

———. 1986, 1987. Fish planting list. Fish Wild. Div., Edmonton.

———. 1988. Boating in Alberta. Fish Wild. Div., Edmonton.

———. 1989. Guide to sportfishing. Fish Wild. Div., Edmonton.

Alberta Municipal Affairs. 1978. Cold Lake regional plan, heritage preservation: Heritage resources background paper. Reg. Plan. Sec., Edmonton.

———. 1979. Marie Lake cottage owner survey. Plan. Serv. Div., Edmonton.

———. 1987[a]. Marie Lake background report February 1987. Prep. for ID No. 18 (S) by Plan. Serv. Div., Edmonton.

———. 1987[b]. Marie Lake review and assessment report March 1987. Prep. for ID No. 18 (S) by Plan. Serv. Div., Edmonton.

———. 1988. Marie Lake area structure plan. Prep. for ID No. 18 (S) by Plan. Serv. Div., Edmonton.

Alberta Recreation, Parks and Wildlife. 1976. Commercial fisheries catch statistics for Alberta, 1942–1975. Fish Wild. Div., Fish. Mgt. Rep. No. 22, Edmonton.

Alberta Research Council. 1972. Geological map of Alberta. Nat. Resour. Div., Alta. Geol. Surv., Edmonton.

Aquatic Environments Limited. 1983. Fisheries studies; main report and detailed data report [Appendices F and G]. *In* Cold Lake-Beaver River water management study, Vol. 4: Fisheries. Alta. Envir., Plan. Div., Edmonton.

Cross, P.M. 1979. Limnological and fisheries surveys of the aquatic ecosystems at Esso Resources' Cold Lake base: Data volume. Aquat. Envir. Ltd., Calgary.

Energy, Mines and Resources Canada. 1981. National topographic series 1:250 000 73L (1981). Surv. Map. Br., Ottawa.

Environment Canada. 1980–1987. Surface water data. Prep. by Inland Waters Directorate. Water Surv. Can., Water Resour. Br., Ottawa.

———. 1982. Canadian climate normals, Vol. 7: Bright sunshine (1951–1980). Prep. by Atm. Envir. Serv. Supply Serv. Can., Ottawa.

Geographic Board of Canada. 1928. Place-names of Alberta. Dept. Interior, Ottawa.

Hanson, J.M. and W.C. Leggett. 1982. Empirical prediction of fish biomass and yield. Can. J. Fish. Aquat. Sci. 39:257–263.

Kocaoglu, S.S. 1975. Reconnaissance soil survey of the Sand River area. Alta. Soil Surv. Rep. No. 34, Univ. Alta. Bull. No. SS–15, Alta. Inst. Pedol. Rep. No. S–74–34 1975. Univ. Alta., Edmonton.

Lasouski, R. 1989. Can. Forces Base Cold L., Medley. Pers. comm.

Longmore, L.A. and C.E. Stenton. 1983. Fish and fisheries: Status and utilization [Appendix H]. *In* Cold Lake-Beaver River water management study, Vol. 5: Fisheries and wildlife. Alta. Envir., Plan. Div., Edmonton.

McGregor, C.A. 1983. Summary [Appendix K] and Detailed report [Appendix L]. *In* Cold Lake-Beaver River water management study, Vol. 7: Ecological inventory of lake shorelines. Alta. Envir., Plan. Div., Edmonton.

McMillan, W.J. 1977. An interpretation concept plan for Cold Lake Provincial Park. MSc thesis. Univ. Calg., Calgary.

Ozoray, G.F. and A.T. Lytviak. 1980. Hydrogeology of the Sand River area, Alberta. Earth Sci. Rep. 79–1. Alta. Res. Counc., Edmonton.

Rippon, B. 1983. Water related wildlife resources [Appendix I]. *In* Cold Lake-Beaver River water management study, Vol. 5: Fisheries and wildlife. Alta. Envir., Plan. Div., Edmonton.

Shaw, J.F.H. and E.E. Prepas. 1989. Potential significance of phosphorus release from shallow sediments of deep Alberta lakes. ms submitted to Limnol. Oceanogr.

Slaght, D. 1989. Alta. For. Ld. Wild., Alta. For. Serv., Lac La Biche. Pers. comm.

Strong, W.L. and K.R. Leggat. 1981. Ecoregions of Alberta. Alta. En. Nat. Resour., Resour. Eval. Plan. Div., Edmonton.

Sullivan, M. 1989. Alta. For. Ld. Wild., Fish Wild. Div., St. Paul. Pers. comm.

Trew, D.O. 1989. Alta. Envir., Envir. Assess. Div., Envir. Qlty. Monit. Br., Edmonton. Pers. comm.

———, E.I. Yonge and R.P. Kaminski. 1983. Lake trophic assessment [Appendix M]. *In* Cold Lake-Beaver River water management study, Vol. 8: Water quality. Alta. Envir., Plan. Div., Edmonton.

Watters, D.V. 1979. Marie Lake 65–2, 3–W4. Alta. Rec. Parks Wild., Fish Wild. Div. Unpubl. rep., Edmonton.

MOORE LAKE

MAP SHEETS: 73L/9, 10
LOCATION: Tp64 R4 W4
LAT/LONG: 54°31'N 110°31'W

Moore Lake is a very popular recreational lake, both on a local and a regional basis. It is located in Alberta's Lakeland Region, and is valued for its clear water and lovely natural shoreline. Because of its high backshore, Moore Lake remains calm on windy days, and therefore is an excellent lake for water skiing. The lake is situated about 280 km northeast of Edmonton in Improvement District No. 18 (South), and borders on the Municipal District of Bonnyville. The town of Bonnyville to the south of the lake, and the towns of Cold Lake and Grand Centre to the southeast, are the principal urban centres in the area. To reach the lake from Edmonton, take Highways 28 and 28A northeast to Bonnyville, then Highway 41 north to the locality of La Corey. Turn east onto Highway 55 and drive for about 13 km. A sign on the highway indicates the north turn to a local road that leads to the south shore of Moore Lake and two provincial recreation areas. Other parts of the lakeshore are not accessible by road (Fig. 1).

The lake was named for Dr. Bromley Moore, a former President of the College of Physicians and Surgeons and a friend of the surveyor Marshall Hopkins (Alta. Cult. Multicult. n.d.). Locally, it is also known as Crane Lake, and residents have petitioned to have the name officially changed (Alta. Mun. Aff. 1988).

Woodland Cree occupied the region when the fur traders first arrived. The Beaver River, to the south of Moore Lake, was part of a major fur trade route from Lac Isle-à-la-Crosse, Saskatchewan to the Athabasca River. The first fur-trading post in the area was Cold Lake House. It was established by the North West Company in 1781 on the Beaver River near the present-day hamlet of Beaver Crossing (Alta. Mun. Aff. 1978). The history of the area near Moore Lake has not been documented.

During the 1980s, concerns about future development pressures and potential lake-user conflicts led Improvement District No. 18 (South) to request that Alberta Municipal Affairs prepare a background report and lake management plan for Moore Lake (Alta. Mun. Aff. 1987[a]; 1987[b]). The plan determines the extent of future land developments, allocates land use, and determines ways to minimize environmental impacts and conflicts in the use of the lakeshore. It also recommends preferred lake uses and ways to minimize lake-user conflicts. In 1988, an area structure plan for Moore Lake was adopted by the Minister of Municipal Affairs (Alta. Mun. Aff. 1988). The area structure plan provides guidelines for Improvement District No. 18 (South), the Municipal District of Bonnyville, and federal and provincial government agencies for land developments that affect the lake.

Most of Moore Lake's shoreline is Crown land. Patented land is located along the north, west and south shores at the west end of the lake (Fig. 2). In 1987, there were 70 developed lots and 110 undeveloped lots in the subdivisions on the south and west shores (Alta. Mun. Aff. 1987[a]). Sixty-nine of the developed lots were on the south shore. Almost 4 km of shoreline have been developed; this area includes almost 11 ha of municipal and environmental reserves, which are primarily located between the lake and the registered lots.

There are two provincial recreation areas on the south shore of Moore Lake (Fig. 2). Both are operated by Alberta Recreation and Parks and are open year-round. Moore Lake East Provincial Recreation Area covers 1.3 ha of land and has 34 unserviced campsites. Moore Lake West Provincial Recreation Area covers 1.5 ha and has 26 unserviced campsites. Both parks provide picnic tables and shel-

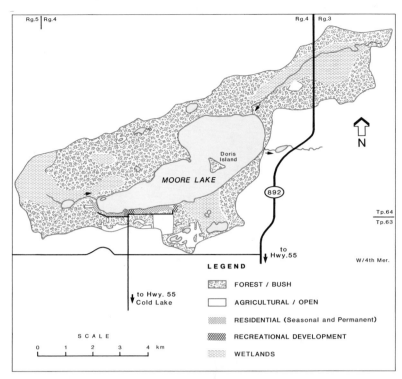

Figure 1. Features of the drainage basin of Moore Lake.
SOURCES: Alta. Envir. n.d.[b]; En. Mines Resour. Can. 1971; 1978. Updated with 1982 and 1986 aerial photos.

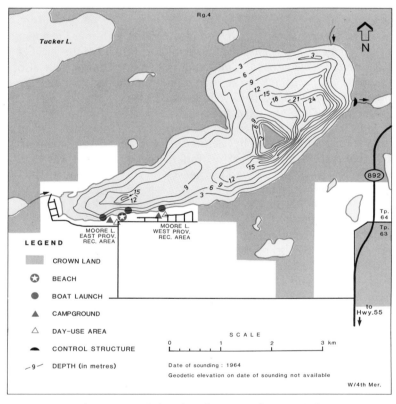

Figure 2. Bathymetry and shoreline features of Moore Lake.
BATHYMETRY SOURCE: Alta. Envir. n.d.[c].

Table 1. Characteristics of Moore Lake drainage basin.

area (excluding lake) (km²)[a]	37.1
soil[b]	Orthic Gray Luvisols, Eluviated Dystric Brunisols
bedrock geology[c]	La Biche Formation (Upper Cretaceous): shale, ironstone partings and concretions; marine
terrain[b]	level to moderately rolling
ecoregion[d]	Dry Mixedwood Subregion of Boreal Mixedwood
dominant vegetation[d]	trembling aspen
mean annual inflow (m³)[a, e]	1.86 x 10⁶
mean annual sunshine (h)[f]	2 240

NOTE: [e]excluding groundwater inflow
SOURCES: [a]Alta. Envir. n.d.[b]; [b]Kocaoglu 1975; [c]Alta. Res. Counc. 1972; [d]Strong and Leggat 1981; [f]Envir. Can. 1982

Table 2. Characteristics of Moore Lake.

elevation (m)[a, b]	549.35 to 549.91
surface area (km²)[b, c]	9.28
volume (m³)[b, c]	77.4 x 10⁶
maximum depth (m)[b, c]	26.0
mean depth (m)[b, c]	8.3
shoreline length (km)[d]	16.7
mean annual lake evaporation (mm)[e]	634
mean annual precipitation (mm)[e]	439
mean residence time (yr)[e, f]	>100
control structure[g]	earthen dike

NOTES: [a]range over period of water level record; elevation on date of sounding not available; [b]on date of sounding: (month unknown) 1964; [f]excluding groundwater inflow
SOURCES: [c]Alta. Envir. n.d.[c]; [d]Alta. For. Ld. Wild. n.d.; [e]Alta. Envir. n.d.[b]; [g]Ducks Unltd. (Can.) n.d.

ters, firepits, pump water, boat launches, beaches and swimming areas. There are two commercial recreational developments on the south shore, as well. One of them, Bodina Resort, is located just west of Moore Lake West Recreation Area. The boat launch at this resort is owned by Alberta Recreation and Parks and is available for public use (Alta. Mun. Aff. 1987[a]).

During summer weekends, all of the recreation areas receive heavy use. Surveys of cottage owners in 1977 and 1986 indicated that popular summer recreational activities at the lake were swimming, fishing, sightseeing, general relaxation, power boating, water skiing and picnicking (Alta. Mun. Aff. 1979; 1987[b]). There are no boating restrictions specific to Moore Lake, but general federal regulations apply (Alta. For. Ld. Wild. 1988). Motor boating and water skiing are hampered by the presence of Doris Island and by shallow areas in the west basin where there is extensive plant growth. Because of permanent residences on the lake, access roads are ploughed in winter. Popular winter activities cited by cottage owners were sightseeing, general relaxation, cross-country skiing, ice fishing, snowmobiling, skating, snowshoeing and hunting.

The water in Moore Lake is quite transparent during most of the open-water season, but turns green in late summer and early fall. Sport fish species in the lake are walleye, northern pike, yellow perch and lake whitefish. Significant growth of aquatic vegetation is limited to only a few areas, such as in the west basin; the lack of extensive vegetation limits fish spawning and feeding habitat in the lake. The sport fishery in Moore Lake's inlet and outlet streams is closed for a period during April and May each year (Alta. For. Ld. Wild. 1989).

Drainage Basin Characteristics

Moore Lake is a headwater lake with a small drainage basin that is only four times the size of the lake (Tables 1, 2). The only inlets are two minor streams, one each on the northeast and west shores (Fig. 1). The outlet flows from the east shore into nearby Hilda and Ethel lakes and eventually into the Beaver River.

Moore Lake is situated on a rolling morainal plain in the Dry Mixedwood Subregion of the Boreal Mixedwood Ecoregion (Kocaoglu 1975; Strong and Leggat 1981). Land north of the lake is level to moderately rolling (0 to 15% slope), whereas to the south it is level to gently rolling (0 to 9% slope). The majority of the drainage basin is forested (Fig. 1). Soils are mainly moderately well-drained Orthic Gray Luvisols, which support a forest cover of trembling aspen. These soils developed on fine loamy, moderately to strongly calcareous glacial till and are found on the upper and middle portions of slopes. Large areas of Eluviated Dystric Brunisols also occur, particularly along the eastern shore and the outflow, along the central portion of the southern shore, and northwest of the west basin. These rapidly drained soils, which occur on midslopes, formed on sandy glaciofluvial and aeolian parent material. The main tree species growing on Brunisols is jack pine. Poorly drained Organic soils (Mesisols), which are dispersed throughout the watershed in depressional areas, support a cover of black spruce, willows and sedges. Large wetlands are located along the two inflows and south of the lake (Fig. 1).

Agricultural activity in the drainage basin is limited by adverse topography, undesirable soil structure, low or excessive moisture-holding capacity of the soil, and a relatively short growing season (Alta. Mun. Aff. 1987[a]). Most of the cultivated land is located south of the lake. The main agricultural activity is grazing. The grazing land has been partially cleared and seeded with tame grass, but is assessed as unimproved pasture. A limited number of grazing permits and leases have been issued for Crown land in the drainage basin (Alta. Mun. Aff. 1987[a]).

Moore Lake is underlain by the Muriel Lake aquifer (Alta. Mun. Aff. 1987[a]). Currently, the principal water sources for regional water needs are the aquifers and not the lake. The largest water users in the area are the oil sands industries. Oil sands and petroleum and natural gas leases in the Moore Lake drainage basin are held by several companies, including Esso Resources and Husky Oil. The oil sands permits allow the companies to test and set up drilling operations for subsurface oil deposits, including those under the lake surface. There are no significant gas pools in the area. As a result of Alberta Environment's studies of the water resources in the Cold Lake-Beaver River basin in the early 1980s, a long-term plan for water resources management in the Cold Lake region was adopted by the government in 1985 (Alta. Envir. 1985). Under the provisions of this plan, Moore Lake will not become a major water supply for the oil industry. Major industrial water users will be required to obtain their water supply from a pipeline from the North Saskatchewan River.

Lake Basin Characteristics

Moore Lake is a medium-sized, deep water body (Table 2, Fig. 2). The lake has two basins which are separated by Doris Island. The eastern basin slopes quite steeply to a maximum depth of 26 m northeast of the island. The western basin, with a maximum depth of 15 m, is relatively shallow. Its deepest locations are south of the island and north of the recreation areas. The lake basin drops off very steeply southeast of Doris Island.

In 1952, Ducks Unlimited (Canada) and the provincial government built a rock and timber dam on the lake's outlet. The purpose of the structure was to raise the lake level, improve duck-breeding habitat below the dam and ensure year-round water flow in the creek. By 1982, the old dam was in disrepair and Ducks Unlimited (Canada) had built a new earthen dyke upstream of the old structure (Ducks Unltd. (Can.) n.d.).

The elevation of Moore Lake has been monitored since 1969 (Fig. 3). The maximum elevation (549.91 m) was recorded in June 1974, a year of high precipitation. Since 1974, there has been a general decline in lake levels. The minimum elevation (549.35 m), which was recorded in November 1987, was 0.56 m lower than the maximum elevation. This change in elevation would have little effect on the

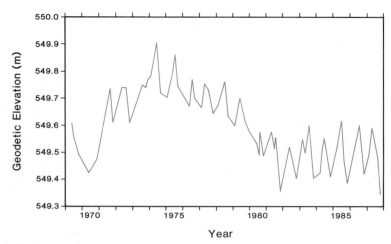

Figure 3. Water level of Moore Lake, 1969 to 1987.
SOURCES: Alta. Envir. n.d.[c]; Envir. Can. 1980–1987.

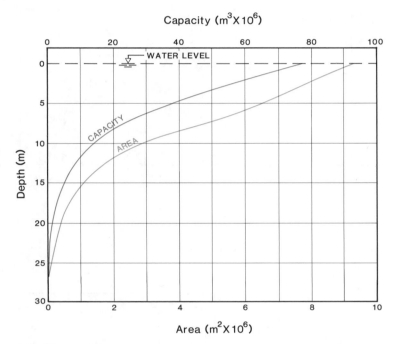

Figure 4. Area/capacity curve for Moore Lake.
SOURCE: Alta. Envir. n.d.[c].

surface area of the lake (Fig. 4). From 1980 to 1987, the range in lake levels was 0.27 m.

Water Quality

Water quality in Moore Lake was sampled by Alberta Environment frequently from 1978 to 1981 and once in 1986, and by the University of Alberta twice in 1981 (Alta. Envir. n.d.[a]; Prepas 1983; Prepas and Trew 1983; Trew et al. 1983). The total dissolved solids concentration is moderately high for a freshwater lake (Table 3). The dominant cation in Moore Lake is sodium, whereas in most other lakes in the area it is calcium. Because the ionic composition of groundwater in the immediate area is similar to the composition of Moore Lake water, it is likely that Moore Lake has substantial groundwater inflow (Ozoray et al. 1980).

The deeper areas of Moore Lake are thermally stratified during summer. In 1980, the epilimnion extended to a depth of 8 to 9 m (Fig. 5). Surface water temperatures exceeded 18°C from mid-June until late August during 1980 and 20°C in July and August 1981. Moore Lake did not mix completely during May 1980, and the bottom water was anoxic by early June. From late June until early September, the water below a depth of 12 m was anoxic (Fig. 6). The lake was well–mixed by October 1980; dissolved oxygen concentrations of 8 mg/L were measured near the bottom. From January to March 1980, under-ice dissolved oxygen concentrations were

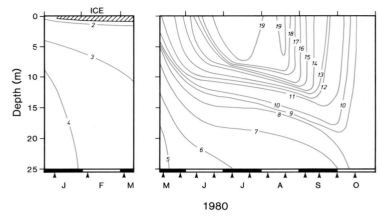

Figure 5. Temperature (°C) of Moore Lake, 1980. Arrows indicate sampling dates.
SOURCE: Alta. Envir. n.d.[a].

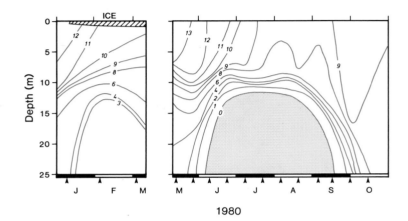

Figure 6. Dissolved oxygen (mg/L) in Moore Lake, 1980. Arrows indicate sampling dates.
SOURCE: Alta. Envir. n.d.[a].

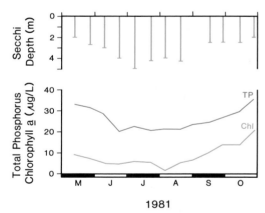

Figure 7. Total phosphorus, chlorophyll *a* and Secchi depth in Moore Lake, 1981.
SOURCE: Alta. Envir. n.d.[a].

Table 3. Major ions and related water quality variables for Moore Lake. Average concentrations in mg/L; pH in pH units. Composite samples from the euphotic zone collected 13 times from 12 May to 14 Oct. 1980. S.E. = standard error.

	Mean	S.E.
pH (range)	8.4–8.9	—
total alkalinity ($CaCO_3$)	348	4.1
specific conductivity (μS/cm)	717	6.1
total dissolved solids (calculated)	400[a]	2.1
total hardness ($CaCO_3$)	201	2.2
dissolved organic carbon	15[b]	2.8
HCO_3	386	8.8
CO_3	19	2.7
Mg	40	0.8
Na	88	1.7
K	7	0.1
Cl	20	0.1
SO_4	18	1.0
Ca	15[c]	0.9

NOTES: [a]n = 11; [b]n = 9; [c]n = 12
SOURCE: Alta. Envir. n.d.[a], Naquadat station 01AL06AC4090

Table 4. Nutrient, chlorophyll *a* and Secchi depth data for Moore Lake. Average concentrations in μg/L. Composite samples from the euphotic zone collected 13 times from 12 May to 14 Oct. 1980 and 13 times from 12 May to 27 Oct. 1981. S.E. = standard error.

	1980		1981	
	Mean	S.E.	Mean	S.E.
total phosphorus	—	—	26	1.5
total dissolved phosphorus	—	—	11	0.7
soluble reactive phosphorus	—	—	3[c]	0.6
total Kjeldahl nitrogen	1 163	62.6	935	37.8
$NO_3 + NO_2$–nitrogen	<2[a]	—	—	—
NH_4–nitrogen	<29	—	<21	—
iron	—	—	<28[d]	—
chlorophyll *a*	7.9[b]	1.07	8.2	1.44
Secchi depth (m)	2.7[b]	0.23	3.3[b]	0.29

NOTES: [a]n = 6; [b]n = 12; [c]n = 11; [d]n = 8
SOURCE: Alta. Envir. n.d.[a], Naquadat station 01AL06AC4090

Table 5. Theoretical total phosphorus loading to Moore Lake from external sources.

Source		Phosphorus (kg/yr)	Percentage of Total
watershed	forested/bush	315	52
	agricultural/cleared	36	6
	residential	6	1
sewage	cottage/campground	59	10
precipitation/dustfall		189	31
	TOTAL	605	100
annual areal loading (g/m² of lake surface)	0.06		

SOURCE: Trew 1989

Table 6. Percentage composition of major algal groups by total biomass in Moore Lake, 1980 and 1981. Composite samples collected from the euphotic zone.

ALGAL GROUP	1980					1981				
	28 May	23 June	05 Aug.	03 Sep.	14 Oct.	12 May	23 June	08 Aug.	16 Sep.	27 Oct.
Total Biomass (mg/L)	40.66	1.64	22.84	7.30	29.23	41.19	1.05	42.56	2.61	7.36
Percentage Composition:										
Cyanophyta	76	29	24	10	35	13	35	6	22	63
	Oscillatoria —————————————————————————→						*Oscillatoria*		*Oscillatoria* ———→	
Chlorophyta	3	14	26	5	15	3	4	10	7	5
			Oocystis							
Chrysophyta	9	8	5	1	9	14	18	5	5	6
Bacillariophyta	11	43	40	1	39	47	31	31	30	24
		Fragilaria ———→ *Synedra*			*Stephanodiscus* *Synedra*		*Fragilaria* ———→		*Stephano‑ discus*	*Fragilaria*
Cryptophyta	2	4	6	4	2	21	13	3	36	2
						Cryptomonas ———————————→				
Pyrrhophyta	0	1	0	79	0	2	0	45	0	0
				Ceratium				*Peridinium*		

source: Alta. Envir. n.d.[a].

greater than 2 mg/L in the deepest water (Fig. 6). In January 1981, however, the bottom water was anoxic and in March and April 1981, water at depths greater than 18 m was anoxic.

Moore Lake is mesotrophic. In both 1980 and 1981, chlorophyll *a* values averaged 8 µg/L, and in 1981, total phosphorus concentrations averaged 26 µg/L (Table 4). Phosphorus data are not available for 1980. Chlorophyll *a* concentrations were highest during October of both years; in 1981, the highest value exceeded 20 µg/L (Fig. 7). A chlorophyll *a* maximum was also observed in May. In May and October 1981, the elevated chlorophyll *a* levels coincided with peak total phosphorus values. This synchrony of phosphorus and chlorophyll *a* levels is consistent with a lake that is phosphorus limited. When water over the bottom sediments is anoxic, as can happen during both winter and summer, phosphorus is released from the sediments into the overlying water. When the water column mixes in spring and fall, this accumulated phosphorus is mixed into the upper layers where it is used by algae.

Total phosphorus loading to Moore Lake from external sources has been estimated to be 605 kg/year (Table 5). More than half (52%) of this load is carried in runoff from forested land in the watershed, and almost one-third (31%) is present in precipitation that falls on the lake. Although not measured, sewage effluent from cottages and the two provincial campgrounds may account for 10% of the total phosphorus load. This estimate is based on coefficients derived from studies on other lakes. In 1981, internal phosphorus loading from the shallow sediments in Moore Lake was estimated to be 2.4 mg/m^2 per day from June through August (Shaw and Prepas 1989). This indicates that as much as 22 kg per day, or 670 kg per month, could enter the surface waters by this internal pathway, and that during summer internal loading probably provides the largest input of phosphorus to Moore Lake.

Biological Characteristics

Plants

Phytoplankton biomass and taxonomic composition were determined monthly from May to October in 1980 and 1981 by Alberta Environment (Table 6). Total biomass fluctuated widely: from more than 40 mg/L during May 1980, May 1981, and August 1981 to less than 2 mg/L during June of both years. Diatoms (Bacillariophyta), especially *Fragilaria crotonensis*, *Stephanodiscus* spp., and *Synedra delicatissima angustissima*, formed more than 20% of the total biomass in 80% of the samples. Blue-green algae (Cyanophyta), mostly *Oscillatoria* spp., formed more than 20% of the biomass on 7 of the 10 sampling dates. Cryptomonads (Cryptophyta: mainly *Cryptomonas* spp.) were important in Moore Lake during May and September 1981. Green algae (Chlorophyta: mainly *Oocystis*

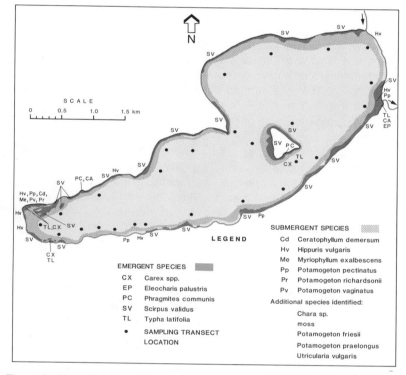

Figure 8. Species composition and distribution of aquatic macrophytes in Moore Lake, 1978.
SOURCE: Alta. Envir. n.d.[a].

borgei) formed one-quarter of the biomass during August 1980; and dinoflagellates (Pyrrhophyta) such as *Ceratium hirundinella* and *Peridinium apiculatum* were the dominant group during September 1980 and August 1981, respectively.

The distribution of emergent and submergent macrophytes was surveyed by Alberta Environment during 1978 (Fig. 8). Submergent macrophytes ringed the shoreline but the distribution of emergent species was more patchy. Common great bulrush (*Scirpus validus*) was the most widespread emergent. Ten species of submergent plants were identified, but their relative abundance was not estimated.

Invertebrates

The zooplankton community was sampled for Esso Resources Ltd. five times from March to December 1978 with a 64– to 70–µm–mesh net (Cross 1979). The total density of crustacean zooplankton in the offshore waters was highest (312 animals/L) in

Table 7. Estimated angler numbers, effort and harvest from Moore Lake. Estimates based on creel survey data collected from 17 May to 26 Aug. 1986. WE = walleye; NP = northern pike; YP = yellow perch.

	WE	NP	YP	Total
number of anglers[a]	—	—	—	8 749
angler-hours[b]	—	—	—	20 131
per cent of fish released	0	50	47	—
total number fish harvested[c]	97	3 223	14 323	17 643
total yield (kg)	198	3 697	1 862	5 757
mean weight (g)	2 046	1 147	130	—
harvest/angler-hour[b, c]	0.01	0.16	0.72	0.89
harvest/angler[a, c]	0.01	0.38	1.65	2.04

NOTES: [a]observed no. anglers = 2 329; [b]observed hours = 5 336; [c]based on observed no. fish kept: WE = 27, NP = 881, YP = 3 841
SOURCE: Alta. For. Ld. Wild. n.d.

October. The dominant copepod was *Diacyclops bicuspidatus thomasi*; adults reached a density of 141/L in October and December. Adult *Diaptomus sicilis* were also present, at densities of 4 to 19 animals/L. Of the 5 species of cladocerans identified, *Chydorus sphaericus* had a maximum density of 51 animals/L in July, *Daphnia galeata mendotae* reached a density of 15/L in December, and *Bosmina longirostris* increased to a density of 12/L in December. The dominant rotifers were *Keratella cochlearis* and *Kellicottia longispina*. The total number of rotifers per litre varied from 85/L in March to 946/L in October.

A preliminary survey of benthic invertebrates in the 10– to 18–m depth zone was carried out from March to December 1978 (Cross 1979). Typical of Alberta lakes, dipteran larvae were numerically dominant on four of five sampling dates, especially older instars of phantom midges (*Chaoborus* spp.). Scuds (*Hyalella azteca*) were abundant in the littoral zone in May, July and October. They are usually found mainly in this zone, but during July and October significant numbers were collected in water 10– to 13–m deep.

Fish

The fish fauna of Moore Lake includes cisco, northern pike, yellow perch, walleye, burbot, white sucker, lake chub, spottail shiner, brook stickleback, ninespine stickleback and Iowa darter (Cross 1979; Longmore and Stenton 1983). The lake is managed for recreational and domestic fisheries. There are no data for the domestic fishery, and commercial fishing was allowed only during the 1947/48 and 1955/56 seasons (Alta. Rec. Parks Wild. 1976).

Sport fishing is an important recreational activity on Moore Lake. In a 1986 survey, most cottage owners rated the fishing as fair to good (Alta. Mun. Aff. 1987[a]). Fish and Wildlife Division conducted a creel survey from 17 May to 26 August 1986 (Table 7). It was estimated that more than 20 000 hours were spent fishing by almost 8 800 anglers. The average harvest was 0.01 walleye/angler-hour, 0.16 northern pike/angler-hour, and 0.72 yellow perch/angler-hour. On a regional basis, these rates are low for walleye and northern pike, but higher than average for yellow perch (Alta. For. Ld. Wild. n.d.). The walleye in Moore Lake are very large—on average, 2 kg. Prior to 1988, the walleye population had gaps in the age-structure and no strong year classes (Berry 1989). In 1988, the lake was stocked with 850 000 walleye fry on a trial basis.

Wildlife

Moore Lake is not a key waterfowl lake, largely because the shoreline provides little nesting habitat (Ducks Unltd. (Can.) n.d.). Red-necked Grebes, Bufflehead, American Widgeons and Lesser Scaup are the most common species. Other species present include Mallards, Blue-winged Teal, Green-winged Teal, Gadwall, Common Loons, and Ring-billed Gulls. Ospreys, Bald Eagles, and Great Blue Herons are commonly seen and have nested on the lake, and White Pelicans forage there (Rippon 1983; Alta. Mun. Aff. 1987[a]).

Big-game hunting is an important recreational activity in the Moore Lake area. White-tailed deer are abundant, mule deer are present, and moose are found at low densities. Black bears have been observed along the north shore of the lake. Of the fur-bearing animals, beaver are most abundant and widespread and coyotes, red foxes, muskrats, and pine martens are present. Upland game birds, primarily Ruffed and Sharp-tailed Grouse, are found in trembling aspen woodlands that have a dense understory (Rippon 1983; Alta. Mun. Aff. 1987[a]).

M.E. Bradford

References

Alberta Culture and Multiculturalism. n.d. Hist. Resour. Div., Hist. Sites Serv. Unpubl. data, Edmonton.
Alberta Environment. n.d.[a]. Envir. Assess. Div., Envir. Qlty. Monit. Br. Unpubl. data, Edmonton.
———. n.d.[b]. Tech. Serv. Div., Hydrol. Br. Unpubl. data, Edmonton.
———. n.d.[c]. Tech. Serv. Div., Surv. Br. Unpubl. data, Edmonton.
———. 1985. Cold Lake-Beaver River long term water management plan. Plan. Div., Edmonton.
Alberta Forestry, Lands and Wildlife. n.d. Fish Wild. Div. Unpubl. data, Edmonton.
———. 1988. Boating in Alberta. Fish Wild. Div., Edmonton.
———. 1989. Guide to sportfishing. Fish Wild. Div., Edmonton.
Alberta Municipal Affairs. 1978. Cold Lake regional plan, heritage preservation, heritage resources background paper. Plan. Serv. Div., Plan. Br., Edmonton.
———. 1979. Moore Lake cottage owner survey. Plan. Serv. Div., Plan. Br., Edmonton.
———. 1987[a]. Moore Lake background report February, 1987. Prep. for ID No. 18 (S) by Plan. Serv. Div., Plan. Br., Edmonton.
———. 1987[b]. Moore Lake lake management plan, review and assessment report March 1987. Prep. for ID No. 18 (S) by Plan. Serv. Div., Plan. Br., Edmonton.
———. 1988. Moore (Crane) Lake area structure plan. Prep. for ID No. 18 (S) by Plan. Serv. Div., Plan. Br., Edmonton.
Alberta Recreation, Parks and Wildlife. 1976. Commercial fisheries catch statistics for Alberta, 1942–1975. Fish Wild. Div., Fish. Mgt. Rep. No. 22, Edmonton.
Alberta Research Council. 1972. Geological map of Alberta. Nat. Resour. Div., Alta. Geol. Surv., Edmonton.
Berry, D. 1989. Alta. For. Ld. Wild., Fish Wild. Div., Edmonton. Pers. comm.
Cross, P.M. 1979. Limnological and fishery surveys of the aquatic ecosystems at Esso Resources' Cold Lake lease: Data volume. Aquat. Envir. Ltd., Calgary.
Ducks Unlimited (Canada). n.d. Unpubl. data, Edmonton.
Energy, Mines and Resources Canada. 1971, 1978. National topographic series 1:50 000 73L/8 (1971), 73L/9 (1971), 73L/10 (1971), 73L/7 (1978). Surv. Map. Br., Ottawa.
Environment Canada. 1980–1987. Surface water data. Prep. by Inland Waters Directorate. Water Surv. Can., Water Resour. Br., Ottawa.
———. 1982. Canadian climate normals, Vol. 7: Bright sunshine (1951–1980). Prep. by Atm. Envir. Serv. Supply Serv. Can., Ottawa.
Kocaoglu, S.S. 1975. Reconnaissance soil survey of the Sand River area. Alta. Soil Surv. Rep. No. 34, Univ. Alta. Bull. No. SS–15, Alta. Inst. Pedol. Rep. No. S–74–34 1975. Univ. Alta., Edmonton.
Longmore, L.A. and C.E. Stenton. 1983. Fish and fisheries; status and utilization [Appendix H]. *In* Cold Lake-Beaver River water management study, Vol. 5: Fisheries and wildlife. Alta. Envir., Plan. Div., Edmonton.

Ozoray, G., E.J. Wallick and A.T. Lytviak. 1980. Hydrogeology of the Sand River area, Alberta. Earth Sci. Rep. No. 79–1. Alta. Res. Counc., Edmonton.

Prepas, E.E. 1983. Orthophosphate turnover time in shallow productive lakes. Can. J. Fish. Aquat. Sci. 40:1412–1418.

———— and D.O. Trew. 1983. Evaluation of the phosphorus-chlorophyll relationship for lakes off the Precambrian Shield in western Canada. Can. J. Fish. Aquat. Sci. 40:27–35.

Rippon, B. 1983. Water related wildlife resources [Appendix I]. *In* Cold Lake-Beaver River water management study, Vol. 5: Fisheries and wildlife. Alta. Envir., Plan. Div., Edmonton.

Shaw, J.F.H. and E.E. Prepas. 1989. Potential significance of phosphorus release from shallow sediments of deep Alberta lakes. ms submitted to Limnol. Oceanogr.

Strong, W.L. and K.R. Leggat. 1981. Ecoregions of Alberta. Alta. En. Nat. Resour., Resour. Eval. Plan. Div., Edmonton.

Trew, D.O., E.I. Yonge and R.P. Kaminski. 1983. Lake trophic assessment [Appendix M]. *In* Cold Lake-Beaver River water management study, Vol. 8: Water quality. Alta. Envir., Plan. Div., Edmonton.

Trew, D.O. 1989. Alta. Envir., Envir. Assess. Div., Envir. Qlty. Monit. Br., Edmonton. Pers. comm.

MOOSE LAKE

F. Schulte

MAP SHEETS: 73L/2, 6, 7
LOCATION: Tp60, 61 R6, 7 W4
LAT/LONG: 54°14'N 110°55'W

Moose Lake is one of the most popular and scenic lakes in the Lakeland Region of Alberta. Its sandy beaches and good fishing draw hundreds of people to its excellent parks during summer. The lake is situated in the Municipal District of Bonnyville, about 240 km northeast of Edmonton and 3.5 km west of the town of Bonnyville. Access to several points along the north shore, including Moose Lake Provincial Park (Fig. 1), is available from Secondary Road 660. Access to the east and south shores is available from Highway 28 west of Bonnyville and Highway 28A.

The lake's name is a translation of the French name, *Lac d'Orignal*. Although moose are rarely found in the area now, the former abundance of the animal no doubt inspired the name. In 1789, Angus Shaw of the North West Company built a trading post, Fort Lac d'Orignal (Shaw House), on the northwest shore of Moose Lake (Geog. Bd. Can. 1928). The first settlers, French Canadians from Beaumont, Alberta, began to homestead in the Bonnyville area in 1907 and 1908, and large numbers of settlers began to arrive after 1912 (Alta. Mun. Aff. 1978; Glendon Hist. Soc. 1985). In 1928, the railroad was extended from St. Paul to Bonnyville, thus ensuring the continued growth and settlement of the area. In the early 1900s, commercial fishing was an important area industry, and by 1936, three large fish-packing plants were in operation. Several mink farms were located around Moose Lake, but they are no longer present.

Much of the lake's shoreline is extensively developed, particularly along the east shores of Vezeau Bay and Bonnyville Beach Bay (Fig. 2). The first subdivision of land was at Bonnyville Beach in 1945, and rapid development occurred after 1960 (Runge 1977). At present, two summer villages are located on the east shore (Fig. 2). The summer village of Bonnyville Beach was incorporated in 1958, and the summer village of Pelican Narrows was incorporated in 1979. There were a total of about 130 dwellings in the 2 summer villages in 1988, of which 37% were permanent residences. A number of subdivisions are also situated along the shore. They comprise a total of 794 lots, but not all of these are developed. There are five institutional camps located on Franchere Bay and the west shore of Island Bay and the Bonnyville Golf and Country Club is situated south of Vezeau Bay beside Chatwin Lake.

There are five public campgrounds and day-use areas around the lake, including Moose Lake Provincial Park on the north shore (Fig. 2). The provincial park was opened in 1967; its facilities include 59 campsites, tap water, beaches, a change house, a boat launch and hiking trails. Franchere Bay Provincial Recreation Area on the west end of Franchere Bay is operated by Alberta Recreation and Parks. Its facilities include 200 campsites, a beach, picnic shelters, tap water and a boat launch. Alberta Recreation and Parks also operates Eastbourne Provincial Recreation Area on the south side of the lake. This facility has 13 campsites, pump water, a picnic shelter and a boat launch. Pelican Point Park, situated on the southeast corner of Franchere Bay, is operated by the Municipal District of Bonnyville. It has 40 campsites, picnic tables, pump water and a launch for small boats. The Vezeau Beach Recreation Area on the southeast corner of Vezeau Bay was transferred to the Municipal District in 1988. It is small and has an undefined area for camping, a picnic shelter, a boat launch and a pier (Alta. Hotel Assoc. 1989).

Moose Lake receives intense recreational use during summer, particularly on weekends. In 1983, cottagers accounted for 47 to 67% of the total recreational use (Marshall Macklin Monaghan

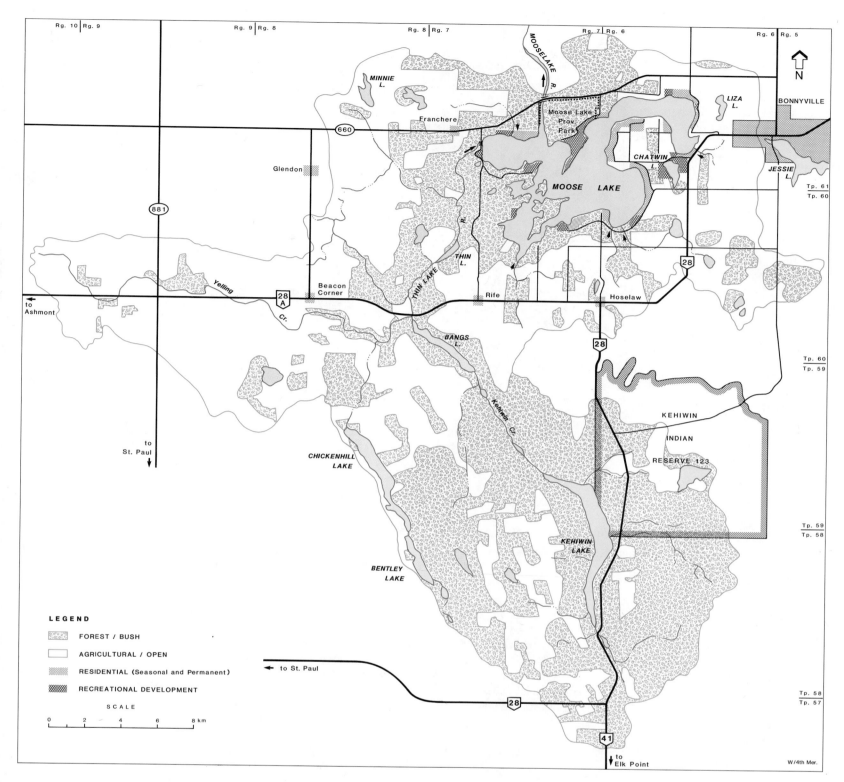

Figure 1. Features of the drainage basin of Moose Lake.
SOURCES: Alta. Envir. n.d.[d]; En. Mines Resour. Can. 1974; 1981. Updated with 1982 aerial photos.

Table 1. Characteristics of Moose Lake drainage basin.

area (excluding lake) (km²)[a]	755
soil[b]	Orthic Gray Luvisols
bedrock geology[c]	Lea Park Formation (Upper Cretaceous): shale, ironstone concretions; marine
terrain[b]	level to gently rolling
ecoregion[d]	Dry Mixedwood Subregion of Boreal Mixedwood
dominant vegetation[e]	trembling aspen and balsam poplar
mean annual inflow (m³)[a, f]	37.7 x 10⁶
mean annual sunshine (h)[g]	2 240

NOTE: [f]excluding groundwater inflow
SOURCES: [a]Alta. Envir. n.d.[d]; [b]Kocaoglu 1975; [c]Alta. Res. Counc. 1972; [d]Strong and Leggat 1981; [e]Alta. Envir. 1983; [g]Envir. Can. 1982

Table 2. Characteristics of Moose Lake.

elevation (m)[a, b]	533.60
surface area (km²)[a, b]	40.8
volume (m³)[a, b]	230 x 10⁶
maximum depth (m)[c]	19.8
mean depth (m)[a, b]	5.6
shoreline length (km)[b]	64.1
mean annual lake evaporation (mm)[d]	634
mean annual precipitation (mm)[d]	454
mean residence time (yr)[d, e]	7.5
control structure[f]	concrete weir and vertical slot fishway
top of weir elevation (m)[f]	533.23

NOTES: [a]on date of sounding: Aug. 1962; [e]excluding groundwater inflow
SOURCES: [b]Alta. Envir. n.d.[e]; [c]Runge 1977; [d]Alta. Envir. n.d.[d]; [f]Alta. Envir. n.d.[a]

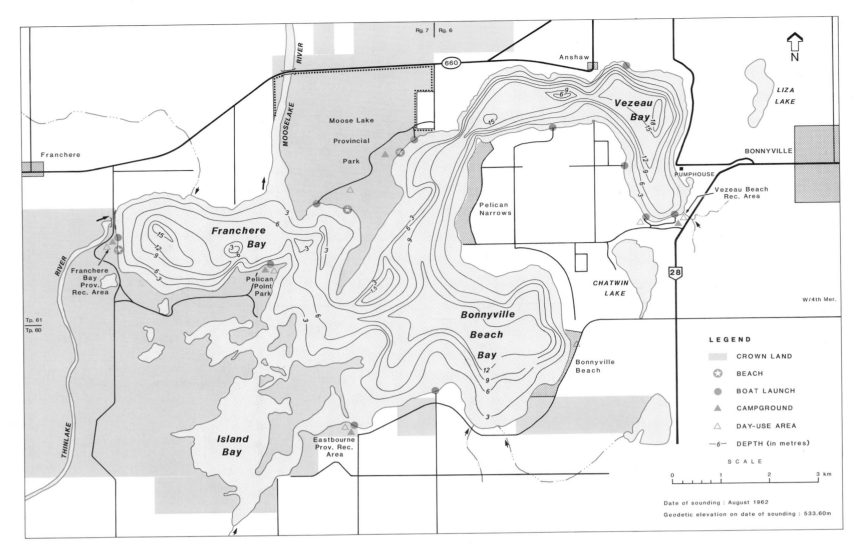

Figure 2. Bathymetry and shoreline features of Moose Lake.
BATHYMETRY SOURCE: Alta. Envir. n.d.[e].

West. Ltd. 1983). The most popular recreational activities are swimming, fishing, camping and boating. In designated areas, either all vessels are prohibited or power driven vessels are subject to a maximum speed of 12 km/hour (Alta. For. Ld. Wild. 1988).

Moose Lake has dense blooms of blue-green algae during late summer and fall. The lake supports a commercial fishery, primarily for lake whitefish and a popular sport fishery for walleye, northern pike and yellow perch. There are no special sport fishing regulations for Moose Lake, but general provincial limits and regulations apply (Alta. For. Ld. Wild. 1989). The western region of the lake, particularly Island Bay, is important fish spawning and waterfowl habitat. White Pelicans are conspicuous inhabitants of the lake in summer.

Drainage Basin Characteristics

The drainage basin of Moose Lake is 19 times larger than the area of the lake (Tables 1, 2). Runoff from about 75% of the watershed flows into Franchere Bay via the Thinlake River (Fig. 1). The Thinlake River is joined by Yelling Creek, which receives water from Chickenhill and Bentley lakes and drains the western portion of the watershed; runoff from the southern portion of the watershed enters Kehiwin and Bangs lakes and then flows into the Thinlake River above Thin Lake. Water from the rest of the drainage basin drains to Moose Lake via five intermittent streams. Moose Lake's outlet is the Mooselake River, which flows northwest from the north side of Franchere Bay to the Beaver River.

The terrain near the lake varies from level to gently undulating (0 to 5% slope) to gently rolling (5 to 9% slope). In the remainder of the watershed, the land is generally undulating, with some areas of moderately rolling hills (9 to 15% slope) in the eastern region (Kocaoglu 1975).

Surficial deposits around the north, west and east sides of the lake

are glaciofluvial, consisting of sand and pockets of gravel (Kocaoglu 1975). Parts of the southern and extreme western regions of the drainage basin are ground moraine composed of small knobs, ridges and crevasse fillings. Kehiwin Creek and Kehiwin Lake occupy a major meltwater channel that is partly filled with glacial till and alluvial deposits. Most of the remaining area is ground moraine that forms a nearly featureless glacial till plain.

The dominant soils throughout most of the drainage basin are moderately well-drained Orthic Gray Luvisols, with moderately well-drained Dark Gray Luvisols in the western region. Rough, broken land with steep slopes is characteristic of the area along Kehiwin and Bangs lakes, and rapidly drained loamy sand and sandy loam-textured Eluviated Eutric and Dystric Brunisols are located along the north, west and south shores of Moose Lake (Kocaoglu 1975). These soils are not satisfactory for intense development because they have a poor ability to maintain ground cover. Poorly drained Organic soils consisting of Terric, Terric Fibric and Typic Mesisols are located along the northern part of the Thinlake River and the west shore of Island Bay (Runge 1977). Nearly all of the shoreline of Moose Lake is sand, and sandy beaches are present in developed areas (McGregor 1983).

About 46% of the drainage basin is open or has been cleared of its natural forest cover for agriculture (Fig. 1). Most of the remaining forest is located north and west of Moose Lake and in the southern portion of the drainage basin. It consists of a mixture of trembling aspen, balsam poplar, white birch, white spruce and balsam fir (Alta. Envir. 1983). There are areas of climax forest within Moose Lake Provincial Park; the long point of land at the south end of the park, for example, has escaped damage by fire. With its dense undergrowth and large spruce and aspen, this area differs greatly from the adjacent land (Alta. Rec. Parks n.d.).

There are no active commercial forestry operations in the Moose Lake area (Runge 1977). Most agriculture in the upland region around the lake is mixed farming; it is concentrated along the north and east sides of Vezeau Bay and along the south shore of the lake. Forage crops are grown near the lake, and barley and oats are important crops throughout the watershed. There are several small livestock operations near the lake; two are located about 1.5 km south of Vezeau Bay (Hockridge 1988).

Urban land use occupies about 1.6% of the drainage basin area; it consists of the two summer villages and several subdivisions on the shore of Moose Lake, and the western part of Bonnyville, to the east of the lake. In 1977, Moose Lake became subject to the Regulated Lake Shoreland Development Operation Regulations. The regulations prohibited most development at the lake until a lake management plan and an area structure plan were prepared by Alberta Municipal Affairs and adopted by the Municipal District of Bonnyville and the summer villages of Bonnyville Beach and Pelican Narrows. The lake management plan determines the extent of future land developments, allocates land use and determines ways to minimize environmental impacts and conflicts in uses of the lakeshore. It recommends lake uses and ways to minimize lake-user conflicts (Alta. Mun. Aff. 1977; 1979).

A large portion of the shoreland is Crown land, most of which is located in the provincial park and on the west shore (Fig. 2). The islands in the lake, which cover 3.42 km² and are also owned by the Crown, have been reserved for recreation since 1969; in 1983, they received the status of Protective Notation (Alta. For. Ld. Wild. 1987).

Part of Kehiwin Indian Reserve 123 is located in the drainage basin south of Moose Lake. The northeast corner of the reserve borders Muriel Lake. Members of the Kehiwin Band, who are descended from Plains Cree, numbered 900 in 1984 (Alta. Native Aff. 1986).

Lake Basin Characteristics

Moose Lake is a large water body with a surface area of 41 km² (Table 2). It has an irregular shape with four main bays, and there are several islands located in Island Bay (Fig. 2). The lake as a whole is fairly shallow, with a mean depth of 5.6 m (Table 2). The deepest region, in Vezeau Bay, extends to a depth of almost 20 m; Island Bay is less than 3–m deep.

In 1951, following a period of low water levels, the provincial government installed a steel sheet-pile, rock and timber weir on the Mooselake River about 6.4 km downstream of Moose Lake's outlet. Its purpose was to safeguard fish and waterfowl habitat, to maintain a suitable water level for recreation and to ensure a water supply for Bonnyville (Alta. Envir. n.d.[c]). The lake rose to its highest recorded level of 534.10 m in May 1966, after which the weir deteriorated and the level declined considerably (Fig. 3). By October 1984, the lake had reached its lowest recorded level of 532.60 m. Changes in the area and volume of the lake with variations in water level are illustrated in Figure 4.

In the early 1980s, Alberta Environment initiated studies of the Cold Lake-Beaver River basin to manage the basin's water resources and to resolve concerns regarding high demand on local water supplies. The Cold Lake-Beaver River Long Term Water Management Plan was adopted by the government in October 1985. The plan applies to the surface and groundwater resources in the Cold Lake and lower Beaver River basins. Under this water resources management plan, it was recommended that a control structure be built to stabilize the levels of Moose Lake. In 1986, a new concrete outlet structure was built by Alberta Environment at the same location as the old one. The structure has a main weir, a slightly lower narrow weir to maintain downstream flow, and a vertical slot fishway to allow fish passage upstream into the lake. The weir was designed to stabilize the lake around a target elevation of 533.23 m (Alta. Envir. n.d.[a]). Water withdrawals from Moose Lake are limited to 3 x 10⁶ m³/year (3 000 dam³/year). This allocation is for the current and future needs of the town of Bonnyville, which has withdrawn water from the east shore of Vezeau Bay since 1950. Between 1982 and 1987, the town withdrew an average of 0.82 x 10⁶ m³ per year (Alta. Envir. n.d.[f]).

The estimated residence time of water in Moose Lake is 7.5 years. Because the major inlet and outlet are near each other on Franchere

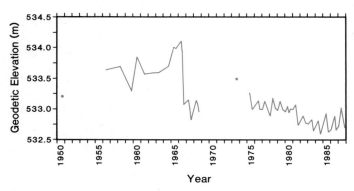

Figure 3. Water level of Moose Lake, 1950 to 1987.
SOURCE: Alta. Envir. n.d.[e].

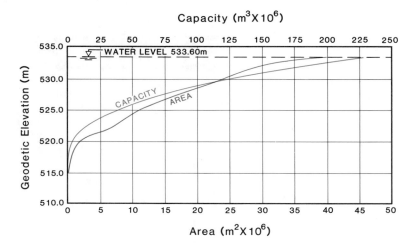

Figure 4. Area/capacity curve for Moose Lake.
SOURCE: Alta. Envir. n.d.[e].

Bay, it is likely that the actual exchange of most water in the lake takes longer.

Water Quality

The water quality of Moose Lake was studied in 1973 and 1974 by researchers at the University of Alberta (Alta. Envir. n.d.[b]; Gallup 1977), and has been studied since 1983 under a joint monitoring program by Alberta Environment and Alberta Recreation and Parks (Alta. Envir. n.d.[b]; 1989). As well, Vezeau Bay was studied in 1980 and 1981 by Alberta Environment (Alta. Envir. n.d.[b]).

Moose Lake is well-buffered, and has a fairly high level of total dissolved solids for a freshwater lake (Table 3). Its water is very hard; the dominant ions are bicarbonate, sulfate and sodium. The lake's transparency is often poor because of dense algal growth.

During summer, the shallow, exposed areas of the lake are usually well-mixed from the surface of the lake to the bottom (Fig. 5). Deeper areas are weakly thermally stratified, but this may be disrupted during strong winds. Vezeau Bay is strongly stratified for most of the open-water period. On days when the lake is well-mixed, the concentration of dissolved oxygen in shallow areas probably remains high throughout the water column, as on 13 August 1987 (Fig. 5). During thermally stratified periods in deeper areas and in Vezeau Bay, anoxic conditions develop above the bottom sediments, as on 31 July 1986. Throughout winter, there is a general decline in the levels of dissolved oxygen, but the lake is not known to winterkill.

The high concentrations of nutrients and chlorophyll a indicate that the lake is eutrophic (Table 4). The average concentration of chlorophyll a varies considerably from year to year; between 1983 and 1988, it ranged from a low of 12.5 µg/L in 1985 to a high of 21.5 µg/L in 1987. High variability is often characteristic of eutrophic lakes, and there is no indication that the water quality of Moose Lake is changing. Most phosphorus in the lake originates either from runoff from the drainage basin (Table 5) or from the bottom sedi-

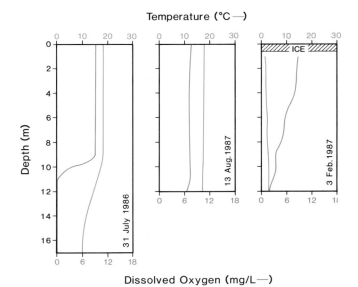

Figure 5. Temperature and dissolved oxygen in Moose Lake, 1986 and 1987.
SOURCE: Alta. Envir. n.d.[b].

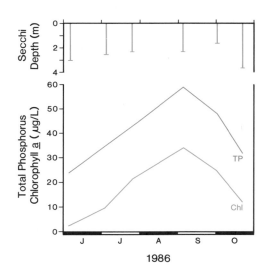

Figure 6. Total phosphorus, chlorophyll *a* and Secchi depth in Moose Lake, 1986.
SOURCE: Alta. Envir. n.d.[b].

Table 3. Major ions and related water quality variables for Moose Lake. Average concentrations in mg/L; pH in pH units. Composite samples from the euphotic zone collected 3 times from 04 June to 01 Oct. 1986. S.E. = standard error.

	Mean	S.E.
pH (range)	8.4–8.8	—
total alkalinity (CaCO$_3$)	254	1.4
specific conductivity (μS/cm)	657	8.3
total dissolved solids (calculated)	389	5.6
total hardness (CaCO$_3$)	206	4.1
HCO$_3$	280	5.6
CO$_3$	15	2.7
Mg	35	0.6
Na	65	1.2
K	12	0.1
Cl	13	0.3
SO$_4$	87	3.1
Ca	25	0.9

SOURCE: Alta. Envir. n.d.[b], Naquadat station 01AL06AC2101

Table 4. Nutrient, chlorophyll *a* and Secchi depth data for Moose Lake. Average concentrations in μg/L. Composite samples from the euphotic zone collected 6 times from 04 June to 21 Oct. 1986 and 5 times from 24 May to 04 Oct. 1988. S.E. = standard error.

	1986		1988	
	Mean	S.E.	Mean	S.E.
total phosphorus	40	5.0	42	2.8
iron	<20[a]	—	—	—
chlorophyll *a*	17.6	4.70	16.0	4.67
Secchi depth (m)	2.6	0.29	2.5	0.28

NOTE: [a]n = 3
SOURCE: Alta. Envir. n.d.[b], Naquadat station 01AL06AC2101

Table 5. Theoretical total phosphorus loading to Moose Lake from external sources.

Source		Phosphorus (kg/yr)	Percentage of Total
immediate watershed	forested/bush	1 998	19
	agricultural/cleared	5 683	55
	residential/cottage	1 247	12
sewage[a]		78	<1
precipitation/dustfall		898	9
inflow from other lakes		370	4
	TOTAL	10 274	100
annual areal loading (g/m^2 of lake surface)	0.25		

NOTE: [a]not measured: assumes 4% of all sewage effluent from residences and camps enters the lake, as in Mitchell 1982
SOURCE: Alta. Envir. 1989

ments. The extensive areas of cleared and agricultural land in the drainage basin contribute an estimated 56% of the external phosphorus load; the internal load, which may be substantial, has not been estimated.

The seasonal pattern of phosphorus and chlorophyll concentrations in Moose Lake is characteristic of many shallow, eutrophic lakes in Alberta (Fig. 6). Both trophic indicators are lowest in June and reach maximum levels by late summer. A small spring peak of chlorophyll probably occurs in May when diatoms are abundant. The phosphorus maximum in late summer is typical of lakes with large internal phosphorus loads.

Biological Characteristics

Plants

There have been no extensive studies of the phytoplankton in Moose Lake. Fish and Wildlife Division briefly surveyed the phytoplankton in midsummer 1967 (McDonald 1967). Blue-green (*Anabaena* sp.) and green algae were most abundant.

The aquatic vegetation of Moose Lake has not been surveyed in detail. The sandy shoreline restricts emergent growth except in protected areas. Aquatic vegetation is dense along the provincial park peninsula, near the origin of the Mooselake River, the southern side

of Bonnyville Beach Bay and in Island Bay (Runge 1977). The macrophyte species in the lake are typical of many lakes in Alberta: common cattails (*Typha latifolia*) and bulrush (*Scirpus* sp.) are the dominant emergent types, and pondweeds (*Potamogeton* spp.) and northern watermilfoil (*Myriophyllum exalbescens*) are the most common submergent types (McGregor 1983).

Invertebrates

The zooplankton of Moose Lake was sampled by Fish and Wildlife Division in 1967, and the benthic invertebrate fauna was sampled in

Table 6. Estimated angler numbers, effort and harvest from Moose Lake. Estimates based on creel survey data collected from 07 May to 26 Aug. 1986. Every weekend day and 40 to 60% of weekdays were surveyed. WE = walleye; NP = northern pike; YP = yellow perch.

	WE	NP	YP	Total
number of anglers[a]	—	—	—	28 944
angler-hours[b]	—	—	—	63 684
total number fish harvested[c]	6 526	14 124	25 271	46 021
total yield (kg)	4 070	11 991	5 863	21 924
mean weight (g)	624	849	232	—
harvest/angler-hour[b, c]	0.10	0.22	0.39	—
harvest/angler[a, c]	0.21	0.48	0.86	—

NOTES: [a]observed no. anglers = 6 013; [b]observed hours = 13 180; [c]based on observed no. fish kept:
WE = 1 325, NP = 2 867, YP = 5 199
SOURCE: Alta. For. Ld. Wild. n.d.

July 1966 (McDonald 1967). The zooplankton was dominated by copepods (*Cyclops* sp.) and cladocerans (*Daphnia* sp). Benthic invertebrates were collected in four 15–cm Ekman dredge hauls taken at each of 25 random locations between depths of 1.8 and 17 m. Sand was the predominant substrate type; it was covered by various amounts of silt, shells and detritus. There was an average of 2 720 organisms/m², which comprised a volume of 60.8 cm³. Organisms were most abundant in the littoral zone; no organisms were present in the samples from 15– and 17–m depths. Scuds (Amphipoda) were most abundant in the shallowest areas (less than 3–m deep), whereas midge larvae (Diptera: Chironomidae) were most abundant at depths greater than 5 m. Other organisms collected were clams (Pelecypoda), snails (Gastropoda), leeches (Hirudinea), caddis fly larvae (Trichoptera), flatworms (Turbellaria) and aquatic earthworms (Oligochaeta).

Fish

Moose Lake is very productive habitat for fish, and supports large stocks of cisco, lake whitefish, walleye, yellow perch and northern pike. Other species of fish in the lake are brook stickleback, burbot, Iowa darter, spottail shiner and white sucker (McDonald 1967).

Seine samples taken during a Fish and Wildlife Division survey in 1967 indicated large numbers of yellow perch and spottail shiners near shore. Walleye were the most abundant fish caught by gill netting in deeper water, followed by cisco, northern pike, white suckers, lake whitefish, burbot and yellow perch (McDonald 1967).

Northern pike and yellow perch spawn in macrophyte beds in the Thinlake and Mooselake rivers, in Island Bay and in small reed beds on the south and east sides of Moose Lake Provincial Park. Lake whitefish and walleye spawn in sandy locations offshore of Bonnyville Beach Bay and near some of the islands in Island Bay. Walleye also spawn in the Thinlake and Mooselake rivers (Runge 1977).

Moose Lake is managed for commercial, domestic and recreational fisheries. A commercial fishery has operated since the early 1900s, but records are available only for the period since 1942 (Alta. For. Ld. Wild. n.d.; Alta. Rec. Parks Wild. 1976). The commercial season opens after ice breakup in May. Cisco were very abundant in the catch before 1970/71, but changes in commercial net sizes reduced the catches of cisco, northern pike and walleye, so now the catch is dominated by lake whitefish (Runge 1977). Between 1968/69 and 1987/88, the average annual harvests of commercially important species were 9 672 kg of lake whitefish, 3 410 kg of cisco, 462 kg of walleye and 444 kg of northern pike, an average total annual harvest of 13 987 kg. The maximum recorded annual harvests for each species during this period were 19 177 kg of lake whitefish (1977/78), 24 802 kg of cisco (1969/70), 1 814 kg of walleye (1970/71), and 1 589 kg of northern pike (1970/71). There are no catch data for the domestic fishery, but an average of 67 licences were issued between 1984/85 and 1988/89 (Walker 1989).

Sport fishing is very popular at Moose Lake. The main species caught are yellow perch, northern pike and walleye. A creel survey conducted during 1986 indicated that the most numerous species harvested was yellow perch, followed by northern pike and walleye (Table 6). The catch of these species was considerably higher than the harvest: 60% of the perch, 35% of the pike and 18% of the walleye caught were released. The harvest of yellow perch was higher in Moose Lake (0.39 fish/angler-hour) than in 19 other lakes surveyed in the region (0.32 fish/angler-hour), but the harvest rates for walleye (0.10 fish/angler-hour) and northern pike (0.22 fish/angler-hour) were the same as those in the other lakes.

Wildlife

Good waterfowl habitat is present on Moose Lake, especially in Island Bay. Common species of waterfowl include Mallard, Lesser Scaup, American Widgeon and Blue-winged Teal (Rippon 1983). In 1977, Red-breasted Mergansers were reported to nest along the Mooselake River and Western Grebes and Common Loons frequented the lake (Runge 1977). Great Blue Herons nested on islands in Island Bay in the 1970s, but the colony is no longer active. Gulls are commonly seen around the lake, and the White Pelican is a prominent species seen feeding there. The main limitations to waterfowl are the scarcity of emergent aquatic vegetation around much of the lake, except for Island Bay, and the high level of recreational development (Ducks Unltd. (Can.) n.d.).

P.A. Mitchell and L. Hart Buckland-Nicks

References

Alberta Environment. n.d.[a]. Devel. Op. Div., Constr. Br. Unpubl. data, Edmonton.
———. n.d.[b]. Envir. Assess. Div., Envir. Qlty. Monit. Br. Unpubl. data, Edmonton.
———. n.d.[c]. Records Mgt. Div. Unpubl. data, Edmonton.
———. n.d.[d]. Tech. Serv. Div., Hydrol. Br. Unpubl. data, Edmonton.
———. n.d.[e]. Tech. Serv. Div., Surv. Br. Unpubl. data, Edmonton.
———. n.d.[f]. Water Resour. Admin. Div., Water Rights Br. Unpubl. data, Edmonton.
———. 1983. Cold Lake-Beaver River water management study, Vol. 1: Main report. Plan. Div., Edmonton.
———. 1989. Moose Lake. Envir. Assess. Div., Envir. Qlty. Monit. Br., Edmonton.
Alberta Forestry, Lands and Wildlife. n.d. Fish Wild. Div. Unpubl. data, Edmonton.
———. 1987. A summary of Alberta's natural areas reserved and established. Pub. Ld. Div., Ld. Mgt. Devel. Br. Unpubl. rep., Edmonton.
———. 1988. Boating in Alberta. Fish Wild. Div., Edmonton.
———. 1989. Guide to sportfishing. Fish Wild. Div., Edmonton.
Alberta Hotel Association. 1989. Alberta campground guide 1989. Prep. for Travel Alta., Edmonton.
Alberta Municipal Affairs. 1977. Moose Lake management study. Plan. Serv. Div., Reg. Plan. Sec., Edmonton.
———. 1978. Cold Lake regional plan, heritage preservation: Heritage resources background paper. Reg. Plan. Sec., Edmonton.
———. 1979. Moose Lake area structure plan. Plan. Serv. Div., Reg. Plan. Sec., Edmonton.
Alberta Native Affairs. 1986. A guide to native communities in Alberta. Native Aff. Secret., Edmonton.
Alberta Recreation and Parks. n.d. Parks Div. Unpubl. data, Edmonton.
Alberta Recreation, Parks and Wildlife. 1976. Commercial fisheries catch statistics for Alberta, 1942–1975. Fish Wild. Div., Fish. Mgt. Rep. No. 22, Edmonton.

Alberta Research Council. 1972. Geological map of Alberta. Nat. Resour. Div., Alta. Geol. Surv., Edmonton.

Ducks Unlimited (Canada). n.d. Unpubl. data, Edmonton.

Energy, Mines and Resources Canada. 1974, 1981. National topographic series 1:250 000 73E (1974), 73L (1981). Surv. Map. Br., Ottawa.

Environment Canada. 1982. Canadian climate normals, Vol. 7: Bright sunshine (1951–1980). Prep. by Atm. Envir. Serv. Supply Serv. Can., Ottawa.

Gallup, D.N. 1977. The limnology of Moose Lake. Alta. Envir., Poll. Contr. Div. Unpubl. rep., Edmonton.

Geographic Board of Canada. 1928. Place-names of Alberta. Dept. Interior, Ottawa.

Glendon Historical Society. 1985. So soon forgotten—a history of Glendon and districts. Glendon Hist. Soc., Glendon.

Hockridge, R. 1988. Alta. Agric., Bonnyville. Pers. comm.

Kocaoglu, S.S. 1975. Reconnaissance soil survey of the Sand River area. Alta. Soil Surv. Rep. No. 34, Univ. Alta. Bull. No. SS–15, Alta. Inst. Pedol. Rep. No. S–74–34 1975. Univ. Alta., Edmonton.

Marshall Macklin Monaghan Western Limited. 1983. Water based recreation [Appendix J]. *In* Cold Lake-Beaver River water management study, Vol. 6: Recreation. Alta. Envir., Plan. Div., Edmonton.

McDonald, D. 1967. Moose Lake. Alta. For. Ld. Wild., Fish Wild. Div. Unpubl. rep., Edmonton.

McGregor, C.A. 1983. Summary [Appendix K] and Detailed report [Appendix L]. *In* Cold Lake-Beaver River water management study, Vol. 7: Ecological inventory of lake shorelines. Alta. Envir., Plan. Div., Edmonton.

Mitchell, P.A. 1982. Evaluation of the "septic snooper" on Wabamun and Pigeon lakes. Alta. Envir., Poll. Contr. Div., Water Qlty. Contr. Br., Edmonton.

Rippon, B. 1983. Water related wildlife resources [Appendix I]. *In* Cold Lake-Beaver River water management study, Vol. 5: Fisheries and wildlife. Alta. Envir., Plan. Div., Edmonton.

Runge, R. 1977. Moose Lake management study. Alta. Mun. Aff., Plan. Serv. Div., Plan. Br., Edmonton.

Strong, W.L. and K.R. Leggat. 1981. Ecoregions of Alberta. Alta. En. Nat. Resour., Resour. Eval. Plan. Div., Edmonton.

Walker, G. 1989. Alta. For. Ld. Wild., Fish Wild. Div., St. Paul. Pers. comm.

MURIEL LAKE

D. LeClair

MAP SHEET: 73L/2
LOCATION: Tp59, 60 R5, 6 W4
LAT/LONG: 54° 8'N 110°41'W

Muriel Lake is a large lake with lovely beaches and fairly clear water. It is located in the Municipal District of Bonnyville about 13 km south of the town of Bonnyville and 250 km northeast of the city of Edmonton. To reach the lake from Edmonton, take Highways 28 and 28A north and east to Bonnyville. At the junction of Highways 28 and 41 within the town (55 Street), turn south onto a road known locally as the Gurneyville Road. This road joins Secondary Road 657 just south of the locality of Gurneyville, on the western side of the lake (Fig. 1), and provides access to Muriel Lake Provincial Recreation Area. An alternate route, which provides access to the eastern side of the lake and Muriel Lake Park, is to drive east through Bonnyville on Secondary Road 659 and turn south onto Secondary Road 657 at Charlotte Lake. This north-south portion of Secondary Road 657 will be renumbered to 891 in about 1990, when the road is extended south to the hamlet of Lindbergh (Campeau 1989).

The origin of Muriel Lake's name is not known. The first fur-trading post in the area was established in 1781 by the North West Company near the present-day hamlet of Beaver Crossing, about 35 km northeast of Muriel Lake. A second post, Fort Lac d'Orignal (Shaw House), was established in 1789 on the north shore of nearby Moose Lake. The first settlers came to the Bonnyville area in 1907, and a store, post office and sawmill were established about 10 km east of Bonnyville in 1908. By 1909, two schools were operating in the area (Alta. Mun. Aff. 1978). The local economy in the early 1900s was based on the timber industry, and two sawmills were located at Muriel Lake, one at the northeastern tip and the other on the large island/peninsula on the eastern shore (Fig. 1). In the 1920s, an extensive fire destroyed the timber and the economic base switched to agriculture. The locality of Gurneyville, on the western shore, and the locality of Muriel Lake, northeast of the lake, provided post offices and general stores for local residents. At present, Gurneyville has a gas station, post office and general store, but the post office at Muriel Lake is closed and no one lives there now (Alta. Cult. Multicult. n.d.; Alta. Mun. Aff. 1979). There are several subdivisions around the lakeshore and on the backshore, mostly on the south and east sides of the lake. By 1988, almost half of the 391 registered lots had been developed (Alta. Mun. Aff. 1988). Kehiwin Indian Reserve 123 is located on 8 200 ha of land southwest of the lake. The Kehiwin Band, which was named in 1876 when Chief Kehiwin signed Treaty No. 6, are descendants of Plains Cree (Alta. Native Aff. 1986). A 1984 census recorded 900 band members.

In 1988, landowners near the lake were surveyed for the background report to the Muriel Lake Area Structure Plan review (Alta. Mun. Aff. 1988; 1989). Most respondents (87%) were concerned about water levels in the lake. Other problems cited were poor fishing (54%), shoreline weeds (31%), weeds in the lake (26%) and algae (20%). Water quality was rated, on average, as good to excellent. In a 1976 survey of cottage owners, only 17% of respondents cited poor fishing as a problem, 10% cited algal growth, and only a few people complained of weeds. Variations in the weather, and therefore, changes in the lake level and the concentration of algae, were probably responsible for the differences between the results of the two surveys. In summer, the favourite recreational activities of cottage owners in the 1976 survey were swimming, fishing, power boating, sightseeing, and water skiing. Only 25% of respondents used their cottages in winter and these people mostly went snowmobiling and ice fishing (Alta. Mun. Aff. 1976).

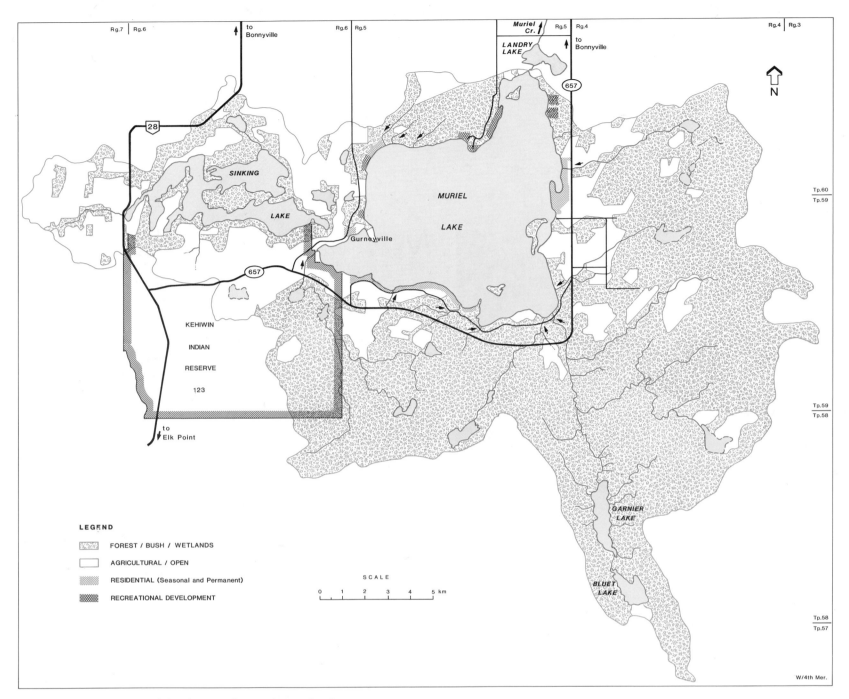

Figure 1. Features of the drainage basin of Muriel Lake.
SOURCES: Alta. Envir. n.d.[b]; En. Mines Resour. Can. 1971; 1976. Updated with 1982 and 1986 aerial photos.

The largest recreational facility on Muriel Lake is Muriel Lake Park, which is operated by the Municipal District of Bonnyville. It is located on the large bay at the northeast end of the lake (Fig. 2). Signs on Secondary Road 657 direct visitors to the area. The park is open from mid-May to mid-September and offers 105 campsites, 3 group camping areas with 36 sites, a sewage disposal station, pump water, a concession, a boat launch and dock, and a day-use area with picnic tables, a playground, a beach and a swimming area. The municipal district also owns a boat launch on the eastern shore, in Beaumieux Resort subdivision. It can be reached by a local road from Secondary Road 657. There are no boating restrictions specific to Muriel Lake, but general federal regulations apply (Alta. For. Ld. Wild. 1988).

Alberta Recreation and Parks operates Muriel Lake Provincial Recreation Area, located on the western shore (Fig. 2). It is open from Victoria Day to Thanksgiving Day and has 19 campsites, pump water, picnic tables, a picnic shelter, a beach and a boat launch.

There are three commercial campgrounds and two institutional camps at Muriel Lake. The institutional camps, which are located on Crown land at the northeast tip of the lake, are the Fort Kent Catholic Boys Camp and Recreation Centre, and the Lakeland Division of the Girl Guides of Canada.

The concentration of algae in Muriel Lake is quite low, and the water is usually moderately transparent. Aquatic vegetation covers an extensive area, particularly along the south and east sides of the lake, but emergent vegetation is not abundant in most areas. The species of sport fish in the lake are northern pike, yellow perch and walleye. There are no sport fishing regulations specific to the lake, but provincial limits and regulations apply. The northern pike may contain natural levels of mercury higher than levels recommended for human consumption. Pregnant women should not eat the fish, and others should not eat more than one meal of the fish per week (Alta. For. Ld. Wild. 1989). The lake also supports commercial and domestic fisheries.

Drainage Basin Characteristics

Muriel Lake drains an area of 384 km^2 (Table 1), but because of the large size of the lake (64.1 km^2, Table 2), the ratio of drainage basin area to lake area is only 6 to 1. Most water flows into the lake from the south and east via several creeks (Fig. 1). The largest inflow is a small creek that drains Bluet Lake and Garnier Lake to the south. The area around Sinking Lake, to the west of Muriel Lake, is considered part of the gross drainage basin, but it is unlikely that water levels are ever high enough to allow water to flow from this area into

Table 1. Characteristics of Muriel Lake drainage basin.

area (excluding lake) (km²)[a]	384
soil[b]	Orthic Gray Luvisols
bedrock geology[c]	Lea Park Formation (Upper Cretaceous): shale, ironstone concretions; marine
terrain[b]	gently undulating to moderately rolling
ecoregion[d]	Dry Mixedwood Subregion of Boreal Mixedwood
dominant vegetation[d]	trembling aspen
mean annual inflow (m³)[a, e]	14.4 x 10⁶
mean annual sunshine (h)[f]	2 240

NOTE: [e]excluding groundwater inflow
SOURCES: [a]Alta. Envir. n.d.[b]; [b]Kocaoglu 1975; [c]Alta. Res. Counc. 1972; [d]Strong and Leggat 1981; [f]Envir. Can. 1982

Table 2. Characteristics of Muriel Lake.

elevation (m)[a, b]	558.90 to 560.43
surface area (km²)[b, c]	64.1
volume (m³)[b, c]	424 x 10⁶
maximum depth (m)[b, c]	10.7
mean depth (m)[b, c]	6.6
shoreline length (km)[d]	50
mean annual lake evaporation (mm)[e]	634
mean annual precipitation (mm)[e]	419
mean residence time (yr)[e, f]	>100
control structure	none

NOTES: [a]range over period of water level record; elevation on date of sounding not available; [c]on date of sounding: Aug. 1962; [f]excluding groundwater inflow
SOURCES: [b]Alta. Envir. n.d.[c]; [d]Alta. Mun. Aff. 1979; [e]Alta. Envir. n.d.[b].

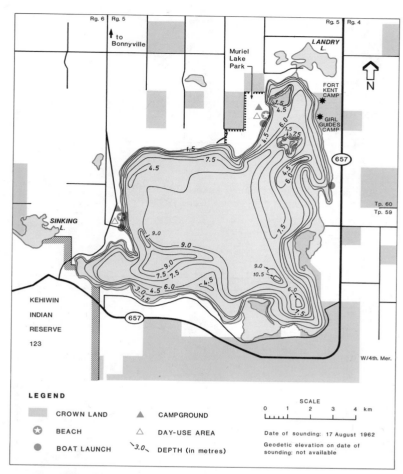

Figure 2. Bathymetry and shoreline features of Muriel Lake.
BATHYMETRY SOURCE: Alta. Envir. n.d.[c].

Muriel Lake. The outlet from Muriel Lake, Muriel Creek, flows intermittently from the northeastern bay to nearby Landry Lake, and eventually to the Beaver River.

The landforms in the drainage basin are quite varied. The largest area, which comprises land northwest, north, east and southeast of the lake, is rolling morainal plain (Kocaoglu 1975). It is characterized by undulating to gently rolling topography featuring minor ridges and knobs intermixed with numerous wet depressions and small peat bogs. The soils are mainly moderately well-drained Orthic Gray Luvisols that developed on fine loamy glacial till. South of Secondary Road 657 lies an area of moderately rolling hummocky morainal plain, which is characterized by rough, irregular knob and kettle topography. Again, soils are mainly Orthic Gray Luvisols. The portion of the watershed that is part of Indian Reserve 123 is undulating morainal plain. It is relatively level, with occasional low ridges and knolls. The main soils in this area are well-drained Orthic Dark Gray Chernozemics that developed on fine loamy glacial till.

The drainage basin is part of the Dry Mixedwood Subregion of the Boreal Mixedwood Ecoregion (Strong and Leggat 1981). The main tree species are trembling aspen on well-drained to moderately well-drained sites, jack pine on rapidly drained to well-drained sites, white spruce on imperfectly drained sites, and black spruce, willows and sedges on poorly to very poorly drained sites. Balsam poplar, trembling aspen, white spruce and lesser amounts of white birch and willow grow around the lakeshore (Alta. Mun. Aff. 1979; McGregor 1983).

Most agricultural activity in the watershed is on land near Muriel and Sinking lakes (Fig. 1). Grazing is the main activity, and most crops are grown for forage (Alta. Mun. Aff. 1979).

Most of the lakeshore is privately owned (Fig. 2). A large parcel of Crown land located south of the lake is covered by grazing leases or permits, but is also reserved for future recreational purposes. A provincial park on this land has been discussed, but no definite plans or approvals have been made (Alta. Mun. Aff. 1979). All islands in the lake belong to the province and are reserved for recreation.

After the first subdivisions on Muriel Lake were approved in 1965, 16 lots were created on the south shore. By 1975, 337 lots were registered, of which 110 were developed. In 1977, the Muriel Lake area became subject to the Regulated Lake Shoreland Development Operation Regulations, which were administered by Alberta Environment. The regulations prohibited most developments at the lake until a lake management plan and an area structure plan were prepared and adopted by the Municipal District of Bonnyville (Alta. Mun. Aff. 1979; 1980). Lake management plans determine the extent of future land developments, allocate land use and determine ways to minimize environmental impacts and conflicts in uses of the lakeshore. They recommend preferred lake uses and ways to minimize lake-user conflicts. The two plans were completed and adopted in 1980 and updated in 1989 (Alta. Mun. Aff. 1988; 1989). By 1988, 54 additional lots had been created, for a total of 391 lots within a distance of 1.5 km from the lake. By 1988, 168 of the 297 lakefront lots and 18 of the 94 backshore lots had been developed. Almost 56% of the total number of lots are located on the south side of the lake, another 40% are located on the east side, and about 4% are located at the northwest end (Alta. Mun. Aff. 1988).

Lake Basin Characteristics

Muriel Lake is a large but rather shallow water body (Table 2, Fig. 2). The maximum depth of 10.7 m is located in a small hole north of the island in the southeast bay. Most of the central part of the lake basin is about 9 m deep. The basin drops off most steeply along the west-central and north-central shores. The lake has three islands, with locations and shapes that vary with water levels. When water levels are lower, as in 1962 when the bathymetry was surveyed (Fig. 2), there are two islands in the northeast bay, a peninsula along the eastern shore, and an island in the southeast bay that has a long sand spit extending from its southeast corner. When water levels are sufficiently high, as in 1986 (Fig. 1), the more southerly island in the northeast basin floods and the peninsula on the eastern shore becomes an island.

The shoreline consists primarily of rocks or boulders, but there are

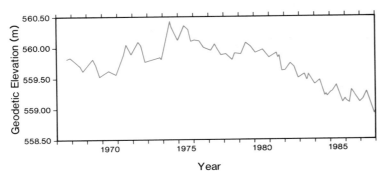

Figure 3. Water level of Muriel Lake, 1967 to 1987.
SOURCES: Alta. Envir. n.d.[c]; Envir. Can. 1981–1987.

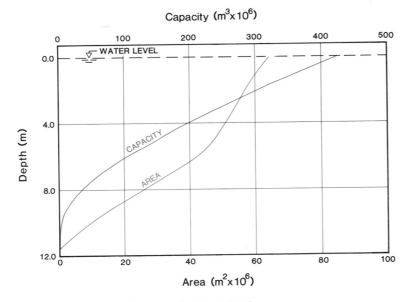

Figure 4. Area/capacity curve for Muriel Lake.
SOURCE: Alta. Envir. n.d.[c].

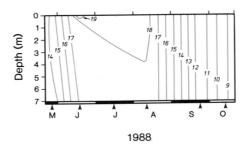

1988

Figure 5. Temperature (°C) of Muriel Lake, 1988. Arrows indicate sampling dates.
SOURCE: Alta. Envir. n.d.[a].

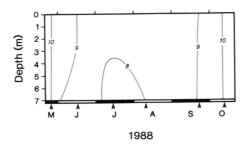

1988

Figure 6. Dissolved oxygen (mg/L) in Muriel Lake, 1988. Arrows indicate sampling dates.
SOURCE: Alta. Envir. n.d.[a].

Table 3. Major ions and related water quality variables for Muriel Lake. Average concentrations in mg/L; pH in pH units. Composite samples from the euphotic zone collected 6 times from 26 May to 12 Oct. 1988. S.E. = standard error.

	Mean	S.E.
pH (range)	8.2–9.6	—
total alkalinity (CaCO₃)	556	3.1
specific conductivity (μS/cm)	1 143	3.2
total dissolved solids (calculated)	714	4.2
total hardness (CaCO₃)	427	7.1
total particulate carbon	2	0.4
dissolved organic carbon	26	1.3
HCO₃	535	1.9
CO₃	70	1.2
Mg	98	1.9
Na	118	0.6
K	21	2.0
Cl	17	0.2
SO₄	116	0.8
Ca	11	0.3

SOURCE: Alta. Envir. n.d.[a], Naquadat station 01AL06AC2005

Table 4. Nutrient, chlorophyll *a* and Secchi depth data for Muriel Lake. Average concentrations in μg/L. Composite samples from the euphotic zone collected 6 times from 25 May to 12 Oct. 1988. S.E. = standard error.

	Mean	S.E.
total phosphorus	36	2.2
total dissolved phosphorus	12	0.8
total Kjeldahl nitrogen	1 532	51.2
NO₃ + NO₂–nitrogen	<2	—
NH₄–nitrogen	21	3.4
iron	<22	—
chlorophyll *a*	6.7	0.26
Secchi depth (m)	2.2	0.21

SOURCE: Alta. Envir. n.d.[a], Naquadat station 01AL06AC2005

also several attractive sandy beaches (Alta. Mun. Aff. 1979). The rocky shores are often accompanied by steep banks, although much of the backshore flattens out to undulating topography.

Water levels have been monitored since 1967 (Fig. 3). The lake reached its maximum recorded level (560.43 m) in 1974, a very wet year. After 1974, water levels steadily declined to a minimum of 558.90 m in 1987. This fluctuation of 1.53 m changed the area of the lake by several square kilometres (Fig. 4).

In the early 1980s, Alberta Environment initiated studies of the Cold Lake-Beaver River basin to provide data for management of the basin's water resources and to resolve concerns regarding high demand from oil sands plants on local water supplies. Under the long-term water management plan adopted by the government in 1985, no large withdrawals from Muriel Lake will be allowed. Oil sands plants will be required to obtain their water supply from a pipeline from the North Saskatchewan River.

Water Quality

Water quality in Muriel Lake was studied by Alberta Environment intensively during 1975, 1976, 1978 and 1988, and once in March 1986 (Alta. Envir. n.d.[a]; Mitchell 1979). The water is well buffered, very hard and slightly saline (Table 3). The dominant ions are bicarbonate, sodium and sulphate.

Muriel Lake is typical of many of Alberta's shallow lakes: in spring, the water column warms rapidly; during summer, thermal stratification is weak or nonexistent; and during fall, the water column is well mixed. In 1988, the maximum surface temperature recorded was 19°C in June (Fig. 5). Levels of dissolved oxygen were uniformly high throughout the water column during the open-water season in 1988 (Fig. 6). Under ice in March 1986, levels of dissolved oxygen fell to less than 5 mg/L at depths greater than 5 m. Concentrations near the surface, however, remained above 10 mg/L.

Muriel Lake is mesotrophic. In 1988, the chlorophyll *a* concentration averaged 6.7 μg/L and levels were quite constant during the open-water period. They ranged between a maximum of 7.8 μg/L in May to a minimum of 6.1 μg/L in July (Fig. 7). Ten years earlier, in 1978, chlorophyll *a* levels were slightly lower. They averaged 3.2 μg/L and varied between a minimum of 1.3 μg/L in June and a maximum of 5.7 μg/L in August. These variations between years are expected. They are often caused by changes in the weather, and do not imply a deterioration in water quality. The chlorophyll *a* levels in Muriel Lake are actually quite low relative to the concentration of total phosphorus, and it is possible that algal biomass in the lake is depressed by salinity. In 1988, total phosphorus reached its highest level in July (Fig. 7) and averaged 36 μg/L over the season (Table 4). Phosphorus data are not available for 1978.

Biological Characteristics

Plants

The phytoplankton in Muriel Lake was sampled briefly during July and August in 1966 (McDonald 1967) and monthly in 1976 and 1978 (Mitchell 1979). In 1976, blue-green (Cyanophyta: *Lyngbya* sp.) and golden-brown algae (Chrysophyta: *Dinobryon* sp.) were the dominant groups in May, diatoms (Bacillariophyta: *Fragilaria crotonensis*) and dinoflagellates (Pyrrhophyta: *Ceratium hirundinella*) formed most of the volume in June, and diatoms (*F. crotonensis*), unidentified filamentous blue-green algae, and a green alga (Chlorophyta: *Closterium* sp.) were prominent in late summer. The main species were similar in 1978 except that the diatom *Stephanodiscus astraea* and the green alga *Pediastrum sculptatum* formed most of the volume in June and the blue-green *Anabaena* sp. and the diatom *Asterionella formosa* were the dominant species during late summer.

Aquatic plants grew to a depth of 7 m in Muriel Lake in September 1978 and the littoral zone covered almost 50% of the lake's area. The littoral zone in some areas extended as far as 750 m from shore (Mitchell 1979). Four species of emergent plants and five species of submergent plants were identified (Fig. 8). Emergent vegetation is largely restricted to protected areas because the lake is exposed to wind. As well, the northwest shore, although somewhat protected, has no emergent stands because of its rocky or sandy substrate. The dominant emergent species in 1978 were common great bulrush (*Scirpus validus*) in the water, and common cattail (*Typha latifolia*) and sedges (*Carex* spp.) closer to shore. The dominant submergent species was large-sheath pondweed (*Potamogeton vaginatus*), and stonewort (*Chara* sp.) was distributed sparsely throughout the littoral area. The filamentous alga *Cladophora* was abundant on plants growing in water about 3–m deep.

Invertebrates

The benthic fauna of Muriel Lake has not been surveyed in detail. The zooplankton community was examined by Alberta Environment during 1976 and 1978 (Mitchell 1979). The most abundant copepods were *Diaptomus sicilis* and *Diacyclops bicuspidatus thomasi*, the dominant cladocerans were *Daphnia galeata mendotae* and *Diaphanosoma leuctenbergianum*, and the dominant rotifers were *Keratella cochlearis* and *Conochilus* sp.

Fish

The fish fauna of Muriel Lake includes northern pike, walleye, lake whitefish, yellow perch, burbot, white sucker, spottail shiner, and

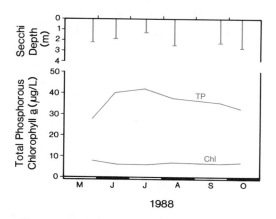

Figure 7. Total phosphorus, chlorophyll *a* and Secchi depth in Muriel Lake, 1988.
SOURCE: Alta. Envir. n.d.[a].

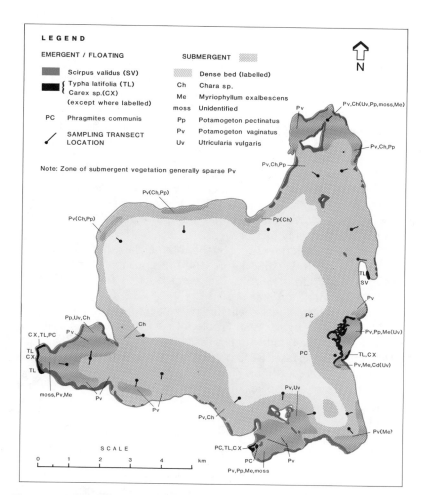

Figure 8. Species composition and distribution of aquatic macrophytes in Muriel Lake, September 1978.
SOURCE: Mitchell 1979.

Iowa darter. Lake whitefish were stocked in 1937 (Alta. For. Ld. Wild. n.d.). Walleye populations have been augmented by stocking at a rate of 535 adults from Moose Lake in 1964, 58 000 9.5–cm–long juveniles in 1984, 169 000 fingerlings in 1986, and 131 500 fingerlings in 1987 (McDonald 1967; Alta. En. Nat. Resour. 1984; Alta. For. Ld. Wild. 1986; 1987).

Muriel Lake is managed for domestic, commercial and sport fisheries. There are no data available for the domestic fishery. The primary commercial species is lake whitefish, which generally has formed about 95% of the total catch (Alta. For. Ld. Wild. n.d.; Alta. Rec. Parks Wild. 1976). The largest whitefish catch was 109 150 kg, taken in the 1957/58 season. The average whitefish catch from 1942/43 to 1963/64 was 40 000 kg/year. The whitefish population began to show signs of overexploitation by 1964/65, when the catch declined to 7 500 kg. From 1965/66 to 1974/75, the average catch was 25 000 kg/year. Catch size increased in 1975/76 to 40 460 kg,

Table 5. Estimated angler numbers, effort and harvest from Muriel Lake. Estimates based on creel survey data collected from 17 May to 27 Aug. 1986. NP = northern pike; YP = yellow perch.

	NP	YP	Total
number of anglers[a]	—	—	5 872
angler-hours[b]	—	—	10 762
total number fish harvested[c]	3 853	742	4 595
total yield (kg)	4 125	111	4 236
mean weight (g)	1 161	150	—
catch/angler-hour	0.57	0.18	—
percentage released	38	62	—
harvest/angler-hour[b, c]	0.33	0.07	0.40
harvest/angler[a, c]	0.59	0.12	0.71

NOTES: [a]observed no. anglers = 702; [b]observed hours = 1 278; [c]based on observed no. fish kept: NP = 417, YP = 85
SOURCE: Alta. For. Ld. Wild. n.d.

but declined again from 1976/77 to 1981/82, to an average of 20 870 kg/year. In 1982/83, the whitefish catch declined to less than 10 000 kg, and from 1983/84 to 1986/87, the catch and effort were greatly reduced. During the latter period, fewer than 20 licences were issued each year and the annual whitefish catch ranged from 263 to 13 223 kg. In 1987/88, only seven licences were issued, but the whitefish catch increased to 22 347 kg.

Small numbers of northern pike have always been caught in the commercial fishery. The largest catch was 6 810 kg in 1949/50 and the average catch from 1942/43 to 1987/88 was 1 230 kg/year. Catches were lower than average during the period from 1983/84 to 1987/88, at only 565 kg/year.

Walleye are seldom caught by the commercial fishery. The historic maximum catch was 636 kg in 1945/46 and none were reported from 1946/47 to 1966/67. The average catch from 1980/81 to 1987/88 was 12 kg/year.

The sport fishery was evaluated by a creel survey conducted from 17 May to 27 August 1986 (Table 5). An estimated 5 872 anglers fished for 10 762 hours. Anglers caught an average of 0.57 pike/angler-hour, but released 38% of their catch, resulting in a harvest rate of 0.33 pike/angler-hour. This rate was higher than the average harvest rate of 0.22 pike/angler-hour reported for 22 lakes in the area (Alta. For. Ld. Wild. n.d.). Anglers caught yellow perch at a rate of 0.18 perch/angler-hour, but since they released 62% of their catch, the harvest rate was only 0.07/angler-hour. This rate was substantially below the average harvest rate for the area of 0.32 perch/angler-hour. No lake whitefish or walleye were reported in the catch. It is not known from these data whether the walleye stocking program increased walleye abundance, because the fish stocked in 1984 were too small for anglers in 1986. Rough water, caused by the large surface area exposed to strong winds, reduces the number of opportunities to fish in Muriel Lake.

Wildlife

High quality waterfowl habitat constitutes only 10% of the shoreland around Muriel Lake. Much of the best habitat is located at nearby Landry Lake (Alta. Mun. Aff. 1979; 1988). A colony of Western Grebes and 20 to 25 pairs of Common Loons nest on Muriel Lake. There were 12 Great Blue Heron nests in 1975, but none were seen in 1988. White Pelicans use the lake for feeding and California and Ring-billed gulls are common on or near the southern island. White-tailed deer are common around the lake, as are moose on the eastern shore.

M.E. Bradford and J.M. Hanson

References

Alberta Culture and Multiculturalism. n.d. Hist. Resour. Div., Hist. Sites Serv. Unpubl. data, Edmonton.
Alberta Energy and Natural Resources. 1984. Fish planting list. Fish Wild. Div., Edmonton.
Alberta Environment. n.d.[a]. Envir. Assess. Div., Envir. Qlty. Monit. Br. Unpubl. data, Edmonton.
———. n.d.[b]. Tech. Serv. Div., Hydrol. Br. Unpubl. data, Edmonton.
———. n.d.[c]. Tech. Serv. Div., Surv. Br. Unpubl. data, Edmonton.
Alberta Forestry, Lands and Wildlife. n.d. Fish Wild. Div. Unpubl. data, Edmonton.
———. 1986, 1987. Fish planting list. Fish Wild. Div., Edmonton.
———. 1988. Boating in Alberta. Fish Wild. Div., Edmonton.
———. 1989. Guide to sportfishing. Fish Wild. Div., Edmonton.
Alberta Municipal Affairs. 1976. Cottage owner survey Moose and Muriel Lakes MD of Bonnyville. Plan. Serv. Div., Edmonton.
———. 1978. Cold Lake regional plan, heritage preservation: Heritage resources background paper. Plan. Serv. Div., Edmonton.
———. 1979. Muriel Lake management study. Prep. for MD Bonnyville by Plan. Serv. Div., Edmonton.
———. 1980. Muriel Lake area structure plan. Prep. for MD Bonnyville by Plan. Serv. Div., Edmonton.
———. 1988. Muriel Lake area structure plan background report. Prep. for MD Bonnyville by Plan. Serv. Div., Edmonton.
———. 1989. Muriel Lake area structure plan. 3rd draft. Prep. for MD Bonnyville by Plan. Serv. Div., Edmonton.
Alberta Native Affairs. 1986. A guide to native communities in Alberta. Native Aff. Secret., Edmonton.
Alberta Recreation, Parks and Wildlife. 1976. Commercial fisheries catch statistics for Alberta, 1942–1975. Fish Wild. Div., Fish. Mgt. Rep. No. 22, Edmonton.
Alberta Research Council. 1972. Geological map of Alberta. Nat. Resour. Div., Alta. Geol. Surv., Edmonton.
Campeau, R. 1989. MD Bonnyville, Bonnyville. Pers. comm.
Energy, Mines and Resources Canada. 1971, 1976. National topographic series 1:50 000 73L/1 (1971), 73L/2 (1971), 73E/15 (1976). Surv. Map. Br., Ottawa.
Environment Canada. 1981–1987. Surface water data. Prep. by Inland Waters Directorate. Water Surv. Can., Water Resour. Br., Ottawa.
———. 1982. Canadian climate normals, Vol. 7: Bright sunshine (1951–1980). Prep. by Atm. Envir. Serv. Supply Serv. Can., Ottawa.
Kocaoglu, S.S. 1975. Reconnaissance soil survey of the Sand River area. Alta. Soil Surv. Rep. No. 34, Univ. Alta. Bull. No. SS–15, Alta. Inst. Pedol. Rep. No. S–74–34 1975. Univ. Alta., Edmonton.
McDonald, D. 1967. Muriel Lake Twp. 59, Rge. 5, W4th. Alta. Ld. For., Fish Wild. Div. Unpubl. rep., Edmonton.
McGregor, C.A. 1983. Summary [Appendix K] and Detailed report [Appendix L]. *In* Cold Lake-Beaver River water management study, Vol. 7: Ecological inventory of lake shorelines. Alta. Envir., Plan. Div., Edmonton.
Mitchell, P.A. 1979. Skeleton, Garner, Muriel Lakes water quality studies. Alta. Envir., Poll. Contr. Div., Water Qlty. Contr. Br., Edmonton.
Strong, W.L. and K.R. Leggat. 1981. Ecoregions of Alberta. Alta. En. Nat. Resour., Resour. Eval. Plan. Div., Edmonton.

NORTH BUCK LAKE

MAP SHEETS: 83I/9, 10
LOCATION: Tp65, 66 R17, 18 W4
LAT/LONG: 54°41′N 112°32′W

The attractive natural qualities of North Buck Lake and area have made it a local and regional focal point for recreational and residential development. North Buck Lake is situated on the border of the County of Athabasca and Improvement District No. 18 (South), immediately north of the hamlet of Caslan and 180 km northeast of the city of Edmonton. To reach the lake from Edmonton, take Highway 28 north to Highway 63. Travel north on Highway 63 to its junction with Secondary Road 663, then turn east and drive until you reach Caslan. Turn north on Secondary Road 855, which skirts the east side of the lake (Fig. 1). An access road from Secondary Road 855 leads to North Buck Lake Provincial Recreation Area (Fig. 2).

The origin of the lake's name is not known. Locally, the name is frequently shortened to Buck Lake (Chipeniuk 1975). "North" may have been added to distinguish between this lake and the Buck Lake located about 100 km southwest of Edmonton (Holmgren and Holmgren 1976).

The history of the region near North Buck Lake was influenced by the fur trade. A trading post at Athabasca Landing (now the town of Athabasca), 45 km west of the lake, was reached by the Athabasca Trail, which ran north from Fort Edmonton. The trading post served as a gateway to the north via the Athabasca River. A trading post at Lac La Biche, 40 km east of North Buck Lake, was established in 1798. It was accessible from Athabasca Landing via the Athabasca and La Biche rivers. Settlement of the Lac La Biche area began in 1857 and proceeded slowly until the Northern Alberta Railroad arrived from Edmonton in 1914. To the west, the Canadian National Railway was completed from Edmonton to Athabasca in 1912 (Kjearsgaard 1972). By the early 1900s, the only developments on North Buck Lake were a trading post and the homes of several Métis families (Alta. Cult. Multicult. n.d.; Chipeniuk 1975). In 1917, the Wagner and Lyons Fish Company began to fish the lake commercially. During the 1930s, land east of the lake was opened for homesteading.

By the 1970s, North Buck Lake had become a very popular recreational lake. As the demand for recreational and residential development increased, the need for a management plan was recognized. In 1985, development of all lands within 1.5 km of the lake was restricted until a water quality study was completed by Alberta Environment and a lakeshore management plan was completed by the County of Athabasca and Improvement District No. 18 (South) with the assistance of Alberta Municipal Affairs. Lakeshore management plans determine the extent of future land developments, allocate land use and determine ways to minimize environmental impacts and conflicts in uses of the lakeshore. They recommend preferred lake uses and ways to minimize lake-user conflicts. Following completion of the lakeshore management plan, work began on a planning strategy, which was adopted as an area structure plan in March 1988 (N Buck L. Plan Commit. 1987; Alta. Mun. Aff. 1988; N Buck/Chump L. Plan Commit. 1988). Also in 1985, Alberta Energy and Natural Resources addressed problems of Crown land management through the initiation of an Integrated Crown Land and Resource Use Management Strategy for the Caslan/North Buck Lake area. Concurrently, Public Lands Division developed a management plan for a natural area to be located on the western side of North Buck Lake and on land surrounding Chump Lake.

A 1987 survey of lake-user groups found that North Buck Lake

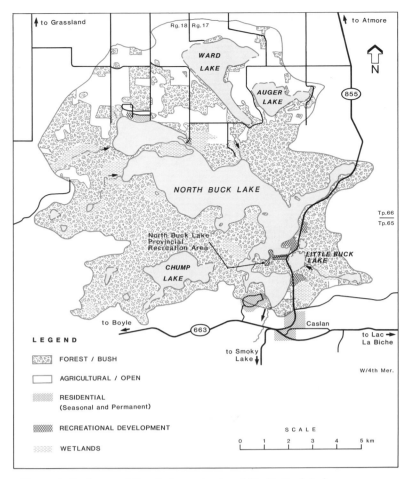

Figure 1. Features of the drainage basin of North Buck Lake.
SOURCES: Alta. Envir. n.d.[b]; En. Mines Resour. Can. 1972; 1973.
Updated with 1983 aerial photos.

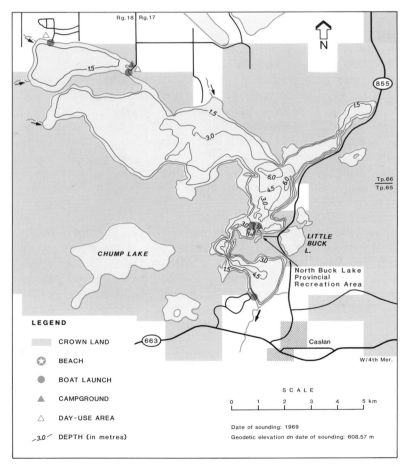

Figure 2. Bathymetry and shoreline features of North Buck Lake.
BATHYMETRY SOURCE: Alta. Envir. n.d.[c].

Table 1. Characteristics of North Buck Lake drainage basin.

area (excluding lake) (km²)[a]	100
soil[b]	Eluviated Dystric and Eutric Brunisols, Orthic Gray Luvisols
bedrock geology[c]	Lea Park Formation (Upper Cretaceous): shale, ironstone concretions; marine
terrain[b]	flat to moderately rolling
ecoregion[d]	Dry Mixedwood Subregion of Boreal Mixedwood
dominant vegetation[d]	trembling aspen
mean annual inflow (m³)[a, e]	3.25×10^6
mean annual sunshine (h)[f]	2 264

NOTE: [e]excluding groundwater inflow
SOURCES: [a]Alta. Envir. n.d.[b]; [b]Kjearsgaard 1972; [c]Alta. Res. Counc. 1972; [d]Strong and Leggat 1981; [f]Envir. Can. 1982

Table 2. Characteristics of North Buck Lake.

elevation (m)[a, b]	608.57
surface area (km²)[a, b]	19.0
volume (m³)[a, b]	47.3×10^6
maximum depth (m)[a, b]	6.1
mean depth (m)[a, b]	2.49
shoreline length (km)[c]	41.8
mean annual lake evaporation (mm)[d]	636
mean annual precipitation (mm)[d]	517
mean residence time (yr)[d, e]	40.5
control structure	none

NOTES: [a]on date of sounding: (month unknown) 1969; [e]excluding groundwater inflow
SOURCES: [b]Alta. Envir. n.d.[c]; [c]N Buck L. Plan Commit. 1987; [d]Alta. Envir. n.d.[b].

was most valued for fishing, the beauty of the natural setting, clean water and good boating (N Buck L. Plan Commit. 1987). Favourite activities of lake users are camping, general relaxation, fishing, swimming, boating and water skiing. There are no boating restrictions over most of the lake, but in posted areas, either all boats are prohibited or power boats are subject to a maximum speed of 12 km/hour (Alta. For. Ld. Wild. 1988). There are no sport fishing regulations specific to the lake but provincial limits and regulations apply (Alta. For. Ld. Wild. 1989).

The largest recreational facility on the lake is North Buck Lake Recreation Area. It is located on a peninsula on the southeast side of the lake, 4 km north of Caslan along Secondary Road 855 (Fig. 2). It is the second most popular provincial recreation area in northern Alberta (N Buck L. Plan Commit. 1987). Day-use services at the recreation area are provided year-round and camping services are provided from Victoria Day to Thanksgiving Day. In 1988, the facilities consisted of 100 unserviced campsites, 2 water pumps, picnic tables, a beach, a dock, 2 boat launches and 1 000 m of lake frontage. Upgrading is planned for the near future, when the recreation area will be expanded to include the rest of the peninsula. Eventually, additional expansion may include land on the western side of the lake across from the existing campground. Recreational activities in the new areas will focus on walk-in picnicking, beach development, hiking, walk-in/boat-in camping and cross-country skiing (N Buck L. Plan Commit. 1987).

Two recreational areas operated by the County of Athabasca are located along the north basin of the lake (Fig. 2). The first is a small campground with approximately 10 informal campsites, a boat launch, firepits and picnic tables, which is located at the north end of the narrows. The second is a day-use area with several picnic tables, firepits and a boat launch, which is located at the extreme northwestern tip of the lake. A playground is planned for the day-use area in the future (Driesen 1988). Improvement District No. 18 (South) maintains a public boat launch, parking lot and swimming area in the subdivision on the southern bay.

There are one private and two commercially operated recreation areas on the lake: the citizens of Caslan hold a recreational lease on land just north of the provincial recreation area, and the two commercial campgrounds are located north and south of the provincial recreation area, on the eastern shore of the lake near Secondary Road 855.

The water in North Buck Lake is quite clear during most of the year, but high concentrations of blue-green algae may colour the water green during late summer. Aquatic vegetation grows densely around much of the shoreline and provides habitat for wildlife and waterfowl production and spawning areas for yellow perch and northern pike.

Drainage Basin Characteristics

The drainage basin surrounding North Buck Lake is 5 times the size of the lake (Tables 1, 2). There are no major inflows, only four intermittent streams that flow into the northwest and central basins (Fig. 1). The outlet stream flows from the southern tip of the lake to the Amisk River.

Most of the land north and northwest of the lake is level to gently undulating (0 to 5% slope), whereas land to the northeast and southwest is gently rolling (5 to 9% slope). The primary soils are Eluviated Eutric and Dystric Brunisols and important secondary soils are Orthic Gray Luvisols. A complex of Eluviated Eutric Brunisols and Orthic Gray Luvisols is located in the southwestern and north-central parts of the watershed. Eluviated Dystric Brunisols are located mainly in the northeastern and southwestern sections and Orthic Gray Luvisols are located east and northwest of the lake. The few partially cultivated areas in the northwestern portion of the watershed are Orthic Gray Luvisols, which have a poor to fair arability rating (Kjearsgaard 1972). There are many areas of Organic soils throughout the watershed, particularly between the lake's main and northwest basins and east of the south basin (Fig. 1).

North Buck Lake is located in the Dry Mixedwood Subregion of the Boreal Mixedwood Ecoregion (Strong and Leggat 1981). The main tree species on upland areas is trembling aspen. Balsam poplar is also common, and jack pine and white birch are present in localized areas around the lake. A number of wetlands are located close to the lakeshore and along inflowing streams (Fig. 1). Sand hills located east of the south basin and between North Buck and Chump lakes were historically prime blueberry- and cranberry-producing areas. Berry production has declined because of increased recreation, encroaching underbrush and dryness during critical growing periods (N Buck L. Plan Commit. 1987; Mitchell 1988).

There are three subdivisions on the lakeshore. In July 1987, Blue Heron Estates consisted of 38 developed and 79 undeveloped lots on the northern side of the northwest basin; South Subdivision consisted of 8 developed lots on the eastern shore of the main basin; and Golden Nodding Estates comprised 55 developed and 19 undeveloped lots on the western shore of the south basin (N Buck L. Plan Commit. 1987).

Lake Basin Characteristics

North Buck Lake is a fairly shallow, moderate-sized water body with a very irregular shoreline (Table 2, Fig. 2). The lake has a large main basin and two smaller, shallower basins. The northwest basin has a maximum depth of approximately 1.5 m. It is connected to the main basin by a shallow, weedy narrows. The main basin is generally 3–m deep or less in the northern portion, but as deep as 6 m in the southern portion. The south basin, which is connected to the main basin by a narrow, weedy channel, has a maximum depth of approximately 4.5 m.

Much of the shoreline has a gentle slope or is rounded. Beach areas are associated with the provincial recreation area and opposite the recreation area on the west side of the lake. They are also present

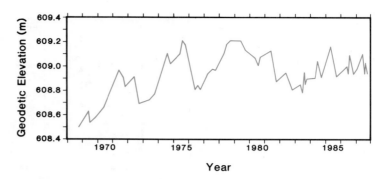

Figure 3. Water level of North Buck Lake, 1968 to 1987.
SOURCE: Alta. Envir. n.d.[c].

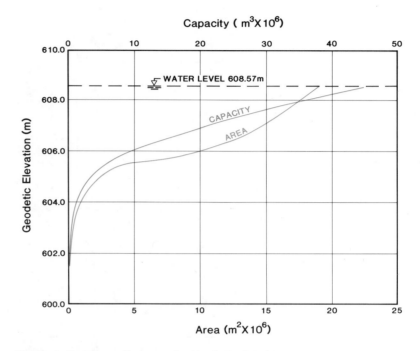

Figure 4. Area/capacity curve for North Buck Lake.
SOURCE: Alta. Envir. n.d.[c].

along the northeast portion of the south basin, along the north shore of the north basin at Blue Heron Estates, and along parts of the north shore of the main basin (N Buck L. Plan Commit. 1987).

The lake's water level has been recorded since 1968 (Fig. 3). The difference between the historic minimum (608.50 m in 1968) and the historic maximum (609.21 m in 1978) is 0.71 m. This range in water levels would have little effect on the area of the lake (Fig. 4). The maximum fluctuation between 1980 and 1988 was 0.38 m.

Water Quality

The main basin of North Buck Lake was sampled monthly by Alberta Environment between May and October 1986 and once in January 1987 (Alta. Envir. n.d.[a]). The lake has hard, well-buffered, fresh water and the dominant ions are bicarbonate and calcium (Table 3).

During July 1986, the water column was weakly thermally stratified. It became well-mixed for the remainder of the open-water period (Fig. 5). Levels of dissolved oxygen were high at all depths during the ice-free season but had declined to 0 mg/L below a depth of 5 m by late January 1987 (Fig. 6). Dissolved oxygen concentrations above 5 m, however, probably were sufficient to sustain the fish population for the rest of the winter.

North Buck Lake is eutrophic. During August 1986, chlorophyll a concentrations reached a maximum of almost 42 µg/L (Fig. 7). This peak corresponded to a total phosphorus peak of 40 µg/L in the euphotic zone and a phytoplankton biomass of 10 mg/L. Total phosphorus concentrations during the open-water season in 1986 averaged 30 µg/L (Table 4). Phosphorus loading from sources external to the lake has been estimated for North Buck Lake (Table 5). The

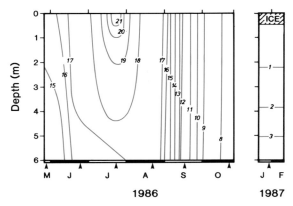

Figure 5. Temperature (°C) of North Buck Lake, 1986 to 1987. Arrows indicate sampling dates. SOURCE: Alta. Envir. n.d.[a].

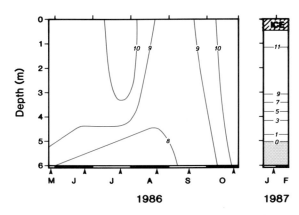

Figure 6. Dissolved oxygen (mg/L) in North Buck Lake, 1986 to 1987. Arrows indicate sampling dates. SOURCE: Alta. Envir. n.d.[a].

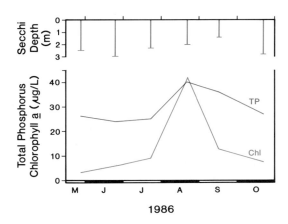

Figure 7. Total phosphorus, chlorophyll *a* and Secchi depth in North Buck Lake, 1986. SOURCE: Alta. Envir. n.d.[a].

Table 3. Major ions and related water quality variables for North Buck Lake. Average concentrations in mg/L; pH in pH units. Composite samples from the euphotic zone collected 6 times from 27 May to 21 Oct. 1986. S.E. = standard error.

	Mean	S.E.
pH (range)	7.9–8.7	—
total alkalinity ($CaCO_3$)	162	1.9
specific conductivity ($\mu S/cm$)	326	3.8
total dissolved solids (calculated)	172	1.8
total hardness ($CaCO_3$)	147	4.2
total particulate carbon	1[a]	0.3
dissolved organic carbon	33	19.8
HCO_3	188	3.9
CO_3	<5	—
Mg	18	0.9
Na	10	0.2
K	6	0.1
Cl	<1	—
SO_4	11	0.8
Ca	30	0.9

NOTE: [a]n = 5
SOURCE: Alta. Envir. n.d.[a], Naquadat station 01AL06AA2710

Table 4. Nutrient, chlorophyll *a* and Secchi depth data for North Buck Lake. Average concentrations in $\mu g/L$. Composite samples from the euphotic zone collected 6 times from 27 May to 21 Oct. 1986. S.E. = standard error.

	Mean	S.E.
total phosphorus	30	2.7
total dissolved phosphorus	8	0.5
total Kjeldahl nitrogen	1 050	40.8
$NO_3 + NO_2$–nitrogen	<2	—
NH_4–nitrogen	20	8.2
iron	<20	—
chlorophyll *a*	13.3	5.82
Secchi depth (m)	2.3	0.24

SOURCE: Alta. Envir. n.d.[a], Naquadat station 01AL06AA2710

Table 5. Theoretical total phosphorus loading to North Buck Lake from external sources.

Source		Phosphorus (kg/yr)	Percentage of Total
watershed	forested/bush	336	28
	agricultural/cleared	374	31
sewage[a]		—	—
precipitation/dustfall		498	41
	TOTAL	1 208	100
annual areal loading (g/m² of lake surface)	0.06		

NOTE: [a]negligible
SOURCE: Mitchell 1988

Table 6. Percentage composition of major algal groups by total biomass in North Buck Lake, 1986. Composite samples collected from the euphotic zone.

ALGAL GROUP	27 May	24 June	22 July	21 Aug.	16 Sep.	21 Oct.
Total Biomass (mg/L)	1.07	4.08	4.75	10.11	1.95	1.28
Percentage Composition:						
Cyanophyta	1	39	60	62	23	5
		Anabaena ——————————————→			*Oscillatoria*	
Chlorophyta	40	35	16	5	12	17
	Oocystis ————→					
Euglenophyta	0	0	0	0	0	3
Chrysophyta	19	3	3	2	6	12
Bacillariophyta	30	17	13	4	24	40
	Melosira				*Melosira*	*Asterionella*
Cryptophyta	10	2	2	6	30	20
Pyrrhophyta	0	4	7	21	5	3
					Cryptomonas ——→	

SOURCE: Alta. Envir. n.d.[a]

lake's watershed is small compared to its surface area, so phosphorus loading through runoff is low. The major sources of phosphorus are precipitation and dustfall (41%), runoff from agricultural land (31%) and runoff from forested land (28%). Loading from cottage septic systems and residential land is assumed to be negligible (less than 1% of the total external load) because of the small number of cottages on the lakeshore. The areal loading rate for North Buck Lake (0.06 g/m² of lake surface) is similar to the rates calculated for Lake Wabamun (0.08 g/m²) and Moore Lake (0.06 g/m²), and much lower than those calculated for Baptiste Lake (0.36 g/m²) and Lac la Nonne (0.41 g/m²).

Biological Characteristics

Plants

The phytoplankton community in North Buck Lake was studied by Alberta Environment from May to October in 1986 (Alta. Envir. n.d.[a]). Total biomass was quite low (1 to 5 mg/L) on all sampling dates except 21 August, when it exceeded 10 mg/L (Table 6). In May, green algae (Chlorophyta) such as *Oocystis lacustris* and diatoms (Bacillariophyta) such as *Melosira islandica helvetica* formed most of the biomass. From June through August, however, the blue-greens (Cyanophyta) *Anabaena flos-aquae* and *A. planctonica* were the dominant species. By mid-September, another blue-green (*Oscillatoria agardhii*), two diatoms (*Melosira islandica helvetica* and *M. granulata*) and two cryptophytes (*Cryptomonas erosa* and *C. Marsonii*) were the most important species. During October, the diatom *Asterionella formosa* was the dominant species but *Cryptomonas* sp. remained important .

There is little information on the aquatic macrophytes in North Buck Lake. Their general distribution is indicated in Figure 8.

Invertebrates

There are no data on the invertebrates in North Buck Lake.

Fish

Seven species of fish have been reported in North Buck Lake: northern pike, yellow perch, lake whitefish, walleye, cisco, burbot and white sucker. Walleye was indigenous to the lake, but most of the stock disappeared during the 1950s. Walleye fingerlings were planted in 1984, 1986 and 1987, at an average rate of 64 400 per year (Alta. En. Nat. Resour. 1984; Alta. For. Ld. Wild. 1986; 1987). A few walleye were sighted in 1988, but they were not a catchable size. The population will not reproduce for 7 to 9 years after the first planting. The important spawning areas for yellow perch and north-

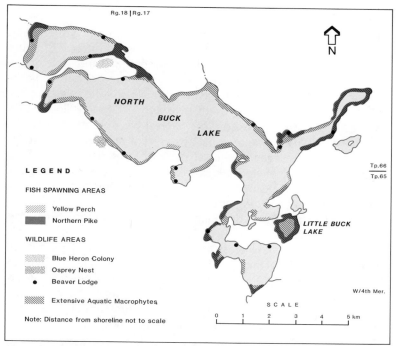

Figure 8. Distribution of aquatic macrophytes, fish spawning areas and wildlife areas in North Buck Lake, 1987.
SOURCE: N Buck L. Plan Commit. 1987.

ern pike are shown in Figure 8. Nearby Little Buck Lake is an important northern pike spawning and rearing area. This lake is joined to North Buck Lake by a culvert under Secondary Road 855 (Sullivan 1987).

North Buck Lake is managed for commercial, sport and domestic fisheries. There are no data available for domestic catches. The commercial fishery has operated since 1917 but records were not kept until 1942. Lake whitefish is the main catch and cisco, northern pike and burbot are secondary in importance. Historically, the largest catches were: 17 177 kg of lake whitefish in 1946/47, 14 540 kg of cisco in 1952/53, 29 548 kg of northern pike in 1947/48 and 3 200 kg of burbot in 1966/67. Between 1981/82 and 1987/88 the average annual harvests were: 10 132 kg of whitefish, 181 kg of cisco, and 214 kg of northern pike. Between 1981/82 and 1985/86, the average burbot catch was 440 kg. Yellow perch were harvested until 1965/66 and walleye until 1969/70. After 1970, only occasional walleye were taken. The largest walleye harvest since 1970 was 54 kg taken in 1987/88 after the stocking program had begun (Alta. For. Ld. Wild. n.d.; Alta. Rec. Parks Wild. 1976).

A creel survey of the sport fishery at North Buck Lake was conducted during 1984 (Sullivan 1985). Northern pike and yellow perch

Table 7. Estimated angler numbers, effort and harvest from North Buck Lake. Estimates based on creel survey data collected from 15 May to 31 Aug. 1984. A total of 36 weekdays and 31 weekend days and holidays were surveyed; 39 weekdays were not included. Information was collected from 07:00 to 23:00. NP = northern pike; YP = yellow perch.

	NP	YP	Total
number of anglers[a]	—	—	11 623
angler-hours[b]	—	—	24 771
total number fish harvested[c]	9 878	5 504	15 382
total yield (kg)	6 668	1 326	7 994
mean weight (g)	677	241	—
catch/angler-hour	0.77	0.48	1.25
harvest/angler-hour[b, c]	0.50	0.29	0.78
harvest/angler[a, c]	1.06	0.61	1.67

NOTES: [a]observed no. anglers = 5 208; [b]observed hours = 11 099; [c]based on observed no. fish kept: NP = 5 511, YP = 3 174
SOURCE: Sullivan 1985

were the main catches; no walleye were taken during the survey period. It was estimated that 11 623 anglers fished for 24 771 hours (Table 7). Approximately 35% of the northern pike and 40% of the yellow perch caught were released. The average harvest/angler-hour for 21 lakes in the Northeast Region surveyed between 1984 and 1987 was 0.22 for northern pike and 0.32 for yellow perch (Sullivan 1989). In comparison, the harvest per unit effort at North Buck Lake was twice the regional average for pike and very similar to the regional average for perch (Table 7). Almost half (49%) of the anglers interviewed at North Buck Lake caught at least one pike, but relatively few (14%) caught at least one perch. The largest catches of pike were taken during the latter half of May and the largest catches of perch during early June. The lake is noted for the small size of its pike and large size of its perch. North Buck Lake received the second heaviest angling pressure of seven Northeast Region lakes surveyed during 1984, and produced the largest number of pike and the second largest number of perch. Only Lac Ste. Anne was fished for more hours. Because of its smaller size, however, North Buck Lake received more than double the angling pressure (15.7 angler-hours/ha) than did Lac Ste. Anne (6.4 angler-hours/ha).

Wildlife

There is little information on the wildlife in the area. A Great Blue Heron colony is located at the north end of the lake (Fig. 8). In 1985, there were 27 active nests (N Buck L. Plan Commit. 1987). An

Osprey nesting site is located on the northwest side of the main basin. Upland game bird species in the area include Ruffed, Spruce and Sharp-tailed grouse.

Moose and white-tailed deer are the most common ungulates and mule deer are seen occasionally. The furbearer harvest consists mainly of muskrat, beaver, coyote, mink and squirrel. Other species taken occasionally are ermine, fisher, fox, lynx and marten (N Buck L. Plan Commit. 1987).

M.E. Bradford

References

Alberta Culture and Multiculturalism. n.d. Hist. Resour. Div., Hist. Sites Serv. Unpubl. data, Edmonton.
Alberta Energy and Natural Resources. 1984. Fish planting list. Fish Wild. Div., Edmonton.
Alberta Environment. n.d.[a]. Envir. Assess. Div., Envir. Qlty. Monit. Br. Unpubl. data, Edmonton.
———. n.d.[b]. Tech. Serv. Div., Hydrol. Br. Unpubl. data, Edmonton.
———. n.d.[c]. Tech. Serv. Div., Surv. Br. Unpubl. data, Edmonton.
Alberta Forestry, Lands and Wildlife. n.d. Fish Wild. Div. Unpubl. data, Edmonton.
———. 1986, 1987. Fish planting list. Fish Wild. Div., Edmonton.
———. 1988. Boating in Alberta. Fish Wild. Div., Edmonton.
———. 1989. Guide to sportfishing. Fish Wild. Div., Edmonton.
Alberta Municipal Affairs. 1988. North Buck/Chump (Johnson) Lakes area structure plan 1988. Prep. by Alta. Mun. Aff., Plan. Br., Edmonton for Co. Athabasca No. 12, Athabasca and ID No. 18 (S), Lac La Biche.
Alberta Recreation, Parks and Wildlife. 1976. Commercial fisheries catch statistics for Alberta, 1942–1975. Fish Wild. Div., Fish. Mgt. Rep. No. 22, Edmonton.
Alberta Research Council. 1972. Geological map of Alberta. Nat. Resour. Div., Alta. Geol. Surv., Edmonton.
Chipeniuk, R.C. 1975. Lakes of the Lac La Biche district. R.C. Chipeniuk, Lac La Biche.
Driesen, A. 1988. Athabasca Regional Recreation and Further Education, Athabasca. Pers. comm.
Energy, Mines and Resources Canada. 1972, 1973. National topographic series 1:50 000 83I/9 (1972), 83I/10 (1973). Surv. Map. Br., Ottawa.
Environment Canada. 1982. Canadian climate normals, Vol. 7: Bright sunshine (1951–1980). Prep. by Atm. Envir. Serv. Supply Serv. Can., Ottawa.
Holmgren, E.J. and P.M. Holmgren. 1976. Over 2000 place names of Alberta. 3rd ed. West. Producer Prairie Books, Saskatoon.
Kjearsgaard, A.A. 1972. Reconnaissance soil survey of the Tawatinaw map sheet (83–I). Alta. Soil Surv. Rep. No. 29, Univ. Alta. Bull. No. SS–12, Alta. Inst. Pedol. Rep. No. S–72–29. Univ. Alta., Edmonton.
Mitchell, P.A. 1988. Alta. Envir., Envir. Assess. Div., Envir. Qlty. Monit. Br., Edmonton. Pers. comm.
North Buck Lake Plan Committee. 1987. North Buck/Chump (Johnson) Lakes management study: Background report. First draft, Sep. 1987. Prep. for Co. Athabasca, Athabasca and ID No. 18 (S), Lac La Biche.
North Buck/Chump (Johnson) Lakes Plan Committee. 1988. North Buck/Chump (Johnson) Lake management study: Proposed lake planning strategy. Prep. for Co. Athabasca, Athabasca and ID No. 18 (S), Lac La Biche.
Strong, W.L. and K.R. Leggat. 1981. Ecoregions of Alberta. Alta. En. Nat. Resour., Resour. Eval. Plan. Div., Edmonton.
Sullivan, M.G. 1985. Characteristics and impacts of the sports fishery at North Buck Lake during May–August 1984. Alta. En. Nat. Resour., Fish Wild. Div. Unpubl. rep., St. Paul.
———. 1989. Alta. For. Ld. Wild., Fish Wild. Div., St. Paul. Pers. comm.

PINEHURST LAKE

MAP SHEET: 73L/11
LOCATION: Tp65, 66 R9, 10 W4
LAT/LONG: 59°39'N 111°26'W

Pinehurst Lake is a popular destination for anglers, hunters and campers who visit Alberta's Lakeland Region. It is valued for its beautiful beaches and natural shoreline. The lake is located in Improvement District No. 18 (South), about 245 km northeast of the city of Edmonton. The town of Lac La Biche, which is the nearest large population centre, is about 60 km to the northwest. To reach the lake from Edmonton, take Highway 28 north and east to the village of Vilna, then Highway 36 north to Highway 55. Drive east on Highway 55 for 5 km, then turn onto a gravelled local road that runs north for 2.5 km and then west for 30 km. The road ends at the Pinehurst Lake Forest Recreation Area on the western shore of the lake (Fig. 1).

The name Pinehurst is derived from the jack pine tree and from the English word "hurst", which means "a wooded hillock". This term refers to the long ridge that runs along the northwest shore of the lake. At one time, jack pine may have grown along the ridge, but forest fires have removed most of this species. The name of Pinehurst Lake's outlet, Punk Creek, is a translation of the Cree word *pusakan*. Punk referred to poplar or birch wood that was used to start a fire with flint and steel (Chipeniuk 1975).

A number of trappers and fishermen lived around the lake and on the islands during the first half of the twentieth century. The commercial fishery began around 1909, when two Norwegian brothers began fishing the lake. They transported their catch to the town of Vegreville by horse-drawn sleigh. A trading post, store and post office were built on the eastern shore at Snug Cove in the late 1940s. The post office closed in 1951 for lack of business. In 1947, the cisco population at nearby Lac La Biche declined drastically, leaving area mink ranchers without a convenient source of mink food. The ranchers decided to transport cisco from Pinehurst Lake, so they built an airstrip on land just east of Snug Cove. The airstrip is now unused and overgrown by trembling aspen (Chipeniuk 1975).

Pinehurst Lake Forest Recreation Area is the only developed recreational facility at the lake (Fig. 2). It is operated by the Alberta Forest Service and is open from May to September. There are 65 campsites, pump water, a beach and a boat launch. There are no boating restrictions specific to Pinehurst Lake, but general federal regulations apply (Alta. For. Ld. Wild. 1988). The two islands on the east side of the lake were reserved for recreation in 1969, and at present, they have the status of Protective Notation. This means that they have recognized potential as natural areas but they have not been formally established as such (Alta. For. Ld. Wild. 1987). About 98% of the shoreline is Crown land; the only 2 parcels of private land are located on the eastern shore south of the outlet. The management intent for the Pinehurst Lake area, as cited in the Lakeland Sub-Regional Integrated Resource Plan, is for its development as a major recreation destination area (Alta. En. Nat. Resour. 1985). Future developments could include both public and commercially operated facilities.

The water in Pinehurst Lake turns green during the open-water season. The density of aquatic vegetation is generally low to moderate except in several bays and around the islands, where density is high. Sport fishing for walleye, northern pike and yellow perch is one of the most popular activities at the lake. There are no sport fishing regulations specific to Pinehurst Lake, but provincial limits and regulations apply (Alta. For. Ld. Wild. 1989). The lake has not been fished commercially since the 1976/77 season because of the high density of parasites in the lake whitefish and cisco.

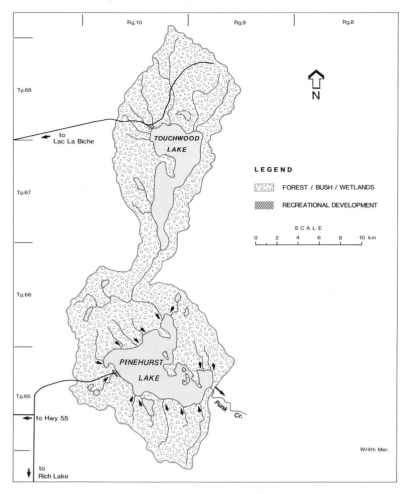

Figure 1. Features of the drainage basin of Pinehurst Lake.
SOURCES: Alta. Envir. n.d.[b]; En. Mines Resour. Can. 1981. Updated with 1982 aerial photos.

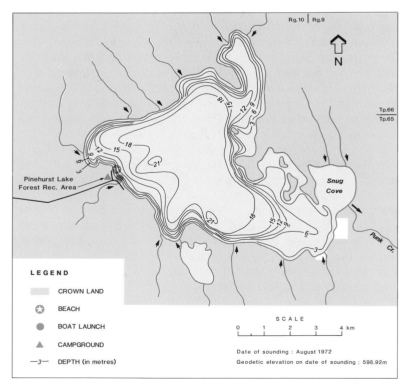

Figure 2. Bathymetry and shoreline features of Pinehurst Lake.
BATHYMETRY SOURCE: Alta. Envir. n.d.[c].

Table 1. Characteristics of Pinehurst Lake drainage basin.

area (excluding lake) (km²)[a]	285
soil[b]	Orthic Gray Luvisols, Brunisols, Organics
bedrock geology[c]	La Biche Formation (Upper Cretaceous): shale, ironstone partings and concretions; marine
terrain[b]	undulating to moderately rolling
ecoregion[d]	Dry and Moist subregions of Boreal Mixedwood
dominant vegetation[d]	trembling aspen, balsam poplar
mean annual inflow (m³)[a, e]	18.1×10^6
mean annual sunshine (h)[f]	2 240

NOTE: [e]excluding groundwater inflow
SOURCES: [a]Alta. Envir. n.d.[b]; [b]Kocoaglu 1975; [c]Alta. Res. Counc. 1972; [d]Strong and Leggat 1981; [f]Envir. Can. 1982

Table 2. Characteristics of Pinehurst Lake.

elevation (m)[a, b]	598.92
surface area (km²)[a, b]	40.7
volume (m³)[a, b]	496×10^6
maximum depth (m)[a, b]	21.3
mean depth (m)[a, b]	12.2
shoreline length (km)[c]	49.8
mean annual lake evaporation (mm)[d]	640
mean annual precipitation (mm)[d]	528
mean residence time (yr)[d, e]	36.5
control structure	none

NOTES: [a]on date of sounding: Aug. 1972; [e]excluding groundwater inflow
SOURCES: [b]Alta. Envir. n.d.[c]; [c]Mills 1987; [d]Alta. Envir. n.d.[b].

Drainage Basin Characteristics

Pinehurst Lake has a large drainage basin that is about 7 times the size of the lake (Tables 1, 2). A large portion of the inflow to Pinehurst Lake comes from Touchwood Lake via a permanent stream (Fig. 1). Other inflow is provided by more than a dozen small, intermittent streams. The outlet, Punk Creek, flows from the southeast shore to the Beaver River via the Sand River.

The portion of the drainage basin to the south, west and the northwest of Pinehurst Lake and to the north and east of Touchwood Lake is part of a hummocky morainal plain (Kocaoglu 1975). It is characterized by rough, irregular knob and kettle topography that is gently to moderately rolling. The knobs and ridges, which are composed mainly of glacial till, are interspersed with undrained depressions. The remainder of the drainage basin is part of a rolling morainal plain. It is characterized by undulating to gently rolling topography that features minor ridges and knobs intermixed with numerous wet depressions and small peat bogs. The soils in both areas are mainly moderately well-drained Orthic Gray Luvisols formed on fine loamy, weakly calcareous till. Organic (Mesisols and Fibrisols) and Gleysolic soils occupy poorly drained depressions, and well-drained Brunisols are present on knolls or ridges where thick sand and gravel deposits cap the till.

Almost the entire drainage basin is covered by forest, bush and wetlands (Fig. 1). Land to the north and east of Pinehurst Lake is part of the Moist Mixedwood Subregion of the Boreal Mixedwood Ecoregion, whereas land to the west and south of the lake is part of the Dry Mixedwood Subregion (Strong and Leggat 1981). The main difference between the two subregions is that both trembling aspen and balsam poplar are the dominant trees on moderately well-drained Gray Luvisols in the dry subregion, whereas trembling aspen alone is the dominant tree on well-drained to moderately well-drained Gray Luvisols in the moist subregion. In both subregions, jack pine grows on well-drained Brunisols, white spruce grows on imperfectly drained Gleysols and Gray Luvisols, and black spruce, willows and sedges grow on poorly to very poorly drained Organics and Gleysols.

Near the lake, the shoreland is extensively forested with trembling aspen, and poorly drained areas and sedge bogs are common. Beach sand is present along various sections of the shoreline, particularly at the east and south ends of the lake and along parts of the peninsula that lies between the islands (Hay and Haag 1985). Steep escarpments are located along sections of the southeast, east and north-central shoreland, along the peninsula bordering Snug Cove and on the land immediately north of this peninsula.

There is no agricultural activity and no country residential subdivision development in the drainage basin. The few cottages on Pinehurst Lake are located on private land south of Punk Creek. Recreational development is limited to the Alberta Forest Service recreation areas on both Pinehurst and Touchwood lakes.

Lake Basin Characteristics

Pinehurst Lake has a complex shoreline that includes several large bays (Fig. 2). The lake covers an area of 40.7 km^2 and has a maximum depth of 21.3 m (Table 2). Two islands are located in the bay on the northeast side of the lake and one is located north of the peninsula on the northeast shore. The bays at the east end of the lake are very shallow (less than 6–m deep) and the bottom of the basin slopes gently. The bay at the north end is somewhat deeper (less than 12–m deep) and its sides slope more steeply. The steepest slopes are present along the northwest, northeast and south sides of the lake. A large area in the centre of the basin is quite level, and ranges in depth from 18 to 21.3 m. Near shore, the bottom sediments are organic material or sand and rock, and at depths greater than 10 m, they are generally organic material (McDonald 1964).

The elevation of Pinehurst Lake has been monitored since 1968 (Fig. 3). The historic maximum elevation, 599.37 m, was recorded in September 1971, and the historic minimum, 598.53 m, was recorded in February 1983. Changes in the lake's area and capacity with fluctuations in water level are given in Figure 4.

Water Quality

Water quality in Pinehurst Lake was studied by Alberta Environment in August 1978, February 1979, twice in 1985, approximately monthly in 1986, and in February 1987 (Alta. Envir. n.d.[a]). As well, Fish and Wildlife Division took occasional samples in 1964, 1969, 1973, 1978, 1979, 1985 and 1986 (Mills 1987).

The lake has fresh water that is hard and well-buffered (Table 3). The dominant ions are bicarbonate and calcium. The deeper areas of the lake are thermally stratified from May to October (Fig. 5). In 1986, the concentration of dissolved oxygen in the deeper water was lower than at the surface on all sampling dates (Fig. 6). In March 1986, and from late July to late September, water below depths of 17 to 20 m was anoxic.

Pinehurst Lake is eutrophic. In 1986, the maximum chlorophyll a concentration was 18.1 µg/L, recorded in May (Fig. 7). The average Secchi depth that year (1.1 m) was somewhat shallow considering that the average concentration of chlorophyll a was 14.6 µg/L (Table 4). In 1986, the patterns of total phosphorus and chlorophyll a were similar during the open-water period. Both variables were elevated in May, July and October (Fig. 7). The spring and fall maxima are typical of stratified lakes. Phosphorus released from the sediments when the bottom water becomes anoxic during midsummer and late winter is mixed into the overlying water during spring and fall turnover and becomes available to algae. The midsummer peak of phosphorus can be attributed to increased phosphorus loading from the unusually high levels of precipitation (148 mm) in July 1986 (Envir. Can. 1986).

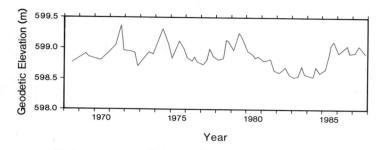

Figure 3. Water level of Pinehurst Lake, 1968 to 1987.
SOURCE: Alta. Envir. n.d.[c].

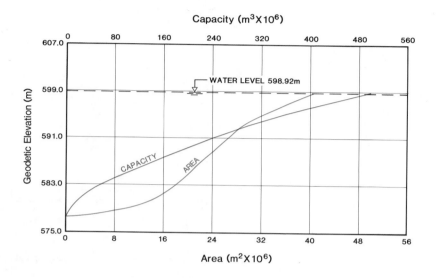

Figure 4. Area/capacity curve for Pinehurst Lake.
SOURCE: Alta. Envir. n.d.[c].

Table 3. Major ions and related water quality variables for Pinehurst Lake. Average concentrations in mg/L; pH in pH units. Composite samples from the euphotic zone collected 6 times from 28 May to 23 Oct. 1986. S.E. = standard error.

	Mean	S.E.
pH (range)	7.9–8.7	—
total alkalinity (CaCO$_3$)	149	0.5
specific conductivity (µS/cm)	280	3.2
total dissolved solids (calculated)	152	0.5
total hardness (CaCO$_3$)	133	2.0
total particulate carbon	3[a]	0.4
dissolved organic carbon	13	0.2
HCO$_3$	170	4.1
CO$_3$	<6	—
Mg	13	0.5
Na	8	0.2
K	4	0
Cl	<1	—
SO$_4$	<5	—
Ca	32	0.3

NOTE: [a]n = 5
SOURCE: Alta. Envir. n.d.[a], Naquadat station 01AL06AB4050

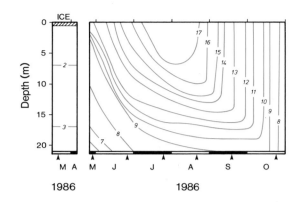

Figure 5. Temperature (°C) of Pinehurst Lake, 1986.
Arrows indicate sampling dates.
SOURCE: Alta. Envir. n.d.[a].

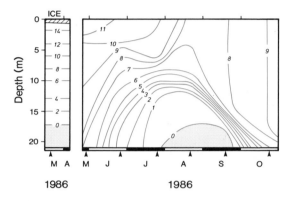

Figure 6. Dissolved oxygen (mg/L) in Pinehurst Lake, 1986. Arrows indicate sampling dates.
SOURCE: Alta. Envir. n.d.[a].

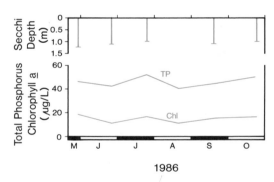

Figure 7. Total phosphorus, chlorophyll *a* and Secchi depth in Pinehurst Lake, 1986.
SOURCE: Alta. Envir. n.d.[a].

Table 4. Nutrient, chlorophyll *a* and Secchi depth data for Pinehurst Lake. Average concentrations in μg/L. Composite samples from the euphotic zone collected 6 times from 28 May to 23 Oct. 1986. S.E. = standard error.

	Mean	S.E.
total phosphorus	46	1.9
total dissolved phosphorus	10	1.1
total Kjeldahl nitrogen	1 213	25.1
$NO_3 + NO_2$–nitrogen	<2	—
NH_4–nitrogen	17	2.1
iron	<20	—
chlorophyll *a*	14.6	1.27
Secchi depth (m)	1.1	0.04

SOURCE: Alta. Envir. n.d.[a], Naquadat station 01AL06AB4050

Biological Characteristics

Plants

The phytoplankton community was sampled by Alberta Environment in January 1985 and monthly from May to October in 1986 (Alta. Envir. n.d.[a]). The highest biomass (12.93 mg/L) was recorded in the January sample; the dominant species on that date was the blue-green species *Oscillatoria agardhii*, which accounted for 95% of the total biomass. During the open-water period in 1986, biomass was highest in July, August and October (Table 5). Note the total dominance of the blue-green alga *O. agardhii* on all sampling dates. This species formed 86 to 98% of the total biomass on all dates except 28 May, when it accounted for 58% of the total biomass. In May, other species that formed a significant portion of the biomass were the dinoflagellate (Pyrrhophyta) *Gymnodinium helveticum*, the golden-brown alga (Chrysophyta) *Dinobryon sociale* and the cryptophytes *Cryptomonas erosa*, *C. Marsonii* and *C. reflexa*.

Brief surveys of the aquatic macrophytes in Pinehurst Lake were made by Fish and Wildlife Division in 1964 and 1985 (McDonald 1964; Mills 1987). In 1985, macrophyte density was estimated to be low to high, but species were not identified. That year, emergent species were restricted to Snug Cove, the adjacent bay to the west, the two northern bays, and the large bay on the south shore. Submergent species grew around most of the shoreline, but were dense only around the largest island, near the campground, and in the most northerly bay. Species identified in August 1964 were pondweeds (*Potamogeton* spp.), northern watermilfoil (*Myriophyllum exalbescens*), yellow water lily (*Nuphar variegatum*), common cattail (*Typha latifolia*) and rushes (*Juncus* spp.).

Invertebrates

There are no recent data available for the invertebrates in Pinehurst Lake. The plankton was sampled with a net once in 1964 and benthic invertebrates were sampled once in 1964 and once in 1969 by Fish and Wildlife Division (McDonald 1964; Holmes and Milsom 1969). In 1964, the most abundant zooplankton group was Copepoda and the most abundant benthic invertebrates were scuds (Amphipoda) at depths of 2 m and less and midge larvae (Chironomidae) at depths from 4 to 14 m.

Fish

The fish species known to occur in Pinehurst Lake include walleye, northern pike, lake whitefish, cisco, yellow perch, burbot, white sucker and spottail shiner. The lake is currently managed for sport fishing, domestic net fishing and commercial bait fishing. A small number of licences (two in 1984/85) are issued each year for the bait fishery. Licensees seine for spottail shiners, which are then sold to commercial bait outlets (Alta. For. Ld. Wild. n.d.). There was a commercial net fishery on Pinehurst Lake until 1976/77. Interest in

Table 5. Percentage composition of major algal groups by total biomass in Pinehurst Lake, 1986. Composite samples collected from the euphotic zone.

ALGAL GROUP	28 May	25 June	24 July	20 Aug.	18 Sep.	23 Oct.
Total Biomass (mg/L)	5.19	6.54	11.04	11.74	8.26	10.81
Percentage Composition:						
Cyanophyta	59	90	90	92	94	98
	Oscillatoria agardhii ———————————————————→					
Chrysophyta	10	1	1	4	1	0
Bacillariophyta	2	2	1	0	1	0
Cryptophyta	12	4	5	1	2	0
Pyrrhophyta	18	4	4	3	2	1

SOURCE: Alta. Envir. n.d.[a]

Table 6. Estimated angler numbers, effort and harvest from Pinehurst Lake. Estimates based on creel survey data collected from 15 May to 27 Aug. 1985. A total of 38 weekdays and 33 weekend days and holidays were surveyed; 37 weekdays were not included. Information was collected from 07:00 to 23:00. WE = walleye; NP = northern pike; YP = yellow perch.

	WE	NP	YP	Total
number of anglers[a]	—	—	—	13 988
angler-hours[b]	—	—	—	37 040
total number fish harvested[c]	6 250	4 107	2 644	13 001
total yield (kg)	3 943	8 174	342	12 459
mean weight (g)	631	1 990	129	—
catch/angler-hour	0.25	0.18	0.16	0.59
harvest/angler-hour[b, c]	0.17	0.11	0.08	0.36
harvest/angler[a, c]	0.45	0.30	0.20	0.95

NOTES: [a]observed no. anglers = 10 353; [b]observed hours = 27 415; [c]based on observed no. fish kept:
  WE = 4 620, NP = 3 076, YP = 2 112
SOURCE: Sullivan 1987

commercial fishing in the lake declined during the early 1970s, primarily because of the poor quality of the fish and low prices (Brown 1980). Lake whitefish and cisco in the lake are heavily infested with cysts of the tapeworm *Triaenophorus crassus* and are suitable only for animal food. Test nettings to assess the potential for a whitefish roe fishery in 1981 and 1985 indicated too many sport fish would be caught if the commercial net fishery resumed (Mills 1987).

Records for the commercial net fishery in Pinehurst Lake have been kept since 1942/43 (Alta. For. Ld. Wild. n.d.; Alta. Rec. Parks Wild. 1976). The primary target species of the fishery were cisco, northern pike and lake whitefish. The greatest commercial harvest of all species was 592 564 kg taken during the 1947/48 season, the first year of the cisco fishery. The average total catch from 1948/49 to 1972/73 was 80 226 kg/year. Commercial fishing essentially ended in 1972/73, when almost 52 000 kg of fish were harvested. No licences were issued during the next two seasons, and catches declined to only 115 kg of fish in 1975/76 and 272 kg in 1976/77.

Records for the domestic net fishery are limited. From 1983/84 to 1985/86, the average annual reported harvest was 2 578 kg of whitefish, 338 kg of walleye and northern pike, and 48 kg of cisco (Mills 1987).

The summer sport fishery in Pinehurst Lake was evaluated by Fish and Wildlife Division in 1985 (Table 6). Harvests by the winter sport fishery and the domestic fishery were estimated for the period from 1983/84 to 1985/86 (Mills 1987). During the summer of 1985, almost 14 000 anglers fished for over 37 000 hours (Table 6). This represents an intense angling effort. Virtually all of the effort was near shore; it amounted to 88.2 angler-hours/ha of sport fish habitat—the second highest effort recorded for 13 lakes surveyed during 1984 and 1985. Summer anglers harvested 12 459 kg of sport fish, winter anglers harvested about 8 300 kg, and the domestic fishery harvested about 680 kg. The total catch of 21 440 kg represents 40.8 kg/ha of sport fish habitat, or 5.2 kg/ha for the whole lake, which is a very high harvest rate.

Summer anglers harvested 6 250 walleye, or 0.17 fish/angler-hour. This is above the average harvest rate of 0.10 walleye/angler-hour recorded for 22 lakes surveyed in the region (Alta. For. Ld. Wild. n.d.). The 3 943 kg of walleye harvested during the summer, plus 2 000 kg in the winter sport fishery and 338 kg in the domestic fishery, is a total harvest of 6 281 kg of walleye, or 12 kg/ha of sport fish habitat (1.5 kg/ha for whole lake). The walleye population shows clear indications of overexploitation, with a trend toward younger (3– to 5–years–old), smaller fish (Mills 1987).

Summer anglers caught 4 107 northern pike, or 0.11 fish/angler-hour. This is well below the average harvest rate of 0.22 pike/angler-hour recorded for 22 lakes surveyed in the region. The average size of the pike kept was 2.0 kg. The summer harvest was 8 174 kg, the winter sport fishing harvest was about 6 000 kg and the domestic catch was about 340 kg. The total harvest of 14 500 kg represents 27.7 kg/ha of sport fish habitat, or 3.5 kg/ha for the whole lake.

Summer anglers kept 2 644 yellow perch, or 0.08 fish/angler-hour. This is very low compared to the average rate of 0.32 perch/angler-hour recorded for 22 lakes surveyed in the region. The perch catch was 342 kg in summer and about 300 kg in winter—a total of 642 kg, or 1.2 kg/ha of sport fish habitat (0.2 kg/ha for the whole lake). Part of the reason for the low harvest is that the perch averaged only 129 g despite being 4– to 7–years–old. Such slow growth is typical for food-limited perch populations (Hanson and Leggett 1985; Heath and Roff 1987).

Wildlife

There are few data for the wildlife at Pinehurst Lake. Great Blue Herons and White Pelicans have been reported there (Alta. For. Ld. Wild. n.d.).

M.E. Bradford and J.M. Hanson

References

Alberta Energy and Natural Resources. 1985. Lakeland sub-regional integrated resource plan. Resour. Eval. Plan. Div., Edmonton.

Alberta Environment. n.d.[a]. Envir. Assess. Div., Envir. Qlty. Monit. Br. Unpubl. data, Edmonton.

⸺. n.d.[b]. Tech. Serv. Div., Hydrol. Br. Unpubl. data, Edmonton.

⸺. n.d.[c]. Tech. Serv. Div., Surv. Br. Unpubl. data, Edmonton.

Alberta Forestry, Lands and Wildlife. n.d. Fish Wild. Div. Unpubl. data, Edmonton.

⸺. 1987. A summary of Alberta's natural areas reserved and established. Pub. Ld. Div., Ld. Mgt. Devel. Br. Unpubl. rep., Edmonton.

⸺. 1988. Boating in Alberta. Fish Wild. Div., Edmonton.

⸺. 1989. Guide to sportfishing. Fish Wild. Div., Edmonton.

Alberta Recreation, Parks and Wildlife. 1976. Commercial fisheries catch statistics for Alberta, 1942–1975. Fish Wild. Div., Fish. Mgt. Rep. No. 22, Edmonton.

Alberta Research Council. 1972. Geological map of Alberta. Nat. Resour. Div., Alta. Geol. Surv., Edmonton.

Brown, D. 1980. Growth, maturity and fecundity of lake whitefish, *Coregonus clupeaformis*, Pinehurst Lake, Alberta. Alta. For. Ld. Wild., Fish Wild. Div. Unpubl. rep., St. Paul.

Chipeniuk, R.C. 1975. Lakes of the Lac La Biche district. R.C. Chipeniuk, Lac La Biche.

Energy, Mines and Resources Canada. 1981. National topographic series 1:250 000 73L (1981). Surv. Map. Br., Ottawa.

Environment Canada. 1982. Canadian climate normals, Vol. 7: Bright sunshine (1951–1980). Prep. by Atm. Envir. Serv. Supply Serv. Can., Ottawa.

⸺. 1986. Climate of Alberta, report for 1986. Prep. by Atm. Envir. Serv. Alta. Envir., Edmonton.

Hanson, J.M. and W.C. Leggett. 1985. Experimental and field evidence for inter- and intraspecific competition in two freshwater fishes. Can. J. Fish. Aquat. Sci. 42:280–286.

Hay, W.K. and R.W. Haag. 1985. Pinehurst Lake implementation plan: Baseline data assessment. Alta. En. Nat. Resour., Resour. Eval. Br. Unpubl. rep., Edmonton.

Heath, D. and D.A. Roff. 1987. Test of genetic differentiation in growth of stunted and nonstunted populations of yellow perch and pumpkinseed. Trans. Am. Fish. Soc. 116:98–102.

Holmes, D.W. and B.K. Milsom. 1969. Pinehurst Lake. Alta. Ld. For., Fish Wild. Div. Unpubl. rep., Edmonton.

Kocaoglu, S.S. 1975. Reconnaissance soil survey of the Sand River area (73L). Alta. Soil Surv. Rep. No. 34, Univ. Alta. Bull. No. SS–15, Alta. Inst. Pedol. Rep. No. S–74–34 1975. Univ. Alta., Edmonton.

McDonald, D. 1964. Lake survey report: Pinehurst Lake (65–10–W4). Alta. Ld. For., Fish Wild. Div. Unpubl. rep., Edmonton.

Mills, J.B. 1987. Pinehurst Lake Lsd 15–Sec 27–Twp 65–Rge 10–W4M limnological survey phase I and II. Alta. For. Ld. Wild., Fish Wild. Div. Unpubl. rep., St. Paul.

Strong, W.L. and K.R. Leggat. 1981. Ecoregions of Alberta. Alta. En. Nat. Resour., Resour. Eval. Plan. Div., Edmonton.

Sullivan, M.G. 1987. Characteristics and impact of the sports fishery at Pinehurst Lake during May-August 1985. Alta. For. Ld. Wild., Fish Wild. Div. Unpubl. rep., St. Paul.

SEIBERT LAKE

MAP SHEETS: 73L/11, 14
LOCATION: Tp66, 67 R9, 10 W4
LAT/LONG: 54°43'N 111°18'W

Pristine, isolated Seibert Lake is set in the wilderness of the Lakeland Region. It is valued for the high-quality angling for large northern pike that it provides. Seibert Lake is located in Improvement District No. 18 (South), 265 km northeast of the city of Edmonton and about 100 km east of the town of Lac La Biche. To reach the lake from Edmonton, take Highways 28 and 28A northeast to Secondary Road 881. Drive north to Highway 55, then turn east and drive for about 6 km until you reach an improved road that runs north. This 22–km–long road leads to Seibert Lake Forest Recreation Area on the southeast shore of the lake (Fig. 1). The final two-thirds of the road twists and turns and is classed as unimproved. During wet weather, a four-wheel drive vehicle with a winch may be necessary, and during winter, the road is not plowed regularly.

Seibert Lake Forest Recreation Area is operated by Alberta Forestry, Lands and Wildlife. It is open from May to September and offers 33 campsites, pump water, a beach, a boat launch, and a day-use area with picnic tables and a picnic shelter (Fig. 2).

Seibert Lake was named for F.V. Seibert, who explored a large area of northern Alberta and surveyed the township in which the lake is located (Holmgren and Holmgren 1976). The lake is known locally as Worm Lake, a translation from the Cree *Mohteo Sakhahigan* or *Munghoos Sakhahigan.* The name refers to cysts of the tapeworm *Triaenophorus crassus* found in the lake whitefish (Chipeniuk 1975).

A trading post and several sawmills were located on the south shore of Seibert Lake at various times during the period from the 1930s to the 1950s (Chipenuik 1975). The lake was fished commercially from the early 1900s to 1957. In 1915, a northern pike reported to weigh 18 kg was caught in a gill net and during the 1930s, pike in the range of 8 to 14 kg were frequently reported caught (Chipeniuk 1975).

Seibert Lake was designated a Trophy Lake in 1970. Anglers who fish in trophy waters must hold a Trophy Waters Fishing Licence in addition to their sport fishing licence. Exceptions are people under the age of 16 or over the age of 65. The daily catch and possession limit for northern pike, at two per angler, differs from the regular provincial limit. As well, fishing for bait fish and the use of bait fish are not allowed. Seibert Lake's inlet and outlet streams are closed to fishing during a designated period in April and May (Alta. For. Ld. Wild. 1989). There are no boating restrictions specific to Seibert Lake, but general federal regulations apply (Alta. For. Ld. Wild. 1988).

Drainage Basin Characteristics

Seibert Lake's drainage basin is less than twice the size of the lake (Tables 1, 2). Several intermittent streams flow into the lake at various points along the shore (Fig. 1). The outlet, an unnamed creek, flows into the Sand River to the east and then into the Beaver River.

Seibert Lake is underlain by the Cretaceous-age shales and ironstone of the La Biche Formation (Table 1). The lake lies on a rolling morainal plain characterized by level to gently rolling topography. Minor ridges and knobs are intermixed with numerous wet depressions and small peat bogs. Elevations range from 739 m above sea level at the northern tip of the watershed to 621 m near the lakeshore. The drainage basin is part of the Moist Mixedwood Sub-

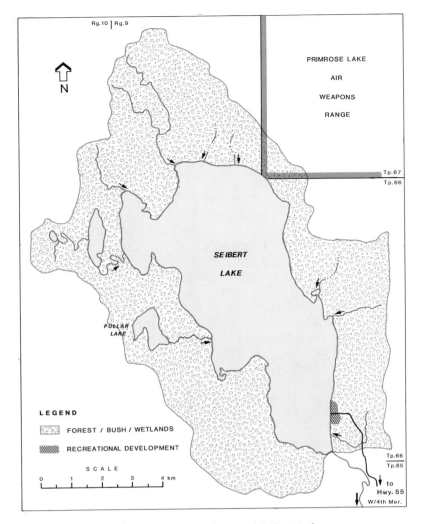

Figure 1. Features of the drainage basin of Seibert Lake.
SOURCES: Alta. Envir. n.d.[b]; En. Mines Resour. Can. 1970; 1979.
Updated with 1982 aerial photos.

Table 1. Characteristics of Seibert Lake drainage basin.

area (excluding lake) (km²)[a]	67.6
soil[b]	Orthic Gray Luvisol, Eluviated Eutric Brunisol, Mesisol
bedrock geology[c]	La Biche Formation (Upper Cretaceous): shale, ironstone partings and concretions; marine
terrain[b]	level to gently rolling
ecoregion[d]	Moist Mixedwood Subregion of Boreal Mixedwood
dominant vegetation[d]	trembling aspen, balsam poplar
mean annual inflow (m³)[a, e]	5.53 x 10⁶
mean annual sunshine (h)[f]	2 240

NOTE: [e]excluding groundwater inflow
SOURCES: [a]Alta. Envir. n.d.[b]; [b]Kocaoglu 1975; [c]Alta. Res. Counc. 1972; [d]Strong and Leggat 1981; [f]Envir. Can. 1982

Table 2. Characteristics of Seibert Lake.

elevation (m)[a]	approximately 621.2
surface area (km²)[b, c]	37.9
volume (m³)[b, c]	263 x 10⁶
maximum depth (m)[b, c]	11.0
mean depth (m)[b, c]	6.9
shoreline length (km)[d]	35
mean annual lake evaporation (mm)[e]	640
mean annual precipitation (mm)[e]	528
mean residence time (yr)[e, f]	>100
control structure	none

NOTES: [b]on date of sounding: May 1973; [f]excluding groundwater inflow
SOURCES: [a]En. Mines Resour. Can. 1979; [c]Alta. Envir. n.d.[c]; [d]Alta. Mun. Aff. 1984; [e]Alta. Envir. n.d.[b]

region of the Boreal Mixedwood Ecoregion (Strong and Leggat 1981). The dominant soils in the watershed are moderately well-drained to well-drained Orthic Gray Luvisols (Kocaoglu 1975). These fine-loamy, moderately to strongly calcareous soils, which developed on glacial till, support a forest cover of trembling aspen and balsam poplar. A large area of Eluviated Eutric Brunisols of a loamy coarse sand texture is located north of the lake. These rapidly drained soils formed on sandy glaciofluvial materials and support a tree cover of jack pine. Organic soils, particularly Mesisols, are present throughout the drainage basin in depressional to level areas. They support a cover of black spruce, willows and sedges.

Seibert Lake's entire watershed, except for the recreation area, is in its natural state. All of the land belongs to the Crown. Agricultural and residential developments have not taken place to date, and will not be allowed in the future under the Lakeland Sub-Regional Integrated Resource Plan (Alta. En. Nat. Resour. 1985). Other activities restricted by this management plan are commercial, industrial and non-renewable resource developments. Planning objectives are to manage the lake for high-quality angling for trophy-sized northern pike and to provide recreational opportunities for water-based and upland wilderness activities.

Lake Basin Characteristics

Seibert Lake has a surface area of almost 38 km² and a maximum depth of 11 m (Table 2). The deepest spot is located in a small hole in the centre of the single basin (Fig. 2). Most of the lake is 9–m deep or less. The sides of the basin slope gradually to the lake bottom, which is quite flat, and there are no islands. A 1971 study noted that sand and gravel made up most of the bottom sediments to a depth of 4.5 m (Mackowecki 1973[a]). Below 6 m, gray silt was the char-

acteristic bottom type. The elevation of Seibert Lake has not been monitored.

Water Quality

Water quality data for Seibert Lake are limited. Alberta Environment sampled the lake in March of both 1979 and 1986, and a University of Alberta researcher conducted a brief survey during July 1971 (Alta. Envir. n.d.[a]; Mackowecki 1973[a]).

The water in Seibert Lake is fresh, well-buffered and very hard (Table 3). The major ions are bicarbonate, magnesium and sodium. In July 1971, the water temperature was a uniform 16°C from surface to bottom. In March 1986, the dissolved oxygen concentration was 12.5 mg/L at the surface and 0 mg/L at the bottom (Fig. 3). Anoxic conditions in the deepest water were also observed in March 1979.

It is not possible to properly categorize the trophic status of Seibert Lake with the data available. However, the relatively low total phosphorus concentration (9 µg/L) measured in March 1986 (Table 4) indicates that the lake is likely low in productivity.

Biological Characteristics

Plants

The phytoplankton community in Seibert Lake has not been sampled quantitatively. McDonald (1964) noted the presence of *Anabaena* sp., *Microcystis* sp. and *Aphanocapsa* sp. on 29 July 1964.

Aquatic vegetation was surveyed qualitatively by a researcher at the University of Alberta in July and August of 1971 and 1972 (Mackowecki 1973[a]). Three emergent, 2 free-floating, 3 floating-

Table 3. Major ions and related water quality variables for Seibert Lake. Average concentrations in mg/L; pH in pH units. Samples were collected once from 1–, 4– and 8–m depths on 20 Mar. 1986. Ice depth = 87 cm.

pH	7.8
total alkalinity ($CaCO_3$)	307
specific conductivity (μS/cm)	547
total dissolved solids (calculated)	301
total hardness ($CaCO_3$)	234
HCO_3	340
CO_3	17
Mg	44
Na	30
K	14
Cl	3
SO_4	<5
Ca	21

SOURCE: Alta. Envir. n.d.[a], Naquadat station 01AL06AB4001

Table 4. Nutrient data for Seibert Lake. Average concentrations in μg/L. Samples were collected once from 1–, 4– and 8–m depths on 20 Mar. 1986.

total phosphorus	9
total Kjeldahl nitrogen	1 140
$NO_3 + NO_2$–nitrogen	79
NH_4–nitrogen	160

SOURCE: Alta. Envir. n.d.[a], Naquadat station 01AL06AB4001

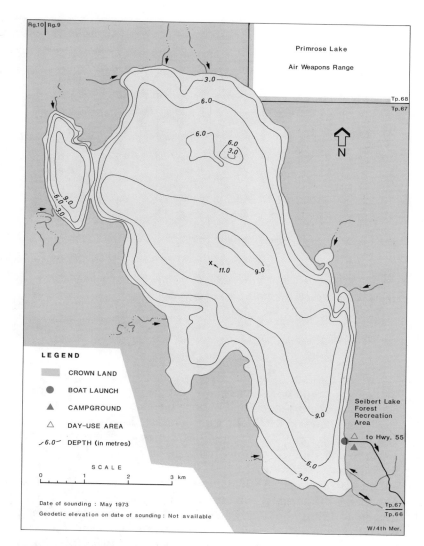

Figure 2. Bathymetry and shoreline features of Seibert Lake.
BATHYMETRY SOURCE: Alta. Envir. n.d.[c].

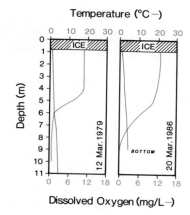

Figure 3. Temperature and dissolved oxygen in Seibert Lake, 1979 and 1986.
SOURCE: Alta. Envir. n.d.[a].

leaved, and 10 submergent species were identified (Table 5). Emergent vegetation, mostly common great bulrush (*Scirpus validus*), almost rings the lake. Yellow water lily (*Nuphar variegatum*) was mostly confined to the ends of bays. Stonewort (*Chara* sp.) was the most widespread submergent plant, followed by large-sheath pondweed (*Potamogeton vaginatus*), white-stem pondweed (*P. praelongus*) and northern watermilfoil (*Myriophyllum exalbescens*). Submergent vegetation grew to a depth of at least 4.8 m, which is 30% of the lake's area (Fig. 4).

Invertebrates

The zooplankton and benthic invertebrates in Seibert Lake were sampled by a researcher from the University of Alberta in 1971 and 1972 (Mackowecki 1973[a]). In July 1971 samples, the most abundant large zooplankton were copepods (mainly *Cyclops* sp. and some *Limnocalanus* sp.) and cladocerans (*Daphnia* sp. and *Diaphanasoma* sp.); ostracods were found occasionally.

Benthic invertebrate samples were collected, in duplicate, at 1.5–m depth intervals along transects at each of 14 sites in July 1971. A further 72 sites were sampled in duplicate at the 3–m depth during July and August of 1971 and 1972. The mean total biomass (wet weight) was 15.9 g/m² (n = 35) for the littoral zone (1.5– to 4.5–m depths) and 4.2 g/m² (n = 28) for the sublittoral zone (6.5– to 9–m depths). These biomass estimates are fairly typical of mesotrophic lakes in Alberta. The dominant littoral species, based on numbers, were scuds (Amphipoda: *Hyalella azteca* and *Gammarus lacustris*), mayfly nymphs (Ephemeroptera: mostly *Ephemera* sp.) and midge larvae (Chironomidae). The dominant sublittoral organisms were midge larvae, scuds and fingernail clams (Sphaeriidae: *Pisidium* sp.).

Fish

The fish species found in Seibert Lake are northern pike, walleye, yellow perch, lake whitefish, burbot, white sucker, Iowa darter,

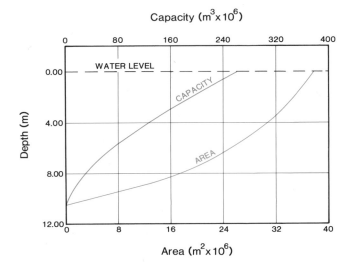

Capacity (m³x10⁶)

Figure 4. Area/capacity curve for Seibert Lake.
SOURCE: Alta. Envir. n.d.[c].

Table 5. Species of aquatic macrophytes in Seibert Lake. Survey conducted during July and August in 1971. Arranged in alphabetical order.

emergent	sedge	*Carex* sp.
	common great bulrush	*Scirpus validus*
	common cattail	*Typha latifolia*
free-floating	star duckweed	*Lemna trisulca*
	bladderwort	*Utricularia* sp.
submergent	coontail	*Ceratophyllum demersum*
	stonewort	*Chara* sp.
	aquatic moss	*Drepanocladus* sp.
	mare's tail	*Hippuris* sp.
	northern watermilfoil	*Myriophyllum exalbescens*
	variable pondweed	*Potamogeton gramineus*
	white-stem pondweed	*P. praelongus*
	Richardson pondweed	*P. richardsonii*
	large-sheath pondweed	*P. vaginatus*
	flat-stemmed pondweed	*P. zosteriformis*
floating-leaved	floating-leaf pondweed	*P. natans*
	yellow pond lily	*Nuphar variegatum*
	smartweed	*Polygonum* sp.

SOURCE: Mackowecki 1973[a]

spottail shiner and brook stickleback. Fathead minnow were recovered from a walleye stomach, but none were collected by seining in 1971 (Mackowecki 1973[a]). Cisco are listed in the commercial fishing records for 1947/48 to 1949/50 but were not recorded in the 1955/56 and 1956/57 seasons, nor were they collected in multiple-mesh test nets set in August 1972. Seibert Lake supported a small, intermittent commercial fishery from the early 1900s to 1957, but at present it is managed for sport fishing only (Alta. For. Ld. Wild. n.d.; Chipeniuk 1975; Alta. Rec. Parks Wild. 1976). Commercial fishing was discontinued after 1957, largely because the lake whitefish were heavily infested with cysts of *Triaenophorus crassus* (McDonald 1964; Alta. Rec. Parks Wild. 1976).

Data for the sport fishery are limited. Questionnaires were sent to all purchasers of Trophy Lake licences from 1970/71 to 1972/73 and, based on the numbers of questionnaires returned, Mackowecki (1973[b]) concluded that anglers at Seibert Lake harvested 277 northern pike in 1970/71, 615 northern pike in 1971/72 and 949 northern pike in 1972/73. Based on a mean weight of 3.4 kg, the anglers in 1972/73 harvested 3 231 kg of pike, which was near the maximal level of harvest at which the population could be maintained. The numbers of large pike in Seibert Lake are currently in decline (Norris 1989).

Walleye are the only other game fish in Seibert Lake. Anglers harvested 1 538 walleye in 1970/71, 2 430 walleye in 1971/72 and 2 636 walleye in 1972/73. These walleye averaged about 800 g in weight, so in 1972/73, the catch weighed about 2 100 kg (Mackowecki 1973[b]). Lake whitefish are caught incidentally by walleye anglers. Their primary role in Seibert Lake appears to be as food for large pike.

Wildlife

There is no information available on the wildlife at Seibert Lake.
M.E. Bradford and J.M. Hanson

References

Alberta Energy and Natural Resources. 1985. Lakeland sub-regional integrated resource plan. Resour. Eval. Plan. Div., Edmonton.
Alberta Environment. n.d.[a]. Envir. Assess. Div., Envir. Qlty. Monit. Br. Unpubl. data, Edmonton.
———. n.d.[b]. Tech. Serv. Div., Hydrol. Br. Unpubl. data, Edmonton.
———. n.d.[c]. Tech. Serv. Div., Surv. Br. Unpubl. data, Edmonton.
Alberta Forestry, Lands and Wildlife. n.d. Fish Wild. Div. Unpubl. data, Edmonton.
———. 1988. Boating in Alberta. Fish Wild. Div., Edmonton.
———. 1989. Guide to sportfishing. Fish Wild. Div., Edmonton.
Alberta Municipal Affairs. 1984. Improvement District No.18 (South) lake planning framework. Plan. Serv. Div., Edmonton.
Alberta Recreation, Parks and Wildlife. 1976. Commercial fisheries catch statistics for Alberta, 1942–1975. Fish Wild. Div., Fish. Mgt. Rep. No. 22, Edmonton.
Alberta Research Council. 1972. Geological map of Alberta. Nat. Resour. Div., Alta. Geol. Surv., Edmonton.
Chipeniuk, R.C. 1975. Lakes of the Lac La Biche district. R.C. Chipeniuk, Lac La Biche.
Energy, Mines and Resources Canada. 1970, 1979. National topographic series 1:50 000 73L/14 (1970), 73L/11 (1979). Surv. Map. Br., Ottawa.
Environment Canada. 1982. Canadian climate normals, Vol. 7: Bright sunshine (1951–1980). Prep. by Atm. Envir. Serv. Supply Serv. Can., Ottawa.
Holmgren, E.J. and P.M. Holmgren. 1976. Over 2000 place names of Alberta. 3rd ed. West. Producer Prairie Books, Saskatoon.
Kocaoglu, S.S. 1975. Reconnaissance soil survey of the Sand River area (73L). Alta. Soil Surv. Rep. No. 34, Univ. Alta. Bull. No. SS–15, Alta. Inst. Pedol. Rep. No. S–74–34 1975. Univ. Alta., Edmonton.
Mackowecki, R. 1973[a]. The trophy pike, *Esox lucius*, of Seibert Lake. MSc thesis. Univ. Alta., Edmonton.
———. 1973[b]. The trophy pike of Seibert Lake. Alta. Ld. For., Fish Wild. Div. Rep. No. 10, Edmonton.
McDonald, D. 1964. Lake survey report: Seibert Lake, also Worm Lake (66–9–W4). Alta. Ld. For., Fish Wild. Div., Edmonton.
Norris, H. 1989. Alta. For. Ld. Wild., Fish Wild. Div., St. Paul. Pers. comm.
Strong, W.L. and K.R. Leggat. 1981. Ecoregions of Alberta. Alta. En. Nat. Resour., Resour. Eval. Plan. Div., Edmonton.

SKELETON LAKE

MAP SHEET: 83I/10
LOCATION: Tp65 R18, 19 W4
LAT/LONG: 54°37'N 112°44'W

Skeleton Lake is a local and regional focal point for water-based recreation. Consequently, this popular lake is quite extensively developed and is used each year by hundreds of Albertans. It is located in the County of Athabasca, 160 km northeast of the city of Edmonton and 6.5 km northeast of the village of Boyle. To reach the lake from Edmonton, take Highway 28 northeast to Highway 63. Travel north on Highway 63 to its junction with Secondary Road 663, then turn east and drive until you are about 5 km past Boyle. Local roads from Secondary Road 663 lead north to the summer villages of Mewatha Beach and Bondiss, on the southern shore of the lake (Fig. 1).

The lake's name is a translation of the Cree *Cheply Sakhahigan*, which means "place of the skeletons" (Holmgren and Holmgren 1976). A Cree chief is buried near the entrance to the Boyle Old-timers Golf Course along the eastern shore of the lake (Alta. Mun. Aff. 1979).

The early local history of the area reflects, to a large extent, the harvest of natural resources such as fur, fish and timber (Alta. Mun. Aff. 1979). Large stands of spruce around the lake attracted logging activity—one sawmill operated on the lakeshore sometime after 1915 and another operated at Bondiss from 1923 to 1940. Log booms were frequently seen on the lake during this period. The Northern Alberta Railway reached the vicinity in 1914, bringing homesteaders and providing the means to ship lumber and fish to local markets. The area immediately north of Boyle was settled mostly by immigrants from the Ukraine (Alta. Cult. Multicult. n.d.). The major economic activity in the region eventually became mixed farming.

The more recent history of the area reflects the importance of the lake's recreational resources. In 1946, a private resort opened at the end of the southeast bay on the site of one of the former sawmills, and later, the summer village of Bondiss grew around the resort. Seasonal cottage development is the predominant form of recreational land use at Skeleton Lake. In addition to the summer villages of Bondiss and Mewatha Beach, several subdivisions are located on the lakeshore. As well, the Edmonton Region Boy Scouts Association has a camp on the eastern shore of the lake that provides canoe training and wilderness outings for members. A public golf course is located just south of this camp (Fig. 2).

Public access to Skeleton Lake is available, but there are no provincial campgrounds or large recreation areas. There are two public boat launches in subdivisions in the north basin (Fig. 2), but no day-use area. Another boat launch is located in the south basin, just south of the narrows. The summer village of Mewatha Beach has a day-use area with picnic tables, fire pits, toilets, a water pump, and a shallow, sandy beach with a designated swimming area. A public boat launch is located nearby, in a public reserve south of the day-use area. The summer village of Bondiss offers two day-use areas. One is located south of the golf course (Fig. 2) and has a boat launch, picnic tables, campstoves, toilets and a playground. The second area is located on the point of land that juts into the southeast bay. It was being developed in 1988; when finished, it will have picnic tables, toilets and a playground. Two commercial campgrounds, one within Bondiss and the other just west of the boundary of Bondiss on the southern shore, offer a variety of facilities to overnight campers and day users.

The most popular recreational activities at the lake during summer

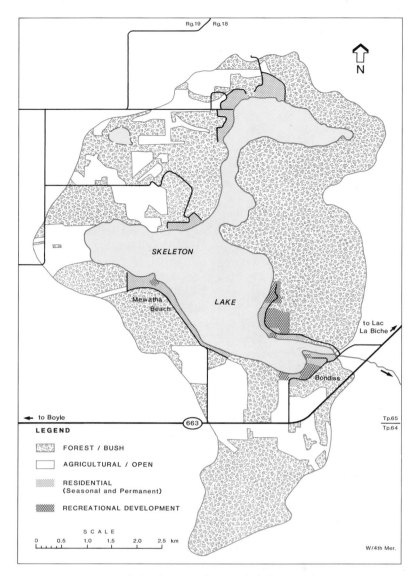

Figure 1. Features of the drainage basin of Skeleton Lake.
SOURCES: Alta. Envir. n.d.[b]; En. Mines Resour. Can. 1973. Updated with 1983 aerial photos.

Table 1. Characteristics of Skeleton Lake drainage basin.

area (excluding lake) (km²)[a]	31.7
soil[b]	Orthic Gray Luvisols
bedrock geology[c]	Lea Park Formation (Upper Cretaceous): shale, ironstone concretions; marine
terrain[b]	gently undulating to strongly rolling
ecoregion[d]	Dry Mixedwood Subregion of Boreal Mixedwood
dominant vegetation[b, d]	trembling aspen
mean annual inflow (m³)[a, e]	1.78 x 10⁶
mean annual sunshine (h)[f]	2 264

NOTE: [e]excluding groundwater inflow
SOURCES: [a]Alta. Envir. n.d.[b]; [b]Pedol. Consult. 1978; [c]Alta. Res. Counc. 1972; [d]Strong and Leggat 1981; [f]Envir. Can. 1982

Table 2. Characteristics of Skeleton Lake.

elevation (m)[a, b]	623.77
surface area (km²)[a, b]	7.89
volume (m³)[a, b]	51.4 x 10⁶
maximum depth (m)[a, b]	17
mean depth (m)[a, b]	6.5
shoreline length (km)[c]	24.7
mean annual lake evaporation (mm)[d]	636
mean annual precipitation (mm)[d]	517
mean residence time (yr)[d, e]	61.5
control structure	none

NOTES: [a]on date of sounding: Aug. 1965; [e]excluding groundwater inflow
SOURCES: [b]Alta. Envir. n.d.[c]; [c]Alta. Mun. Aff. 1979; [d]Alta. Envir. n.d.[b]

are fishing for northern pike and yellow perch, swimming, sightseeing, general relaxation, power boating and water skiing. In winter, ice fishing and general relaxation are the favoured activities (Alta. Mun. Aff. 1979). Boat speeds are restricted to 12 km/hour in posted areas. As well, power boats towing water skiers or surfboarders are prohibited in the narrow channel that joins the north and south basins (Alta. For. Ld. Wild. 1988). There are no sport fishing regulations specific to Skeleton Lake, but provincial limits and regulations apply (Alta. For. Ld. Wild. 1989).

Skeleton Lake is very fertile. Blooms of blue-green algae turn the water green in both basins during summer, but average concentrations of algae in the south basin are higher than in the north basin. Large aquatic plants are common along the entire shoreline and are particularly dense throughout the narrow channel that joins the two basins.

Drainage Basin Characteristics

The area of land that drains into Skeleton Lake is about four times the size of the lake (Tables 1, 2). Precipitation, surface runoff and groundwater are the sources of inflow. Several small intermittent streams flow into the lake, mainly from Organic soil areas. The outlet is a small creek located at the southeast end of the lake (Fig. 1) that drains eastward to Amisk Lake; it is often blocked by beaver dams.

The topography of the drainage basin is quite variable. The land is undulating (2 to 5% slope) in the southern and western portions and moderately to strongly rolling (10 to 30% slope) in the eastern and northern areas. Steep escarpments are present along the south shore of the north basin near the narrows (Pedol. Consult. 1978).

The majority of the watershed is underlain by the marine shales and ironstone concretions of the Lea Park Formation, which is capped by several metres of morainal drift, or glacial till. The till is clay-loam textured, and has slow to very slow permeability rates. It is frequently overlain by a thin, sandy glaciofluvial veneer (Pedol. Consult. 1978).

Skeleton Lake is located in the Dry Mixedwood Subregion of the Boreal Mixedwood Ecoregion (Strong and Leggat 1981). The dominant soils in the drainage basin are moderately well-drained Orthic Gray Luvisols that developed on clay-loam textured till (Pedol. Consult. 1978). They are often found in association with well-drained Orthic Gray Luvisols that developed on the sandy veneers overlying the till. Both soils are located throughout the watershed on undulating to strongly rolling land. They support a tree cover that consists primarily of trembling aspen and secondarily of white spruce, balsam poplar and white birch. Isolated areas of rapidly drained Orthic Regosols are located on level to undulating land along the southern portions of the lake. These soils developed on sand that has been exposed by the receding water levels. When vegetated, they support a cover of balsam poplar, white spruce and shrubs. Organic deposits are significant throughout the watershed. Soils developed on sedge peat support sedges, reeds and coarse grasses, with occasional bluffs of willow and white birch, whereas soils developed on moss peat support an association of black spruce, Labrador tea and *Sphagnum* moss.

Most agricultural activity in the drainage basin takes place in the southern and northwestern sections. The main crops are forage and coarse grains, with some improved land devoted to pasture. Resource extraction is limited. A gas plant is located west of Mewatha Beach (Alta. Mun. Aff. 1979). The lakeshore has been extensively developed for residential use. The first cottage subdivision was established in 1958 when eight lots were subdivided at Bondiss. In 1960, 132 lots were subdivided along the southwestern shore at Mewatha Beach. By 1978, a total of 479 lots had been created on the lakeshore; 75% of them had been developed for cottage use

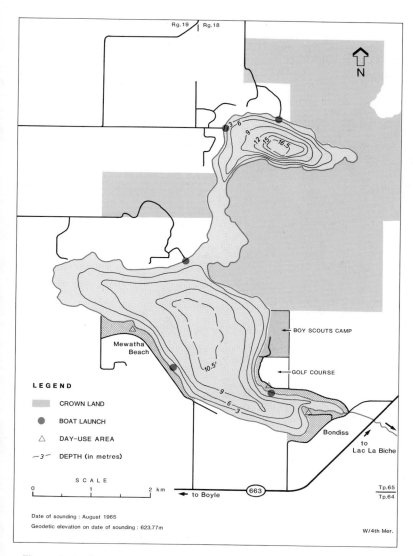

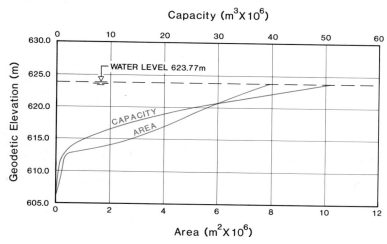

Figure 3. Area/capacity curve for Skeleton Lake.
SOURCE: Alta. Envir. n.d.[c].

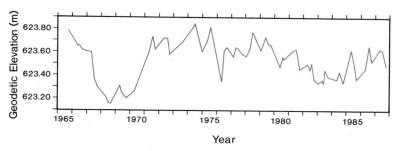

Figure 4. Water level of Skeleton Lake, 1965 to 1987.
SOURCE: Alta. Envir. n.d.[c].

Figure 2. Bathymetry and shoreline features of Skeleton Lake.
BATHYMETRY SOURCE: Alta. Envir. n.d.[c].

(Alta. Mun. Aff. 1979). In response to the increasing development pressures, Skeleton Lake was placed under the jurisdiction of the Regulated Lake Shoreland Development Operation Regulations, which were administered by Alberta Environment. These regulations restricted lakeshore development until a lake management plan was completed and an area structure plan was adopted by the County of Athabasca (Alta. Mun. Aff. 1979; 1980). The purpose of the area structure plan was to provide goals, objectives and policies that would ensure responsible future management of the lake and its surrounding shoreland. In 1988, the plan was in the process of being revised. As of January 1989, a total of 513 lots had been registered at the lake, and 85% had been developed (Alta. Mun. Aff. n.d.).

Lake Basin Characteristics

Skeleton Lake is divided into two basins (Fig. 2). The north basin is separated from the south basin by a shallow, weedy narrows. During the late 1940s, when lake levels were low, the two basins were separated by exposed land at the narrows. The north basin is small and deep, with steeply sloping sides that reach a maximum depth of about 17 m (Table 2). The larger south basin slopes gradually to a maximum depth of only 11 m. The littoral zone extends to a depth of about 3 m (Mitchell 1979) and occupies about 28% of the lake's area (Fig. 3).

The elevation of Skeleton Lake has been monitored since 1965 (Fig. 4). The water level declined during the late 1960s to the historic minimum of 623.15 m in September 1968. The lake level rose during the early 1970s to the historic maximum level of 623.85 m in July 1974. This is a maximum fluctuation of 0.70 m.

Skeleton Lake provides drinking water for the village of Boyle. A pumping station is located in the summer village of Mewatha Beach.

The annual water allocation for Boyle is 185 000 m³. Between 1985 and 1987, the village withdrew an average of 174 000 m³/year (Alta. Envir. n.d.[d]).

Water Quality

The water quality of Skeleton Lake was studied monthly by Alberta Environment in 1978, 1979, 1985 and 1986 (Alta. Envir. n.d.[a]; Mitchell 1979; Alta. Envir. 1985), and in 1989 by volunteer citizens from the summer village of Bondiss (Mitchell 1989). The studies from the two earlier years provided a data base for the development of the Skeleton Lake Area Structure Plan. Similarly, the later studies were requested so that changes in water quality over the six-year interval could be detected and recommendations incorporated into the 1988 area structure plan. The lake was also sampled once in August 1984 and once in March 1985 by researchers at the University of Alberta (Prepas n.d.).

Skeleton Lake has fresh water with high levels of bicarbonate; the dominant cations are calcium and magnesium (Table 3). The ionic composition of both basins is very similar, but they have different temperature patterns. The north basin, which is deep and protected from wind, is thermally stratified throughout the ice-free period, whereas the south basin mixes periodically and stratifies only during relatively calm periods (Fig. 5). In the north basin during summer, thermal stratification results in anoxic conditions below a depth of about 9 m (Fig. 6). In the south basin during summer, dissolved oxygen gradually becomes depleted with depth, and in each year sampled, the concentration of dissolved oxygen in water near the sediments declined to less than 1 mg/L. During winter, both basins became anoxic below depths of about 9 to 10 m (Fig. 6). The upper layers of water, however, were well oxygenated.

Table 3. Major ions and related water quality variables for Skeleton Lake. Average concentrations in mg/L; pH in pH units. Composite samples from the euphotic zone collected 6 times from the north basin between 22 May and 01 Oct. 1985 and 7 times from the south basin between 22 May and 31 Oct. 1985. S.E. = standard error.

	North		South	
	Mean	S.E.	Mean	S.E.
pH (range)	8.4–8.8	—	8.5–8.8	—
total alkalinity (CaCO₃)	170	1.2	178	0.6
specific conductivity (μS/cm)	318	3.5	333	0.8
total dissolved solids (calculated)	172	1.0	181	0.9
total hardness (CaCO₃)	135	1.1	143	2.0
total particulate carbon	1	0.1	2	0.3
dissolved organic carbon	15	0.3	14	0.3
HCO₃	198	3.3	208	1.9
CO₃	<5	—	<6	—
Mg	19	0.4	19	0.4
Na	13	0.2	14	0.3
K	8	0.02	9	0.05
Cl	<2	—	<2	—
SO₄	<5	—	<5	—
Ca	23	0.4	26	0.9

SOURCE: Alta. Envir. n.d.[a], Naquadat stations 01AT06AA2501 (north), 01AT06AA2301 (south)

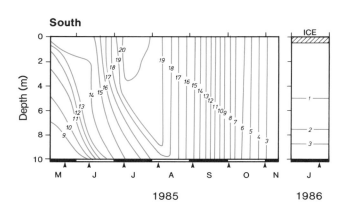
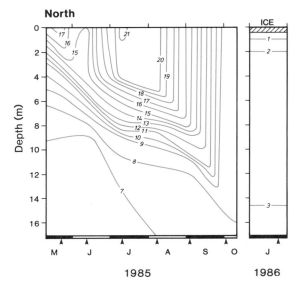

Figure 5. Temperature (°C) of Skeleton Lake, north and south basins, 1985 and 1986. Arrows indicate sampling dates. SOURCE: Alta. Envir. n.d.[a].

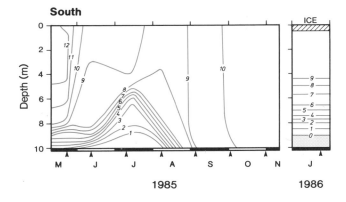
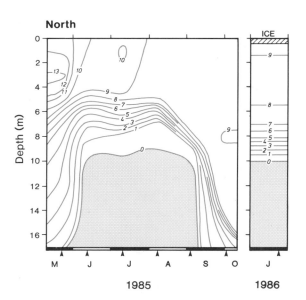

Figure 6. Dissolved oxygen (mg/L) in Skeleton Lake, north and south basins, 1985 and 1986. Arrows indicate sampling dates. SOURCE: Alta. Envir. n.d.[a].

Table 4. Nutrient, chlorophyll _a_ and Secchi depth data for Skeleton Lake. Average concentrations in μg/L. Samples from the euphotic zone collected 6 times from 22 May to 01 Oct. 1985 and 6 times from 27 May to 21 Oct. 1986. S.E. = standard error.

| | NORTH | | | | SOUTH | | | |
| | 1985 | | 1986 | | 1985[a] | | 1986 | |
	Mean	S.E.	Mean	S.E.	Mean	S.E.	Mean	S.E.
total phosphorus	—	—	36	4.9	—	—	47	3.6
total dissolved phosphorus	—	—	10	1.5	—	—	11	0.8
total Kjeldahl nitrogen	1 160	25.8	1 140	15.5	1 139	45.6	1 318[b]	91.4
$NO_3 + NO_2$–nitrogen	<3	—	<4	—	<3	—	<3[b]	—
NH_4–nitrogen	21	10.2	32	11.8	13	1.0	37[b]	10.4
iron	<47	—	<20	—	<46	—	<26[b]	—
chlorophyll _a_	9.2	1.11	10.7	2.52	15.7	2.60	24.2	5.63
Secchi depth (m)	2.5	0.43	2.5	0.38	2.0	0.14	1.6	0.20

NOTES: [a]n = 7 (includes 31 Oct.); [b]n = 5
SOURCE: Alta. Envir. n.d.[a], Naquadat stations 01AT06AA2501 (north), 01AT06AA2301 (south)

Table 5. Theoretical external total phosphorus loading to Skeleton Lake.

	Source	Phosphorus (kg/yr)	Percentage of Total
watershed	forested/bush	224	33
	agricultural/cleared	137	20
	residential/cottage	106	16
sewage[a]		10	2
precipitation/dustfall		205	30
	TOTAL	682	100

annual areal loading (g/m² of lake surface) 0.086

NOTE: [a]unmeasured: assumes 4% of all sewage effluent from residences and camps enters the lake, as in Mitchell 1982
SOURCE: Mitchell 1989

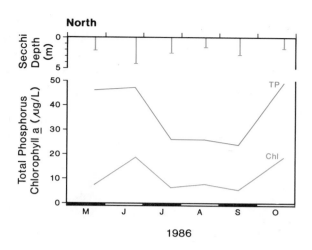

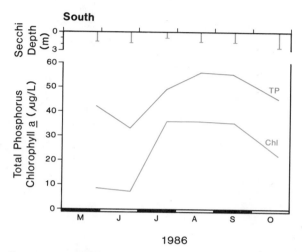

Figure 7. Total phosphorus, chlorophyll _a_ and Secchi depth in Skeleton Lake, north and south basins, 1986. SOURCE: Alta. Envir. n.d.[a].

The trophic status of the two basins also differ: the north basin is mesotrophic, whereas the south basin is eutrophic. The north basin has about half as much chlorophyll _a_, less total phosphorus, and generally more transparent water than the south basin (Table 4). The basins also exhibit different patterns of chlorophyll _a_ over the ice-free period. In the strongly thermally stratified north basin, chlorophyll _a_ levels are highest in May or June and in October (Fig. 7). In the shallower south basin, chlorophyll _a_ levels are high continuously from July through October. The different pattern occurs because the south basin mixes periodically during summer. Mixing circulates phosphorus-rich water overlying the sediments into the upper water, where it replenishes the nutrient supply to growing algae. In the north basin, nutrients are trapped in the bottom water except when the lake mixes in spring and fall.

The productivity of Skeleton Lake has remained stable over the period between the two studies. The average concentrations of chlorophyll _a_ and the average Secchi depth in 1985/86 were very similar to those values recorded in 1978/79:

| | North Basin | | South Basin | |
	1978/79	1985/86	1978/79	1985/86
chlorophyll _a_ (μg/L)	10.1	10.0	20.8	19.2
Secchi depth (m)	2.6	2.5	1.8	1.9

Although chlorophyll _a_ levels in the two study periods are similar, there are differences among the four years sampled. In 1978 and 1986, considerably higher concentrations of algae were measured than in 1979 and 1985. Values for 1985 and 1986 are given in Table 4. These variations are probably related to weather conditions, since several lakes in central Alberta have exhibited similar patterns.

The theoretical external supply of phosphorus to Skeleton Lake is estimated to be 682 kg/year (Table 5). The largest contributions are made by surface runoff from forested land (33%) and precipitation and dustfall (30%). The phosphorus supply that enters the lake in sewage effluent from residential areas and campgrounds has not been measured, but it is estimated to be about 2% of the external total phosphorus load. Phosphorus loading from internal sources such as bottom sediments and groundwater has not been estimated, but is probably high in the south basin.

Biological Characteristics

Plants

The phytoplankton in the two basins of Skeleton Lake was studied monthly by Alberta Environment during 1978, 1985 and 1986, and by researchers at the University of Alberta on 14 August 1984 and 12 March 1985 (Alta. Envir. n.d.[a]; Prepas n.d.; Mitchell 1979). The average algal biomass in Skeleton Lake differs between years. In 1985 and 1986, chlorophyll _a_ concentrations indicated that a greater average biomass of algae was present in 1986 than in 1985 (Table 4); actual biomass measurements supported this conclusion. In 1986, the average algal biomass was 37% higher in the north basin and 60% higher in the south basin than in 1985. Average algal biomass differs between basins, as well. In 1986 (Table 6), the

Table 6. Percentage composition of major algal groups by total biomass in Skeleton Lake, 1986. Composite samples collected from the euphotic zone.

ALGAL GROUP	27 May	24 June	22 July	19 Aug.	16 Sep.	21 Oct.
North Basin						
Total Biomass (mg/L)	0.95	3.65	1.92	2.10	0.92	1.15
Percentage Composition:						
Cyanophyta	1	44	50	45	51	21
		Anabaena ————————————————→				*Lyngbya*
Chlorophyta	4	8	8	5	17	14
Euglenophyta	0	0	0	2	2	0
Chrysophyta	33	1	4	1	5	0
	Ochromonas					
Bacillariophyta	4	39	0	0	4	21
		Melosira				*Cyclotella*
Cryptophyta	54	4	8	15	10	42
	Cryptomonas					*Cryptomonas Rhodomonas*
Pyrrhophyta	4	4	29	32	11	2
			Ceratium ————→			
South Basin						
Total Biomass (mg/L)	2.54	1.73	9.52	6.02	5.37	3.47
Percentage Composition:						
Cyanophyta	9	13	59	52	34	11
			Anabaena ————→			
Chlorophyta	5	4	4	2	8	9
Euglenophyta	0	0	4	0	0	0
Chrysophyta	8	1	0	2	1	0
Bacillariophyta	64	33	11	25	7	53
	Stephanodiscus ————————————————————————————→					
Cryptophyta	12	10	2	4	9	26
						Cryptomonas
Pyrrhophyta	1	57	21	15	4	1
		Ceratium ————→				

SOURCE: Alta. Envir. n.d.[a]

Table 7. Estimated angler numbers, effort and harvest from Skeleton Lake. Estimates based on creel survey data collected from 17 May to 27 Aug. 1985. A total of 38 weekdays and 33 weekend days and holidays were surveyed; 37 weekdays were not included. Information was collected from 07:00 to 23:00. WE = walleye; NP = northern pike; YP = yellow perch.

	WE	NP	YP	Total
number of anglers[a]	—	—	—	5 349
angler-hours[b]	—	—	—	11 131
total number fish harvested[c]	<10	1 837	5 699	7 536[d]
total yield (kg)	—	1 653	985	2 638
mean weight (g)	—	900	173	—
catch/angler-hour	—	0.26	1.04	1.30
harvest/angler-hour[b, c]	—	0.16	0.53	0.69
harvest/angler[a, c]	—	0.33	1.11	1.44

NOTES: [a]observed no. anglers = 1 889; [b]observed hours = 3 925; [c]based on observed no. fish kept: WE = 2, NP = 617, YP = 2 099; [d]excluding WE
SOURCE: Sullivan 1987

average biomass in the south basin (4.78 mg/L) during the open-water season was almost 3 times the biomass in the north basin (1.78 mg/L).

The species composition of algae in the two basins is similar. In 1986 (Table 6), species of blue-green algae (Cyanophyta) such as *Anabaena flos-aquae*, *A. spiroides*, *Aphanizomenon flos-aquae* and *Lyngbya limnetica* were dominant in both basins on most sampling dates from June to October. Species of green algae (Chlorophyta) and Euglenophyta were not common in either basin, and golden-brown species (Chrysophyta: *Ochromonas globosa*) formed

more than 20% of the biomass only in the north basin in late May. Diatoms (Bacillariophyta) formed more than 20% of the biomass in the north basin in June (*Melosira islandica*) and October (*Cyclotella* sp.) and in the south basin in May, June, August and October (*Stephanodiscus niagarae*). Cryptophytes (mostly *Cryptomonas erosa*, *C. Marsonii*, *C. ovata* and *Rhodomonas minuta nannoplanctic*) were an important part of the biomass in May only in the north basin and in October in both basins. Pyrrhophyta, particularly *Ceratium hirundinella*, were common in July and August in the north basin and in June and July in the south basin.

Aquatic macrophytes were surveyed by Alberta Environment in September 1978 (Fig. 8). Much of the shoreline in the south basin was not surveyed because dense blue-green algal growth obscured observation. Therefore, blank areas on Figure 8 do not necessarily indicate an absence of plants. The dominant species of emergent vegetation in the main basin was bulrush (*Scirpus* sp.). Small stands of common cattail (*Typha latifolia*) grew in protected areas and cattails, or cattails associated with sedge (*Carex* sp.), lined the edges of the narrows. A large bed of bulrushes grew in the centre of the channel and a large stand of reed grass (*Phragmites communis*) occupied the southern entrance to the narrows. Dominant species of submergent vegetation included large-sheath pondweed (*Potamogeton vaginatus*), Sago pondweed (*P. pectinatus*), Richardson pondweed (*P. richardsonii*), coontail (*Ceratophyllum demersum*), northern watermilfoil (*Myriophyllum exalbescens*), star duckweed (*Lemna trisulca*) and stonewort (*Chara* sp.). Most species were observed growing to greater depths in the clearer water of the north basin than in the south basin.

Invertebrates

The relative abundance of zooplankton in Skeleton Lake was studied by Alberta Environment in 1978 (Mitchell 1979). Fifteen zooplankton species were identified in the north basin, and 21 species in the south basin. The most abundant species throughout the lake were two copepods, *Diaptomus sicilis* and *Diacyclops bicuspidatus thomasi*. In the north basin, the cladocerans *Daphnia galeata mendotae* and *D. retrocurva* were abundant as well. The small cladoceran *Chydorus sphaericus*, which inhabits shallow, weedy areas in early summer and deeper water during blue-green algal blooms, was abundant in the productive south basin. Rotifers did not form a large portion of the zooplankton numbers, although they were relatively abundant in May and June. The dominant species were *Kellicottia longispina*, *Keratella cochlearis* and *Sychaeta* sp.

Recent data for the benthic invertebrate community are not available.

Fish

Eight species of fish are known to inhabit Skeleton Lake: lake whitefish, northern pike, walleye, cisco, burbot, yellow perch, white sucker and spottail shiner (Alta. For. Ld. Wild. n.d.). The lake is managed for domestic, commercial and recreational fisheries. There are no data available for the domestic fishery.

Commercial fishing records for Skeleton Lake date back to 1944. Until the mid–1950s, the main catch was cisco, and harvests were as high as 29 940 kg, as in 1953/54. The lake was closed to fishing from 1956 to 1959. By the early 1960s, the focus of the fishery changed from cisco to lake whitefish (Alta. Rec. Parks Wild. 1976; Brown 1980). Whitefish harvests have ranged from a 1963/64 high of 14 218 kg to a 1972/73 low of 181 kg. During the early 1980s, catches of all species were low. In 1983/84 and 1984/85, no licences were issued, and in 1985/86, the single licensee took 260 kg of whitefish and a total of 79 kg of walleye, white suckers, burbot and northern pike. Since 1985/86, the whitefish catch has been used for collection of roe for production of caviar. After the eggs are taken, the rest of the fish is used for animal food (Sullivan 1989). In 1987/88, 10 782 kg of whitefish were taken by 10 licensees (Alta. For. Ld. Wild. n.d.). Both the whitefish and cisco in Skeleton Lake are heavily infested with cysts of the tapeworm *Triaenophorus crassus,* and are not sold for human consumption.

Skeleton Lake has one of the more important and popular sport fisheries in the Lakeland Region of Alberta. Northern pike and yellow perch are the main catches. Prior to 1988, the walleye population was quite small. Little or no recruitment had occurred in recent years and the population appeared to consist only of older individuals. In 1988, Skeleton Lake became a high priority lake in the provincial walleye enhancement program. That year, the lake was stocked with 150 000 5–cm–long walleye fingerlings. Stocking was to continue through 1989 and 1990, after which, the sport catch was to be monitored (Berry 1988).

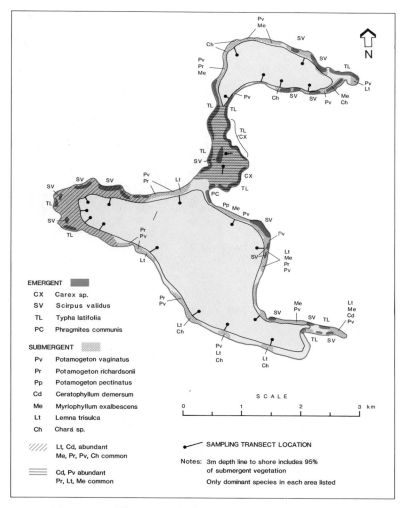

Figure 8. Species composition and distribution of aquatic macrophytes in Skeleton Lake, September 1978.
SOURCE: Mitchell 1979.

A creel survey of the sport fishery was conducted during 1985 (Sullivan 1987). Northern pike and yellow perch were the main catches, and a few walleye were taken. It was estimated that, from May to August, 5 349 anglers fished for 11 131 hours (Table 7). Approximately 39% of the northern pike caught and 49% of the yellow perch caught were released. On a regional basis, the average harvest/angler-hour for 22 lakes in the Northeast Region surveyed between 1984 and 1987 was 0.22 for northern pike and 0.32 for yellow perch (Alta. For. Ld. Wild. n.d.). In comparison, the harvest per unit effort at Skeleton Lake was lower than average for northern pike (0.16 pike/angler-hour) and almost twice the regional average for yellow perch (0.53 perch/angler-hour). Only 21% of the anglers interviewed caught one or more pike and 32% caught one or more perch. The mean size of the pike and perch was considered average. During the survey period, Skeleton Lake received moderate angling pressure of 14.5 angler-hours/ha. Most of the angling effort was concentrated around the shoreline.

Wildlife

The main species of waterfowl present on the lake are grebes, Common Loon, Lesser Scaup, Mallard and Bufflehead. Prime waterfowl nesting and habitat areas are those areas that support abundant emergent vegetation. Although the lake is not a good production area for Mallards, they are quite abundant along the southern and eastern shores (Alta. Mun. Aff. 1979).

The forested shorelands around the lake provide fairly good habitat for white-tailed deer, moose, black bears, coyotes, porcupines, varying hares, skunks, mink, muskrats, beaver and squirrels. Upland game birds that frequent the area are Sharp-tailed and Ruffed grouse (Alta. Mun. Aff. 1979).

M.E. Bradford

References

Alberta Culture and Multiculturalism. n.d. Hist. Resour. Div., Hist. Sites Serv. Unpubl. data, Edmonton.

Alberta Environment. n.d.[a]. Envir. Assess. Div., Envir. Qlty. Monit. Br. Unpubl. data, Edmonton.

————. n.d.[b]. Tech. Serv. Div., Hydrol. Br. Unpubl. data, Edmonton.

————. n.d.[c]. Tech. Serv. Div., Surv. Br. Unpubl. data, Edmonton.

————. n.d.[d]. Water Resour. Admin. Div., Sur. Water Rights Br. Unpubl. data, Edmonton.

————. 1985. Skeleton Lake. Poll. Contr. Div., Water Qlty. Contr. Br., Edmonton.

Alberta Forestry, Lands and Wildlife. n.d. Fish Wild. Div. Unpubl. data, Edmonton.

————. 1988. Boating in Alberta. Fish Wild. Div., Edmonton.

————. 1989. Guide to sportfishing. Fish Wild. Div., Edmonton.

Alberta Municipal Affairs. n.d. Plan. Serv. Div., Plan. Br. Unpubl. data, Edmonton.

————. 1979. Skeleton Lake management study. Prep. for Co. Athabasca and SV Mewatha Beach, Athabasca by Plan. Serv. Div., Plan. Br., Edmonton.

————. 1980. Skeleton Lake area structure plan. Prep. for Co. Athabasca and SV Mewatha Beach, Athabasca by Plan. Serv. Div., Reg. Plan. Sec., Edmonton.

Alberta Recreation, Parks and Wildlife. 1976. Commercial fisheries catch statistics for Alberta, 1942–1975. Fish Wild. Div., Fish. Mgt. Rep. No. 22, Edmonton.

Alberta Research Council. 1972. Geological map of Alberta. Nat. Resour. Div., Alta. Geol. Surv., Edmonton.

Berry, D. 1988. Alta. For. Ld. Wild., Fish Wild. Div., Edmonton. Pers. comm.

Brown, D. 1980. Growth, maturity and fecundity of lake whitefish, *Coregonus clupeaformis,* Skeleton Lake, Alberta. Alta. En. Nat. Resour., Fish Wild. Div. Unpubl. rep., Edmonton.

Energy, Mines and Resources Canada. 1973. National topographic series 1:50 000 83I/10 (1973). Surv. Map. Br., Ottawa.

Environment Canada. 1982. Canadian climate normals, Vol. 7: Bright sunshine (1951–1980). Prep. by Atm. Envir. Serv. Supply Serv. Can., Ottawa.

Holmgren, E.J. and P.M. Holmgren. 1976. Over 2000 place names of Alberta. 3rd ed. West. Producer Prairie Books, Saskatoon.

Mitchell, P.A. 1979. Skeleton, Garner, Muriel Lakes water quality studies. Alta. Envir., Poll. Contr. Div., Water Qlty. Contr. Br., Edmonton.

————. 1982. Evaluation of the "septic snooper" on Wabamun and Pigeon lakes. Alta. Envir., Poll. Contr. Div., Water Qlty. Contr Br., Edmonton.

————. 1989. Alta. Envir., Envir. Assess. Div., Envir. Qlty. Monit. Br., Edmonton. Pers. comm.

Pedology Consultants. 1978. Soil survey and land suitability of the Skeleton Lake study area. Prep. for Alta. Envir., Plan. Div., Edmonton.

Prepas, E.E. n.d. Univ. Alta., Dept. Zool. Unpubl. data, Edmonton.

Strong, W.L. and K.R. Leggat. 1981. Ecoregions of Alberta. Alta. En. Nat. Resour., Resour. Eval. Plan. Div., Edmonton.

Sullivan, M.G. 1987. Characteristics and impacts of the sport fishery at Skeleton Lake during May-August 1985. Alta. For. Ld. Wild., Fish Wild. Div. Unpubl. rep., Edmonton.

————. 1989. Alta. For. Ld. Wild., Fish Wild. Div., St. Paul. Pers. comm.

TOUCHWOOD LAKE

MAP SHEET: 73L/14

LOCATION: Tp66–68 R9, 10 W4

LAT/LONG: 54°49'W 111°24'N

Touchwood Lake is a beautiful wilderness lake set in heavily forested, rolling hills. It is located in the Lakeland Region of Improvement District No. 18 (South), 265 km northeast of Edmonton and 45 km east of the town of Lac La Biche, which is the closest large population centre. To drive to the lake from the town of Lac La Biche, take Secondary Road 868 around the southeast bay of Lac La Biche for about 15 km until you see the sign indicating the road to Touchwood Lake. Drive east on this improved road for 30 km to the Touchwood Lake Forest Recreation Area on the northwest shore of the lake (Fig. 1).

The word "touchwood" refers to birch punk, which was used to start fires with flint and steel. In Cree, *Pusakan Sakhahigan* means "Punk" or "Touchwood" Lake. The Cree had, however, used this term to refer to nearby Pinehurst Lake. They had called Touchwood Lake *Nameygos Sakhahegan*, which means Trout Lake, in reference to the abundant large lake trout found there (Chipeniuk 1975). By the late 1920s, however, the trout population had apparently been decimated by the commercial fishery, and in spite of stocking during the 1960s and 1980s, no trout have been reported in the commercial or recreational fisheries (Norris 1989). There are no records of permanent or semipermanent residents living at Touchwood Lake. Cabins on the southwest shore were reported to be used during the 1930s by brewers of illegal "moonshine" (Chipeniuk 1975).

Access to the lake is available only at Touchwood Lake Forest Recreation Area (Fig. 2). This Alberta Forest Service campground is open from May to September. It offers 91 campsites, pump water, a beach and a boat launch, but there is no day-use area. There are no boating restrictions over most of Touchwood Lake, but in posted areas such as the designated swimming area, all boats are prohibited (Alta. For. Ld. Wild. 1988).

A 107–ha parcel of land at Touchwood Lake has been reserved for recreation by Alberta Forestry, Lands and Wildlife. It also holds the status of Protective Notation, which means that the potential of the land as a natural area has been recognized but a natural area has not been established (Alta. For. Ld. Wild. 1987[b]). The land is located mainly on, and north of, the peninsula on the western shore. It includes mature white spruce and white spruce/balsam fir forests, beach ridges with lodgepole pine/jack pine stands and white spruce/trembling aspen forests. Access to the area is by boat only; picnic tables are provided.

Concentrations of algae in Touchwood Lake are low throughout the open-water period, so the water is transparent. The density of aquatic vegetation is sparse to moderate, with many unvegetated areas along the lakeshore. Walleye and northern pike are the main species caught by the popular sport fishery. There are no special sport fishing regulations for Touchwood Lake, but provincial limits and regulations apply (Alta. For. Ld. Wild. 1989). The lake also supports commercial and domestic fisheries for lake whitefish.

Drainage Basin Characteristics

Touchwood Lake is a headwater lake. It drains quite a large area, but because of the lake's large size, the drainage basin is less than 4 times the size of the lake (Tables 1, 2). Most of the dozen inlet streams flow into the north and west sides of the lake (Fig. 1). The outlet stream flows to Pinehurst Lake, 6 km to the south, and eventually to the Beaver River via Punk Creek and the Sand River.

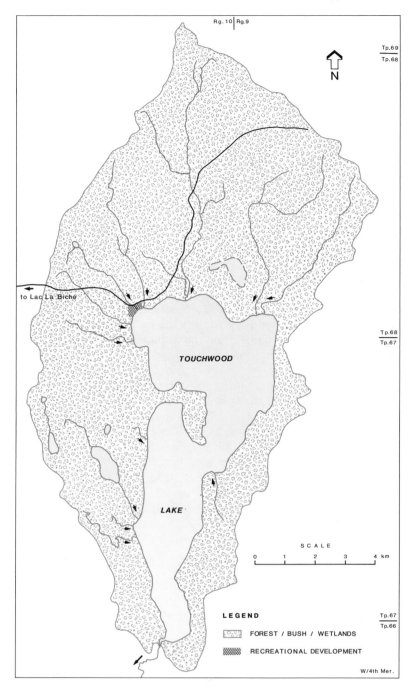

Figure 1. Features of the drainage basin of Touchwood Lake.
SOURCES: Alta. Envir. n.d.[b]; En. Mines Resour. Can. 1970; 1979.
Updated with 1982 aerial photos.

Table 1. Characteristics of Touchwood Lake drainage basin.

area (excluding lake) (km²)[a]	111
soil[b]	Orthic Gray Luvisols, Eluviated Eutric Brunisols, Humic Luvic Gleysols, Mesisols
bedrock geology[c]	La Biche Formation (Upper Cretaceous): shale, ironstone partings and concretions; marine
terrain[b]	level to moderately rolling
ecoregion[d]	Moist and Wet Mixedwood subregions of Boreal Mixedwood
dominant vegetation[d]	trembling aspen, balsam poplar, lodgepole pine
mean annual inflow (m³)[a, e]	9.43 x 10⁶
mean annual sunshine (h)[f]	2 240

NOTE: [e]excluding groundwater inflow
SOURCES: [a]Alta. Envir. n.d.[b]; [b]Kocaoglu 1975; [c]Alta. Res. Counc. 1972; [d]Strong and Leggat 1981; [f]Envir. Can. 1982

Table 2. Characteristics of Touchwood Lake.

elevation (m)[a, b]	630.90 to 631.95
surface area (km²)[b, c]	29.0
volume (m³)[b, c]	430 x 10⁶
maximum depth (m)[b, c]	40
mean depth (m)[b, c]	14.8
shoreline length (km)[d]	36.6
mean annual lake evaporation (mm)[e]	640
mean annual precipitation (mm)[e]	528
mean residence time (yr)[e, f]	69.5
control structure	none

NOTES: [a]range over period of water level record; [b]on date of sounding: Nov. 1964; [f]excluding groundwater inflow
SOURCES: [c]Alta. Envir. n.d.[c]; [d]Mills 1987; [e]Alta. Envir. n.d.[b]

The watershed is underlain by the shale and ironstone of the La Biche Formation. The land is generally level to moderately rolling and the relief is about 214 m. The elevation of the land is highest at the extreme northern tip of the drainage basin (846 m) and lowest along the lakeshore (632 m). North and northeast of the lake, the land is part of a hummocky morainal plain that is characterized by rough, irregular knob and kettle topography (Kocaoglu 1975). The knobs and ridges consist mainly of glacial till and secondarily of glaciofluvial sand and gravel. The remainder of the drainage basin is part of a rolling morainal plain that features minor ridges and knobs intermixed with many wet depressions and small peat bogs.

Soils throughout the drainage basin are mainly moderately well-drained Orthic Gray Luvisols (Kocaoglu 1975). These soils formed on fine loamy, weakly to strongly calcareous glacial till. Secondary soils are well-drained Eluviated Eutric Brunisols on undulating to gently rolling land, poorly drained Humic Luvic Gleysols on level land, and poorly to very poorly drained Mesisols on depressional to level land.

The drainage basin north of the lake is part of the Wet Mixedwood Subregion of the Boreal Mixedwood Ecoregion (Strong and Leggat 1981). The dominant trees are an association of trembling aspen, balsam poplar and lodgepole pine on moderately well-drained Gray Luvisols. The southern portion of the drainage is part of the Moist Mixedwood Subregion. The main trees are trembling aspen and balsam poplar on moderately well-drained Gray Luvisols. Other species present in both subregions are jack pine on Eutric Brunisols, white spruce on imperfectly drained Gleysols and Gray Luvisols, and black spruce, willows and sedges on Gleysols and/or Organic soils.

All of the land in the drainage basin belongs to the Crown. In the Lakeland Sub-Regional Integrated Resource Plan, the primary management objective for the Touchwood Lake area is to develop it as

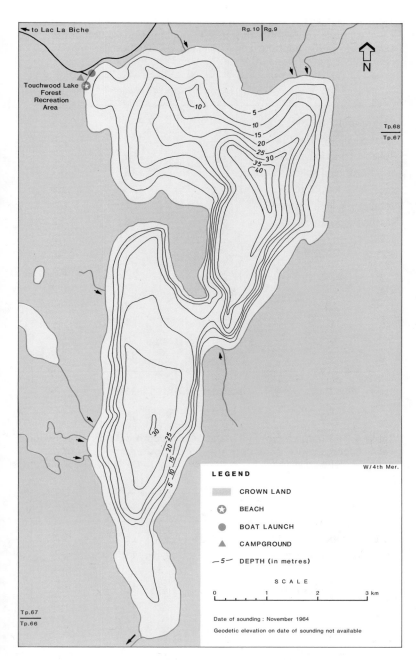

Figure 2. Bathymetry and shoreline features of Touchwood Lake.
BATHYMETRY SOURCE: Alta. Envir. n.d.[c].

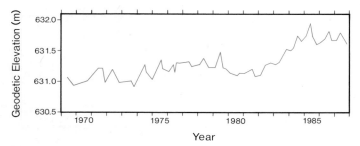

Figure 3. Water level of Touchwood Lake, 1969 to 1987.
SOURCE: Alta. Envir. n.d.[c].

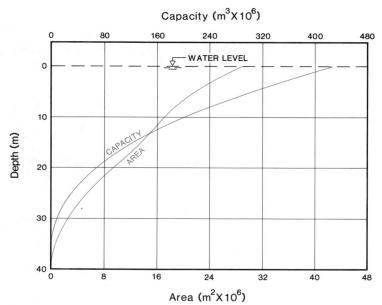

Figure 4. Area/capacity curve for Touchwood Lake.
SOURCE: Alta. Envir. n.d.[c].

a major recreation destination area for water-based and upland recreation activities (Alta. En. Nat. Resour. 1985[a]). Under this plan, no improved grazing, industrial development, or exploration and development of oil sands, minerals or coal are allowed in the watershed. Commercial, residential and cottage development may be permitted.

Lake Basin Characteristics

Touchwood Lake is one of the largest bodies of water in the Lakeland Region. It is separated into two basins by a large peninsula (Fig. 2). The north basin, with a maximum depth of 40 m, is the deepest of the two. The lake bottom in the northern portion of this basin slopes relatively gradually, but toward the "narrows" the sides of the basin are quite steep. This steepness continues throughout the south basin, with the exception of the southern tip of the lake.

The elevation of Touchwood Lake has been monitored since 1969 (Fig. 3). The historic minimum, 630.90 m, was recorded in September 1973, and the maximum, 631.95 m, was recorded in May 1985. A fluctuation of this size (1.05 m) would cause the lake's surface area to vary by about 3% (Fig. 4).

Water Quality

The water quality of Touchwood Lake was assessed by Alberta Environment monthly from May to November 1986, and once each in March 1986 and February 1987 (Alta. Envir. n.d.[a]). The water is fresh, well-buffered and hard and the dominant ions are bicarbonate and calcium (Table 3).

In 1986, Touchwood Lake was weakly thermally stratified at the end of May, strongly stratified from June to early September and well-mixed in the autumn (Fig. 5). During 1986, dissolved oxygen concentrations in the upper layers of the water column were sufficient for fish survival, but there was substantial dissolved oxygen depletion in the deeper water. Concentrations of less than 2 mg/L were found at depths greater than 14 m in September (Fig. 6). The dissolved oxygen concentration was a uniform 9 mg/L from surface to bottom during November. Dissolved oxygen was depleted near the bottom sediments during the winter months, but concentrations were higher than 4 mg/L throughout most of the water column on both dates sampled (Fig. 6).

Touchwood Lake is mesotrophic. In 1986, the average chlorophyll *a* concentration was quite low and the water was generally very transparent (Table 4). The highest total phosphorus and chlorophyll *a* concentrations in 1986 were recorded in late May. The chlorophyll *a* concentration declined from a May high of 12 μg/L to 2 μg/L in mid-August, then increased slightly in October (Fig. 7). Phosphorus concentrations decreased from a maximum of 28 μg/L in May to 18 μg/L in June, increased moderately in July and then decreased again until September. Chlorophyll *a* concentrations and Secchi depth did not reflect the elevated phosphorus concentrations in October and early November. Secchi depths increased from 3 m in late May to 11 m in early November. The amount of phosphorus released from the bottom sediments in the euphotic zone was estimated for the period from June through August in 1986 (Shaw and

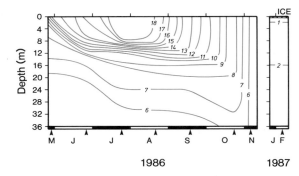

Figure 5. Temperature (°C) of Touchwood Lake, 1986 and 1987. Arrows indicate sampling dates.
SOURCE: Alta. Envir. n.d.[a].

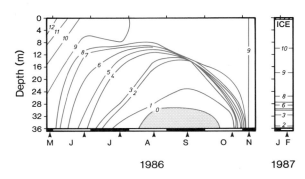

Figure 6. Dissolved oxygen (mg/L) in Touchwood Lake, 1986 and 1987. Arrows indicate sampling dates.
SOURCE: Alta. Envir. n.d.[a].

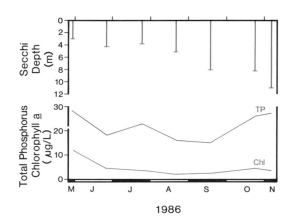

Figure 7. Total phosphorus, chlorophyll *a* and Secchi depth in Touchwood Lake, 1986.
SOURCE: Alta. Envir. n.d.[a].

Table 3. Major ions and related water quality variables for Touchwood Lake. Average concentrations in mg/L; pH in pH units. Composite samples from the euphotic zone collected 7 times from 28 May to 05 Nov. 1986. S.E. = standard error.

	Mean	S.E.
pH (range)	7.8–8.5	—
total alkalinity (CaCO$_3$)	143	0.6
specific conductivity (μS/cm)	268	2.5
total dissolved solids (calculated)	146	0.7
total hardness (CaCO$_3$)	128	1.8
total particulate carbon	1[a]	0.1
dissolved organic carbon	36	0.8
HCO$_3$	170	2.3
CO$_3$	<3	—
Mg	11	0.3
Na	7	0.2
K	3	0
Cl	<1	—
SO$_4$	<5	—
Ca	33	0.3

NOTE: [a]n = 6
SOURCE: Alta. Envir. n.d.[a], Naquadat station 01AL06AB2500

Table 4. Nutrient, chlorophyll *a* and Secchi depth data for Touchwood Lake. Average concentrations in μg/L. Composite samples from the euphotic zone collected 7 times from 28 May to 05 Nov. 1986. S.E. = standard error.

	Mean	S.E.
total phosphorus	22	2.1
total dissolved phosphorus	11	2.5
total Kjeldahl nitrogen	761	111.4
NO$_3$ + NO$_2$–nitrogen	<10	—
NH$_4$–nitrogen	<26	—
chlorophyll *a*	4.6	1.27
Secchi depth (m)	6.3	1.10

SOURCE: Alta. Envir. n.d.[a], Naquadat station 01AL06AB2500

Prepas 1989). This estimate (3.3 mg/m^2 per day, or 92 kg per day to the whole lake) indicates that shallow sediments are probably a major source of phosphorus for algal growth in Touchwood Lake.

Biological Characteristics

Plants

The phytoplankton community of Touchwood Lake was examined by Alberta Environment monthly during the open-water season in 1986 (Alta. Envir. n.d.[a]). Total phytoplankton biomass followed the same seasonal pattern as chlorophyll *a* concentration. Biomass was highest in late May (1.91 mg/L), decreased until mid-August, and then increased slightly in late October (Table 5). Diatoms (Bacillariophyta) formed most of the biomass from May to July (*Cyclotella comta*) and again in November (*Fragilaria crotonensis* and *F. capucina*). Golden-brown algae (Chrysophyta: *Ochromonas* sp. and *Chrysochromulina parva*) were the dominant group in June and blue-green algae (Cyanophyta: *Aphanizomenon flos-aquae*) were the dominant group during August and September. Cryptomonads

(Cryptophyta) accounted for most of the biomass in May (*Cryptomonas erosa*), June (*Katablepharis ovalis*), July (*C. Marsonii*), September (*C. erosa* and *Rhodomonas minuta*), October and November (*C. erosa*).

A brief survey of aquatic macrophytes was carried out by Fish and Wildlife Division on 31 July 1984 (Mills 1987). The dominant emergent species was bulrush (*Scirpus* sp.), with occasional patches of common cattail (*Typha latifolia*). Pondweeds (*Potamogeton* spp.) were present near shore and patches of coontail (*Ceratophyllum demersum*) grew at the north end of the lake.

Invertebrates

The zooplankton and benthic invertebrates in Touchwood Lake have not been surveyed.

Fish

The fish fauna of Touchwood Lake includes walleye, northern pike, yellow perch, lake whitefish, cisco, burbot, longnose sucker, white sucker and spottail shiner (Mills 1987). Lake trout were abundant before 1927 but subsequent commercial fishing apparently eliminated them from the lake. In an attempt to reestablish the species, lake trout were stocked at a rate of 31 000 fingerlings in 1967, 61 000 fingerlings in 1968, 90 400 juveniles in 1985, and 90 000 juveniles

Table 5. Percentage composition of major algal groups by total biomass in Touchwood Lake, 1986. Composite samples collected from the euphotic zone.

ALGAL GROUP	28 May	25 June	23 July	20 Aug.	17 Sep.	22 Oct.	05 Nov.
Total Biomass (mg/L)	1.91	0.59	0.44	0.45	0.41	0.70	0.53
Percentage Composition:							
Cyanophyta	1.0	0	18.5	70.0	50.0	7.7	8.6
				Aphanizomenon———→			
Chlorophyta	0.5	1.2	6.9	1.6	3.2	7.2	1.4
Chrysophyta	4.2	26.1	4.5	3.7	1.6	1.2	0.4
		Ochromonas					
		Chrysochromulina					
Bacillariophyta	64.2	32.0	20.2	0.5	0.8	7.5	27.9
	Cyclotella————————→						*Fragilaria*
Cryptophyta	29.8	38.0	42.4	9.5	39.0	76.4	61.7
	Cryptomonas Katablepharis Cryptomonas			*Cryptomonas*————————→			
				Rhodomonas			
Pyrrhophyta	0.3	2.7	7.5	14.6	5.4	0	0

SOURCE: Alta. Envir. n.d.[a]

Table 6. Estimated angler numbers, effort and harvest from Touchwood Lake. Estimates based on creel survey data collected from 15 May to 31 Aug. 1984 and 20 May to 15 Aug. 1988.

	Walleye		Northern Pike		Yellow Perch		Total	
	1984	1988	1984	1988	1984	1988	1984	1988
number of anglers[a]	—	—	—	—	—	—	6 790	7 156
angler-hours[b]	—	—	—	—	—	—	18 582	18 423
total number fish harvested[c]	1 750	908	4 984	1 185	191	—	6 925	2 093
total yield (kg)	1 309	571	7 538	2 270	19	—	8 866	2 841
mean weight (g)	748	629	1 512	1 322	100	—	—	—
catch/angler-hour	0.15	0.06	0.64	0.18	0.01	—	0.89	0.24
harvest/angler-hour[b, c]	0.09	0.05	0.26	0.09	0.01	—	0.36	0.14
harvest/angler[a, c]	0.23	0.14	0.41	0.24	0.03	—	0.67	0.38

NOTES: [a]observed no. anglers = 5 346 (1984), 4 840 (1988); [b]observed hours = 14 524 (1984), 12 604 (1988); [c]based on observed no. fish kept: walleye = 1 255 (1984), 683 (1988), northern pike = 2 167 (1984), 1 185 (1988), yellow perch = 148 (1984), 10 (1988)
SOURCES: Alta. For. Ld. Wild. n.d.; Sullivan 1986

in both 1986 and 1987 (Alta. For. Ld. Wild. n.d.; 1986; 1987[a]; Alta. En. Nat. Resour. 1985[b]). No lake trout have been caught by anglers surveyed during creel censuses or by the commercial fishery (Norris 1989).

Touchwood Lake is managed for domestic, commercial and recreational fisheries. Catch data for the domestic fishery are not available. The commercial fishery has operated since the 1920s and records have been kept since 1942 (Alta. For. Ld. Wild. n.d.; Alta. Rec. Parks Wild. 1976). The total commercial catch for the period from 1942/43 to 1973/74 varied between a maximum of 103 786 kg in 1947/48 and a minimum of 957 kg in 1959/60. The average catch for this period was 20 946 kg/year. Some of the variation in annual catch was due to variations in the total effort and the effort to catch cisco, as well as incomplete records of catch. Between 1974/75 and 1987/88, the total catch (excluding burbot, suckers and yellow perch) of lake whitefish, walleye, northern pike and cisco varied between 89 kg in 1978/79 and 12 300 kg in 1987/88. The average catch for the period was 2 803 kg/year. The high catch for 1987/88 was largely due to the increased harvest of lake whitefish for a roe fishery; whitefish accounted for 84% of the total catch in this year.

On average, lake whitefish formed 67% of the total catch (including burbot, suckers and yellow perch) from 1942/43 to 1973/74 (range 32 to 100%). The average whitefish catch for this period was 11 075 kg/year. The whitefish catch declined to 917 kg/year for the period from 1974/75 to 1985/86 because of reduced effort, and increased to 5 720 kg in 1986/87 and to 10 343 kg in 1987/88. The

maximum recorded catch of 56 000 kg was taken during the 1952/53 season. The low effort for whitefish during the 1970s and early 1980s was primarily due to the difficulty in finding a market for fish containing high numbers of cysts of the tapeworm *Triaenophorus crassus*.

Cisco are no longer harvested from Touchwood Lake. They were taken from 1947/48 to 1949/50 and from 1965/66 to 1967/68. Cisco were used for animal food on the mink ranches at Lac La Biche. When the mink ranching industry declined there was a decline in the harvest of this species.

The average commercial harvest of walleye was 1 100 kg/year from 1942/43 to 1967/68, 150 kg/year from 1968/69 to 1979/80 and 430 kg/year from 1980/81 to 1986/87. The maximum catch was 4 651 kg in 1942/43. The 1 100 kg of walleye caught in 1987/88 represented 9% of the total catch that year.

The commercial harvest of northern pike averaged 5 363 kg/year from 1942/43 to 1967/68, 883 kg/year from 1968/69 to 1979/80, 307 kg/year from 1980/81 to 1986/87 and 895 kg in 1987/88.

The sport fishery in Touchwood Lake was evaluated by means of creel surveys conducted by Fish and Wildlife Division during the summer months of 1984 and 1988 (Table 6). In addition, Mills (1987) provides estimates of the winter sport fishery. Walleye and northern pike are the species most highly sought by anglers, yellow perch are caught incidentally by walleye anglers and the catch of whitefish is negligible. Angling effort (angler-hours) was almost identical in both years surveyed.

In the summer of 1984, anglers caught 0.15 walleye/angler-hour and kept 1 750 fish, which is a harvest rate of 0.09 walleye/angler-hour. Over the year, anglers harvested 1 309 kg of walleye during summer and about 500 kg in winter. When combined with the average commercial harvest of 450 kg of walleye per year from 1980 to 1984, the total harvest was about 2 260 kg/year, or 0.78 kg/ha. In the summer of 1988, the walleye catch rate declined to 0.06 fish/angler-hour and the average size of fish caught was smaller than in 1984 (Table 6).

In the summer of 1984, anglers caught 0.64 northern pike/angler-hour and kept 4 984 fish, which is a harvest rate of 0.26 pike/angler-hour. Anglers harvested about 7 500 kg of pike during the summer and about 3 000 kg of pike during the winter (Mills 1987). When combined with the average commercial harvest of 144 kg/year from 1980 to 1984, the total pike harvest was 10 682 kg/year, or 3.68 kg/ha. In the summer of 1988, the catch rate declined to 0.18 pike/angler-hour and the mean weight of fish harvested was somewhat smaller than in 1984 (Table 6).

Wildlife

The wildlife on and around Touchwood Lake has not been studied. Birds reported to use the lake include Common Loons, White Pelicans, Belted Kingfishers and Double-crested Cormorants (Alta. For. Ld. Wild. 1987[b]).

M.E. Bradford and J.M. Hanson

References

Alberta Energy and Natural Resources. 1985[a]. Lakeland sub-regional integrated resource plan. Resour. Eval. Plan. Div., Edmonton.
———. 1985[b]. Fish planting list. Fish Wild. Div., Edmonton.
Alberta Environment. n.d.[a]. Envir. Assess. Div., Envir. Qlty. Monit. Br. Unpubl. data, Edmonton.
———. n.d.[b]. Tech. Serv. Div., Hydrol. Br. Unpubl. data, Edmonton.
———. n.d.[c]. Tech. Serv. Div., Surv. Br. Unpubl. data, Edmonton.
Alberta Forestry, Lands and Wildlife. n.d. Fish Wild. Div. Unpubl. data, Edmonton.
———. 1986, 1987[a]. Fish planting list. Fish Wild. Div., Edmonton.
———. 1987[b]. A summary of Alberta's natural areas reserved and established. Pub. Ld. Div., Ld. Mgt. Devel. Br. Unpubl. rep., Edmonton.
———. 1988. Boating in Alberta. Fish Wild. Div., Edmonton.
———. 1989. Guide to sportfishing. Fish Wild. Div., Edmonton.
Alberta Recreation, Parks and Wildlife. 1976. Commercial fisheries catch statistics for Alberta, 1942–1975. Fish Wild. Div., Fish. Mgt. Rep. No. 22, Edmonton.
Alberta Research Council. 1972. Geological map of Alberta. Nat. Resour. Div., Alta. Geol. Surv., Edmonton.
Chipeniuk, R.C. 1975. Lakes of the Lac La Biche district. R.C. Chipeniuk, Lac La Biche.
Energy, Mines and Resources Canada. 1970, 1979. National topographic series 1:50 000 73L/14 (1970), 73L/11 (1979). Surv. Map. Br., Ottawa.
Environment Canada. 1982. Canadian climate normals, Vol. 7: Bright sunshine (1951–1980). Prep. by Atm. Envir. Serv. Supply Serv. Can., Ottawa.
Kocaoglu, S.S. 1975. Reconnaissance soil survey of the Sand River area. Alta. Soil Surv. Rep. No. 34, Univ. Alta. Bull. No. SS–15, Alta. Inst. Pedol. Rep. No. S–74–34 1975. Univ. Alta., Edmonton.
Mills, J.B. 1987. Touchwood Lake LSD 6–Sec 24–Twp 67–Rge 10–W4M limnological survey phase I and II. Alta. For. Ld. Wild., Fish Wild. Div. Unpubl. rep., St. Paul.
Norris, H. 1989. Alta. For. Ld. Wild., Fish Wild. Div., St. Paul. Pers. comm.
Shaw, J.F.H. and E.E. Prepas. 1989. Potential significance of phosphorus release from shallow sediments of deep Alberta lakes. ms submitted to Limnol. Oceanogr.
Strong, W.L. and K.R. Leggat. 1981. Ecoregions of Alberta. Alta. En. Nat. Resour., Resour. Eval. Plan. Div., Edmonton.
Sullivan, M.G. 1986. Characteristics and impact of the sports fishery at Touchwood Lake during May-August 1984. Alta. For. Ld. Wild., Fish Wild. Div. Unpubl. rep., St. Paul.

TUCKER LAKE

MAP SHEET: 73L/10
LOCATION: Tp64 R4, 5 W4
LAT/LONG: 54°32′N 110°36′W

Tucker Lake is an isolated water body surrounded by low, rolling, aspen-covered hills. It is located in Improvement District No. 18 (South), about 280 km northeast of the city of Edmonton. The town of Bonnyville to the south, and the towns of Cold Lake and Grande Centre to the southeast, are the principal urban centres in the area. To reach the lake from Edmonton, take Highways 28 and 28A northeast to Bonnyville, then Highway 41 north to the locality of La Corey. Turn east onto Highway 55 and drive for about 5.5 km to the first north turn after Jackfish Creek. Drive north on this gravel road for 3 km, east for 0.75 km, north for 3.25 km, then turn east onto the final 6 km of road, which leads to the western shore of Tucker Lake (Fig. 1). Poor access to the lake has been a major factor limiting its recreational use, and at present, no facilities have been developed. Sport fishing for northern pike and yellow perch during spring and early summer, with associated swimming and camping, are the primary recreational activities at Tucker Lake. Boats can be launched from the end of the entrance road. There are no boating regulations specific to the lake, but general federal regulations apply (Alta. For. Ld. Wild. 1988).

The origin of the name "Tucker" is not known. Locally, the lake is called Little Jackfish Lake, probably because of the abundant but small northern pike that inhabit its waters (Chipeniuk 1975).

Woodland Cree occupied the region when fur traders first arrived late in the eighteenth century. The Beaver River, south of Tucker Lake, was part of a major fur-trade route from Isle-à-la-Crosse, Saskatchewan, to the Athabasca River. The first trading post in the area was Cold Lake House, 30 km to the southeast. It was established by the North West Company in 1781 on the Beaver River near the present-day hamlet of Beaver Crossing (Alta. Mun. Aff. 1978). The history of the area near Tucker Lake has not been documented.

There are no cottages on the lake, and almost the entire shoreline is Crown land. One quarter section of private land abuts the northwest bay, and several other privately held sections are located northwest of the lake.

The water in Tucker Lake is usually quite clear during spring and early summer, but turns green from dense blooms of blue-green algae during midsummer and autumn. Aquatic macrophytes grow around most of the shoreline, and are densest at the northeast end of the lake. Sport fishing pressure is light, and the commercial fishery, which catches northern pike, is small. The provincial record for yellow perch is held by a 1.0 kg, 38.1–cm–long perch caught in Tucker Lake in 1967. Sport fishing regulations prohibit fishing in Tucker Lake's inlet and outlet streams for a period during April and May each year to protect spawning pike (Alta. For. Ld. Wild. 1989).

Drainage Basin Characteristics

Tucker Lake has a large drainage basin that is 47 times the size of the lake (Tables 1, 2). The entire watershed lies to the north of the lake, and all streams flow into the north shore (Fig. 1). The largest of the four inflowing streams is Jackfish Creek, which drains Bourque Lake and flows into the northwest side of Tucker Lake.

Tucker Lake's drainage basin is part of a rolling morainal plain that is characterized by generally flat and undulating to gently rolling topography (Kocaoglu 1975). Several isolated areas are moderately rolling. The land features minor ridges and knobs intermixed with numerous wet depressions and small peat bogs. The most common

323

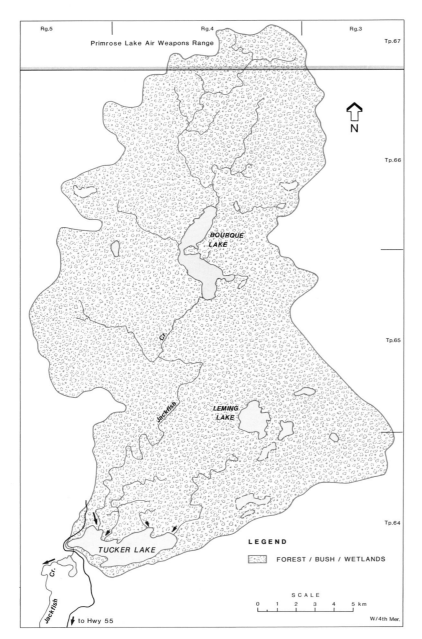

Figure 1. Features of the drainage basin of Tucker Lake.
SOURCES: Alta. Envir. n.d.[b]; En. Mines Resour. Can. 1970; 1971.
Updated with 1982 aerial photos.

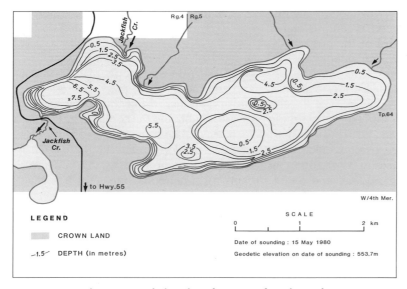

Figure 2. Bathymetry and shoreline features of Tucker Lake.
BATHYMETRY SOURCE: Alta. Envir. n.d.[c].

Table 1. Characteristics of Tucker Lake drainage basin.

area (excluding lake) (km²)[a]	312
soil[b]	Orthic Gray Luvisols, Dystric and Eutric Brunisols
bedrock geology[c]	La Biche Formation (Upper Cretaceous): shale, ironstone partings and concretions; marine
terrain[b]	level to moderately rolling
ecoregion[d]	Dry (south) and Moist (north) Mixedwood subregions of Boreal Mixedwood
dominant vegetation[d]	trembling aspen, balsam poplar
mean annual inflow (m³)[a, e]	15.0×10^6
mean annual sunshine (h)[f]	2 240

NOTE: [e]excluding groundwater inflow
SOURCES: [a]Alta. Envir. n.d.[b]; [b]Kocaoglu 1975; [c]Alta. Res. Counc. 1972; [d]Strong and Leggat 1981; [f]Envir. Can. 1982

Table 2. Characteristics of Tucker Lake.

elevation (m)[a, b]	553.70
surface area (km²)[a, b]	6.65
volume (m³)[a, b]	19.0×10^6
maximum depth (m)[a, b]	7.5
mean depth (m)[a, b]	2.9
shoreline length (km)[c]	16.7
mean annual lake evaporation (mm)[d]	634
mean annual precipitation (mm)[d]	439
mean residence time (yr)[d, e]	1.5
control structure[f]	dilapidated fixed-crest weir

NOTES: [a]on date of sounding: 15 May 1980; [e]excluding groundwater inflow
SOURCES: [b]Alta. Envir. n.d.[c]; [c]En. Mines Resour. Can. 1971; [d]Alta. Envir. n.d.[b]; [f]Ducks Unltd. (Can.) n.d.

soils in the drainage basin are moderately well-drained, fine loamy Orthic Gray Luvisols that developed on moderately to strongly calcareous glacial till. Soils along the southwestern and western shores of Tucker Lake and around the northern half of Bourque Lake are mainly Eluviated Dystric and Eutric Brunisols and Brunisolic Gray Luvisols. These are rapidly drained, loamy sand textured soils that formed on sandy fluvial or aeolian material. Along Jackfish Creek north of Tucker Lake, soils are poorly to rapidly drained undifferentiated Gleysols that formed on sandy to fine-clay alluvium. Poorly to very poorly drained Organic soils, mainly Mesisols, are common in depressional to level areas.

Tucker Lake's watershed lies in the Boreal Mixedwood Ecoregion (Strong and Leggat 1981). The area north of the lake is part of the Moist Mixedwood Subregion, and the small area south of the lake is part of the Dry Mixedwood Subregion. The difference between the two subregions is the codominance of balsam poplar and trembling aspen on moderately well-drained Gray Luvisols in the moist subregion, and the dominance of only trembling aspen on well-drained to moderately well-drained Gray Luvisols in the dry subregion. In both areas, jack pine grows on rapidly to well-drained Eutric Brunisols, white spruce grows on imperfectly drained Gleysols and Gray Luvisols, and black spruce, willows and sedges grow on poorly to very poorly drained Gleysols and Organics.

Close to the lake, the shoreline is lightly tree-covered, with some open areas, on the west and southwest sides, where the topography is level to undulating (Alta. For. Ld. Wild. n.d.). The remainder of the lakeshore has a moderately dense tree cover. The west half of the south shore is moderately to strongly rolling and the north shore is level to undulating (Kocaoglu 1975). The tree cover extends down to the water's edge, and beaches along most of the shoreline are confined to a narrow fringe. Part of the south shore on the east half of the lake is sandy, with some beach areas (Alta. For. Ld. Wild. n.d.).

Table 3. Major ions and related water quality variables for Tucker Lake. Average concentrations in mg/L; pH in pH units. Composite samples from the euphotic zone collected 7 times from 13 May to 29 Sep. 1981. S.E. = standard error.

	Mean	S.E.
pH (range)	7.1–8.3	—
total alkalinity ($CaCO_3$)	200	5.7
specific conductivity (µS/cm)	374	11.1
total dissolved solids (calculated)	199	5.8
total hardness ($CaCO_3$)	168[a]	1.9
total particulate carbon	3[b]	2.8
dissolved organic carbon	12	0.4
HCO_3	243	6.8
CO_3	0.4	0.43
Mg	24	0.7
Na	21	0.3
K	3	0.1
Cl	2	0.1
SO_4	4	0.5
Ca	26	2.6

NOTES: [a]n = 5, 12 May to 08 July 1980; [b]n = 13, 12 May to 27 Oct. 1982
SOURCE: Alta. Envir. n.d.[a], Naquadat station 01AL06AC5490

Most of the watershed remains in its natural, forest-covered state (Fig. 1). A very small amount of land has been cleared for agriculture directly north of the western tip of the lake, just outside of the drainage basin boundary. There are no permanent or seasonal residences on or near the lakeshore and no recreational developments. The oil and gas industry is active in the area. The pipelines of Esso Resources' Cold Lake Heavy Oil Project transect the watershed (Yonge and Trew 1989) and Husky Oil has developed a pilot recovery plant north of the lake.

Lake Basin Characteristics

Tucker Lake is a medium-sized, shallow lake (Table 2) with a firm, sandy bottom. In contrast to many shallow lakes, the morphometry of Tucker Lake is quite complex. The deepest spot (7.5 m) in the lake is a small hole in the centre of the western bay (Fig. 2). The largest portion of this bay extends to a depth of 6.5 m. The remainder of the lake bottom ranges from 2.5 to 4.5 m in depth, with several elevated areas in the eastern half of the lake that are only 0.5 m below the lake surface.

Water levels in Tucker Lake have not been monitored. Because the sides of most of the lake basin slope gently, changes in water levels would cause marked changes in the surface area and volume of the lake (Fig. 3).

Ducks Unlimited (Canada) and the provincial government built a fixed-crest timber weir across the outlet in 1952 to raise the lake level by about 0.3 m (Ducks Unltd. (Can.) n.d.). This would ensure greater water flow in Jackfish Creek and therefore maintain the marshes downstream, which were good duck habitat. By 1982, the dam was in disrepair, and after 1985, Ducks Unlimited (Canada) withdrew their involvement with Tucker Lake.

Subsequent to studies of lakes in the Cold Lake-Beaver River basin during the early 1980s, Alberta Environment adopted a long term plan for water resources management in the Cold Lake region in 1985. Under this plan, no large water withdrawals from Tucker Lake will be allowed; oil sands plants will obtain their water supply from a pipeline from the North Saskatchewan River (Alta. Envir. 1985).

Water Quality

Water quality in Tucker Lake was studied by Alberta Environment intensively from 1980 to 1982 and occasionally in 1986 (Alta. Envir. n.d.[a]; Prepas and Trew 1983; Yonge and Trew 1989). The lake

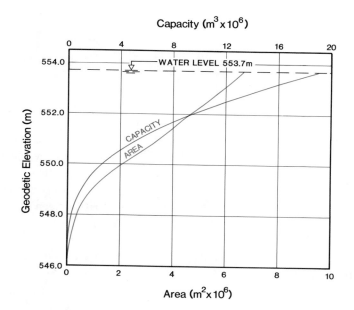

Figure 3. Area/capacity curve for Tucker Lake.
SOURCE: Alta. Envir. n.d.[c].

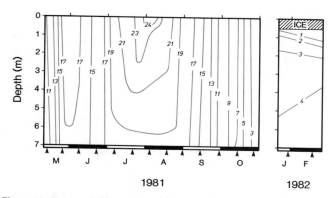

Figure 4. Temperature (°C) of Tucker Lake, 1981 and 1982. Arrows indicate sampling dates.
SOURCE: Alta. Envir. n.d.[a].

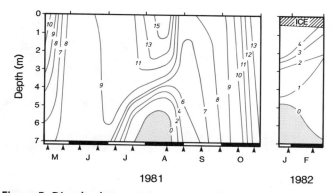

Figure 5. Dissolved oxygen (mg/L) in Tucker Lake, 1981 and 1982. Arrows indicate sampling dates.
SOURCE: Alta. Envir. n.d.[a].

water is fresh, hard and well-buffered (Table 3). The dominant ions are bicarbonate, calcium, magnesium and sodium.

Most of the lake is well mixed during the open-water season. The deepest part of the lake basin was thermally stratified during July and August in 1981 (Fig. 4) and in June 1982, but was well mixed throughout the summer in 1980. The maximum surface temperature in 1981 was over 24°C in early August.

The deepest part of Tucker Lake typically becomes anoxic for a time between January and March and between May and August each year. In 1981, the water was anoxic below 5 m from late July through August (Fig. 5). Periods of oxygen depletion in the rest of the lake, which is shallower than 5 m, are only transient. The shallow

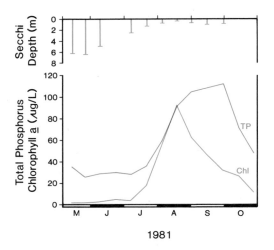

Figure 6. Total phosphorus, chlorophyll *a* and Secchi depth in Tucker Lake, 1981.
SOURCE: Alta. Envir. n.d.[a].

Table 4. Nutrient, chlorophyll *a* and Secchi depth data for Tucker Lake. Average concentrations in µg/L. Composite samples from the euphotic zone collected 13 times from 13 May to 26 Oct. 1981 and 13 times from 12 May to 27 Oct. 1982. S.E. = standard error.

	1981		1982	
	Mean	S.E.	Mean	S.E.
total phosphorus	60	9.3	67	6.3
total dissolved phosphorus	23	1.4	22[a]	2.1
soluble reactive phosphorus	7	0.7	10	1.7
total Kjeldahl nitrogen	1 310[a]	126.6	1 235	83.6
$NO_3 + NO_2$–nitrogen	—	—	<16	—
NH_4–nitrogen	110[a]	23.4	135	71.5
iron	<53[b]	—	127[d]	44.6
chlorophyll *a*	25.7[a]	8.32	19.4	4.75
Secchi depth (m)	2.5[c]	0.78	1.9[e]	0.80

NOTES: [a]n = 12; [b]n = 6; [c]n = 10; [d]n = 4; [e]n = 7
SOURCE: Alta. Envir. n.d.[a], Naquadat station 01AL06AC5490

eastern half of the lake was sampled to a depth of 3 m during the open-water season in 1982. It was completely mixed and well oxygenated at all times. On 17 August 1981, the concentration of dissolved oxygen in the 0– to 1–m depth zone in the west basin rose to supersaturated levels of almost 16 mg/L. These high levels occurred in conjunction with an extremely dense bloom of blue-green algae that weighed almost 205 mg/L. In January and February of 1982, the water in the deepest area of the lake was anoxic below 4.5 m, and dissolved oxygen levels at the surface were about 4 mg/L (Fig. 5).

Tucker Lake is hyper-eutrophic. Maximum chlorophyll *a* levels vary considerably between years. The highest concentration of chlorophyll *a* was 93 µg/L, recorded on 17 August 1981 during the bloom of blue-green algae (Fig. 6). In 1980, the highest level recorded was 28 µg/L in July and September, and in 1982 the maximum level was 57 µg/L in September. Average chlorophyll *a* levels were 17 µg/L in 1980, 26 in 1981 and 19 in 1982 (Table 4). The concentration of total phosphorus increased sharply during August and reached a maximum in September of both 1981 (Fig. 6) and 1982. During the period from 1980 to 1982, the highest concentration recorded was 112 µg/L in late September of 1981. In general, total phosphorus and chlorophyll *a* in Tucker Lake are correlated during the summer, indicating that the algae are phosphorus-limited (Prepas 1983).

A total phosphorus budget for Tucker Lake was calculated for the period from 10 May to 27 October in 1982 (Table 5). As well, total phosphorus loading from internal sources only was calculated for a similar period in 1981. The study focused on patterns of internal loading and deposition to the sediments. From July to September in both years, internal sources of phosphorus were very significant. In 1982, 75% (10.82 kg/day) of the mean daily total phosphorus load from May to October originated from internal sources (Table 5). Phosphorus returned to the sediments during periods when the lake was well mixed in spring and autumn. In 1981, the internal load was considerably higher (19.60 kg/day), but the external load was not measured. In 1982, inflow from Bourque Lake via Jackfish Creek accounted for 29% of the total phosphorus load, and inflow from diffuse runoff and the creek at the eastern end of the lake accounted for 9%. Precipitation, at 3%, was the smallest input. From January to March in 1982, phosphorus accumulation under ice was relatively low.

In the summer of 1986, bottom sediment chemistry, porewater chemistry and groundwater inflow and outflow were monitored at Tucker Lake by researchers from the University of Alberta (J. Shaw et al. 1989; J. Shaw and Prepas 1990[a]; 1990[b]; R. Shaw and Prepas 1990). One of their goals was to estimate the relative contribution of groundwater to the water budget and the contribution of bottom sediments and groundwater to the phosphorus budget at Tucker Lake. Soluble reactive phosphorus in the porewater was

Table 5. Theoretical total phosphorus loading to Tucker Lake, 10 May to 27 October 1982.

Source		Phosphorus (kg/day)	Percentage of Total
immediate watershed	forest/bush	0.82	6
precipitation/dustfall		0.24	2
inflow from Bourque Lake		2.61	18
	SUBTOTAL	3.67	26
sediment release[a]		10.82	75
	TOTAL	14.49	101

NOTE: [a]06 July to 15 Sep. 1982
SOURCE: Yonge and Trew 1989

collected from the top 10 cm of of sediment along a transect at depths of 2.5, 4, 5 and 7 m. In comparison with eight other Alberta lakes, the average porewater soluble reactive phosphorus concentration (356 ± 75 µg/L) was low. In addition, a relatively high proportion of particulate sediment phosphorus was available for transport from the particulate sediments to the overlying water. There was a strong positive gradient of soluble reactive phosphorus between the porewater, water within 10 cm of the bottom sediments and the surface water, indicating transport of phosphorus from the bottom sediments to the surface waters, even at shallow depths. Groundwater inflow was low. Rates over a 100–m transect were generally less than 1 x 10^{-8} m/second and decreased linearly with distance from shore. The average flow rate was 2.8 x 10^{-9} m/second. Groundwater was estimated as 1% of the total annual inflow of water, by far the lowest of the nine lakes studied. Transport of phosphorus from the sediments in the euphotic zone and from groundwater was estimated to be 2.81 kg/day. Although measurable, phosphorus input from these sources is likely a small portion of the total internal loading to this lake (Table 5).

Biological Characteristics

Plants

The phytoplankton community in Tucker Lake was studied intensively by Alberta Environment during the open-water period in 1981, 1982 and 1983 (Alta. Envir. n.d.[a]). The average biomass varied considerably among years: 10.12 mg/L in 1980, 29.74 mg/L in 1981 and 5.21 mg/L in 1982. In each year, the highest biomass was recorded during the period between late July and late October when species of blue-green algae usually accounted for more than 75% of the biomass. Low oxygen concentrations over the bottom sediments

Table 6. Percentage composition of major algal groups by total biomass in Tucker Lake, 1981. Composite samples collected from the euphotic zone.

ALGAL GROUP	13 May	25 May	08 June	22 June	04 July	20 July	04 Aug.	17 Aug.	31 Aug.	14 Sep.	29 Sep.	13 Oct.	26 Oct.
Total Biomass (mg/L)	2.96	0.57	1.46	0.59	0.26	38.95	40.60	204.54	3.27	66.1	04.81	3.35	19.21
Percentage Composition:													
Cyanophyta	0	0	1	2	13	52	83	98	97	87	98	97	20
						Anabaena —————————————————→				*Oscillatoria* —————————→			
Chlorophyta	2	7	4	4	13	4	16	0	2	1	0	2	13
Chrysophyta	28	6	0	4	44	36	1	2	1	0	1	0	9
	Dinobryon				*Dinobryon*	*Uroglena*							
Bacillariophyta	0	37	14	53	8	5	0	0	0	6	0	0	15
			Asterionella										
			Nitzschia										
Cryptophyta	70	49	80	36	23	4	0	0	0	6	0	1	44
	Cryptomonas ————————————————→												*Rhod.*
	Rhodomonas												*Crypt.*

NOTES: *Rhod.* = *Rhodomonas*; *Crypt.* = *Cryptomonas*
SOURCE: Alta. Envir. n.d.[a]

and high phosphorus concentrations are responsible for the predominance of blue-green algae during this period (Trimbee and Prepas 1987; 1988).

From May to July in 1981 (Table 6), the dominant groups were golden-brown algae (Chrysophyta), particularly *Dinobryon divergens* in May and early July and *Uroglena americana* in late July; diatoms (Bacillariophyta), particularly *Asterionella formosa* in May and June and *Nitzschia* in late June; and Cryptophyta, particularly *Rhodomonas minuta* in May and *Cryptomonas* spp. from May to July. These two species were also important in late October. During the blue-green bloom from July to September, *Anabaena flos-aquae* and, secondarily, *A. spiroides* were the dominant species. When total biomass declined after mid-September, the blue-green alga *Oscillatoria agardhii* became the most important species.

Macrophytes in Tucker Lake were described briefly in 1982 (McGregor 1983). Vegetation grew around the entire shoreline and was densest in the northeast part of the lake, where water depth is shallow and the bottom sediments are highly organic. Common great bulrush (*Scirpus validus*) and yellow water lily (*Nuphar variegatum*) were the most extensive emergent and floating species, and sedge (*Carex* sp.) and reed grass (*Phragmites* sp.) were also identified. Coontail (*Ceratophyllum demersum*) was the most widespread submergent species, and northern watermilfoil (*Myriophyllum exalbescens*) and three pondweeds—Richardson (*Potamogeton richardsonii*), flat-stemmed (*P. zosteriformis*) and Sago (*P. pectinatus*)—were also identified. In 1982, macrophytes grew to a depth of 5 m. A further study in July 1986 recorded macrophytes growing to a depth of 2.5 m (Chambers and Prepas 1988).

Invertebrates

A survey of the zooplankton and benthic invertebrate communities in Tucker Lake was conducted for Esso Resources Canada during 1978 (Cross 1979). Based on five zooplankton samples collected from 2 March to 12 December, the dominant cladocerans were *Bosmina longirostris* (range: 6 to 2 225/L) and *Daphnia pulex*-type (range: 5.5 to 103/L). The dominant copepods were *Diacylops bicuspidatus thomasi* (range: 37 to 485/L) and *Diaptomus oregonensis* (range: 0 to 330/L), and the dominant rotifer was *Keratella cochlearis* (range: 18 to 4 437/L).

A total of 18 dredge samples were collected in the sublittoral zone (4.8–m to 6–m deep) from 2 March to 12 December 1978. By number, the dominant group of benthic invertebrates was midge larvae (Chironomidae), with small numbers of scuds (Amphipoda: *Hyalella azteca*), snails (Gastropoda: mostly *Valvata* spp.) and fingernail clams (Sphaeriidae) also recorded. As well, a total of 9 dredge samples were collected in the littoral zone (2.5–m to 4.8–m deep). Scuds (*Hyalella azteca* and *Gammarus lacustris*) were numerically dominant. The data for both sublittoral and littoral zones are too few to allow estimation of the total abundance, total biomass or relative abundance of the benthic invertebrates in Tucker Lake.

Fish

The fish fauna of Tucker Lake includes northern pike, lake whitefish, yellow perch, walleye, burbot, white sucker, ninespine stickleback and Iowa darter. The lake is managed for domestic, recreational and commercial fisheries. The extent of the domestic and sport harvests is unknown. Some aspects of the fishery were examined during the limnological and fisheries surveys for the proposed heavy oil development near Cold Lake, Alberta (McCart et al. 1979).

The commercial catch has been recorded since 1944 (Alta. For. Ld. Wild. n.d.; Alta. Rec. Parks Wild. 1976). Northern pike are the primary target of the commercial fishery, with smaller amounts of lake whitefish, yellow perch, white sucker and burbot also taken. From 1944/45 to 1959/60, the commercial fishery operated in only 7 of 15 years. From 1959/60 to 1975/76, the average total catch was 8 732 kg/year. The greatest catch, 13 845 kg, was taken in 1970/71. The average catch from 1980/81 to 1987/88, 4 214 kg/year, was much lower, largely due to reduced effort, but partly because yellow perch, suckers and burbot were not recorded after 1976.

The largest catch of northern pike, 11 972 kg, was taken in 1972/73. From 1959/60 to 1974/75 the average pike catch was 8 146 kg/year, or 90% of the total catch. From 1975/76 to 1987/88, the pike harvest averaged 4 776 kg/year, or almost 100% of the total catch. Appreciable amounts of yellow perch were harvested from Tucker Lake from 1967/68 to 1975/76. The average perch harvest during that period was 1 280 kg/year, which was 12% of the average total catch. The maximum catch of yellow perch was 2 494 kg, taken in 1970/71. The lake whitefish harvest in Tucker Lake averaged 30 kg/year between 1967/68 and 1976/77 and totalled 6 kg from 1980/81 to 1987/88. The commercial catch of white sucker and burbot either was sporadic or not recorded in most years. The greatest catch (both species combined) was 794 kg, taken in 1964/65.

Wildlife

The wildlife in and around Tucker Lake has not been studied in detail. A Ducks Unlimited (Canada) report noted that there were few upland and overwater nest sites, a shortage of loafing areas, and sparse emergent vegetation (Ducks Unltd. (Can.) n.d.). A variety of duck species, Red-necked Grebe and American Coot have been observed using the lake as a fall staging area. As well, a number of active beaver lodges have been observed on the lake (Rippon 1983).

M.E. Bradford and J.M. Hanson

References

Alberta Environment. n.d.[a]. Envir. Assess. Div., Envir. Qlty. Monit. Br. Unpubl. data, Edmonton.

————. n.d.[b]. Tech. Serv. Div., Hydrol. Br. Unpubl. data, Edmonton.

————. n.d.[c]. Tech. Serv. Div., Surv. Br. Unpubl. data, Edmonton.

————. 1985. Cold Lake-Beaver River long term water management plan. Plan. Div., Edmonton.

Alberta Forestry, Lands and Wildlife. n.d. Fish Wild. Div. Unpubl. data, Edmonton.

————. 1988. Boating in Alberta. Fish Wild. Div., Edmonton.

————. 1989. Guide to sportfishing. Fish Wild. Div., Edmonton.

Alberta Municipal Affairs. 1978. Cold Lake regional plan, heritage preservation: Heritage resources background paper. Reg. Plan. Sec., Edmonton.

Alberta Recreation, Parks and Wildlife. 1976. Commercial fisheries catch statistics for Alberta, 1942–1975. Fish Wild. Div., Fish. Mgt. Rep. No. 22, Edmonton.

Alberta Research Council. 1972. Geological map of Alberta. Nat. Resour. Div., Alta. Geol. Surv., Edmonton.

Chambers, P.A. and E.E. Prepas. 1988. Underwater spectral attenuation and its effect on the maximum depth of angiosperm colonization. Can. J. Fish. Aquat. Sci. 45:1010–1017.

Chipeniuk, R.C. 1975. Lakes of the Lac La Biche district. R.C. Chipeniuk, Lac La Biche.

Cross, P.M. 1979. Limnological and fishery surveys of the aquatic ecosystems at Esso Resources' Cold Lake lease: Data volume. Aquat. Envir. Ltd., Calgary.

Ducks Unlimited (Canada). n.d. Unpubl. data, Edmonton.

Energy, Mines and Resources Canada. 1970, 1971. National topographic series 1:50 000 73L/15 (1970), 73L/9 (1971), 73L/10 (1971), 73L/16 (1971). Surv. Map. Br., Ottawa.

Environment Canada. 1982. Canadian climate normals, Vol. 7: Bright sunshine (1951–1980). Prep. by Atm. Envir. Serv. Supply Serv. Can., Ottawa.

Kocaoglu, S.S. 1975. Reconnaissance soil survey of the Sand River area. Alta. Soil Surv. Rep. No. 34, Univ. Alta. Bull. No. SS–15, Alta. Inst. Pedol. Rep. No. S–74–34 1975. Univ. Alta., Edmonton.

McCart, P.J., P.M. Cross, R. Green and D.W. Mayhood. 1979. Limnological and fishery surveys of the aquatic ecosystems at Esso Resources' Cold Lake lease. Aquat. Envir. Ltd., Calgary.

McGregor, C.A. 1983. Summary [Appendix K] and Detailed report [Appendix L]. *In* Cold Lake-Beaver River water management study, Vol. 7: Ecological inventory of lake shorelines. Alta. Envir., Plan. Div., Edmonton.

Prepas, E.E. 1983. Orthophosphate turnover time in shallow productive lakes. Can. J. Fish. Aquat. Sci. 40:1412–1418.

———— and D.O. Trew. 1983. Evaluation of the phosphorus-chlorophyll relationship for lakes off the Precambrian Shield in western Canada. Can. J. Fish. Aquat. Sci. 40:27–35.

Rippon, B. 1983. Water related wildlife resources [Appendix I]. *In* Cold Lake-Beaver River water management study, Vol. 5: Fisheries and wildlife. Alta. Envir., Plan. Div., Edmonton.

Shaw, J.F.H. and E.E. Prepas. 1990[a]. Exchange of phosphorus from shallow sediments at nine Alberta lakes. J. Envir. Qlty.

————. 1990[b]. Relationships between phosphorus in shallow sediments in the trophogenic zone of seven lakes. Water Res. [in press]

Shaw, J.F.H., R.D. Shaw and E.E. Prepas. 1989. Advective transport of phosphorus from lake bottom sediments into lakewater. ms to be submitted.

Shaw, R.D. and E.E. Prepas. 1990[c]. Groundwater-lake interactions: II. Nearshore seepage patterns and the contribution of groundwater to lakes in central Alberta. J. Hydrol. [in press]

Strong, W.L. and K.R. Leggat. 1981. Ecoregions of Alberta. Alta. En. Nat. Resour., Resour. Eval. Plan. Div., Edmonton.

Trimbee, A.M. and E.E. Prepas. 1987. Evaluation of total phosphorus as a predictor of the relative biomass of blue-green algae with emphasis on Alberta lakes. Can. J. Fish. Aquat. Sci. 44:1337–1342.

————. 1988. The effect of oxygen depletion on the timing and magnitude of blue-green algal blooms. Verh. Internat. Verein. Limnol. 23:220–226.

Yonge, E.I. and D.O. Trew. 1989. A total phosphorus budget for a shallow, naturally eutrophic lake: Tucker Lake, Alberta. Alta. Envir., Envir. Assess. Div., Envir. Qlty. Monit. Br. Unpubl. rep., Edmonton.

WOLF LAKE

MAP SHEETS: 73L/10, 11
LOCATION: Tp65 R7 W4
LAT/LONG: 54°41′N 110°57′W

Wolf Lake is a beautiful wilderness lake located in Improvement District No. 18 just south of the Primrose Lake Air Weapons Range (Fig. 1). It is popular for its northern pike and walleye fishery, low-density campground and minimal boat traffic. The lake is situated approximately 70 km north of the town of Bonnyville and 310 km northeast of the city of Edmonton. To reach the lake from Edmonton, take Highway 28 northeast to Bonnyville, then Highway 41 north to the hamlet of La Corey. Drive west on Highway 55 until you are 5.5 km west of the hamlet of Iron River, then turn north onto an all weather road that eventually winds its way to Wolf Lake. Occasional signs along this road point the way to Wolf Lake Forest Recreation Area on the south shore of the lake (Fig. 2).

The lake's name is a translation from the Cree *Mahikan Sakhahegan*. In 1911, wolves near the lake were reported to have chased a fur-buyer's sleigh for quite a distance (Chipeniuk 1975). During the 1980s, wolves were still resident in the area.

The Wolf Lake Métis Settlement was created around 1940 to provide Métis trappers with a central area in which to live. The settlement was near traditional trapping grounds as well as local villages and schools. In 1953, the federal government established the Primrose Lake Air Weapons Range north of Wolf Lake and the Métis lost their traplines in that area. They turned to logging for a source of income, but by the early 1960s, most of the marketable timber had been removed. The settlement disbanded at that time and many people moved to the Cold Lake area (Chipeniuk 1975).

A road to the lake was built in 1963 by the Department of Lands and Forests. A campground, Wolf Lake Forest Recreation Area, is located on the south shore (Fig. 2). It is open from 1 May to 30 September and provides 64 campsites, pump water, a sewage disposal facility, a boat launch and a sandy beach. The campground is heavily forested and has been left, as much as possible, in its natural state. There is no defined swimming area and no day-use area, but day-users are welcome to use the facilities at a campsite. Fishing, camping, swimming, sightseeing and relaxing are the most popular activities at the lake and motor boating, water skiing, canoeing and picnicking are enjoyed as well. There are no boating restrictions over most of the lake, but in posted areas such as the swimming area, all boats are prohibited (Alta. For. Ld. Wild. 1988). Fall and winter recreational use of the area is limited to moose hunting, snowmobiling and ice fishing (Marshall Macklin Monaghan West. Ltd. 1983).

The average concentrations of algae in Wolf Lake are quite low, but the water turns green in early spring and midsummer. Large areas of dense aquatic vegetation are present in some parts of the lake, whereas other areas support a low density of plants. In addition to the popular sport fishery for walleye and northern pike, a commercial fishery and a small domestic fishery operate on the lake. Wolf Lake and its tributary streams are closed to fishing during April and May each year (Alta. For. Ld. Wild. 1989).

Drainage Basin Characteristics

The drainage basin of Wolf Lake is 22 times the size of the lake (Tables 1, 2). Most of the watershed is located northeast of the lake and is drained by the Wolf River, which flows into the northwest basin of the lake (Fig. 1). Three smaller streams, one of which drains Sinclair Lake, flow into the northeast basin. As well, nearby Corner

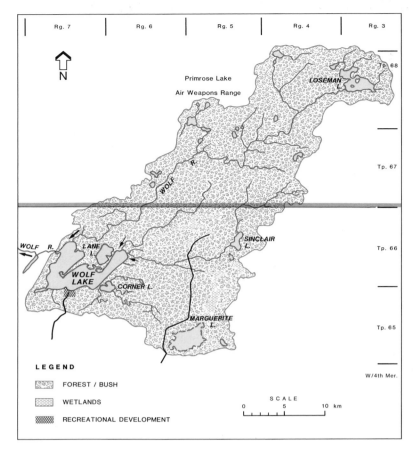

Figure 1. Features of the drainage basin of Wolf Lake.
SOURCES: Alta. Envir. n.d.[b]; En. Mines Resour. Can. 1970; 1971; 1979.
Updated with 1982 aerial photos.

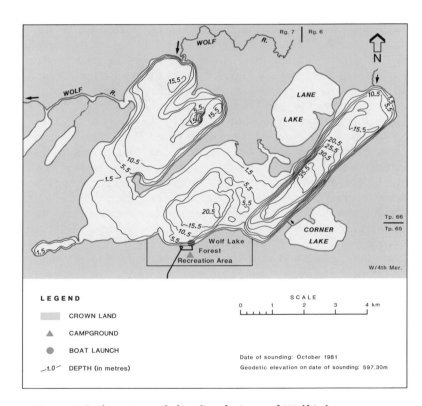

Figure 2. Bathymetry and shoreline features of Wolf Lake.
BATHYMETRY SOURCE: Alta. Envir. n.d.[c].

Table 1. Characteristics of Wolf Lake drainage basin.

area (excluding lake) (km²)[a]	693
soil[b]	Orthic Gray Luvisols
bedrock geology[c]	La Biche Formation (Upper Cretaceous): shale, ironstone partings and concretions; marine
terrain[b]	undulating to gently rolling
ecoregion[d]	Moist Mixedwood Subregion of Boreal Mixedwood
dominant vegetation[d]	trembling aspen, balsam poplar
mean annual inflow (m³)[a, e]	55.9 x 10⁶
mean annual sunshine (h)[f]	2 240

NOTE: [e]excluding groundwater inflow
SOURCES: [a]Alta. Envir. n.d.[b]; [b]Kocaoglu 1975; [c]Alta. Res. Counc. 1972; [d]Strong and Leggat 1981; [f]Envir. Can. 1982

Table 2. Characteristics of Wolf Lake.

elevation (m)[a, b]	597.30
surface area (km²)[a, b]	31.5
volume (m³)[a, b]	289 x 10⁶
maximum depth (m)[a, b]	38.3
mean depth (m)[a, b]	9.2
shoreline length (km)[c]	49.8
mean annual lake evaporation (mm)[d]	634
mean annual precipitation (mm)[d]	439
mean residence time (yr)[d, e]	6
control structure	none

NOTES: [a]on date of sounding: Oct. 1981; [e]excluding groundwater inflow
SOURCES: [b]Alta. Envir. n.d.[c]; [c]En. Mines Resour. Can. 1971; 1979; [d]Alta. Envir. n.d.[b]

Lake flows into the southeast part of Wolf Lake via a short stream, and Lane Lake is joined to the central basin by a wetland area during periods of high water. The outlet, the Wolf River, flows east to the Sand River, which eventually joins the Beaver River.

The soils around Wolf Lake were described in 1975, except for the portion of the watershed that lies within the Primrose Lake Air Weapons Range (Kocaoglu 1975). The watershed is part of a land unit called rolling morainal plain. The undulating to gently rolling landscape features minor ridges and knobs intermixed with many wet depressions and small peat bogs. The predominant soils are Orthic Gray Luvisols. These moderately well-drained soils, which formed on fine-loamy, moderately to strongly calcareous glacial till, are located on the upper and middle portions of slopes. Large areas of poorly drained Organic soils (Fibrisols, Humisols and Mesisols) are located in low-lying depressions and drainageways in the eastern and southeastern parts of the watershed, and between Lane Lake and the central basin of Wolf Lake.

Wolf Lake is located in the Moist Mixedwood Subregion of the Boreal Mixedwood Ecoregion (Strong and Leggat 1981). The dominant trees on moderately well-drained Gray Luvisols are trembling aspen and balsam poplar. Jack pine grows on rapidly to well-drained Eutric Brunisols, and in moister locations, white spruce grows on imperfectly drained Gray Luvisols and Gleysols. In wet areas, black spruce and willows grow on poorly drained Organics and Gleysols, and sedges grow on very poorly drained Organics.

All of the land in the drainage basin is owned by the federal or provincial governments. Access to the federal land is restricted. Portions of the provincial land are leased to the oil industry or for grazing, which is the only agricultural activity in the watershed. A provincial grazing reserve is located near Marguerite Lake, and individual parcels of land in the watershed are leased for grazing as well. The shoreline of Wolf Lake is undeveloped except for the 1.5–km section at the recreation area. BP Canada Inc. and Petro-Canada hold approximately 30 000 ha of oil sands leases in the watershed.

Table 3. Major ions and related water quality variables for Wolf Lake. Average concentrations in mg/L; pH in pH units. Composite samples from the euphotic zone collected 9 times from 11 May to 26 Oct. 1981. S.E. = standard error.

	Mean	S.E.
pH (range)	7.4–8.5	—
total alkalinity ($CaCO_3$)	156	1
specific conductivity (μS/cm)	300	8
total dissolved solids (calculated)	156	2
total hardness ($CaCO_3$)	138	2
dissolved organic carbon	13[a]	0.3
HCO_3	189	1.4
CO_3	0.3	0.33
Mg	16	0.4
Na	11	0.1
K	2	0.1
Cl	1	0.1
SO_4	2	0.2
Ca	30	1.5

NOTE: [a]n = 12

SOURCE: Alta. Envir. n.d.[a], Naquadat station 01AL06AB5190

The leased area is bounded by Marguerite Lake to the south, the Primrose Lake Air Weapons Range to the north, Sinclair Lake to the east, and Wolf Lake to the west (BP Can. Inc. 1985). The first three wells were drilled in 1964 and a pilot project was started later that year. Since 1982, a commercial project, Wolf Lake Phase I, has been operating. Expansion was planned throughout the 1980s. Water for the projects is obtained from groundwater aquifers.

Lake Basin Characteristics

Wolf Lake is large (31.5 km², Table 2) and has three distinct basins (Fig. 2). The northwest basin slopes rapidly to a maximum depth of 15.5 m; most of it is deeper than 10 m. The central basin has a maximum depth of 20.5 m, but a large part of it is less than 6 m deep. The eastern basin is long and narrow and contains the deepest part of the lake. It drops off steeply to a maximum depth of about 38 m. The composition of the sediment in the littoral zone of Wolf Lake is estimated to be 30% organic/silt and 70% sand (McGregor 1983; Trew 1983).

In the early 1980s, Alberta Environment initiated studies of the Cold Lake-Beaver River Basin in order to manage the basin's water resources and to resolve concerns regarding high demand on local water supplies. A long-term plan for water resources management in the Cold Lake region was adopted by the government in October 1985 (Alta. Envir. 1985). The plan applies to the surface and ground-water resources in the Cold Lake and lower Beaver River basin and, for Wolf Lake, stipulates that below a minimum water elevation of 597.20 m, industrial withdrawals will be reduced or suspended. In the future, oil sands plants in the region will obtain their water supply from the North Saskatchewan River via a water pipeline. At present, no water withdrawals are made from Wolf Lake, but under the Cold Lake-Beaver River basin water management plan, withdrawals from Wolf Lake are limited to 0.850 x 10⁶ m³/year. This limit could be raised to 6.30 x 10⁶ m³/year if a control structure were constructed on the outlet to the lake.

The elevation of Wolf Lake has been monitored since 1968 (Fig. 3). The difference between the historic minimum (597.09 m), recorded in October 1969, and the maximum (597.65 m), recorded in June 1974, is 0.56 m. A fluctuation of this size would change the lake's area by about 3.5 km² (Fig. 4).

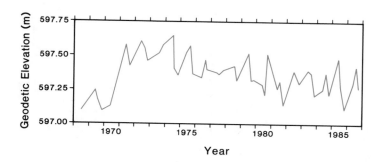

Figure 3. Water level of Wolf Lake, 1968 to 1986. SOURCE: Alta. Envir. n.d.[c].

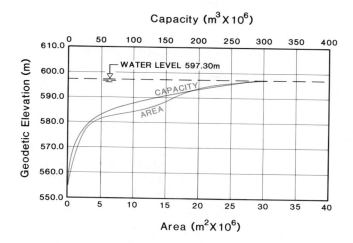

Figure 4. Area/capacity curve for Wolf Lake. SOURCE: Alta. Envir. n.d.[c].

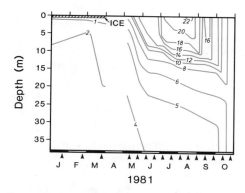

Figure 5. Temperature (°C) of Wolf Lake, 1981. Arrows indicate sampling dates. SOURCE: Alta. Envir. n.d.[a].

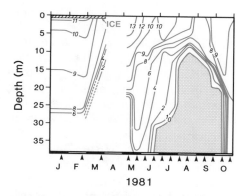

Figure 6. Dissolved oxygen (mg/L) in Wolf Lake, 1981. Maximum sampling depth from Jan. to Mar. was 20 to 28 m. Arrows indicate sampling dates. SOURCE: Alta. Envir. n.d.[a].

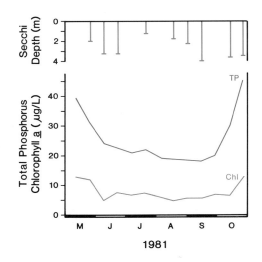

Figure 7. Total phosphorus, chlorophyll *a* and Secchi depth in Wolf Lake, 1981.
SOURCE: Alta. Envir. n.d.[a].

Table 4. Nutrient, chlorophyll *a* and Secchi depth data for Wolf Lake. Average concentrations in μg/L. Composite samples from the euphotic zone collected 12 times from 11 May to 26 Oct. 1981. S.E. = standard error.

	Mean	S.E.
total phosphorus	25	2.6
total dissolved phosphorus	10	1.3
soluble reactive phosphorus	3	0.4
total Kjeldahl nitrogen	911	49
$NO_3 + NO_2$–nitrogen	<8	—
NH_4–nitrogen	<35	—
iron	<26[a]	—
chlorophyll *a*	7.9[b]	1.31
Secchi depth (m)	2.8	0.32

NOTES: [a] n = 7; [b] n = 13
SOURCE: Alta. Envir. n.d.[a], Naquadat station 01AL06AB5190

Water Quality

The water quality of Wolf Lake was studied by Alberta Environment from January through October in 1981 and in March and July in 1986 (Alta. Envir. n.d.[a]). The water is fresh, hard and well-buffered and the dominant ions are calcium and bicarbonate (Table 3).

Wolf Lake is deep and strongly thermally stratified (Fig. 5). During spring turnover in 1981, the water column in the deepest basin did not mix to the bottom. Consequently, the concentration of dissolved oxygen was very low (less than 2 mg/L) in the deeper water during May (Fig. 6). By late June, the hypolimnion was anoxic, and remained so throughout summer. By the end of October, the water column was isothermal but not fully saturated with dissolved oxygen. Under ice in 1981, dissolved oxygen concentrations were high at the surface and declined to 6 mg/L at the deepest sampling point (Fig. 6). The water column was sampled only to depths of 20 to 28 m during this period, so the dissolved oxygen concentration below these depths is not known. In some years, as in March 1986, the deepest water was sampled and did become anoxic by late winter.

Wolf Lake is mesotrophic. Like many other deep lakes in Alberta, the highest concentrations of total phosphorus (45 μg/L) and chlorophyll *a* (13 μg/L) are present after spring and fall turnover (Fig. 7). Except during midsummer, the water is quite clear. The average Secchi transparency in 1981 was 2.8 m, and the average concentration of chlorophyll *a* was 7.9 μg/L (Table 4).

Biological Characteristics

Plants

The phytoplankton community was sampled by Alberta Environment on 30 July 1986 (Alta. Envir. n.d.[a]). The total biomass was small (1.4 mg/L dry weight). The dominant algal group, Pyrrhophyta, accounted for almost 42% of the biomass, and two species, *Ceratium hirundinella* and *Peridinium africanum remotum*, were most important. Species of blue-green algae were next in abundance; they formed 22% of the total biomass.

The macrophyte community was studied by Alberta Energy and Natural Resources in August 1981 (McGregor 1983). Plants grew mainly in the shallow central basin, particularly along the northern shore and in the southwestern bay. In this bay the zone of vegetation extended 500–1 000 m from shore. In the other two basins, large areas without vegetation were located along parts of the northern and eastern shores. Common great bulrush (*Scirpus validus*), an emergent species, grew in most vegetated areas. Common cattail (*Typha latifolia*), sedge (*Carex* sp.) and yellow water lily (*Nuphar variegatum*) were found only along the northern and southern shores of the central basin and northern reed grass (*Calamagrostis inexpansa*) grew in one small area along the southern shore. The

most common submergent plant was northern watermilfoil (*Myriophyllum exalbescens*). Other submergent species included largesheath pondweed (*Potamogeton vaginatus*), whitestem pondweed (*P. praelongus*), *P. friesii*, stonewort (*Chara* sp.) and coontail (*Ceratophyllum demersum*).

Invertebrates

No data are available for the zooplankton in Wolf Lake.

Benthic invertebrates were sampled in July 1965 (McDonald 1967) and August 1968 (Robertson 1970). In 1968, the standing crop was estimated to be 47.5 kg/ha wet weight, or 7.3 kg/ha dry weight. This figure is quite low in comparison to other lakes, such as Whitefish and Moose, in the same general area. Approximately 80% of the biomass in Wolf Lake was collected at depths of 3 m and less, where the bottom type is sand and debris. Midge larvae (Chironomidae) and scuds (Amphipoda: *Gammarus* and *Hyalella*) formed the largest portion of the biomass; below 3 m, midge larvae dominated.

Fish

Twelve species of fish have been identified in Wolf Lake: northern pike, walleye, lake whitefish, cisco, burbot, yellow perch, white sucker, longnose sucker, Iowa darter, spottail shiner, brook stickleback and ninespine stickleback (Robertson 1970; Aquat. Envir. Ltd. 1983). The lake whitefish and cisco are infested with cysts of the tapeworm *Triaenophorus crassus* (Alta. Rec. Parks Wild. 1976). The lake is managed for domestic, commercial and recreational fisheries. The size and species composition of the domestic catch is not known, but the number of licences issued for the domestic fishery is quite small: 5 in 1984/85, 8 in 1985/86 and 12 in 1986/87 (Norris 1988).

A commercial fishery has operated since at least 1942, when records were first kept (Alta. For. Ld. Wild. n.d.; Alta. Rec. Parks Wild. 1976). Northern pike, lake whitefish and walleye are the most important species harvested. Cisco, burbot and suckers are also taken. Historically, the largest total catch of all species (43 306 kg) was taken in 1965/66. Between 1980/81 and 1987/88, the total catch of whitefish, walleye, northern pike and cisco averaged 10 044 kg/year. It ranged from a low of 8 378 kg in 1983/84 to a high of 11 934 kg in 1986/87. The composition of the catch during this period was 58% whitefish, 34% northern pike, 6% walleye and 2% cisco. The size of the cisco catch has decreased sharply since the 1969/70 season. The average cisco catch between 1964/65 and 1969/70 was 18 766 kg/year; this declined sharply between 1980/81 and 1987/88 to an average of only 212 kg/year. Cisco are used as mink food, and the decline in fishing effort for cisco is the result of a declining mink ranching industry and, therefore, a decline in the demand for fish.

Sport fishing is the main activity of visitors to the lake. Anglers

Table 5. Estimated angler numbers, effort and harvest from Wolf Lake. Estimates based on creel survey data collected from 20 May to 14 Aug. 1988. WE = walleye; NP = northern pike; YP = yellow perch.

	WE	NP	YP	Total
number of anglers[a]	—	—	—	6 149
angler-hours[b]	—	—	—	14 119
total number fish harvested[c]	518	4 811	58	5 387
total yield (kg)	436	5 963	—	6 399[d]
mean weight (g)	842	1 240	—	—
catch/angler-hour	0.05	0.76	—	0.81[d]
harvest/angler-hour[b, c]	0.04	0.34	0.01	0.39
harvest/angler[a, c]	0.08	0.79	0.01	0.88

NOTES: [a]observed no. anglers = 4 340; [b]observed hours = 10 042; [c]based on observed no. fish kept: WE = 358, NP = 3 441, YP = 51; [d]excluding YP
SOURCE: Alta. For. Ld. Wild. n.d.

were surveyed during 1979, 1980, 1982 and 1988 (Alta. For. Ld. Wild. n.d.). In 1988, an estimated 6 149 anglers spent 14 119 hours fishing (Table 5). Walleye were harvested at a rate of 0.04 fish/angler-hour, which is considerably lower than the regional average of 0.10 walleye/angler-hour. The harvest rate of northern pike (0.34 fish/angler-hour), on the other hand, was higher than the regional average of 0.22 pike/angler-hour. Of the total number of fish caught, 22% of the walleye and 45% of the northern pike were released. Catches of yellow perch were incidental.

Wildlife

Wolf Lake and its watershed provide a wide variety of habitat types for wildlife in a relatively remote setting. The lake is diverse in depth, shoreline configuration, backshore topography and vegetation. It has several inflowing streams, and two smaller lakes, Lane and Corner, are nearby.

The most abundant waterfowl at Wolf Lake are dabbling and diving ducks, including Mallards, Widgeons, Common Goldeneye, Blue-winged Teal and Bufflehead. American Coots and Red-necked Grebes are also numerous. An interesting feature of the lake is the presence of several bird colonies. In 1981, these colonies included 145 Western Grebe nests, 20 Great Blue Heron nests, and approximately 100 Common Tern nests. As well, a pair of Ospreys and a pair of Turkey Vultures nested in the southwestern bay. Nearby Lane Lake and the marshy north shore of Wolf Lake's central basin support colonies of Eared Grebe and Common Tern (Rippon 1983).

The interspersion of wetlands with upland areas in the watershed has created prime habitat for fur-bearing species such as beaver, mink, muskrat, otter, coyote, weasel, fox, squirrel, lynx, wolf and skunk (BP Exploration Can. Ltd. 1982). In 1980 there were 9 beaver lodges and 15 muskrat houses on Wolf Lake (Rippon 1983). The area surrounding the eastern arm of the lake has been identified as a key winter range area for moose (BP Exploration Can. Ltd. 1982). The Primrose Lake Air Weapons Range provides a refuge for animals such as moose because no hunting is allowed. Other ungulates sighted in the drainage basin include white-tailed deer, mule deer, woodland caribou and elk.

M.E. Bradford

References

Alberta Environment. n.d.[a]. Envir. Assess. Div., Envir. Qlty. Monit. Br. Unpubl. data, Edmonton.
———. n.d.[b]. Tech. Serv. Div., Hydrol. Br. Unpubl. data, Edmonton.
———. n.d.[c]. Tech. Serv. Div., Surv. Br. Unpubl. data, Edmonton.
———. 1985. Cold Lake-Beaver River long term water management plan. Plan. Div., Edmonton.
Alberta Forestry, Lands and Wildlife. n.d. Fish Wild. Div. Unpubl. data, Edmonton.
———. 1988. Boating in Alberta. Fish Wild. Div., Edmonton.
———. 1989. Guide to sportfishing. Fish Wild. Div., Edmonton.
Alberta Recreation, Parks and Wildlife. 1976. Commercial fisheries catch statistics for Alberta, 1942–1975. Fish Wild. Div., Fish. Mgt. Rep. No. 22, Edmonton.
Alberta Research Council. 1972. Geological map of Alberta. Nat. Resour. Div., Alta. Geol. Surv., Edmonton.
Aquatic Environments Limited. 1983. Fisheries studies; detailed data report [Appendix G]. In Cold Lake-Beaver River water management study, Vol. 4: Fisheries. Alta. Envir., Plan. Div., Edmonton.
BP Canada Inc. 1985. Wolf Lake development plan. BP Can. Inc., Calgary.
BP Exploration Canada Ltd. 1982. Wolf Lake project: Environmental information document. Envir. Aff. Health Safety Group, Calgary.
Chipeniuk, R.C. 1975. Lakes of the Lac La Biche district. R.C. Chipeniuk, Lac La Biche.
Energy, Mines and Resources Canada. 1970, 1971, 1979. National topographic series 1:50 000 73L/15 (1970), 73L/10 (1971), 73L/16 (1971), 73L/11 (1979). Surv. Map. Br., Ottawa.
Environment Canada. 1982. Canadian climate normals, Vol. 7: Bright sunshine (1951–1980). Prep. by Atm. Envir. Serv. Supply Serv. Can., Ottawa.
Kocaoglu, S.S. 1975. Reconnaissance soil survey of the Sand River area. Alta. Soil Surv. Rep. No. 34, Univ. Alta. Bull. No. SS–15, Alta. Inst. Pedol. Rep. No. S–74–34 1975. Univ. Alta., Edmonton.
Marshall Macklin Monaghan Western Limited. 1983. Water based recreation [Appendix J]. In Cold Lake-Beaver River water management study, Vol. 6: Recreation. Alta. Envir., Plan. Div., Edmonton.
McDonald, D.G. 1967. Wolf Lake. Alta. Ld. For., Fish Wild. Div. Unpubl. rep., Edmonton.
McGregor, C.A. 1983. Detailed report [Appendix L]. In Cold Lake-Beaver River water management study, Vol. 7: Ecological inventory of lake shorelines. Alta. Envir., Plan. Div., Edmonton.
Norris, H.J. 1988. Alta. For. Ld. Wild., Fish Wild. Div., St. Paul. Pers. comm.
Rippon, B. 1983. Water related wildlife resources [Appendix I]. In Cold Lake-Beaver River water management study, Vol. 5: Fisheries and wildlife. Alta. Envir., Plan. Div., Edmonton.
Robertson, M.R. 1970. Wolf Lake. Alta. Ld. For., Fish Wild. Div. Unpubl. rep., Edmonton.
Strong, W.L. and K.R. Leggat. 1981. Ecoregions of Alberta. Alta. En. Nat. Resour., Resour. Eval. Plan. Div., Edmonton.
Trew, D.O. 1983. Impacts of lake level fluctuations on trophic status [Appendix N]. In Cold Lake-Beaver River water management study, Vol. 8: Water quality. Alta. Envir., Plan. Div., Edmonton.

NORTH SASKATCHEWAN REGION

The North Saskatchewan and Battle River basins in central Alberta provide abundant recreational opportunities for the people of Edmonton and surrounding communities. The basins' lakes range from deep, fresh Hubbles and Eden lakes to shallow, salty Miquelon and Peninsula lakes. In between are numerous relatively shallow freshwater lakes that are highly developed and heavily used for recreation. To the south and east of these basins is the Sounding Creek Basin, which is isolated from major river systems. It drains an area of low precipitation and shallow, often saline lakes.

The North Saskatchewan River Basin, with an area of 56 700 km^2 within Alberta, is the third largest river basin in the province. The river originates in the Rocky Mountains among glaciers of the Columbia Icefield, and then flows east and north toward the town of Drayton Valley. Through this land the river traverses five ecoregions: the Alpine and Subalpine at the highest elevations, Montane in the Kootenay Plains area, Boreal Uplands at Nordegg, and finally Boreal Foothills at the towns of Rocky Mountain House and Drayton Valley. Within these ecoregions, the lakes discussed in the *Atlas* are Crimson, Buck and Twin, which are all in the Boreal Foothills Ecoregion. Surrounding these lakes are the diverse forest vegetation and Gray Luvisolic soils typical of the boreal foothills. Trembling aspen, balsam poplar, lodgepole pine and white spruce are the dominant species of trees.

The slope of the North Saskatchewan River decreases gradually as it flows eastward past Drayton Valley, and the river passes through the Boreal Mixedwood Ecoregion. Within the basin, this ecoregion extends eastward to the town of Stony Plain and south to encompass Pigeon and Battle lakes in the Battle River Basin. At one time, the area was covered in trembling aspen and balsam poplar, but now much of it has been cleared for agriculture and for the extraction of gas, oil and coal. Recreation is concentrated at some of the most heavily used lakes in the province: Wabamun, Ste. Anne, Isle, Jackfish, Sandy and Pigeon lakes. An isolated portion of the Boreal Mixedwood Ecoregion lies in the Cooking Lake moraine to the east of the city of Edmonton. There are several recreational lakes within the moraine, including Cooking, Hastings and Miquelon.

The Battle River Basin, with its headwaters in Battle Lake, drains an area of 25 000 km^2. The river flows southeast from Battle Lake, collects water from Pigeon Lake Creek, turns northeast at the town of Ponoka and then receives water from Coal Lake. The river passes into Driedmeat Lake, which has been stabilized with a weir. The Battle and North Saskatchewan rivers flow eastward through the Aspen Parkland Ecoregion, cross the border into Saskatchewan, and join near the city of North Battleford. Eventually, the Saskatchewan River system joins the Nelson River system, which flows into Hudson Bay.

The Aspen Parkland within the North Saskatchewan and Battle River basins of Alberta is characterized by a mixture of rough fescue grassland and trembling aspen. The Chernozemic soils that have developed under the grassland are highly productive, and the area is extensively used for tilled crops. Some of the lakes in the region are saline, such as Oliva and Peninsula, but the water in many lakes to the north of these, for example Lac St. Cyr and Bonnie Lake, is fresh. Also in this ecoregion is Beaverhill Lake, an internationally recognized staging area for migratory birds.

The Aspen Parkland Ecoregion grades to the drier Mixed Grass and Short Grass ecoregions within the Sounding Creek Basin, which

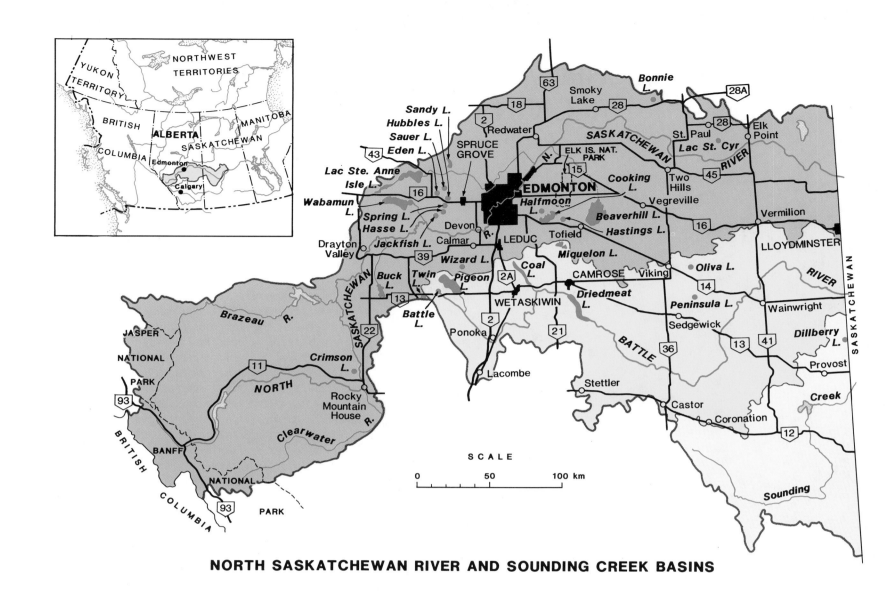

NORTH SASKATCHEWAN RIVER AND SOUNDING CREEK BASINS

Wabamun Lake. Photo by P.A. Mitchell

Pigeon Lake. Photo by P.A. Mitchell

Battle Lake. Photo by D. Huet

Sandy Lake. Photo by Alberta Environment

is located to the south of the Battle River Basin. In the northern portion of the Sounding Creek Basin, where Dillberry Lake is located, the dominant vegetation is rough fescue grass, dotted with shrubs and trembling aspen where moisture is sufficient. In the southern part of the basin, spear and grama grasses predominate. Dryland farming and cattle production are the main land uses.

The Battle River Basin was the scene of white people's first arrival in what is now Alberta. In 1754, Anthony Henday walked into the area to explore and to determine the potential for expanding the fur trade west. Thus began a long and colourful history of white settlement in the North Saskatchewan River Basin. The fur trading posts that were established along the North Saskatchewan River, including Edmonton House in 1795 and Rocky Mountain House in 1799, attracted settlers and farmers. In 1843, a Catholic mission was established on Lac Ste. Anne, and a Protestant mission on Pigeon Lake a few years later. Edmonton became a focal point for much of the development in the basin, and it remains so today.

The total population in the basins of the North Saskatchewan and Battle rivers and Sounding Creek was about one million people in the mid–1980s. Most of these people are concentrated in the Edmonton area and, consequently, attractive lakes within easy driving distance of the city have been developed extensively. Picnicking, swimming, fishing and camping are favourite activities at these lakes. Wabamun Lake is especially popular for sailing, and there are several sailing clubs on the lake. Wizard Lake attracts water skiing enthusiasts. Several lakes—Pigeon, Wabamun, Ste. Anne, Hasse, Crimson, Dillberry and Miquelon—have developed public beaches, and crowds of people flock to them on summer weekends to enjoy the relatively clear water.

Fishing is a major activity in Alberta lakes, and the lure of stocked rainbow trout draws anglers to several pothole lakes near Edmonton. Many of these lakes now offer picnicking, swimming, and other family-oriented facilities in either private or public developments. Examples of rainbow trout stocked lakes with recreational facilities include Eden, Spring, Hasse, Dillberry and Twin lakes. Within these drainage basins, four lakes included in the *Atlas* are fished commercially: Wabamun, Buck, Ste. Anne and Pigeon. The target commercial species is lake whitefish.

The 28 lakes described in the *Atlas* in these river basins provide the angler, recreationist and lake scientist with a diverse, fascinating, cross-section of lake types. Whatever the lake visitors' interest, they will find a lake in these basins to suit them.

P.A. Mitchell

BEAVERHILL LAKE

MAP SHEETS: 83H/7, 8, 9, 10
LOCATION: Tp51, 52 R17, 18 W4
LAT/LONG: 53°27'N 112°32'W

Beaverhill Lake is one of the most important bird habitats in Alberta. It is recognized as an internationally significant water body for shorebirds and waterfowl, in particular, as a staging area for migratory birds flying to and from the arctic. During May and September each year, the lake hosts thousands of birds. In the spring, most of the birds move on, but many others stay and nest. Beaverhill Lake and the surrounding area have been Ducks Unlimited (Canada) projects since early 1969. In 1981, the Canadian Nature Federation designated the lake as a National Nature Viewpoint in recognition of its importance to birds and birdwatchers, and in 1982, the lake became part of the Wetlands for Tomorrow Program. This is a joint program between Ducks Unlimited (Canada) and Fish and Wildlife Division for the management and enhancement of waterfowl populations and habitats. In June 1987, the lake was designated a Ramsar site. The Ramsar Convention of 1971 is an international agreement that identifies and protects wetlands of importance to migratory birds. By 1988, the convention had been ratified by 45 countries. The secretariat for the convention is the Switzerland-based International Union for the Conservation of Nature and Natural Resources.

Beaverhill Lake is situated in the counties of Beaver and Lamont. It is easily accessible from the city of Edmonton, as it is located only 65 km east of the city, just north of Highway 14 and east of Secondary Road 834. The closest population centre is the town of Tofield, 4 km southwest of the lake on Highway 14 (Fig. 1).

The lake's name is a translation of the Cree name, *amisk-wa-chi-sakhahigan* (Holmgren and Holmgren 1976). The lake appears on the Thompson map of 1814 as Beaver Lake. This map also shows the nearby Beaver Hills, now known as the Cooking Lake Moraine, which were named for the large number of beaver found there.

According to legend, the lake was a favourite camping spot for Cree when they came to the area to hunt buffalo. In the late 1800s and early 1900s, settlements were established in four areas near the lake. The western shore was first settled by Métis, who came to hunt buffalo in the early 1870s (Touchings 1976). Many of the Métis families later filed for homesteads and began farming. White settlers arrived in the area during the 1880s and occupied land along the western shore. One of the first settlers to acquire land legally was Robert Logan, who operated a store and trading post and owned land near the lake. The district soon became known as Logan, and the Logan post office was established in 1892. Robert Logan's son, John, promoted the lake as a pleasure resort, and operated a steamboat that carried vacationers across the water (Lister 1979). The second area, Beaverlake Settlement, was located on the northeast shore just east of the lake's outlet, Beaverhill Creek. This area was settled sometime after 1873, and by 1892, the settlement boasted a school and a one-man detachment of the North West Mounted Police. The third area, Bathgate, was located on the southeast shore; it was settled around 1900. The Bathgate post office opened in 1906 but closed in 1927 after the community failed to expand. The fourth settlement was the village of Tofield, located 4 km southwest of the lake. It was the fastest growing community in the area in the 1900s. In 1907, Tofield was incorporated as a village, and in 1909, after the arrival of the Grand Trunk Pacific Railroad, it became a town (Touchings 1976). At the present time, Tofield is the only one of the four communities that still exists.

The birds of Beaverhill Lake have been studied by many ornithologists since the beginning of the twentieth century. In particular,

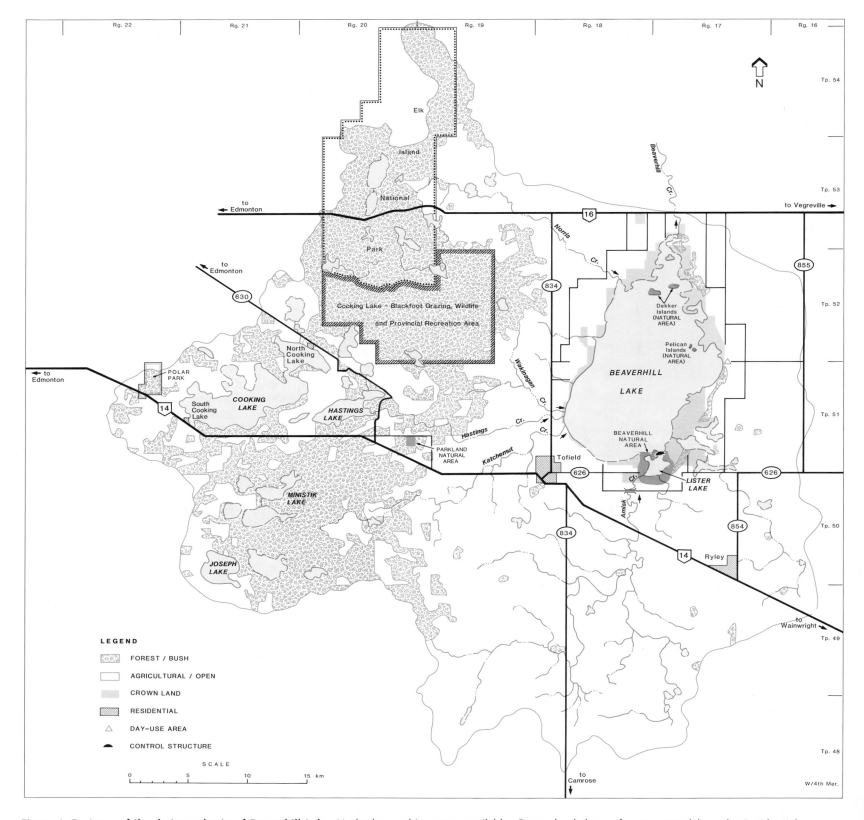

Figure 1. Features of the drainage basin of Beaverhill Lake. No hydrographic survey available. Crown land shown for area near lake only. Residential development not shown.
SOURCES: Alta. Envir. n.d.[b]; En. Mines Resour. Can. 1983. Updated with 1983 and 1987 aerial photos.

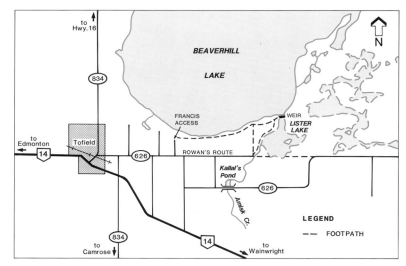

Figure 2. Access to the southern portion of Beaverhill Lake.

long-term observations were made by the late Professor William Rowan and the late Robert Lister, both from the Zoology Department of the University of Alberta. Beginning in 1920, Rowan spent 37 years collecting, sketching and banding birds and making extensive notes on their behaviour. He combined two contradictory attitudes toward wildlife: that of the hunter/collector and that of the naturalist/conservationist. In 1925, the lake was declared a Public Shooting Ground, but by 1948, when the Edmonton Bird Club was founded, most visitors to the lake were more interested in identifying and observing birds than shooting them (Lister 1979). The Edmonton Bird Club has contributed much to the knowledge of the species of birds at the lake. In 1983, another group of birding enthusiasts began the Beaverhill Lake Bird Banding Station to encourage research and to provide instruction in ornithology. The group was named the Beaverhill Bird Observatory in 1985. Members carry out many projects, including daily counts of birds, construction of nesting boxes, banding, and research on the behaviour and habitat of individual species (Ebel 1988).

During the 1970s, management of the Beaverhill Lake area became a subject of concern to the Fish and Wildlife and Public Lands divisions of Alberta Forestry, Lands and Wildlife, Alberta Agriculture, local leaseholders and the general public. In 1981, the Beaverhill Lake Integrated Resource Plan was approved (Alta. En. Nat. Resour. 1981). It allocated the approximately 4 450 ha of Crown land around the lake according to 5 land-use themes: agriculture, agriculture-wildlife, wildlife-agriculture, wildlife and recreation. Theme areas are used to prepare a local development plan for each disposition. The local development plan then forms the basis for range improvement agreements between the government and the lessee or permittee, or for wildlife habitat enhancement or recreation projects.

In 1987, Alberta Forestry, Lands and Wildlife established the Beaverhill Natural Area to protect parts of Beaverhill Lake and the surrounding area (Alta. For. Ld. Wild. 1987). The natural area comprises the Dekker and Pelican islands at the north end of Beaverhill Lake and land surrounding Robert Lister Lake, also known as "A" Lake (Fig. 1). It is managed through the cooperation of the Fish and Wildlife and Public Lands divisions of Alberta Forestry, Lands and Wildlife, Ducks Unlimited (Canada) and the Beaverhill Bird Observatory. Although the natural area is conserved and managed to maintain its wilderness and wildlife qualities, recreational and educational use is encouraged. Popular activities are birdwatching, photography and hiking.

There are several points of access to the shore of Beaverhill Lake, but most of them must be reached on foot. The route to the southern side of the lake begins in Tofield (Fig. 2). Turn left off Highway 14 and then immediately right onto the Tofield access road. Turn left again at the gas station. The Beaverhill Lake Nature Centre is located next to the gas station. It provides field checklists for birds, nesting boxes, seed and tourist information. Once over the railroad tracks, turn east onto Rowan's Route, which is also called 51 Avenue within Tofield, and Secondary Road 626 outside the town. About 5 km east of Tofield, a north-south road allowance provides a short, direct route to Francis Point on the southern side of the lake. The turnoff is marked with a sign. At the far eastern end of Rowan's Route is the access to Robert Lister Lake and the natural area. When you have driven almost 9 km from Tofield, turn north off the road. Close the gate upon entering the pasture, then drive northeast over a cart-track that ends in an informal parking area at another gate. Motor vehicles are not allowed past the parking area. There is a large sign on the other side of this gate that shows a map of Beaverhill Lake. A cart track leads from the sign along the western shore of Robert Lister Lake, and terminates at a Ducks Unlimited (Canada) weir. Another trail runs from the weir along the southern shore of Beaverhill Lake to Francis Point.

Robert Lister Lake is an impoundment developed by Ducks Unlimited (Canada) to control water levels and provide nesting habitat for waterfowl. Approximately 26 islands have been built around the southern and eastern sides of the lake; they have been well used by nesting ducks and geese since their construction. The headland on the western side of the weir is one of the best locations for viewing

Table 1. Characteristics of Beaverhill Lake drainage basin.

area (excluding lake) (km²)[a]	1 970
soil[b]	Black Chernozemics, Black Solonetzics and Orthic Gray Luvisols
bedrock geology[c]	Belly River Formation (Upper Cretaceous): sandstone, siltstone, mudstone, ironstone beds; nonmarine Bearpaw Formation (Upper Cretaceous): shale, thin ironstone and bentonite beds; marine
terrain[b]	gently to strongly rolling
ecoregion[d]	Boreal Mixedwood and Aspen Parkland
dominant vegetation[d]	trembling aspen
mean annual inflow (m³)[a, e]	28.1 x 10⁶
mean annual sunshine (h)[f]	2 168

NOTE: [e]excluding groundwater inflow
SOURCES: [a]Alta. Envir. n.d.[b]; [b]Howitt 1988; [c]Alta. Res. Counc. 1972; [d]Strong and Leggat 1981; [f]Envir. Can. 1982

shorebirds. The Beaverhill Lake Banding Station is situated near the western side of the weir, as well.

Kallal's Ponds are located at the Kallal Dam on Amisk Creek, just south of Robert Lister Lake (Fig. 2). During migration, waterfowl, blackbirds, marsh-dwelling birds and sandpipers congregate on the ponds (Heath et al. 1984). Another area enhanced by Ducks Unlimited (Canada) is a marsh called "C" Lake, which is located near the southeastern shore of Beaverhill Lake, approximately 2.2 km northeast of the weir on Lister Lake. To create waterfowl nesting habitat, about eight islands were built around the perimeter of the marsh. The marsh is connected to Beaverhill Lake by a drainage ditch.

Access to the Beaverhill Lake Recreation Area, midway along the eastern shore, can be gained from Secondary Road 855 (Fig. 1). This area is operated by the County of Beaver, and has a picnic shelter and outdoor toilets. In 1988, however, they were in need of repair. Motor boats are not allowed on Beaverhill Lake, but canoes and rowboats are permitted (Alta. For. Ld. Wild. 1988). The lake is popular for waterfowl hunting, but hunting restrictions are in effect over the southern half of the lake. Hunting game birds on the southern portion of the lake and the southern islands, or hunting within 0.8 km of the edge of the water of that portion of the lake, is prohibited until 1 November each year (Alta. For. Ld. Wild. 1989).

Drainage Basin Characteristics

A large portion of Beaverhill Lake's drainage basin lies within the Cooking Lake Moraine (Alta. Envir. 1977). This landform occupies most of the central and western parts of the watershed. It is characterized by knob and kettle topography that gives it a gently to strongly rolling appearance. The knobs range from 5 to 15 m in height, and many of the kettles contain water. In general, the moraine slopes downward to the northeast. The eastern and southern parts of the drainage basin are a poorly drained ground moraine plain. Intermittent and permanent sloughs and lakes are present throughout this area.

The Cooking Lake Moraine contains the largest tracts of continuously forested land within a 30–km radius of Edmonton (Alta. Envir. 1977). The moraine is part of the Boreal Mixedwood Ecoregion (Strong and Leggat 1981). The soils are mainly Orthic Gray Luvisols and the forest cover is mostly deciduous, with trembling aspen the dominant tree (Table 1). White spruce is the climax species but, because of land clearing during the late 1800s, timber harvesting and fire, few mature stands of spruce remain. Mature trembling aspen forest predominates in the southern part of the moraine, as well as in Elk Island National Park and the Cooking Lake-Blackfoot Grazing, Wildlife and Provincial Recreation Area in the northern part of the moraine.

The ground moraine plain in the eastern and southern parts of the drainage basin has relatively little tree cover. This area is part of the Aspen Parkland Ecoregion, and the natural vegetation consists of trembling aspen interspersed with patches of grassland (Strong and Leggat 1981). Much of the land, however, has been cultivated since the early 1900s. The soils are fertile Black Chernozemics that are used to grow barley, oats and canola crops (Alta. En. Nat. Resour. 1981; Howitt 1988).

Approximately 90% of the 4 450 ha of Crown land surrounding the lake is leased for agriculture, primarily grazing, and the private land nearby is used to grow crops. In 1981, there were 35 grazing leases, 5 grazing permits, 7 cultivation permits and 6 farm development leases assigned to approximately 44 farmers and ranchers who own adjacent lands. A recreational lease for the Beaverhill Lake Recreation Area on the eastern shore is held by the County of Beaver. As well, there were 12 producing and 13 potential natural gas well sites in the area in 1981 (Alta. En. Nat. Resour. 1981).

The development of country residential subdivisions in the western portion of the drainage basin increased dramatically during the 1970s and 1980s. Closer to the lake, however, residential development has been minimal.

Most of the creeks draining into Beaverhill Lake flow intermittently. Amisk Creek drains the southern part of the watershed and flows over two Ducks Unlimited (Canada) weirs into Robert Lister Lake. Norris, Wakinagan, Hastings and Katchemut creeks drain the Cooking Lake Moraine and flow intermittently into the western side of Beaverhill Lake. The outlet, Beaverhill Creek, is overgrown with cattails and flows only during periods of very high water. It eventually drains into the North Saskatchewan River.

Lake Basin Characteristics

The large size (139 km²) and shallow depth of Beaverhill Lake, as well as the presence of several islands, are some of the physical features that attract birds to the lake. There are no depth contours available, but the shape of the lake basin is that of a large, shallow pan with a maximum depth of 2.3 m (Table 2). The number and size of the islands at the north end of the lake, which include the Dekker and Pelican islands (Fig. 1), vary with the water level.

The character of the shoreline is variable. The southern shore is quite straight and has narrow, sandy beaches, whereas the northern shore is muddy and irregular in shape, and is characterized by reed-choked bays and rock-strewn points. The lake is bordered by willow and trembling aspen in the east and south, but in the west and north the landscape is open and consists of pasture and gently sloping fields (Dekker 1982).

The elevation of Beaverhill Lake has been monitored since 1968 (Fig. 3). The minimum recorded level (668.23 m) occurred in that year, and the maximum level (669.60 m) was recorded in 1974. An interesting anecdotal history of long-term water levels in Beaverhill Lake is given by Lister (1979). In 1885, the lake's elevation was so low that buffalo had to drink from springs in the centre of the basin, and willow and poplar trees grew on the accrued land. By 1895, the water level had risen high enough to flood the trees, and Great Blue Herons nested in their dry, dead branches. The period between 1899 and 1903 was very rainy, and the lake level of approximately 670.9 m achieved in 1902 may have been the highest of the past century. From 1905 to 1910, the lake receded, and much of the previously submerged land was cultivated. Water levels remained stable until the rainy fall of 1915, when they began, once again, to rise. The highest level for this period was approximately 670.3 m in 1917 (Zelt and Glasgow 1976). By 1922, the lake had receded to levels similar to those of 1910. In 1929, the elevation dropped about 1.5 m, and the following winter most of the fish population died. Water levels remained low for more than two decades, and in 1950 and 1951, the lake almost dried up completely. By 1974, the elevation had risen to 669.60 m, but it declined again during the late 1970s, and has remained quite stable since that time (Fig. 3).

At various times, Lister Lake has been either an integral part of Beaverhill Lake, a dry mud flat, or various stages in between. In 1917, it was a large, wide bay at the southeast end of the lake (Zelt and Glasgow 1976), whereas in the 1950s, a car could be driven

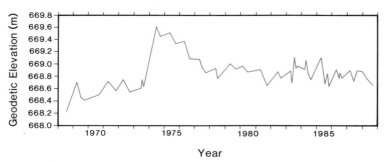

Figure 3. Water level of Beaverhill Lake, 1968 to 1986. SOURCE: Alta. Envir. n.d.[c].

Table 2. Characteristics of Beaverhill Lake.

surface area (km²)[a]	139
volume (m³)	unknown
maximum depth (m)[b]	2.3
mean depth (m)	unknown
shoreline length (km)[a]	79.5
mean annual lake evaporation (mm)[c]	655
mean annual precipitation (mm)[c]	453
mean residence time (yr)[c, d]	>100
control structure	Ducks Unlimited (Canada) weir between Beaverhill Lake and Robert Lister Lake

NOTE: [d]excluding groundwater inflow
SOURCES: [a]En. Mines Resour. Can. 1983; [b]Alta. Envir. n.d.[a]; [c]Alta. Envir. n.d.[b].

Table 3. Major ions and related water quality variables for Beaverhill Lake. Average concentrations in mg/L; pH in pH units. Samples from two depths were collected 3 times from 01 June to 29 July 1976. S.E. = standard error.

	Mean	S.E.
pH (range)	8.3–8.8	—
total alkalinity (CaCO₃)	402	11.0
specific conductivity (µS/cm)	1 302	105.4
total dissolved solids (calculated)	874	17.0
total hardness (CaCO₃)	317	8.6
HCO₃	472	19.8
CO₃	9	5.7
Mg	54	2.8
Na	188	6.0
K	35	1.1
Cl	13	0.2
SO₄	301	9.4
Ca	38	2.5

SOURCE: Alta. Envir. n.d.[a], Naquadat station 01AT05EB2020

across its dry bottom (Lister 1979). In 1970, it was a water-filled slough, and Ducks Unlimited (Canada) built a weir between it and Beaverhill Lake (Fig. 1). To encourage waterfowl production, they also constructed artificial islands and nesting platforms. High water levels during the spring of 1974 washed out the weir, but it was reconstructed soon after. The present structure is an earthen berm with a concrete spillway.

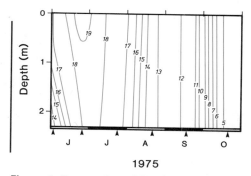

Figure 4. Temperature (°C) of Beaverhill Lake, 1975. Arrows indicate sampling dates. SOURCE: Alta. Envir. n.d.[a].

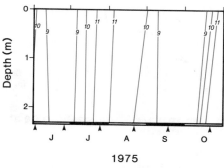

Figure 5. Dissolved oxygen (mg/L) in Beaverhill Lake, 1975. Arrows indicate sampling dates. SOURCE: Alta. Envir. n.d.[a].

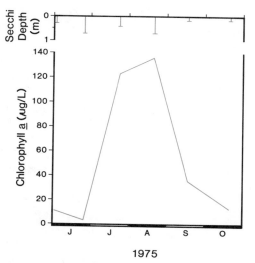

Figure 6. Chlorophyll *a* and Secchi depth in Beaverhill Lake, 1975. SOURCE: Alta. Envir. n.d.[a].

Water Quality

The water quality of Beaverhill Lake was studied by researchers at the University of Alberta during 1971 and from 1974 to 1976 (Alta. Envir. n.d.[a]).

The water is well-buffered and slightly saline (Table 3). The dominant ions are bicarbonate, sulphate and sodium. The lake is so shallow that it is mixed constantly by wind during the open-water period. In 1975, the water column was weakly thermally stratified during June, but isothermal for the rest of the open-water period (Fig. 4). The concentration of dissolved oxygen was high during the summer and fall of 1975 (Fig. 5), but declined over winter until, by February 1976, the concentration was 2.4 mg/L at the surface and 1.8 mg/L at a depth of 0.5 m.

Beaverhill Lake is hyper-eutrophic. In 1975, the average Secchi depth was only 0.4 m and the average chlorophyll *a* concentration was 54 µg/L. The highest chlorophyll level (137 µg/L) was recorded in August (Fig. 6). Data for total phosphorus concentrations are not available, but the high chlorophyll levels suggest that total phosphorus levels would be very high as well. Major potential sources of phosphorus are runoff from agricultural land, particularly pasture land near the shore, inputs by the tens of thousands of birds that use the lake, return of phosphorus from sediments to the water column, and phosphorus released by senescing macrophytes.

Biological Characteristics

Plants

Qualitative studies of the plant community in Beaverhill Lake were conducted by researchers at the University of Alberta from 1974 to 1976 (Alta. Envir. n.d.[a]). Of the eight algal genera identified, three were green algae (Chlorophyta: *Ankistrodesmus* sp., *Chlamydomonas* sp., *Crucigenia* sp.) and three were blue-green algae (Cyanophyta: *Anabaena* spp., *Aphanizomenon* sp., *Microcystis* sp.). Macrophytes were sampled in June 1975. The three emergent species identified were common great bulrush (*Scirpus validus*), sedges (*Carex* spp.) and rushes (*Juncus* spp.), and the two submergent species were large-sheath pondweed (*Potamogeton vaginatus*) and mare's tail (*Hippurus vulgaris*).

Invertebrates

The zooplankton community was sampled regularly from November 1974 to July 1976 by the University of Alberta (Alta. Envir. n.d.[a]). During the open-water period in 1976, the average biomass was 2.5 g/m². Copepods, in particular *Diaptomus* sp., were present in large numbers on all sampling dates except 2 June. On that date, the planktonic rotifer *Conochilus unicornis* was dominant numerically. In August, *Daphnia pulicaria* shared dominance with *Diaptomus* sp.

There are no data available for the benthic invertebrate community.

Fish

There are no sport fish in Beaverhill Lake. Because of the lake's shallow depth, dissolved oxygen becomes depleted over winter and most fish are unable to survive. Historically, northern pike, whitefish and suckers inhabited the lake, which supported a good fishery when water levels were high. At present, however, only minnows and sticklebacks can survive the winter (Lister 1979; Dekker 1982).

Wildlife

Beaverhill Lake is one of the major staging areas in western North America for waterfowl and shorebirds bound to and from the western Arctic. By 1988, 272 species of birds had been reported in the area of the lake (Ebel n.d.). Of these, 145 species are known to breed locally. Dekker (1982) gives an excellent overview of the timing of various migrations and the locations of locally nesting birds and migrants. In years with an early spring, the first Canada Geese arrive before mid-March. Locally breeding pairs are followed by transient "honkers", then later by White-fronted and Snow geese. Their numbers can reach tens of thousands at peak periods. Most Sandhill Cranes arrive in late April or early May, and stragglers continue to come for two weeks. Shorebirds, including Greater and Lesser yellowlegs, Short-billed and Long-billed dowitchers, Hudsonian Godwits and Pectoral Sandpipers, congregate on flooded fields and wet meadows before the lake is free of ice. As meltwater pools evaporate, flocks of waders congregate on mudflats along the lakeshore. The number and variety of shorebirds increase toward mid-May, when great numbers collect on pastureland to feed on newly hatched midges. Different areas of the lake are used by various species of waders. Sandpipers are found in the greatest numbers along the open western shore, whereas Sanderlings are attracted to the wave-swept strip of sand along the southern shore. Dowitchers, yellowlegs and Stilt Sandpipers favour shallow bays, Black-bellied Plovers, Knots and Ruddy Turnstones frequent rock-strewn points along the eastern shore, and American Golden Plovers and Buff-breasted Sandpipers use the nearby grasslands. After the northern shorebirds depart, locally breeding waders, such as American Avocets, Marbled Godwits, Willets, Wilson's Phalaropes, Killdeer, and a few Piping Plovers, remain.

Other birds that nest at the lake include Canvasbacks, Pintails, Mallards, Ruddy Ducks, American Coots and grebes. The distribution of ducks, geese and swans was surveyed during the fall of 1973 and the spring and summer of 1974 by the Canadian Wildlife Service (Kemper 1976). The greatest number of birds are present during spring and fall, but because Beaverhill Lake is a major duck moulting area, duck numbers increase substantially in July and August when birds that have nested in nearby potholes move from the potholes to the lake to moult. Other ducks breed on the lake itself, and their numbers increase when ducklings hatch. Most of the ducks are dabblers rather than divers; they primarily frequent the marshy shorelines at the northern end of the lake during July and August.

During summer, thousands of Red-winged and Yellow-headed blackbirds and Franklin's gulls raise their young in the cover of bulrushes. Ring-billed and California gulls, terns, Black-crowned Night Herons, Great Blue Herons, White Pelicans and Double-crested Cormorants nest on islands (Dekker 1982). Two groups of islands are part of the natural area. The Dekker Islands (Fig. 1) consist of three islands at the northern end of the lake. The two southern islands are included in the natural area; the largest of these two islands has hosted a nesting colony of Great Blue Herons, but since 1980, the colony has been inactive (Folinsbee 1988). The Pelican Islands are a group of very small islands near the eastern shore. Their number varies depending on water levels. They support nesting colonies of pelicans and cormorants. Access to the Pelican Islands is prohibited by The Wildlife Act (Alta. En. Nat. Resour. 1981).

While local birds are still raising young, migrants from the north begin to arrive. Least Sandpipers appear by mid-July, followed by Semipalmated Sandpipers and a few plovers. Northern Phalaropes start to build up substantial flocks far out on the lake during summer, although they do not reach the large numbers seen in late May. By early August, parts of the lake are crowded with Dowitchers, yellowlegs, Stilt and Pectoral sandpipers (Dekker 1982).

Rare birds that have been sighted at the lake include Surfbirds, Sharp-tailed Sandpipers, Ruffs, Western Sandpipers, Wandering Tattlers, Black-necked Stilts, Common Egrets, Sabine's Gulls, Black Brants and Long-tailed Jaegers (Dekker 1982). During the summer of 1988, about 15 juvenile Trumpeter Swans were recorded on the lake.

Birds of prey such as Red-tailed, Swainson's and Cooper's hawks are plentiful in late summer and fall, and Parasitic Jaegers are recorded in most years. Shorebird numbers begin to decline by October, although some remain until freeze-up. Small passerines such as longspurs and buntings, on the other hand, are more plentiful than ever in October (Dekker 1982). From September to early October, very high concentrations of ducks mass along the southern shore where a bait station is located. The station, which is operated by Fish and Wildlife Division, feeds grain to ducks to minimize damage to nearby crops. Public access to the station is prohibited. The best staging areas for geese are along the northern and western sides of the lake, although smaller flocks use pastures along the southwestern and southeastern shores. Whistling Swans are the last large group to arrive. Thousands of these birds line the shores and dredge

for the roots of aquatic plants. Many remain until November when ice begins to form (Dekker 1982).

Beaverhill Lake is an important area for ungulates. The northern, eastern and southern shores provide wintering habitat for white-tailed and mule deer (Alta. En. Nat. Resour. 1981). A census of the muskrat population conducted during the autumn of 1974 recorded 65 muskrat houses along the shoreline, and the population was estimated to be at least 390 muskrats (Zelt and Glasgow 1976).

M.E. Bradford

References

Alberta Energy and Natural Resources. 1981. Integrated resource plan: Beaverhill Lake, Vol. 1: Land use plan, Vol. 2: Background information. Resour. Eval. Plan. Div., Edmonton.

Alberta Environment. n.d.[a]. Envir. Assess. Div., Envir. Qlty. Monit. Br. Unpubl. data, Edmonton.

———. n.d.[b]. Tech. Serv. Div., Hydrol. Br. Unpubl. data, Edmonton.

———. n.d.[c]. Tech. Serv. Div., Surv. Br. Unpubl. data, Edmonton.

———. 1977. Cooking Lake area study, Vol. I: Planning report. Plan. Div., Edmonton.

Alberta Forestry, Lands and Wildlife. 1987. A summary of Alberta's natural areas reserved and established. Pub. Ld. Div., Ld. Mgt. Devel. Br. Unpubl. rep., Edmonton.

———. 1988. Boating in Alberta. Fish Wild. Div., Edmonton.

———. 1989. Guide to game bird hunting. Fish Wild. Div., Edmonton.

Alberta Research Council. 1972. Geological map of Alberta. Nat. Resour. Div., Alta. Geol. Surv., Edmonton.

Dekker, D. 1982. An introduction to Beaverhill Lake. Alta. Nat. 12:1–5.

Ebel, G.R. n.d. Birds of the Beaverhill Lake area: A field checklist. Beaverhill L. Nat. Centre, Tofield.

———. 1988. The Beaverhill Bird Observatory, Edmonton. Pers. comm.

Energy, Mines and Resources Canada. 1983. National topographic series 1:250 000 83H (1983). Surv. Map. Br., Ottawa.

Environment Canada. 1982. Canadian climate normals, Vol. 7: Bright sunshine (1951–1980). Prep. by Atm. Envir. Serv. Supply Serv. Can., Ottawa.

Folinsbee, J. 1988. Alta. For. Ld. Wild., Fish Wild. Div., Dist. Office, Edmonton. Pers. comm.

Heath, R., G.R. Ebel and M. Cox. 1984. Beaverhill Lake gazeteer. The Edm. Bird Club, Edmonton.

Holmgren, E.J. and P.M. Holmgren. 1976. Over 2000 place names of Alberta. 3rd ed. West. Producer Prairie Books, Saskatoon.

Howitt, R.W. 1988. Soil survey of the County of Beaver. Alta. Soil Surv. Rep. No. 47. Alta. Res. Counc., Terrain Sci. Dept., Edmonton.

Kemper, J.B. 1976. Implications for waterfowl and migratory birds [Appendix 7]. In Cooking Lake area study, Vol. IV: Ecology. Alta. Envir., Plan. Div., Edmonton.

Lister, R. 1979. The birds and birders of Beaverhills Lake. The Edm. Bird Club, Edmonton.

Strong, W.L. and K.R. Leggat. 1981. Ecoregions of Alberta. Alta. En. Nat. Resour., Resour. Eval. Plan. Div., Edmonton.

Touchings, D. 1976. Heritage resource inventory of the Cooking Lake study area [Appendix 10]. In Cooking Lake area study, Vol. V: Economic base and heritage resources. Alta. Envir., Plan. Div., Edmonton.

Zelt, K.A. and W.M. Glasgow. 1976. Evaluation of the fish and wildlife resources of the Cooking Lake study area [Appendix 6]. In Cooking Lake area study, Vol. IV: Ecology. Alta. Envir., Plan. Div., Edmonton.

BONNIE LAKE

MAP SHEET: 73L/4
LOCATION: Tp59, 60 R13 W4
LAT/LONG: 54°09'N 111°52'W

Bonnie Lake is a popular recreational lake located in the County of Smoky Lake. It is situated approximately 130 km northeast of the city of Edmonton and 5 km northeast of the village of Vilna, which is the closest population centre. To drive to the lake from Edmonton, take Highway 28 until you are 5.5 km past the turnoff for Vilna (Fig. 1), then turn north and drive 3 km to Bonnie Lake Provincial Recreation Area on the south side of the lake (Fig. 2). Access to other parts of the lakeshore is provided by three other roads that branch north from Highway 28.

The origin of the lake's name is not known. Before settlers arrived, the Bonnie Lake area was inhabited by Cree Indians who followed the buffalo. Settlers of English, Polish, Ukrainian and American descent began farming land in the region in 1904. Vilna was established in 1919 when the railroad arrived, and was incorporated in 1923 (Co. Smoky L. 1968).

Bonnie Lake Provincial Recreation Area is operated by Alberta Recreation and Parks. It is open from the Victoria Day weekend to Thanksgiving Day for camping and year-round for day use. There are 45 campsites, pump water, a beach, a boat launch, a picnic shelter and a playground (Alta. Hotel Assoc. 1989). In addition to the provincial recreation area, there are informal campsites maintained by the County of Smoky Lake on the southeast shore (Fig. 2). The only other public recreational facility is a village of Vilna ball park and informal campground located on leased Crown land immediately southwest of the recreation area (Bonnie L. Plan Commit. 1987[a]).

Scouts Canada (Northern Region) also holds a recreational lease on Crown land on the south shore of the lake (Fig. 2). Their facility operates year-round and consists of a campground and leader-training facility. The remainder of the Crown land is located north of the lake; the portion that fronts on the lake has protective notation, but there is no road access to the area. The portion farther north is held under grazing and farm development leases (Bonnie L. Plan Commit. 1987[a]).

In 1984, Alberta Municipal Affairs recommended that Bonnie Lake be designated for intensive recreational use (Alta. Mun. Aff. 1984). In response to increasing development pressures, a lake management plan was completed in 1986 and an area structure plan was finalized and adopted in 1987 (Bonnie L. Plan Commit. 1987[a]; 1987[b]). The lake management plan determines the development capacity of Bonnie Lake, provides land-use planning policies for the lake, and determines ways to minimize environmental impacts and conflicts in the use of the lakeshore. It also recommends preferred lake uses and ways to minimize lake-user conflicts. In 1989, the only country residential development on the lakeshore was Bonnie Lake Resort, located on the south shore. In 1987, 75 of the 111 lots in the resort had been purchased, 36 residences had been built and 26 sites had trailers (Bonnie L. Plan Commit. 1987[a]). In addition, several single residences were located on the shore.

The water in Bonnie Lake turns green during summer. The extensive beds of aquatic vegetation present in shallow areas provide nesting habitat for several species of waterfowl. The main water-based activities at the lake are motor boating and water skiing. Over most of the lake, there are no boating restrictions, but in posted areas such as the designated swimming area, all boats are prohibited (Alta. For. Ld. Wild. 1988). Until 1987, the lake supported a popular sport fishery for northen pike and yellow perch, but after severe winterkills in 1987 and 1988, the stocking of yellow perch was discontinued for

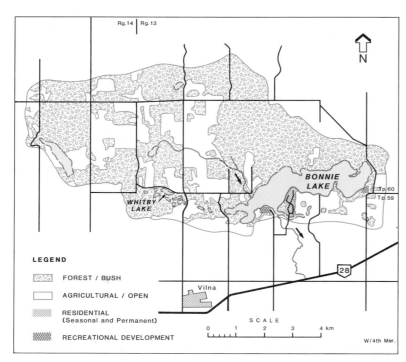

Figure 1. Features of the drainage basin of Bonnie Lake.
SOURCES: Alta. Envir. n.d.[b]; En. Mines Resour. Can. 1972; 1978.
Updated with 1986 aerial photos.

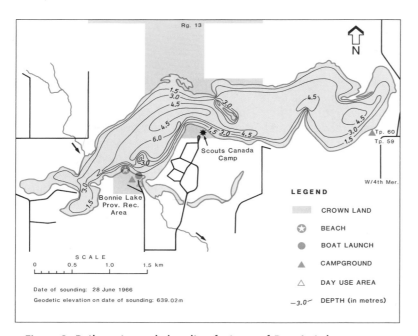

Figure 2. Bathymetry and shoreline features of Bonnie Lake.
BATHYMETRY SOURCE: Alta. Envir. n.d.[c].

Table 1. Characteristics of Bonnie Lake drainage basin.

area (excluding lake) (km²)[a]	49.6
soil[b]	Orthic and Dark Gray Luvisols
bedrock geology[c]	Belly River Formation (Upper Cretaceous): sandstone, siltstone, mudstone, ironstone beds; nonmarine
terrain[d]	level to gently rolling
ecoregion[e]	Aspen Subregion of Aspen Parkland (south), Dry Mixedwood Subregion of Boreal Mixedwood (north)
dominant vegetation[e]	trembling aspen
mean annual inflow (m³)[f, g]	1.28 x 10⁶
mean annual sunshine (h)[h]	2 168

NOTE: [g]excluding groundwater inflow
SOURCES: [a]Alta. Envir. n.d.[c]; [b]Twardy and Reid 1984; [c]Alta. Res. Counc. 1972; [d]Kocaoglu 1975; [e]Strong and Leggat 1981; [f]Alta. Envir. n.d.[b]; [h]Envir. Can. 1982

Table 2. Characteristics of Bonnie Lake.

elevation (m)[a, b]	639.02
surface area (km²)[a, b]	3.77
volume (m³)[a, b]	11.7 x 10⁶
maximum depth (m)[a, b]	6.1
mean depth (m)[a, b]	3.1
shoreline length (km)[c]	18.7
mean annual lake evaporation (mm)[d]	649
mean annual precipitation (mm)[d]	487
mean residence time (yr)[d, e]	21
control structure	none

NOTES: [a]on date of sounding: 28 June 1966; [e]excluding groundwater inflow
SOURCES: [b]Alta. Envir. n.d.[c]; [c]En. Mines Resour. Can. 1978; [d]Alta. Envir. n.d.[b]

undulating morainal plain, which is relatively level. The main soils over most of the drainage basin are moderately well-drained Orthic and Dark Gray Luvisols of a loam type. These soils developed on fine loamy, weakly or strongly calcareous glacial till. Poorly to very poorly drained Organic and Gleysolic soils are located in depressional to level areas, particularly north of the western half of the lake. Chernozemic soils are confined to the southern and northwestern portions of the watershed, and Eluviated Eutric Brunisols are common on well-drained to rapidly drained sands in the southwestern and northern portions (Kocaoglu 1975; Twardy and Reid 1984).

The small portion of the drainage basin south of the lake is part of the Aspen Subregion of the Aspen Parkland Ecoregion. The remainder of the drainage basin is part of the Dry Mixedwood Subregion of the Boreal Mixedwood Ecoregion. The main tree species in both subregions is trembling aspen. In the Boreal Mixedwood Ecoregion, the subordinate species include jack pine on rapidly drained to well-drained Eutric Brunisols, white spruce on imperfectly drained Gray Luvisols and Gleysols, black spruce and willows on poorly drained Organics and Gleysols, and sedges on very poorly drained organic soils (Strong and Leggat 1981).

Almost 70% of Bonnie Lake's drainage basin is forested and less than 2% is cleared for residential development (Fig. 1). Thirty per cent of the watershed, mainly south of the lake and in the central portion of the drainage area, is used for agriculture, mainly livestock grazing, forage crops and coarse grains (Twardy and Reid 1984). Some parcels of land in the northwest and east that were once farmed were abandoned and recolonized by trembling aspen. In some areas, the preglacial sands and gravels that are present along a meltwater channel west of Bonnie Lake have been excavated by commercial operations.

an indefinite period. Bonnie Lake's outlet stream is closed to sport fishing for a period during April and May each year (Alta. For. Ld. Wild. 1989). The main land-based recreational activities near the lake are camping, picnicking and golfing.

Drainage Basin Characteristics

The drainage basin surrounding Bonnie Lake is about 13 times the size of the lake (Tables 1, 2). Water drains into the lake mostly from the northwest via an unnamed creek (Fig. 1) and diffuse runoff. Groundwater also plays an unquantified, but likely important, role in the lake's water balance. The outlet, a tributary of Stoney Creek, flows intermittently in springtime and after major rainstorms (Babin and Trew 1987).

Most of the drainage basin is rolling morainal plain. It is characterized by undulating to gently rolling topography that features minor ridges and knobs intermixed with many wet depressions and small peat bogs. A small portion of the watershed west of the lake is

Lake Basin Characteristics

Bonnie Lake is a shallow, fairly small lake with a surface area of less than 4 km² and a mean depth of about 3 m (Table 2). The lake bed consists of two shallow basins with gradually sloping contours (Fig. 2). The deepest spot in the lake (6.1 m) is located near the provincial recreation area. Numerous arms and bays contribute to a relatively long shoreline. An arm of the lake on the southeast side was isolated from the lake proper for 30 years by a farm road that acted as a dam. In 1979, a culvert was installed, reconnecting the two water bodies so that the arm was no longer stagnant (Bascor Devel. Ltd. 1981).

Bonnie Lake is the municipal water source for the residents of Vilna. The village has been licenced since 1969 to withdraw up to 61 674 m³/year of drinking water from the lake (Alta. Envir. n.d.[d]).

The elevation of Bonnie Lake has been monitored since 1965 (Fig. 3). The highest level (639.76 m) was recorded in 1967, and the lowest level (638.45 m) was recorded in 1988; this is a maximum fluctuation of 1.31 m. Generally, lake elevations from late 1981 to 1989 have been lower than those in the previous 15 years. Runoff data for Waskatenau Creek indicate that Bonnie Lake has received only 48% of the expected median inflow volume since 1981, and these drought conditions are responsible for the low lake levels (O'Leary and Hay 1988). Changes in the lake's surface area and capacity (up to an elevation of 639.02 m) are illustrated in Figure 4.

The shoreline and nearshore areas of Bonnie Lake were studied by Alberta Forestry, Lands and Wildlife during 1988 (O'Leary and Hay 1988). The study evaluated the types of shoreline around the lake and examined the impact of fluctuating water levels on aquatic vegetation and erosion. The most common shoreline, which represented 44% of the area studied, was described as permanent wetland with little or no relief, water depths of less than 1 m, and balsam poplar and willow communities along the shore. This type of shoreline is most common along the north side and at the east and west ends of the lake. Because of the shallow water depth, large mud flats along these areas are often exposed in the spring and fall and the zone of emergent and submergent vegetation is extensive (30– to 50–m wide). The emergent zone was defined as the area that was covered by less than 0.5 m of water for the entire growing season. The second most common shoreline type, which represented 33% of the lake edge, was found mostly along the southern side. It was described as cobbly sand beach, and included the artificially-made beach at the provincial recreation area. Cobbly sandy beach is characterized by gradual to abrupt upland banks and a zone of emergent vegetation that is generally less than 10–m wide, except at the recreation area, where vegetation has been removed. The third shoreline type accounts for 21% of the lake edge, mainly along the northern and southeastern shores. It is characterized by sandy beaches and fairly abrupt but short upland banks. The zone of vegetation along this area is 25– to 40–m wide, the zone of submergent vegetation is less than 5–m wide and the maximum water depth within the emergent zone is less than 0.1 m. The fourth shoreline type was found along only 2% of the lake margin, and was characterized by a cobble/gravel shoreline and no emergent vegetation.

Water Quality

A water quality study of Bonnie Lake was conducted by Alberta Environment during the open-water periods of 1983 and 1989 and in March of 1984 and 1989. As well, samples were taken once each in July and September of 1988 as part of a study of phosphorus release from the sediments of 19 Alberta lakes (Alta. Envir. n.d.[a]; Shaw 1989).

Bonnie Lake has fresh, well-buffered water. The dominant ions are bicarbonate, magnesium and calcium (Table 3). Bonnie Lake displays characteristics common to other shallow Alberta lakes: in the spring, the water column warms rapidly, throughout the summer, the lake is weakly thermally stratified most of the time, and in the fall, the water column cools rapidly (Fig. 5). The lake is usually well oxygenated during the open-water season. In 1983, for example, dissolved oxygen concentrations generally exceeded 9 mg/L,

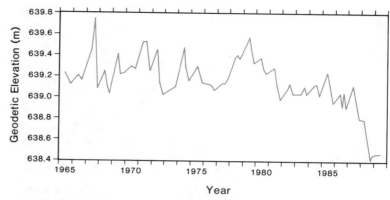

Figure 3. Water level of Bonnie Lake, 1965 to 1989.
SOURCE: Alta. Envir. n.d.[c].

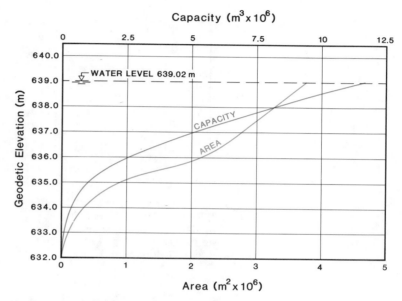

Figure 4. Area/capacity curve for Bonnie Lake.
SOURCE: Alta. Envir. n.d.[c].

Table 3. Major ions and related water quality variables for Bonnie Lake. Average concentrations in mg/L; pH in pH units. Composite samples from the euphotic zone collected 3 or 7 times from 12 May to 24 Oct. 1983. S.E. = standard error.

	Mean	S.E.
pH (range)	8.4–8.6[a]	—
total alkalinity (CaCO₃)	189[a]	2.3
specific conductivity (μS/cm)	397[a]	2.0
total dissolved solids (calculated)	206[a]	4.2
total hardness (CaCO₃)	161[a]	7.0
total particulate carbon	<1[b]	—
dissolved organic carbon	18[b]	0.5
dissolved inorganic carbon	45[b]	0.9
HCO₃	221[a]	5.4
CO₃	<6[a]	—
Mg	24[a]	0.6
Na	16[a]	0.4
K	9[a]	0.1
Cl	2[a]	0.4
SO₄	18[a]	0.9
Ca	25[a]	2.1

NOTES: [a]n = 3; [b]n = 7
SOURCE: Alta. Envir. n.d.[a], Naquadat station 01AL05ED3090

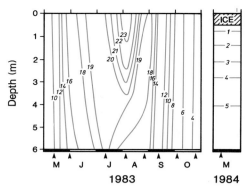

Figure 5. Temperature (°C) of Bonnie Lake, 1983 and 1984. Arrows indicate sampling dates.
SOURCE: Alta. Envir. n.d.[a].

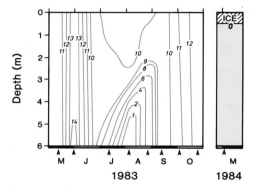

Figure 6. Dissolved oxygen (mg/L) in Bonnie Lake, 1983 and 1984. Arrows indicate sampling dates, shaded area indicates no dissolved oxygen.
SOURCE: Alta. Envir. n.d.[a].

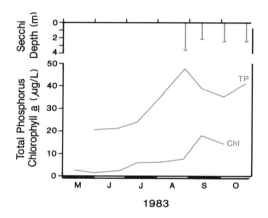

Figure 7. Total phosphorus, chlorophyll *a* and Secchi depth in Bonnie Lake, 1983.
SOURCE: Alta. Envir. n.d.[a].

Table 4. Nutrient, chlorophyll *a* and Secchi depth data for Bonnie Lake. Average concentrations in μg/L. Composite samples from the euphotic zone collected 4 to 9 times from 12 May to 24 Oct. 1983 and 5 times from 18 May to 02 Aug. 1989. S.E. = standard error.

	1983		1989	
	Mean	S.E.	Mean	S.E.
total phosphorus	33[a]	3.5	95	7.3
total dissolved phosphorus	19[a]	2.5	32	2.8
soluble reactive phosphorus	3[b]	0.6	—	—
total Kjeldahl nitrogen	1 250[c]	50.7	2 310	140.0
$NO_3 + NO_2$–nitrogen	9[c]	2.5	9	5.0
NH_4–nitrogen	32[c]	5.3	—	—
iron	—	—	740	—
chlorophyll *a*	7.2[a]	2.11	31.5	5.87
Secchi depth (m)	2.7[d]	0.30	1.1[d]	0.13

NOTES: [a]n = 8; [b]n = 9; [c]n = 7; [d]n = 4
SOURCE: Alta. Envir. n.d.[a], Naquadat station 01AL05ED3090

Table 5. Theoretical total phosphorus loading to Bonnie Lake from external sources.

Source		Phosphorus (kg/yr)	Percentage of Total
watershed	forested/bush	276	26
	agricultural/cleared	592	55
	residential/cottage	64	6
sewage		31	3
precipitation/dustfall		114	10
	TOTAL	1 077	100
annual areal loading (g/m² of lake surface)	0.29		

SOURCES: Bonnie L. Plan Commit. 1987[a]; Babin and Trew 1987

recorded was 268 μg/L, also in September. In 1989, data available from mid-May to early August suggested that the lake was eutrophic. The highest chlorophyll *a* concentration was 54 μg/L, recorded in mid-May, and the highest total phosphorus concentrations were 112 μg/L, recorded in mid-May, and 113 μg/L, recorded in late June. The average Secchi transparency has also declined, from 2.7 m in 1983 to 1.1 m in 1989 (Table 4). The causes of these fluctuations in trophic status are unknown, but as of 1989, Alberta Environment began an investigation into the potential reasons for the changes.

The loading of total phosphorus to Bonnie Lake from external sources is estimated to be 1 077 kg/year, or 0.29 g/m² of lake surface (Table 5). The largest external source is runoff from agricultural land, which accounts for 55% of the total load. Other external sources are runoff from forested land (26%), runoff from urban areas (6%), sewage from cottages and camps (3%) and precipitation and dustfall (10%). The internal loading of total phosphorus from the sediments was calculated from 1983 data, and was estimated to be 271 kg/year (Trew 1989). This figure is likely to have increased significantly in 1988 and 1989.

Biological Characteristics

Plants

The phytoplankton community in Bonnie Lake was studied approximately monthly by Alberta Environment during the open-water season in 1983 (Table 6). Biomass was low throughout the season, ranging from a minimum of 0.04 mg/L in late May to a maximum of 2.63 mg/L in late October.

The species of algae that dominated the phytoplankton community in 1983 consisted mostly of golden-brown algae (Chrysophyta), cryptophytes, and diatoms (Bacillariophyta). Species of *Cryp-*

except for a brief period from late July to mid-August (Fig. 6). During that time the lake was thermally stratified and the water over the sediments became anoxic. In the winter, the entire water column may become anoxic, as in March of both 1984 and 1989. Anoxic conditions during winter have been reported in other years, and have resulted in partial to extensive winterkills of fish in 1969, 1982, 1987, 1988 and 1989 (Sullivan 1989).

The trophic status of Bonnie Lake is difficult to categorize, because the maximum concentration of chlorophyll *a* has varied greatly from 1983 to 1989. In 1983, the lake was mesotrophic: chlorophyll *a* reached a maximum concentration of 18 μg/L in September and total phosphorus reached a maximum concentration of 48 μg/L in August (Fig. 7). The increase in chlorophyll *a* over the summer indicated phosphorus release from the sediments when the bottom water was anoxic. In 1988, Bonnie Lake was hyper-eutrophic. The highest chlorophyll *a* concentration recorded that year was 145 μg/L in September and the highest total phosphorus concentration

Table 6. Percentage composition of major algal groups by total biomass in Bonnie Lake, 1983. Composite samples collected from the euphotic zone.

ALGAL GROUP	10 Mar.	12 May	30 May	23 June	04 Aug.	12 Aug.	26 Aug.	24 Oct.	07 Nov.
Total Biomass (mg/L)	1.32	1.43	0.04	0.33	1.77	1.38	1.06	2.63	1.56
Percentage Composition:									
Cyanophyta	6	2	0	2	1	44 *Anabaena*	8	0	44 *Anab.*[a]
Chlorophyta	6	2	3	4	13	2	50 *Oocystis*	4	11
Chrysophyta	20 *Uroglena*	1	91 *Ochromonas*	6	8	26 *Dinobryon*	0	18	6
Bacillariophyta	16	42 *Synedra*	6	2	36 *Asterionella*	7	13	21 *Asterionella*	18
Cryptophyta	52 *Cryptomonas*→	53	0	79 *Cryptomonas Rhodomonas*————	21	18	26	56 →	7
Pyrrhophyta	0	0	0	8	22 *Ceratium*	3	2	1	13

NOTE: [a]*Anab.* = *Anabaena*
SOURCE: Alta. Envir. n.d.[a]

tomonas were especially prominent in spring and fall, probably because they compete well under low-light conditions. Other common algal species included the colonial forms *Dinobryon* and *Asterionella*. Blue-green algae, mostly *Anabaena flos-aquae* (Cyanophyta), dominated the algal biomass only in mid-August and early November.

A brief survey of aquatic macrophytes was conducted by Fish and Wildlife Division in 1977 (Alta. Rec. Parks Wild. 1977) and by Alberta Forestry, Lands and Wildlife in 1988 (O'Leary and Hay 1988). During both studies, abundant beds of cattails (*Typha latifolia*) and bulrushes (*Scirpus* spp.) were found throughout shallow areas along the shoreline (Fig. 8). Water lilies (*Nuphar* sp.) and submergent macrophytes, including northern watermilfoil (*Myriophyllum exalbescens*) and pondweeds (*Potamogeton* spp.), were also common.

Invertebrates

No data are available on the zooplankton in Bonnie Lake. In a 1969 survey of benthic invertebrates, Fish and Wildlife Division biologists noted that scuds (Amphipoda) and midge larvae (Chironomidae) were present in abundance, but no detailed data were collected (Holmes and Abraham 1969).

Fish

The fish community in Bonnie Lake has included northern pike, yellow perch and spottail shiner, and at times, the lake has supported a popular summer sport fishery. At present, Bonnie Lake is managed for recreational fishing only. There is no domestic fishery, and a commercial fishery for yellow perch and walleye operated for only one year, in 1945; this was the last year that walleye were reported in the lake (Alta. For. Ld. Wild. n.d.; Sullivan 1989).

Bonnie Lake is very shallow, and frequently becomes anoxic under ice cover. Partial to extensive winterkills were reported in 1969, 1982, 1987 and 1988, and winterkill conditions were recorded in 1989. After the extensive winterkill in 1987, the lake was stocked with perch and spottail shiners. Northern pike are not stocked—if the population has survived, it has done so by natural reproduction only. After the next extensive winterkill occurred in the late winter of 1988, the lake was not restocked. As of 1989, the status of the fish populations was uncertain and there were no plans to restock the lake in the near future (Sullivan 1989).

Wildlife

The extensive macrophyte beds in Bonnie Lake provide good habitat for Mallards, American Widgeons, Lesser Scaup, Redheads, Black

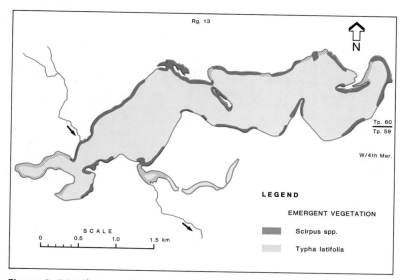

Figure 8. Distribution of emergent macrophytes in Bonnie Lake.
SOURCE: Alta. Rec. Parks Wild. 1977.

Terns, American Coots, Franklin's Gulls, Common Loons and Red-necked Grebes. Great Blue Herons and Ospreys have also been sighted on the lake (Alta. Rec. Parks Wild. 1977).

M.E. Bradford

References

Alberta Environment. n.d.[a]. Envir. Assess. Div., Envir. Qlty. Monit. Br. Unpubl. data, Edmonton.
————. n.d.[b]. Tech. Serv. Div., Hydrol. Br. Unpubl. data, Edmonton.
————. n.d.[c]. Tech. Serv. Div., Surv. Br. Unpubl. data, Edmonton.
————. n.d.[d]. Water Resour. Admin. Div., Records Mgt. Sec. Unpubl. data, Edmonton.
Alberta Forestry, Lands and Wildlife. n.d. Fish Wild. Div. Unpubl. data, Edmonton.
————. 1988. Boating in Alberta. Fish Wild. Div., Edmonton.
————. 1989. Guide to sportfishing. Fish Wild. Div., Edmonton.
Alberta Hotel Association. 1989. Alberta campground guide 1989. Prep. for Travel Alta., Edmonton.
Alberta Municipal Affairs. 1984. County of Smoky Lake #13 lake planning framework. Plan. Br., Edmonton.
Alberta Recreation, Parks and Wildlife. 1977. Lake surveys for wildlife, St. Paul Region: Bonnie Lake. Fish Wild. Div. Unpubl. rep., Edmonton.
Alberta Research Council. 1972. Geological map of Alberta. Nat. Resour. Div., Alta. Geol. Surv., Edmonton.
Babin, J. and D.O. Trew. 1987. A trophic assessment of Bonnie Lake. Alta. Envir., Poll. Contr. Div., Water Qlty. Contr. Br. Unpubl. rep., Edmonton.

Bascor Developments Ltd. 1981. Bonnie Lake south tributary shoreline improvement: Appeal to the Deputy Minister Mr. W. Solodzuk, P. Eng. Bascor Devel. Ltd. Unpubl. rep., Edmonton.

Bonnie Lake Plan Committee. 1987[a]. Bonnie Lake management study. Prep. for Counc. Co. Smoky L. No. 13. Alta. Mun. Aff., Edmonton.

————. 1987[b]. Bonnie Lake management study phase 2—area structure plan bylaw #778–87 (1987). Prep. for Counc. Co. Smoky L. No. 13. Alta. Mun. Aff., Edmonton.

County of Smoky Lake. ca 1968. A century of progress. Co. Smoky L. No. 13, Smoky Lake.

Energy, Mines and Resources Canada. 1972, 1978. National topographic series 1:50 000 83I/1 (1972), 73L/4 (1978). Surv. Map. Br., Ottawa.

Environment Canada. 1982. Canadian climate normals, Vol. 7: Bright sunshine (1951–1980). Prep. by Atm. Envir. Serv. Supply Serv. Can., Ottawa.

Holmes, D.W. and M. Abraham. 1969. ARDA lake survey 73L: Bonnie Lake. Alta. Ld. For., Fish Wild. Div. Unpubl. rep., Edmonton.

Kocaoglu, S.S. 1975. Reconnaissance soil survey of the Sand River area. Alta. Soil Surv. Rep. No. 34, Univ. Alta. Bull. No. SS–15, Alta. Inst. Pedol. Rep. No. S–74–34 1975. Univ. Alta., Edmonton.

O'Leary, D. and W. Hay. 1988. Shoreline assessment of Bonnie Lake. Alta. For. Ld. Wild., Ld. Information Serv. Div., Edmonton.

Shaw, J.F.H. 1989. Increases in lakewater phosphorus concentrations during the summer in shallow Alberta lakes. Prep. for Alta. Envir., Envir. Assess. Div., Envir. Qlty. Monit. Br. by Shaw Envir. Consult. Unpubl. rep., Edmonton.

Strong, W.L. and K.R. Leggat. 1981. Ecoregions of Alberta. Alta. En. Nat. Resour., Resour. Eval. Plan. Div., Edmonton.

Sullivan, M. 1989. Alta. For. Ld. Wild., Fish Wild. Div., St. Paul. Pers. comm.

Trew, D.O. 1989. Alta. Envir., Envir. Assess. Div., Envir. Qlty. Monit. Br., Edmonton. Pers. comm.

Twardy, A.G. and A.L Reid. 1984. Soil survey and land suitability evaluation of the Bonnie Lake study area. Prep. for Alta. Envir., Edmonton by Pedol. Consult., Edmonton.

BUCK LAKE

MAP SHEETS: 83B/15, 83G/2
LOCATION: Tp46 R6 W5
LAT/LONG: 53°00′N 114°45′W

Buck Lake is set amidst gently rolling hills in the County of Wetaskiwin, 105 km southwest of the city of Edmonton and 70 km north of the town of Rocky Mountain House. The nearest large population centre is the town of Drayton Valley, 30 km to the northwest. To reach the lake from Edmonton, drive south on Highway 2 for 65 km, then west on Highway 13 for 80 km. Secondary roads branching from Highway 13 provide access to all sides of the lake (Fig. 1).

Prior to 1900, the region surrounding Buck Lake was covered by a spruce and pine forest and the Cree who lived there called the area *Minnehik*, which means "Place of the Pines" (Buck L. Hist. Book Commit. 1981). Buck Lake was named Bull Lake on the Arrowsmith map of 1859 (Holmgren and Holmgren 1976).

The first white people to visit the area were fur traders. In 1799, John MacDonald travelled up the North Saskatchewan River and built Rocky Mountain House, and a few years later, Boggy Hill trading post was built near the present site of Drayton Valley (Lindsay et al. 1968). J.B. Tyrrell, who traversed the old pack trail from Buck Lake to Rocky Mountain House, wrote in 1887 that the lake was "said to contain large whitefish of particularly fine flavor", which were supplied to the Hudson's Bay Company post at Rocky Mountain House (Tyrrell 1886). The first settlers arrived in the region soon after 1900. Local sawmills were a major employer in the early part of the century, but by the 1930s the larger trees had been harvested (Buck L. Hist. Book Commit. 1981). Intensive drilling for oil and gas followed in the 1950s, and at present, drilling rigs dot the countryside.

The largest recreation facility on the lake, Buck Lake-Calhoun's Bay Provincial Recreation Area, is located on 374 ha of Crown land on the east side of the lake (Fig. 2). It is operated by Alberta Recreation and Parks and offers 75 campsites and pump water (Friebel 1989). The hamlet of Buck Lake, known as Minnehik prior to 1954, is located on the southwest shore (Fig. 2). In 1986, the hamlet had 91 residents. Every year in early July, the hamlet holds a popular rodeo, the Buck Lake Stampede, which is attended by more than 3 000 people. Buck Lake Campground, an Alberta Transportation and Utilities facility, is located in the hamlet. It offers 10 campsites, picnic tables, a picnic shelter, a boat launch and a small beach. As well, Alberta Environment operates a day-use area beside the weir on Bucklake Creek at the north end of the lake. Facilities include picnic tables and a boat launch.

Buck Lake is popular for swimming, boating and year-round fishing. Over most of the lake there are no boating restrictions, but in posted areas either motor boats are restricted to speeds of 12 km/ hour, or all boats are prohibited (Alta. For. Ld. Wild. 1988). Sport fish species found in the lake include lake whitefish, walleye, northern pike and yellow perch. Buck Lake, Rat Lake, and Mink Creek and its tributaries are closed to sport fishing for a period during April and May each year (Alta. For. Ld. Wild. 1989). Since 1967, an annual fish derby organized by the Breton and District Fish and Game Association has been held on the lake during June. The commercial fishery has operated since 1938; its main catch is lake whitefish. Buck Lake also supports a domestic fishery.

Late in summer, the lake becomes quite green as concentrations of blue-green algae in the water increase. As well, aquatic vegetation such as bulrushes and pondweeds grow densely in many areas. These plant beds provide spawning habitat for fish and nesting cover

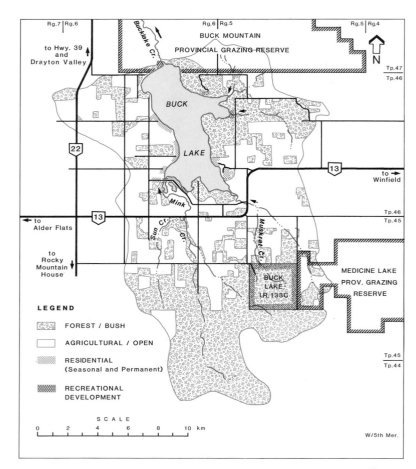

Figure 1. Features of the drainage basin of Buck Lake.
SOURCES: Alta. Envir. n.d.[c]; En. Mines Resour. Can. 1974. Updated with 1984 aerial photos.

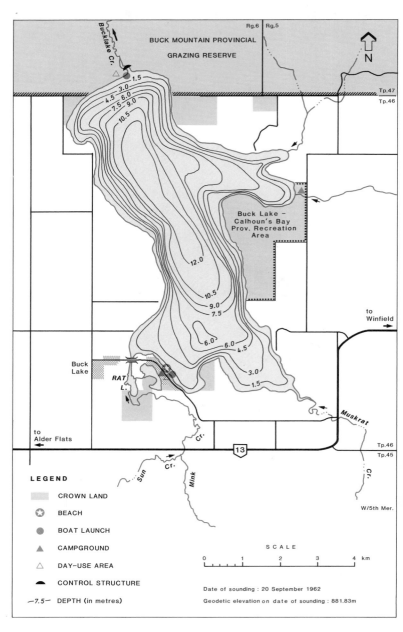

Figure 2. Bathymetry and shoreline features of Buck Lake.
BATHYMETRY SOURCE: Alta. Envir. n.d.[d].

for waterfowl but they are frequently removed by local residents because they interfere with boating and swimming.

Drainage Basin Characteristics

Buck Lake is situated north of the divide between the North Saskatchewan River drainage basin, of which it is part, and the Red Deer River drainage basin to the south. Buck Lake's drainage basin is about 9 times the size of the lake (Tables 1, 2). Most of the water flowing into the lake arrives from the south via Mink and Muskrat creeks (Fig. 1). Mink Creek flows into Rat Lake before entering the southeast bay of Buck Lake. As well, two unnamed creeks flow into the eastern shore. The outlet, Bucklake Creek, flows from the north end of the lake into Modeste Creek and then into the North Saskatchewan River.

The land around Buck Lake is flat to undulating. It rises in gently rolling hills from about 882 m near the water's edge to more than 1 036 m in the southern part of the drainage basin at the divide. The main soils throughout the watershed are moderately well-drained Orthic Gray Luvisols of a clay-loam to loam texture (Lindsay et al. 1968). These soils developed on the glacial till overlying the Paskapoo Formation. The main soils in a large area of land directly south of the lake and a second area to the northwest are Orthic Humic Gleysols and Organics.

Buck Lake's watershed is part of the Boreal Foothills Ecoregion (Strong and Leggat 1981). The dominant trees are trembling aspen, balsam poplar and lodgepole pine on well-drained to moderately well-drained Gray Luvisols. Secondary succession is by white spruce. The main trees on imperfectly drained Gleysolic soils are lodgepole pine, which is invaded by black spruce and, at times, white spruce. On poorly drained to very poorly drained Organics and Gleysols, black spruce, willows and sedges predominate.

Most of the southern portion of the drainage basin is wooded, but in many places the land has been cleared for grazing and cultivation of mixed grains (Fig. 1). The cleared areas generally have an agricultural rating of fair to fairly good arability, whereas the uncleared

areas are rated poor to fair arability or pasture and woodland (Lindsay et al. 1968). Portions of two grazing reserves are present in the watershed: Medicine Lake Provincial Grazing Reserve abuts Buck Lake Indian Reserve 133C in the southeast corner of the drainage basin, and a portion of Buck Mountain Provincial Grazing Reserve is located in the northern section of the drainage basin. Industrial development is related to the coal and petrochemical industries. The Pembina Oilfield is located beneath the watershed and a number of oil and gas wells dot the countryside. Natural gas is extracted at the Buck Lake gas plant, located west of the hamlet.

Almost 40% of the lakeshore is owned by the Crown, mostly along the north and east shores (Fig. 2). Much of the Crown land bordering the north shore is part of Buck Mountain Provincial Grazing Reserve. The County of Wetaskiwin owns land on two sides of the southeast bay. Since the mid–1960s, development of the privately owned portion of the shoreline has increased markedly. In 1966, there were only 29 cottages on the lake, but by 1986, 6 subdivisions had been created. Of the 240 lots in these subdivisions, 75 had been developed, 65 with seasonal residences and 10 with permanent residences (Battle R. Reg. Plan. Commis. n.d.; Co. Wetaskiwin n.d.).

Lake Basin Characteristics

Buck Lake is a large, shallow lake with a single basin that slopes gradually to a maximum depth of 12.2 m in its centre (Fig. 2, Table

Table 1. Characteristics of Buck Lake drainage basin.

area (excluding lake) (km²)[a]	233
soil[b]	Orthic Gray Luvisol, Organic Humic Gleysol, Organic
bedrock geology[c]	Paskapoo Formation (Tertiary): sandstone, siltstone, mudstone; thin limestone, coal and tuff beds; nonmarine
terrain[b]	flat to hilly
ecoregion[d]	Boreal Foothills
dominant vegetation[d]	trembling aspen, balsam poplar, lodgepole pine
mean annual inflow (m³)[a, e]	22.1 x 10⁶
mean annual sunshine (h)[f]	2 315

NOTE: [e]excluding groundwater inflow
SOURCES: [a]Alta. Envir. n.d.[c]; [b]Lindsay et al. 1968; [c]Alta. Res. Counc. 1972; [d]Strong and Leggat 1981; [f]Envir. Can. 1982

Table 2. Characteristics of Buck Lake.

elevation (m)[a, b]	882.03
surface area (km²)[a, b]	25.4
volume (m³)[a, b]	158 x 10⁶
maximum depth (m)[a, b]	12.2
mean depth (m)[a, b]	6.2
shoreline length (km)[c]	32.8
mean annual lake evaporation (mm)[d]	642
mean annual precipitation (mm)[d]	567
mean residence time (yr)[d, e]	8.0
control structure[f]	concrete fixed-crest weir with stop logs and holes for riparian flow
top of stop logs (m)[f]	881.75
bottom of riparian holes (m)[f]	880.65

NOTES: [a]on date of sounding: 20 Sep. 1962; [e]excluding groundwater inflow
SOURCES: [b]Alta. Envir. n.d.[d]; [c]En. Mines Resour. Can. 1974; [d]Alta. Envir. n.d.[c]; [f]Alta. Envir. n.d.[a].

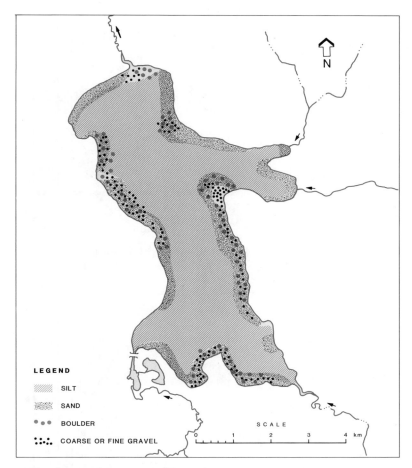

Figure 3. Distribution of sediment types in Buck Lake.
SOURCE: Bidgood 1972.

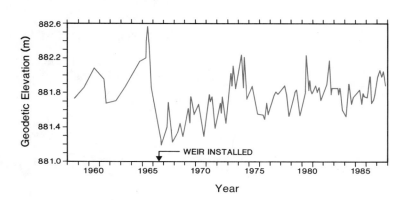

Figure 4. Water level of Buck Lake, 1958 to 1986.
SOURCE: Alta. Envir. n.d.[d].

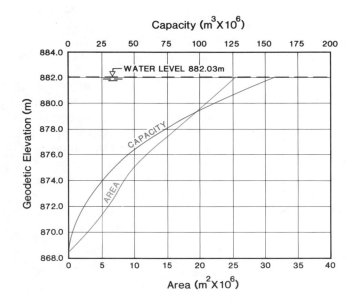

Figure 5. Area/capacity curve for Buck Lake.
SOURCE: Alta. Envir. n.d.[d].

2). The bottom sediments are sand where the water is less than 8–m deep (Fig. 3), and boulder and gravel in localized areas around the perimeter of the lake. In deeper water, the sediments are mainly silt.

The elevation of Buck Lake has been monitored since 1958 (Fig. 4). The maximum elevation, 882.57 m, was recorded in 1965 and the minimum elevation, 881.20 m, was recorded in 1966. This large fluctuation (1.37 m) caused concern among local land-owners, as the hamlet of Buck Lake, which is situated on very flat land, has often been flooded. In response to these concerns, Alberta Environment installed a weir on Bucklake Creek in September 1966. Water levels have stabilized since the weir was built. From 1980 to 1987, the range in lake levels was 0.64 m. A fluctuation of this size would change the lake's area by about 5% (Fig. 5).

Water is withdrawn from the lake by a West Coast Petroleum pumping station on the south shore just east of the hamlet. The station was first licenced in 1984, and is allowed to withdraw a maximum of 1.02 x 10⁶ m³/year. Withdrawals began in 1986, and averaged 0.59 x 10⁶ m³/year in 1986 and 1987 (Alta. Envir. n.d.[e]).

Water Quality

Buck Lake's water quality was monitored by the University of Alberta in 1981 (Prepas 1983) and by Alberta Environment through 1983 and 1984 and during the winter of 1985 (Alta. Envir. n.d.[b]).

The water in Buck Lake is well-buffered and fresh, and the total hardness is relatively low for a prairie lake. The dominant ions are bicarbonate and calcium (Table 3). The lake is shallow and is frequently mixed by wind during the open-water season. Weak thermal

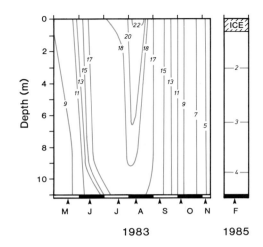

Figure 6. Temperature (°C) of Buck Lake, 1983 and 1985. Arrows indicate sampling dates.
SOURCE: Alta. Envir. n.d.[b].

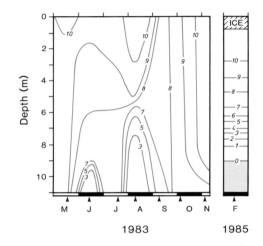

Figure 7. Dissolved oxygen (mg/L) in Buck Lake, 1983 and 1985. Arrows indicate sampling dates.
SOURCE: Alta. Envir. n.d.[b].

Table 3. Major ions and related water quality variables for Buck Lake. Average concentrations in mg/L; pH in pH units. Composite samples from the euphotic zone collected 6 times from 01 May to 20 Sep. 1984. S.E. = standard error.

	Mean	S.E.
pH (range)	7.7–9.0	—
total alkalinity (CaCO₃)	111	1.2
specific conductivity (μS/cm)	228	1.9
total dissolved solids (calculated)	120	1.3
total hardness (CaCO₃)	79	2.7
total particulate carbon	2	0.4
dissolved organic carbon	9	0.5
dissolved inorganic carbon	26	0.7
HCO₃	131	1.8
CO₃	<3	—
Mg	5	0.3
Na	12	0.5
K	4	0
Cl	<2	—
SO₄	<7	—
Ca	23	1.4

SOURCE: Alta. Envir. n.d.[b], Naquadat station 01AL05DE2100

Table 4. Nutrient, chlorophyll *a* and Secchi depth data for Buck Lake. Average concentrations in μg/L. Composite samples from the euphotic zone collected 7 times from 17 May to 03 Nov. 1983 and 6 times from 01 May to 20 Sep. 1984. S.E. = standard error.

	1983		1984	
	Mean	S.E.	Mean	S.E.
total phosphorus	38	9.5	42	10.4
total dissolved phosphorus	16	3.6	13	3.4
soluble reactive phosphorus	10	3.1	—	—
total Kjeldahl nitrogen	750	82.3	770	93.8
NO₃ + NO₂–nitrogen	20	6.5	2	0.5
NH₄–nitrogen	29	11.6	7	0.8
chlorophyll *a*	15.4	4.4	20.8	7.6
Secchi depth (m)	3.4	0.4	2.9	0.5

SOURCE: Alta. Envir. n.d.[b], Naquadat station 01AL05DE2100

stratification occurs periodically during the summer (Fig. 6) and the concentration of dissolved oxygen over the sediments can fall to low levels (Fig. 7). The dissolved oxygen concentration at the surface, however, remains quite high. In winter, the deeper water can become anoxic, as in February 1985, but the dissolved oxygen concentration in the upper layers of water is adequate to support the fish population (Fig. 7).

Buck Lake is eutrophic. Average total phosphorus and chlorophyll *a* concentrations are moderately high (Table 4). In 1983, the highest levels of these two variables were recorded in September (Fig. 8). This indicates that phosphorus is recycled from the sediments in late summer, as was found in the 1981 study. During late summer the water is quite green, but generally the water clarity is very good, as indicated by the high Secchi depth values in 1983 (Fig. 8).

Biological Characteristics

Plants

The phytoplankton community in Buck Lake was sampled by Fish and Wildlife Division in 1948 (Miller and Macdonald 1950) and by Alberta Environment in 1983 (Alta. Envir. n.d.[b]). In 1983, algal biomass was low (less than 2 mg/L) until September, when the

maximum biomass (5.9 mg/L) was recorded (Table 5). Biomass remained high into October and then declined by early November. Cryptophytes were the dominant group from mid-May to mid-July. During May, one species, *Cryptomonas erosa reflexa,* accounted for 47% of the total algal biomass. By June, *C. ovata* had become dominant, and during July, *C. ovata* was codominant with *Ceratium hirundinella,* a dinoflagellate (Pyrrhophyta). *C. hirundinella* is a species often found in alkaline, eutrophic lakes. During August and September, when phosphorus concentrations in the euphotic zone increased dramatically (Fig. 8), blue-greens were the dominant algae (Trimbee and Prepas 1987; 1988). By September, one blue-green species, *Aphanizomenon flos-aquae,* accounted for 90% of the total algal biomass. This species remained very common into October, along with the diatom *Stephanodiscus niagarae* (Bacillariophyta). In November, *S. niagarae* constituted 83% of the total biomass.

The macrophyte community was sampled by a researcher from the University of Alberta in July 1969 (Fig. 9). Rooted emergent species grew mostly at depths of 2 m or less. The most widely distributed species were common great bulrush (*Scirpus validus*) and Sago pondweed (*Potamogeton pectinatus*). Along some parts of the lakeshore, cottage owners used herbicides or mechanical harvesters to remove macrophytes.

Table 5. Percentage composition of major algal groups by total biomass in Buck Lake, 1983. Composite samples collected from the euphotic zone.

ALGAL GROUP	17 May	13 June	17 July	09 Aug.	08 Sep.	04 Oct.	03 Nov.
Total Biomass (mg/L)	0.62	0.23	0.61	1.33	5.90	5.34	2.65
Percentage Composition:							
Cyanophyta	0	<1	6	32	97	36	1
				Anabaena	*Aphanizomenon⟶*		
Chlorophyta	3	6	2	2	1	1	<1
Chrysophyta	19	12	2	16	<1	<1	0
Bacillariophyta	17	6	11	31	1	59	93
				Fragilaria	*Stephanodiscus⟶*		
Cryptophyta	61	73	40	11	<1	0	0
	Cryptomonas⟶						
Pyrrhophyta	0	2	40	8	<1	0	0
			Ceratium				

SOURCE: Alta. Envir. n.d.[b].

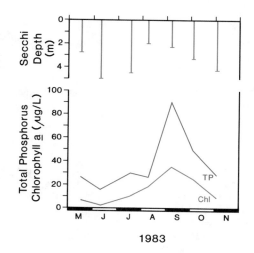

Figure 8. Total phosphorus, chlorophyll *a* and Secchi depth in Buck Lake, 1983. SOURCE: Alta. Envir. n.d.[b].

Invertebrates

The zooplankton in Buck Lake was sampled by Fish and Wildlife Division in 1948 (Miller and Macdonald 1950). A species of *Daphnia* (Cladocera), *Diacyclops bicuspidatus thomasi* (Copepoda) and *Keratella* sp. (= *Anuraea* sp.) (Rotifera) were found in abundance, whereas *Polyarthra* sp. (Rotifera) was seen occasionally.

Monthly or bimonthly samples of the benthic invertebrate community were taken with a 15–cm Ekman dredge between July 1970 and July 1971 (Bidgood 1972). Midge larvae (Chironomidae) were most abundant on silt substrates and scuds (Amphipoda) and aquatic earthworms (Oligochaeta) were most abundant on sand. Caddis fly larvae (Trichoptera), phantom midge larvae (*Chaoborus* sp.), aquatic earthworms, clams (Pelecypoda) and snails (Gastropoda) were also well represented. The largest wet weight biomass of invertebrates was found on sand substrate in the fall. For most months sampled, Buck Lake had higher numbers of benthic invertebrates on all substrate types than Pigeon Lake, which was sampled at the same time.

Fish

Ten species of fish have been reported in Buck Lake: lake whitefish, walleye, northern pike, white sucker, burbot, yellow perch, trout-perch, brook stickleback, Iowa darter and spottail shiner. Lake whitefish in Buck Lake spawn from late September throughout December on a boulder, rubble and sand substrate, which makes up about 15% of the lake bottom (Fig. 3, 9). In spring, walleye use the same spawning grounds that whitefish use in the fall (Bidgood 1972). White sucker and some northern pike migrate up tributary streams to spawn, whereas other pike spawn in the lake.

Fishing is popular on Buck Lake, which is managed for recreational, domestic and commercial fisheries. There are no catch data for the recreational and domestic fisheries. The commercial fishery opened in 1938, but records have been kept only since 1942 (Alta. For. Ld. Wild. n.d.; Alta. Rec. Parks Wild. 1976). The main catch of the fishery has always been lake whitefish, but small numbers of white suckers, burbot, northern pike, yellow perch and walleye are also taken. The largest total catch, 139 000 kg, was taken in 1960/61 by 1 603 licensees. From 1980/81 to 1987/88, an average of 557 licences were issued and the mean total catch was 22 750 kg/year. Most (98%) of this catch was lake whitefish.

Wildlife

Bird species that have been sighted on Buck Lake include Mallard, Gadwall, Blue-winged Teal, Bufflehead, Common Goldeneye, Lesser Scaup, Red-necked Grebe, Western Grebe, American Coot, Ring-billed Gull, Franklin's Gull, Common Tern and Wilson's Phalarope.

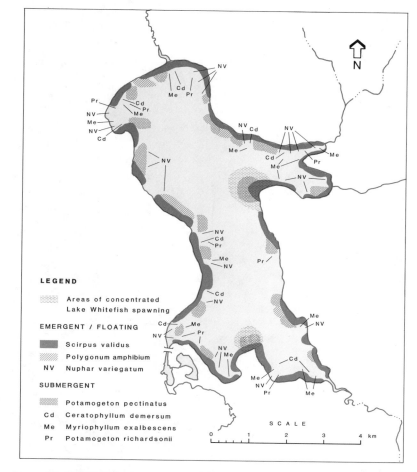

LEGEND

Areas of concentrated Lake Whitefish spawning

EMERGENT / FLOATING

Scirpus validus
Polygonum amphibium
NV Nuphar variegatum

SUBMERGENT

Potamogeton pectinatus
Cd Ceratophyllum demersum
Me Myriophyllum exalbescens
Pr Potamogeton richardsonii

SCALE
0   1   2   3   4 km

Figure 9. Distribution of aquatic macrophytes and whitefish spawning areas in Buck Lake, July 1969. SOURCE: Bidgood 1972.

Osprey nest on the western shore. A major limitation for waterfowl is a shortage of resting areas and an increasing number of disturbances by recreational users of the lake. As well, emergent vegetation and nesting cover continue to be removed from the lakeshore (Ducks Unltd. (Can.) n.d.).

M.E. Bradford

References

Alberta Environment. n.d.[a]. Devel. Op. Div., Project Mgt. Br. Unpubl. data, Edmonton.

———. n.d.[b]. Envir. Assess. Div., Envir. Qlty. Monit. Br. Unpubl. data, Edmonton.

———. n.d.[c]. Tech. Serv. Div., Hydrol. Br. Unpubl. data, Edmonton.

———. n.d.[d]. Tech. Serv. Div., Surv. Br. Unpubl. data, Edmonton.

———. n.d.[e]. Water Resour. Admin. Div., Sur. Water Rights Br. Unpubl. data, Edmonton.

Alberta Forestry, Lands and Wildlife. n.d. Fish Wild. Div. Unpubl. data, Edmonton.

———. 1988. Boating in Alberta. Fish Wild. Div., Edmonton.

———. 1989. Guide to sportfishing. Fish Wild. Div., Edmonton.

Alberta Recreation, Parks and Wildlife. 1976. Commercial fisheries catch statistics for Alberta, 1942–1975. Fish Wild. Div., Fish. Mgt. Rep. No. 22, Edmonton.

Alberta Research Council. 1972. Geological map of Alberta. Nat. Resour. Div., Alta. Geol. Surv., Edmonton.

Battle River Regional Planning Commission. n.d. Unpubl. data, Wetaskiwin.

Bidgood, B.J. 1972. Divergent growth in lake whitefish populations from two eutrophic Alberta lakes. PhD thesis. Univ. Alta., Edmonton.

Buck Lake History Book Committee. 1981. Packhorse to pavement: Buck Lake history. Buck L. Hist. Book Commit., Buck Lake.

County of Wetaskiwin No. 10. n.d. Unpubl. data, Wetaskiwin.

Ducks Unlimited (Canada). n.d. Unpubl. data, Edmonton.

Energy, Mines and Resources Canada. 1974. National topographic series 1:50 000 83B/15 (1974), 83G/2 (1974). Surv. Map. Br., Ottawa.

Environment Canada. 1982. Canadian climate normals, Vol. 7: Bright sunshine (1951–1980). Prep. by Atm. Envir. Serv. Supply Serv. Can., Ottawa.

Friebel, D. 1989. Alta. Rec. Parks, Parks Div., Pigeon L. Pers. comm.

Holmgren, E.J. and P.M. Holmgren. 1976. Over 2000 place names of Alberta. 3rd ed. West. Producer Prairie Books, Saskatoon.

Lindsay, J.D., W. Odynsky, J.W. Peters and W.E. Bowser. 1968. Soil survey of the Buck Lake (NE 83B) and Wabamun Lake (E1/2 83G) areas. Alta. Soil Surv. Rep. No. 24, Univ. Alta. Bull. No. SS–7, Res. Counc. Alta. Rep. No. 87 1968. Univ. Alta., Edmonton.

Miller, R.B. and W.H. Macdonald. 1950. Preliminary biological surveys of Alberta watersheds 1947–1949. Alta. Ld. For., Edmonton.

Prepas, E.E. 1983. Orthophosphate turnover time in shallow productive lakes. Can. J. Fish. Aquat. Sci. 40:1412–1418.

Strong, W.L. and K.R. Leggat. 1981. Ecoregions of Alberta. Alta. En. Nat. Resour., Resour. Eval. Plan. Div., Edmonton.

Trimbee, A.M. and E.E. Prepas. 1987. Evaluation of total phosphorus as a predictor of the relative biomass of blue-green algae with emphasis on Alberta lakes. Can. J. Fish. Aquat. Sci. 44:1337–1342.

———. 1988. The effect of oxygen depletion on the timing and magnitude of blue-green algal blooms. Verh. Internat. Verein. Limnol. 23:220–226.

Tyrrell, J.B. 1886. Canada geological and natural history survey, annual report: Report on a part of northern Alberta. Dawson Brothers, Montreal, Québec.

COOKING LAKE

MAP SHEETS: 83H/6, 7

LOCATION: Tp51 R20 W4

LAT/LONG: 53°25'N 113°03'W

Cooking Lake is a large, shallow lake located about 25 km east of the city of Edmonton in the County of Strathcona. Highway 14 skirts the southern shore and Secondary Roads 629 and 630 skirt the northern and eastern shores (Fig. 1). The closest population centres are three hamlets—South Cooking Lake, North Cooking Lake and Collingwood Cove—located around the lakeshore.

The lake's name is a translation of the Cree *opi-mi-now-wa-sioo*, which means "a cooking place". The lake was a favourite Cree campground (Holmgren and Holmgren 1976; Redecop and Gilchrist 1981).

The hamlet of South Cooking Lake is the oldest settlement on Cooking Lake. In 1892, Sheriff Robertson of Edmonton set up a summer camp for his family there, and in 1893, he built a permanent cottage (Touchings 1976). In 1894, a group of Edmontonians formed a company to develop an exclusive recreation club on Koney Island, in the southwest part of the lake (Fig. 1). By 1905, South Cooking Lake had a store and post office, and in 1909, a school. The hamlet of North Cooking Lake became an important recreation area after 1909, when the Grand Trunk Pacific Railway line from Edmonton was completed. Special weekend trains from Edmonton brought tourists to the north end of the lake, and passenger boats from the hamlet transported the visitors to sandy beaches on the south shore (Redecop and Gilchrist 1981). Subdivision of the shorelands and islands at the north end of the lake was rapid, and there was a large demand for cottages prior to World War I. After the war, demand continued, but at a reduced rate.

The Cooking Lake Moraine was the setting for Alberta's first conservation and reforestation projects. Most of the virgin timber had been removed from the area by the late 1890s, either by fire or by timber cutting. A particularly devastating fire in 1895 was caused by settlers clearing land. In 1899, Alberta's first forest reserve, the Cooking Lake Forest Reserve, was opened. It included all of the present-day Elk Island National Park and the Cooking Lake-Blackfoot Grazing, Wildlife and Provincial Recreation Area (Fig. 1) and extended south and west of Cooking Lake to the area around Ministik Lake. William Stephens, the province's first forest ranger, built a ranger station on the reserve in 1899, and the province's first forest fire lookout tower was constructed there in 1913. In 1910, a tree nursery was started on the shore of Cooking Lake, where the soil was sheltered by tall poplars. The nursery failed, however, when spruce and pine seeds did not germinate. In 1919, the Cooking Lake Forest Reserve also became the site of Alberta's first large-scale forest plantation (Touchings 1976).

The water in Cooking Lake is very fertile, and dense algal blooms occur from mid- to late summer. Consequently, there are few recreational facilities at the lake. In 1988, the only public facility on the lakeshore was South Cooking Lake Park, a County of Strathcona day-use area and boat launch in the hamlet of South Cooking Lake (Fig. 2). The facilities, which include picnic tables, firepits and a picnic shelter, were to be upgraded, starting in 1989. Future plans include a concrete boat launch, a washroom/changeroom building, trail construction and cleanup of the beach area. Access to the northeast end of the lake is available in North Cooking Lake, where a small boat or canoe can be launched. Ministik Campground, which is located just south of Cooking Lake on Highway 14, is operated by Alberta Transportation and Utilities. There are 15 campsites, picnic tables, a picnic shelter and a water pump. The North Cooking Lake Natural

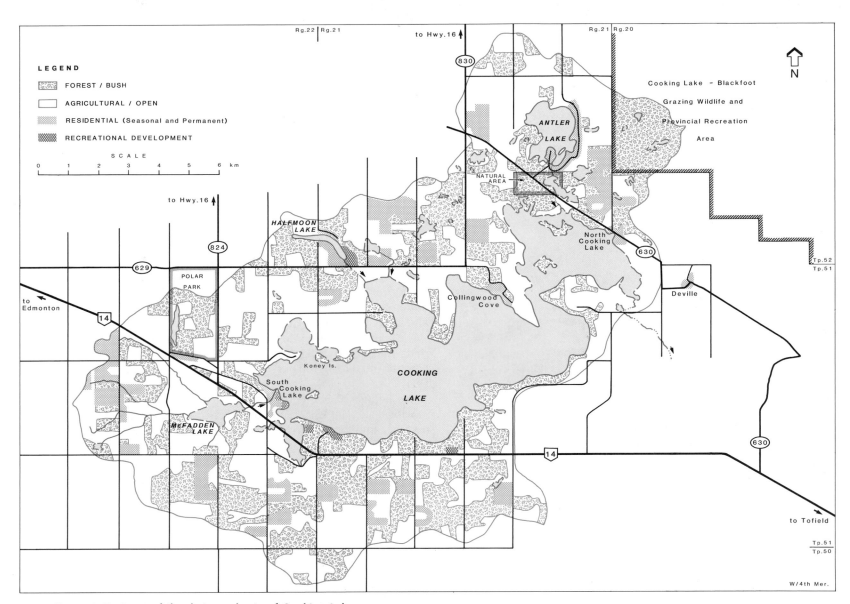

Figure 1. Features of the drainage basin of Cooking Lake.
SOURCES: Alta. Envir. n.d.[b]; En. Mines Resour. Can. 1973; 1974; 1975. Updated with 1983 aerial photos.

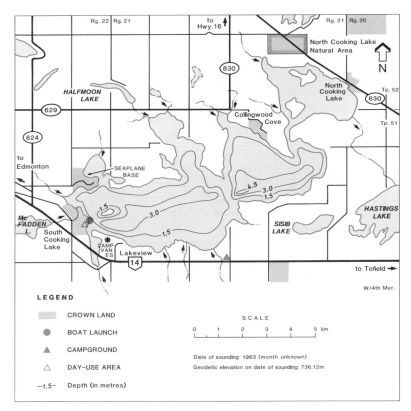

Figure 2. Bathymetry and shoreline features of Cooking Lake.
Bathymetry of northeast basin not surveyed.
BATHYMETRY SOURCE: Alta. Envir. n.d.[c].

Area is located on Secondary Road 630, just north of Cooking Lake (Fig. 2). The land was reserved in 1961 as a wilderness area for hunting and recreation, and was established as a natural area in 1987. It features rolling moraine, ponds and wetlands, and an abundance of waterfowl. There are good opportunities for bird watching, nature observation, hiking and cross-country skiing (Alta. For. Ld. Wild. 1987).

The other recreational facilities at Cooking Lake include Camp Van Es and Lakeview, both located near the peninsula just east of the hamlet of South Cooking Lake (Fig. 2). Camp Van Es is a summer camp operated by the Moravian Church. In 1988, the church received a grant to build a retreat centre at the camp. Lakeview, which is located east of Camp Van Es, was formerly a commercially operated resort that is now owned by the County of Strathcona. In 1988, part of the land was leased to the South Cooking Lake Sail Club, and members plan to build facilities there. The county will sell or lease the remaining land to a private developer.

The Cooking Lake Seaplane Base was established on Crown land on the northwest shore of the lake in 1935 (Fig. 2). It is used for recreational and industrial air traffic. Facilities include a lodge, several buildings, and mooring wharves. An ancillary land runway operated by Alberta Forestry, Lands and Wildlife is also part of the base (Alta. Envir. 1977).

Cooking Lake is most popular for wind surfing, sailing, power boating and bird watching. It is considered regionally significant as a breeding, moulting, staging and migration stopover area for waterfowl (Strathcona Co. 1987). There are no boating regulations specific to the lake, but general federal and provincial regulations apply (Alta. For. Ld. Wild. 1988). Small freshwater invertebrates are

Table 1. Characteristics of Cooking Lake drainage basin.

area (excluding lake) (km²)[a]	158
soil[b]	Orthic Gray Luvisols and Gray Solodized Solonetz
bedrock geology[c]	Horseshoe Canyon Formation (Upper Cretaceous): sandstone, mudstone, shale; ironstone, scattered coal and bentonite beds; mainly nonmarine
terrain[b]	gently rolling to rolling
ecoregion[d]	Moist Mixedwood Subregion of Boreal Mixedwood
dominant vegetation[d]	trembling aspen, balsam poplar
mean annual inflow (m³)[a, e]	7.12 x 10⁶
mean annual sunshine (h)[f]	2 280

NOTE: [e]excluding groundwater inflow
SOURCES: [a]Alta. Envir. n.d.[b]; [b]Bowser et al. 1962; [c]Alta. Res. Counc. 1972; [d]Strong and Leggat 1981; [f]Envir. Can. 1982

Table 2. Characteristics of Cooking Lake.

elevation (m)[a, b]	736.12
surface area (km²)[a, b]	36.0
volume (m³)[a, b]	60.9 x 10⁶
maximum depth (m)[a, b]	4.6
mean depth (m)[a, b]	1.7
shoreline length (km)[c]	72.0
mean annual lake evaporation (mm)[d]	664
mean annual precipitation (mm)[d]	466
mean residence time (yr)[d, e]	>100
control structure	none

NOTES: [a]on date of sounding: (month unknown) 1963; [e]excluding groundwater inflow
SOURCES: [b]Alta. Envir. n.d.[c]; [c]Rasmussen and Gallup 1979; [d]Alta. Envir. n.d.[b].

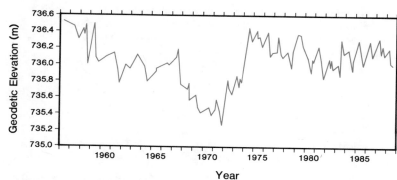

Figure 3. Water level of Cooking Lake, 1956 to 1988.
SOURCES: Alta. Envir. n.d.[c]; Envir. Can. 1972–1988.

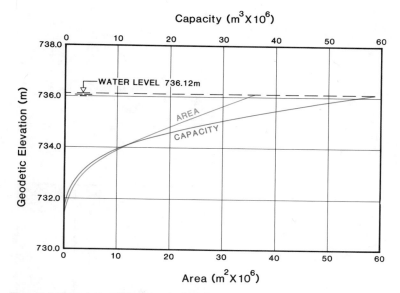

Figure 4. Area/capacity curve for Cooking Lake. Includes area and estimated capacity of northeast basin.
SOURCE: Alta. Envir. n.d.[c].

abundant, but there are no sport fish in the lake because there is not enough oxygen to overwinter fish.

Drainage Basin Characteristics

Cooking Lake's drainage basin is about 4 times the size of the lake (Tables 1, 2). McFadden, Halfmoon and Antler lakes flow intermittently into Cooking Lake via small creeks (Fig. 1). The outlet creek, at the east end of the lake, joins Cooking Lake to Hastings Lake during years when water levels are very high. The precise overflow elevation of Cooking Lake is not known, but water was last known to flow from the lake during the period from 1952 to the mid–1950s, when the lake reached an estimated elevation of 736.7 m (Stanley Assoc. Eng. Ltd. 1976).

The watershed, which is part of the Cooking Lake Moraine, is characterized by knob and kettle topography that gives it an undulating to rolling appearance. Numerous sloughs and peaty depressions occur throughout the area. The main soils are Orthic Gray Luvisols that developed on either glacial till or glaciolacustrine material. Secondary soils are Gray Solodized Solonetz that developed on either glaciolacustrine or residual material (Bowser et al. 1962).

The drainage basin is located within the Moist Mixedwood Subregion of the Boreal Mixedwood Ecoregion. The main trees are trembling aspen and balsam poplar on moderately well-drained Gray Luvisols. Jack pine grows on rapidly drained Eutric Brunisols and white spruce grows on imperfectly drained Gleysols and Gray Luvisols. Poorly drained Organics and Gleysols support a cover of black spruce and willows, and very poorly drained Organics support a cover of sedges (Strong and Leggat 1981). Most of the soils in the drainage basin have a moderate to high capability for cultivation, grazing and pastureland (Alta. Envir. 1977), and a large portion of the land has been cleared for agriculture (Fig. 1).

A considerable portion of the land in the watershed has been developed for country residential subdivisions. During the 1970s and 1980s, the development of subdivisions to the north, south and west of Cooking Lake increased dramatically. Development pressures originate from the population base around Edmonton. Residential developments along the shoreline of Cooking Lake are mainly situated within the hamlets of South Cooking Lake, Collingwood Cove and North Cooking Lake. The only Crown land on the lakeshore is located at the Cooking Lake Seaplane Base.

Lake Basin Characteristics

Cooking Lake has a large surface area and a shallow mean depth (Table 2). There are three basins separated by shallow narrows, and several large, shallow bays (Fig. 2). The west basin had a maximum depth of about 3.0 m when the bathymetry was surveyed in 1963. The central basin is triangular in shape and had a maximum depth of about 4.6 m in that year. The very shallow northeast basin has not been surveyed, but the area and volume were estimated for Table 2 and Figure 4. In 1983, there were four islands in the lake (Fig. 1). During times when water levels are lower, such as the year of the bathymetric survey, the point of land shown as Koney Island in Figure 1 becomes joined to the mainland, as in Figure 2.

Water levels were recorded from 1919 to 1922 and in 1939 and 1941, and have been recorded regularly since 1956 (Fig. 3). An 1897 elevation of approximately 738.2 m was estimated from comments made by a long-term resident of the area. Since 1897, the lake level has declined fairly steadily. By 1919 it had fallen to about 737.4 m, and by 1951, it was estimated to have been 735.5 m. The following year, however, the level rose to an estimated 736.7 m (Stanley Assoc. Eng. Ltd. 1976). Since regular recordings began in 1956, the elevation has dropped from 736.52 m in May 1956, to the historic

Table 3. Major ions and related water quality variables for Cooking Lake. Average concentrations in mg/L; pH in pH units. Composite samples from the euphotic zone collected 6 times from 03 May to 15 Aug. 1983. S.E. = standard error.

	Mean	S.E.
pH (range)	8.6–9.2	—
total alkalinity	414	11.6
specific conductivity (µS/cm)	1 402	42.8
total dissolved solids	1 019[a]	39.2
turbidity (NTU)	14	2.5
colour (Pt)	39	2.7
total hardness (calculated)	277	—
HCO₃	419	12.3
CO₃	42	6.1
Mg	49	1.5
Na	239	9.8
K	44	1.7
Cl	17	0.8
SO₄	284[b]	6.9
Ca	30	2.2

NOTES: [a]n = 5; [b]1987 data, n = 4
SOURCE: Prepas et al. n.d.

Table 4. Nutrient, chlorophyll *a* and Secchi depth data for Cooking Lake. Average concentrations in µg/L. Composite samples from the euphotic zone collected 6 times from 03 May to 15 Aug. 1983 and 6 times from 16 May to 17 Aug. 1987. S.E. = standard error.

	1983[a]		1987[a, c]	
	Mean	S.E.	Mean	S.E.
total phosphorus	232	19.0	270	10.7
total dissolved phosphorus	60	6.7	65[d]	4.7
total Kjeldahl nitrogen	6 299	787.1	6 720	672.3
NO₃ + NO₂–nitrogen	5	1.4	10	3.2
NH₄–nitrogen	52	16.1	27	6.5
iron	181	53.9	—	—
chlorophyll *a*	82.5	14.65	84.2[b]	10.95
Secchi depth (m)	0.6[b]	0.05	0.5[e]	0

NOTES: [b]n = 5; [d]n = 3; [e]n = 2
SOURCES: [a]Prepas et al. n.d.; [c]Alta. Envir. n.d.[a], Naquadat station 01AL05EB1901

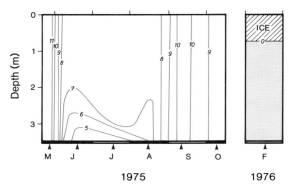

Figure 5. Temperature (°C) of Cooking Lake, 1975 and 1976. Arrows indicate sampling dates.
SOURCE: Rasmussen and Gallup 1979.

Figure 6. Dissolved oxygen (mg/L) in Cooking Lake, 1975 and 1976. Arrows indicate sampling dates.
SOURCE: Rasmussen and Gallup 1979.

recorded minimum of 735.25 m in October 1971 (Fig. 3). High runoff levels in 1974 increased the lake's elevation to 736.45 m. In 1988, the maximum elevation recorded was 736.20 m in May. Changes in the lake's area and capacity with fluctuations in elevation (up to an elevation of 736.12 m) are illustrated in Figure 4.

In 1973, Alberta Environment responded to concerns about water levels in Cooking Lake and other area lakes by initiating the Cooking Lake Area Study (Alta. Envir. 1977). The study concluded that precipitation levels had the greatest effect on the elevations of lakes in the moraine, and that changes in evaporation and runoff were also important (Stanley Assoc. Eng. Ltd. 1976; Alta. Envir. 1977). Long-term precipitation records indicated that, around 1900, area lakes were filled to their greatest recorded capacities when seasonal precipitation reached the level of a 1–in–100–year return period. This event is one that is expected to occur once every 100 years, or 1% of the time. In 1953, most lake levels in the area, including that of Cooking Lake, reached a peak when seasonal precipitation reached the level of a 1–in–50–year return period, which is expected to occur 2% of the time. Precipitation levels in 1953 were the highest recorded since 1901, and 1953 was followed by three consecutive years of higher than average rainfall. Lake levels rose again in 1974, another year of high precipitation levels. During the two periods of decline, from 1902 to 1952 and from 1953 to 1973, the elevation of Cooking Lake fell at an average rate of 6.1 cm/year (Stanley Assoc. Eng. Ltd. 1976). Since 1974, the long-term downward trend appears to have stopped, and lake levels have remained relatively stable (Fig. 3). The Cooking Lake Area Study recommended that water level augmentation plans and lake level control structures be considered on an as-needed basis for each of the study lakes (Alta. Envir. 1977). Water level augmentation has not been implemented and therefore no control structure has been necessary for Cooking Lake, as it rarely overflows.

Water Quality

Water quality in Cooking Lake was studied by researchers with the University of Alberta in 1963 and 1964, from 1971 to 1976, and in 1981, 1983, 1986 and 1987 (Prepas et al. n.d.; Kerekes 1965; Kerekes and Nursall 1966; Gallup and Hickman 1975; Rasmussen and Gallup 1979; Prepas and Trew 1983; Bierhuizen and Prepas 1985; Marino et al. 1990). The lake was also studied by Alberta Environment in 1981 and 1987 (Alta. Envir. n.d.[a]).

Cooking Lake is slightly to moderately saline (Table 3). The water is moderately coloured and low in turbidity and the dominant ions are bicarbonate, sulphate and sodium.

The lake is very shallow, and during summer the water column warms uniformly to more than 20°C by July (Fig. 5). The water is well-oxygenated to the bottom during the open-water season (Fig. 6), but soon after ice formation, the bottom water becomes

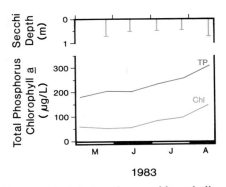

Figure 7. Total phosphorus, chlorophyll _a_ and Secchi depth in Cooking Lake, 1983. SOURCE: Prepas et al. n.d.

Table 5. Percentage composition of major algal groups by total biomass in Cooking Lake, 1987.

ALGAL GROUP	16 May	12 June	16 July	14 Aug.
Total Biomass (mg/L)	3.77	26.84	90.76	137.81
Percentage Composition:				
Cyanophyta	6	32	60	54
		Aphanizomenon ——————————————→		
Chlorophyta	18	41	29	29
		Cosmarium _Scenedesmus_	_Staurastrum_ _Ulothrix_[a] —→	_Closterium_
Bacillariophyta	76	26	6	17
	Pleurosigma	_Synedra_		
Cryptophyta	0	0	5	0

NOTE: [a]_Ulothrix_-type filament
SOURCE: Prepas et al. n.d.

Table 6. Species of aquatic macrophytes in Cooking Lake, June 1975. Arranged in alphabetical order.

emergent	sedge	_Carex_ spp.
	spike rush	_Eleocharis_ spp.
	rush	_Juncus_ sp.
	reed grass	_Phragmites communis_
	bulrush	_Scirpus_ spp.
	common great bulrush	_S. validus_
	common cattail	_Typha latifolia_
free-floating	lesser duckweed	_Lemna minor_
	star duckweed	_Lemna trisulca_
submergent	northern watermilfoil	_Myriophyllum exalbescens_
	Sago pondweed	_Potamogeton pectinatus_
	large-sheath pondweed	_P. vaginatus_
	horned pondweed	_Zannichellia palustris_

SOURCE: Gallup and Hickman 1975

anoxic. In March 1976 and January 1987, the entire water column was anoxic. In 1974 and 1975, the odour of hydrogen sulphide was present from soon after ice formation until ice left the lake.

Cooking Lake is hyper-eutrophic (Table 4). In 1983, total phosphorus concentrations rose gradually over the summer to a high of 310 µg/L in August (Fig. 7), likely due to release from the bottom sediments. The bottom sediments of Cooking Lake have high phosphorus concentrations (Allan and Williams 1978). Increases in the chlorophyll _a_ concentration followed those of phosphorus, and chlorophyll _a_ also reached a maximum in mid-August. In 1987, the average phosphorus concentration was somewhat higher than that recorded for 1983 (Table 4), but maximum values were very similar. Average chlorophyll _a_ concentrations were very similar between the two years, but in 1987, the highest chlorophyll _a_ value measured (120 µg/L) was lower than the highest measured in 1983 (147 µg/L). Although chlorophyll _a_ concentrations are high in Cooking Lake, they would be higher if the salinity were lower.

Biological Characteristics

Plants

The phytoplankton community in Cooking Lake was studied from 1974 to 1976 and from May to August 1987 by the University of Alberta (Alta. Envir. n.d.[a]; Prepas et al. n.d.; Hickman 1978; 1979; Marino et al. 1990). In 1987, biomass increased steadily over the study period, from 3.77 mg/L in May to 137.81 mg/L in August (Table 5). Diatoms (Bacillariophyta), particularly _Pleurosigma_ sp., were the dominant group in May. The blue-green alga _Aphanizomenon flos-aquae_ became prominent during June, then dominated the biomass for the remainder of the study period. Green algae (Chlorophyta), such as _Cosmarium_ sp. and _Scenedesmus quadricau-

da in June, _Staurastrum_ sp. and a _Ulothrix_-type filament in July, and _Staurastrum_ sp. and _Closterium_ sp. in August, were also important.

Macrophytes were studied by the University of Alberta in 1963, 1975 and 1986 (Kerekes 1965; Gallup and Hickman 1975; Chambers and Prepas 1988). In 1975, a total of 13 species were identified (Table 6). Chambers and Prepas have developed a model, based partly on data from this lake, to predict the depth of macrophyte colonization. In Cooking Lake, this depth is estimated to be 2.4 m.

Invertebrates

The zooplankton community was studied by the University of Alberta during 1963 and 1964 and from November 1974 to July 1976 (Alta. Envir. n.d.[a]; Kerekes 1965; Kerekes and Nursall 1966; Gallup and Hickman 1975). In both studies, vertical tows were taken; the later study used 76–µm mesh nets. Seston biomass was determined in 1963 and 1964 and zooplankton biomass was determined from 1974 to 1976. In 1975, the average zooplankton biomass for the period from May to September was 6.9 g/m³ dry weight. This was considerably higher than the biomass in nearby Hastings (1.4 g/m³) and Beaverhill (2.5 g/m³) lakes, which were sampled over a similar period in 1975. In Cooking Lake, biomass decreased between January 1975 (0.6 g/m³) and March (less than 0.1 g/m³), increased steadily until mid-August (10.5 g/m³), then declined until December (2.6 g/m³). The most frequently observed species were the copepods _Diaptomus siciloides_, _Diacyclops bicuspidatus thomasi_, _Acanthocyclops vernalis_ and _Eucyclops agilis_; the cladocerans _Daphnia pulicaria_ and _Diaphanosoma leuctenbergianum_; and the rotifers _Keratella quadrata_, _K. cochlearis_, _Branchionus angularis_, _Filinia longiseta_, _F. terminalis_, _Polyarthra_ sp., _Branchionus_ spp. and _Notholca_ sp.

Benthic invertebrates in Cooking, Hastings and Ministik lakes

Table 7. Biomass of benthic invertebrates in Cooking Lake, 1963.
Samples collected with an Ekman dredge from unspecified depths;
n = 91.

Invertebrate Group	01 July	05 Aug.	07 Sep.	Mean
Chironomidae	9.99	59.01	22.94	30.64
Amphipoda	1.33	1.76	0.60	1.32
Hirudinea	1.38	0.90	1.46	1.25
Sphaeriidae[a]	0.02	<0.01	<0.01	0.01
Oligochaeta	<0.01	—	—	<0.01
Miscellaneous[b]	<0.01	—	<0.01	<0.01
Total Biomass (g/m^2 wet weight)	12.73	61.68	25.01	33.23

NOTES: [a]shell weight deducted; [b]Trichoptera and Hemiptera
SOURCE: Kerekes 1965

were studied by the University of Alberta in July, August and September of 1963 (Kerekes 1965; Kerekes and Nursall 1966). A total of 91 samples were taken at unspecified depths. In Cooking Lake, the average biomass for the survey period was 33.23 g/m^2 wet weight (Table 7). The greatest biomass (61.68 g/m^2) was recorded in August. Midge larvae (Chironomidae) were the most important organisms on all sampling dates. On average, they formed 92% of the biomass and 83% of the total numbers. The average biomass of benthos in Cooking Lake was much smaller than the biomass in nearby Hastings Lake (63.47 g/m^2), but greater than the biomass in Ministik Lake (9.85 g/m^2).

Fish

There are no sport fish in Cooking Lake. In 1963, brook sticklebacks were netted in very low numbers (Kerekes 1965). Anoxic conditions during winter are the major limitation to fish survival. There probably were northern pike and yellow perch in the lake before water levels began to decline (Zelt and Glasgow 1976). These fish would have migrated upstream from nearby Hastings Lake when the creek between the two lakes was flowing.

Wildlife

Wildlife habitat in the Cooking Lake Moraine was evaluated in 1974 by Alberta Environment and in 1987 by the County of Strathcona (Zelt and Glasgow 1976; Griffiths 1987). Although existing forest cover and other natural features are extensive enough to provide excellent habitat for many species, agricultural and other land uses have reduced the quality of the habitat. In 1987, Cooking Lake was identified by the County of Strathcona as a provincially important waterfowl moulting, staging and breeding area. Its sheltered bays and islands provide productive breeding habitat for water-associated birds and mammals. McFadden Lake, which flows into the western shore of Cooking Lake, and Antler Lake, which flows into the northeast basin, have locally significant waterfowl and muskrat habitat. In 1974, there were estimated to be 24 beaver and 516 muskrats in Cooking Lake. The drainage basin is not considered important winter habitat for ungulates.

The presence and distribution of ducks, geese and swans on Cooking Lake was studied by the Canadian Wildlife Service during 1973 and 1974 (Kemper 1976). In comparison to other area lakes, Cooking Lake was not as important for spring migration or nesting. Dabbling ducks accounted for about 15% of all ducks sighted during the spring and early summer breeding period. Mallards were the most common dabbler; Gadwall, Widgeons, Shovellers and Pintails were seen less frequently. Diving ducks, which were the most numerous group, included Redheads, Canvasbacks, Ruddy Ducks, Bufflehead, Common Goldeneye, Lesser Scaup and White-winged Scoters. The latter two species were most numerous. The waterfowl population remained very low until August, when ducks and geese began to arrive. Large rafts of diving ducks were observed in the centre of the lake during the moulting period from August to early September, and swans appeared in late September. Peak numbers of all three groups occurred from late September to early November.

M.E. Bradford

References

Alberta Environment. n.d.[a]. Envir. Assess. Div., Envir. Qlty. Monit. Br. Unpubl. data, Edmonton.
————. n.d.[b]. Tech. Serv. Div., Hydrol. Br. Unpubl. data, Edmonton.
————. n.d.[c]. Tech. Serv. Div., Surv. Br. Unpubl. data, Edmonton.
————. 1977. Cooking Lake area study, Vol. I: Planning report. Plan. Div., Edmonton.
Alberta Forestry, Lands and Wildlife. 1987. A summary of Alberta's natural areas reserved and established. Pub. Ld. Div., Ld. Mgt. Devel. Br. Unpubl. rep., Edmonton.
————. 1988. Boating in Alberta. Fish Wild. Div., Edmonton.
Alberta Research Council. 1972. Geological map of Alberta. Nat. Resour. Div., Alta. Geol. Surv., Edmonton.
Allan, R.J. and J.D.H. Williams. 1978. Trophic status related to sediment chemistry of Canadian prairie lakes. J. Envir. Qlty. 9:199–206.
Bierhuizen, J.F.H. and E.E. Prepas. 1985. Relationship between nutrients, dominant ions, and phytoplankton standing crop in prairie saline lakes. Can. J. Fish. Aquat. Sci. 42:1588–1594.
Bowser, W.E., A.A. Kjearsgaard, T.W. Peters and R.E. Wells. 1962. Soil survey of the Edmonton sheet (83–H). Alta. Soil Surv. Rep. No. 21, Univ. Alta. Bull. No. SS–4. Univ. Alta., Edmonton.
Chambers, P.A. and E.E. Prepas. 1988. Underwater spectral attenuation and its effect on the maximum depth of angiosperm colonization. Can. J. Fish. Aquat. Sci. 45:1010–1017.
Energy, Mines and Resources Canada. 1973, 1974, 1975. National topographic series 1:50 000 83H/11 (1973), 83H/6 (1974), 83H/7 (1975), 83H/10 (1975). Surv. Map. Br., Ottawa.
Environment Canada. 1972–1988. Surface water data. Prep. by Inland Waters Directorate. Water Surv. Can., Water Resour. Br., Ottawa.
————. 1982. Canadian climate normals, Vol. 7: Bright sunshine (1951–1980). Prep. by Atm. Envir. Serv. Supply Serv. Can., Ottawa.
Gallup, D.N. and M. Hickman. 1975. Lakes primary productivity study, Part B: Cooking Lakes watershed. Interim rep. July 1975. Alta. Envir. Unpubl. rep., Edmonton.
Griffiths, D.E. 1987. A survey of wetland wildlife resources, Strathcona County #20, Alberta. Prep. for Co. Strathcona, Sherwood Park.
Hickman, M. 1978. Ecological studies on the epipelic algal community in five prairie-parkland lakes in central Alberta. Can. J. Bot. 56:991–1009.
————. 1979. Phytoplankton of shallow lakes: Seasonal succession, standing crop and the chief determinants of primary productivity, 1. Cooking Lake, Alberta, Canada. Holarctic Ecol. 1:337–350.
Holmgren, E.J. and P.M. Holmgren. 1976. Over 2000 place names of Alberta. 3rd ed. West. Producer Prairie Books, Saskatoon.
Kemper, J.B. 1976. Implications for waterfowl and migratory birds [Appendix 7]. In Cooking Lake area study, Vol. IV: Ecology. Alta. Envir., Plan. Div., Edmonton.
Kerekes, J. 1965. A comparative limnological study of five lakes in central Alberta. MSc thesis. Univ. Alta., Edmonton.
———— and J.R. Nursall. 1966. Eutrophication and senescence in a group of prairie parkland lakes in Alberta, Canada. Verh. Internat. Verein. Limnol. 16:65–73.
Marino, R., R.W. Howarth, J. Shamess and E.E. Prepas. 1990. Molybdenum and sulfate as controls on the abundance of nitrogen-fixing cyanobacteria in Alberta saline lakes. Limnol. Oceanogr. [in press]
Prepas, E.E., J.F.H. Bierhuizen, J. Shamess, P.A. Chambers, R.W. Howarth and R. Marino. n.d. Unpubl. data, Univ. Alta., Edmonton and Cornell Univ., Ithaca, New York.
Prepas, E.E. and D.O. Trew. 1983. Evaluation of the phosphorus-chlorophyll relationship for lakes off the Precambrian Shield in western Canada. Can. J. Fish. Aquat. Sci. 40:27–35.
Rasmussen, H.B. and D.N. Gallup. 1979. A survey of physical, chemical and biological characteristics of a series of lakes of central Alberta. Alta. Envir., Poll. Contr. Div. Unpubl. rep., Edmonton.
Redecop, L. and W. Gilchrist. 1981. Strathcona County—a brief history. W. Gilchrist, Univ. Alta. Printing Serv., Edmonton.
Stanley Associates Engineering Ltd. 1976. Main report, data volume and atlas volume [Appendices 1, 2, 3]. In Cooking Lake area study, Vol. II: Water inventory and demands. Alta. Envir., Plan. Div., Edmonton.
Strathcona County. 1987. Outdoor master plan 1987: Technical report. Rec. Parks Dept., Sherwood Park.
Strong, W.L. and K.R. Leggat. 1981. Ecoregions of Alberta. Alta. En. Nat. Resour., Resour. Eval. Plan. Div., Edmonton.
Touchings, D. 1976. Heritage resource inventory of the Cooking Lake study area [Appendix 10]. In Cooking Lake area study, Vol. V: Economic base and heritage resources. Alta. Envir., Plan. Div., Edmonton.
Zelt, K.A. and W.M. Glasgow. 1976. Evaluation of the fish and wildlife resources of the Cooking Lake study area [Appendix 6]. In Cooking Lake area study, Vol. IV: Ecology. Alta. Envir., Plan. Div., Edmonton.

CRIMSON LAKE

MAP SHEET: 83B/6

LOCATION: Tp40 R8 W5

LAT/LONG: 52°27'N 115°02'W

Crimson Lake is a small, clear, shallow lake attractively set in rolling, pine-covered hills; in the fall, the scenery is further enhanced by blazing orange tamaracks in low-lying areas. The lake can be reached by travelling 8 km west of Rocky Mountain House on Highway 11, then 7 km north on Secondary Road 756. A short access road leads to Crimson Lake Provincial Park (Fig. 1). Crimson Lake was named by an early trapper for the spectacular sunsets he saw reflected in the water (Finlay and Finlay 1987).

Crimson Lake is located in the Municipal District of Clearwater, within the drainage basin of the North Saskatchewan River. This river, which flows 3 km east of the lake, was navigable by canoes and York boats as far as Rocky Mountain House and was the route that brought the fur trade to the area. Anthony Henday of the Hudson's Bay Company explored the area for its potential for furs in 1754; forty years later, nearby Rocky Mountain House was established as the most westerly fur-trading post in Canada at the time. Settlers arrived in the early 1900s, and in 1912, the Canadian Northern Railway crossed the area. By 1917, a small community and school had been established near Crimson Lake (Long 1977; Finlay and Finlay 1987).

In 1945, land surrounding Crimson Lake was reserved for a provincial park. A few years later, Pioneer Ranch Camp was established on the northeast shore (Long 1977). Crimson Lake Provincial Park, which was officially established in 1955, completely surrounds the lake. Facilities are open year-round and include a campground with 161 sites, a day-use area, tap water, public telephones, sewage disposal facilities and change houses (Alta. Hotel Assoc. 1988). There are two boat launches, one for canoes and hand-launched boats in the southeast corner of the lake and one with a concrete ramp farther north along the east shore (Fig. 2). Very clear water and a clean natural sand beach make the area attractive for recreational use; up to 1 500 people have visited the lake on July weekends (Mitchell 1978). The lake is used for power boating, but propellers may become tangled in the dense aquatic vegetation growing in some areas. All boats are restricted from some posted areas and power boats are limited to speeds less than 12 km/hour in other posted areas (Alta. For. Ld. Wild. 1988). The beach is popular and so are swimming and hiking. A large skating rink is kept cleared in the winter and a network of cross-country ski trails is maintained. There are no sport fish in the lake, as they would winterkill in most years. Some provincial park land along the southwest shore is leased for cottages (Fig. 1); six cottages had been built by 1947, 102 had been built by 1977 (Long 1977) and none have been added since.

Drainage Basin Characteristics

The Crimson Lake drainage basin is a narrow band surrounding the lake (Fig. 1). The basin is very small and covers less area than the lake itself (Tables 1, 2). The watershed is part of the Boreal Foothills Ecoregion, the ecoregion with the most diverse tree cover in Alberta (Strong and Leggat 1981). This diversity is typified in the Crimson Lake area, where trembling aspen, balsam poplar, paper birch, lodgepole pine, white spruce, black spruce and fir all occur on moderately well-drained sites. Both white and black spruce are successful in this area and both are potential climax species on the same site. Luvisolic soils have typically developed on moderately well-drained sites. Low or depressional areas are poorly drained and form *Sphag-*

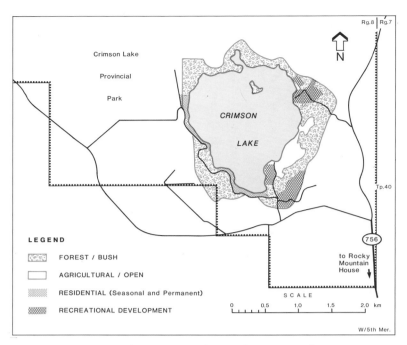

Figure 1. Features of the drainage basin of Crimson Lake.
SOURCES: Alta. Envir. n.d.[b]; En. Mines Resour. Can. 1979. Updated with 1986 aerial photos.

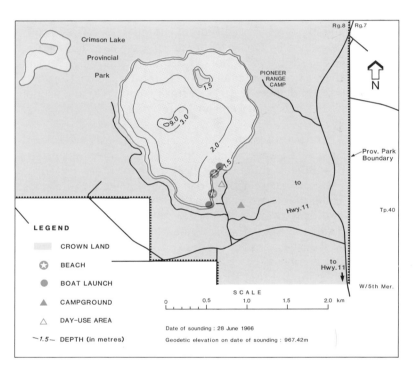

Figure 2. Bathymetry and shoreline features of Crimson Lake.
BATHYMETRY SOURCE: Alta. Envir. n.d.[c].

Table 1. Characteristics of Crimson Lake drainage basin.

area (excluding lake) (km^2)[a]	1.75
soil[b]	Gray Luvisol
bedrock geology[c]	Paskapoo Formation (Tertiary): sandstone, siltstone, mudstone; thin limestone, coal and tuff beds; nonmarine
terrain[b]	gently undulating to hilly
ecoregion[d]	Boreal Foothills
dominant vegetation[b]	trembling aspen, lodgepole pine, white spruce, black spruce, tamarack
mean annual inflow (m^3)[a, e]	0.172 x 10^6
mean annual sunshine (h)[f]	2 125

NOTE: [e]excluding groundwater inflow
SOURCES: [a]Alta. Envir. n.d.[b]; [b]Greenlee 1974; [c]Alta. Res. Counc. 1972; [d]Strong and Leggat 1981; [f]Envir. Can. 1982

Table 2. Characteristics of Crimson Lake.

elevation (m)[a, b]	967.88
surface area (km^2)[a, b]	2.32
volume (m^3)[a, b]	5.21 x 10^6
maximum depth (m)[a, b]	9.1
mean depth (m)[a, b]	2.2
shoreline length (km)[c]	9.25
mean annual lake evaporation (mm)[d]	630
mean annual precipitation (mm)[d]	556
mean residence time (yr)[d, e]	>100

NOTES: [a]on date of sounding: 28 June 1966; [e]excluding groundwater inflow
SOURCES: [b]Alta. Envir. n.d.[c]; [c]Mitchell 1978; [d]Alta. Envir. n.d.[b].

Lake Basin Characteristics

Crimson Lake lies in a shallow, gently-sloping depression (Fig. 2). Approximately 95% of the lake is less than 3-m deep; there is only one small area, about 0.5 ha, that extends to 9 m (Fig. 3). Except for the sandy beach in the south portion, and some areas along the east shore, the bottom of the lake is covered by a deep layer of organic material. With most of the lake bottom in the littoral zone, macrophytes flourish and each year's growth adds another layer to the bottom ooze (Mitchell 1978).

It was noted in 1952 that the water level of Crimson Lake was relatively stable (Miller and Paetz 1953), but more recent records indicate a drop of about 0.9 m between 1965 and the late 1970s. Since then, the lake level has been relatively stable, with annual fluctuations of less than 0.25 m (Fig. 4).

Water Quality

Crimson Lake has been monitored since 1982 under a joint sampling program between Alberta Environment and Alberta Recreation and Parks designed to document long-term patterns in lakes associated with provincial parks (Alta. Envir. n.d.[a]). The lake was also studied by Alberta Environment in 1978 to address the concerns of cottagers (Mitchell 1978).

Crimson Lake has excellent water quality. The water is fresh (total dissolved solids = 137 mg/L, Table 3) and clear and the Secchi depth frequently extends to the lake bottom—that is, to more than 3 m. The dominant ions are bicarbonate, calcium and magnesium.

During the open-water period, the water temperature is usually uniform from the lake surface to a depth of 4 m (Fig. 5). Temperature profiles of the "deep hole" (9 m) were taken five times in the summer of 1978; in early May, late June and late July it was thermally stratified. Dissolved oxygen concentrations remained high all summer, with occasional depletion near depths of 4 m (Fig. 5). In 1978, water in the deepest area was low in dissolved oxygen in May and

num bogs ringed with tamarack and black spruce, or sedge bogs ringed with willows. Soils in these poorly drained areas are Organics and Gleysols. This mix of vegetation creates a great variety of habitats; 266 species of vascular plants, including 13 orchid species, have been reported in the provincial park (Finlay and Finlay 1987).

Pockets of sand are common in the drainage basin and throughout the park. One natural-sand area occurs along the southeast shore of the lake and makes an attractive beach (Greenlee 1974).

There are no permanent inflowing or outflowing streams. Groundwater plays a significant role to maintain the water balance of Crimson Lake.

The drainage basin is entirely Crown land and lies entirely within Crimson Lake Provincial Park. Residential and recreational developments consist of the park campground and day-use areas, cottages on the southwest shore and Pioneer Ranch Camp on the northeast shore. There are a few active oil wells within the park.

Table 3. Major ions and related water quality variables for Crimson Lake. Average concentrations in mg/L; pH in pH units. Composite samples from the euphotic zone collected 3 times from 27 May to 06 Oct. 1986. S.E. = standard error.

	Mean	S.E.
pH (range)	8.6–9.1	—
total alkalinity ($CaCO_3$)	139	13.6
specific conductivity (μS/cm)	257	24.2
total dissolved solids (calculated)	137	14.0
total hardness ($CaCO_3$)	122	15.4
HCO_3	150	20.4
CO_3	10	3.2
Mg	18	0.6
Na	8	0.4
K	2	0.1
Cl	1	0.3
SO_4	<5	—
Ca	19	5.3

SOURCE: Alta. Envir. n.d.[a], Naquadat station 01AL05DC1000

Table 4. Nutrient, chlorophyll *a* and Secchi depth data for Crimson Lake. Average concentrations in μg/L. Composite samples from the euphotic zone collected 3 times from 03 July to 18 Sep. 1984 and 5 times from 27 May to 06 Oct. 1986. S.E. = standard error.

	1984		1986	
	Mean	S.E.	Mean	S.E.
total phosphorus	17.0	1.5	19.0	1.3
chlorophyll *a*	4.8	0.86	4.8	0.60
Secchi depth (m)	3.8	0.75	3.2	0.29

SOURCE: Alta. Envir. n.d.[a], Naquadat station 01AL05DC1000

June, anoxic in late July and partially reoxygenated by late August. Under ice cover, decay of organic debris on the lake bottom consumes oxygen, and the lake is often anoxic by late winter, as in March 1986 (Fig. 5) and February 1978. In other years, however, such as 1987, there was still sufficient oxygen for fish survival in the top 3 m of the water column.

Algal growth in Crimson Lake is not conspicuous and does not create a problem for recreation. The low phosphorus and chlorophyll *a* concentrations throughout the summer (Fig. 6) indicate the lake is mesotrophic. Data from 1984 and 1986 (Table 4) indicate that nutrient and chlorophyll *a* concentrations are fairly consistent from year to year.

A water quality study was conducted by Alberta Environment in 1978 to address concerns expressed by recreational users of the lake (Mitchell 1978). The main complaints regarded the abundance of leeches, the soft oozy bottom and the prolific growth of rooted aquatic plants. One solution proposed by cottagers was to divert a nearby creek to flush the lake. The report concluded that high nutrient levels in the diverted creek water would increase phosphorus loading to the lake and could result in blue-green algal blooms and a shift in the trophic status of the lake to eutrophic. Therefore, a decision was made to maintain the lake in its present state.

Biological Characteristics

Plants

There are no data available on phytoplankton species in Crimson Lake.

Most of Crimson Lake supports luxuriant macrophyte growth. A survey by Alberta Environment in 1978 found that white-stem pondweed (*Potamogeton praelongus*), the most widespread species, dominated most of the lake (Table 5, Fig. 7).

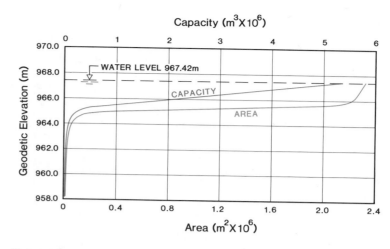

Figure 3. Area/capacity curve for Crimson Lake.
SOURCE: Alta. Envir. n.d.[c].

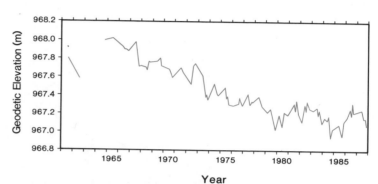

Figure 4. Water level of Crimson Lake, 1961 to 1988.
SOURCE: Alta. Envir. n.d.[c].

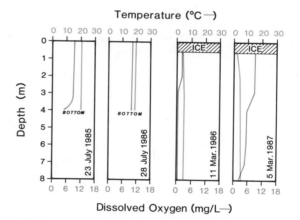

Figure 5. Temperature and dissolved oxygen in Crimson Lake, 1986.
SOURCE: Alta. Envir. n.d.[a].

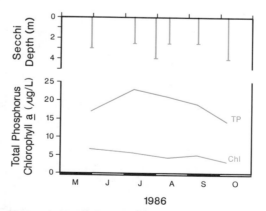

Figure 6. Total phosphorus, chlorophyll *a* and Secchi depth in Crimson Lake, 1986.
SOURCE: Alta. Envir. n.d.[a].

Table 5. Species of aquatic macrophytes in Crimson Lake. Survey conducted in August 1978. Arranged by order of dominance.

emergent	scouring rush	*Equisetum fluviatile*
	common cattail	*Typha latifolia*
	arrowhead	*Sagittaria cuneata*
	sedge	*Carex rostrata*
	spike rush	*Eleocharis acicularis*
	small-fruited bulrush	*Scirpus microcarpus*
	common great bulrush	*S. validus*
	bur-reed	*Sparganium multipedunculatum*
submergent	stonewort	*Chara* sp.
	naiad	*Najas flexilis*
	white-stem pondweed	*Potamogeton praelongus*
	Richardson pondweed	*Potamogeton richardsonii*
	pondweed	*Potamogeton strictifolius*
	flat-stemmed pondweed	*Potamogeton zosteriformis*
floating-leaved	floating-leaf pondweed	*Potamogeton natans*
	yellow water lily	*Nuphar variegatum*

SOURCE: Mitchell 1978

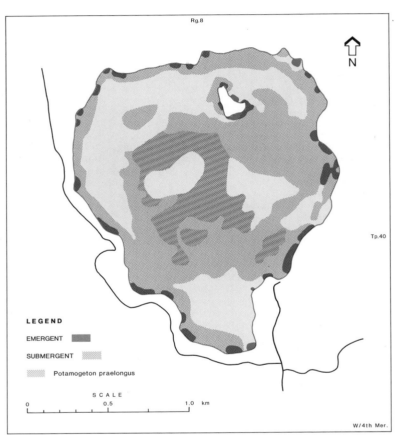

Figure 7. Distribution of macrophytes in Crimson Lake, August 1978. SOURCE: Alta. Envir. n.d.[a].

Invertebrates

During a brief survey in 1952, Miller and Paetz found almost no benthic invertebrates to a depth of 2 m; slightly more were found at 3.5 m and 6.5 m (Miller and Paetz 1953). A single plankton haul collected rotifers (*Keratella* [= *Anuraea* sp.], *Polyarthra* sp. and *Asplanchna* sp.) and crustaceans (*Diacyclops bicuspidatus thomasi*, *Diaptomus* sp., *Daphnia pulex* and *Bosmina* sp.). Free-swimming macroinvertebrates were abundant, including *Gammarus lacustris* and horsehair worms (*Gordius* sp.) in "tremendous numbers". Large clams (*Anodonta* sp.) were found in the sand.

Crimson Lake is notorious for its leech population. In 1952 there were "thousands everywhere in the lake, swimming between surface and bottom" (Miller and Paetz 1953). Other large species burrow in the sand at the water's edge. Most species in the lake feed on other invertebrates or detritus and are harmless to man, but there are some blood-sucking varieties (Mitchell 1978).

Fish

The only fish in Crimson Lake are two species noted for their tolerance of low dissolved oxygen concentrations: brook sticklebacks and fathead minnows (Miller and Paetz 1953; Kraft 1988).

Yellow perch were introduced into Crimson Lake in 1950. They did not establish a reproducing population and probably succumbed to winterkill (Alta. For. Ld. Wild. n.d.). In 1952, Miller and Paetz (1953) concluded that Crimson Lake was "useless for fish", except possibly as a put-and-take fishery, where fairly large sport fish are introduced in the spring and harvested before freeze-up. This approach to a managed fishery was tried by Alberta Fish and Wildlife from 1952 to 1957. Rainbow trout fingerlings were introduced each spring and grew well over the summer. However, catch rates were low and most of the fish remained uncaught and died in the winter (Alta. For. Ld. Wild. n.d.). The lake is too large to stock with trout of catchable size—many fish would be required to ensure a reasonable catch rate, and losses from winterkill would be substantial.

Wildlife

At Crimson Lake, lodgepole pine forests typical of the lower foothills are interspersed with bog vegetation typical of boreal forests to the north and with aspen woodlands typical of the aspen parkland. With this variety of habitats, the wildlife is also diverse. Over 100 species of birds have been seen in the provincial park, including nesting Sandhill Cranes, Mourning Doves, Pygmy Owls and Boreal Owls. Common Loons nest on Crimson Lake, as do Mallards, teal, and Common Goldeneye.

Thirty-one species of mammals inhabit the park, including wolves, black bears and mink. The loud songs of frogs can be heard in the spring; amphibian species include western and Dakota toads and chorus, wood and leopard frogs. The two reptile species present are western and common garter snakes (Finlay and Finlay 1987).

J.M. Crosby

References

Alberta Environment. n.d.[a]. Envir. Assess. Div., Envir. Qlty. Monit. Br. Unpubl. data, Edmonton.

———. n.d.[b]. Tech. Serv. Div., Hydrol. Br. Unpubl. data, Edmonton.

———. n.d.[c]. Tech. Serv. Div., Surv. Br. Unpubl. data, Edmonton.

Alberta Forestry, Lands and Wildlife. n.d. Fish Wild. Div. Unpubl. data, Edmonton.

———. 1988. Boating in Alberta. Fish Wild. Div., Edmonton.

Alberta Hotel Association. 1988. 1988 Alberta campground guide. Prep. for Travel Alta., Edmonton.

Alberta Research Council. 1972. Geological map of Alberta. Nat. Resour. Div., Alta. Geol. Surv., Edmonton.

Energy, Mines and Resources Canada. 1979. National topographic series 1:50 000 83B/6 (1979). Surv. Map. Br., Ottawa.

Environment Canada. 1982. Canadian climate normals, Vol. 7: Bright sunshine (1951–1980). Prep. by Atm. Envir. Serv. Supply Serv. Can., Ottawa.

Finlay, J. and C. Finlay. 1987. Parks in Alberta: A guide to peaks, ponds, parklands & prairies. Hurtig Publ., Edmonton.

Greenlee, G.M. 1974. Soil survey of Crimson Lake Provincial Park and interpretation for use. Alta. Inst. Pedol. Rep. No. M–74–15. Alta. Res. Counc., Edmonton.

Kraft, M. 1988. Alta. For. Ld. Wild., Fish Wild. Div., Rocky Mountain House. Pers. comm.

Long, L. 1977. The Atwaters, p. 312. In F. Fleming [ed.] The days before yesterday—History of Rocky Mountain House district. Rocky Mountain House Reunion Hist. Soc., Rocky Mountain House.

Miller, R.B. and M. Paetz. 1953. Preliminary biological surveys of Alberta watersheds 1950–1952. Alta. Ld. For., Fish Wild. Div., Edmonton.

Mitchell, P.A. 1978. Assessment of the potential for improving water quality in Crimson Lake. Alta. Envir., Poll. Control. Div., Water Qlty. Contr. Br., Edmonton.

Strong, W.L. and K.R. Leggat. 1981. Ecoregions of Alberta. Alta. En. Nat. Resour., Resour. Eval. Plan. Div., Edmonton.

LAKE EDEN

MAP SHEET: 83G/9
LOCATION: Tp53 R2 W5
LAT/LONG: 53°35'N 114°09'W

Lake Eden is a small, deep pothole lake nestled in a sheltered depression in rolling hills west of the city of Edmonton. The lake is located in the County of Parkland. It is a pleasant place to visit on warm summer weekends and is a popular family recreation area. To reach the lake, travel west on Highway 16 until you are 10 km west of the town of Stony Plain, then turn north onto a local road and continue for 2 km. Private roads skirt the lakeshore (Fig. 1).

All of the land around the lake, except for two road easements, is owned by Lake Eden Summer and Winter Resort. Access to the lake and parking are available for a fee at the resort; free public walk-in access is available as well, but there is no parking area. The only facilities on the lake are those offered by the commercially operated resort; included are 220 campsites, picnic tables, beaches and a boat launch. The only power boats allowed on the lake are those with battery-operated motors (Alta. For. Ld. Wild. 1988). In winter, the resort operates a downhill ski area with several tows. The chalet is open to all, as is a fine network of cross-country ski trails.

Lake Eden was named in the early 1950s by the owner of Lake Eden Fur Farm, which was established on land adjacent to the lake (Holmgren and Holmgren 1976).

Algal growth in Lake Eden is not conspicuous, and the clear water is attractive for swimming and wind surfing. The lake is stocked annually with rainbow trout by Fish and Wildlife Division and sport fishing is popular in both summer and winter. Aquatic plants, which grow densely in some areas, can be a nuisance to shore-based anglers, but because the lake slopes steeply, few plants are encountered beyond a short distance from shore. The use of bait fish and the capture of bait fish is not permitted in Lake Eden (Alta. For. Ld. Wild. 1989).

Drainage Basin Characteristics

The drainage basin for Lake Eden is small (1.5 km², Table 1) about 10 times the area of the lake (Table 2, Fig. 1). The terrain is rolling, and hills rise approximately 60 m on all sides of the lake, providing shelter (En. Mines Resour. Can. 1974). The soils in most of the drainage basin are Orthic Gray Luvisols that developed under aspen woodlands on glacial deltaic material (Lindsay et al. 1968). The basin is pocked with small sloughs to the east and south of the lake; soils in these wet areas are Orthic Humic Gleysols. The arability of the soil in the basin is rated as poor to fair. The drainage area is part of the Moist Mixedwood Subregion of the Boreal Mixedwood Ecoregion (Strong and Leggat 1981). The dominant natural vegetation—trembling aspen and balsam poplar, with willow and alder in wetter areas—surrounds most of the lake and covers most of the area north of the lake. Clearing for agricultural crops, mainly grains and canola, has occurred extensively to the south and east of the lake. The area near the lake has been extensively developed by Lake Eden Resort, and includes 30 cottages (12 owned by Lake Eden Resort) that front on the lake, 3 camping areas and a large day-use area.

Lake Basin Characteristics

Lake Eden is irregularly shaped and has 2 basins with similar maximum depths (more than 15 m) (Fig. 2). The lake bottom slopes quite steeply on all sides except in the three bays along the north shore and along the south shore near the narrows. The littoral zone extends to

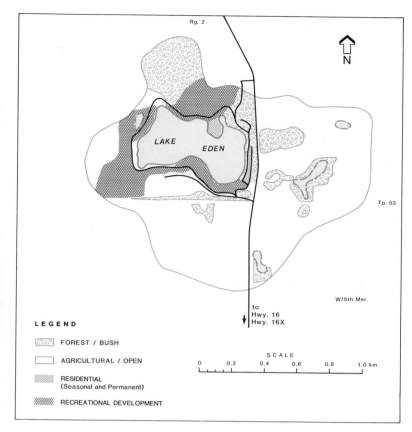

Figure 1. Features of the drainage basin of Lake Eden.
SOURCES: Alta. Envir. n.d.[a]; En. Mines Resour. Can. 1974. Updated with 1987 aerial photos.

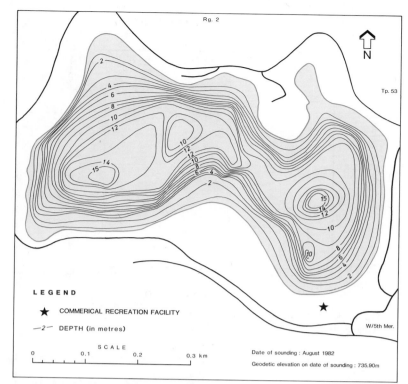

Figure 2. Bathymetry and shoreline features of Lake Eden.
BATHYMETRY SOURCE: Babin 1984.

approximately 5 m (R.L. & L. Envir. Serv. Ltd. 1987) and includes about 37% of the surface area of the lake (Fig. 3). The shoreline is dominated by fibrous organic material. Sand has been brought in to create a beach at the resort at the east end and is present in a small area on the north shore. As in most Alberta lakes, the bottom underlying the deeper areas of the lake is soft organic material (R.L. & L. Envir. Serv. Ltd. 1987).

Lake Eden is a pothole; it has no channelized inlet and no surface outlet. Groundwater inflow and outflow have never been measured, but likely provide a significant amount to the water balance. The lake level has been monitored 4 times a year since 1968 (Fig. 4). Since 1975, the level has fluctuated a maximum of 0.6 m.

Water Quality

Lake Eden was the subject of intensive water quality studies by the University of Alberta from May through July 1981, May 1982 through March 1983 and in March 1986 (Prepas and Babin n.d.; Prepas 1983[a]; 1983[b]; Prepas and Trew 1983; Babin 1984; Prepas and Vickery 1984; Babin and Prepas 1985).

The lake has very fresh water; the salt content (total dissolved solids = 123 mg/L) (Table 3) is the lowest of the 27 lakes in the Edmonton-Athabasca-Beaver River area studied by Prepas and Trew (1983). The dominant ions are bicarbonate and calcium; the alkalinity and hardness are both relatively low for prairie lakes. The water is neither turbid nor coloured.

Although the thermal stratification patterns in Lake Eden are unusual compared to those in larger and windier lakes in Alberta, they are similar to other small and relatively deep lakes in central Alberta. Lake Eden does not mix to any appreciable extent in spring, nor does it mix completely in autumn. The lake is strongly thermally stratified in summer, with only a thin (up to 3 m by July) mixed layer at the surface (Fig. 5). In 1982, dissolved oxygen concentrations below a depth of 9 m were less than 1 mg/L from ice-out in early May through mid-October (Fig. 6). The water near the bottom was anoxic throughout this period. The lake did not mix thoroughly in the autumn but some dissolved oxygen did reach the bottom sediments just before freeze-up. Overwinter dissolved oxygen consumption

Table 1. Characteristics of Lake Eden drainage basin.

area (excluding lake) (km²)[a]	1.50
soil[b]	Orthic Gray Luvisols, Orthic Humic Gleysols
bedrock geology[c]	Wapiti Formation (Upper Cretaceous): sandstone, mudstone, bentonite, scattered coal beds; nonmarine
terrain[b]	rolling
ecoregion[d]	Moist Mixedwood Subregion of Boreal Mixedwood
dominant vegetation[d]	trembling aspen, balsam poplar
mean annual inflow (m³)[a, e]	0.027×10^6
mean annual sunshine (h)[f]	2 264

NOTE: [e]excluding groundwater inflow
SOURCES: [a]Alta. Envir. n.d.[a]; [b]Lindsay et al. 1968; [c]Alta. Res. Counc. 1972; [d]Strong and Leggat 1981; [f]Envir. Can. 1982

Table 2. Characteristics of Lake Eden.

elevation (m)[a, b]	735.90
surface area (km²)[a, c]	0.161
volume (m³)[a, c]	1.12×10^6
maximum depth (m)[c]	15.3
mean depth (m)[c]	6.95
shoreline length (km)[d]	4.5
mean annual lake evaporation (mm)[e]	664
mean annual precipitation (mm)[e]	495
mean residence time (yr)[e, f]	>100
control structure	none

NOTES: [a]on date of sounding: 09 Aug. 1982; [f]excluding groundwater inflow
SOURCES: [b]Alta. Envir. n.d.[b]; [c]Babin 1984; [d]En. Mines Resour. Can. 1974; [e]Alta. Envir. n.d.[a]

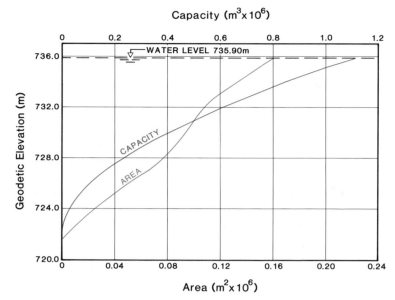

Figure 3. Area/capacity curve for Lake Eden.
SOURCE: Babin 1984.

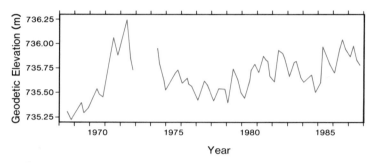

Figure 4. Water level of Lake Eden, 1968 to 1987.
SOURCE: Alta. Envir.

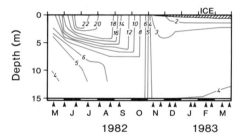

Figure 5. Temperature (°C) of Lake Eden, 1982 and 1983. Arrows indicate sampling dates.
SOURCES: Prepas and Babin n.d.; Prepas 1983[a].

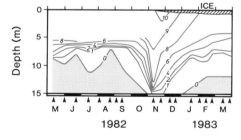

Figure 6. Dissolved oxygen (mg/L) in Lake Eden, 1982 and 1983. Arrows indicate sampling dates.
SOURCES: Prepas and Babin n.d.; Prepas 1983[a].

Table 3. Major ions and related water quality variables for Lake Eden. Average concentrations in mg/L; pH in pH units. Composite samples from the euphotic zone collected various times from 06 May to 21 July 1981 and 6 times from 12 May to 14 Sep. 1982. S.E. = standard error.

	Mean	S.E.
pH	7.5[a], 7.6[b]	—
total alkalinity (CaCO₃)	83	0.2
specific conductivity (µS/cm)	161[c]	5.1
total dissolved solids	123[d]	6.1
turbidity (NTU)	1[e]	0.4
colour (Pt)	6[e]	1.3
total hardness (CaCO₃)	90	0.2
HCO₃	101	1.7
CO₃	0	0
Mg	6[b]	—
Na	4[b]	—
K	13[b]	—
SO₄	3[b]	—
Ca	26[b]	—

NOTES: [a]06 May 1981; [b]11 Mar. 1986; [c]n = 10; [d]n = 9; [e]n = 2
SOURCE: Prepas and Babin n.d.

rates in 1982/83 were relatively low (0.331 g of O_2/m² per day), reflecting the relatively low algal productivity in this lake (Babin and Prepas 1985). Dissolved oxygen concentrations in the upper strata were high enough to support fish, but the bottom water was anoxic from early January until spring.

Phosphorus is released from the anoxic sediments in Lake Eden throughout the period of winter ice cover. In spring, some of the phosphorus is mixed into the upper water of the lake and the total phosphorus concentration in the euphotic zone reaches a maximum in May (Fig. 7). Algal production (as indicated by chlorophyll *a* concentration) in the upper water also peaks at this time. This brief spring algal bloom consumes much of the phosphorus in the upper water of the lake, then both algae and phosphorus precipitate to the bottom when the algae die. Phosphorus moves into the upper layer of the lake from the sediments within the littoral zone at an estimated rate of 1.1 mg/m² per day from June through August (Shaw and Prepas 1989). However, thermal stratification restricts the movement of phosphorus from below the thermocline to the upper water. It has been estimated that phosphorus is transported from the deep water in Lake Eden to the surface water at the very slow rate of 0.03 mg/m² per day. Therefore, the concentrations of total phosphorus and chlorophyll *a* in the euphotic zone decline rapidly soon after spring thaw, then more slowly throughout the summer (Fig. 7). After the spring bloom, the surface water is very clear and Secchi depths are close to 6 m throughout the summer.

While the total phosphorus concentration in the epilimnion is low and decreasing all summer, the situation is quite different below the thermocline. In the lower layer of the lake, the dissolved oxygen concentration is low or zero and phosphorus is released fairly rapidly from the bottom sediment into the overlying water. In 1982, the total phosphorus concentration at a depth of 9 m was between 42 and 67 µg/L from May until mid-September (Prepas 1983[a]), approximately 3 times the concentrations in the top 2 m of the lake as shown in Figure 7. Because sufficient light for algal growth penetrates to approximately 9 m in Lake Eden, it is near this depth that conditions are optimal for algal growth; chlorophyll *a* concentrations at this depth ranged from 15.2 to 43.0 µg/L, approximately 4 times the concentration in the top layer of the lake. It is this sharp vertical gradient in chlorophyll *a* concentrations that explains the difference in mean chlorophyll *a* reported for 1981 and 1982 (Table 4). Small differences in estimates of the depth of the euphotic zone mean that the layer of dense algal growth is sometimes included in the sample and sometimes missed.

In late October, thermal stratification breaks down and some of

Table 4. Nutrient, chlorophyll _a_ and Secchi depth data for Lake Eden. Average concentrations in µg/L. Composite samples from the euphotic zone collected 4 times from 06 May to 21 July 1981 and 6 times from 12 May to 14 Sep. 1982. S.E. = standard error.

	1981		1982	
	Mean	S.E.	Mean	S.E.
total phosphorus	22	2.9	23[b]	3.6
total dissolved phosphorus	7	0.6	—	—
soluble reactive phosphorus	2[a]	0.2	—	—
total Kjeldahl nitrogen	785	87.7	663	58.9
$NO_3 + NO_2$–nitrogen	10	2.8	8	1.7
NH_4–nitrogen	11	6.1	—	—
iron	—	—	126[c]	—
chlorophyll _a_	10.2	1.46	5.1[b]	1.25
Secchi depth (m)	4.2	0.63	4.4	0.53

NOTES: [a]n = 3; [b]n = 7; [c]11 Mar. 1986
SOURCE: Prepas and Babin n.d.

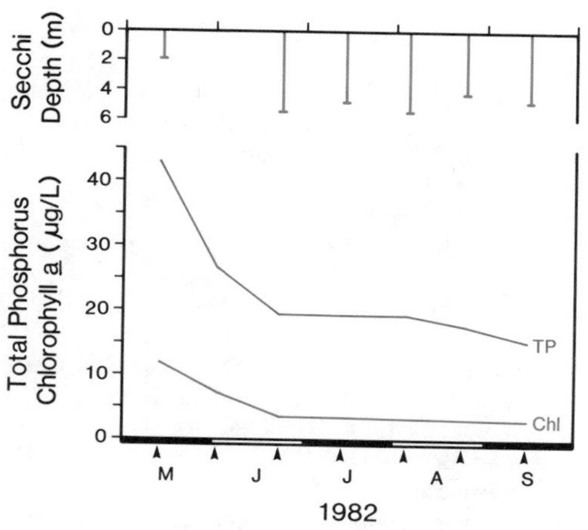

Figure 7. Total phosphorus, chlorophyll _a_ and Secchi depth in Lake Eden, 1982.
SOURCES: Prepas and Babin n.d.; Prepas 1983[a].

Table 5. Species of aquatic macrophytes in Lake Eden, 1986. Arranged in order of abundance.

emergent	common cattail	_Typha latifolia_
	sedge	_Carex_ spp.
	common horsetail	_Equisetum arvense_
	giant bur-reed	_Sparganium eurycarpum_
	arrowhead	_Sagittaria cuneata_
submergent/free-floating	Richardson pondweed	_Potamogeton richardsonii_
	flat-stemmed pondweed	_P. zosteriformis_
	northern watermilfoil	_Myriophyllum exalbescens_
	coontail	_Ceratophyllum demersum_
	Canada waterweed	_Elodea canadensis_
	stonewort	_Chara_ spp.
	small-leaf pondweed	_Potamogeton pusillus_
	floating-leaf pondweed	_P. natans_
	yellow water lily	_Nuphar variegatum_
	common bladderwort	_Utricularia vulgaris_

SOURCE: R.L. & L. Envir. Serv. Ltd. 1987

---

the phosphorus-rich water in the lower part of the lake mixes into the upper layers and there is, potentially, a fall algal bloom near the surface. Under ice, total phosphorus concentrations build up when the dissolved oxygen concentration is low; in March 1983, total phosphorus concentrations ranged from 14 µg/L at the surface to 183 µg/L over the bottom sediments (Prepas and Babin n.d.). Lake Eden is classified as a mesotrophic lake.

Biological Characteristics

Plants

There are no data on the species of algae in Lake Eden.

The aquatic vegetation in Lake Eden was surveyed for Fish and Wildlife Division in 1986 (Table 5). The shallow inshore areas support emergent vegetation dominated by cattails (_Typha latifolia_) and sedges (_Carex_ spp.). The main submergent species were Richardson pondweed (_Potamogeton richardsonii_), flat-stemmed pondweed (_P. zosteriformis_) and northern watermilfoil (_Myriophyllum exalbescens_).

Invertebrates

The zooplankton was sampled in 1981 and 1982 (Prepas 1983[a]). The dominant cladocerans were a small _Daphnia_ species (_D. thorata_ or _D. galeata mendotae_), and a _Ceriodaphnia_ species (_C. lacustris_ or _C. reticulata_). The copepods _Diacyclops bicuspidatus thomasi_ and _Diaptomus oregonensis_ and the phantom midge _Chaoborus_ sp. were also noted. Benthic invertebrates have not been sampled in Lake Eden.

Fish

The indigenous fish community of Lake Eden likely consisted of northern pike, yellow perch, brook stickleback and "shiners" (species unknown) (Alta. For. Ld. Wild. n.d.). The stocking history of Lake Eden (Alta. For. Ld. Wild. n.d.) began in 1953 when walleye were introduced as eyed-eggs following a severe winterkill in 1952/53 which eliminated pike and perch. The walleye did not survive, and in 1954, rainbow trout were introduced. In 1956, northern pike were introduced; the population was augmented by more pike in 1957, 1958 and 1959. As well, perch were stocked in 1959. No fish were added from 1960 to 1966. Dissolved oxygen concentrations fell to less than 0.8 mg/L in March 1967, causing a severe fish kill; no fish were caught by test-netting in the following July. Perch were stocked in the summer of 1967 but apparently failed to thrive. From 1967 to 1982, rainbow trout were stocked annually and provided a moderate sport fishery. Brook trout were stocked once, in 1971. Stocking was suspended in 1983, then resumed in 1985 when free walk-in access to the lake was provided. Annual stocking with rainbow trout has continued since then. Approximately 24 000 fingerlings are added each year and support a moderate sport fishery. There is no commercial or domestic fishery on the lake.

Wildlife

There is no readily available information on wildlife at Lake Eden. Good waterfowl habitat is provided by the rooted vegetation along the shoreline.

J.M. Crosby and E.E. Prepas

References

Alberta Environment. n.d.[a]. Tech. Serv. Div., Hydrol. Br. Unpubl. data, Edmonton.
———. n.d.[b]. Tech. Serv. Div., Surv. Br. Unpubl. data, Edmonton.
Alberta Forestry, Lands and Wildlife. n.d. Fish Wild. Div. Unpubl. data, Edmonton.
———. 1988. Boating in Alberta. Fish Wild. Div., Edmonton.
———. 1989. Guide to sportfishing. Fish Wild. Div., Edmonton.
Alberta Research Council. 1972. Geological map of Alberta. Nat. Resour. Div., Alta. Geol. Surv., Edmonton.
Babin, J. 1984. Winter oxygen depletion in temperate zone lakes. MSc thesis. Univ. Alta., Edmonton.
———— and E.E. Prepas. 1985. Modelling winter oxygen depletion rates in ice-covered temperate zone lakes in Canada. Can. J. Fish. Aquat. Sci. 42:239–249.
Energy, Mines and Resources Canada. 1974. National topographic series 1:50 000 83G/9 (1974). Surv. Map. Br., Ottawa.
Environment Canada. 1982. Canadian climate normals, Vol. 7: Bright sunshine (1951–1980). Prep. by Atm. Envir. Serv. Supply Serv. Can., Ottawa.
Holmgren, E.J. and P.M. Holmgren. 1976. Over 2000 place names of Alberta. 3rd ed. West. Producer Prairie Books, Saskatoon.
Lindsay, J.D., W. Odynsky, J.W. Peters and W.E. Bowser. 1968. Soil survey of the Buck Lake (NE 83B) and Wabamun Lake (E1/2 83G) areas. Alta. Soil Surv. Rep.

No. 24, Univ. Alta. Bull. No. SS–7, Alta. Res. Counc. Rep. No. 87. Univ. Alta., Edmonton.
Prepas, E.E. 1983[a]. The influence of phosphorus and zooplankton on chlorophyll levels in Alberta lakes. Prep. for Alta. Envir., Res. Mgt. Div. Rep. 83/23, Edmonton.
———. 1983[b]. Orthophosphate turnover time in shallow productive lakes. Can. J. Fish. Aquat. Sci. 40:1412–1418.
———— and J. Babin. n.d. Univ. Alta., Dept. Zool. Unpubl. data., Edmonton.
Prepas, E.E. and D.O. Trew. 1983. Evaluation of the phosphorus-chlorophyll relationship for lakes off the Precambrian Shield in western Canada. Can. J. Fish. Aquat. Sci. 40:27–35.
———— and J. Vickery. 1984. The contribution of particulate phosphorus (>250 µm) to the total phosphorus pool in lake water. Can. J. Fish. Aquat. Sci. 41:351–363.
R.L. & L. Environmental Services Ltd. 1987. County of Parkland fisheries inventory—Eden Lake. Prep. for Alta. For. Ld. Wild., Fish Wild. Div. and Alta. Rec. Parks Wild. Foundation, Edmonton.
Shaw, J.F.H. and E.E. Prepas. 1989. Potential significance of phosphorus release from shallow sediments of deep Alberta lakes. ms submitted to Limnol. Oceanogr.
Strong, W.L. and K.R. Leggat. 1981. Ecoregions of Alberta. Alta. En. Nat. Resour., Resour. Eval. Plan. Div., Edmonton.

HALFMOON LAKE

MAP SHEET: 83H/6
LOCATION: Tp52 R21 W4
LAT/LONG: 53°24'N 113°04'W

Halfmoon Lake is a picturesque little crescent of water located just east of the city of Edmonton, in the County of Strathcona. To travel to the lake from Edmonton, drive east on the Sherwood Park Freeway and Wye Road (Secondary Road 630) until you are 3 km east of the hamlet of Sherwood Park; turn south onto Highway 21 and drive for 9.6 km, then turn east onto Secondary Road 629 and drive for 10.5 km until you reach the local road that provides access to the south side of the lake (Fig. 1).

The lake was probably named for its crescent shape; the first documentation of the name appears on a 1915 federal government map. Little is known of the history of the lake, but it is now very popular for recreation as it is easily accessible from Edmonton for a day or evening visit. There is no public campground or day-use area at the lake, but Halfmoon Lake Resort, a commercially operated facility at the south end of the lake, is open from May to October and offers 90 campsites, washroom facilities, a developed beach, a wading pool, groceries, a boat launch and other amenities (Fig. 2). The east and west shores of the lake are developed with 35 country residential lots. There is no Crown land around the lake.

The resort area and beach at the south end of the lake are very heavily used in summer. Popular activities at the lake are swimming, canoeing and water skiing in summer and snowmobiling in winter. There are no boating restrictions over most of the lake, but in posted areas such as the designated swimming area, all boats are prohibited (Alta. For. Ld. Wild. 1988). Algal blooms turn the lake water green from early summer until fall. Large leeches are common. When the algae decay in winter, most of the dissolved oxygen in the lake is consumed; the only fish that can overwinter are brook sticklebacks. Sport fishing is available near the lake in an aerated trout-pond stocked and operated by Halfmoon Lake Resort.

Drainage Basin Characteristics

The drainage basin of Halfmoon Lake covers a small portion (2.43 km^2, Table 1) of the Cooking Lake Moraine. It is formed of rolling glacial till; the land rises from approximately 745 m near the lake to 760 m in the low hills to the west and north of the lake. The drainage basin is small compared to the lake area (6:1) and provides little inflow—only one intermittent stream flows into the lake, at the eastern end. The outflow drains intermittently into Cooking Lake. The amount of groundwater inflow and outflow is not known.

The watershed is part of the Moist Mixedwood Subregion of the Boreal Mixedwood Ecoregion (Strong and Leggat 1981). The dominant trees are trembling aspen and balsam poplar and the soils in the area are Orthic Gray Luvisols. The arability rating of the land is poor to fair (Bowser et al. 1962), and only about one-quarter of the basin has been cleared for agriculture (Fig. 1), mostly for pasture and mixed farming. The eastern portion of the north and south shores has been extensively developed for recreational use and for country residential properties.

Lake Basin Characteristics

Halfmoon Lake is a tiny lake with a surface area of only 0.41 km^2 (Table 2, Fig. 3); it has a single, elongate basin with a maximum depth of 8.5 m (Fig. 2). Approximately 40% of the lake is less than 4–m deep (Fig. 3). The lake bottom slopes moderately steeply at the

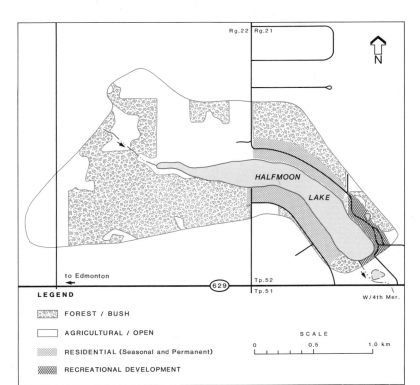

Figure 1. Features of the drainage basin of Halfmoon Lake.
SOURCES: Alta. Envir. n.d.[b]; En. Mines Resour. Can. 1974. Updated with 1982 aerial photos.

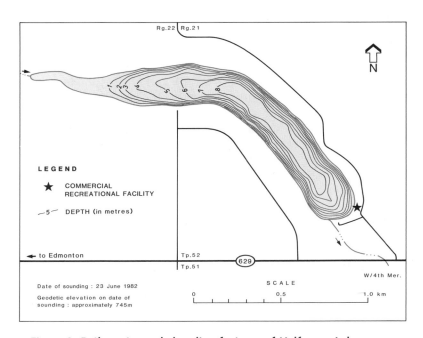

Figure 2. Bathymetry and shoreline features of Halfmoon Lake.
BATHYMETRY SOURCE: Babin 1984.

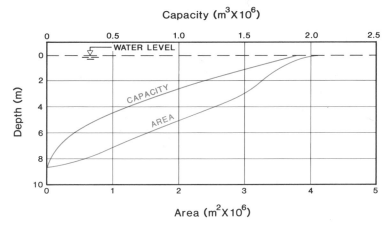

Figure 3. Area/capacity curve for Halfmoon Lake.
SOURCE: Babin 1984.

Table 1. Characteristics of Halfmoon Lake drainage basin.

area (excluding lake) (km²)[a]	2.43
soil[b]	Orthic Gray Luvisols
bedrock geology[c]	Horseshoe Canyon Formation (Upper Cretaceous): sandstone, mudstone, shale; ironstone, scattered coal and bentonite beds; mainly nonmarine
terrain[b]	gently rolling to rolling
ecoregion[d]	Moist Mixedwood Subregion of Boreal Mixedwood
dominant vegetation[d]	trembling aspen, balsam poplar
mean annual inflow (m³)[a, e]	0.114×10^6
mean annual sunshine (h)[f]	2 280

NOTE: [e]excluding groundwater inflow
SOURCES: [a]Alta. Envir. n.d.[b]; [b]Bowser et al. 1962; [c]Alta. Res. Counc. 1972; [d]Strong and Leggat 1981; [f]Envir. Can. 1982

Table 2. Characteristics of Halfmoon Lake.

elevation (m)[a] approximately	745 m
surface area (km²)[b, c]	0.41
volume (m³)[b, c]	1.92×10^6
maximum depth (m)[b, c]	8.5
mean depth (m)[b, c]	4.7
shoreline length (km)[a]	4.4
mean annual lake evaporation (mm)[d]	664
mean annual precipitation (mm)[d]	466
mean residence time (yr)[d, e]	60
control structure	none

NOTES: [b]on date of sounding: 23 June 1982; [e]excluding groundwater inflow
SOURCES: [a]En. Mines Resour. Can. 1974; [c]Babin 1984; [d]Alta. Envir. n.d.[b]

south end and along the north and south sides, but very gradually at the west end. The residence time of water in the lake is long (60 years) based on surface inflows (Table 2). The lake level has not been monitored.

Water Quality

The water quality of Halfmoon Lake has long been a concern. Dissolved oxygen concentrations were monitored by Fish and Wildlife Division from 1955 to 1961, and again in 1967 (Alta. For. Ld. Wild. n.d.). The University of Alberta monitored water quality intensively from 1981 through 1983 (Prepas n.d.; Prepas and Trew 1983; Riley 1983; Babin 1984; Riley and Prepas 1984; Babin and Prepas 1985) and Alberta Environment monitored the lake in 1987. In 1988 and 1989, the lake became the subject of an experimental lake restoration program and was monitored intensively by both the University of Alberta (Prepas n.d.) and Alberta Environment (Alta. Envir. n.d.[a]).

Halfmoon Lake has fresh, well-buffered water. The dominant ions are bicarbonate, calcium and sodium (Table 3). The lake becomes thermally stratified in early summer and remains so until fall. In 1982, thermal stratification was evident by late May and continued until late September (Fig. 4). The bottom water was anoxic by early June in 1982, and remained so until mid-October (Fig. 5). In late fall, although the lake water was the same temperature from top to bottom, winds were light and dissolved oxygen concentrations reached only 48% saturation before freeze-up. Under ice cover, the dissolved oxygen consumption rate was very high (0.462 g O_2/m^2 per day), and by mid-January of 1983, the whole water column was anoxic (Babin and Prepas 1985).

Halfmoon Lake is hyper-eutrophic, and dense algal blooms are common during most of the summer. The total phosphorus concentration in the euphotic zone was high in May 1982 (Fig. 6, Table 4), likely because phosphorus had been released from the bottom sed-

Table 3. Major ions and related water quality variables for Halfmoon Lake. Average concentrations in mg/L; pH in pH units. Composite samples from the euphotic zone collected twice on 22 July and 17 Aug. 1987. S.E. = standard error.

	Mean	S.E.
pH (range)	8.8–9.4	—
total alkalinity (CaCO₃)	139	1.0
specific conductivity (μS/cm)	287	2.0
total dissolved solids (calculated)	156	4.0
turbidity (NTU)	3[a, b]	—
colour (Pt)	12[a, b]	—
total hardness (CaCO₃)	90	4.5
HCO₃	133	4.0
CO₃	18	1.0
Mg	10	0.5
Na	18	0.5
K	12	0.5
Cl	8	1.0
SO₄	<5	—
Ca	19	1.0

NOTE: [a]n = 1, 15 Oct. 1982
SOURCES: Alta. Envir. n.d.[a], Naquadat station 01AL05EB0501; [b]Prepas n.d.

Table 4. Nutrient, chlorophyll *a* and Secchi depth data for Halfmoon Lake. Average concentrations in μg/L. Composite samples from the euphotic zone collected 11 times from 27 May to 11 Oct. 1982 and on 22 July and 17 Aug. 1987. S.E. = standard error.

	1982[a]		1987[d]	
	Mean	S.E.	Mean	S.E.
total phosphorus	124	14.3	99	27.0
total dissolved phosphorus	—	—	27	2.2
total Kjeldahl nitrogen	3 111[b]	294.7	2 180	190.0
NO₃ + NO₂–nitrogen	44[c]	21.2	9	2.0
NH₄–nitrogen	—	—	94	16.0
chlorophyll *a*	50.1	10.87	63.8	43.70
Secchi depth (m)	1.3[c]	0.17	0.8	0

NOTES: [b]n = 8; [c]n = 9
SOURCES: [a]Prepas n.d.; Riley 1983; [d]Alta. Envir. n.d.[a], Naquadat station 01AL05EB0501

iments into the anoxic water column under ice cover. Total phosphorus concentrations increase under ice: on 10 March 1983, the concentration ranged from 157 μg/L just under the ice to 344 μg/L at a depth of 7 m. Algae respond to the abundant phosphorus in the water column with a spring algal bloom—the chlorophyll *a* concentration reached at least 88 μg/L in 1982 (Fig. 6). Throughout the summer, chlorophyll *a* concentrations closely paralleled total phosphorus concentrations in the epilimnion. After the lake became thermally stratified in June 1982, the lower strata quickly became anoxic and total phosphorus concentrations in the hypolimnion rose dramatically. By 11 June, the total phosphorus concentration at 1 m above the lake bottom was 806 μg/L, and by 20 August it had increased to 1 350 μg/L at 1 m above the bottom and 644 μg/L at 2.5 m above the bottom (Riley and Prepas 1984). When thermal stratification broke down in September 1982 and the water column mixed, an immense amount of phosphorus was transferred from the hypolimnion to the surface water, causing the total phosphorus concentration in the epilimnion to increase to 190 μg/L. Algal biomass did not respond to this phosphorus peak, possibly due to the simultaneous mixing of residual herbicides such as copper sulphate, which have been applied to Halfmoon Lake in the past. A similar situation was observed in Figure Eight Lake near Peace River: mixing in the autumn was accompanied by the resuspension of copper

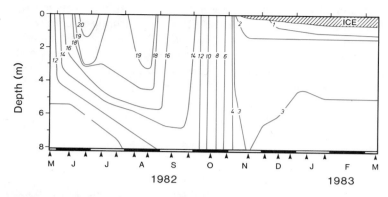

Figure 4. Temperature (°C) of Halfmoon Lake, 1982 and 1983. Arrows indicate sampling dates.
SOURCES: Prepas n.d.; Riley 1983.

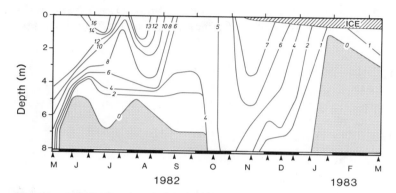

Figure 5. Dissolved oxygen (mg/L) in Halfmoon Lake, 1982 and 1983. Arrows indicate sampling dates.
SOURCES: Riley 1983; Babin 1984.

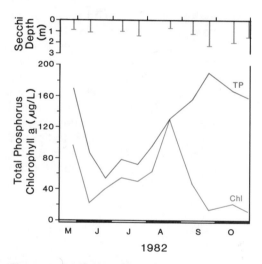

Figure 6. Total phosphorus, chlorophyll *a* and Secchi depth in Halfmoon Lake, 1982.
SOURCE: Riley 1983.

sulphate, which had last been applied several years previously, and algal growth was low despite the high phosphorus concentrations (Prepas et al. 1987).

In 1988, an experimental project to reduce phosphorus and chlorophyll concentrations was initiated by the County of Strathcona, Halfmoon Lake Resort, Alberta Environment and the University of Alberta. Fifty-eight tonnes of calcium carbonate (powdered limestone) and 40 tonnes of calcium hydroxide (hydrated lime) were added in July 1988, and an additional dosage of 138 tonnes of calcium hydroxide was added in August 1989. In 1989 the mean total phosphorus concentration (May to August) was 67 μg/L, maximum total phosphorus concentration was 90 μg/L. This was a lower mean total phosphorus concentration than recorded in 1982 for a similar period (107 μg/L), and a lower maximum total phosphorus concentration than recorded in any of the four previous years on record. Similarly, average chlorophyll *a* concentration was lower in 1989 than in 1982 (30 versus 69 μg/L), although there was a substantial algal bloom in July 1989 (maximum chlorophyll *a* 82 μg/L). A joint research program set up in 1989 between the University of Alberta and the Alberta Environmental Centre is expected to continue for three to five years.

Biological Characteristics

Plants

Halfmoon Lake was one of 31 lakes in the area between Edmonton and the Beaver River that were sampled between mid-July and early August in 1983 (Alta. Envir. n.d.[a]). Halfmoon Lake had the highest chlorophyll *a* concentration (148 μg/L) and the second highest algal biomass (32.0 mg/L; second only to Lac la Nonne) of the 31 lakes. Over 97% of the algal biomass was *Aphanizomenon flos-aquae*.

Aquatic macrophytes grow profusely at the northwest end of the lake but there has been no documentation of the species present there.

Invertebrates

There is no information on invertebrates in Halfmoon Lake. A study to document the invertebrate community was in its initial stages in 1988 (Alta. Envir. n.d.[a]).

Fish

Halfmoon Lake becomes completely anoxic in many winters and no fish species can survive except brook stickleback. However, the popularity of the lake and its proximity to Edmonton has led to persistent efforts by Fish and Wildlife Division to establish a sport fishery (Alta. For. Ld. Wild. n.d.). The lake was stocked with rainbow trout in 1955 and 1956, but angling success was poor in 1956 and no fish were caught by test netting in 1957. Perch were stocked in 1957 and pike in 1958, but no fish were caught by angling in 1959 or by test netting in 1960. A last attempt at stocking perch was made in 1960, but these fish also succumbed to winterkill in the first winter. In 1962, the owner of Halfmoon Lake Resort installed an aerator in the lake to try to keep winter dissolved oxygen concentrations sufficiently high to overwinter sport fish. The aerator operated continuously all winter, but by 11 March 1963, dissolved oxygen concentrations in the lake were very low (0.8 to 1.2 mg/L). In 1966, the resort owner increased the capacity of the aerator, changed the position of the

hoses and started to aerate the lake just before freeze-up. However, the results were similar, and dissolved oxygen dropped to critical concentrations (1.2 to 2.0 mg/L) early in the new year. In 1967, 41 000 rainbow trout fingerlings were planted, but despite aeration, winterkill occurred once again. In 1970, 1 000 yearling northern pike and 1 000 adult yellow perch were stocked, and in 1973, an additional 450 adult pike were added. None of these fish survived the winter following their placement in the lake (Alta. For. Ld. Wild. n.d.).

Wildlife

The shallow weedy area at the northwest end of the lake provides good nesting habitat for waterfowl, but no details of species or densities are available.

J.M. Crosby and E.E. Prepas

References

Alberta Environment. n.d.[a]. Envir. Assess. Div., Envir. Qlty. Monit. Br. Unpubl. data, Edmonton.
———. n.d.[b]. Tech. Serv. Div., Hydrol. Br. Unpubl. data, Edmonton.
Alberta Forestry, Lands and Wildlife. n.d. Fish Wild. Div. Unpubl. data, Edmonton.
———. 1988. Boating in Alberta. Fish Wild. Div., Edmonton.
Alberta Research Council. 1972. Geological map of Alberta. Nat. Resour. Div., Alta. Geol. Surv., Edmonton.
Babin, J. 1984. Winter oxygen depletion in temperate zone lakes. MSc thesis. Univ. Alta., Edmonton.
——— and E.E. Prepas. 1985. Modelling winter oxygen depletion rates in ice-covered temperate zone lakes in Canada. Can. J. Fish. Aquat. Sci. 42:239–249.
Bowser, W.E., A.A. Kjearsgaard, T.W. Peters and R.E. Wells. 1962. Soil survey of the Edmonton sheet (83–H). Alta. Soil Surv. Rep. No. 21, Univ. Alta. Bull. No. SS–4. Univ. Alta., Edmonton.
Energy, Mines and Resources Canada. 1974. National topographic series 1:50 000 83H/6 (1974). Surv. Map. Br., Ottawa.
Environment Canada. 1982. Canadian climate normals, Vol. 7: Bright sunshine (1951–1980). Prep. by Atm. Envir. Serv. Supply Serv. Can., Ottawa.
Prepas, E.E. n.d. Univ. Alta., Dept. Zool. Unpubl. data, Edmonton.
——— and D.O. Trew. 1983. Evaluation of the phosphorus-chlorophyll relationship for lakes off the Precambrian Shield in western Canada. Can. J. Fish. Aquat. Sci. 40:27–35.
Prepas, E.E., T. Murphy and P. Manning. 1987. Report on the 1985 evaluation of Figure Eight Lake, Alberta. Prep. for Alta. Envir., Plan. Div., Edmonton.
Riley, E.T. 1983. Internal phosphorus loading from the sediments and the phosphorus-chlorophyll model in shallow lakes. MSc thesis. Univ. Alta., Edmonton.
——— and E.E. Prepas. 1984. Role of internal phosphorus loading in two shallow, productive lakes in Alberta, Canada. Can. J. Fish. Aquat. Sci. 41:845–855.
Strong, W.L. and K.R. Leggat. 1981. Ecoregions of Alberta. Alta. En. Nat. Resour., Resour. Eval. Plan. Div., Edmonton.

HASSE LAKE

MAP SHEETS: 83G/8, 9
LOCATION: Tp52 R2 W5
LAT/LONG: 53°29′N 114°10′W

Hasse Lake, a quiet little lake in the rolling hills west of the city of Edmonton, is a beautiful spot for canoeing, fishing or bird-watching. To reach the lake, drive 6 km west of the town of Stony Plain on Highway 16 to the turnoff for Edmonton Beach and continue west for 2.5 km. Turn south and drive for 5 km, then turn west onto a winding road and follow it west and south for 10 km to reach Hasse Lake Provincial Park. The route is well marked with signs indicating the provincial park. The lake is located in the County of Parkland.

The lake was named for Frederick Hasse, who started farming beside the lake in 1936. Prior to the arrival of British and European settlers, the region was frequented by Cree and Stoney Indians. Settlement was rapid from 1902 to 1910, and agriculture has been the main land use ever since. Private recreational facilities were developed on Hasse Lake in 1956. Land was later purchased by the provincial government, and in 1970, Hasse Lake Provincial Park was established (Alta. Rec. Parks n.d.).

The provincial park covers 69 ha on the northwest shore of the lake (Fig. 1). Its facilities are for day use only and include a picnic shelter, pump water, a telephone, a playground, walking trails, a small beach, four piers and two floating boardwalks (Fig. 2) (Alta. Hotel Assoc. 1988). There is an area where small boats and canoes can be launched; boat speed is restricted to 12 km/hour on the entire lake and all boats are restricted from posted areas near the beach (Alta. For. Ld. Wild. 1988). The park is open year-round.

Hasse Lake has clear water. Except for the small beach at the provincial park, most of the shoreline is soft and weedy. The lake has been stocked with rainbow trout since 1953 and provides a locally popular sport fishery. Fishing for bait fish and the use of bait fish is prohibited in Hasse Lake (Alta. For. Ld. Wild. 1989). Aquatic plants grow on most of the lake bottom but rarely reach the surface. Emergent plants grow abundantly in shallow areas and provide good nesting habitat for waterfowl.

Drainage Basin Characteristics

The drainage basin of Hasse Lake is small (7.4 km², Table 1), only about 8 times the area of the lake (0.90 km², Table 2). Of this area, only 2.8 km² contributes runoff directly to the lake (Fig. 1). Groundwater input is likely significant, but has never been measured (Prepas n.d.).

The drainage area lies on the eastern edge of the Duffield Moraine, which consists of glacial till laid down during the last glaciation. It is characterized by numerous pothole lakes, like Hasse Lake, and mounds of till that have an average height of 35 m. Slopes in the drainage basin range from 6 to 15%; the area immediately around the lake is less hilly (Lindsay et al. 1968).

The watershed is part of the Moist Mixedwood Subregion of the Boreal Mixedwood Ecoregion (Strong and Leggat 1981). The predominant vegetation is trembling aspen and balsam poplar, with willows in less well-drained areas and sedges in poorly drained boggy areas. Soils are mainly Dark Gray Luvisols, but the soils in the wet area at the northeast corner of the lake are Typic and Terric Fibrisols, which are typical of sedge-dominated bogs (Lindsay et al. 1968). The arability of the soil in the basin is considered to be mostly fair to fairly good. About 65% of the basin has been cleared for agriculture,

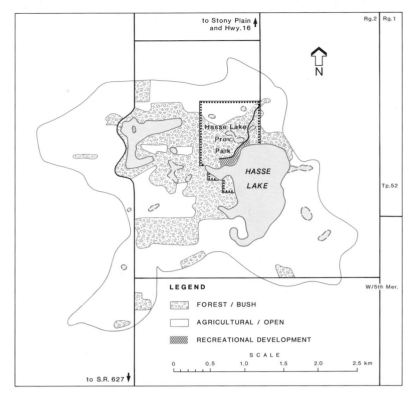

Figure 1. Features of the drainage basin of Hasse Lake.
SOURCES: Alta. Envir. n.d.[a]; En. Mines Resour. Can. 1974; 1975.
Updated with 1987 aerial photos.

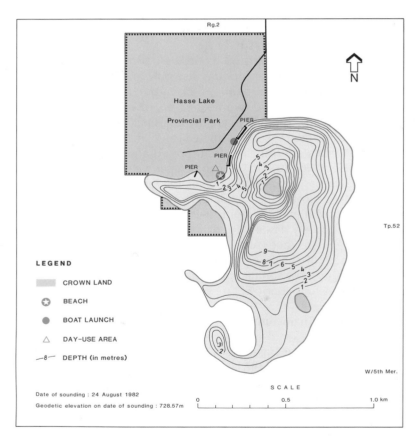

Figure 2. Bathymetry and shoreline features of Hasse Lake.
BATHYMETRY SOURCE: Babin 1984.

Table 1. Characteristics of Hasse Lake drainage basin.

area (excluding lake) (km^2)[a, b]	7.40
soil[c]	Orthic Dark Gray Luvisols
bedrock geology[d]	Wapiti Formation (Upper Cretaceous): sandstone, mudstone, bentonite, scattered coal beds; nonmarine
terrain[c]	rolling to hilly
ecoregion[e]	Moist Mixedwood Subregion of Boreal Mixedwood
dominant vegetation[e]	trembling aspen, balsam poplar
mean annual inflow (m^3)[f, g]	0.145 x 10^6
mean annual sunshine (h)[h]	2 315

NOTES: [b]of this area, only 2.8 km^2 contributes runoff directly to the lake; [g]excluding groundwater inflow
SOURCES: [a]Alta. Envir. n.d.[a]; [c]Lindsay et al. 1968; [d]Alta. Res. Counc. 1972; [e]Strong and Leggat 1981; [f]Alta. Envir. n.d.[b]; [h]Envir. Can. 1982

Table 2. Characteristics of Hasse Lake.

elevation (m)[a, b]	728.57
surface area (km^2)[a, c]	0.90
volume (m^3)[a, c]	3.28 x 10^6
maximum depth (m)[a, c]	9.5
mean depth (m)[a, c]	3.5
shoreline length (km)[c]	5.8
mean annual lake evaporation (mm)[d]	664
mean annual precipitation (mm)[d]	500
mean residence time (yr)[d, e]	>100
control structure	none

NOTES: [a]on date of sounding: 24 Aug. 1982; [e]excluding groundwater inflow
SOURCES: [b]Alta. Envir. n.d.[b]; [c]Babin 1984; [d]Alta. Envir. n.d.[a]

primarily grain crop production or pasture. There are no population centres in the basin.

Lake Basin Characteristics

Hasse Lake is an oval lake with three bays on the west side. The basin slopes gently all around, with the steepest gradient at the north end of the lake (Fig. 2). The deepest spot (9.5 m) is in the middle of the lake. There are two islands, one in the north half of the lake and one in very shallow water just off the southeast shore. The littoral zone extends to a depth of approximately 4.5 m (calculated from Chambers and Prepas 1988) and includes approximately 65% of the lake area (Fig. 3).

The water level of Hasse Lake has varied less than 0.6 m from 1975 to 1987 (Fig. 4). From 1968 to 1973, the level was relatively low; it rose sharply in 1974, a year of heavy snow and near-record spring rains, and has stayed relatively high. There is no defined surface inflow to or outflow from Hasse Lake, but local anecdotes tell of outflow from the lake to the North Saskatchewan River in the first three decades of this century (Stony Plain Dist. Hist. Soc. 1982). The residence time of water in the lake, based on surface inflows, is long, but because the rate of groundwater flow is unknown, the residence time cannot be accurately estimated.

Water Quality

The water quality of Hasse Lake was studied by the University of Alberta from 1981 through 1983 (Prepas n.d.; 1983[a]; 1983[b]; Prepas and Trew 1983; Babin 1984; Prepas and Vickery 1984; Babin and Prepas 1985; Prepas and Shaw 1985).

Hasse is a freshwater, well-buffered lake. The dominant ions are sulphate, bicarbonate, calcium and magnesium (Table 3); their concentrations are relatively high for a freshwater lake and are likely strongly influenced by groundwater inflow (Prepas n.d.).

Table 3. Major ions and related water quality variables for Hasse Lake. Average concentrations in mg/L; pH in pH units. Composite samples from the euphotic zone collected once on 26 Mar. 1986. S.E. = standard error.

	Mean	S.E.
pH (range)	7.9–8.2[a]	—
total alkalinity (CaCO₃)	153[b]	10.6
specific conductivity (μS/cm)	447[c]	3.0
total dissolved solids	344[c]	8.3
turbidity (NTU)	2[d]	—
colour (Pt)	5[d]	—
total hardness (CaCO₃)	228[e]	—
HCO₃	187[b]	13.0
CO₃	0[b]	0
Mg	43	—
Na	19	—
K	17	—
SO₄	170	—
Ca	45	—

NOTES: [a]n = 2, 06 May 1981 and 26 Mar. 1986; [b]n = 2, 27 Sep. 1982 and 26 Mar. 1986; [c]n = 8, 11 May to 27 Sep. 1982; [d]n = 1, 27 Sep. 1982; [e]n = 1, 22 July 1981.
SOURCE: Prepas n.d.

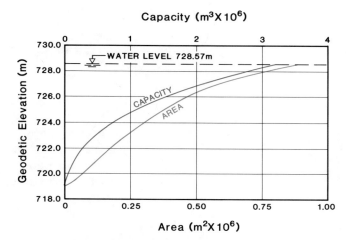

Figure 3. Area/capacity curve for Hasse Lake.
SOURCE: Babin 1984.

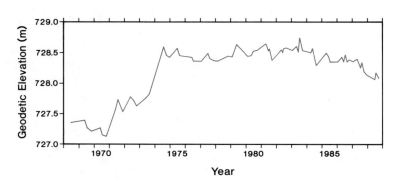

Figure 4. Water level of Hasse Lake, 1968 to 1987.
SOURCE: Alta. Envir. n.d.[b].

The lake is weakly thermally stratified in summer (Fig. 5). Anoxic conditions develop over the bottom sediment by early June and remain so until fall (Fig. 6). These anoxic conditions do not extend high into the water column because there is some mixing in the upper strata. Also, aquatic macrophytes extend across most of the lake bottom and likely inhibit mixing near the sediment-water interface. In the autumn, the entire water column is fairly well mixed, and by freeze-up the lake is usually fully saturated with dissolved oxygen. Throughout the winter, dissolved oxygen decreases at a steady and relatively slow rate, 0.373 g O₂/m² per day (Babin and Prepas 1985). Anoxic conditions develop over the sediments in the latter part of the winter and gradually extend upwards in the water column. Winterkills of fish are not common, but severe ones occurred in each winter from 1967/68 to 1969/70 and in the winter of 1972/73 (Alta. For. Ld. Wild. n.d.).

Hasse Lake is fairly low in nutrients; its trophic status is at the low end of the mesotrophic range. Total phosphorus concentrations in the euphotic zone are highest in the spring and autumn (Fig. 7), when deep water containing a high concentration of phosphorus is mixed throughout the water column. The concentration of total phosphorus is much higher below the thermocline than in the surface waters by early June; total phosphorus concentration in the deep water continues to increase throughout the summer. By late August 1983, the total phosphorus concentration was 292 μg/L at the bottom of the lake but only 19 μg/L at the surface (Fig. 8). Under ice cover on 14 March 1982, the total phosphorus concentration was 91 μg/L at a depth of 9 m (Prepas n.d.).

Since most of the phosphorus in the lake water is trapped in the hypolimnion, chlorophyll *a* concentrations in Hasse Lake are usually fairly low (Fig. 7, Table 4). Algal biomass peaks in the spring when phosphorus-rich water is mixed into the euphotic zone, where light is available. For most of the summer, the water is clear and Secchi depths are usually between 3 and 4 m (Fig. 7).

Biological Characteristics

Plants

There are no data on algal species in Hasse Lake.

Aquatic macrophytes blanket almost the entire bottom of Hasse Lake. They reach to the surface in only a few areas and are not generally a nuisance to boaters; in fact, floating in a canoe and

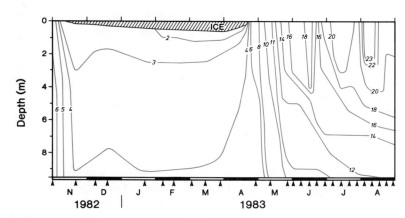

Figure 5. Temperature (°C) of Hasse Lake, 1982 and 1983. Arrows indicate sampling dates.
SOURCES: Prepas n.d.; Prepas and Shaw 1985.

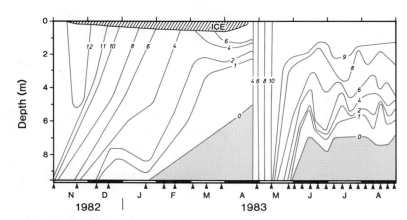

Figure 6. Dissolved oxygen (mg/L) in Hasse Lake, 1982 and 1983. Arrows indicate sampling dates.
SOURCES: Babin 1984; Prepas and Shaw 1985.

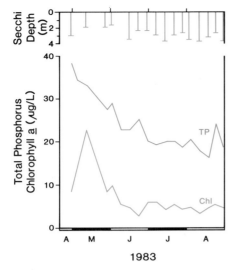

Figure 7. Total phosphorus, chlorophyll *a* and Secchi depth in Hasse Lake, 1983.
SOURCE: Prepas and Shaw 1985.

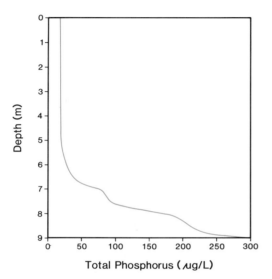

Figure 8. Total phosphorus concentrations in Hasse Lake, 29 August 1983.
SOURCE: Prepas and Shaw 1985.

Table 4. Nutrient, chlorophyll *a* and Secchi depth data for Hasse Lake. Average concentrations in μg/L. Composite samples from the euphotic zone collected 4 times from 06 May to 22 July 1981, 8 times from 11 May to 27 Sep. 1982 and 17 times from 29 Apr. to 29 Aug. 1983. S.E. = standard error.

	1981		1982		1983	
	Mean	S.E.	Mean	S.E.	Mean	S.E.
total phosphorus	21	1.7	26	2.6	23[b]	1.1
total dissolved phosphorus	10	0.7	—	—	—	—
soluble reactive phosphorus	2	0.2	—	—	—	—
total Kjeldahl nitrogen	1 219	73.9	1 240	21.0	—	—
NO_3 + NO_2-nitrogen	5	1.1	16	9.3	—	—
NH_4-nitrogen	31	11.6	—	—	—	—
iron	—	—	—	—	38[c]	—
chlorophyll *a*	4.9	2.31	—	—	6.6	1.11
Secchi depth (m)	4.3[a]	0.74	3.3	0.23	2.7[d]	0.16

NOTES: [a]n = 5; [b]n = 15; [c]n = 1, 26 Mar. 1986; [d]n = 16, from light meter data
SOURCES: Prepas n.d.; 1983[a]; 1983[b]; Prepas and Shaw 1985

Table 5. Species of aquatic macrophytes in Hasse Lake. Survey conducted on 08 Sep. 1986. Arranged by dominance.

emergent	common great bulrush	*Scirpus validus*
	sedge	*Carex* spp.
	common cattail	*Typha latifolia*
	common horsetail	*Equisetum arvense*
	arrowhead	*Sagittaria cuneata*
	reed grass	*Phragmites communis*
submergent	common bladderwort	*Utricularia vulgaris*
	stonewort	*Chara* spp.
	northern watermilfoil	*Myriophyllum exalbescens*
	Sago pondweed	*Potamogeton pectinatus*
	coontail	*Ceratophyllum demersum*
	large-sheath pondweed	*Potamogeton vaginatus*
	Richardson pondweed	*P. richardsonii*
	mare's tail	*Hippuris vulgaris*
floating-leaved	yellow water lily	*Nuphar variegatum*

SOURCE: R.L. & L. Envir. Serv. Ltd. 1987

looking through the clear water to the underwater garden below can be a very pleasant way to spend a summer day.

A brief survey of aquatic vegetation in Hasse Lake was conducted for Fish and Wildlife Division in 1986 (R.L. & L. Envir. Serv. Ltd. 1987). Emergent plants ring the lake except for the small area of beach in the provincial park. Cattails, bulrushes and sedges were the dominant emergent species. Stonewort was the most prevalent submergent species; northern watermilfoil, coontail and Sago pondweed were also present at most sites, but at lower densities than stonewort (Table 5).

Invertebrates

The zooplankton community was sampled on three dates in 1981 and 1982 by the University of Alberta (Prepas 1983[a]). Cladocerans (*Daphnia pulicaria*, *D. galeata mendotae* and *Daphnia* sp.) were the most abundant group on all dates.

The benthic invertebrates in Hasse Lake have not been documented.

Fish

Hasse Lake has only two indigenous species of fish: fathead minnow and brook stickleback. Other species present are rainbow trout, which are stocked by Fish and Wildlife Division, and the mysteriously introduced threespine stickleback, which first appeared in 1980.

Prior to 1930, local residents reported northern pike, yellow perch and suckers in the lake (Stony Plain Dist. Hist. Soc. 1982). The pike and perch provided a modest sport fishery until the winter of 1952/53, when they were eliminated in a severe winterkill. Fish and Wildlife Division stocked the lake with rainbow trout in 1953, 1955 and 1956, and with brook trout in 1954. The trout fishery was slow and public pressure was exerted to stock the lake with perch and pike. Perch were stocked in 1957, pike and walleye were introduced in 1959, and more pike were added in 1960. A successful fishery was not established and many fish died in a partial winterkill in 1967/68. Rotenone was applied to the lake in 1968 to kill all pike, perch and suckers. From 1970 to 1988 (except 1983) the lake has been stocked annually with fingerling rainbow trout. As well, brook trout were added in 1970 and 1971 but they did not become established. The rainbow trout do not spawn successfully in Hasse Lake (Alta. For. Ld. Wild. n.d.; R.L. & L. Envir. Serv. Ltd. 1987).

Hasse Lake provides a popular trout fishery in both summer and winter. An extensive creel survey conducted between March 1982 and January 1984 revealed a success rate of 0.14 trout/angler-hour; 18% of the 3 787 anglers interviewed caught at least one fish. The total hours fished over the course of the survey were estimated to be 185 635. The total number of trout caught was estimated to be 25 977, with 40% caught in winter. The oldest trout caught were age 5; the longest was an age-5 female with a fork length of 618 mm and a weight of 3.2 kg (Berry 1986).

Hasse Lake is unique in Alberta because it harbours a vigourous population of threespine stickleback. This species is usually found in coastal British Columbia, near Hudson's Bay and in the Maritimes; it is rarely found at elevations over 100 m. The discovery of threespine stickleback in Hasse Lake in 1980 was the first in the interior plains of North America. It was probably introduced by an unknown person in 1976 or 1977 (Nelson and Harris 1987). This species inhabits dense aquatic vegetation and has thrived in Hasse Lake; in 1986, it accounted for 95% of the fish caught by seining. The highest catch rate was 150 fish/100 m^2 (R.L. & L. Envir. Serv. Ltd. 1987).

Research into the feeding patterns of fish in Hasse Lake conducted by the University of Alberta in the mid–1980s found: 1) no cannibalism of adult trout on newly introduced trout fry, 2) little or no overlap in the diet of threespine stickleback, brook stickleback and yearling rainbow trout, and 3) only minor overlap in the diets of young-of-the-year trout and adult trout. The newly stocked trout feed on brook stickleback by early August and young-of-the-year threespine stickleback by late August. Adult threespine stickleback are the main prey of larger trout (Smith n.d.).

Wildlife

Hasse Lake provides good habitat for nesting waterfowl, including Common Loons (Finlay and Finlay 1987), but there are few data regarding numbers or species.

J.M. Crosby

References

Alberta Environment. n.d.[a]. Tech. Serv. Div., Hydrol. Br. Unpubl. data, Edmonton.
———. n.d.[b]. Tech. Serv. Div., Surv. Br. Unpubl. data, Edmonton.
Alberta Forestry, Lands and Wildlife. n.d. Fish Wild. Div. Unpubl. data, Edmonton.
———. 1988. Boating in Alberta. Fish Wild. Div., Edmonton.
———. 1989. Guide to sportfishing regulations. Fish Wild. Div., Edmonton.
Alberta Hotel Association. 1988. 1988 Alberta campground guide. Prep. for Travel Alta., Edmonton.
Alberta Recreation and Parks. n.d. Parks Div. Unpubl. data, Edmonton.
Alberta Research Council. 1972. Geological map of Alberta. Nat. Resour. Div., Alta. Geol. Surv., Edmonton.

Babin, J. 1984. Winter oxygen depletion in temperate zone lakes. MSc thesis. Univ. Alta., Edmonton.
——— and E.E. Prepas. 1985. Modelling winter oxygen depletion rates in ice-covered temperate zone lakes in Canada. Can. J. Fish. Aquat. Sci. 42:239–249.
Berry, D.K. 1986. Angler harvest and population estimate of rainbow trout in Hasse Lake, Alberta. Alta. For. Ld. Wild., Fish Wild. Div., Edmonton.
Chambers, P.A. and E.E. Prepas. 1988. Underwater spectral attenuation and its effect on the maximum depth of angiosperm colonization. Can. J. Fish. Aquat. Sci. 45:1010–1017.
Energy, Mines and Resources Canada. 1974, 1975. National topographic series 1:50 000 83G/9 (1974), 83G/8 (1975). Surv. Map. Br., Ottawa.
Environment Canada. 1982. Canadian climate normals, Vol. 7: Bright sunshine (1951–1980). Prep. by Atm. Envir. Serv. Supply Serv. Can., Ottawa.
Finlay, J. and C. Finlay. 1987. Parks in Alberta: A guide to peaks, ponds, parklands & prairies. Hurtig Publ., Edmonton.
Lindsay, J.D., W. Odynsky, J.W. Peters and W.E. Bowser. 1968. Soil survey of the Buck Lake (NE 83B) and Wabamun Lake (E1/2 83G) areas. Alta. Soil Surv. Rep. No. 24, Univ. Alta. Bull. No. SS–7, Alta. Res. Counc. Rep. No. 87. Univ. Alta., Edmonton.
Nelson, J.S. and M.A. Harris. 1987. Morphological characteristics of an introduced threespine stickleback, *Gasterosteus aculeatus*, occurrence in the interior plains of North America. Envir. Biol. of Fishes 18:173–181.
Prepas, E.E. n.d. Univ. Alta., Dept. Zool. Unpubl. data, Edmonton.
———. 1983[a]. The influence of phosphorus and zooplankton on chlorophyll levels in Alberta lakes. Prep. for Alta. Envir., Res. Mgt. Div. Rep. 83/23, Edmonton.
———. 1983[b]. Orthophosphate turnover time in shallow productive lakes. Can. J. Fish. Aquat. Sci. 40:1412–1418.
——— and J.F.H. Shaw. 1985. Phosphorus dynamics in five shallow Alberta lakes: Hasse, Mayatan, Mink N., Mink S., and Wizard. Prep. for Alta. Envir., Res. Mgt. Div., Edmonton.
Prepas, E.E. and D.O. Trew. 1983. Evaluation of the phosphorus-chlorophyll relationship for lakes off the Precambrian Shield in western Canada. Can. J. Fish. Aquat. Sci. 40:27–35.
Prepas, E.E. and J. Vickery. 1984. The contribution of particulate phosphorus (>250 μm) to the total phosphorus pool in lake water. Can. J. Fish. Aquat. Sci. 41:351–363.
R.L. & L. Environmental Services Ltd. 1987. County of Parkland fisheries inventory—Hasse Lake. Prep. for Alta. For. Ld. Wild., Fish. Wild. Div. and Alta. Rec. Parks Wild. Foundation, Edmonton.
Smith, T. n.d. Univ. Alta., Dept. Zool. Unpubl. data, Edmonton.
Stony Plain and District Historical Society. 1982. Along the fifth—A history of Stony Plain and district. Stony Plain Dist. Hist. Soc., Stony Plain.
Strong, W.L. and K.R. Leggat. 1981. Ecoregions of Alberta. Alta. En. Nat. Resour., Resour. Eval. Plan. Div., Edmonton.

HASTINGS LAKE

MAP SHEETS: 83H/7
LOCATION: Tp51 R20 W4
LAT/LONG: 53°25'N 113°55'W

Hastings Lake, with its natural shoreline and many islands, is a popular lake for boating and bird watching. It is a regionally significant nesting, moulting, staging and migration area for diving ducks, and its islands provide nesting habitat for Canada Geese. The lake is located 40 km east of the city of Edmonton in the County of Strathcona. To reach the north side of the lake from Edmonton, take Highway 14 east to the hamlet of Sherwood Park, then continue east and southeast on Secondary Road 630, locally known as Wye Road. About 3 km southeast of the hamlet of Deville, turn south on Range Road 203 and drive 0.5 km to the lakeshore (Fig. 1). Access is also available at the end of Range Road 204 on the north shore and in the hamlet of Hastings Lake on the south shore. Small boats or canoes can be hand launched from all three access points, but it would be difficult to back a trailer down into the water. Boats can also be launched at a commercial recreational facility on the north shore at the end of Range Road 205 (Fig. 2). There are no boating restrictions specific to Hastings Lake, but general federal regulations are in effect (Alta. For. Ld. Wild. 1988).

The Cree name for the lake is *a-ka-ka-kwa-tikh*, which means "the lake that does not freeze" (Holmgren and Holmgren 1976). Apparently, springs that flow into the lake bottom prevent parts of the lake from icing over in winter (Bowick 1988). In 1884, the lake and its outlet were renamed by J.B. Tyrrell for Tom Hastings, a member of Tyrrell's geological survey party (Holmgren and Holmgren 1976).

The first settlers at Hastings Lake were Jonas Ward and August Gladue, who arrived sometime during the late 1800s (Touchings 1976). A Grand Trunk Railway station was built at the hamlet of Deville, 2.5 km north of the lake, in 1909, and a post office was established there soon after. In 1912, the school district of Deville was created, and a school was built in the hamlet.

By the late 1890s, most of the virgin timber had been removed from the area surrounding Hastings Lake, either by fire or by timber cutting. In 1893, a sawmill operated just south of the lake (Redecop and Gilchrist 1981). In 1899, Alberta's first forest reserve, the Cooking Lake Forest Reserve, was opened. It included all of Hastings Lake's drainage basin as well as land north and south of the drainage basin (Touchings 1976).

Most of the people who use Hastings Lake are local residents, and recreational facilities for visitors are limited. The only campground is Kawtikh Recreational Retreat on the north shore, a commercially operated facility that opened in 1988. There are 40 rustic campsites, a playground, a picnic area and a boat launch (Fig. 2). A parcel of county land is located on the lakeshore between Range roads 204 and 205, but it has not been developed for recreation. A quarter section of Crown land, east of the county land and immediately west of Range Road 204, was reserved for a natural area in 1974, but as of 1988 it had not been officially designated as such (Alta. For. Ld. Wild. 1987). The area is used for picnicking, bird watching and wildlife viewing. Grazing is permitted and the land is fenced, but access to the lakeshore is available and small boats can be launched at the end of the range road. The remainder of the shoreland, with the exception of some reserve land within the hamlet of Hastings Lake, is privately owned. West of the hamlet, there is a private camp owned by the Legion of Frontiersmen and a private sailing club, the Cutty Sark Club. Within the hamlet, there is a summer camp operated by the Hastings Lake and Lutheran Bible Camp Association. The

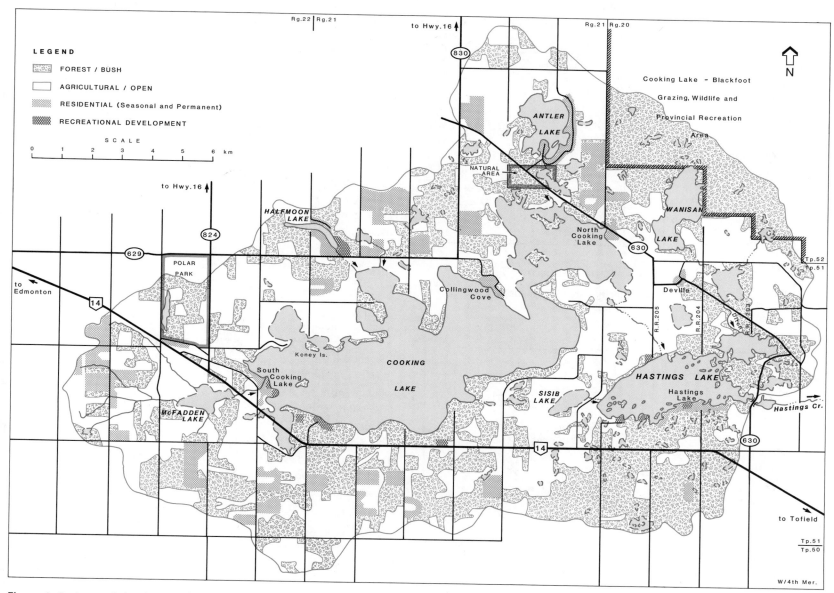

Figure 1. Features of the drainage basin of Hastings Lake.
SOURCES: Alta. Envir. n.d.[b]; En. Mines Resour. Can. 1973; 1974; 1975. Updated with 1983 aerial photos.

most popular recreational activities at Hastings Lake are bird watching, sailing, canoeing, rowing and power boating.

Hastings lake is very fertile. During July and August, blue-green algae often reach bloom proportions. In some years, these blooms have been responsible for poisoning domestic animals and wildlife. The lake is marginal for overwinter fish survival, but yellow perch were stocked from 1982 to 1985, and by 1989, the perch catch rate was reported to be good. As of 1989, there were no plans to continue stocking. There are no sport fishing regulations specific to Hastings Lake, but general provincial limits and regulations apply (Alta. For. Ld. Wild. 1989).

Drainage Basin Characteristics

The drainage basin around Hastings Lake is 31 times larger than the lake (Tables 1, 2). A large portion of the watershed is covered by other lakes, including Cooking, Antler, Halfmoon, McFadden, Sisib and Wanisan, but there is little or no flow between these lakes. When lake levels are sufficiently high, Cooking and Sisib lakes are connected to Hastings Lake by short creeks. As well, a small, unnamed lake north of the northeast basin of Hastings Lake is connected to Hastings Lake by a ditch. Water was last known to flow from Cooking to Hastings Lake during the period from 1952 to about 1957, when the level of Cooking Lake reached an estimated 736.7 m (Stanley Assoc. Eng. Ltd. 1976). When water levels are sufficiently high, the outlet for Hastings Lake, Hastings Creek, flows eastward into Beaverhill Lake. The precise overflow elevations of Cooking and Hastings lakes have not been determined.

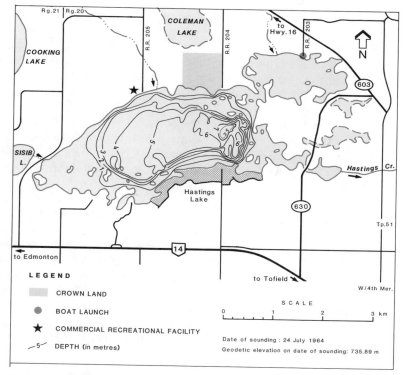

Figure 2. Bathymetry and shoreline features of Hastings Lake.
BATHYMETRY SOURCE: Alta. Envir. n.d.[c].

Capacity (m³X10⁶)

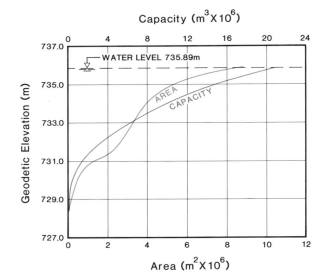

Figure 3. Area/capacity curve for Hastings Lake.
SOURCE: Alta. Envir. n.d.[c].

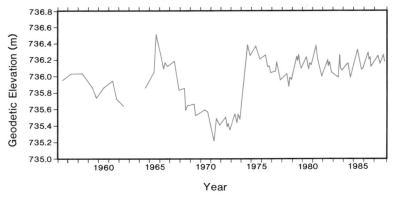

Year

Figure 4. Water level of Hastings Lake during the ice-free season, 1956 to 1987.
SOURCES: Alta. Envir. n.d.[c]; Envir. Can. 1972–1987.

Table 1. Characteristics of Hastings Lake drainage basin.

area (excluding lake) (km²)[a, b]	269
soil[c]	Orthic Gray Luvisols, Gray Solodized Solonetz
bedrock geology[d]	Horseshoe Canyon Formation (Upper Cretaceous): sandstone, mudstone, shale; ironstone, scattered coal and bentonite beds; mainly nonmarine
terrain[c]	undulating to rolling
ecoregion[e]	Boreal Mixedwood
dominant vegetation[e]	trembling aspen, balsam poplar
mean annual inflow (m³)[a, f]	1.73 x 10⁶
mean annual sunshine (h)[g]	2 280

NOTES: [b]includes Cooking Lake drainage basin even though Cooking Lake has not spilled recently; [f]does not include groundwater inflow
SOURCES: [a]Alta. Envir. n.d.[b]; [c]Bowser et al. 1962; [d]Alta. Res. Counc. 1972; [e]Strong and Leggat 1981; [g]Envir. Can. 1982

Table 2. Characteristics of Hastings Lake.

elevation (m)[a, b]	735.89
surface area (km²)[a, b]	8.71
volume (m³)[a, b]	20.9 x 10⁶
maximum depth (m)[a, b]	7.3
mean depth (m)[a, b]	2.4
shoreline length (km)[c]	35.5
mean annual lake evaporation (mm)[d]	664
mean annual precipitation (mm)[d]	466
mean residence time (yr)[d ,e]	>100
control structure	none

NOTES: [a]on date of sounding: 24 July 1964; [e]does not include groundwater inflow
SOURCES: [b]Alta. Envir. n.d.[c]; [c]Rasmussen and Gallup 1979; [d]Alta. Envir. n.d.[b]

The watershed of Hastings Lake is part of the Cooking Lake Moraine. It is characterized by knob and kettle topography, which gives it an undulating to gently rolling appearance (Bowser et al. 1962). Numerous sloughs and peaty depressions are present throughout the area. A large ridge south of the lake rises to an elevation of 785 m above sea level, or about 48 m above the shore of Hastings Lake. The primary soils are Orthic Gray Luvisols that developed on either glacial till or glaciolacustrine material. Secondary soils are Gray Solodized Solonetz that developed on either glaciolacustrine or residual material.

The drainage basin is part of the Boreal Mixedwood Ecoregion. The most common trees on moderately well-drained Gray Luvisols are trembling aspen and balsam poplar. Jack pine grows on rapidly to well-drained Eutric Brunisols, and white spruce is the climax species on imperfectly drained Gray Luvisols and Gleysols. Poorly drained Organics and Gleysols support black spruce and willows, and very poorly drained Organic soils support sedges (Strong and Leggat 1981). A large portion of the drainage basin has been cleared for agriculture and country residential subdivisions (Fig. 1). Most of the soils northeast and west of Hastings Lake, particularly land surrounding Cooking Lake, have a moderate to high capability for cultivation, grazing and pasture (Alta. Envir. 1977). Directly north and south of Hastings Lake, the soils have a low rating for agriculture. Except for the hamlet of Hastings Lake, most residential development in the watershed has taken place around Cooking, Antler and Halfmoon lakes.

Lake Basin Characteristics

Hastings Lake is a shallow, medium-sized water body that consists of two basins separated by a narrow channel. The smaller, northeast basin is known locally as Little Hastings Lake. The shoreline of the

lake is irregular, and there are numerous bays along its length. The lake has more than 20 islands, mostly located in the main basin; their number and size vary with the water level. When the main basin was surveyed in July 1964, its maximum depth was 7.3 m (Fig. 2). There are no contours available for the northeast basin, but its area and capacity were estimated and included in Figure 3.

Lake levels were recorded from 1919 to 1922, and have been monitored regularly since 1956; as well, levels were estimated for 1939, 1941 and 1949 (Alta. Envir. n.d.[c]; Stanley Assoc. Eng. Ltd. 1976). During the earlier period (1919 to 1922), the highest lake level recorded was 735.56 m in May 1920. The level declined continuously until 1949, when it reached its estimated historic minimum of 733.39 m. By 1956, when regular recording began, the level had risen by an estimated 2.57 m, to 735.96 m (Fig. 4). The highest water level ever recorded in Hastings Lake was 736.53 m, in July 1965. During the late 1960s and early 1970s the lake level declined again, to the second lowest recorded level of 735.22 m, in April 1971. Precipitation levels were high during 1974, and the lake level rose to 736.27 m in October. Since the mid–1970s, there has been no obvious trend, either upward or downward, in the elevation of Hastings Lake (Fig. 4). In 1987, the maximum elevation was 736.31 m in September.

In 1973, Alberta Environment responded to concerns about water levels in Hastings Lake and other area lakes by initiating the Cooking Lake Area Study (Alta. Envir. 1977). The study concluded that precipitation had the greatest effect on the elevations of lakes in the moraine, and that changes in evaporation and runoff were also important (Stanley Assoc. Eng. Ltd. 1976; Alta. Envir. 1977). The elevation of Hastings Lake is not available, but long-term precipitation records indicated that, around 1900, area lakes were filled to their greatest recorded capacities. These high lake levels occurred when seasonal precipitation reached the level of a one–in–100–year return period. This event is one that is expected to occur once every 100 years, or 1% of the time (Stanley Assoc. Eng. Ltd. 1976). In 1953, most lake levels in the area reached a peak when seasonal precipitation reached the level of a 1–in–50–year return period, which is expected to occur 2% of the time. Precipitation levels in 1953 were the highest recorded since 1901, and 1953 was followed by three consecutive years of higher than average rainfall. Unlike other area lakes, the level of Hastings Lake did not reach a peak in 1953, but continued to rise until 1957, probably as a result of inflow from Cooking Lake (Stanley Assoc. Eng. Ltd. 1976). Hastings Lake also differed from the other moraine lakes on a long-term basis, because its level in the mid–1970s, after a period of high precipitation in 1974, was similar to that estimated for the turn of the century, whereas the levels of the other area lakes had dropped significantly since 1900. The Cooking Lake Area Study recommended that water level augmentation plans and lake level control structures be considered on an as-needed basis for each of the study lakes (Alta. Envir. 1977). Water importation has not been implemented, and therefore no control structure has been necessary for Hastings Lake, as it rarely overflows.

Water Quality

Water quality in Hastings Lake was studied by researchers with the University of Alberta in 1963 and 1964, from 1974 to 1976, and in 1981 (Prepas n.d.; Kerekes 1965; Kerekes and Nursall 1966; Gallup and Hickman 1975; Schwartz and Gallup 1978; Rasmussen and Gallup 1979; Prepas 1983[a]; Prepas and Trew 1983). The lake was also studied by Alberta Environment from 1971 to 1973 and in 1981 and 1987 (Alta. Envir. n.d.[a]).

The water is slightly saline, very hard and well-buffered (Table 3), and turbidity (4 NTU) and colour (19 mg/L Pt) are low (Prepas and Trew 1983). The dominant ions are bicarbonate, sulphate and sodium.

Hastings Lake is typical of many shallow lakes: it is well mixed throughout most of the open-water season and becomes thermally stratified only during calm periods (Fig. 5). In June, July and September of 1975, dissolved oxygen concentrations declined to less than 5 mg/L in water overlying the sediments, but the rest of the water column was well oxygenated throughout the open-water period (Fig. 6). On 18 August 1987, the concentration of dissolved oxygen declined to less than 2.7 mg/L at all depths. Under ice cover in the winter of 1975/76, dissolved oxygen became depleted, until by March 1976, the concentration was less than 1.4 mg/L throughout the water column. Samples taken in January 1987 indicated that dissolved oxygen levels were very similar to those recorded in January 1976 (Fig. 6).

Hastings Lake is hyper-eutrophic. During the spring and summer of 1981, the chlorophyll *a* concentration fluctuated between 20 and 66 μg/L until late August, when it rose to 239 μg/L (Fig. 7). It is likely that this late-summer algal bloom resulted from internal loading of phosphorus. In shallow lakes, phosphorus is frequently released from the deeper sediments during calm periods in summer, and from shallow sediments throughout the summer. The total phosphorus concentration in the euphotic zone of Hastings Lake increased between June and early August in 1981, but no phosphorus data are available for late August when the chlorophyll *a* level was so extraordinarily high. Average values of chlorophyll *a* vary greatly among different years. In 1975, the mean chlorophyll *a* concentration over the open-water period was 54 μg/L (±16.96), with a peak value of 108 μg/L. These values are considerably lower than those recorded in 1981 and 1987 (Table 4, Fig. 7).

Biological Characteristics

Plants

The phytoplankton community in Hastings Lake was studied by researchers with the University of Alberta from 1963 to 1964 and from 1973 to 1976 (Kerekes 1965; Kerekes and Nursall 1966; Hickman 1978; Hickman and Jenkerson 1978; Jenkerson and Hickman

Table 3. Major ions and related water quality variables for Hastings Lake. Average concentrations in mg/L; pH in pH units. Composite samples from the euphotic zone collected on 28 July and 18 Aug. 1987. S.E. = standard error.

	Mean	S.E.
pH (range)	8.8–9.0	—
total alkalinity (CaCO₃)	238	8.0
specific conductivity (μS/cm)	917	4.5
total dissolved solids (calculated)	573	4.0
total hardness (CaCO₃)	258	6.0
total particulate carbon	7	3.0
dissolved organic carbon	36	0.1
HCO₃	238	33.5
CO₃	26	11.5
Mg	46	0.5
Na	98	2.0
K	29	0.5
Cl	10	0.5
SO₄	221	3.5
Ca	29	1.5

SOURCE: Alta. Envir. n.d.[a], Naquadat station 01AL05EB2040

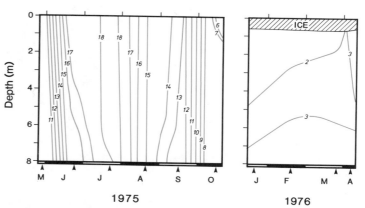

Figure 5. Temperature (°C) of Hastings Lake, 1975 and 1976. Arrows indicate sampling dates.

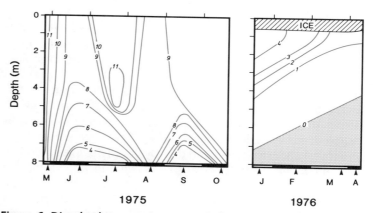

Figure 6. Dissolved oxygen (mg/L) in Hastings Lake, 1975 and 1976. Arrows indicate sampling dates.
SOURCE: Rasmussen and Gallup 1979.

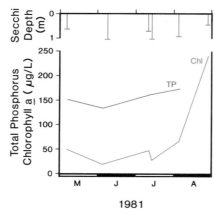

Figure 7. Total phosphorus, chlorophyll *a* and Secchi depth in Hastings Lake, 1981.
SOURCES: Alta. Envir. n.d.[a]; Prepas n.d.

Table 4. Nutrient, chlorophyll *a* and Secchi depth data for Hastings Lake. Average concentrations in µg/L. Composite samples from the euphotic zone collected 6 times from 06 May to 27 Aug. 1981 and on 28 July and 18 Aug. 1987. S.E. = standard error.

	1981[a, b]		1987[b]	
	Mean	S.E.	Mean	S.E.
total phosphorus	156[c]	6.6	116	1.5
total dissolved phosphorus	61[d]	12.3	41	5.5
soluble reactive phosphorus	2[e]	1.2	—	—
total Kjeldahl nitrogen	—	—	3 730[f]	—
NO$_3$ + NO$_2$–nitrogen	—	—	12	7.0
NH$_4$–nitrogen	—	—	515	298.0
iron	—	—	<20	—
chlorophyll *a*	75.7	33.33	72.5	52.00
Secchi depth (m)	0.8	0.09	0.9	0.30

NOTES: [c]n = 5; [d]n = 3; [e]n = 2; [f]n = 1
SOURCE: [a]Prepas n.d.; [b]Alta. Envir. n.d.[a], Naquadat station 01AL05EB2040

Table 5. Species of aquatic macrophytes in Hastings Lake, 1963, 1964 and 1975. Arranged in alphabetical order.

emergent	sedge	*Carex* spp.
	rush	*Juncus* sp.
	reed grass	*Phragmites communis*
	widgeon grass	*Ruppia maritima*
	arrowhead	*Sagittaria cuneata*
	bulrush	*Scirpus* spp.
	common great bulrush	*S. validus*
	common cattail	*Typha latifolia*
free-floating	lesser duckweed	*Lemna minor*
	star duckweed	*Lemna trisulca*
submergent	coontail	*Ceratophyllum demersum*
	northern watermilfoil	*Myriophyllum exalbescens*
	pondweed	*Potamogeton filiformis*
	Richardson pondweed	*P. richardsonii*
	Sago pondweed	*P. pectinatus*
	large-sheath pondweed	*P. vaginatus*
floating-leaved	water smartweed	*Polygonum amphibium*

SOURCES: Kerekes 1965; Gallup and Hickman 1975

1983), by a researcher at the University of Zürich, Switzerland in 1978 (Schanz 1982), and by Alberta Environment on 29 September 1983 (Alta. Envir. n.d.[a]). Algal cell counts indicated that in May 1976, the green alga *Chlamydomonas globosa* (Chlorophyta) was the dominant species. Blue-green species (Cyanophyta) such as *Microcystis aeruginosa*, *Anabaena circinalis* and *Oscillatoria* sp. were the dominant species during summer, autumn and early winter. They were succeeded by flagellated algae and small chlorococcalean algae (Chlorophyta) under ice cover, and then by flagellates in early spring. On 29 September 1983, 62 algal species were identified and the total phytoplankton biomass was calculated to be 12.45 mg/L. Diatoms, particularly *Stephanodiscus niagarae* (Bacillariophyta), accounted for 47% of the total biomass, and blue-green algal species, particularly *Microcystis aeruginosa* and *Oscillatoria agardhii*, formed 28% of the biomass.

The incidence of toxic populations of blue-green algae (Cyanophyta) was monitored by researchers with the University of Alberta during July and August in 1975, 1976 and 1977 (Carmichael and Gorham 1981). Toxic strains of three species of blue-green algae—*Microcystis aeruginosa*, *Aphanizomenon flos-aquae* and *Anabaena flos-aquae* — are most commonly implicated in poisonings of livestock and wildlife world wide. In Hastings Lake, all three species were detected, but only the toxin from *Microcystis aeruginosa* was found to be responsible for the toxicity observed during the study. Toxic blooms often do not result in poisoning because they are blown by wind from one side of the lake to the other. Thus, a

poisoning could occur at one point on one day, but might not recur there.

Qualitative studies of macrophytes in Hastings Lake were made in 1963 and 1964 and in June 1975 by researchers with the University of Alberta (Kerekes 1965; Kerekes and Nursall 1966; Gallup and Hickman 1975). Seventeen species were identified (Table 5), but distribution and abundance were not determined.

Invertebrates

The zooplankton community was studied by researchers with the University of Alberta in 1963 and 1964, from November 1974 to July 1976, and on 10 July 1981 (Alta. Envir. n.d.[a]; Kerekes 1965; Kerekes and Nursall 1966; Gallup and Hickman 1975; Schwartz and Gallup 1978; Prepas 1983[b]). In the study from 1974 to 1976, vertical tows were taken with 76-µm mesh nets. The average biomass for the period from May to October 1975 was 1.4 g/m^3 dry weight. This was lower than the biomass in nearby Cooking (6.9 g/m^3) and Beaverhill (2.5 g/m^3) lakes, which were sampled over a similar period in 1975. In Hastings Lake, biomass decreased between May (1.3 g/m^3) and June (0.9 g/m^3), increased to a peak in August (2.9 g/m^3), then declined steadily until October (0.5 g/m^3). The biomass of individual species was not measured, but organisms were counted. Numerically, the most important species were the cladocerans *Diaphanosoma leuctenbergianum*, *Chydorus sphaericus* and *Daphnia pulicaria*; the calanoid copepods *Diaptomus*

Table 6. Biomass of benthic invertebrates in Hastings Lake, 1963. Samples collected from unspecified depths with an Ekman dredge; n = 86.

Invertebrate Group	24 June	31 July	06 Sep.	Mean
Chironomidae	11.10	70.20	95.03	58.78
Amphipoda	1.68	2.37	2.80	2.28
Hirudinea	1.42	0.09	4.30	1.94
Sphaeriidae	0.65	0.03	0.02	0.23
Trichoptera	0.73	—	—	0.24
Total Biomass (g/m² wet weight)	15.58	72.69	102.15	63.47

SOURCE: Kerekes 1965

siciloides and *D. oregonensis*; the cyclopoid copepods *Diacyclops bicuspidatus thomasi* and *Acanthocyclops vernalis*; and the rotifers *Keratella cochlearis*, *K. quadrata* and *Pompholyx* sp.

Benthic invertebrates in Cooking, Hastings and Ministik lakes were studied by researchers with the University of Alberta in June, July and September 1963 (Kerekes 1965; Kerekes and Nursall 1966). In Hastings Lake, a total of 86 samples were taken with an Ekman dredge at unspecified depths. The average biomass for the survey period was 66.47 g/m² wet weight (Table 6). The greatest biomass (102.15 g/m²) was recorded in September. Chironomids, which formed the largest part of the biomass on all sampling dates, accounted for an average of 93% of the biomass and 86% of the total numbers. The average biomass of benthos in Hastings Lake was much larger than the biomass in nearby Cooking (33.23 g/m²) and Ministik (9.85 g/m²) lakes.

Fish

Hastings Lake has a long history of fish stocking. The lake was first stocked with yellow perch in 1925. By the winter of 1930/31, perch were caught in large numbers. Declining water levels during the drought years of the 1930s eventually resulted in serious oxygen depletion throughout the water column during winter. In 1934/35, a severe winterkill decimated the fish population, which probably had included northern pike as well as yellow perch. Between 1935 and 1977, Hastings Lake was stocked 15 times with yellow perch, 5 times with pike, once with walleye, and once with spottail shiners (Alta. For. Ld. Wild. n.d.; Zelt and Glasgow 1976). Stocking resumed in 1982, when 10 000 yellow perch were planted, and continued through 1983 (36 000 perch), 1984 (8 900 perch) and 1985 (250 perch). Although the habitat is marginal for overwinter survival, the yellow perch population had survived from 1984 to 1989. In March 1989, anglers reported a good fishery, with perch weights up to 225 g and lengths up to 20 cm. As of 1989, there were no plans to resume stocking (Stenton 1989; Watters 1989).

Wildlife

Wildlife habitat in the Cooking Lake Moraine was evaluated in 1974 by Fish and Wildlife Division and in 1987 by the County of Strathcona (Zelt and Glasgow 1976; Griffiths 1987). Although existing forest cover and other natural features are extensive enough to provide excellent habitat for many species, agriculture and other land uses have reduced the quality of the habitat. The remaining forested areas between Ministik Lake and the Cooking Lake-Blackfoot Grazing, Wildlife and Provincial Recreation Area are important as a travel corridor for ungulates and other wildlife. The large block of forested land in the Hastings Lake watershed is, on a regional basis, a key area for white-tailed deer and moose. During the winter of 1974, white-tailed deer were seen frequently on the southern shore of Hastings Lake, and coyotes were observed on the eastern shore. Also in 1974, there were an estimated 102 muskrats and 32 beaver living in the lake.

Waterfowl on Hastings Lake were studied by the Canadian Wildlife Service during 1973 and 1974 (Kemper 1976). Hastings Lake is regionally important as a nesting, moulting, staging and migration area for diving ducks (Strathcona Co. 1987). Ducks that breed on the lake began arriving in mid-April. More than 97% of the ducks at the lake in 1974 were divers and less than 3% were dabblers. Lesser Scaup and White-winged Scoter were the most numerous divers, and Redheads, Canvasbacks, Ruddy Ducks, Bufflehead and Common Goldeneye were seen less frequently. Dabblers included Mallards, Gadwalls, Widgeons, Blue-winged and Green-winged teal, Shovelers and Pintails (Kemper 1976). Duck numbers remained fairly constant from mid-May until August, when they began to increase as many ducks arrived to moult. Peak duck numbers for the fall staging period were significant for the size of the lake. The peak occurred in late September and early October, after which numbers declined until freeze-up.

Canada geese that breed on the lake began arriving in late April in 1974. The number of geese continued to increase throughout late May and June as goslings joined the population. Geese were present in fairly constant numbers from June until the end of September, when the local birds migrated south. Numbers increased again from mid- to late October as migratory flocks passed through. Swans were recorded on Hastings Lake only during the fall of 1973. Other birds that nest on the lake are Great Blue Herons, Black-crowned Night Herons and American Bitterns. Bald Eagles have been seen on the lake in the fall (Deville-N Cooking L. Hist. Soc. 1982).

M.E. Bradford

References

Alberta Environment. n.d.[a]. Envir. Assess. Div., Envir. Qlty. Monit. Br. Unpubl. data, Edmonton.

———. n.d.[b]. Tech. Serv. Div., Hydrol. Br. Unpubl. data, Edmonton.

———. n.d.[c]. Tech. Serv. Div., Surv. Br. Unpubl. data, Edmonton.

———. 1977. Cooking Lake area study, Vol. I: Planning report. Plan. Div., Edmonton.

Alberta Forestry, Lands and Wildlife. n.d. Fish Wild. Div. Unpubl. data, Edmonton.

———. 1987. A summary of Alberta's natural areas reserved and established. Pub. Ld. Div., Ld. Mgt. Devel. Br. Unpubl. rep., Edmonton.

———. 1988. Boating in Alberta. Fish Wild. Div., Edmonton.

———. 1989. Guide to sportfishing. Fish Wild. Div., Edmonton.

Alberta Research Council. 1972. Geological map of Alberta. Nat. Resour. Div., Alta. Geol. Surv., Edmonton.

Bowick, C. 1988. Kawtikh Rec. Retreat, Hastings L. Pers. comm.

Bowser, W.E., A.A. Kjearsgaard, T.W. Peters and R.E. Wells. 1962. Soil survey of the Edmonton sheet (83–H). Alta. Soil Surv. Rep. No. 21, Univ. Alta. Bull. No. SS–4. Univ. Alta., Edmonton.

Carmichael, W.W. and P.R. Gorham. 1981. The mosaic nature of toxic blooms of cyanobacteria. *In* W.W. Carmichael [ed.] The water environment: Algal toxins and health. Plenum Press, New York.

Deville-North Cooking Lake Historical Society. 1982. Land among the lakes. Deville-N Cooking L. Hist. Soc., Deville.

Energy, Mines and Resources Canada. 1973, 1974, 1975. National topographic series 1:50 000 83H/11 (1973), 83H/6 (1974), 83H/7 (1975), 83H/10 (1975). Surv. Map. Br., Ottawa.

Environment Canada. 1972–1987. Surface water data. Prep. by Inland Waters Directorate. Water Surv. Can., Water Resour. Br., Ottawa.

———. 1982. Canadian climate normals, Vol. 7: Bright sunshine (1951–1980). Prep. by Atm. Envir. Serv. Supply Serv. Can., Ottawa.

Gallup, D.N. and M. Hickman. 1975. Lakes primary productivity study, Part B: Cooking Lakes watershed. Interim rep. July 1975. Alta. Envir. Unpubl. rep., Edmonton.

Griffiths, D.E. 1987. A survey of wetland wildlife resources, Strathcona County #20, Alberta. Prep. for Co. Strathcona, Sherwood Park.

Hickman, M. and C.G. Jenkerson. 1978. Phytoplankton primary productivity and population efficiency studies in a prairie-parkland lake near Edmonton, Alberta, Canada. Int. Revue Ges. Hydrobiol. 63:1–24.

Holmgren, E.J. and P.M. Holmgren. 1976. Over 2000 place names of Alberta. 3rd ed. West. Producer Prairie Books, Saskatoon.

Jenkerson, C.G. and M. Hickman. 1983. The spatial and temporal distribution of an epiphytic algal community in a shallow prairie-parkland lake. Holarctic Ecol. 6:41–58.

Kemper, J.B. 1976. Implications for waterfowl and migratory birds [Appendix 7]. *In* Cooking Lake area study, Vol. IV: Ecology. Alta. Envir., Plan. Div., Edmonton.

Kerekes, J. 1965. A comparative limnological study of five lakes in central Alberta. MSc thesis. Univ. Alta., Edmonton.

——— and J.R. Nursall. 1966. Eutrophication and senescence in a group of prairie parkland lakes in Alberta, Canada. Verh. Internat. Verein. Limnol. 16:65–73.

Prepas, E.E. n.d. Univ. Alta., Dept. Zool. Unpubl. data, Edmonton.

————. 1983[a]. Orthophosphate turnover time in shallow productive lakes. Can. J. Fish. Aquat. Sci. 40:1412–1418.

————. 1983[b]. The influence of phosphorus and zooplankton on chlorophyll levels in Alberta lakes. Prep. for Alta. Envir., Res. Mgt. Div. Rep. 83/23, Edmonton.

———— and D.O. Trew. 1983. Evaluation of the phosphorus-chlorophyll relationship for lakes off the Precambrian Shield in western Canada. Can. J. Fish. Aquat. Sci. 40:27–35.

Rasmussen, H.B. and D.N. Gallup. 1979. A survey of physical, chemical and biological characteristics of a series of lakes of central Alberta. Alta. Envir., Poll. Contr. Div. Unpubl. rep., Edmonton.

Redecop, L. and W. Gilchrist. 1981. Strathcona County—a brief history. W. Gilchrist, Univ. Alta. Printing Serv., Edmonton.

Schanz, F. 1982. Bioassays and the algal populations of Hastings Lake, Alberta, Canada. Water Res. 16:441–447.

Schwartz, F.W. and D.N. Gallup. 1978. Some factors controlling the major ion chemistry of small lakes: Examples from the prairie parkland of Canada. Hydrobiologia 58:65–81.

Stanley Associates Engineering Ltd. 1976. Main report, data volume and atlas volume [Appendices 1, 2, 3]. *In* Cooking Lake area study, Vol. II: Water inventory and demands. Alta. Envir., Plan. Div., Edmonton.

Stenton, E. 1989. Alta. For. Ld. Wild., Fish Wild. Div., Edmonton. Pers. comm.

Strathcona County. 1987. Outdoor master plan 1987: Technical report. Rec. Parks Dept., Sherwood Park.

Strong, W.L. and K.R. Leggat. 1981. Ecoregions of Alberta. Alta. En. Nat. Resour., Resour. Eval. Plan. Div., Edmonton.

Touchings, D. 1976. Heritage resource inventory of the Cooking Lake study area [Appendix 10]. *In* Cooking Lake area study, Vol. V: Economic base and heritage resources. Alta. Envir., Plan. Div., Edmonton.

Watters, D. 1989. Alta. For. Ld. Wild., Fish Wild. Div., Edm. Reg. Off. Pers. comm.

Zelt, K.A. and W.M. Glasgow. 1976. Evaluation of the fish and wildlife resources of the Cooking Lake study area [Appendix 6]. *In* Cooking Lake area study, Vol. IV: Ecology. Alta. Envir., Plan. Div., Edmonton.

HUBBLES LAKE

MAP SHEET: 83G/9
LOCATION: Tp53 R1 W5
LAT/LONG: 58°34'N 114°05'W

Hubbles Lake is a peaceful, clear little lake nestled in trees in the rolling country just west of the town of Stony Plain. To reach the east end of the lake, drive 5 km west of Stony Plain on Highway 16, then 3.0 km north on a local road (Fig. 1). Hubbles Lake is located in the County of Parkland.

The lake was named for the founder of a resort on the southeast shore in the early 1950s (Holmgren and Holmgren 1976). All of the land around the lake is privately owned except for two undeveloped road allowance easements. There is no public access to the lake, but two commercially operated resorts offer campgrounds with a total of 280 sites, boat launches and beach areas. One resort is at the southeast end of the lake and one is on the northwest shore (Fig. 2). About 40% of the shoreline has been developed as resort area or for private cottages and residences.

Hubbles Lake is popular for camping, picnicking and beach activities. Canoeing is also popular, partly because only electric motors are allowed on the lake (Alta. For. Ld. Wild. 1988). The water in the lake is very clear and quantities of algae are usually low compared to the other lakes in the area. The clear water and surprising depth of Hubbles Lake (30 m) make it a popular destination for SCUBA divers. Northern pike and yellow perch support a moderate sport fishery. Provincial sport fishing regulations apply to Hubbles Lake, but as of 1989, there were no specific restrictions (Alta. For. Ld. Wild. 1989).

Drainage Basin Characteristics

The Hubbles Lake drainage basin is 20 times the area of the lake (Fig. 1, Tables 1, 2), but only 1.36 km² of the basin contributes runoff to the lake (Alta. Envir. n.d.[b]). Therefore, the effective drainage basin is very small, less than 4 times the area of the lake. The lake is a pothole, so it has no defined inlet or outlet stream. Groundwater inflow likely provides a significant amount of water to the lake (Prepas n.d.).

Hubbles Lake is nestled in hummocky terrain. Surficial deposits consist of glacial till overlying bedrock of Upper Cretaceous age (Alta. Res. Counc. 1972). The land north of the lake is hilly, with slopes over 15%; south of the lake, it is rolling, with slopes of 9 to 15% (Lindsay et al. 1968). The highest hill in the basin is south of the lake; it rises 26 m to an elevation of 755 m.

The drainage area is in the Moist Mixedwood Subregion of the Boreal Mixedwood Ecoregion (Strong and Leggat 1981). Vegetation is primarily trembling aspen and secondarily balsam poplar. Willow, alders and birch grow in less well-drained areas and peat moss and sedges grow in wetter areas such as the low-lying area at the southwest end of the lake (R.L. & L. Envir. Serv. Ltd. 1987). Soils are Orthic Gray and Orthic Dark Gray Luvisols, which typically develop under deciduous trees. The arability rating is good to very good. An area of Organic soils composed of an accumulation of *Sphagnum* peat is found in the depressional area southeast of the lake (Lindsay et al. 1968).

Approximately 60% of the drainage basin has been cleared for agriculture, primarily cereal crop production or mixed farming. Numerous residential acreages have been developed in the basin and approximately 40% of the shoreline has been developed for cottages and resorts (R.L. & L. Envir. Serv. Ltd. 1987).

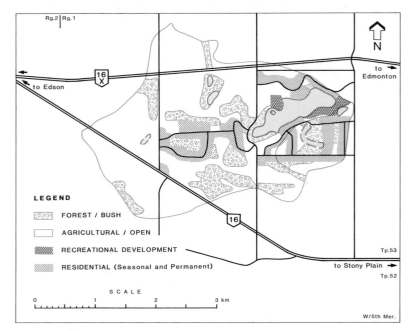

Figure 1. Features of the drainage basin of Hubbles Lake.
SOURCES: Alta. Envir. n.d.[b]; En. Mines Resour. Can. 1974. Updated with 1987 aerial photos.

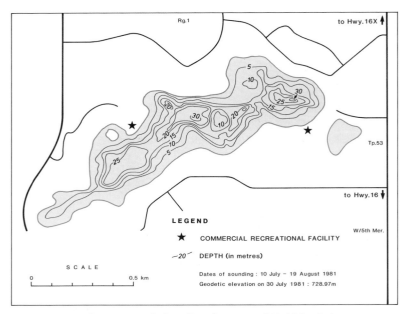

Figure 2. Bathymetry and shoreline features of Hubbles Lake.
BATHYMETRY SOURCE: Prepas n.d.

Lake Basin Characteristics

Hubbles is a tiny lake with a surface area of only 0.40 km² (Table 2). It has an irregular, elongate shape and an irregular bottom with several deep holes, two of which are 30–m deep and two of which are 25–m deep (Fig. 2). The maximum length of the lake is 1.61 km and the maximum width is 0.48 km. There is one small island near the north shore. The littoral zone, which extends to a depth of about 4.9 m (calculated from Chambers and Prepas 1988), is 34% of the lake area (Fig. 3). The substrate is rich organic material at depths below 5 m. In shallower areas, the substrate is mainly fibrous organic material, with sandy areas along the east end of the lake and along parts of the north and south shores and clay in one area along the north shore (R.L. & L. Envir. Serv. Ltd. 1987).

The water level of Hubbles Lake has varied only 0.30 m since mid–1974 (Fig. 4). From 1968 to 1973, the level was as much as 1.25 m lower than levels in the late 1970s and in the 1980s. The level rose in 1974, a year of exceptionally heavy snow accumulation and torrential spring rain. Because there is no surface outlet, the residence time of the lake water is likely very long, but as the amount of groundwater inflow or outflow is not known, the water residence

Table 1. Characteristics of Hubbles Lake drainage basin.

area (excluding lake) (km²)[a, b]	8.33
soil[c]	Orthic Gray Luvisols, Orthic Dark Gray Luvisols
bedrock geology[d]	Wapiti Formation (Upper Cretaceous): sandstone, mudstone, bentonite, scattered coal beds; nonmarine
terrain[c]	rolling to hilly
ecoregion[e]	Moist Mixedwood Subregion of Boreal Mixedwood
dominant vegetation[e]	trembling aspen, balsam poplar
mean annual inflow (m³)[a, f]	0.067 x 10⁶
mean annual sunshine (h)[g]	2 315

NOTES: [b]of this area, only 1.36 km² contributes surface runoff to the lake;
[f]excluding groundwater inflow
SOURCES: [a]Alta. Envir. n.d.[b]; [c]Lindsay et al. 1968; [d]Alta. Res. Counc. 1972;
[e]Strong and Leggat 1981; [g]Envir. Can. 1982

Table 2. Characteristics of Hubbles Lake.

elevation (m)[a, b]	728.98
surface area (km²)[a, b]	0.40
volume (m³)[a, b]	4.0 x 10⁶
maximum depth (m)[a, b]	30
mean depth (m)[a, b]	10.1
shoreline length (km)[c]	3.9
mean annual lake evaporation (mm)[d]	664
mean annual precipitation (mm)[d]	495
mean residence time (yr)[d, e]	>100
control structure	none

NOTES: [a]on date of sounding: 30 July 1981; [e]excluding groundwater inflow
SOURCES: [b]Prepas n.d.; [c]En. Mines Resour. Can. 1974; [d]Alta. Envir. n.d.[b]

time cannot be accurately calculated. Based on surface flows, it is estimated to be more than 100 years (Table 2).

Water Quality

Because Hubbles Lake is small, deep, and protected from wind by hills and trees, the water does not mix from top to bottom in most years. Consequently, the water quality of the lake is quite unusual and the nutrient and algal dynamics were a focus for intensive study by the University of Alberta in the summers of 1980 and 1981 and in the fall and winter of 1982/83 (Prepas n.d.; 1983[a]; 1983[b]; Prepas and Trew 1983; Babin 1984; Prepas and Vickery 1984; Babin and Prepas 1985).

Hubbles is a well-buffered, freshwater lake with major ion concentrations that are relatively high for fresh water. Sulphate, bicarbonate, calcium and magnesium are the dominant ions (Table 3), and their proportions and concentration likely reflect local groundwater conditions.

Lakes in temperate areas such as Alberta often mix vertically when the temperature of the water column is uniform. This often occurs in spring and usually in autumn. Many of Alberta's lakes are so shallow or in such windy areas that they mix occasionally in summer. In contrast, Hubbles Lake is small, quite deep and well sheltered from wind. When the ice melts, usually in mid-April, the lake water warms rapidly at the surface. In 1981, the lake was strongly stratified as early as 3 May (Fig. 5) and there was no evidence of mixing below 8 m. The lake remained strongly thermally stratified until late October. During this period, there was no dissolved oxygen from the lower reaches of the thermocline to the bottom of the lake (Fig. 6). The lake mixed briefly in early November 1981, but ice covered the lake by midmonth, so the mixing time was brief. In November 1982, the lake did not mix completely and at no time was dissolved oxygen detectable at depths below 23 m (Fig. 6). The average dissolved oxygen concentration in the whole lake at freeze-up was only 53%

Table 3. Major ions and related water quality variables for Hubbles Lake. Average concentrations in mg/L; pH in pH units. Composite samples from the euphotic zone collected twice, 04 May and 05 Aug. 1981. S.E. = standard error.

	Mean	S.E.
pH	7.7[a]	—
total alkalinity (CaCO$_3$)	138	0.9
specific conductivity (μS/cm)	418[b]	41.7
total dissolved solids	383[c]	11.3
turbidity (NTU)	0.5	0.47
colour (Pt)	4	1.3
total hardness (CaCO$_3$)	275	3.1
HCO$_3$	163	5.3
CO$_3$	2	2.0
Mg	35[a]	—
Na	9[a]	—
K	11[a]	—
SO$_4$	185[a]	—
Ca	47[a]	—

NOTES: [a]n = 1, 11 Mar. 1986; [b]n = 3; [c]n = 2
SOURCE: Prepas n.d.

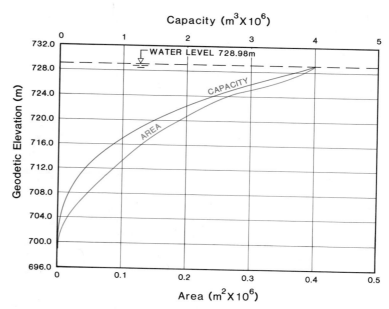

Figure 3. Area/capacity curve for Hubbles Lake.
SOURCE: Prepas n.d.

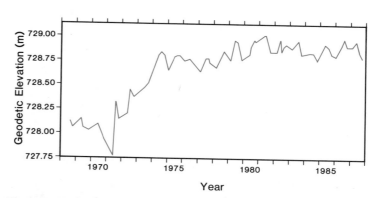

Figure 4. Water level of Hubbles Lake, 1978 to 1986.
SOURCE: Alta. Envir. n.d.[c].

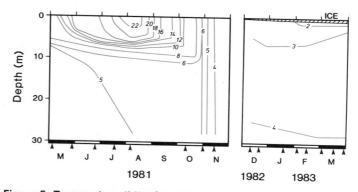

Figure 5. Temperature (°C) of Hubbles Lake, 1981 to 1983. Arrows indicate sampling dates.
SOURCE: Prepas n.d.

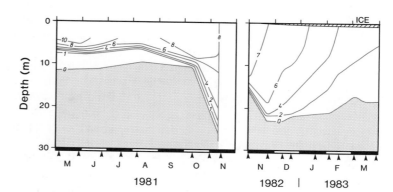

Figure 6. Dissolved oxygen (mg/L) in Hubbles Lake, 1981 to 1983. Arrows indicate sampling dates.
SOURCES: Prepas n.d.; Babin 1984.

of saturation (Babin and Prepas 1985). By late March 1983, there was little dissolved oxygen remaining in the lake (Fig. 6). Winterkills of northern pike and perch occur frequently (Alta. For. Ld. Wild. n.d.). Oxygen depletion rates under ice are difficult to evaluate as the sediments are rarely oxygenated.

The algae in Hubbles Lake are inconspicuous and the water is clear, with Secchi depths reaching 5 m in midsummer (Fig. 7, Table 4). The lake is ranked at the low end of the mesotrophic range. Total phosphorus concentrations in the euphotic zone are highest in spring and autumn when some phosphorus is mixed from the lower strata into the upper strata (Fig. 7). Chlorophyll *a* in the euphotic zone reaches a maximum in autumn in response to the autumn phosphorus peak; for example, in 1981, the highest chlorophyll *a* concentration of the year, 25 μg/L, was recorded on 14 November, only days before freeze-up. Chlorophyll *a* concentrations appear to stay relatively high in the upper 4 m of the water column long after ice cover, as on 10 December 1982, when chlorophyll *a* was still 9.3 μg/L. Chlorophyll *a* concentrations decreased through the winter to a low of 3.2 μg/L on 2 March 1983 (Babin 1984).

When the hypolimnion is anoxic, total phosphorus is released from the bottom sediment and accumulates in the overlying water. Immediately below the thermocline, total phosphorus concentrations are 4 times greater than they are above the thermocline (Prepas and Trew 1983). Phosphorus is the nutrient primarily responsible for controlling algal biomass in Alberta lakes. In Hubbles Lake, a delicate balance is established between abundant phosphorus available in the deep water and the diminished light available at that depth. As is shown in Figure 8, there is adequate light and abundant phosphorus at a depth of 8 m; this is the optimum place for algae to grow and consequently, there is a peak of chlorophyll *a* at this depth. There was a smaller maximum at 5 m where more light was available and the total phosphorus concentration was 50% greater than at the surface.

Total phosphorus is also released from the sediment into the overlying anoxic water in winter. On 16 March 1983, the total phosphorus concentration at a depth of 26 m was 470 μg/L, whereas it was 19 μg/L just below the ice (Prepas n.d.).

Biological Characteristics

Bacteria

Purple sulphur-fixing bacteria accumulate in Hubbles Lake where there is a rapid gradient of temperature, oxygen and nutrients,

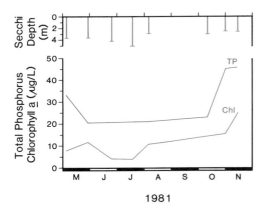

Figure 7. Total phosphorus, chlorophyll *a* and Secchi depth in Hubbles Lake, 1981.
SOURCE: Prepas n.d.

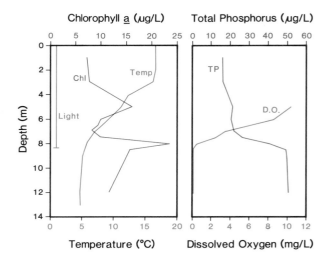

Figure 8. Vertical stratification of temperature, chlorophyll *a*, dissolved oxygen and phosphorus in Hubbles Lake, 28 May 1981. Light indicator marks depth of 1% incident light penetration.
SOURCE: Prepas and Trew 1983.

Table 4. Nutrient, chlorophyll *a* and Secchi depth data for Hubbles Lake. Average concentrations in μg/L. Composite samples from the euphotic zone collected 4 times from 19 June to 08 Aug. 1980 and 4 times from 04 May to 05 Aug. 1981. S.E. = standard error.

	1980		1981	
	Mean	S.E.	Mean	S.E.
total phosphorus	30	2.9	24	3.0
total dissolved phosphorus	—	—	9[b]	1.2
soluble reactive phosphorus	0.6[a]	0.05	1[c]	—
total Kjeldahl nitrogen	—	—	1 020	58.1
$NO_3 + NO_2$–nitrogen	—	—	6	1.2
NH_4–nitrogen	—	—	73	32.7
iron	—	—	36[d]	—
chlorophyll *a*	10.3	0.11	7.7[e]	1.59
Secchi depth (m)	5.2	0.53	3.9[e]	0.35

NOTES: [a]n = 2; [b]n = 3; [c]n = 1; [d]n = 1, 11 Mar. 1986; [e]n = 5
SOURCE: Prepas n.d.

Invertebrates

The zooplankton was sampled from May through September in 1980 and from May through August 1981 by researchers at the University of Alberta (Prepas 1983[a]; Prepas and Vickery 1984). In both years, the larger zooplankters were concentrated in the surface waters in May and September, and moved into deeper water (5– to 10–m depths) from June through August. On 24 June 1981, a species of large cladoceran (*Daphnia pulex*) was the most abundant zooplankter, followed by phantom midge larvae (*Chaoborus* sp.) and the cladoceran (*Ceriodaphnia* sp.). The copepods *Diaptomus oregonensis* and *Macrocyclops albidus* were also present. There are no data on the benthic invertebrates in Hubbles Lake.

Fish

There are reports of only two species of fish in Hubbles Lake: northern pike and yellow perch. No forage fish were caught during shoreline seining in 1986 for a Fish and Wildlife Division study (R.L. & L. Envir. Serv. Ltd. 1987). It is not known whether pike or perch were indigenous to the lake. Adult pike were stocked by Fish and Wildlife Division annually from 1957 to 1960. Perch were stocked in 1959. Both pike and perch spawn successfully in the lake but partial winterkills are fairly common (Alta. For. Ld. Wild. n.d.).

In an attempt to improve or create habitat for pike and perch, 2 000 old tires were chained together and sunk in the lake in 1967 as a community centennial project (Alta. For. Ld. Wild. n.d.). The success of this venture has not been evaluated.

Wildlife

There is no available information on wildlife at Hubbles Lake.

J.M. Crosby and E.E. Prepas

usually at about 7– to 9–m depths. Water samples from this stratum appear pink because of the high concentration of bacteria, and SCUBA divers descending in the lake notice a sudden decrease in light below this layer (Prepas n.d.).

Plants

The phytoplankton in Hubbles Lake was sampled on 19 July 1981 by Alberta Environment (Alta. Envir. n.d.[a]). The total phytoplankton biomass in Hubbles Lake (0.105 mg/L) was the lowest of all 31 lakes in the Edmonton-Cold Lake area sampled between 4 July and 25 August 1981. The assemblage was dominated by Cryptophyta (*Cryptomonas Marsonii*), which formed 45% of the biomass. The remainder of the biomass was 30% diatoms (mostly *Asterionella formosa*), 20% Chrysophyta (*Dinobryon sociale*) and 5% Chlorophyta.

The aquatic macrophytes in Hubbles Lake form a narrow band around most of the shore. Most of the inshore areas less than 1–m deep support a narrow band of emergents dominated by common cattails (*Typha latifolia*) and sedges (*Carex* sp.), with patches of common great bulrush (*Scirpus validus*), arrowhead (*Sagittaria cuneata*) and giant bur-reed (*Sparganium eurycarpum*). Stonewort (*Chara* sp.) is the most abundant species of submergent vegetation along most of the shoreline. Northern watermilfoil (*Myriophyllum exalbescens*) and Sago pondweed (*Potamogeton pectinatus*) occur commonly but at low densities (R.L. & L. Envir. Serv. Ltd. 1987). Substantial areas of aquatic vegetation have been removed by cottage and resort owners.

References

Alberta Environment. n.d.[a]. Envir. Assess. Div., Envir. Qlty. Monit. Br. Unpubl. data, Edmonton.
———. n.d.[b]. Tech. Serv. Div., Hydrol. Br. Unpubl. data, Edmonton.
———. n.d.[c]. Tech. Serv. Div., Surv. Br. Unpubl. data, Edmonton.
Alberta Forestry, Lands and Wildlife. n.d. Fish Wild. Div. Unpubl. data, Edmonton.
———. 1988. Boating in Alberta. Fish Wild. Div., Edmonton.
———. 1989. Guide to sportfishing. Fish Wild. Div., Edmonton.
Alberta Research Council. 1972. Geological map of Alberta. Nat. Resour. Div., Alta. Geol. Surv., Edmonton.
Babin, J. 1984. Winter oxygen depletion in temperate zone lakes. MSc thesis. Univ. Alta., Edmonton.
——— and E.E. Prepas. 1985. Modelling winter oxygen depletion rates in ice-covered temperate zone lakes in Canada. Can. J. Fish. Aquat. Sci. 42:239–249.

Chambers, P.A. and E.E. Prepas. 1988. Underwater spectral attenuation and its effect on the maximum depth of angiosperm colonization. Can. J. Fish. Aquat. Sci. 45:1010–1017.

Energy, Mines and Resources Canada. 1974. National topographic series 1:50 000 83G/9 (1974). Surv. Map. Br., Ottawa.

Environment Canada. 1982. Canadian climate normals, Vol. 7: Bright sunshine (1951–1980). Prep. by Atm. Envir. Serv. Supply Serv. Can., Ottawa.

Holmgren, E.J. and P.M. Holmgren. 1976. Over 2000 place names of Alberta. 3rd ed. West. Producer Prairie Books, Saskatoon.

Lindsay, J.D., W. Odynsky, J.W. Peters and W.E. Bowser. 1968. Soil survey of the Buck Lake (NE 83B) and Wabamun Lake (E1/2 83G) areas. Alta. Soil Surv. Rep. No. 24, Univ. Alta. Bull. No. SS–7, Alta. Res. Counc. Rep. No. 87. Univ. Alta., Edmonton.

Prepas, E.E. n.d. Univ. Alta., Dept. Zool. Unpubl. data, Edmonton.

———. 1983[a]. The influence of phosphorus and zooplankton on chlorophyll levels in Alberta lakes. Prep. for Alta. Envir., Res. Mgt. Div. Rep. 83/23, Edmonton.

———. 1983[b]. Orthophosphate turnover time in shallow productive lakes. Can. J. Fish. Aquat. Sci. 40:1412–1418.

——— and D.O. Trew. 1983. Evaluation of the phosphorus-chlorophyll relationship for lakes off the Precambrian Shield in western Canada. Can. J. Fish. Aquat. Sci. 40:27–35.

Prepas, E.E. and J. Vickery. 1984. The contribution of particulate phosphorus (>250 μm) to the total phosphorus pool in lake water. Can. J. Fish. Aquat. Sci. 41:351–363.

R.L. & L. Environmental Services Ltd. 1987. County of Parkland fisheries inventory—Hubbles Lake. Prep. for Alta. For. Ld. Wild., Fish Wild. Div. and Alta. Rec. Parks Wild. Foundation, Edmonton.

Strong, W.L. and K.R. Leggat. 1981. Ecoregions of Alberta. Alta. En. Nat. Resour., Resour. Eval. Plan. Div., Edmonton.

ISLE LAKE

MAP SHEET: 83G/10
LOCATION: Tp53 R5 W5
LAT/LONG: 53°38'N 114°44'W

Scenic Isle Lake is located in the counties of Parkland and Lac Ste. Anne. It is situated about 80 km west of the city of Edmonton, immediately north of Highway 16. The hamlet of Gainford is located on the southwestern shore (Fig. 1). Unpaved Secondary Road 633 follows the northern shore of the lake and joins Highway 33 just southeast of Lac Ste. Anne.

The lake's name refers to the presence of several islands. In the past Isle Lake was called Lac des Isles and Lac des Islets (Holmgren and Holmgren 1976); now it is known locally as Lake Isle.

In 1870, the Hudson's Bay Company built a trading post beside Lac Ste. Anne, about 14 km northeast of Isle Lake (Lindsay et al. 1968). The wooded region around Isle Lake was settled after 1905 when lands became available for agriculture. The first subdivision was registered at Gainford in 1942 and the most rapid development of land around the lake occurred between 1955 and 1964. In 1980, there were 18 registered subdivisions with a total of 1 038 lots; 736 lots were developed (Edm. Reg. Plan. Commis. 1983). Several of these subdivisions are incorporated into two summer villages, Silver Sands and South View, on the eastern end of the lake (Fig. 2).

Access to the lake is available at numerous municipal reserves that provide boat launches, parks, access points or walkways (Edm. Reg. Plan. Commis. 1983). Gainford Park day-use area, operated by the County of Parkland, provides picnic tables and a gravel boat launch. As well, there are two public campgrounds (Fig. 2). Gainford Campground, operated by Alberta Transportation and Utilities, is located on Highway 16, about 1 km west of Gainford; it has eight campsites, a picnic shelter, picnic tables and a water pump. The Kokomoko Recreation Area, which is owned by the County of Parkland, is located on the southern shore. Its facilities include 10 campsites, picnic tables and a gravel boat launch. There are also a number of church operated and commercially operated recreational facilities that have campgrounds and trailer parks with boat launching, swimming and picnicking facilities. Camp He-Ho-Ha on the southern shore is operated by the Alberta Rehabilitation Council for the Disabled; it provides outdoor recreation facilities for handicapped children. Swimming, boating and fishing are favoured recreational activities at Isle Lake. In posted areas of the lake boats may be prohibited or subject to a maximum speed of 12 km/hour (Alta. For. Ld. Wild. 1988).

A small proportion of the land adjacent to Isle Lake, and all of the islands in the lake, are Crown land (Fig. 2). Most of it is maintained in its natural state except for the portion containing Camp He-Ho-Ha (Edm. Reg. Plan. Commis. 1983). Two quarter sections south of Camp He-Ho-Ha were established as a Natural Area for recreation in 1971 and some trails have been developed there (Alta. For. Ld. Wild. 1987).

Isle Lake commonly has blooms of blue-green algae during summer, and aquatic vegetation grows extensively throughout much of the lake. Although low levels of dissolved oxygen sometimes cause summer and winter fish kills, northern pike and walleye support a popular sport fishery. All tributary streams to, and the outlet from, the lake are closed to fishing for a period in spring (Alta. For. Ld. Wild. 1989). The actual closing and opening dates may vary from year to year.

Drainage Basin Characteristics

The drainage basin of Isle Lake is about 11 times the size of the lake (Tables 1, 2). Most surface water flows into the lake from the south-

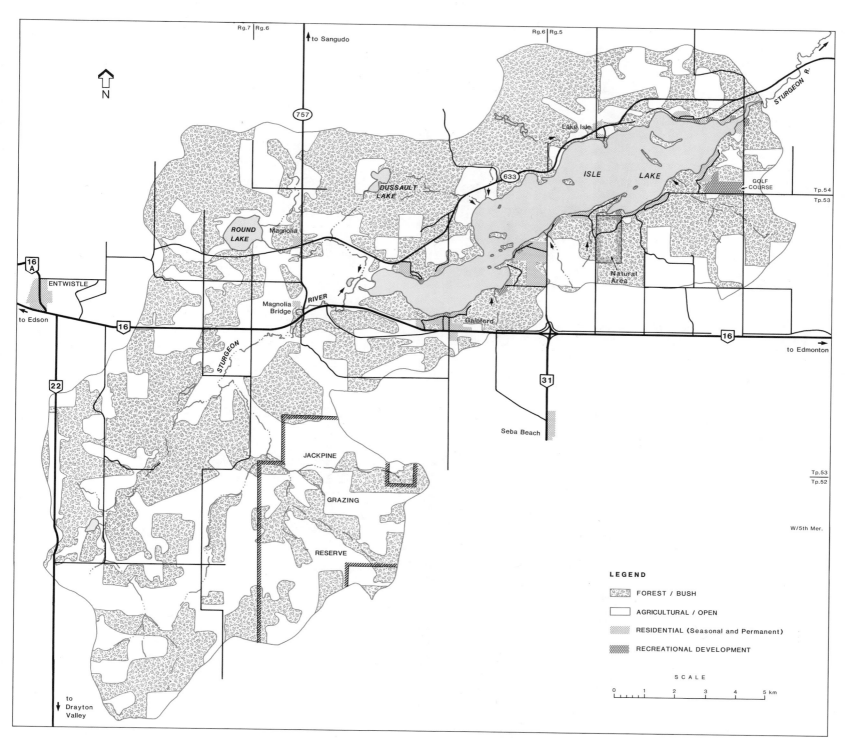

Figure 1. Features of the drainage basin of Isle Lake.
SOURCES: Alta. Envir. n.d.[b]; En. Mines Resour. Can. 1974. Updated with 1985 aerial photos.

west through the Sturgeon River (Fig. 1). The outflow from Dussault and Round lakes, situated northwest of Isle Lake, drains into the Sturgeon River shortly before the river enters Isle Lake. Several intermittent streams drain the remainder of the drainage basin. The lake's outlet, the Sturgeon River, is located at the eastern end; it flows eastward to the North Saskatchewan River via Lac Ste. Anne, Matchayaw Lake and Big Lake.

A detailed study of the water resources of the Sturgeon River basin was completed in 1977 (Alta. Envir. 1977). The report examined flooding problems, water-based recreation, fish and wildlife resources and water supply concerns.

Four bedrock formations underlie Isle Lake. The lowermost, Horseshoe Canyon Formation, is lithologically complex, which results in groundwater conditions that differ markedly from area to area. Overlying the Horseshoe Canyon Formation are the relatively impermeable Whitemud and Battle formations. The Paskapoo Formation lies nearest the surface and offers the most reliable source of groundwater; this formation contains the Ardley coal zone, which is mined at nearby Wabamun Lake. Saskatchewan sands and gravels

overlie the bedrock and are characterized by extremely good water availability (Edm. Reg. Plan. Commis. 1983).

Most of the drainage basin is characterized by gently rolling (5 to 9% slope) to moderately rolling (9 to 15% slope) terrain. There is a strongly rolling region (greater than 15% slope) just southwest of the lake (Lindsay et al. 1968). Surficial deposits appear closely related to the underlying bedrock. The undulating ground moraine that covers most of the drainage basin is composed of glacial till, and lesser amounts of glaciolacustrine deposits are present. Organic deposits occur in depressions throughout the basin, and beach sands occur around the shoreline (Twardy and Brocke 1978).

The dominant soils in the watershed are moderately well-drained Orthic Gray Luvisols, which are developed on a variety of glacial materials, but mainly till. Moderately well-drained Dark Gray Luvisols developed on glaciolacustrine or glaciofluvial materials are also present in the western portion of the area; these are some of the better agricultural soils near Isle Lake. Eluviated Eutric Brunisols developed on very coarse materials are present south and northeast of the lake. Small areas of Organic soils, characterized by more than 50

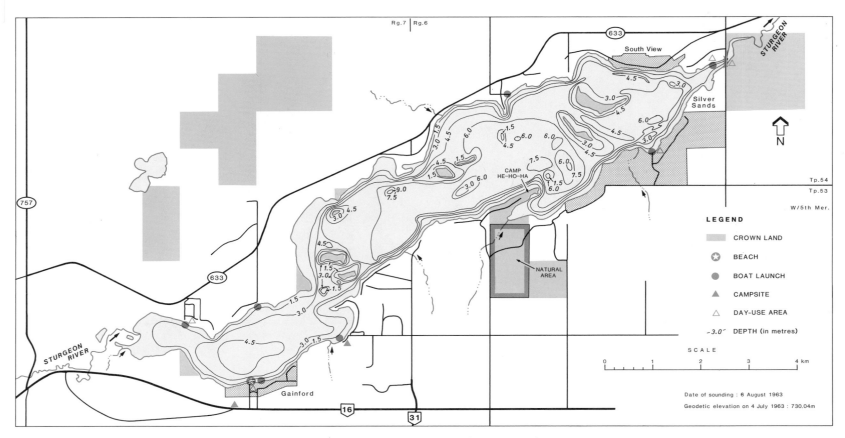

Figure 2. Bathymetry and shoreline features of Isle Lake. BATHYMETRY SOURCE: Alta. Envir. n.d.[c].

cm of compacted sedge or moss peat, occur throughout the drainage basin (Twardy and Brocke 1978).

Sand and gravel are the most important nonrenewable resources presently extracted in the watershed. Coal, oil and natural gas deposits are not yet being exploited to any great extent (Edm. Reg. Plan. Commis. 1983).

About 54% of the drainage basin is forested and 45% is open or has been cleared for agriculture (Fig. 1). The remaining 1% has been developed for cottages and permanent residences. Trembling aspen is the dominant tree on well-drained sites, and balsam poplar, white spruce and willow grow in more poorly drained areas (Edm. Reg. Plan. Commis. 1983). A sedge fen is located around the inlet of the Sturgeon River. Most of the natural vegetation immediately surrounding the lake is relatively undisturbed (R.L. & L. Envir. Serv. Ltd. 1987). Beef cattle production is a prominent agricultural activity in the region (Olson 1988), and part of the Jackpine Grazing Reserve is located in the southern portion of the drainage basin.

Most of the lakeshore is privately owned. In 1977, Isle Lake became subject to the Regulated Lake Shoreland Development Operations Regulations, which were administered by Alberta Environment. The regulations prohibited most developments at the lake until an area redevelopment plan and area structure plan were prepared at the direction of the councils of the counties of Lac Ste. Anne and Parkland and the summer villages of Southview and Silver Sands (Yell. Reg. Plan. Commis. 1984). Such plans determine the extent of future land developments, allocate land use and determine ways to minimize environmental impacts and conflicts in uses of the lakeshore. They recommend preferred lake uses and ways to minimize lake-user conflicts.

Lake Basin Characteristics

Isle Lake is long, narrow and fairly shallow (Fig. 2). It is a medium-sized lake, with a surface area of 23 km². The maximum depth, near the middle of the lake, is only about 7.5 m. The lake is divided into a small, shallow western basin and a slightly larger and deeper eastern basin. There are about eight islands in the eastern basin. The littoral zone extends to 3.8 m (as calculated from Chambers and Prepas 1988) and occupies 40% of the surface area of the lake (Fig. 3).

Table 1. Characteristics of Isle Lake drainage basin.

area (excluding lake) (km²)[a]	246
soil[b]	Orthic Gray and Dark Gray Luvisols
bedrock geology[c]	Horseshoe Canyon Formation (Upper Cretaceous): sandstone, mudstone, shale; ironstone, scattered coal and bentonite beds; mainly nonmarine Whitemud Formation (Upper Cretaceous): sandstone, clay; nonmarine Battle Formation (Upper Cretaceous): mudstone, tuff beds; nonmarine Paskapoo Formation (Tertiary): sandstone, siltstone, mudstone; thin limestone, coal and tuff beds; nonmarine Wapiti Formation (Upper Cretaceous): sandstone, mudstone, bentonite, scattered coal beds; nonmarine
terrain[b]	gently rolling to rolling
ecoregion[d]	Moist Mixedwood Subregion of Boreal Mixedwood
dominant vegetation[d]	trembling aspen, balsam poplar
mean annual inflow (m³)[a, e]	12.3 x 10⁶
mean annual sunshine (h)[f]	2 264

NOTE: [e]excluding groundwater inflow
SOURCES: [a]Alta. Envir. n.d.[b]; [b]Lindsay et al. 1968; [c]Alta. Res. Counc. 1972; Edm. Reg. Plan. Commis. 1983; [d]Strong and Leggat 1981; [f]Envir. Can. 1982

The lake bottom is quite irregular. Slopes are steep near shore but the bottom is fairly flat in deeper water, except for scattered knobs and islands. Sand is located around much of the perimeter of the lake and around several of the islands. There are also small localized regions of gravel, rubble and boulders, and clay and fibrous organic substrates in small patches along the shore (R.L. & L. Envir. Serv. Ltd. 1987). Sediment cores were examined in 1977 to determine the environmental history of the lake and its drainage basin; erosion rates have remained fairly constant, and the lake has probably been eutrophic for the last 4 000 years (Klarer and Hickman 1977).

Table 2. Characteristics of Isle Lake.

elevation (m)[a, b]	730.05
surface area (km²)[a, b]	23.0
volume (m³)[a, b]	94.8 x 10⁶
maximum depth (m)[a, b]	7.5
mean depth (m)[a, b]	4.1
shoreline length (km)[a, b]	41.1
mean annual lake evaporation (mm)[c]	642
mean annual precipitation (mm)[c]	539
mean residence time (yr)[c, d]	9.5
control structure	none

NOTES: [a]on date of sounding: Aug. 1963; [d]excluding groundwater inflow
SOURCES: [b]Alta. Envir. n.d.[c]; [c]Alta. Envir. n.d.[b].

Table 3. Major ions and related water quality variables for Isle Lake. Average concentrations in mg/L; pH in pH units. Composite samples from the euphotic zone collected 6 times from 04 May To 20 Sep. 1983 and 6 times from 09 May to 25 Oct. 1984. S.E. = standard error.

	Mean	S.E.
pH (range)	8.1–9.2	—
total alkalinity (CaCO₃)	143	1.9
specific conductivity (μS/cm)	283	5.5
total dissolved solids (calculated)	155	2.8
total hardness (CaCO₃)	98	3.4
total particulate carbon	3	0.7
dissolved organic carbon	13	0.2
HCO₃	163	6.9
CO₃	<6	—
Mg	7	0.2
Na	18	0.3
K	6	0.1
Cl	3	0.2
SO₄	<8	—
Ca	27	1.1

SOURCE: Alta. Envir. n.d.[a], Naquadat stations 01AT05EA1500, 01AT05EA2009

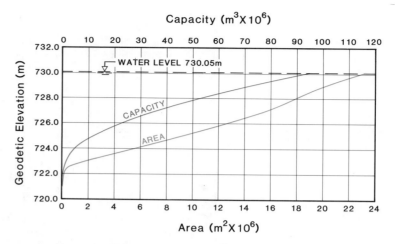

Figure 3. Area/capacity curve for Isle Lake.
SOURCE: Alta. Envir. n.d.[c].

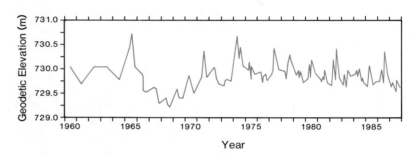

Figure 4. Water level of Isle Lake, 1960 to 1987.
SOURCE: Alta. Envir. n.d.[c]; Envir. Can. 1972–1987.

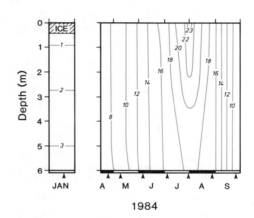

Figure 5. Temperature (°C) of Isle Lake, 1984.
Arrows indicate sampling dates.
SOURCE: Alta. Envir. n.d.[a].

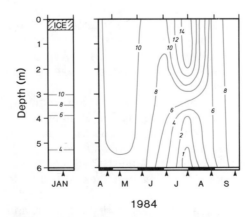

Figure 6. Dissolved oxygen (mg/L) in Isle Lake, 1984. Arrows indicate sampling dates.
SOURCE: Alta. Envir. n.d.[a].

As with other lakes in the area, the water level fluctuation in Isle Lake has elicited complaints from property owners. Between 1960 and 1987 the water level varied over a range of 1.5 m, from a recorded high of 730.72 m in 1965 to a recorded low of 729.22 m in 1968 (Fig. 4). A few complaints about the low water level in 1968 were registered, but high water levels have generated more concern. Alberta Environment studied the feasibility of regulating the water levels of Isle Lake and Lac Ste. Anne in 1979 and 1980. Regulation of water levels in Isle Lake was not considered feasible (Alta. Envir. 1980).

Water Quality

Alberta Environment studied the water quality of Isle Lake between 1983 and 1985 (Alta. Envir. n.d.[a]; 1989; Mitchell 1984). Data were also collected on 20 August 1986 (R.L. & L. Envir. Serv. Ltd. 1987).

Isle Lake is a freshwater lake; the dominant ions are calcium and bicarbonate (Table 3). The clarity of the water is fairly poor because algal growth is heavy during the open-water period.

Because the lake is shallow, large and exposed to the prevailing westerly winds, its waters mix from the surface to the bottom on most days during the open-water season. The water column is weakly thermally stratified on hot, calm days (Fig. 5). During the period between June and August in 1984 (Fig. 6), dissolved oxygen levels were lower over the bottom sediments than in water at the surface; in late summer, concentrations dropped to 1 mg/L near the bottom. Summerkills of fish have been reported in Isle Lake. In January 1984,

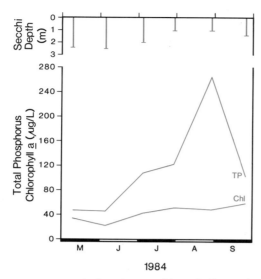

Figure 7. Total phosphorus, chlorophyll *a* and Secchi depth in Isle Lake, 1984.
SOURCE: Alta. Envir. n.d.[a].

Table 4. Nutrient, chlorophyll *a* and Secchi depth data for Isle Lake. Average concentrations in µg/L. Composite samples from the euphotic zone collected 7 times from 04 May to 17 Oct. 1983 and 7 times from 24 Apr. to 25 Sep. 1984. S.E. = standard error.

	1983		1984	
	Mean	S.E.	Mean	S.E.
total phosphorus	93	24.3	109	32.7
total dissolved phosphorus	46	15.5	65	35.5
soluble reactive phosphorus	32	13.4	–	–
total Kjeldahl nitrogen	1 393	196.5	1 389	167.6
$NO_3 + NO_2$–nitrogen	13	3.8	<11	–
NH_4–nitrogen	156	122.7	60	30.5
iron	158	54.1	<63	–
chlorophyll *a*	39.2	11.33	39.3	5.99
Secchi depth (m)	2.1	0.37	1.8	0.24

SOURCE: Alta. Envir. n.d.[a], Naquadat station 01AT05EA1500

Table 5. Theoretical external total phosphorus loading to Isle Lake.

	Source	Phosphorus (kg/yr)	Percentage of Total
watershed	forested/bush	1 327	17
	agricultural/cleared	5 524	72
	residential/cottage	273	4
sewage[a]		51	1
precipitation/dustfall		498	6
	TOTAL	7 673	100
annual areal loading (g/m² of lake surface)　0.33			

NOTE: [a]unmeasured: assumes 4% of all sewage from residences and camps enters the lake
SOURCE: adapted from Alta. Envir. 1989

dissolved oxygen ranged from 10.9 mg/L at 1 m to 3.5 mg/L at the bottom (Fig. 6). Winter dissolved oxygen data compiled for seven occasions from 1971 to 1985 indicated that dissolved oxygen concentrations in the lake are frequently very low during winter (R.L. & L. Envir. Serv. Ltd. 1987). Partial winterkills of fish sometimes occur.

Isle Lake is classified as hyper-eutrophic. Phosphorus concentrations are very high: in 1984, the peak concentration of total phosphorus exceeded 270 µg/L (Fig. 7). These high phosphorus concentrations may result from external sources such as runoff from the relatively large watershed of the lake and extensive areas of cleared and agricultural land, and the large number of cattle in the drainage basin (Table 5). A 1981 estimate of phosphorus loading to Isle Lake reached similar conclusions (Reynoldson 1981). The release of phosphorus from the sediments is also an important source. For example, in 1984, the quantity of total phosphorus estimated to result from internal loading is about twice the annual external load reported in Table 5.

The high nutrient levels in Isle Lake are reflected in its high algal productivity, as indicated by chlorophyll *a* (Table 4). In 1984, phosphorus concentrations rose sharply in late August (Fig. 7). The most likely source of this phosphorus was the lake bottom sediments. The level of chlorophyll *a* increased gradually over the summer and transparency declined. These patterns appear to be quite typical for this lake.

Biological Characteristics

Plants

Heavy blooms of blue-green algae (Cyanophyta) develop in Isle Lake during July and August. These blooms were noted as long ago as 1952 (Miller and Paetz 1953). Die-offs of the blooms often produce unpleasant odours in late summer and may reduce oxygen levels, which contribute to summerkills of fish.

The composition and biomass of the phytoplankton community was studied by Alberta Environment in 1983 (Table 6). In May, the dominant groups were Pyrrhophyta (*Peridinium cinctum*) and the diatoms *Stephanodiscus hantzschia* and *Asterionella formosa*. Blue-green algae were dominant from June to August, likely due to the high phosphorus concentrations (Trimbee and Prepas 1987). In June, *Gloeotrichia echinulata* and *Aphanizomenon flos-aquae* were the dominant species. *A. flos-aquae* was most abundant in July and developed into an intense bloom during August. In the fall, diatoms, particularly *Stephanodiscus niagarae*, accounted for most of the algal biomass.

Aquatic macrophytes grow extensively in Isle Lake because it is shallow and nutrient-rich. These plants are important as cover,

spawning habitat and food sources for fish, but they interfere with swimming, boating and angling. In 1973, the vegetation offshore of Kokomoko Recreation Area was removed by various chemical treatments, with variable success (Worthington 1973). During a survey in September 1986 (R.L. & L. Envir. Serv. Ltd. 1987), narrow bands of emergent species dominated by common great bulrush (*Scirpus validus*) were found along shallow areas of the shore and around islands (Fig. 8). Common cattail (*Typha latifolia*) and sedge (*Carex* sp.) also were common. Submergent species were abundant between depths of 1 m and 5 m, particularly in the western basin, where they extended 200 m to 300 m from shore.The most abundant submergent species were northern watermilfoil (*Myriophyllum exalbescens*), which grew along most of the shoreline, and Richardson pondweed (*Potamogeton richardsonii*).

Invertebrates

During a study conducted by Fish and Wildlife Division from June to August 1969, zooplankton was found to be most abundant in early June. The cladoceran *Daphnia* sp. was present from June to August; the most numerous copepod was *Cyclops* sp. and the most abundant rotifer was *Keratella* sp. (Lane 1971).

Benthic invertebrates were sampled during a fisheries study in 1969 (Lane 1971). From an analysis of 47 dredge samples from various depths and bottom types, the average dry weight of bottom fauna was determined to be 5.6 g/m² (Table 7). This was considered to be very high and indicative of the eutrophic condition of Isle Lake. The most numerically abundant invertebrates were midge larvae (Chironomidae) which made up about 55% of the total number in samples; scuds (Amphipoda) accounted for about 26%, and phantom midge larvae (*Chaoborus* sp.) for 10%. Chironomidae were most numerous on fine-grained substrates in deep water, whereas

Table 6. Percentage composition of major algal groups by total biomass in Isle Lake, 1983.
Composite samples collected from the euphotic zone.

ALGAL GROUP	04 May	31 May	28 June	27 July	24 Aug.	20 Sep.	17 Oct.
Total Biomass (mg/L)	7.67	3.38	0.70	1.32	14.35	1.75	9.31
Percentage Composition:							
Cyanophyta	<1	<1	72	68	99	31	9
			Aphanizomenon———→		*Oscillatoria*		
			Gloeotrichia	*Coelosphaerium*———→			
Chlorophyta	2	<1	2	1	<1	1	<1
Chrysophyta	2	5	5	2	0	<1	<1
Bacillariophyta	40	86	14	20	<1	58	89
	Steph.	*Asterionella*		*Fragilaria*		*Steph.*———→	
Cryptophyta	13	8	7	<1	1	9	2
	Cryptomonas						
Pyrrhophyta	43	<1	0	8	<1	0	0
	Peridinium						

NOTE: *Steph.* = *Stephanodiscus*
SOURCE: Alta. Envir. n.d.[a]

Table 7. Benthic invertebrate fauna of Isle Lake, 1969. Average number per m² and average wet and dry weight. Samples collected with a 15–cm Ekman dredge from various depths and substrate types, June to Aug. n = 47.

TAXA		No./m²	
Annelida:	Hirudinea		13
	Oligochaeta		98
Mollusca:	Pelecypoda		
	Sphaeriidae		40
	Gastropoda		13
Crustacea:	Amphipoda		
	Hyalella azteca		200
	Gammarus lacustris		302
Insecta:	Diptera		
	Chironomidae		1 062
	Chaoborus sp.		191
	Ceratopogonidae		27
mean total number			1 946
mean wet weight (g/m²)		43	
mean dry weight (g/m²)		5.6	
mean volume (mL/m²)		70	

SOURCE: Lane 1971

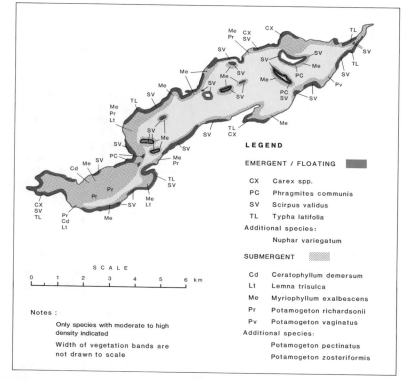

Figure 8. Species composition and distribution of aquatic macrophytes in Isle Lake, September 1986.
SOURCE: adapted from R.L. & L. Envir. Serv. Ltd. 1987.

amphipods were most abundant in shallow water (less than 4 m deep).

Fish

Isle Lake is productive for fish. Species that have been reported in the lake are northern pike, yellow perch, walleye, burbot, white suckers, brook stickleback, spottail shiners and fathead minnows (Lane 1971; R.L. & L. Envir. Serv. Ltd. 1987). In 1986 the most numerous species were brook stickleback, northern pike and white suckers (R.L. & L. Envir. Serv. Ltd. 1987). Walleye were very abundant in commercial catches during the 1920s but declined by 1945 (Dempsey 1945). Walleye eggs were planted in the lake in 1953 to supplement the indigenous population but the success of the project was not determined (R.L. & L. Envir. Serv. Ltd. 1987). Partial summerkills of fish were reported in Isle Lake in May 1957, August 1968, July 1970, August 1974 and July 1978 (Hawryluk 1980). Partial winterkills occurred in 1957/58 and 1971/72 (R.L. & L. Envir. Serv. Ltd. 1987). Northern pike spawn in weedy areas in the western basin of Isle Lake and in the Sturgeon River. Walleye spawn in gravel/cobble

areas near the three largest islands in the eastern basin, just west of the "narrows" between the basins, and along the southern shore next to Sunset Beach. Known spawning areas for yellow perch include the inlet and outlet of the Sturgeon River, and the bay at Isle Cove on the southern shore (R.L. & L. Envir. Serv. Ltd. 1987).

Commercial fishing took place on Isle Lake before 1938 and in 1947/48 (Hawryluk 1980). In 1971/72 the lake was fished commercially to salvage fish before a predicted winterkill (R.L. & L. Envir. Serv. Ltd. 1987). That season's total harvest of 8 193 kg consisted of 4 153 kg of white suckers, 3 504 kg of northern pike, 291 kg of walleye, 235 kg of burbot, and 10 kg of yellow perch (Alta. Rec. Parks Wild. 1976). Commercial fishing has not taken place since 1972.

Isle Lake is managed for domestic and recreational fisheries, but there have been no domestic permits issued since 1984 (Watson 1989). Sport fishing is an important activity, both in summer and winter. A 1969 creel survey estimated that, between May and October, 6 851 anglers fished the lake for 21 237 hours. The catch was dominated by northern pike (92%). Walleye accounted for only 7% of the harvest and the catch of yellow perch was negligible. The catch per unit effort was 0.82 fish/angler-hour, which was considered to be a high success rate. Successful walleye fishing occurred primarily during spring and fall. Most anglers use boats because dense macrophyte beds interfere with fishing from the shore (Lane 1971).

Wildlife

Isle Lake and its shore region provide very important wildlife habitat. Part of the southern shore is excellent raptor nesting and breeding territory; Ospreys nest by the lake. Important areas for waterfowl are located at the outlet and at the western end of the lake, including the marsh by the Sturgeon River inlet. The islands and shallow, weedy areas in the lake and along its shore also provide good breeding, nesting and brood-rearing habitat. In addition, Isle Lake is an important waterfowl staging area for fall migration. Common ducks include Bufflehead, Common Goldeneye, Lesser Scaup and Mallards. A nesting colony of Great Blue Herons was noted in 1981. Beaver habitat is located on the western and northern shores of the lake (Edm. Reg. Plan. Commis. 1983).

L. Hart Buckland-Nicks and P.A. Mitchell

References

Alberta Environment. n.d.[a]. Envir. Assess. Div., Envir. Qlty. Monit. Br. Unpubl. data, Edmonton.

———. n.d.[b]. Tech. Serv. Div., Hydrol. Br. Unpubl. data, Edmonton.

———. n.d.[c]. Tech. Serv. Div., Surv. Br. Unpubl. data, Edmonton.

———. 1977. Interim report—Sturgeon River basin study. Plan. Div., Edmonton.

———. 1980. Isle Lake/Lac Ste. Anne regulation feasibility study—summary report. Plan. Div., Edmonton.

———. 1989. Lake Isle. Envir. Assess. Div., Envir. Qlty. Monit. Br., Edmonton.

Alberta Forestry, Lands and Wildlife. 1987. A summary of Alberta's natural areas reserved and established. Pub. Ld. Div., Ld. Mgt. Devel. Br. Unpubl. rep., Edmonton.

———. 1988. Boating in Alberta. Fish Wild. Div., Edmonton.

———. 1989. Guide to sportfishing. Fish Wild. Div., Edmonton.

Alberta Recreation, Parks and Wildlife. 1976. Commercial fisheries catch statistics for Alberta, 1942–1975. Fish Wild. Div., Fish. Mgt. Rep. No. 22, Edmonton.

Alberta Research Council. 1972. Geological map of Alberta. Nat. Resour. Div., Alta. Geol. Surv., Edmonton.

Chambers, P.A. and E.E. Prepas. 1988. Underwater spectral attenuation and its effect on the maximum depth of angiosperm colonization. Can. J. Fish. Aquat. Sci. 45:1010–1017.

Dempsey, H.V. 1945. A biological examination of Isle Lake. Alta. Ld. Mines, Fish Game Admin. Unpubl. rep., Edmonton.

Edmonton Regional Planning Commission. 1983. Lake Isle management study. Edm. Reg. Plan. Commis., Edmonton.

Energy, Mines and Resources Canada. 1974. National topographic series 1:50 000 83G/7 (1974), 83G/10 (1974). Surv. Map. Br., Ottawa.

Environment Canada. 1972–1987. Surface water data. Prep. by Inland Waters Directorate. Water Surv. Can., Water Resour. Br., Ottawa.

———. 1982. Canadian climate normals, Vol. 7: Bright sunshine (1951–1980). Prep. by Atm. Envir. Serv. Supply Serv. Can., Ottawa.

Hawryluk, R.W. 1980. An overview of fisheries data for Lake Isle. Alta. En. Nat. Resour., Fish Wild. Div. Unpubl. rep., Edmonton.

Holmgren, E.J. and P.M. Holmgren. 1976. Over 2000 place names of Alberta. 3rd ed. West. Producer Prairie Books, Saskatoon.

Klarer, D.M. and M. Hickman. ca 1977. A paleolimnological study of Lake Isle, Alberta. Prep. for Alta. Envir., Water Qlty. Cont. Br., Edmonton.

Lane, C.B. 1971. A survey of the fishery resources of Isle, Lac Ste. Anne and Matchayaw or Devils Lake, 1969. Alta. Ld. For., Fish Wild. Div. Unpubl. rep., Edmonton.

Lindsay, J.D., W. Odynsky, J.W. Peters and W.E. Bowser. 1968. Soil survey of the Buck Lake (NE 83B) and Wabamun Lake (E1/2 83G) areas. Alta. Soil Surv. Rep. No. 24, Univ. Alta. Bull. No. SS–7, Alta. Res. Counc. Rep. No. 87. Univ. Alta., Edmonton.

Miller, R.B. and M. Paetz. 1953. Preliminary biological surveys of Alberta watersheds 1950–1952. Alta. Ld. For., Fish Wild. Div., Edmonton.

Mitchell, P.A. 1982. Evaluation of the "septic snooper" on Wabamun and Pigeon lakes. Alta. Envir., Poll. Contr. Div., Water Qlty. Contr. Br., Edmonton.

———. 1984. Water quality in Lake Isle—1983. Alta. Envir., Poll. Contr. Div., Water Qlty. Contr. Br., Edmonton.

Olson, M. 1988. Alta. Agric., Sangudo Dist. Office. Pers. comm.

Reynoldson, T.B. 1981. A reassessment of phosphorus inputs to Lake Isle, or Lake Isle revisited. Alta. Envir., Poll. Contr. Div., Water Qlty. Contr. Br., Edmonton.

R.L. & L. Environmental Services Ltd. 1987. County of Parkland fisheries inventory—Isle Lake. Prep. for Alta. For. Ld. Wild., Fish Wild. Div. and Alta. Rec. Parks Wild. Foundation, Edmonton.

Strong, W.L. and K.R. Leggat. 1981. Ecoregions of Alberta. Alta. En. Nat. Resour., Resour. Eval. Plan. Div., Edmonton.

Trimbee, A.M. and E.E. Prepas. 1987. Evaluation of total phosphorus as a predictor of the relative importance of blue-green algae with emphasis on Alberta lakes. Can. J. Fish. Aquat. Sci. 44:1337–1342.

Twardy, A.G. and L.K. Brocke. 1978. Soil survey and land suitability evaluation of the Isle Lake study area. Prep. for Alta. Envir. by Pedol. Consult., Edmonton.

Watson, M. 1989. Alta. For. Ld. Wild., Fish Wild. Div., Edmonton. Pers. comm.

Worthington, B. 1973. Control of aquatic weeds—Lake Isle 1973—Submergent and emergent aquatics. Alta. Agric., Weed Contr. Field Serv. Br. Unpubl. rep., Edmonton.

Yellowhead Regional Planning Commission. 1984. Lake Isle area structure plan/area redevelopment plan. Mun. Plan. Sec., Onoway.

JACKFISH LAKE

MAP SHEETS: 83G/8, 9
LOCATION: Tp52 R2 W5
LAT/LONG: 53°29'N 114°15'W

Jackfish Lake is an attractive recreational lake located in the County of Parkland, approximately 60 km west of the city of Edmonton and 25 km west of the town of Stony Plain. To reach the lake from Edmonton, take Highway 16 west for 50 km to Secondary Road 770 and drive south for about 10 km to the east side of the lake. Several local roads provide access to residential developments along the lakeshore (Fig. 1). Public access to the water is available only at the county-owned Jackfish Lake Recreation Area on the eastern shore (Fig. 2). Facilities include a day-use area with 16 picnic sites, parking and a boat launch.

The origin of the lake's name and the local history of the area near the lake have not been documented, but the name likely came from the target of the sport fishery, the northern pike, which are popularly known as jackfish.

Blue-green algae turn the water in Jackfish Lake green in July and August and aquatic vegetation grows densely in shallow areas. The major recreational activities are picnicking, water skiing, boating, and fishing for northern pike, yellow perch and walleye. Swimming is popular, but there is no sandy beach. Provincial sport fishing regulations prohibit fishing for bait fish or the use of bait fish in Jackfish Lake (Alta. For. Ld. Wild. 1989). Conflicts have occurred between recreational groups on this busy lake—anglers and swimmers need quiet areas away from power boats and water skiers. The county has been looking for a solution to this problem, but by 1988 no decisions had been reached and no boating restrictions were in place (Alta. For. Ld. Wild. 1988). Regulations proposed include a 12 km/hour speed limit in front of the boat launch and designation of a swimming area where no boats are allowed.

Drainage Basin Characteristics

Jackfish Lake has a small drainage basin that is about 5 times the size of the lake (Tables 1, 2). There are no defined inlets to the lake, so most inflow comes from precipitation and groundwater. The outlet flows intermittently. Most of the land in the watershed is gently undulating, but localized areas are hummocky and consist of steep-sided knolls with slopes greater than 15%. Slopes are steep along most of the shoreline of the lake and around the larger sloughs nearby (Bird and Hale 1976). Elevations range from 762 m on the eastern side of the drainage basin to 730 m on the shore of Jackfish Lake. Most of the surficial deposits are clay, silt and fine sand either in stratified layers or in a homogeneous mixture. Soils are mainly well-drained Orthic Gray and Dark Gray Luvisols that formed on deltaic parent material (Lindsay et al. 1968). Shallow deposits of Organic soils have accumulated in some of the larger sloughs and in areas adjacent to the shore of the lake (Bird and Hale 1976).

Jackfish Lake's drainage basin is part of the Moist Mixedwood Subregion of the Boreal Mixedwood Ecoregion (Strong and Leggat 1981). Approximately 60% of the drainage basin has been cleared for agricultural use, but extensive wooded areas remain close to the lake (Fig. 1). Most of the natural vegetation has been disturbed by human activity and is in a state of regeneration. The dominant species are trembling aspen and balsam poplar, which are interspersed with willow, birch and white spruce (R.L. & L. Envir. Serv. Ltd. 1987). A large part of the cleared land is used for annual crops and livestock pasture. At the north end of the lake, livestock are pastured and watered along the shore.

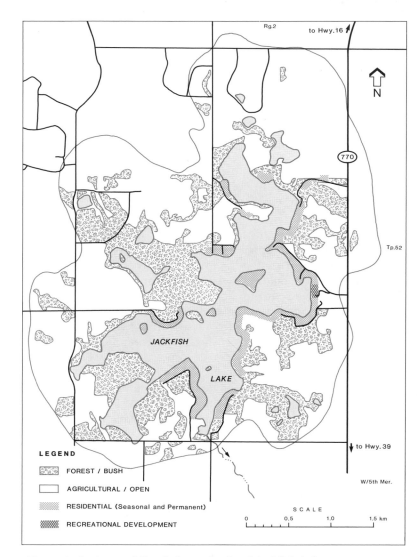

Figure 1. Features of the drainage basin of Jackfish Lake.
SOURCES: Alta. Envir. n.d.[b]; En. Mines Resour. Can. 1974; 1975.
Updated with 1982 aerial photos.

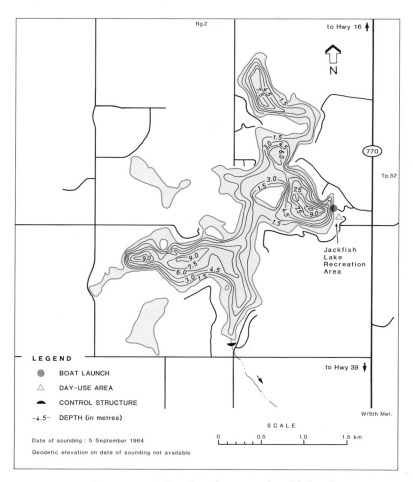

Figure 2. Bathymetry and shoreline features of Jackfish Lake.
BATHYMETRY SOURCE: Alta. Envir. n.d.[c].

Table 1. Characteristics of Jackfish Lake drainage basin.

area (excluding lake) (km²)[a]	12.6
soil[b]	Orthic and Dark Gray Luvisols, Gleysols
bedrock geology[c]	Wapiti Formation (Upper Cretaceous): sandstone, mudstone, bentonite, scattered coal beds; nonmarine
terrain[b]	undulating to gently rolling
ecoregion[d]	Moist Mixedwood Subregion of Boreal Mixedwood
dominant vegetation[d]	trembling aspen, balsam poplar
mean annual inflow (m³)[a, e]	0.392 x 10⁶
mean annual sunshine (h)[f]	2 315

NOTE: [e]excluding groundwater inflow
SOURCES: [a]Alta. Envir. n.d.[b]; [b]Lindsay et al. 1968; [c]Alta. Res. Counc. 1972; [d]Strong and Leggat 1981; [f]Envir. Can. 1982

Table 2. Characteristics of Jackfish Lake.

elevation (m)[a]	approximately 730
surface area (km²)[a, b]	2.39
volume (m³)[a, b]	8.18 x 10⁶
maximum depth (m)[a, b]	9.0
mean depth (m)[a, b]	3.4
shoreline length (km)[c]	18.1
mean annual lake evaporation (mm)[d]	664
mean annual precipitation (mm)[d]	500
mean residence time (yr)[d, e]	>100
control structure[f]	fixed-crest weir
top of weir (m)[f]	729.72

NOTES: [a]on date of sounding: 05 Sep. 1964; [e]excluding groundwater inflow
SOURCES: [b]Alta. Envir. n.d.[c]; [c]En. Mines Resour. Can. 1974; 1975; [d]Alta. Envir. n.d.[b]; [f]Twach 1988

Approximately 42% of the shoreline, including islands, is developed. Eight subdivisions and a number of leased properties have been developed near the lake and on three of the five islands around the lake. The remaining, undeveloped islands are popular picnicking spots for visitors. In 1981, there were about 235 residences and trailers at the lake, of which only 20% were permanent.

Lake Basin Characteristics

Jackfish Lake is a small (2.4 km², Table 2), shallow lake with a very irregular shoreline (Fig. 2). The five islands in the lake have a combined surface area of approximately 0.1 km². The lake bottom is also irregular: there are three distinct basins, two of which are 9–m deep. In shallower areas, the sediment is mainly sand, although localized areas of clay are also present. There are a few areas of gravel and rubble substrate suitable for walleye spawning (R.L. & L. Envir. Serv. Ltd. 1987).

For many years prior to 1983, Jackfish Lake had no defined outlet. Historically, a stream had flowed from the southeast basin, but the outlet had been blocked for many years. Residents at the lake were concerned about high water levels in the early 1980s because the lake's elevation had been rising steadily for more than a decade (Fig. 3). From 1970 to 1982, the water level rose by 1.4 m. Changes in the lake's area and capacity with variations in water level are shown in Figure 4. In the winter of 1982/83, the County of Parkland reestablished outflow by clearing the old stream bed and constructing a culvert under a road near the southeast basin (Twach 1988). During the winter of 1982/83, the county built a concrete cut-off wall that forms a low fixed-crest weir at the inlet to the culvert. Water drains over the top of the weir when lake levels surpass 729.72 m. Since 1983, however, the lake's elevation has declined slightly, and consequently, water has flowed from the lake only intermittently.

Table 3. Major ions and related water quality variables for Jackfish Lake. Average concentrations in mg/L; pH in pH units. Composite samples from the euphotic zone collected 13 times from 15 May to 28 Oct. 1980. S.E. = standard error.

	Mean	S.E.
pH (range)	7.1–8.1	—
total alkalinity ($CaCO_3$)	98	4.0
specific conductivity ($\mu S/cm$)	867	8.2
total dissolved solids (calculated)	569[a]	7.4
total hardness ($CaCO_3$)	396[a]	11.6
dissolved organic carbon	11[b]	1.0
HCO_3	117	3.2
CO_3	0	0
Mg	49	0.5
Na	20	0.2
K	15	0.4
Cl	2	0.1
SO_4	346	2.4
Ca	76	1.7

NOTES: [a]n = 5; [b]n = 9
SOURCE: Alta. Envir. n.d.[a], Naquadat station 01AL05DE4591

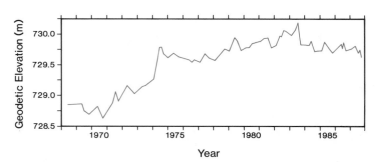

Figure 3. Water level of Jackfish Lake, 1968 to 1986.
SOURCE: Alta. Envir. n.d.[c].

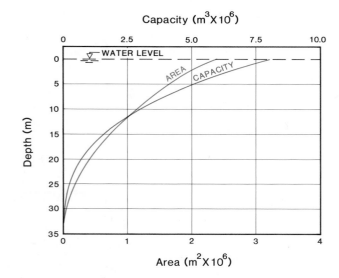

Figure 4. Area/capacity curve for Jackfish Lake.
SOURCE: Alta. Envir. n.d.[c].

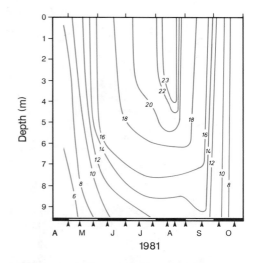

Figure 5. Temperature (°C) of Jackfish Lake, 1981. Arrows indicate sampling dates.
SOURCE: Alta. Envir. n.d.[a].

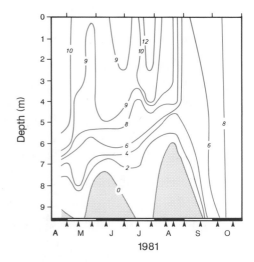

Figure 6. Dissolved oxygen (mg/L) in Jackfish Lake, 1981. Arrows indicate sampling dates.
SOURCE: Alta. Envir. n.d.[a].

Water Quality

The water quality of Jackfish Lake was examined by Alberta Environment in 1980 and 1981 (Alta. Envir. n.d.[a]; 1989). As well, dissolved oxygen concentrations were measured by Fish and Wildlife Division in March 1983. Although the lake water is fresh, the level of total dissolved solids is slightly higher than in most freshwater lakes, but well within the range of the smaller lakes in the County of Parkland. The water is very hard, but the alkalinity is relatively low for a prairie lake (Table 3). The dominant ions are calcium and sulphate. The high sulphate levels probably reflect the influence of groundwater inflow.

The water column probably did not mix completely in the spring of 1981, as indicated by the weak thermal stratification (Fig. 5) and the anoxia near the bottom sediments (Fig. 6) in early May. Thermal stratification and anoxia below depths of 6 to 7.5 m continued through the summer until September. After turnover in late September, the water column was almost fully saturated with dissolved oxygen. Under ice cover in March 1983, the water was anoxic below 4 m in all basins, and surface concentrations of dissolved oxygen did not exceed 2.2 mg/L.

Large fluctuations in total phosphorus concentrations were recorded throughout the summer of 1981 (Fig. 7). Chlorophyll *a* concentrations were less erratic; the highest peak (17 μg/L) occurred in early May after partial mixing of the water column took place. The trophic status of Jackfish Lake is not easily determined, but the lake is probably best characterized as eutrophic. Maximum chlorophyll *a* levels vary considerably from year to year. For example, the highest value in 1980 was 32 μg/L in September, almost double the 1981 peak level, detected in May. Average chlorophyll *a* levels (Table 4) were also higher in 1980 (12.6 μg/L) than in 1981 (9.2 μg/L).

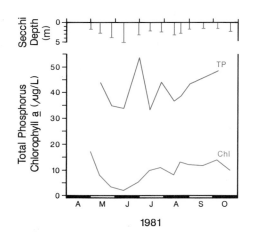

Figure 7. Total phosphorus, chlorophyll *a* and Secchi depth in Jackfish Lake, 1981.
SOURCE: Alta. Envir. n.d.[a].

Table 4. Nutrient, chlorophyll *a* and Secchi depth data for Jackfish Lake. Average concentrations in μg/L. Composite samples from the euphotic zone collected 13 times from 15 May to 28 Oct. 1980 and 12 times from 12 May to 05 Oct. 1981. S.E. = standard error.

	1980		1981	
	Mean	S.E.	Mean	S.E.
total phosphorus	—	—	39[a]	2.9
total dissolved phosphorus	—	—	13[a]	1.3
soluble reactive phosphorus	—	—	3[b]	0.6
total Kjeldahl nitrogen	1 259	76	1 174	41
$NO_3 + NO_2$–nitrogen	<5	—	<3	—
NH_4–nitrogen	41	5.4	64	12.6
iron	<32	—	<22	—
chlorophyll *a*	12.6	2.74	9.2	1.10
Secchi depth (m)	3.0	0.34	2.4	0.34

NOTES: [a]n = 11; [b]n = 7
SOURCE: Alta. Envir. n.d.[a], Naquadat station 01AL05DE4591

Table 5. Theoretical total phosphorus loading to Jackfish Lake from external sources.

Source		Phosphorus (kg/yr)	Percentage of Total
watershed	forested/bush	37	11
	agricultural/cleared	157	47
	residential/cottage	58	18
sewage[a]		25	8
precipitation/dustfall		55	17
	TOTAL	332	101
annual areal loading (g/m² of lake surface) 0.12			

NOTE: [a]unmeasured: assumes 4% of all sewage effluent from residences and camps enters the lake, as in Mitchell 1982
SOURCE: Mitchell 1988

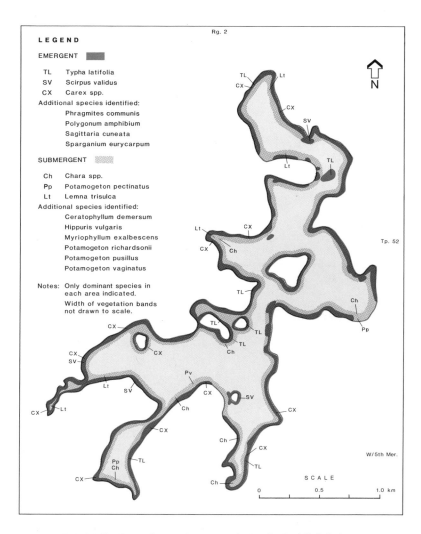

Figure 8. Distribution of aquatic macrophytes in Jackfish Lake, September 1986.
SOURCE: modified from R.L. & L. Envir. Serv. Ltd. 1987.

The external load of total phosphorus to Jackfish Lake is estimated to be 332 kg/year, or 0.12 g/m² of lake area (Table 5). This rate is lower than those calculated for hyper-eutrophic lakes such as Lac la Nonne (0.41 g/m² per year), but is higher than less productive lakes such as Marie (0.08 g/m² per year). Most of the external phosphorus loading to Jackfish Lake originates from runoff from agricultural land, runoff from residential developments, and precipitation and dustfall. Runoff from forested areas and inputs of sewage effluent provided smaller amounts of phosphorus. Loading from sewage was not measured on Jackfish Lake—it was calculated from data collected for other Alberta lakes. Phosphorus inputs from groundwater and sediment release have not been quantified, but they are likely to be important.

Biological Characteristics

Plants

The phytoplankton community has not been studied in detail. The relative abundance of net phytoplankton was determined by Fish and Wildlife Division on 9 August 1966 (Hunt 1966). The blue-green genera *Lyngbya*, *Coelosphaerium*, *Anacystis* and *Anabaena* were most abundant, whereas diatoms and desmids were present but not abundant.

A survey of the aquatic macrophyte community was conducted for the provincial government in September 1986 (Fig. 8). The emergent vegetation in the shallow inshore areas was dominated by sedges (*Carex* spp.) and common cattail (*Typha latifolia*), with numerous patches of common great bulrush (*Scirpus validus*). Areas from 1– to 5–m deep supported extensive growths of submergent plants. The dominant species, stonewort (*Chara* spp.), was present around the entire perimeter of the lake. Sago pondweed (*Potamogeton pectinatus*), northern watermilfoil (*Myriophyllum exalbescens*) and large-sheath pondweed (*Potamogeton vaginatus*) were present at low densities over most of the littoral zone, and star duckweed (*Lemna trisulca*) was frequently encountered in scattered clusters.

Invertebrates

The zooplankton community was sampled with a net by Fish and Wildlife Division on 9 August 1966 (Hunt 1966). The most abundant animals were the crustacean *Diaptomus* and the rotifer *Keratella*. During the same survey, the benthic community was sampled at 8 depths between 3.5 m and 9 m (sample size unknown). At the 3.5–m depth, snails (Gastropoda: Planorbidae and Lymnaedae), scuds (Amphipoda: Gammaridae) and midge larvae (Diptera: Chironomidae) were most abundant, and small numbers of caddis fly larvae (Trichoptera) and leeches (Hirudinea) were present. At depths greater than 5 m, phantom midge larvae (Diptera: *Chaoborus*) were most abundant.

Fish

The fish species present in Jackfish Lake are northern pike, yellow perch, walleye, brook stickleback, spottail shiner and Iowa darter. Populations of northern pike and yellow perch are large enough to sustain a sport fishery. Walleye are present in limited numbers, perhaps because of angling pressure and lack of suitable spawning habitat (R.L. & L. Envir. Serv. Ltd. 1987).

In a 1986 survey for the provincial government (R.L. & L. Envir. Serv. Ltd. 1987), northern pike was the dominant species captured in gill nets (71% of the total catch). The length-at-age of northern pike in Jackfish Lake was similar to that of populations in Lesser Slave, Hilda, Hubbles and Mere lakes. The oldest pike sampled were 7 years old, with an average length of 618 mm and an average weight of 1 654 g. Ample spawning habitat for northern pike and yellow perch is provided by the extensive beds of aquatic macrophytes along the lakeshore. Yellow perch in Jackfish Lake were smaller at a given age than perch from Mere, Hubbles and Muir lakes. The growth of Jackfish Lake perch was typical of other stunted populations; that is, the fish were less than 160 mm in total length by age 3. The oldest perch caught was a seven-year-old specimen that was 177–mm long.

In 1982, a creel survey at Jackfish Lake was conducted over a seven-day period in June (Alta. For. Ld. Wild. n.d.). The 42 anglers interviewed fished for 51 hours and caught 19 northern pike (0.37 fish/hour), 11 yellow perch (0.21 fish/hour) and 2 walleye (0.04 fish/hour). Most of the anglers fished from large boats rather than from shore.

Wildlife

There is no information available on the wildlife at Jackfish Lake.

M.E. Bradford

References

Alberta Environment. n.d.[a]. Envir. Assess. Div., Envir. Qlty. Monit. Br. Unpubl. data, Edmonton.
———. n.d.[b]. Tech. Serv. Div., Hydrol. Br. Unpubl. data, Edmonton.
———. n.d.[c]. Tech. Serv. Div., Surv. Br. Unpubl. data, Edmonton.
———. 1989. Jackfish Lake. Envir. Assess. Div., Envir. Qlty. Monit. Br., Edmonton.
Alberta Forestry, Lands and Wildlife. n.d. Fish Wild. Div. Unpubl. data, Edmonton.
———. 1988. Boating in Alberta. Fish Wild. Div., Edmonton.
———. 1989. Guide to sportfishing. Fish Wild. Div., Edmonton.
Alberta Research Council. 1972. Geological map of Alberta. Nat. Resour. Div., Alta. Geol. Surv., Edmonton.
Bird and Hale Ltd. 1976. Development capability study for Jackfish and Mayatan Lakes. Prep. for Alta. Envir., Ld. Conserv. Reclamation Div., Reg. Ld. Use Br., Edmonton.
Energy, Mines and Resources Canada. 1974, 1975. National topographic series 1:50 000 83G/9 (1974), 83G/8 (1975). Surv. Map. Br., Ottawa.
Environment Canada. 1982. Canadian climate normals, Vol. 7: Bright sunshine (1951–1980). Prep. by Atm. Envir. Serv. Supply Serv. Can., Ottawa.
Hunt, C. 1966. Preliminary lake survey: Jackfish Lake. Alta. Ld. For., Fish Wild. Div., Edmonton.
Lindsay, J.D., W. Odynsky, J.W. Peters and W.E. Bowser. 1968. Soil survey of the Buck Lake (NE 83B) and Wabamun Lake (E1/2 83G) areas. Alta. Soil Surv. Rep. No. 24, Univ. Alta. Bull. No. SS–7, Res. Counc. Alta. Rep. No. 87 1968. Univ. Alta., Edmonton.
Mitchell, P.A. 1982. Evaluation of the "septic snooper" on Wabamun and Pigeon lakes. Alta. Envir., Poll. Contr. Div., Water Qlty. Contr. Br., Edmonton.
———. 1988. Alta. Envir., Envir. Assess. Div., Envir. Qlty. Monit. Br. Pers. comm.
R.L. & L. Environmental Services Ltd. 1987. County of Parkland fisheries inventory: Jackfish Lake. Prep. for Alta. For. Ld. Wild., Fish Wild. Div. and Alta. Rec. Parks, Rec. Devel. Div., Rec. Parks Wild. Foundation, Edmonton.
Strong, W.L. and K.R. Leggat. 1981. Ecoregions of Alberta. Alta. En. Nat. Resour., Resour. Eval. Plan. Div., Edmonton.
Twach, J. 1988. Co. Parkland No. 31, Stony Plain. Pers. comm.

LAC ST. CYR

E. Stockerl and R. Kent

MAP SHEET: 73E/14
LOCATION: Tp56, 57 R8, 9 W4
LAT/LONG: 53°54'N 111°12'W

Lac St. Cyr is a small, attractive lake located in the County of St. Paul, southeast of the town of St. Paul. To reach the lake, take Secondary Road 881 south from St. Paul for 10.5 km, then turn east on Secondary Road 646 for 2 km to a dirt track leading to the southwest side of the lake (Fig. 1). There is a county-owned launching area for small boats there (Fig. 2), but no other recreational facilities. A former resort on the southeastern bay was a private retreat centre in 1989, and not available to the public.

Because it is close to town, Lac St. Cyr is popular with residents of St. Paul. There are about 18 cottages in a subdivision of 28 lots on the south shore. Fishing for yellow perch and northern pike can be quite good at times. There are no special sport fishing regulations for the lake, but provincial limits and regulations apply (Alta. For. Ld. Wild. 1989). Sand is present around the shoreline and the clear water encourages boating and swimming. The best beach is at the private retreat. There are no specific boating regulations for Lac St. Cyr, but general federal regulations apply (Alta. For. Ld. Wild. 1988).

The lake has been used as a water supply for the town of St. Paul since 1951. By 1978, the lake level had declined about 3 m from levels in the 1950s. Concern expressed by the town and by recreational users prompted Alberta Environment to construct a diversion from the North Saskatchewan River to supplement the lake volume. Pumping commenced in 1978. It is restricted to fall and early winter, because studies suggested that the impact on the water quality of the lake would be least during those seasons. As of 1986, there had been little significant change in water quality in Lac St. Cyr as a result of the diversion and the water level had increased. Although blue-green algae tint the water green in July and August, the water is usually quite clear. Aquatic vegetation is prolific in shallow areas. The deep north basin tends to have somewhat better water quality than the shallow western and eastern basins.

Drainage Basin Characteristics

The drainage basin is about 11 times larger than the area of the lake (Tables 1, 2). About one-third of the land has been cleared for agriculture; barley, oats, wheat, canola, field peas and hay are grown in the area (Piquette 1988). The dominant natural vegetation—trembling aspen, balsam poplar, white spruce and willow—is typical of the dry mixedwood forest. Balsam poplar is prevalent along the backshore and on the largest island.

The terrain around the lake is gently to strongly rolling (6 to 30% slope). The dominant soils in the watershed are Gray Luvisols developed on fine loamy glacial till and coarse loamy glaciofluvial deposits. Soils found in minor amounts (less than 20% of the area) are Dark Gray Luvisols or Dark Gray Chernozemics developed on fine loamy till. The Gray soils have low natural fertility, whereas the Dark Gray soils are more fertile (Brierley et al. 1988).

There are no major natural surface inflows to the lake, and the outlet, at an elevation of 647.7 m, has not flowed for many years (Doell and Tamjeedi 1978). At one time, the outlet drained toward Siler Lake and then to the North Saskatchewan River.

Lake Basin Characteristics

Lac St. Cyr is a small lake with an irregular outline (Fig. 2). The northern basin is the deepest (maximum depth of 21 m, Table 2),

Table 1. Characteristics of Lac St. Cyr drainage basin.

area (excluding lake) (km²)[a]	28.1
soil[b]	Orthic Gray Luvisols
bedrock geology[c]	Belly River Formation (Upper Cretaceous): sandstone, siltstone, mudstone, ironstone beds; nonmarine
terrain[b]	rolling to hilly
ecoregion[d]	Dry Mixedwood Subregion of Boreal Mixedwood
dominant vegetation[d]	trembling aspen, balsam poplar, white spruce, willow
mean annual inflow (m³)[a, e]	0.449 x 10⁶
mean annual sunshine (h)[f]	2 240

NOTE: [e]does not include groundwater inflow or diversion from the North Saskatchewan River
SOURCES: [a]Alta. Envir. n.d.[b]; [b]Wyatt et al. 1944; [c]Alta. Res. Counc. 1972; [d]Strong and Leggat 1981; [f]Envir. Can. 1982

Table 2. Characteristics of Lac St. Cyr.

elevation (m)[a, b]	645.14
surface area (km²)[a, b]	2.46
volume (m³)[a, b]	12.5 x 10⁶
maximum depth (m)[a, b]	21
mean depth (m)[a, b]	5.1
shoreline length (km)[c]	11.62
mean annual lake evaporation (mm)[d]	636
mean annual precipitation (mm)[d]	454
mean residence time (yr)[d, e]	>100
control structure	pumped diversion from the North Saskatchewan River

NOTES: [a]on date of sounding: July 1972; [e]does not include groundwater inflow, diversion inflow or withdrawals
SOURCES: [b]Alta. Envir. n.d.[c]; [c]En. Mines Resour. Can. 1976; [d]Alta. Envir. n.d.[b]

Figure 1. Features of the drainage basin of Lac St. Cyr.
SOURCES: Alta. Envir. n.d.[b]; En. Mines Resour. Can. 1976. Updated with 1984 and 1987 aerial photos.

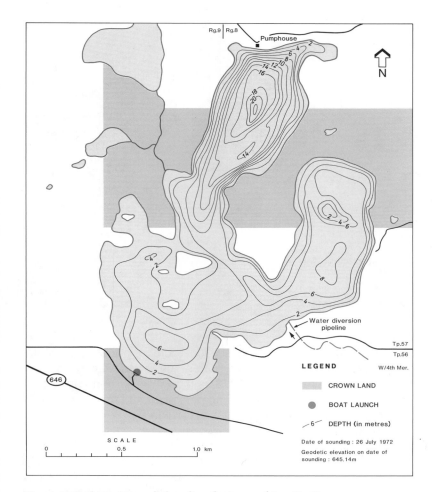

Figure 2. Bathymetry and shoreline features of Lac St. Cyr.
BATHYMETRY SOURCE: Alta. Envir. n.d.[c].

and the bottom slopes steeply toward the deep area. The western portion of the lake is the shallowest; much of it is littoral and aquatic vegetation is abundant. The eastern bay slopes gently to a maximum depth of about 8 m. The islands in the lake are very low and all but the largest would be inundated with a small rise in lake level.

The highest water level recorded in Lac St. Cyr was 647.06 m in 1959 and the lowest was 644.21 m in 1978 (Fig. 3). The decline over these years amounts to 2.85 m. To supplement the lake, Alberta Environment has operated a diversion from the North Saskatchewan River since 1978. Between 1978 and 1985, the average annual diversion volume was 0.987 x 10⁶ m³ and the Town of St. Paul withdrew an annual average volume of 0.882 x 10⁶ m³ (Alta. Envir. n.d.[b]). The lake's water level has increased since the diversion began. The establishment of an optimum level was based on a compromise among property holders on the lake (Doell and Tamjeedi 1978). The quantity pumped is designed to increase the water level to the optimum level and to maintain this level by replacing the portion removed as water supply.

Much of the bottom sediment in the shallower areas is sandy, but silt and organic material are present along the shore in the deep north basin; aquatic plant growth extended to a depth of 4 m in 1984 (Stockerl and Kent 1984). This colonized area represents 43% of the area of the lake (Fig. 4).

Water Quality

The water quality of Lac St. Cyr was studied by Alberta Environment from 1977 to 1980 and in 1983 and 1986 to determine the effect of the diversion from the North Saskatchewan River (Alta. Envir. n.d.[a]; Reynoldson 1977; Mitchell 1987).

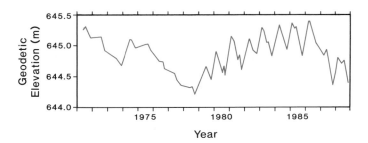

Figure 3. Water level of Lac St. Cyr, 1971 to 1987.
SOURCE: Alta. Envir. n.d.[c].

Table 3. Major ions and related water quality variables for the east basin of Lac St. Cyr. Average concentrations in mg/L; pH in pH units. Grab samples from 1 m depth collected 13 times from 08 May to 24 Oct. 1978 and 6 times from 21 May to 01 Oct. 1986. S.E. = standard error.

	1978		1986	
	Mean	S.E.	Mean	S.E.
pH (range)	8.0–9.1	—	7.7–8.2	—
total alkalinity (CaCO$_3$)	153	2.9	156	1.5
specific conductivity (μS/cm)	296	6.2	337	2.4
total dissolved solids (calculated)	163	2.9	179	2.2
total hardness (CaCO$_3$)	132	3.3	149	4.2
total organic carbon	11	1.7	9	0.4
HCO$_3$	171	5.8	180	2.8
CO$_3$	8	1.3	<5	—
Mg	21	0.3	19	0.3
Na	6	0.1	8	0.3
K	15	0.7	9	0.1
Cl	2	0.2	3	0.3
SO$_4$	<9	—	18	1.8
Ca	17	1.4	29	1.4

SOURCE: Alta. Envir. n.d.[a], Naquadat station 01AL05ED3100

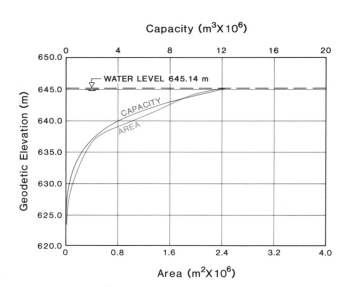

Figure 4. Area/capacity curve for Lac St. Cyr.
SOURCE: Alta. Envir. n.d.[c].

Table 4. Nutrient, chlorophyll *a* and Secchi depth data for the north and east basins of Lac St. Cyr. Average concentrations in μg/L. Grab samples from 1 m depth collected 7 times from 04 May to 27 Oct. 1983 and 6 times from 21 May to 01 Oct. 1986. S.E. = standard error.

	NORTH BASIN				EAST BASIN			
	1983		1986		1983		1986	
	Mean	S.E.	Mean	S.E.	Mean	S.E.	Mean	S.E.
total phosphorus	35	7.2	23	1.6	28	3.8	25	2.6
total dissolved phosphorus	15[a]	2.4	8	0.3	16[a]	2.0	8	0.4
total Kjeldahl nitrogen	960	54	752	30	883	37	765	34
NO$_3$ + NO$_2$ –nitrogen	<28[b]	—	<2.5	—	<23[b]	—	<2	—
NH$_4$–nitrogen	90	24.1	22	11.7	36[b]	10.3	22	12.3
iron	<22[b]	—	<25	—	<33[b]	—	<30	—
chlorophyll *a*	4.5	1.49	7.0	2.70	5.7	2.10	7.5	1.77
Secchi depth (m)	6.4	1.00	4.3	0.50	6.1	0.81	4.3[c]	0.33

NOTES: [a]n = 3; [b]n = 6; [c]n = 4
SOURCE: Alta. Envir. n.d.[a], Naquadat stations 01AL05ED3120 (north), 01AL05ED3100 (east)

As a result of the diversion, the ionic composition of the lake has shifted to resemble that of river water. The total salinity of the river and lake were similar before 1978, but now calcium and sulphate are significantly higher in the lake and potassium and magnesium have decreased (Table 3). Bicarbonate and calcium are the dominant ions.

The deep north basin thermally stratifies between May and September (Fig. 5), whereas the shallower east basin is only weakly thermally stratified in midsummer. The remainder of the lake mixes on windy days all summer. The north basin does not mix completely in spring most years, so the anoxia that builds up over winter in the bottom half of the water column remains until fall turnover, when complete or partial mixing occurs (Fig. 6). Anoxia develops at the bottom during summer stratification in other parts of the lake, but the bottom water is reoxygenated during windy periods. Fish kills as a result of a lack of oxygen are unlikely in summer or winter because of the lake's depth.

The water in Lac St. Cyr is often very transparent. One of the deepest Secchi depths recorded from Alberta lakes was measured in this lake (11 m, June 1983). The lake has low levels of phosphorus

Table 5. Summer average chlorophyll *a* concentrations (μg/L) for the north and east basins of Lac St. Cyr, 1977 to 1980, 1983 and 1986. Grab samples from the euphotic zone collected from May to Oct. each summer. S.E. = standard error.

		North Basin		East Basin	
Year	n	Mean	S.E.	Mean	S.E.
1977	9	5.8	0.84	9.2	0.92
1978[a]	13	5.5	0.88	5.9	1.10
1979	13	7.7	1.33	10.7	1.93
1980	12	6.1	1.11	6.6	1.10
1983	7	4.9	1.34	5.8	2.01
1986	6	7.0	2.74	7.2	1.78

NOTE: [a]year diversion began
SOURCE: Alta. Envir. n.d.[a], Naquadat stations 01AL05ED3120 (north), 01AL05ED3100 (east)

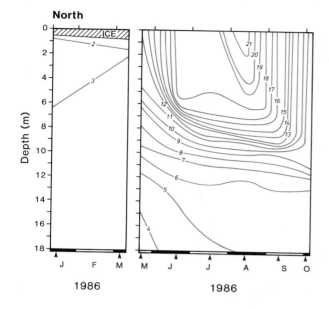

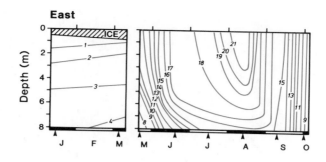

Figure 5. Temperature of Lac St. Cyr, north and east basins, 1986. Arrows indicate sampling dates.
SOURCE: Alta. Envir. n.d.[a].

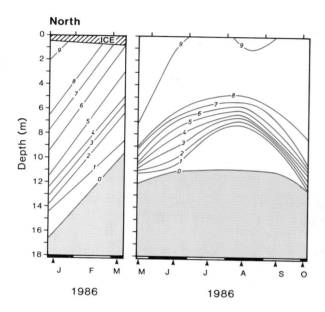

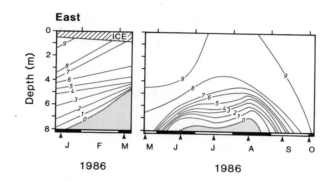

Figure 6. Dissolved oxygen in Lac St. Cyr, north and east basins, 1986. Arrows indicate sampling dates.
SOURCE: Alta. Envir. n.d.[a].

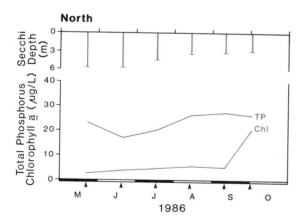

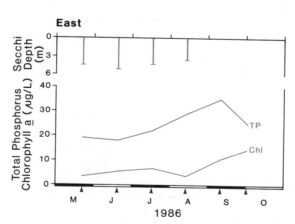

Figure 7. Total phosphorus, chlorophyll *a* and Secchi depth in Lac St. Cyr, north and east basins, 1986.
SOURCE: Alta. Envir. n.d.[a].

and chlorophyll *a* (Table 4); it is classified as mesotrophic. Average chlorophyll *a* data for the open-water season for pre- and post-diversion periods are presented in Table 5. There is little difference among average chlorophyll *a* values for any of these years. Up to the end of 1986, the diversion had had no obvious effect on water quality in the lake, even though phosphorus levels in the river water are about 4 times higher than those in the lake water and the annual external phosphorus supply has increased by 25% (Table 6).

The patterns of chlorophyll *a* and phosphorus fluctuations over the summer are typical of many lakes in Alberta (Fig. 7). In the north basin, chlorophyll *a* levels remain low until fall, when nutrient-rich water from the hypolimnion mixes into the upper water and stimulates algal growth. Mixing usually occurs earlier in the shallow east basin than in the north basin. In some years, chlorophyll *a* concentrations peaked in August in the east basin, which is typical of shallow lakes that mix intermittently.

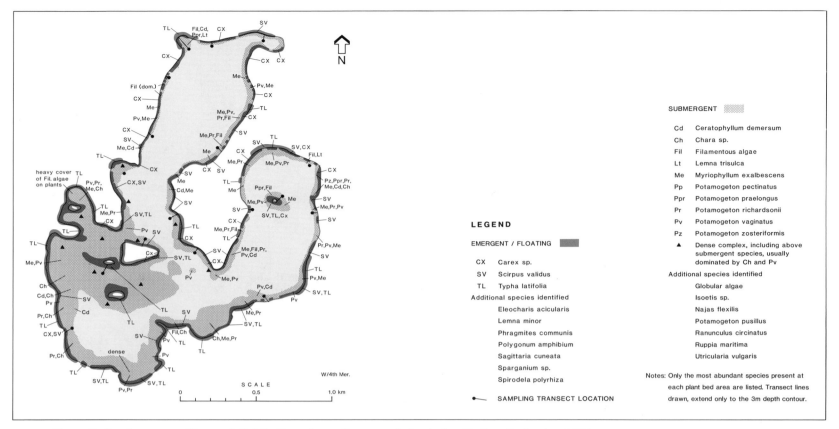

Figure 8. Species composition and distribution of aquatic macrophytes in Lac St. Cyr, September 1984.
SOURCE: Stockerl and Kent 1984.

Table 6. Theoretical external total phosphorus supply to Lac St. Cyr after diversion.

Source		Phosphorus (kg/yr)	Percentage of Total
watershed	forested/bush	151	24
	agricultural/cleared	260	41
	residential/cottage	50	8
sewage[a]		—	—
precipitation/dustfall		54	8
diversion input		119	19
	TOTAL	634	100
annual areal loading (g/m² of lake surface)		0.26	

NOTE: [a]negligible
SOURCE: Mitchell 1987

Biological Characteristics

Plants

The phytoplankton was studied by Alberta Environment in 1983 as part of the diversion impact assessment (Alta. Envir. n.d.[a]). The total biomass is low compared to that in more productive lakes. Blue-green algae are dominant in summer (Table 7) but they rarely have become so abundant that the population would be called a "bloom". There was little difference in biomass and composition between the two basins.

Macrophytes were surveyed by Alberta Environment in 1978 before the start-up of the diversion, and again in 1984 (Stockerl and Kent 1984; Mitchell 1987). Northern watermilfoil (*Myriophyllum exalbescens*) was dominant in 1978, whereas large-sheath pondweed (*Potamogeton vaginatus*) and stonewort (*Chara* sp.) were the dominant species in 1984 (Fig. 8). Populations were very dense in shallow areas in the southern and western parts of the lake during both survey years. Filamentous algal mats associated with

stands of *Potamogeton* spp. were prevalent in 1978 and in 1984, but appeared to be more abundant in 1984.

Invertebrates

There are no data available on the zooplankton of Lac St. Cyr.

Benthic invertebrates were collected with an Ekman dredge in October 1976 from each basin of the lake (Alta. Envir. n.d.[a]; Reynoldson 1977). Flatworms (*Dugesia tigrina*) were dominant in the shallowest areas near shore; leeches (*Nephelopsis obscura, Glossiphonia complanata* and *Helobdella stagnalis*) and caddis fly larvae (Trichoptera: *Leptocella* sp.) were also abundant. In the deepest area of the north basin, the phantom midge larva (Chaoborinae: *Chaoborus* sp.) was dominant, but midge larvae (Chironominae and Tanypodinae) and aquatic earthworms (Oligochaeta) were common as well. *Chaoborus* sp. was also very abundant in the deeper water of the other basins.

Fish

Little is known of the fish and fishery of Lac St. Cyr. Yellow perch and northern pike are present in the lake, and "pickerel" (probably walleye) were stocked as eggs in May 1959. No significant walleye population developed from this stocking (Alta. For. Ld. Wild. n.d.). The lake was reported to be used fairly heavily by pleasure boaters and casual anglers in 1970 (Smith and McMillan 1970). Large yellow perch are the main target for the local sport fishery. The lake is not fished commercially.

Wildlife

Lac St. Cyr is not particularly valuable for wildlife; waterfowl production is low compared to that on surrounding pothole lakes (Doell and Tamjeedi 1978). No documentation of species nesting on the lake exists.

P.A. Mitchell

Table 7. Percentage composition of major algal groups by total biomass in Lac St. Cyr, north and east basins, 1983. Grab samples collected at top, center and bottom of water column.

ALGAL GROUP	May		June		July		Aug.		Sep.		Oct.	
	N	E	N	E	N	E	N	E	N	E	N	E
Total Biomass (mg/L)	1.23	1.49	1.21	0.22	1.94	1.99	0.98	1.89	1.05	1.77	0.28	0.24
Percentage Composition:												
Cyanophyta	0	<1	45	29	72	94	48	62	50	53	18	14
			Aphan.	*Lyngbya*	*Aphan.*	*Aphan.*	*Lyngbya*	*Anabaena*	*Coel.*	*Anabaena*		
				Anabaena	*Anabaena*			*Lyngbya*				
Chlorophyta	9	28	23	19	6	1	2	1	1	2	0	1
		Sphaer.	*Ankyra*									
Euglenophyta	10	0	0	0	0	0	0	0	0	0	0	0
Chrysophyta	9	20	0	<1	<1	<1	1	<1	3	1	0	4
		Dinobryon										
Bacillariophyta	61	34	1	6	4	<1	16	1	6	28	29	10
	Cyclotella	*Cyclotella*								*Fragilaria*	*Fragilaria*	
Cryptophyta	11	17	31	45	14	4	26	5	38	9	53	71
			Crypt.	*Crypt.*			*Crypt.*		*Crypt.*		*Crypt.*	*Crypt.*
Pyrrhophyta	0	0	0	0	3	1	7	31	2	7	0	0
								Ceratium				

NOTE: *Sphaer.* = *Sphaerocystis*; *Aphan.* = *Aphanizomenon*; *Crypt.* = *Cryptomonas*; *Coel.* = *Coelosphaerium*
SOURCE: Alta. Envir. n.d.[a]

References

Alberta Environment. n.d.[a]. Envir. Assess. Div., Envir. Qlty. Monit. Br. Unpubl. data, Edmonton.
———. n.d.[b]. Tech. Serv. Div., Hydrol. Br. Unpubl. data, Edmonton.
———. n.d.[c]. Tech. Serv. Div., Surv. Br. Unpubl. data, Edmonton.
Alberta Forestry, Lands and Wildlife. n.d. Fish Wild. Div. Unpubl. data, Edmonton.
———. 1988. Boating in Alberta. Fish Wild. Div., Edmonton.
———. 1989. Guide to sportfishing. Fish Wild. Div., Edmonton.
Alberta Research Council. 1972. Geological map of Alberta. Nat. Resour. Div., Alta. Geol. Surv., Edmonton.
Brierley, A., W.L. Nikiforuk and L.A. Andriashek. 1988. Soil survey of the County of St. Paul. Interim maps. Alta. Res. Counc., Edmonton.
Doell, B.C. and A. Tamjeedi. 1978. Lac St. Cyr stabilization study. Alta. Envir., Plan. Div., Edmonton.
Energy, Mines and Resources Canada. 1976. National topographic series 1:50 000 73E/14 (1976). Surv. Map. Br., Ottawa.

Environment Canada. 1982. Canadian climate normals, Vol. 7: Bright sunshine (1951–1980). Prep. by Atm. Envir. Serv. Supply Serv. Can., Ottawa.
Mitchell, P.A. 1987. Lac St. Cyr: The impact of river diversion on water quality. Alta. Envir., Poll. Contr. Div., Water Qlty. Contr. Br., Edmonton.
Piquette, K. 1988. Alta. Agric., St. Paul. Pers. comm.
Reynoldson, T. 1977. A preliminary assessment of the effects of diversion on Lac St. Cyr. Alta. Envir., Poll. Contr. Div., Water Qlty. Contr. Br., Edmonton.
Smith, A. and B. McMillan. 1970. Lac St. Cyr. Alta. Ld. For., Fish Wild. Div. Unpubl. rep., Edmonton.
Stockerl, E.C. and R.L. Kent. 1984. Lac St. Cyr aquatic macrophyte survey 1984. Prep. for Alta. Envir., Poll. Contr. Div., Water Qlty. Contr. Br., Edmonton.
Strong, W.L. and K.R. Leggat. 1981. Ecoregions of Alberta. Alta. En. Nat. Resour., Resour. Eval. Plan. Div., Edmonton.
Wyatt, F.A., J.D. Newton, W.E. Bowser and W. Odynsky. 1944. Soil survey of Wainwright-Vermilion sheet. Alta. Soil Surv. Rep. No. 13, Univ. Alta. Bull. No. 42. Univ. Alta., Edmonton.

LAC STE. ANNE

MAP SHEETS: 83G/9, 10

LOCATION: Tp54, 55 R3, 4 W5

LAT/LONG: 53°42'N 114°25'W

West of the city of Edmonton lies a large, popular recreational lake known as Lac Ste. Anne. It is a special lake for many people because of its long history and spiritual symbolism, and because of its recreational attractiveness. Located in the County of Lac Ste. Anne, it is reached easily from Edmonton: take Highway 16 west to the Highway 43 turnoff, then turn north and drive for 10 km. Take Secondary Road 633 west for 10 km to the summer village of Alberta Beach on the east end of the lake (Fig. 1). There are access points all around the lake, but Alberta Beach is a centre of activity for most visitors on summer weekends.

The recorded history of Lac Ste. Anne goes back to 1843 when Father Jean Baptiste Thibault established a mission on the south shore where Mission Creek enters the lake. Before Father Thibault renamed the lake for his patron saint, it was called by the Cree name *Manitou Sakhahigan*, which means "Lake of the Spirit" (Holmgren and Holmgren 1976). Long before Europeans arrived, the lake was visited by the Cree and other native people because the water was thought to have healing properties (Alta. Cult. Multicult. n.d.). Even today, native people from a wide area gather at the mission site for a few days in July to celebrate the Christian faith and bathe in the waters of Lac Ste. Anne, as they have since 1889.

The Alexis Indian Reserve 133 is located on the northwest shore of the lake. The Alexis Band of Stoney Indians settled on their traditional hunting grounds at Lac Ste. Anne after Treaty No. 6 was signed in 1876 (Alta. Native Aff. 1986).

The summer village of Alberta Beach was established by the Canadian Northern Railway shortly after the turn of the century. Castle Island, at the east end of the lake, was bought by Viscount Charles de Gaze; he started building a stone castle on the island in 1890, but it was never completed. Eventually the island was subdivided and incorporated into a summer village (Alta. Beach Dist. Pioneers Archives Soc. 1982). Now there are seven summer villages and a number of subdivisions around the lakeshore (Fig. 2).

Lac Ste. Anne becomes quite green in midsummer, but this does not deter the crowds of people who swim at the sandy beach along the east shore. Fishing for northern pike, lake whitefish, walleye and yellow perch is an equally popular activity. Lac Ste. Anne, all inlet streams and the outlet are closed to fishing during designated periods in spring (Alta. For. Ld. Wild. 1989). Since about 1986, a popular and productive winter sport fishery for perch has developed, and perch up to 0.7 kg have been caught (Watters 1989). The lake supports commercial and domestic fisheries as well as the sport fishery.

Other activities include sightseeing, power boating, sailing, water skiing and wind surfing in summer, and snowmobiling and cross-country skiing in winter. Large boats may be launched at Alberta Beach and at the narrows, and there are several other boat access points around the shore (Fig. 2). In posted areas, all boats are prohibited, or power-driven boats are subject to a maximum speed of 12 km/hour (Alta. For. Ld. Wild. 1988).

Camping facilities at Lac Ste. Anne include two public campgrounds and several commercial campgrounds. The public campground at Alberta Beach is operated by the summer village and has a beach, a public boat launch, boat rentals, a concession, flush toilets and showers, with 80 serviced campsites and about 20 unserviced campsites. It is open from mid-May to the end of September. An Alberta Transportation and Utilities campground is located along Highway 43 near the hamlet of Gunn (Fig. 2); it has pump water, a

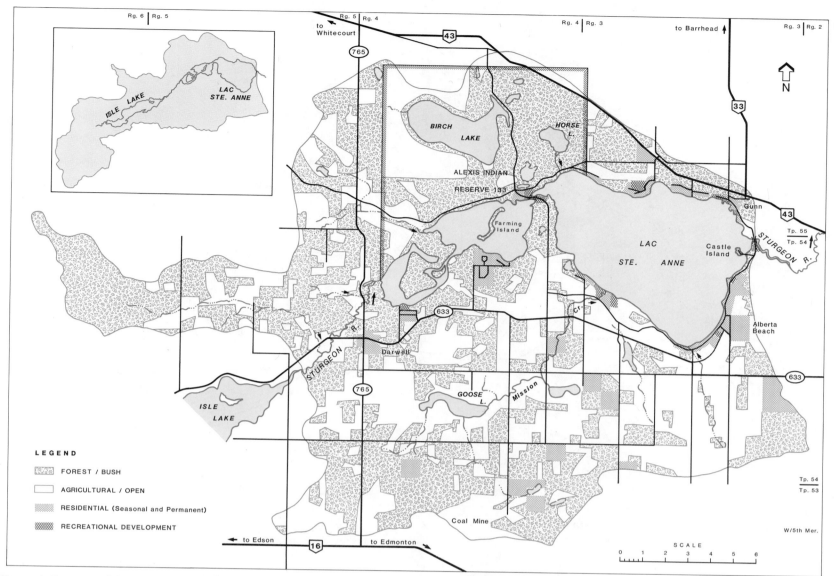

Figure 1. Features of the immediate drainage basin of Lac Ste. Anne. Inset shows entire drainage basin.
SOURCES: Alta. Envir. n.d.[b]; En. Mines Resour. Can. 1974; 1975. Updated with 1985 aerial photos.

Table 1. Characteristics of Lac Ste. Anne drainage basin.

area (excluding lake) (km²)[a]	619
soil[b]	Orthic and Dark Gray Luvisols
bedrock geology[c]	Wapiti Formation (Upper Cretaceous): sandstone, mudstone, bentonite, scattered coal beds; nonmarine
terrain[b]	undulating to strongly rolling
ecoregion[d]	Moist Mixedwood Subregion of Boreal Mixedwood
dominant vegetation[d]	trembling aspen, balsam poplar
mean annual inflow (m³)[a, e]	26.4 x 10⁶
mean annual sunshine (h)[f]	2 264

NOTE: [e]excluding groundwater inflow
SOURCES: [a]Alta. Envir. n.d.[b]; [b]Macyk and Veauvy 1977; [c]Alta. Res. Counc. 1972; [d]Strong and Leggat 1981; [f]Envir. Can. 1982

Table 2. Characteristics of Lac Ste. Anne.

elevation (m)[a, b]	723.21
surface area (km²)[a, b]	54.5
volume (m³)[a, b]	263 x 10⁶
maximum depth (m)[a, b]	9.0
mean depth (m)[a, b]	4.8
shoreline length (km)[c]	63.6
mean annual lake evaporation (mm)[d]	642
mean annual precipitation (mm)[d]	549
mean residence time (yr)[d, e]	12
control structure[f]	partial weir

NOTES: [a]on date of sounding: June 1965; [e]excluding groundwater inflow
SOURCES: [b]Alta. Envir. n.d.[c]; [c]En. Mines Resour. Can. 1974; [d]Alta. Envir. n.d.[b]; [f]Card 1969

kitchen shelter and 25 campsites. A grocery store and other consumer services are located at Alberta Beach and at Gunn. Also near Gunn is a University of Alberta biological station. A large area of Crown land south of the narrows and an area south of Horse Island at the west end are reserved for a provincial park, but as of 1989, the park was still in the planning stage.

Drainage Basin Characteristics

The drainage basin of Lac Ste. Anne is more than 11 times larger than the area of the lake and includes Isle and Birch lakes (Fig. 1, Tables

1, 2). The main inlet is the Sturgeon River, which flows from Isle Lake into the southwestern arm at the west end of Lac Ste. Anne. Other inflowing creeks are small and flow only intermittently. The outflow is the Sturgeon River, which leaves the lake at the eastern end, north of Alberta Beach. The Sturgeon River eventually flows into Big Lake and the North Saskatchewan River.

The terrain in the drainage basin is undulating to strongly rolling, typical of hummocky moraine. The dominant soils are Orthic Gray Luvisols that developed on medium-textured to moderately fine-textured glacial till. These soils have severe or very severe limitations for agriculture. Soils presently under cultivation are Dark Gray Luvi-

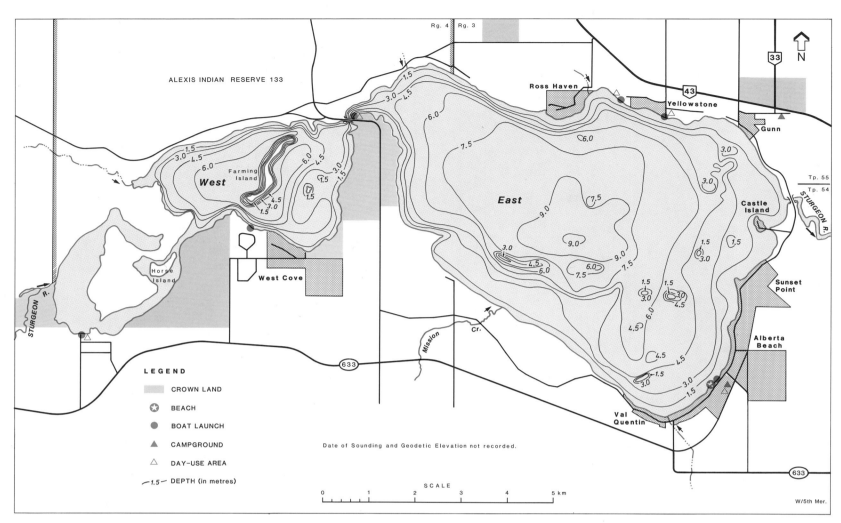

Figure 2. Bathymetry and shoreline features of Lac Ste. Anne.
BATHYMETRY SOURCE: Alta. Envir. n.d.[c].

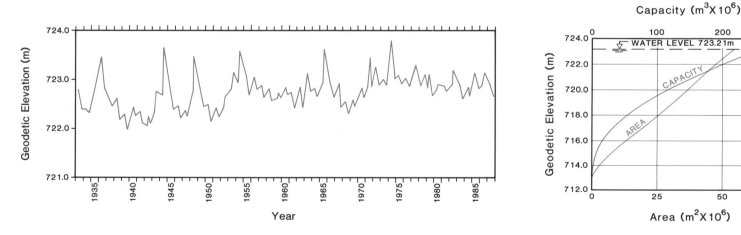

Figure 3. Water level of Lac Ste. Anne, 1933 to 1987.
SOURCE: Alta. Envir. n.d.[c].

Figure 4. Area/capacity curve for Lac Ste. Anne.
SOURCE: Alta. Envir. n.d.[c].

sols, which have less severe limitations for agriculture. Sand lenses occur throughout the watershed, and beach sands are present at the east end of the lake and at a few other areas along the shoreline (Macyk and Veauvy 1977).

The vegetation in the watershed is typical of the region. Trembling aspen grows on higher ground, and balsam poplar grows near the lakeshore. In 1971, 46% of the land surrounding Lac Ste. Anne was forested, mostly with deciduous mixed forest. Willow and black spruce grew in wet areas, and there were small areas of coniferous-dominated forest (Renewable Resour. Consult. Serv. Ltd. 1971). Air photos taken in the 1980s show a similar percentage of forested land.

Crops grown within the basin include canola, peas, oats and barley on the land east and south of the east basin, and hay and pasture in the western and northern parts of the watershed (Olson 1988). A small portion of TransAlta Utilities' Whitewood coal mine

extends into the southern part of the basin. Cottage development around the shoreline, with over 2 000 cottages, is dense compared to that around most Alberta lakes.

Lake Basin Characteristics

Lac Ste. Anne is made up of two basins connected by a narrow passage, which is spanned by a bridge. The east basin is about 9.5–km long and contains the deepest water (9 m; Fig. 2). The west basin is smaller and has a maximum depth of 6 m. The narrow, coiled, sloughlike southwestern arm was not sounded when the bathymetric survey was made, but it is very shallow, perhaps only a metre or so in depth. Lac Ste. Anne is about 15–km long including the southwestern arm, and 7–km wide at its widest point. In both basins, the bottom slopes gradually toward the centre; in the west basin the slope is fairly steep in the area of Farming Island.

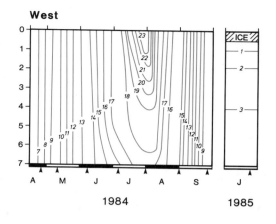

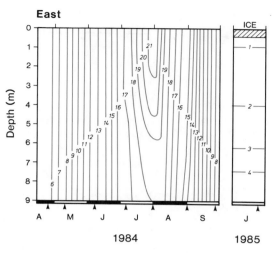

Figure 5. Temperature (°C) of Lac Ste. Anne, west and east basins, 1984. Arrows indicate sampling dates.
SOURCE: Alta. Envir. n.d.[a].

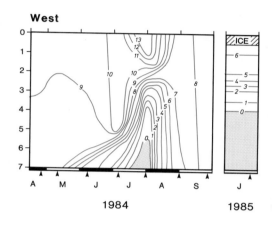

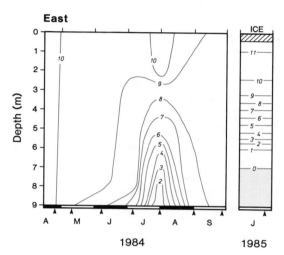

Figure 6. Dissolved oxygen (mg/L) in Lac Ste. Anne, west and east basins, 1984. Arrows indicate sampling dates.
SOURCE: Alta. Envir. n.d.[a].

A rock-and-timber weir was built on the outlet in 1951 by the provincial government (Card 1969), but since then it has been partially removed. The downstream channel controls the level of the lake, but the weir does help to maintain minimum lake levels.

Water levels have been recorded since 1933 (Fig. 3). The average water level increased very slightly after the weir was built. The level has fluctuated between elevations of 721.99 m in 1939 and 723.79 m in 1974, a difference of 1.8 m. Between 1980 and 1987, however, the level has varied by only 0.57 m. Because the lake bottom slopes gradually, a small change in water level results in a relatively large change in surface area (Fig. 4).

Water Quality

Lac Ste. Anne was sampled monthly in 1984 and 1985 by Alberta Environment (Alta. Envir. n.d.[a]; 1989) and weekly during the summer of 1988 by Alberta Environment and volunteer citizens from several summer villages on the lakeshore (Nelson and Mitchell 1988).

Lac Ste. Anne is a freshwater lake (Table 3); total dissolved solids are low, and the dominant ions are bicarbonate and calcium. Concentrations of most major ions are slightly lower in the west basin than in the east basin.

The water column in both basins mixes periodically throughout the summer, but on calm days the lake may thermally stratify, as occurred at the beginning of August 1984 (Fig. 5). This results in rapid oxygen depletion at the bottom, so that at times the water over the sediments is anoxic (Fig. 6). In winter, oxygen depletion in the west basin is rapid. In January 1985, the deepest water in both basins

Table 3. Major ions and related water quality variables for Lac Ste. Anne. Average concentrations in mg/L; pH in pH units. Composite samples from the euphotic zone collected 7 times from 25 Apr. to 26 Sep. 1984. S.E. = standard error.

	West		East	
	Mean	S.E.	Mean	S.E.
pH (range)	8.1–9.0	—	8.2–8.7	—
total alkalinity (CaCO₃)	144	5.0	152	2.6
specific conductivity (μS/cm)	288	11.4	305	5.0
total dissolved solids (calculated)	156	6.5	165	2.8
total hardness (CaCO₃)	98	5.8	112	2.8
total particulate carbon	3	0.5	2	0.3
dissolved organic carbon	11	1.8	9	1.5
HCO₃	162	8.6	176	4.7
CO₃	<5	—	<6	—
Mg	8	0.2	9	0.1
Na	16	0.7	16	0.7
K	7	0.1	7	0.2
Cl	2	0.1	2	0
SO₄	8	0.8	10	0.8
Ca	27	2.5	30	1.1

SOURCE: Alta. Envir. n.d.[a], Naquadat stations 01AT05EA2044 (east), 01AT05EA2045 (west)

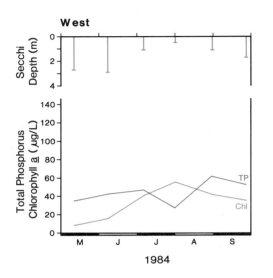
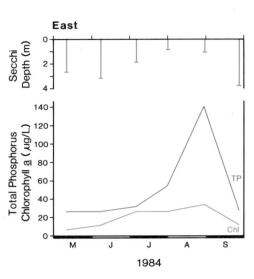

Figure 7. Total phosphorus, chlorophyll *a* and Secchi depth in Lac Ste. Anne, west and east basins, 1984.
SOURCE: Alta. Envir. n.d.[a].

was anoxic, but the dissolved oxygen concentration at the surface in the east basin was almost twice that in the west basin.

Lac Ste. Anne is eutrophic. As algal blooms proliferate in late summer, the water becomes turbid with algae, and Secchi depths decline (Fig. 7). The west basin generally has higher concentrations of chlorophyll *a* (Table 4) than the east basin, although in 1984, average phosphorus levels were similar. Total phosphorus concentrations in the east basin peaked in late August (Fig. 7). The source of much of this nutrient is the bottom sediments, which typically release phosphorus as the water warms and bacterial activity reduces oxygen levels at the bottom of the lake. In 1984, the internal load was estimated to exceed 6 000 kg of total phosphorus, which is nearly equivalent to the phosphorus supply from external sources (Table 5). The large total supply from internal and external sources results in a highly productive lake.

Biological Characteristics

Plants

The phytoplankton of Lac Ste. Anne was assessed during the Alberta Environment water quality study in 1984 and 1985 (Alta. Envir. n.d.[a]). Two or three species of *Anabaena*, a blue-green alga, were dominant in late summer in both 1984 and 1985. In July 1984, *A. planktonica* was the most abundant species in the east basin (Table 6), whereas *A. spiroides* and *A. flos-aquae* were the most abundant species in the west basin. Diatoms were prevalent in spring and fall both years; *Stephanodiscus niagarae* and *Melosira granulata* were important species. The species composition of phytoplankton in the two basins was generally similar in summer 1984 and 1985, except that there were large blooms of the diatom *S. niagarae* in the west basin but not in the east basin; the total biomass was greater in the west basin on most sampling dates.

Emergent aquatic vegetation was surveyed as part of a 1971 wildlife and fisheries study in the Sturgeon River basin (Renewable Resour. Consult. Serv. Ltd. 1971). In the shallow southwestern arm of the west basin, common cattail (*Typha latifolia*) and sedge (*Carex* sp.) were by far the most abundant types of plants along the shore and only about 2% of the shoreline was devoid of vegetation. Submergent vegetation was sparse in this area, although duckweed (*Lemna* sp.) was common. In the main part of the west basin, bulrush (*Scirpus* sp.) was more abundant than in shallow areas to the west, and submergent species were abundant. In the main basin, 63% of the shoreline was occupied by bulrush, and bur-reed (*Sparganium* sp.) was also abundant. Submergent species present were those typical of many lakes in the area: various species of pondweed (*Potamogeton* spp.), northern watermilfoil (*Myriophyllum exalbescens*), coontail (*Ceratophyllum demersum*) and duckweed (*Lemna* sp.).

Table 4. Nutrient, chlorophyll *a* and Secchi depth data for Lac Ste. Anne. Average concentrations in µg/L. Composite samples from the euphotic zone collected 7 times from 25 Apr. to 26 Sep. 1984. S.E. = standard error.

	West		East	
	Mean	S.E.	Mean	S.E.
total phosphorus	44	4.1	48	16.0
total dissolved phosphorus	12	0.6	18	8.6
total Kjeldahl nitrogen	1 181	164.7	919	56.4
NO_3 + NO_2–nitrogen	<5	—	<3[a]	—
NH_4–nitrogen	44	27.7	24	6.9
iron	<61	—	<27	—
chlorophyll *a*	32.7	7.48	17.9	4.06
Secchi depth (m)	1.6	0.33	2.2	0.40

NOTE: [a]n = 6
SOURCE: Alta. Envir. n.d.[a], Naquadat stations 01AT05EA2044 (east), 01AT05EA2045 (west)

Table 5. Theoretical total phosphorus loading to Lac Ste. Anne from external sources.

Source		Phosphorus (kg/yr)	Percentage of Total
immediate watershed	forested/bush	1 768	25
	agricultural/cleared	2 740	38
	residential/cottage	553	8
sewage[a]		153	2
precipitation/dustfall		1 190	16
inflow from other lakes		767	11
	TOTAL	7 171	100

annual areal loading (g/m² of lake surface) 0.13

NOTE: [a]unmeasured: assumes 4% of all sewage effluent from residences and camps enters the lake, as in Mitchell 1982
SOURCE: Alta. Envir. 1989

Invertebrates

There are no recent data on the zooplankton of Lac Ste. Anne. A fisheries study in 1969 (Lane 1971) included identification to genus and an estimate of abundance; the genera found (*Daphnia*, *Cyclops* and *Diaptomus*) are typical of many other lakes in the area.

Benthic invertebrate samples were collected in 1969 (Table 7) from several depths and substrate types (Lane 1971). The am-

Table 6. Percentage composition of major algal groups by total biomass in Lac Ste. Anne, west and east basins, 1984. Composite samples collected from the euphotic zone.

ALGAL GROUP	25 Apr. W	25 Apr. E	09 May W	09 May E	07 June W	07 June E	05 July W	05 July E	31 July W	31 July E	30 Aug. W	30 Aug. E	26 Sep. W	26 Sep. E
Total Biomass (mg/L)	3.18	2.08	6.10	1.59	2.39	2.80	15.22	9.89	32.59	26.80	5.73	5.77	20.14	3.68
Percentage Composition:														
Cyanophyta	0	0	0	1	32	50	85	66	95	93	66	43	5	52
					Anabaena ——————————————————————————————————→									
Chlorophyta	7	21	2	16	9	2	4	1	0	1	3	5	2	10
		Paulschultzia												
Euglenophyta	0	0	0	0	0	0	0	0	0	0	0	5	0	0
Chrysophyta	6	13	2	16	9	0	1	0	0	1	1	2	0	5
Bacillariophyta	42	33	92	52	47	45	7	30	1	0	18	24	91	30
	Stephanodiscus ————————————————————————————→												*Steph.*	
	Synedra					*Fragilaria*	*Fragilaria* ——→				*Melosira* ————————→			
Cryptophyta	44	32	3	13	3	1.5	2	0	1	2	7	4	2	1
	Cryptomonas ——→													
Pyrrhophyta	0	1	0	2	0	2	2	3	2	4	6	17	0	2

NOTE: *Steph.* = *Stephanodiscus*
SOURCE: Alta. Envir. n.d.[a]

phipods *Hyalella azteca* and *Gammarus lacustris* were abundant over sandy substrates in the east basin at depths of less than 4 m. These species were much less abundant in west basin samples, perhaps because the substrate is clay or silt even in shallow water. Amphipods formed the largest percentage of organisms in whitefish stomachs assessed during the same study. Midge larvae (Chironomidae) were numerically dominant and were found on fine-grained substrates to the maximum depth in both basins. The phantom midge *Chaoborus* sp. accounted for 18% of the average total number of organisms in west basin samples, but was rare in east basin samples.

Fish

The game fish in Lac Ste. Anne include northern pike, walleye, yellow perch and lake whitefish; other species in the lake include white sucker, burbot, spottail shiner and brook stickleback (Lane 1971). Fish and Wildlife Division manages Lac Ste. Anne for sport, commercial and domestic fishing. Sport fishing is very popular, largely because the lake is so close to Edmonton.

The fisheries resources of Lac Ste. Anne were surveyed in 1969 (Lane 1971). For a series of 18– to 24–hour test nettings during June to August, the average total catch of fish per 275 m of net was 93.3 fish, weighing a total of 72 kg. The average total number of lake whitefish, perch and walleye caught in the east basin was 43% greater than in the west basin. The average total annual harvest of fish until 1969 (number of years not provided) was estimated at 56 700 kg for the sport, commercial and domestic fisheries combined. Fifty percent were whitefish, 40% were pike and 10% were walleye. The sport fishery accounted for about half of the total harvest. Perch were considered unimportant except as a food base for pike and walleye.

Between 1982 and 1988, the average annual commercial harvest was 21 762 kg for whitefish, 3 188 kg for northern pike and 281 kg for walleye. The annual harvest varied little over these years. There is no information on harvest by the domestic fishery (Alta. For. Ld. Wild. n.d.).

An intensive creel survey was conducted at Alberta Beach between 15 May and 31 August 1984 to assess the magnitude of the sport fish harvest (Table 8). It was estimated that the total walleye harvest was 3 360 fish (2 856 kg) including 1 440 fish caught during a fishing derby. The harvest per unit effort for walleye was 0.12/angler-hour for the entire summer; it was highest in May (0.31/angler-hour) and nil in July and August. In comparison, the harvest per unit effort for walleye in 21 lakes in northern Alberta between 1984 and 1988 was 0.09/angler-hour (Sullivan 1988). The total northern pike

Table 7. Benthic invertebrate fauna of Lac Ste. Anne, 1969. Average number per m² and average total wet and dry weight. Samples collected with a 15–cm Ekman dredge from various depths and substrate types, June to Aug.

	East Basin	West Basin
Amphipoda		
Hyalella azteca	697	4.4
Gammarus lacustris	658	—
Annelida		
Hirudinea	62	4.4
Oligochaeta	102	76
Mollusca		
Sphaeriidae	98	62
Gastropoda	98	—
Trichoptera	4.4	—
Diptera		
Chironomidae	960	964
Chaoborus sp.	2.7	253
Ceratopogonidae	4.4	53
Miscellaneous	8.8	1.8
Mean Total Number	2 695	1 418
Mean Wet Weight (g/m²)	66.5	46.6
Mean Dry Weight (g/m²)	8.7	6.1
Mean Volume (mL)	84	68
Number of Samples	50	26

SOURCE: Lane 1971

harvest, including fish caught during the derby, was 6 700 pike (6 400 kg). The pike catch rate over the entire survey period was 0.40/angler-hour and the harvest rate was 0.21/angler-hour, in comparison to a harvest rate of 0.23 for the 21 lakes surveyed between 1984 and 1988. The catch per unit effort in 1984 was highest in late May and lowest in early August. Only 26 yellow perch and 4 lake whitefish were observed harvested during the survey period; whitefish are caught more frequently in winter and early spring than in summer.

Researchers at the University of Alberta biological station at Lac Ste. Anne have studied the environmental physiology of fish in the lake for many years (Mackay 1989). Over 50 research papers and theses have been produced, including such topics as the activity and

Table 8. Estimated angler numbers, effort and harvest from Lac Ste. Anne. Estimates based on creel survey data collected from 15 May to 31 Aug. 1984. A total of 32 weekdays and 29 weekend days and holidays were surveyed; 39 weekdays were not included. Information was collected from 07:00 to 23:00. Data exclude 2–day fish derby. WE = walleye; NP = northern pike; YP = yellow perch.

	WE	NP	YP	Total
number of anglers[a]	—	—	—	5 423
angler-hours[b]	—	—	—	16 452
total number fish harvested[c]	1 922	3 082	26	5 030
total yield (kg)	1 634	2 928	—	4 562
mean weight (g)	850	950	—	—
catch/angler-hour	0.13	0.40	—	0.53
harvest/angler-hour[b, c]	0.12	0.21	—	0.33
harvest/angler[a, c]	0.37	0.64	—	1.01

NOTES: [a]observed no. anglers = 878; [b]observed hours = 2 664; [c]based on observed no. fish kept: WE = 325, NP = 564, YP = 26
SOURCE: Sullivan 1986

feeding patterns of northern pike (Diana et al. 1977; Diana 1979; 1980), aging techniques and growth in yellow perch (Norris 1984), food and distribution of yellow perch and walleye (Langer 1974) and growth and reproductive success in burbot (Boag 1989). These studies have shown that feeding activity in northern pike is greatest in late May and June as water temperatures are increasing and spawning is completed. Pike are inactive more than 90% of the time, but they move extensively in the lake during periods of activity, and may move a kilometre or more in a day. Low water temperatures do not slow their movement, but do decrease their feeding. Perch in Lac Ste. Anne are slow-growing and short-lived, and may become stunted unless predation (by anglers or natural predators like pike) is high. In the early 1980s, the perch population showed all the characteristics of stunting: slow growth, high mortality and early sexual maturity at a small size. But in later years there seemed to be a change in the population because anglers were catching larger perch again.

Wildlife

The wildlife of Lac Ste. Anne was studied in 1971 as part of a wildlife and fisheries study in the Sturgeon River basin (Renewable Resour. Consult. Serv. Ltd. 1971). A total of 1 394 dabbling and diving ducks were observed during a 1–week boat survey in May. The majority of breeding birds were Mallards, American Widgeon and Blue-winged Teal. Diving ducks such as Lesser Scaup and Common Goldeneye were much less abundant than dabbling ducks. The main basin had higher numbers of pairs and broods than the areas west of the narrows. It was suggested that the solid band of cattail in the far western section was less favourable habitat than the bulrush and bur-reed emergent vegetation in the eastern basin. Other species of water birds observed during the study included Western, Red-necked, Eared and Horned grebes, American Coot and Great Blue Heron. There were two nesting colonies of Western Grebes on the lake.

Beaver, muskrats and mink are present in the Lac Ste. Anne area, and the habitat is suitable for white-tailed and mule deer and moose (Renewable Resour. Consult. Serv. Ltd. 1971).

P.A. Mitchell

References

Alberta Beach and District Pioneers and Archives Society. 1982. Spirit and trails of Lac Ste. Anne. Alta. Beach Dist. Pioneers Archives Soc., Alberta Beach.

Alberta Culture and Multiculturalism. n.d. Hist. Resour. Div., Hist. Sites Serv. Unpubl. data, Edmonton.

Alberta Environment. n.d.[a]. Envir. Assess. Div., Envir. Qlty. Monit. Br. Unpubl. data, Edmonton.

———. n.d.[b]. Tech. Serv. Div., Hydrol. Br. Unpubl. data, Edmonton.

———. n.d.[c]. Tech. Serv. Div., Surv. Br. Unpubl. data, Edmonton.

———. 1989. Lac Ste. Anne. Envir. Assess. Div., Envir. Qlty. Monit. Br., Edmonton.

Alberta Forestry, Lands and Wildlife. n.d. Fish Wild. Div. Unpubl. data, Edmonton.

———. 1988. Boating in Alberta. Fish Wild. Div., Edmonton.

———. 1989. Guide to sportfishing. Fish Wild. Div., Edmonton.

Alberta Native Affairs. 1986. A guide to native communities in Alberta. Native Aff. Secret., Edmonton.

Alberta Research Council. 1972. Geological map of Alberta. Nat. Resour. Div., Alta. Geol. Surv., Edmonton.

Boag, T.D. 1989. Aspects of growth and fecundity in burbot, *Lota lota* L., from two Alberta lakes. MSc thesis. Univ. Alta., Edmonton.

Card, J.R. 1969. Lake level stabilization Lac Ste. Anne: Consideration of simple outlet control structure. Alta. Envir., Water Resour. Div., Edmonton.

Diana, J.S. 1979. An energy budget for northern pike (*Esox lucius*) in Lac Ste. Anne. PhD thesis. Univ. Alta., Edmonton.

———. 1980. Diel activity pattern and swimming speeds in northern pike (*Esox lucius*) in Lac Ste. Anne, Alberta. Can. J. Fish. Aquat. Sci. 37:1454–1458.

———, W.C. Mackay and M. Ehrman. 1977. Movements and habitat preference of northern pike (*Esox lucius*) in Lac Ste. Anne, Alberta. Trans. Am. Fish. Soc. 106:560–565.

Energy, Mines and Resources Canada. 1974, 1975. National topographic series 1:50 000 83G/9 (1974), 83G/10 (1974), 83G/15 (1975), 83G/16 (1975). Surv. Map. Br., Ottawa.

Environment Canada. 1982. Canadian climate normals, Vol. 7: Bright sunshine (1951–1980). Prep. by Atm. Envir. Serv. Supply Serv. Can., Ottawa.

Holmgren, E.J. and P.M. Holmgren. 1976. Over 2000 place names of Alberta. 3rd ed. West. Producer Prairie Books, Saskatoon.

Lane, C.B. 1971. A survey of the fishery resources of Isle, Lac Ste. Anne and Matchayaw or Devil's Lake, 1969. Alta. Ld. For., Fish Wild. Div., Surv. Rep. No. 14, Edmonton.

Langer, O.E. 1974. Seasonal variation of food, mouth anatomy and distribution of adult yellow perch (*Perca fluviatilis flavescens*) and yellow walleye (*Stizostedion vitreum vitreum*) in Lac Ste. Anne. MSc thesis. Univ. Alta., Edmonton.

Mackay, W.C. 1989. Univ. Alta., Dept. Zool., Edmonton. Pers. comm.

Macyk, T.M. and C.F. Veauvy. 1977. Detailed soil survey of the Lac Ste. Anne area. Alta. Inst. Pedol. Rep. No. M–77–9. Alta. Res. Counc., Edmonton.

Mitchell, P.A. 1982. Evaluation of the "septic snooper" on Wabamun and Pigeon lakes. Alta. Envir., Poll. Contr. Div., Water Qlty. Contr. Br., Edmonton.

Nelson, L.R. and P.A. Mitchell. 1988. Volunteer citizen's lake monitoring program (1988)—Lac Ste. Anne and Pigeon Lakes. Alta. Envir., Envir. Assess. Div., Envir. Qlty. Monit. Br., Edmonton.

Norris, H.J. 1984. A comparison of aging techniques and growth of yellow perch (*Perca flavescens*) from selected Alberta lakes. MSc thesis. Univ. Alta., Edmonton.

Olson, M. 1988. Alta. Agric., Sangudo Dist. Off., Sangudo. Pers. comm.

Renewable Resources Consulting Services Ltd. 1971. An ecological study of the wildlife and fisheries in the Pembina and Sturgeon River basins. Prep. for Alta. Envir., Water Resour. Div., Edmonton.

Strong, W.L. and K.R. Leggat. 1981. Ecoregions of Alberta. Alta. En. Nat. Resour., Resour. Eval. Plan. Div., Edmonton.

Sullivan, M.G. 1986. Characteristics and impact of the sports fishery at Lac Ste. Anne during May-August 1984. Alta. For. Ld. Wild., Fish Wild. Div., Edmonton.

———. 1988. Alta. For. Ld. Wild., Fish Wild. Div., St. Paul. Pers. comm.

Watters, D. 1989. Alta. For. Ld. Wild., Fish Wild. Div., Edm. Reg. Off., Edmonton. Pers. comm.

SANDY LAKE

D. LeClair

MAP SHEET: 83G/16
LOCATION: Tp55, 56 R1 W5
LAT/LONG: 53°47'N 114°02'W

Sandy Lake is a shallow, extensively developed recreational lake that is popular for its yellow perch fishery. Two summer villages, Sandy Beach and Sunrise Beach, and Pine Sands Subdivision are located on the lakeshore. The lake is situated 55 km northwest of Edmonton in the County of Lac Ste. Anne and the Municipal District of Sturgeon. The town of Morinville, 20 km east of the lake, is the closest large population centre. To drive to the lake from Edmonton, take Highway 2 north to Morinville, then Secondary Road 642 west to the causeway that crosses the lake (Fig. 1).

The lake's name is descriptive of the sandy shoreline and basin. Captain John Palliser noted the lake on his 1865 map, and his assistant, Dr. James Hector, referred in 1859 to "the Sandy Lakes" that were part of the route from Fort Edmonton to Fort Assiniboine (Holmgren and Holmgren 1976).

The Sandy Lake area was probably used by native people prior to European settlement. In 1876, Treaty No. 6 was signed by Plains Cree at Fort Carleton, Saskatchewan. The treaty resulted in the creation of Alexander Indian Reserve 134, located immediately east of Sandy Lake (Fig. 1). Members of the Alexander Band are descended from these nomadic people, who had followed buffalo herds prior to moving to the reserve. The reserve covers 7 244 ha and had a population of 731 people in 1984 (Alta. Native Aff. 1986).

The first settlers arrived in the area late in the 1800s, probably during the 1880s. The main land use at that time was agricultural, but by the 1920s, recreational development became important as well. In 1923, the first subdivision was established on Sandy Lake (Edm. Reg. Plan. Commis. 1979). Development continued fairly steadily until, by 1988, there were more than 1 000 lots within 1.5 km of the shoreline (Edm. Reg. Plan. Commis. n.d.; Yell. Reg. Plan. Commis. n.d.).

There are no public campgrounds at Sandy Lake, but 2 commercially operated campgrounds, with a total of 212 campsites, provide camping and other facilities. As well, an Alberta Transportation day-use area is located on the east side of the lake just north of the causeway (Fig. 2). Facilities include picnic tables, a picnic shelter, toilets, a beach and a boat launch. Another public boat launch, owned by the summer village of Sandy Beach, is located on the western shore just south of the causeway. Recreational activities enjoyed at Sandy Lake include fishing, swimming, power boating and camping in summer, and tobogganing, cross-country skiing, ice fishing and snowmobiling in winter. The single institutional camp on the lake is owned by the Girl Guides of Canada. It is located on the east side of the north basin (Fig. 2).

The two sport fish species in Sandy Lake are yellow perch and northern pike. There are no sport fishing regulations specific to the lake, but general provincial limits and regulations apply (Alta. For. Ld. Wild. 1989). All boats are restricted from entering some posted areas of the lake and power boats are limited to speeds of 12 km/hour or less in other posted areas (Alta. For. Ld. Wild. 1988).

Sandy Lake is very fertile and the water is green during much of the open-water season. The water in the south basin is somewhat clearer and contains less algae than the water in the north basin. Aquatic macrophytes, which grow along most of the shoreline, are particularly abundant at the north end of the lake. Because it is fertile and shallow, the lake has a potential for fish kills in summer and winter. Fish kills have occurred only occasionally, however, most recently during the winter of 1988/89.

Table 1. Characteristics of Sandy Lake drainage basin.

area (excluding lake) (km²)[a]	48.4
soil[b]	Orthic Gray Luvisols, Gray Solodized Solonetz
bedrock geology[c]	Wapiti Formation (Upper Cretaceous): sandstone, mudstone, bentonite, scattered coal beds; nonmarine
terrain[b]	undulating to strongly rolling
ecoregion[d]	Moist Mixedwood Subregion of Boreal Mixedwood
dominant vegetation[b, d]	trembling aspen, balsam poplar
mean annual inflow (m³)[a, e]	1.82 x 10⁶
mean annual sunshine (h)[f]	2 264

NOTE: [e]excluding groundwater inflow
SOURCES: [a]Alta. Envir. n.d.[b]; [b]Twardy and Brocke 1976; [c]Alta. Res. Counc. 1972; [d]Strong and Leggat 1981; [f]Envir. Can. 1982

Table 2. Characteristics of Sandy Lake.

elevation (m)[a, b]	697.54
surface area (km²)[a, b]	11.4
volume (m³)[a, b]	29.4 x 10⁶
maximum depth (m)[a, b]	4.4
mean depth (m)[a, b]	2.6
shoreline length (km)[c]	27.8
mean annual lake evaporation (mm)[d]	664
mean annual precipitation (mm)[d]	504
mean residence time (yr)[d, e]	>100
control structure	none

NOTES: [a]on date of sounding: 14 Aug. 1976; [e]excluding groundwater inflow
SOURCES: [b]Alta. Envir. n.d.[c]; [c]En. Mines Resour. Can. 1975; [d]Alta. Envir. n.d.[b]

Table 3. Major ions and related water quality variables for Sandy Lake. Average concentrations in mg/L; pH in pH units. Composite samples from the euphotic zone collected 7 times from 04 May to 19 Oct. 1988. S.E. = standard error.

	North Basin		South Basin	
	Mean	S.E.	Mean	S.E.
pH (range)	8.6–9.1	—	8.6–9.1	—
total alkalinity (CaCO₃)	304	3.8	322	1.6
specific conductivity (μS/cm)	583	6.1	603	3.0
total dissolved solids (calculated)	340	4.1	354	1.5
total hardness (CaCO₃)	73	2.0	78	1.7
total particulate carbon	15	3.7	4	0.7
dissolved organic carbon	41	1.1	32	1.1
HCO₃	335	10.8	349	7.5
CO₃	19	4.5	22	3.5
Mg	10	0.2	11	0.2
Na	109	1.2	114	1.0
K	13	0.5	14	0.4
Cl	4	0	4	0.1
SO₄	<8	—	<5	—
Ca	13	0.7	13	0.5

SOURCE: Alta. Envir. n.d.[a], Naquadat stations 01AL05EA3400 (north), 01AL05EA3500 (south)

Drainage Basin Characteristics

Sandy Lake drains a small area that is only about 4 times larger than the lake (Tables 1, 2). There are several small water bodies in the drainage basin, but only one drains into Sandy Lake via a stream. This intermittent stream enters the north shore of the lake. There is no active outflow channel, but at high water levels a creek flows from the southeast end of the lake to the Sturgeon River. It last flowed in 1976 (Alta. Envir. n.d.[c]).

The land in the drainage basin is undulating to strongly rolling with few level areas (Twardy and Brocke 1976). Elevations range from about 700 m above sea level at the lakeshore and over much of the watershed, to 745 m on the Alexander Indian Reserve.

The drainage basin is part of the Moist Mixedwood Subregion of the Boreal Mixedwood Ecoregion (Strong and Leggat 1981). Soils are mainly moderately well-drained to well-drained Orthic Gray Luvisols and moderately well-drained to imperfectly drained Gray Solodized Solonetz. Both soils developed on moderately fine textured to medium-textured glacial till. The main tree species on these soils is trembling aspen. Along the shore of Sandy Lake, receding water levels have exposed beach sand soils. These soils are rapidly drained, coarse-textured Orthic Regosols that support a tree cover of trembling aspen, balsam poplar, willow and alder. Organic soils are present throughout the watershed in level to depressional areas where surface water accumulates. They mainly support a vegetative cover of black spruce and tamarack or sedges, grasses, willows and birch (Twardy and Brocke 1976).

Most of the northern half and some of the southern half of the drainage basin has been cleared for agriculture (Fig. 1). Much of the land throughout the drainage basin, however, has moderately severe to severe limitations to agriculture and therefore is not considered prime agricultural land (Twardy and Brocke 1976). Most of the land is suitable for forage production and improved pasture and a smaller amount is suitable only for unimproved pasture.

Nonrenewable resource extraction is not an important industry in the watershed. In 1979, oil and gas were being produced from the Alexander Field, which is located immediately northeast of the lake (Edm. Reg. Plan. Commis. 1979). Coal deposits are present, but their recovery is not economical at present.

Recreation is a major land use in the drainage basin. Except for three small parcels of Crown land, all of the land near the lake is privately owned or lies within the Alexander Indian Reserve (Fig. 2). Between 1923, when the first subdivision was created, and 1977, 953 registered lots were approved in an area that extends approximately 1.5 km from the lakeshore. In August 1977, the Sandy Lake area became subject to the Regulated Lake Shoreland Development Operation Regulations. These regulations restricted major developments until a lakeshore management plan and an area structure plan were prepared. Lake management plans determine the extent of future land developments, allocate land use, and determine ways to minimize environmental impacts and conflicts in the use of the lakeshore. They also recommend preferred lake uses and ways to minimize lake-user conflicts. The area structure plan was adopted by the County of Lac Ste. Anne and the Municipal District of Sturgeon as part of their land-use bylaws in 1981 (Edm. Reg. Plan. Commis. 1979; 1980; 1981). Between 1978 and 1988, 66 lots were registered, resulting in a total of 1 019 lots in the Sandy Lake area (Edm. Reg. Plan. Commis. n.d.; Yell. Reg. Plan. Commis. n.d.). Most of these lots are located on the east and west shores of the north basin in the summer village of Sandy Beach, and on the west shore of the south basin in the summer village of Sunrise Beach.

Lake Basin Characteristics

Sandy Lake is a medium-sized water body that is divided into two basins by a narrows and a causeway (Fig. 2, Table 2). The smaller north basin is shallowest and has a maximum depth of 2.3 m. The south basin reaches a maximum depth of 4.4 m.

The elevation of Sandy Lake has been monitored since 1959 (Fig. 3). The lake generally was at a lower level between 1959 and 1973 than it was between 1974 and 1987. The historic minimum

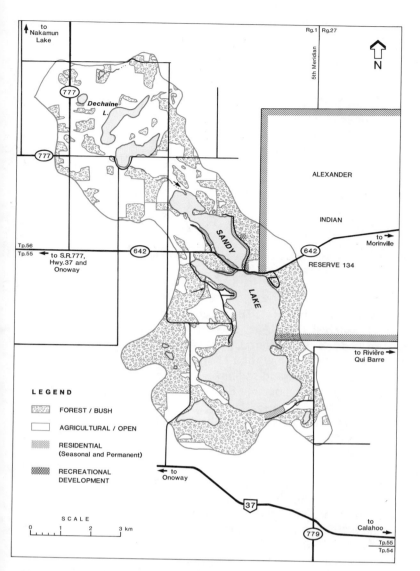

Figure 1. Features of the drainage basin of Sandy Lake.
SOURCES: Alta. Envir. n.d.[b]; En. Mines Resour. Can. 1973; 1974; 1975; 1980. Updated with 1987 aerial photos.

Table 4. Nutrient, chlorophyll *a* and Secchi depth data for Sandy Lake. Average concentrations in μg/L. Composite samples from the euphotic zone collected 7 times from 04 May to 19 Oct. 1988. S.E. = standard error.

	North Basin		South Basin	
	Mean	S.E.	Mean	S.E.
total phosphorus	221	35.2	88	9.4
total dissolved phosphorus	33	2.8	30	1.5
total Kjeldahl nitrogen	3 736	242.5	2 876	120.2
$NO_3 + NO_2$–nitrogen	3	0.4	9	4.6
NH_4–nitrogen	111	62.2	105	39.0
iron	400[a]	99.4	153[a]	17.6
chlorophyll *a*	67.8	13.53	29.9	5.50
Secchi depth (m)	0.6	0.11	1.5	0.25

NOTE: [a]n = 6
SOURCE: Alta. Envir. n.d.[a], Naquadat stations 01AL05EA3400 (north), 01AL05EA3500 (south)

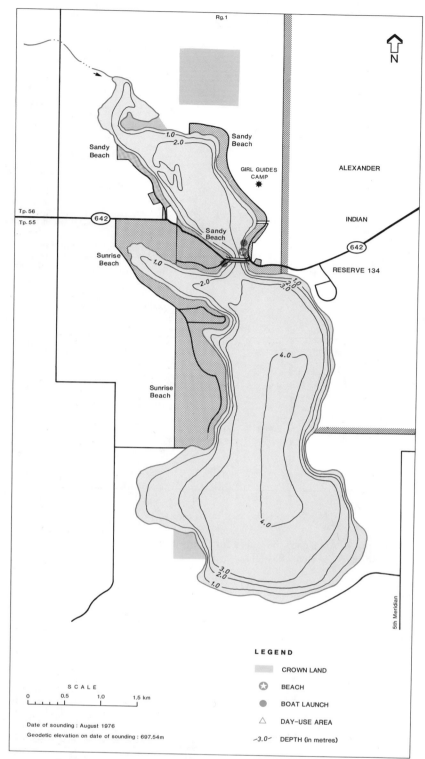

Figure 2. Bathymetry and shoreline features of Sandy Lake.
BATHYMETRY SOURCE: Alta. Envir. n.d.[c].

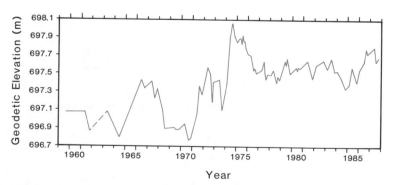

Figure 3. Water level of Sandy Lake, 1959 to 1987.
SOURCE: Alta. Envir. n.d.[c].

level, 696.76 m, was recorded in 1970, and the historic maximum level, 698.06 m, was recorded in 1974, a year of high precipitation. This historic fluctuation of 1.30 m would result in a change in the lake's area on the order of 20% (Fig. 4).

Water Quality

Water quality in Sandy Lake was monitored by Alberta Environment approximately monthly during the open-water season, and once in

Table 5. Theoretical total phosphorus loading to Sandy Lake from external sources.

		North Basin		South Basin	
		Phosphorus (kg/yr)	% of Total	Phosphorus (kg/yr)	% of Total
immediate watershed	forested/bush	62	8	146	18
	agricultural/cleared	347	47	420	51
	residential/cottage	42	6	42	5
sewage[a]		16	2	11	1
precipitation/dustfall		52	7	200	25
inflow from other lake		219	30	—	—
	TOTAL	738	100	819	100
annual areal loading (g/m² of lake surface)		0.32		0.09	

NOTE: [a]unmeasured: assumes 4% of all sewage effluent from residences and camps enters the lake, as in Mitchell 1982
SOURCES: Mitchell 1983; 1989

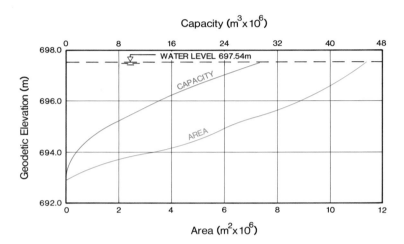

Figure 4. Area/capacity curve for Sandy Lake.
SOURCE: Alta. Envir. n.d.[c].

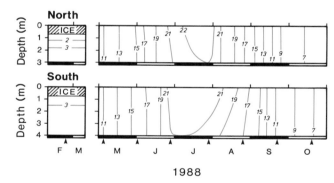

1988

Figure 5. Temperature (°C) of Sandy Lake, north and south basins, 1988. Arrows indicate sampling dates.
SOURCE: Alta. Envir. n.d.[a].

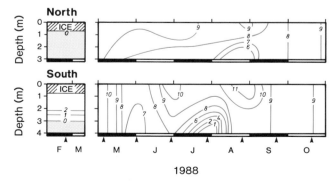

1988

Figure 6. Dissolved oxygen (mg/L) in Sandy Lake, north and south basins, 1988. Arrows indicate sampling dates.
SOURCE: Alta. Envir. n.d.[a].

late winter, in each of 1978, 1979, 1988 and 1989 (Alta. Envir. n.d.[a]; Mitchell 1983; Alta. Envir. 1984).

The lake has well-buffered, fresh water with a calcium concentration that is relatively low for a prairie lake (Table 3). The dominant ions are bicarbonate and sodium.

Sandy Lake is shallow and does not thermally stratify during the open-water period (Fig. 5). During 1988, the concentration of dissolved oxygen in the north basin became slightly depleted near the sediments during August (Fig. 6). Depletion was more severe in the south basin, where the concentration declined to about 1 mg/L near the sediments in late July. Dissolved oxygen concentrations often become very low during winter. In the north basin in March 1988 and February 1989, the entire water column was anoxic. In the south basin, the concentrations immediately below the ice were 2.1 mg/L in March 1988 and 2.7 mg/L in February 1989. On both dates, the water in the south basin was anoxic at depths of 3 m or more. A severe fish kill occurred in March 1989.

The two basins of Sandy Lake differ in trophic status. The north basin, which is most fertile (Table 4), is hyper-eutrophic and the south basin is eutrophic. In 1988, the maximum chlorophyll *a* concentration in the north basin was 125 µg/L and the maximum total phosphorus concentration was 410 µg/L (Fig. 7). These variables were considerably lower in the south basin in 1988: chlorophyll *a* reached a maximum of 53 µg/L and total phosphorus reached a maximum value of 125 µg/L (Fig. 7). In both basins, these maxima occurred during September.

Chlorophyll *a* concentrations can vary considerably among years. This point is illustrated by average open-water chlorophyll *a* data (µg/L) for Sandy Lake (Alta. Envir. n.d.[a]):

	North Basin	South Basin
1978	59	35
1979	30	11
1988	68	30

In both basins, the chlorophyll *a* concentration was, on average, about 2 to 3 times higher in 1978 and 1988 than in 1979. The wide variation between years is probably related to differences in climatic conditions. The difference between basins reflects differences in total phosphorus loading.

Total phosphorus loading to Sandy Lake from external sources is estimated to be 1 557 kg/year (Table 5). The supply of phosphorus to the north basin (738 kg/year) is smaller than the supply to the south basin (819 kg/year), but when the supply is expressed per unit of lake surface, the annual areal loading to the smaller north basin (0.32 g/m² of lake surface) is considerably higher than the annual areal loading to the south basin (0.09 g/m² of lake surface). In both basins, the largest external source of total phosphorus (approximately 50%) is runoff from agricultural and cleared land. In the north

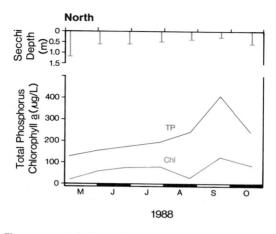

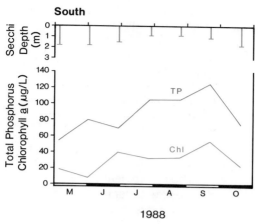

Figure 7. Total phosphorus, chlorophyll *a* and Secchi depth in Sandy Lake, north and south basins, 1988.
SOURCE: Alta. Envir. n.d.[a].

basin, inflow from the upstream lake is the second largest contributor (30%), whereas in the south basin, precipitation and dustfall provide the second highest load (25%). Sewage inputs, at 2% and less, are minor. Sewage inputs were not measured directly at Sandy Lake; they were calculated from data collected for other lakes. Total phosphorus loading from internal sources such as sediments has not been estimated for Sandy Lake. The high phosphorus peaks recorded in both basins in September 1988 (Fig. 7) suggest that internal loading is substantial and would account for a large part of the total phosphorus loading to the surface waters.

Biological Characteristics

Plants

The phytoplankton in Sandy Lake has not been studied intensively. One sample was taken from the south basin on 18 August 1983 by Alberta Environment (Alta. Envir. n.d.[a]). The biomass of 17.91 mg/L comprised 75% diatoms (Bacillariophyta), 13% green algae (Chlorophyta) and 7% blue-green algae (Cyanophyta). The diatom *Stephanodiscus niagarae* accounted for 72% of the total biomass.

A survey of aquatic macrophytes was conducted by Alberta Environment in August 1979 (Fig. 8). The most widespread emergent species were common cattail (*Typha latifolia*), common bulrush (*Scirpus acutus*) and common great bulrush (*Scirpus validus*), which were particularly dense in the south basin. Other species frequently recorded were sedges (*Carex* spp.) and reed grass (*Phragmites communis*). Sweet flag (*Acorus calamus*), giant bur-reed (*Sparganium eurycarpum*) and yellow water lily (*Nuphar variegatum*) were also identified. Pondweeds (*Potamogeton* spp.) were the most widespread submergent macrophytes. In addition to the six pondweed species identified, northern watermilfoil (*Myriophyllum exalbescens*), stonewort (*Chara* sp.) and coontail (*Ceratophylllum demersum*) were common, and widgeon grass (*Ruppia occidentalis*), water crowfoot (*Ranunculus* sp.) and naiad (*Najas flexilis*) were noted occasionally.

Invertebrates

The zooplankton and benthic invertebrates in Sandy Lake have not been studied.

Fish

Sandy Lake is managed for sport fishing. No catch data are available, but the fishery is most popular for northern pike in spring and yellow perch in winter. Fishing derbies for both species are held during winter. From 1954 to 1959, the lake was stocked each year with northern pike and/or yellow perch (Alta. For. Ld. Wild. n.d.). During the 1950s, pearl dace were reported present, and in 1984, a few walleye were caught in the deepest part of the lake. These walleye

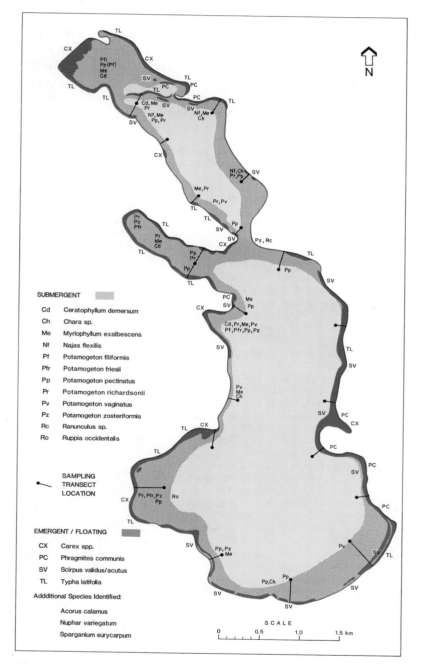

Figure 8. Species composition and distribution of aquatic macrophytes in Sandy Lake, August 1979.
SOURCE: Alta. Envir. n.d.[a].

were likely a remnant population, as they have not been reported since 1984, and there is little walleye spawning habitat available (Watters 1989).

Sandy Lake has a history of summer and winter fish kills, as, for example, in June of 1959 and 1964, in the winter of 1970/71, in April of 1987 and in late winter of 1989. The 1989 incident was a severe kill that affected both northern pike and yellow perch. Test nets in May 1989 caught some pike but no perch (Watters 1989).

Wildlife

The extreme north end of Sandy Lake is rated very good to excellent for waterfowl production (Alta. For. Ld. Wild. n.d.). Nesting cover is plentiful and loafing areas are available. Ducks sighted on this basin include Blue-winged Teal, Lesser Scaup, American Widgeons, Mallards, Shovellers, Pintails, Gadwalls, Bufflehead and Ring-necked Ducks. Great Blue Herons are also present. Waterfowl production at the far end of the north basin, although good, is limited by the overgrown nature of the shoreline and a lack of offshore emergent aquatic vegetation (Ducks Unltd. (Can.) n.d.). The remainder of the north basin and all of the south basin have a relatively poor rating for waterfowl production.

M.E. Bradford

References

Alberta Environment. n.d.[a]. Envir. Assess. Div., Envir. Qlty. Monit. Br. Unpubl. data, Edmonton.

———. n.d.[b]. Tech. Serv. Div., Hydrol. Br. Unpubl. data, Edmonton.

———. n.d.[c]. Tech. Serv. Div., Surv. Br. Unpubl. data, Edmonton.

———. 1984. Sandy Lake. Alta. Envir., Poll. Contr. Div., Water Qlty. Contr. Br., Edmonton.

Alberta Forestry, Lands and Wildlife. n.d. Fish Wild. Div. Unpubl. data, Edmonton.

———. 1988. Boating in Alberta. Fish Wild. Div., Edmonton.

———. 1989. Guide to sportfishing. Fish Wild. Div., Edmonton.

Alberta Native Affairs. 1986. A guide to native communities in Alberta. Native Aff. Secret., Edmonton.

Alberta Research Council. 1972. Geological map of Alberta. Nat. Resour. Div., Alta. Geol. Surv., Edmonton.

Ducks Unlimited (Canada). n.d. Unpubl. data, Edmonton.

Edmonton Regional Planning Commission. n.d. Unpubl. data, Edmonton.

———. 1979. Sandy Lake: Background information and management philosophy. Edm. Reg. Plan. Commis., Edmonton.

———. 1980. Sandy Lake: Management plan alternatives. Edm. Reg. Plan. Commis., Edmonton.

———. 1981. Sandy Lake area structure plan. Prep. for Co. Lac Ste. Anne, MD Sturgeon and SV Sandy Beach by Edm. Reg. Plan. Commis., Edmonton.

Energy, Mines and Resources Canada. 1973, 1974, 1975, 1980. National topographic series 1:50 000 83H/13 (1973), 83G/9 (1974), 83G/16 (1975), 83H/12 (1980). Surv. Map. Br., Ottawa.

Environment Canada. 1982. Canadian climate normals, Vol. 7: Bright sunshine (1951–1980). Prep. by Atm. Envir. Serv. Supply Serv. Can., Ottawa.

Holmgren, E.J. and P.M. Holmgren. 1976. Over 2000 place names of Alberta. 3rd ed. West. Producer Prairie Books, Saskatoon.

Mitchell, P.A. 1982. Evaluation of the "septic snooper" on Wabamun and Pigeon lakes. Alta. Envir., Poll. Contr. Div., Water Qlty. Contr. Br., Edmonton.

———. 1983. Trophic status of Sandy and Nakamun Lakes. Alta. Envir., Poll. Contr. Div., Water Qlty. Contr. Br. Unpubl. rep., Edmonton.

———. 1989. Alta. Envir., Envir. Assess. Div., Envir. Qlty. Monit. Br., Edmonton. Pers. comm.

Strong, W.L. and K.R. Leggat. 1981. Ecoregions of Alberta. Alta. En. Nat. Resour., Resour. Eval. Plan. Div., Edmonton.

Twardy, A.G. and L.K. Brocke. 1976. Soil survey and land suitability evaluation of the Sandy Lake-Nakamun Lake study area. Prep. for Alta. Envir. by Pedol. Consult., Edmonton.

Watters, D. 1989. Alta. For. Ld. Wild., Fish Wild. Div., Dist. Office, Edmonton. Pers. comm.

Yellowhead Regional Planning Commission. n.d. Unpubl. data, Onoway.

SAUER LAKE

MAP SHEET: 83G/9
LOCATION: Tp53 R1 W5
LAT/LONG: 53°37′N 114°05′W

Sauer is a charming, tiny lake set among the rolling hills west of the city of Edmonton in the County of Parkland. It is a quiet spot for canoeing or fishing for rainbow trout. To reach Sauer Lake from Edmonton, drive west on Highway 16 to the town of Stony Plain, then turn north onto Secondary Road 779 and drive for 6 km, then drive west on Chickakoo Lake Road for 4.2 km, then north for 1.8 km. Public walk-in access to the lake is available along a road allowance that leads from the road on the east side of the lake. Hand-carried boats can be launched there. Only electric-powered motors are allowed on Sauer Lake (Alta. For. Ld. Wild. 1988). There are no public facilities such as camping areas, toilets or picnic tables, nor are there any commercially operated resort facilities. Day-use facilities are available at Chickakoo Lake, less than 1 km away. The land around Sauer Lake is all privately owned, but as of 1988 there was no development at the lake and all of the shoreline was treed and undisturbed (Fig. 1). The lake was named after George Sauer, who homesteaded on the shore around the turn of the century (Alta. Cult. Multicult. n.d.).

The majority of users who come to Sauer Lake are anglers seeking the rainbow trout stocked annually by Fish and Wildlife Division. No fishing with, or for, bait fish is permitted (Alta. For. Ld. Wild. 1989). Sauer Lake has very clear water and algae are not usually conspicuous. Aquatic plants ring the lake, but as the lake is deep they do not interfere with angling from boats.

Drainage Basin Characteristics

The tiny drainage basin of Sauer Lake is only 5 times the lake area (Tables 1, 2). The lake has no defined inlet or outlet and groundwater plays a major role in maintaining lake levels.

The watershed lies within the Moist Mixedwood Subregion of the Boreal Mixedwood Ecoregion near its interface with the Aspen Parkland Ecoregion (Strong and Leggat 1981). Surficial materials are Pleistocene-age, pitted deltaic material and the terrain is hilly, with some slopes exceeding 15%. Hills rise approximately 25 m above the lake (En. Mines Resour. Can. 1974). The soils are Orthic Gray Luvisols (Lindsay et al. 1968) and the dominant vegetation is trembling aspen and balsam poplar, with willow and alder bordering the lake. The drainage basin has not been cleared except for a small area south of the lake that is being developed as a subdivision. As of 1988, no residences had been built.

Lake Basin Characteristics

Sauer Lake is an elongated, oval shape with three tiny bays at the south end. The main body of the lake has 2 deep areas, one 14–m deep and one 12–m deep (Fig. 2). The lake is 0.58–km long and has a maximum width of 0.38 km. The lake basin slopes steeply on all sides except near the three little bays at the south end. Aquatic plants grow to a depth of 5 m (Chambers and Prepas 1988). Approximately 67% of the lake area is less than this depth (Fig. 3).

The water level of Sauer Lake has not been monitored. Because there is no surface outflow from the lake, the residence time is likely very long. A good estimate of the water residence time of Sauer Lake would require an estimate of groundwater inflow and outflow.

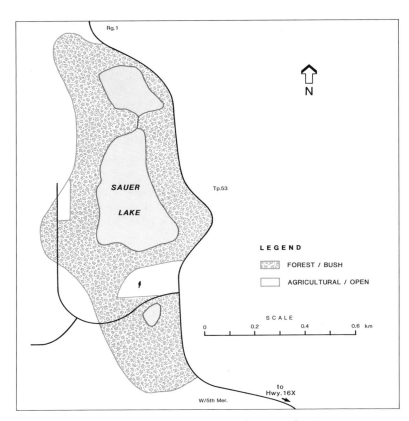

Figure 1. Features of the drainage basin of Sauer Lake.
SOURCES: Alta. Envir. n.d.; En. Mines Resour. Can. 1974. Updated with
1987 aerial photos.

Figure 2. Bathymetry and shoreline features of Sauer Lake.
BATHYMETRY SOURCE: Babin 1984.

Table 1. Characteristics of Sauer Lake drainage basin.

area (excluding lake) (km²)[a]	0.49
soil[b]	Orthic Gray Luvisols
bedrock geology[c]	Wapiti Formation (Upper Cretaceous): sandstone, mudstone, bentonite, scattered coal beds; nonmarine
terrain[b]	hilly
ecoregion[d]	Moist Mixedwood Subregion of Boreal Mixedwood
dominant vegetation[d, e]	trembling aspen, balsam poplar
mean annual inflow (m³)[a, f]	0.0172 x 10⁶
mean annual sunshine (h)[g]	2 264

NOTE: [f]excluding groundwater inflow
SOURCES: [a]Alta. Envir. n.d.; [b]Lindsay et al. 1968; [c]Alta. Res. Counc. 1972; [d]Strong
and Leggat 1981; [e]R.L. & L. Envir. Serv. Ltd. 1987; [g]Envir. Can. 1982

Water Quality

The water quality of Sauer Lake was monitored by researchers from
the University of Alberta from May through July in 1981, from May
1982 through March 1983 and in March and August of 1986 (Prepas and Babin n.d.; Prepas 1983; Prepas and Trew 1983; Babin
1984; Prepas and Vickery 1984[a]; 1984[b]; Babin and Prepas 1985)
and by Fish and Wildlife Division (R.L. & L. Envir. Serv. Ltd. 1987).

Sauer Lake contains fresh water; concentrations of alkalinity and
hardness are relatively low compared to those in other Alberta lakes
(Table 3). The dominant ions are bicarbonate and calcium.

Sauer Lake is strongly thermally stratified all summer (Fig. 4). The
top of the thermocline is at a depth of about 3 m by late June; it
descends to about 7 m by October. In 1982, the water was anoxic
below 12 m when sampling began in early May just after the ice
melted; it was anoxic below 8 m from the first of June through
August and dissolved oxygen concentrations were less than 1 mg/L
below 6 m during the same period. In years when there is little wind
in the autumn and the onset of ice cover is rapid, Sauer Lake likely
does not mix completely and the bottom water may be anoxic all
year. In 1982, some mixing did occur in the autumn, and by late
November temperature and dissolved oxygen were uniform from
the lake surface to the bottom before freeze-up. However, mixing
did not continue for a sufficiently long period to fully oxygenate the
lake. By freeze-up, the water was only 72% saturated with dissolved
oxygen. Under-ice oxygen-depletion rates were moderately high
(0.363 g O_2/m² per day); by mid-February 1983, dissolved oxygen
levels had dropped to less than 1 mg/L throughout the water
column. Fish cannot survive these conditions and winterkills are
common in Sauer Lake. In Figure 5, note that the dissolved oxygen
concentration increased through March of 1983. This was due to an
algal bloom that developed under the ice; chlorophyll *a* concentrations peaked at 23 μg/L, higher than values reached through the
entire preceding summer (Fig. 6).

The temperature patterns of lakes have a strong effect on the
distribution of phosphorus throughout the water column. In lakes
like Sauer, with strong thermal stratification, the amount of phosphorus moving from the sediment into the water is different between shallow and deep areas. In 1982, it was estimated that 0.7 mg
total phosphorus/m² per day returned from the sediments in shallow
areas (less than 8–m deep) into the water of the euphotic zone
(Shaw and Prepas 1989). In deeper areas of Sauer Lake, there is
well-developed anoxia in the bottom stratum, and phosphorus is
released from the sediment more quickly than at the shallow sites.
By 4 August 1982, the total phosphorus concentration below a
depth of 8 m averaged 138 μg/L; in the top few meters it was 20
μg/L (Prepas 1983). There is virtually no mixing across the thermocline (Shaw and Prepas 1989). Thus, when phosphorus in the surface
water is taken up by small organisms, it is precipitated to the hypolimnion in waste products or when the small organisms die. Therefore, total phosphorus in the upper layer of the lake is at its highest
concentration after partial mixing in spring, then it decreases

Table 2. Characteristics of Sauer Lake.

elevation (m)[a]	approximately 740
surface area (km²)[b, c]	0.085
volume (m³)[b, c]	0.352 x 10⁶
maximum depth (m)[b, c]	14
mean depth (m)[b, c]	4.2
shoreline length (km)[a]	1.8
mean annual lake evaporation (mm)[d]	664
mean annual precipitation (mm)[d]	495
mean residence time (yr)[d, e]	>100
control structure	none

NOTES: [b]on date of sounding: 17 June 1982; [e]excluding groundwater inflow
SOURCES: [a]En. Mines Resour. Can. 1974; [c]Babin 1984; [d]Alta. Envir. n.d.

Table 3. Major ions and related water quality variables for Sauer Lake. Average concentrations in mg/L; pH in pH units. Composite samples from the euphotic zone collected at various times during the open-water seasons of 1981 and 1982, and in Mar. and Aug. 1986. S.E. = standard error.

	Mean	S.E.
pH (range)	7.7–8.1[a]	—
total alkalinity (CaCO₃)	97[b]	9.0
specific conductivity (μS/cm)	174[c]	7.6
total dissolved solids	135[d]	0.8
turbidity (NTU)	1.3[a]	0.1
colour (Pt)	8[a]	1.4
total hardness (CaCO₃)	94[e]	16.0
HCO₃	119	11.0
CO₃	0	0
Mg	9[e]	0.5
Na	4[e]	0.3
K	8[e]	1.2
Cl	1[f]	—
SO₄	5[e]	0.6
Ca	22[e]	5.5

NOTES: [a]n = 3; [b]n = 4; [c]n = 12; [d]n = 11; [e]n = 2; [f]n = 1
SOURCES: Prepas and Babin n.d.; R.L. & L. Envir. Serv. Ltd. 1987

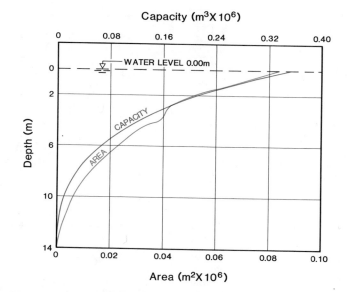

Figure 3. Area/capacity curve for Sauer Lake.
SOURCE: Babin 1984.

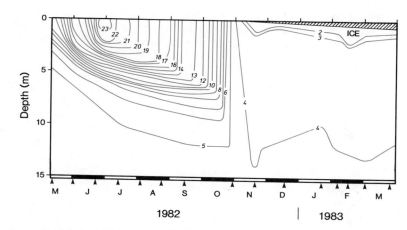

Figure 4. Temperature (°C) of Sauer Lake, 1982 to 1983. Arrows indicate sampling dates.
SOURCE: Prepas and Babin n.d.

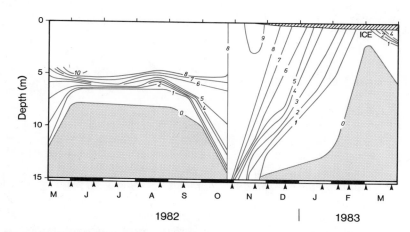

Figure 5. Dissolved oxygen (mg/L) in Sauer Lake, 1982 to 1983. Arrows indicate sampling dates.
SOURCES: Prepas and Babin n.d.; Babin 1984.

throughout the summer (Fig. 6). As the total phosphorus concentration above the thermocline drops, so does the chlorophyll *a* concentration, and water clarity (measured by Secchi depth) increases. However, light can penetrate the water column to depths below the thermocline and into the upper portion of the phosphorus-rich hypolimnion. It is at this depth (approximately 8 m in Sauer Lake) that a fine balance of high phosphorus concentrations and sufficient light provides the best conditions in the lake for algae to grow; it is here that chlorophyll *a* and bacteria concentrations are highest. For example, on 29 July 1981, the chlorophyll *a* concentration from the surface to a depth of 4 m was only 1.3 μg/L, whereas the concentration of a sample incorporating water from the surface to 9 m was 9.2 μg/L. Thus, although Sauer Lake is mesotrophic and fairly nutrient-rich (Table 4), most of the algal biomass is well below the surface and the upper water remains clear and attractive for recreation.

In the winter, the bottom stratum is again anoxic and phosphorus is released from the sediment to the water. In March 1983, the total phosphorus concentration in the surface water was only 28 μg/L, while at 13 m it was 164 μg/L. Some of this phosphorus mixes into the surface water soon after the spring thaw.

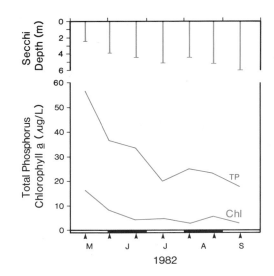

Figure 6. Total phosphorus, chlorophyll *a* and Secchi depth in Sauer Lake, 1982.
SOURCE: Prepas 1983.

Table 4. Nutrient, chlorophyll *a* and Secchi depth data for Sauer Lake. Average concentrations in µg/L. Composite samples from the euphotic zone collected 4 times from 06 May to 29 July 1981 and 7 times from 12 May to 14 Sep. 1982. S.E. = standard error.

	1981		1982	
	Mean	S.E.	Mean	S.E.
total phosphorus	40	6.1	30	5.1
total dissolved phosphorus	10	1.3	—	—
soluble reactive phosphorus	2[a]	—	—	—
total Kjeldahl nitrogen	1 207	46.6	1 147[d]	48.4
$NO_3 + NO_2$–nitrogen	9	3.6	10[d]	2.5
NH_4–nitrogen	9	3.8	—	—
iron	114[a, c]	—	43[a, d]	—
chlorophyll *a*	4.5	1.79	6.2	1.78
Secchi depth (m)	3.7	0.57	4.6	0.42

NOTES: [a]n = 1; [b]n = 6; [c]11 Mar. 1986; [d]16 Aug. 1986
SOURCES: Prepas and Babin n.d.; R.L. & L. Envir. Serv. Ltd. 1987

Biological Characteristics

Plants

There are no data on the species of algae in Sauer Lake.

The entire shoreline of Sauer Lake supports emergent vegetation to a depth of 1 m. Common cattail (*Typha latifolia*) and common horsetail (*Equisetum arvense*) dominate. Submergent plants grow to a depth of 5 m (Chambers and Prepas 1988). Richardson pondweed (*Potamogeton richardsonii*), flat-stemmed pondweed (*P. zosteriformis*) and stonewort (*Chara* sp.) are the most abundant species. At the south end of the lake, the weed beds are extensive and provide good wildlife habitat.

Invertebrates

The zooplankton in Sauer Lake was sampled from May through July in 1981 and from May through September in 1982 (Prepas 1983; Prepas and Vickery 1984[a]). The cladoceran *Daphnia galeata mendotae* was the dominant species. The copepods *Mesocyclops edax* and *Diacyclops bicuspidatus thomasi* were very abundant in 1981 and *Diaptomus oregonensis* was common in both years. As in many lakes, the abundance of zooplankton is variable from year to year;

in Sauer Lake, the total weight of zooplankton in 1982 was consistently more than 50% greater than that in 1981.

Benthic invertebrates in Sauer Lake have not been sampled.

Fish

Only two species of fish are indigenous to Sauer Lake: redbelly dace and brook stickleback. The only other fish in the lake are rainbow trout, which have been stocked annually, except from 1957 to 1959 and from 1963 to 1964, by Fish and Wildlife Division. Because winterkill is common, Sauer Lake is managed as a put-and-take fishery. Each spring, approximately 9 000 yearlings (15+ cm) are put in the lake, with the expectation that most will be taken in the sport fishery in the same year (Alta. For. Ld. Wild. n.d.).

Angling pressure is moderately high and success rates are also high. In a 1982 creel survey, 232 anglers caught 438 trout at an average rate of 0.66 trout per hour. This is a much higher rate than the estimated 0.24 trout/hour at nearby Big Chickakoo Lake or 0.12 trout/hour at Hasse Lake (Berry 1986[a]; 1986[b]; 1986[c]).

There are no commercial or domestic fisheries on Sauer Lake.

Wildlife

There is no detailed information on waterfowl use of Sauer Lake. The south end appears to be good waterfowl habitat and Common Loons nest on the lake.

J.M. Crosby and E.E. Prepas

References

Alberta Culture and Multiculturalism. n.d. Hist. Resour. Div., Hist. Sites Serv. Unpubl. data, Edmonton.
Alberta Environment. n.d. Tech. Serv. Div., Hydrol. Br. Unpubl. data, Edmonton.
Alberta Forestry, Lands and Wildlife. n.d. Fish Wild. Div. Unpubl. data, Edmonton.
———. 1988. Boating in Alberta. Fish Wild. Div., Edmonton.
———. 1989. Guide to sportfishing. Fish Wild. Div., Edmonton.
Alberta Research Council. 1972. Geological map of Alberta. Nat. Resour. Div., Alta. Geol. Surv., Edmonton.
Babin, J. 1984. Winter oxygen depletion in temperate zone lakes. MSc thesis. Univ. Alta., Edmonton.
——— and E.E. Prepas. 1985. Modelling winter oxygen depletion rates in ice-covered temperate zone lakes in Canada. Can. J. Fish. Aquat. Sci. 42:239–249.
Berry, D.K. 1986[a]. Catch rate and trout harvest for the "put and take" sportfishery at Sauer Lake, Alberta, 1982. Alta. For. Ld. Wild., Fish Wild. Div., Edmonton.
———. 1986[b]. An assessment of the spring sportfishery at Big Chickakoo Lake, Alberta, 1982. Alta. For. Ld. Wild., Fish Wild. Div., Edmonton.
———. 1986[c]. Angler harvest and population estimate of rainbow trout in Hasse Lake, Alberta, 1982–83. Alta. For. Ld. Wild., Fish Wild. Div., Edmonton.
Chambers, P.A. and E.E. Prepas. 1988. Underwater spectral attenuation and its effect on the maximum depth of angiosperm colonization. Can. J. Fish. Aquat. Sci. 45:1010–1017.
Energy, Mines and Resources Canada. 1974. National topographic series 1:50 000 83G/9 (1974). Surv. Map. Br., Ottawa.
Environment Canada. 1982. Canadian climate normals, Vol. 7: Bright sunshine (1951–1980). Prep. by Atm. Envir. Serv. Supply Serv. Can., Ottawa.
Lindsay, J.D., W. Odynsky, J.W. Peters and W.E. Bowser. 1968. Soil survey of the Buck Lake (NE 83B) and Wabamun Lake (E1/2 83G) areas. Alta. Soil Surv. Rep. No. 24, Univ. Alta. Bull. No. SS–7, Alta. Res. Counc. Rep. No. 87. Univ. Alta., Edmonton.
Prepas, E.E. 1983. The influence of phosphorus and zooplankton on chlorophyll levels in Alberta lakes. Prep. for Alta. Envir., Res. Mgt. Div. Rep. 83/23, Edmonton.
——— and J. Babin. n.d. Univ. Alta., Dept. Zool. Unpubl.data, Edmonton.
Prepas, E.E. and D.O. Trew. 1983. Evaluation of the phosphorus-chlorophyll relationship for lakes off the Precambrian Shield in western Canada. Can. J. Fish. Aquat. Sci. 40:27–35.
Prepas, E.E. and J. Vickery. 1984[a]. The contribution of particulate phosphorus (>250 µm) to the total phosphorus pool in lake water. Can. J. Fish. Aquat. Sci. 41:351–363.
———. 1984[b]. Seasonal changes in total phosphorus and the role of internal loading in western Canadian lakes. Verh. Internat. Verein. Limnol. 223:303–308.
R.L. & L. Environmental Services Ltd. 1987. County of Parkland fisheries inventory: Sauer Lake. Prep. for Alta. For. Ld. Wild., Fish Wild. Div., Edmonton.
Shaw, J.F.H. and E.E. Prepas. 1989. Potential significance of phosphorus release from shallow sediments of deep Alberta lakes. ms submitted to Limnol. Oceanogr.
Strong, W.L. and K.R. Leggat. 1981. Ecoregions of Alberta. Alta. En. Nat. Resour., Resour. Eval. Plan. Div., Edmonton.

SPRING LAKE

MAP SHEET: 83G/9
LOCATION: Tp52 R1 W5
LAT/LONG: 53°31'N 114°08'W

Spring Lake is a small, picturesque lake located 28 km west of the city of Edmonton in the County of Parkland. Because of the lake's close proximity to Edmonton and the town of Stony Plain, which is the closest population centre, the lake is popular with cottagers, resort patrons and day-users, and it receives moderate to heavy recreational use during summer. To reach the lake, exit Highway 16 at the turnoff for the summer village of Edmonton Beach, about 6 km west of Stony Plain. Continue west for another 2.5 km, turn south and drive 3 km to Edmonton Beach Resort (Fig. 1). Permission for walk-in public access to the lakeshore for fishing can be obtained at the resort, but free public facilities are not provided.

The area surrounding Spring Lake was homesteaded in 1894. In the early 1900s, the lake became popular among residents of Edmonton and the surrounding areas, and small acreage and cottage lots were sold; Edmonton Beach was established by cottagers and was incorporated as a summer village in 1959 (Stony Plain Dist. Hist. Soc. 1982).

In 1894, Spring Lake was called Schimpf's Lake. In the years that followed, the name was changed several times as ownership of the surrounding land changed; the lake has been called McCoppen's, Cottage and Barrie's lake (Stony Plain Dist. Hist. Soc. 1982). In the 1940s, the lake level began to decline. Underground springs were thought to feed the lake and attempts to find and clear the springs with dynamite prompted a final name change, to Spring Lake. The lake itself is also referred to as Edmonton Beach.

Edmonton Beach Resort is a commercially operated facility located on the southeast corner of the lakeshore (Fig. 2). Popular activities include swimming, hiking and fishing. The resort provides 336 campsites, a beach, a boat launch, boat rentals, a playground, a sewage disposal station and tap water (Alta. Hotel Assoc. 1989). Power-driven vessels are permitted on the lake, but are restricted to maximum speeds of 12 km/hour (Alta. For. Ld. Wild. 1988).

Spring Lake is shallow and moderately productive. Algal biomass is low and the water is fairly clear, but aquatic vegetation flourishes in shallow areas. The lake is stocked annually with rainbow trout and the sport fishery is popular, particularly with members of the Edmonton Trout Club, who have been fishing at Spring Lake for 30 years. Fishing for bait fish and the use of bait fish is prohibited (Alta. For. Ld. Wild. 1989).

Drainage Basin Characteristics

The drainage basin is approximately 16 times larger than the lake surface (Tables 1, 2). There are no defined permanent inlets to, or outlets from, the lake (Miller and Macdonald 1950). Historically, inflow came from an intermittent tributary that drained a series of small sloughs in the northwest section of the drainage basin.

The undulating to gently rolling terrain was formed on a pitted delta; surficial deposits include sand, silt and sand, clay, gravel, glacial till pockets and stones (Andriashek et al. 1979). The main soils are Orthic Gray Luvisols (Strong and Leggat 1981).

Spring Lake is part of the Moist Mixedwood Subregion of the Boreal Mixedwood Ecoregion (Strong and Leggat 1981). The predominant land use within the watershed is agriculture. Most land is cultivated for cereal crop production, but some areas are reserved for pasture. Areas of natural, undeveloped forest are present throughout the drainage basin (Fig. 1). The dominant tree cover is trembling aspen and balsam poplar, with occasional stands of white spruce.

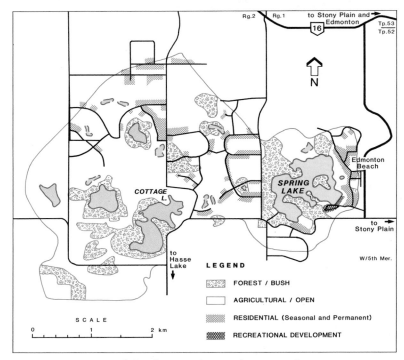

Figure 1. Features of the drainage basin of Spring Lake.
SOURCES: Alta. Envir. n.d.[b]; En. Mines Resour. Can. 1974. Updated with 1982 and 1987 aerial photos.

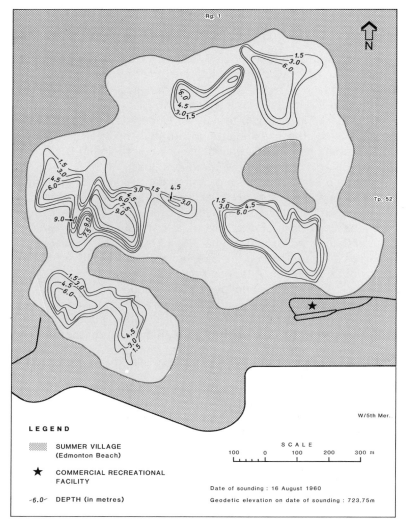

Figure 2. Bathymetry and shoreline features of Spring Lake.
BATHYMETRY SOURCE: Alta. Envir. n.d.[c].

Table 1. Characteristics of Spring Lake drainage basin.

area (excluding lake) (km²)[a]	12.5
soil[b]	Orthic Gray Luvisols
bedrock geology[c]	Wapiti Formation (Upper Cretaceous): sandstone, mudstone, bentonite, scattered coal beds; nonmarine
terrain[d]	undulating to gently rolling
ecoregion[b]	Moist Mixedwood Subregion of Boreal Mixedwood
dominant vegetation[b]	trembling aspen, balsam poplar
mean annual inflow (m³)[a, e]	0.131 x 10⁶
mean annual sunshine (h)[f]	2 315

NOTE: [e]excluding groundwater inflow
SOURCES: [a]Alta. Envir. n.d.[b]; [b]Strong and Leggat 1981; [c]Alta. Res. Counc. 1972; [d]R.L. & L. Envir. Serv. Ltd. 1987; [f]Envir. Can. 1982

Table 2. Characteristics of Spring Lake.

elevation (m)[a, b]	723.75
surface area (km²)[a, b]	0.80
volume (m³)[a, b]	1.55 x 10⁶
maximum depth (m)[a, b]	9.1
mean depth (m)[a, b]	1.9
shoreline length (km)[c, d]	6.0
mean annual lake evaporation (mm)[e]	664
mean annual precipitation (mm)[e]	500
mean residence time (yr)[e, f]	>100
control structure	none

NOTES: [a]on date of sounding: 16 Aug. 1960; [d]includes island; [f]excluding groundwater inflow
SOURCES: [b]Alta. Envir. n.d.[c]; [c]En. Mines Resour. Can. 1974; [e]Alta. Envir. n.d.[b]

Around the lake perimeter, the forest is mainly on the western shore, at the Edmonton Beach Resort and along a thin strip on the eastern shore. Closer to the water's edge, on imperfectly to poorly drained sites, stands of willow and alder are prevalent (R.L. & L. Envir. Serv. Ltd. 1987).

The summer village of Edmonton Beach completely surrounds Spring Lake and all of the shoreland is privately owned (Fig. 2). Cottage development is most intensive along the eastern side of the lake, but the southern and western shores are also developed. There is considerable residential development, particularly acreages, to the west and east of the lake (Fig. 1)—seven subdivisions, as well as the summer village, are registered in the watershed (R.L. & L. Envir. Serv. Ltd. 1987).

Lake Basin Characteristics

Spring Lake is 2.4–km long and 2.2–km wide; a large island is located in the eastern half of the lake and a shallow sill separates the southwestern bay from the rest of the lake (Fig. 2). The lake has a very irregular bottom; much of it is less than 1.5–m deep, but five holes exceed 6 m in depth. The maximum depth is 9.1 m, but because of the extensive littoral zone, the mean depth is less than 2 m (Table 2). An irregular shoreline, the large island, and the extensive tree growth around much of the lakeshore provide protection from wind.

Water levels were recorded in 1937 and from 1939 to 1944, and have been monitored regularly since 1956 (Fig. 3). Since 1939, the lake level has fluctuated between a high of 726.36 m, recorded in 1939, and a low of 722.99 m, recorded in 1968. During years of high water levels, cottages were located adjacent to the water's edge. As the lake's elevation declined, however, a wide buffer strip of grasses formed between the cottages and the water's edge, particularly along the northern and eastern shores. As well, two peninsulas were exposed along the south side of the lake (Fig. 1). Since the 1960s, however, the lake level has remained fairly stable (Fig. 3). Preliminary

Table 3. Major ions and related water quality variables for Spring Lake.
Average concentrations in mg/L; pH in pH units. Composite samples
from the euphotic zone collected 7 times from 18 May to 01 Nov. 1983.
S.E. = standard error.

	Mean	S.E.
pH (range)	7.3–9.5	—
total alkalinity (CaCO₃)	178[a]	3.6
specific conductivity (μS/cm)	600[a]	5.6
total dissolved solids (calculated)	341[b]	4.4
turbidity (NTU)	1[c, d]	—
colour (Pt)	10[c, d]	—
total hardness (CaCO₃)	245[a]	1.3
total particulate carbon	1[e]	0.2
dissolved organic carbon	14[e]	0.4
HCO₃	208[a]	3.6
CO₃	<5[a]	—
Mg	40[a]	0.7
Na	23[a]	0.5
K	10[a]	0.1
Cl	<2[a]	—
SO₄	128[a]	4.2
Ca	33[a]	1.3

NOTES: [a]n = 5; [b]n = 4; [c]n = 11; [e]n = 6
SOURCES: Alta. Envir. n.d.[a], Naquadat station 01AL05EA1000; [d]R.L. & L. Envir.
    Serv. Ltd. 1987

Table 4. Nutrient, chlorophyll *a* and Secchi depth data for Spring Lake.
Average concentrations in μg/L. Composite samples from the euphotic
zone collected 7 times from 18 May to 01 Nov. 1983. S.E. = standard
error.

	Mean	S.E.
total phosphorus	21	1.0
total dissolved phosphorus	12	0.4
soluble reactive phosphorus	2	0.5
total Kjeldahl nitrogen	1 197[a]	26.0
NO₃ + NO₂–nitrogen	<5[a]	—
NH₄–nitrogen	40[a]	11.2
iron	<56[b]	—
chlorophyll *a*	8.0	1.50
Secchi depth (m)	4.4	0.46

NOTES: [a]n = 6; [b]n = 5
SOURCE: Alta. Envir. n.d.[a], Naquadat station 01AL05EA1000

data collected in 1986 suggested that groundwater inflow to Spring
Lake was 0.6 to 6.2 x 10⁻⁸ m/second (Shaw and Prepas 1989).
Groundwater appears to be an important contribution of inflow to
the lake. Changes in the lake's area and capacity with fluctuations
in the water level (up to an elevation of 723.75 m) are illustrated in
Figure 4.

Water Quality

The water quality of Spring Lake was studied during the open-water
period in 1983 (Alta. Envir. n.d.[a]) and 1986 (R.L. & L. Envir. Serv.
Ltd. 1987) and under ice in January 1984 (Alta. Envir. n.d.[a]). As
well, winter dissolved oxygen concentrations were studied by Fish
and Wildlife Division for 21 years between 1956 and 1985 (Alta. For.
Ld. Wild. n.d., summarized in R.L. & L. Envir. Serv. Ltd. 1987).

The lake is well-buffered and the dominant ions are bicarbonate,
magnesium and sulphate (Table 3). The water is usually clear; the
low turbidity and Secchi depths to 6 m indicate that the euphotic
zone often extends to the bottom of the lake, except in the deepest
areas (Table 4).

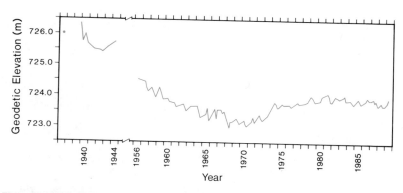

Figure 3. Water level of Spring Lake, 1937 to 1989.
SOURCE: Alta. Envir. n.d.[c].

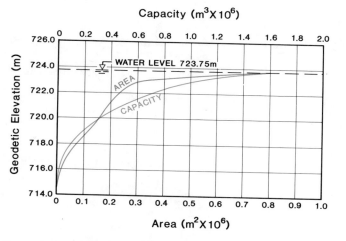

Figure 4. Area/capacity curve for Spring Lake.
SOURCE: Alta. Envir. n.d.[c].

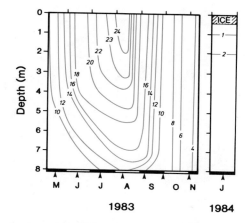

**Figure 5. Temperature (°C) of Spring Lake,
1983 and 1984.** Arrows indicate sampling
dates.
SOURCE: Alta. Envir. n.d.[a].

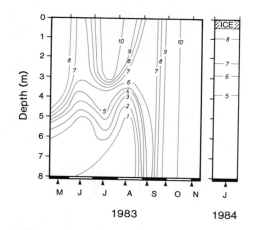

**Figure 6. Dissolved oxygen (mg/L) in Spring
Lake, 1983 and 1984.** Arrows indicate
sampling dates.
SOURCE: Alta. Envir. n.d.[a].

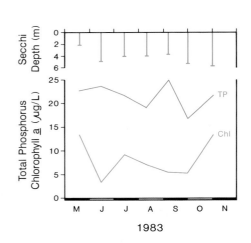

Figure 7. Total phosphorus, chlorophyll *a* and Secchi depth in Spring Lake, 1983.
SOURCE: Alta. Envir. n.d.[a].

Table 5. Percentage composition of major algal groups by total biomass in Spring Lake, 1983. Composite samples collected from the euphotic zone.

ALGAL GROUP	18 May	14 June	13 July	10 Aug.	06 Sep.	30 Sep.[a]	01 Nov.
Total Biomass (mg/L)	1.34	0.25	2.48	0.88	0.58	0.91	2.40
Percentage Composition:							
Cyanophyta	0	30	0	17	0	0	0
		Oscillatoria					
Chlorophyta	2	26	7	2	4	<1	29
		Sphaerocystis					*Mougeotia*
Chrysophyta	78	5	33	15	14	7	21
	Uroglena		*Uroglena*				*Uroglena*
	Dinobryon						
Bacillariophyta	0	9	4	<1	5	53	28
						Asterionella⟶	
							Gomphonema
Cryptophyta	18	19	23	62	43	38	22
			Cryptomonas⟶				*Rhodomonas*
Pyrrhophyta	2	10	34	3	34	1	0
			Peridinium		*Ceratium*		

NOTE: [a]Euglenophyta less than 1% of biomass
SOURCE: Alta. Envir. n.d.[a]

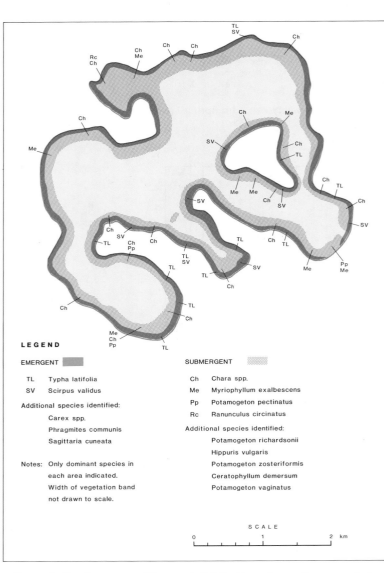

LEGEND

EMERGENT		SUBMERGENT	
TL	Typha latifolia	Ch	Chara spp.
SV	Scirpus validus	Me	Myriophyllum exalbescens
		Pp	Potamogeton pectinatus
Additional species identified:		Rc	Ranunculus circinatus
	Carex spp.		
	Phragmites communis	Additional species identified:	
	Sagittaria cuneata		Potamogeton richardsonii
			Hippuris vulgaris
Notes:	Only dominant species in		Potamogeton zosteriformis
	each area indicated.		Ceratophyllum demersum
	Width of vegetation band		Potamogeton vaginatus
	not drawn to scale.		

SCALE
0   1   2 km

Figure 8. Species composition and distribution of aquatic macrophytes in Spring Lake, September 1983.
SOURCE: R.L. & L. Envir. Serv. Ltd. 1987.

The deepest part of Spring Lake was thermally stratified from early June until early September in 1983 (Fig. 5). During this period, the concentration of dissolved oxygen in the deeper water decreased to less than 1 mg/L (Fig. 6). From June to August in 1986, water over the sediments in this deep area was anoxic. The lake mixes thoroughly in the fall and the water column becomes well-oxygenated, as in September 1983 (Fig. 6). During most winters, the deeper water is anoxic by March, and dissolved oxygen concentrations throughout the rest of the water column are low.

Spring Lake is classified as mesotrophic. In 1983, the highest concentrations of chlorophyll *a* were detected in May and October (Fig. 7). Phosphorus and chlorophyll concentrations likely show unusually rapid changes with depth in the euphotic zone of Spring Lake, and thus more detailed data are required to interpret seasonal patterns.

Biological Characteristics

Plants

The phytoplankton in Spring Lake was sampled monthly during 1983 by Alberta Environment (Table 5). The total biomass was low throughout the sampling period, ranging from a low of 0.25 mg/L to a high of 2.48 mg/L. The dominant or codominant group throughout the sampling period was Cryptophyta, generally *Cryptomonas erosa*, *C. ovata* and *Rhodomonas minuta*. Species of blue-green algae (Cyanophyta) were not an important part of the biomass except in mid-June, when *Oscillatoria agardhii* was the dominant species. Green algae (Chlorophyta) were important only in mid-June (*Sphaerocystis schroeteri*) and early November (*Mougeotia* sp.) and diatoms (Bacillariophyta) accounted for a large part of the biomass only in late September (*Asterionella formosa*) and early November (*A. formosa*, *Gomphonema sphaerophorum* and *G. truncatum*). Golden-brown algae (Chrysophyta), particularly *Uroglena americana* and *Dinobryon divergens*, were prevalent in May, July and November and Pyrrhophyta (*Ceratium hirundinella* and *Peridinium cinctum*) were prominent in July and September.

Macrophytes were abundant throughout the shallow inshore areas of Spring Lake during a survey conducted by R.L. & L. Environmental Services Ltd. on 6 September 1986 (Fig. 8). The dominant emergent plants were cattail (*Typha latifolia*) and bulrush (*Scirpus validus*), interspersed with occasional patches of sedges (*Carex* spp.), reed grass (*Phragmites communis*) and arrowhead (*Sagittaria cuneata*). The deeper littoral areas supported thick mats of stonewort (*Chara* spp.), a submergent species, which extended in places, 30 m out from shore. Two other submergent plants, northern watermilfoil (*Myriophyllum exalbescens*) and Sago pondweed (*Potamogeton pectinatus*) were less dense and distributed sparsely throughout the lake.

Invertebrates

A brief survey of the invertebrate population in Spring Lake was conducted in 1949 (Miller and Macdonald 1950). No recent data are available.

Fish

Four species of fish are present in Spring Lake: fathead minnow, brook stickleback, yellow perch and rainbow trout. Fathead minnow and brook stickleback are indigenous. Arctic grayling were planted in 1954, but the stock was depleted by 1958 and the species is no longer present (Alta. For. Ld. Wild. n.d.).

Spring Lake is managed as a sport fishery only. There is no commercial or domestic fishery. Yellow perch were first stocked in the early 1950s; initially, the population expanded but was stunted. Since the 1950s, however, periodic partial winterkills reduced the size of the population and thus alleviated stunting. The population maintains itself by natural reproduction and supports a good fishery. Perch growth appears to be comparable to that in other Alberta lakes (Alta. For. Ld. Wild. n.d.; R.L. & L. Envir. Serv. Ltd. 1987).

Rainbow trout have been planted annually in the lake since 1953 (except for 1957). In 1960, test nets caught five rainbow trout; their growth was described as below average for a pothole lake (Alta. For. Ld. Wild. n.d.). The rainbow trout population is severely limited, perhaps because of low dissolved oxygen concentrations or competition for food between the trout fingerlings and yellow perch. The present management policy is to stock a small number of relatively large rainbow trout on an annual basis; between 1965 and 1986, an average of 8 900 trout were planted, ranging in size from 6 to 15 cm (Alta. For. Ld. Wild. n.d.; 1987; R.L. & L. Envir. Serv. Ltd. 1987). Since 1980, fish greater than 10 cm in length have been planted, which ensures that fish of catchable size are immediately available and further reduces losses from winterkill. The low stocking rate, when compared to other Alberta lakes, is appropriate since the lake is vulnerable to winterkills and has limited public access.

Wildlife

Detailed data are not available for the wildlife population at Spring Lake; however, beaver lodges have been seen on the lake (R.L. & L. Envir. Serv. Ltd. 1987).

L.G. McIntyre

References

Alberta Environment. n.d.[a]. Envir. Assess. Div., Envir. Qlty. Monit. Br. Unpubl. data, Edmonton.

——. n.d.[b]. Tech. Serv. Div., Hydrol. Br. Unpubl. data, Edmonton.

——. n.d.[c]. Tech. Serv. Div., Surv. Br. Unpubl. data, Edmonton.

Alberta Forestry, Lands and Wildlife. n.d. Fish Wild. Div. Unpubl. data, Edmonton.

——. 1987. Fish planting list. Fish Wild. Div., Edmonton.

——. 1988. Boating in Alberta. Fish Wild. Div., Edmonton.

——. 1989. Guide to sportfishing. Fish Wild. Div., Edmonton.

Alberta Hotel Association. 1989. Alberta campground guide 1989. Prep. for Travel Alta., Edmonton.

Alberta Research Council. 1972. Geological map of Alberta. Nat. Resour. Div., Alta. Geol. Surv., Edmonton.

Andriashek, L.D., M.M. Fenton and J.D. Root. 1979. Surficial geology of the Wabamun Lake area (NTS 83G). Prep. by Alta. Res. Counc., Edmonton.

Energy, Mines and Resources Canada. 1974. National topographic series 1:50 000 83G/9 (1974). Surv. Map. Br., Ottawa.

Environment Canada. 1982. Canadian climate normals, Vol. 7: Bright sunshine (1951–1980). Prep. by Atm. Envir. Serv. Supply Serv. Can., Ottawa.

Miller, R.B. and W.H. Macdonald. 1950. Preliminary biological surveys of Alberta watersheds, 1947–1949. Alta. Ld. For., Fish Wild. Div., Edmonton.

R.L. & L. Environmental Services Ltd. 1987. County of Parkland fisheries inventory: Spring Lake. Prep. for Alta. Fish Wild. Div. and Alta. Rec. Parks and Wild. Foundation, Edmonton.

Shaw, R.D. and E.E. Prepas. 1989. Groundwater-lake interactions: II. Nearshore seepage patterns and the contribution of groundwater to lakes in central Alberta. J. Hydrol. [in press]

Stony Plain and District Historical Society. 1982. Along the fifth—A history of Stony Plain and district. Stony Plain Hist. Soc., Stony Plain.

Strong, W.L. and K.R. Leggat. 1981. Ecoregions of Alberta. Alta. En. Nat. Resour., Resour. Eval. Plan. Div., Edmonton.

TWIN LAKE

MAP SHEET: 83B/16
LOCATION: Tp46 R3 W5
LAT/LONG: 52°57′N 114°22′W

Tiny, sparkling Twin Lake is located 115 km southwest of the city of Edmonton in the County of Wetaskiwin. From Edmonton, take Highway 2 south to Highway 13, then travel west on Highway 13 past Pigeon Lake. Twin Lake is 3 km east of the hamlet of Winfield, just south of Highway 13. As the name implies, there are two lakes at this location, often referred to as West and East Twin or Twin Lakes. These two lakes are separated by a distance of less than 700 m; both have clear water. West Twin is relatively deep and is referred to in this chapter as Twin Lake (Fig. 1), whereas East Twin is extremely shallow and will be discussed only in reference to the deeper lake.

Twin Lake is located in a treed area; it is an idyllic location for picnics, quiet camping and fishing. A campground with 60 sites is located on the north shore of the lake and along the road connecting the two lakes (Fig. 2). The campground has firewood, pump water and a picnic area (Walker 1988) and is maintained by the County of Wetaskiwin. A small boat can be launched at the gravel boat launch on the north side; gasoline motors are prohibited (Alta. For. Ld. Wild. 1988). A soft mud bottom discourages swimming from the shoreline, although gravel added at the east end has improved shore access for swimmers. The lake water is excellent for swimming and the lake is one of the best in Alberta for SCUBA diving (Conroy Club and Yeoford Ladies Club 1973). The lake is stocked with catchable size rainbow trout. Although provincial fishing regulations apply, there are no specific regulations for Twin Lake (Alta. For. Ld. Wild. 1989).

Drainage Basin Characteristics

The drainage basin of Twin Lake is mostly forested (Table 1). White spruce predominate in upland areas, black spruce and tamarack predominate in lower areas and white birch, lodgepole pine, balsam poplar and trembling aspen are found throughout. Some areas in the southwest corner of the drainage basin are cleared for agriculture; the agricultural capacity of soils in this corner are rated as fair to fairly good (Lindsay et al. 1968). All of the land directly around the lake is owned by the Crown. The only development near both lakes is the campground.

Two intermittent streams flow into Twin Lake through culverts from East Twin Lake (Smith 1982). The main inflow from East Twin Lake enters on the east side of Twin Lake and the second one flows occasionally into the north side. A third stream flows through a tiny unnamed lake in the southeast part of the drainage basin and into the southeast corner of Twin Lake (Fig. 1).

Twin Lake is located near a topographic divide between three major river basins: the North Saskatchewan, the Battle and the Red Deer. The outflow stream from the lake, a fork of Poplar Creek, flows northwest from the lake (Fig. 2) and eventually enters the North Saskatchewan River 25 km east of Drayton Valley.

Lake Basin Characteristics

The oval lake basin is 35–m deep (Table 2) and the sides are steep, particularly along the south shore (Fig. 2).

The water level of Twin Lake has been recorded since October 1968 (Fig. 3). Water levels dropped a full metre, from a high of 920.0 m when records began, to 919.0 m in February 1981. Later

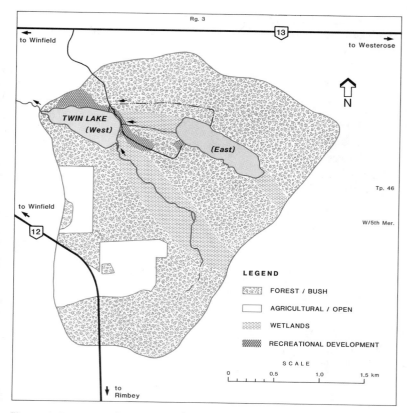

Figure 1. Features of the drainage basin of Twin Lake.
SOURCES: Alta. Envir. n.d.[a]; En. Mines Resour. Can. 1975. Updated with 1987 aerial photos.

Table 1. Characteristics of Twin Lake drainage basin.

area (excluding lake) (km²)[a]	7.12
soil[b]	Dark Gray Luvisols, Organics and Orthic Gray Luvisols
bedrock geology[c]	Paskapoo Formation (Tertiary): sandstone, siltstone, mudstone; thin limestone, coal and tuff beds; nonmarine
terrain[b]	level to rolling
ecoregion[d]	Boreal Foothills; bordering on Moist Mixedwood Subregion of Boreal Mixedwood
dominant vegetation[d]	lodgepole pine, trembling aspen, balsam poplar
mean annual inflow (m³)[a, e]	0.39 x 10⁶
mean annual sunshine (h)[f]	2 315

NOTE: [e]excluding groundwater inflow
SOURCES: [a]Alta. Envir. n.d.[a]; [b]Lindsay et al. 1968; [c]Alta. Res. Counc. 1972; [d]Strong and Leggat 1981; [f]Envir. Can. 1982

Table 2. Characteristics of Twin Lake.

elevation (m)[a, b]	919.18
surface area (km²)[a, c]	0.24
volume (m³)[a, c]	3.69 x 10⁶
maximum depth (m)[c]	35
mean depth (m)[c]	15.7
shoreline length (km)[d]	1.9
mean annual lake evaporation (mm)[e]	664
mean annual precipitation (mm)[e, f]	534
mean residence time (yr)[e]	10
control structure	none

NOTES: [a]on date of sounding: 30 July 1980; [f]excluding groundwater inflow
SOURCES: [b]Alta. Envir. n.d.[b]; [c]Babin 1984; [d]En. Mines Resour. Can. 1975; [e]Alta. Envir. n.d.[a]

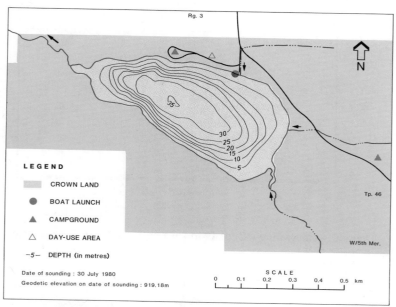

Figure 2. Bathymetry and shoreline features of Twin Lake.
BATHYMETRY SOURCE: Prepas et al. n.d.

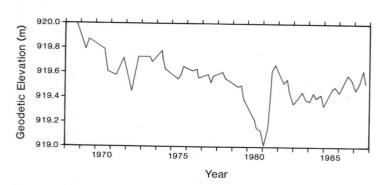

Figure 3. Water level of Twin Lake, 1968 to 1987.
SOURCE: Alta. Envir. n.d.[b].

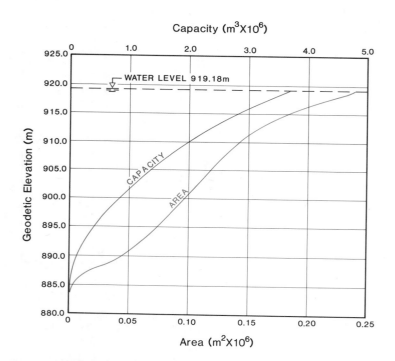

Figure 4. Area/capacity curve for Twin Lake.
SOURCE: Prepas et al. n.d.

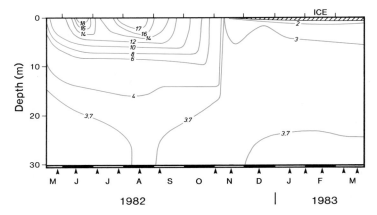

Figure 5. Temperature (°C) of Twin Lake, 1982 to 1983. Arrows indicate sampling dates.
SOURCE: Prepas et al. n.d.

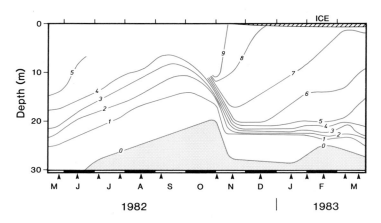

Figure 6. Dissolved oxygen (mg/L) in Twin Lake, 1982 to 1983. Arrows indicate sampling dates.
SOURCES: Prepas et al. n.d.; Babin 1984.

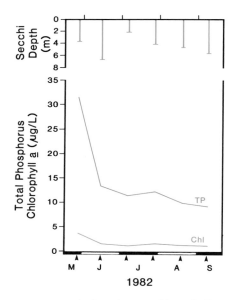

Figure 7. Total phosphorus, chlorophyll *a* and Secchi depth in Twin Lake, 1982.
SOURCES: Prepas et al. n.d.; Prepas 1983[c].

Table 3. Major ions and related water quality variables for Twin Lake. Average concentrations in mg/L; pH in pH units. One composite sample from a depth of 2 m collected on 13 Mar. 1986. S.E. = standard error.

	Mean	S.E.
pH	7.8	—
total alkalinity (CaCO$_3$)	178[a]	20.7
specific conductivity (μS/cm)	291[b]	10.6
total dissolved solids	188[b]	8.5
turbidity (NTU)	0.6[c]	0.30
colour (Pt)	19[c]	3.6
total hardness (CaCO$_3$)	159[d]	11.7
HCO$_3$	217[a]	25.2
CO$_3$	0.1[a]	0.1
Mg	15	—
Na	19	—
K	3	—
SO$_4$	6	—
Ca	44	—

NOTES: [a]n = 2, summers 1981, 1982; [b]n = 6, 26 May to 08 Sep. 1982; [c]n = 3, summers 1981, 1982, 1983; [d]n = 2, summers 1980, 1981
SOURCE: Prepas et al. n.d.

Table 4. Nutrient, chlorophyll *a* and Secchi depth data for Twin Lake. Average concentrations in μg/L. Composite samples from the euphotic zone collected 3 times from 11 May to 01 July 1981 and 6 times from 26 May to 08 Sep. 1982. S.E. = standard error.

	1981		1982	
	Mean	S.E.	Mean	S.E.
total phosphorus	13[a]	1.6	15	3.4
total dissolved phosphorus	7	0.4	7[b]	—
soluble reactive phosphorus	2[b]	—	—	—
total Kjeldahl nitrogen	323	24.8	299	9.2
NO$_3$ + NO$_2$–nitrogen	19	10.0	6	1.9
NH$_4$–nitrogen	5	2.4	—	—
iron	—	—	29[c]	—
chlorophyll *a*	2.0[a]	0.48	1.7	0.41
Secchi depth (m)	4.2[a]	0.32	4.3	0.64

NOTES: [a]n = 7, 08 May to 25 Aug. 1980; [b]n = 1; [c]n = 1, 13 Mar. 1986
SOURCE: Prepas et al. n.d.

in 1981, water levels rebounded, and in recent years, they have fluctuated around 919.5 m. A beaver dam, which extends across the outlet, controls lake water levels.

Changes in the lake's area and capacity, to an elevation of 919.18 m, are shown in Figure 4.

Water Quality

The water quality of Twin Lake was studied in the summers of 1980 and 1981, and from May 1982 through March 1983 by researchers at the University of Alberta (Prepas et al. n.d.; Prepas 1983[a]; 1983[b]; 1983[c]; Prepas and Trew 1983; Babin 1984; Prepas and Vickery 1984[a]; 1984[b]; Babin and Prepas 1985).

Twin Lake has hard water; the dominant ions are bicarbonate and calcium (Table 3). The water is moderately coloured, but not turbid. Due to the lake's relatively high elevation (919 m), the surface water temperatures in summer are about 4°C cooler than many other small lakes in central Alberta. The water is strongly thermally stratified in summer (Fig. 5). The lake is sheltered by trees and by relatively steep banks, particularly on the south side. Given the lake depth and protection from the wind, thermal mixing is weak and dissolved oxygen concentrations are strongly stratified year-round (Fig. 6).

Dissolved oxygen depletion rates were measured in the hypolimnion in the summer of 1980 (0.312 g O_2/m² per day), and under ice cover in the winter of 1982/83 (0.193 g O_2/m² per day). These rates are low and reflect, at least partially, low algal productivity in the lake.

Twin Lake is oligotrophic. In summer, total phosphorus typically falls below 10 μg/L and chlorophyll *a* concentrations are generally below 2 μg/L (Table 4). Total phosphorus concentrations in the surface waters are highest in spring (Fig. 7) and late fall. These maxima are caused by the mixing of water from the phosphorus-rich hypolimnion throughout the lake during overturn. In September 1982, total phosphorus concentrations reached 190 μg/L over the bottom sediments and 50 μg/L at 13 m below the surface. By March 1983, total phosphorus concentrations had reached 30 μg/L in the surface waters and 400 μg/L over the bottom sediments. Detailed phosphorus budgets provided no evidence that phosphorus from bottom sediments was recycled into the trophogenic zone of Twin Lake (Shaw and Prepas 1989). This is a very unusual situation in an Alberta lake. The phosphorus concentrations in the surface waters of Twin Lake are unusually low and the calcium concentrations are unusually high for a lake in central Alberta (Tables 3, 4). Twin may be a lake where phosphorus released from the bottom sediments is not available for algal production due to coprecipitation with iron and/or calcium.

The water quality of East Twin Lake was measured once in August 1980. Although it was generally similar to that in Twin Lake, the water in East Twin was less coloured, and open-water phytoplankton levels were one-third those recorded for the deeper lake. The shallow lake has a rich benthic algal community.

Biological Characteristics

Plants

There are no data on the plants in Twin Lake.

Invertebrates

The zooplankton was sampled at various intervals from May through September, from 1980 to 1982 (Prepas et al. n.d.; Prepas 1983[c]; Prepas and Vickery 1984[a]). The zooplankton biomass was relatively high: 15% of the total phosphorus pool in the trophogenic zone. The dominant species in the summers of 1981 and 1982 were *Daphnia pulex/pulicaria*, *Diaptomus leptopus*, *Diacyclops bicuspidatus thomasi* and *Chaoborus* sp.

There are no data on benthic invertebrates in Twin Lake.

Fish

Four species of fish have been recorded in the lake. Northern pike, burbot, and yellow perch are native, whereas rainbow trout has been introduced. Forage fish and suckers are present, but species have not been identified.

From 1964 through 1966, the lake was stocked with kokanee salmon (Alta. For. Ld. Wild. n.d.), but few, if any, salmon were caught subsequently. From 1969 through 1975, an average of 13 000 yearling rainbow trout were introduced each year. This program was halted because few or none of the small trout survived, likely due to predation by northern pike. Fish and Wildlife Division considered treating both Twin lakes and the inlet stream at the southeast corner with rotenone, to remove the northern pike (Smith 1982), but this treatment was not carried out. Instead, a program of stocking adult rainbow trout was initiated in 1984. An annual aver-age of 480 trout were planted from 1984 through 1988. The program of stocking catchable size trout has been very successful and will likely continue in Twin Lake, but only as large trout become available (Lowe 1988).

The distribution of northern pike in Twin Lake was studied by divers using SCUBA in 1980 (Chapman and Mackay 1984). During summer, when the water was thermally stratified, most pike (81%) observed by divers were in the top 2 m of water, and only 1% were below a depth of 4 m. Smaller pike (greater than 25-cm standard length) were found more frequently in the top 2 m of water than larger pike. In the autumn, very few pike were observed, and those that were seen were at depths of less than 2 m.

Wildlife

Mallards, Gadwall, Common Goldeneye and Bufflehead nest on the lake. Common Loons are seen on the lake in spring (Alta. For. Ld. Wild. n.d.).

E.E. Prepas

References

Alberta Environment. n.d.[a]. Tech. Serv. Div., Hydrol. Br. Unpubl. data, Edmonton.
———. n.d.[b]. Tech. Serv. Div., Surv. Br. Unpubl. data, Edmonton.
Alberta Forestry, Lands and Wildlife. n.d. Fish Wild. Div. Unpubl. data, Edmonton.
———. 1988. Boating in Alberta. Fish Wild. Div., Edmonton.
———. 1989. Guide to sportfishing. Fish Wild. Div., Edmonton.
Alberta Research Council. 1972. Geological map of Alberta. Nat. Resour. Div., Alta. Geol. Surv., Edmonton.
Babin, J. 1984. Winter oxygen depletion in temperate zone lakes. MSc thesis. Univ. Alta., Edmonton.
——— and E.E. Prepas. 1985. Modelling winter oxygen depletion rates in ice-covered temperate zone lakes in Canada. Can. J. Fish. Aquat. Sci. 42:239–249.
Chapman, C.A. and W.C. Mackay. 1984. Direct observation of habitat utilization by northern pike. Copeia:255–258.
Conroy Club and Yeoford Ladies Club. ca 1973. Trail blazers. Conroy Club Yeoford Ladies Club, Winfield.
Energy, Mines and Resources Canada. 1975. National topographic series 1:50 000 83B/16 (1975). Surv. Map. Br., Ottawa.
Environment Canada. 1982. Canadian climate normals, Vol. 7: Bright sunshine (1951–1980). Prep. by Atm. Envir. Serv. Supply Serv. Can., Ottawa.
Lindsay, J.D., W. Odynsky, J.W. Peters and W.E. Bowser. 1968. Soil survey of the Buck Lake (NE 83B) and Wabamun Lake (E1/2 83G) areas. Alta. Soil Surv. Rep. No. 24, Univ. Alta. Bull. No. SS–7, Alta. Res. Counc. Rep. No. 87. Univ. Alta., Edmonton.
Lowe, D. 1988. Alta. For. Ld. Wild., Fish Wild. Div., Red Deer. Pers. comm.
Prepas, E.E. 1983[a]. Orthophosphate turnover time in shallow productive lakes. Can. J. Fish. Aquat. Sci. 40:1412–1418.
———. 1983[b]. Total dissolved solids as a predictor of lake biomass and productivity. Can. J. Fish. Aquat. Sci. 40:92–95.
———. 1983[c]. The influence of phosphorus and zooplankton on chlorophyll levels in Alberta lakes. Prep. for Alta. Envir., Res. Mgt. Div. Rep. 83/23, Edmonton.
——— and D.O. Trew. 1983. Evaluation of the phosphorus-chlorophyll relationship for lakes off the Precambrian Shield in western Canada. Can. J. Fish. Aquat. Sci. 40:27–35.
Prepas, E.E. and J. Vickery. 1984[a]. The contribution of particulate phosphorus (>250 μm) to the total phosphorus pool in lake water. Can. J. Fish. Aquat. Sci. 41:351–363.
———. 1984[b]. Seasonal changes in total phosphorus and the role of internal loading in western Canadian lakes. Verh. Internat. Verein. Limnol. 223:303–308.
Prepas, E.E., I. Wisheu and J. Babin. n.d. Univ. Alta, Dept. Zool. Unpubl. data, Edmonton.
Shaw, J.F.H. and E.E. Prepas. 1989. Potential significance of phosphorus release from shallow sediments of deep Alberta lakes. ms submitted to Limnol. Oceanogr.
Smith, T. 1982. Memorandum to C. Ladd on West Twin Lake rehabilitation. Alta. En. Nat. Resour., Fish Wild. Div., Red Deer.
Strong, W.L. and K.R. Leggat. 1981. Ecoregions of Alberta. Alta. En. Nat. Resour., Resour. Eval. Plan. Div., Edmonton.
Walker, G. 1988. Co. Wetaskiwin, Wetaskiwin. Pers. comm.

WABAMUN LAKE

MAP SHEETS: 83G/7, 9, 10
LOCATION: Tp52, 53 R4, 5 W5
LAT/LONG: 53°33'N 114°36'W

Wabamun Lake, one of the best-known and most-studied lakes in Alberta, lies 60 km west of the city of Edmonton on Highway 16. From Edmonton, the first turnoff to the lake provides access to the summer village of Kapasiwin and Wabamun Lake Provincial Park on Moonlight Bay (Fig. 1). The other main access points are reached by turnoffs to the village of Wabamun on the north shore and to Seba Beach on the west end of the lake. Local roads run along much of the lakeshore; on the south side, a gravel road parallels the lakeshore beside active coal mines.

Wabamun is a Cree word meaning "mirror" (Holmgren and Holmgren 1976). The lake was once called White Whale Lake for the large whitefish caught in its waters; this name appears on maps from the late 1800s (Hills of Hope Hist. Commit. 1976). The lake's name reverted back to the original Cree name sometime near the turn of the century.

The Paul Band Reserve is situated on the eastern edge of the lake. By 1876, the Stoney Indian Nation had separated into smaller bands; one of them, the Paul Band, hunted in the area northwest of Edmonton. They signed Treaty No. 6 in 1876 and settled on the shores of Wabamun Lake. In 1984, the population of the band was 875 (Alta. Native Aff. 1986).

The community of Wabamun was established in 1912. Cottage subdivisions were built at Lakeview on Moonlight Bay and at Kapasiwin; these became two of the first summer villages in Alberta. The railway that passed through Wabamun ran excursion trains on weekends, and visitors were accommodated at a large hotel.

The first coal mines in the watershed began as underground operations in 1910 and as strip mines in 1948. Two power generating plants have been built on Wabamun Lake by TransAlta Utilities Corporation to take advantage of the abundant supply of local coal. The Wabamun plant, near the village of Wabamun, began operation in 1956, and the Sundance plant, on the opposite shore, began in 1970. A third plant, Keephills, is located just outside the watershed southeast of the lake, but its cooling pond lies within the watershed boundary. The Wabamun plant uses lake water for cooling, and heated effluent is returned to the lake via a canal. As a result, a large portion of Kapasiwin Bay remains ice-free in winter. The Sundance plant also used lake water for cooling when it began operation, but now uses a large cooling pond near the lakeshore. Make-up water for this pond is pumped from the North Saskatchewan River, and blow-down water is returned to the river. The effect of the two power plants near the lakeshore, their associated coal mines and the heated effluent on water quality in Wabamun Lake has stimulated much controversy (Reid, Crowther Partners Ltd. 1973; Noton 1974; Beak Consult. Ltd. 1980; Habgood 1983).

The popular opinion that the lake has poor water quality probably stems from the nuisance growth of an aquatic plant called Canada waterweed or Elodea (*Elodea canadensis*), which was not observed in the lake before 1968. It became the dominant aquatic plant in the eastern end by the early 1970s, and snarled fishing lines, wound in propellers, and washed onto beaches. The cooling water discharges from both power plants were implicated as the cause, although this was never confirmed. By 1975, the Sundance effluent was diverted to a large cooling pond near the lake, and in 1977, the Elodea population began to decline. Now it is rare in the lake except near the Wabamun plant cooling water discharge canal and two small areas at Seba Beach (Terrestrial Aquat. Envir. Managers, Ltd. 1987).

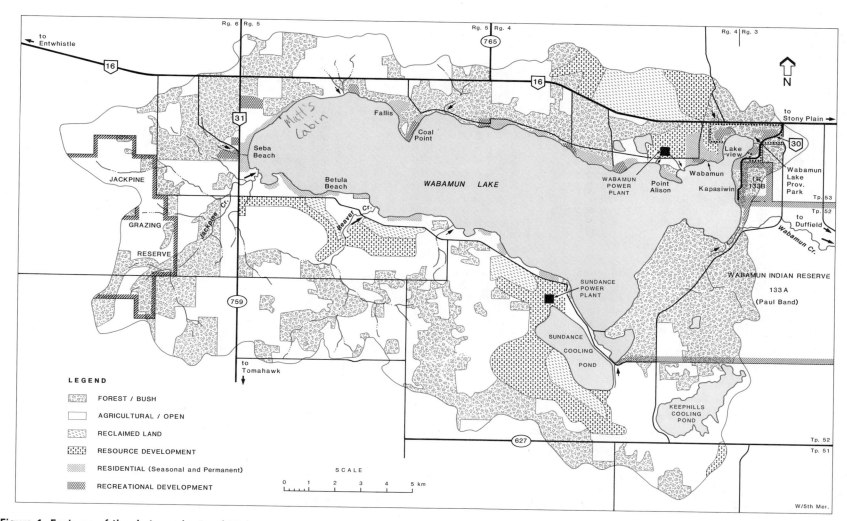

Figure 1. Features of the drainage basin of Wabamun Lake.
SOURCES: Alta. Envir. n.d.[b]; En. Mines Resour. Can. 1974; 1975. Updated with 1985 and 1987 aerial photos.

TransAlta Utilities Corporation is required to cut aquatic vegetation in a designated area of Kapasiwin Bay.

There is abundant natural aquatic vegetation along shorelines and in bays, but the water in Wabamun Lake is often fairly clear, and blue-green algal blooms are rare. Wabamun Lake Provincial Park, located on Moonlight Bay, is a focus of activity on warm summer weekends. The boat launch at the park is one of the best on the lake, although sailboats with tall masts cannot pass under the CN railway trestle across the mouth of the bay. The park has several campgrounds with a total of 318 campsites, extensive day-use areas, showers, hiking trails and a sandy swimming beach. It is open in winter for day-use (Alta. Hotel Assoc. 1989). There are commercially operated campgrounds at the west end of the lake, and the Ernest Poole Scout camp on the north shore offers camping to nonmembers by reservation. The County of Parkland operates three day-use areas on the north shore: Ascot Beach, Rich's Point and Coal Point. All have picnic areas, but only Ascot Beach and Rich's Point have boat launches. There are boat launches, piers and day-use areas at Seba Beach and at the village of Wabamun. The village also offers a small campground north of the lake access.

Sport fishing is one of the most popular activities on the lake. In summer, fishing is often excellent for northern pike, and increasingly so for walleye. In winter, ice fishing for lake whitefish draws hundreds of anglers on mild weekends, and large pike may be taken from the inlet and outlet canals at the Wabamun power plant. A few fishermen launch small boats in the outlet canal in winter to fish the open water created by the heated effluent. Yellow perch are also in the lake, but they are the least important of the game fish because of their small size and low numbers. There are no special sport fishing regulations applicable to Wabamun Lake, but provincial limits apply. The lake's inlet creeks and outlet are closed to fishing for a period in spring (Alta. For. Ld. Wild. 1989).

Wabamun Lake, with three sailing clubs, is an important sailing lake, perhaps because of the strong winds that sweep down the lake

Table 1. Characteristics of Wabamun Lake drainage basin.

area (excluding lake) (km²)[a]	259
soil[b]	Solonetzic south of lake, Gray Luvisols north of lake
bedrock geology[c]	Paskapoo Formation (Tertiary): sandstone, siltstone, mudstone; thin limestone, coal and tuff beds; nonmarine
	Battle Formation (Upper Cretaceous): mudstone, tuff beds; nonmarine
	Whitemud Formation (Upper Cretaceous): sandstone, clay; nonmarine
	Wapiti Formation (Upper Cretaceous): sandstone, mudstone, bentonite, scattered coal beds; nonmarine
terrain[b]	level to rolling
ecoregion[d]	Moist Mixedwood Subregion of Boreal Mixedwood
dominant vegetation[d]	trembling aspen, balsam poplar
mean annual inflow (m³)[a, e]	13.1×10^6
mean annual sunshine (h)[f]	2 315

NOTE: [e]excluding groundwater inflow
SOURCES: [a]Alta. Envir. n.d.[b]; [b]Lindsay et al. 1968; [c]Alta. Res. Counc. 1972; [d]Strong and Leggat 1981; [f]Envir. Can. 1982

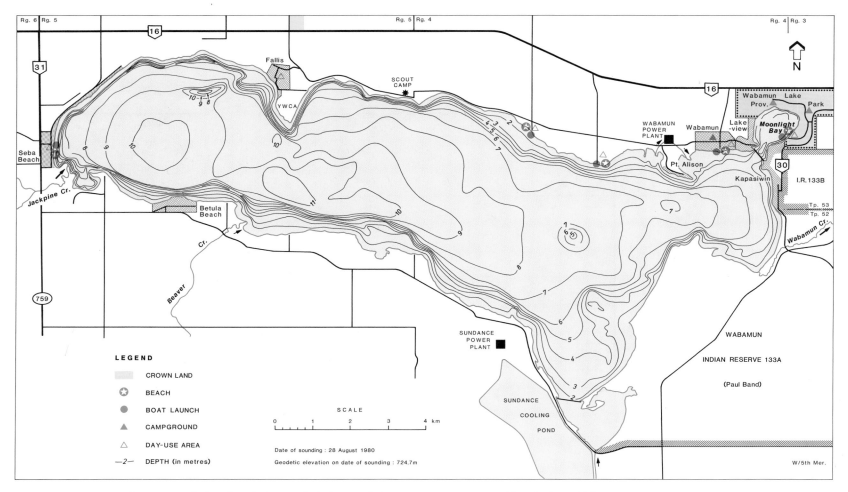

Figure 2. Bathymetry and shoreline features of Wabamun Lake. BATHYMETRY SOURCE: Alta. Envir. n.d.[c].

at times. Wind surfing is also common near the village of Wabamun and near Seba Beach. Other activities include power boating, water skiing and swimming. In certain areas of the lake, power-driven boats are subject to a maximum speed of 12 km/hour (Alta. For. Ld. Wild. 1988). The Naval Reserve of the Canadian Armed Forces keeps a tugboat on the lake in the inlet canal at the Wabamun Power Plant. It is used for training in basic seamanship and engineering for recruits and officers (Pelletier 1989).

Drainage Basin Characteristics

The drainage basin surrounding Wabamun Lake is about 3 times larger than the area of the lake (Fig. 1, Table 1). About half of the land in the basin is cleared or used for agriculture, particularly for hay, barley, forage oats and cattle production (Reid, Crowther Partners Ltd. 1973). Coal is strip-mined extensively north and south of the lake by companies associated with TransAlta Utilities Corporation to supply the coal-fired generating plants located in the basin. As coal excavation moves west, the mined-out land is reclaimed, primarily for agricultural purposes.

Cottage development is dense compared to that on many Alberta lakes. In 1981, there were 1 513 developed lots around the lakeshore, excluding those in the village of Wabamun, of which 1 071 were occupied. About 10% of these had permanent residences (Andries and Schinkel 1981). Half of these cottages are within the summer villages of Seba Beach, Kapasiwin, Point Alison, Lakeview and Betula Beach (Fig. 1); the remaining cottages are under the jurisdiction of the County of Parkland. The village of Wabamun had a population of 589 in 1987 (Ivan 1988). Many people living in the village work at the Wabamun power plant or its coal mines. Services such as a gas station, grocery store, hotel, restaurant and hardware store are available in the village. Another location on the lake for some of these services is Seba Beach, and there is a small store at Kapasiwin.

The terrain in the watershed is gently rolling to undulating, and hills to the south of the lake rise to an elevation of 844 m. Fallis, or

Coal Point, in the Fallis area, rises from the water's edge as a vertical cliff. The native vegetation is dominated by trembling aspen, balsam poplar and willow, with white spruce in undisturbed areas. Coal mining is gradually altering the landscape in the watershed, but reclamation efforts include recontouring and the return of native vegetation, as well as agricultural development.

Surficial deposits to the south and west of the lake are discontinuous glacial till or bedrock of Paleocene age. Where till occurs, it contains a large proportion of bedrock material. Coal is mined in this area; coal seams occur in the lowermost portion of the Paskapoo Formation or in the uppermost Cretaceous bedrock. In areas along the shoreline where coal outcrops, beach sands are black. To the north of the lake, till thickness generally exceeds a depth of 2 m. Surficial deposits to the east of the lake consist of fine-grained glaciolacustrine materials. Bedrock underlying this area is of Cretaceous age, whereas to the south and west of the lake the underlying bedrock is of Paleocene age (Andriashek et al. 1979).

Soils in the watershed are predominantly Gray Luvisols developed on till; a few small areas of Organic soils are present (Lindsay et al. 1968). The Luvisolic soils have moderately severe to severe limitations for agriculture, mainly because the soil structure is undesirable or they absorb water slowly (Can. Dept. Reg. Econ. Expansion 1972).

There are at least 35 drainage courses that convey runoff to the lake. Most of these flow only during snowmelt in spring and during summer rainstorms, but several on the north side have a continuous base flow from groundwater. The seven largest streams account for about 70% of the total volume of runoff to the lake (Mitchell 1985). Mine drainage enters the lake on the north side after settling in several ponds. On the south side, mine drainage enters the Sundance cooling pond, which drains to the North Saskatchewan River. The lake's outlet, Wabamun Creek, flows intermittently toward the North Saskatchewan River.

Table 2. Characteristics of Wabamun Lake.

elevation (m)[a, b]	724.70
surface area (km²)[a, b]	81.8
volume (m³)[a, b]	513 x 10⁶
maximum depth (m)[a, b]	11
mean depth (m)[a, b]	6.3
shoreline length (km)[c]	57.3
mean annual lake evaporation (mm)[d]	642
mean annual precipitation (mm)[d]	534
mean residence time (yr)[d, e]	>100
control structure	none

NOTES: [a]on date of sounding: Aug. 1980; [e]excluding groundwater inflow
SOURCES: [b]Alta. Envir. n.d.[c]; [c]Habgood 1983; [d]Alta. Envir. n.d.[b]

Table 3. Major ions and related water quality variables for Wabamun Lake, main basin. Average concentrations in mg/L; pH in pH units. Composite samples from the euphotic zone collected 19 times from 03 May 1983 to 21 Oct. 1985. S.E. = standard error.

	Mean	S.E.
pH (range)	7.9–9.6	—
total alkalinity (CaCO₃)	193	0.6
specific conductivity (µS/cm)	417	2.4
total dissolved solids (calculated)	235	0.9
total hardness (CaCO₃)	111	1.5
total particulate carbon	2	0.2
dissolved organic carbon	11	0.1
HCO₃	220	2.0
CO₃	<8	—
Mg	12	0.2
Na	46	0.4
K	8	0.1
Cl	3	0.2
SO₄	26	0.5
Ca	24	0.4

SOURCE: Alta. Envir. n.d.[a], Naquadat station 01AL05DE2294

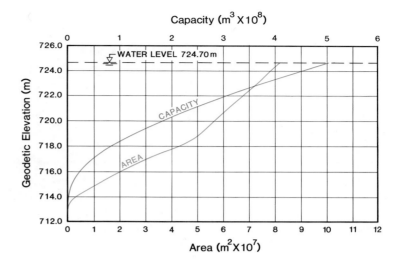

Figure 3. Area/capacity curve for Wabamun Lake.
SOURCE: Alta. Envir. n.d.[c].

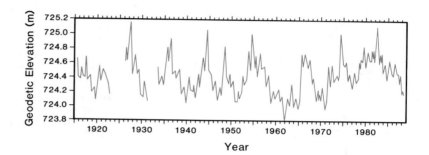

Figure 4. Water level of Wabamun Lake, 1915 to 1987.
SOURCE: Envir. Can. 1915–1987.

The water level of Wabamun Lake has long been the subject of concern and controversy among lake users. Water levels have been recorded continuously since 1933, with additional records back to 1915 (Fig. 4). From 1915 to 1987, the range in fluctuation was about 1.4 m, with an annual fluctuation of about 1 m. Since 1912, a number of control structures designed to regulate water levels have been built at the outlet and subsequently destroyed. As of 1989, investigations were under way by Alberta Environment to determine a suitable elevation for a new control structure.

Water Quality

The water quality of Wabamun Lake has been studied off and on since 1968. Investigations included the effects of the thermal discharges from the two power plants (Nursall et al. 1972; Gallup and Hickman 1973; 1975; Beak Consult. Ltd. 1980); the ion chemistry (Schwartz and Gallup 1978); and groundwater (Crowe and Schwartz 1982). Additional reports and studies are listed in a comprehensive literature review (Habgood 1983). Studies by Alberta Environment on the limnology of the lake and its nutrient sources began in 1980 (Mitchell 1985) and have been ongoing (Alta. Envir. n.d.[a]; Mitchell 1984).

The water in Wabamun Lake is fresh; bicarbonate and sodium are the dominant ions (Table 3). Groundwater is thought to play a role in the ion chemistry of the lake, but the volume of groundwater inflow and outflow has been the subject of controversy. The proportion of ions in groundwater in coal seams below the lake bed, and in surficial inflow streams with a groundwater base flow, are both similar to that in the lake water. The maintenance of fresh water in the lake depends on groundwater outflow as well as inflow.

The temperature of the water is usually similar from the top to the bottom of the water column (Fig. 5) because the surface area is large relative to the depth, and the lake is oriented with the prevailing wind. As a result, the entire water column is normally well-oxygenated from May through October (Fig. 6). Very rarely, rapid surface

Lake Basin Characteristics

Wabamun Lake is a large, shallow lake that is 19.2–km long and 6.6–km wide (Fig. 2, Table 2). Its orientation with the prevailing wind and its long fetch are a great advantage to sailors, but wave action is heavy at times.

The bottom of the lake is fairly flat, with a gradual slope toward the deepest area at the western end. In comparison, the slopes along the edges of the lake are steep. Popular opinion is that a very deep hole is present off of Fallis (Coal) Point because a sailboat sank and was lost in the area, but such a depression was not revealed during the 1980 hydrographic survey.

The littoral zone in Wabamun Lake extends to the 5–m depth contour (Haag and Gorham 1979) and includes 31% of the lake bottom (Fig. 3). This is a somewhat deeper littoral area than that in most central Alberta lakes. Sandy areas are found at depths less than 2 m, with soft clay or organic sediments over most of the lake bottom (R.L. & L. Envir. Serv. Ltd. 1987). Hamilton and Reynoldson (1981) found that the highest percentage of organic matter (41%) was in sediments collected from the west end at depths of 10 m and the lowest percentage (9%) was in sandy sediments from near the Sundance area at a depth of 4 m.

There are natural beaches along much of the shoreline, but emergent vegetation restricts their use. The most popular beaches for swimming are the artificially-made one at the provincial park and the natural one at Seba Beach.

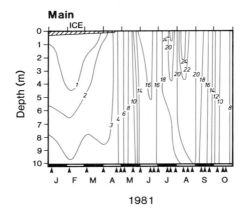

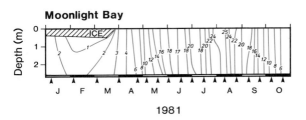

Figure 5. Temperature (°C) of Wabamun Lake, main bay and Moonlight Bay, 1981. Arrows indicate sampling dates.
SOURCE: Alta. Envir. n.d.[a].

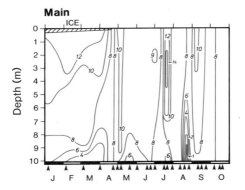

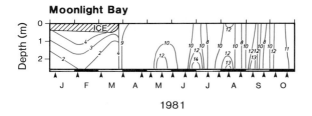

Figure 6. Dissolved oxygen (mg/L) in Wabamun Lake, main bay and Moonlight Bay, 1981. Arrows indicate sampling dates.
SOURCE: Alta. Envir. n.d.[a].

Table 4. Nutrient, chlorophyll *a* and Secchi depth data for Wabamun Lake, main basin. Average concentrations in µg/L. Composite samples from the euphotic zone collected 14 times from 22 Apr. to 19 Oct. 1981 and 7 times from 03 May to 17 Oct. 1983. S.E. = standard error.

	1981		1983	
	Mean	S.E.	Mean	S.E.
total phosphorus	34	1.7	30	1.5
total dissolved phosphorus	11	1.1	10	0.5
soluble reactive phosphorus	4	0.6	3	0.4
total Kjeldahl nitrogen	1 040	47.8	767	37.0
NO$_3$ + NO$_2$–nitrogen	4	0.6	5	3.3
NH$_4$–nitrogen	76	23.0	17	4.7
iron	<20	—	<20	—
chlorophyll *a*	12.6	1.36	10.4	1.81
Secchi depth (m)	1.9	0.14	2.3	0.34

SOURCE: Alta. Envir. n.d.[a], Naquadat stations 01AL05DE2291, 01AL05DE2292, 01AL05DE2294

Table 5. A comparison of average summer chlorophyll *a* and total phosphorus concentrations in Wabamun Lake, 1980 to 1989. Composite samples collected from the euphotic zone each year from 18 June to 18 Sep. S.E. = standard error; n = sample size.

Year	n	Chlorophyll *a* (µg/L)	S.E.	Phosphorus (µg/L)	S.E.
1980	6	13.0	2.6	29.8	2.4
1981	7	12.6	1.5	33.0	1.5
1982	4	11.1	3.8	30.0	3.0
1983	3	12.4	2.7	30.5	2.7
1984	3	13.5	1.9	32.9	2.6
1985	3	11.5	1.6	—	—
1986	4	10.6	2.3	32.8	1.8
1987	3	14.3	3.5	36.3	0.9
1988	4	11.6	2.5	34.4	2.9
1989	3	10.9	1.3	33.4	1.0

SOURCE: Alta. Envir. n.d.[a]

warming promotes temporary thermal stratification, and dissolved oxygen levels decline near the bottom. Under ice in winter, the main basin of the lake remains well-oxygenated near the surface, although oxygen levels gradually decline at the bottom. Levels in Moonlight Bay declined to 1.9 mg/L by February in 1980, but they remained somewhat higher in the winter of 1981. As a result of its shallowness and abundant summer plant growth, total oxygen depletion under ice in Moonlight Bay probably occurs in some years. Heated effluent from the Wabamun Power Plant maintains an open area in Kapasiwin Bay in winter; this changes shape and size with weather conditions, but winter dissolved oxygen levels in the east end of the lake undoubtedly are higher as a result. Lake water temperature at the mouth of the cooling canal can be as high as 33°C in summer and 21°C in winter (Beak Consult. Ltd. 1980).

Wabamun Lake is mildly eutrophic. The water has a greenish-brown tinge most of the summer, but the quantity of algae is low enough that water-based activities are enjoyable (Table 4). Average concentrations of total phosphorus and chlorophyll *a* in Wabamun

Table 6. Measured average total phosphorus loading to Wabamun Lake, 1980 and 1981.

Source		Phosphorus (kg/yr)	Percentage of Total
watershed	streams	2 030	14
	diffuse runoff	1 210	9
	ash lagoon effluent	743	5
precipitation/dustfall		1 882	13
sewage[a]		75	1
sediment release		8 000	56
groundwater		260	2
	TOTAL	14 200	100

annual areal loading (g/m² of lake surface) 0.17

NOTE: [a]unmeasured: assumes 4% of all sewage effluent from residences and camps enters the lake, as in Mitchell 1982
SOURCE: Mitchell 1985

Table 7. Percentage composition of major algal groups by total biomass in Wabamun Lake, 1983. Composite samples collected from the euphotic zone.

ALGAL GROUP	03 May	31 May	28 June	27 July	24 Aug.	20 Sep.	17 Oct.
Total Biomass (mg/L)	2.15	0.272	2.24	5.37	7.21	11.9	3.04
Percentage composition:							
Cyanophyta	0	13	18	44	54	6	18
				Microcystis	*Aphanoth.*		
				Anabaena———————→			
Chlorophyta	16	23	15	14	11	1	4
		Pediastrum					
Chrysophyta	24	33	2	4	0	0	<1
	Heteroch.	*Dinobryon*					
Bacillariophyta	43	28	47	30	13	88	72
	Cyclotella	*Fragilaria*————————————→				*Melosira*	*Asterionella*
		Melosira————————————→				*Stephan.*	*Fragilaria*
Cryptophyta	17	1	8	5	17	3	5
Pyrrhophyta	0	2	10	3	5	2	0

NOTE: *Aphanoth.* = *Aphanothece*; *Heteroch.* = *Heterochromonas*; *Stephan.* = *Stephanodiscus*.
SOURCE: Alta. Envir. n.d.[a]

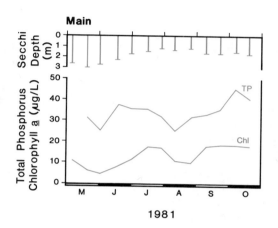
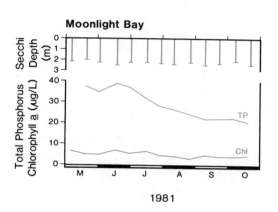

Figure 7. Total phosphorus, chlorophyll *a* and Secchi depth in Wabamun Lake, main bay and Moonlight Bay, 1981. SOURCE: Alta. Envir. n.d.[a].

Lake are similar from year to year (Table 5); these levels were somewhat higher in 1987 when blue-green algal blooms were prevalent.

The patterns of total phosphorus and chlorophyll *a* concentrations over the summer are also fairly similar from year to year; those illustrated for the main basin in Figure 7 are typical. There is evidence that phosphorus release from the bottom sediments occurs, even though the water column is usually well-oxygenated. In Moonlight Bay, phosphorus and chlorophyll *a* levels were minimal in midsummer in 1981, probably as a result of dense macrophyte growth. In general, the limnology of Moonlight Bay is different from that of the main basin of the lake.

The average transparency of the lake is somewhat less than in other lakes with similar levels of chlorophyll. Windy periods tend to resuspend organic material from the bottom of the lake and decrease transparency.

Most of the external supply of phosphorus that enters the lake in a year is derived from the watershed via streams and diffuse runoff (Table 6). The supply in precipitation and dust that falls directly onto the lake is also relatively large. Although many people are concerned about the impact of sewage effluent on the lake, it is apparent from the information in Table 6 that this source is minor compared to the other sources. The release of phosphorus from the bottom sediments probably has as great an influence on water quality in Wabamun Lake as any other factor.

Biological Characteristics

Plants

Phytoplankton biomass was measured monthly by Alberta Environment during each open-water period from 1980 through 1986 (Alta. Envir. n.d.[a]). Table 7 presents data for 1983, which was a fairly typical year for patterns of dominance and variation in biomass.

Diatoms (Bacillariophyta) were usually dominant in spring and fall, with blue-greens (Cyanophyta: *Anabaena* spp. and *Aphanizomenon flos-aquae*) dominant in July and August. Blue-greens never reached bloom proportions through the first seven years of study. In 1987, however, large populations of *Lyngbya Birgei*, *Gloeotrichia echinulata* and *Anabaena flos-aquae* developed in July. These blue-green species have been present in the phytoplankton in midsummer most years, but in very low proportions. It is likely that the potential for blue-green algal blooms is present each year, but climatic conditions determine whether such blooms actually develop.

In some years, diatoms were dominant throughout the summer. In 1985, for example, *Stephanodiscus niagarae* attained a large biomass by the end of June, and this continued through mid-September. The well-mixed water column may allow diatoms to persist in Wabamun Lake, whereas in other lakes, they settle out when the water column stratifies (Reynolds 1980). A diatom bloom, which appears brown-green, generally does not cause public concern as does a similar biomass of one of the common nuisance species of blue-green algae.

Macrophytes are abundant in Wabamun Lake and probably always have been. The first plant survey, in 1961 (Dobson and Stanley 1961), documented species similar to those in the lake today, with the exception of *Elodea canadensis*, which was not observed in the lake in 1961, but became dominant in Kapasiwin Bay by 1970. It was speculated that the success of this species resulted from the open water created by the thermal effluent, rather than from the warm water itself. TransAlta Utilities Corporation conducted a major study on macrophyte growth in Wabamun Lake from 1973 to 1979 (Beak Consult. Ltd. 1980) and continued mapping the macrophyte beds until 1987 (Terrestrial Aquat. Envir. Managers, Ltd. 1987). Elodea breaks dormancy earlier than native species; by the time other species break dormancy in late April, Elodea plants are large and overshadow them (Allen and Gorham 1973; Haag and Gorham 1979; Beak Consult. Ltd. 1980). Elodea populations declined sharply in 1974, but this species is still present in the lake near the outlet canal of the Wabamun power plant at Seba Beach, and in a few other small areas.

The macrophytes in Wabamun Lake were surveyed during the period from 1973 to 1977 by researchers at the University of Alberta (Haag and Gorham 1979). Macrophytes were distributed on the basis of sediment texture and exposure to wind and wave action. Exposed habitats were most prevalent along the north and south shores; emergent plants were absent from most exposed sites. Common great bulrush (*Scirpus validus*) increased in importance as exposure decreased, and extended to a depth of 1.5 m. Dominant submergent species in exposed areas included stonewort (*Chara* sp.) and northern watermilfoil (*Myriophyllum exalbescens*). In areas of lesser exposure and finer-grained sediments, large-sheath pondweed (*Potamogeton vaginatus*), Richardson pondweed (*P. richardsonii*) and northern watermilfoil dominated the macrophyte community. Persistent populations of Sago pondweed (*P. pectinatus*) were confined to fine-textured sediments. Sheltered habitats had higher total plant cover and greater diversity of species than exposed habitats. There was a considerable turnover of species composition at the 30 transect locations studied, even during a single growing season.

TransAlta Utilities Corporation has cut and removed submergent macrophytes from Kapasiwin Bay since 1972. The average annual total wet weight of plants removed during the period from 1972 to 1974 was 2 763 metric tonnes, but between 1975 and 1988, the average annual wet weight was 287 metric tonnes. Plants are harvested from a maximum area of 128 ha, but the average area harvested each year since 1975 has been 51 ha. The peak harvest (4 682 tonnes) was taken in 1973 and the lowest harvest (83 tonnes) was taken in 1982. The greatest weight of plants harvested per hectare is consistently in the area where heated effluent from the Wabamun power plant enters the lake (TransAlta Util. Corp. 1988).

Invertebrates

Alberta Environment collected zooplankton samples twice monthly during the open-water season in 1980 and 1981 and monthly in 1982 (Alta. Envir. n.d.[a]). The zooplankton in the main basin of Wabamun Lake was numerically dominated by the cladocerans *Bosmina longirostris* and *Daphnia galeata mendotae*, and immature stages of calanoid and cyclopoid copepods, until mid-July in all three years. After mid-July until October, *B. longistrostris* and *D. galeata mendotae* declined, to be replaced by *Chydorus sphaericus*, *Daphnia retrocurva* and *Diaphanosoma leuctenbergianum*. Immature copepods were abundant throughout the open-water season; two species of calanoid copepods (*Diaptomus oregonensis* and *D. siciles*) and three species of planktonic cyclopoid copepods (*Diacyclops bicuspidatus thomasi*, *Acanthocyclops vernalis* and *Mesocyclops edax*) contributed to pulses of nauplii and copepodids. The large numbers of grazers in the main basin affected the levels of chlorophyll at times, and were themselves affected by the types of algae that became dominant.

In Moonlight Bay, there were more zooplankton species that were typically littoral than were observed in the main basin. Immature cyclopoid copepods were abundant throughout the sampling period

Table 8. Estimated angler hours, effort and harvest of lake whitefish from Wabamun Lake.

Year	Period	Total Angler Hours	Total Number Fish Caught	Catch Rate
1982/83	Nov.–Apr.	364 817	192 054	0.53
1983	Mar.–Apr.	157 349	115 608	0.61
1984	Mar.	31 348	15 204	0.48
1985	Jan.–Apr.	85 304	32 314	0.38
1986	Mar.	33 734	16 530	0.49

SOURCE: R.L. & L. Envir. Serv. Ltd. 1987

in 1980 and 1981. *Bosmina longirostris* was the dominant cladoceran; it did not decline in Moonlight Bay in midsummer as it did in the main basin, nor did *Chydorus sphaericus* become dominant. The relationship between zooplankton grazing and chlorophyll levels was less apparent in Moonlight Bay than in the main basin.

The macroinvertebrate fauna of Wabamun Lake was studied intensively between May 1972 and September 1975 as a thesis project at the University of Alberta (Rasmussen 1979). Nearly 200 different types of bottom-dwelling and vegetation-inhabiting organisms were observed; most of these were identified to species. Chironomidae (midge) larvae dominated the invertebrate fauna. The fauna of the most organic and nutrient-rich sediments was dominated by larvae of large-sized species of *Chironomus*. The benthos of moderately organic areas was dominated by smaller-sized species of *Chironomus*, and the least organic sediments supported species of *Polypedilum*, *Cladotanytarsus* and *Tanytarsus*. In the deepest portions of the lake (9 to 11 m), *Chironomus* spp. were prevalent, but the species were different than those found in shallower areas. Near the mouth of the heated discharge canal, tubificid oligochaetes were dominant in the sediment and snails (Gastropoda) were dominant on vegetation. The maximum annual standing crop of Chironomidae was greatest in areas affected by the thermal discharge.

Fish

Wabamun Lake is managed for sport, commercial and domestic fisheries. A comprehensive assessment of the fish and fisheries of the lake was completed in 1986 by a consultant for Fish and Wildlife Division; the following is based largely on this study (R.L. & L. Envir. Serv. Ltd. 1987). Four species of sport fish inhabit the lake: lake whitefish, northern pike, yellow perch and walleye. Other fish species include burbot, white sucker, brook stickleback, spottail shiner and Iowa darter.

Angling is an important recreational pursuit in Wabamun Lake. The winter fishery for whitefish is more popular than the summer fishery for northern pike and walleye. The sport fishery is allocated 68 040 kg of the total harvest quota of 113 400 kg for whitefish; the weighted mean catch rate since 1982 is 0.55 fish per hour (Table 8, Berry 1986; Ash and Hildebrand 1986). Catch rates are highest when the sport fishery is dominated by young whitefish.

Northern pike grow fairly slowly in Wabamun Lake compared to their growth in nearby Hubbles, Jackfish, Isle and Mink lakes; the reasons for the slow growth are unknown.

Walleye were reportedly present in the lake in 1912, but apparently died out after that time. They were reintroduced as 1–cm fry annually between 1983 and 1986, after which, stocking was suspended to determine if the new population would reproduce naturally. Some stocked fish from each year survived, but as of 1988 it was too early to tell whether reproduction would occur. Growth rates are high, and anglers report that walleye fishing is good (Berry 1988).

Yellow perch are considered too small and too low in abundance to be an important sport fish in Wabamun Lake. Along with spottail shiners and other small fish, they provide a forage base for northern pike and walleye.

Lake whitefish are considered the most important commercial

species in the lake. Although eyed-eggs were introduced in the mid–1940s to supplement the population, it was later concluded that the spawning potential of the natural population was sufficient (Miller and Paetz 1953). The population structure of whitefish is related to the emergence of strong year-classes, which become vulnerable first to the sport fishery, then to the commercial fishery as they grow larger. Most female whitefish spawn when they are five years old; males generally reach sexual maturity somewhat earlier. The spawning period extends from early to mid-October to early December, when water temperatures drop below 9°C. Most of the spawning habitat (mixed rock and sand) is at the east end of the lake (Ash 1974).

The predominant food of larger whitefish in Wabamun Lake is chironomid larvae and fingernail clams, and small yellow perch in the fall. In areas affected by thermal effluent, *Elodea* shoots, snails and chironomid larvae are the main food items; even though *Elodea* was a dominant item in guts, it is the animals associated with the shoots, rather than the shoots themselves, that are digested (Mackay 1988).

The length of time permitted for the commercial fishery each year depends on the abundance of fish that are large enough to be caught in a 14–cm mesh net; the quota may be reached in one day when fish are abundant. Records of the commercial harvest of whitefish since the winter of 1968/69 indicate that the average harvest over the period to 1987/88 was 50 459 kg. The largest catch during this period was 209 902 kg in the winter of 1987/88 and the smallest catch was 7 529 kg in 1980/81. Over the six-year period from 1982 to 1988, the commercial fishery accounted for about half of the total harvest of whitefish. Wabamun Lake also supports a native domestic fishery; it is allocated 11 340 kg of whitefish annually. Actual catch sizes are unknown (Alta. For. Ld. Wild. n.d.).

Wildlife

Upland game birds and big game are present in the Wabamun Lake drainage basin. As the watershed is cleared for mining and agriculture, white-tailed deer increase in numbers while other species of big game decrease (Andries and Schinkel 1981). Marshy areas around the shoreline are used for nesting by waterfowl such as Western and Red-necked grebes, Mallards, American Coots, and Lesser Scaup. There has probably been a reduction in suitable waterfowl habitat over the past 50 years as emergent vegetation was cleared. Some species of ducks and occasionally swans overwinter in the open area produced by the heated effluent of the Wabamun plant and in the Sundance and Keephills cooling ponds. Osprey have been observed nesting on the TransAlta Utilities Corporation power pylons at the southeast end of the lake.

P.A. Mitchell

References

Alberta Environment. n.d.[a]. Envir. Assess. Div., Envir. Qlty. Monit. Br. Unpubl. data, Edmonton.
——. n.d.[b]. Tech. Serv. Div., Hydrol. Br. Unpubl. data, Edmonton.
——. n.d.[c]. Tech. Serv. Div., Surv. Br. Unpubl. data, Edmonton.
Alberta Forestry, Lands and Wildlife. n.d. Fish Wild. Div. Unpubl. data, Edmonton.
——. 1988. Boating in Alberta. Fish Wild. Div., Edmonton.
——. 1989. Guide to sportfishing. Fish Wild. Div., Edmonton.
Alberta Hotel Association. 1989. Alberta campground guide 1989. Prep. for Travel Alta., Edmonton.
Alberta Native Affairs. 1986. A guide to native communities in Alberta. Native Aff. Secret., Edmonton.
Alberta Research Council. 1972. Geological map of Alberta. Nat. Resour. Div., Alta. Geol. Surv., Edmonton.
Allen, E. and P. Gorham. 1973. Changes in the submerged macrophyte communities of Lake Wabamun as a result of thermal discharge, p. 314–324. In E.R. Reinelt, A.H. Laycock and W.M. Schultz [ed.] Proceedings of a symposium of lakes in western Canada. Univ. Alta., Water Resour. Centre, Edmonton.
Andriashek, L.D., M.M. Fenton and J.D. Root. 1979. Surficial geology, Wabamun Lake, Alberta, NTS 83G. Alta. Res. Counc., Edmonton.
Andries, K. and D. Schinkel. 1981. The regional significance of Wabamun Lake as a recreation resource. Alta. Rec. Parks, Outdoor Rec. Plan. Br., Edmonton.
Ash, G. 1974. The effects of heated water discharge upon lake whitefish (*Coregonus clupeaformis* [Mitchill]) in Wabamun Lake, Alberta. Proceedings of the 10th symposium (1975). Water Poll. Res. Can.:9–16.

——— and L. Hildebrand. 1986. Winter creel survey of Wabamun Lake, Alberta, 1 Jan. to 9 Apr. 1986. Prep. for Alta. For. Ld. Wild. and Rec. Parks Wild. Foundation, Edmonton by R.L. & L. Envir. Serv. Ltd., Edmonton.
Beak Consultants Ltd. 1980. The effect of thermal discharges on the aquatic plants and other biota of Wabamun Lake, Alberta. Prep. for Calg. Power Ltd., Calgary.
Berry, D.K. 1988. Alta. For. Ld. Wild., Fish Wild. Div., Edmonton. Pers. comm.
Berry, K.B. 1986. Wabamun Lake sportfishery results of creel surveys and sportfishing monitoring from 1982 to 1984. Alta. En. Nat. Resour., Fish Wild. Div., Edmonton.
Canada Department of Regional Economic Expansion. 1972. Canada land inventory, soil capability for agriculture: Wabamun Lake 83G. Catalogue No. RE64/2–83G. Information Can., Ottawa.
Crowe, A. and F.W. Schwartz. 1982. The groundwater component of the Wabamun Lake eutrophication study. Alta. Envir., Poll. Contr. Div., Water Qlty. Contr. Br., Edmonton.
Dobson, H. and B. Stanley. 1961. Aquatic plants in Wabamun Lake. Calg. Power Ltd. Unpubl. rep., Calgary.
Energy, Mines and Resources Canada. 1974, 1975. National topographic series 1:50 000 83G/8 (1974), 83G/7 (1975), 83G/9 (1975), 83G/10 (1975). Surv. Map. Br., Ottawa.
Environment Canada. 1915–1987. Surface water data. Prep. by Inland Waters Directorate. Water Surv. Can., Water Resour. Br., Ottawa.
——. 1982. Canadian climate normals, Vol. 7: Bright sunshine (1951–1980). Prep. by Atm. Envir. Serv. Supply Serv. Can., Ottawa.
Gallup, D.N. and M. Hickman. 1973. Temperature and oxygen distribution in the mixing zone of a thermal discharge to Lake Wabamun, Alberta, p. 285–303. In E.R. Reinelt, A.H. Laycock and W.M. Schultz [ed.] Proceedings of a symposium of lakes in western Canada. Univ. Alta., Water Resour. Centre, Edmonton.
——. 1975. Effects of the discharge of thermal effluent from a power station on Lake Wabamun, Alberta. Canada—limnological features. Hydrobiologia 46:45–69.
Haag, R.W. and P.R. Gorham. 1979. Community dynamics of submerged macrophytes in Lake Wabamun, Alberta. Alta. Envir., Poll. Contr. Div., Water Qlty. Contr. Br. Unpubl. rep., Edmonton.
Habgood, H. 1983. Lake Wabamun literature review. Prep. for L. Wabamun Watershed Advisory Commit., Edmonton.
Hamilton, H. and T.B. Reynoldon. 1981. Lake Wabamun eutrophication study: Interim report on 1980 lake sediment studies. Alta. Envir., Poll. Contr. Div., Water Qlty. Contr. Br. Unpubl. rep., Edmonton.
Hills of Hope Historical Committee. 1976. Hills of hope. Carvel Unifarm, Spruce Grove.
Holmgren, E.J. and P.M. Holmgren. 1976. Over 2000 place names of Alberta. 3rd ed. West. Producer Prairie Books, Saskatoon.
Ivan, M. 1988. Village of Wabamun. Pers. comm.
Lindsay, J.D., W. Odynsky, J.W. Peters and W.E. Bowser. 1968. Soil survey of the Buck Lake (NE 83B) and Wabamun Lake (E1/2 83G) areas. Alta. Soil Surv. Rep. No. 24, Univ. Alta. Bull. No. SS–7, Alta. Res. Counc. Rep. No. 87. Univ. Alta., Edmonton.
Mackay, W.C. 1988. Univ. Alta., Dept. Zool., Edmonton. Pers. comm.
Miller, R.B. and M.J. Paetz. 1953. Report on Lake Wabamun, October, 1952. Alta. Ld. For., Fish Wild. Div. Edmonton.
Mitchell, P.A. 1984. The importance of sediment release in the assessment of a shallow, eutrophic lake for phosphorus control, p. 129–133. In Proceedings of the 3rd annual conference on lake and reservoir management, North American Lake Management Society. USEPA 440/5–84–001. Washington.
——. 1985. Preservation of water quality in Lake Wabamun. Alta. Envir., Poll. Contr. Div., Water Qlty. Contr. Br., Edmonton.
Noton, L.R. 1974. Phytoplankton productivity in Lake Wabamun, Alberta and the effect of thermal effluent. MSc thesis. Univ. Alta., Edmonton.
Nursall, J.R., J.B. Nuttall and P. Fritz. 1972. The effect of thermal effluent in Lake Wabamun, Alberta. Verh. Internat. Verein. Limnol. 18:269–277.
Pelletier, Lieutenant. 1989. Can. Armed Forces. Pers. comm.
Rasmussen, J.B. 1979. The macroinvertebrate fauna and thermal regime of Lake Wabamun, a lake receiving thermal effluent. MSc thesis. Univ. Alta., Edmonton.
Reid, Crowther and Partners Ltd. 1973. Lake Wabamun Study. Prep. for Alta. Envir., Edmonton.
Reynolds, C.S. 1980. Phytoplankton assemblages and their periodicity in stratifying lake systems. Holarctic Ecol. 3:141–159.
R.L. & L. Environmental Services Ltd. 1987. County of Parkland fisheries inventory: Lake Wabamun. Prep. for Alta. For. Ld. Wild., Fish Wild. Div. and Rec. Parks Wild. Foundation, Edmonton.
Schwartz, F. and D.N. Gallup. 1978. Some factors controlling the major ion chemistry of small lakes: Examples from the prairie-parkland of Canada. Hydrobiologia 58:65–81.
Strong, W.L. and K.R. Leggat. 1981. Ecoregions of Alberta. Alta. En. Nat. Resour., Resour. Eval. Plan. Div., Edmonton.
Terrestrial and Aquatic Environmental Managers, Ltd. 1987. Distribution and abundance of aquatic macrophytes in Wabamun Lake, 1986. Prep. for TransAlta Util. Corp., Calgary.
TransAlta Utilities Corporation. 1988. Wabamun thermal plant. Unpubl. data, Wabamun Lake.

WIZARD LAKE

MAP SHEET: 83H/4
LOCATION: Tp48 R27, 28 W4
LAT/LONG: 53°07'N 113°55'W

Wizard Lake is a long, serpentine lake lying in a heavily forested, deep glacial meltwater channel 50 km southwest of the city of Edmonton. The valley provides excellent shelter from winds, making this lake very popular for water skiing. To reach Wizard Lake from Edmonton, take Highway 2 south to the city of Leduc, turn west onto Highway 39 and drive for 16 km to the town of Calmar, then take Secondary Road 795 south for 17 km to the turnoff for the east end of the lake (Fig. 1). The northern shore of the lake is in the County of Leduc and the southern shore is in the County of Wetaskiwin.

The Indian name for this lake meant "Lizard Lake" (Alta. Cult. Multicult. n.d.). Until the late 1960s the popular name for the lake was Conjuring Lake (Alta. Cult. Multicult. n.d.). Indian legends said strange noises in the lake came from "conjuring creatures" (Stout 1956). The creek draining the lake is still called Conjuring Creek. Homesteaders began to arrive in 1904 and a sawmill opened near the lake in the same year, only to close in 1905 when the railway was not built across the area as expected (Stout 1956). An underground coal mine operated on the south shore until the 1940s; the two mine entrances still exist (Riddett 1988). Land was set aside on the north shore for a park in the 1920s; it has now been developed by the County of Leduc as Wizard Lake Jubilee Park.

There are 61 cottages on the south shore at the east end of the lake, 56 lots in a subdivision above the valley and 24 acreages in an area at the west end (Riddett 1988). In 1988, none of the acreages had been developed. On the north shore, there are 110 developed cottage lots fronting on the lakeshore just west of Wizard Lake Jubilee Park (Pinkowski 1989).

Public access to the lake is best at Wizard Lake Jubilee Park (Fig. 2). Facilities include a summer campground with 114 sites, tap water, a sewage disposal station, a public telephone, a beach, a playground and a boat launch. A small grocery store and concession also operate at the park.

Intensive use of the lake, especially on summer weekends, led to conflict between water skiers, high-speed power boat operators, canoeists and anglers. In 1977, the Wizard Lake area became subject to the Regulated Lake Shoreland Development Operation Regulations, which were administered by Alberta Environment. The regulations prohibited most developments at the lake until a lake management plan and an area structure plan were prepared and adopted by the counties of Leduc and Wetaskiwin. A lake management plan was prepared by 1979, which included a summary of regulations and policies (Edm. and Battle R. Reg. Plan. Commis. 1979[a]; 1979[b]; 1980). One of the recommendations in the plan was to divide the lake into two zones. The boat speed in the west half of the lake was to be limited to 12 km/hour to facilitate access by anglers, yet minimize conflict with canoeists and wildlife. The boat speed in the east half was to be limited to 65 km/hour to allow water skiing, yet minimize excessively fast power boat activities that might endanger other users. These recommendations had not been implemented as of 1988, but there are posted areas on the lake where power boats are prohibited or restricted to 12 km/hour (Alta. For. Ld. Wild. 1988).

Fishing for yellow perch and northern pike is popular at Wizard Lake, as are water skiing, canoeing, sailing, SCUBA diving and observing wildlife. Provincial limits for the number and size of fish caught apply to the sport fishery but there are no regulations specific

Table 1. Characteristics of Wizard Lake drainage basin.

area (excluding lake) (km²)[a]	29.8
soil[b]	West half: Orthic Gray Luvisols; East half: Orthic Black Chernozemics
bedrock geology[c]	Paskapoo Formation (Tertiary): sandstone, siltstone, mudstone; thin limestone, coal and tuff beds; nonmarine
terrain[b]	gently rolling till plain, cut by deep preglacial channel
ecoregions[d]	West half: Moist Mixedwood Subregion of Boreal Mixedwood; East half: Aspen Subregion of Aspen Parkland
dominant vegetation[b]	trembling aspen, white spruce, willow
mean annual inflow (m³)[e, f]	1.54 x 10⁶
mean annual sunshine (h)[g]	2 315

NOTE: [f]excluding groundwater inflow
SOURCES: [a]Alta. Envir. n.d.[b]; [b]Bowser et al. 1962; Twardy et al. 1979; [c]Alta. Res. Counc. 1972; [d]Strong and Leggat 1981; [f]Alta. Envir. n.d.[b]; [g]Envir. Can. 1982

Table 2. Characteristics of Wizard Lake.

elevation (m)[a, b]	784.01
surface area (km²)[a, b]	2.48
volume (m³)[a, b]	14.8 x 10⁶
maximum depth (m)[a, b]	11
mean depth (m)[a, b]	6.2
shoreline length (km)[c]	18.0
mean annual lake evaporation (mm)[d]	664
mean annual precipitation (mm)[d]	492
mean residence time (yr)[d, e]	13.5
mean outflow (m³)[b]	1.06 x 10⁶
control structure	none

NOTES: [a]on date of sounding: 13 Sep. 1982; [e]excluding groundwater inflow
SOURCES: [b]Babin 1984; [c]En. Mines Resour. Can. 1974; [d]Alta. Envir. n.d.[b]

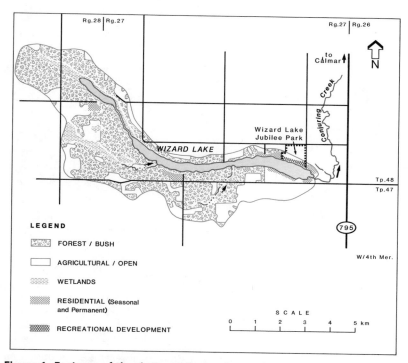

Figure 1. Features of the drainage basin of Wizard Lake.
SOURCES: Alta. Envir. n.d.[b]; En. Mines Resour. Can. 1974. Updated with 1985 aerial photos.

to Wizard Lake (Alta. For. Ld. Wild. 1989). The water is fairly clear in spring and early summer but blue-green algal blooms turn the water green by midsummer.

Drainage Basin Characteristics

The drainage basin of Wizard Lake lies mostly on an undulating glacial till plain. The Wizard Lake Valley was formed in several stages. Prior to glaciation, a channel was cut in the bedrock (Edm. and Battle R. Reg. Plan. Commis. 1979[a]). Next, glaciation deposited till over the area and meltwater from the retreating glacial ice sheet flowed southeastward, following the old channel, eroding the till and leaving the contemporary 30–m deep valley (Twardy et al. 1979). Hills rise to an elevation of 846 m on the southern edge of the drainage basin and to 823 m on the northern edge (En. Mines Resour. Can. 1974).

The bedrock is composed of sandstone, mudstone and siltstone (Table 1) with thin limestone, coal and tuff beds in some areas. Highly weathered beds of these formations can be found at shallow depths (1 to 2 m) below the soil surface and as outcrops on the valley slopes (Twardy et al. 1979).

The eastern half of the drainage basin is in the Aspen Parkland Ecoregion, whereas the western half is in the Moist Mixedwood Subregion of the Boreal Mixedwood Ecoregion (Strong and Leggat 1981). The natural vegetation near the lake is typical of both these regions; trembling aspen is dominant and paper birch, white spruce, willow and balsam poplar grow in wetter areas or on north-facing slopes. The difference between the ecoregions is seen in the occurrence of fescue grassland, which is found in dry areas of the Aspen

Parkland but not in the Boreal Mixedwood. Before settlement, areas of natural grassland likely occurred at the east end of the Wizard Lake drainage basin, but these areas have since been cultivated. Another difference between the ecoregions is apparent in the soils. The eastern portion is underlain by Chernozemic soils, which form under grasslands; the western portion is underlain by Dark Gray Chernozemics grading to Dark Gray Luvisols, soils which typically form under aspen forests (Bowser et al. 1962; Twardy et al. 1979).

About 7% of the drainage basin is composed of low lying fens and bogs, the former being more common. Fens, such as the area extending northwest from the lake, are generally wet, accumulate sedge peat and have a cover or border of willow, sedges and slough grass; they are underlain by Gleysolic soils. Bogs have an accumulation of moss peat and are covered or bordered by black spruce, tamarack, Labrador tea and mosses; soils in bogs are Humic Mesisols. In the Wizard Lake basin, peat accumulations of up to 4–m deep have been found (Twardy et al. 1979).

The valley of the lake is still forested, but some of the surrounding plain has been cleared for cereal crop production and mixed farming (Fig. 1). Approximately 65% of the basin is forest or bush, 25% is cleared for agriculture, 7% is lake or sloughs and 3% is cleared for urban development. Several subdivisions, loacated on the eastern portion of the lakeshore and on the upland area, have been developed in the last 20 years. There are several oil and gas wells in the basin. There is no Crown land on the shore of Wizard Lake.

Water enters Wizard Lake via two intermittent creeks on the south shore (Fig. 1) or as indirect runoff. The lake is drained by Conjuring Creek which flows north to join the North Saskatchewan River north of the village of Calmar.

Lake Basin Characteristics

Wizard Lake is 11.5–km long; it stretches 8 km from the east end to the narrow neck, then another 3.5 km along the neck and the shallow northwest bay. The maximum width of the lake is 0.55 km. The lake has a simple basin with sides that slope steeply to a maximum depth of 11 m (Fig. 2; Table 2). The ends are more gently sloping, especially at the northwest end near the shallow neck. The littoral zone extends to approximately 4.1 m (Chambers and Prepas 1985) and approximately 33% of the lake is shallower than this depth (Fig. 3).

The lake level is fairly variable; it ranged over 0.9 m, from a low in 1968 to a high in 1981 (Fig. 4). Annual fluctuations of 0.5 m

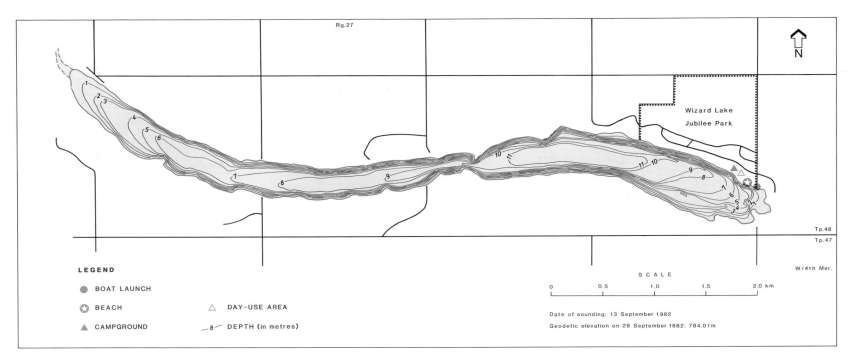

Figure 2. Bathymetry and shoreline features of the main basin of Wizard Lake. BATHYMETRY SOURCE: Babin 1984.

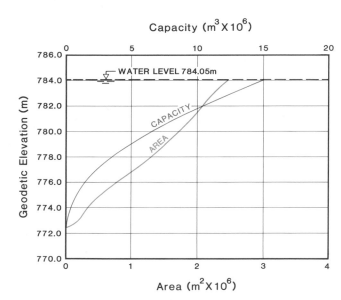

Figure 3. Area/capacity curve for Wizard Lake.
SOURCE: Babin 1984.

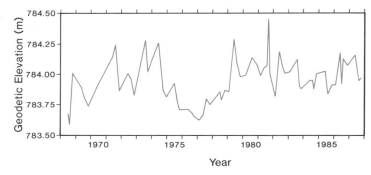

Figure 4. Water level of Wizard Lake, 1969 to 1988.
SOURCE: Alta. Envir. n.d.[c].

Table 3. Major ions and related water quality variables for Wizard Lake. Average concentrations in mg/L; pH in pH units. Composite samples from the euphotic zone collected 5 times from 11 May to 12 Aug. 1981 and once on 13 Mar. 1986. S.E. = standard error.

	Mean	S.E.
pH	7.7[a]	—
total alkalinity (CaCO$_3$)	177[b]	3.0
specific conductivity (μS/cm)	269	13.1
total dissolved solids	208	13.4
turbidity (NTU)	3[c]	1.5
colour (Pt)	14[c]	3.0
total hardness (CaCO$_3$)	127[c]	8.3
HCO$_3$	215[b]	3.8
CO$_3$	0.4[b]	0.2
Mg	8[a]	—
Na	24[a]	—
K	8[a]	—
SO$_4$	4[a]	—
Ca	36[a]	—

NOTES: [a]n = 1, 13 Mar. 1986; [b]n = 2; [c]n = 3
SOURCE: Prepas n.d.

commonly occurred through the 1970s, but since 1982, levels have been more stable, with annual fluctuations of about 0.25 m. The mean residence time of water in the lake is approximately 14 years (Alta. Envir. n.d.[b]). In 1988, the counties of Leduc and Wetaskiwin were investigating the feasibility of stabilizing the level of Wizard Lake (Alta. Envir. n.d.[d]).

Water Quality

Wizard lake was monitored for water quality in 1978 and 1979 by Alberta Environment (Alta. Envir. n.d.[a]). From 1981 through 1983 it was monitored by the University of Alberta and in 1984 it was intensively studied by the University of Alberta as part of a project to examine the dynamics of phosphorus in moderately productive, shallow lakes (Prepas n.d.; 1983[a]; 1983[b]; Prepas and Trew 1983; Babin 1984; Prepas and Vickery 1984; Babin and Prepas 1985; Prepas and Shaw 1985).

Wizard Lake is a well-buffered freshwater lake. The dominant ions are sodium, calcium and bicarbonate (Table 3). The lake is

Table 4. Nutrient, chlorophyll *a* and Secchi depth data for Wizard Lake. Average concentrations in µg/L. Composite samples from the euphotic zone collected 5 times from 11 May to 12 Aug. 1981, 7 times from 26 May to 27 Sep. 1982 and 17 times from 09 May to 27 Aug. 1984. S.E. = standard error.

	1981[a]		1982[a]		1984[b]	
	Mean	S.E.	Mean	S.E.	Mean	S.E.
total phosphorus	42	7.2	52	3.7	40	3.1
total dissolved phosphorus	10	0.5	—	—	12[e]	0.9
soluble reactive phosphorus	2[c]	0.3	—	—	—	—
total Kjeldahl nitrogen	1 050	118	1 189	65.6	935[f]	28.5
$NO_3 + NO_2$–nitrogen	8	2.4	12	3.2	1[f]	0.3
NH_4–nitrogen	12	6.4	—	—	—	—
iron	—	—	—	—	68[a, g]	—
chlorophyll *a*	20.3	6.21	17.7	3.38	11.0	1.49
Secchi depth (m)	1.8	0.32	1.8[d]	0.19	2.9[h]	0.18

NOTES: [c] n = 3; [d] n = 6; [e] n = 12; [f] n = 13; [g] n = 1, 13 Mar. 1986; [h] from light meter data
SOURCES: [a] Prepas n.d.; [b] Prepas and Shaw 1985

shallow and, despite the protection given by its high valley walls, the water frequently mixes vertically throughout the summer. In 1984, mixing periods occurred from 29 May to 5 June, from 25 June to 9 July, from 16 to 23 July, and from 7 to 20 August (Fig. 5, 6). Although the lake was only weakly and infrequently stratified, dissolved oxygen depletion progressed in the deeper water and the water near the bottom became anoxic in August 1984. Four stations that are shallower than the one shown in Figure 6 (8.5–, 8.0–, 7.5– and 5.5–m depths) were also monitored weekly through the summer of 1984. Anoxic conditions developed by early August near the bottom of the deeper three of these sites. Total anoxia was not observed at the 5.5–m deep station, but the dissolved oxygen concentration dropped to 0.1 mg/L by 13 August.

In the winter of 1982/83, dissolved oxygen concentrations decreased continuously at a rate of 0.533 g/m² per day (Babin and Prepas 1985). This relatively high rate reflects the high productivity in this lake. By late February 1983, dissolved oxygen concentrations were very low throughout the water column at the deep station, with no dissolved oxygen in the lowest 0.5 m and only 3.0 mg/L near the surface (Fig. 6). Fish survival may be compromised at these concentrations but no fish kills have been recorded in Wizard Lake (Watters 1989).

The dissolved oxygen profiles from the deepest part of a lake may not be representative of oxygen concentrations throughout the lake. Oxygen profiles were taken at six sites in Wizard Lake on 7 March 1983 (Babin and Prepas 1985). The dissolved oxygen concentrations were higher at all levels a four of the shallower stations (8–, 6–, 5– and 2–m depths) compared to the concentrations measured at the deepest site (11 m). The estimated average dissolved oxygen concentration was 47% higher when data from all 6 stations were used, rather than data from only the deepest station.

Under ice chlorophyll *a* profiles in Wizard Lake were taken 7 times between 26 November 1982 and 22 March 1983 (Babin 1984). Concentrations were greatest near the surface and were highest on 26 November (9.2 µg/L). They decreased throughout the winter to 17 February (1.9 µg/L), then rose until 22 March (7.6 µg/L).

Wizard Lake is nutrient-rich (Table 4) and a dense blue-green algal bloom usually forms after midsummer. This lake is classified as eutrophic. The major nutrient that controls the amount of algae in lakes in Alberta is usually phosphorus (Prepas and Trew 1983; Prepas 1983[b]); Figure 7 illustrates that the concentration of total phosphorus in the euphotic zone and chlorophyll *a* are closely correlated during summer.

Phosphorus enters lakes from several external sources (Table 5). In the Wizard Lake basin, runoff is the major contributor with 1 ha of agricultural land contributing about 5 times as much phosphorus as 1 ha of forest, and 1 ha of urban land delivering 10 times as much as forest. Sloughs act as phosphorus traps; if the slough at the

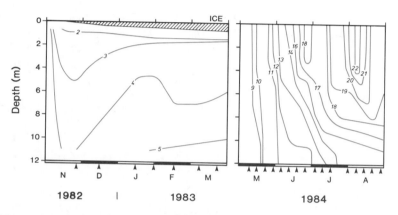

Figure 5. Temperature (°C) of Wizard Lake, 1982 to 1984. Arrows indicate sampling dates.
SOURCES: Prepas n.d.; Prepas and Shaw 1985.

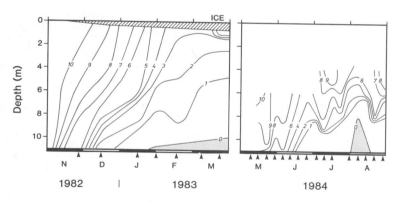

Figure 6. Dissolved oxygen (mg/L) in Wizard Lake, 1982 to 1984. Arrows indicate sampling dates.
SOURCES: Babin 1984; Prepas and Shaw 1985.

northwest end of the lake were dry, the phosphorus contribution from that area of the watershed would be more than 4 times the 52 kg listed in Table 5. Rainfall and dustfall directly on the lake are significant contributors; sewage from cottages and camps is a minor contribution (Alta. Envir. n.d.[a]).

That prairie lakes have an important internal source of phosphorus has been recognized for the last decade. In Wizard Lake, like most shallow, productive prairie lakes, total phosphorus concentrations increase throughout the summer to peak in late August (Fig. 7). This phosphorus increase comes from sources within the lake itself; the phosphorus stored in the bottom sediment is released to the overlying water and then mixed into the surface waters where it is used by algae.

Table 5. Theoretical total phosphorus loading to Wizard Lake.

Source		Phosphorus (kg/yr)	Percentage of Total
External Load[a]			
immediate watershed	forested/bush	111	14
	agricultural/cleared	313	41
	residential/cottage	228	29
sewage[b]		11	1
precipitation/dustfall		61	8
inflow via upstream slough		52	7
Total External Load		776	100
annual areal loading (g/m² of lake surface)	0.31		
Internal Load			
sediment release, summer[c, d]		2 133	—
	TOTAL LOAD	3 207	

NOTES: [b]unmeasured: assumes 4% of all sewage effluent from cottages and camps enters the lake, as in Mitchell 1982; [c]values estimated for 01 June to 31 Aug. 1984 based on 8.4 mg/m² per day
SOURCES: [a]Alta. Envir. n.d.[a]; [d]Prepas and Shaw 1985

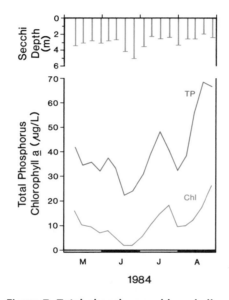

Figure 7. Total phosphorus, chlorophyll *a* and Secchi depth in Wizard Lake, 1984.
SOURCE: Prepas and Shaw 1985.

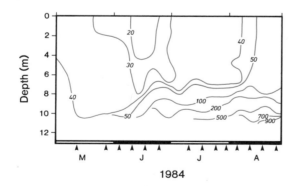

Figure 8. Total phosphorus concentrations in Wizard Lake, 1984. Arrows indicate sampling dates.
SOURCE: Prepas and Shaw 1985.

Five sites in Wizard Lake were studied intensively in 1984 to determine the rate at which phosphorus was released from the sediments under shallow and deep water. Phosphorus concentrations became very high (900 μg/L) in the anoxic water over the bottom sediments at the deepest site (Fig. 8). A similar general pattern was apparent at the shallower stations, but the phosphorus concentration rarely exceeded 300 μg/L. The rate of phosphorus release from the sediment was calculated to be 27.2 mg/m² per day at the deep site. The average rate for the whole lake was estimated to be 8.4 mg/m² per day. At this rate, 2 133 kg of phosphorus entered the lake water from the sediment in the June through August period—an amount more than double all external inputs combined (Table 5). Also, in the winter, phosphorus moves from the sediment into the overlying water. On 22 March 1983, the concentration of total phosphorus was 147 μg/L in the water near the bottom, but only 30.4 μg/L just under the ice. Approximately 60% of the total phosphorus was dissolved.

The good correlation between phosphorus and chlorophyll *a* concentrations in Figure 7 suggests that phosphorus released from the sediment is almost all available for use by algae. These observations were confirmed by experiments with labelled phosphorus (Prepas and Shaw 1985).

Biological Characteristics

Plants

Phytoplankton was sampled in Wizard Lake by Alberta Environment monthly from 12 February to 25 September 1979 (Beliveau and Furnell 1980) and on 18 July 1983 (Alta. Envir. n.d.[a]). In 1979, the volume of algae peaked in late August (80% Cyanophyta), with a lower peak in late September (45% Bacillariophyta, 34% Cyanophyta). In July 1983, 49% of the phytoplankton biomass was bluegreens (Cyanophyta: primarily *Aphanizomenon flos-aquae*), 19% was diatoms (Bacillariophyta: primarily *Melosira granulata*), 10% was Cryptophyta (primarily *Cryptomonas rostratiformis*) and the remainder was fairly equally divided among the green algae (Chlorophyta), golden-brown algae (Chrysophyta) and Pyrrhophyta. High total phosphorus concentrations and low dissolved oxygen concentrations over the bottom sediments are responsible for the preponderance of blue-green algae in summer in Wizard Lake (Trimbee and Prepas 1987; 1988).

Aquatic macrophytes were surveyed in detail during August 1979 (Fig. 9). The ends of the lake support the densest growth, with emergent beds of bulrushes (*Scirpus* spp.), common cattails (*Typha latifolia*) and sedges (*Carex* spp.), patches of yellow water lily (*Nuphar variegatum*), and submergent beds composed of pondweeds (*Potamogeton* spp.) and stonewort (*Chara* sp.). Macrophytes form a narrow band along the rest of the shoreline which slopes more steeply to deep water.

Invertebrates

The zooplankton community was sampled in 1981 and 1982 by the University of Alberta (Prepas n.d.; 1983[b]). The dominant organisms were two species of *Daphnia* (*D. galeata mendotae* and *D. retrocurva*), a large cladoceran (*Leptodora kindtii*), two other cladocerans (*Chydorus sphaericus* and *Diaphanosoma leuchtenbergianum*), two species of calanoid copepods (*Acanthodiaptomus denticornis* and *Diaptomus oregonensis*) and three species of cyclopoid copepods (*Mesocyclops edax*, *Diacyclops bicuspidatus thomasi* and *Acanthocyclops vernalis*).

Benthic invertebrates have not been sampled in Wizard Lake.

Fish

Wizard Lake provides a moderately popular sport fishery for northern pike; yellow perch are also occasionally caught by anglers. Other species of fish in the lake include white sucker and spottail shiner. In 1948, yellow perch were scarce and exhibited very poor growth rates (Miller and Macdonald 1950). Over a million walleye eyed-eggs

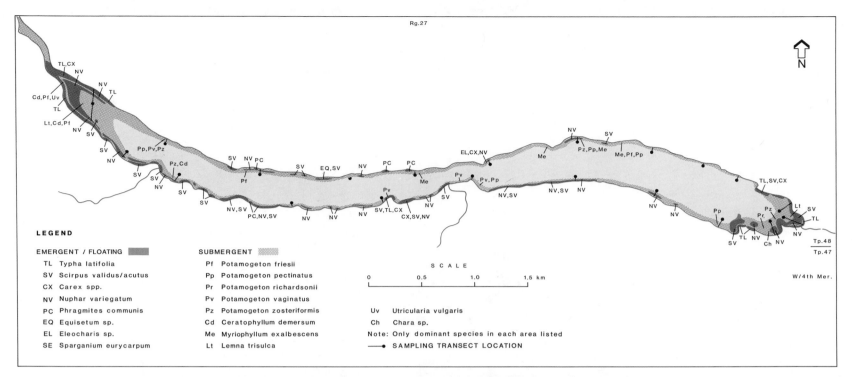

Figure 9. Species composition and distribution of aquatic macrophytes in the main basin of Wizard Lake, August 1979.
SOURCE: Alta. Envir. n.d.[a].

were planted in Wizard Lake between 1949 and 1953; in 1967, no walleye could be found and none have been caught since (Alta. For. Ld. Wild. n.d.). No winterkills have been noted at Wizard Lake (Watters 1989).

Wildlife

The main part of Wizard Lake provides poor waterfowl habitat because of the steep banks and intensive recreational use. The northwest end and the adjoining marsh area provide fairly good duck habitat. Muskrat and beaver occur there too. White-tailed deer are common, especially at the northwest end of the lake. Ruffed Grouse are found in the wooded areas, and Sharp-tailed Grouse can be found at the margins of pasture and bush land (Edm. and Battle R. Reg. Plan. Commis. 1979[a]).

J.M. Crosby and E.E. Prepas

References

Alberta Culture and Multiculturalism. n.d. Hist. Resour. Div., Hist. Sites Serv. Unpubl. data, Edmonton.
Alberta Environment. n.d.[a]. Envir. Assess. Div., Envir. Qlty. Monit. Br. Unpubl. data, Edmonton.
——. n.d.[b]. Tech. Serv. Div., Hydrol. Br. Unpubl. data, Edmonton.
——. n.d.[c]. Tech. Serv. Div., Surv. Br. Unpubl. data, Edmonton.
——. n.d.[d]. Water Resour. Admin. Div., Edm. Reg. Unpubl. data, Edmonton.
Alberta Forestry, Lands and Wildlife. n.d. Fish Wild. Div. Unpubl. data, Edmonton.
——. 1988[a]. Boating in Alberta. Fish Wild. Div., Edmonton.
——. 1988[b]. Guide to sportfishing regulations. Fish Wild. Div., Edmonton.
Alberta Research Council. 1972. Geological map of Alberta. Nat. Resour. Div., Alta. Geol. Surv., Edmonton.
Babin, J. 1984. Winter oxygen depletion in temperate zone lakes. MSc thesis. Univ. Alta., Edmonton.
—— and E.E. Prepas. 1985. Modelling winter oxygen depletion rates in ice-covered temperate zone lakes in Canada. Can. J. Fish. Aquat. Sci. 42:239–249.
Beliveau, D. and A. Furnell. 1980. Phytoplankton data summary 1976–1980. Alta. Envir., Poll. Contr. Div., Water Qlty. Contr. Br. Unpubl. rep., Edmonton.
Bowser, W.E., A.A. Kjearsgaard, T.W. Peters and R.E. Wells. 1962. Soil survey of the Edmonton sheet (83–H). Alta. Soil Surv. Rep. No. 21, Univ. Alta. Bull. No. SS–4. Univ. Alta., Edmonton.
Chambers, P.A. and E.E. Prepas. 1988. Underwater spectral attenuation and its effect on the maximum depth of angiosperm colonization. Can. J. Fish. Aquat. Sci. 45:1010–1017.

Edmonton and Battle River Regional Planning Commissions. 1979[a]. Wizard Lake management plan: Background information and management philosophy. Battle R. Reg. Plan. Commis., Wetaskiwin and Edm. Reg. Plan. Commis., Edmonton.
——. 1979[b]. Wizard Lake management plan: Management plan alternatives. Battle R. Reg. Plan. Commis., Wetaskiwin and Edm. Reg. Plan. Commis., Edmonton.
——. 1980. Wizard Lake management plan: A summary of regulations and policies. Battle R. Reg. Plan. Commis., Wetaskiwin and Edm. Reg. Plan. Commis., Edmonton.
Energy, Mines and Resources Canada. 1974. National topographic series 1:50 000 83H/4 (1974). Surv. Map. Br., Ottawa.
Environment Canada. 1982. Canadian climate normals, Vol. 7: Bright sunshine (1951–1980). Prep. by Atm. Envir. Serv. Supply Serv. Can., Ottawa.
Miller, R.B. and W.H. Macdonald. 1950. Conjuring Lake. Alta. Ld. Mines, Fish Wild. Div. Unpubl. rep., Edmonton.
Mitchell, P.A. 1982. Evaluation of the "septic snooper" in Wabamun and Pigeon lakes. Alta. Envir., Poll. Contr. Div., Water Qlty. Contr. Br., Edmonton.
Pinkowski, K. 1989. Co. Leduc, Leduc. Pers. comm.
Prepas, E.E. n.d. Univ. Alta., Dept. Zool. Unpubl. data, Edmonton.
——. 1983[a]. The influence of phosphorus and zooplankton on chlorophyll levels in Alberta lakes. Prep. for Alta. Envir., Res. Mgt. Div. Rep. 83/23, Edmonton.
——. 1983[b]. Orthophosphate turnover time in shallow productive lakes. Can. J. Fish. Aquat. Sci. 40:1412–1418.
—— and J.F.H Shaw. 1985. Phosphorus dynamics in five shallow Alberta lakes: Hasse, Mayatan, Mink N., Mink S., and Wizard. Prep. for Alta. Envir., Res. Mgt. Div., Edmonton.
Prepas, E.E. and D.O. Trew. 1983. Evaluation of the phosphorus-chlorophyll relationship for lakes off the Precambrian Shield in western Canada. Can. J. Fish. Aquat. Sci. 40:27–35.
Prepas, E.E. and J. Vickery. 1984. The contribution of particulate phosphorus (>250 μm) to the total phosphorus pool in lake water. Can. J. Fish. Aquat. Sci. 41:351–363.
Riddett, R. 1988. Battle R. Reg. Plan. Commis., Wetaskiwin. Pers. comm.
Stout, C.H. [ed.] ca 1956. Frontier days in Leduc and district. Leduc Hist. Soc. and 75th Anniversary Commit., Leduc.
Strong, W.L. and K.R. Leggat. 1981. Ecoregions of Alberta. Alta. En. Nat. Resour., Resour. Eval. Plan. Div., Edmonton.
Trimbee, A.M. and E.E. Prepas. 1987. Evaluation of total phosphorus as a predictor of the relative biomass of blue-green algae with emphasis on Alberta lakes. Can. J. Fish. Aquat. Sci. 44:1337–1342.
——. 1988. The effect of oxygen depletion on the timing and magnitude of blue-green algal blooms. Verh. Internat. Verein. Limnol. 23:220–226.
Twardy, A.C., L.J. Knapik and L.A. Leskiw. 1979. Soil survey and land suitability evaluation of the Wizard Lake study area. Prep. for Alta. Envir., Ld. Reclamation Div. by Pedol. Consult., Edmonton.
Watters, D. 1989. Alta. For. Ld. Wild., Fish Wild. Div., Edmonton. Pers. comm.

BATTLE LAKE

MAP SHEET: 83B/16
LOCATION: Tp46 R2 W5
LAT/LONG: 52°58'N 114°11'W

Lovely Battle Lake is set in a narrow valley surrounded by heavily treed hills. It is located 102 km southwest of Edmonton in the County of Wetaskiwin and can be reached by travelling south for 68 km on Highway 2, then west for 35 km on Highway 13. The hamlet of Battle Lake is situated less than a kilometre east of the lake (Fig. 1).

The lake's name is a translation from Cree and refers to the frequent territorial conflicts between the Blackfoot and Cree in the region near the Battle River (Alta. Cult. Multicult. n.d.). Settlers began arriving in the area around 1900, and established a church and general store near the southeast end of the lake (Conroy Club and Yeoford Ladies Club 1973). By 1904, loggers were active and the lake and river were used to float lumber and logs downstream to Ponoka and Hobbema (MacGregor 1976). A sawmill located near the lake operated in the 1920s; logging in the area ended in 1944 (Falun Hist. Soc. 1974).

The proximity of Battle Lake to popular resort lakes such as Pigeon and Wizard has encouraged the County of Wetaskiwin to plan shoreline development carefully, with the objective of preserving the natural wooded beauty of the lakeshore. Consequently, low-volume, well-dispersed activities such as hiking, nature viewing, angling and cross-country skiing are encouraged. Power boats are permitted on the lake, but they are subject to a maximum speed of 12 km/hour (Alta. For. Ld. Wild. 1988).

Public access to Battle Lake is available at a County of Wetaskiwin campground on the southeast side of the north shore (Fig. 2). The campground, which opened in August 1989, has 26 campsites, a tenting area, a day-use area with picnic tables and firepits, a boat launch and walking trails. Improvements planned for 1990 are flush toilets, tap water and a playground. The county also owns land at the lake's outlet, the Battle River, and holds a recreational lease on the quarter section of Crown land immediately west of the outlet (Fig. 2). Two additional areas of Crown land, located on the northwest side of the south shore, have protective notations and are reserved for natural areas by Alberta Forestry, Lands and Wildlife (Alta. For. Ld. Wild. 1987). The remainder of the shoreline is privately owned. The only institutional camp on the lake is owned by the Girl Guides of Canada. It consists of 0.78 ha of land on the south shore (Fig. 2).

The water in Battle Lake is fairly clear, but occasional algal blooms colour the water green in late summer. The lake supports a sport fishery for northern pike, yellow perch and lake whitefish and a domestic fishery for lake whitefish. There are no sport fishing regulations specific to Battle Lake, but provincial limits and general regulations apply (Alta. For. Ld. Wild. 1989).

Drainage Basin Characteristics

Battle Lake's drainage basin is almost 23 times larger than the lake (Tables 1, 2). Elevations range from 1 000 m at the western edge of the watershed to 837 m at the lakeshore. The lake basin lies in a deep, steep-sided valley that was a glacial meltwater channel that drained Lake Edmonton during the Pleistocene epoch (Battle R. Reg. Plan. Commis. 1974). Battle Lake is the headwater of the Battle River, which flows from the southeast end of the lake. The main inlet, Battle Creek, is less than 2–m deep and flows into the northwest end of the lake. Several smaller, intermittent creeks and springs are located on the north and south shores.

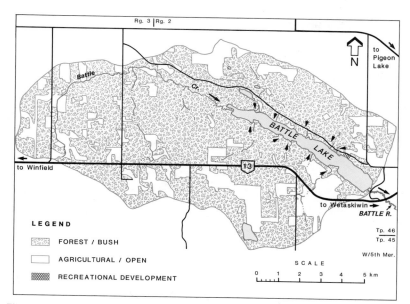

Figure 1. Features of the drainage basin of Battle Lake.
SOURCES: Alta. Envir. n.d.[b]; En. Mines Resour. Can. 1974; 1975.
Updated with 1984 aerial photos.

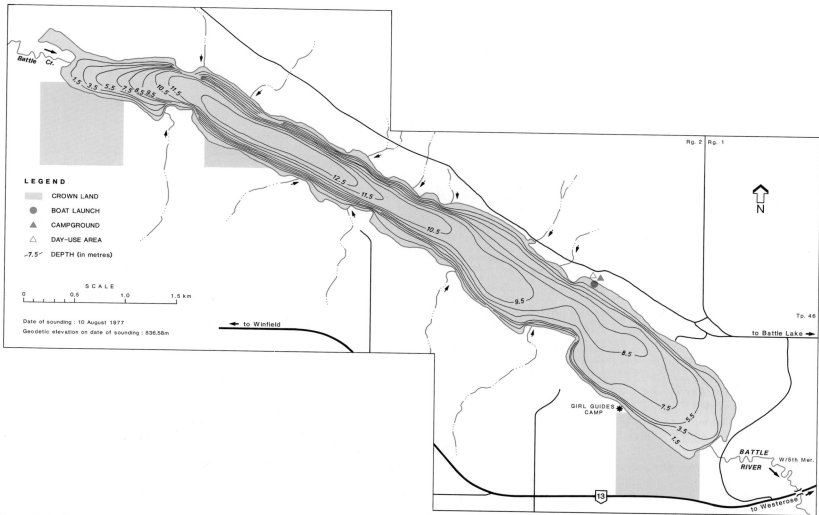

Figure 2. Bathymetry and shoreline features of Battle Lake.
SOURCE: Alta. Envir. n.d.[c].

Battle Lake's watershed lies in the Moist Mixedwood Subregion of the Boreal Mixedwood Ecoregion (Strong and Leggat 1981). The main soils are moderately well-drained Orthic Gray Luvisols that developed on glacial till of the Paskapoo Formation (Lindsay et al. 1968). More than three-quarters of the drainage basin is forested (Fig. 2). The cover is medium to heavy and consists of trembling aspen, balsam poplar, and white and black spruce, with the addition of birch, willow and alder in the lake valley. The forestry potential of the area is moderate to poor, because of either local excess or deficiency of soil moisture. Growth is slow and trees do not reach full

size (Battle R. Reg. Plan. Commis. 1974). A County of Wetaskiwin land-use bylaw encourages retention of tree cover.

Most of the remaining quarter of the drainage basin is used for agriculture; only a small portion has been cleared for urban or cottage development. Near the lake, the valley sides are too steep to permit agriculture, and Organic and alluvial soils in flatter areas in the valley are suitable only for production of hay (Battle R. Reg. Plan. Commis. 1974). Pasture along Battle Creek is subject to frequent flooding.

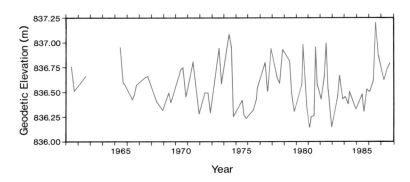

Figure 3. Water level of Battle Lake, 1961 to 1986.
SOURCE: Alta. Envir. n.d.[c].

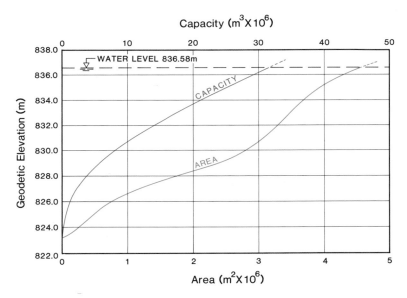

Figure 4. Area/capacity curve for Battle Lake. To obtain correct geodetic elevation add 0.15 m to elevations shown.
SOURCE: Alta. Envir. n.d.[c].

Lake Basin Characteristics

Battle Lake consists of a long, narrow single basin that has a maximum depth of 13.1 m (Fig. 2). The sides of the basin slope steeply in the central portion of the lake and more gradually at the northwest and southeast ends. The lake bottom consists mainly of sand and a few gravel shoals to depths of 4.5 m, and of mud in the deeper areas (Christiansen 1978). The shoreline also consists of sand, except at the northwest end, where it is muddy. The beach area is narrow, and almost disappears when water levels are high (Alta. For. Ld. Wild. n.d.). The elevation of Battle Lake was recorded occasionally in 1961 and 1962 and has been monitored regularly since 1965 (Fig. 3). The difference between the maximum elevation (837.23 m), recorded in July 1986, and the minimum elevation (836.10 m), recorded in February 1981, is 1.13 m. Changes in the lake's area and capacity with fluctuations in water level are shown in Figure 4.

Water Quality

Battle Lake was sampled by Fish and Wildlife Division in 1948, 1979, and 1980 (Alta. For. Ld. Wild. n.d.; Clarkson 1979; Rhude 1980), by the University of Alberta in May 1981 (Prepas 1983) and by Alberta Environment in 1983 and 1984 (Alta. Envir. n.d.[a]). The water is fresh, hard and well-buffered and the dominant ions are bicarbonate and calcium (Table 3).

Battle Lake is moderately deep and is sheltered from wind by its steep banks. The water column is usually thermally stratified to some degree during summer. The July 1948 and July 1979 observations detected a marked thermocline and dissolved oxygen concentrations of less than 2 mg/L in deeper water overlying the sediments. In July 1984, the water was weakly thermally stratified (Fig. 5) and dis-

Table 1. Characteristics of Battle Lake drainage basin.

area (excluding lake) (km²)[a]	103
soil[b]	Orthic Gray Luvisols
bedrock geology[c]	Paskapoo Formation (Tertiary): sandstone, siltstone, mudstone; thin limestone, coal and tuff beds; nonmarine
terrain[b]	level to hilly
ecoregion[d]	Moist Mixedwood Subregion of Boreal Mixedwood
dominant vegetation[d]	trembling aspen, balsam poplar
mean annual inflow (m³)[a, e]	6.19×10^6
mean annual sunshine (h)[f]	2 315

NOTE: [e]excluding groundwater inflow
SOURCES: [a]Alta. Envir. n.d.[b]; [b]Lindsay et al. 1968; [c]Alta. Res. Counc. 1972; [d]Strong and Leggat 1981; [f]Envir. Can. 1982

Table 2. Characteristics of Battle Lake.

elevation (m)[a, b]	836.72
surface area (km²)[a, b]	4.56
volume (m³)[a, b]	31.6×10^6
maximum depth (m)[a, b]	13.1
mean depth (m)[a, b]	6.9
shoreline length (km)[c]	17.6
mean annual lake evaporation (mm)[d]	664
mean annual precipitation (mm)[d]	534
mean residence time (yr)[d, e]	6
control structure	none

NOTES: [a]on date of sounding: Aug. 1977; [e]excluding groundwater inflow
SOURCES: [b]Alta. Envir. n.d.[c]; [c]En. Mines Resour. Can. 1975; [d]Alta. Envir. n.d.[b]

solved oxygen concentrations were only 1 mg/L at a depth of 11 m (Fig. 6). Although the water column was isothermal by September 1984, it was only partially saturated with dissolved oxygen. By February 1985, the water at a depth of 10 m was anoxic (Fig. 6). It is quite common for small areas of the lake to remain open in winter because springs flowing out of the banks bring in warmer water.

Battle Lake is eutrophic. There was a considerable difference between the maximum chlorophyll *a* concentrations recorded in 1983 and 1984. In 1983, the highest concentration recorded was 38.2 μg/L in early October, whereas in 1984, the maximum value was 16.3 μg/L, recorded in late August (Fig. 7). Despite the differences in maximum chlorophyll *a* concentrations, the maximum (6.5, 6.4 m) and average (3.7, 3.8 m, Table 4) Secchi depths were very similar for both years. As in other shallow Alberta lakes, phosphorus concentrations in the euphotic zone of Battle Lake are highest in September. This suggests the release of phosphorus from the bottom sediments during late summer and mixing of phosphorus-rich bottom water into the surface water when the lake mixes.

Biological Characteristics

Plants

The phytoplankton community was studied by Alberta Environment monthly during the open-water period in 1983 (Table 5). Biomass was less than 5 mg/L on all sampling dates except 5 October, when it reached 10 mg/L. The average biomass over the study period was 3 mg/L. Diatoms (Bacillariophyta) formed 32% of the biomass in May (mainly *Asterionella formosa*) and 86 to 99% of the biomass in October and November (mainly *Stephanodiscus niagarae*). Golden-brown algae (Cryptophyta: mainly *Cryptomonas ovata*, *C. erosa* and *Rhodomonas minuta*) were important from mid-May to mid-July and dinoflagellates (Pyrrhophyta: mainly *Ceratium hirundinella*) formed more than 20% of the biomass from mid-July to early Au-

Table 3. Major ions and related water quality variables for Battle Lake. Average concentrations in mg/L; pH in pH units. Composite samples from the euphotic zone collected 6 times from 01 May to 20 Sep. 1984. S.E. = standard error.

	Mean	S.E.
pH (range)	8.1–8.4	—
total alkalinity (CaCO₃)	182	0.9
specific conductivity (µS/cm)	352	2.5
total dissolved solids (calculated)	190	1.4
total hardness (CaCO₃)	134	2.2
total particulate carbon	1	0.2
dissolved organic carbon	9	0.4
HCO₃	215	2.5
CO₃	<4	—
Mg	10	0.2
Na	20	0.4
K	3	0.1
Cl	<2	—
SO₄	9	0.6
Ca	37	0.7

SOURCE: Alta. Envir. n.d.[a], Naquadat station 01AL05FA1000

Table 4. Nutrient, chlorophyll *a* and Secchi depth data for Battle Lake. Average concentrations in µg/L. Composite samples from the euphotic zone collected 7 times from 17 May to 03 Nov. 1983 and 6 times from 01 May to 20 Sep. 1984. S.E. = standard error.

	1983 Mean	S.E.	1984 Mean	S.E.
total phosphorus	29	5.9	33	5.7
total dissolved phosphorus	13	2.9	10	4.1
soluble reactive phosphorus	7	4.2	—	—
total Kjeldahl nitrogen	655[a]	61.7	610	45
NO₃ + NO₂–nitrogen	4	2.0	2	1.5
NH₄–nitrogen	31	11.8	13	3.9
iron	104[b]	22.5	<25	—
chlorophyll *a*	13.1	4.88	9.4	2.51
Secchi depth (m)	3.7	0.61	3.8	0.71

NOTES: [a]n = 6; [b]n = 5
SOURCE: Alta. Envir. n.d.[a], Naquadat station 01AL05FA1000

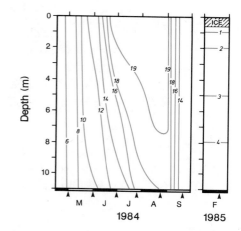

Figure 5. Temperature (°C) of Battle Lake, 1984 and 1985. Arrows indicate sampling dates.
SOURCE: Alta. Envir. n.d.[a].

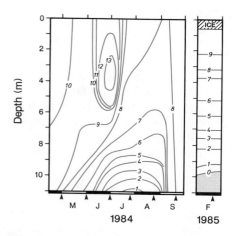

Figure 6. Dissolved oxygen (mg/L) in Battle Lake, 1984 and 1985. Arrows indicate sampling dates. Shaded area indicates 0 mg/L.
SOURCE: Alta. Envir. n.d.[a].

Figure 7. Total phosphorus, chlorophyll *a* and Secchi depth in Battle Lake, 1984.
SOURCE: Alta. Envir. n.d.[a].

gust. Green algae did not form more than 9% of the biomass on any sampling date. Blue-greens (Cyanophyta: mainly *Anabaena flos-aquae*, *Microcystis aeruginosa* and *Aphanizomenon flos-aquae*) were the dominant group from mid-July to early September. Anoxic conditions over the bottom sediments and subsequent release of sediment-bound phosphorus are important factors that stimulate the production of blue-green algae in this lake (Trimbee and Prepas 1987; 1988).

In a 1979 survey, Fish and Wildlife Division noted that the macrophyte community was mainly restricted to a narrow fringe along both shores and to the shallow inlet and outlet at either end of the lake (Clarkson 1979). The dominant emergent vegetation was bulrush (*Scirpus* spp.) and common cattail (*Typha latifolia*). In deeper water, yellow water lily (*Nuphar variegatum*) was plentiful and northern watermilfoil (*Myriophyllum exalbescens*) was common, but lower in density. Horsetail (*Equisetum* sp.) was noted in one location only. During a brief survey by Alberta Environment in June 1988, species noted included the emergent species arrowhead (*Sagittaria cuneata*) and the submergent species stonewort (*Chara* sp.), northern watermilfoil and Richardson (*Potamogeton richardsonii*), large-sheath (*P. vaginatus*) and Sago (*P. pectinatus*) pondweeds (Mitchell 1988).

Table 5. Percentage composition of major algal groups by total biomass in Battle Lake, 1983. Composite samples collected from the euphotic zone.

ALGAL GROUP	17 May	13 June	18 July	09 Aug.	08 Sep.	05 Oct.	08 Nov.
Total Biomass (mg/L)	0.34	0.84	0.61	1.67	2.71	10.21	4.45
Percentage Composition:							
Cyanophyta	0	0	40	44	71	13	1
			Anabaena	*Microcystis*	*Aphan.*		
Chlorophyta	9	2	2	1	1	0	0
Chrysophyta	16	18	1	0	4	0	0
Bacillariophyta	32	14	1	5	14	86	99
	Asterionella					*Stephanodiscus*——→	
Cryptophyta	37	66	35	15	9	1	0
	Cryptomonas——————→						
	Rhodomonas						
Pyrrhophyta	6	0	21	35	1	0	0
			Ceratium————→				

NOTE: *Aphan.* = *Aphanizomenon*
SOURCE: Alta. Envir. n.d.[a]

Invertebrates

The invertebrate community was sampled in 1948 and 1979 by Fish and Wildlife Division (Miller and Macdonald 1950; Clarkson 1979). In 1979, aquatic earthworms (Oligochaeta) and leeches (Hirudinea) were very abundant, and caddis fly larvae (Trichoptera), back swimmers (Hemiptera: Notonectidae), scuds (Amphipoda: *Gammarus* spp.) and mayfly nymphs (Ephemeroptera) were less abundant.

Fish

Five species of fish have been reported in Battle Lake: yellow perch, northern pike, white sucker, lake whitefish and burbot. Walleye eggs were planted in 1951 and 1953; although some fish survived, lack of suitable spawning substrate prevented reproduction, and only a few walleye were captured between 1960 and 1979 (Clarkson 1979). Battle Lake is managed for domestic and recreational fisheries. The main catch of the domestic fishery is lake whitefish. There is no information available for the recreational fishery. A commercial fishery for lake whitefish and northern pike operated from 1949 to 1969 (Alta. Rec. Parks Wild. 1976). It closed after the whitefish catch declined from an average of 15 560 kg/year in the 1950s to 2 885 kg/year in 1966/67 and 15 kg/year in 1968/69.

A partial winterkill occurred in Battle Lake in March 1980. Although several hundred fish died, a test netting in May 1980 caught representatives of all five species normally found in the lake (Rhude 1980). Local residents maintained that the winterkill was an isolated event.

Wildlife

The natural state of the shoreline and the presence of a marshy area at the southeast end of the lake provide habitat for several species of ducks, a Great Blue Heron colony, Common Loons, Ospreys, grebes and Belted Kingfishers. Trumpeter Swans have been sighted on the lake as well (Battle R. Reg. Plan. Commis. 1974; Clarkson 1979).

M.E. Bradford

References

Alberta Culture and Multiculturalism. n.d. Hist. Resour. Div., Hist. Sites Serv. Unpubl. data, Edmonton.
Alberta Environment. n.d.[a]. Envir. Assess. Div., Envir. Qlty. Monit. Br. Unpubl. data, Edmonton.
———. n.d.[b]. Tech. Serv. Div., Hydrol. Br. Unpubl. data, Edmonton.
———. n.d.[c]. Tech. Serv. Div., Surv. Br. Unpubl. data, Edmonton.
Alberta Forestry, Lands and Wildlife. n.d. Fish Wild. Div. Unpubl. data, Edmonton.
———. 1987. A summary of Alberta's natural areas reserved and established. Pub. Ld. Div., Ld. Mgt. Devel. Br. Unpubl. rep., Edmonton.
———. 1988. Boating in Alberta. Fish Wild. Div., Edmonton.
———. 1989. Guide to sportfishing. Fish Wild. Div., Edmonton.
Alberta Recreation, Parks and Wildlife. 1976. Commercial fisheries catch statistics for Alberta, 1942–1975. Fish Wild. Div., Fish. Mgt. Rep. No. 22, Edmonton.
Alberta Research Council. 1972. Geological map of Alberta. Nat. Resour. Div., Alta. Geol. Surv., Edmonton.
Battle River Regional Planning Commission. 1974. The Battle Lake study. Battle R. Reg. Plan. Commis., Wetaskiwin.
Christiansen, D.G. 1978. Preliminary draft of the Battle River basin study: Pigeon Lake, Battle Lake, Samson Lake, Coal Lake, Driedmeat Lake, Forestburg Reservoir. Alta. Rec. Parks Wild., Fish Wild. Div., Edmonton.
Clarkson, P. 1979. Survey of Battle Lake (Twp. 46, Rge. 2, W5). Alta. En. Nat. Resour., Fish Wild. Div., Edmonton.
Conroy Club and Yeoford Ladies Club. 1973. Trail blazers. Conroy Club and Yeoford Ladies Club, Winfield.
Energy, Mines and Resources Canada. 1974, 1975. National topographic series 1:50 000 83G/1 (1974), 83B/16 (1975). Surv. Map. Br., Ottawa.
Environment Canada. 1982. Canadian climate normals, Vol. 7: Bright sunshine (1951–1980). Prep. by Atm. Envir. Serv. Supply Serv. Can., Ottawa.
Falun Historical Society. 1974. Freeway west. Falun Hist. Soc., Falun.
Lindsay, J.D., W. Odynsky, T.W. Peters and W.E. Bowser. 1968. Reconnaissance soil survey of the Buck Lake (NE 83B) and Wabamun Lake (E1/2 83G) areas. Alta. Soil Surv. Rep. No. 24 1968, Univ Alta. Bull. No. SS–7, Res. Counc. Alta. Rep. No. 87. Univ. Alta., Edmonton.
MacGregor, J.G. 1976. The Battle River valley. West. Producer Prairie Books, Saskatoon, Sask.
Miller, R.B. and W.H. Macdonald. 1950. Preliminary biological surveys of Alberta watersheds, 1947–1949. Alta. Ld. For., Fish Wild. Div., Edmonton.
Mitchell, P.A. 1988. Alta. Envir., Envir. Assess. Div., Envir. Qlty. Monit. Br., Edmonton. Pers. comm.
Prepas, E.E. 1983. Orthophosphate turnover time in shallow productive lakes. Can. J. Fish. Aquat. Sci. 40:1412–1418.
Rhude, L. 1980. Evaluation of the Battle Lake winterkill of 1980. Alta. En. Nat. Resour., Fish Wild. Div., Red Deer.
Strong, W.L. and K.R. Leggat. 1981. Ecoregions of Alberta. Alta. En. Nat. Resour., Resour. Eval. Plan. Div., Edmonton.
Trimbee, A.M. and E.E. Prepas. 1987. Evaluation of total phosphorus as a predictor of the relative importance of blue-green algae with emphasis on Alberta lakes. Can. J. Fish. Aquat. Sci. 44:1337–1342.
———. 1988. The effect of oxygen depletion on the timing and magnitude of blue-green algal blooms. Verh. Internat. Verein. Limnol. 23:220–226.

COAL LAKE

MAP SHEET: 83H
LOCATION: Tp46, 48 R23 W4
LAT/LONG: 53°08'N 113°21'W

Coal Lake is a long, sinuous lake located approximately 60 km southeast of the city of Edmonton. Most of the lake is in the County of Wetaskiwin, but the northern portion is in the County of Leduc. Coal Lake lies in a portion of the glacial meltwater channel that drained glacial Lake Edmonton after the last ice age about 12 000 years ago. Beginning east of Nisku, the channel can be traced as it winds southeastward through a chain of lakes—Saunders, Ord, three unnamed ephemeral lakes, Coal and Driedmeat. Coal Lake is attractively bordered by treed valley walls rising 45 m above the lake. Access to the water is available at Alberta Environment day-use areas at each end of the lake. The southern day-use area can be reached by driving west from the city of Wetaskiwin on Highway 13 for 13 km and turning north onto Secondary Road 822 (Fig. 1) just west of the hamlet of Gwynne. The northern day-use area is located where Secondary Road 616 (Cloverlawn Road) crosses the lake (Fig. 2). Both day-use areas include boat launches, parking areas and picnic tables. There is no campground at Coal Lake.

Coal Lake was named in 1892 by J.D.A. Fitzpatrick, a Dominion Land Surveyor, for the coal beds present in many places along the northeast shore (Millet Dist. Hist. Soc. 1978). It is likely the same lake that is labelled "Long Lake" on the Palliser map of 1859 (Holmgren and Holmgren 1976). Despite the obvious beds of coal, there has never been any commercial mining near the lake. However, local farmers mined small quantities of coal along the shore until the early 1950s.

Coal Lake has been used as a municipal water supply by the City of Wetaskiwin since 1968 (City Wetaskiwin n.d.). Prior to the construction of a dam in 1972, the lake was much shallower, with a maximum depth of 2.5 m. In dry years, algal blooms in the lake caused intolerable taste and "curious colour" in the city drinking water (Battle R. Reg. Plan. Commis. 1974). In 1972, Alberta Environment built a dam across the valley 100 m downstream of the natural sill; this rerouted Pipestone Creek to flow into Coal Lake (Fig. 2). The lake surface is now 3 m higher, the water quality has improved and the lake is a reliable source of water for Wetaskiwin. The lake still supports a dense blue-green algal bloom through most of the summer.

Year-round sport fishing for northern pike is popular at Coal Lake. There are no sport fishing regulations specific to the lake, but general provincial regulations apply (Alta. For. Ld. Wild. 1989). The lake is also popular for power boating and snowmobiling. General federal boating regulations apply to the lake, but there are no specific restrictions (Alta. For. Ld. Wild. 1988). A hiking trail developed by the Waskahegan Trail Association follows the western shore (Battle R. Reg. Plan. Commis. 1974).

Drainage Basin Characteristics

The drainage basin of Coal Lake was about 100 km² prior to dam construction in 1972. Since 1972, Pipestone Creek has flowed into Coal Lake and the watershed now includes the Pipestone-Bigstone Creek drainage basin and totals 1 250 km² (Fig. 1, Table 1). Water flows out of Coal Lake via Pipestone Creek to the Battle River, 10 km to the southeast.

The drainage basin is located in the Aspen Parkland Ecoregion (Strong and Leggat 1981). Almost all of the land above the top of the valley has been cleared and is farmed intensively for grain and

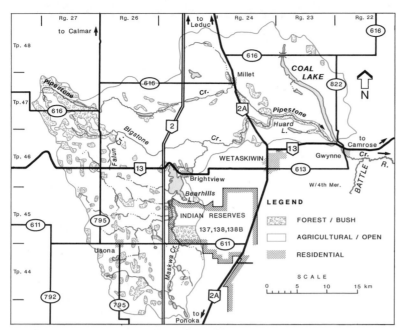

Figure 1. Features of the drainage basin of Coal Lake.
SOURCES: Alta. Envir. n.d.[d]; En. Mines Resour. Can. 1970; 1983.
Updated with 1983 and 1984 aerial photos.

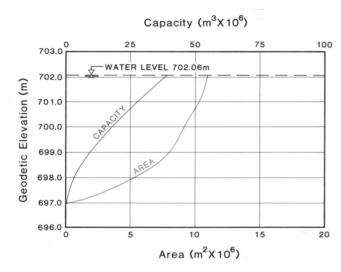

Figure 3. Area/capacity curve for Coal Lake.
SOURCE: Alta. Envir. n.d.[e].

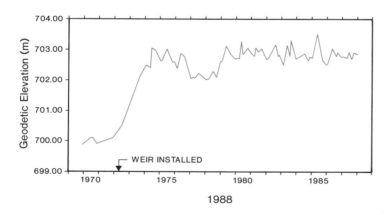

Figure 4. Water level of Coal Lake, 1969 to 1985.
SOURCE: Envir. Can. 1969–1985.

Table 1. Characteristics of Coal Lake drainage basin.

area (excluding lake) (km²)[a]	1 250
soil[b]	Solonetzic Black Chernozemics
bedrock geology[c]	Horseshoe Canyon Formation (Upper Cretaceous): sandstone, mudstone, shale; ironstone, scattered coal and bentonite beds; mainly nonmarine
terrain[b]	undulating, cut by glacial meltwater channel
ecoregion[d]	Aspen Parkland
dominant vegetation[d]	trembling aspen
mean annual inflow (m³)[a, e]	48.5 x 10⁶
mean annual sunshine (h)[f]	2 315

NOTE: [e]excluding groundwater inflow
SOURCES: [a]Alta. Envir. n.d.[d]; [b]Bowser et al. 1947; [c]Alta. Res. Counc. 1972; [d]Strong and Leggat 1981; [f]Envir. Can. 1982

Table 2. Characteristics of Coal Lake.

elevation (m)[a, b]	702.06
surface area (km²)[a, b]	10.9
volume (m³)[a, b]	38.8 x 10⁶
maximum depth (m)[a, b]	5.5
mean depth (m)[a, b]	3.5
shoreline length (km)[c]	43.0
mean annual lake evaporation (mm)[d]	664
mean annual precipitation (mm)[d]	449
mean residence time (yr)[d, e]	0.85
control structure[f]	earth embankment with concrete overflow dam and submerged culvert
dam crest elevation (m)[f]	705.9
full supply level (m)[f]	702.8
lowest possible controlled drawdown (m)[f]	699.82

NOTES: [a]on date of sounding: Aug. 1978; [e]excluding groundwater inflow
SOURCES: [b]Alta. Envir. n.d.[e]; [c]En. Mines Resour. Can. 1983; [d]Alta. Envir. n.d.[d]; [f]Alta. Envir. n.d.[a]

livestock production (Battle R. Reg. Plan. Commis. 1974). The terrain outside of the valley is level or undulating to gently rolling. Within the glacial channel that extends upstream and downstream of Coal Lake, some of the valley floor is leased for hay production or grazing and the valley sides support trembling aspen, balsam poplar, willows and shrubs. The dominant soils are Solonetzic Black Chernozemics on the uplands and Solodized Solonetz on the valley floor (Bowser et al. 1947). The valley walls are fairly steep and erode easily if the vegetation is removed (Battle R. Reg. Plan. Commis. 1974). The tributary creeks have carved deep coulees, and alluvial fans have formed in the lake at the inlets.

There are many farms and several small population centres within the drainage basin, including the hamlets of Gwynne, Bright View and Usona and the village of Millet. The city of Wetaskiwin is only 10 km southwest of the lake but is outside the drainage basin. All of the land bordering Coal Lake is Crown land (Fig. 2).

Lake Basin Characteristics

Coal Lake is 18–km long, but only 0.7–km wide at its widest point. The lake has a steeply sloping bottom (Fig. 2). The substrate is primarily firm sand and clay to a water depth of 2.0 m; in water deeper than 2 m, the substrate is soft flocculent mud (Integrated Envir. Sci. Inc. 1984). When the lake is at an elevation of 703 m, approximately 20% of the lake is less than 2.0–m deep (Fig. 3), which is the limit of dense aquatic plant growth. Since 1972, the lake level has been regulated by an earthen embankment and dam with a low-level riparian outlet and a concrete overflow spillway (Table 2).

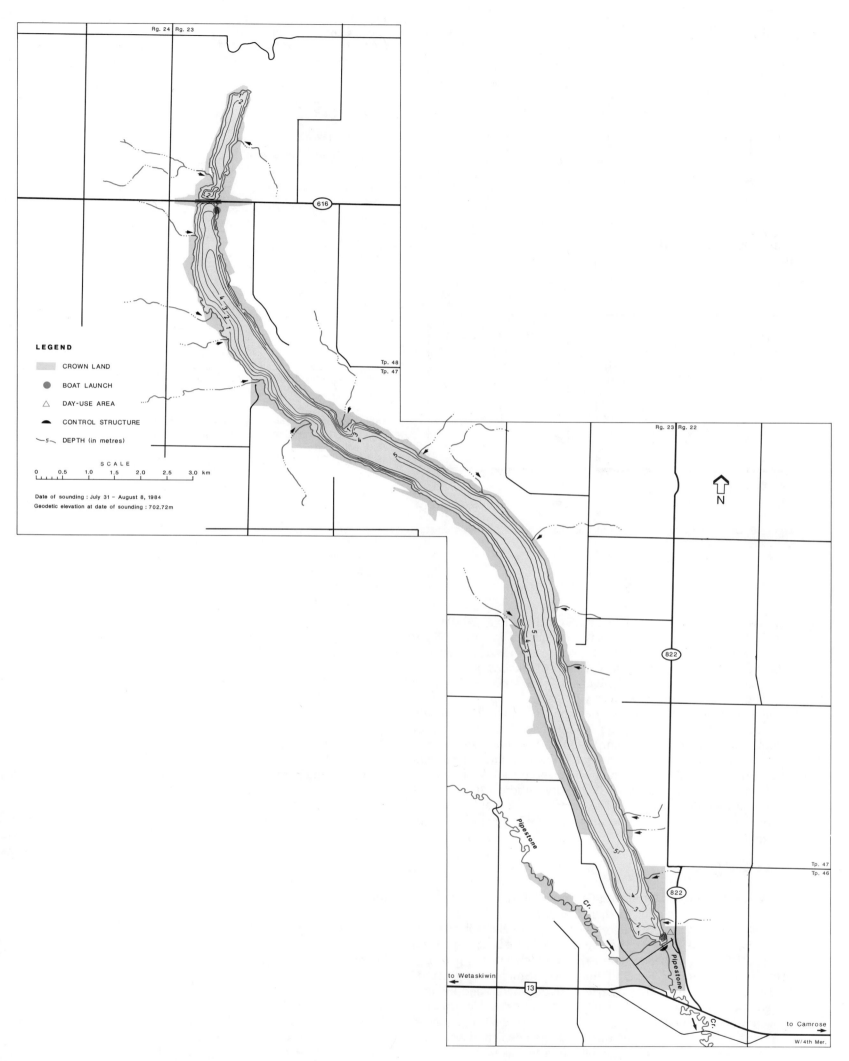

Figure 2. Bathymetry and shoreline features of Coal Lake.
BATHYMETRY SOURCE: adapted from Integrated Envir. Sci. Inc. 1984.

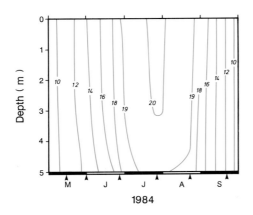

Figure 5. Temperature (°C) of Coal Lake, 1984. Arrows indicate sampling dates.
SOURCE: Alta. Envir. n.d.[b].

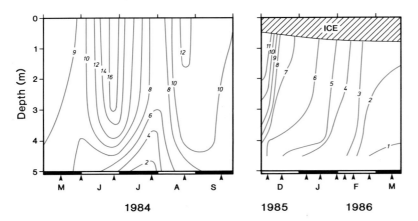

Figure 6. Dissolved oxygen (mg/L) in Coal Lake, 1984. Arrows indicate sampling dates.
SOURCE: Alta. Envir. n.d.[b]; n.d.[c].

Table 3. Major ions and related water quality variables for Coal Lake. Average concentrations in mg/L; pH in pH units. Composite samples from the euphotic zone collected 6 times from 14 May to 21 Sep. 1984 and 6 times from 15 May to 23 Oct. 1985. S.E. = standard error.

	Mean	S.E.
pH (range)	8.2–9.5	—
total alkalinity (CaCO₃)	201	2.2
specific conductivity (μS/cm)	469	6.1
total dissolved solids (calculated)	273	3.9
total hardness (CaCO₃)	122	2.9
total particulate carbon	3	0.8
dissolved organic carbon	49	1.7
HCO₃	226	4.8
CO₃	<9	—
Mg	12	0.3
Na	53	1.0
K	12	0.4
Cl	7	0.2
SO₄	41	2.7
Ca	31	1.1

SOURCE: Alta. Envir. n.d.[b], Naquadat station 01AL05FA0100

Table 4. Nutrient, chlorophyll *a* and Secchi depth data for Coal Lake. Average concentrations in μg/L. Composite samples from the euphotic zone collected 6 times from 14 May to 21 Sep. 1984 and 6 times from 15 May to 23 Oct. 1985. S.E. = standard error.

	1984		1985	
	Mean	S.E.	Mean	S.E.
total phosphorus	176	49.9	—	—
total dissolved phosphorus	109	36.4	—	—
total Kjeldahl nitrogen	1 840	225.9	1 398	83.5
NO₃ + NO₂–nitrogen	16	5.6	30	14.4
NH₄–nitrogen	138	74.6	166	66.5
iron	168	45.0	187	30.2
chlorophyll *a*	43.8	13.47	43.0	11.97
Secchi depth (m)	2.4	0.61	1.2	0.34

SOURCE: Alta. Envir. n.d.[b], Naquadat station 01AL05FA0100

This dam raised the lake level by 3 m. From 1974 to 1986 the level has fluctuated 1.2 m (Fig. 4). The average annual volume of water that passes through the lake is sufficient to exchange the volume every year (Table 2), but because Pipestone Creek flows into the lake very near the outlet, most of the water is "short-circuited" and the effective residence time is likely very long.

Alberta Environment built the dam on Coal Lake to meet two objectives: to ensure an adequate supply of good quality water for Wetaskiwin (Battle R. Reg. Plan. Commis. 1974) and to create a reservoir to augment flows in the Battle River in times of drought (Alta. Envir. n.d.[a]). The Wetaskiwin diversion intake is on the southwest shore of the lake. In 1986, the city withdrew 10.3 x 10⁶ m³ of water (City Wetaskiwin n.d.). The capacity for flow augmentation has been used only twice: in the summer of 1977 and in the winter of 1985/86.

Water Quality

Coal Lake was sampled by Alberta Environment from 1982 to 1985 (Alta. Envir. n.d.[b]; n.d.[c]; Sloman 1984).

Coal Lake is a well-buffered, freshwater lake (total dissolved solids average 273 mg/L, Table 3). The dominant ions are bicarbonate and sodium. The lake is shallow and is likely thermally stratified only occasionally in summer (Fig. 5). It may become more strongly stratified in areas of dense macrophyte growth where wind-induced currents are attenuated. In late July 1984, the dissolved oxygen concentration declined to 1.6 mg/L at the bottom while it remained at 8.0 mg/L at the surface (Fig. 6). The oxygen depletion was likely due to the decay of a dense algal bloom in the lake.

In winter, dissolved oxygen levels near the dam were only 4.0 mg/L at the surface and 2.0 mg/L at the bottom by mid-February in both 1983 and 1986 (Fig. 6). The northern end of the lake just

south of Secondary Road 616 had fairly high dissolved oxygen concentrations all winter. On 23 February 1983, for example, concentrations were 8.1 mg/L at the surface and 5.8 mg/L at the bottom. The water remained open near this site all winter of both years.

Coal Lake is hyper-eutrophic and supports a conspicuous, dense algal bloom during most of the summer (Table 4). The mean open-water total phosphorus concentration is higher (176 μg/L) than that recorded in 36 other lakes that have been similarly studied by Alberta Environment (Alta. Envir. n.d.[b]). The total phosphorus concentration in Coal Lake increased over the open-water period from less than 50 μg/L in May to a maximum of 342 μg/L in late August (Fig. 7). This suggests that phosphorus was released from the sediments, as occurs in many central Alberta lakes.

Biological Characteristics

Plants

The species composition and biomass of the phytoplankton community was examined by Alberta Environment in 1984 and in 1985 (Table 5). In 1984, there was a dense bloom of blue-green algae (Cyanophyta) dominated by *Aphanizomenon flos-aquae* through June and July. This was followed in September by a strong bloom of diatoms (Bacillariophyta) dominated by *Stephanodiscus niagarae*. In

Table 5. Percentage composition of major algal groups by total biomass in Coal Lake, 1984. Composite samples collected from the euphotic zone.

ALGAL GROUP	14 May	30 May	26 June	26 July	22 Aug.	21 Sep.
Total Biomass (mg/L)	1.17	0.67	14.23	29.75	9.03	21.77
Percentage Composition:						
Cyanophyta	0	7	98	86	28	1
			Aphanizomenon————————→		*Microcystis*	
Chlorophyta	5	20	0	0	0	<1
		Closterium				
Bacillariophyta	87	56	<1	13	72	97
	Stephanodiscus————————→				*Stephanodiscus*————————→	
Cryptophyta	8	17	2	1	0	2

SOURCE: Alta. Envir. n.d.[b]

Table 6. Species of aquatic macrophytes in Coal Lake. Survey conducted between 31 July and 08 Aug. 1984. Arranged by dominance.

emergent	sedge	*Carex* spp.
	bulrush	*Scirpus* sp.
	common cattail	*Typha latifolia*
	bur-reed	*Sparganium* sp.
free-floating	coontail	*Ceratophyllum demersum*
	star duckweed	*Lemna trisulca*
submergent	Richardson pondweed	*Potamogeton richardsonii*
	large-sheath pondweed	*P. vaginatus*
	Sago pondweed	*P. pectinatus*
	small-leaf pondweed	*P. pusillus*
	northern watermilfoil	*Myriophyllum exalbescens*
	pondweed	*Potamogeton friesii*
	flat-stemmed pondweed	*P. zosteriformis*
	white-stem pondweed	*P. praelongus*
	musk grass	*Chara globularis*
floating-leaved	arrowhead	*Sagittaria cuneata*
	yellow water lily	*Nuphar variegatum*

SOURCE: Integrated Envir. Sci. Inc. 1984

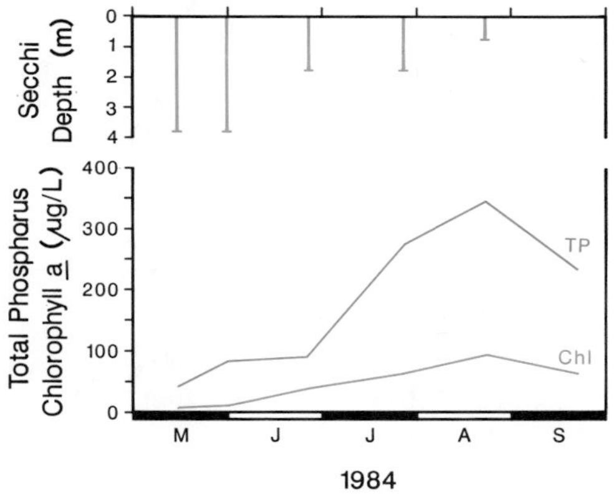

Figure 7. Total phosphorus, chlorophyll *a* and Secchi depth in Coal Lake, 1984.
SOURCE: Alta. Envir. n.d.[b].

comparison, data from 1985 suggest that a blue-green bloom occurred from June to late August, dominated first by *Anabaena flosaquae* in June, then by *Microcystis aeruginosa*. The diatom bloom that year, as in 1984, was dominated by *Stephanodiscus niagarae*; it peaked in August and continued through September. The phytoplankton was sampled once under ice-cover, on 20 February 1985. At that time, algal biomass was 0.3 mg/L; diatoms (*Stephanodiscus niagarae*) and cryptophytes (*Cryptomonas rostratiformis*) were codominant.

Macrophytes in Coal Lake were mapped in detail for Alberta Environment in 1984 (Table 6). Emergent species were most conspicuous at the southern end of the lake and in the northern section. In the main portion of the lake, cattle grazing and active soil slumping limited emergent growth to small pockets of *Carex* spp. Submergent species covered 112.6 ha, or 11% of the lake's area. The dominant species were pondweeds (*Potamogeton richardsonii*, *P. vaginatus* and *P. pectinatus*). Submergent macrophytes grew densely in a narrow band, 5– to 20–m wide, along almost the entire shoreline. The plants were generally limited to water 1.5– to 2.0–m deep and grew up to the surface. More extensive and widespread growth was found at both ends of the lake and near the inlet streams.

Invertebrates

There are no data on the invertebrates in Coal Lake.

Fish

Prior to dam construction, Coal Lake supported few sport fish because of severe winterkills (Battle R. Reg. Plan. Commis. 1974). It now supports a popular local sport fishery for northern pike, and was stocked with yellow perch by Fish and Wildlife Division in 1983, 1984 and 1985 (Alta. En. Nat. Resour. 1983–1985). In May 1984, Fish and Wildlife Division set three gangs of test nets for 24 hours and caught 602 white suckers, 234 northern pike and 14 yellow perch (Alta. For. Ld. Wild. n.d.). Migration of fish into Coal Lake from the Battle River is now blocked by the Coal Lake dam, but fish can still pass downstream over the dam. Pipestone Creek immediately downstream of Coal Lake is a primary spawning area for northern pike and white suckers from the Battle River (Fernet et al. 1985). Forage fish in the lake include lake chub, emerald shiner, longnose dace and brook stickleback (Fernet et al. 1985).

Wildlife

The best areas of Coal Lake for waterfowl production are the shallow northern portion and the area near the dam at the south end. The shore on the rest of the lake is too steep to provide good nesting habitat (Boyko 1987). Large numbers of ducks and Common Loons feed on the lake and numerous waterfowl stop there on migration. A nesting colony of Great Blue Herons is located on the outlet creek. Muskrats and beaver are frequently seen.

J.M. Crosby

References

Alberta Energy and Natural Resources. 1983–1985. Fish planting list. Fish Wild. Div., Edmonton.

Alberta Environment. n.d.[a]. Devel. Op. Div. Unpubl. data, Edmonton.

————. n.d.[b]. Envir. Assess. Div., Envir. Qlty. Monit. Br. Unpubl. data, Edmonton.

————. n.d.[c]. Plan. Div., Plan. Serv. Br. Unpubl. data, Edmonton.

————. n.d.[d]. Tech. Serv. Div., Hydrol. Br. Unpubl. data, Edmonton.

————. n.d.[e]. Tech. Serv. Div., Surv. Br. Unpubl. data, Edmonton.

Alberta Forestry, Lands and Wildlife. n.d. Fish Wild. Div. Unpubl. data, Edmonton.

————. 1988. Boating in Alberta. Fish Wild. Div., Edmonton.

————. 1989. Guide to sportfishing. Fish Wild. Div., Edmonton.

Alberta Research Council. 1972. Geological map of Alberta. Nat. Resour. Div., Alta. Geol. Surv., Edmonton.

Battle River Regional Planning Commission. 1974. Coal Lake—A study of conflicting uses. Prep. for Co. Wetaskiwin, Wetaskiwin.

Bowser, W.E., R.L. Erdman, F.A. Wyatt and J.D. Newton. 1947. Soil survey of Peace Hills sheet. Alta. Soil Surv. Rep. No. 14, Univ. Alta. Bull. No. 48. Univ. Alta., Edmonton.

Boyko, D. 1987. Alta. For. Ld. Wild., Fish Wild. Div., Wetaskiwin Dist. Office. Pers. comm.

City of Wetaskiwin. n.d. Eng. Dept. Unpubl. data, Wetaskiwin.

Energy, Mines and Resources Canada. 1970, 1983. National topographic series 1:250 000 83A (1970), 83H (1983). Surv. Map. Br., Ottawa.

Environment Canada. 1969–1985. Surface water data. Prep. by Inland Waters Directorate. Water Surv. Can., Water Resour. Br., Ottawa.

————. 1982. Canadian climate normals, Vol. 7: Bright sunshine (1951–1980). Prep. by Atm. Envir. Serv. Supply Serv. Can., Ottawa.

Fernet, D.A., G.A. Ash and S.M. Matkowski. 1985. Investigations of the Battle River fishery relative to the potential effects of flow augmentation. Prep. for Alta. Envir., Plan. Div. by Envir. Mgt. Assoc., Calgary and R.L. & L. Envir. Serv. Ltd., Edmonton.

Holmgren, E.J. and P.M. Holmgren. 1976. Over 2000 place names of Alberta. 3rd ed. West. Producer Prairie Books, Saskatoon.

Integrated Environmental Sciences Inc. 1984. Aquatic macrophyte surveys of Coal Lake, Driedmeat Lake and the Battle Reservoir. Prep. for Alta. Envir., Plan. Div., Edmonton.

Millet and District Historical Society. 1978. Tales and trails of Millet, Vol. 1. Millet Dist. Hist. Soc., Millet.

Sloman, K.W. 1984. Dissolved oxygen in the Battle River system, winter 1982/83. Alta. Envir., Plan. Div., Edmonton.

Strong, W.L. and K.R. Leggat. 1981. Ecoregions of Alberta. Alta. En. Nat. Resour., Resour. Eval. Plan. Div., Edmonton.

DRIEDMEAT LAKE

MAP SHEET: 83A

LOCATION: Tp44, 45 R19 W4

LAT/LONG: 52°52′N 112°45′W

Driedmeat Lake is a long, narrow lake that was originally formed above a natural constriction of the Battle River; it is now stabilized by a weir. The lake is located 17 km south of the city of Camrose in the County of Camrose (Fig. 1). Driedmeat Lake is situated in a glacial meltwater channel incised 40 m into the surrounding plain. From the top of the valley, the view of the lake is very attractive; from the lake, the impression is one of being surrounded by rolling, wooded hills.

Before the arrival of the white man, the area near the lake was used by Blackfoot and Cree Indians. The word "driedmeat".comes from the Cree word for drying buffalo meat and making pemmican. The lake took its name from Driedmeat Hill, just east of the centre of the lake (Gould 1939). The hill has recently been disturbed by gravel extraction, but Saskatoon berries, an ingredient of pemmican, still grow luxuriantly in the area. The Cree tended to stay to the east of the Battle River and the Blackfoot to the west; the river provided a natural barrier and was the site of numerous skirmishes, hence the name Battle River.

By 1900, settlers had arrived to farm the rich soil in the area (MacGregor 1972). Roads were hard to maintain, especially in the spring when snowmelt and rain turned the dirt tracks to gumbo. At that time, the lake was an important transportation corridor. About 1903, a 30–foot motorboat powered by a woodburning steam engine provided ferry service along the lake (Edberg Hist. Soc. Book Club 1981).

Access to the lake is available at Tillicum Beach Park, a County of Camrose campground that is open from May to September. The park is located halfway along the eastern shore (Fig. 2). The facilities available include 31 random campsites, a boat launch, a beach, tap water, flush toilets, a picnic shelter, food service, ball diamonds and a playground; in winter, a skating rink is maintained. The only commercial resort on the lake and a few cottages are located just north of Tillicum Beach. Another access point, where canoes and small boats can be launched, is located at the south end of the lake where Highway 56 crosses the Battle River near the weir (Fig. 2).

Aquatic vegetation, which grows luxuriantly at both ends of Driedmeat Lake, provides excellent waterfowl habitat but inhibits boat traffic. Recreational activities enjoyed at the lake include fishing, swimming, canoeing, power boating and wildlife viewing. There are no boating restrictions specific to Driedmeat Lake, but general federal regulations apply (Alta. For. Ld. Wild. 1988). Provincial sport fishing regulations apply and angling is not permitted within 25 m of the weir at the south end of the lake (Alta. For. Ld. Wild. 1989). The lake is rich in nutrients and supports dense algal blooms during most of the summer.

Drainage Basin Characteristics

The drainage basin of Driedmeat Lake is very large (7 220 km², Table 1). It encompasses the upstream portion of the Battle River basin, which extends west of Battle Lake and includes Pigeon Lake, Miquelon Lake and areas south of the town of Lacombe (Fig. 1).

The watershed is mostly in the Aspen Parkland Ecoregion, except for a small area at the far western border, which is in the Boreal Mixedwood Ecoregion (Strong and Leggat 1981). Most of the eastern two-thirds of the drainage basin has been cleared for grain production, with some hay and pasture production in the north. The

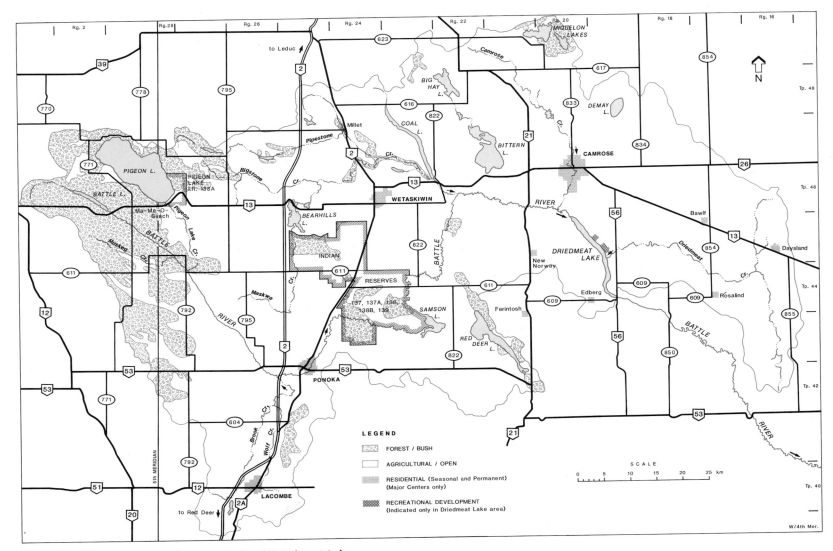

Figure 1. Features of the drainage basin of Driedmeat Lake.
SOURCES: Alta. Envir. n.d.[d]; En. Mines Resour. Can. 1963; 1970; 1976; 1983. Updated with 1980 aerial photos.

western 5% of the basin is mostly forested, and the remainder is partially wooded and partially cleared for mixed farming. The vegetation in the valley close to Driedmeat Lake is dominated by trembling aspen, with willows growing near the water. Some areas at the upstream end of the lake have been cleared for hay production and pasture. Soils are dominated by Solodic and Solodized Solonetz Black Chernozemics; Orthic Gray Luvisols are present in the far western portion of the basin (Bowser et al. 1947).

There are two cities (Camrose and Wetaskiwin) and numerous towns (including Lacombe and Ponoka) and villages in the drainage basin (Fig. 1). The Battle River upstream of Driedmeat Lake provides water for, and receives waste effluent from, many of these communities (Nanuk Eng. and Hydroqual Consult. Inc. 1986). The city of Camrose has withdrawn water directly from Driedmeat Lake for municipal use since 1950 (City Camrose n.d.). As of 1988, approximately 1.9×10^6 m³ are withdrawn annually from the east side of the lake, north of Tillicum Beach. Sewage from Camrose passes through lagoons, and the effluent is then discharged into Camrose Creek, which flows into the Battle River just upstream of Driedmeat Lake (Fig. 1).

Lake Basin Characteristics

Driedmeat Lake is a long stretch of the Battle River that is wider (0.7 km) and deeper (maximum depth 3.7 m, Table 2) than the rest of the river. The sediments under about one-quarter of the lake at each end are soft organic mud; under the rest of the lake to a water depth of 2.0 m, the sediments are firm sand or clay with some gravel. In areas deeper than 2.0 m, the substrate is soft mud (Integrated Envir. Sci. Inc. 1984). The lake bottom slopes very gradually at both ends, and somewhat more steeply along the sides near the middle (Fig. 2).

Table 1. Characteristics of Driedmeat Lake drainage basin.

area (excluding lake) (km²)[a]	7 220
soil[b]	Black Solodic Chernozemics, Orthic Gray Luvisols
bedrock geology[c]	Belly River Formation (Upper Cretaceous): sandstone, siltstone, mudstone, ironstone beds; nonmarine
terrain[b]	flat to undulating, incised water courses
ecoregion[d]	Aspen Parkland (east), Boreal Mixedwood (west)
dominant vegetation[d]	trembling aspen
mean annual inflow (m³)[a, e]	171×10^6
mean annual sunshine (h)[f]	2 317

NOTE: [e]excluding groundwater inflow
SOURCES: [a]Alta. Envir. n.d.[d]; [b]Bowser et al. 1947; [c]Alta. Res. Counc. 1972; [d]Strong and Leggat 1981; [f]Envir. Can. 1982

The water level was highly variable prior to 1975 (Fig. 3). The extreme peak in 1974 was caused by the melting of the heavy snowfall of 1973/74 and by the very heavy spring rainfall in 1974. In 1975, Alberta Environment installed a sheet-pile fixed-crest weir with an elevation of 684.6 m. Its purpose was to stabilize water levels and to provide more reliable storage to augment downstream flows in times of severe drought (Alta. Envir. n.d.[a]). Although the lake level has become more stable with the weir in place, it still fluctuates. For example, between 1975 and 1987, the lake level varied by 1.9 m, and during 1982 alone, it fluctuated by 1.6 m.

Driedmeat Lake is part of the Battle River, so the average water retention time is short (0.25 year, Table 2) but highly variable,

Table 2. Characteristics of Driedmeat Lake.

elevation (m)[a, b]	684.44
surface area (km²)[a, b]	16.5
volume (m³)[a, b]	41.9 x 10⁶
maximum depth (m)[a, b]	3.7
mean depth (m)[a, b]	2.2
shoreline length (km)[c]	41.2
mean annual lake evaporation (mm)[d]	664
mean annual precipitation (mm)[d]	453
mean residence time (yr)[d, e]	0.25
control structure[f]	fixed-crest weir with step-pool fish ladder
fixed sill elevation (m)[f]	684.6

NOTES: [a]on date of sounding: 05 Aug. 1984; [e]excluding groundwater inflow
SOURCES: [b]Alta. Envir. n.d.[e]; [c]Integrated Envir. Sci. Ltd. 1984; [d]Alta. Envir. n.d.[d]; [f]Alta. Envir. n.d.[a]

Table 3. Major ions and related water quality variables for Driedmeat Lake. Average concentrations in mg/L; pH in pH units. Composite samples from the euphotic zone collected 6 times from 07 May to 27 Sep. 1984. S.E. = standard error.

	Mean	S.E.
pH (range)	8.1–9.5	—
total alkalinity (CaCO₃)	219	3.9
specific conductivity (µS/cm)	579	13.1
total dissolved solids (calculated)	344	6.3
total hardness (CaCO₃)	163	6.9
total particulate carbon	8	1.9
dissolved organic carbon	19	1.5
HCO₃	227	18.7
CO₃	20	7.9
Mg	18	0.4
Na	61	2.8
K	9	0.2
Cl	14	0.6
SO₄	75	3.6
Ca	35	2.7

SOURCE: Alta. Envir. n.d.[b], Naquadat station 01AL05FA2005

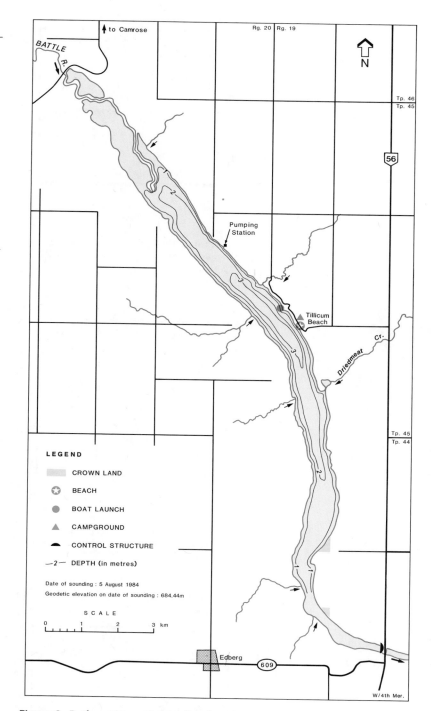

Figure 2. Bathymetry and shoreline features of Driedmeat Lake.
BATHYMETRY SOURCE: Integrated Envir. Sci. Inc. 1984.

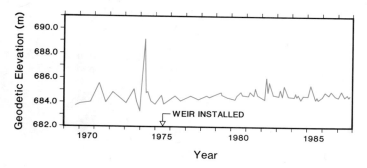

Figure 3. Water level of Driedmeat Lake, 1969 to 1985.
SOURCE: Alta. Envir. n.d.[e].

depending on the flow of the river. In 1968, for example, the total discharge of the Battle River was 14.2 x 10⁶ m³, and the retention time of water in the lake was one year; in 1974, however, the mean annual discharge was 662.0 x 10⁶ m³ and the retention time averaged only 7.3 days (Envir. Can. 1969–1985).

The weir at the lake's outlet is fitted with an eight-bay step-pool fish ladder with adjustable stop-logs (Alta. Envir. n.d.[a]) to facilitate passage of northern pike into Driedmeat Lake. When the lake elevation is below the top of the weir, flow through the fish ladder provides 0.2 m³/second continuous flow to the Battle River.

Water Quality

The water quality of Driedmeat Lake was monitored by Alberta Environment in 1984 as part of a study to determine the effect of flow augmentation on the Battle River (Alta. Envir. n.d.[b]; Nanuk Eng. and Hydroqual Consult. Inc. 1986). Under-ice oxygen conditions have been monitored in detail by Alberta Environment throughout the Battle River, including Driedmeat Lake, over three winters: 1982/83 (Sloman 1984), 1984/85 (Fernet et al. 1985) and 1985/86 (Alta. Envir. n.d.[c]).

Driedmeat Lake contains fresh water (total dissolved solids average 344 mg/L, Table 3). The dominant ions are bicarbonate, sodium, sulphate and calcium.

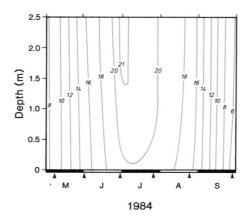

Figure 4. Temperature (°C) of Driedmeat Lake, 1984. Arrows indicate sampling dates.
SOURCE: Alta. Envir. n.d.[b].

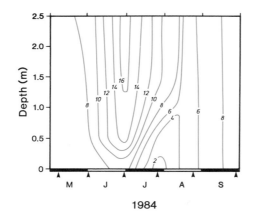

Figure 5. Dissolved oxygen (mg/L) in Driedmeat Lake, 1984. Arrows indicate sampling dates.
SOURCE: Alta. Envir. n.d.[b].

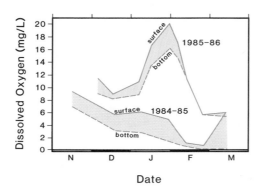

Figure 6. Winter dissolved oxygen in Driedmeat Lake, 1984/85 (a typical year) and 1985/86 (under-ice algal bloom).
SOURCES: Alta. Envir. n.d.[c]; Fernet et al. 1985.

Table 4. Chlorophyll *a* concentrations (μg/L) in Driedmeat Lake during an under-ice algal bloom, 1986.

Depth (m)	15 Jan.	05 Feb.	12 Feb.	25 Feb.	13 Mar.
0.7	38	45	128	59	368
1.0	39	32	134	47	459
1.5	60	28	69	33	443
2.0	32	42	38	10	220
2.5	37	20	34	9	206
3.0	50	9	20	11	125

SOURCE: Prepas and Crosby n.d.

Table 5. Nutrient, chlorophyll *a* and Secchi depth data for Driedmeat Lake. Average concentrations in μg/L. Composite samples from the euphotic zone collected 6 times from 07 May to 27 Sep. 1984. S.E. = standard error.

	Mean	S.E.
total phosphorus	453	133.7
total dissolved phosphorus	301	100.2
total Kjeldahl nitrogen	3 133	574.8
$NO_3 + NO_2$–nitrogen	69	39.7
NH_4–nitrogen	182	121.3
iron	166	45.7
chlorophyll *a*	87	29.3
Secchi depth (m)	1.5[a]	0.6

NOTE: [a]n = 4
SOURCE: Alta. Envir. n.d.[b], Naquadat station 01AL05FA2005

Driedmeat Lake is so shallow that it is well-mixed from surface to bottom throughout the open-water period (Fig. 4). Even in July and August of 1984, the temperature difference from top to bottom was less than 2°C. A vertical gradient in dissolved oxygen was maintained throughout most of June, July and August in 1984 (Fig. 5). On 25 July the dissolved oxygen concentration was 10 mg/L at the surface but only 1 mg/L near the substrate. This measurement was taken at a site near the centre of the lake. In the large areas of the lake at each end, where aquatic plants grow very densely and form mats on the surface, dissolved oxygen concentrations from just below the mats down to the substrate are often less than 1 mg/L, as in July 1975 (Crosby n.d.). As a result, dissolved oxygen concentrations in the Battle River below Driedmeat Lake are often low enough to cause fish kills despite aeration by the weir and fishway (Fernet et al. 1985).

In winter, dissolved oxygen concentrations in Driedmeat Lake are often very low and cause frequent and extensive fish kills (Alta. For. Ld. Wild. n.d.; Rhude 1980; Fernet et al. 1985). The data for 1984/85 (Fig. 6) are likely typical of most winters; the under-ice decay of macrophytes and algae rapidly consumes dissolved oxygen. Similarly, throughout the Battle River system, dissolved oxygen concentrations are frequently too low by late January (less than 2 mg/L) to support fish. The winter of 1985/86 was exceptional because an algal bloom developed in Driedmeat Lake in December; it lasted until March and produced dissolved oxygen concentrations as high as 20.1 mg/L immediately under the ice and 16.4 mg/L on the bottom of the lake (Fig. 6). Chlorophyll *a* concentrations peaked at 459 μg/L at a depth of 1.0 m (0.3 m below the bottom of the ice) on 13 March 1986 (Table 4). However, even when dissolved oxygen concentrations are low throughout most of the lake, an area near the mouth of the unnamed creek north of Driedmeat Creek has adequate dissolved oxygen for fish throughout the winter.

Driedmeat Lake is hyper-eutrophic. In 1984, the mean summer total phosphorus concentration (453 μg/L, Table 5) was almost 4 times higher than that of any of 36 other lakes studied by Alberta Environment (Alta. Envir. n.d.[b]). The total phosphorus concentration increased over the summer to a maximum of 1 016 μg/L (Fig. 7). This pattern of increasing phosphorus concentration over

Table 6. Percentage composition of major algal groups by total biomass in Driedmeat Lake, 1984. Composite samples collected from the euphotic zone.

ALGAL GROUP	07 May	30 May	29 June	26 July	21 Aug.	21 Sep.
Total Biomass (mg/L)	0.39	0.36	98.04	34.30	35.07	20.36
Percentage Composition:						
Cyanophyta	1	6	100	96	98	23
			Aphanizomenon ———————————————→			
Chlorophyta	5	18	0	0	1	15
Chrysophyta	0	0	0	0	0	5
Xanthophyta	0	0	0	1	0	5
Bacillariophyta	60	3	0	1	1	50
	Stephanodiscus					*Stephanodiscus*
Cryptophyta	34	73	0	1	0	7
	Cryptomonas ———————————————→					

SOURCE: Alta. Envir. n.d.[b]

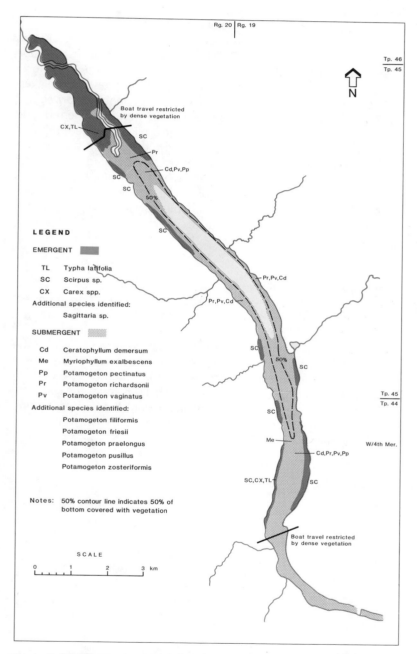

Figure 7. Total phosphorus, chlorophyll *a* and Secchi depth in Driedmeat Lake, 1984.
SOURCE: Alta. Envir. n.d.[b].

the summer is typical of shallow eutrophic and hyper-eutrophic lakes in central Alberta. Phosphorus is likely transferred from the bottom sediments to the water during this period.

A dense algal bloom develops throughout the lake in early June and remains all summer (Fig. 7). In 1984, peak chlorophyll *a* concentrations over 160 µg/L were recorded in late June and August. During blooms, the Secchi transparency is less than one metre (Fig. 7) and a noxious-smelling scum, which discourages swimming, forms on the water and drifts onto shore areas.

Biological Characteristics

Plants

A conspicuous feature of Driedmeat Lake is the blue-green algal bloom that turns the water to "pea soup" from early June to mid-September. During this period in 1984 (Table 6), over 97% of the algal biomass in the lake was one species, *Aphanizomenon flos-aquae* (Cyanophyta). By 21 September, the diatom (Bacillariophyta) *Stephanodiscus hantzschia* was the dominant alga, followed by the blue-green alga *Aphanizomenon flos-aquae* and the green alga (Chlorophyta) *Actinastrum Hantzschii*.

In the winter of 1985/86, the exceptionally dense algal bloom that occurred under-ice in Driedmeat Lake from December until March was dominated by Cryptophyta (*Cryptomonas* sp., *Peridinium* sp. and *Dinobryon* sp.). Protozoans were also very abundant at this time (Prepas and Crosby n.d.).

Aquatic macrophytes are another notable feature of Driedmeat Lake, especially in the northern and southern thirds of the lake, where aquatic plants form mats on the surface and make boat travel sluggish, if not impossible. Fourteen species of aquatic macrophytes were identified by Alberta Environment during a 1984 survey of Driedmeat Lake (Fig. 8). The most abundant plants were pondweeds (*Potamogeton richardsonii*, *P. vaginatus* and *P. pectinatus*) and coontail (*Ceratophyllum demersum*). Approximately 67% of the lake area supported vegetation; plants grew in water depths of up to 2.5 m and reached the surface in almost all areas. Most macrophytes were tall and slender; a short understory was absent, likely because of shading by the taller species. An earlier survey, completed in 1975, reported similar macrophyte distribution and abundance patterns (Krochak 1988).

Invertebrates

There are no data available on the zooplankton in Driedmeat Lake. Benthic invertebrates were sampled by Fish and Wildlife Division at six sites on 27 August 1985 in water depths ranging from 1.0 to 3.0 m. Midge larvae (Chironomidae) dominated by number at five sites and aquatic earthworms (Oligochaeta) dominated at the 1.5–m site (Alta. For. Ld. Wild. n.d.).

Figure 8. Distribution and species composition of aquatic macrophytes in Driedmeat Lake, August 1984.
SOURCE: modified from Integrated Envir. Sci. Inc. 1984.

Fish

Driedmeat Lake is popular for angling for northern pike in summer and for ice-fishing in winter. Other species found in the lake include longnose dace, lake chub, emerald shiner, spottail shiner, white sucker and brook stickleback (Fernet et al. 1985). Migration of additional species that are abundant in the lower reaches of the Battle River is blocked by the dam that creates Battle River Reservoir near Forestburg. Fish can move from the river upstream of Forestburg into Driedmeat Lake through the step-pool fishway in the Driedmeat Lake weir.

Driedmeat Lake provides essential fish overwintering habitat, as much of the Battle River becomes anoxic in winter. Although dissolved oxygen in the lake is often very low and extensive winterkills are common (Alta. For. Ld. Wild. n.d.; Rhude 1980; Fernet et al. 1985), there is an oxygen-rich refuge in the lake near the mouth of the unnamed creek north of Driedmeat Creek. In April, northern pike and white suckers move up the Battle River from Driedmeat Lake to spawn. Pike are known to spawn in Camrose Creek and Pipestone Creek and might spawn in other inflowing streams as well (Rhude1980; Fernet et al. 1985). Summerkills are common in Driedmeat Lake and immediately below the weir.

A three-year mark-recapture study by Fish and Wildlife Division estimated that there were 46 800 ± 18 000 pike in the lake (Rhude 1980). Measurements indicated that the growth rate of pike in Driedmeat Lake was slow compared to that in other Alberta lakes. By age three, male pike averaged 374 mm in forklength and weighed 338 g (n = 57), and females averaged 409 mm in forklength and weighed 471 g (n = 21). By age six, male pike averaged 467 mm forklength and weighed 752 g (n = 45); there were no data for six-year-old females. Pike in Driedmeat Lake matured at a smaller size than in other lakes; most spawning pike were at least four years old but were less than 500–mm long. The slow growth may be due to stress from high temperatures and low dissolved oxygen concentrations throughout the Battle River system.

Wildlife

Driedmeat Lake provides important nesting habitat for waterfowl and is an important fall staging area for swans and Canada geese (Ducks Unltd. (Can.) 1982). Flocks of White Pelicans feed on the lake.

In 1939, the provincial government was petitioned to have the lake classified as a bird sanctuary (Gould 1939). The region is now a Restricted Wildlife Area, which means that hunting of waterfowl and upland game birds is not allowed within 0.8 km of the lake until 1 November each year. From November until the end of hunting season, hunting is permitted to encourage waterfowl to continue their migration.

J.M. Crosby

References

Alberta Environment. n.d.[a]. Devel. Op. Div., Project Mgt. Br. Unpubl. data, Edmonton.
———. n.d.[b]. Envir. Assess. Div., Envir. Qlty. Monit. Br. Unpubl. data, Edmonton.
———. n.d.[c]. Plan. Div., Impact Assess. Br. Unpubl. data, Edmonton.
———. n.d.[d]. Tech. Serv. Div., Hydrol. Br. Unpubl. data, Edmonton.
———. n.d.[e]. Tech. Serv. Div., Surv. Br. Unpubl. data, Edmonton.
Alberta Forestry, Lands and Wildlife. n.d. Fish Wild. Div. Unpubl. data, Edmonton.
———. 1988. Boating in Alberta. Fish Wild. Div., Edmonton.
———. 1989. Guide to sportfishing. Fish Wild. Div., Edmonton.
Alberta Research Council. 1972. Geological map of Alberta. Nat. Resour. Div., Alta. Geol. Surv., Edmonton.
Bowser, E.W., R.L. Erdman, F.A. Wyatt and J.D. Newton. 1947. Soil survey of Peace Hills sheet. Alta. Soil Surv. Rep. No. 14, Univ. Alta. Bull. No. 48. Univ. Alta., Edmonton.
City of Camrose. n.d. Eng. Dept. Unpubl. data, Camrose.
Crosby, J. n.d. Univ. Alta. Unpubl. data, Edmonton.
Ducks Unlimited (Canada). 1982. Project Inspection report (05 Nov. 1982). Unpubl. rep., Camrose.
Edberg Historical Society Book Club. 1981. Trails, trials and triumphs of Edberg and community: A history of Edberg, Driedmeat Lake, Viewpoint, Silver Creek, Little Beaver, Big Four, Stockholm, Meeting Creek, Matlock, Little Rock, Dorenlee, Ferry Point and Rosebush. Edberg Hist. Soc. Book Club, Edberg.
Energy, Mines and Resources Canada. 1963, 1970, 1976, 1983. National topographic series 1:250 000 83B (1963), 83A (1970), 83G (1976), 83H (1983). Surv. Map. Br., Ottawa.
Environment Canada. 1969–1985. Surface water data. Prep. by Inland Waters Directorate. Water Surv. Can., Water Resour. Br., Ottawa.
———. 1982. Canadian climate normals, Vol. 7: Bright sunshine (1951–1980). Prep. by Atm. Envir. Serv. Supply Serv. Can., Ottawa.
Fernet, D.A., G.A. Ash and S.M. Matkowski. 1985. Investigations of the Battle River fishery relative to the potential effects of flow augmentation. Prep. for Alta. Envir., Plan. Div., Edmonton by Envir. Mgt. Assoc. Ltd., Calgary and R.L. & L. Envir. Serv. Ltd., Edmonton.
Gould, C. 1939. Report on Driedmeat Lake—A proposed bird sanctuary or game preserve—During the year 1939. Alta. Agric., Game Fish. Br., Edmonton.
Integrated Environmental Sciences Inc. 1984. Aquatic macrophyte surveys of Coal Lake, Driedmeat Lake and the Battle Reservoir. Prep. for Alta. Envir., Plan. Div., Edmonton.
Krochak, D. 1988. Integrated Envir. Sci. Inc., Saskatoon. Pers. comm.
Lowe, D. 1988. Alta. For. Ld. Wild., Fish Wild. Div., Red Deer. Pers. comm.
MacGregor, J.G. 1972. A history of Alberta. Hurtig Publ., Edmonton.
Nanuk Engineering and Hydroqual Consultants Inc. 1986. Battle River basin study phase III, water balance and water quality assessment. Prep. for Alta. Envir., Plan. Div., Edmonton.
Prepas, E.E. and J.M. Crosby. n.d. Univ. Alta. Unpubl. data., Edmonton.
Rhude, L. 1980. Driedmeat Lake—Northern pike tagging study 1977-1979. Alta. En. Nat. Resour., Fish Wild. Div., Red Deer.
Sloman, K. 1984. Dissolved oxygen in the Battle River system, winter 1982/83. Alta. Envir., Plan. Div., Edmonton.
Strong, W.L. and K.R. Leggat. 1981. Ecoregions of Alberta. Alta. En. Nat. Resour., Resour. Eval. Plan. Div., Edmonton.

MIQUELON LAKE

MAP SHEETS: 83H/2, 7

LOCATION: Tp49 R20, 21 W4

LAT/LONG: 53°21'N 112°55'W

Shallow, salty Miquelon Lake is located within the County of Camrose in central Alberta, about 35 km southeast of the city of Edmonton. It lies on the southern edge of the Cooking Lake Moraine. The lake was once part of a considerably larger lake that receded and left three isolated basins. These are often referred to as "the Miquelon Lakes" (Fig. 1, inset), but this discussion will focus on the largest basin, henceforth called "Miquelon Lake". To get to the lake from Edmonton, take Highway 14 to Highway 21, turn south and drive for 20 km, then turn east onto Secondary Road 623 and drive for 17 km. This road leads to the entrance to Miquelon Lake Provincial Park, which is located on the south and east shores of the lakes.

Miquelon Lake has been used for recreation by local residents since the turn of the twentieth century, especially after a railway line was established between Camrose and Tofield in 1909. The access and facilities at the lake were greatly improved when Miquelon Lake Provincial Park was established in 1958. The park now has 275 campsites, tap water, a sandy swimming beach, a telephone, boat launches, hiking trails and day-use areas (Alta. Hotel. Assoc. 1989). A golf course is nearby. Around the turn of the twentieth century, much of the Miquelon Lakes and much of the surrounding land were designated as the Miquelon Lake Bird Sanctuary. Now some of this land is part of the provincial park, but the remaining Crown land near the lakes and the lakes themselves retain the sanctuary status.

At present, Miquelon Lake is heavily used for recreation, especially on warm, sunny weekends. Game fish are no longer present in the lake, but a pond in the provincial park is stocked annually with a small number of catchable-sized rainbow trout. The beach area at the park is generally clean and attractive for swimming. The saline water tends to inhibit the growth of algae, and the lake is often very clear. Swimming, sailing, wind surfing and water skiing are favourite activities. Boats are restricted to a 12 km/hour maximum speed limit in the park area, and all boats are prohibited in certain waterfowl nesting areas and along the beach (Alta. For. Ld. Wild. 1988).

There has been no surface outflow from Miquelon Lake since the 1920s, and the lake level has declined considerably. In 1927, the outlet creek, which flowed from the most southern of the three Miquelon lakes was deepened to divert water for the town of Camrose water supply. The flow in the diversion ditch ran only about three years, even though the ditch was deepened when flow declined (Hanson 1981). It is not known why the level of the lake has gone down, but climatic factors probably have played a major role (Woodburn 1977).

Drainage Basin Characteristics

The drainage basin of Miquelon Lake is only about 4 times larger than the area of the lake (Tables 1, 2). The land surrounding Miquelon Lake is the knob and kettle terrain typical of morainal deposits (Battle R. Reg. Plan. Commis. 1973). The overall relief varies only about 30 m; the highest point of land is located south of the provincial park. The predominant soils surrounding the lake are fairly well-drained Orthic Gray Luvisols that have severe limitations for forage crop production. These soils have developed from glacial till that originates mainly from the underlying bedrock (Bowser et al. 1962). Trembling aspen, balsam poplar, white spruce and other species of trees historically covered the drainage area, but clearing

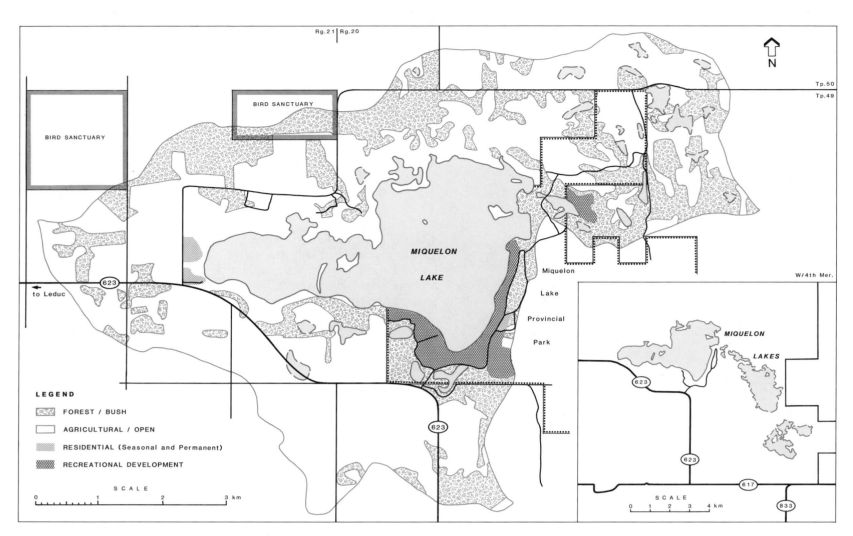

Figure 1. Features of the drainage basins of the Miquelon Lakes. Inset shows the three lakes known as the Miquelon Lakes.
SOURCES: Alta. Envir. n.d.[b]; En. Mines Resour. Can. 1975; 1983. Updated with 1983 aerial photos.

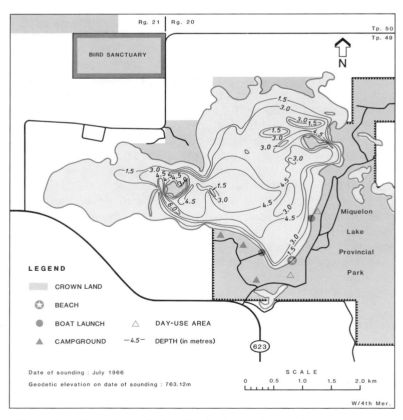

Figure 2. Bathymetry and shoreline features of Miquelon Lake.
BATHYMETRY SOURCE: Alta. Envir. n.d.[c].

for agriculture and numerous fires at the turn of the century extensively reduced the forest cover. Since then, natural regrowth has restored much of the native vegetation, particularly in Miquelon Lake Provincial Park.

Livestock operations and cereal crop farming are pursued in the basin, particularly in areas west of the lake (Fig. 1). In addition to the provincial park, development includes two registered cottage subdivisions on the western shore. There are also a number of country residential lots in the basin (Battle R. Reg. Plan. Commis. 1973).

At present, there are no permanent inlet streams to Miquelon Lake and there has been no surface outflow for more than 50 years. If outflow were to occur, the former outlet from the most southern lake would drain into the Battle River through Stoney Creek and Camrose Creek, but the present Miquelon Lake (the northwestern lake), would probably drain to Larry Lake to the northwest, then to Oliver Lake and eventually to the North Saskatchewan River (Battle R. Reg. Plan. Commis. 1973).

Lake Basin Characteristics

Miquelon Lake had a maximum depth of approximately 6 m when the lake was sounded in 1966. Much of the lake is less than 1.5–m deep, particularly in the western bay (Fig. 2, Table 2).

The level of the lake has been recorded since 1972 (Fig. 3). The fluctuation in water level between 1972 and 1987 exceeded 1 m, but there was no trend toward declining levels over the last 10 years of this record. In 1974, an increase in water level of about 1 m occurred after heavy spring runoff. Changes in the lake's area and capacity (up to an elevation of 763.12 m) are illustrated in Figure 4.

The character of Miquelon Lake has been strongly influenced by its fluctuating water level. Anecdotal evidence indicates that Beaverhill Lake, which is also in the Cooking Lake Moraine, was nearly dry in 1885 (Lister 1979). Levels increased and declined in subsequent

Table 1. Characteristics of Miquelon Lake drainage basin.

area (excluding lake) (km²)[a]	35.4
soil[b]	Orthic Gray Luvisols
bedrock geology[c]	Horseshoe Canyon Formation (Upper Cretaceous): sandstone, mudstone, shale; ironstone, scattered coal and bentonite beds; mainly nonmarine
terrain[b]	rolling to gently rolling
ecoregion[d]	Dry Mixedwood Subregion of Boreal Mixedwood
dominant vegetation[d]	trembling aspen
mean annual inflow (m³)[a, e]	1.72 x 10⁶
mean annual sunshine (h)[f]	2 317

NOTE: [e]excluding groundwater inflow
SOURCES: [a]Alta. Envir. n.d.[b]; [b]Bowser et al. 1962; [c]Alta. Res. Counc. 1972; [d]Strong and Leggat 1981; [f]Envir. Can. 1982

Table 2. Characteristics of Miquelon Lake.

elevation (m)[a, b]	763.12
surface area (km²)[a, b]	8.72
volume (m³)[a, b]	23.8 x 10⁶
maximum depth (m)[a, b]	6
mean depth (m)[a, b]	2.7
shoreline length (km)[c]	19.5
mean annual evaporation (mm)[d]	664
mean annual precipitation (mm)[d]	466
mean residence time (yr)[d, e]	>100
control structure	none

NOTES: [a]on date of sounding: July 1966; [e]excluding groundwater inflow
SOURCES: [b]Alta. Envir. n.d.[c]; [c]En. Mines Resour. Can. 1975; [d]Alta. Envir. n.d.[b]

Table 3. Major ions and related water quality variables for Miquelon Lake. Average concentrations in mg/L; pH in pH units. Composite samples from the euphotic zone collected 6 times from 03 May to 15 Aug. 1983. S.E. = standard error.

	Mean	S.E.
pH (range)	9.3–9.4	—
total alkalinity (CaCO₃)	1 407	20.3
specific conductivity (µS/cm)	6 530	151.8
total dissolved solids	5 402	92.1
total hardness (calculated)	883	—
HCO₃	1 083	13.2
CO₃	306	15.5
Mg	206	11.9
Na	1 473	14.1
K	110	6.6
Cl	99	2.5
SO₄	2 413	58.8
Ca	14	0.7

SOURCES: Prepas et al. n.d.; Bierhuizen and Prepas 1985

years, but heavy rains in 1900 and 1901 restored the lakes in the moraine to high levels. At that time, the three Miquelon Lakes were joined and outflow from the lake probably occurred (Nyland 1970). Since then, there have been periodic droughts (for example, in 1928, in the 1930s, and in 1950, 1957 and 1961), and changes in land use in the moraine. There is insufficient information to determine whether changes in the groundwater inflow have contributed to the declining level, although it is known that the lake is spring-fed (EPEC Consult. 1971).

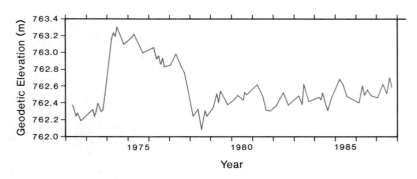

Figure 3. Water level of Miquelon Lake, 1972 to 1987.
SOURCE: Alta. Envir. n.d.[c].

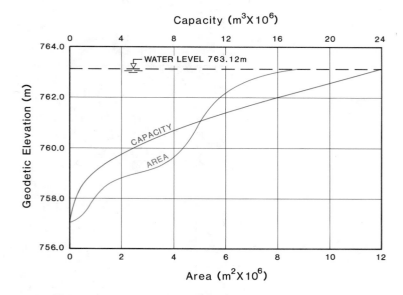

Figure 4. Area/capacity curve for Miquelon Lake.
SOURCE: Alta. Envir. n.d.[c].

Water Quality

The water quality of Miquelon Lake was studied by the University of Alberta from 1973 to 1976 (Alta. Envir. n.d.[a]), and during 1983, 1986 and 1987 (Prepas et al. n.d.; Bierhuizen and Prepas 1985; Marino et al. 1990). Concentrations of total dissolved solids (TDS) in Miquelon Lake are about 10 times higher than the arbitrary criterion of 500 mg/L TDS used to distinguish saline lakes from freshwater lakes. Sulphate, sodium and carbonate/bicarbonate are the dominant ions (Table 3). Total dissolved solids and sulphate are higher when the water level is low. Saline groundwater is present in the area, but evaporation probably plays a major role in concentrating salts in the lake. In 1974, a heavy spring runoff raised the lake level and diluted its salt content (TDS = 4 309 mg/L, Table 4). Since 1976, the dissolved solids have become more concentrated again (TDS = 5 402 mg/L in 1983).

The water temperature tends to be uniform from the lake surface to the bottom in the summer and the entire water column mixes on windy days (Fig. 5). The dissolved oxygen concentrations tend to remain high much of the time (Fig. 6), although during periods of temporary stratification, oxygen depletion near the bottom may occur. In winter, the lake remains fairly well oxygenated, but under certain conditions the entire water column may become anoxic, as in March 1974.

Because the salinity in Miquelon Lake is high, algal production, as measured by chlorophyll a, is depressed (Table 5). Phosphorus concentrations are so high that if the lake water were fresh, Miquelon Lake probably would have heavy blooms of blue-green algae. However, chlorophyll a levels in Miquelon Lake rank with those of some of the least-productive lakes in the province. Chlorophyll levels in Miquelon Lake are highest in spring and sometimes in fall, rather

Table 4. A comparison of average summer chlorophyll *a*, Secchi transparency and total dissolved solids in Miquelon Lake, 1973 to 1976. Grab samples collected at 0.5– or 1–m intervals from the euphotic zone from May to Aug. each summer. S.E. = standard error.

Year	n	Chl *a* (mg/L)	S.E.	Secchi (m)	S.E.	TDS (mg/L)	S.E.
1973	4	3.12	0.93	2.8	0.18	6 079	74.9
1974	5	3.29	2.06	3.1	0.42	4 309	86.4
1975	5	2.48	0.88	3.4	0.41	4 580	35.8
1976	3	1.82	0.52	3.4	0.58	4 764	62.3

SOURCE: Alta. Envir. n.d.[a]

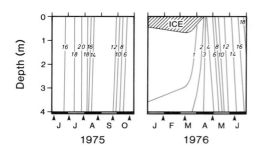

Figure 5. Temperature (°C) of Miquelon Lake, 1975 to 1976. Arrows indicate sampling dates. SOURCE: Alta. Envir. n.d.[a].

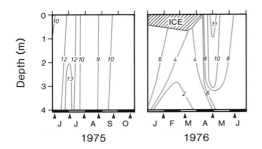

Figure 6. Dissolved oxygen (mg/L) in Miquelon Lake, 1975 to 1976. Arrows indicate sampling dates.
SOURCE: Alta. Envir. n.d.[a].

Table 5. Phosphorus, nitrogen and chlorophyll *a* data for Miquelon Lake. Average concentrations in μg/L. Composite samples from the euphotic zone collected 6 times from 03 May to 15 Aug. 1983 and 4 times from 16 May to 14 Aug. 1987. S.E. = standard error.

	1983		1987	
	Mean	S.E.	Mean	S.E.
total phosphorus	131	4.4	302	11.4
total dissolved phosphorus	105	5.8	267[b]	—
total Kjeldahl nitrogen	5 696	545.5	5 569	327.1
NH₄–nitrogen	16[a]	6.8	57	48.3
NO₃ + NO₂–nitrogen	3	0.9	21	15.5
iron	109	23.4	—	—
chlorophyll *a*	4.6	1.23	6.8	1.59

NOTES: [a]n = 5; [b]n = 1
SOURCES: Prepas et al. n.d.; Bierhuizen and Prepas 1985

than in midsummer (Fig. 7) as in most shallow freshwater lakes in Alberta.

It is difficult to establish the trophic category of this lake. The high phosphorus and nitrogen concentrations suggest a eutrophic lake, but chlorophyll concentrations and the clarity of the water suggest that it is mesotrophic.

Biological Characteristics

Plants

The phytoplankton of Miquelon Lake was studied by the University of Alberta in 1964 and 1987 (Prepas et al. n.d.; Kerekes 1965; Marino et al. 1990). Species diversity of the phytoplankton community is low in Miquelon Lake (Table 6). Only 8 species were identified in 1964 and 10 in 1987. Two of the species identified in the 1964 study are restricted to brackish water, and consequently were not found in neighboring freshwater lakes. The only genus common to both studies was the blue-green alga *Gomphosphaeria* sp. (Cyanophyta). It was the only species of blue-green algae noted in 1987, and occurred only in the May sample. *Monoraphidium contortum* occurred in all samples in 1987.

A survey of macrophytes was conducted by researchers with the University of Alberta during a water quality study in 1973 and 1974 (Table 7). Although phytoplankton biomass is low in Miquelon Lake, visual observations suggest that much of the plant production takes place on the bottom of the lake, as attached algae and macrophytes.

The dominant species of macrophyte is widgeon grass (*Ruppia occidentalis*), which is highly tolerant of saline conditions. In 1973, it grew densely throughout the lake, but was especially abundant at depths of 1 to 2 m. The only other species of submergent macrophyte noted in 1973 was Sago pondweed, *Potamogeton pectinatus*. The dominant emergent species were several types of bulrush. The most common species, identified as *Scirpus pungens*, formed 62% of the emergent vegetation, and was found in water less than 0.5–m deep.

Invertebrates

The biomass of zooplankton was estimated for Miquelon Lake by a researcher with the University of Alberta in 1975 and 1976 (Alta. Envir. n.d.[a]). The calanoid copepod *Diaptomus sicilis* was usually dominant throughout the year and it reached a peak biomass in midsummer. A species of large *Daphnia*, probably *D. pulicaria*, and a saline-tolerant rotifer, *Hexarthra* sp., were also abundant in midsummer. The crustaceans are grazers, and probably have a major impact on algal populations in June and July, as evidenced by minimum chlorophyll levels during these months for most of the years that the lake was studied. *Daphnia pulicaria* and *Diaptomus sicilis* were abundant through the winter in 1974/75, but the following winter, neither species was observed in the lake by March.

The benthic invertebrate fauna of Miquelon Lake and four other lakes in the Cooking Lake Moraine was studied in 1964 by a researcher at the University of Alberta (Kerekes 1965). Of these lakes, Miquelon was the most saline, and the biomass of benthic organisms and the level of organic matter in the bottom sediments were lowest. Midge larvae (Chironomidae) were dominant in 1964 and also in samples collected for Alberta Environment in 1975 and 1976 (Table 8).

Fish

The brook stickleback is reported to be the only species of fish remaining in Miquelon Lake (Battle R. Reg. Plan. Commis. 1973;

Table 6. Percentage composition of major algal groups by total biomass in Miquelon Lake, 1987. Composite samples collected from the euphotic zone.

ALGAL GROUP	16 May	12 June	16 July	04 Aug.
Total Biomass (mg/L)	0.76	3.18	1.65	0.15
Percentage Composition:				
Cyanophyta	18	0	0	0
Chlorophyta	32	94	98	26
	Monoraphidium	*Eudorina*	*Trachelomonas*	*Chlamydomonas*
			Monoraphidium———→	
Chrysophyta	10	0	<1	0
Bacillariophyta	0	4	2	0
Cryptophyta	40	2	0	74
	Rhodomonas			*Rhodomonas*

SOURCE: Prepas et al. n.d.

Table 7. Species of aquatic macrophytes in Miquelon Lake. Survey conducted during the summers of 1973 and 1974.

submergent	widgeon grass	*Ruppia occidentalis*
	Sago pondweed	*Potamogeton pectinatus*
emergent	three-square rush	*Scirpus pungens*
	prairie bulrush	*S. paludosus*
	common great bulrush	*S. validus*
	sedge	*Carex rostrata*
	common cattail	*Typha latifolia*
	spike rush	*Eleocharis palustris* var. *major*
	reed grass	*Phragmites communis*
	slough grass	*Beckmannia syzigachne*
	dock	*Rumex* sp.
	wire rush	*Juncus balticus* var. *littoralis*
	slender arrow-grass	*Triglochen palustris*

SOURCE: Alta. Envir. n.d.[a]

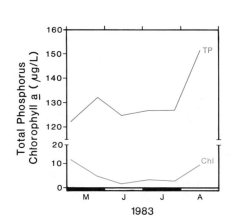

Figure 7. Total phosphorus, chlorophyll *a* and Secchi depth in Miquelon Lake, 1983.
SOURCE: Prepas et al. n.d.

Jensen 1987; Lowe 1987). At the turn of the century, when the outlet was flowing, northern pike and suckers moved up the creek connecting the lake to the Battle River, and yellow perch were abundant. Adult yellow perch were stocked in the lake in 1955, 1956 and possibly 1958. Nets set in the lake in 1964 caught stickleback and only three or four yellow perch (Alta. For. Ld. Wild. n.d.). It is not clear why perch and pike are no longer in the lake, but it may be related to occasional winter kills and isolation from population sources. As well, the high salinity may reduce the survival of the spawn of these species.

Wildlife

The Miquelon Lakes were set aside in 1915 as a bird sanctuary. The Cooking Lake Moraine is excellent habitat for waterfowl and upland game birds as well as moose and deer. When fish were more numerous in the lake, pelicans and cormorants nested on the islands, particularly on the larger one near the north shore, known as Pelican Island (Hanson 1981). Now, Ring-billed and California gulls colonize the islands in the western arm of the lake by the thousands, and ducks and geese nest along the shoreline (Finlay and Finlay 1987).

P.A. Mitchell

Table 8. Abundance (numbers/m²) of benthic invertebrates in Miquelon Lake. Samples collected in July 1964, 1975 and 1976 with an Ekman dredge in about 4 m of water.

Taxa	22 July 1964	28 July 1975	06 July 1976
Diptera			
Chironomidae	1 900		
Chironomus utahensis		4 312	88
Procladius sp.		1 034	1 320
other		836	374
Culicidae (*Chaoborus flavicans*)	0	242	22
Amphipoda	181	0	176
Oligochaeta	9	0	0
Hemiptera	25	0	0
Ephemeroptera (*Caenis* sp.)	0	0	1 474
other	0	22	176
TOTAL	2 115	6 446	3 630

SOURCES: Alta. Envir. n.d.[a]; Kerekes 1965

References

Alberta Environment. n.d.[a]. Envir. Assess. Div., Envir. Qlty. Monit. Br. Unpubl. data, Edmonton.
———. n.d.[b]. Tech. Serv. Div., Hydrol. Br. Unpubl. data, Edmonton.
———. n.d.[c]. Tech. Serv. Div., Surv. Br. Unpubl. data, Edmonton.
Alberta Forestry, Lands and Wildlife. n.d. Fish Wild. Div. Unpubl. data, Edmonton.
———. 1988. Boating in Alberta. Fish Wild. Div., Edmonton.
Alberta Hotel Association. 1989. Alberta campground guide 1989. Prep. for Travel Alta., Edmonton.

Alberta Research Council. 1972. Geological map of Alberta. Nat. Resour. Div., Alta. Geol. Surv., Edmonton.

Battle River Regional Planning Commission. 1973. Miquelon Lakes planning report. Prep. for Co. Camrose No. 22, Camrose.

Bierhuizen, J.F.H. and E.E. Prepas. 1985. Relationship between nutrients, dominant ions, and phytoplankton standing crop in prairie saline lakes. Can. J. Fish. Aquat. Sci. 42:1588–1594.

Bowser, W.E., A.A. Kjearsgaard, T.W. Peters and R.E. Wells. 1962. Soil survey of the Edmonton sheet (83–H). Alta. Soil Surv. Rep. No. 21, Univ. Alta. Bull. No. SS–4. Univ. Alta., Edmonton.

Energy, Mines and Resources Canada. 1975, 1983. National topographic series 1:50 000 83H/2 (1975), 83H/7 (1975) and 1:250 000 83H (1983). Surv. Map. Br., Ottawa.

Environment Canada. 1982. Canadian climate normals, Vol. 7: Bright sunshine (1951–1980). Prep. by Atm. Envir. Serv. Supply Serv. Can., Ottawa.

EPEC Consulting. 1971. An economic analysis of the Cooking and Hastings Lakes. Prep. for Alta. Envir., Water Resour. Div., Edmonton.

Finlay, J. and C. Finlay. 1987. Parks in Alberta: A guide to peaks, ponds, parklands & prairies. Hurtig Publ., Edmonton.

Hanson, R.W. 1981. Harvest of memories: History of Kingman and districts, p. 159–164. *In* Kingman Silver Club. Kingman.

Jensen, M. 1987. Alta. Rec. Parks, Miquelon L. Pers. comm.

Kerekes, J. 1965. A comparative limnological study of five lakes in central Alberta. MSc thesis. Univ. Alta., Edmonton.

Lister, R. 1979. The birds and birders of Beaverhills Lake. The Edm. Bird Club, Edmonton.

Lowe, D. 1987. Alta. For. Ld. Wild., Fish Wild. Div., Red Deer. Pers. comm.

Marino, R., R.W. Howarth, J. Shamess and E.E. Prepas. 1990. Molybdenum and sulfate as controls on the abundance of nitrogen-fixing cyanobacteria in Alberta saline lakes. Limnol. Oceanogr. [in press]

Nyland, E. 1970. Miquelon Lake? Alberta Lands-Forests-Parks-Wildlife 13:18–25. Alta. Ld. For., Edmonton.

Prepas, E.E., J.F.H. Bierhuizen, J. Shamess, R.W. Howarth and R. Marino. n.d. Unpubl. data, Univ. Alta., Edmonton and Cornell Univ., Ithaca, New York.

Strong, W.L. and K.R. Leggat. 1981. Ecoregions of Alberta. Alta. En. Nat. Resour., Resour. Eval. Plan. Div., Edmonton.

Woodburn, R.L. 1977. Surplus patterns and water supply alternatives: Cooking Lake moraine. MSc thesis. Univ. Alta., Edmonton.

OLIVA LAKE

E.E. Prepas

MAP SHEET: 73E/4
LOCATION: Tp47 R11 W4
LAT/LONG: 53°05'N 111°36'W

Oliva Lake is an extremely saline lake located in the County of Beaver, 144 km southeast of Edmonton. It is situated 15 km east of the town of Viking, just south of Secondary Road 619 (Fig. 1). The south side of Oliva Lake can be reached from a gravel road. The lake is surrounded by cleared land and mixed forest and there is one cottage on the south side. The water is clear and the lake is used for boating by local residents. There are no boating restrictions specific to this lake, but general federal regulations apply (Alta. For. Ld. Wild. 1988). There are no fish in Oliva Lake.

The first settlers arrived in the region surrounding the hamlet of Kinsella, to the southeast of Oliva Lake, in 1904. Grain and mixed farming and livestock rearing have since developed in this area, where a good quality native grass grows (Kinsella Hist. Book Commit. 1983).

Oliva Lake represents a distinct lake type found in eastern Alberta. It is 2 to 3 times more saline than sea water. The salinity in the lake is the result of high carbonate, sodium and sulphate content; these minerals come from saline groundwater in the region (Currie and Zacharko 1976). The lakeshore is encrusted with salt, which is replaced by gravel away from the shore. The width of the white crust increases over the summer. Saline lakes with similar ion content are common in eastern Alberta—Oliva Lake is an extreme example of what increased concentrations of certain ions do to lake functions. Characteristics such as temperature, nutrient concentrations, plants and animals differ from those in less saline lakes. The temperature of the water under ice drops below 0°C, and in summer the water is warmest at the bottom because it is saltier at the bottom than at the surface. Few species of plants and animals live in Oliva Lake. Although concentrations of phosphorus and nitrogen are the highest recorded for an Alberta lake, plant growth is very limited. However, a few inhabitants, such as the brine shrimp (*Artemia salina*), reach enormous densities and can turn the water a reddish colour.

Drainage Basin Characteristics

Although the drainage basin of Oliva Lake is large (256 km², Fig. 1), most of it does not contribute water to the lake, so the contributing drainage area is small (6.3 km², Table 1). The land surrounding the lake is privately owned and is used for cattle grazing. Cattle graze mostly around the northeast shore of the lake.

Although there are no saline soils in the small contributing drainage basin (Wyatt et al. 1944), there is saline groundwater in the region and a marine shale formation to the west (Currie and Zacharko 1976). Interactions between saline groundwater and Oliva Lake contribute to the lake's salinity.

Lake Basin Characteristics

Oliva Lake is small (Table 2); it is 1.3–km long and has a maximum width of 0.6 km. The lake basin is bowl-shaped; the deepest part (1.7 m) is towards the west end (Fig. 2). There are no long-term records of water level fluctuations; however, relative water levels were measured from May 1983 through August 1984. During this period, the maximum fluctuation in lake level was 0.32 m; the highest water level was in July 1983 and the lowest was in August 1984 (Campbell 1986). There are no permanent inlets to, or outlets from, the lake. Oliva Lake is an evaporation basin, and this may

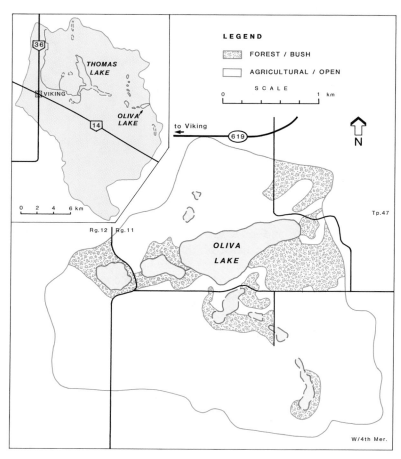

Figure 1. Features of the drainage basin of Oliva Lake.
SOURCES: Alta. Envir. n.d.; En. Mines Resour. Can. 1976. Updated with
1983 aerial photos.

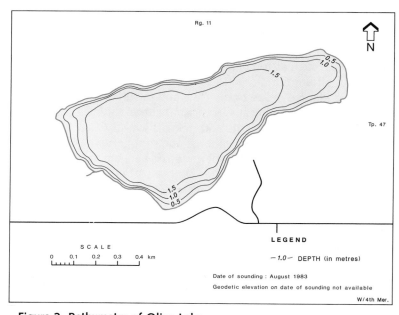

Figure 2. Bathymetry of Oliva Lake.
SOURCE: Campbell 1986.

contribute to its high level of total dissolved solids. However,
groundwater is the primary variable controlling the concentration of
total dissolved solids.

Water Quality

Oliva Lake was sampled from 1982 through 1984 and again in 1986
and 1987 by researchers with the University of Alberta (Prepas et al.
n.d.; Bierhuizen and Prepas 1985; Campbell 1986; Campbell and
Prepas 1986).

Most shallow freshwater lakes in Alberta are easily mixed by wind.
Consequently, key variables such as total dissolved solids, tempera-

Table 1. Characteristics of Oliva Lake drainage basin.

drainage area (excluding lake) (km²)[a]	gross: 256
	actual contributing: 6.3
soil[b]	Orthic Black Chernozemics
bedrock geology[c]	Belly River Formation (Upper Cretaceous): sandstone, siltstone, mudstone, ironstone beds; nonmarine
terrain[b]	gently rolling to rolling
ecoregion[d]	Aspen Subregion of Aspen Parkland
dominant vegetation[d]	aspen and rough fescue grassland
mean annual inflow (m³)[a, e]	0.091 x 10⁶
mean annual sunshine (h)[f]	2 168

NOTE: [e]excluding groundwater inflow
SOURCES: [a]Alta. Envir. n.d.; [b]Wyatt et al. 1944; [c]Alta. Res. Counc. 1972; [d]Strong
and Leggat 1981; [f]Envir. Can. 1982

Table 2. Characteristics of Oliva Lake.

surface area (km²)[a, b]	0.52
volume (m³)[a, b]	0.650 x 10⁶
maximum depth (m)[b]	1.7
mean depth (m)[b]	1.3
shoreline length (km)[c]	3.4
mean annual lake evaporation (mm)[d]	637
mean annual precipitation (mm)[d]	430
mean residence time[d, e]	>100
control structure	none

NOTES: [a]on date of sounding: Aug. 1983; [e]excluding groundwater inflow
SOURCES: [b]Campbell 1986; [c]En. Mines Resour. Can. 1976; [d]Alta. Envir. n.d.

ture and dissolved oxygen are similar from the lake surface to near
the bottom sediments during the ice-free season. However, when
Oliva Lake was monitored in 1984, it was chemically stratified most
of the time (Fig. 3). During summer, this unusual concentration of
mineral salts just over the sediments resulted in the heat from the sun
being trapped in the bottom layer; bottom-water temperatures sur-
passed 26°C, whereas surface waters reached only 24°C (Fig. 4). In
addition, bottom-water dissolved oxygen concentrations dropped to
less than 3 mg/L in contrast to those of the surface, which were
between 6 and 7 mg/L (Fig. 5).

Mineral salts in Oliva Lake precipitate and form a hard white crust
over the entire lake bottom and along the entire shoreline. The
dominant minerals are sulphate, sodium and carbonate (Table 3).
The pH of the water is extremely high. Open-water pH values often
exceeded 10 and rarely dropped below 9.7.

The high mineral content of Oliva Lake water reduces dissolved
oxygen concentrations in summer and water temperatures under
ice. During summer, dissolved oxygen concentrations at the surface
were well below saturation for fresh water (Fig. 5). In contrast,
dissolved oxygen concentrations in March 1984 were fairly high for
such a shallow lake. Although the cause of these relatively high
winter dissolved oxygen concentrations is unknown, low summer
primary productivity (Table 4), low under-ice temperatures (down to
−1.5°C, Fig. 4), and sediments with low bacterial activity, may be
contributing factors.

In all four years studied, phosphorus and nitrogen concentrations
were extremely high in the surface waters of Oliva Lake (Table 4).
These high nutrient concentrations were accompanied by very low
chlorophyll *a* concentrations (approximately 4 µg/L) in the surface
waters in summer (Table 4, Fig. 6). In contrast, a freshwater lake with
similar total nitrogen and phosphorus concentrations would be very
green, with chlorophyll *a* levels in excess of 300 µg/L (Campbell and
Prepas 1986). High soluble reactive phosphorus concentrations

Table 3. Major ions and related water quality variables for Oliva Lake. Average concentrations in mg/L; pH in pH units. Composite samples from the euphotic zone collected 6 times from 07 May to 29 Aug. 1983. S.E. = standard error.

	Mean	S.E.
pH (range)	9.7–10.2[a, b]	—
total alkalinity (CaCO₃)	24 979	1 154
specific conductivity (μS/cm)	59 674[b, c]	1 960
total dissolved solids	84 314[b, d]	7 057
turbidity (NTU)	2[b, e]	0.2
colour (Pt)	28[b, f]	1.6
total hardness (calculated)	606	—
HCO₃	5 368	332
CO₃	12 335	600
Mg	138	28.2
Na	21 851	1 252
K	396	30.0
Cl	459	56.2
SO₄	16 530[g]	2 037
Ca	15	2.1

NOTES: [a]14 May to 01 Oct. 1983, 07 May to 27 Aug. 1984 (n = 16); [c]as in [a] (but n = 19), corrected as per Bierhuizen and Prepas 1985; [d]overestimate (n = 5); [e]14 May to 01 Oct. (n = 9); [f]as in [e] (but n = 8); [g]Aug. 1986, May to Aug. 1987 (n = 5)
SOURCES: Prepas et al. n.d.; [b]Campbell 1986

Table 4. Nutrient, chlorophyll a and Secchi depth data for Oliva Lake. Average concentrations in μg/L. Composite samples from the euphotic zone collected 9 times from 14 May to 01 Oct. 1983 and 11 times from 17 May to 27 Aug. 1984. S.E. = standard error.

	1983		1984	
	Mean	S.E.	Mean	S.E.
total phosphorus	12 772	407	13 345	687
total dissolved phosphorus	12 364	430	12 792	646
soluble reactive phosphorus	—	—	12 607[e]	1 078
total Kjeldahl nitrogen	9 884[a]	2 555	11 516[e]	1 014
NO₃ + NO₂–nitrogen	2[a]	1.9	0[e]	0
NH₄–nitrogen	376[b]	70	—	—
iron	574[c, d]	93.5	—	—
chlorophyll a	4.2	1.4	3.9	1.1
Secchi depth (m)	1.5	0.03	1.6	0.02

NOTES: [a]n = 6; [b]n = 5; [c]17 May to 29 Aug. 1983, n = 6; [e]n = 3
SOURCES: [d]Prepas et al. n.d.; Campbell 1986

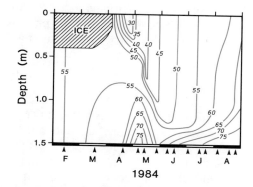

Figure 3. Conductivity (μS/cm x 1000) in Oliva Lake, 1984. Conductivity is an estimate of salinity or total dissolved solids. SOURCE: Campbell 1986.

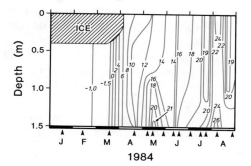

Figure 4. Temperature (°C) in Oliva Lake, 1984. Arrows indicate sampling dates. SOURCE: Campbell 1986.

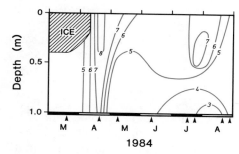

Figure 5. Dissolved oxygen (mg/L) in Oliva Lake, 1984. Arrows indicate sampling dates. SOURCE: Campbell 1986.

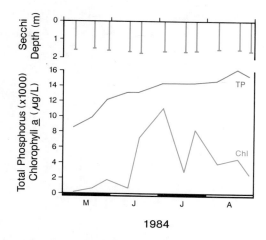

Figure 6. Total phosphorus, chlorophyll a and Secchi depth in Oliva Lake, 1984. Secchi depths of 1.7 m (or more) are on lake bottom. SOURCE: Campbell 1986.

(greater than 12 000 μg/L) and the complete lack of uptake of available phosphorus indicate that algae in this lake are limited by ions other than phosphorus or inhibited by the extreme concentrations of some ions. In contrast, algal biomass in less saline freshwater lakes in Alberta is controlled by phosphorus (Prepas 1983; Prepas and Trew 1983). The salinity of this lake is so extreme that it would be difficult to determine which ions inhibit algal growth.

The water in Oliva Lake is relatively clear; it is not uncommon to be able to see the bottom of the entire lake (Fig. 6). Although the extremely high nutrient levels make it difficult to classify, chlorophyll a concentrations and water transparency indicate that this lake is mesotrophic.

Biological Characteristics

In general, saline lakes such as Oliva have limited biological productivity; few species of plants and animals can survive and only some of those appear to do very well. Much is to be learned about factors controlling production in inland saline lakes.

The plants and animals in Oliva Lake were studied in 1983 and 1984 (Campbell 1986; Campbell and Prepas 1986), and the phytoplankton was studied again from May to August 1987 (Prepas et al. n.d.).

Plants

Identification of algae is very difficult in saline lakes such as Oliva, because the samples tend to have high densities of unidentified detrital and crystalline material. Over the three years that the planktonic algae were studied, only a small number of species were found in Oliva Lake; in 1983 and 1984, these included a cryptomonad (*Cryptomonas* sp.) and small diatoms (Bacillariophyta) such as *Fragilaria* spp. and *Navicula* spp. From May to July 1987, no phytoplankton species could be identified amid the other small particles in the sample. The chlorophyll *a* concentration was low during this period (mean = 2.7 μg/L). In August 1987, the only identifiable algae were two blue-green (Cyanophyta) species, *Aphanizomenon flos-aquae* and *Aphanothece clathrata*. The total biomass of these two species was small (0.87 mg/L). The chlorophyll *a* concentration in August 1987 was the highest measured that summer (10.4 μg/L), and this may have made algal identification easier. The dominant plant living on the lake sediments (phytobenthos) was a filamentous green algae (Chlorophyta) that was relatively dense. Two species of macrophytes grow in the lake: widgeon grass (*Ruppia occidentalis*), which usually grows in saline waters, and sedge (*Carex* sp.). The phytobenthos biomass was greater than the macrophyte biomass.

Bacteria

From April to August 1984, the mean summer bacterial density in the open water of Oliva Lake was 23×10^6 cells/mL. A subsequent study indicated that this was probably an underestimate of true bacterial densities (Harvey 1987). The concentration of bacteria in Oliva Lake was 5 to 10 times higher than in freshwater lakes (Bird and Kalff 1984). Bacterial numbers in Oliva Lake are similar to those in other saline lakes. The reason for these high bacterial densities in saline lakes is unknown.

Invertebrates

Two species of rotifer were found in Oliva Lake: *Branchionus plicatilis*, a member of a genus often found in hard waters, and *Hexarthra* sp., which is common in saline lakes (Pennak 1978). Summer visitors cannot miss the dense red clouds of brine shrimp (*Artemia salina*). No other zooplankton species were found there. The mean dry weight of zooplankton during the growing season (8.2 mg/L) in Oliva Lake was more than 10 times higher than that predicted from measured chlorophyll *a* concentrations and from data collected on freshwater lakes (Campbell and Prepas 1986). Bacteria and detritus

are likely major sources of food for small invertebrates in this saline lake. Of the benthic invertebrates, shore-fly larvae (Ephydridae) were abundant during summer. These larvae are typically found in saline and alkaline waters (Pennak 1978).

Fish

There are no fish in Oliva Lake. There is little potential for fish production due to the lake's extremely high salinity and pH and the dominance of the sulphate anion, rather than chloride, as in the ocean.

Wildlife

There are no data on the wildlife near Oliva Lake.

E.E. Prepas

References

Alberta Environment. n.d. Tech. Serv. Div., Hydrol. Br. Unpubl. data, Edmonton.

Alberta Forestry, Lands and Wildlife. 1988. Boating in Alberta. Fish Wild. Div., Edmonton.

Bierhuizen, J.F.H. and E.E. Prepas. 1985. Relationship between nutrients, dominant ions, and phytoplankton standing crop in prairie saline lakes. Can. J. Fish. Aquat. Sci. 42:1588–1594.

Bird, D.F. and J. Kalff. 1984. Empirical relationships between bacterial abundance and chlorophyll concentrations in fresh and marine waters. Can. J. Fish. Aquat. Sci. 41:1015–1023.

Campbell, C.E. 1986. A study of low chlorophyll levels relative to high phosphorus and nitrogen levels in prairie saline lakes. MSc thesis. Univ. Alta., Edmonton.

———— and E.E. Prepas. 1986. Evaluation of factors related to the unusually low chlorophyll levels in prairie saline lakes. Can. J. Fish. Aquat. Sci. 43:846–854.

Currie, D.V. and N. Zacharko. 1976. Hydrogeology of the Vermilion area. Alta. Res. Counc. Rep. 75–5, Edmonton.

Energy, Mines and Resources Canada. 1974, 1976, 1981. National topographic series 1:50 000 73E/4 (1976) and 1:250 000 73E (1974), 73D (1981). Surv. Map. Br., Ottawa.

Environment Canada. 1982. Canadian climate normals, Vol. 7: Bright sunshine (1951–1980). Prep. by Atm. Envir. Serv. Supply Serv. Can., Ottawa.

Harvey, R.W. 1987. A fluorochrome-staining technique for counting bacteria in saline, organically enriched, alkaline lakes. Limnol. Oceanogr. 32:993–995.

Kinsella History Book Committee. 1983. Hoofprints and homesteading: A history of Kinsella and area. Kinsella Hist. Book Commit., Kinsella.

Pennak, R.W. 1978. Fresh-water invertebrates of the United States. 2nd ed. John Wiley & Sons, Toronto.

Prepas, E.E. 1983. Orthophosphate turnover time in shallow productive lakes. Can. J. Fish. Aquat. Sci. 40:1412–1418.

————, J.F.H. Bierhuizen, C.E. Campbell, J. Shamess, R.W. Howarth and R. Marino. n.d. Unpubl. data, Univ. Alta., Edmonton and Cornell Univ., Ithaca, New York.

Prepas, E.E. and D.O. Trew. 1983. Evaluation of the phosphorus-chlorophyll relationship for lakes off the Precambrian Shield in western Canada. Can. J. Fish. Aquat. Sci. 40:27–35.

Strong, W.L. and K.R. Leggat. 1981. Ecoregions of Alberta. Alta. En. Nat. Resour., Resour. Eval. Plan. Div., Edmonton.

Wyatt, F.A., J.D. Newton, W.E. Bowser and W. Odynsky. 1944. Soil Survey of Wainwright-Vermilion sheet. Alta. Soil Surv. Rep. No. 13, Univ. Alta. Bull. No. 42. Univ. Alta., Edmonton.

PENINSULA LAKE

E.E. Prepas

MAP SHEET: 73D
LOCATION: Tp45 R11 W4
LAT/LONG: 52°52'N 111°29'W

Peninsula Lake is a small, shallow, salty lake located in the County of Flagstaff, 160 km southeast of the city of Edmonton. From Edmonton, take Highway 14 east to the hamlet of Kinsella. The lake is 3 km east of Secondary Road 870, halfway between Kinsella, on Highway 14, and the village of Lougheed, on Highway 13 (Fig. 1). The east side of the lake can be reached from a gravel road. Between this road and the lake there is a small gravel beach where small boats can be launched. There are no boating restrictions specific to this lake, but general federal regulations apply (Alta. For. Ld. Wild. 1988).

Homesteaders arrived in the district of Kinsella, to the north of Peninsula Lake, in 1904. Grain, mixed farming and livestock ranching developed in this region, where an exceptionally good quality native grass grows (Kinsella Hist. Book Commit. 1983).

Peninsula Lake is one of a number of saline lakes in eastern Alberta. Its salinity causes characteristics such as temperature, nutrient concentrations and plant and animal communities to be different from those in freshwater lakes. Salinity in this lake is characterized by high sulphate, sodium and bicarbonate/carbonate concentrations; these minerals come from saline groundwater in the region. In winter, the temperature of water under the ice drops to 0°C, uncommonly low for Alberta lakes. Although levels of nutrients are high, plant growth is sparse. A few planktonic invertebrates are exceptionally abundant, but there are fewer species than in freshwater lakes. There are no fish in the lake.

The lake is surrounded by trembling aspen. There are no recreational facilities or cottages on the shore, and this absence of development, in conjunction with clear water, makes the lake an attractive place for boating and canoeing.

Drainage Basin Characteristics

The drainage basin of Peninsula Lake is large compared to the lake (ratio of 31 to 1; Fig. 1, Tables 1, 2). However, a large portion of the drainage basin is likely noncontributing. Although soils in the watershed are nonsaline (MacMillan et al. 1988), there are saline soils in surrounding areas and saline groundwater in the drainage basin. The agricultural capacity of soils around the lake is rated as fairly good to good. At present, most of the land is cultivated primarily for canola and flax, or is grazed by cattle (Campbell 1986). The land surrounding the lake is privately owned.

Lake Basin Characteristics

Peninsula Lake is small (Table 2); it has a maximum length of 2.3 km and a maximum width of 0.9 km. The lake has one bowl-shaped basin with the deepest area (3.1 m) located near the southeast end. When water levels are sufficiently low, a narrow peninsula is formed on the south side, connecting the shore with a tiny island (Fig. 2).

The water level was monitored from May 1983 through August 1984. During this period it was very stable; the water fluctuated a maximum of 0.17 m, with a minimum level recorded in June 1983 and a maximum in July 1984 (Campbell 1986). Data on water well and surface water fluctuations in the region would be required to put these data in perspective with long-term patterns. Because there is usually no outflow from the lake (Table 2), it is functionally an evaporative basin. This fact, coupled with saline groundwater in the

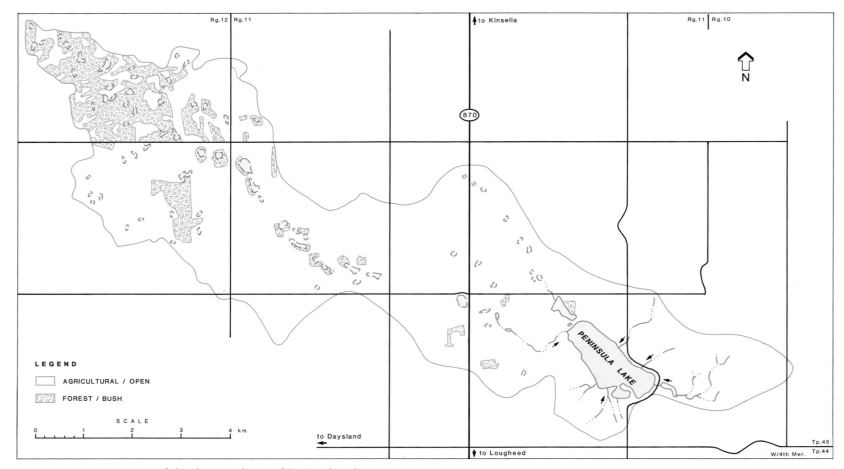

Figure 1. Features of the drainage basin of Peninsula Lake.
SOURCES: Alta. Envir. n.d.; En. Mines Resour. Can. 1978. Updated with 1982 aerial photos.

Table 1. Characteristics of Peninsula Lake drainage basin.

area (excluding lake) (km²)[a]	43.9
soil[b]	Orthic Black Chernozemics
bedrock geology[c]	Belly River Formation (Upper Cretaceous): sandstone, siltstone, mudstone, ironstone beds; nonmarine
terrain[b]	undulating to rolling
ecoregion[d]	Aspen Parkland
dominant vegetation[d]	trembling aspen and rough fescue grassland
mean annual inflow (m³)[a, e]	0.303 x 10⁶
mean annual sunshine (h)[f]	2 168

NOTE: [e]excluding groundwater inflow
SOURCES: [a]Alta. Envir. n.d.; [b]MacMillan et al. 1988; [c]Alta. Res. Counc. 1972;
[d]Strong and Leggat 1981; [f]Envir. Can. 1982

Table 2. Characteristics of Peninsula Lake.

surface area (km²)[a, b]	1.39
volume (m³)[a, b]	2.94 x 10⁶
maximum depth (m)[a, b]	3.1
mean depth (m)[a, b]	2.1
shoreline length (km)[b]	6.15
mean annual lake evaporation (mm)[c]	637
mean annual precipitation (mm)[c]	421
mean residence time[c, d]	>100
control structure	none

NOTES: [a]on date of sounding: Aug. 1983; [d]excluding groundwater inflow
SOURCES: [b]Campbell 1986; [c]Alta. Envir. n.d.

region (Currie and Zacharko 1976; MacMillan et al. 1988), explains the lake's high concentration of total dissolved solids.

Water Quality

Peninsula Lake was sampled for water quality characteristics from 1982 through 1984 and again in 1986 and 1987 by researchers with the University of Alberta (Prepas et al. n.d.; Bierhuizen and Prepas 1985; Campbell 1986; Campbell and Prepas 1986).

Peninsula Lake water is well-mixed by the wind during most of the ice-free season. As illustrated with data from 1984, temperature and dissolved oxygen concentrations are fairly uniform during the open-water period (Fig. 3, 4). High concentrations of total dissolved solids (9 600 mg/L, Table 3), made up primarily by sulphate, sodium and bicarbonate/carbonate ions, have an influence on under-ice water temperatures and dissolved oxygen concentrations in this lake. The temperature of the water column drops to 0°C under ice (Fig. 3); this is an unusually low temperature for a lake and is a result of the high salt content. Dissolved oxygen concentrations are lower in the surface waters during the open-water period than in freshwater lakes in Alberta (Fig. 4), due to the reduced solubility of oxygen as the concentration of salts in the water increases. In contrast, dissolved oxygen concentrations under ice in late winter 1984 were remarkably high for such a shallow lake (Fig. 4). The reason for these relatively high winter dissolved oxygen concentrations is unknown. They may result from the combination of low summer productivity (Table 4), low under-ice water temperatures, and sediments with minimal bacterial activity.

Phosphorus and nitrogen were present in extremely high concentrations in Peninsula Lake (Table 4), similar to those in other saline lakes in Alberta. In contrast to freshwater lakes with similar nutrient concentrations, chlorophyll *a* concentrations in this lake were low (7.3 to 10.6 µg/L); freshwater lakes with similar nitrogen and phosphorus concentrations would be very green in summer (chlorophyll *a* concentrations greater than 300 µg/L; Campbell and Prepas 1986). The single high chlorophyll *a* concentration in late July 1984 (Fig. 5) is unusual and there is no explanation for its short duration.

Table 3. Major ions and related water quality variables for Peninsula Lake. Average concentrations in mg/L. Composite samples from the euphotic zone collected 5 times from 17 May to 27 Aug. 1983. S.E. = standard error.

	Mean	S.E.
pH (range)	9.2–9.4[a, b]	—
total alkalinity (CaCO₃)	2 111	7.3
specific conductivity (μS/cm)	12 600[a, c]	234.0
total dissolved solids	9 600[d]	125.7
turbidity (NTU)	12[a, e]	0.9
colour (Pt)	46[a, e]	1.3
total hardness (calculated)	511	—
HCO₃	1 727	29.2
CO₃	416	55.8
Mg	107	10.1
Na	3 363	84.7
K	109	7.0
Cl	178	2.6
SO₄	4 842[d]	36.2
Ca	28	4.2

NOTES: [b]11 May to 01 Oct. 1983 and 07 May to 27 Aug. 1984, n = 16; [c]as in [b] (but n = 20); [d]n = 4; [e]11 May to 01 Oct. 1983, n = 9
SOURCES: Prepas et al. n.d.; [a]Campbell 1986

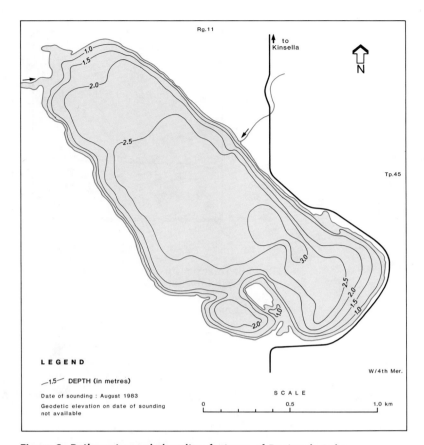

Figure 2. Bathymetry and shoreline features of Peninsula Lake. BATHYMETRY SOURCE: Campbell 1986.

When compared to Alberta lakes with similar chlorophyll *a* concentrations, the transparency of the water in Peninsula Lake (Fig. 5) is low, perhaps because it is highly coloured (Chambers and Prepas 1988).

Although difficult to classify because of its salinity, Peninsula Lake would be mesotrophic based on chlorophyll *a* concentrations.

Biological Characteristics

Saline lakes such as Peninsula are less productive biologically than their freshwater counterparts; fewer species of plants and animals live there. The biomass of primary producers (for example, algae) appears to be constrained more by moderately high levels of salinity than some trophic levels (such as bacteria or invertebrates). Much is to be learned about factors controlling biological processes in these distinct lakes.

Plants and animals in Peninsula Lake were studied in 1983 and 1984 (Campbell 1986), and the phytoplankton was studied again in 1987 (Prepas et al. n.d.; Marino et al. 1990).

Plants

Phytoplankton identification in saline lakes such as Peninsula is made very difficult by high densities of unidentified detrital and crystalline material. In 1983 and 1984, the dominant phytoplankton in Peninsula Lake were the blue-green algae (Cyanophyta) *Microcystis aeruginosa* and *Lyngbya Birgei*. The dominant alga living on the sediments (phytobenthos) was *Rhizoclonium hieroglyphicum*. In 1987, the phytoplankton were sampled 4 times; the average chlorophyll *a* concentration was 5.5 μg/L. In May, 90% of the community was made up of a small alga (Cryptophyta), *Rhodomonas minuta*, and 10% was a green alga (Chlorophyta), *Monoraphidium contortum*. By July, a golden-brown alga (Chrysophyta), *Chrysomonad* sp., was the only identifiable species. By August, two species of blue-green algae (Cyanophyta: *Oscillatoria angustissima* and *Chroococcus dispersus*) made up 75% of the biomass and *R. minuta* made up the remaining 22% of the biomass. Algal biomass varied from 0.044 mg/L in July to 0.062 mg/L in May, to 0.15 mg/L in August 1987. No algal species could be identified in June 1987. Only a few species of macrophytes grow in the lake: widgeon grass (*Ruppia occidentalis*), which is indigenous to saline waters, and one or more species of sedge (*Carex* spp.).

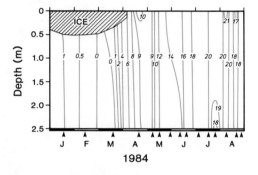

Figure 3. Temperature (°C) of Peninsula Lake, 1984. Arrows indicate sampling dates. SOURCE: Campbell 1986.

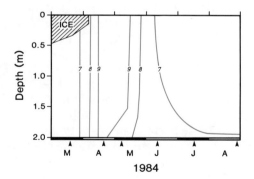

Figure 4. Dissolved oxygen (mg/L) in Peninsula Lake, 1984. Arrows indicate sampling dates. SOURCE: Campbell 1986.

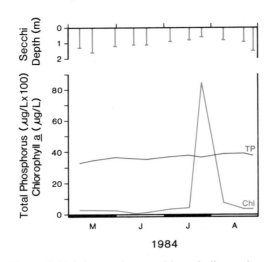

Figure 5. Total phosphorus, chlorophyll *a* and Secchi depth in Peninsula Lake, May to Aug. 1984.
SOURCE: Campbell 1986.

Table 4. Nutrient, chlorophyll *a* and Secchi depth data for Peninsula Lake. Average concentrations in μg/L. Composite samples from the euphotic zone collected 9 times from 11 May to 01 Oct. 1983 and 11 times from 07 May to 27 Aug. 1984. S.E. = standard error.

	1983		1984	
	Mean	S.E.	Mean	S.E.
total phosphorus	3 495	42.1	3 658	60.5
total dissolved phosphorus	3 335	38.3	3 475	63.9
soluble reactive phosphorus	—	—	3 589[e]	182.6
total Kjeldahl nitrogen	4 647[a]	166.1	4 092[e]	361.4
NO$_3$ + NO$_2$–nitrogen	31[a]	16.0	86.4[e]	46.0
NH$_4$–nitrogen	52[b]	16.6	—	—
iron	1 454[c, d]	260.1	—	—
chlorophyll *a*	7.3	1.71	10.6	7.41
Secchi depth (m)	0.7	0.08	1.1	0.09

NOTES: [a] n = 5; [b] n = 4; [d] 17 May to 27 Aug. 1983, n = 5; [e] n = 3
SOURCES: [c] Prepas et al. n.d.; Campbell 1986

Bacteria

From April to August 1984, the mean summer bacterial density in the open water of Peninsula Lake was 13 x 10^6 cells/mL; a subsequent study indicated that this is probably an underestimate of true bacterial densities (Harvey 1987). This concentration is about twice as high as the concentration predicted from data collected on freshwater lakes relative to measured chlorophyll *a* concentrations (Bird and Kalff 1984), but similar to values reported for other saline lakes. These data suggest that there is more organic substrate for bacteria in the open water of saline lakes, as compared with freshwater lakes with similar chlorophyll levels. These bacteria are part of the normal process of decomposition, but there are more of them in saline lakes.

Invertebrates

Only three species of zooplankton were found in Peninsula Lake: the copepods *Diaptomus nevadensis* and *D. sicilis*, and the waterflea *Daphnia similis*. The mean dry weight or biomass of zooplankton during the growing season (1.4 mg/L) was 10 times higher than the biomass predicted from data collected on freshwater lakes, relative to measured chlorophyll *a* concentrations. Bacteria and detritus are likely the main source of food for zooplankton. An amphipod (*Hyalella azteca*) was the only macroinvertebrate found in significant numbers.

Fish

Although there are, at present, no freshwater fish species that could reproduce in Peninsula Lake, there may be potential for salt-tolerant fish to live in this and similar lakes. More work is needed to determine which species adapt to water where sulphate ions are the dominant anion. Fish from brackish marine areas have adapted to similar degrees of salinity, but there, chloride ions are relatively more important and sulphate ions are less important.

Wildlife

There is no information on the wildlife at Peninsula Lake.

E.E. Prepas

References

Alberta Environment. n.d. Tech. Serv. Div., Hydrol. Br. Unpubl. data, Edmonton.

Alberta Forestry, Lands and Wildlife. 1988. Boating in Alberta. Fish Wild. Div., Edmonton.

Alberta Research Council. 1972. Geological map of Alberta. Nat. Resour. Div., Alta. Geol. Surv., Edmonton.

Bierhuizen, J.F.H. and E.E. Prepas. 1985. Relationship between nutrients, dominant ions, and phytoplankton standing crop in prairie saline lakes. Can. J. Fish. Aquat. Sci. 42:1588–1594.

Bird, D.F. and J. Kalff. 1984. Empirical relationships between bacterial abundance and chlorophyll concentrations in fresh and marine waters. Can. J. Fish. Aquat. Sci. 41:1015–1023.

Campbell, C.E. 1986. A study of low chlorophyll levels relative to high phosphorus and nitrogen levels in prairie saline lakes. MSc thesis. Univ. Alta., Edmonton.

———— and E.E. Prepas. 1986. Evaluation of factors related to the unusually low chlorophyll levels in prairie saline lakes. Can. J. Fish. Aquat. Sci. 43:846–854.

Chambers, P.A. and E.E. Prepas. 1988. Underwater spectral attenuation and its effect on the maximum depth of angiosperm colonization. Can. J. Fish. Aquat. Sci. 45:1010–1017.

Currie, D.V. and N. Zacharko. 1976. Hydrogeology of the Vermilion area. Alta. Res. Counc. Rep. 75–5, Edmonton.

Energy, Mines and Resources Canada. 1978. National topographic series 1:50 000 73D/13 (1978), 73D/14 (1978). Surv. Map. Br., Ottawa.

Environment Canada. 1982. Canadian climate normals, Vol. 7: Bright sunshine (1951–1980). Prep. by Atm. Envir. Serv. Supply Serv. Can., Ottawa.

Harvey, R.W. 1987. A fluorochrome-staining technique for counting bacteria in saline, organically enriched, alkaline lakes. Limnol. Oceanogr. 32:993–995.

Kinsella History Book Committee. 1983. Hoofprints and homesteading: A history of Kinsella and area. Kinsella Hist. Book Commit., Kinsella.

MacMillan, R.A., W.L. Nikiforuk and A.T. Rodvang. 1988. Soil survey of the County of Flagstaff. Alta. Soil Surv. Rep. No. 51. Alta. Res. Counc., Edmonton.

Marino, R., R.W. Howarth, J. Shamess and E.E. Prepas. 1990. Molybdenum and sulfate as controls on the abundance of nitrogen-fixing cyanobacteria in Alberta saline lakes. Limnol. Oceanogr. [in press]

Prepas, E.E., J.F.H. Bierhuizen, C.E. Campbell, J. Shamess, R.W. Howarth and R. Marino. n.d. Unpubl. data, Univ. Alta., Edmonton and Cornell Univ., Ithaca, New York.

Strong, W.L. and K.R. Leggat. 1981. Ecoregions of Alberta. Alta. En. Nat. Resour., Resour. Eval. Plan. Div., Edmonton.

PIGEON LAKE

MAP SHEETS: 83A/13, 83B/16, 83G/1, 83H/4
LOCATION: Tp46, 47 R1 W5
LAT/LONG: 53°01′N 114°02′W

Pigeon Lake is a large, very popular recreational lake located in the counties of Wetaskiwin and Leduc, within easy driving distance from the cities of Edmonton, Leduc and Wetaskiwin. It is located about 60 km southwest of Edmonton and can be reached by taking Highway 2 south of the city, then following Highway 13 west to Ma-Me-O Beach on the south end of the lake. Several secondary roads provide good access to most of the lakeshore (Fig. 1).

The lake was once known as "Woodpecker Lake", a translation from the Cree name *Hmi-hmoo*, but by 1858, the name Pigeon Lake was in use (Holmgren and Holmgren 1976). The name probably originates from the huge flocks of Passenger Pigeons that once ranged over the area (Falun Hist. Soc. 1974). In 1847, Reverend Robert Rundle established Rundle Mission on the northwest shore; this agricultural settlement, which was Alberta's first Protestant mission, is commemorated by a cairn at Mission Beach (Warburg Dist. Hist. Soc. 1977). A Hudson's Bay Company trading post was built on the west shore in 1868, but operated only until 1875 (Falun Hist. Soc. 1974). In 1896, Pigeon Lake Indian Reserve was established on the southeast shore. Later, the summer village of Ma-Me-O Beach was developed at the south end of the lake on land obtained from the Indian reserve in 1924. *Ma-Me-O* is a Cree word meaning "white pigeon". Logging, commercial fishing and farming were important livelihoods of residents of the area in the early 1900s. Near the hamlet of Mulhurst, a sawmill operated year-round, and a fish-packing plant operated during winter (Millet Dist. Hist. Soc. 1978).

At present, Pigeon Lake is one of the most intensively used recreational lakes in Alberta. There are over 2 300 private cottage lots in 10 summer villages and 9 unincorporated subdivisions (Fig. 2) (Battle R. Reg. Plan. Commis. 1985). Approximately 10% of the cottages are permanent homes. In 1985, the hamlet of Mulhurst on the northeast shore had a population of 295 people and the hamlet of Westerose on the southeast shore had a population of 87 people (Co. Wetaskiwin 1988). As well, there are about 200 people living on the Pigeon Lake Indian Reserve (Four Bands Admin. 1988). They are members of the Louis Bull, Ermineskin, Samson and Montana bands.

Two provincial parks are located on Pigeon Lake. Ma-Me-O Beach Provincial Park, located within the summer village, was established in 1957 (Alta. Rec. Parks n.d.). It is the smallest provincial park in Alberta (area of 0.016 km²). The park is open from the Victoria Day weekend to 15 September and provides day-use services only. Facilities include a picnic shelter, a playground, toilets and pump water. A sandy beach is nearby. Pigeon Lake Provincial Park was established on the west side of the lake in 1967 (Alta. Rec. Parks n.d.). Alberta Recreation and Parks acquired nearby Zeiner Park (formerly operated by the County of Leduc) in 1981 and incorporated it into the provincial park (Fig. 2). There are 180 campsites in the main campground and 116 sites at Zeiner Campground; facilities include beaches, boat launches, change houses, docks, flush and vault toilets, picnic shelters, a concession, group camping, sewage disposal, tap water, walking trails, a telephone and playgrounds. The park offers camping from early May to mid-October, and is open for day-use activities year-round (Wilson 1988).

Another public recreational facility at Pigeon Lake is the Mission Beach Campground at Mission Beach. It is operated by Alberta Transportation and has nine campsites, picnic tables, one picnic shelter and a water pump (Danchuk 1988). Additional public access

Figure 1. Features of the drainage basin of Pigeon Lake.
SOURCES: Alta. Envir. n.d.[c]; En. Mines Resour. Can. 1974; 1975. Updated with 1987 aerial photos.

Table 1. Characteristics of Pigeon Lake drainage basin.

area (excluding lake) (km²)[a]	187
soil[b]	Orthic Gray Luvisols
bedrock geology[c]	Paskapoo Formation (Tertiary): sandstone, siltstone, mudstone; thin limestone, coal and tuff beds; nonmarine
terrain[b]	level to gently rolling
ecoregion[d]	Dry Mixedwood Subregion of Boreal Mixedwood
dominant vegetation[d]	trembling aspen
mean annual inflow (m³)[a, e]	17.0 x 10⁶
mean annual sunshine (h)[f]	2 315

NOTE: [e]excluding groundwater inflow
SOURCES: [a]Alta. Envir. n.d.[c]; [b]Bowser et al. 1947; 1962; Lindsay et al. 1968; [c]Alta. Res. Counc. 1972; [d]Strong and Leggat 1981; [f]Envir. Can. 1982

points, with boat launches, are available at Mulhurst and at the summer village of Ma-Me-O Beach. Commercial recreational facilities at the lake include two campgrounds located in the Indian reserve at either side of the summer village of Ma-Me-O Beach and golf courses located at Mulhurst and near Westerose. Institutional facilities consist of eight youth and church group camps situated along the lakeshore.

Water sports such as swimming, power boating, sailing, windsurfing, water skiing and sport fishing are popular. In posted areas of the

lake, all boats are prohibited or subject to a maximum speed of 12 km/hour (Alta. For. Ld. Wild. 1988).

The water quality of Pigeon Lake is typical of large, shallow lakes in central Alberta. The water is green for much of the summer, but nuisance algal blooms are rare. The lake supports active commercial and domestic fisheries, and sport fishing for yellow perch, walleye and northern pike is popular year-round. A portion of Pigeon Lake Creek downstream from the lake is closed to fishing during designated periods in spring (Alta. For. Ld. Wild. 1989).

Drainage Basin Characteristics

Pigeon Lake has a relatively small watershed that is only twice the size of the lake (Fig. 1, Tables 1, 2). Water flows into the lake through several intermittent streams that drain the western and northwestern portions of the drainage basin. The outlet is Pigeon Lake Creek, which flows from the south end of the lake in a southeasterly direction to the Battle River.

The relief in the drainage basin is fairly low; most areas range from level to undulating (0 to 5% slope) particularly near the lake, to gently rolling (5 to 9% slope) (Lindsay et al. 1968). Surficial deposits in the drainage basin are predominantly glacial till that originated from the Paskapoo bedrock formation underlying the area. The dominant soils are Orthic Gray Luvisols, which are present throughout the drainage basin. These are moderately well-drained soils developed on glacial till. Soils to the north and west have moderately severe limitations for crop production (Can. Dept. Reg. Econ. Expansion 1972). Pockets of Organic soil formed from undifferentiated moss and sedge parent material are scattered throughout the water-

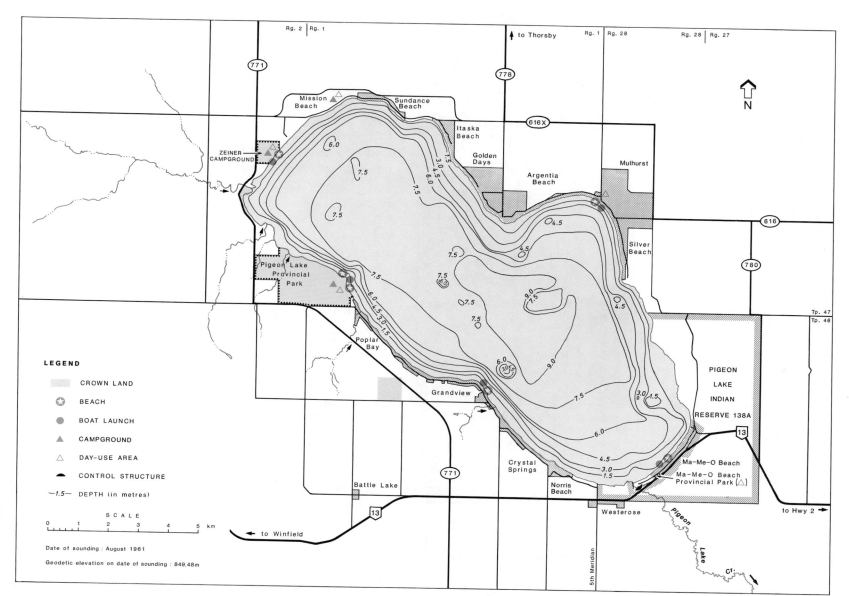

Figure 2. Bathymetry and shoreline features of Pigeon Lake.
BATHYMETRY SOURCE: Alta. Envir. n.d.[d].

shed and along the lakeshore. At the southeast end of the lake, in the region of Pigeon Lake Creek and Ma-Me-O Beach, Eluviated Black Chernozemic soils have developed on alluvial-aeolian material (Bowser et al. 1947).

The forest cover in the drainage basin is dominated by trembling aspen. Balsam poplar grows in poorly drained locations, such as along some areas of the lakeshore. Approximately 50% of the drainage basin is forest-covered, 46% is cleared for agriculture and 4% is developed for cottage and residential use (Fig. 1). Crops on cultivated land are mainly feed grains and hay. There are a number of cow-calf operations in the watershed and several small feed lots, but there is little cattle grazing within 3 km of the lake (Pinkoski 1988). There are two oil fields adjacent to Pigeon Lake: the Pembina Field covers the northwestern region of the drainage basin and the Bonnie Glen Field is located in the southeastern portion (Pigeon L. Study Group 1975).

The only Crown land around the lake is in the two provincial parks and in a quarter section west of the lake. The latter has the status of Protective Notation and is reserved for recreation (Alta. For. Ld. Wild. 1987).

Lake Basin Characteristics

Pigeon Lake is large and roughly oval, with one simple basin that is fairly shallow. The lake bottom slopes gently to a maximum depth of about 9 m near the centre (Fig. 2). The littoral zone extends to a depth of 4.5 m (Haag and Noton 1981) and occupies 25% of the surface area of the lake. A large proportion of the sediments in the littoral zone are coarse-textured (Haag and Noton 1981; Fig. 3).

Table 2. Characteristics of Pigeon Lake.

elevation (m)[a, b]	849.48
surface area (km²)[a, b]	96.7
volume (m³)[a, b]	603 x 10⁶
maximum depth (m)[a, b]	9.1
mean depth (m)[a, b]	6.2
shoreline length (km)[c]	46
mean annual lake evaporation (mm)[d]	664
mean annual precipitation (mm)[d]	534
mean residence time (yr)[d, e]	>100
control structure[f]	two bay weir with stop logs and Denil II fish ladder
sill elevation (m)[f]	849.8

NOTE: [a]on date of sounding: Aug. 1961; [e]excluding groundwater inflow
SOURCES: [b]Alta. Envir. n.d.[d]; [c]En. Mines Resour. Can. 1974; 1975; [d]Alta. Envir. n.d.[c]; [f]Alta. Envir. n.d.[a]

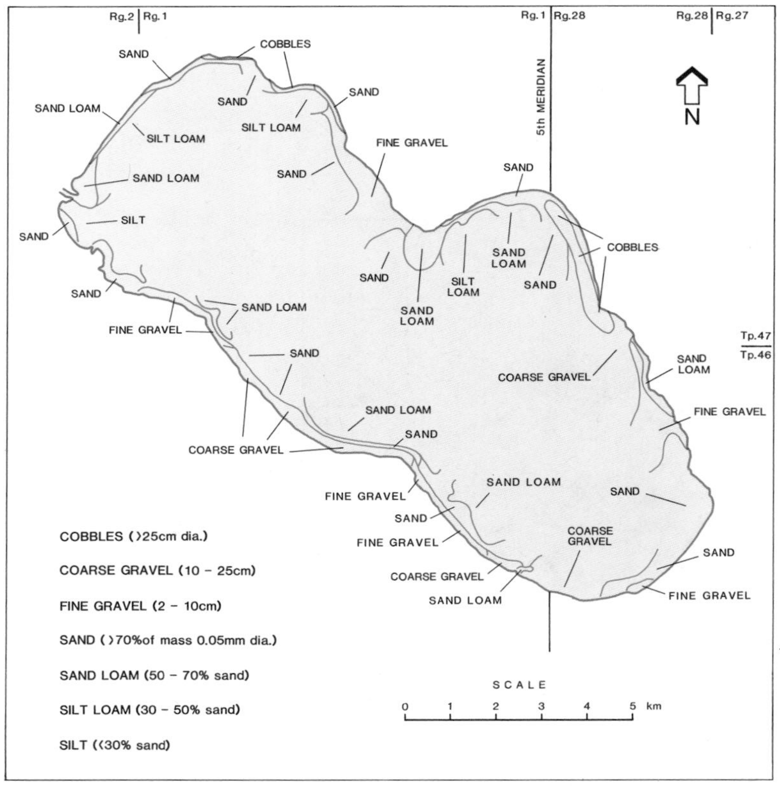

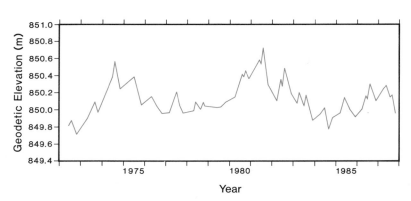

Figure 3. Distribution of littoral sediments (1981)[a] and shoreline characteristics[b] of Pigeon Lake.
SOURCES: [a]Haag and Noton 1981; [b]Pigeon L. Study Group 1975.

Figure 4. Water level of Pigeon Lake, 1972 to 1987.
SOURCE: Envir. Can. 1972–1987.

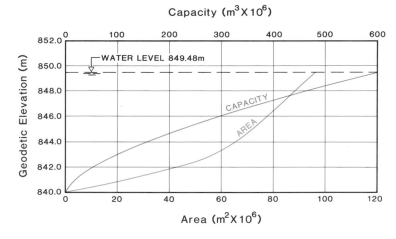

Figure 5. Area/capacity curve for Pigeon Lake.
SOURCE: Alta. Envir. n.d.[d].

Table 3. Major ions and related water quality variables for Pigeon Lake. Average concentrations in mg/L; pH in pH units. Composite samples from the euphotic zone collected 3 times from 29 May to 07 Sep. 1983 and 4 times from 17 June to 05 Sep. 1984. S.E. = standard error.

	Mean	S.E.
pH (range)	8.2–8.6	—
total alkalinity (CaCO$_3$)	152	1.2
specific conductivity (µS/cm)	283	5.3
total dissolved solids (calculated)	155[a]	1.5
total hardness (CaCO$_3$)	107	2.5
HCO$_3$	179	3.4
CO$_3$	<4	—
Mg	10	0.2
Na	16	0.4
K	5	0.1
Cl	<1	—
SO$_4$	<5	—
Ca	26[a]	0.9

NOTE: [a]n = 6
SOURCE: Alta. Envir. n.d.[b], Naquadat station 01AL05FA1500

Table 4. Nutrient, chlorophyll *a* and Secchi depth data for Pigeon Lake. Average concentrations in µg/L. Composite samples from the euphotic zone collected 3 times from 29 May to 07 Sep. 1983 and 6 times from 10 June to 03 Oct. 1984. S.E. = standard error.

	1983 Mean	1983 S.E.	1984 Mean	1984 S.E.
total phosphorus	29	7.9	35	3.8
total Kjeldahl nitrogen	910[a]	—	—	—
iron	—	—	<20[b]	—
chlorophyll *a*	11.6	6.50	14.1	3.77
Secchi depth (m)	2.9	0.92	2.0	0.16

NOTES: [a]n = 1; [b]n = 4
SOURCE: Alta. Envir. n.d.[b], Naquadat station 01AL05FA1500

Wave-deposited sand occurs at the southeast end, offshore from Ma-Me-O Beach.

Wide, sandy beaches occur along 28% of the shoreline, such as at Ma-Me-O Beach, Zeiner Park, Itaska Beach and between Silver Beach and Argentia Beach (Pigeon L. Study Group 1975). About 42% of the shoreline has a gentle gradient, but lacks a sandy beach. Low-lying regions of wetland with very gentle slopes occur along 19% of the shore, such as at the northwest end near Zeiner Campground. The remaining 11% consists of a steeply sloping backshore with no beach area, as is found in the area of Crystal Springs.

A wooden control structure, with a sill elevation of about 850 m, was first built by the federal government on the outlet of Pigeon Lake at Pigeon Lake Creek in 1914 (Alta. Envir. 1982). It was rebuilt in 1939/40 and had a fixed-sill level of 849.78 m. The purpose of the weir was to regulate the flow through Pigeon Lake Creek during late summer to prevent the flooding of hay fields. By 1980, lakeshore residents expressed concerns about high lake levels (Fig. 4). In 1981, the lake level fell from 850.65 m to 850.21 m after the outlet structure and creek channel were cleared and maintained. In 1986, Alberta Environment replaced the old weir with a new two-bay structure with two stop logs and a Denil II fish ladder (Alta. Envir. n.d.[a]). The weir is usually operated with one stop log in place to maintain the lake level at an elevation of 849.95 m. Between 1972 and 1987, the water level fluctuated over a range of about 1 m, which is a typical fluctuation for many lakes in central Alberta. The area and volume of the lake would change relatively little as a result of this fluctuation (Fig. 5).

Table 5. Theoretical total external phosphorus loading to Pigeon Lake.

Source		Phosphorus (kg/yr)	Percentage of Total
watershed	forested/bush	900	16
	agricultural/cleared	1 702	30
	residential/cottage	770	14
sewage[a]		133	2
precipitation/dustfall		2 127	38
	TOTAL	5 632	100
annual areal loading (g/m² of lake surface)	0.06		

NOTE: [a]unmeasured: assumes 4% of all sewage effluent from residences and camps enters the lake, as in Mitchell 1982
SOURCE: Alta. Envir. 1989

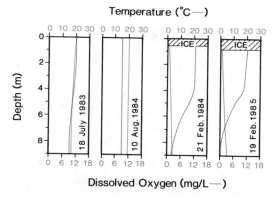

Figure 6. Temperature and dissolved oxygen in Pigeon Lake, 1983, 1984, and 1985.
SOURCE: Alta. Envir. n.d.[b].

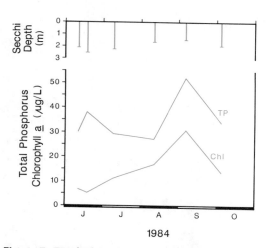

Figure 7. Total phosphorus, chlorophyll *a* and Secchi depth in Pigeon Lake, 1984.
SOURCE: Alta. Envir. n.d.[b].

Water Quality

The water quality of Pigeon Lake was studied by the University of Alberta between 1973 and 1975 (Alta. Envir. n.d.[b]), and since 1983 there has been an ongoing monitoring program conducted jointly by Alberta Environment and Alberta Recreation and Parks (Alta. Envir. n.d.[b]; 1989). The lake was also sampled by Alberta Environment in 1988 as part of a pilot project using cottage owners to collect water samples (Nelson and Mitchell 1988). In 1982, a water quality study was commissioned by the Battle River Regional Planning Commission (Hardy Assoc. (1978) Ltd. 1983).

Pigeon Lake is a well-buffered, freshwater lake; bicarbonate and calcium are the dominant ions (Table 3).

The water mixes from the lake surface to the bottom on windy days during most of the open-water period, and the temperature is usually uniform. Dissolved oxygen concentrations remain high throughout the water column (Fig. 6). By late winter, dissolved oxygen may be depleted near the bottom, but winterkill of fish is unlikely because there is sufficient dissolved oxygen in the upper portion of the water column.

Pigeon Lake is mildly eutrophic (Table 4). There is considerable year-to-year variation in the average levels of total phosphorus and chlorophyll *a*. Total phosphorus and chlorophyll *a* concentrations increase during summer to peak levels in late August (Fig. 7). This pattern is typical of shallow lakes in Alberta and is probably caused by a recycling of phosphorus into the water column from the bottom sediments. This internal supply of phosphorus may be very significant in maintaining summer algal populations in Pigeon Lake. Precipitation and dustfall onto the lake surface provide a large part (38%) of the total external phosphorus supply, but the largest portion is derived from various types of land-use in the watershed (Table 5).

Biological Characteristics

Plants

There are no data on the phytoplankton in Pigeon Lake.

The distribution of aquatic macrophytes was surveyed in 1981 as part of an Alberta Environment study to determine the effects of lake level stabilization (Fig. 8). Plant cover was generally low along most of the shoreline at depths less than 1.5 m and was highest where fine sediments accumulated. The most frequently occurring species were northern watermilfoil (*Myriophyllum exalbescens*), stonewort (*Chara* sp.), and Richardson pondweed (*Potamogeton richardsonii*). Northern watermilfoil tended to grow in areas of low turbulence, and was found at slightly greater depths than Richardson pondweed. Cottage owners consider Richardson pondweed a nuisance because of its high density in shallow water. Also abundant was widgeon grass (*Ruppia occidentalis*). The high frequency of widgeon grass was surprising, because it is usually found in saline water. The dominant emergent species was common great bulrush (*Scirpus validus*). It was found in shoreline areas without lakefront cottages; its distribution is limited by substrate type and cutting by cottage-owners.

Invertebrates

A graduate student at the University of Alberta examined the zooplankton and benthic invertebrate fauna of Pigeon Lake (Bidgood 1972). The standing crop of zooplankton was examined monthly at one station from June 1970 to June 1971. Copepods were abundant throughout the open-water period, particularly in May and June. The most common copepod was *Diacyclops bicuspidatus thomasi*. *Diaptomus* sp. was also common. Cladocerans were less numerous; the highest numbers occurred in midsummer. One species of *Daphnia* was dominant, and another cladoceran, the large *Leptodora kindtii*, was also present.

Sand, silt and rubble substrates in Pigeon Lake were sampled monthly for benthic invertebrates between July 1970 and June 1971 with a 15–cm Ekman dredge. The highest number of invertebrates was observed in March; the dominant organism was *Hyalella azteca*, an amphipod, which was found mainly on sandy substrates (3–m deep). Midge larvae (Chironomidae) were abundant on silt substrates in August.

Fish

Pigeon Lake is managed for commercial, domestic and recreational fisheries. Species of fish in the lake include lake whitefish, white sucker, burbot, yellow perch, walleye, northern pike, spottail shiner, emerald shiner, trout-perch and Iowa darter (Alta. For. Ld. Wild. n.d.; Bidgood 1972). Walleye were present in commercial catches prior to 1963/64, but subsequently the population died out. They were stocked in 1979, 1980, 1982, 1983 and 1984 and a small population has become established once again (Alta. For. Ld. Wild. n.d.). Important spawning areas for lake whitefish are on boulder, rubble and sand substrate, particularly at the southeast end of the

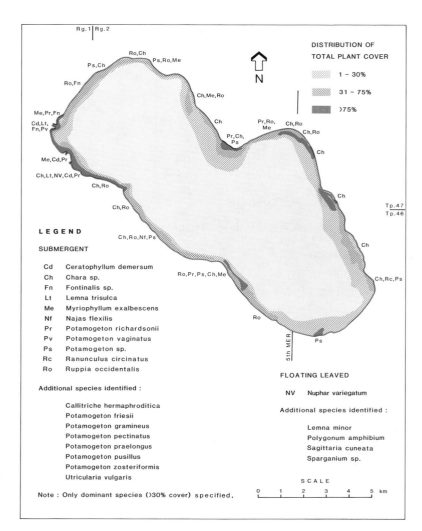

Figure 8. Distribution of floating and submergent macrophytes in Pigeon Lake, August 1981.
SOURCE: Haag and Noton 1981.

lake offshore from the Indian reserve (Bidgood 1972). Partial summerkills of yellow perch have been recorded, such as in May 1965. The cause of mortality was not determined, although both disease and temperature shock were suggested (Alta. For. Ld. Wild. n.d.).

Pigeon Lake has been fished commercially for lake whitefish since 1918. The fishery averaged 81 194 kg of fish annually between 1918 and 1939. Between 1939 and 1946, an unlimited catch was allowed, to determine the effects of over-exploitation of the whitefish population (Miller 1947; 1956). The annual harvest exceeded 181 400 kg until 1946, after which the fishery collapsed. After several seasons with restricted quotas, normal quotas were restored in 1951/52. The population apparently recovered, but following large harvests (averaging 141 515 kg annually) between 1954/55 and 1960/61, yields began to decline. A reduction in mesh size resulted in increased yields, but in the 1960s many of the lake whitefish harvested were below the minimum allowable commercial size of 0.7 kg (Alta. For. Ld. Wild. n.d.).

Between 1968 and 1972 a researcher at the University of Alberta conducted a study to identify factors causing a decrease in size-at-age of lake whitefish since 1956 (Bidgood 1972). The size of six age-classes of fish collected from Pigeon Lake were significantly lower than those of similarly collected fish from Buck Lake (30 specimens for each age class from each lake). It was concluded that growth rates of Pigeon Lake whitefish declined as their abundance increased because the populations of their main predators, northern pike and walleye, had declined. It was thought that competition for food directly affected the size-at-age of the whitefish. It was further speculated that aquatic vegetation removal by cottage owners reduced predator populations. No significant improvement in the size-at-age of lake whitefish has occurred since that time (Buchwald 1988).

Between 1968/69 and 1987/88, the average annual commercial harvests were 89 844 kg of lake whitefish, 54 kg of walleye (cap-

tured in 5 years only) and 3 463 kg of northern pike. Burbot and white suckers are a small part of the commercial catch. The yield of northern pike has increased considerably since 1974/75 and walleye have been present in the catch since 1983/84. The commercial fishery is prohibited in waters within 800 m of the lakeshore to protect northern pike, and from the northwest corner of the lake to reduce conflict with the popular winter sport fishery (Alta. For. Ld. Wild. n.d.; Buchwald 1988). The Indian domestic fishery is fairly active on Pigeon Lake. In 1987/88 there were 33 domestic licences issued, but there are no catch statistics available (Stenton 1989).

The winter recreational fishery has become very popular since the 1960s (Alta. For. Ld. Wild. n.d.). In 1972/73, 9 244 kg of lake whitefish were caught by anglers between January and April, a catch rate of 0.50 fish/angler-hour. In 1973/74, 4 940 kg were caught from December to April, a catch rate of 0.34 fish/angler-hour. Lake whitefish accounted for over 95% of the total number of fish caught. The most popular location for angling was the north end near Gilwood Beach (Kraft and Shirvell 1975).

Wildlife

Pigeon Lake does not provide good waterfowl habitat because shallow, marshy areas are scarce, but the lake is important as a staging area during fall migration (Hardy Assoc. (1978) Ltd. 1983). Nesting colonies of gulls and terns have been reported; a Great Blue Heron colony in Pigeon Lake Provincial Park contained 16 active nests in 1987 (Buchwald 1988).

L. Hart Buckland-Nicks and P.A. Mitchell

References

Alberta Environment. n.d.[a]. Devel. Op. Div. Unpubl. data, Edmonton.
——. n.d.[b]. Envir. Assess. Div., Envir. Qlty. Monit. Br. Unpubl. data, Edmonton.
——. n.d.[c]. Tech. Serv. Div., Hydrol. Br. Unpubl. data, Edmonton.
——. n.d.[d]. Tech. Serv. Div., Surv. Br. Unpubl. data, Edmonton.
——. 1982. Pigeon Lake regulation feasibility study. Plan. Div., Edmonton.
——. 1989. Pigeon Lake. Envir. Assess. Div., Envir. Qlty. Monit. Br., Edmonton.
Alberta Forestry, Lands and Wildlife. n.d. Fish Wild. Div. Unpubl. data, Edmonton.
——. 1987. A summary of Alberta's natural areas reserved and established. Pub. Ld. Div., Ld. Mgt. Devel. Br. Unpubl. rep., Edmonton.
——. 1988. Boating in Alberta. Fish Wild. Div., Edmonton.
——. 1989. Guide to sportfishing. Fish Wild. Div., Edmonton.
Alberta Recreation and Parks. n.d. Parks Div. Unpubl. data, Edmonton.
Alberta Research Council. 1972. Geological map of Alberta. Nat. Resour. Div., Alta. Geol. Surv., Edmonton.
Battle River Regional Planning Commission. 1985. The Pigeon Lake management plan. Battle R. Reg. Plan. Commis., Wetaskiwin.
Bidgood, B.F. 1972. Divergent growth in lake whitefish populations from two eutrophic Alberta lakes. PhD thesis. Univ. Alta., Edmonton.
Bowser, W.E., R.L. Erdman, F.A. Wyatt and J.D. Newton. 1947. Soil survey of Peace Hills sheet. Alta. Soil Surv. Rep. No. 14, Univ. Alta. Bull. No. 48. Univ. Alta., Edmonton.
Bowser, W.E., A.A. Kjearsgaard, T.W. Peters and R.E. Wells. 1962. Soil survey of the Edmonton sheet (83–H). Alta. Soil Surv. Rep. No. 21, Univ. Alta. Bull. No. SS–4, Agric. Can., Res. Counc. Alta. Univ. Alta., Edmonton.
Buchwald, V. 1988. Alta. For. Ld. Wild., Fish Wild. Div., Red Deer. Pers. comm.
Canada Department of Regional Economic Expansion. 1972. Canada land inventory, soil capability for agriculture: Wabamun Lake 83G. Catalogue No. RE64/2–83G. Information Can., Ottawa.
County of Wetaskiwin. 1988. County official. Pers. comm.
Danchuk, K. 1988. Alta. Transp., Op. Br., Edmonton. Pers. comm.
Energy, Mines and Resources Canada. 1974, 1975. National topographic series 1:50 000 83A/13 (1974), 83G/1 (1974), 83H/4 (1974), 83B/16 (1975). Surv. Map. Br., Ottawa.
Environment Canada. 1972–1987. Surface water data. Prep. by Inland Waters Directorate. Water Surv. Can., Water Resour. Br., Ottawa.
——. 1982. Canadian climate normals, Vol. 7: Bright sunshine (1951–1980). Prep. by Atm. Envir. Serv. Supply Serv. Can., Ottawa.
Falun Historical Society. 1974. Freeway west. The Falun Hist. Soc., Falun.
Four Bands Administration. 1988. Hobbema. Pers. comm.
Haag, R. and L. Noton. 1981. Pigeon Lake macrophyte and littoral sediment survey. Prep. for Alta. Envir., Plan. Div., Edmonton.
Hardy Associates (1978) Ltd. 1983. Pigeon Lake water quality study. Battle R. Reg. Plan. Commis., Wetaskiwin.
Holmgren, E.J. and P.M. Holmgren. 1976. Over 2000 place names of Alberta. 3rd ed. West. Producer Prairie Books, Saskatoon.

Kraft, M.E. and C.S. Shirvell. 1975. The sportfishery harvest of lake whitefish from Pigeon lake during the winters of 1972–73 and 1973–74. Alta. Rec. Parks Wild., Fish Wild. Div., Edmonton.

Lindsay, J.D., W. Odynsky, J.W. Peters and W.E. Bowser. 1968. Soil survey of the Buck Lake (NE 83B) and Wabamun Lake (E1/2 83G) areas. Alta. Soil Surv. Rep. No. 24, Univ. Alta. Bull. No. SS–7, Alta. Res. Counc. Rep. No. 87. Univ. Alta., Edmonton.

Miller, R.B. 1947. The effects of different intensities of fishing on the whitefish populations of two Alberta lakes. J. Wild. Mgt. 2:289–301.

——— . 1956. The collapse and recovery of a small whitefish fishery. J. Fish. Res. Bd. Can. 13:135–146.

Millet and District Historical Society. 1978. Tails and trails of Millet, Vol. 1. Millet Dist. Hist. Soc., Millet.

Mitchell, P.A. 1982. Evaluation of the "septic snooper" on Wabamun and Pigeon lakes. Alta. Envir., Poll. Contr. Div., Water Qlty. Contr Br., Edmonton.

Nelson, L.R. and P.A. Mitchell. 1988. Volunteer citizen's lake monitoring program (1988)—Lac Ste. Anne and Pigeon Lake. Alta. Envir., Envir. Assess. Div., Envir. Qlty. Monit. Br., Edmonton.

Pigeon Lake Study Group. 1975. The Pigeon Lake study. Edm. Reg. Plan. Commis., Edmonton and Battle R. Reg. Plan. Commis., Wetaskiwin.

Pinkoski, K. 1988. Alberta Agric., Leduc. Pers. comm.

Stenton, E. 1989. Alta. For. Ld. Wild., Fish Wild. Div., Edmonton. Pers. comm.

Strong, W.L. and K.R. Leggat. 1981. Ecoregions of Alberta. Alta. En. Nat. Resour., Resour. Eval. Plan. Div., Edmonton.

Warburg and District Historical Society. 1977. Golden memories. Warburg Dist. Hist. Soc., Warburg.

Wilson, K. 1988. Alta. Rec. Parks, Parks Div., Edmonton. Pers. comm.

DILLBERRY LAKE

Alberta Tourism

MAP SHEETS: 73C/12, 73D/9
LOCATION: Tp41, 42 R28 W3
Tp41, 42 R1 W4
LAT/LONG: 52°35'N 110°00'W

D illberry Lake is a small lake set in rolling aspen parkland on the Alberta-Saskatchewan border. It is situated in the Municipal District of Wainwright, approximately 80 km southeast of the town of Wainwright and 80 km south of the city of Lloydminster. The closest population centre is the village of Chauvin, 20 km northeast of the lake. To travel to Dillberry Lake from Lloydminster, take Highway 17 south to Dillberry Lake Provincial Park, which borders on the Alberta side of the lake (Fig. 1).

The origin of the lake's name has not been documented. Before Europeans arrived, the area surrounding the lake was inhabited by Cree, Blackfoot, Sarcee and Assiniboine Indians. Anthony Henday, the first European to explore Alberta, entered the province in 1754 at a point about 40 km north of Dillberry Lake. Settlers arrived in the region about 1909 and grazing leases were issued, but the land that later became Dillberry Lake Provincial Park was never homesteaded. By 1930, the lake had become a popular recreational area, and in 1932, land was reserved for the park. Cottages were built on the western shore of the lake, and a subdivision was surveyed in 1933. The park was formally established in 1957 and expanded in 1965. By the early 1970s, there were 37 cottages near the lake within the park boundary (Alta. Rec. Parks n.d.). No further development was allowed until late 1988, when leases were offered for several existing lots (Loomis 1988).

Dillberry Lake Provincial Park encompasses all of the Alberta side of Dillberry Lake, parts of Killarney and Leane lakes, and most of Long Lake (Fig. 1). All of the recreational facilities within the park are located adjacent to Dillberry Lake (Fig. 2). There are 235 campsites, showers, sewage disposal facilities, playgrounds, a concession, a picnic area, swimming and beach areas, a boat launch and walking trails. Points of interest in the park include unique wind-blown sand dunes, vegetation characteristic of both prairie and parkland, and at least 139 species of birds (Finlay and Finlay 1987). Fishing, power boating, water skiing, canoeing, sailing, observing wildlife, cross-country skiing and swimming are some of the activities available to park visitors. Over most of the lake there are no boating restrictions, but in posted areas such as designated swimming areas, all boats are prohibited, and in other posted areas, motor boats are subject to a maximum speed of 12 km/hour (Alta. For. Ld. Wild. 1988).

Dillberry lake is shallow and has clear, fresh water with low concentrations of algae even in midsummer. Aquatic vegetation grows abundantly in the shallow southern bay and in a narrow fringe along parts of the shoreline. The lake is regularly stocked with rainbow trout, which, along with yellow perch, support a popular sport fishery. Fishing for bait fish and the use of bait fish are not allowed in Dillberry Lake (Alta. For. Ld. Wild. 1989).

Drainage Basin Characteristics

Although Dillberry Lake has a small drainage basin of only 12 km², the drainage basin is almost 15 times the size of the lake (Tables 1, 2). Most of the watershed lies within Saskatchewan and water drains into the lake primarily from the southeast (Fig. 1). There is no defined inlet or outlet, so water enters as diffuse runoff, precipitation and, probably, groundwater.

The land in the watershed is flat to moderately rolling, with low local relief provided by kame hills and kettle hole depressions. A kame is a mound of stratified drift deposited by glacial meltwater.

Table 1. Characteristics of Dillberry Lake drainage basin.

area (excluding lake) (km²)[a]	11.8
soil[b]	Black and Dark Brown Chernozemics
bedrock geology[c]	Belly River Formation (Upper Cretaceous): sandstone, siltstone, mudstone, ironstone beds; nonmarine
terrain[d]	flat to moderately rolling
ecoregion[b]	Groveland Subregion of Aspen Parkland
dominant vegetation[b]	rough fescue, trembling aspen
mean annual water inflow (m³)[a, e]	0.171 x 10⁶
mean annual sunshine (h)[f]	2 490

NOTE: [e]excluding groundwater inflow
SOURCES: [a]Alta. Envir. n.d.[b]; [b]Strong and Leggat 1981; [c]Alta. Res. Counc. 1972; [d]Noton 1988; [f]Envir. Can. 1982

Table 2. Characteristics of Dillberry Lake.

elevation (m)[a, b]	619.88
surface area (km²)[a, b]	0.80
volume (m³)[a, b]	2.240 x 10⁶
maximum depth (m)[a, b]	10.7
mean depth (m)[a, b]	2.8
shoreline length (km)[c]	5.2
mean annual lake evaporation (mm)[d]	637
mean annual precipitation (mm)[d]	422
mean residence time (yr)[d, e]	>100
control structure	none

NOTES: [a]on date of sounding: 25 June 1971; [e]excluding groundwater inflow
SOURCES: [b]Alta. Envir. n.d.[c]; [c]Andriuk and Nordstrom 1978; [d]Alta. Envir. n.d.[b]

Surficial deposits are primarily sand, silt and clay. The soils, which are nonsaline, sandy, low in organic matter, and well-drained to rapidly drained, are easily eroded by wind and water (Renew. Resour. Consult. Serv. Ltd. 1974[a]).

The drainage basin is part of the Groveland Subregion of the Aspen Parkland Ecoregion (Strong and Leggat 1981). The vegetation typically consists of expanses of prairie grasses interspersed with groves of trembling aspen. Sand dune complexes are present, as well. Trembling aspen usually grows on well-drained moister sites such as north-facing slopes, seepage areas and creek banks, whereas balsam poplar usually grows on poorly drained soils that border ponds and lakes. Rough fescue grassland and low shrub communities cover well-drained south-facing slopes. Although rough fescue is the dominant grass species, its abundance has been reduced by intensive grazing; this has permitted secondary species to increase in importance (Renew. Resour. Consult. Serv. 1974[a]). The Dillberry Lake area is one of the few locations in Alberta where poison ivy is found. It grows profusely in several areas, including the northwest side of the lake (Finlay and Finlay 1987).

Sand dune communities differ from those growing on other soils in the area (Renew. Resour. Consult. Serv. 1974[a]). In areas that are eroding actively, vegetative cover is sparse. Sand flats and stabilized depressions, on the other hand, are covered by herbaceous species and low shrubs such as creeping juniper and common bearberry. Dune slopes that face north and east are stabilized by a forest cover of trembling aspen that often is severely stunted, and have an understory dominated by choke cherry and saskatoon. Dune crests and south-facing slopes are dominated by grasses, and also support prickly pear cacti.

In Alberta, most of the Dillberry Lake watershed lies within the provincial park. A large area is used for recreational purposes such as camping, day use and cottages. On the Saskatchewan side, land is used extensively for cattle grazing, and cattle use the lake for water.

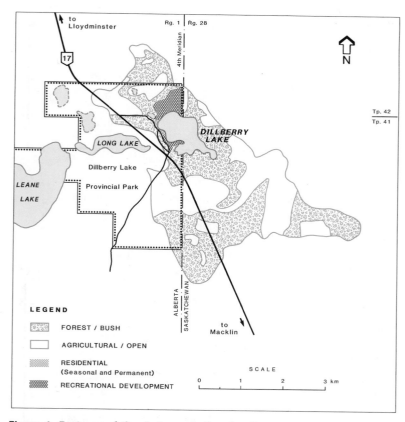

Figure 1. Features of the drainage basin of Dillberry Lake.
SOURCES: Alta. Envir. n.d.[b]; En. Mines Resour. Can. 1976; 1978. Updated with 1987 aerial photos.

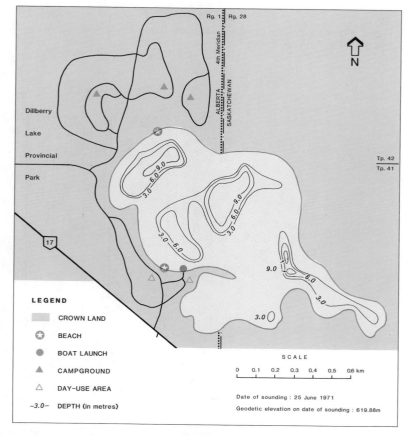

Figure 2. Bathymetry and shoreline features of Dillberry Lake.
BATHYMETRY SOURCE: Alta. Envir. n.d.[c].

Lake Basin Characteristics

Dillberry Lake has a small surface area of only 0.8 km² (Table 2). The lake bottom is irregular: most of it is less than 3-m deep but there are four areas with maximum depths of 6 to 10.7 m (Fig. 2). Because there is no surface outlet, the residence time of water in the lake is very long (Table 2).

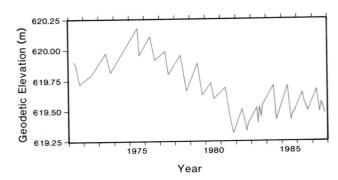

Figure 3. Water level of Dillberry Lake, 1971 to 1987.
SOURCE: Alta. Envir. n.d.[c].

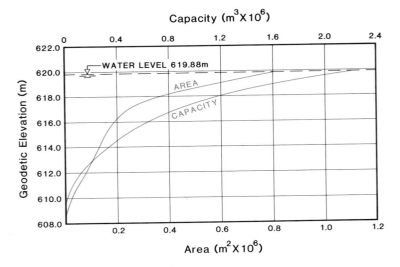

Figure 4. Area/capacity curve for Dillberry Lake.
SOURCE: Alta. Envir. n.d.[c].

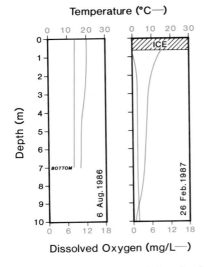

Figure 5. Temperature and dissolved oxygen in Dillberry Lake, 1986 and 1987.
SOURCE: Alta. Envir. n.d.[a].

The elevation of Dillberry Lake has been monitored since 1971 (Fig. 3). The difference between the historic maximum (620.18 m, recorded in 1975) and minimum (619.31 m, recorded in 1981) values is 0.87 m. During the 1980s, lake levels have generally been lower than those recorded during the 1970s. In unusually dry years, only the deeper parts of the lake contain water (Andriuk and Nordstrom 1978). Changes in the lake's area and capacity with fluctuations in water level are illustrated in Figure 4.

Water Quality

The water quality in Dillberry Lake has been monitored jointly by Alberta Environment and Alberta Recreation and Parks since 1984.

Samples were taken approximately monthly during the open-water season and once each winter (Alta. Envir. n.d.[a]). Dillberry Lake has fresh water, whereas most other lakes nearby are saline. The water is well-buffered and the dominant ions are magnesium, calcium and bicarbonate (Table 3). The chemical composition of the lake water is influenced by groundwater and diffuse runoff. When groundwater in the area of the lake was analysed in 1974, the major groundwater source to the lake was identified as a calcium-bicarbonate type from shallow drift aquifers (Renew. Resour. Consult. Serv. Ltd. 1974[a]).

Dillberry Lake is typical of shallow water bodies: it is easily mixed by wind and rarely stratifies during summer. Levels of dissolved oxygen were high throughout the water column in August 1986 (Fig. 5) and August 1985. During winter, dissolved oxygen decreases gradually with depth. In February 1987, the concentration decreased from 8 mg/L immediately under the ice to 1 mg/L at a depth of 10 m. The concentration of dissolved oxygen throughout most of the water column in 1987 was sufficient to overwinter fish. Dillberry Lake has been stocked with rainbow trout since 1955 without any evidence of winterkill.

Dillberry Lake is oligotrophic—chlorophyll *a* levels are low and transparency is high (Table 4). During the period from 1984 to 1985, the highest chlorophyll *a* concentration recorded was 5.8 µg/L in September 1984 (Fig. 6). It is typical of lakes with relatively low nutrient levels that transparency and concentrations of total phosphorus and chlorophyll *a* vary little over the summer. Between May and October each year from 1984 to 1988, chlorophyll values in Dillberry Lake varied by only 2 to 3 µg/L and total phosphorus concentrations varied by 6 µg/L or less. As well, there was little difference in average chlorophyll and phosphorus values between years. Variations in Secchi transparency over the open-water season can sometimes be caused by wind activity disturbing the bottom sediments. For example, the shallow Secchi depth recorded on 9 August 1984 (Fig. 6) occurred after a storm during the previous night mixed sediment into the overlying water. Over the period of record, the average Secchi depth for the open-water season ranged from a minimum of 3.3 m in 1988 to a maximum of 4.7 m in 1985. The loading of total phosphorus to Dillberry Lake has not been estimated, but possible external sources of phosphorus include cattle, sewage from cottages and camps, land clearing and shoreline erosion.

Biological Characteristics

Plants

The phytoplankton community was sampled for Alberta Recreation and Parks on 13 August and 16 July in 1974 (Renew. Resour. Consult. Serv. Ltd. 1974[b]). Vertical net hauls were taken in July and unconcentrated surface samples were taken in August. In the later sample, unidentified species of very small plankton were most numerous, and cryptomonads (*Rhodomonas* sp.) and chlorophytes (*Coelastrum* sp.) were secondary in importance.

Emergent macrophytes were studied briefly by Fish and Wildlife Division in 1955 and 1965 (Paetz 1955; Hunt 1965). Emergent macrophytes grew densely in the shallow bay at the southern end of the lake. Otherwise, they were limited to areas off the points of land on the northern and southern shores and to a narrow band around part of the lake. The littoral zone has a sandy bottom that discourages the growth of rooted aquatic plants in most areas. Submergent species were not examined in the older studies, but observations made in 1988 indicated that they generally were not abundant (Noton 1988).

Invertebrates

Recent data on the invertebrate community are not available. Fish and Wildlife Division recorded observations made during June 1955 and July 1965 (Paetz 1955; Hunt 1965). As well, in July 1974, two vertical net hauls of zooplankton were taken at two depths (Renew. Resour. Consult. Serv. Ltd. 1974[b]). The greatest numbers of organisms per cubic metre (2 459) in 1974 were found at a depth of 8.5 m. Calanoid copepods were most abundant; they accounted for

Table 3. Major ions and related water quality variables for Dillberry Lake. Average concentrations in mg/L; pH in pH units. Composite samples from the euphotic zone collected 3 times from 10 June to 08 Oct. 1984, on 27 May and 16 July 1985, and on 27 May and 28 July 1986. S.E. = standard error.

	Mean	S.E.
pH (range)	8.1–8.7[a]	—
total alkalinity (CaCO$_3$)	181	1.0
specific conductivity (μS/cm)	337	2.7
total dissolved solids (calculated)	178	1.4
total hardness (CaCO$_3$)	149	2.7
HCO$_3$	205	2.4
CO$_3$	<8	—
Mg	23	0.5
Na	13	0.6
K	4	0.1
Cl	2	0.3
SO$_4$	<5	—
Ca	22	0.8

NOTE: [a]n = 2, 15 Aug. 1985 and 06 Aug. 1986
SOURCE: Alta. Envir. n.d.[a], Naquadat station 01AL05GA3000

Table 4. Nutrient, chlorophyll _a_ and Secchi depth data for Dillberry Lake. Average concentrations in μg/L. Composite samples from the euphotic zone collected 5 times from 10 June to 08 Oct. 1984 and 4 times from 12 May to 25 Aug. 1986. S.E. = standard error.

	1984		1986	
	Mean	S.E.	Mean	S.E.
total phosphorus	16	0.7	14[a]	1.5
chlorophyll _a_	3.6	0.58	3.2	0.70
Secchi depth (m)	3.7	0.42	4.6	0.38

NOTE: [a]n = 3
SOURCE: Alta. Envir. n.d.[a], Naquadat station 01AL05GA3000

75% of the total numbers at 1.7 m and 85% at 8.5 m. Cyclopoid copepods were not present in the shallower sample and cladocerans were of secondary importance in both samples. During the same study, the number of benthic invertebrates in two Ekman dredge samples taken at 1.7–m and 8.5–m depths was recorded. Scuds (Amphipoda) and midge larvae (Chironomidae) were most abundant at the shallower depth, whereas clams (Pelecypoda) were most abundant in the deeper sample.

Fish

Yellow perch, rainbow trout and Iowa darter inhabit Dillberry Lake. Rainbow trout is an introduced species that was planted first in August 1955 (Paetz 1955). There are no suitable spawning areas in the lake, so trout are planted on a regular basis. From 1981 to 1987, the lake was stocked 7 times with an average of 30 000 10–cm–long rainbow trout (Alta. En. Nat. Resour. 1981–1985; Alta. For. Ld. Wild. 1986; 1987). The lake is managed for recreational fishing, and is popular with local anglers. Fishing intensity, which is moderate, is greatest in winter when trout stocked the previous summer have grown to a size suitable for eating (Walker 1988). There are no commercial or domestic fisheries on the lake.

Wildlife

Dillberry Lake itself is not used extensively by waterfowl, but the drainage basin provides a varied selection of habitats that range from aquatic to terrestrial and arid prairie to forest. At least 139 bird species have been recorded in Dillberry Lake Provincial Park. The large mud flats on nearby alkaline Killarney lake are used by migrat-

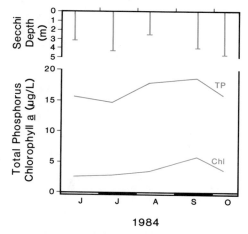

Figure 6. Total phosphorus, chlorophyll _a_ and Secchi depth in Dillberry Lake, 1984.
SOURCE: Alta. Envir. n.d.[a].

ing shorebirds in fall. Leane and Long lakes (Fig. 1) provide habitat for nesting waterfowl and marsh birds such as Eared Grebes, Common Loons, Yellow-headed Blackbirds and Long-billed Marsh Wrens, as well as prairie grassland species such as Sprague's Pipit and Horned Lark. Great Blue Herons from a colony at Freshwater Lake to the northeast come to the park to feed, and Sharp-tailed Grouse use several areas in, or adjacent to, the park as dancing grounds (Finlay and Finlay 1987).

Within the park, 21 species of mammals have been reported. They include white-tailed jackrabbit and long-tailed weasels, Franklin's ground squirrels, and mule and white-tailed deer. Six species of amphibians and reptiles are found, including chorus and northern leopard frogs, Canadian toads and garter snakes (Finlay and Finlay 1987).

M.E. Bradford

References

Alberta Energy and Natural Resources. 1981–1985. Fish planting list. Fish Wild. Div., Edmonton.

Alberta Environment. n.d.[a]. Envir. Assess. Div., Envir. Qlty. Monit. Br. Unpubl. data, Edmonton.

———. n.d.[b]. Tech. Serv. Div., Hydrol. Br. Unpubl. data, Edmonton.

———. n.d.[c]. Tech. Serv. Div., Surv. Br. Unpubl. data, Edmonton.

Alberta Forestry, Lands and Wildlife. 1986, 1987. Fish planting list. Fish Wild. Div., Edmonton.

———. 1988. Boating in Alberta. Fish Wild. Div., Edmonton.

———. 1989. Guide to sportfishing. Fish Wild. Div., Edmonton.

Alberta Recreation and Parks. n.d. Parks Div. Unpubl. data, Edmonton.

Alberta Research Council. 1972. Geological map of Alberta. Nat. Resour. Div., Alta. Geol. Surv., Edmonton.

Andriuk, C. and W. Nordstrom. 1978. Discussion on the water quality situation at Dillberry Lake in east central Alberta, 1978. Alta. Rec. Parks Wild., Parks Plan. Design Br. Unpubl. rep., Edmonton.

Energy, Mines and Resources Canada. 1976, 1978. National topographic series 1:50 000 73C/12 (1976), 73D/9 (1978). Surv. Map. Br., Ottawa.

Environment Canada. 1982. Canadian climate normals, Vol. 7: Bright sunshine (1951–1980). Prep. by Atm. Envir. Serv. Supply Serv. Can., Ottawa.

Finlay, J. and C. Finlay. 1987. Parks in Alberta: A guide to peaks, ponds, parklands & prairies. Hurtig Publ., Edmonton.

Hunt, C. 1965. Lake survey report. Alta. Ld. For., Fish. Wild. Div. Unpubl. rep., Edmonton.

Loomis, S. 1988. Alta. Rec. Parks, Prog. Devel. Br., Edmonton. Pers. comm.

Noton, L. 1988. Alta. Envir., Envir. Assess. Div., Envir. Qlty. Monit. Br., Edmonton. Pers. comm.

Paetz, M.J. 1955. Report on Dillberry Lake. Alta. Ld. For., Fish Wild. Div. Unpubl. rep., Edmonton.

Renewable Resources Consulting Services Ltd. 1974[a]. Preliminary report: Dillberry Lake resource inventory and analysis. Prep. for Alta. Rec. Parks, Parks Div., Edmonton.

———. 1974[b]. Dillberry Lake resource inventory and analysis. Prep. for Alta. Rec. Parks, Parks Div., Edmonton.

Strong, W.L. and K.R. Leggat. 1981. Ecoregions of Alberta. Alta. En. Nat. Resour., Resour. Eval. Plan. Div., Edmonton.

Walker, G. 1988. Alta. For. Ld. Wild., Fish Wild. Div., St. Paul. Pers. comm.

SOUTH SASKATCHEWAN REGION

The drainage basins of the South Saskatchewan River and the Milk River occupy slightly more than the southern fifth of the povince—a glorious area of jagged mountains, glistening glaciers, blue lakes and forested foothills in the west, and an endless expanse of golden grain and arid grasslands in the east. The South Saskatchewan River originates among the peaks of the continental divide along Alberta's western edge; the Milk River starts in the foothills just south of the American border. Despite the proximity of their origins, the destinies of these two rivers are very different. The South Saskatchewan River flows eastward across the prairie to join the North Saskatchewan River in Saskatchewan. From here the Saskatchewan River continues east to Lake Winnipeg which is drained by the Nelson River flowing north to enter Hudson Bay. The Milk River also flows eastward through the arid plains of southern Alberta, but then it bends south to join the Missouri River in Montana, which then joins the Mississippi River to roll south to the Gulf of Mexico.

South Saskatchewan River Basin

The South Saskatchewan River has three major tributaries: the Red Deer River, which originates just east of Lake Louise ski area in Banff National Park; the Bow River, which originates on Bow Glacier north of Lake Louise; and the Oldman River, which originates in the mountains west of Pincher Creek. The river formed by the confluence of the Bow and Oldman is called the South Saskatchewan River; the Red Deer River joins it just east of the Saskatchewan border. The combined area that these four rivers drain is the South Saskatchewan River Basin and includes about one-fifth of Alberta. Approximately 41% of this area drains to the Red Deer River, 21% to the Bow, 22% to the Oldman, and 16% to the South Saskatchewan.

Population and Geography

The population density in the South Saskatchewan Basin is greater than that of most of Alberta. As of 1988, over a million people, or 46% of Alberta's population, lived in the basin; 87% of them in a 100–km–wide corridor between Red Deer, Calgary and Lethbridge. Approximately 2 billion m^3 of water are withdrawn from the rivers in the basin each year. Irrigation accounts for 96% of the water consumption in the basin, municipal use for 3% and industry for 1%. The average annual discharge of the South Saskatchewan River below its confluence with the Red Deer River is approximately 7 billion m^3.

The geography of the South Saskatchewan basin is remarkably varied. In the west, the rocky peaks along the Continental Divide rise as high as 3 600 m above sea level. Snow accumulates and many of the mountains are dotted with glaciers. Coniferous forests cover the valleys and slopes of the mountains and the western region of foothills. The lower foothills are covered with mixed coniferous-deciduous forests and open patches of grassland. The remainder of the basin, south of the Red Deer River and east of the mountains, is prairie grassland. The flat terrain, rich soil, and long frost-free growing season was the major attraction for settlers coming to the area at the turn of the century. Most of the prairie is now extensively cultivated for grain crops.

There is great variation in the amount of precipitation that falls in the basin. In an average year, the mountains and foothills receive

SOUTH SASKATCHEWAN AND MILK RIVER BASINS

over 700 mm of precipitation; a large proportion falls as snow. This area has a net moisture surplus, which means precipitation exceeds eaporation and excess water is available for runoff. The western part of the prairie grasslands receives about 520 mm of precipitation. Evaporation exceeds precipitation and the area is very dry with an average moisture deficit of about 170 mm. The eastern part of the basin receives only about 300 mm of precipitation and has a net moisture deficit of 350 mm; this is the driest region in Alberta.

Approximately 75% of the flow in the rivers in the South Saskatchewan Basin comes from mountain snowmelt. About half of the annual flow in the rivers surges through the system in only two months, from mid-May to mid-July. For the rest of the year, natural flows in the rivers can be very low. Given the rich, easily cultivated soils of the prairie and the long, warm growing season, it is easy to understand the attraction the area had for farmers. The limiting factor is water: as rain, as lakes and as flow in the rivers. The obvious solution to the early settlers of southern Alberta was irrigation—not only using the water where and when it was available, but also

storing water that could later be redistributed as needed. The story of settlement in the South Saskatchewan Basin becomes the story of irrigation, of canals, of reservoirs....

Irrigation

The first irrigation project in Alberta was in 1879 when a settler named John Glenn dug a ditch to divert water from Fish Creek to irrigate 6 ha of hay meadow. By 1920, private companies, including the Canadian Pacific Railway, had built extensive canal systems and major reservoirs, including Chestermere Lake, McGregor Lake and Little Bow Lake Reservoir; about 72,000 ha of land in the basin was under irrigation. The spread of irrigation farming slowed under the stress of drought, depression and World War II. However, after the war, the Prairie Farm Rehabilitation Administration (PFRA) of the federal government undertook several major projects including Travers Reservoir; Milk River Ridge Reservoir; St. Mary Reservoir and improvements to its extensive canal system; and Waterton

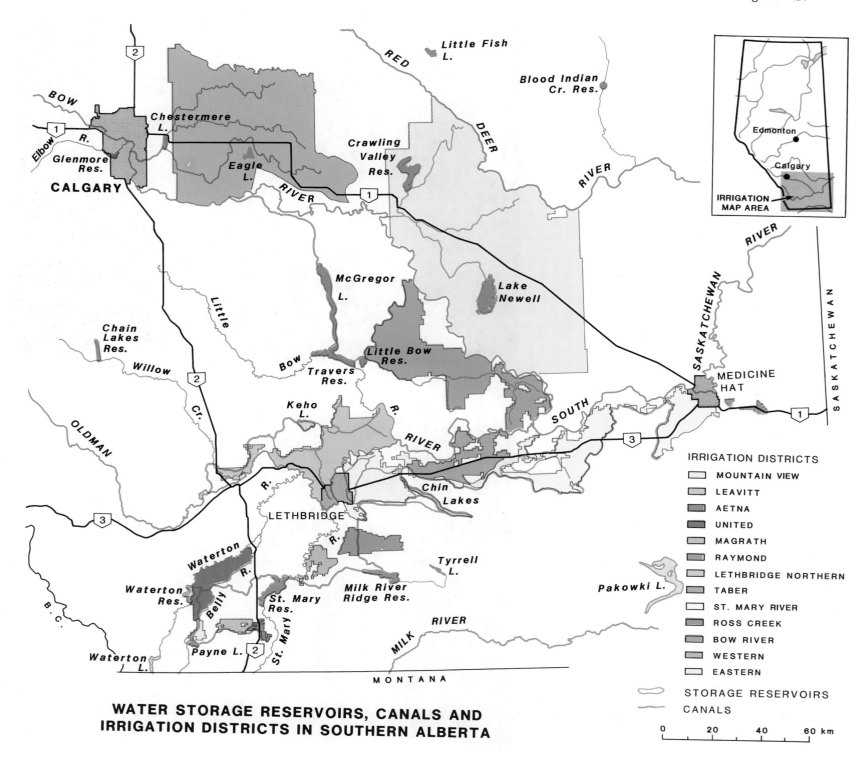

**WATER STORAGE RESERVOIRS, CANALS AND
IRRIGATION DISTRICTS IN SOUTHERN ALBERTA**

Reservoir, which is used to supply water to St. Mary Reservoir. By 1960, the area under irrigation had increased to 240 000 ha. In 173, the federal government turned all its projects over to the provincial government. By 1980, the irrigated area had increased to 336 000 ha. In the 1980s, three new large offstream reservoirs were built; Badger Lake, Crawling Valley and Forty-Mile Coulee. Two new onstream reservoirs were also built or were under construction: Gleniffer Lake, with the primary objective to regulate flow of the Red Deer River; and the Oldman Dam to store water for irrigation. By 1990, the South Saskatchewan Basin contained 8 onstream reservoirs, 17 large offstream reservoirs, 22 smaller reservoirs and approximately 8 000 km of major or local canals.

Ever since 1894, when the Dominion government passed the Northwest Irrigation Act, the Crown (then federal, now provincial) has had control over the development and use of all water in the basin and now all withdrawals must be licenced by the province. Irrigation involves three basic steps: diversion of water from its source, such as a river; conveyance of the water to the farm; and application of the water to the land. Most of the major headworks systems which divert water from a river to a canal are now owned and operated by Alberta Environment, or by an irrigation district, as

is the case with the Eastern Irrigation District (EID) and the United Irrigation District (UID). There are 13 irrigation districts that supply water to 90% of irrigated land in Alberta. The district builds and maintains canals to deliver water to headgates at each farm. Each farmer is responsible for the equipment to distribute the water on their land.

Irrigated land is frequently in a different sub-basin than the source of the water it receives. For example, 28% of the water diverted from the Bow River goes to irrigate farms in the Red Deer basin and 15% goes to farms in the Oldman Basin. Similarly, 35% of the water taken from the Oldman River is used on land that drains directly to the South Saskatchewan River.

Hydroelectric power generation

As the rivers of the South Saskatchewan Basin flow down the mountains, they release tremendous energy. This energy was first harnessed by Calgary Power Ltd. (now TransAlta Utilities Corporation) soon after the turn of the century. The first two plants, one on a canal in Calgary, and one at Horseshoe Falls near Seebe, were "run-of-the-river" plants and did not involve reservoirs. The first dam on

Spray Lakes. Photo by P.A. Mitchell

Glenmore Reservoir. Photo by P.A. Mitchell

Lake Minnewanka was providing power by 1923. In 1929 the Ghost Reservoir was built, and in 1932, Upper Kananaskis Lake was raised ad regulated to feed generators at the Seebe plant on the Bow River. The most rapid expansion of hydroelectric power developments in Alberta occurred soon after the Second World War. The Minnewanka Dam was raised, and the present-day Cascade Power Plant was built by 1942. By 1952 the dam on Lower Kananaskis Lake was raised and generating plants were installed at both Upper and Lower Kananaskis Lakes, Spray Lakes Reservoir with its three generating plants had been built, and Barrier Lake and Bearspaw Reservoir had been created and generators installed.

Today, TransAlta Utilities Corporation owns and operates 11 hydroelectric plants on the Bow River upstream of Calgary. Total generating capability is 325 megawatts, about 10% of the company's total potential and about 5% of the total power generated in Alberta (the other 95% is derived from coal-fired thermal generating plants).

Recreation, Fish and Wildlife

The reservoirs of southern Alberta provide not only irrigation water and hydropower, they also provide a focus for water-based recreation in a hot, dry region where natural lakes are few, and may turn to dry, alkali flats in years of drought. The water quality is generally excellent for recreation in most of this basin's lakes and reservoirs that are presented in the *Atlas*. The clearest water is found in oligotrophic or oligo-mesotrophic lakes. Of the 15 water bodies in these categories in the *Atlas*, 12 are in the South Saskatchewan River Basin. Several of these clear lakes are in the mountains, such as Crowsnest, Upper and Lower Kananaskis Lakes, and Spray Lakes and Chain Lakes reservoirs. The others are reservoirs with rapid flow-through of water derived from mountain run-off, such as Gleniffer Lake and Ghost, Glenmore, Travers, St. Mary, Little Bow Lake and Milk River Ridge reservoirs. Only 19% of the *Atlas* lakes in this basin

Crawling Valley Reservoir. Photo by P.A. Mitchell

Gull Lake. Photo by D. Huet

are eutrophic or hyper-eutrophic, compared to 53% of those considered in the *Atlas* from all over the province. Most of these productive wter bodies are prairie lakes, or reservoirs with little flow-through, for example Pine and Eagle lakes, Lake Newell and Blood Indian Creek Reservoir.

This basin has the warmest climate, the highest population density and the lowest availability of lakes; therefore, almost all water bodies are popular for recreation. There are parks, day-use areas and boat launches on almost every lake and reservoir. Many lakes and reservoirs provide angling for northern pike and yellow perch and many are stocked with trout for sport fishing. In the mountain lakes, such as Kananaskis, Crowsnest, and Spray Lakes Reservoir, the reward for the angler may lie more in the spectacular scenery than in the catch, but stocked rainbow trout grow rapidly in the warm, productive, prairie reservoirs such as Blood Indian Creek and Crawling Valley reservoirs, and Tyrrell Lake. For example, rainbow trout in Tyrrell Lake grow at one of the fastest rates in North America, and Blood Indian Creek Reservoir is regarded by many Albertans as the best trout fishery in the province. Many of the larger reservoirs, such as McGregor Lake and Travers Reservoir, support commercial fisheries for lake whitefish. Beach and cottage activities are popular on the natural lakes in the northern part of the basin—Gull, Sylvan, Buffalo and Pine. Sailing is very popular on Glenmore Reservoir and Chestermere Lake; windsurfing and iceboating are favourite activities on Ghost Reservoir.

Alberta reservoirs also provide habitat for wildlife. Migratory waterfowl use them, primarily for staging and resting areas during their long flights north or south. Some waterfowl stay to nest, especially on the islands in Milk River Ridge and Little Bow Lake reservoirs, and Lake Newell. The uncultivated coulees and slopes around the southern irrigation reservoirs are home for white-tailed deer, antelope, upland game birds, songbirds and small mammals.

The South Saskatchewan River Basin plays a vital role in Alberta, providing water to irrigate half a million hectares of land, supplying water for the domestic needs of over one million people, generating electrical power, and providing recreation and sport fishing for Albertans and tourists from the rest of Canada and the world.

The Milk River Basin

The Milk River rises in the foothills of Montana as two major forks, the North Milk River and the south fork of the Milk River. The North Milk River carries water diverted to it from the St. Mary River in Montana and therefore its flow is often surprisingly high during the hot, dry summers of southern Alberta. The south fork carries only natural flow; in summer the volume is occasionally so low that water movement is negligible. The Milk River traverses eastward across the southernmost part of Alberta, then re-enters the United States near the tiny hamlet of Wild Horse. The southern flank of the Cypress Hills is drained by a few streams that cross into the United States before joining the Milk River, which then continues eastward to join the Missouri River, then the Mississippi River which enters the Gulf of Mexico at New Orleans.

The population of the Alberta portion of the Milk River Basin was less than 2 000 in 1988. The town of Milk River and the village of Coutts are the largest population centres.

The basin in Alberta is almost all flat to undulating dry grasslands, cut by the Milk River and indented by dry coulees carved by glacial meltwater. However, the northernmost part of the basin which straddles the Alberta-Saskatchewan border includes a strikingly green, forested surprise—the Cypress Hills. Rising to nearly 1 500 m, this is the highest Canadian land between Labrador and the Rocky Mountains. These hills were never glaciated, the soil is rich and rainfall is adequate to support forests of pine and spruce. As Captain Palliser wrote in his journal in 1859, "These hills are a perfect oasis in the desert we have travelled."

Outside of the Cypress Hills, water is scarce in the Milk River Basin. There are few sloughs and no significant lakes. There is more moisture in Cypress Hills area, but even here there are few lakes, and the only one in the *Atlas*, Reesor, is maintained by flow diverted from nearby Battle Creek.

The Milk River Basin is not an area where water-based recreation abounds. It does, however, present an expanse of vast open spaces, a dramatic canyon, rolling grasslands and spectacular prairie vistas. To visit the basin is to relive the history of the prairies. Standing on a grassy knoll staring into a golden sunset conjures visions of the past: of buffalo, of whisky-traders, of the Northwest Mounted Police, of the incredible isolation and hardships of the early settlers. A sojourn here is not soon forgotten.   J.M. Crosby

BLOOD INDIAN CREEK RESERVOIR

L. Noton

MAP SHEETS: 72M/3, 6
LOCATION: Tp26 R9 W4
LAT/LONG: 51°15'N 111°13'W

Blood Indian Creek Reservoir is a long, narrow impoundment that fills a creek valley in the arid, treeless plains of southeastern Alberta. In an area where one can travel through seemingly endless miles of dry grassland, this small reservoir provides a welcome and delightful oasis. To reach the north end of the reservoir from the town of Hanna, take Highway 9 east for 44 km to the village of Youngstown, then travel south on Secondary Road 884 for 29 km (Fig. 1). An alternate route approaches from the south, via the hamlet of Pollockville and Secondary Road 565. The reservoir is located in Special Area No. 3.

Blood Indian Creek Reservoir was named for the creek it impounds. The origin of the name may be for the Blood Indian tribe that travelled the area (Alta. Cult. Multicult. n.d.), or it may be for a battle between Blood and Blackfoot Indians in which the Bloods were defeated and the creek "flowed with their blood" (Holmgren and Holmgren 1976). In 1957, the Special Areas Board asked the Prairie Farm Rehabilitation Administration to construct a reservoir on Blood Indian Creek to provide water for stock downstream and for future irrigation of small plots adjacent to the creek (Can. Dept. Reg. Econ. Expansion 1978). The reservoir was built by the Prairie Farm Rehabilitation Administration in 1965 and turned over to the Special Areas Board in 1967.

The area around Blood Indian Creek Reservoir is in one of the driest regions in Canada. Precipitation is light and evaporation rates are double those of precipitation. Creeks run only in spring or after unusually heavy rainfall. Lakes are small and sparsely distributed, so any water body is eagerly sought out by local recreationists. However, Blood Indian Creek Reservoir is not only locally important. In 1982, more than half of the 6 500 people who visited the reservoir travelled more than 200 km to it. Once there, visitors stayed longer (2.7 days) than the average visit to the rest of Alberta's provincial parks (1.8 days) (DGK Plan. Assoc. Ltd. 1983). The main attraction is the remarkable rainbow trout fishery managed by Fish and Wildlife Division. Angler success is high and trout up to 1 kg are not uncommon. Fishing for bait fish and the use of bait fish are not permitted (Alta. For. Ld. Wild. 1989).

The Special Areas Board operates a park that surrounds the reservoir. It includes 150 random campsites, 3 boat launches, picnic tables and pump water (Fig. 2). The operation of power boats to tow persons on anything, including water skis and surf boards, is prohibited on the whole lake (Alta. For. Ld. Wild. 1988). Improvements to the park were made in the mid–1980s, including the addition of a small beach, sewage disposal facilities for recreational vehicles, improved roads, fish-cleaning facilities, and hundreds of newly planted trees.

The water is clear and free of algae but aquatic plants impede angling from the shore in some areas. Although Blood Indian Creek Reservoir is best known for its excellent trout fishery, it is also a very pretty place to stay. Visitors can explore an unplowed, arid, short-grass prairie area that is typical of southern Alberta but very different from the foothill and mountain areas that are most often thought of as representative of this province.

Drainage Basin Characteristics

The drainage basin of Blood Indian Creek Reservoir is very large (116 km², Table 1) compared to the size of the reservoir (1.03 km²,

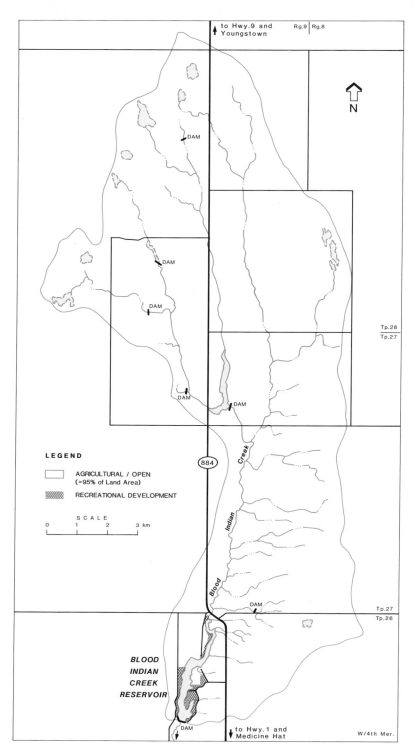

Figure 1. Features of the drainage basin of Blood Indian Creek Reservoir.
SOURCES: Alta. Envir. n.d.[b]; En. Mines Resour. Can. 1975. Updated with 1986 aerial photos.

LEGEND

☐ AGRICULTURAL / OPEN (>95% of Land Area)

▨ RECREATIONAL DEVELOPMENT

SCALE
0 1 2 3 km

Table 1. Characteristics of Blood Indian Creek Reservoir drainage basin.

area (excluding lake) (km²)[a]	116
soil[b]	Brown Solodized Solonetz
bedrock geology[c]	Bearpaw Formation (Upper Cretaceous): shale, thin ironstone and bentonite beds; marine
terrain[b]	undulating to rolling
ecoregion[d]	Short Grass
dominant vegetation[d]	grama grass, spear grass, buckbrush
mean annual sunshine (h)[e]	2 334

SOURCES: [a]Alta. Envir. n.d.[b]; [b]Kjearsgaard 1988; [c]Alta. Res. Counc. 1972; [d]Strong and Leggat 1981; [e]Envir. Can. 1982

Table 2. Characteristics of Blood Indian Creek Reservoir.

control structure[a]	zoned earthfill dam
dam height (m)[a]	15.5
crest length (m)[a]	716
full supply level (FSL) (m)[a, b]	761.39
volume at FSL (m³)[a, b]	6.4 x 10⁶
live storage at FSL (m³)[a, b]	4.80 x 10⁶
surface area at FSL (km²)[a, b]	1.03
maximum drawdown (m)	unknown
mean annual drawdown (m)	unknown
maximum depth at FSL (m)[a, b]	13.3
mean depth at FSL (m)[a, b]	4.6
shoreline length (km)[c]	22.9
lake length at FSL (km)[a]	3.90
lake width at FSL (km)[a]	0.55
mean annual lake evaporation (mm)[d]	727
mean annual precipitation (mm)[d]	354
mean residence time (yr)[d]	24.5
mean annual inflow volume (1985–1988) (m³)[d, e]	0.704 x 10⁶

NOTES: [a]on date of sounding: 21 Aug. 1973; [e]excluding groundwater inflow
SOURCES: [b]Can. Dept. Reg. Econ. Expansion 1978; [c]En. Mines Resour. Can. 1975; [d]Alta. Envir. n.d.[b]

Table 2). It extends north of the reservoir (Fig. 1) and is located within the Short Grass Ecoregion (Strong and Leggat 1981). The drainage area is an undulating to rolling morainal plain. Soils are mostly weakly calcareous, moderately saline Brown Solodized Solonetz (Kjearsgaard 1988). There is an area in the northern portion of the basin where Orthic Brown Chernozemics predominate.

The Short Grass Ecoregion has the lowest precipitation, both summer and winter, and highest evaporation rates in the province (Table 2). Therefore, vegetation must be extremely hardy to withstand aridity as well as very cold winters with sudden chinooks. The natural vegetation is dominated by grama, wheat and spear grasses with buckbrush and wolf willow in coulees and a few trembling aspen, willow and birch in poorly drained areas (Strong and Leggat 1981). One of Alberta's less common species, prickly pear cactus (*Opuntia polycantha*), is present on the dry slopes near the reservoir (DGK Plan. Assoc. Ltd. 1983). Some of the basin has been plowed for grain crop production, but most of the land is pasture or natural grassland. The area surrounding the reservoir is all Crown land (Fig. 2), and most of it has been leased for grazing. There are no population centres in the basin.

Blood Indian Creek supplies almost all of the inflow to the reservoir. There are numerous small impoundments for local stock water supplies upstream of Blood Indian Creek Reservoir (Fig. 1). Almost all of the runoff enters the reservoir in March and April and the creek dries up in most summers. The spring inflow volume is extremely variable; in 1986 it was 0.065 x 10⁶ m³, in 1985 it was 4.01 x 10⁶ m³ (Agric. Can. 1985–1988).

Table 3. Major ions and related water quality variables for Blood Indian Creek Reservoir. Average concentrations in mg/L; pH in pH units. Composite samples from the euphotic zone collected 6 times from 07 June to 19 Oct. 1983. S.E. = standard error.

	Mean	S.E.
pH (range)	8.3–9.0	—
total alkalinity ($CaCO_3$)	334	3.2
specific conductivity (μS/cm)	2 261[a]	41.0
total dissolved solids (calculated)	1 565	35.9
turbidity (NTU)	4	0.6
total hardness ($CaCO_3$)	157	3.7
HCO_3	356	9.9
CO_3	25	3.8
Mg	19	0.9
Na	472	11.9
K	10	0.5
Cl	10	0.5
SO_4	817	22.6
Ca	31	0.5

NOTE: [a]n = 5
SOURCE: Alta. Envir. n.d.[a], Naquadat station 05AL05CK1000

Reservoir Basin Characteristics

Blood Indian Creek Reservoir is a long (3.9 km), narrow (0.5 km) impoundment with several narrow arms that reach into side coulees (Fig. 2). The maximum depth of 13.3 m is located at the south end near the dam. The reservoir was created when the Prairie Farm Rehabilitation Administration built a zoned earthfill dam across the creek in 1965 (Table 2). The dam is equipped with a drop-inlet operating spillway that can pass water at a rate of 18 m³/second. In the left abutment of the dam there is a 30—m—wide emergency spillway. The total flow that can be passed is 85 m³/second when runoff is extremely high (Can. Dept. Reg. Econ. Expansion 1978).

The water level has not been monitored except during the March to June period from 1985 to 1988 (Agric. Can. 1985–1988); changes in the lake's area and capacity, to an elevation of 761.39 m, are shown in Figure 3. Spring runoff is usually adequate to raise the level to near the full supply level (761.40 m). Water is released from the dam only if the full supply level is over-topped or when downstream users need additional water for stock watering. No records are kept of releases, but they usually occur once or twice a year. When water is released, the level of the reservoir drops quickly. For example, water was released from 24 to 29 June 1987 and the reservoir level dropped 0.5 m. (Special Areas Bd. n.d.). No exceptional drawdowns have occurred in the last 15 years (Lowe 1989).

Water Quality

The water quality of Blood Indian Creek Reservoir was studied in 1983 by Alberta Environment (Alta. Envir. n.d.[a]). The reservoir is a well-buffered, moderately saline water body (1 565 mg/L total dissolved solids, Table 3). The dominant ions are sulphate, sodium and bicarbonate.

The reservoir is exposed to strong winds, but since it is deep compared to its area, the water column becomes stratified during summer. Temperature and dissolved oxygen data are available for an area of the reservoir that is only 6—m deep (Fig. 4, 5). Weak thermal stratification was indicated in July 1983, and the reservoir remained stratified until at least mid-August. Dissolved oxygen depletion was evident near the bottom at this relatively shallow site, and was likely more severe at the bottom of deeper areas. Dissolved oxygen concentrations in the upper 6 m were consistently well above the limit for trout throughout the summer. Winter dissolved oxygen concentrations in the upper 2 m have been checked twice by Fish and

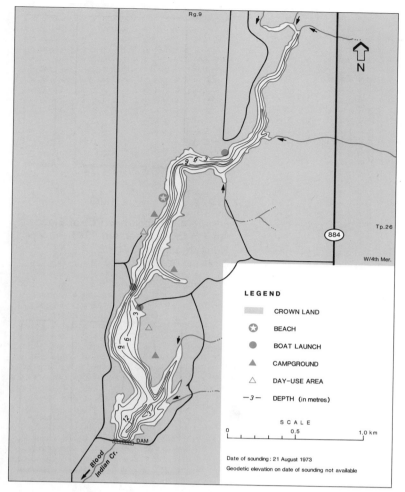

Figure 2. Bathymetry and shoreline features of Blood Indian Creek Reservoir.
BATHYMETRY SOURCE: Alta. Envir. n.d.[c].

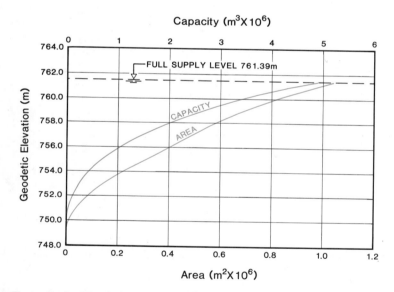

Figure 3. Area/capacity curve for Blood Indian Creek Reservoir.
SOURCE: Can. Dept. Reg. Econ. Expansion 1978.

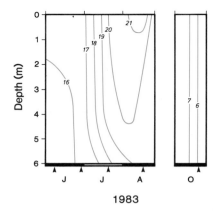

Figure 4. Temperature (°C) of Blood Indian Creek Reservoir, 1983. Arrows indicate sampling dates.
SOURCE: Alta. Envir. n.d.[a].

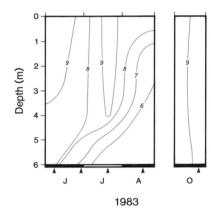

Figure 5. Dissolved oxygen (mg/L) in Blood Indian Creek Reservoir, 1983. Arrows indicate sampling dates.
SOURCE: Alta. Envir. n.d.[a].

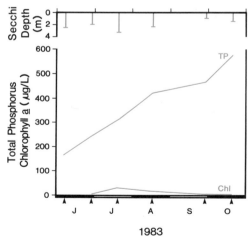

Figure 6. Total phosphorus, chlorophyll *a* and Secchi depth in Blood Indian Creek Reservoir, 1983.
SOURCE: Alta. Envir. n.d.[a].

Table 4. Nutrient, chlorophyll *a* and Secchi depth data for Blood Indian Creek Reservoir. Average concentrations in μg/L. Composite samples from the euphotic zone collected 6 times from 07 June to 19 Oct. 1983. S.E. = standard error.

	Mean	S.E.
total phosphorus	366	61.3
total Kjeldahl nitrogen	1 433	117.9
NO_3 + NO_2–nitrogen	48	20.7
NH_4–nitrogen	97	27.6
chlorophyll *a*	19.8	11.01
Secchi depth (m)	2.1	0.33

SOURCE: Alta. Envir. n.d.[a], Naquadat station 05AL05CK1000

Wildlife Division (Alta. For. Ld. Wild. n.d.). Levels were above 7.0 mg/L in both 1979 and 1980. Winterkill of trout has not been reported for this reservoir (Lowe 1989).

The trophic status of Blood Indian Creek Reservoir is difficult to assess. The total phosphorus concentrations in the euphotic zone are extremely high. In 1983, they had risen to more than 550 μg/L by October (Table 4, Fig. 6). The increase in total phosphorus through the summer is probably due to release of phosphorus from the bottom sediments. The high total phosphorus concentrations indicate the reservoir might be hyper-eutrophic. However, the chlorophyll *a* concentrations are only moderate, indicating a lake at the lower end of the eutrophic range. In 1983, they reached a maximum of 30 μg/L in July. A similar pattern was found in 20 other saline lakes in Alberta, and it was concluded that salinity inhibited the production of algae in lakes with specific conductivity over 1 000 μS/cm (Bierhuizen and Prepas 1985).

Biological Characteristics

Plants

There are no data on species of algae in Blood Indian Creek Reservoir. Bulrushes (*Scirpus* spp.) line the shore in the northern portions of the reservoir (DGK Plan. Assoc. Ltd. 1983). Submergent macrophytes grow abundantly in some areas, especially along the west side and at the north end, and are a nuisance to shore-based anglers (Lowe 1989). There are no data on species of submergent macrophytes in the reservoir.

Invertebrates

There are no data on the invertebrates in Blood Indian Creek Reservoir.

Fish

Blood Indian Creek Reservoir is one of the best lakes for trout fishing in Alberta (Lowe 1989). Rainbow trout were first stocked by Fish and Wildlife Division in 1966, and approximately 130 000 fingerlings have been stocked every year since (Alta. For. Ld. Wild. n.d.). Winterkill does not occur and many of the trout caught are several years old; they do not, however, spawn in the reservoir. Because there are no suckers in the reservoir, there is little competition for food and trout growth rates are rapid. The major prey for trout are amphipods (*Gammarus* sp.); longnose dace and brook stickleback are of lesser importance (DGK Plan. Assoc. Ltd. 1983). Fishing is popular in summer and winter and angler success is high. Ice-fishing huts are allowed to remain on the lake all winter, but permits for them must be obtained from the Special Areas office in Hanna.

In August 1983, the fishery was closed because several trout with skin lesions were found. The lesions were attributed to a bacteria that attacks trout when water temperatures are high. The fish with lesions are edible if they are well cooked, but caution should be used when handling them with bare hands, especially if your hands have cuts or scrapes (Larson 1989). Some trout with lesions were caught in 1984 and 1985, but no occurrences have been reported since (Lowe 1989).

Wildlife

Blood Indian Creek Reservoir is used for nesting by a moderate number of waterfowl, including a small number of Canada Geese. It is fairly important for fall staging; up to 10 000 Canada and Snow geese have been reported in some years (Ducks Unltd. (Can.) n.d.). Shorebirds such as Long-billed Curlews, Hudsonian Godwits and Piping Plovers nest in the area (DGK Plan. Assoc. Ltd. 1983).

The prairie grassland around the reservoir provides habitat for pronghorn antelope, coyotes and Richardson's ground squirrels. Upland game birds such as Sharp-tailed Grouse, Ruffed Grouse and Hungarian Partridges also live in the area. Hunting is not allowed near the reservoir (Alta. For. Ld. Wild. n.d.).

J.M. Crosby

References

Agriculture Canada. 1985–1988. Spring runoff monitoring program: Annual reports. Prairie Farm Rehabilitation Admin., Eng. Serv., Regina, Sask.

Alberta Culture and Multiculturalism. n.d. Hist. Resour. Div., Hist. Sites Serv. Unpubl. data, Edmonton.

Alberta Environment. n.d.[a]. Envir. Assess. Div., Envir. Qlty. Monit. Br. Unpubl. data, Edmonton.

———. n.d.[b]. Tech. Serv. Div., Hydrol. Br. Unpubl. data, Edmonton.

———. n.d.[c]. Tech. Serv. Div., Surv. Br. Unpubl. data, Edmonton.

Alberta Forestry, Lands and Wildlife. n.d. Fish Wild. Div. Unpubl. data, Edmonton.

———. 1988. Boating in Alberta. Fish Wild. Div., Edmonton.

———. 1989. Guide to sportfishing. Fish Wild. Div., Edmonton.

Alberta Research Council. 1972. Geological map of Alberta. Nat. Resour. Div., Alta. Geol. Surv., Edmonton.

Bierhuizen, J.F.H. and E.E. Prepas. 1985. Relationship between nutrients, dominant ions, and phytoplankton standing crop in prairie saline lakes. Can. J. Fish. Aquat. Sci. 42:1588–1594.

Canada Department of Regional Economic Expansion. 1978. Engineering and water management study of community dams—Berry Creek, Blood Indian Creek and Bullpound Creek basins. Prairie Farm Rehabilitation Admin., Calgary.

DGK Planning Associates Ltd. 1983. Blood Indian Reservoir site development study. Prep. for Alta. Envir., Plan. Div., Edmonton.

Ducks Unlimited (Canada). n.d. Unpubl. data, Edmonton.

Energy, Mines and Resources Canada. 1975. National topographic series 1:50 000 72M/3 (1975), 72M/6 (1975). Surv. Map. Br., Ottawa.

Environment Canada. 1982. Canadian climate normals, Vol. 7: Bright sunshine (1951–1980). Prep. by Atm. Envir. Serv. Supply Serv. Can., Ottawa.

Holmgren, E.J. and P.M. Holmgren. 1976. Over 2000 place names of Alberta. 3rd ed. West. Producer Prairie Books, Saskatoon.

Kjearsgaard, A.A. 1988. Reconnaissance soil survey of the Oyen map sheet—72 M. Alta. Inst. Pedol. Rep No. S–76–36, Ld. Resour. Res. Centre Contribution No. 85–56. Agric. Can. Res. Br., Edmonton.

Larson, B. 1989. Alta. For. Ld. Wild., Fish Wild. Div., Edmonton. Pers. comm.

Lowe, D. 1989. Alta. For. Ld. Wild., Fish Wild. Div., Red Deer. Pers. comm.

Special Areas Board. n.d. Unpubl. data, Hanna.

Strong, W.L. and K.R. Leggat. 1981. Ecoregions of Alberta. Alta. En. Nat. Resour., Resour. Eval. Plan. Div., Edmonton.

BUFFALO LAKE

MAP SHEET: 83A
LOCATION: Tp40 R21, 22 W4
LAT/LONG: 52°28'N 112°54'W

Buffalo Lake is a large, shallow lake in central Alberta, 40 km northeast of Red Deer in the counties of Camrose, Stettler and Lacombe (Fig. 1). To reach Buffalo Lake from the town of Lacombe, drive east on Highway 12 for 68 km to the hamlet of Erskine, then turn north on Secondary Road 835 and drive for 15 km to Rochon Sands Provincial Park. Access routes to other recreation areas are shown on Figures 1 and 2.

There are four public recreation areas on Buffalo Lake (Fig. 2). Rochon Sands Provincial Park offers a campground with 69 sites, tap water, a telephone, a boat launch, change houses, a sand beach, picnic shelters, a playground and sewage disposal facilities. The Narrows Recreation Area on the southwest end of the lake is operated by Alberta Recreation and Parks. It offers a 72–site campground, pump water and picnic shelters. Buffalo Lake Recreation Area (previously Boss Hill Park) is on the east end of the lake. This area is also operated by Alberta Recreation and Parks and offers a campground with 25 sites, pump water, a sand beach, change houses, picnic shelters, a playground and a boat launch. Pelican Point Park is on the north shore near the east end of the lake. It is operated by the County of Camrose and offers a 100–site campground, pump water, a sand beach, change houses, a boat launch, a playground and a concession (Alta. Hotel Assoc. 1988).

The lake is naturally divided into four areas (Fig. 2). Main Bay at the east end is the largest and deepest (maximum depth of 6.5 m) and supports most of the recreational activity on the lake. Secondary Bay, to the west of Main Bay, is smaller and so shallow (maximum depth of 2.5 m) that it was possible to drive wagons across it when water levels were extremely low in the 1930s. The Narrows is the channel west of Secondary Bay and is a popular fishing area. Parlby Bay is the small bay west of the Narrows; because it is very shallow (maximum depth of 1.1 m) and densely filled with aquatic plants, it provides excellent waterfowl habitat.

The lake was labelled Buffalo Lake on David Thompson's map of 1814. It was so named for its resemblance to the profile of a buffalo with the legs to the north and the head to the east (Alta. Cult. Multicult. n.d.). Palliser named it Bull Lake on his 1860 map, but Thompson's name is still retained (Holmgren and Holmgren 1976). The trembling aspen and fescue grassland habitat around the lake likely attracted herds of buffalo. The lake was also a favourite Cree and Blackfoot camping area (Lamerton Hist. Soc. 1974). In 1858, Father Lacombe, then a young missionary, travelled for two days in bitter weather to help a group of Blackfoot Indians dying of scarlet fever in their encampment on the east shore of Buffalo Lake. After treating them for 20 days, he too almost died from the fever, but later recovered to become a leading figure in Alberta's history (Lamerton Hist. Soc. 1974). Buffalo Lake Settlement on the southwest side of the lake was one of the earliest settlements in central Alberta. It was established in 1883, well before the mainstream of settlers arrived between 1891 and 1905 (Lamerton Hist. Soc. 1974). The beach within Rochon Sands Provincial Park was a popular picnic spot for the early settlers, who called it "Hannah's Beach". The name of the area was later changed to Rochon Sands, when land owned by Mr. Rochon was subdivided (Finlay and Finlay 1987). The land for the provincial park was set aside in 1933 and 1934, and the park was officially established in 1957 (Alta. Rec. Parks n.d.).

By 1923, 23 cottages had been built on the lake; this remained unchanged until 1951 (Red Deer Reg. Plan. Commis. 1977). By

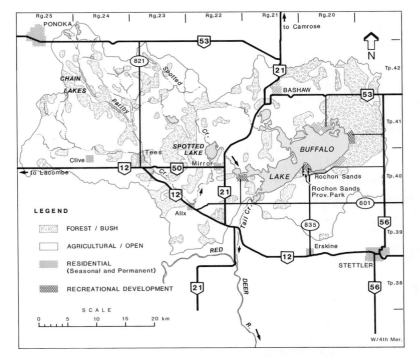

Figure 1. Features of the drainage basin of Buffalo Lake.
SOURCES: Alta. Envir. n.d.[c]; En. Mines Resour. Can. 1970. Updated with 1984 aerial photos.

Table 1. Characteristics of Buffalo Lake drainage basin.

area (excluding lake) (km^2)[a]	1 440
soil[b]	Orthic Black Chernozemic
bedrock geology[c]	Horseshoe Canyon Formation (Upper Cretaceous): sandstone, mudstone, shale; ironstone, scattered coal and bentonite beds; mainly nonmarine
terrain[b]	gently rolling to rolling
ecoregion[d]	Aspen Parkland
dominant vegetation[d]	trembling aspen, rough fescue grassland
mean annual inflow (m^3)[e, f]	23.6 x 10^6
mean annual sunshine (h)[g]	2 125

NOTE: [f]includes groundwater inflow, which has been estimated to be between 6 x 10^6 m^3 (Clare and Ko 1982) and 13 x 10^6 m^3 (Shaw and Prepas 1989[a])
SOURCES: [a]Alta. Envir. n.d.[c]; [b]Bowser et al. 1947; 1951; [c]Alta. Res. Counc. 1972; [d]Strong and Leggat 1981; [e]Alta. Envir. n.d.[b]; [g]Envir. Can. 1982

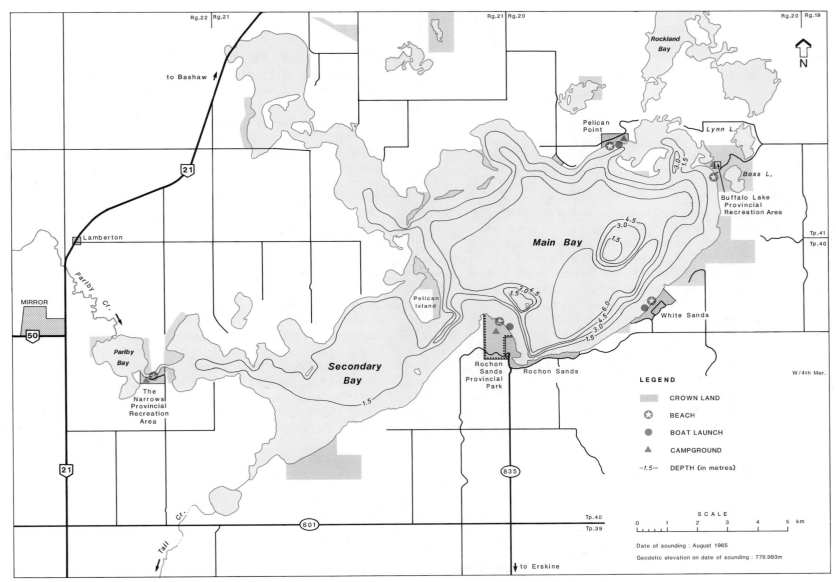

Figure 2. Bathymetry and shoreline features of Buffalo Lake.
BATHYMETRY SOURCE: Alta. Envir. n.d.[d].

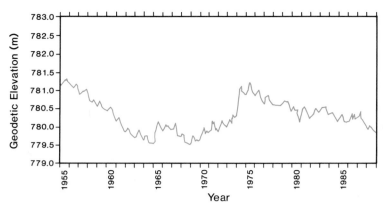

Figure 3. Water level of Buffalo Lake, 1955 to 1988.
SOURCE: Envir. Can. 1955–1988.

Table 2. Characteristics of Buffalo Lake.

elevation (m)[a, b]	779.98
surface area (km²)[a, b]	93.5
volume (m³)[a, b]	248 x 10⁶
maximum depth (m)[a, b]	6.5
mean depth (m)[a, b]	2.8
shoreline length (km)[c]	126
mean annual lake evaporation (mm)[d]	665
mean annual precipitation (mm)[d]	413
mean residence time (yr)[d, e]	>100
control structure	none

NOTES: [a]on date of sounding: 04 Aug. 1965; [e]excluding groundwater inflow
SOURCES: [b]Alta. Envir. n.d.[d]; [c]En. Mines Resour. Can. 1970; [d]Alta. Envir. n.d.[c]

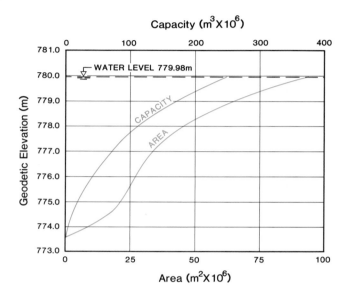

Figure 4. Area/capacity curve for Buffalo Lake.
SOURCE: Alta. Envir. n.d.[d].

1982, there were 650 cottages in 4 subdivisions and 2 summer villages, all located on Main Bay (Fig. 2). Two new subdivisions remained undeveloped as of 1982 (HLA Consult. 1982).

The water in Buffalo Lake is moderately saline. It is generally quite clear, but algae may become conspicuous in late summer, especially in the western half of the lake. Buffalo Lake is popular for boating, swimming and beach activities. All boats are restricted from some posted areas and power vessels are restricted to speeds of 12 km/hour or less in other posted areas of the lake (Alta. For. Ld. Wild. 1988). Northern pike provide a locally important sport fishery. The Narrows (Fig. 2), which is the most popular area for angling, is closed to fishing from late March to late May each year to protect spawning pike. Angling in inflowing Parlby Creek is restricted during the same period (Alta. For. Ld. Wild. 1989). The lake is one of the most important waterfowl breeding and staging areas in Alberta.

Drainage Basin Characteristics

The drainage basin of Buffalo Lake is large (1 440 km²); it consists of a gently rolling glacial till plain that slopes from an elevation of 975 m on the western boundary to 780 m at the lake. Much of the basin, particularly north and east of the lake, is knob and kettle terrain. It formed when large chunks of ice, left in the gravel by the retreating ice sheet, melted and left holes or "kettles". These depressions, which are now filled with water, are pothole lakes, and the surrounding gravel hills are "knobs". These small lakes form pockets of dead storage that do not contribute surface runoff to Buffalo Lake (Bowser et al. 1947; 1951).

The drainage basin lies within the Aspen Parkland Ecoregion; the dominant native vegetation is trembling aspen, wild rose and saska-

toon, with rough fescue grassland on drier, south-facing slopes. Approximately 65% of the basin has been cleared for agriculture. Rich Black Chernozemic soils and adequate precipitation make the western portion of the watershed one of the most productive areas of Alberta for wheat, oat and canola production (Strong and Leggat 1981).

Most of the lakeshore is privately owned; areas of Crown land are shown on Figure 2. The drainage basin includes the town of Bashaw, the villages of Mirror, Alix and Clive and the hamlet of Tees. There is some gas exploration and extraction in the basin.

Lake Basin Characteristics

The surface area of Buffalo Lake is moderate-sized relative to its drainage basin (Tables 1, 2). The lake is 20.5–km long and 8.2–km wide at its widest point. It has an irregular shape, and is divided into two large basins and one small basin (Fig. 2).

Main Bay is the largest basin. It slopes gently to a maximum depth of 6.5 m. The nearshore areas are mostly sand, and there are extensive sand beaches along the south and east sides of the bay. The lake bottom near the north shore is also sandy, but plant growth in protected bays has left some organic debris (Haag and Noton 1981). There are two islands in Main Bay: one large one to the northeast and a tiny one near Rochon Sands Provincial Park that disappears when water levels are high.

Secondary Bay is about one-third the area of Main Bay. The lake bottom slopes very gradually to a maximum depth of 2.5 m. The shoreline along the north side of the bay is sand, with silt increasing from 0% on shore to 60% at a depth of 1.5 m. The lake bottom along the south shore is coarser sand, with fine-textured sediment in sheltered areas (Haag and Noton 1981). Pelican Island, a large, low, sand and gravel island, separates Main Bay from Secondary Bay.

Parlby Bay is the smallest bay. It lies west of Secondary Bay and is joined to it by the Narrows, a 15–m–wide, 1.0–km–long channel. The maximum depth of Parlby Bay is 1.1 m. The sediments are much finer than in the rest of the lake and include a large proportion of clay (Haag and Noton 1981). Aquatic plants grow across the entire bottom of the bay, and motor boat travel is impossible during the summer.

Almost all surface inflow to the lake enters at the west end of Parlby Bay through Parlby Creek (Fig. 2). There are a few intermittent streams around the shore, but the volume they contribute to the lake is negligible (Alta. Envir. 1982; Clare and Ko 1982). In 1985, an Alberta Environment drainage and flood control project to deepen and straighten Parlby Creek was started at the mouth of the creek. By 1989, it had progressed upstream of Spotted Lake. Control structures will allow annual backflooding of hay meadows at the landowners' request and will provide habitat for pike spawning. Other structures at Spotted Lake can be operated to maximize pike spawning habitat and waterfowl brood production without interfering with hay harvesting (Alta. Envir. 1985).

Groundwater inflow to Buffalo Lake is significant in maintaining the water balance. Areas of artesian upwelling of groundwater are

Table 3. Major ions and related water quality variables for Buffalo Lake. Average concentrations in mg/L; pH in pH units. Composite samples from the euphotic zone collected 7 times from 13 May to 15 Aug. 1983. S.E. = standard error.

	Main Bay		Secondary Bay		Parlby Bay	
	Mean	S.E.	Mean	S.E.	Mean	S.E.
pH (range)	8.9–9.3	—	8.9–9.2	—	8.2–9.3	—
total alkalinity (CaCO$_3$)	979	25.8	846	32.0	292	9.6
specific conductivity (μS/cm)	2 357	20.0	2 009	61.9	613	22.4
total dissolved solids (calculated)	1 595	23.8	1 346[a]	62.3	371	10.6
colour (Pt)[b]	12	0.5	34	3.8	—	—
turbidity (NTU)	4	0.9	8	0.8	4	1.1
total hardness (CaCO$_3$)	240	25.4	221	21.4	180	15.3
HCO$_3$	922	20.1	818	25.7	294	25.8
CO$_3$	134	7.2	105	8.6	31	8.2
Mg	53	6.3	47	5.0	26	0.7
Na	501	8.8	421	23.4	70	3.2
K	37	1.0	33	1.6	7	0.2
Cl	12	0.3	11	0.3	5	0.2
SO$_4$	394	5.2	338	13.3	49	3.2
Ca	9	0.6	12	0.9	30	5.7

NOTE: [a]n = 6
SOURCES: Alta. Envir. n.d.[a], Naquadat stations 01AL05CD2012 (Main Bay), 01AL05CD2013 (Secondary Bay), 01AL05CD2015 (Parlby Bay); [b]Prepas et al. n.d.

evident at the west end of the lake and along the north shore of Secondary Bay, as well as within the lake (Gabert 1975; Norecol Envir. Consult. Ltd. 1984). In 1980, Alberta Environment established a network of wells and piezometers on the land surrounding Buffalo Lake. After 2 years of observation, they estimated the annual groundwater inflow to Buffalo Lake to be about 6.0 x 10^6 m^3 (Clare and Ko 1982). Actual measurements with seepage meters on the bottom of the Main Bay of Buffalo Lake were taken in 1986 and 1987 by the University of Alberta (Shaw and Prepas 1989[a]; 1989[b]). Groundwater inflow inflow rates were found to be very high (8.7 to 16.4 x 10^{-8} m/second), from 2 to 24 times greater than that in 8 other Alberta lakes surveyed. The study estimated that the annual volume of groundwater inflow to Buffalo Lake equalled the annual volume of surface inflow (approximately 13 x 10^6 m^3/year). Subsequent evaluation of the hydrogeologic regime, undertaken as part of an Environmental Impact Assessment of Buffalo Lake stabilization, has resulted in an estimate of 6.2 x 10^6 m^3/year of annual groundwater inflow (Envir. Mgt. Assoc. 1990).

There has been no surface outflow from Buffalo Lake since 1929 (Alta. Envir. 1979). The natural sill elevation of the outlet is approximately 782.0 m, well above lake levels since 1950. Groundwater outflow is indicated, as the salinity of the lake is not as high as would be expected if evaporation were the only route for water to leave the lake (Norecol Envir. Consult. Ltd. 1984; Crosby 1987), however, no areas have been found where water in Buffalo Lake seeps downward into underlying geologic material (Envir. Mgt. Assoc. 1990).

In 1983, a study of water mixing within Buffalo Lake concluded that the water in each bay circulated in a clockwise direction. Mixing between the bays occurred when there was a southwest or northeast wind (about one day in three). It was estimated that water entering Parlby Bay moved into Main Bay within a month (Norecol Envir. Consult. Ltd. 1984).

The water level of Buffalo Lake has been monitored since 1955 (Fig. 3). The level dropped 1.9 m from a high in 1955 (781.4 m) to the historic low in 1964 (779.5 m). After 1968, levels rose until 1975 and slowly dropped until 1988. The largest change in one year occurred in 1974, a year of deep snowfall and heavy spring rain, when the lake rose 1.1 m. Because the lake basin slopes so gently, even small changes in lake levels cause extensive changes in beach width or flood nearshore developments (Fig. 4). Changes in lake

levels complicate recreational and cottage development; in the 1970s, demand for lake level stabilization led to extensive engineering and environmental feasibility studies by Alberta Environment (Lin 1979; Alta. Envir. 1979; 1982; Haag and Noton 1981; IBI Group 1981; Acres Consult. Serv. Ltd. 1982; Clare and Ko 1982; Hardy Assoc. Ltd. 1982; Norecol Envir. Consult. Ltd. 1984; Crosby 1987). The only feasible option from an engineering perspective was to pump water from the Red Deer River to Buffalo Lake. The studies raised concerns that the water quality of the lake would change and algal and macrophyte growth would increase if relatively nutrient-rich, less saline river water were mixed into the lake (Crosby 1987). A subsequent evaluation (Alta. Envir. 1989) predicted that nutrient loads would not increase significantly with the addition of Red Deer River water, but that salinity levels would decrease and algal biomass would increase. In late 1989, Alberta Environment called for a formal Environmental Impact Assessment of the Buffalo Lake stabilization project. The assessment, to be completed in March 1990, will include an evaluation of the effect that potential water quality changes could have on macrophyte and algal growth (Envir. Mgt. Assoc. 1990).

Water Quality

The water quality of Buffalo Lake was monitored from 1980 to 1983 as part of Alberta Environment's investigation of the feasibility of lake level stabilization (Alta. Envir. n.d.[a]; Crosby 1987). Groundwater quality was monitored as part of this program, as well (Clare and Ko 1982; Norecol Envir. Consult. Ltd. 1984). The lake's water quality has been monitored jointly since 1984 by Alberta Environment and Alberta Recreation and Parks (Alta. Envir. n.d.[a]), and in 1983, 1986 and 1987 by the University of Alberta as part of a program to determine factors controlling algal growth in saline lakes (Bierhuizen and Prepas n.d.; 1985; Prepas et al. n.d.).

Buffalo Lake is a well-buffered, moderately saline lake; its dominant ions are sodium, sulphate and bicarbonate. The salinity and the concentration of most ions in the lake increase along a gradient from west to east (Table 3). Only one ion, calcium, was higher in Parlby Bay, to the west, than in Secondary Bay, which in turn had higher calcium values than those in Main Bay (Table 3). The gradient can be attributed to the different sources of water in Buffalo Lake. Water quality in Parlby Bay is strongly influenced by inflowing Parlby Creek.

Table 4. Nutrient, chlorophyll *a* and Secchi depth data for three bays in Buffalo Lake. Average concentrations in µg/L. Composite samples from the euphotic zone collected 10 times from 04 June to 22 Oct. 1983 and 5 times from 19 May to 17 Sep. 1986. S.E. = standard error.

| | 1983 | | | | | | 1986[a] | | | |
| | Main | | Secondary | | Parlby | | Main | | Secondary | |
	Mean	S.E.	Mean	S.E.	Mean	S.E.	Mean	S.E.	Mean	S.E.
total phosphorus	59	2.4	76	5.3	84	17.2	58	5.0	78	9.4
total dissolved phosphorus	44	2.2	45	1.3	50	6.0	—	—	—	—
total Kjeldahl nitrogen	2 807	114.8	2 401	104.2	—	—	—	—	—	—
$NO_3 + NO_2$–nitrogen	3	1.0	2	0.8	—	—	—	—	—	—
NH_4–nitrogen	26	5.1	24	10.0	—	—	—	—	—	—
chlorophyll *a*	4.9	1.50	6.9	2.18	<11.0	—	6	1.9	15	4.7
Secchi depth (m)	—	—	—	—	—	—	2.9	0.59	2.0	0.02

NOTE: [a]samples not collected from Parlby Bay
SOURCES: Alta. Envir. n.d.[a], Naquadat stations 01AL05CD2012 (Main Bay 1983), 01AL05CD2029 (Main Bay 1986), 01AL05CD2013 (Secondary Bay 1983),
 01AL05CD2011 (Secondary Bay 1986), 01AL05CD2015 (Parlby Bay); all nitrogen data from Prepas et al. n.d.

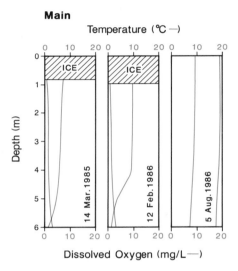

Figure 5. Temperature (°C) and dissolved oxygen (mg/L) in Buffalo Lake, Main Bay, 1985 and 1986.
SOURCE: Alta. Envir. n.d.[a].

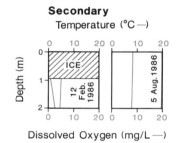

Figure 6. Temperature (°C) and dissolved oxygen (mg/L) in Buffalo Lake, Secondary Bay, 1986.
SOURCE: Alta. Envir. n.d.[a].

The ionic composition of Main Bay, on the other hand, is very different from Parlby Creek but is similar to the groundwater in the area. The ionic composition of the water in Secondary Bay is also similar to the groundwater, but is somewhat diluted by Parlby Creek inflow.

Buffalo Lake is not a simple "evaporating pan" despite the absence of surface outflow to provide flushing. Rather, the salinity of the lake is not much different than it was 3 000 years ago. A 1982 study examined a sediment core containing pollen grains deposited during the period from 7 400 years ago to the present (Hickman et al. 1983). Pollen deposited in the most recent 3 000 years indicated that the water has been less saline for the last 3 000 years than it was between 7 400 and 3 000 years BP.

Buffalo Lake is shallow and exposed to winds; it is well-mixed vertically and usually is not thermally stratified in summer (Fig. 5). The Main Bay, however, might stratify briefly during prolonged calm weather. Secondary Bay is likely well-mixed throughout the open-water season (Fig. 6).

In winter, dissolved oxygen concentrations in Main Bay are high (over 6 mg/L) down to a depth of 4 m. Below this, there is some oxygen depletion but anoxic conditions have not been found. In winter, dissolved oxygen concentrations in Secondary Bay are surprisingly high and there is no evidence of oxygen depletion near the sediment-water interface. These low oxygen depletion rates are in contrast to the rapid consumption of dissolved oxygen in other shallow but more productive lakes on the prairies.

A vertical salinity gradient is evident in Main Bay in the winter. Profiles taken between January and the end of March consistently indicated that the conductivity at the bottom was 100 to 500 µS/cm greater than near the top (Sloman 1983; Alta. Envir. 1984).

Buffalo Lake is mesotrophic, although the total phosphorus concentration in the lake is moderately high. The phosphorus gradient from west to east (Table 4) is opposite to the gradient for most other ions (Table 3). During the open-water season, the highest average total phosphorus concentration is in Parlby Bay (84 µg/L in 1983), the next highest is in Secondary Bay (76 µg/L), and the lowest is in Main Bay (59 µg/L). Chlorophyll *a* concentrations tend to be higher in Secondary Bay than in Main Bay (Table 4, Fig. 7). Both total phosphorus and chlorophyll *a* concentrations increase over the summer to maxima in August and September. Even in September when the water turns murky green, chlorophyll *a* concentrations are consistently lower than would be expected from the total phosphorus concentrations. A 1983 study, which included Buffalo Lake and 17 other moderately saline Alberta lakes, found a definite inhibition of algal production in lakes where the specific conductivity was over 1 000 µS/cm (Bierhuizen and Prepas 1985). This inhibition became more pronounced as salinity increased, and was related to high levels of most of the dominant ions, including sulphate. A subsequent study indicated that molybdate to sulphate ratios might explain the depressed phytoplankton biomass in lakes such as Buffalo (Marino et al. 1990).

Table 5. Percentage composition of major algal groups by total biomass in Buffalo Lake, 1987. Composite samples collected from the euphotic zone.

ALGAL GROUP	14 May	10 June	14 July	13 Aug.
Total Biomass (mg/L)	1.31	1.16	5.02	6.01
Percentage Composition:				
Cyanophyta	22 *Gomphosphaeria*	1	92 *Gomphosphaeria*	62 *Anabaena*
Chlorophyta	88 *Closterium*	83 *Oocystis*	4	7
Bacillariophyta	0	0	4	31 *Fragilaria*
Cryptophyta	0	16	0	0

SOURCES: Prepas et al. n.d.; Marino et al. 1990

Table 6. Species of aquatic macrophytes and their frequency of occurrence in Buffalo Lake. Survey conducted between 15 July and 04 Aug. 1981, based on 405 sampling points. Arranged in decreasing order of abundance.

			Percentage of Sites
submergent	widgeon grass	*Ruppia occidentalis*	75
	Sago pondweed	*Potamogeton pectinatus*	43
	large-sheath pondweed	*P. vaginatus*	13
	aquatic moss	*Fontinalis* sp.	7
	star duckweed	*Lemna trisulca*	6
	northern watermilfoil	*Myriophyllum exalbescens*	6
	stonewort	*Chara globularis*	5
	common bladderwort	*Utricularia vulgaris*	3
	coontail	*Ceratophyllum demersum*	2
	stonewort	*Chara* spp.	1
	small-leaf pondweed	*P. pusillus*	1
	Richardson pondweed	*P. richardsonii*	1
	aquatic moss	*Ricciocarpus natans*	1
emergent	common great bulrush	*Scirpus validus*	most common
	three-square rush	*S. pungens*	common
	northern reed grass	*Calamagrostis inexpansa*	common
	Baltic rush	*Juncus balticus*	common
	sedge	*Carex* sp.	rare
	link	*Scolochloa festucacea*	rare
	arrow-grass	*Triglochen maritima*	rare
	common cattail	*Typha latifolia*	rare

SOURCE: adapted from Haag and Noton 1981

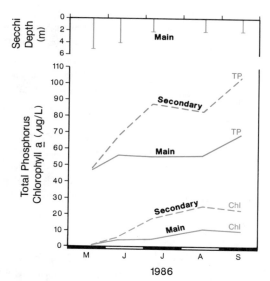

Figure 7. Total phosphorus and chlorophyll *a* in Main and Secondary bays, and Secchi depth in Main Bay, of Buffalo Lake, 1986.
SOURCE: Alta. Envir. n.d.[a].

Biological Characteristics

Plants

The algae in the Main Bay of Buffalo Lake was sampled on 11 September 1972 (Crosby 1972), monthly from June 1973 to August 1974 (Hickman n.d.), from January to March 1976 (Heinrichs 1976), on 29 August 1986 (Alta. Envir. n.d.[a]) and in July and August 1987 (Table 5). During the years sampled, the late-summer bloom was consistently dominated by blue-green algae (Cyanophyta). *Anabaena flos-aquae* was the most abundant species in most years; the codominant species were *Microspora tumidula* in 1972, *Synechocystis* sp. in 1973, *Oocystis parva* in 1974, and *Gomphosphaeria aponina* and *G. lacustris* in 1987. Some interesting species of algae have been reported in Buffalo Lake: *Chaetoceros elmorei*, which is often the most abundant diatom, is indicative of brackish water, and *Characiopsis spinifer*, a chlorophyte, was found for the first time in Alberta in a January 1976 sample.

Aquatic macrophytes were surveyed at 405 locations in Buffalo Lake between 15 July and 4 August 1981 (Table 6). In Main Bay, rooted macrophytes grew to a depth of 3.5 m. Widgeon grass (*Ruppia occidentalis*) and Sago pondweed (*Potamogeton pectinatus*) were the only species to flourish. The dominance of these salt-tolerant species and the absence of species typical of fresh water such as northern watermilfoil (*Myriophyllum exalbescens*) and

Richardson pondweed (*P. richardsonii*) reflects the high salinity and high concentrations of bicarbonate and sulphate ions in the Main Bay. Large-sheath pondweed (*Potamogeton vaginatus*) occurred occasionally and stonewort (*Chara* sp.) rarely. Common great bulrush (*Scirpus validus*) was sparsely distributed, mostly in sheltered bays on the north and west shores.

In Secondary Bay, plants grew to the maximum depth of the bay (2.5 m). Species composition in the eastern portion of the bay was typical of saline water, and was similar to that in Main Bay. However, there were some plants with a lower tolerance to salinity, such as common bladderwort (*Utricularia vulgaria*), star duckweed (*Lemna trisulca*) and northern watermilfoil (*Myriophyllum exalbescens*), which were found in the bay nearest the Narrows where the water is less saline. Boat travel was restricted by the density of plants in the shallow areas of some bays, especially towards the Narrows where the water salinity is lower than in the eastern portion of the bay.

In Parlby Bay, macrophytes grew throughout the bay and the community was typical of fresh water. There was no widgeon grass and this was the only bay in which Richardson pondweed, small-leaf pondweed (*P. pusillus*) and coontail (*Ceratophyllum demersum*) were found. Northern watermilfoil and stonewort were much denser here than at the eastern end of the Narrows. Boat traffic was severely impeded in most of the bay.

Invertebrates

There are no data available for zooplankton in Buffalo Lake.

Benthic invertebrates were sampled on 20 June 1967. Midge larvae (*Chironomus* sp.) were the dominant group (Hunt 1970).

Fish

Buffalo Lake supports only four species of fish: northern pike, burbot, white sucker and brook stickleback. All of these species are native to the lake and are tolerant of high salinity and alkalinity. Fish and Wildlife Division stocked the lake with yellow perch in the 1950s and with walleye as eyed-eggs in 1960; neither species survived (Alta. For. Ld. Wild. n.d.; Hunt 1970; Buchwald 1976).

The alkalinity of the water in Main Bay (979 mg/L) and Secondary Bay (846 mg/L) approaches or exceeds the limit for survival of pike eggs and fry (950 mg/L). Studies indicate that most of the pike from Buffalo Lake move west through the Narrows to Parlby Bay, then continue up Parlby Creek to spawn in flooded hay meadows. Some spawning occurs in Parlby Bay. Winter fish kills are not common in Buffalo Lake; a partial one was reported in the area of the Narrows in May 1961 (Hunt 1970).

Test netting in the Main Bay in 1967 and 1976 indicated an increase in the size of the pike population over this period. In 1967, 1 pike was caught per 18.3 m of net set; in 1976, 1 pike was caught per 9.1 m of net. The pike caught in these two years were weighed, measured and their age determined. The pike caught in 1976 were significantly smaller at all ages than fish caught in 1967. The catch of white suckers exceeded that of pike in both years (Buchwald 1976).

It is hoped that an Alberta Environment project to channelize Parlby Creek will have a beneficial effect on pike in Buffalo Lake by facilitating access to Spotted Lake for spawning. Control structures can be operated to hold water in Spotted Lake until fry have hatched and are an adequate size to travel to Buffalo Lake (Alta. Envir. 1985).

Wildlife

In central Alberta, Buffalo Lake is second only to Beaverhill Lake in its importance for waterfowl brood production, moulting and fall staging, and for nesting of colonial birds (Can. Wild. Serv. 1979; Hardy Assoc. Ltd. 1982). Breeding surveys were conducted in 1976 and 1981 (Alta. For. Ld. Wild. n.d.); staging surveys were conducted by Canadian Wildlife Service annually from 1960 to 1969, by Ducks Unlimited (Canada) in 1979 (Ducks Unltd. (Can.) n.d.) and by Fish and Wildlife Division in 1981 (Anderson 1981; Hardy Assoc. Ltd. 1982).

Production of ducklings in Buffalo Lake is estimated to be 7 000/year. Dabbling ducks include Mallards, Pintails, Gadwalls, American Widgeons, Blue-winged Teal, Green-winged Teal and Shovellers; diving ducks include Lesser Scaup, Redheads, Canvasbacks, Ring-necked Ducks, Bufflehead, Common Goldeneye and White-winged Scoters. Colonies of Great Blue Herons, Ring-billed Gulls, California Gulls, Forester's Terns, Common Terns and Eared Grebes also nest at Buffalo Lake. The Ring-billed Gull colony is one of the three largest colonies in Alberta, and Buffalo Lake is one of only three lakes in Alberta known to support a colony of Forester's Terns (Salt and Wilk 1972). In the autumn, up to 17 000 ducks, 3 500 swans and 12 000 geese (mostly Canada Geese and Snow Geese) use Buffalo Lake for staging before migration. No shooting of migratory game birds is permitted on Buffalo Lake or within 1 km of its shoreline.

Avian botulism has been a problem in Buffalo Lake for many years, especially in the bay that extends toward the town of Bashaw (Barnhard and Russell 1981). The most recent outbreak, in 1981, infected and killed hundreds of waterfowl and required intensive cleanup by Fish and Wildlife Division to restrict further spread.

Muskrats are plentiful in Buffalo Lake, especially along the north and west shores. The area supports numerous white-tailed deer; mule deer are less common and moose are occasionally seen. A Buck for Wildlife project is in place on 228 ha on the south shore of Secondary Bay to preserve and enhance habitat for waterfowl, Ring-necked Pheasants and other wildlife (Alta. For. Ld. Wild. n.d.).

J.M. Crosby

References

Acres Consulting Services Ltd. 1982. Buffalo Lake regulation study, Phase II (addendum)—Modes of operation. Prep. for Alta. Envir., Plan. Div., Edmonton.

Alberta Culture and Multiculturalism. n.d. Hist. Resour. Div., Hist. Sites Serv. Unpubl. data, Edmonton.

Alberta Environment. n.d.[a]. Envir. Assess. Div., Envir. Qlty. Monit. Br. Unpubl. data, Edmonton.

———. n.d.[b]. Plan. Div., Plan. Serv. Br. Unpubl. data, Edmonton.

———. n.d.[c]. Tech. Serv. Div., Hydrol. Br. Unpubl. data, Edmonton.

———. n.d.[d]. Tech. Serv. Div., Surv. Br. Unpubl. data, Edmonton.

———. 1979. Buffalo Lake regulation study, Phase I. Plan. Div., Edmonton.

———. 1982. Buffalo Lake regulation study, Phase II. Plan. Div., Edmonton.

———. 1984. Buffalo Lake, conductivity profiles under ice, 1982–83. Plan. Div., Edmonton.

———. 1985. Parlby Creek-Buffalo Lake water management project. Design Const. Div., Edmonton.

———. 1989. Water quality evaluation of Buffalo Lake stabilization project. Plan. Div., Edmonton.

Alberta Forestry, Lands and Wildlife. n.d. Fish Wild. Div. Unpubl. data, Edmonton.

———. 1988. Boating in Alberta. Fish Wild. Div., Edmonton.

———. 1989. Guide to sportfishing. Fish Wild. Div., Edmonton.

Alberta Hotel Association. 1988. 1988 Alberta campground guide. Prep. for Travel Alta., Edmonton.

Alberta Recreation and Parks. n.d. Parks Div. Unpubl. data, Edmonton.

Alberta Research Council. 1972. Geological map of Alberta. Nat. Resour. Div., Alta. Geol. Surv., Edmonton.

Anderson, P. 1981. Waterfowl surveys and habitat evaluation for waterfowl on Buffalo Lake: Wildlife investigations progress report. Alta. En. Nat. Resour., Fish Wild. Div., Edmonton.

Barnhard, T. and R. Russell. 1981. Preliminary multi-use proposal for the Parlby Creek-Buffalo Lake area. Prep. for Alta. Envir., Plan. Div. by Ducks Unltd. (Can.), Edmonton.

Bierhuizen, J.F.H. and E.E. Prepas. n.d. Univ. Alta., Dept. Zool. Unpubl. data, Edmonton.

———. 1985. Relationship between nutrients, dominant ions, and phytoplankton standing crop in prairie saline lakes. Can. J. Fish. Aquat. Sci. 42:1588–1594.

Bowser, W.E., R.L. Erdman, F.A. Wyatt and J.D. Newton. 1947. Soil survey of Peace Hills sheet. Alta. Soil Surv. Rep. No. 14, Univ. Alta. Bull. No. 48. Univ. Alta., Edmonton.

Bowser, W.E., T.W. Peters and J.D. Newton. 1951. Soil survey of Red Deer sheet. Alta. Soil Surv. Rep. No. 16, Univ. Alta. Bull. No. 51. Univ. Alta., Edmonton.

Buchwald, V. 1976. Buffalo Lake survey, 1976. Alta. Rec. Parks Wild., Fish Wild. Div., Red Deer.

Canadian Wildlife Service. 1979. Migratory birds habitat priorities, prairie provinces. Can. Wild. Serv., Edmonton.

Clare, S.J. and C.A. Ko. 1982. Groundwater study, Buffalo Lake stabilization, Phase II. Alta. Envir., Earth Sci. Div., Edmonton.

Crosby, J.M. 1972. An early fall survey of aquatic algal communities in Alberta. Univ. Calg. Unpubl. rep., Calgary.

———. 1987. Studies into the effect of proposed Buffalo Lake stabilization on algal growth. Alta. Envir., Plan. Div., Edmonton.

Ducks Unlimited (Canada). n.d. Unpubl. data, Edmonton.

Energy, Mines and Resources Canada. 1970. National topographic series 1:250 000 83A (1970). Surv. Map. Br., Ottawa.

Environment Canada. 1955–1988. Surface water data. Prep. by Inland Waters Directorate. Water Surv. Can., Water Resour. Br., Ottawa.

———. 1982. Canadian climate normals, Vol. 7: Bright sunshine (1951–1980). Prep. by Atm. Envir. Serv. Supply Serv. Can., Ottawa.

Environmental Management Associates. 1990. Environmental impact assessment for Parlby Creek/Buffalo Lake Development Project—Buffalo Lake stabilization component. Prep. for Alta. Envir., Plan. Div., Edmonton. [in prep.]

Finlay, J. and C. Finlay. 1987. Parks in Alberta: A guide to peaks, ponds, parklands & prairies. Hurtig Publ., Edmonton.

Gabert, G.M. 1975. Hydrogeology of Red Deer and vicinity, Alberta. Alta. Res. Counc. Bull. No. 31, Edmonton.

Haag, R. and L. Noton. 1981. Buffalo Lake macrophyte and littoral sediment survey. Prep. for Alta. Envir., Plan. Div., Edmonton.

Hardy Associates Ltd. 1982. Environmental summary report, Buffalo Lake stabilization project. Prep. for Alta. Envir., Plan. Div., Edmonton.

Heinrichs, R. 1976. Winter algal populations of three reservoirs and a lake in Alberta. Univ. Calg. Unpubl. rep., Calgary.

Hickman, M. n.d. Univ. Alta. Unpubl. data, Edmonton.

———, E. Bombin and M. Bombin. 1983. A paleoenvironmental history derived from a core taken from Buffalo Lake, Alberta. Prep. for Alta. Envir., Plan. Div., Edmonton by Univ. Alta., Dept. Bot., Edmonton.

HLA Consultants. 1982. An economic analysis of Buffalo Lake stabilization. Prep. for Alta. Envir., Plan. Div., Edmonton.

Holmgren, E.J. and P.M. Holmgren. 1976. Over 2000 place names of Alberta. 3rd ed. West. Producer Prairie Books, Saskatoon.

Hunt, C.W. 1970. Buffalo Lake: Preliminary survey, 1967–1968. Alta. Ld. For., Fish Wild. Div., Red Deer.

IBI Group. 1981. Buffalo Lake stabilization study—Recreation component. Prep. for Alta. Envir., Plan. Div., Edmonton.

Lamerton Historical Society. 1974. Land of the lakes: A story of the settlement and development of the country west of Buffalo Lake. Lamerton Hist. Soc., Lacombe.

Lin, W. 1979. Generation of hydrological data and stabilization alternatives for Buffalo Lake. Alta. Envir., Earth Sci. Div., Edmonton.

Marino, R., R.W. Howarth, J. Shamess and E.E. Prepas. 1990. Molybdenum and sulfate as controls on the abundance of nitrogen-fixing cyanobacteria in Alberta saline lakes. Limnol. Oceanogr. [in press]

Norecol Environmental Consultants Ltd. 1984. Buffalo Lake water quality modelling study, Vol. 1. Prep. for Alta. Envir., Plan. Div., Edmonton.

Prepas, E.E., J.F.H. Bierhuizen, R.W. Howarth and R. Marino. n.d. Unpubl. data, Univ. Alta., Edmonton and Cornell Univ., Ithaca, New York.

Red Deer Regional Planning Commission. 1977. Buffalo Lake management plan: A summary statement. Red Deer Reg. Plan. Res. Sec., Red Deer.

Salt, W.R. and A.L. Wilk. 1972. The Birds of Alberta. Queen's Printer, Edmonton.

Shaw, R.D. and E.E. Prepas. 1989[a]. Groundwater-lake interactions: II Nearshore seepage patterns and the contribution of groundwater to lakes in central Alberta. J.Hydrol. [in press]

———. 1989[b]. Anomalous short-term influx of water into seepage meters. Limnol. Oceanogr. 34:1343–1351.

Sloman, K. 1983. Buffalo Lake conductivity testing, fall 1983 and winter 1982–83. Alta. Envir., Plan. Div., Edmonton.

Strong, W.L. and K.R. Leggat. 1981. Ecoregions of Alberta. Alta. En. Nat. Resour., Resour. Eval. Plan. Div., Edmonton.

CRAWLING VALLEY RESERVOIR

MAP SHEET: 82I/16
LOCATION: Tp22, 23 R17, 18 W4
LAT/LONG: 50°56'N 112°21'W

Crawling Valley Reservoir is a large, newly created offstream storage reservoir in the Eastern Irrigation District and the County of Newell. The reservoir is almost 18–km long; the best access to the reservoir is at a recreation area on the west shore at the south end, near the main dam. To reach the south end of the reservoir from the city of Calgary, take Highway 1 east until you are just north of the town of Bassano, then turn off Highway 1 and continue travelling east for 5 km, then north for 3 km and east for 2 km (Fig. 1). The campground and day-use area were built by a group of local citizens, the Crawling Valley Recreation Society, who were assisted by Alberta Environment, Alberta Recreation and Parks, the Eastern Irrigation District and the County of Newell. Facilities include 60 campsites in 1988 and 60 more campsites slated for completion in 1989, and a day-use area with picnic tables, tap water, a telephone and a boat launch. A 1.6 ha subimpoundment of the reservoir was built at the recreation area to provide stable water levels for swimming and sand was brought in for a beach. There are no boating restrictions specific to Crawling Valley Reservoir, but general federal regulations are in effect (Alta. For. Ld. Wild. 1988).

The recent history of the Crawling Valley area goes back to the 1870s when the Canadian Pacific Railway (CPR) built its trans-Canada railway line across the prairies. The Canadian government gave the CPR alternate sections of land along the right-of-way. In southern Alberta, the CPR exchanged the alternate sections for two large blocks of land, one near the town of Brooks and one near the town of Strathmore. In 1910, the CPR built the Bassano Dam on the Bow River southwest of Brooks to supply irrigation water to the area around the locality of Gem. To get the water from the Bow River to where it was needed, the North Branch Canal was built, but water had to cross 20–m–deep Crawling Valley. To do this, a trestled wood-stave flume was built in 1912 and water was flowing through the system by 1914. In 1926, the flume needed to be replaced and the use of Crawling Valley as a storage site was first considered. However, the flume was replaced in 1929 with a semicircular wood-stave flume and the idea of a reservoir was dropped; the same flume provided reliable service until 1985, when Crawling Valley Reservoir was built and took over the flume's function.

Settlement of the area accelerated after the irrigation system became operational in 1914, but World War I soon followed, then an agricultural recession, then the depression and drought of the "Dirty Thirties". Farmers who had bought land from the CPR could not make enough profit to meet their payments. Meanwhile, the CPR was suffering heavy operating losses and saw little hope for recovery of its investment in the irrigation project. When the farmers offered to assume responsibility for the irrigation works, the CPR welcomed the suggestion. On 1 May 1935, the CPR transferred the irrigation works, the existing land contracts, all unsold lands and $300 000 to the farmer's organization, and the Eastern Irrigation District was formed (Gross and Nicoll Kramer 1985). The block of land near Strathmore followed suit; in 1944 it became the Western Irrigation District.

In 1942, Ducks Unlimited (Canada) saw the potential for waterfowl production in the area. They built a low dam north of the Crawling Valley flume, and from 1943 until 1985 a volume of up to one million cubic metres of water was diverted annually from the canal near the flume to create Barkenhouse Lake. Crawling Valley Reservoir now includes this area.

Table 1. Characteristics of Crawling Valley Reservoir drainage basin.

area (excluding lake) (km²)[a]	802
soil[b]	Solonetzic Brown and Solonetzic Dark Brown Chernozemics; saline Rego Gleysols and Brown Solodized Solonetz in valley
bedrock geology[c]	East: Horseshoe Canyon Formation (UpperCretaceous): sandstone, mudstone, shale; ironstone, scattered coal and bentonite beds; mainly nonmarine West: Bearpaw Formation (Upper Cretaceous): shale, thin ironstone and bentonite beds; marine
terrain[b]	undulating
ecoregion[d]	Mixed Grass; Short Grass in southeast portion
dominant vegetation[d]	spear, grama, wheat grasses
mean annual sunshine (h)[e]	2 334

SOURCES: [a]Alta. Envir. n.d.[b]; [b]Kjearsgaard et al. 1983; [c]Alta. Res. Counc. 1972; [d]Strong and Leggat 1981; [e]Envir. Can. 1982

In 1954, in response to the increased demand for irrigation water along the North Branch Canal, the Eastern Irrigation District requested that Agriculture Canada's Prairie Farm Rehabilitation Administration investigate the feasibility of building Crawling Valley Reservoir. Plans for a dam 300 m north of the existing flume were drawn up, but due to lack of funds, the dam was not built. From 1975 to 1977, the Planning Division of Alberta Environment investigated potential storage sites in the Eastern Irrigation District and identified Crawling Valley as one that would help meet demands. In 1980, funds for the project were allocated under the Alberta Environment Irrigation Headworks and Main Irrigation Systems Improvement Program, funded by the Alberta Heritage Savings Trust Fund. Engineering expertise was provided by the Prairie Farm Rehabilitation Administration. Construction began in 1983 and water first entered the reservoir in the fall of 1984 (Alta. Envir. 1984; Gross and Nicoll Kramer 1985). The reservoir is owned and operated by the Eastern Irrigation District. It now provides adequate water to the existing irrigation development, which covers 8 700 ha, and will allow future expansion for irrigation of a total of 22 000 ha (Alta. Envir. 1984).

Crawling Valley Reservoir has been stocked with rainbow, brook and brown trout, and in 1988, it provided an outstanding sport fishery. Angling is not permitted within 100 m of the inlet to the reservoir, and because trout spawn in the inlet canal, fishing is prohibited in the Eastern Irrigation District North Branch Canal between its origin near the Bow River and Crawling Valley Reservoir (Alta. For. Ld. Wild. 1989). Concentrations of algae in the reservoir are moderate and the reservoir has good potential for recreational use.

Drainage Basin Characteristics

Crawling Valley was created as a meltwater channel when the Laurentide ice sheet melted at the end of the last continental glaciation. The sinuous north-to-south valley lies approximately 20 m below the adjacent uplands. The northern end of the drainage basin is only 4 km south of the Red Deer River, but the natural drainage was via Matzhiwin Creek which flows south for 45 km then east for another 40 km before it drains into the Red Deer River just upstream of Dinosaur Provincial Park.

Although the reservoir's natural drainage basin is large (802 km², Table 1), most of the area is hummocky moraine, which traps runoff so only 40 km² of the drainage basin contributes runoff to the valley, even during a 1–in–20–year flood (Agric. Can. 1982). Natural inflow via Matzhiwin Creek (Fig. 1) is usually negligible and provides less than 1% of the water in Crawling Valley Reservoir. Almost all of the inflow comes via the North Branch Canal from the Bow River up-

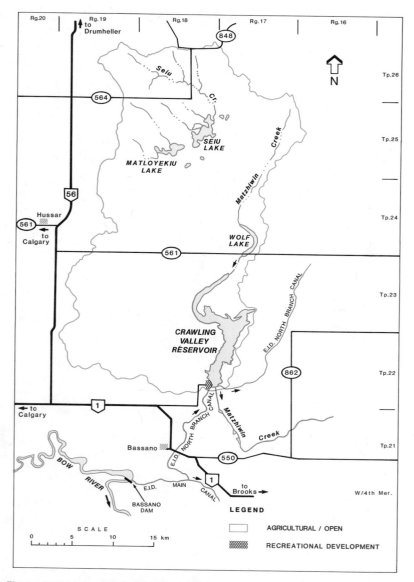

Figure 1. Features of the drainage basin of Crawling Valley Reservoir. SOURCES: Alta. Envir. n.d.[a]; En. Mines Resour. Can. 1977; 1978. Land use classification derived from topographic maps; aerial photos not available.

stream of the Bassano Dam (East. Irrig. Dist. n.d.) and the outflow leaves the reservoir via a continuation of the North Branch Canal. Seepage from the dam maintains a year-round flow of approximately 0.01 m³/second in Matzhiwin Creek downstream of the reservoir (East. Irrig. Dist. n.d.).

The bedrock under the valley is the nonmarine sandstone and sandy shales of the Horseshoe Canyon Formation overlain by marine shales of the Bearpaw Formation. Between the Bearpaw Formation bedrock and the overlying glacial till, there is a thick gravel deposit of preglacial age that was buried on the floor of an ancestral river valley, the Calgary Valley, which flowed in a northeast direction. This basal gravel extends below the full length of the reservoir and is, for the most part, overlain by approximately 16 m of impervious till and alluvial clay.

The northern part of the reservoir and the western portion of the drainage basin are part of the Mixed Grass Ecoregion, whereas the southern part of the reservoir and the eastern portion of the basin are part of the Short Grass Ecoregion (Strong and Leggat 1981). The natural vegetation is a complex of grama, wheat and spear grasses, with buckbrush and willow in depressions and in damp areas. Cushion cactus was found on slopes in the valley in 1982 (Alta. Envir. 1984). Large areas of original grassland still exist around the reservoir and on the uplands, but much of the basin has been cultivated for improved pasture or grain production (mostly wheat) on nonirrigated land. Alfalfa is the most important crop on irrigated land.

Soils in the northern portion of the drainage basin are mostly Solonetzic Dark Brown Chernozemics that developed on glacial till;

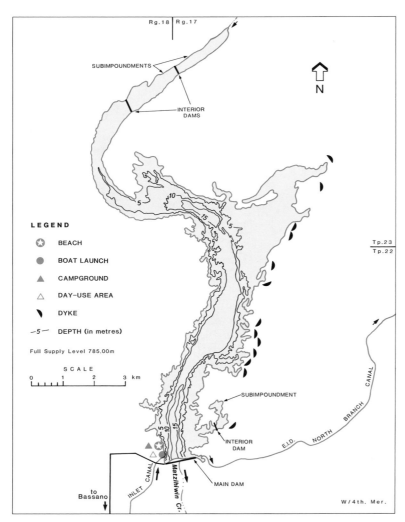

Figure 2. Bathymetry and shoreline features of Crawling Valley Reservoir.
BATHYMETRY SOURCE: Alta. Envir. 1984.

Capacity (m³X 10⁶)

Figure 3. Area/capacity curve for Crawling Valley Reservoir.
SOURCE: Agric. Can. n.d.

Table 2. Characteristics of Crawling Valley Reservoir.

control structure[a]	Main dam; 13 dykes on east side; 3 interior dams to create subimpoundments
dam height (m)[b]	18.7
crest length (m)[b]	1 710
full supply level (FSL) (m)[a]	785.00
volume at FSL (m³)[a]	130×10^6
live storage at FSL (m³)[a]	113.0×10^6
surface area at FSL (km²)[a]	25.1
maximum drawdown (m)[a]	8.0
mean annual drawdown (1988) (m)[a]	0.6
maximum depth at FSL (m)[a]	16
mean depth at FSL (m)[a]	5.2
shoreline length at FSL (km)[b]	approximately 150
lake length at FSL (km)[a]	17.6
lake width at FSL (km)[a]	4.0
mean annual lake evaporation (mm)[c]	750
mean annual precipitation (mm)[c]	353
mean residence time (yr)[c, d]	1.4
mean (Apr.–Sep.) inflow volume (1987–1988) (m³)[c, d]	103×10^6
mean (Apr.–Sep.) outflow volume (1987–1988) (m³)[c]	93.0×10^6

NOTE: [d]natural runoff estimated to be less than 1% of this volume; volume excludes groundwater inflow
SOURCES: [a]East. Irrig. Dist. n.d.; [b]Alta. Envir. 1984; [c]Alta. Envir. n.d.[b]

south of the middle of the reservoir there is a complex of Solonetzic Brown Chernozemics and Orthic Brown Chernozemics (Kjearsgaard et al. 1983). In Crawling Valley, there are poorly drained lacustrine deposits where Rego-Gleysols and saline Rego-Gleysols have developed. At the north end of the reservoir there are areas of Brown Solodized Solonetzic soils (Alta. Envir. 1984). Salt-crusted alkali flats were present in the northern third of the reservoir area before it was flooded.

The major land use in the drainage basin is low-intensity farming, both dryland and irrigated. There are several active gas wells in the area but no population centres.

Reservoir Characteristics

Crawling Valley Reservoir is a long, sinuous water body that stretches for almost 18 km, has a maximum width of 4 km and covers an area of 25 km² (Table 2, Fig. 2). Because the reservoir flooded a valley with innumerable side coulees, the shoreline is very complex and is approximately 150–km long. The reservoir is quite shallow (maximum depth = 16 m) and the bottom slopes gently except in the immediate area of the dam. Approximately 60% of the reservoir is less than 5–m deep (Fig. 3).

The main dam, built at the south end of the reservoir in 1983 and 1984, is 1 710–m long and 18.7–m high. The full supply level of the reservoir is 785.0 m, but if there were extremely high precipitation in the basin, water levels could rise to 787.5 m (Fig. 3). To limit flooding along the eastern shore at a water level of 787.5 m, thirteen dykes were built across coulees on the east side of the reservoir. When the reservoir was filled, it covered Barkenhouse Lake and the "South Reservoir", a pond just south of Barkenhouse Lake. These water bodies provided important habitat for nesting and migrating waterfowl. To replace the valuable waterfowl habitat that would be flooded by Crawling Valley Reservoir, three interior dams were built to create three subimpoundments (Fig. 2). These dams allow water to flow into the subimpoundments when reservoir water levels are high; control structures operated by Ducks Unlimited (Canada) and the Eastern Irrigation District are closed to prevent water from flowing out of the subimpoundments when the reservoir is drawn down. Water can be pumped into the subimpoundments from the reservoir

Table 3. Major ions and related water quality variables for Crawling Valley Reservoir. Average concentrations in mg/L; pH in pH units. Composite samples from the euphotic zone collected 3 times from 18 June to 24 Sep. 1986. S.E. = standard error.

	North		Middle		South	
	Mean	S.E.	Mean	S.E.	Mean	S.E.
total alkalinity ($CaCO_3$)	156	7.4	148	7.4	143	5.7
specific conductivity ($\mu S/cm$)	357	8.4	347	9.3	328	15.2
total dissolved solids (calculated)	238	7.4	227	7.1	214	4.4
total hardness ($CaCO_3$)	182	1.4	177	1.6	170	1.1
dissolved organic carbon	5	0.4	4	0.4	4	0.3
HCO_3	191	9.0	181	9.0	174	6.9
CO_3	<1	—	<1	—	<1	—
Mg	16	0.3	16	0.2	15	0
Na	18	2.0	17	1.5	14	1.0
K	3	0.1	2	0.2	2	0.1
Cl	7	0.2	6	0.1	6	0.2
SO_4	51	3.6	49	2.7	45	1.2
Ca	46	0.2	45	0.5	43	0.4

SOURCE: Alta. Envir. n.d.[a], Naquadat stations 05AL05CJ4000 (north), 05AL05CJ4002 (middle), 05AL05CJ4004 (south)

Table 4. Nutrient, chlorophyll *a* and Secchi depth data for Crawling Valley Reservoir. Average concentrations in $\mu g/L$. Composite samples from the euphotic zone collected 3 times from 18 June to 24 Sep. 1986. S.E. = standard error.

	North		Middle		South	
	Mean	S.E.	Mean	S.E.	Mean	S.E.
total phosphorus	66	11.1	59	8.7	46	7.8
total dissolved phosphorus	30	11.4	27	11.9	25	11.6
total Kjeldahl nitrogen	833	190.6	767	161.8	653	99.6
$NO_3 + NO_2$–nitrogen	85	29.9	123	23.7	206	59.0
NH_4–nitrogen	83	43.7	93	43.7	150	75.1
iron	60	23.1	73	14.5	57	24.0
chlorophyll *a*	16.0	2.97	12.1	1.61	8.5	4.24
Secchi depth (m)	2.6	0.61	2.6	0.64	2.6	0.89

SOURCE: Alta. Envir. n.d.[a], Naquadat stations 05AL05CJ4000 (north), 05AL05CJ4002 (middle), 05AL05CJ4004 (south)

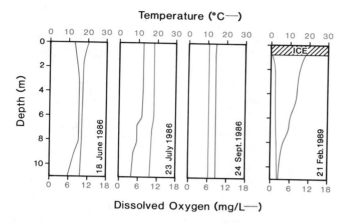

Figure 4. Temperature and dissolved oxygen in the central area of Crawling Valley Reservoir, 1986.
SOURCE: Alta. Envir. n.d.[a].

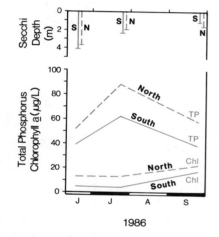

Figure 5. Total phosphorus, chlorophyll *a* and Secchi depth in the north and south ends of Crawling Valley Reservoir, 1986.
SOURCE: Alta. Envir. n.d.[a].

in early spring to raise the water level before the nesting season. Natural islands in the south subimpoundment provide secure nesting sites and Ducks Unlimited (Canada) has built islands to increase nesting sites in the northern subimpoundments (Schmidt 1989).

More than 99% of the water entering the reservoir comes from the Bow River via the Eastern Irrigation District North Branch Canal. This canal empties into the reservoir at the southwest corner and water drains from the reservoir at the southeast corner via a portal at an elevation of 777 m. The reservoir is operated to fill from April through June. Water is then withdrawn from July through September. If water is available, some filling may occur in the autumn. There is no flow in the canals from late October through March and natural runoff is negligible. The reservoir has been operated since 1986; summer drawdown over the three years from 1986 to 1988 averaged 1.5 m (East. Irrig. Dist. n.d.).

The residence time of the water in the reservoir is estimated to be 1.4 years, but as most of the flow "short-circuits" through the south end, the actual residence time is likely much shorter in the southern end and much longer in the northern end of the reservoir.

Water Quality

Water first entered Crawling Valley Reservoir in the fall of 1984 and the reservoir was full by the summer of 1985. Water quality was monitored by Alberta Environment on three occasions in the summer of 1986 and approximately monthly in 1989 (Alta. Envir. n.d.[a]).

As of 1986, the reservoir was filled with fresh, well-buffered water. The dominant ions were bicarbonate, sulphate and calcium. The concentrations of total dissolved solids and most ions were highest at the north end (Table 3). On 18 June and 23 July 1986 the water column was weakly thermally stratified (Fig. 4). In July, dissolved oxygen concentrations near the bottom were low. In February 1989, the dissolved oxygen concentration was high (10.8 mg/L) near the surface but fairly low (1.9 mg/L) near the bottom (Fig. 4). Trout winterkills have not been reported, indicating that dissolved oxygen does not become severely depleted under ice.

Only one year after the reservoir was filled, the water was moderately nutrient-rich and the concentration of nutrients increased from south to north (Table 4). Three sites were monitored: one at the north end of the reservoir, one at the south end and one in the middle. At all three sites, the concentration of total phosphorus was highest on 23 July and chlorophyll *a* was highest on 24 September (Fig. 5). The data indicate that Crawling Valley Reservoir was mesotrophic in 1986. It is likely that the water will become more nutrient-rich over the first five to seven years after initial filling of the reservoir as nutrients are leached from the inundated soils; there were reports of excessively "green" water in the northern half in 1988 (Kemper 1989). After this period of trophic upsurge, the nutrient level may drop, depending in part on flushing rates and water level fluctuations.

Biological Characteristics

There is no detailed information on the algae or macrophytes in Crawling Valley Reservoir. By 1988, submergent macrophytes, including northern watermilfoil (*Myriophyllum exalbescens*) and Sago (*Potamogeton pectinatus*) and Richardson (*P. richardsonii*) pondweeds had densely colonized the three subimpoundments (Schmidt 1989).

Invertebrates

There are no data on the zooplankton or benthic invertebrates in Crawling Valley Reservoir.

Amphibians

Before Crawling Valley Reservoir was filled, Barkenhouse Lake and the South Reservoir supported a population of tiger salamanders (*Ambystoma tigrinum melanosticum*), which live in shallow areas where macrophytes grow densely. This population was thought to be neotenic, a condition where reproductively mature salamanders retain larval characteristics such as external gills and do not metamorphose into the adult form. Such variants are not common in Alberta (Alta. Envir. 1984). The fate of salamanders in the area is not known; in other stocked lakes and reservoirs, for example Tyrrell Lake, the salamanders fall prey to trout and populations are quickly decimated.

Fish

Prior to reservoir filling, Barkenhouse Lake and the South Reservoir supported a resident population of fathead minnows and brook stickleback, species that are tolerant of low dissolved oxygen concentrations. Longnose sucker, white sucker and shorthead redhorse, which were also found, may have been migrants from the North Branch Canal. The fish in the Bow River have access to Crawling Valley Reservoir from the North Branch Canal; northern pike, rainbow trout and the three species of suckers have been caught in the canal (Alta. Envir. 1984).

Fish and Wildlife Division stocked Crawling Valley Reservoir with 324 000 rainbow trout, 108 000 brook trout and 375 brown trout in 1985, the year the reservoir was first filled. In each of 1987 and 1988, 434 000 rainbow trout were stocked (Alta. En. Nat. Resour. 1985; Alta. For. Ld. Wild. 1986–1988). In 1988, the sport fishery was excellent and very popular, attracting anglers from as far away as Edmonton. There has been no evidence of winterkill and trout growth rates appear to be high; rainbow trout up to 8 kg were frequently caught in 1988. In the spring of 1988, rainbow trout were seen attempting to spawn in the upper reaches of the North Branch Canal. Fish and Wildlife Division spread gravel in the canal in late 1988 to improve the habitat for spawning (Fitch 1989). By summer of 1989, trout were less frequently caught and pike were the most commonly caught sport fish (Bishop 1989).

Wildlife

Crawling Valley Reservoir inundated Barkenhouse Lake, a Ducks Unlimited (Canada) project that had provided excellent habitat for migrating and nesting waterfowl, including eight species of dabbling ducks, nine species of diving ducks, Canada Geese, American Bitterns and colonial nesters such as Western and Eared grebes, Double-crested Cormorants, California Gulls and Common Terns. Black-crowned Night Herons and Ring-billed Gulls were probably nesting there as well (Alta. Envir. 1984). By 1988, the subimpoundments in the reservoir were developing into excellent waterfowl habitat. Submergent macrophytes had developed and emergent species were becoming established. In 1989, it was expected that some areas would be fenced off to prevent cattle from trampling the shoreline of the northern subimpoundment and nesting waterfowl would be surveyed by Ducks Unlimited (Canada). In 1988, thousands of birds stopped on Crawling Valley Reservoir during migration (Schmidt 1989).

In 1982, a survey of Crawling Valley was conducted for Alberta Environment (Alta. Envir. 1984). Sixteen species of shorebirds were reported, including Long-billed Curlews and Avocets, as well as 2 species of upland game birds, 6 species of raptors and 21 species of passerines. The valley has changed since 1982, but the reservoir and the subimpoundments have been designed to replace lost habitat.

Eleven species of mammals were observed in the 1982 survey. Pronghorn antelope use the valley year-round and mule deer are present but not abundant. Furbearers include weasels, coyotes, muskrats, white-tailed jackrabbits, mink, red foxes and badgers. Richardson's ground squirrels, deer mice and prairie voles are common.

J.M. Crosby

References

Agriculture Canada. n.d. Prairie Farm Rehabilitation Admin. Unpubl. data, Lethbridge.
———. 1982. Crawling Valley storage project—Predesign report. Prairie Farm Rehabilitation Admin. Can. Dept. Reg. Econ. Expansion, Lethbridge.
Alberta Energy and Natural Resources. 1985. Fish planting list. Fish Wild. Div., Edmonton.
Alberta Environment. n.d.[a]. Envir. Assess. Div., Envir. Qlty. Monit. Br. Unpubl. data, Edmonton.
———. n.d.[b]. Tech. Serv. Div., Hydrol. Br. Unpubl. data, Edmonton.
———. 1984. Crawling Valley Reservoir: Environmental effects and mitigation, Vol. I: Main report. Plan. Div., Edmonton.
———. 1986–1988. Fish planting list. Fish Wild. Div., Edmonton.
———. 1988. Boating in Alberta. Fish Wild. Div., Edmonton.
———. 1989. Guide to sportfishing. Fish Wild. Div., Edmonton.
Alberta Research Council. 1972. Geological map of Alberta. Nat. Resour. Div., Alta. Geol. Surv., Edmonton.
Bishop, F. 1989. Alta. For. Ld. Wild., Fish Wild. Div., Lethbridge. Pers. comm.
Eastern Irrigation District. n.d. Unpubl. data, Brooks.
Energy, Mines and Resources Canada. 1977, 1978. National topographic series 1:250 000 82I (1977), 82P (1978). Surv. Map. Br., Ottawa.
Environment Canada. 1982. Canadian climate normals, Vol. 7: Bright sunshine (1951–1980). Prep. by Atm. Envir. Serv. Supply Serv. Can., Ottawa.
Fitch, L. 1989. Alta. For. Ld. Wild., Fish Wild. Div., Lethbridge. Pers. comm.
Gross, R. and L. Nicoll Kramer. 1985. Tapping the Bow. East. Irrig. Dist., Brooks.
Kemper, J.B. 1989. Alta. Envir., Envir. Assess. Div., Envir. Qlty. Monit. Br., Edmonton. Pers. comm.
Kjearsgaard, A.A., T.W. Peters and W.W. Pettapiece. 1983. Soil survey of the County of Newell, Alberta. Alta. Soil Surv. Rep. No. 41, Alta. Inst. Pedol. Rep. No. S–82–41, Ld. Resour. Res. Inst. Contribution No. LRRI 83–48. Agric. Can., Res. Br., Edmonton.
Schmidt, K. 1989. Ducks Unltd. (Can.), Brooks. Pers. comm.
Strong, W.L. and K.R. Leggat. 1981. Ecoregions of Alberta. Alta. En. Nat. Resour., Resour. Eval. Plan. Div., Edmonton.

GLENIFFER LAKE

MAP SHEET: 83B
LOCATION: Tp35 R2, 3 W5
LAT/LONG: 52°03'N 114°10'W

Gleniffer Lake is one of Alberta's newest reservoirs. Created in 1983 by the impoundment of the Red Deer River by Dickson Dam, Gleniffer Lake fills the Red Deer River Valley 20 km west of the town of Innisfail in the County of Red Deer (Fig. 1). The closest population centre is the hamlet of Dickson, 1 km north of the reservoir. To reach Gleniffer Lake from Red Deer, drive 22 km south on Highway 2 to the town of Innisfail, then drive approximately 22 km west on Highway 54; turn south onto a section road and drive for 4 km to the Dickson Dam, which can be crossed by automobile. Routes to various sites on the reservoir are shown in Figure 2.

Gleniffer Lake is named after the tiny post office that was located near the present dam site. Dickson Dam takes its name from the nearby hamlet of Dickson, which was named after Mr. Benedickson, a settler who arrived from Norway near the turn of the century (Holmgren and Holmgren 1976).

The need for a reservoir on the Red Deer River became apparent in the late 1950s with the expansion of communities along the Red Deer River in central Alberta. This expansion led to increased water demand and a need for flow stability. Residents and industrial users also became concerned about water quality in the Red Deer River downstream of the city of Red Deer, especially at times when flows dropped as low as 2 m³/second. In winter, dissolved oxygen concentrations in the river from near Red Deer to the Saskatchewan border dropped well below levels that could support fish (Beak Consult. Ltd. 1977). Alberta Environment initiated technical studies in 1971, and after seven years of engineering and environmental studies and a series of public hearings, a decision was made to build Dickson Dam. Construction began in 1980 and the reservoir started to fill in the summer of 1983.

The reservoir now provides three major benefits to downstream users: an assured year-round water supply, improved water quality in the Red Deer River and flood control. A minimum flow of 16 m³/second is assured and dissolved oxygen concentrations have improved, so the potential for year-round fish survival has also improved. Other benefits of the reservoir include recreation and the potential for small-scale hydroelectric generation.

Gleniffer Lake is very clear and attractive for recreational fishing and boating, but variable water levels make the shoreline and beaches less appealing than those in natural lakes. The Alberta government operates a visitor centre on the dam, six day-use areas that provide access to the lake and two day-use areas for access to the river below the dam (Fig. 2). Boat launches on the reservoir are available at North Dyke, South Dyke and Cottonwood day-use areas, and canoes can also be launched at Portage day-use area. There is a boat launch on the river below the dam at South Valley day-use area. Swimming is good at Dickson Point, and at South Dyke and North Dyke day-use areas. Fishing is permitted in the trout pond at Dickson Point and there is a children's fish pond at Cottonwood day-use area. Posted areas of the reservoir designate areas where no boats are permitted (Alta. For. Ld. Wild. 1988).

The only public campsite at the lake is a group campground (by reservation only) on the south shore. There are two commercially operated campgrounds; one on the north shore between the North Dyke and Dickson Point day-use areas, and one on the south shore near the South Dyke day-use area. Red Lodge Provincial Park on the Little Red Deer River is approximately 12 km south of the reservoir; it has 130 sites, tap water and a telephone. There is one subdivision on the lake, midway along the south shore.

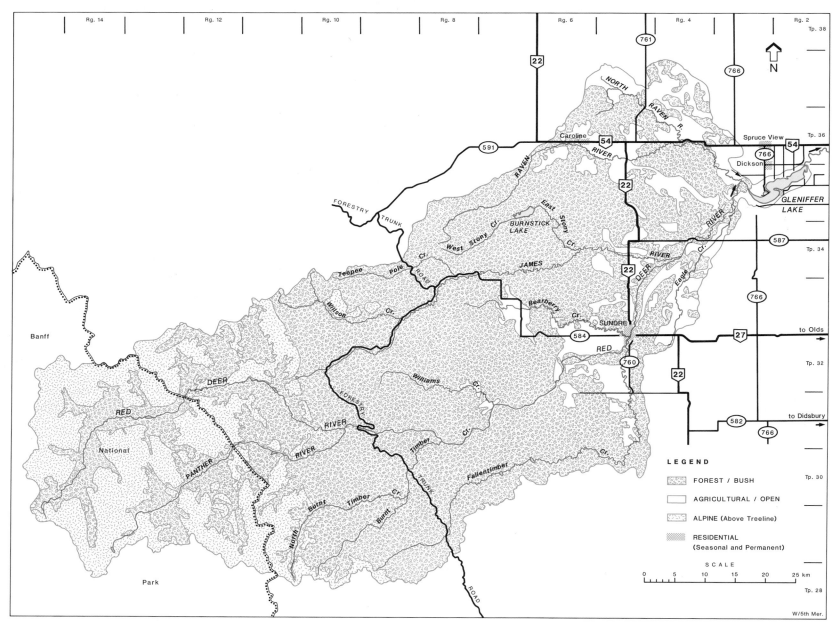

Figure 1. Features of the drainage basin of Gleniffer Lake.
SOURCES: Alta. Envir. n.d.[c]; En. Mines Resour. Can. 1963; 1966; 1967. Updated with 1984 aerial photos.

Gleniffer Lake has very clear water, but it can become turbid with suspended silt during filling in the spring or following heavy rainfalls. It supports a recreational fishery for pike, mountain whitefish and trout. Fish and Wildlife Division has stocked the lake annually since 1983 with rainbow trout. Cutthroat trout were also introduced in 1983 and brown trout in 1984. Dickson Pond, an oxbow on the north shore that can be isolated from the reservoir, is also stocked with rainbow trout, as is a children's fish pond at the South Valley day-use site. Provincial sport fishing regulations apply to Gleniffer Lake. Walleye and sauger from the Red Deer River downstream of Dickson Dam may contain mercury levels that exceed recommended safe levels for human consumption. Pregnant women should not eat these fish; others should not eat more than one meal of these walleye or sauger per week (Alta. For. Ld. Wild. 1989).

Drainage Basin Characteristics

Gleniffer Lake is an onstream storage reservoir; its watershed is that of the entire Red Deer River upstream of Dickson Dam (Fig. 1). This drainage basin is very large (5 610 km²; Table 1) and extends west to Douglas Lake in Banff National Park, just east of the Lake Louise Ski Area. Here, in the Alpine Ecoregion, mountains up to 3 000 m above sea level hold glaciers that melt to provide runoff all summer. Vegetation at this high elevation is dominated by heaths, willow, dwarf birch and krumholz fir and soils are poorly developed Regosols (Strong and Leggat 1981). The Subalpine Ecoregion is located at lower elevations than the Alpine Ecoregion. The dominant vegeta-

tion is lodgepole pine and Engelmann spruce; soils are Eutric Brunisols. The middle two-thirds of the basin drops from the Subalpine Ecoregion through the low mountains and hills of the Boreal Uplands and Boreal Foothills ecoregions, the latter of which extends as far east as the North Raven River. Here the vegetation is primarily white spruce, lodgepole pine, trembling aspen and balsam poplar; soils are Orthic Gray Luvisols. Land use includes logging, oil and gas extraction and summer grazing for cattle. Approximately 60% of this area is covered with trembling aspen, white spruce and lodgepole pine, with black spruce and tamarack in low areas, and 40% of the area has been cleared for grazing and mixed farming. Oil and gas wells are numerous. Most of the area east of the North Raven River and immediately surrounding Gleniffer Lake is in the Aspen Subregion of the Aspen Parkland Ecoregion and has been cleared for grain crop production and mixed farming. Soils in this area are Orthic and Eluviated Black Chernozemics, which developed on glacial till (Peters and Bowser 1960). In 1975, only 19% of the 270 km² surrounding the reservoir site had not been cleared; 81% of this was forested with deciduous or mixed wood, 10% was black spruce bog, 8% was coniferous forest and 1% was covered with shrubs (D.A. Westworth Assoc. Ltd. et al. 1982). The lowest elevation in the basin is on the shore of Gleniffer Lake, 948.0 m at full supply level.

There are only two population centres in the basin; the town of Sundre and the village of Caroline. All of the shoreline of the reservoir is Crown land, but in some areas it forms only a very narrow band; larger areas of Crown land are shown on Figure 2.

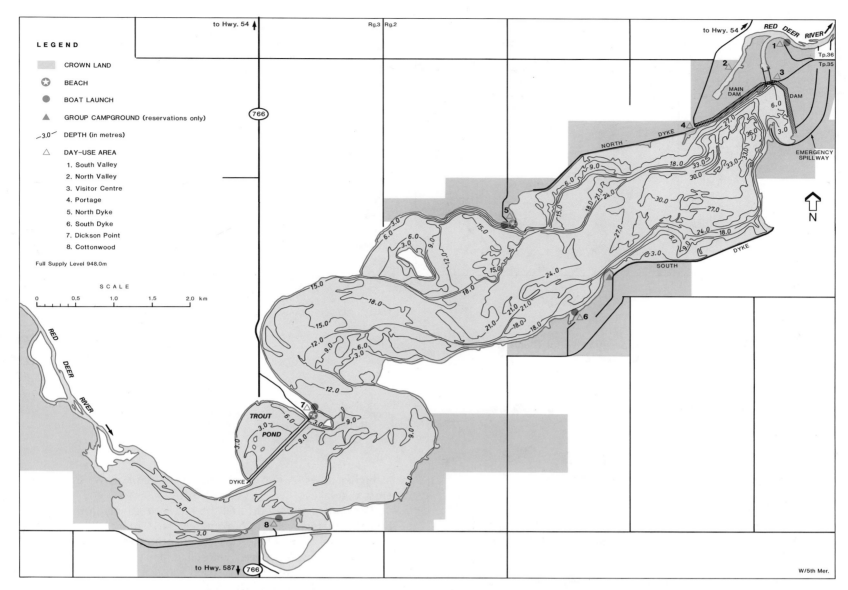

Figure 2. Bathymetry and shoreline features of Gleniffer Lake. BATHYMETRY SOURCE: Alta. Envir. n.d.[d].

Table 1. Characteristics of Gleniffer Lake drainage basin.

area (excluding lake) (km^2)[a]	5 610
soil[b]	Orthic and Eluviated Black Chernozemics in east; Orthic Gray Luvisols and Eutric Brunisols in west
bedrock geology[c]	Paskapoo Formation (Tertiary): sandstone, siltstone, mudstone; thin limestone, coal and tuff beds; nonmarine
terrain[d]	gently rolling in east to mountainous in west
ecoregion[d]	Aspen Parkland in east; Boreal Foothills, Boreal Uplands, Subalpine to Alpine in west
dominant vegetation[d]	trembling aspen and rough fescue in east; trembling aspen, lodgepole pine, white spruce and black spruce in centre; lodgepole pine, white spruce, black spruce, Engelmann spruce and heath in west
mean annual sunshine (h)[e]	2 100

SOURCES: [a]Alta. Envir. n.d.[c]; [b]Peters and Bowser 1960; [c]Alta. Res. Counc. 1972; [d]Strong and Leggat 1981; [e]Envir. Can. 1982

Table 2. Characteristics of Gleniffer Lake.

control structure[a]	Dickson Dam plus north dyke (3.1 km) and south dyke (3.7 km)
first fill[a]	1983
dam height (m)[a]	40
crest elevation (m)[a]	952
crest length (m)[a]	650
full supply level (FSL) (m)[a]	948.0
volume at FSL (m^3)[b]	205 x 10^6
useable storage (m^3)[a]	203.0 x 10^6
flooded area at FSL (km^2)[b]	17.6
maximum drawdown (m)[c]	21.4
mean annual drawdown (1983–1987) (m)[c]	7.75
maximum depth at FSL (m)[d]	33.0
mean depth at FSL (m)[a]	11.6
shoreline length at FSL (km)[d]	40
lake length at FSL (km)[d]	11.0
lake width at FSL (km)[d]	2.1
mean annual lake evaporation (mm)[e]	640
mean annual precipitation (mm)[e]	467
mean residence time (yr)[e]	0.2
mean annual inflow (m^3)[e]	1 090 x 10^6
mean annual discharge (1975–1982) (m^3)[f]	941.2 x 10^6
minimum discharge rate (m^3/s)[a]	16.1

SOURCES: [a]Alta. Envir. n.d.[a]; [b]Alta. Envir. n.d.[d]; [c]Envir. Can. 1983–1987; [d]R.L. & L. Envir. Serv. Ltd. 1985; [e]Alta. Envir. n.d.[c]; [f]Envir. Can. 1985

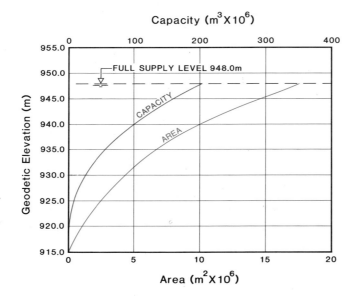

Figure 3. Area/capacity curve for Gleniffer Lake.
SOURCE: Alta. Envir. n.d.[d].

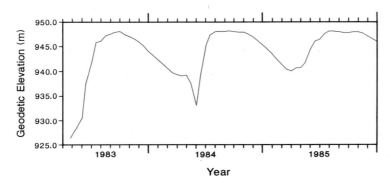

Figure 4. Water level of Gleniffer Lake, 1983 to 1987.
SOURCE: Envir. Can. 1983–1987.

Reservoir Characteristics

Gleniffer Lake has a very small surface area (17.6 km²) relative to the size of its drainage basin (5 610 km²). At full supply level, the reservoir is 11.0–km long and 2.1–km wide and follows the contours of the Red Deer River Valley. Its steep sides drop sharply to a wide, flat bottom. The deepest point (33 m) is just upstream of the dam (Fig. 2).

When the reservoir is drawn down 15 m to an elevation of 933 m (as it was in May of 1984), the surface area drops to about 6 km², exposing over 11 km² of mud flats (Fig. 3). Such fluctuating water levels make it unlikely that a littoral zone with aquatic plants will develop. However, on the north side of the reservoir near the western end, a pond created in an old oxbow of the river has been separated from the main body of the reservoir with a dyke and weir. The water level in the pond can be held constant when the reservoir is drawn down, and aquatic plants have already colonized the area. The maximum depth of the pond (7.0 m) and the low productivity of the water provide good conditions to overwinter trout.

Dickson Dam is a multizoned earthfill structure (Table 2). With 3.6 x 10⁶ m³ of fill, it is one of the largest dams of its type in Alberta. Two dykes border the reservoir at the east end; the north one is 3.1–km long and the south one is 3.7–km long (Fig. 2). Two tunnels under the dam can provide continuous riparian flow of 16 m³/second year-round and can pass flows up to 84 m³/second. The service spillway passes flow in excess of 84 m³/second and can handle flows that would occur in a flood that might be expected only once in every 10 000 years. In the event of a larger flood, the emergency spillway near the east end of the dam would carry the overflow. The two low-level tunnels are equipped to be fitted with turbines in future; they could generate 4 MW at 16 m³/second flow and up to 20 MW

Table 3. Major ions and related water quality variables for Gleniffer Lake. Average concentrations in mg/L; pH in pH units. Composite samples from the euphotic zone collected 8 times from the east end and 6 times from the west end from 28 May to 24 Oct. 1984. S.E. = standard error.

	East		West	
	Mean	S.E.	Mean	S.E.
pH (range)	8.0–8.4[a]	—	8.2–8.3[c]	—
total alkalinity (CaCO₃)	149	4.4	147	3.3
specific conductivity (μS/cm)	347	9.6	344	2.5
total dissolved solids (calculated)	198[b]	3.1	202	4.9
total hardness (CaCO₃)	177	3.9	181	5.7
dissolved organic carbon	2[a]	0.2	2[c]	0.1
HCO₃	174	6.3	173	5.4
CO₃	<4	—	2.8	2.0
Mg	14	0.4	14	0.5
Na	4	0.2	3	0.1
K	1	0.02	0.9	0.01
Cl	0.7[b]	0.07	0.6	0.08
SO₄	41	0.7	42	1.2
Ca	47	1.1	49	1.5

NOTES: [a]n = 7; [b]n = 6; [c]n = 5
SOURCE: Alta. Envir. n.d.[b], Naquadat stations 05AL05CB2000 (east), 05AL05CB2002 (west)

at higher flows. A two-lane road on the dam allows the public to cross the valley.

The dam is operated to fill the reservoir rapidly in the spring to bring the water level to approximately 946.0 m by 1 July (Alta. Envir. n.d.[a]). The level is held close to this throughout the summer to maximize recreational use, yet still retain some capacity to hold floodwater. The reservoir is filled close to its full supply level (947.8 m) by fall (Fig. 4). Water is released at a minimum of 16.0 m³/second all winter, leading to the lowest annual reservoir levels by March or April (Nguyen 1980).

The volume of flow through the reservoir is high; average residence time of the water is 70 days (0.2 years, Table 2). In years of high flow in the Red Deer River, the mean residence time could be as short as 30 days.

Water Quality

The water quality of Gleniffer Lake has been monitored by Alberta Environment since the reservoir was first filled in the summer of 1983 (Alta. Envir. n.d.[b]).

Gleniffer Lake is a well-buffered, freshwater reservoir; its dominant ions are bicarbonate, sulphate and calcium. There is little difference in ionic composition between the west end where the Red Deer River enters the reservoir, and the east end near the dam (Table 3).

The shallower west end is frequently mixed by wind and the inflowing river currents; in 1984, the water column was only weakly thermally stratified in July and August (Fig. 5). The water in this area was well-oxygenated throughout the summer and fall (Fig. 6). The deep east end was thermally stratified from mid-June to the end of August 1984 (Fig. 5). At the same time, dissolved oxygen concentrations were low below 10 m; the water within 5 m of the substrate was anoxic by late July (Fig. 6). In the summers of 1986 and 1987, the deep end was stratified only occasionally and anoxic conditions were not found even at the greatest depth.

Phosphorus concentrations during the open-water period follow a pattern of high levels in spring, possibly due to the inflow of nutrient-rich runoff in the Red Deer River; then a late summer or autumn peak (Fig. 7). The autumn peak occurs when thermal stratification breaks down at the deep east end of the reservoir and the lower stratum of water, which is enriched with nutrients released from anoxic sediment, mixes with the upper stratum of water.

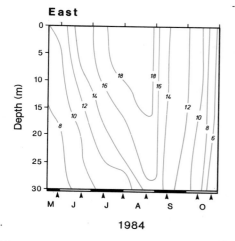

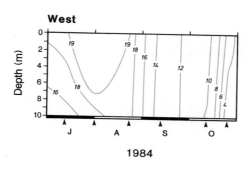

Figure 5. Temperature (°C) of Gleniffer Lake, east and west ends, 1984.
Arrows indicate sampling dates.
SOURCE: Alta. Envir. n.d.[b].

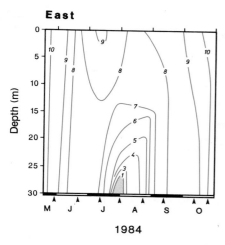

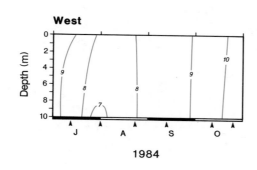

Figure 6. Dissolved oxygen (mg/L) in Gleniffer Lake, east and west ends, 1984. Arrows indicate sampling dates.
SOURCE: Alta. Envir. n.d.[b].

Table 4. Nutrient, chlorophyll *a* and Secchi depth data for Gleniffer Lake. Average concentrations in µg/L. Composite samples from the euphotic zone collected 8 times from the east end and 6 times from the west end from 28 May to 24 Oct. 1984 and 7 times from 13 May to 28 Oct. 1986. S.E. = standard error.

| | 1984 | | | | 1986 | | | |
| | East | | West | | East | | West | |
	Mean	S.E.	Mean	S.E.	Mean	S.E.	Mean	S.E.
total phosphorus	8	1.1	7	0.5	12	1.9	18	3.1
total dissolved phosphorus	—	—	3	0.3	<3	—	<3	—
total Kjeldahl nitrogen	400	112.1	587	161.6	357	41.3	389	35.7
NO$_3$ + NO$_2$ –nitrogen	32[a]	7.4	20	4.0	31	8.2	35	7.1
iron	<30	—	<20	—	—	—	—	—
chlorophyll *a*	1.4	0.20	0.6	0.08	1.9	0.22	1.1	0.13
Secchi depth (m)	4.3[a]	1.07	4.1[b]	0.74	2.4	0.71	1.4	1.50

NOTES: [a]n = 6; [b]n = 4
SOURCE: Alta. Envir. n.d.[b], Naquadat stations 05AL05CB2000 (east), 05AL05CB2002 (west)

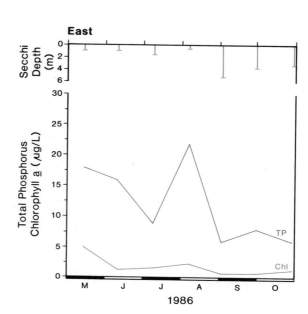

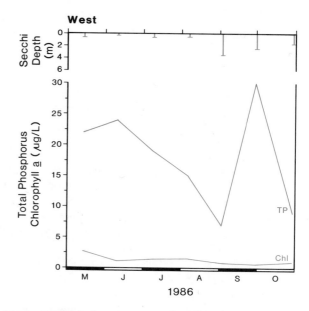

Figure 7. Total phosphorus, chlorophyll *a* and Secchi depth in Gleniffer Lake, 1986.
SOURCE: Alta. Envir. n.d.[b].

Table 5. Percentage composition of major algal groups by total biomass in the east end of Gleniffer Lake, 1986. Composite samples collected from the euphotic zone.

ALGAL GROUP	13 May	10 June	08 July	06 Aug.	02 Sep.	29 Sep.	02 Oct.
Total Biomass (mg/L)	0.350	0.097	0.175	0.207	0.066	0.076	0.093
Percentage Composition:							
Cyanophyta	0	0	3	0	0	0	0
Chlorophyta	0	13	6	1	7	1	0
Chrysophyta	32 *Heterochromonas globosa*	20 *Ochromonas sp.*	23 *Dinobryon divergens*	17	19	11	14
Bacillariophyta	43 *Cyclotella ocellata*	16	7	1	23 *Synedra ulna*	8	10
Cryptophyta	22 *Cryptomonas erosa*	46 *Rhodomonas minuta*	59 *C. erosa*————→	68	51 *R. minuta*	71 *Cryptomonas sp.*	72 *C. erosa*
Pyrrhophyta	3	6	2	13	0	9	3

SOURCE: Alta. Envir. n.d.[b]

Table 6. Species of fish in Gleniffer Lake. Arranged by taxonomic order according to Scott and Crossman 1973.

cutthroat trout	quillback
rainbow trout	longnose sucker
brown trout	white sucker
bull trout	mountain sucker
lake whitefish	shorthead redhorse
mountain whitefish	burbot
goldeye	brook stickleback
mooneye	trout-perch
northern pike	sauger
lake chub	walleye
spottail shiner	sculpin
longnose dace	

SOURCES: Alta. For. Ld. Wild. n.d.; D.A. Westworth Assoc. et al. 1982; R.L. & L. Envir. Serv. Ltd. 1985; Roberts 1987

Chlorophyll *a* levels are consistently low (Table 4, Fig. 7). The low Secchi depth in spring and early summer (Fig. 7) is attributable to suspended sediment in the water, not algae. Gleniffer Lake is considered to be oligotrophic.

Biological Characteristics

Plants

Phytoplankton species composition and density in Gleniffer Lake were monitored by Alberta Environment at three sites monthly during the ice-free period since the reservoir was first filled in 1983, until 1986 (Alta. Envir. n.d.[b]). In general, the low phytoplankton abundance and species composition is indicative of cold, clean nutrient-poor water. For example, in 1986 (Table 5), phytoplankton biomass at the east end of the reservoir peaked in May and was dominated by diatoms (*Cyclotella ocellata*) and chrysophytes (*Heterochromas globosa*). During the rest of the open-water period the algal community was strongly dominated by cryptophytes (*Cryptomonas erosa* and *Rhodomonas minuta*).

There is no detailed information on macrophytes in Gleniffer Lake. Because of annual drawdowns, it is unlikely that areas of abundant macrophytes will develop, except in the trout pond near Dickson Point where dyking prevents water withdrawal during drawdown.

Invertebrates

There are no data on zooplankton or benthic invertebrates in Gleniffer Lake.

Fish

Twenty-three species of fish have been collected from Gleniffer Lake (Table 6); of these, mountain whitefish, northern pike and white suckers are the most common. An average of 223 000 rainbow trout were stocked annually from 1983 to 1986. In 1987, approximately 250 adult trout were introduced. Cutthroat trout were stocked in 1983 and brown trout in 1984. The Red Deer River immediately downstream of the dam was stocked with rainbow trout annually from 1983 to 1987, as was the trout pond near the Dickson Point Day-Use Area. In 1988, approximately 152 000 walleye were introduced into the reservoir (Alta. En. Nat. Resour. 1983; 1985; Alta. For. Ld. Wild. 1986–1988). As of 1989, Fish and Wildlife Division planned to stock a similar number of walleye in each of 1989 and 1990.

In the summer of 1987, during a creel census conducted by Fish and Wildlife Division, 116 anglers at Gleniffer Lake were interviewed. They reported a catch rate of 0.05 fish per hour of angling; 55% of the catch was northern pike, 37% was rainbow trout and 5% was brown trout. A 1986 creel census of 219 anglers on the river below the dam reported 0.02 fish caught per hour; 47% were rainbow trout, 21% were mountain whitefish, 9% were walleye, 8% were sauger, 6% were brown trout and 2% were cutthroat trout. A creel census at the trout pond near Dickson Point reported a catch rate of 0.24 fish per hour, all rainbow trout (Alta. For. Ld. Wild. n.d.).

Fish and Wildlife Division test-netted the reservoir every autumn from 1983 to 1987. In 1987, 245 fish were caught: 50% longnose sucker, 32% white sucker, 10% northern pike, 3% rainbow trout, 3% shorthead redhorse and 1% or less of each of mountain whitefish and burbot (Alta. For. Ld. Wild. n.d.).

Spawning areas of the fish in the reservoir are not known. Winter drawdown limits the habitat within the reservoir for fall spawners and restricts growth of macrophyte beds, which are often used by pike. Suitable habitat does exist upstream on the Red Deer River and in tributaries (D.A. Westworth Assoc. Ltd. et al. 1982). The dam completely blocks fish movement, so species of fish trapped below the dam (mountain whitefish, mooneye, goldeneye), which previously spawned in tributaries above the dam (such as the Raven River), have had to find new spawning areas (Alta. For. Ld. Wild. n.d.; D.A. Westworth Assoc. Ltd. et al. 1982). Fish in the river downstream of the dam appear to have adapted and significant reductions in the populations have not been noticed (Alta. For. Ld. Wild. n.d.).

Accumulation of mercury in fish following the filling of new reservoirs commonly occurs in Canada and throughout the world. The mercury content of fish in the reservoir and in the Red Deer River downstream of the dam has been monitored since 1983 (Moore et al. 1986; Weaver 1989). As of 1988, there was no large increase in the mercury residues in fish compared to levels found before the reservoir was filled. In most instances, the difference in mercury concentrations in muscle tissue from fish of the same length were not statistically significant. Except for large individuals, concentrations rarely exceeded 0.5 μg/g in any species.

Wildlife

There is no readily available information on wildlife at Gleniffer Lake.
J.M. Crosby

References

Alberta Energy and Natural Resources. 1983, 1985. Fish planting list. Fish Wild. Div., Edmonton.
Alberta Environment. n.d.[a]. Devel. Op. Div., Project Mgt. Br. Unpubl. data, Edmonton.
——. n.d.[b]. Envir. Assess. Div., Envir. Qlty. Monit. Br. Unpubl. data, Edmonton.
——. n.d.[c]. Tech. Serv. Div., Hydrol. Br. Unpubl. data, Edmonton.
——. n.d.[d]. Tech. Serv. Div., Surv. Br. Unpubl. data, Edmonton.
Alberta Forestry, Lands and Wildlife. n.d. Fish Wild. Div. Unpubl. data, Edmonton.
——. 1986–1988. Fish planting list. Fish Wild. Div., Edmonton.
——. 1988. Boating in Alberta. Fish Wild. Div., Edmonton.
——. 1989. Guide to sportfishing. Fish Wild. Div., Edmonton.
Alberta Research Council. 1972. Geological map of Alberta. Nat. Resour. Div., Alta. Geol. Surv., Edmonton.
Beak Consultants Ltd. 1977. Red Deer River water quality study. Prep. for Alta. Envir., Plan. Div., Edmonton.
D.A. Westworth and Associates Ltd., R.L. & L. Environmental Services Ltd. and E 5 Ranching and Consulting. 1982. An assessment of fish and wildlife use and enhancement alternatives for the Dickson Dam reservoir. Prep. for Alta. En. Nat. Resour., Fish Wild. Div. and Alta. Envir., Plan. Div., Edmonton.
Energy, Mines and Resources Canada. 1963, 1966, 1967. National topographic series 1:250 000 83B (1963), 82N (1966), 82O (1967). Surv. Map. Br., Ottawa.
Environment Canada. 1982. Canadian climate normals, Vol. 7: Bright sunshine (1951–1980). Prep. by Atm. Envir. Serv. Supply Serv. Can., Ottawa.
——. 1983–1987. Surface water data. Prep. by Inland Waters Directorate. Water Surv. Can., Water Resour. Br., Ottawa.
——. 1985. Historical streamflow summary: Alberta to 1984. Prep. by Inland Waters Directorate. Water Surv. Can., Water Resour. Br., Ottawa.
Holmgren, E.J. and P.M. Holmgren. 1976. Over 2000 place names of Alberta. 3rd ed. West. Producer Prairie Books, Saskatoon.
Moore, J.W., S. Ramamoorthy and A. Sharma. 1986. Mercury residues in fish from twenty-four lakes and rivers in Alberta. Alta. Envir. Centre, Vegreville.
Nguyen, T. 1980. Design of the operational strategy for the Dickson Reservoir. Alta. Envir., Tech. Serv. Div., Edmonton.
Peters, T.W. and W.E. Bowser. 1960. Soil survey of Rocky Mountain House sheet. Alta. Soil Surv. Rep. No. 19, Univ. Alta. Bull. No. SS–1. Univ. Alta., Edmonton.
R.L. & L. Environmental Services Ltd. 1985. A compendium of existing environmental data on Alberta reservoirs. Prep. for Alta. Envir. Res. Trust, Edmonton.
Roberts, W. 1987. Univ. Alta., Dept. Zool., Edmonton. Pers. comm.
Scott, W.B. and E.J. Crossman. 1973. Freshwater fishes of Canada. Fish. Res. Bd. Can. Bull. No. 184, Ottawa.
Strong, W.L. and K.R. Leggat. 1981. Ecoregions of Alberta. Alta. En. Nat. Resour., Resour. Eval. Plan. Div., Edmonton.
Weaver, R.S. 1989. Alta. Envir., Alta. Envir. Centre, Vegreville. Pers. comm.

GULL LAKE

MAP SHEETS: 83A, B
LOCATION: Tp40, 41 R28 W4
Tp41, 42 R1 W5
LAT/LONG: 52°34'N 114°00'W

Gull Lake is a large, shallow lake located west of the town of Lacombe in the counties of Ponoka and Lacombe. Because it is situated between the cities of Edmonton and Calgary, Gull Lake is easily accessible to large numbers of people. Its clear water and sandy beaches contribute to its popularity, and the lake is heavily used on warm, sunny weekends. To reach the lake, take Highway 2 from Edmonton or Calgary to Lacombe, then turn west on Highway 12 and drive for 14 km to the summer village of Gull Lake (Fig. 1).

Homesteaders first settled the region south and west of Gull Lake in about 1895; many of these people came from the United States. By 1902, most of the land had been settled and a lumber industry had been established. A 26–m–long steamboat built in 1898 was used in a sawmill operation at Birch Bay on the northwest shore of Gull Lake (Coulton 1975). Passengers were often carried on this and other steamboats on the lake.

In 1908, Gull Lake served briefly as a hydroelectric reservoir when the Blindman River Electric Power Company Ltd. built a concrete dam on the outlet. Water from the lake was intended to supplement the flow of the Blindman River for power generation, but the dam was destroyed by dynamite in 1910. In ensuing years, the water level of the lake declined, and in 1921, the first formal complaint regarding the low water level was received by the Commissioner of Irrigation in Calgary. The same year, the summer village of Gull Lake built an earth and concrete dam at the outlet, which is now located about 1.6 km from the present shoreline (Bailey 1970).

Between 1924 and 1968, the water level in Gull Lake dropped an average of 6 cm per year, causing great concern among recreational users. In 1967, the Water Resources Division of Alberta Agriculture undertook a series of preliminary studies to try to solve the problem. In 1969 a Gull Lake Study Task Force, formed by personnel from various government agencies, was directed to investigate alternative proposals for stabilizing Gull Lake. Engineering, economic and land use studies were completed in 1970. The decision was made to divert water from the Blindman River through a pipeline and canal to supplement inflow. Pumping began in the spring of 1977, but at present, pumping occurs only when the lake level declines below a designated elevation (Richmond 1988).

Aspen Beach Provincial Park, established in 1932, was one of the first parks in the Alberta park system (Finlay and Finlay 1987). It is located on the southwest shore of Gull Lake. This attractive park, with an area of 2.15 km², has 4 campgrounds with 572 sites, a group camping area, a boat launch, beaches, day-use areas, flush toilets and showers. In addition, there are several campgrounds operated by private owners or nonprofit organizations around the lakeshore. Activities at the lake include sailing, power boating, swimming, fishing and windsurfing. In posted areas of the lake, either all boats are prohibited or power-driven boats are subject to a maximum speed of 12 km/hour (Alta. For. Ld. Wild. 1988).

Gull Lake is used moderately for sport fishing, but there is no commercial or domestic fishery. Northern pike and walleye are the most sought-after sport fish, although lake whitefish are also present in the lake. Walleye have been stocked in Gull Lake in recent years. The diversion canal into the lake is closed to fishing year-round; there are no specific fishing regulations for the lake, but provincial limits apply (Alta. For. Ld. Wild. 1989).

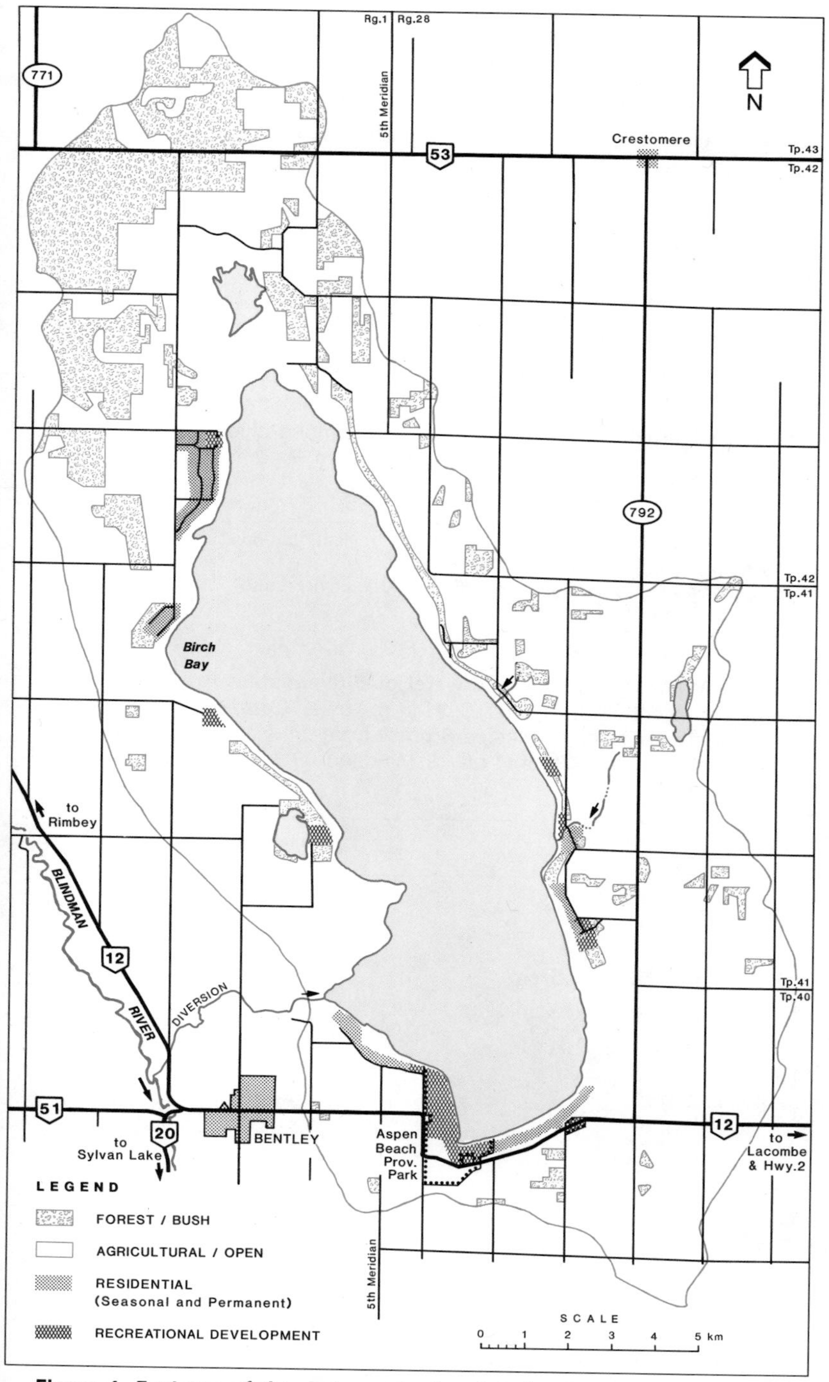

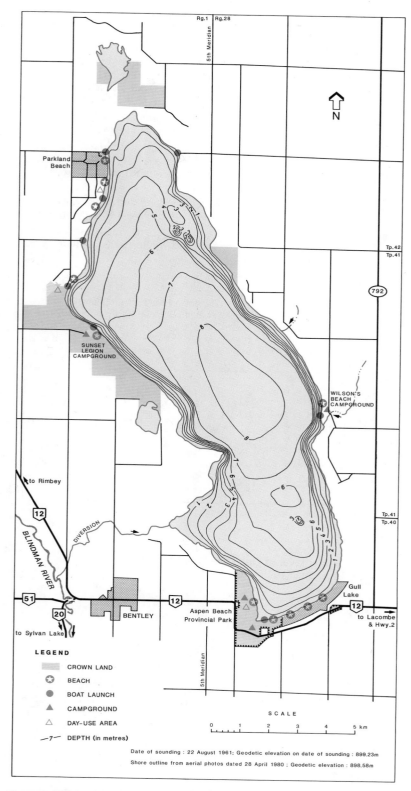

Figure 1. Features of the drainage basin of Gull Lake.
SOURCES: Alta. Envir. n.d.[b]; En. Mines Resour. Can. 1974; 1975.
Updated with 1980 aerial photos.

Figure 2. Bathymetry and shoreline features of Gull Lake.
BATHYMETRY SOURCE: Alta. Envir. n.d.[c].

Drainage Basin Characteristics

The area of the watershed surrounding Gull Lake is about twice the area of the lake (Fig. 1, Tables 1, 2). There are no permanently flowing inlet streams, and the lake's natural outlet in the southwest corner has been dry for many years (Red Deer Reg. Plan. Commis. 1979).

Along the western side of the drainage basin and in the northern one third, soils are Orthic Gray Luvisols that developed on glacial till. Immediately north of the lake, soils are Organics, interspersed with Dark Gray Luvisols that developed on lacustrine material. Eluviated Black Chernozemic soils are present along a narrow strip on the western side of the lake, south of the lake and along the eastern side. The Luvisolic soils have an arability rating of fairly good to good, whereas the Chernozemic soils are rated good to excellent. Near the lake and in the southern part of the watershed, the topography is level, but to the west and east, slopes range from 5 to 15% (Bowser et al. 1947; 1951; Lindsay et al. 1968).

Much of the land in the drainage basin has been cleared for agriculture; cattle production and cereal crops are the main agricultural uses. The native vegetation is typical of the Aspen Parkland and Boreal Mixedwood ecoregions: the dominant trees are trembling aspen, balsam poplar, white spruce and willow.

The fairly extensive recreational development at Gull Lake is concentrated on the southern and southeastern shores, although other parts of the shoreline are also developed. By 1978, about 25% of the shoreline had been developed (Red Deer Reg. Plan. Commis. 1979). The number of cottages along the shore of Gull Lake within the County of Ponoka was estimated to be 157 in 1987 including those in the summer village of Parkland Beach, which was established in 1983 (Heilman 1989). In 1980, it was estimated there were about 330 cottages along the shore within the County of Lacombe, including those in the summer village of Gull Lake (Williams 1989). The summer village of Gull Lake had a population of 102 in 1986.

Lake Basin Characteristics

Gull Lake has one large, shallow basin (Fig. 2). It is oriented in the direction of the prevailing northwest wind, and therefore the water

Table 1. Characteristics of Gull Lake drainage basin.

area (excluding lake) (km²)[a]	206
soil[b]	Eluviated Black and Orthic Dark Gray Chernozemics, Orthic Gray and Dark Gray Luvisols and Orthic Humic Gleysols
bedrock geology[c]	Paskapoo Formation (Tertiary): sandstone, siltstone, mudstone; thin limestone, coal and tuff beds; nonmarine
terrain[b]	undulating (south) to gently rolling (north)
ecoregion[d]	Aspen Parkland and Moist Mixedwood Subregion of Boreal Mixedwood
dominant vegetation[d]	trembling aspen, rough fescue grassland, white spruce, balsam poplar
mean annual inflow (mm)[a, e]	14.3 x 10⁶
mean annual sunshine (h)[f]	2 125

NOTE: [e]excludes annual diversion from Blindman River and groundwater inflow
SOURCES: [a]Alta. Envir. n.d.[b]; [b]Lindsay et al. 1968; [c]Alta. Res. Counc. 1972; [d]Strong and Leggat 1981; [f]Envir. Can. 1982

Table 2. Characteristics of Gull Lake.

elevation (m)[a, b]	899.23
surface area (km²)[a, b]	80.6
volume (m³)[a, b]	437 x 10⁶
maximum depth (m)[a, b]	8.0
mean depth (m)[a, b]	5.4
shoreline length (km)[c]	58.0
mean annual evaporation (mm)[d]	640
mean annual precipitation (mm)[d]	462
mean residence time (yr)[d, e]	>100
operational structure[f]	pumped diversion via canal from Blindman River
elevation of lake outlet (m)[g]	902.2

NOTES: [a]on date of sounding: Aug. 1961; [e]excludes annual diversion from Blindman River and groundwater inflow
SOURCES: [b]Alta. Envir. n.d.[c]; [c]Bailey 1970; [d]Alta. Envir. n.d.[b]; [f]Alta. Envir. n.d.[d]; [g]Rozeboom and Figliuzzi 1985

Table 3. Major ions and related water quality variables for Gull Lake. Average concentrations in mg/L; pH in pH units. Composite samples from the euphotic zone collected 8 times from 24 May to 13 Sep. 1983, 29 May to 20 Aug. 1984 and on 28 May and 09 July 1985. S.E. = standard error.

	Mean	S.E.
pH (range)	9.0–10.1	—
total alkalinity (CaCO₃)	623	4.9
specific conductivity (μS/cm)	1 144	8.7
total dissolved solids (calculated)	713	6.6
total hardness (CaCO₃)	266	4.9
HCO₃	603	6.1
CO₃	77	1.8
Mg	60	1.4
Na	183	3.0
K	18	0.3
Cl	4	0.3
SO₄	67	0.9
Ca	8	0.5

SOURCE: Alta. Envir. n.d.[a], Naquadat station 01AL05CC2050

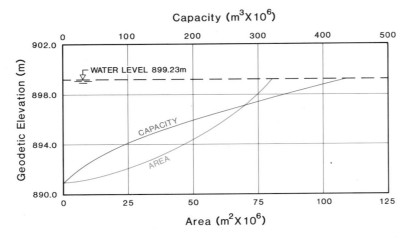

Figure 3. Water level of Gull Lake, 1938 to 1987.
SOURCE: Envir. Can. 1938–1987.

Figure 4. Area/capacity curve for Gull Lake.
SOURCE: Alta. Envir. n.d.[c].

becomes very rough when the wind blows from the northwest or southeast. The greatest depth of the lake, 8 m, covers a large area of the bottom in the centre of the basin. The lake bottom slopes very gradually toward the centre, except along the east and west shores, which are steeper. The shoreline is sandy, but soft organic sediments have accumulated in the shallow water of protected bays.

The water level in Gull Lake was first recorded in 1924, when the lake was at an elevation of 901.45 m. The elevation was also recorded from 1938 to 1946, in 1949, and has been monitored regularly since 1953 (Fig. 3). Between 1924 and 1975, the decline in lake elevation amounted to 2.6 m (Rozeboom and Figliuzzi 1985). The

main reason for the decline was thought to be an increase in the ratio of evaporation to precipitation, but changing groundwater patterns also may have contributed (Bailey 1970). In 1977, Alberta Environment began diverting water from the Blindman River into Gull Lake through a channel dug into the bed of the old outlet creek. The diversion is facilitated by three pumps with a combined maximum pumping capacity of 0.85 m³/second. The maximum amount of water that could be diverted in a full pumping season is about 11 x 10⁶ m³, or 2% of the lake volume. This volume of water would raise the level of the lake about 14 cm (Rozeboom and Figliuzzi 1985) (Fig. 4). Although pumping may occur anytime between March and October, the diversion is limited by the availability of water in the Blindman River. During dry periods, when the water level in the lake is declining, the volume of water in the river tends to be low as well, and pumping is limited. Pumping also does not take place whenever the target elevation is attained, as occurred most of the time between 1982 and 1986 (Richmond 1988). The target elevation of 899.16 m, which was based on recreation studies conducted in about 1969, is lower than lake elevations recorded in the 1920s (Bailey 1970).

Water Quality

Gull Lake was studied by researchers at the University of Alberta in 1973 and 1974 (Alta. Envir. n.d.[a]), and Alberta Environment as-

Table 4. Nutrient, chlorophyll *a* and Secchi depth data for Gull Lake. Average concentrations in μg/L. Composite samples from the euphotic zone collected 6 times from 24 May to 13 Oct. 1983 and 5 times from 29 May to 25 Sep. 1984. S.E. = standard error.

| | 1983 | | 1984 | |
	Mean	S.E.	Mean	S.E.
total phosphorus	36	4.1	41	5.4
total Kjeldahl nitrogen	1 540	72.6	—	—
$NO_3 + NO_2$–nitrogen	10	5.3	—	—
NH_4–nitrogen	32	4.6	—	—
iron	57	18.7	<20[a]	—
chlorophyll *a*	7.3	1.43	6.0	1.04
Secchi depth (m)	2.9	0.54	3.1[b]	0.60

NOTES: [a]n = 2; [b]n = 4
SOURCE: Alta. Envir. n.d.[a], Naquadat stations 01AL05CC2050, 01AL05CC2011

Table 5. Theoretical external phosphorus supply to Gull Lake since beginning of diversion.

	Source	Phosphorus (kg/yr)	Percentage of Total
watershed	forested/bush	434	7
	agricultural/cleared	3 032	51
	residential/cottage	102	2
precipitation/dustfall		1 760	29
sewage[a]		35	<1
Blindman diversion[b]		615	10
	TOTAL	5 978	100
annual areal loading (g/m² of lake surface) 0.07			

NOTE: [a]unmeasured: assumes 4% of all sewage effluent from residences and camps enters the lake, as in Mitchell 1982; [b]assumes full pumping season
SOURCE: Alta. Envir. 1989

sessed the impact of the Blindman River diversion on the water quality of Gull Lake between October 1977 and February 1980 (Mitchell 1981) and again in 1989 (Alta. Envir. n.d.[a]). The lake has also been sampled intermittently since 1983 as part of an ongoing monitoring program conducted jointly by Alberta Environment and Alberta Recreation and Parks (Alta. Envir. 1989).

Gull Lake is slightly saline; the total dissolved solids concentrations (TDS) averaged 713 mg/L between 1983 and 1985 (Table 3). Bicarbonate, sodium and sulphate are the dominant ions. Total dissolved solids concentrations declined slightly between 1977 and 1983 as a result of diversion water inflow that was low in salinity (TDS = 250 mg/L), but concentrations increased in the lake after pumping was discontinued between 1983 and 1986. These fluctuations are within the natural variation observed in lake TDS data prior to the diversion.

This large, shallow lake mixes completely during most of the summer, and temperature remains uniform from the surface to the bottom (Fig. 5). As a result, levels of dissolved oxygen are high throughout the water column (Fig. 6). In winter, dissolved oxygen concentrations decline gradually. Although dissolved oxygen was often negligible a metre or two above the bottom by early March in the years sampled (1978 to 1980 and 1984 to 1986), the upper portion of the water column always had sufficient oxygen to support fish; no winterkills of fish have been reported in Gull Lake.

The relatively low concentrations of chlorophyll *a* in Gull Lake indicate that it is mesotrophic (Table 4), although the phosphorus levels suggest a more productive lake. It appears that the lake's salinity depresses algal biomass (chlorophyll *a*) to some extent, as was found in other saline lakes in Alberta (Bierhuizen and Prepas 1985). The diversion had no detectable effect on chlorophyll levels in Gull Lake up to 1986. Although the concentration of phosphorus in the diversion water is about twice that in the lake water, the supply

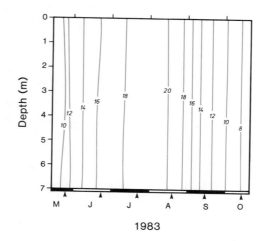

Figure 5. Temperature (°C) of Gull Lake, 1983. Arrows indicate sampling dates.
SOURCE: Alta. Envir. n.d.[a].

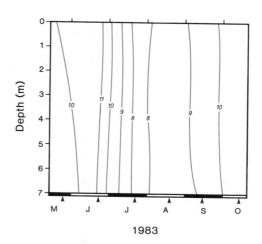

Figure 6. Dissolved oxygen (mg/L) in Gull Lake, 1983. Arrows indicate sampling dates.
SOURCE: Alta. Envir. n.d.[a].

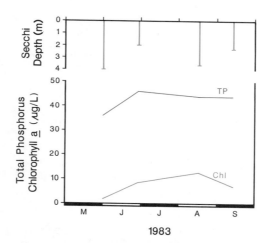

Figure 7. Total phosphorus, chlorophyll *a* and Secchi depth in Gull Lake, 1983.
SOURCE: Alta. Envir. n.d.[a].

of phosphorus to the lake (Table 5) would increase only by about 11% per year during a full pumping season. Runoff over agricultural land during spring snowmelt and summer rainfall contributes the highest percentage of total phosphorus to the lake.

It is probable that some portion of the supply of total phosphorus to Gull Lake is derived from its bottom sediments, as occurs in most shallow, productive lakes in Alberta. Increases in phosphorus and chlorophyll levels in summer (Fig. 7) may be the result of such phosphorus release. This potential source of phosphorus to the lake

Table 6. Percentage composition of major algal groups by total biomass in Gull Lake. Composite samples from the euphotic zone collected 6 times from 24 May to 13 Oct. 1983.

ALGAL GROUP	24 May	22 June	21 July	18 Aug.	14 Sep.	13 Oct.
Total Biomass (mg/L)	0.23	0.31	2.64	2.70	2.04	0.46
Percentage Composition:						
Cyanophyta	0	3	20 *Lyngbya*	8	46 *Gomphosphaeria* *Microcystis*	18
Chlorophyta	49 *Ankyra* *Staurastrum*	33 *Sphaerocystis*	26 *Mougeotia* ⟶	24	25 *Closterium*	10
Chrysophyta	0	9	2	<1	<1	0
Bacillariophyta	0	51 *Amphora* *Asterionella*	47 *Fragilaria* *Stephanodiscus*	34	28 ⟶	67
Cryptophyta	46 *Cryptomonas* *Rhodomonas*	4	2	<1	1	5
Pyrrhophyta	5	0	3	33 *Ceratium*	0	0

SOURCE: Alta. Envir. n.d.[a]

Table 7. Species of aquatic macrophytes in Gull Lake in 1973 and 1974. Arranged by dominance.

submergent	large-sheath pondweed	*Potamogeton vaginatus*
	northern watermilfoil	*Myriophyllum exalbescens*
	Sago pondweed	*Potamogeton pectinatus*
	stonewort	*Chara* sp.
	horned pondweed	*Zanichellia palustris*
emergent	common great bulrush	*Scirpus validus*
	common cattail	*Typha latifolia*
	sedge	*Carex atherodes*
	sedge	*C. rostrata*
	sedge	*C. aquatilis*
	common spike rush	*Eleocharis calva*
	creeping spike rush	*E. palustris* var. *major*
	northern reed grass	*Calamagrostis inexpansa* var. *brevior*
	three-square rush	*Scirpus pungens*
	slough grass	*Beckmannia syzigachne*
	reed canary grass	*Phalaris arundinacea*
	wild mint	*Mentha arvensis* var. *villosa*
	water hemlock	*Cicuta maculata*
	wire rush	*Juncus balticus* var. *littoralis*

SOURCE: Alta. Envir. n.d.[a]

has not been quantified, nor has the phosphorus in local groundwater that may enter the lake.

Biological Characteristics

Plants

The phytoplankton of Gull Lake was studied briefly during a Fish and Wildlife Division survey in 1969 (Kraft 1977) and by Alberta Environment during a water quality assessment in 1983 (Alta. Envir. n.d.[a]). In 1969, green (Chlorophyta) and blue-green (Cyanophyta) algae were most abundant in June and blue-greens (*Anabaena flos-aquae*) dominated the phytoplankton community by mid-August. In 1983 (Table 6), the biomass of phytoplankton was low through May and June, and green algae, diatoms (Bacillariophyta) and crypto-phytes (Cryptophyta) were the dominant groups. The prevalent species included *Ankyra judayii*, *Staurastrum* sp., *Rhodomonas minuta*, *Sphaerocystis schroeteri*, *Amphora ovalis* and *Asterionella formosa*. By mid-July, the total biomass had increased considerably, and the dominant species were the diatoms *Fragilaria crotonensis* and *Stephanodiscus niagarae*, the green alga *Mougeotia* sp., and the blue-green alga *Lyngbya Birgei*. *Mougeotia* sp. maintained a high population through August, but *Fragilaria crotonensis* was re-

placed by *F. capucina*, and *Ceratium hirundinella*, a species of Pyrrhophyta, became dominant. In September and October, the species with the highest biomass was *Fragilaria crotonensis*, followed by *Closterium acutum* and *Gomphosphaeria aponina*.

The macrophyte community of Gull Lake was surveyed in 1973 and 1974 by researchers at the University of Alberta (Table 7). Gull Lake supports extensive submergent macrophyte beds, as might be expected in such a shallow lake, but emergent species such as common cattail (*Typha latifolia*), common great bulrush (*Scirpus validus*) and sedge (*Carex* sp.) were found along only 30% of the shoreline. Limited emergent vegetation was also found during a fish habitat study conducted by Fish and Wildlife Division in 1969 (Fig. 8). Other lakes surveyed during 1973 and 1974 had more extensive emergent beds. Cattail was the most common emergent plant in Gull Lake, whereas in neighbouring lakes, bulrush tended to be most abundant. The submergent zone in Gull Lake was dominated by large-sheath pondweed (*Potamogeton vaginatus*), and in many areas it was the sole species present. It grew abundantly to a depth of 4 m. In shallow areas (less than 1–m deep) northern water-milfoil (*Myriophyllum exalbescens*) and Sago pondweed (*Potamogeton pectinatus*) were common.

Table 8. Average number of benthic invertebrates in Gull Lake. Samples collected by Ekman dredge from June and Aug. 1969 at 4 depths between 0 m and 6 m, from 4 locations on the north, south, east and west sides of the lake. Abundance expressed as mean number/m².

Taxa	June	Aug.
Amphipoda	4 101	710
Trichoptera	43	0
Ephemeroptera	7	5
Diptera	387	603
Pelecypoda	32	11
Hirudinea: Rhynchobdellida	41	5
TOTAL	4 611	1 334

NOTE: n = 16 for both June and Aug.
SOURCE: Kraft 1977

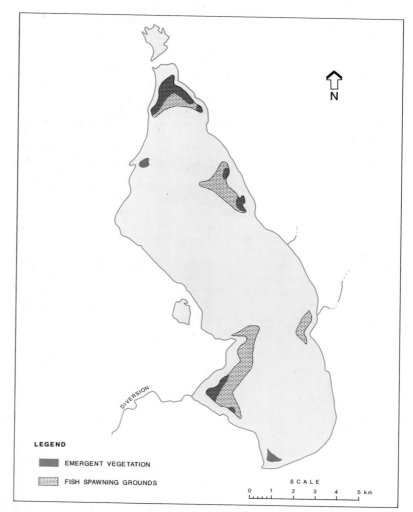

Figure 8. Areas of critical fish habitat in Gull Lake.
SOURCE: Red Deer Reg. Plan. Commis. 1979.

Invertebrates

The zooplankton of Gull Lake was studied by Alberta Environment in 1978 and 1979 as part of an assessment of the impact of the diversion on water quality (Alta. Envir. n.d.[a]; Mitchell 1981). The large grazers, *Daphnia pulicaria* and *Diaptomus sicilis*, were abundant in the spring and early summer of both years, but their populations were smaller through the remainder of the summer to the end of October. Large numbers of the rotifer *Conochilus* sp. were present in July. Seven other species of rotifers were observed sporadically throughout the summer. The predaceous copepod *Diacyclops bicuspidatus thomasi* was most abundant in spring and early summer, but was present throughout the entire open-water season. *Mesocyclops edax* was abundant in midsummer.

Benthic invertebrates were sampled by Fish and Wildlife Division in June and August of 1969 (Kraft 1977). About 98% of the organisms collected were scuds (Amphipoda) and midge larvae (Chironomidae) (Table 8). The greatest number of scuds were collected from depths between 0 and 3 m, whereas the greatest number of midge larvae were found at depths between 3 and 4.5 m.

Fish

White suckers, northern pike, walleye, burbot, lake whitefish, spottail shiners and brook stickleback are known to inhabit Gull Lake (Alta. For. Ld. Wild. n.d.; Paetz and Nelson 1970). One specimen of yellow perch was captured during a Fish and Wildlife Division test netting of the lake in 1969. It was speculated that this was a remnant of a stocking program conducted during the 1960s (Kraft 1977). Yellow perch were also stocked in 1975 and 1977, but none were captured during a Fish and Wildlife Division netting program in 1983, so the species may not have become established in Gull Lake (Kozak 1984).

Gull Lake is managed for sport fishing only. The most sought-after fish are walleye and northern pike. Angling pressure is greatest in spring and then tapers off during summer. In 1969, walleye were most abundant along the east side of the lake in the area known as Wilson's Beach. Most walleye caught in test nets were age six through nine years, even though most of the nets set were of small mesh size (4 and 6 cm). It was thought that the small proportion of young fish was a result of age-class failures (Kraft 1977). Walleye were stocked in 1987, 1988 and 1989 to augment the natural population. After several years, the success of the program will be evaluated (Alta. For. Ld. Wild. n.d.).

Northern pike were found to be sparse during a Fish and Wildlife Division survey in 1969. They were most abundant at the north end of the lake where aquatic vegetation is abundant. Eighty percent of the northern pike captured were 40 to 50 cm in fork length; the largest fish caught weighed 6.8 kg and had a fork length of nearly 1 m. The growth rate of pike in Gull Lake was similar to that of pike captured in test nets in other central Alberta lakes. Their main food was burbot (Kraft 1977).

Lake whitefish were transplanted to Gull Lake from Pigeon Lake in 1975, 1976 and 1977 and have now become established (Alta. For. Ld. Wild. n.d.). In 1983, a test netting program was conducted to evaluate the whitefish population. Most of the fish caught were three, four or five years old. Whitefish in Gull Lake were a greater size at a particular age than those in Pigeon Lake, but smaller at age than those collected from Buck Lake (Kozak 1984).

Wildlife

Gull Lake is one of the few lakes in the region that supports large populations of waterfowl. The lake serves as a staging area during fall migration, and the marshy north end supports Ring-billed Gulls, Black Terns, Common Goldeneye, American Widgeons, Mallards, Blue-winged Teal, White-winged Scoters, Common Mergansers, Common Loons and Red-winged Blackbirds (Red Deer Reg. Plan. Commis. 1979).

P.A. Mitchell and L. Hart Buckland-Nicks

References

Alberta Environment. n.d.[a]. Envir. Assess. Div., Envir. Qlty. Monit. Br. Unpubl. data, Edmonton.
――――. n.d.[b]. Tech. Serv. Div., Hydrol. Br. Unpubl. data, Edmonton.
――――. n.d.[c]. Tech. Serv. Div., Surv. Br. Unpubl. data, Edmonton.
――――. n.d.[d]. Devel. Op. Div., Project Mgt. Br. Unpubl. data, Edmonton.
――――. 1989. Gull Lake. Envir. Assess. Div., Envir. Qlty. Monit. Br., Edmonton.
Alberta Forestry, Lands and Wildlife. n.d. Fish Wild. Div. Unpubl. data, Edmonton.
――――. 1988. Boating in Alberta. Fish Wild. Div., Edmonton.
――――. 1989. Guide to sportfishing. Fish Wild. Div., Edmonton.
Alberta Research Council. 1972. Geological map of Alberta. Nat. Resour. Div., Alta. Geol. Surv., Edmonton.
Bailey, R.E. 1970. Gull Lake study. Prep. for Gull L. Coordinating Commit. by Alta. Agric., Water Resour. Div., Edmonton.

Bierhuizen, J.F.H. and E.E. Prepas. 1985. Relationship between nutrients, dominant ions, and phytoplankton standing crop in prairie saline lakes. Can. J. Fish. Aquat. Sci. 42:1588–1594.

Bowser, W.E., R.L. Erdman, F.A. Wyatt and J.D. Newton. 1947. Soil survey of the Peace Hills sheet. Alta. Soil Surv. Rep. No. 14, Univ. Alta. Bull. No. 48. Univ. Alta., Edmonton.

Bowser, W.E., T.W. Peters and J.D. Newton. 1951. Soil survey of the Red Deer sheet. Alta. Soil Surv. Rep. No. 16, Univ. Alta. Bull. No. 51. Univ. Alta., Edmonton.

Coulton, R.L. 1975. A guide to the historic sites of the Gull Lake region of Alberta. R.L. Coulton, Bentley.

Energy, Mines and Resources Canada. 1974, 1975. National topographic series 1:50 000 83B/8 (1974), 83A/5 (1975), 83A/12 (1975), 83B/9 (1975). Surv. Map. Br., Ottawa.

Environment Canada. 1938–1987. Surface water data. Prep. by Inland Waters Directorate. Water Surv. Can., Water Resour. Br., Ottawa.

———. 1982. Canadian climate normals, Vol. 7: Bright sunshine (1951–1980). Prep. by Atm. Envir. Serv. Supply Serv. Can., Ottawa.

Finlay, J. and C. Finlay. 1987. Parks in Alberta: A guide to peaks, ponds, parklands & prairies. Hurtig Publ., Edmonton.

Heilman, R. 1989. Battle R. Reg. Plan. Commis., Wetaskiwin. Pers. comm.

Kozak, H.M. 1984. A comparison of the growth rate and aging techniques of lake whitefish (*Coregonus clupeaformis*) in Gull Lake. Alta. En. Nat. Resour., Fish Wild. Div., Edmonton.

Kraft, M.E. 1969. Survey for aquatic plant control. Alta. Ld. For., Fish Wild. Div., Edmonton.

———. 1977. Biological survey of Gull Lake, 1969. Alta. Rec. Parks Wild., Fish Wild. Div., Edmonton.

Lindsay, J.D., W. Odynsky, J.W. Peters and W.E. Bowser. 1968. Soil survey of the Buck Lake (NE 83B) and Wabamun Lake (E1/2 83G) areas. Alta. Soil Surv. Rep. No. 24, Univ. Alta. Bull. No. SS–7, Alta. Res. Counc. Rep. No. 87. Univ. Alta., Edmonton.

Mitchell, P.A. 1981. Gull Lake—Effects of diversion on water quality. Alta. Envir., Poll. Contr. Div., Water Qlty. Contr. Br., Edmonton.

———. 1982. Evaluation of the "septic snooper" on Wabamun and Pigeon lakes. Alta. Envir., Poll. Contr. Div., Water Qlty. Contr. Br., Edmonton.

Paetz, M.J. and J.S. Nelson. 1970. The fishes of Alberta. The Queen's Printer, Edmonton.

Red Deer Regional Planning Commission. 1979. Gull Lake management plan. Reg. Plan. Res. Sec., Red Deer.

Richmond, D. 1988. Alta. Envir., Devel. Op. Div., Project Mgt. Br., Edmonton. Pers. comm.

Rozeboom, W.A. and S.J. Figliuzzi. 1985. Gull Lake hydrology study. Alta. Envir., Tech. Serv. Div., Hydrol. Br., Edmonton.

Strong, W.L. and K.R. Leggat. 1981. Ecoregions of Alberta. Alta. En. Nat. Resour., Resour. Eval. Plan. Div., Edmonton.

Williams, A. 1989. Red Deer Reg. Plan. Commis., Red Deer. Pers. comm.

LITTLE FISH LAKE

MAP SHEET: 82P/8
LOCATION: Tp28 R16, 17 W4
LAT/LONG: 51°22′N 112°14′W

Little Fish Lake lies among rolling, grassy hills in the dry, windswept prairies of southern Alberta. The lake is located on the western edge of Special Area No. 2, about 185 km northeast of the city of Calgary. To reach the lake from the city of Drumheller, take Highway 10 south for 15 km and continue east along Secondary Road 573 for 25 km to Little Fish Lake Provincial Park (Fig. 1). An alternate route is to follow Secondary Road 576 east from the city for 35 km, turn south on Secondary Road 851 and continue for 10.5 km to the provincial park. The closest population centre is the hamlet of East Coulee, about 15 km east of the lake.

The original name of Little Fish Lake was Lake of Little Fishes (Roen 1972). Native people dried and smoked fish from the lake for a winter food supply. Settlers also caught fish from the lake as an important food supplement. In early historic times the Blackfoot and Crow people both claimed the nearby Hand Hills area as a favorite buffalo-hunting ground, and territorial disputes were frequent. An old Indian trail that crossed the mouth of Willow Creek and led to Little Fish Lake still existed in 1972 (Roen 1972). The mixed-grass vegetation made the region ideal for cattle ranching and cattle grazed on the open range at the turn of the century. In 1909, the area was opened to homesteaders and the range land was fenced. In 1989, cattle grazing remained the primary land use in the region.

In 1934, land around Little Fish Lake was reserved for a park (Alta. Rec. Parks n.d.[a]). A local organization built Fish Lake Hall shortly after, and the hall and lake were used by local residents for a number of years. Interest in the park revived in the 1950s, and in 1957, Little Fish Lake Provincial Park was established. Activities enjoyed at the park are camping, picnicking, power boating and wind surfing. The park covers 0.61 km², and its facilities consist of 100 random campsites, picnic sites, a playground, a beach, a boat launch and tap water. In posted areas, all vessels are prohibited or power boats are restricted to maximum speeds of 12 km/hour (Alta. For. Ld. Wild. 1988). There are no sport fishing regulations specific to Little Fish Lake, but Fish Creek and its tributaries are closed to sport fishing from 1 November to 15 June each year (Alta. For. Ld. Wild. 1989[b]).

Little Fish Lake is an important staging area for waterfowl during fall migration. The lake is shallow, slightly saline, and very productive; algal blooms flourish in summer. Since the early 1980s, declining water levels and poor water quality have had a detrimental effect on recreational use of the lake (Monenco Consult. Ltd. 1987). Swimming in Little Fish Lake is not recommended because algal blooms occasionally become toxic during late summer (Charlton and Brennan 1986). Also, the yellow perch population has decreased considerably and, as of 1988, Fish and Wildlife Division suspended the perch stocking program (Lowe 1988). In 1987, Alberta Environment investigated the possibility of diverting water into the lake to regulate water levels and improve water quality (Monenco Consult. Ltd. 1987). However, the study suggested that additional water quality data should be collected to augment the available baseline information and that the current low water levels were a natural extreme. Water diversion into Little Fish Lake was not recommended.

Drainage Basin Characteristics

Little Fish Lake is located on the southern edge of the Hand Hills, an ancient plateau that rises 225 m above the surrounding prairie (Thormin 1980). The terrain consists of rolling hills and steep-sided

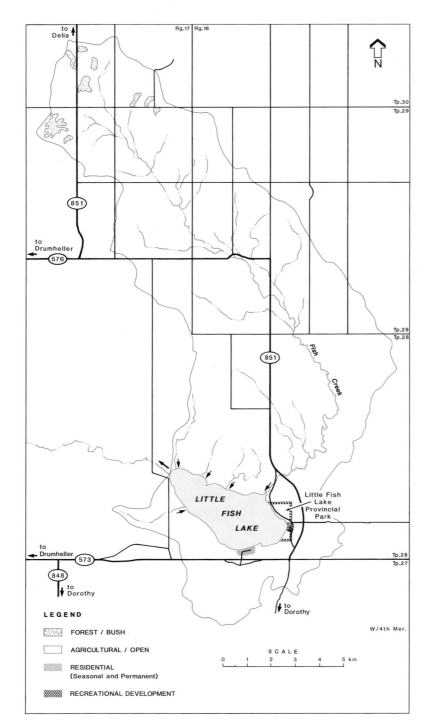

Figure 1. Features of the drainage basin of Little Fish Lake.
SOURCES: Alta. Envir. n.d.[b]; En. Mines Resour. Can. 1977. Updated with 1981 aerial photos.

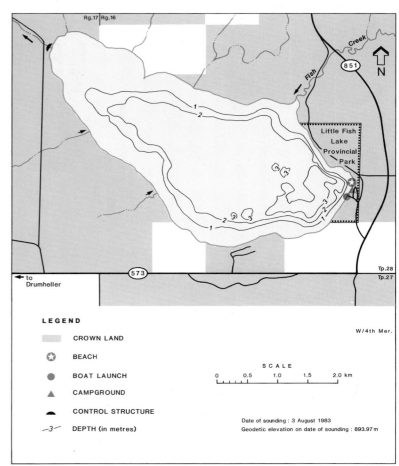

Figure 2. Bathymetry and shoreline features of Little Fish Lake.
BATHYMETRY SOURCE: Alta. Envir. n.d.[c].

Table 1. Characteristics of Little Fish Lake drainage basin.

area (excluding lake) (km²)[a]	157
soil[b]	Orthic Dark Brown Chernozemics
bedrock geology[c]	Horseshoe Canyon Formation (Upper Cretaceous): sandstone, mudstone, shale; ironstone, scattered coal and bentonite beds; mainly nonmarine
terrain[d]	rolling to hilly
ecoregion[e]	Mixed Grass
dominant vegetation[e]	spear, grama and wheat grasses
mean annual inflow (m³)[a, f]	2.50 x 10⁶
mean annual sunshine (h)[g]	2 334

NOTE: [f]excluding groundwater inflow
SOURCES: [a]Alta. Envir. n.d.[b]; [b]Wallis and Wershler 1985; [c]Alta. Res. Counc. 1972; [d]Wyatt et al. 1943; [e]Strong and Leggat 1981; [g]Envir. Can. 1982

Table 2. Characteristics of Little Fish Lake.

elevation (m)[a, b]	893.87
surface area (km²)[a, b]	7.09
volume (m³)[a, b]	12.5 x 10⁶
maximum depth (m)[a, b]	3.0
mean depth (m)[a, b]	1.76
shoreline length (km)[c]	14.3
mean annual lake evaporation (mm)[d]	725
mean annual precipitation (mm)[d]	372
mean residence time (yr)[d, e]	>100
control structure[f]	fixed-crest earthfill weir
weir height (m)[f]	unknown

NOTES: [a]on date of sounding: 03 Aug. 1983; [e]excluding groundwater inflow
SOURCES: [b]Alta. Envir. n.d.[c]; [c]En. Mines Resour. Can. 1977; [d]Alta. Envir. n.d.[b]; [f]Ducks Unltd. (Can.) n.d.

coulees (Table 1). Ground moraine and gravelly/sandy glaciofluvial materials are the major surficial deposits (Wallis and Wershler 1985); a commercial gravel pit operates south of the lake.

Water flows into Little Fish Lake primarily from the north via Fish Creek and several intermittent streams (Fig. 1). The outflow is a tributary of Willow Creek, which eventually flows into the Red Deer River, but since the early 1960s, there has been no surface outflow from the lake (Monenco Consult. Ltd. 1987).

Little Fish Lake is part of the Mixed Grass Ecoregion (Strong and Leggat 1981). The natural vegetation mainly consists of several species of grasses, including grama, spear, June and wheat grasses, which are underlain by Orthic Dark Brown Chernozemic soils, the dominant soils in the region. The grasslands are very productive and well adapted to grazing. Agricultural land use in the area is primarily cattle grazing and secondarily hay production (Wallis and Wershler 1985). Shrub communities grow in depressions, coulees and seepage sites, and include clumps of snowberry, wild rose, sage, willow, buckbrush and saskatoon (Ducks Unltd. (Can.) n.d.). A small area in

Table 3. Major ions and related water quality variables for Little Fish Lake. Average concentrations in mg/L; pH in pH units. Composite samples from the euphotic zone collected 6 times from 06 June to 18 Oct. 1983. S.E. = standard error.

	Mean	S.E.
pH (range)	8.8–9.1	—
total alkalinity (CaCO₃)	909	17.1
specific conductivity (μS/cm)	1 697	45.1
total dissolved solids (calculated)	1 107	24.0
turbidity (NTU)	24	3.8
colour (Pt)	62	9.5
total hardness (CaCO₃)	262	24.8
HCO₃	827	17.4
CO₃	138	15.6
Mg	54	6.2
Na	309	5.6
K	66	1.7
Cl	23	0.7
SO₄	89	5.2
Ca	16	0.5

SOURCE: Alta. Envir. n.d.[a], Naquadat station 01AL05CG2000

the north-central region of the watershed is part of the Hand Hills Ecological Reserve. Ecological reserves are maintained in their natural state and are used for nature appreciation, photography and wildlife viewing (Alta. Rec. Parks n.d.[b]). The Hand Hills reserve is representative of natural prairie grasslands and is part of the largest area of northern fescue grassland left in the world. Rough fescue is the dominant grass and oat grass and bluegrass are secondary species. The forb community is lush, and is composed of *Hedysarum* spp., lily and Indian paint-brush (Wallis and Wershler 1985). Sedges grow around the lake.

Shoreline development at Little Fish Lake is limited to a small group of summer cottages on the south shore and the provincial park on the east shore. Most of the land adjacent to the lake is Crown land (Fig. 2) and is leased for cattle grazing. Cattle have access to the lake on the north and west shores, and in these areas, the shoreline is heavily grazed (Hammer 1988).

Lake Basin Characteristics

The surface area of Little Fish Lake occupies about 5% of the drainage basin area (Table 2). The lake is 5.3–km long and 2.7–km wide. The oval-shaped basin slopes gently to the deepest areas (3 m), which are located offshore of the provincial park (Fig. 2). The west and central areas of the lake are no deeper than 2 m. The lake sediments are sandy near the eastern shore, with mud, gravel and rock in other regions (Alta. For. Ld. Wild. n.d.).

In 1939, the elevation of Little Fish Lake, reported to be 897.3 m, appeared to have declined since the topographic survey of the lake area in 1920 (Alta. For. Ld. Wild. n.d.). In the mid–1960s, water levels were high and outflow caused erosion at the lake's outlet. Consequently, in 1966, Ducks Unlimited (Canada) constructed a 27.4–m–long, fixed-crest earthfill weir with a natural spillway (Ducks Unltd. (Can.) n.d.). The structure was intended to prevent further reductions in water level and to create shallow bays to enhance waterfowl production. The level of the lake, however, has decreased continuously since it was first monitored in 1973 (Fig. 3). Between 1975 and 1989, the surface elevation declined by about 3.4 m. The historic maximum water level, recorded on 11 June 1975, is 895.98 m, and the historic minimum water level, recorded on 26 July 1989, is 892.54 m. Figure 4 illustrates changes in the lake's area and capacity as the water level changes (up to an elevation of 893.87 m). The current low water levels should not be considered permanent, but rather a natural extreme brought about by the climatic conditions that have prevailed over the past few years. Surface runoff and precipitation have decreased while evaporation

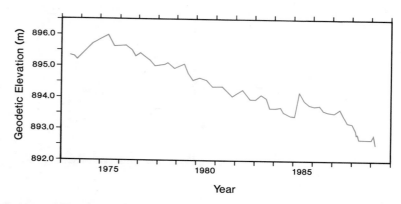

Figure 3. Water level of Little Fish Lake, 1973 to 1989. SOURCE: Alta. Envir. n.d.[c].

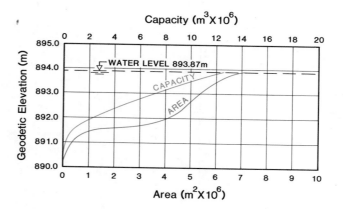

Figure 4. Area/capacity curve for Little Fish Lake. SOURCE: Alta. Envir. n.d.[c].

losses have increased, resulting in lowered lake levels. Alberta Environment studied the feasibility of diverting water into Little Fish Lake from either the Red Deer River or the Sheerness pipeline water supply, but the project benefit:cost ratio did not warrant lake regulation (Monenco Consult. Ltd. 1987). There is insufficient information to determine the role that groundwater plays in the lake's water balance.

Water Quality

Little Fish Lake was studied by Alberta Environment in 1983 as part of a preliminary investigation of water quality in southern Alberta lakes and reservoirs (Charlton and Brennan 1986) and again in 1985 (Alta. Envir. n.d.[a]). The lake is alkaline and slightly saline, and the dominant ions are bicarbonate, carbonate and sodium (Table 3). The salinity may be increasing because of evaporative concentration as water levels decline (Monenco Consult. Ltd. 1987).

The entire water column mixed fairly continuously during the summer of 1983. Consequently, the water temperature was uniform throughout the lake, except for July when the water column was weakly thermally stratified (Fig. 5). Dissolved oxygen levels remained high during the summer although the lake was weakly stratified from June through August (Fig. 6). In winter, dissolved oxygen concentrations vary considerably from year to year (Lowe 1988). Levels were relatively high in March 1986 (8.5 to 10.0 mg/L at a depth of 3 m), but considerably lower in February 1987 (1.1 to 2.3 mg/L at a depth of 1.8 m). In March 1980 the water column was almost anoxic (0.8 mg/L).

Little Fish Lake is hyper-eutrophic; concentrations of phosphorus and chlorophyll *a* are among the highest reported in studies on other lakes in the province (Alta. Envir. n.d.[a]). In 1983, the midsummer and late fall maxima of chlorophyll *a* and total phosphorus (Fig. 7, Table 4) may have resulted from phosphorus recycling from bottom sediments. However, little is known about internal loading of phosphorus in saline as compared with freshwater lakes. Because algal concentrations were high, the water was very murky throughout the

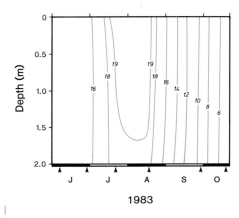

Figure 5. Temperature (°C) of Little Fish Lake, 1983. Arrows indicate sampling dates. SOURCE: Alta. Envir. n.d.[a].

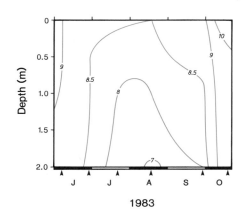

Figure 6. Dissolved oxygen (mg/L) in Little Fish Lake, 1983. Arrows indicate sampling dates.
SOURCE: Alta. Envir. n.d.[a].

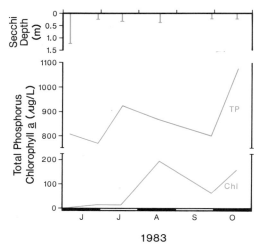

Figure 7. Total phosphorus, chlorophyll *a* and Secchi depth in Little Fish Lake, 1983.
SOURCE: Alta. Envir. n.d.[a].

Table 4. Nutrient, chlorophyll *a* and Secchi depth data for Little Fish Lake. Average concentrations in μg/L. Composite samples from the euphotic zone collected 6 times from 06 June to 18 Oct. 1983. S.E. = standard error.

	Mean	S.E.
total phosphorus	876	46.7
total Kjeldahl nitrogen	3 160	284.1
$NO_3 + NO_2$–nitrogen	30[a]	16.2
chlorophyll *a*	77.1	33.70
Secchi depth (m)	0.4	0.16

NOTE: [a]n = 5
SOURCE: Alta. Envir. n.d.[a], Naquadat station 01AL05CG2000

open-water period, and Secchi depths were low. Even so, salinity may have depressed algal production to some extent (Bierhuizen and Prepas 1985).

Biological Characteristics

Plants

In 1983, the algal community in Little Fish Lake was studied by Alberta Environment (Charlton and Brennan 1986). Blue-green algae reached nuisance proportions in 1983 and 1984. Also, concerns were expressed by local residents when three dogs died after ingesting thick algal scum near the shore in 1982 (Alta. Envir. n.d.[a]). Such toxic algal blooms are rare and unpredictable, and occur when common species of blue-green algae develop a toxic strain. In 1983, blue-green algae (Cyanophyta) were numerically dominant during August and September; the most common species were *Microcystis aeruginosa* and *Aphanizomenon flos-aquae*. These species were toxic during September when they were senescing.

Macrophytes are present only in small areas of the lake; plant growth is probably limited by lack of light penetration, wave action and the sandy substrate. In 1966, the species of submergent plants observed were northern watermilfoil (*Myriophyllum exalbescens*), Sago pondweed (*Potamogeton pectinatus*) and Richardson pondweed (*Potamogeton richardsonii*). The spike rush (*Eleocharis* sp.), an emergent plant, was found in shallow bays. In 1982, the most prominent submergent plant was large-sheath pondweed (*Potamogeton vaginatus*) (Ducks Unltd. (Can.) n.d.).

Invertebrates

There are no data available on invertebrate species in Little Fish Lake.

Fish

Early in the twentieth century, fish were reported to be plentiful in Little Fish Lake. In the 1920s, people came from as far away as 30 km to catch fish with "fish nets, hay forks and horsefly nets", and wagonloads of fish were removed from the lake each year (Roen 1972). Since then, however, the fish population has declined dramatically. For example, northern pike and white suckers were abundant in 1939 but northern pike have since disappeared (Alta. For. Ld. Wild. n.d.). The last sauger was netted in 1970 (Wiebe 1978). Walleye eggs were stocked in 1978 and walleye fry in 1979, but the species did not survive. As well, yellow perch were stocked in 1956, 1958, 1960 and 1981 (Alta. For. Ld. Wild. n.d.; Alta. Rec. Parks Wild. 1978; Alta. En. Nat. Resour. 1979; 1981).

In May 1983, 42 yellow perch and 102 white suckers were caught in test nets, and in July, the lake was stocked with 2 816 yellow perch (Alta. En. Nat. Resour. 1983; Lowe 1988). In June 1985, however, only four perch and one white sucker were caught in test nets. The success of fish-planting operations in Little Fish Lake is limited by the low dissolved oxygen levels during summer and winter. Fish restocking programs will not be continued until water levels increase and stabilize (Lowe 1988).

Wildlife

At least 15 species of ducks and shorebirds are regular summer residents on and around Little Fish Lake and nearby ponds. Ducks include Green-winged Teal, Mallards, Pintails, Blue-winged Teal, Shovellers, Gadwall, American Widgeons, Lesser Scaup, Ruddy Ducks and American Coots (Wallis and Wershler 1985; Finlay and Finlay 1987). More than 30 additional species of waterbirds have been recorded as summer visitors or migrants to Little Fish Lake (Wallis and Wershler 1985). Although the sparse growth of aquatic plants limits nesting areas, the lake is an important staging area for waterfowl during migration. Canada Geese have been seen on the lake (Ducks Unltd. (Can.) n.d.) and the northwest shore is a regular resting site for flocks of hundreds to thousands of Snow Geese during fall migration (Wallis and Wershler 1985). Ross's Geese, White Pelicans, Common Loons, Whistling Swans and Common Mergansers also use the lake (Finlay and Finlay 1987). Little Fish Lake and the region within 0.8 km of the entire lakeshore is a Restricted Wildlife Area. Hunting of game birds is prohibited until 1 November each year (Alta. For. Ld. Wild. n.d.[a]). This restriction helps to minimize the impact of hunting on migration.

Shorebirds sighted at Little Fish Lake include Spotted Sandpipers, Wilson's Phalaropes, Willets, Marbled Godwits, Killdeer, American Avocets and Piping Plovers. The latter three species are found only at the northwest end of the lake. Upland Sandpipers nest well back from the lake on the sparsely vegetated backshore, while American Avocets nest closer to the water and on the islands that form periodically; Piping Plovers nest on pebbly portions of the shoreline.

Chestnut-collared Longspurs, Clay-coloured and Vesper sparrows, Sprague's Pipits, Prairie Falcons, Ferruginous and Swainson's hawks, and Sharp-tailed Grouse have been seen in the area (Finlay and Finlay 1987).

Mammals sighted near Little Fish Lake include pronghorn antelope, mule deer, white-tailed jackrabbits, Richardson's ground squirrels, badgers, coyotes and long-tailed weasels. Plains and western garter snakes have been seen in the grasslands (Finlay and Finlay 1987).

L.G. McIntyre

References

Alberta Energy and Natural Resources. 1979, 1981, 1983. Fish planting list. Fish Wild. Div., Edmonton.

Alberta Environment. n.d.[a]. Envir. Assess. Div., Envir. Qlty. Monit. Br. Unpubl. data, Edmonton.

———. n.d.[b]. Tech. Serv. Div., Hydrol. Br. Unpubl. data, Edmonton.

———. n.d.[c]. Tech. Serv. Div., Surv. Br. Unpubl. data, Edmonton.

Alberta Forestry, Lands and Wildlife. n.d. Fish Wild. Div. Unpubl. data, Edmonton.

———. 1988. Boating in Alberta. Fish Wild. Div., Edmonton.

———. 1989[a]. Guide to game bird hunting. Fish Wild. Div., Edmonton.

———. 1989[b]. Guide to sportfishing. Fish Wild. Div., Edmonton.

Alberta Lands and Forests. 1956, 1958, 1960. Fish planting list. Fish Wild. Div., Edmonton.

Alberta Recreation and Parks. n.d.[a]. Parks Div. Unpubl. data, Edmonton.

———. n.d.[b]. Ecological reserves. Now ... and forever. Advisory Commit. on Wilderness Areas and Ecol. Reserves, Edmonton.

Alberta Recreation, Parks and Wildlife. 1978. Fish planting list. Fish Wild. Div., Edmonton.

Alberta Research Council. 1972. Geological map of Alberta. Nat. Resour. Div., Alta. Geol. Surv., Edmonton.

Bierhuizen, J.F.H. and E.E. Prepas. 1985. Relationship between nutrients, dominant ions, and phytoplankton standing crop in prairie saline lakes. Can. J. Fish. Aquat. Sci. 42:1588–1594.

Charlton, S.E.D. and K.A. Brennan. 1986. Water quality among southern Alberta lakes and reservoirs. Alta. Envir., Poll. Contr. Div., Water Qlty. Contr. Br. Unpubl. rep., Calgary.

Ducks Unlimited (Canada). n.d. Unpubl. data, Edmonton.

Energy, Mines and Resources Canada. 1977. National topographic series 1:50 000 82P/8 (1977). Surv. Map. Br., Ottawa.

Environment Canada. 1982. Canadian climate normals, Vol. 7: Bright sunshine (1951–1980). Prep. by Atm. Envir. Serv. Supply Serv. Can., Ottawa.

Finlay, J. and C. Finlay. 1987. Parks in Alberta: A guide to peaks, ponds, parklands & prairies. Hurtig Publ., Edmonton.

Hammer, F. 1988. Alta. Rec. Parks, Parks Div., Midland Prov. Park. Pers. comm.

Lowe, D. 1988. Alta. For. Ld. Wild., Fish Wild. Div., Red Deer. Pers. comm.

Monenco Consultants Limited. 1987. Little Fish Lake regulation study. Prep. for Alta. Envir., Plan. Div., Calgary.

Roen, H.B. 1972. The grass roots of Dorothy. Northwest Printing and Lithographing, Calgary.

Strong, W.L. and K.R. Leggat. 1981. Ecoregions of Alberta. Alta. En. Nat. Resour., Resour. Eval. Plan. Div., Edmonton.

Thormin, T. 1980. Hand Hills, p. 131–132. In D.A.E. Spalding [ed.] A nature guide to Alberta. Prov. Museum Publ. No. 5. Hurtig Publ., Edmonton.

Wallis, C. and C. Wershler. 1985. Little Fish Lake resource assessment for ecological reserves planning in Alberta. Alta. En. Nat. Resour., Tech. Rep. No. T/82, Edmonton.

Wiebe, A.P. 1978. Survey of Little Fish Lake. Alta. Rec. Parks Wild., Fish Wild. Div., Calgary.

Wyatt, F.A., J.D. Newton, W.E. Bowser and W. Odynsky. 1943. Soil survey of Rosebud and Banff sheets. Alta. Soil Surv. Rep. No. 12, Univ. Alta. Bull. No. 40. Univ. Alta., Edmonton.

PINE LAKE

MAP SHEETS: 83A/3, 4
LOCATION: Tp36 R24, 25 W4
LAT/LONG: 52°04'N 113°27'W

Pine Lake is a long, narrow lake set in an attractively wooded valley 35 km southeast of the city of Red Deer. Its location midway between the cities of Calgary and Edmonton makes it a very popular destination for recreational users throughout the summer and for ice fishing in the winter. To reach Pine Lake from Red Deer, take Highway 2 south for 8 km, then turn east on Highway 42 and drive for about 25 km to the north end of the lake (Fig. 1).

The name "Pine Lake" recalls a very colourful chapter in Alberta's history. In about 1830, Blackfoot Indians raided a sleeping band of Cree Indians on the east shore of the lake and killed every man, woman and child in the camp. Only one Cree warrior survived, having been away hunting at the time. This lone man painted his face black in mourning, then set out to avenge his family and comrades. Stealthily creeping into camp at night or ambushing individuals, he managed to kill and scalp many of his enemies. For years afterwards both tribes avoided the lake in the belief that the region was haunted by ghosts of the murdered Cree. A contorted old pine tree grew near the shore and the lake was named Ghostpine or Devil's Pine Lake. Stories also report a headless horseman rising out of the swamp southeast of Pine Lake, then galloping along high banks in the light of the full moon (Elnora Hist. Commit. 1972; Holmgren and Holmgren 1976). The name "Devil's Pine Lake" is on an 1892 survey map and in an 1894 Northwest Mounted Police report, but when the post office opened in 1895, that name was thought to be "too cumbersome" and it was shortened to Pine Lake (Elnora Hist. Commit. 1972). The creek draining the lake is still named Ghostpine.

Settlers arrived in the area in the early 1890s, and the recreational potential of Pine Lake was soon recognized; it is now one of Alberta's most intensively developed lakes. In 1984, approximately 35% of the shoreline was developed, including five institutional camps and eight commercial operations with motel, hotel and campsite facilities. There were also 121 seasonal cottage lots (96 developed), 93 grouped country residential lots and 20 isolated country residential lots (Marshall Macklin Monaghan West. Ltd. 1984). Only 1% of the shore is Crown land and the only public access to the lake is at a small Alberta Transportation and Utilities day-use area at the north end of the lake (Fig. 2). This area includes a picnic shelter and a boat launch. There are five other boat launches on the lake at commercially operated resorts. There are no government-operated campgrounds on Pine Lake, but there are 6 commercially operated campgrounds offering a total of 1 080 campsites (Alta. Hotel Assoc. 1988).

The water in Pine Lake is nutrient-rich and becomes green with algae by midsummer. The lake is very popular for water skiing, power boating, swimming, and fishing for northern pike and yellow perch, especially during midsummer weekends. Conflicting opinions on "appropriate use" of the lake and levels of overcrowding led to the development of a management plan for the lake in 1977 (Red Deer Reg. Plan. Commis. 1977). One recommendation was for strict control of boating, including zoning the lake for maximum speeds. Another recommendation was for monitoring of water quality, which was thought to be deteriorating. Subsequently, the lake's water quality was studied in 1978, 1979, 1984 and 1989 by Alberta Environment. As of 1988, however, boating conflicts had not been resolved. Regulations in effect that year prohibited all boats from the swimming areas and restricted power boat speeds to 12 km/hour in posted areas (Alta. For. Ld. Wild. 1988). To protect the northern pike

Table 1. Characteristics of Pine Lake drainage basin.

area (excluding lake) (km²)[a]	150
soil[b]	Orthic Black, Dark Brown and Dark Gray Chernozemics
bedrock geology[c]	Paskapoo Formation (Tertiary): sandstone, siltstone, mudstone; thin limestone, coal and tuff beds; nonmarine
terrain[d]	gently rolling to rolling
ecoregion[d]	Groveland Subregion of Aspen Parkland
dominant vegetation[d]	trembling aspen, rough fescue
mean annual inflow (m³)[a, e]	2.77 × 10⁶
mean annual sunshine (h)[f]	2 125

NOTE: [e]excluding groundwater inflow
SOURCES: [a]Alta. Envir. n.d.[b]; [b]Bowser et al. 1951; Pedol. Consult. 1980; [c]Alta. Res. Counc. 1972; [d]Strong and Leggat 1981; [f]Envir. Can. 1982

Table 2. Characteristics of Pine Lake.

elevation (m)[a, b]	889.34
surface area (km²)[a, b]	3.89
volume (m³)[a, b]	20.6 × 10⁶
maximum depth (m)[a, b]	12.2
mean depth (m)[a, b]	5.3
shoreline length (km)[c]	19.9
mean annual lake evaporation (mm)[d]	640
mean annual precipitation (mm)[d]	522
mean residence time (yr)[d, e]	9.0
control structure	none

NOTES: [a]on date of sounding: June 1967; [e]excluding groundwater inflow
SOURCES: [b]Alta. Envir. n.d.[c]; [c]En. Mines Resour. Can. 1974; [d]Alta. Envir. n.d.[b]

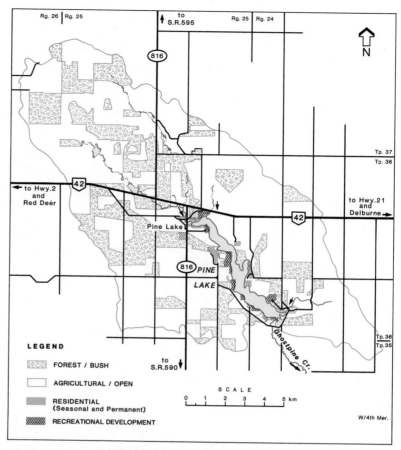

Figure 1. Features of the drainage basin of Pine Lake.
SOURCES: Alta. Envir. n.d.[b]; En. Mines Resour. Can. 1974. Updated with 1980 aerial photos.

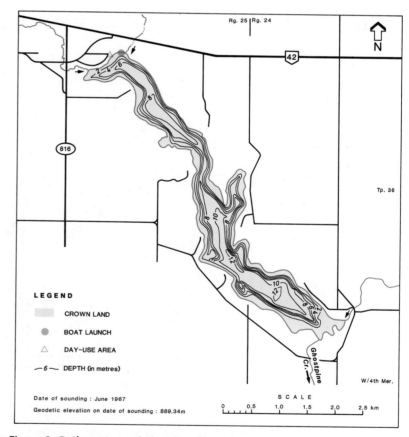

Figure 2. Bathymetry and shoreline features of Pine Lake.
BATHYMETRY SOURCE: Alta. Envir. n.d.[c].

population, angling is not permitted in Ghostpine Creek or any of the streams flowing into Pine Lake for a designated period each spring (Alta. For. Ld. Wild. 1989).

Drainage Basin Characteristics

The drainage basin area of Pine Lake is very large, almost 40 times the area of the lake (Tables 1, 2). Much of the northwest portion of the basin is a type of hummocky moraine called knob and kettle terrain, a patchwork of tiny pothole lakes that formed when lumps of glacial ice disrupted the even deposition of glacial till. When the ice lumps finally melted they left the potholes, or kettles. The heaps of gravel that accumulated around the ice lumps now form small hills, or knobs. In this type of terrain, much of the runoff is trapped in the potholes and seldom reaches major water bodies like Pine Lake. Therefore, the effective basin for Pine Lake may be much smaller than the apparent basin. The low ridge of hills along the southwest edge of the basin rises 110 m above the lake to an elevation of 1 000 m and the hills on the northeast edge rise to about 960 m. The bedrock in the area is Paskapoo Formation, which underlies a thick layer of glacial till in most of the basin, but outcrops on some steep slopes and escarpments bordering the lake (Pedol. Consult. 1980).

The drainage basin is part of the Groveland Subregion of the Aspen Parkland Ecoregion (Strong and Leggat 1981). Soils are typically well-drained Orthic Dark Brown and Black Chernozemics, some Dark Gray Chernozemics with Gleysols in low-lying, poorly drained areas and Organic soils in wet sedge-marsh areas (Bowser 1951; Pedol. Consult. 1980; Strong and Leggat 1981). The native vegetation is predominantly rough fescue grass on dry, south-facing areas and aspen-dominated woodlands on some north slopes and level areas. White spruce grow on cool, damp, north-facing slopes and willows and sedges grow around wetlands. In 1988, half of the basin

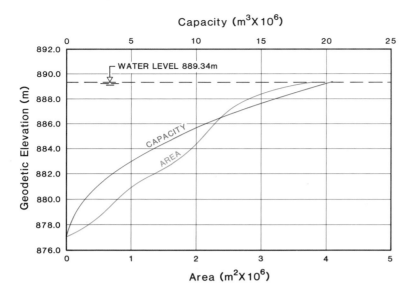

Figure 3. Area/capacity curve for Pine Lake.
SOURCE: Alta. Envir. n.d.[c].

Table 3. Major ions and related water quality variables for Pine Lake. Average concentrations in mg/L; pH in pH units. Composite samples from the euphotic zone collected from 3 sites 4 times from 12 July to 17 Sep. 1984. S.E. = standard error.

	Mean	S.E.
pH (range)	7.9–8.9	—
total alkalinity (CaCO₃)	319	2.3
specific conductivity (μS/cm)	726	3.4
total dissolved solids (calculated)	450	1.4
total hardness (CaCO₃)	160	2.8
HCO₃	343	6.8
CO₃	23	3.5
Mg	25	0.8
Na	108	1.9
K	10	0.1
Cl	6	0.1
SO₄	84	0.3
Ca	23	0.4

SOURCE: Alta. Envir. n.d.[a], Naquadat stations 01AT05CE2300 (north end), 01AT05CE2200 (middle), 01AT05CE2031 (south end)

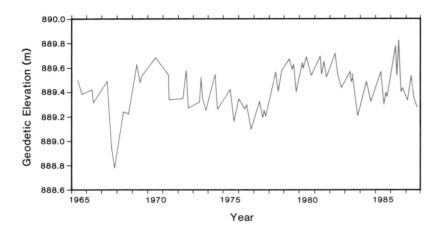

Figure 4. Water level of Pine Lake, 1966 to 1987.
SOURCE: Envir. Can. 1965–1987.

had been cleared for agriculture, primarily for cereal crop production or mixed farming, and 48% remained uncleared. Approximately one percent of the basin had been developed for cottages and commercial resorts; almost all of this development is along the shore of the lake.

Lake Basin Characteristics

Pine Lake is a serpentine lake with a maximum length of 6.4 km and a maximum width of 0.8 km lying in a narrow glacial meltwater channel. There are two basins: the north basin has a maximum depth of 9.1 m and the south basin has two areas with maximum depths greater than 12 m (Fig. 2). There is a shallow shelf around most of the shore where the water is less than 1.5–m deep. The maximum depth of aquatic plant colonization in this lake is approximately 4 m (Hamilton 1980); 25% of the area of the lake is shallower than this depth (Fig. 3).

A large proportion of the littoral zone has a gravel or sand substrate (Hamilton 1980). Beaches are scarce (850 m total length), are generally narrow and weedy, and tend to be located in small bays (Marshall Macklin Monaghan West. Ltd. 1984). Sand has been imported to many of the beaches near resorts. The shoreline has eroded in several locations and some property owners have installed structures to retard the process.

Pine Lake is fed by several intermittent streams, most of which enter the northern half of the lake. Groundwater inflow to the lake has not been quantified but is likely significant. The outlet stream, Ghostpine Creek, flows out of the south end of the lake, then into Threehills Creek just before Threehills Creek enters the Red Deer River near the city of Drumheller. The residence time of water in the lake is estimated to be nine years (Table 2). However, as some inflow enters the lake near the outlet at the south end, the effective residence time in most of the lake may be longer.

The level of Pine Lake is fairly stable compared to that of many Alberta lakes. From 1966 through 1987, the maximum historic elevation, recorded in 1986, was 1.06 m above the short-lived minimum elevation recorded in 1967 (Fig. 4). From 1977 to 1987 the level varied only 0.6 m. Pine Lake's users, particularly cottage and resort owners, have periodically expressed concern that water levels are either too high or too low. Studies conducted for Alberta Environment have recommended that if a decision is made to regulate the lake, the target lake level should be close to the natural elevation (Hamilton and Bayne 1984; Marshall Macklin Monaghan West. Ltd. 1984).

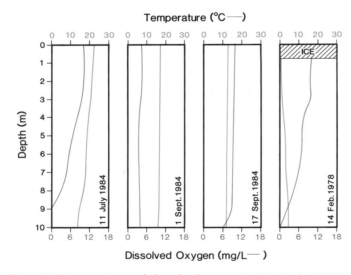

Figure 5. Temperature and dissolved oxygen in Pine Lake, 1978 and 1984.
SOURCE: Alta. Envir. n.d.[a].

Table 4. Nutrient, chlorophyll _a_ and Secchi depth data for Pine Lake.
Average concentrations in µg/L. Composite samples from the euphotic zone collected 5 times from 01 May to 30 Sep. 1979 and 4 times from 3 sites from 12 July to 17 Sep. 1984. S.E. = standard error.

	1979		1984	
	Mean	S.E.	Mean	S.E.
total phosphorus	—	—	56	5.5
total Kjeldahl nitrogen	1 293	81.8	1 302	131.1
$NO_3 + NO_2$–nitrogen	13	5.6	<10	—
NH_4–nitrogen	—	—	59	22.2
iron	38	5.7	28	6.6
chlorophyll _a_	11.3	2.34	26.3	3.97
Secchi depth (m)	3.4	0.75	1.8	0.32

SOURCE: Alta. Envir. n.d.[a], Naquadat stations 01AT05CE2300 (north end), 01AT05CE2200 (middle), 01AT05CE2031 (south end)

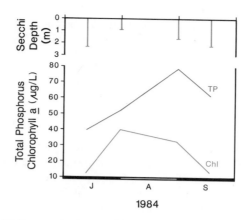

Figure 6. Total phosphorus, chlorophyll _a_ and Secchi depth in Pine Lake, 1984.
SOURCE: Alta. Envir. n.d.[a].

Water Quality

The water quality of Pine Lake has been a concern to recreational users since the early 1970s and was the major impetus for the Pine Lake Management Plan (Red Deer Reg. Plan. Commis. 1977). Water quality was monitored by Alberta Environment in 1978, 1979, 1984 and 1989 (Alta. Envir. n.d.[a]; Hamilton 1980; Hamilton and Bayne 1984). The disposal of sewage from commercial and institutional resorts was also investigated (Alta. Envir. 1972), as were feedlots near the shore (Masuda 1974).

Pine is a freshwater lake. The water is well-buffered and the dominant ions are bicarbonate, sodium and sulphate (Table 3).

The lake water is thermally stratified during calm periods in the summer, as on 11 July 1984 (Fig. 5). When the lake is stratified, the dissolved oxygen concentration decreases in the water near the bottom, and the water may become anoxic in the lowest metre or two. When the lake mixes during windy periods, this anoxic water mixes with the upper layers. This can result in fairly low dissolved oxygen concentrations throughout the water column, as on 1 September 1984 (Fig. 5). Prolonged windy periods increase the dissolved oxygen concentration throughout the water column, as on 17 September 1984. In the winter, dissolved oxygen is depleted by bacterial decomposition of organic matter in the sediment. Anoxic conditions develop near the bottom of the lake but the dissolved oxygen concentration in the upper part of the water column remains fairly high (14 February 1978, Fig. 5). Winter or summer fishkills due to low dissolved oxygen concentrations are not a problem in Pine Lake (Hamilton 1980; Lowe 1989).

Pine Lake is eutrophic. By midsummer, chlorophyll _a_ concentrations are high and the water is a murky green (Table 4, Fig. 6). The total phosphorus concentration rises through the summer as a result of phosphorus released from the sediment, especially during periods when water near the sediment becomes anoxic. In 1984, chlorophyll _a_ concentrations in Pine Lake were almost double those in 1978 or 1979 (Hamilton and Bayne 1984). Low dissolved oxygen concentrations over the sediment and subsequent high phosphorous concentrations in the water column are factors that enhance blue-green algal abundance in Pine Lake (Trimbee and Prepas 1987; 1988). Although the water quality of the lake apparently worsened from 1978 to 1984 despite the rise in water levels, it is not yet possible to determine if this is indicative of a long-term trend or if one of the years represented an extreme year in the normal variation of algal populations.

Most of the phosphorus entering the lake from external sources likely comes in the runoff from cleared agricultural land. The input from septic systems on the lakeshore is difficult to assess, partly due to the uncertain efficiency of sewage disposal systems of cottages and resorts on the lake. A brief 1973 survey of three feedlots adjacent to the lake found that although streams flowing into the lake were high in nutrients, little enrichment could be detected within the

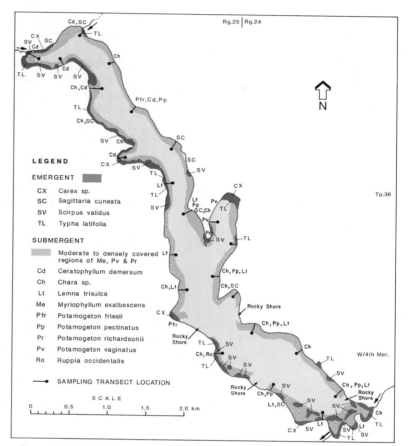

Figure 7. Species composition and distribution of aquatic macrophytes in Pine Lake, August 1979.
SOURCE: Hamilton 1980.

lake; however, sampling was done during a dry period when runoff was low (Masuda 1974). Much of the phosphorus in the lakewater is likely released from the sediment, especially when the water near the substrate becomes anoxic.

Biological Characteristics

Plants

During an Alberta Environment study in 1978, the abundance of each group of algae was determined for three sites in Pine Lake on six sampling dates (Hamilton 1980). The dominant species were those common in eutrophic lakes. The spring algal peak in May was primarily composed of diatoms (*Asterionella formosa*, *Fragilaria* spp., *Melosira* sp. and *Stephanodiscus hantzschia*) and cryptomonads (*Cryptomonas* sp.). The summer peak was dominated by blue-green algae (*Anabaena* sp. and *Aphanizomenon flos-aquae*) and diatoms.

Aquatic macrophytes were mapped by Alberta Environment in August 1979 (Fig. 7). The macrophyte community in Pine Lake is extensive; only a few rocky areas in the southern portion are devoid of plants. Submergent species grew to a depth of 4 m. Northern watermilfoil (*Myriophyllum exalbescens*), large-sheath pondweed (*Potamogeton vaginatus*) and Richardson pondweed (*P. richardsonii*) were the dominant species. Emergent vegetation occurs along most of the western shore; the most common species is cattail (*Typha latifolia*).

Invertebrates

One zooplankton sample was collected by vertical haul net in August 1979 by Alberta Environment. Dominant species were *Daphnia galeata mendotae*, *Ceriodaphnia lacustris*, *Chydorus sphaericus*, *Mesocyclops edax* and *Diaptomus oregonensis*.

There are no data on the benthic invertebrates in Pine Lake.

Fish

There are nine species of fish in Pine Lake: northern pike, yellow perch, walleye, burbot, white sucker, lake chub, fathead minnow, Iowa darter and brook stickleback (Norris 1984; Roberts 1987). The lake supports a sport fishery but not commercial or domestic fisheries.

Northern pike and yellow perch are the mainstay of the sport fishery. Test nets in January 1985 caught six pike and eight perch. The largest pike was 51.4 cm and the largest perch was 27.0 cm. Yellow perch are so abundant in Pine Lake that they are occasionally netted there for stocking in other Alberta lakes. Walleye, which were stocked annually from 1960 to 1963 and 1971 to 1974, are thriving and becoming increasingly available to anglers (Alta. For. Ld. Wild. n.d.). In 1985, Fish and Wildlife Division caught 85 walleye in one sweep of a 30-m seine. There were representatives of most year-classes in the haul, indicating that walleye are reproducing successfully in Pine Lake (Lowe 1989). To speed the establishment of a good walleye sport fishery, an additional 115 000 fingerlings were introduced in 1988.

Localized fish kills of yellow perch were reported in Pine Lake in the 1980s. The cause was found to be caudal peduncle disease, a condition caused by the myxobacterium, *Cytophagia psychrophila*. It strikes perch during and following spawning in late April and May. Affected perch develop red sores in the vicinity of the base of the tail, and severely afflicted fish die. The disease seems to disappear when the water warms in late May (Lowe 1989).

Wildlife

Pine Lake provides moderate waterfowl nesting habitat, especially at the south end and in weedy bays. Intense recreational development has restricted waterfowl use of the central portion of the lake.

J.M. Crosby

References

Alberta Environment. n.d.[a]. Envir. Assess. Div., Envir. Qlty. Monit. Br. Unpubl. data, Edmonton.
———. n.d.[b]. Tech. Serv. Div., Hydrol. Br. Unpubl. data, Edmonton.
———. n.d.[c]. Tech. Serv. Div., Surv. Br. Unpubl. data, Edmonton.
———. 1972. Sewage treatment and disposal report. Poll. Contr. Div., Mun. Eng. Br., Edmonton.
Alberta Forestry, Lands and Wildlife. n.d. Fish Wild. Div. Unpubl. data, Edmonton.
———. 1988. Boating in Alberta. Fish Wild. Div., Edmonton.
———. 1989. Guide to sportfishing. Fish Wild. Div., Edmonton.
Alberta Hotel Association. 1988. 1988 Alberta campground guide. Prep. for Travel Alta., Edmonton.
Alberta Research Council. 1972. Geological map of Alberta. Nat. Resour. Div., Alta. Geol. Surv., Edmonton.
Bowser, W.E., T.W. Peters and J.D. Newton. 1951. Soil survey of Red Deer sheet. Alta. Soil Surv. Rep. No. 16, Univ. Alta. Bull. No. 51. Univ. Alta., Edmonton.
Elnora History Committee. 1972. Buried treasures: The history of Elnora, Pine Lake and Huxley. Elnora Hist. Commit., Elnora.
Energy, Mines and Resources Canada. 1974. National topographic series 1:50 000 83A/3 (1974), 83A/4 (1974). Surv. Map. Br., Ottawa.
Environment Canada. 1965–1987. Surface water data. Prep. by Inland Waters Directorate. Water Surv. Can., Water Resour. Br., Ottawa.
———. 1982. Canadian climate normals, Vol. 7: Bright sunshine (1951–1980). Prep. by Atm. Envir. Serv. Supply Serv. Can., Ottawa.
Hamilton, H.R. 1980. Pine Lake water quality report. Alta. Envir., Poll. Contr. Div., Calgary.
——— and D. Bayne. 1984. Water quality implications of regulating the water level of Pine Lake. Alta. Envir., Poll. Contr. Div., Calgary.
Holmgren, E.J. and P.M. Holmgren. 1976. Over 2000 place names of Alberta. 3rd ed. West. Producer Prairie Books, Saskatoon.
Lowe, D. 1989. Alta. For. Ld. Wild., Fish Wild. Div., Red Deer. Pers. comm.
Marshall Macklin Monaghan Western Limited. 1984. Pine Lake regulation study: Recreation assessment. Prep. for Alta. Envir., Plan. Div., Edmonton.
Masuda, A. 1974. Pine Lake survey. Alta. Envir., Poll. Contr. Div., Edmonton.
Norris, H.J. 1984. A comparison of aging techniques and growth of yellow perch (*Perca flavescens*) from selected Alberta lakes. MSc thesis. Univ. Alta., Edmonton.
Pedology Consultants. 1980. Soil survey and land suitability evaluation of the Pine Lake study area. Prep. for Alta. Envir., Ld. Conserv. Reclamation Div., Edmonton.
Red Deer Regional Planning Commission. 1977. Pine Lake management plan—A summary statement. Red Deer Reg. Plan. Commis., Reg. Plan. Res. Sec., Red Deer.
Roberts, W. 1987. Univ. Alta., Dept. Zool., Edmonton. Pers. comm.
Strong, W.L. and K.R. Leggat. 1981. Ecoregions of Alberta. Alta. En. Nat. Resour., Resour. Eval. Plan. Div., Edmonton.
Trimbee, A.M. and E.E. Prepas. 1987. Evaluation of total phosphorus as a predictor of the relative biomass of blue-green algae with emphasis on Alberta lakes. Can. J. Fish. Aquat. Sci. 44:1337–1342.
———. 1988. The effect of oxygen depletion on the timing and magnitude of blue-green algal blooms. Verh. Internat. Verein. Limnol. 23:220–226.

SYLVAN LAKE

MAP SHEET: 83B/8
LOCATION: Tp39 R1, 2 W5
LAT/LONG: 52°18'N 114°06'W

Sylvan Lake is a large, beautiful lake lying in a shallow basin just west of the city of Red Deer. Its clear water, sandy beaches and proximity to Edmonton, Red Deer and Calgary make it one of the most popular recreational lakes in Alberta. To reach the east end of the lake, the town of Sylvan Lake and Sylvan Lake Provincial Park, travel west from Red Deer on Highway 11A for 15 km. Highway 11A continues westward on the south side of the lake and Highway 20 provides access to Jarvis Bay Provincial Park on the northeast shore (Fig. 1). Sylvan Lake includes portions of the counties of Lacombe and Red Deer.

When the first settlers arrived at Sylvan Lake in 1899, the lake was named Snake Lake from the Indian name *Kinabik*, which referred to the numerous garter snakes in the area. The name was officially changed to Sylvan Lake in 1903 (Gaetz 1948). "Sylvan" is from the Latin *sylvanus*, which means "of a forest".

By 1904, the first cottages, a hotel, a store and a post office had been built at the southeast end of the lake and the area started to become a summer resort (Alta. Rec. Parks n.d.; Gaetz 1948). A lumber mill operated near the lake in the early 1900s and the forest gradually disappeared as trees were cut for lumber. By 1923, there were 185 permanent residents in the village of Sylvan Lake; this number had grown to 700 by 1934 (Dawe n.d.) and 3 937 in 1988 (T. Sylvan L. 1988). The first cottage subdivision was started in 1932 (Alta. Rec. Parks n.d.). The same year, Sylvan Lake Provincial Park was established on the shore of the lake near the town. Provincial park status was removed in 1966 and the park was operated by the municipality until 1980, when it was reinstated as a provincial park (Alta. Rec. Parks n.d.). A second area, Jarvis Bay Provincial Park, was established in 1965 to provide camping facilities on the lake.

Sylvan Lake Provincial Park covers 85 ha and includes a portion of the lake and a narrow strip of beautiful sandy beach between the lake and Highway 11A, which borders the town of Sylvan Lake (Fig. 2). Picnic tables, tap water, change houses, public telephones, playgrounds and a pier are all provided. Boat traffic is prohibited along most of the sand beach and along the northern portion of the park, boat speed is restricted to 12 km/hour (Alta. For. Ld. Wild. 1988). Jarvis Bay Provincial Park is located on Highway 20, 7 km north of the town of Sylvan Lake. It provides 167 campsites, tap water, showers, hiking trails and a public telephone, but there is no beach or boat launch. Access on the north shore is provided at a day-use area operated by a group of citizens, the North Sylvan Public Access Association. Facilities include a concrete boat launch and picnic tables. There are seven privately owned campgrounds within 2 km of the town of Sylvan Lake. The town includes a marina, boat rental businesses, a waterslide and numerous hotels and restaurants. There is a boat launch at the marina, for which a fee is charged, and there are several access points for small boats around the lakeshore.

The shore of Sylvan Lake is quite intensively developed. There are four summer villages, the town of Sylvan Lake and six subdivisions on the lake. In 1977, the cottage density was estimated to be 33 cottages per km of shoreline (MTB Consult. Ltd. 1982). Approximately 16% of the shoreline, including road allowances, is Crown land (Fig. 2), 11% is occupied by 9 institutional camps and 73% is private land (Red Deer Reg. Plan. Commis. 1985). Sylvan Lake Natural Area is an 11–ha area on the northwest shore of the lake where a small portion of the shore is protected in its natural state (Alta. For. Ld. Wild. 1987).

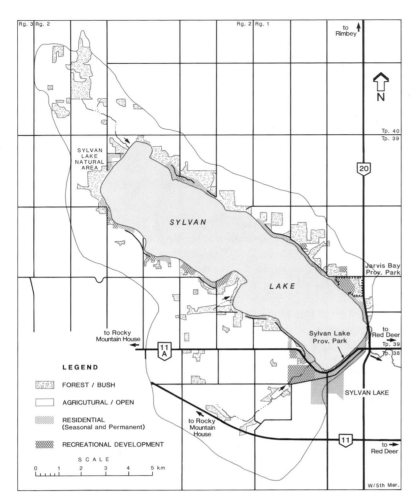

Figure 1. Features of the drainage basin of Sylvan Lake.
SOURCES: Alta. Envir. n.d.[c]; En. Mines Resour. Can. 1974. Updated with 1984 aerial photos.

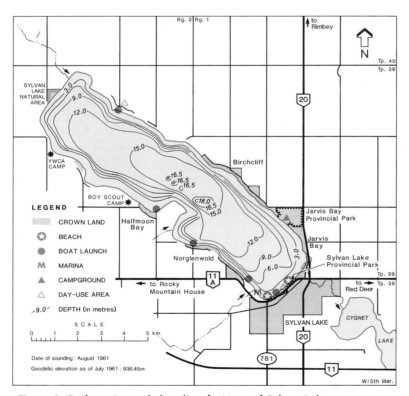

Figure 2. Bathymetry and shoreline features of Sylvan Lake.
BATHYMETRY SOURCE: Alta. Envir. n.d.[c].

Table 1. Characteristics of Sylvan Lake drainage basin.

area (excluding lake) (km²)[a]	102
soil[b]	Orthic Gray and Dark Gray Luvisols
bedrock geology[c]	Paskapoo Formation (Tertiary): sandstone, siltstone, mudstone; thin limestone, coal and tuff beds; nonmarine
terrain[d]	undulating to rolling
ecoregion[d]	Moist Mixedwood Subregion of Boreal Mixedwood
dominant vegetation[d]	trembling aspen, now cleared for agriculture
mean annual inflow (m³)[a, e]	6.54 x 10⁶
mean annual sunshine (h)[f]	2 125

NOTE: [e]excluding groundwater inflow
SOURCES: [a]Alta. Envir. n.d.[b]; [b]Peters and Bowser 1960; Pedocan Ld. Eval. Ltd. 1985; [c]Alta. Res. Counc. 1972; [d]Strong and Leggat 1981; [f]Envir. Can. 1982

Sylvan Lake has clear water, little algal growth and few areas of dense aquatic macrophytes. Although summerkills occur occasionally, the lake supports a popular year-round sport fishery for pike, perch and, in recent years, walleye. Provincial sport fishing regulations apply to Sylvan Lake; no fishing is permitted in the lake or any tributaries or the outlet stream for a designated period in April and May (Alta. For. Ld. Wild. 1989).

Drainage Basin Characteristics

The drainage basin of Sylvan Lake is only 2.5 times the area of the lake (Tables 1, 2). The basin includes an area of rolling hills to the northwest that decline gently to undulating to flat terrain at the east end of the lake. The lake lies in a preglacial valley, which slopes toward the southeast. Bedrock, of the Paskapoo Formation (Table 1), is less than 15 m below the surface over most of the area and strongly influences landforms north of the lake, where it is often within 1 m of the surface. The glacial till southeast of the lake is up to 60–m deep (Pedocan Ld. Eval. Ltd. 1985). The dominant soils in the watershed are Orthic Gray Luvisols developed on weakly calcareous glacial till. The soils around Sylvan Lake are in a transitional zone from Black Chernozemics south of the lake to Gray Luvisols north of the lake. There is a small area of Chernozemic soils off the northwest end of the lake and a pocket of Organic soils and peat in the Sylvan Lake Natural Area (Peters and Bowser 1960; Pedocan Ld. Eval. Ltd. 1985).

Most of the drainage basin was originally forested with trembling aspen (Strong and Leggat 1981). Now, some forest areas remain close to the lake, but approximately 90% of the drainage basin has been cleared for agriculture (Fig. 1). Cereal grain, canola production and mixed farming are the main land uses.

Lake Basin Characteristics

Sylvan Lake is a single rectangular basin that is 13.2–km long and 3.2–km wide (Fig. 2). The lake bottom slopes very gently at the southeast end but more steeply along the northeast and southwest sides. The lake bottom is generally flat, with a small area at the centre declining to the lake's maximum depth of 18.3 m (Fig. 2). At an elevation of 936.5 m, 20% of the lake is occupied by the littoral zone (Fig. 3), which is less than 3.5–m deep.

The lake's shoreline is mostly sand or a mixture of rock and gravel (Jones et al. 1976), but the bottom is soft in sheltered bays. Vertical sandstone banks rise to a height of 20 m along the northeast shore (Strome 1978). As with most Alberta lakes, the substrate in deeper water is soft organic-based ooze.

The inflowing streams flow only intermittently. The outlet stream flowed during part of only three years between 1955 and 1976; it enters Cygnet Lake (Fig. 1), then flows southeast to the Red Deer River. Sylvan Lake is also supplied by numerous submerged springs

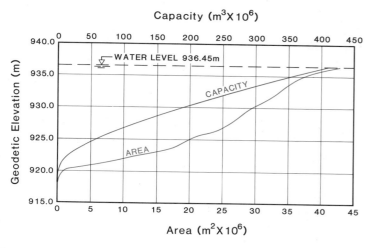

Figure 3. Area/capacity curve for Sylvan Lake.
SOURCE: Alta. Envir. n.d.[c].

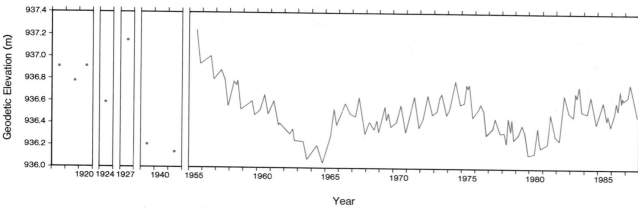

Figure 4. Water level of Sylvan Lake, 1918 to 1987.
SOURCE: Envir. Can. 1918–1987.

Table 2. Characteristics of Sylvan Lake.

elevation (m)[a, b]	936.45
surface area (km²)[a, b]	42.8
volume (m³)[a, b]	412 x 10⁶
maximum depth (m)[a, b]	18.3
mean depth (m)[a, b]	9.6
shoreline length (km)[c]	36.0
mean annual lake evaporation (mm)[d]	640
mean annual precipitation (mm)[d]	504
mean residence time (yr)[d, e]	>100
control structure[b]	none

NOTES: [a]on date of sounding: 29 Aug. 1961; [e]excluding groundwater inflow
SOURCES: [b]Alta. Envir. n.d.[c]; [c]En. Mines Resour. Can. 1974; [d]Alta. Envir. n.d.[b]

Table 3. Major ions and related water quality variables for Sylvan Lake.
Average concentrations in mg/L; pH in pH units. Composite samples from the euphotic zone collected 3 times from 27 May to 12 Aug. 1986. S.E. = standard error.

	Mean	S.E.
pH (range)	8.8–9.0	—
total alkalinity (CaCO₃)	325	1.8
specific conductivity (μS/cm)	597	3.5
total dissolved solids (calculated)	338	1.6
total hardness (CaCO₃)	198	6.9
HCO₃	354	3.7
CO₃	21	1.2
Mg	37	1.3
Na	64	0.6
K	7	0.1
Cl	<1	—
SO₄	16	2.1
Ca	18	0.6

SOURCE: Alta. Envir. n.d.[a], Naquadat station 01AL05CC2220

(Red Deer Reg. Plan. Commis. 1977; Stolte and Herrington 1980).

The water level of Sylvan Lake is quite stable; from 1957 to 1987 the range was only 0.7 m. The present water levels are similar to levels recorded between 1918 and 1941 (Fig. 4).

Water Quality

The water quality in Sylvan Lake is monitored jointly by Alberta Environment and Alberta Recreation and Parks. As well, temperature profiles were taken on 10 dates between May and October in 1973 and 1974 (Alta. Envir. n.d.[a]).

Sylvan Lake is a well-buffered, freshwater lake; its dominant ions are bicarbonate, sodium and magnesium (Table 3). The high sodium and magnesium concentrations support the concept of substantial groundwater inflow. The lake, which is large and exposed to winds,

Temperature (°C —→)

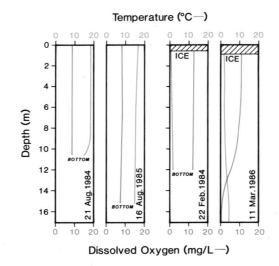

Figure 5. Temperature and dissolved oxygen in Sylvan Lake, 1984 and 1986.
SOURCE: Alta. Envir. n.d.[a].

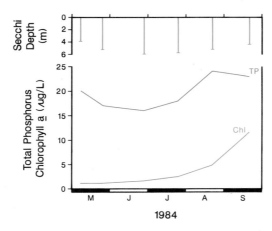

Figure 6. Total phosphorus, chlorophyll *a* and Secchi depth in Sylvan Lake, 1984.
SOURCE: Alta. Envir. n.d.[a].

Table 4. Nutrient, chlorophyll *a* and Secchi depth data for Sylvan Lake. Average concentrations in μg/L. Composite samples from the euphotic zone collected 6 times from 07 May to 20 Sep. 1984, and 6 times from 27 May to 20 Sep. 1986. S.E. = standard error.

	1984		1986	
	Mean	S.E.	Mean	S.E.
total phosphorus	20	1.3	21	2.1
iron	<20[a]	—	<20[b]	—
chlorophyll *a*	3.8	1.66	3.7	1.10
Secchi depth (m)	5.0	0.30	4.7	0.58

NOTES: [a]n = 2; [b]n = 3
SOURCE: Alta. Envir. n.d.[a], Naquadat station 01AL05CC2220

Aquatic macrophytes were surveyed in July and August 1976 during a fisheries study for Alberta Environment (Jones et al. 1976). Macrophytes occurred in patches in sheltered areas around the lake and grew densely in the northwest end. The most common emergent species were bulrush (*Scirpus* sp.) and common cattail (*Typha latifolia*). Submergent macrophytes, which grew to a depth of 3.5 m, included pondweeds (*Potamogeton* spp.), water buttercup (*Ranunculus circinata*), Canada waterweed (*Elodea canadensis*) and the macroalga stonewort (*Chara* sp.). Aquatic vegetation is not a problem for lake users in most areas; in fact, the lack of cover has been thought to limit spawning areas for pike (Miller 1942; Jones et al. 1976).

Invertebrates

There are no data on the zooplankton in Sylvan Lake.
Benthic invertebrates were sampled in July 1976 by a consultant for Alberta Environment (Table 6). The dominant organism in the littoral zone was the amphipod *Hyalella azteca*; in some vegetated areas it reached densities of up to 12 000 animals/m² and represented 92% of the invertebrate community. The dominant invertebrates in the profundal zone were midge larvae (Chironomidae), which made up over half of the community. Sphaeriid clams (Pelecypoda) were abundant in both the profundal and littoral regions. Earlier accounts from 1939 and 1942 mentioned the abundance of both clams and snails in Sylvan Lake (Alta. For. Ld. Wild. n.d.; Miller 1942). In 1946, the snails *Lymnaea stagnalis* and *Physa* sp. from the Sylvan Lake pier area were infected with tiny immature forms of a parasitic worm, called cercaria, which can cause "swimmer's itch" (Miller 1946). Blue-green algae can also cause skin irritation in some people. Swimmer's itch occurs periodically in Sylvan Lake, particularly during warm, sunny summers (Smith 1988).

Fish

There are at least seven species of fish in Sylvan Lake. Northern pike are indigenous to the lake and support an active year-round sport fishery. Yellow perch were introduced annually to the lake by Fish and Wildlife Division from 1940 to 1945 (Hunt 1978). They are now a self-sustaining population; individuals grow to an admirable size and are a very popular target for anglers, particularly during winter (Table 7). In 1986, Alberta angling records reported that an exceptionally large perch of 53 cm and 1.6 kg was taken from Sylvan Lake. Walleye were stocked in 1926, 1929, 1934, 1938, 1943, 1945 and from 1960 to 1963. They have now established a self-sustaining population and contribute to the sport fishery (Lowe 1988). Burbot are also caught by anglers. Lake trout were stocked in 1943 and 1944 but none survived. Spottail shiners were stocked from 1942 to 1945 to increase the forage fish population. Native forage species likely include brook stickleback and fathead minnows (Lowe 1988). In 1987 and 1988, a total of 3 445 adult lake whitefish from Pigeon Lake were stocked in Sylvan Lake to provide a forage species for walleye and northern pike and eventually to contribute to winter sport fishing. It will be the early 1990s before it is known whether

was well-mixed when sampled in August of 1984 and 1985 (Fig. 5). In 1974, the lake was weakly thermally stratified on 11 June and 2 and 30 July, but was well mixed on all other dates. In 1974, dissolved oxygen was measured only on 30 July; at this time the concentration from the surface to a depth of 12 m was greater than 8 mg/L; at 15 m (bottom) it was 1.5 mg/L. In winter, dissolved oxygen depletion is apparent below a depth of about 8 m; in March 1986, the water was anoxic within 1 m of the substrate at a depth of 16 m (Fig. 5).

Sylvan Lake is mesotrophic. Changes in phosphorus and chlorophyll *a* concentrations in Sylvan Lake over the summer are similar to those in other well-mixed lakes in Alberta. The phosphorus concentration peaks in August and the chlorophyll *a* concentration peaks in late August or September (Fig. 6). The average concentrations of phosphorus and chlorophyll *a* are relatively low (Table 4) and the water is clear (Secchi depths are rarely less than 4 m).

Biological Characteristics

Plants

The composition and abundance of phytoplankton in Sylvan Lake were studied in July and August 1976 during an Alberta Environment planning study (Table 5). Seventy-four species were identified. Throughout July and early August the phytoplankton community was dominated by golden-brown algae (Chrysophyta). In late August, blue-green algae (Cyanophyta), particularly *Aphanizomenon flos-aquae*, were very abundant. Colonies of the blue-green alga *Nostoc* sp. were commonly observed rolling in shallow water like green grapes on the sand.

Table 5. Percentage composition of major algal groups by density in Sylvan Lake, 1976.
Composite samples collected from 1–m depth.

ALGAL GROUP	07 July	20 July	05 Aug.	17 Aug.
Total Density (cells/mL)	1 938	3 089	5 122	8 192
Percentage Composition:				
Cyanophyta	26 *Anabaena sp.*	12	16	57 *Aphanizomenon flos-aquae*
Chlorophyta	26 *Sphaerocystis schroeteria*	8	5	14
Chrysophyta	40 *Pseudopedinella sp.*	55 *Chrysochromulina parva* ———→	58	7
Bacillariophyta	8	23 *Melosira granulata*	9	20 *Asterionella formosa Cyclotella sp.*
Cryptophyta	<1	2	12	2

SOURCE: adapted from Jones et al. 1976

Table 6. The abundance of major benthic macroinvertebrates in Sylvan Lake, July 1976. Samples collected by Ekman dredge.

Taxa	Littoral Zone[a] No./m²	%	Profundal Zone[b] No./m²	%
Oligochaeta	651	7.2	95	3.6
Nematoda	523	5.8	117	4.4
Hirudinea	134	1.5	0	0
Amphipoda	6 424	71.6	206	7.7
Ephemeroptera	4	<0.1	0	0
Odonata	5	<0.1	0	0
Trichoptera	50	0.5	0	0
Coleoptera	1	<0.1	0	0
Diptera				
Chaoboridae	0	0	50	1.9
Chironomidae	347	3.9	1 535	57.7
Ceratopogonidae	3	<0.1	0	0
Mollusca				
Pelecypoda	805	9.0	656	24.7
Gastropoda	25	0.3	0	0
Total (No./m²)	8 972		2 659	

NOTES: [a]5 sites sampled, all with different substrates—4 had aquatic vegetation;
[b]1 site sampled; substrate was soft mud
SOURCE: adapted from Jones et al. 1976

Table 7. Age-length relationships of yellow perch in Sylvan Lake, 1976. Fish were captured by gillnets, minnow seines and angling during July and Aug. Length data are mean fork lengths (mm).

Age Class	n	Length	Range
0	203	36.6	27—51
1	35	55.2	47—68
2	18	86.6	72—105
3	29	114.3	99—139
4	18	155.8	136—177
5	—	—	—
6	12	251.4	223—264
7	14	263.4	234—275
8	7	282.0	266—292
9	1	307.0	—

SOURCE: Jones et al. 1976

they have become successfully established (Lowe 1988). There is no commercial or domestic fishery on Sylvan Lake.

Summerkills of young perch occasionally occur in the shallow bays of Sylvan Lake (Smith 1988). In 1976, 100 to 200 dead young-of-the-year perch were found along a portion of the north shore of the lake; it was estimated that a total of 100 000 were killed at that time (Jones et al. 1976). No winterkills have been reported.

The abundance of fish in Sylvan Lake is thought to be limited by a shortage of weed beds, a lack of cover and a shortage of spawning grounds (Miller 1942; Jones et al. 1976). In the early 1940s, projects to improve habitat included building underwater brush shelters (Miller 1942).

Wildlife

Sylvan Lake has few areas that are suitable for breeding or nesting waterfowl or for other aquatic wildlife (Red Deer Reg. Plan. Commis. 1977; Strome 1978). In most areas the shore is too steep or has been altered by human use. However, Cygnet Lake, 2 km downstream of Sylvan Lake, provides excellent waterfowl habitat. A control struc-

ture was built on Cygnet Lake in 1975/76 and habitat improvement was undertaken by Ducks Unlimited (Canada). An agreement was made in 1976 between Alberta Environment and Alberta Recreation, Parks and Wildlife to maintain the water level of Cygnet Lake with necessary deficits to be made up with water from Sylvan Lake. A 1978 study concluded that release of water from Sylvan Lake to Cygnet Lake could compromise recreational use of Sylvan Lake, so no releases have been made (Strome 1978). The Sylvan Lake Natural Area, at the northwest end of the lake, provides excellent birdwatching in upland habitat, along the shoreline and in marshes.

J.M. Crosby

References

Alberta Environment. n.d.[a]. Envir. Assess. Div., Envir. Qlty. Monit. Br. Unpubl. data, Edmonton.
———. n.d.[b]. Tech. Serv. Div., Hydrol. Br. Unpubl. data, Edmonton.
———. n.d.[c]. Tech. Serv. Div., Surv. Br. Unpubl. data, Edmonton.
Alberta Forestry, Lands and Wildlife. n.d. Fish Wild. Div. Unpubl. data, Edmonton.
———. 1987. A summary of Alberta's natural areas reserved and established. Pub. Ld. Div., Ld. Mgt. Devel. Br. Unpubl. rep., Edmonton.
———. 1988. Boating in Alberta. Fish Wild. Div., Edmonton.
———. 1989. Guide to sportfishing. Fish Wild. Div., Edmonton.
Alberta Recreation and Parks. n.d. Parks Div. Unpubl. data, Edmonton.
Alberta Research Council. 1972. Geological map of Alberta. Nat. Resour. Div., Alta. Geol. Surv., Edmonton.
Dawe, R.W. n.d. History of Red Deer, Alberta. Kiwanis Club of Red Deer, Red Deer.
Energy, Mines and Resources Canada. 1974. National topographic series 1:50 000 83B/8 (1974). Surv. Map. Br., Ottawa.

Environment Canada. 1918–1987. Surface water data. Prep. by Inland Waters Directorate. Water Surv. Can., Water Resour. Br., Ottawa.

———. 1982. Canadian climate normals, Vol. 7: Bright sunshine (1951–1980). Prep. by Atm. Envir. Serv. Supply Serv. Can., Ottawa.

Gaetz, A.L. 1948. The Park Country: A history of Red Deer and district. A.L. Gaetz, Red Deer.

Hunt, C. 1978. Evaluation of walleye planting: Sylvan Lake. Alta. Rec. Parks Wild., Fish Wild. Div., Red Deer.

Jones, M.L., J.D. Beste and P.T. Tsui. 1976. Sylvan Lake stabilization study: Fisheries report. Prep. by Aquat. Envir. Ltd. for Alta. Envir., Plan. Div., Edmonton.

Lowe, D. 1988. Alta. For. Ld. Wild., Fish Wild. Div., Red Deer. Pers. comm.

Miller, R.B. 1942. Biological survey of Sylvan Lake, Alberta. Alta. Ld. Mines, Fish Game Admin., Edmonton.

———. 1946. Swimmers itch at Sylvan Lake, Alberta. Alta. Ld. Mines, Fish Game Admin., Edmonton.

MTB Consultants Ltd. 1982. Dickson Reservoir: Recreation planning study. Prep. for Alta. Envir., Plan. Br., Edmonton.

Pedocan Land Evaluation Ltd. 1985. Soil survey and land suitability evaluation of the Sylvan Lake area. Prep. for Alta. Envir., Envir. Assess. Div., Edmonton.

Peters, T.W. and W.E. Bowser. 1960. Soil survey of the Rocky Mountain House sheet. Alta. Soil Surv. Rep. No. 19, Univ. Alta. Bull. No. SS–1. Univ. Alta., Edmonton.

Red Deer Regional Planning Commission. 1977. Sylvan Lake management plan: A summary statement. Reg. Plan. Res. Sec., Red Deer.

———. 1985. Sylvan Lake shoreline access study: Background information. Reg. Plan. Res. Sec., Red Deer.

Smith, T. 1988. Alta. For. Ld. Wild., Fish Wild. Div., Red Deer. Pers. comm.

Stolte, W.J. and R. Herrington. 1980. A study of the hydrologic regime of the Battle River Basin. Rep. No. RMD–80/4. Prep. for Alta. Envir., Res. Mgt. Div., Edmonton by Dept. Civil Eng., Univ. Sask., Saskatoon.

Strome, A.R. 1978. Sylvan Lake regulation study. Alta. Envir., Plan. Div., Edmonton.

Strong, W.L. and K.R. Leggat. 1981. Ecoregions of Alberta. Alta. En. Nat. Resour., Resour. Eval. Plan. Div., Edmonton.

Town of Sylvan Lake. 1988. Town office, Sylvan L. Pers. comm.

CHESTERMERE LAKE

MAP SHEET: 82P/4
LOCATION: Tp24 R28 W4
LAT/LONG: 51°02'N 113°49'W

Chestermere Lake is a small offstream reservoir situated 7 km east of Calgary on Highway 1 in Municipal District No. 44 (Fig. 1). Its proximity to over one-half million people and its ease of access result in tremendous recreational pressure. It is popular for sailing, windsurfing, swimming, skin-diving, fishing and skating.

The derivation of the lake's name is uncertain. The reservoir was built by the Canadian Pacific Railway (CPR) for irrigation purposes. One of the company directors at the time was Lord Chester. The name may also come from the Latin *castra* meaning "camp" and *mere* meaning "lake" (Holmgren and Holmgren 1976). Before settlers arrived, Blackfoot Indians roamed over the dry plains. The first ranches were developed near the Bow River to the south, but cattle and horses grazed as far north as the Chestermere area. Homesteaders arrived between 1883 and 1900 to fence the open prairie and break the rich land (Peake 1982).

When the CPR built its trans-Canada railway line in the 1880s, the Canadian government gave the company alternate sections of land along the right-of-way. In southern Alberta, the CPR exchanged the alternate sections for two large blocks of land; one near the town of Brooks and one near the town of Strathmore, which is just east of Chestermere Lake (Thompson 1971). The CPR developed these blocks into agricultural showcases and sent brochures to Europe to inspire immigration. Hundreds of Russian, Dutch, French and Scandinavian people soon arrived. Mortgages were signed with the CPR, and in return the CPR agreed to supply irrigation water at 50¢ per acre. By 1943, the CPR was losing money in the Strathmore block and offered to cancel the mortgages if the farmers would cancel their water rights. Not all farmers agreed to this, and in 1944 the CPR cancelled the mortgages and gave the farmers $400 000 plus all the irrigation equipment in place at the time. The block of land at Strathmore became the Western Irrigation District (WID). Similar events had occurred in the Brooks block, which became the Eastern Irrigation District in 1935 (Chestermere Hist. Soc. 1971; Thompson 1971).

Part of the irrigation system built for the Strathmore area by the CPR in 1910 included a weir on the Bow River within Calgary and a canal and two dams and headgates on a natural slough which became the impoundment now known as Chestermere Lake. The original purpose of the lake was to act as a balancing reservoir to quickly meet fluctuating demands in the irrigation system. Now the reservoir is operated for both irrigation and recreation. The WID still operates the reservoir. Water flows into secondary canals at the north and south ends of the reservoir to irrigate over 36 000 ha of land and to supply stockwater to more than 800 farms (West. Irrig. Dist. n.d.).

The secondary canals and reservoir right-of-way are owned by the WID. The land around Chestermere Lake is almost all privately owned and most of it is within the summer village of Chestermere Lake (Fig. 2). In 1988 there were 443 developed lots, of which 340 front on the shore; 200 were permanent residences. The best public access is at John Peake Memorial Park on the northwest end of the lake, just north of the Highway 1A crossing (Fig. 2). This day-use area, operated by the summer village of Chestermere Lake, provides a boat launch, washrooms and picnic tables for a small fee. In 1988, a beach was developed at the park. There are two other small day-use areas on municipal reserve land. Anniversary Park is on the west shore, and Sunset Park is on the east. Both offer picnic tables and washrooms and both are very popular with windsurfers. The

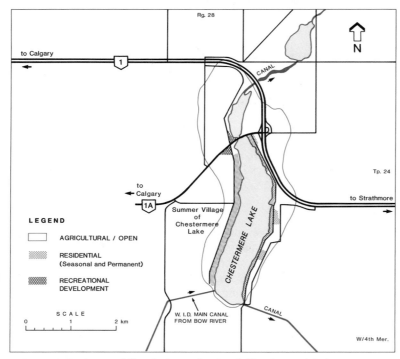

Figure 1. Features of the drainage basin of Chestermere Lake.
SOURCES: Alta. Envir. n.d.[c]; En. Mines Resour. Can. 1980. Updated with 1985 aerial photos.

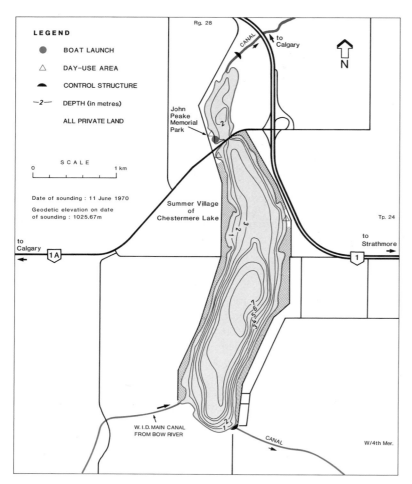

Figure 2. Bathymetry and shoreline features of Chestermere Lake.
BATHYMETRY SOURCE: Alta. Envir. n.d.[d].

Table 1. Characteristics of Chestermere Lake drainage basin.

area (excluding reservoir) (km²)[a]	5.00
soil[b]	Orthic Black Chernozemics
bedrock geology[c]	Paskapoo Formation (Tertiary): sandstone, siltstone, mudstone; thin limestone, coal and tuff beds; nonmarine
terrain[b]	level to gently rolling
ecoregion[d]	Fescue Grass
dominant vegetation[d]	rough fescue, Parry oat grass (now mostly cleared)
mean annual sunshine (h)[e]	2 314

SOURCES: [a]Alta. Envir. n.d.[c]; [b]MacMillan 1987; [c]Alta. Res. Counc. 1972; [d]Strong and Leggat 1981; [e]Envir. Can. 1982

maximum speed for power boats on the entire reservoir is limited to 12 km/hour (Alta. For. Ld. Wild. 1988).

The water in Chestermere Lake is usually clear and algal blooms are not often a problem. However, aquatic plants are widespread and are a nuisance to boaters and anglers. Sport fishing for perch and pike is popular both in summer and winter. Provincial sport fishing regulations are in effect, but there are no additional regulations specific to Chestermere Lake (Alta. For. Ld. Wild. 1989).

Drainage Basin Characteristics

The natural drainage basin of Chestermere Lake is very small, barely larger than the area of the lake (Tables 1, 2). Natural runoff had provided only enough water to create a small slough before water was diverted from the Bow River.

Chestermere Lake lies in a shallow depression on a level to gently rolling glacial till plain in the Fescue Grassland Ecoregion. The dominant soils in the basin are Orthic Black Chernozemics, which have developed under grasslands and have almost no restrictions for agriculture although there are occasional patches of surface salts. The soils in the valley north of the Highway 1A crossing are a mixture of Humic Gleysols and Solodized Solonetz that have developed on glaciolacustrine clays overlying glacial till (MacMillan 1987). The natural vegetation of the region was dominated by rough fescue with secondary quantities of Parry oat grass. Now there is little natural grassland left in the area as most of this ecoregion has been cultivated for grain crop production or mixed farming. Shrubs such as rose, saskatoon and buckbrush grow in seepage sites and on the north slopes of coulees (Strong and Leggat 1981). The Chestermere drainage basin has also been altered by the major complex of Highways 1 and 1A near the lake (Fig. 1).

Reservoir Characteristics

Chestermere Lake was built to be an offstream reservoir to balance flows to the WID. It is a small impoundment, only 5.12–km long and 0.77–km wide (Table 2), and provides little storage. The lake basin is an elongate oval that slopes very gently from the north end to a maximum depth of 7 m (Fig. 2). The slopes along the east and west shores and along the south weir are slightly steeper.

The shoreline north of Highway 1A is sandy; emergent vegetation is dense and the backshore is marshy. In 1988, a beach was being developed at the day-use area. The shoreline south of Highway 1A is almost entirely man-made; the east and west shores are held by concrete, stone or wood retaining walls and a weir crosses the south end. There is some natural sandy shore near the outlet of the WID Main Canal in the southeast corner of the reservoir and some natural marshy shore at the municipal reserve on the east shore. The lake bottom is soft mud (Thompson 1971).

More than 99% of the water entering Chestermere Lake is diverted from the Bow River where the WID weir crosses the river just downstream from the Calgary Zoo. Alberta Environment owns and operates the weir and the WID Main Canal which flows through the

Table 2. Characteristics of Chestermere Lake reservoir.

control structures[a]	dam and control gate at south end; control gate at north end
dam height (m)[a]	5.0
crest length (m)[a]	636.4
full supply level (FSL) (m)[b]	1 025.67
volume at FSL (m^3)[b]	9.16 x 10^6
surface area at FSL (km^2)[b]	2.65
maximum drawdown (m)[b]	2.19
mean annual drawdown (1980–1988) (m)[b]	1.80
maximum depth at FSL (m)[c]	7.0
mean depth at FSL (m)[b]	3.47
shoreline length at FSL (km)[d]	11.4
lake length at FSL (km)[c]	5.12
lake width at FSL (km)[c]	0.77
mean annual lake evaporation (mm)[b]	712
mean annual precipitation (mm)[b]	426
mean (01 Apr.–31 Oct.) residence time (1980–1988) (yr)[e]	0.03
mean (01 Apr.–31 Oct.) inflow volume (1980–1988) (m^3)[e, f]	179.0 x 10^6

NOTE: [f]of this amount 0.04 x 10^6 m^3 is natural runoff, 179 x 10^6 m^3 is via the WID canal; excluding groundwater inflow
SOURCES: [a]Alta. Envir. n.d.[e]; [b]Alta. Envir. n.d.[c]; [c]Thompson 1971; [d]En. Mines Resour. Can. 1980; [e]Alta. Envir. n.d.[a]

Table 3. Major ions and related water quality variables for Chestermere Lake. Average concentrations in mg/L; pH in pH units. Composite samples from the euphotic zone collected 11 times from 24 May to 02 Nov. 1983. S.E. = standard error.

	Mean	S.E.
pH (range)	7.0–8.5[a]	—
total alkalinity (CaCO$_3$)	111	3.4
specific conductivity (μS/cm)	303	20.1
total dissolved solids (calculated)	166	11.1
turbidity (NTU)	2	0.2
total hardness (CaCO$_3$)	139	5.6
dissolved organic carbon	2[a]	0.4
HCO$_3$	136	4.1
CO$_3$	0	0
Mg	12	0.5
Na	7	2.0
K	1	0.1
Cl	4	1.2
SO$_4$	38	4.3
Ca	35	1.4

NOTE: [a]n = 8, 26 Apr. to 02 Oct. 1984
SOURCE: Alta. Envir. n.d.[b], Naquadat station 05AL05BM6000

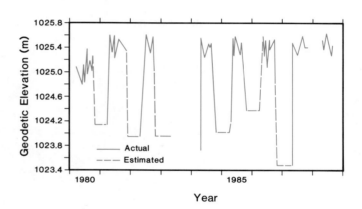

Figure 3. Water level of Chestermere Lake, 1980 to 1988.
SOURCES: Alta. Envir. n.d.[a]; West. Irrig. Dist. n.d.

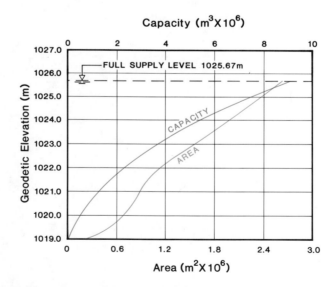

Figure 4. Area/capacity curve for Chestermere Lake.
SOURCE: Alta. Envir. n.d.[d].

city of Calgary and then into the southwest corner of Chestermere Lake. Approximately 55% of the outflow leaves in a secondary canal from the southeast corner and 45% leaves via a secondary canal at the north end (Fig. 2). The volume of flow is high; from April to October an average of 179.0 x 10^6 m^3 flows through the lake, resulting in a mean residence time of only 11 days (Table 2). When flow rates are high, the retention time drops to 4.7 days. From October to April the canals are closed and almost no water flows into or out of the lake (West. Irrig. Dist. n.d.).

The lake level is controlled and is therefore predictable (Fig. 3). From 1980 to 1988, the summer levels varied about 0.4 m each year. In October the level is drawn down about 1.5 m to protect retaining walls around the lake. The winter level is stable until late April when diversion starts and the lake is filled rapidly. The lake was drawn down approximately 1.5 m in the winter of 1987/88, but because no measurements were taken this does not appear on Figure 3. During the winter, the area of the lake is about 75% of the area at the full supply level (Fig. 4).

Water Quality

The water quality of Chestermere Lake was monitored by Alberta Environment in 1971 and 1972 (Masuda 1972), in 1978 (Exner 1978) and in 1983 and 1984 (Alta. Envir. n.d.[b].).

The water quality of Chestermere Lake is strongly influenced by the water quality of the Bow River. Chestermere is a well-buffered, freshwater lake; its dominant ions are calcium, sulphate and bicarbonate (Table 3). The lake mixes occasionally during the summer, but stratifies temporarily during hot, calm weather (Fig. 5). In 1983, the dissolved oxygen concentration was high and uniform from top to bottom except during a brief period of thermal stratification in late July and early August. At this time, there was noticeable dissolved oxygen depletion below 4 m (Fig. 6). Winter dissolved oxygen concentrations have not been monitored but winter fish kills are not a problem in the lake (Lowe 1988).

Chestermere Lake has moderately high nutrient levels. Phosphorus was the focus of a study in 1978 because the average concentration in the lake (28 to 36 μg/L, Table 4) is much higher than the average concentration in the Bow River at the WID Main Canal diversion (7 μg/L, Exner 1978), which provides almost all the water in the lake. In spring, before diversion begins, the total phosphorus

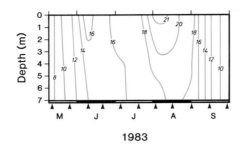

Figure 5. Temperature (°C) of Chestermere Lake, 1983. Arrows indicate sampling dates. SOURCE: Alta. Envir. n.d.[b].

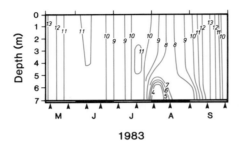

Figure 6. Dissolved oxygen (mg/L) in Chestermere Lake, 1983. Arrows indicate sampling dates. SOURCE: Alta. Envir. n.d.[b].

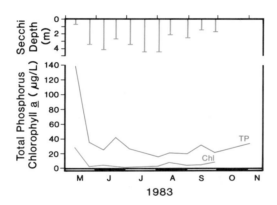

Figure 7. Total phosphorus, chlorophyll *a* and Secchi depth in Chestermere Lake, 1983. SOURCE: Alta. Envir. n.d.[b].

Table 4. Nutrient, chlorophyll *a* and Secchi depth data for Chestermere Lake. Average concentrations in μg/L. Composite samples from the euphotic zone collected 11 times from 24 May to 02 Nov. 1983 and 8 times from 26 Apr. to 02 Oct. 1984. S.E. = standard error.

	1983		1984	
	Mean	S.E.	Mean	S.E.
total phosphorus	36[a]	9.6	28	6.0
total Kjeldahl nitrogen	443	68.1	482	67.4
NH₄–nitrogen	<24	—	<16	—
iron	<19	—	<21	—
chlorophyll a	5.5	2.22	6.5	2.93
Secchi depth (m)	2.9	0.38	2.7	0.61

NOTE: [a]n = 12, 10 May to 02 Nov. 1983
SOURCE: Alta. Envir. n.d.[b], Naquadat station 05AL05BM6000

concentration in the lake is high (139 μg/L, Fig. 7). Total phosphorus levels drop quickly when the diversion from the Bow River starts, but levels stay higher than expected given the rapid flushing rate of approximately once every 11 days. Detailed sampling along the WID canal in 1978 showed distinct increases in total phosphorus below stormwater inputs within the city of Calgary. Since then, only one additional storm drain has been built to empty into the canal; a moratorium on the addition of any more storm drains was imposed in 1983 (Colborne 1988). The total phosphorus concentration was also high in Nose Creek, which enters the Bow River immediately upstream and on the same bank as the WID canal diversion. The total phosphorus concentration of water leaving Chestermere Lake at the north end was considerably lower than that of water entering the lake in the WID Main Canal, likely due to phosphorus uptake by the lush macrophyte beds and algae in the lake.

Chestermere Lake is mesotrophic. Chlorophyll *a* concentrations are highest in early spring when the total phosphorus concentration is highest, but drop when water diversion starts and then rise again in late summer (Fig. 7).

Biological Characteristics

Plants

There are no data regarding species of algae in Chestermere Lake. Diatoms (Bacillariophyta) were consistently abundant in three samples collected between 6 May and 16 June in 1969, and green algae (Chlorophyta) were common (Thompson 1971).

Macrophytes grow profusely throughout most of Chestermere Lake except in the deeper water in the southern half. The dominant genus is *Potamogeton* (pondweed). In autumn 1988, local residents contracted a private company to mechanically remove the weeds and their roots from a 0.25 ha area. It was hoped that growth would be appreciably reduced for at least two years (Lajeunesse 1988).

Invertebrates

Three plankton samples were taken between 6 May and 16 June in 1969 by Fish and Wildlife Division (Thompson 1971). The zooplankton was dominated by the cladoceran *Daphnia* sp. and the copepod *Cyclops* sp.

Twenty-five bottom samples were taken by a 15–cm Ekman dredge in May 1969; 22 were within the littoral zone at a water depth less than 4.5 m (Thompson 1971). The average dry-weight biomass of benthic invertebrates was 26.7 g/m². Numerically, midge larvae (Chironomidae) were most abundant (37%), aquatic earthworms (Oligochaeta) were 30% of the total, scuds (Amphipoda) were 24% and clams (Pelecypoda) were 5%.

Fish

There are at least four species of fish in Chestermere Lake: yellow perch, northern pike, white suckers and longnose suckers. Rainbow trout occasionally migrate into the lake via the WID canal but they are not common (Thompson 1971). Angling for pike and perch is popular. There is no commercial or domestic fishery on Chestermere Lake.

Wildlife

There are no data regarding wildlife at Chestermere Lake. The intense recreational use and predominance of retaining walls along the shore do not provide good wildlife habitat.

J.M. Crosby

References

Alberta Environment. n.d.[a]. Devel. Op. Div., Irrig. Headworks Br. Unpubl. data, Edmonton.
——. n.d.[b]. Envir. Assess. Div., Envir. Qlty. Monit. Br. Unpubl. data, Edmonton.
——. n.d.[c]. Tech. Serv. Div., Hydrol. Br. Unpubl. data, Edmonton.
——. n.d.[d]. Tech. Serv. Div., Surv. Br. Unpubl. data, Edmonton.
——. n.d.[e]. Water Resour. Mgt. Div., Dam Safety Br. Unpubl. data, Edmonton.
Alberta Forestry, Lands and Wildlife. n.d. Fish Wild. Div. Unpubl. data, Edmonton.

——. 1988. Boating in Alberta. Fish Wild. Div., Edmonton.
——. 1989. Guide to sportfishing. Fish Wild. Div., Edmonton.
Alberta Research Council. 1972. Geological map of Alberta. Nat. Resour. Div., Alta. Geol. Surv., Edmonton.
Chestermere Historical Society. 1971. Saddles, sleighs and sadirons. Chestermere Hist. Soc., Chestermere.
Colborne, B. 1988. City of Calgary, Eng. Sewer Div., Calgary. Pers. comm.
Energy, Mines and Resources Canada. 1980. National topographic series 1:50 000 82P/4 (1980). Surv. Map. Br., Ottawa.
Environment Canada. 1982. Canadian climate normals, Vol. 7: Bright sunshine (1951–1980). Prep. by Atm. Envir. Serv. Supply Serv. Can., Ottawa.
Exner, K. 1978. 1978 investigation into the water quality of the Western Irrigation District distribution system to Chestermere Lake. Alta. Envir., Poll. Contr. Div., Edmonton.
Holmgren, E.J. and P.M. Holmgren. 1976. Over 2000 place names of Alberta. 3rd ed. West. Producer Prairie Books, Saskatoon.
Lajeunesse, B. 1988. Alta. For. Ld. Wild., Fish Wild. Div., Red Deer. Pers comm.
Lowe, D. 1988. Alta. For. Ld. Wild., Fish Wild. Div., Red Deer. Pers. comm.
MacMillan, R.A. 1987. Soil survey of the Calgary urban perimeter. Alta. Res. Counc., Dept. Terrain Sci., Edmonton.
Masuda, A. 1972. Chestermere Lake survey 1971–1972. Alta. Envir., Poll. Contr. Div., Edmonton.
Peake, E. 1982. Growing through time: Stories of Chestermere Lake. SV Chestermere L., Chestermere Lake.
Strong, W.L. and K.R. Leggat. 1981. Ecoregions of Alberta. Alta. En. Nat. Resour., Resour. Eval. Plan. Div., Edmonton.
Thompson, G.E. 1971. The limnology and fishery management of Chestermere Lake, Alberta. Alta. Ld. For., Fish Wild. Div., Calgary.
Western Irrigation District. n.d. Unpubl. data, Strathmore.

EAGLE LAKE

MAP SHEETS: 82I/14, 82P/3
LOCATION: Tp23, 24 R24, 25 W4
LAT/LONG: 51°00'N 113°19'W

Eagle Lake is set in gently rolling prairie near the town of Strathmore, approximately 40 km east of the city of Calgary. To reach the lake from Calgary, travel east on Highway 1 until you are 8 km east of Strathmore, then turn south onto the road that leads to the locality of Namaka. Drive 6 km, and you will reach a commercial recreation area on the east shore of the lake (Fig. 1, 2). The lake is located in the County of Wheatland.

The Blackfoot name for Eagle Lake, *Pataomoxecing*, means "many eagles" (Geog. Bd. Can. 1928). On nearby Eagle Hill, just southeast of the lake, Indians would lie in baited holes waiting for eagles to land; when an eagle approached the bait, the hunter would grab its legs and pull its tail feathers out to use for headdresses (Namaka Commun. Hist. Commit. 1983).

Settlement began when the Canadian Pacific Railroad came through the area in 1883. In the same year, Strathmore was founded on the west side of Eagle Lake; it was moved 6 km along the track to the present townsite in 1904. Before refrigerators were common, hundreds of tons of ice were cut from the lake each winter. Covered in sawdust and stored in buildings, the ice was available all summer. A heavy snow accumulation in the spring of 1948 caused serious flood damage to a secondary rail line cutting across the southern end of the lake. In the same year, the railway company built a control structure and dug a drainage ditch from Eagle Lake to Namaka Lake to lower the water level of Eagle Lake and prevent future flooding. This secondary rail line was abandoned in 1982, but the berm still crosses the lake except for a 4–m–wide channel (Fig. 2), which at one time was spanned by a bridge. The control structure on the outlet canal is now operated by the Western Irrigation District (WID). In 1958, a small-scale sand dredging operation commenced on the southeast shore. Sand was hard to find in quantity so the business was abandoned in 1970 (Namaka Commun. Hist. Commit. 1983).

There is no Crown land around the lake. The major land use is irrigation farming or grazing. A subdivision of 100 lots is situated on the northwest shore; by 1988, 20 lots had been developed (Clark 1988). There is a commercially operated campground on land owned by the County of Wheatland on the east shore of the lake (Fig. 2). The campground has 80 campsites, tap water, a beach and a boat launch (Alta. Hotel Assoc. 1988). There are no boating restrictions specific to the lake (Alta. For. Ld. Wild. 1988), but sudden strong winds can make boating treacherous.

Eagle Lake is very nutrient rich and has dense blooms of blue-green algae all summer. Submergent aquatic plants form a ring around the lake, extending about 100 m from shore. The lake supports a moderate sport fishery. Walleye were stocked from 1966 to 1972 and from 1978 to 1980 and are now the major species in the sport fishery; pike are also caught (Sosiak 1988). Provincial regulations regarding the size and number of fish caught apply, but there are no additional regulations specific to Eagle Lake (Alta. For. Ld. Wild. 1989).

Drainage Basin Characteristics

The drainage basin of Eagle Lake is fairly small, being only 10 times the area of the lake (Tables 1, 2). The basin is in the Fescue Grassland Ecoregion, an area that lies between the moister Aspen Parkland and the drier Mixed Grass ecoregions. Fescue grassland is typified by gently rolling terrain, Black and Dark Brown Chernozemic soils and

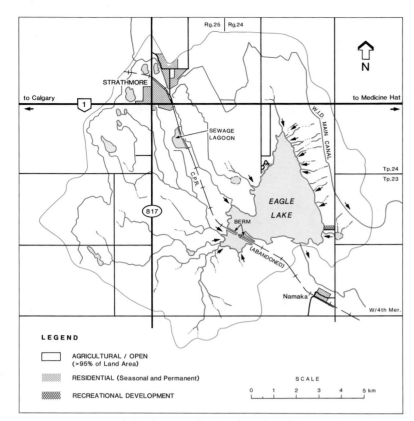

Figure 1. Features of the drainage basin of Eagle Lake.
SOURCES: Alta. Envir. n.d.[b]; En. Mines Resour. Can. 1977. Updated with 1981 aerial photos.

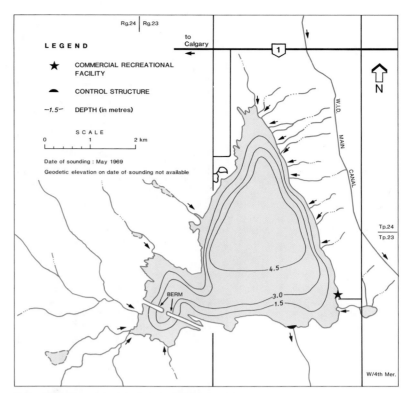

Figure 2. Bathymetry and shoreline features of Eagle Lake.
BATHYMETRY SOURCE: Thompson 1971.

vegetation dominated by rough fescue grass, with Parry oat grass in secondary quantities. Shrubs grow on moister sites such as on north-facing slopes and around seepage sites (Strong and Leggat 1981). The Eagle Lake drainage basin is a gentle depression with relief of only 50 m to the top of Eagle Hill, the highest point in the basin at approximately 970 m. Most of the watershed has been cleared for irrigation farming, but grazing is the primary use around the lake (Charlton et al. 1982). The drainage basin also includes the town of Strathmore; its sewage effluent is retained in lagoons, and until 1988 the effluent was released into a creek draining into the southwest bay of the lake (Fig. 1). In 1988 and 1989, the effluent was used by a private landowner for irrigation.

Inflowing streams to Eagle Lake are mostly intermittent. Most of them are dry by late spring and flow only during periods of very heavy rain. Inflow to the lake is augmented by irrigation return flows and seepage from the WID Main Canal; this volume is approximately equal to the volume derived from natural runoff. One permanent stream enters the southwest corner of the lake (Thompson 1971).

Lake Basin Characteristics

Eagle Lake is a simple, shallow depression that slopes gently to a maximum depth of 4.9 m (Fig. 2). The near-shore sediment is fairly sandy, with soft mud at the northern end, in the southwest bay and in bays along the western shore (Thompson 1971).

The control structure on the outlet helps to keep the water level of Eagle Lake quite stable, but there are no data on water levels. The outflow from the lake is irregular. In 1988, water flowed out of the lake all year; the volume was estimated to be approximately 2×10^6 m³ (Hamilton 1989).

Water Quality

Eagle Lake water quality was sampled by Alberta Environment in 1982, 1983, 1985, 1986 and 1988 (Alta. Envir. n.d.[a]). Fish and Wildlife Division briefly surveyed the lake in 1969 (Thompson 1971).

Eagle Lake is a moderately saline, well-buffered lake. The water is very hard and the dominant ions are sodium, bicarbonate and sulphate (Table 3). Comparison of the 1988 data to that of a Sep-

Table 1. Characteristics of Eagle Lake drainage basin.

area (excluding lake) (km²)[a]	120
soil[b]	Black and Dark Brown Chernozemics
bedrock geology[c]	Paskapoo Formation (Tertiary): sandstone, siltstone, mudstone; thin limestone, coal and tuff beds; nonmarine
terrain[d]	gently rolling
ecoregion[d]	Fescue Grassland
dominant vegetation[d]	rough fescue grass, Parry oat grass; now cleared for agriculture
mean annual inflow (m³)[e, f]	6.5×10^6
mean annual sunshine (h)[g]	2 314

NOTE: [f]excluding groundwater inflow
SOURCES: [a]Alta. Envir. n.d.[b]; [b]Wyatt et al. 1943; [c]Alta. Res. Counc. 1972; [d]Strong and Leggat 1981; [e]Hamilton 1989; [g]Envir. Can. 1982

Table 2. Characteristics of Eagle Lake.

elevation (m)[a]	approximately 922
surface area (km²)[b, c]	11.8
volume (m³)[d]	31.2×10^6
maximum depth (m)[d]	4.9
mean depth (m)[b, d]	2.6
shoreline length (km)[d]	23.2
mean annual lake evaporation (mm)[b]	712
mean annual precipitation (mm)[b]	376
mean residence time (yr)[e, f]	15.3
control structure[g]	weir and control gate

NOTES: [c]on date of sounding: May-June 1969; [f]excluding groundwater inflow
SOURCES: [a]En. Mines Resour. Can. 1977; [b]Alta. Envir. n.d.[b]; [d]Charlton et al. 1982; [e]Hamilton 1989; [g]Alta. Dept. Agric. 1970

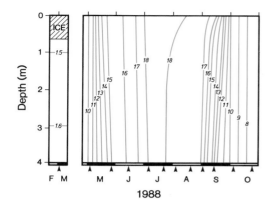

Figure 3. Temperature (°C) of Eagle Lake, 1988. Arrows indicate sampling dates.
SOURCE: Alta. Envir. n.d.[a].

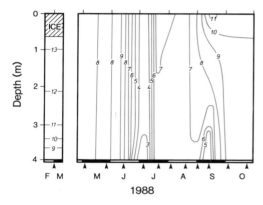

Figure 4. Dissolved oxygen (mg/L) in Eagle Lake, 1988. Arrows indicate sampling dates.
SOURCE: Alta. Envir. n.d.[a].

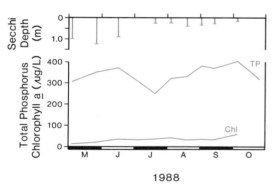

Figure 5. Total phosphorus, chlorophyll *a* and Secchi depth in Eagle Lake, 1988.
SOURCE: Alta. Envir. n.d.[a].

Table 3. Major ions and related water quality variables for Eagle Lake. Average concentrations in mg/L. Composite samples from the euphotic zone collected 11 times from 03 May to 24 Oct. 1988. S.E. = standard error.

	Mean	S.E.
pH (range)	8.7–9.1	—
total alkalinity (CaCO₃)	527	4.7
specific conductivity (μS/cm)	1 828	8.8
total dissolved solids (calculated)	1 231	7.6
turbidity (NTU)	33	5.9
total hardness (CaCO₃)	297	5.7
dissolved organic carbon	21	0.3
HCO₃	538	9.9
CO₃	52	3.0
Mg	55	1.1
Na	333	1.5
K	15	1.5
Cl	30	3.3
SO₄	449	7.2
Ca	29	0.5

SOURCE: Alta. Envir. n.d.[a], Naquadat station 01AL05BM2100

Table 4. Nutrient, chlorophyll *a* and Secchi depth data for Eagle Lake. Average concentrations in μg/L. Composite samples from the euphotic zone collected 3 times from 25 June to 23 Sep. 1986 and 11 times from 03 May to 24 Oct. 1988. S.E. = standard error.

	1986		1988	
	Mean	S.E.	Mean	S.E.
total phosphorus	333	20.3	336	13.1
total dissolved phosphorus	300[a]	—	217	11.2
total Kjeldahl nitrogen	2 230	180.3	2 322	43.1
NO₃ + NO₂–nitrogen	101	50.5	<53	—
NH₄–nitrogen	103	23.3	116	25.5
iron	213	64.9	—	—
chlorophyll *a*	46.2	17.53	32.7[b]	3.82
Secchi depth (m)	0.4	0.08	0.5[c]	0.13

NOTES: [a]n = 1; [b]n = 10; [c]n = 9
SOURCE: Alta. Envir. n.d.[a], Naquadat stations 01AL05BM2101 (1986), 01AL05BM2100 (1988)

tember 1969 sample indicates that the salinity of Eagle Lake has increased over the last 20 years, possibly due to the input of irrigation return flows. In 1969, total alkalinity was 353 mg/L, hardness 180 mg/L, chloride 2 mg/L and sulphate 390 mg/L. By 1988, total alkalinity had increased to 527 mg/L, total hardness to 297 mg/L, chloride to 30 mg/L and sulphate to 449 mg/L.

Eagle Lake is shallow and exposed to winds; it probably mixes all summer except for brief periods. In 1988, it was isothermal for most of the open-water season (Fig. 3). Dissolved oxygen concentrations were depleted throughout the water column in early July, possibly due to algal die-off, and near the lake bottom in mid-September when the lake was very weakly thermally stratified (Fig. 4). Dissolved oxygen concentrations under ice have been measured only once, in March 1988 (Fig. 4); at that time, they were surprisingly high.

Total phosphorus concentrations in Eagle Lake are very high (Table 4, Fig. 5). In 1988, the total phosphorus concentration reached a peak in June. The phosphorus concentration fell until late July, then rose following a period of low dissolved oxygen concentration throughout the entire water column. The phosphorus concentration peaked a second time in early October, after a brief period of weak thermal stratification in September. The pattern in 1985 was similar to that in 1988; the total phosphorus concentration increased from early May (290 µg/L) to late September (380 µg/L). The pattern in 1986 was quite different; the total phosphorus concentration was highest in mid-June (370 µg/L), then fell steadily to a low in late September (300 µg/L).

Chlorophyll *a* concentrations indicate the heavy bloom of blue-green algae that occurs throughout the summer (Fig. 5). Chlorophyll *a* concentrations tend to parallel fluctuations in phosphorus concentration, but chlorophyll *a* concentrations are not as high as might be expected from the high phosphorus levels. It is quite likely that the high salinity, particularly the sulphate concentration, suppresses algal production, a characteristic of other moderately saline lakes in Alberta (Bierhuizen and Prepas 1985). The high phosphorus concentrations, heavy blue-green algal blooms and very low Secchi depths (Fig. 5) all indicate that Eagle Lake is hyper-eutrophic.

Biological Characteristics

Plants

There are no detailed data on phytoplankton species in Eagle Lake. In 1969, the blue-green algal bloom that dominated the lake all summer was largely composed of *Aphanizomenon* sp. (Thompson 1971).

Submergent macrophytes form a dense ring around the lake, extending out from shore for approximately 100 m (Thompson 1971; Trew 1988). The bay south of the old railroad berm becomes choked with aquatic plants, and boat traffic is impossible there in summer. Cattails (*Typha* sp.) and bulrushes (*Scirpus* spp.) are present mostly in the southwest bay and in bays along the west shore.

Invertebrates

The zooplankton and benthic invertebrate fauna of Eagle Lake were surveyed by Fish and Wildlife Division in 1969 (Thompson 1971). Cladocerans (*Daphnia* sp.) and copepods (*Cyclops* sp.) were the most abundant zooplankters.

In 25 bottom samples (13 at 0– to 2–m depth, 4 at 2– to 4–m depth, 8 at 4– to 5–m depth), an average of 15.8 g/m² (dry weight) of benthic invertebrates were found (Thompson 1971). By number, 80% were large midge larvae (Chironomidae), 15% were scuds (Amphipoda) and 2% were aquatic earthworms (Oligochaeta). Distribution did not appear to be affected by depth.

Fish

Eagle Lake contains six species of fish indigenous to the lake: northern pike, yellow perch, white sucker, longnose sucker, brook stickleback and fathead minnow. Walleye were introduced as eyed-eggs annually from 1966 to 1972, and as fingerlings annually from 1978 to 1980. Walleye now constitute the major target of the sport fishery in Eagle Lake and test netting in 1986 confirmed that they are reproducing successfully (Alta. For. Ld. Wild. n.d.).

Angling is popular from boats or from the old railroad causeway and at the campground. Angling from other points around the shore is difficult due to the dense growth of macrophytes that rings the lake. Despite the high algal production and shallow depth, major winterkills of fish have not been recorded in Eagle Lake (Sosiak 1988).

Wildlife

Eagle Lake provides good nesting habitat for dabbling and diving ducks, especially along the west shore and in the south bay. The lake is also a good place to spot numerous shorebirds: American Avocets, Marbled Godwits and yellowlegs are often seen (Sosiak 1988).

J.M. Crosby

References

Alberta Department of Agriculture. 1970. Preliminary report on Eagle Lake Reservoir. Water Resour. Div., Edmonton.

Alberta Environment. n.d.[a]. Envir. Assess. Div., Envir. Qlty. Monit. Br. Unpubl. data, Edmonton.

———. n.d.[b]. Tech. Serv. Div., Hydrol. Br. Unpubl. data, Edmonton.

Alberta Forestry, Lands and Wildlife. n.d. Fish Wild. Div. Unpubl. data, Edmonton.

———. 1988. Boating in Alberta. Fish Wild. Div., Edmonton.

———. 1989. Guide to sportfishing. Fish Wild. Div., Edmonton.

Alberta Hotel Association. 1989. Alberta campground guide 1989. Prep. for Travel Alta., Edmonton.

Alberta Research Council. 1972. Geological map of Alberta. Nat. Resour. Div., Alta. Geol. Surv., Edmonton.

Bierhuizen, J.F.H. and E.E. Prepas. 1985. Relationship between nutrients, dominant ions, and phytoplankton standing crop in prairie saline lakes. Can. J. Fish. Aquat. Sci. 42:1588–1594.

Charlton, S.E.D., D. Hammond and H.R. Hamilton. 1982. Trophic status of Eagle Lake. Alta. Envir., Poll. Contr. Div., Water Qlty. Contr. Br., Calgary.

Clark, B. 1988. Co. Wheatland, Strathmore. Pers. comm.

Energy, Mines and Resources Canada. 1977. National topographic series 1:50 000 82I/14 (1977), 82P/3 (1977). Surv. Map. Br., Ottawa.

Environment Canada. 1982. Canadian climate normals, Vol. 7: Bright sunshine (1951–1980). Prep. by Atm. Envir. Serv. Supply Serv. Can., Ottawa.

Geographic Board of Canada. 1928. Place-names of Alberta. Dept. Interior, Ottawa.

Hamilton, H.R. 1989. Hydroqual Consult. Ltd., Calgary. Pers. comm.

Namaka Community Historical Committee. 1983. Trails to Little Corner. Namaka Commun. Hist. Commit., Namaka.

Sosiak, A. 1988. Alta. Envir., Envir. Assess. Div., Envir. Qlty. Monit. Br., Calgary. Pers. comm.

Strong, W.L. and K.R. Leggat. 1981. Ecoregions of Alberta. Alta. En. Nat. Resour., Resour. Eval. Plan. Div., Edmonton.

Thompson, G.E. 1971. The limnology and fishery management of Eagle Lake, Alberta. Alta. Ld. For., Fish Wild. Div., Edmonton.

Trew, D.O. 1988. Alta. Envir., Envir. Assess. Div., Envir. Qlty. Monit. Br., Edmonton. Pers. comm.

Wyatt, F.A., T.W. Peters and W.E. Bowser. 1943. Soil survey of Blackfoot and Calgary sheets. Alta. Soil Surv. Rep. No. 39, Univ. Alta. Bull. No. SS–2. Univ. Alta., Edmonton.

GHOST RESERVOIR

D. Huet

MAP SHEET: 82O/2
LOCATION: Tp26 R6 W5
LAT/LONG: 51°12'N 114°45'W

Ghost Reservoir is a long, cold, windswept impoundment of the Bow River located on the edge of the foothills approximately 45 km west of Calgary. It was built in 1929 by Calgary Power Ltd., now TransAlta Utilities Corporation, and is still used for hydroelectric power generation. The reservoir lies in an area with beautiful mountain views and provides clean, clear water for recreationists. It is situated on Highway 1A, approximately 22 km west of the town of Cochrane (Fig. 1) in the Municipal District of Bighorn. Ghost Dam and Ghost Reservoir Provincial Recreation Area are located at the eastern end of the reservoir.

The reservoir and dam are named for the Ghost River, which flows into the east end of the reservoir. It was designated "Dead Man River" on Palliser's map of 1860, but the name was changed to "Ghost" to recall tales of a ghost prowling up and down the river valley, picking up skulls of fallen Blackfoot Indians who had been killed in battle by Cree Indians (Holmgren and Holmgren 1976). In 1873, two dedicated Methodist ministers, the Reverend George McDougall and his son, the Reverend John McDougall, set up a mission across the river from the present site of the locality of Morley to promote the cause of their church. At the same time, they brought the first cattle to the area and started the first ranch in the southern foothills. In 1874, the Hudson's Bay Company built a trading post on the hill above the mouth of the Ghost River to trade with the Indians drawn to the McDougalls' mission. A tireless crusader, George McDougall became lost in January 1876 in a blizzard near Nose Hill in Calgary and perished (MacGregor 1972). He was buried beside his church, which still stands on the north shore of Ghost Reservoir where the mountains to the west and the sweeping west wind can evoke the ghosts of the past to imaginative visitors.

In 1929, Calgary Power Ltd. leased reserve land from the Morley Indians to build the Ghost Dam across the Bow River just below the confluence of the Ghost River to create Ghost Reservoir (Snow 1977). A power transmission line was built from the Ghost power plant to Edmonton; for years, this line was the backbone of Alberta's electrical system (MacGregor 1972). Now, the main purpose of the reservoir is to provide power to Albertans during times of peak daily demand.

Despite limitations imposed by large water level fluctuations, cold water temperatures and wind, the reservoir is popular for power boating, windsurfing and sport fishing. There are no boating or fishing regulations specific to the reservoir, but the Ghost River and its tributaries are closed to angling from 1 November to 15 June and a bait ban is in effect in all flowing waters from 1 November to 15 August (Alta. For. Ld. Wild. 1988; 1989). These regulations may change from year to year. In winter, the reservoir is popular for ice fishing and ice boating.

The best access to the reservoir is at Ghost Reservoir Provincial Recreation Area, previously known as Lakeside Park and Campground, which is just southwest of the bridge crossing the Ghost River (Fig. 2). Facilities include day-use services year-round and a summer campground with 51 sites, a day-use area, tap and pump water, sewage disposal facilities, a boat launch, a telephone and a gravel beach. The shoreline around most of the reservoir is gravel. The water is clear and algae are inconspicuous year-round.

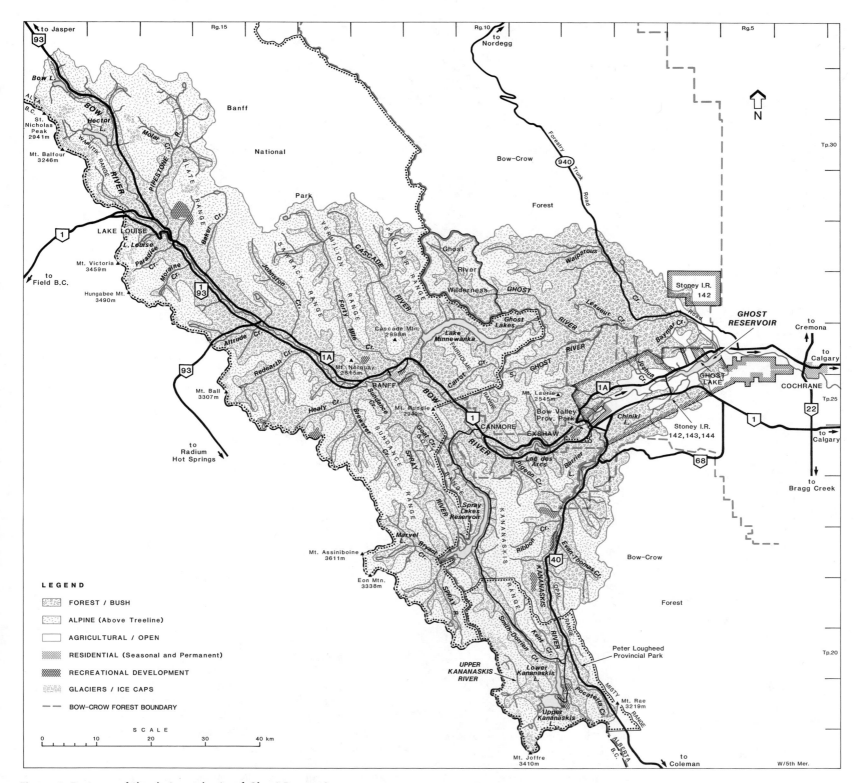

Figure 1. Features of the drainage basin of Ghost Reservoir.
SOURCES: Alta. Envir. n.d.[b]; En. Mines Resour. Can. 1966; 1967; 1975; 1977. Updated with 1982 aerial photos.

Drainage Basin Characteristics

The drainage basin of Ghost Reservoir is that of the Bow River (Fig. 1). It is very large (6 460 km^2; Table 1), almost 600 times the area of the reservoir (11.6 km^2, Table 2), and fans out to the west, reaching up to the continental divide from the glaciers and peaks around the Kananaskis Lakes and north to the glaciers above Bow Lake. The highest elevation in the basin is 3 611 m on the top of Mt. Assiniboine, south of Banff (Fig. 1). In the immediate vicinity of the reservoir, hills rise 200 m to the north and 320 m to the south.

The drainage area includes portions of six ecoregions: Montane, Boreal Foothills, Aspen Parkland, Boreal Uplands, Subalpine and Alpine (McGregor 1979; 1984; Strong and Leggat 1981). The Montane Ecoregion surrounds the reservoir, extends up the Bow Valley past Banff, and includes the headwaters of the Ghost River. This ecoregion is found in only 0.5% of the province; it is typified by the

presence of Douglas fir and varies in elevation from 1 200 to 2 000 m. From the reservoir to the mountains, and on south-facing slopes in the mountains, the firs are interspersed with fescue grassland and the soils are Black Chernozemics. In damper and cooler areas, the density of trembling aspen, lodgepole pine and white spruce increases and the soils are Eutric Brunisols. The Boreal Foothills Ecoregion extends over most of the basin of the Ghost River and is typified by the codominance of trembling aspen, balsam poplar and lodgepole pine. Luvisolic soils are most common. Just before the Ghost River enters the reservoir, it flows through a tiny area of Aspen Parkland Ecoregion, where trembling aspen is interspersed with fescue grasslands on Chernozemic soils. North of the Boreal Foothills Ecoregion, along the midsection of Waiparous Creek, is the most southern extension of the Boreal Uplands Ecoregion in Alberta. This ecoregion is located in the mountains and foothills above the Boreal Foothills and below the Subalpine Ecore-

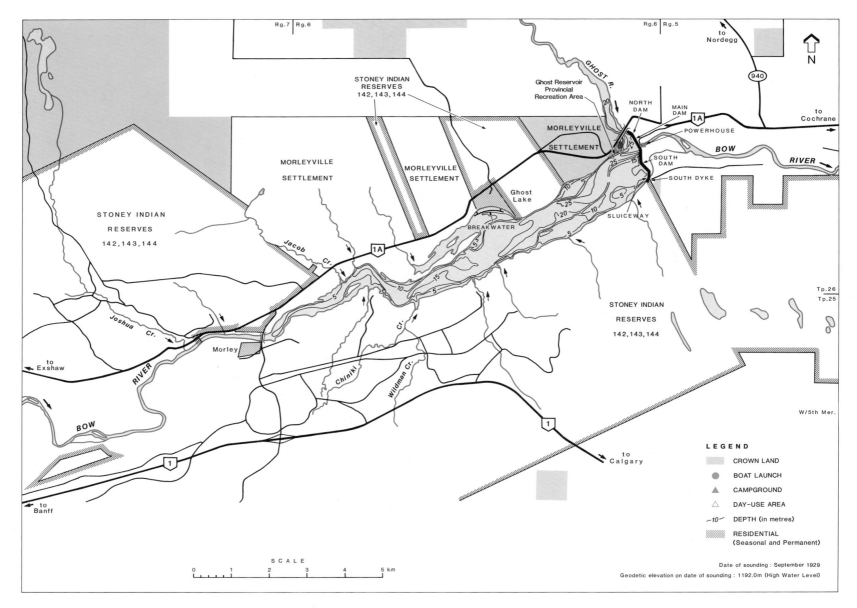

Figure 2. Bathymetry and shoreline features of Ghost Reservoir.
BATHYMETRY SOURCE: TransAlta Util. Corp. n.d.

Table 1. Characteristics of Ghost Reservoir drainage basin.

area (excluding lake) (km²)[a]	6 460
soil[b]	Black Chernozemics, Eutric Brunisols
bedrock geology[c, d]	Alberta Group (Upper Cretaceous): shale, sandstone; marine Brazeau Formation (Upper Cretaceous): sandstone, mudstone, tuff and thin coal beds; nonmarine
terrain[b]	rolling to mountainous
ecoregion[b]	Montane; Boreal Foothills; Aspen Parkland; Boreal Uplands; Subalpine; Alpine
dominant vegetation[b]	fescue, Douglas fir; trembling aspen, balsam poplar, lodgepole pine; trembling aspen; lodgepole pine, white spruce, black spruce; lodgepole pine, white spruce, fir; heaths, lichens
mean annual sunshine (h)[e]	2 314

NOTE: [d]in vicinity of reservoir only
SOURCES: [a]Alta. Envir. n.d.[b]; [b]Strong and Leggat 1981; [c]Alta. Res. Counc. 1972; [e]Envir. Can. 1982

gion. Lodgepole pine is the dominant species, with white or black spruce as climax cover; soils are Luvisols and Brunisols. The Subalpine Ecoregion in the watershed extends from the upper reaches of the Montane and Boreal Uplands ecoregions up to the treeline, which is approximately 2 000 m above sea level in this area. Grasslands on Chernozemic soils develop on steep south-facing slopes; trembling aspen on Chernozemic soils dominates on less-steep south-facing slopes; lodgepole pine, white spruce and fir on Eutric Brunisolic soils dominate in damper, cooler areas; and alder and willow on Regosolic and Gleysolic soils are found along water courses and in depressional areas. The Alpine Ecoregion, indicated on Figure 1, is located above the treeline. Although less than 3% of the province is in this ecoregion, about one-quarter of it is within the Bow River drainage basin. Shrub communities grow in the lower reaches; heaths and dryads are the dominant vegetation at higher elevations and lichens, bare rocks and glaciers occupy the highest areas. Soil development is minimal; those that have developed are Brunisols in well-drained areas and Regosols in poorly drained areas.

The few parcels of private land in the drainage basin lie along the north shore of the reservoir, including the summer village of Ghost Lake, and in the Bow Corridor between the hamlet of Exshaw and the Banff National Park gates, including the Stoney Indian Reserve. Most of the basin is Crown land; a large portion is within Banff National Park, smaller portions are within Peter Lougheed Provincial Park, the Ghost River Wilderness Area and the Bow-Crow Forest Reserve (Fig. 1). Land use in the basin is mostly recreation and preservation. There is some timber harvesting and oil and gas extraction within the forest reserve and on the Morley Indian Reserve. The

Table 2. Characteristics of Ghost Reservoir.

full supply level (FSL) (m)[a]	1 191.16 (open water) 1 191.77 (ice cover)
volume at FSL (m³)[a]	159.1 x 10⁶
live storage at FSL (m³)[a]	70.07 x 10⁶
surface area at FSL (km²)[a]	11.0
maximum drawdown (m)[a]	10.7
mean annual drawdown (1956–1987) (m)[b]	5.3
maximum depth at FSL (m)[c]	34
mean depth at FSL (m)[c]	14.5
shoreline length at FSL (km)[c]	32
lake length at FSL (km)[d]	13.5
lake width at FSL (km)[d]	1.4
mean annual lake evaporation (mm)[e]	664
mean annual precipitation (mm)[e]	537
mean residence time (yr)[a, f, g]	0.03
mean annual inflow volume (1912–1986) (m³)[f, g]	2 700 x 10⁶
mean annual outflow volume (1912–1986) (m³)[f, g]	2 690 x 10⁶

NOTE: [g]excluding groundwater inflow
SOURCES: [a]Monenco Ltd. 1985; [b]TransAlta. Util. Corp. n.d.; [c]CH₂M Hill Can. Ltd. 1980; [d]En. Mines Resour. Can. 1975; [e]Alta. Envir. n.d.[b]; [f]Envir. Can. 1987

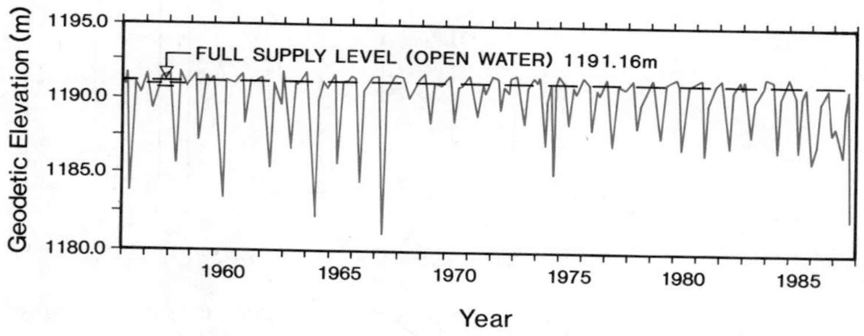

Figure 3. Water level of Ghost Reservoir, 1956 to 1987.
SOURCE: TransAlta Util. Corp. n.d.

Table 3. Control structures on Ghost Reservoir.

	Dam Height (m)	Crest Elevation (m)	Crest Length (m)
North Earthfill Dam	22.3	1 194.21	228
Main Concrete Dam	34.1	1 192.38[a]	283
South Earthfill Dam	21.3	1 194.21	610
South Sluiceway	—	1 192.38[a]	90
South Dyke	7.3	1 194.21	152

NOTE: [a]slopes to 1 194.21 m
SOURCE: Monenco Ltd. 1985

population of the basin is very low and is centred in the towns of Canmore and Banff, in the village of Lake Louise and on the Indian reserve.

Several small, intermittent creeks drain into the reservoir, but the Bow River provides about 93% of the inflow and the Ghost River provides about 7% (Envir. Can. 1987). All outflow is via the Bow River.

Reservoir Characteristics

Ghost Reservoir is a long (13.5 km), narrow (maximum width of 1.4 km) impoundment with one long arm where the Ghost River enters (Fig. 2). The slope of the basin is variable and depends on the meanders of the original Bow River channel. Slopes at the west end of the reservoir are generally gentle and when the water level is low, which it is almost every spring, extensive mud flats are exposed. During chinooks, the west wind lifts silt off these flats and forms dust clouds that occasionally can be seen as far away as Calgary. Most of the shoreline at the eastern end of the reservoir is barren cobble and gravel.

The dam that created the reservoir was built in 1929 by Calgary Power Ltd. Over the years it has been repaired, changed and augmented (Monenco Ltd. 1985), so the present structures are complex (Table 3). Proceeding from north to south, there is an earthfill dam, then a concrete gravity dam fitted with 4 generators that have a total generating capacity of 50 355 kW, then another earthfill dam, then a sluiceway to pass flows greater than those that can be passed through the generators, and finally a dyke to the south shore. The

generators can pass flows up to 230 m³/second. In approximately one year of three, usually in June, July or August, the flow of the Bow River exceeds this amount and water flows through the south sluiceway, which can handle flows of 1 560 m³/second at full supply level and 2 600 m³/second before the water level reaches the top of the dam. If flows ever exceed the capacity of the sluiceway, water can leave the reservoir via an emergency spillway on the main concrete dam at rates up to 1 200 m³/second.

Starting in 1986, TransAlta Utilities Corporation upgraded the dam by replacing the stop-logs in the south sluiceway and in the emergency spillway with electronically controlled steel gates to lessen the time required to release high flows from the reservoir. The stop-logs took days to remove—the new gates can be opened in minutes. To accomplish this, the reservoir was drawn down to 1 183 m and was not filled until mid–1989, when construction was finished.

The dam is operated to generate electrical power. The reservoir is drawn down in April so the water elevation is 1 188 m by 10 May. At that time, the gates in the south sluiceway are set at 1 188.5 m if the mountain snowpack is normal, or 1 187.5 m if the snowpack is above normal. The gates are not changed until June unless a flood causes the reservoir to rise to 1 190 m. If the water is still rising, the south sluiceway gates are opened farther. If the elevation reaches 1 195 m, the gates in the emergency spillway on the main dam are opened. When spring runoff is over, the sluiceway is operated to allow the reservoir to rise to 1 190 m by 1 July and to 1 191 m by mid- to late August. For the rest of the autumn, daily releases approximately equal the inflow. The reservoir is drawn down

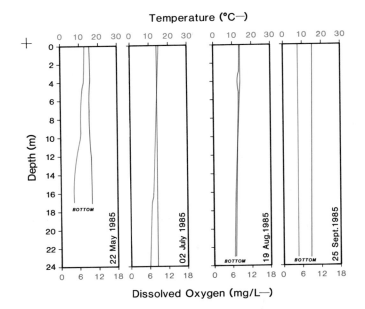

Figure 4. Temperature and dissolved oxygen in Ghost Reservoir, 1985.
SOURCE: Alta. Envir. n.d.[a].

Table 4. Major ions and related water quality variables for Ghost Reservoir. Average concentrations in mg/L; pH in pH units. Composite samples from the euphotic zone collected 4 times from 22 May to 29 Sep. 1985. S.E. = standard error.

	Mean	S.E.
pH (range)	7.3–7.9	—
total alkalinity ($CaCO_3$)	112	3.5
specific conductivity (µS/cm)	277	14.4
total dissolved solids (calculated)	152	5.6
turbidity (NTU)	2	0.8
total hardness ($CaCO_3$)	135	4.4
dissolved organic carbon	<1	—
HCO_3	137	4.3
CO_3	<1	—
Mg	10	0.2
Na	2	0.2
K	0.4	0.02
Cl	1	0.2
SO_4	31	1.6
Ca	37	1.9

SOURCE: Alta. Envir. n.d.[a], Naquadat stations 05AL05BE1000, 05AL05BE1001

Table 5. Nutrient, chlorophyll *a* and Secchi depth data for Ghost Reservoir. Average concentrations in µg/L. Composite samples from the euphotic zone collected 4 times from 22 May to 29 Sep. 1985. S.E. = standard error.

	Mean	S.E.
total phosphorus	7	1.5
total dissolved phosphorus	4	0.3
total Kjeldahl nitrogen	432	171.6
$NO_3 + NO_2$–nitrogen	30	5.6
NH_4–nitrogen	30	7.1
iron	<20	—
chlorophyll *a*	2.0	1.12
Secchi depth (m)	6.4	1.65

SOURCE: Alta. Envir. n.d.[a], Naquadat stations 05AL05BE1000, 05AL05BE1001

through the winter. At all times, a minimum riparian flow of 6 m³/second is maintained to the Bow River; most of the balance of water is released between about 7 a.m. and 8 p.m. (Monenco Ltd. 1985). The flushing rate of Ghost Reservoir averages 22 days. In June, the inflow increases and the flushing rate averages less than 10 days.

The water level of Ghost Reservoir has been monitored by TransAlta Utilities Corporation since 1956 (Fig. 3). Levels reflect the operating regime discussed above. The reservoir is drawn down an average of 5.3 m over winter. A maximum drawdown of 10.7 m is occasionally necessary to inspect or repair the control structures.

Water Quality

The quality of water in Ghost Reservoir was monitored by Alberta Environment four times from May through September 1985 (Alta. Envir. n.d.[a]).

The water in Ghost Reservoir is fresh and moderately well-buffered; the dominant ions are bicarbonate and calcium (Table 4). The reservoir was weakly thermally stratified on the May, July and August sample dates (Fig. 4). Dissolved oxygen concentrations were high from the surface to the bottom of the water column on all dates except 19 August 1985 when there was some dissolved oxygen depletion at the bottom.

Total phosphorus and chlorophyll *a* concentrations are extremely low and the water is clear (Table 5). In 1985, Secchi depths were shallowest (3.0 m) on 22 May when the reservoir was filling and the water was turbid with suspended silt, and greatest (10.3 m) on 19 August. Ghost Reservoir is oligotrophic.

Biological Characteristics

Plants

The phytoplankton in Ghost Reservoir was sampled by Alberta Environment approximately monthly at 8 depths on 18 dates from March 1976 through November 1977 (Beliveau and Furnell 1980). Twenty-five species were identified. The highest concentration of algae (5.9 mg/L) was found on 1 November 1976 and the second and third highest densities were found on 1 September 1976 and 8 November 1977, respectively. Ninety per cent of the November 1977 peak were diatoms (Bacillariophyta), whereas 82% of the September 1976 peak were blue-green algae (Cyanophyta). In 1977, a spring peak on 26 May was 78% Chrysophyta, whereas in

1976, a smaller spring peak on 29 April was 91% blue-greens. In 1977, the algae were strongly dominated by diatoms, cryptophytes, and chrysophytes until late July.

Macrophytes are very sparse in Ghost Reservoir; the gravel shore and fluctuations in water levels maintain a barren shoreline.

Invertebrates

There are no recent data on zooplankton or benthic invertebrates in Ghost Reservoir.

Fish

Nine species of fish are known to inhabit Ghost Reservoir: lake trout, brown trout, mountain whitefish, lake whitefish, longnose sucker, white sucker, burbot, brook stickleback and longnose dace (Alta. For. Ld. Wild. n.d.). Rainbow and cutthroat trout were stocked annually from 1934 to 1941 and may still be present in very low numbers, but none have been captured recently. Some lake trout were present in the reservoir in 1947, but these were likely migrants from Lake Minnewanka or other lakes along the Bow River (Rawson 1948). The current lake trout population in Ghost Reservoir may be largely due to the 89 000 lake trout introduced in 1948 and 1949 and the 100 000 eyed-eggs introduced in 1952 (Kraft 1989).

On 21 September 1987, 475 m of test-gang gill nets were set for 24 hours (Alta. For. Ld. Wild. n.d.). The composition of the total catch of 411 fish was: 62% longnose suckers, 22% lake trout, 6% mountain whitefish, 5% lake whitefish, 2% white sucker, 2% burbot and 1% brown trout. The largest lake trout was over 7 kg, the largest lake whitefish was 4.4 kg and the largest mountain whitefish was over 1 kg.

Angling on the reservoir is popular, especially near the Ghost River inflow, where hills shelter the water from the strong west wind. The fishery is managed exclusively for recreational fishing.

Wildlife

Ghost Reservoir does not provide good nesting habitat for waterfowl because of the fluctuating water level and the absence of shoreline vegetation. Canada Geese are often seen at the western end of the reservoir during spring migration.

Habitat around the reservoir is suitable for white-tailed and mule deer, coyotes, badgers, Richardson's ground squirrels, Western Meadowlarks and Mountain Bluebirds.

J.M. Crosby

References

Alberta Environment. n.d.[a]. Envir. Assess. Div., Envir. Qlty. Monit. Br. Unpubl. data, Edmonton.

———. n.d.[b]. Tech. Serv. Div., Hydrol. Br. Unpubl. data, Edmonton.

Alberta Forestry, Lands and Wildlife. n.d. Fish Wild. Div. Unpubl. data, Edmonton.

———. 1988. Boating in Alberta. Fish Wild. Div., Edmonton.

———. 1989. Guide to sportfishing. Fish Wild. Div., Edmonton.

Alberta Research Council. 1972. Geological map of Alberta. Nat. Resour. Div., Alta. Geol. Surv., Edmonton.

Beliveau, D. and A. Furnell. 1980. Phytoplankton data summary 1976–1980. Alta. Envir., Poll. Contr. Div., Water Qlty. Contr. Br. Unpubl. rep., Edmonton.

CH₂M Hill Canada Ltd. 1980. Water recreation resources study. Prep. for City Calg., Parks Rec. Dept., Calgary.

Energy, Mines and Resources Canada. 1966, 1967, 1975, 1977. National topographic series 1:250 000 82N (1966), 82O (1967), 82J (1977) and 1:50 000 82O/2 (1975). Surv. Map. Br., Ottawa.

Environment Canada. 1982. Canadian climate normals, Vol. 7: Bright sunshine (1951–1980). Prep. by Atm. Envir. Serv. Supply Serv. Can., Ottawa.

———. 1987. Historical streamflow summary: Alberta to 1986. Prep. by Inland Waters Directorate. Water Surv. Can., Water Resour. Br., Ottawa.

Holmgren, E.J. and P.M. Holmgren. 1976. Over 2000 place names of Alberta. 3rd ed. West. Producer Prairie Books, Saskatoon.

Kraft, M. 1989. Alta. For. Ld. Wild., Fish Wild. Div., Rocky Mountain House. Pers. comm.

MacGregor, J.G. 1972. A history of Alberta. Hurtig Publ., Edmonton.

McGregor, C.A. 1979. Ecological land classification and evaluation, Ghost River. Alta. En. Nat. Resour., Resour. Eval. Plan. Div., Edmonton.

———. 1984. Ecological land classification and evaluation, Kananaskis Country. Alta. En. Nat. Resour., Resour. Eval. Plan. Div., Edmonton.

Monenco Limited. 1985. TransAlta Utilities Corporation dam safety evaluation for Ghost development, Vol. 1. Prep. for TransAlta Util. Corp., Calgary.

Rawson, D.S. 1948. Biological investigations on the Bow and Kananaskis rivers in 1947, with special reference to the effects of power development on the availability of game fish in this area. Alta. Ld. Mines, Fish Wild. Div., Edmonton.

Snow, Chief J. 1977. These mountains are our sacred places. Samuel-Stevens Publ., Toronto.

Strong, W.L. and K.R. Leggat. 1981. Ecoregions of Alberta. Alta. En. Nat. Resour., Resour. Eval. Plan. Div., Edmonton.

TransAlta Utilities Corporation. n.d. Unpubl. data, Calgary.

GLENMORE RESERVOIR

MAP SHEETS: 82J/16, 82O/1
LOCATION: Tp23 R1, 2 W5
LAT/LONG: 50°59'N 114°08'W

Calgary is very fortunate to have within its city limits such a sparkling blue gem as Glenmore Reservoir (Fig. 1). This impoundment of the Elbow River not only provides more than half of the city water supply, but it also provides delightful relief from the urban landscape. Surrounded by parks and golf courses, it is a focus for recreation for many of the over half-million residents of this city. The reservoir is in the southwest portion of the city and is reached via 37 Street SW and 24 Street NW on the north side, via 14 Street SW and Heritage Drive on the east side and by 90 Avenue SW and 24 Street SW on the south side (Fig. 1, inset).

The Glenmore area was named by Sam Livingston, one of the first settlers in the area. He built his home in the Elbow Valley in the 1860s and named the valley *Glenmore*, which is Gaelic for "big valley" and was the name of his home in Ireland (Calg. Field Nat. Soc. 1975). In 1932, the city of Calgary purchased the land for the reservoir and the Sarcee Indians transferred part of their reserve to the city, including the area of floodplain bounded by the last major meander of the Elbow River upstream of the reservoir. This area is named Weaselhead after the Sarcee Chief who lived there for about 50 years in the late nineteenth and early twentieth centuries (Calg. Field Nat. Soc. 1975). On 31 January 1933, the Glenmore Dam across the Elbow River was completed, and by that summer, Glenmore Reservoir had been created to provide a stable water supply for Calgary.

All but the northeast bay of Glenmore Reservoir is surrounded by city parks (Fig. 2). North and South Glenmore and Heritage parks provide picnic tables, shelters and washroom facilities; Weaselhead Park is less developed but it is criss-crossed by a network of hiking and bicycle trails. Heritage Park is a replica of an early twentieth century community, with a fur-trade post, a bustling town, a farming community and a sternwheeler that churns through the water of Glenmore Reservoir. South Glenmore Park includes facilities for equestrian events which take place almost every week in summer. Two golf courses, one private and one public, border the northeast bay. Overnight accommodation is not available in the immediate vicinity of the reservoir, but all amenities, including campgrounds, are available within the surrounding city.

Boat access to the reservoir is available at public boat docks on the shore just south of Heritage Park, at the Calgary Sailing School on the south shore and at the Calgary Canoe and Rowing Club on the north shore. As the major use of the reservoir is to supply drinking water for Calgary, maintaining clean water in the reservoir is the top priority. Swimming and wading are prohibited and no pets are allowed in the water. No boating was permitted until 1963; now, some boating is permitted but by-laws are in place to ensure that the water is not contaminated (City Calg. 1989). Restrictions include:

- the prohibition of any motorized boats, inflatable boats or rafts, sailboards, sailboats longer than 8 m and sailboats equipped to pump out wastes;
- launching and docking are allowed at only the three public boat dock areas;
- no boating is permitted between the Glenmore Trail Causeway and Glenmore Dam;
- boating is allowed only during daylight hours;
- no polluting or littering from boats or docks is allowed;
- no pets are allowed in boats.

Sport fishing for trout, pike and perch is moderately popular in Glenmore Reservoir and provincial sport fishing regulations apply.

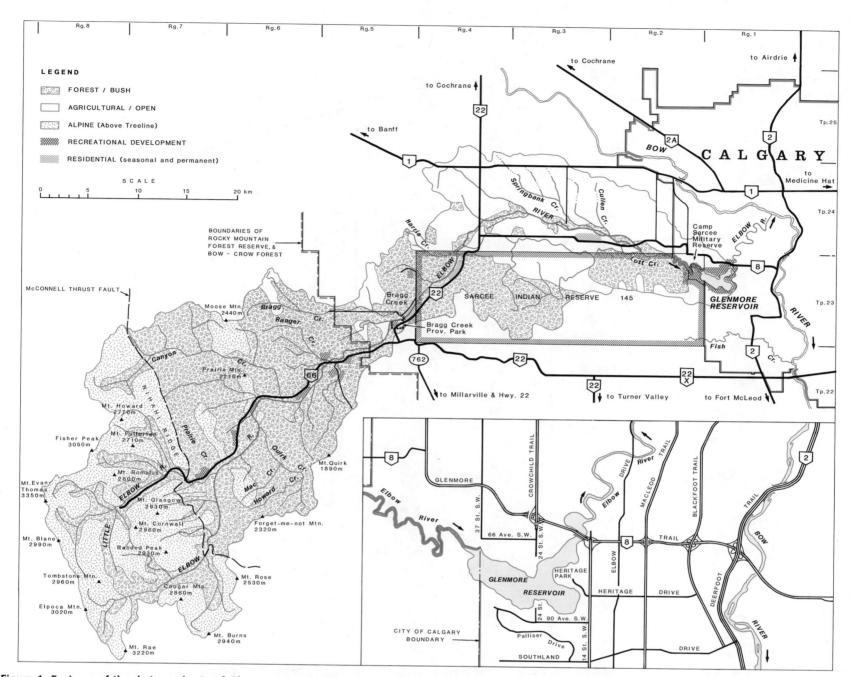

Figure 1. Features of the drainage basin of Glenmore Reservoir. Within the city of Calgary limits, recreational development is shown only for the area immediately surrounding the reservoir. Inset shows access to reservoir.
SOURCES: Alta. Envir. n.d.[a]; En. Mines Resour. Can. 1967; 1971; 1977; 1980. Updated with 1982 aerial photos.

Fishing is prohibited in the Elbow River upstream of the reservoir and in all tributaries to the Elbow River from 1 November through 15 June (Alta. For. Ld. Wild. 1989).

Glenmore is a clear, cold reservoir with low algal concentrations. Aquatic plants grow in the marshy areas at the west end of the reservoir and in a few sheltered areas around the shore.

Drainage Basin Characteristics

The drainage basin for Glenmore Reservoir is that of the Elbow River; it extends westward to the top of the front range of the Rocky Mountains (Fig. 1). It is very large (1 210 km²), over 300 times the area of the reservoir (3.8 km²) (Tables 1, 2).

The drainage basin includes portions of four ecoregions: Aspen Parkland, Boreal Foothills, Subalpine and Alpine (Strong and Leggat 1981). The drainage area within the Aspen Parkland Ecoregion includes the immediate vicinity of the reservoir and the area of rolling hills extending westward to within a few kilometers of Bragg Creek. The soils are mostly Black Chernozemics with Humic Gleysols in poorly drained depressions. The Elbow River lies in an old braided channel with recent deposits of sandy to coarse loam mixed with ribbons and bars of glaciofluvial gravel. Regosolic soils have devel-

Table 1. Characteristics of Glenmore Reservoir drainage basin.

area (excluding lake) (km²)[a]	1 210
soil[b, c]	Black Chernozemics, Orthic Gray Luvisols, Eutric Brunisols
bedrock geology[d]	Porcupine Hills Formation (Tertiary): sandstone, mudstone; nonmarine
terrain[b]	rolling to mountainous
ecoregion[b, e]	Aspen Parkland; Boreal Foothills; Subalpine; Alpine
dominant vegetation[b, e]	trembling aspen/fescue; trembling aspen/pine; pine/white spruce; heaths
mean annual sunshine (h)[f]	2 314

SOURCES: [a]Alta. Envir. n.d.[a]; [b]McGregor 1984; [c]MacMillan 1987; [d]Alta. Res. Counc. 1972; [e]Strong and Leggat 1981; [f]Envir. Can. 1982

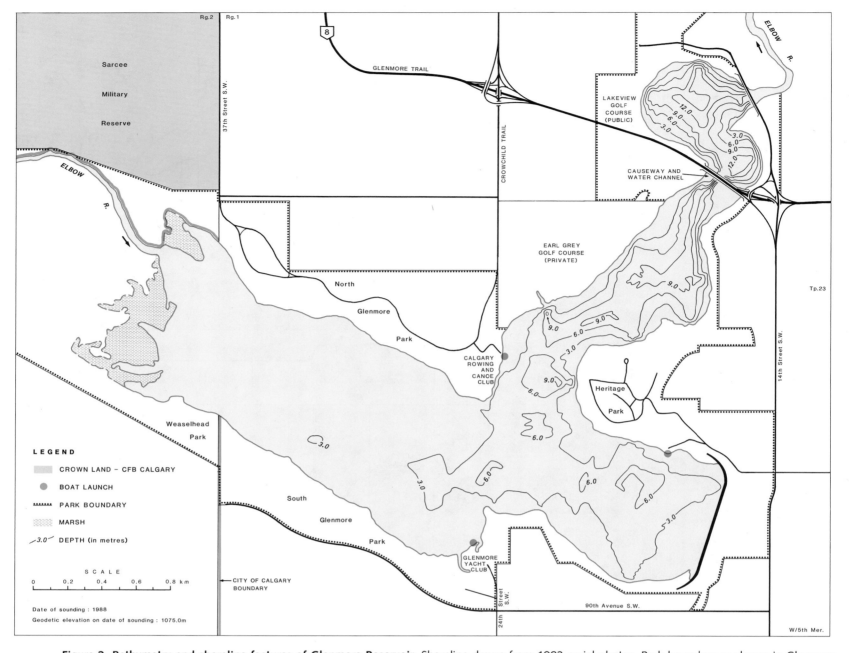

Figure 2. Bathymetry and shoreline features of Glenmore Reservoir. Shoreline drawn from 1982 aerial photos. Park boundary as shown in Glenmore Park proposed master plan (City Calg. 1983).
BATHYMETRY SOURCE: City Calg. n.d.

oped in some areas, Humic Gleysols are present in poorly drained areas and gravel is exposed in others (MacMillan 1987). The dominant vegetation in this portion of the drainage basin was originally fescue grasslands with trembling aspen, saskatoon and buckbrush in coulees and on north-facing slopes. Much of this region has now been broken for agriculture, primarily mixed farming and improved grazing.

To the west of the Aspen Parkland lies a portion of the Boreal Foothills Ecoregion. This ecoregion encompasses the area around Bragg Creek and continues west to just beyond Ranger Creek and almost as far west as Mount Quirk. Slopes are as steep as 45% and hills rise 150 m above the valley. Higher areas are composed of morainal and colluvial deposits; soils are Orthic and Eluviated Eutric Brunisols and Orthic Gray Luvisols that support closed forests of trembling aspen, pine and spruce (McGregor 1984). In the Elbow Valley, a coarse loamy fluvial veneer overlies glaciofluvial gravel. Terraces and floodplains are gullied. Black Chernozemics are present in well-drained areas and peaty Gleysols are present in poorly drained areas (Scheeler and Veauvy 1977).

Most of the area between the Boreal Foothills Ecoregion and the McConnell Thrust Fault is in the Subalpine Ecoregion (McGregor 1984). Slopes are 30% to over 100% and mountain tops rise over 600 m above the valleys. The soils are primarily Orthic Eutric Brunisols and Orthic Regosols under forests of pine and spruce.

The boundary between the Subalpine and Alpine ecoregions is almost contiguous with the McConnell Thrust Fault, the most easterly fault of the Rocky Mountains. This fault resulted in Cambrian strata being lifted 2 km and moved eastward 30 to 75 km; it is conspicuous today at Mount Yamnuska, which is north of the Bow River, and along Nihahi Ridge in the Elbow Valley. In the Alpine Ecoregion, slopes exceed 100% and mountains rise over 1 000 m above the valleys. The highest point in the basin is Mount Rae, at 3 225 m. Bedrock is exposed in many places and there is poor or no soil development. Orthic and Cumulic Regosols support dwarf scrub in some areas (McGregor 1984).

The major land uses in the basin are urban development near the reservoir, mixed farming and grazing almost as far west as Bragg Creek and recreation west of Bragg Creek. The area west of the Calgary city limits has been developed into numerous residential acreages. The western half of the basin is part of Kananaskis Country and includes numerous campgrounds, day-use areas, hiking and equestrian trails and an off-highway vehicle area at McLean Creek.

The Elbow River provides almost all the inflow to Glenmore Reservoir; there are no other natural defined inflows. Twenty-five storm sewers drain urban areas and flow into the reservoir; six of them are major ones. Four of the large storm sewers enter on the south shore, one enters south of Heritage Park and one enters on the north shore (Hargesheimer and Lewis 1988).

Table 2. Characteristics of Glenmore Reservoir.

control structures	Glenmore Dam and 1–km dyke on southeast bay
dam height (m)[a]	18.3
crest length (m)[a]	320
full supply level (FSL) (m)[b]	1 076.9
volume at FSL (m³)[b]	23.4 x 10⁶
surface area at FSL (km²)[b]	3.84
maximum drawdown (1976–1987) (m)[c]	5.38
mean annual drawdown (1976–1987) (m)[c]	3.48
maximum depth at FSL (m)[b]	21.1
mean depth at FSL (m)[b]	6.1
shoreline length at FSL (km)[d]	15.5
lake length at FSL on NE-SW axis (km)[b]	4.5
lake width at FSL on NW-SE axis (km)[b]	4.75
mean annual lake evaporation (mm)[e]	712
mean annual precipitation (mm)[e]	426
mean residence time (yr)[e, f]	0.07
mean annual inflow (m³)[e, f]	299 x 10⁶
annual withdrawal for Calgary water supply (1987) (m³)[b]	101.8 x 10⁶
mean annual outflow to the Elbow River (1908–1986) (m³)[c]	258.0 x 10⁶

NOTE: [f]excluding groundwater inflow
SOURCES: [a]Monenco Consult. Ltd. 1980; [b]City Calg. n.d.; [c]Envir. Can. 1976–1987; [d]En. Mines Resour. Can. 1971; 1980; [e]Alta. Envir. n.d.[a]

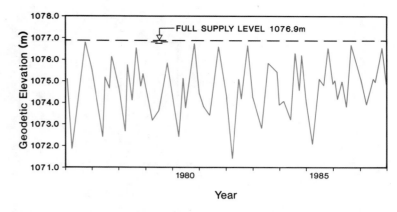

Figure 3. Water level of Glenmore Reservoir, 1976 to 1987.
SOURCE: Envir. Can. 1976–1987.

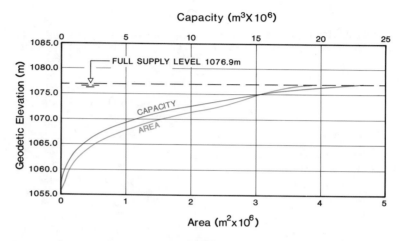

Figure 4. Area/capacity curve for Glenmore Reservoir.
SOURCE: Alta. Envir. n.d.[b].

Reservoir Characteristics

Glenmore Reservoir is an irregularly-shaped impoundment with three arms; the Elbow River enters the northwest arm, the southeast arm fills an old oxbow, and the Elbow River leaves via the Glenmore Dam at the end of the northeast arm. The reservoir is 4.5–km long on its northeast-southwest axis and 4.75–km long on its northwest-southeast axis (Table 2, Fig. 2).

Glenmore Dam is a concrete gravity structure that was built in 1932 and 1933. A road crosses on top of the dam, but as of 1988, this road was closed to motor vehicles. Glenmore Trail crosses the northeast arm of the reservoir on a causeway and a 45–m–long bridge. Approximately one third of the water leaving the reservoir flows through a water intake 6.1 m below the crest level of the dam and provides up to 70% of the city of Calgary's water supply. (The balance of Calgary's water supply is taken from the Bow River just downstream of Bearspaw Reservoir.) The remaining two thirds of the water leaving the reservoir flows through tailrace ports that extend from 1.5 to 7.6 m above the reservoir bottom. The outflowing water forms the Elbow River, which joins the Bow River near the Calgary Zoo (Marshall Macklin Monaghan Ltd. 1985[b]). Another structure, a 1–km–long earthen dyke, retains the southeast arm of the reservoir.

The bottom of the reservoir slopes very gently along most of the northwest arm, but slopes more steeply around the rest of the reservoir, especially in the northeast arm where the bottom drops steeply to the reservoir's maximum depth of 21.1 m.

The water level of the reservoir from 1976 to 1987 is illustrated in Figure 3. The water level is lowered in spring to provide Calgary with some flood protection in the case of sudden snowmelt or heavy rains in the mountains and foothills. The reservoir is filled to its full supply level of 1 076.9 m by about 1 July. Throughout the summer, the level is held as close to the full supply level as the inflow will allow. The level then drops during the winter as inflow is low and water continues to be withdrawn to meet municipal demand. The lowest water level between 1976 and 1987 occurred in 1982 when the water surface was 5.5 m below the full supply level. At this time, the area of the reservoir was approximately 50% of the area at full supply level (Fig. 4).

Water Quality

The water quality of Glenmore Reservoir and its inflowing storm sewers was monitored intensively by the City of Calgary from 1982 through August 1986 (Marshall Macklin Monaghan Ltd. 1985[a]; 1985[b]; Hargesheimer and Lewis 1988) and is still monitored in an ongoing program.

Glenmore is a freshwater reservoir. The water is well-buffered and the dominant ions are bicarbonate, sulphate and calcium (Table 3). More than twenty temperature and dissolved oxygen profiles were taken at each of four sites in the reservoir from April through September in 1985. Throughout this period, there was no evidence of stratification at three of the sites (5– to 7–m deep). At the fourth site, just west of the causeway, weak thermal stratification was apparent for a period of a few days in each of April, May and July (as on 11 July 1985, Fig. 5). Dissolved oxygen concentrations were always near saturation at all sites and at all depths.

The water in Glenmore Reservoir is very clear and Secchi depths are as deep as 7.5 m. Throughout the summer in 1984 and 1985, most of the reservoir bottom was visible from the surface, although heavy rains increased the turbidity for a few days. Chlorophyll a concentrations were almost always low but average values increased from 1984 to 1986 (Table 4). Total phosphorus was analyzed in 395 samples that were collected from Glenmore Reservoir and the upstream portion of the Elbow River. The analytical technique used was sensitive to phosphorus levels over 10 µg/L, but over half of the samples from the reservoir and river were below this detection limit and most of the other samples were barely above it. The low phosphorus concentrations and fairly low mean chlorophyll a concentrations indicate that Glenmore Reservoir is on the borderline between oligotrophic and mesotrophic.

The chemical composition of the base flow in each of the five major storm sewers that empty into Glenmore Reservoir was deter-

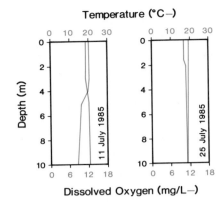

Figure 5. Temperature and dissolved oxygen in Glenmore Reservoir, 1985.
SOURCE: Hargesheimer and Lewis 1988.

Table 3. Major ions and related water quality variables for Glenmore Reservoir. Average concentrations in mg/L; pH in pH units. Samples from the surface collected 15 times from Jan. 1982 to Aug. 1986. S.E. = standard error.

	Mean	S.E.
pH (range)	7.8–8.5	—
total alkalinity (CaCO$_3$)	150	20.2
specific conductivity (μS/cm)	376	49.8
total dissolved solids (calculated)	216[a, b]	31.5
turbidity (NTU)	2[c]	2.2
total hardness (CaCO$_3$)	207	27.6
total organic carbon	2[c]	0.9
HCO$_3$	178[c]	23.2
CO$_3$	2[c]	1.5
Mg	16	1.8
Na	3	0.8
K	1	0.3
Cl	2	1.3
SO$_4$	60	11.0
Ca	56	7.8

NOTES: [a]n = 9, June 1982 to July 1983; [c]n = 229, Jan. 1982 to Aug. 1986
SOURCES: [b]Marshall Macklin Monaghan Ltd. 1985[b]; Hargesheimer and Lewis 1988

Table 4. Nutrient, chlorophyll *a* and Secchi depth data for Glenmore Reservoir. Average concentrations in μg/L. Composite samples from the euphotic zone collected from Jan. 1982 to Aug. 1986. S.E. = standard error.

	Year	Mean	Maximum	S.E.
total phosphorus	1982/83[a]	8	—	5.2
total Kjeldahl nitrogen	1982/83[a]	313	—	101.2
chlorophyll *a*	1982/83[a]	1.2	—	0.69
chlorophyll *a*	1984[b, c]	1.3	4.7	0.69
chlorophyll *a*	1985[b, d]	2.3	11.6	2.02
chlorophyll *a*	1986[b, c]	3.2	10.9	3.12

NOTES: [a]n = 9, June 1982 to July 1983 (open water only); [c]n = 128, Apr. to Dec; [d]n = 110, Jan. to Dec.; [e]n = 50, Jan. to Aug.
SOURCES: Marshall Macklin Monaghan Ltd. 1985[b]; [b]Hargesheimer and Lewis 1988

mined approximately every two weeks from May 1985 through May 1986 (Hargesheimer and Lewis 1988). The storm sewers were not sampled during the spring runoff or during storm events. Phosphorus, arsenic, cadmium, chromium, lead and barium were usually below detection limits in the reservoir but above detection in the base flow of the storm sewers. Organic chemicals such as insecticides, herbicides and other agricultural and industrial compounds were also monitored in the reservoir and in storm sewer base flow. Nine phenolic compounds (such as phenol; 2, 4–D and 2, 4, 5–T) were examined. Phenol was found in 96% of the reservoir samples, and three other phenolics were also frequently found. Twenty-four base-neutral compounds (polyaromatic hydrocarbons, chlorinated organics and industrial residues) were examined in more than 150 reservoir and storm sewer samples. All compounds were consistently higher in the storm sewer samples than in the reservoir samples where they were frequently below detection.

As of July 1989, the City of Calgary was planning to divert the storm effluent from the major storm sewer on the north shore to a retention pond by 1990. The city was also considering the feasibility of options to direct the other five major storm sewers away from the reservoir (Hargesheimer 1989).

Biological Characteristics

Plants

There are no data available on the species of algae or macrophytes in Glenmore Reservoir.

Invertebrates

Zooplankton was briefly sampled in November 1970 (Anderson 1974). The maximum density found was 45 organisms per litre. Six species of cladocerans and four species of copepods were identified.

There are no data on benthic invertebrates in Glenmore Reservoir.

Fish

Six species of fish have been found in Glenmore Reservoir: mountain whitefish, brown trout, northern pike, yellow perch, longnose suckers and white suckers. On 23 and 24 August 1988, Fish and Wildlife Division set two 225–m test nets for a 22–hour period (Alta. For. Ld. Wild. n.d.). A total of 100 fish were caught: 32 northern pike, 25 yellow perch, 6 brown trout, 31 longnose suckers and 6 white suckers. The sport fish caught included large representatives of each species—a 95–cm pike, a 31–cm perch and a 66–cm brown trout. Mountain whitefish are occasionally caught by anglers.

Fish and Wildlife Division stocked the reservoir with rainbow trout, lake trout and kokanee in the mid–1960s (Alta. Ld. For. 1964–1966). These plantings were not successful and the reservoir has not been stocked since.

Sport fishing is only moderately popular in Glenmore Reservoir, more likely due to boating restrictions than to the quality and availability of fish (Lowe 1989).

Wildlife

It is fortunate that the recreation and aesthetic value of the land surrounding Glenmore Reservoir was recognized decades ago and parkland now surrounds the impoundment. The eastern portion has been developed into golf courses, Heritage Park and the Yacht Club, but nearly 280 ha of land south and west of the reservoir has been preserved in its natural state and provides excellent and diverse habitat for wildlife. Plant and animal species likely to be encountered are well described by the Calgary Field Naturalists' Society (1975).

Glenmore Reservoir is extensively used by waterfowl during spring migration. The first ducks arriving near the end of March are Common Mergansers, Common Goldeneye and Mallards. They are soon joined by Canada Geese, Pintails, Blue-winged Teal, Lesser Scaup, American Widgeons, Shovelers and Bufflehead. White-winged Scoters are commonly seen and Surf Scoters are seen more rarely. In 1971, Black Scoters were sighted at the reservoir, the first sighting of this species in Alberta. Whistling Swans and American Coots visit by the hundreds, and Western, Horned and Eared grebes frequent the area.

By the end of May, most of the waterfowl have left, but they return in August with the addition of Hooded Mergansers, but without Whistling Swans, which take a different route south. Only a few Mallards, Pintails, Blue-winged Teal, American Widgeons and occasionally Canada Geese stay to breed, mostly at the western end of the reservoir.

The mudflats at the western end of the reservoir are usually exposed in spring and provide food for thousands of migrating shorebirds as they pass through the area. Black-bellied Plovers, Long-billed Curlews, Willets, Greater and Lesser yellowlegs, Long-billed Dowitchers, Marbled Godwits, Common Snipes and Solitary, Baird's, Least and Semipalmated sandpipers feed on exposed portions of the mudflats.

In winter, large numbers of ducks, mostly Mallards, stay in the open water downstream of the dam. In the winter of 1987/88, approximately 15 000 were seen; in 1988/89, there were 2 500 (Alta. For. Ld. Wild. n.d.).

Mammals seen in the western end of the reservoir include mule and white-tailed deer, black bears, mink, beaver and muskrats (Alta. For. Ld. Wild. n.d.).

J.M. Crosby

References

Alberta Environment. n.d.[a]. Tech. Serv. Div., Hydrol. Br. Unpubl. data, Edmonton.
———. n.d.[b]. Tech. Serv. Div., Surv. Br. Unpubl. data, Edmonton.
Alberta Forestry, Lands and Wildlife. n.d. Fish Wild. Div. Unpubl. data, Edmonton.
———. 1989. Guide to sportfishing regulations. Fish Wild. Div. Edmonton.
Alberta Lands and Forests. 1964–1966. Fish planting list. Fish Wild. Div., Edmonton.
Alberta Research Council. 1972. Geological map of Alberta. Nat. Resour. Div., Alta. Geol. Surv. Edmonton.
Anderson, R.S. 1974. Crustacean plankton communities of 340 lakes and ponds in and near the National Parks of the Canadian Rocky Mountains. J. Fish. Res. Bd. Can. 31:855–869.
Calgary Field Naturalists' Society. 1975. Calgary's natural areas: A popular guide. Calg. Field Nat. Soc., Box 981, Calgary.
City of Calgary. n.d. Eng. Dept. Unpubl. data, Calgary.
———. 1983. Glenmore Park proposed master plan. Rec. Dept., Calgary.
———. 1989. Welcome to Glenmore Reservoir. Parks Rec. Dept., Calgary.
Energy, Mines and Resources Canada. 1967, 1971, 1977, 1980. National topographic series 1:250 000 82O (1967), 82I (1977), 82J (1977) and 1:50 000 82J/16 (1971), 82O/1 (1980). Surv. Map. Br., Ottawa.
Environment Canada. 1976–1987. Surface water data. Prep. by Inland Waters Directorate. Water Surv. Can., Water Resour. Br., Ottawa.
———. 1982. Canadian climate normals, Vol. 7: Bright sunshine (1951–1980). Prep. by Atm. Envir. Serv. Supply Serv. Can., Ottawa.
Hargesheimer, E.E. 1989. City Calg., Eng. Dept., Waterworks Div., Calgary. Pers. comm.
——— and C.M. Lewis. 1988. Water quality in the Glenmore and Bearspaw Reservoirs. City Calg., Eng. Dept., Waterworks Div., Calgary.
Lowe, D. 1989. Alta. For. Ld. Wild., Fish Wild. Div., Red Deer. Pers. comm.
MacMillan, R.A. 1987. Soil survey of the Calgary urban perimeter. Alta. Soil Surv. Rep. No. 45, Alta. Res. Counc. Bull. No. 54. Alta. Res. Counc., Terrain Sci. Dept., Edmonton.
Marshall Macklin Monaghan Limited. 1985[a]. Elbow River watershed study, phase 2 report, Vol. 2: Water management in other areas: Land use inventory, recreation and stormwater assessment. Prep. for City Calg. by Marshall Macklin Monaghan Ltd., Calgary.
———. 1985[b]. Elbow River watershed study, phase 2 report, Vol. 3: Final report on water quality program, dye dispersion study, and statistical analyses. Prep. for City Calg. by Envirocon Ltd., Calgary and by Marshall Macklin Monaghan Ltd., Don Mills.
McGregor, C.A. 1984. Ecological land classification of Kananaskis Country. Alta. En. Nat. Resour., Resour. Eval. Plan. Div., Edmonton.
Monenco Consultants Limited. 1980. City of Calgary Glenmore Dam safety evaluation, phase I study, Vol. 1: Study data and results. Prep. for City Calg., Eng. Dept., Calgary.
Scheeler, M.D. and C.F. Veauvy. 1977. Detailed soil survey of Bragg Creek area. Alta. Inst. Pedol. Rep. No. M–77–8. Univ. Alta., Edmonton.
Strong, W.L. and K.R. Leggat. 1981. Ecoregions of Alberta. Alta. En. Nat. Resour., Resour. Eval. Plan. Div., Edmonton.

KANANASKIS LAKES
Upper and Lower

MAP SHEET: 82J/11
LOCATION: Tp19, 20 R9 W5
LAT/LONG: 50°40'N 115°10'W

The Kananaskis Lakes are beautiful, clear lakes in a striking setting of towering, ice-capped mountains. Located along the continental divide, there are numerous peaks over 3 000 m, many with glaciers, within 10 km of the lakes. The area can be reached from the city of Calgary by travelling 80 km west on Highway 1, then 56 km south on Highway 40 to Peter Lougheed Provincial Park, which includes the lakes (Fig. 1). The turnoff to the lakes is well marked.

The Kananaskis River was named by Captain Palliser in 1858 for an Indian, Joseph Kin-oh-ah-kis. A legend tells that it was at the confluence of the Kananaskis and Bow rivers that Kin-oh-ah-kis displayed supernatural powers upon regaining consciousness and recovering from an axe blow to the head (Appleby 1975). Coincidentally, the Stoney word *Kin-oh-ah-kis* means "meeting of the waters" (Finlay and Finlay 1987). The Kananaskis Lakes are near the Kananaskis River's headwaters and were named after the river. The valley was used occasionally by Sarcee and Stoney Indians; in 1845, when the first white man, James Sinclair, traversed the valley, only a small group of Indians lived in the area. Sinclair came with 15 white families in Red River carts and 250 head of horses and cattle. They were accompanied by 100 Cree warriors for protection from attacks by the Blackfoot, but the Cree deserted the group near Morley. The group's guide, the Cree chief Macipictoon stayed with the settlers. Difficult terrain forced them to abandon their carts near the Kananaskis Lakes. Continuing on foot over Kananaskis Pass, they eventually made it to the State of Washington. All of the settlers survived the trek, as did most of the livestock (Finlay and Finlay 1987). Trappers later came to the area; one of these, George Pocaterra, built a cabin not far from the lakes in 1906. Pocaterra Creek and Pocaterra Dam were named after him.

After the railway came through the Bow Valley in 1883, logging began in the Kananaskis Valley. The Eau Claire and Bow River Lumber Company established a logging camp at the site of the present Eau Claire Campground (15 km north of the lakes) and a sawmill operated at Upper Kananaskis Lake from 1932 to 1944. Large fires swept through the valley in 1910, 1919, 1929 and 1936 (Oltmann 1976).

Before the lakes were developed for power production, they were connected by a 1–km stretch of river (Fig. 2). Water dropped from the upper lake in a 3–m–high waterfall, then fell in another cascade below the lower lake to form the Kananaskis River. Calgary Power Ltd. (now TransAlta Utilities Corporation) began investigating the power potential of the lakes in 1912, but it was 1932 before the first dam was built on the upper lake. Until 1955, only the upper lake was managed, and then only to augment winter flow on the Bow River to drive the generators at Seebe and Ghost Reservoir. Power generation at the Kananaskis Lakes began after 1955 when the Interlakes Plant was built below the upper lake and the Pocaterra Plant was built below the newly-constructed Pocaterra Dam, which raised the level of the lower lake (TransAlta Util. Corp. n.d.).

The Kananaskis-Coleman Road (now Highway 40) was completed in 1952 to encourage recreational activity, but use of the area was low until 1976, when the road was paved and Kananaskis Provincial Park was established (Fig. 1). The park, which covers 509 km^2 around the lakes, was renamed Peter Lougheed Provincial Park on 1 January 1986 in honour of the man who was Alberta's premier from 1971 to 1985.

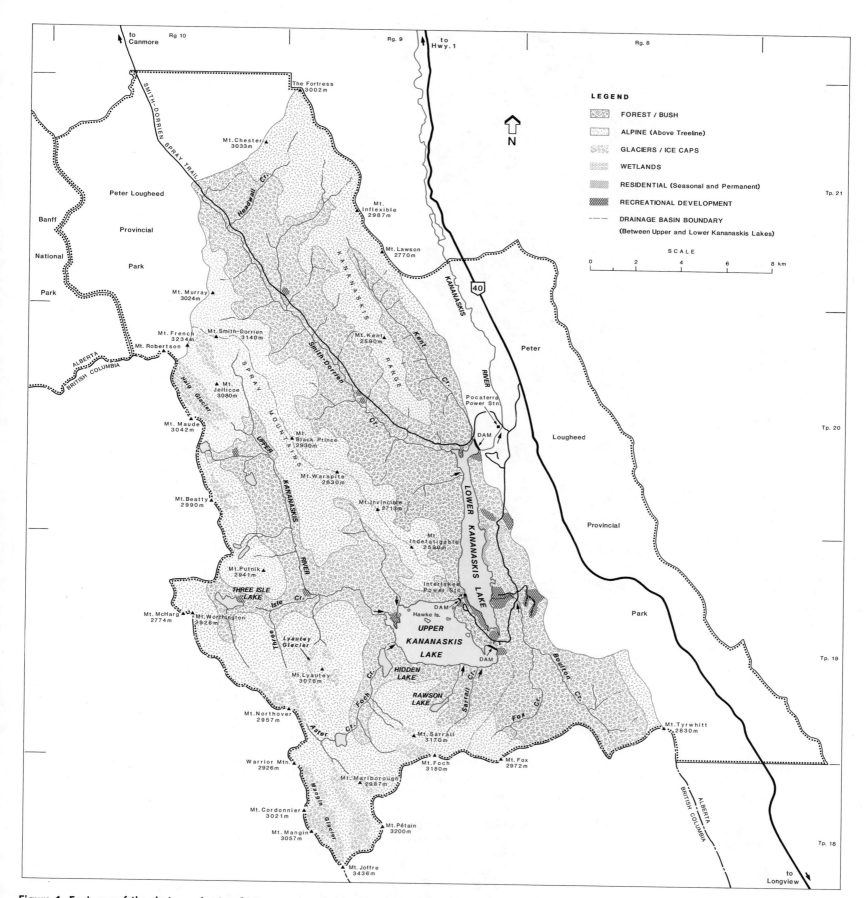

Figure 1. Features of the drainage basin of Upper and Lower Kananaskis lakes.
SOURCES: Alta. Envir. n.d.[b]; En. Mines Resour. Can. 1977. Updated with 1982 aerial photos. Elevation of some peaks from Thorington (1966).

The park provides 14 campgrounds, 9 of which are close to the lakes (Fig. 2). There is a total of 452 sites in 5 road-access campgrounds: Boulton (open year-round), Lower Lake, Interlakes, Elkwood and Canyon (open in summer only). Facilities provided include tap water, picnic shelters, playgrounds, sewage disposal stations, a cafeteria and a grocery store (Alta. Hotel Assoc. 1989). As well, there are 44 walk-in tent sites at Mount Sarrail campground, 2 group campgrounds (Lower Lake and Pocaterra) and an 11–site campground for handicapped persons (William Watson). There are

also six backcountry campgrounds, but only one (Point) is near the Kananaskis Lakes. The park also provides low-cost lodge facilities for senior citizens and handicapped individuals and their families at William Watson Lodge.

There are six day-use sites near the lakes. Boat launches near the Kananaskis Main Dam on the upper lake and near Canyon Campground on the lower lake provide access to the water. Difficulty using the boat launches increases as the lake levels drop; boat access is impossible at the very low water levels that occur in the spring.

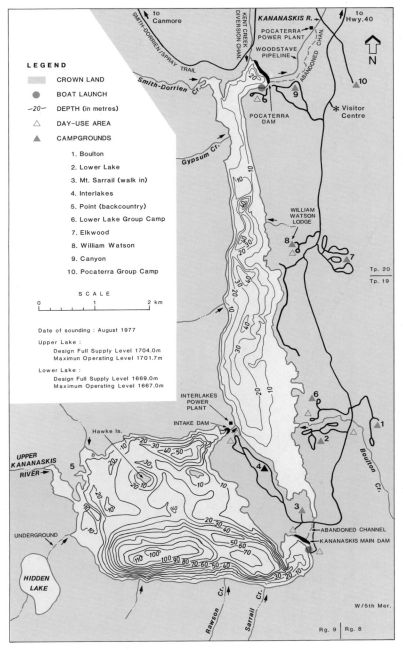

Figure 2. Bathymetry and shoreline features of Upper and Lower Kananaskis lakes.
BATHYMETRY SOURCE: Alta. Envir. n.d.[c].

Table 1. Characteristics of Kananaskis Lakes drainage basin.

area (excluding lakes) (km^2)[a, b]	307, of this 139 km^2 to upper lake
soil[c]	Eutric Brunisols; Orthic Regosols, bedrock
bedrock geology[d]	Mesozoic Era: sandstone, siltstone, shale, carbonates Upper Paleozoic Era: carbonates, shale
terrain[c]	mountainous; slopes >100%
ecoregion[c, e]	Subalpine; Alpine
dominant vegetation[c]	white spruce; heaths
mean annual inflow (m^3)[a, f]	102 x 10^6 (upper lake) 246 x 10^6 (lower lake)
mean annual sunshine (h)[g]	1 970

NOTE: [b]present conditions—French Creek diverted to Mud Lake, Mud Lake diverted to Spray Lakes Reservoir, Kent Creek diverted to Lower Kananaskis Lake; [f]excluding groundwater inflow
SOURCES: [a]Alta Envir. n.d.[b]; [c]McGregor 1984; [d]Alta. Res. Counc. 1972; [e]Strong and Leggat 1981; [g]Envir. Can. 1982

been studied intensively by numerous scientific disciplines. A computerized bibliography is maintained by Alberta Recreation and Parks (More 1988). It is updated continuously—in 1988, it included over 2 000 titles.

Drainage Basin Characteristics

The Kananaskis Lakes drainage basin lies adjacent to the continental divide in one of the most mountainous areas of Alberta. The basin is relatively large—24 times the combined area of the lakes (Tables 1, 2). Fairly high precipitation and numerous glaciers provide ample runoff to the lakes.

The drainage basin lies in the Alpine and Subalpine ecoregions (Strong and Leggat 1981; McGregor 1984). Approximately 70% of the basin, mostly along the western half, is in the Alpine Ecoregion. It is an area of bedrock peaks, colluvial slopes and little or no soil. Slopes exceed 100% and peaks reach altitudes up to 3 500 m above sea level. Vegetation is limited to tiny forbs and grasses growing in cracks in the rocks or in alpine meadows. Glaciers cover much of the area. The valleys and the area around the lakes are in the Subalpine Ecoregion. Colluvial materials form slopes and morainal deposits predominate in the area immediately around the lakes and to the east of them. Vegetation is primarily closed or open white spruce and Engelmann spruce and lodgepole pine forests (McGregor 1984). Soils under the coniferous forests are predominantly Orthic Eutric Brunisols and Orthic Regosols. There is a low-lying area west of the upper lake where some Humic Gleysols have formed in low, damp areas. The part of the basin east of the lakes is covered by a blanket of coarse morainal glacial till with ice margin channels filled with organic materials. The soils in the drier areas are Brunisols and Podzolic Gray Luvisols, whereas in the low, boggy areas they are Typic Mesisols and Humic Gleysols (McGregor 1984).

The entire drainage basin is Crown land and lies within Peter Lougheed Provincial Park. Areas close to the lakes have been developed for recreation and there are about 65 cottages on leased land along the east shore of the lower lake (Fig. 1).

Lake Basin Characteristics

Upper Kananaskis Lake

Upper Kananaskis Lake is deep (maximum depth of 108 m) and irregularly shaped. Because it lies on an uneven area of bedrock and morainal material, the bathymetry also is irregular (Fig. 2). The north and south shores slope steeply to 56 m and 108 m, respectively. The midline of the lake on an east-west axis is shallower and dotted with shoals and islands, many of which are submerged at the operational full supply level (FSL).

The sides of the lake basin between the limits of the FSL and the mean drawdown level are barren bedrock, cobble or gravel. When

Boat speed is limited to 12 km/hour or less in posted areas on both lakes (Alta. For. Ld. Wild. 1988). Caution on the lakes is advised, as the water is very cold and sudden storms can occur at any time of year.

Recreational activities in the provincial park include hiking on well-designed and well-mapped trails, backcountry camping, bicycling on excellent bike trails, fishing, climbing and viewing the spectacular scenery. An impressive visitor centre provides information on the natural features of the park as well as details on facilities. Both Upper and Lower Kananaskis Lakes are stocked with rainbow trout, but the low nutrient level and low temperature of the water results in slow growth rates and low catch rates (Stelfox 1989). Fishing for bait fish and the use of bait fish are not permitted in the lakes. As well, the use of any bait is not permitted in any flowing water from mid-August to early November and no rainbow or cutthroat trout under 25 cm caught in flowing water may be kept (Alta. For. Ld. Wild. 1989). Although the water in the lakes is very clear and attractive, it is usually too cold for swimming. In summer, water temperatures rarely exceed 14°C (Alta. Envir. n.d.[a]).

The ecology of Peter Lougheed Provincial Park has been the subject of numerous provincial government studies, especially since the mid–1970s. The area is near the environmental research stations of the University of Alberta and the University of Calgary and has

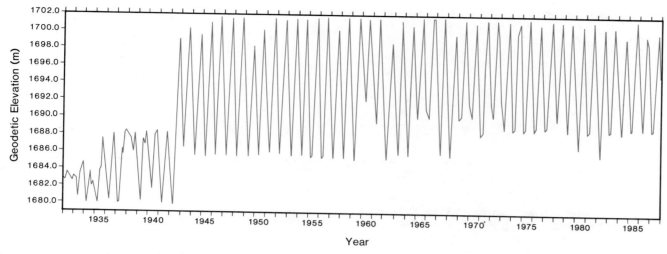

Figure 3. Water level of Upper Kananaskis Lake, 1932 to 1987.
SOURCE: Envir. Can. 1932–1987.

Table 2. Characteristics of Upper and Lower Kananaskis lakes.

	Upper	Lower
control structures[a]	Kananaskis Main Dam; Intake Dam	Pocaterra Dam
dam heights (m)[a]	25; 25	20
crest lengths (m)[a]	400; 150	600
design full supply level (FSL) (m)[a, b]	1 704.0	1 669.0
maximum operating level (MOL) (m)[a]	1 701.7	1 667.0
volume at MOL ($\times 10^6$ m^3)[a]	245	70.0
live storage at MOL ($\times 10^6$ m^3)[a]	120	56.0
surface area at MOL (km^2)[c]	7.80	5.25
maximum drawdown (m)[a]	16.5	13.5
mean annual drawdown (m)[d]	13.7 (1943–1987)	10.5 (1955–1986)
maximum depth at MOL (m)[a]	108	42.1
mean depth at MOL (m)[a, c]	32.0	13.1
shoreline length at MOL (km)[e]	37.3[f]	47.7
lake length at MOL (km)[a]	5.0	8.8
lake width at MOL (km)[a]	3.5	1.4
mean annual lake evaporation (mm)[g]	640	640
mean annual precipitation (mm)[g]	622	622
mean residence time (yr)[g, h]	1.6	0.31
mean annual outflow volume ($\times 10^6$ m^3)	153 (1932–1984)[a]	223 (1975–1982)[d]

NOTES: [b]the FSLs of 1 704.0 and 1 669.0 m have never been utilized; [f]includes shoreline lengths of three largest islands; [h]excluding groundwater inflow
SOURCES: [a]TransAlta Util. Corp. n.d.; [c]Alta. Envir. n.d.[c]; [d]Envir. Can. 1932–1987; [e]En. Mines Resour. Can. 1977; [g]Alta. Envir. n.d.[b]

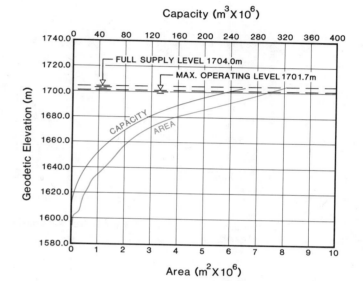

Figure 4. Area/capacity curve for Upper Kananaskis Lake.
SOURCE: Alta. Envir. n.d.[c].

the water level drops, there appear ghostly stumps of trees cut before the level was first raised. Low nutrients, cold water temperatures and extreme fluctuations in water level have inhibited any aquatic plant development around the lake. Fine-grained clay and silt form the sediment on the bottom of the reservoir below the lower limit of water fluctuation (Fillion 1963).

Inflow to the lake is primarily from the Upper Kananaskis River and numerous other small streams (Fig. 1, 2). Inflow from Hidden Lake is underground. The water level of Upper Kananaskis Lake is regulated by TransAlta Utilities Corporation to meet demand for electric power generation (Fig. 3). The first dam and timber spillway were built in 1932/33, raising the maximum lake level from 1 683 m to 1 688 m. By removal of timber stop-logs, 10.0 m of storage could be released each winter to augment flows of the Bow River and drive the generators at Seebe and Ghost Reservoir. In 1942, a higher earthfill dam, Kananaskis Main Dam, was built across the outlet and another dam, Intake Dam, was built at the northeast corner of the lake. These dams raise the upper lake level 13.7 m above the natural level to a maximum operating level of 1 701.7 m; the potential full

supply level of 1 704 m has never been utilized (Table 2, Fig. 3). The lake could then be drawn down 16.5 m each winter, reducing the lake area by about 22% (Fig. 4). From 1942 to 1955, water was released through a steel-gated pipeline at the Intake Dam, still only to augment winter flow on the Bow River. In 1955, the Interlakes Power Plant was built on the shore of Lower Kananaskis Lake and the steel pipeline was extended to the new generators. Since 1955, all outflow from Upper Kananaskis Lake has passed through Interlakes Plant (TransAlta Util. Corp. n.d.).

Most water entering Upper Kananaskis Lake is stored from spring until October. Almost all drawdown is from November to February; some outflow is released between March and October depending on lake levels, runoff and demand for power (TransAlta Util. Corp. n.d.).

Lower Kananaskis Lake

Lower Kananaskis Lake lies against the steep slopes of Mount Indefatigable (Fig. 1). It is a narrow, elongate lake with a maximum width of 1.4 km and a maximum length of 8.8 km (Table 2). On the west

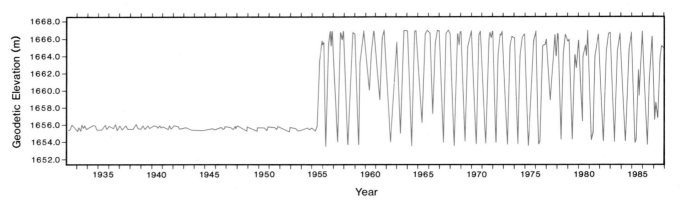

Figure 5. Water level of Lower Kananaskis Lake, 1932 to 1987.
SOURCE: Envir. Can. 1932–1987.

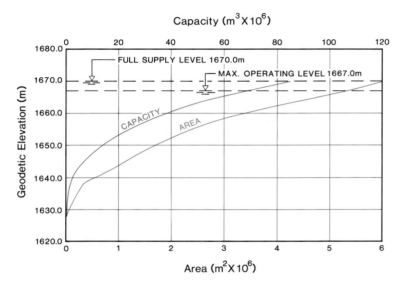

Figure 6. Area/capacity curve for Lower Kananaskis Lake.
SOURCE: Alta. Envir. n.d.[c].

side, the bottom slopes steeply along most of its length; areas with maximum depths of 42 m are found along the middle third of the lake (Fig. 2). The lake bottom on the east side is made up of rolling morainal deposits (McGregor 1984) and slopes are gentle, especially in the southern third of the lake.

The shores of the lake are barren rock, boulders and gravel along the west side, and gravel and mud along the east side. There are numerous islands and shoals along the east side; variable water levels can make boating hazardous in these areas.

In 1955, Calgary Power Ltd. built Pocaterra Dam across the Kananaskis River below the confluence of Smith-Dorrien Creek, about 1 km north of the end of the original lake. This earthfill dam allowed the water level to rise 11 m. A channel was dug from the original lake to the outlet to allow the lake to be drawn down about 2 m below the original level. When it is drawn down to its average low water level of 1 653 m, the lake area is reduced to 44% of the area at FSL (Fig. 6), exposing large areas of lake bottom at the north and south ends (TransAlta Util. Corp. n.d.).

Most inflow enters Lower Kananaskis Lake from Upper Kananaskis Lake via Interlakes Power Plant. Boulton, Gypsum and Smith-Dorrien creeks also enter the lake. The watershed of Smith-Dorrien Creek was diminished in 1959 when two tributaries, French and Burstall creeks, were diverted out of the Kananaskis basin into the Spray Reservoir basin. Kent Creek was diverted in 1956 so it now flows into the lower lake rather than into the Kananaskis River downstream from the lakes (Fig. 2).

The outflow from Lower Kananaskis Lake is through a wood-stave pipeline to Pocaterra Power Plant. Drawdown of the lower lake is not begun until the upper lake storage is withdrawn, usually by February. Drawdown of the lower lake usually is complete by late April, then the lake is filled through spring and summer (Fig. 5). The lower lake is maintained near full supply level from August through January (TransAlta Util. Corp. n.d.). The Kananaskis power plants are used for winter "peak-power production" to supply electricity during times of the day when demand is highest, that is, early morning and evening. Therefore, water is released twice a day, resulting in a large daily variation in the flow of the Kananaskis River downstream. Some water is released from the lakes into the Kananaskis River from April to October; the amount depends on runoff, snowpack and demand for power generation. Water is also occasionally released in response to requests for increased flow for recreation events such as kayaking races.

Water Quality

The water quality of the Kananaskis Lakes was monitored by Alberta Environment in the summer of 1984 (Alta. Envir. n.d.[a]). Fish and Wildlife Division occasionally monitor winter oxygen concentrations (Alta. For. Ld. Wild. n.d.).

The Kananaskis Lakes are freshwater lakes with concentrations of total dissolved solids and alkalinity (Table 3) that are lower than those of most other Alberta lakes in the foothills and on the prairies. The lakes are well-buffered, and the dominant ions are calcium and bicarbonate. The lower lake has a higher concentration of most ions and total dissolved solids than the upper lake. This is probably due to the influence of Smith-Dorrien Creek and Boulton Creek, which drain morainal areas with more fine particulates and better developed soil and vegetation than the barren slopes and glaciers above the upper lake.

Both lakes are thermally stratified all summer (Fig. 7, 8). Dissolved oxygen is close to saturation levels throughout the water column. The dissolved oxygen concentration is higher below the thermocline because more gas can dissolve in cold water than warm water. There is some evidence of oxygen depletion near the bottom of the lower lake, which has greater organic sediment deposits than the upper lake. Upper Kananaskis Lake has never been sampled to its full depth of 108 m, but there is little evidence of dissolved oxygen depletion down to 50 m. Dissolved oxygen concentrations under ice are only slightly depleted in the upper 20 m; samples from below this depth have not been collected (Alta. For. Ld. Wild. n.d.).

Both lakes are very low in nutrients (Table 4, Fig. 9, 10). The lower lake is slightly richer, again likely because of the inflow from Smith-Dorrien and Boulton creeks. The slightly higher phosphorus concentration in June in the lower lake is likely due to snowmelt runoff and flooding of exposed sediments (Fig. 9, 10). Chlorophyll *a* levels are consistently low in both lakes, and the water is clear. The reduced clarity in the lower lake in June is likely a result of suspended silt due to runoff and flooding of exposed lake bottom. Both lakes are oligotrophic.

Table 3. Major ions and related water quality variables for the Upper and Lower Kananaskis lakes. Average concentrations in mg/L; pH in pH units. Composite samples from the euphotic zone collected 3 times from 18 July to 20 Sep. 1984 (upper lake) and 4 times from 19 June to 20 Sep. 1984 (lower lake). S.E. = standard error.

	Upper Lake		Lower Lake	
	Mean	S.E.	Mean	S.E.
pH (range)	7.1–8.6	—	7.7–8.6	—
total alkalinity (CaCO₃)	82	0.6	110	3.0
specific conductivity (μS/cm)	168	6.7	255	12.0
total dissolved solids (calculated)	90	0.7	139	6.3
total hardness (CaCO₃)	88	0.6	132	4.3
HCO₃	98	1.4	130	6.1
CO₃	1	1.0	2	2.1
Mg	4	0.2	9	0.7
Na	0.3	0.03	0.5[c]	0.12
K	0.2	0.01	0.3	0.05
Cl	0.5	0.07	<0.5	—
SO₄	7	0.6	24	3.9
Ca	29	0.2	37	1.1

NOTES: [a]n = 1; [b]n = 2; [c]n = 3

SOURCE: Alta. Envir. n.d.[a], Naquadat stations 05AL05BF1000 (Upper), 05AL05BF2000 (Lower)

Table 4. Nutrient, chlorophyll *a* and Secchi depth data for the Upper and Lower Kananaskis lakes. Average concentrations in μg/L. Composite samples from the euphotic zone collected 3 times from 18 July to 20 Sep. 1984 (upper lake) and 4 times from 19 June to 20 Sep. 1984 (lower lake). S.E. = standard error.

	Upper Lake		Lower Lake	
	Mean	S.E.	Mean	S.E.
total phosphorus	5	0.1	6	0.6
total Kjeldahl nitrogen	273	81.9	293	78.6
NO₃ + NO₂–nitrogen	15	4.8	<25	—
NH₄–nitrogen	<13	—	<10[a]	—
iron	<23	—	<18	—
chlorophyll *a*	2.9	0.14	1.6	0.39
Secchi depth (m)	5.7	0.51	4.3	0.54

NOTE: [a]n = 3

SOURCE: Alta. Envir. n.d.[a], Naquadat stations 05AL05BF1000 (Upper), 05AL05BF2000 (Lower)

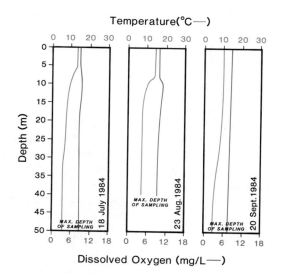

Figure 7. Temperature and dissolved oxygen in Upper Kananaskis Lake, 1984.
SOURCE: Alta. Envir. n.d.[a].

Figure 8. Temperature and dissolved oxygen in Lower Kananaskis Lake, 1984.
SOURCE: Alta. Envir. n.d.[a].

Biological Characteristics

Plants

The rocky shore, extensive drawdown and cold temperature of both Kananaskis Lakes results in a barren shoreline with almost no submergent or emergent aquatic vegetation.

The phytoplankton has not been studied recently. Early studies in 1936 (Rawson 1937) and 1946 (Rawson 1947) noted a "scarcity of algae". Only one species of green algae, *Dictyosphaerium* sp., and two diatoms, *Asterionella* sp. and *Fragilaria* sp., were found, and then only in small numbers. A few *Ceratium* sp. were taken at depths of 20 to 50 m. Samples collected in 1954 were similar (Miller 1955).

Invertebrates

The zooplankton was first sampled in 1936 (Rawson 1937). Density was very low and only ten species were found; copepods were predominant and small species of *Diaptomus* and *Cyclops* were common. A large, red species of *Diaptomus* was taken in small numbers. The only cladoceran found was *Daphnia pulex* and the only rotifer was *Notholca* sp. In 1946, the same species were found (Rawson 1947). In June 1954, the plankton was very sparse; the

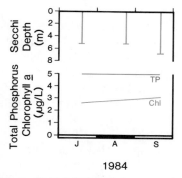

Figure 9. Total phosphorus, chlorophyll *a* and Secchi depth in Upper Kananaskis Lake, 1984.
SOURCE: Alta. Envir. n.d.[a].

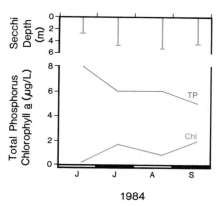

Figure 10. Total phosphorus, chlorophyll *a* and Secchi depth in Lower Kananaskis Lake, 1984.
SOURCE: Alta. Envir. n.d.[a].

zooplankton was mostly *Diaptomus* sp. (Miller 1955). In October 1967, thousands of opossum shrimp, *Mysis relicta*, a small freshwater shrimp about 2.5–cm long, were released by Fish and Wildlife Division into the Upper and Lower Kananaskis lakes in the hope that they would improve the food supply for trout. The source of these shrimp was Kootenay Lake, British Columbia, where they had been introduced from the Waterton Lakes in 1949. It took a few years for the shrimp to become well established but in a survey in 1982 they were found to be the food most extensively used by rainbow trout (Alta. For. Ld. Wild. n.d.). The best way to see the shrimp is to open the stomach of a fresh-caught trout. The red colour of the fish flesh is partly due to its diet of these rosy crustaceans.

Benthic invertebrates were sampled in both lakes in 1936 (Rawson 1937), 1946 (Rawson 1947), 1952 (Thomas 1957), 1954 (Miller 1955), and 1961 and 1962 (Fillion 1963; 1966). The response of the benthic fauna to large annual water level fluctuations has been similar to that observed in Barrier Lake, 30 km downstream on the Kananaskis River, and other similar reservoirs with large annual water level fluctuations (Nursall 1969; Geen 1974). The Lower Kananaskis Lake was sampled before it was regulated, the dominant organisms were pea clams (*Pisidium* sp.), which formed 50% of the total number of organisms (1 672/m³). Midge larvae (Chironomidae) composed 29% of the community, aquatic earthworms (Oligochaeta) composed 11% and scuds (Amphipoda) 9%. Density was greatest in the substrate in the upper 10 m of the reservoir. The lower lake was again sampled in 1961, after the lake level was affected by greater water level fluctuations. Midge larvae strongly dominated the total number of organisms (85%), whereas the number of clams dropped to 8%, aquatic earthworms to 9% and amphipods (a preferred food for trout) were nearly eliminated. The number of animals per sample increased to 2 707/m², but the strong shift from relatively large pea clams to tiny chironomids resulted in a drop in biomass. The zone of the lake originally in the upper littoral zone was the most productive before regulation, now the substrate that is exposed annually is virtually barren; the maximum density of organisms was found just below the lower limit of drawdown. Some animals, mostly chironomids, were found to the maximum depth of both reservoirs.

Fish

Five species of fish are known to occur in Upper Kananaskis Lake: rainbow trout, lake chub, longnose dace, longnose sucker and white sucker. Seven species of fish are known to occur in Lower Kananaskis Lake: rainbow trout, bull trout, lake chub, longnose dace, brook stickleback, longnose sucker and white sucker.

The Kananaskis Lakes have been stocked sporadically by Fish and Wildlife Division since 1914 and have been stocked inadvertently by anglers using live bait, which is now illegal. It is therefore difficult to be certain which species are native to the lakes. Upper Kananaskis Lake was likely barren of fish prior to stocking (Nursall 1969). In 1860, Palliser reported seeing cutthroat trout and Dolly Varden char, now called bull trout, in Lower Kananaskis Lake. In 1914, cutthroat trout were introduced unsuccessfully to the upper lake (Nelson 1962). Rainbow trout or cutthroat trout, or hybrids of the two, were introduced to both lakes in 1935, 1936, 1941, 1944 and 1950 (Nelson 1962). Rainbow trout were stocked as yearlings in 1959, 1960 and almost every year since 1965 (Alta. For. Ld. Wild. n.d.). Species introduced by use as live bait include lake chub, longnose dace, longnose sucker and white sucker. Brook stickleback and bull trout are found only in the lower lake (Nelson 1962; 1965). Hybrids between lake chub and longnose dace are common in both lakes (Butcher 1979) and hybrids between longnose and white suckers occur in Upper Kananaskis Lake (Nelson 1973).

The Kananaskis Lakes support a popular sport fishery for trout, but the popularity may be attributed more to the spectacular scenery than to the success of angling. In 1968, test netting caught 60 suckers but only 7 trout (Alta. For. Ld. Wild. n.d.); no small trout were caught, indicating poor spawning success. Gill netting in 1986 caught 99% suckers and 1% rainbow trout (Stelfox 1989). In a creel census during a one-day fishing derby in June 1981, 246 anglers

fishing a total of 1 476 hours caught only 43 trout (0.03 trout/hour), a very low success rate (Alta. For. Ld. Wild. n.d.). Although survival of stocked trout is very low, the growth rates of the survivors are similar to those of rainbow trout in the Bow River, but slower than those in prairie pothole lakes. Opossum shrimp are the major food source for trout in the Kananaskis Lakes; suckers probably provide intense competition for the other potential food source, midge larvae (Stelfox 1989).

The potential for enhancing spawning habitat for trout in the Kananaskis Lakes was assessed in 1981 (Dickson et al. 1981). The authors were "extremely pessimistic about the possibility of establishing self-sustaining populations of trout or char in the Kananaskis Lakes". Approximately 69 000 rainbow trout fry were released into Smith-Dorrien Creek in August 1980 in the hope that adults would return there from Lower Kananaskis Lake to spawn (Alta. For. Ld. Wild. n.d.). Spawning success in Smith-Dorrien Creek likely is negligible due to extremely low temperatures and scouring of the creek bed in the spring spate (Stelfox 1989).

Wildlife

The wildlife in the Kananaskis area is typical of mountain wilderness. Fifty-four species of mammals live in the area (Finlay and Finlay 1987). Mule deer, moose and black bears are common. Grizzly bears frequent the lower slopes of Mount Indefatigable, which provides excellent habitat. Mountain goats and bighorn sheep can be seen high on the mountain slopes, and wolves and cougars are occasionally seen or heard. The Kananaskis Lakes are not used extensively by waterfowl or aquatic mammals because of the absence of aquatic vegetation.

Bird life in the area is abundant and varied; 235 species have been reported in the provincial park (Wiseley 1979). Of these, 135 species nest in the park and surrounding Kananaskis Country (Finlay and Finlay 1987). Both Golden and Bald eagles nest here, as do Great Horned, Hawk, Barred, Boreal and Saw-whet owls. Rufous and Calliope hummingbirds have been found nesting, as have six species of swallow, including Violet-green and Tree. Three species of chickadee occur, including Black-capped, Mountain and Boreal. The more uncommon warblers that nest in the area include Orange-crowned, Nashville, Mourning, MacGillivray's and Wilson's (Finlay and Finlay 1987). Even the diverse insect community has been well documented (Bird 1977; Kondla 1979).

J.M. Crosby

References

Alberta Environment. n.d.[a]. Envir. Assess. Div., Envir. Qlty. Monit. Br. Unpubl. data, Edmonton.
———. n.d.[b]. Tech. Serv. Div., Hydrol. Br. Unpubl. data, Edmonton.
———. n.d.[c]. Tech. Serv. Div., Surv. Br. Unpubl. data, Edmonton.
Alberta Forestry, Lands and Wildlife. n.d. Fish Wild. Div. Unpubl. data, Edmonton.
———. 1988. Boating in Alberta. Fish Wild. Div., Edmonton.
———. 1989. Guide to sportfishing. Fish Wild. Div., Edmonton.
Alberta Hotel Association. 1989. Alberta campground guide 1989. Prep. for Travel Alta., Edmonton.
Alberta Research Council. 1972. Geological map of Alberta. Nat. Resour. Div., Alta. Geol. Surv., Edmonton.
Appleby, E. 1975. Canmore: The story of an era. E. Appleby, Canmore.
Bird, C.D. 1977. The lichens, bryophytes and butterflies of the proposed park in the Kananaskis Lakes area (checklist). Prep. for Alta. Rec. Parks Wild., Calgary.
Butcher, G.A. 1979. Ecology and taxonomy of hybridizing cyprinid fishes from Upper and Lower Kananaskis Reservoirs, Alberta. MSc thesis. Univ. Alta., Edmonton.
Dickson, T.A., P.J. McCart and J. McCart. 1981. Upper and Lower Kananaskis Lakes fisheries enhancement study. Prep. for Alta. En. Nat. Resour., Fish Wild. Div., Edmonton.
Energy, Mines and Resources Canada. 1977. National topographic series 1:50 000 82J/11 (1977), 82J/14 (1977). Surv. Map. Br., Ottawa.
Environment Canada. 1932–1987. Surface water data. Prep. by Inland Waters Directorate. Water Surv. Can., Water Resour. Br., Ottawa.
———. 1982. Canadian climate normals, Vol. 7: Bright sunshine (1951–1980). Prep. by Atm. Envir. Serv. Supply Serv. Can., Ottawa.
Fillion, D.B. 1963. The benthic fauna of three mountain reservoirs in Alberta. MSc thesis. Univ. Alta., Edmonton.
———. 1966. The abundance and distribution of benthic fauna of three mountain reservoirs on the Kananaskis River, Alberta. J. App. Ecol. 4:1–11.

Finlay, J. and C. Finlay. 1987. Parks in Alberta: A guide to peaks, ponds, parklands & prairies. Hurtig Publ., Edmonton.

Geen, G.H. 1974. Effects of hydroelectric development in western Canada on aquatic ecosystems. J. Fish. Res. Bd. Can. 31:913–927.

Kondla, N. 1979. Skippers and butterflies of Kananaskis Provincial Park. Blue Jay 37:73–75.

McGregor, C.A. 1984. Ecological land classification of Kananaskis Country. Alta. En. Nat. Resour., Resour. Eval. Plan. Div., Edmonton.

Miller, R.B. 1955. Effect of Pocaterra power development on Lower Kananaskis Lake. Alta. Ld. For., Fish Wild. Div., Edmonton.

More, G. 1988. Kananaskis Country computerized bibliography system. Alta. Rec. Parks, Canmore.

Nelson, J.S. 1962. Effects on fishes of changes within the Kananaskis River system. MSc thesis. Univ. Alta., Edmonton.

———. 1965. Effects of fish introductions and hydroelectric development on fishes in the Kananaskis River system, Alberta. J. Fish. Res. Bd. Can. 22:721–753.

———. 1973. Occurrence of hybrids between longnose sucker and white sucker in Upper Kananaskis Reservoir, Alberta. J. Fish. Res. Bd. Can. 30:557–560.

Nursall, J.R. 1969. Faunal changes in oligotrophic man-made lakes: Experience on the Kananaskis River system, p. 163–175. In L.E. Obeng [ed.] Man-made lakes: The Accra Symposium. Ghana Univ. Press, Ghana.

Oltmann, C.R. 1976. The valley of rumours...The Kananaskis. Ribbon Cr. Publ. Co., Seebe.

Rawson, D.S. 1937. Biological examination of the Kananaskis Lakes, Alberta. Prep. for Alta. Ld. Mines, Fish. Serv., Edmonton.

———. 1947. Deterioration of recently established trout populations in lakes of the Canadian Rockies. Can. Fish Culturist 2:14–21.

Stelfox, J. 1989. Alta. For. Ld. Wild., Fish Wild. Div., Calgary. Pers. comm.

Strong, W.L. and K.R. Leggat. 1981. Ecoregions of Alberta. Alta. En. Nat. Resour., Resour. Eval. Plan. Div., Edmonton.

Thomas, R.C. 1957. Effect of Pocaterra power development on Lower Kananaskis Lake. Alta. Ld. For., Fish Wild. Div., Edmonton.

Thorington, J.M. 1966. A climber's guide to the Rocky Mountains of Canada. American Alpine Club, New York, N.Y.

TransAlta Utilities Corporation. n.d. Unpubl. data, Calgary.

Wiseley, A.N. 1979. A review of birds and their habitats in Kananaskis Country. Alta. En. Nat. Resour., Fish Wild. Div., Edmonton.

LAKE NEWELL

Alberta Recreation and Parks/B. Crawford

MAP SHEETS: 72L/5, 12, 82I/8
LOCATION: Tp16, 17 R14, 15 W4
LAT/LONG: 50°25′N 111°57′W

Lake Newell is one of Alberta's largest reservoirs. It is situated in the County of Newell about 200 km southeast of the city of Calgary and 125 km northwest of the city of Medicine Hat. Kinbrook Island Provincial Park is located on the eastern side of the lake (Fig. 1). The closest population centre is the town of Brooks, located about 14 km north of the provincial park. To reach the park from either Calgary or Medicine Hat, take Highway 1 to Brooks, then Secondary Road 873 south to the park entrance road.

Early settlement of what is now the County of Newell followed the arrival of the Canadian Pacific Railway (CPR) in 1883 (Gross and Nicoll Kramer 1985). Rainfall was limited, so the first settlers were mostly ranchers rather than farmers. In 1903, the railway company became owner of most of the land in the area, which it named the Eastern Section. To bring settlers to the land, the company initiated construction of an irrigation system in 1910. The Bassano Dam, located on the Bow River about 6 km southwest of the present-day town of Bassano, was the focal point of the project. All water for the irrigation system is diverted from the Bow River by means of this structure. Dam construction began in 1910 and was completed in 1914. Most homesteaders settled in the area between 1915 and 1919, many of them buying land from the CPR. During the agricultural depression of the 1920s and the general depression and drought of the 1930s, many people abandoned their farms and others could not meet mortgage payments to the railway. Meanwhile, the CPR was suffering heavy operating losses and hopes dwindled for recovering their investment in the irrigation project. When the farmers offered to assume responsibility for the irrigation works, the CPR welcomed the suggestion. In 1935, the CPR transferred the irrigation works, the existing land contracts and $300 000 to the farmers' organization and the Eastern Irrigation District was formed (Gross and Nicoll Kramer 1985). The Eastern Irrigation District covers about 604 000 ha of land, and its boundaries are almost the same as those of the County of Newell. Individual water users in the irrigation district own 345 000 ha of land, and the remaining 259 000 ha is collectively owned by the 1 180 water users in the district's membership (Gross and Nicoll Kramer 1985).

Construction of Lake Newell, the Main Canal and the East Branch Canal was concurrent with construction of the Bassano Dam. The area where the lake is now located was originally a large depression holding a small lake, Crooked Lake, which was fed by a small intermittent stream (Alta. Rec. Parks n.d.). When the reservoir was completed in 1914, it was named for T.H. Newell, an American irrigation expert who had bought half a township of land west of Crooked Lake in 1911 (Gross and Nicoll Kramer 1985). The water level of Lake Newell was raised in 1939 in order to extend irrigation to the Rolling Hills District, southeast of the lake (Alta. Rec. Parks n.d.). The outlet structures and the East Branch Canal inlet were further modified in 1978 to raise the lake's water level by another 0.91 m to increase live storage. Between 1988 and 1992, the East Branch Canal will be enlarged to increase inflow. This will stabilize lake levels and increase outflow for a planned expansion of irrigation (Clark 1989).

The history of Kinbrook Island Provincial Park dates back to 1944, when the Kinsmen Club of Brooks obtained a recreational lease for Kinbrook Island, which they named for their club. Recreational facilities were developed, and in 1951, the island became a provincial park. In 1952, the park was enlarged to include all of the other islands in the lake so that nesting sites for White Pelicans, Double-

Table 1. Characteristics of Lake Newell drainage basin.

area (excluding lake) (km²)[a]	84.6
soil[b]	Brown Solodized Solonetz and Orthic Brown Chernozemic
bedrock geology[c]	Oldman Formation (Upper Cretaceous): sandstone, siltstone, mudstone, shale, ironstone beds; nonmarine
terrain[b]	undulating to gently rolling or low hummocky
ecoregion[d]	Short Grass
dominant vegetation[b, d]	grama, spear and wheat grasses
mean annual sunshine (h)[e]	2 334

SOURCES: [a]Alta. Envir. n.d.[b]; [b]Kjearsgaard et al. 1983; [c]Alta. Res. Counc. 1972; [d]Strong and Leggat 1981; [e]Envir. Can. 1982

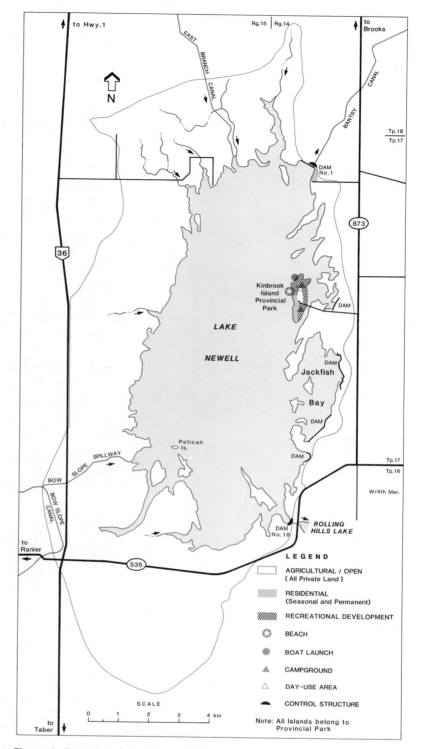

Figure 1. Features of the drainage basin of Lake Newell.
SOURCES: Alta. Envir. n.d.[b]; En. Mines Resour. Can. 1975; 1976. Updated with 1981 aerial photos.

crested Cormorants and Canada Geese would be preserved. Pelican Island, at the southwest end of the lake, is now a seasonal sanctuary, and access is prohibited from 15 April to 15 September each year. The rest of the park is open year-round. The park has 209 campsites, sewage disposal facilities, tap water, playgrounds, two boat launches, picnic areas and shelters, a concession and a swimming area. During summer, popular activities in the park and on the lake are swimming, motor boating, sailing, fishing for northern pike and lake whitefish, birdwatching, windsurfing and canoeing. Several sailing regattas and fishing derbies are held during the season. Boating is prohibited in some posted areas, such as designated swimming areas, and power boats are restricted to a maximum speed of 12 km/hour in other areas (Alta. For. Ld. Wild. 1988). In winter, ice fishing, ice sailing and skating are popular activities. There are no special regulations for the sport fishery, but provincial limits and regulations apply (Alta. For. Ld. Wild. 1989).

The water in Lake Newell turns green during July and August, but the concentration of algae during the remainder of the open-water season is frequently quite low and the water is moderately transparent. Large annual water level fluctuations result in low densities of aquatic vegetation near shore. In addition to the sport fishery, the lake supports a commercial fishery for lake whitefish and northern pike.

Drainage Basin Characteristics

The natural drainage basin around Lake Newell is very small and covers an area only 1.3 times the size of the lake (Tables 1, 2). Five intermittent streams flow into the north and west sides of the reservoir (Fig. 1) but almost all of the water in the reservoir originates from the Bow River at the Bassano Dam diversion. Water from the Bow River is diverted into the Main Canal and then the East Branch Canal. It flows to the lake by two routes: the main volume flows from the East Branch Canal directly into the north end of the lake and a smaller volume flows from the East Branch Canal through the Bow Slope Canal and the Bow Slope Spillway into the southeast end of the lake (Fig. 1). Lake Newell has two outlets: the Bantry Canal at the northeast end delivers water to the North and West Bantry Canal Systems, and the outlet at the southeast end flows into Rolling Hills Lake.

Lake Newell and its canal system are situated within the Kininvie Plain district of the Alberta Plains physiographic region (Kjearsgaard et al. 1983). The Kininvie Plain is primarily an undulating moraine with a few areas of higher relief. The elevation of Lake Newell's natural drainage basin ranges from 768 m near the lake to 800 m at the northwest corner of the drainage basin. The Kininvie Plain is capped with either a blanket or a veneer of glacial till, through which the underlying sedimentary rock material outcrops in localized areas, as at the northern end of Lake Newell. The weakly consolidated sedimentary rock near the lake belongs to the Oldman Formation. The remainder of the lake's natural drainage basin is also underlain by this formation, and is covered by till.

Soils in the north, west and southeast portions of the natural drainage basin and along the north half of the eastern shore are mostly moderately well-drained, loam-textured Brown Solodized Solonetz (Kjearsgaard et al. 1983). Because of their development on moderately saline parent materials, these soils have little or no potential for cultivated agriculture. The land is, however, used for grazing. Well-drained, loam-textured Orthic Brown Chernozemics are located in the southern and southeastern portions of the natural drainage basin. Although these soils have good agricultural potential for dryland and irrigated agriculture, they are grazed, but not farmed, at present. Natural vegetation is typical of the Short Grass Ecoregion: grama grass is dominant in drier areas and spear and wheat grasses become more abundant as moisture increases (Strong and Leggat 1981).

Except for the islands in the lake, all of the land in the drainage basin is privately owned. The largest land owner is the Eastern Irrigation District, which leases much of its land to cattle grazing associations. The watershed lies on top of a major gas field, and there is considerable activity related to gas extraction.

Table 2. Characteristics of Lake Newell.

control structures[a]	Dam #1: earthfill with triple undershot gate Dam #18: earthfill with double undershot gate Plus 17 small dams along the east shore
dam height (m)[b]	Dam #1: 8.53 Dam #18: 3.96
crest length (m)[b]	Dam #1: 716.28 Dam #18: 161.54
full supply level (FSL) (m)[a, c]	767.59
volume at FSL (m³)[d, e]	321 x 10⁶
live storage at FSL (m³)[a, c]	217 x 10⁶
surface area at FSL (km²)[a, c]	66.4
mean depth (m)	4.8
maximum drawdown (m)[a]	3.99
mean annual drawdown (1980–1987) (m)[f]	1.42
maximum depth at FSL (m)[a, c]	19.8
shoreline length at FSL (km)[a, c]	69.5
lake length at FSL (km)[a]	13.0
lake width at FSL (km)[a]	4.0
mean annual lake evaporation (mm)[g]	750
mean annual precipitation (mm)[g]	338
mean residence time (yr)[g]	1.5
mean annual inflow volume (1985–1988) (m³)[a, h]	295 x 10⁶
mean annual outflow volume (1985–1988) (m³)[a]	241 x 10⁶

NOTES: [c]after lake level raised in 1978; [e]at FSL 767.81 m; [h]excluding groundwater inflow
SOURCES: [a]East. Irrig. Dist. n.d.; [b]Alta. Envir. n.d.[d]; [d]R.L. & L. Envir. Serv. Ltd. 1985; [f]Alta. Envir. n.d.[c];
[g]Alta. Envir. n.d.[b]

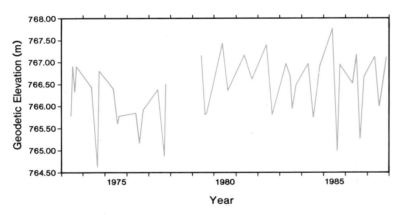

Figure 2. Water level of Lake Newell, ice-free season, 1973 to 1987.
SOURCE: Alta. Envir. n.d.[c].

Table 3. Major ions and related water quality variables for Lake Newell. Average concentrations in mg/L; pH in pH units. Composite samples from the euphotic zone collected 14 times from 17 May to 18 Oct. 1983. S.E. = standard error.

	Mean	S.E.
pH (range)	7.5–8.4[a]	—
total alkalinity (CaCO₃)	123	2.2
specific conductivity (μS/cm)	344	6.4
total dissolved solids (calculated)	186	3.2
turbidity (NTU)	2[b]	0.3
total hardness (CaCO₃)	152	3.2
HCO₃	149	2.7
CO₃	0	0
Mg	15	0.2
Na	10	0.3
K	1	0
Cl	5	0.3
SO₄	43	0.7
Ca	37[c]	0.1

NOTES: [a]n = 8; [b]n = 11; [c]n = 12
SOURCE: Alta. Envir. n.d.[a], Naquadat stations 05AL05BN0100, 05AL05BN9000

There has been little residential development near the lake. A subdivision is located at Dam No. 1 at the northeast corner of the lake (Fig. 1). A second subdivision, with 57 lots, is located within the provincial park.

Reservoir Characteristics

Lake Newell has the largest area (66.4 km², Table 2) of any reservoir in Alberta (Gross and Nicoll Kramer 1985). The lake has never been sounded, so there are no bathymetric contours available.

A total of 19 structures along the eastern shore control the lake's water level. The two main dams are located at the far northeast and southeast corners of the lake (Fig. 1). Dam No. 1, which is also called North Headgate or Bantry Headgate, is the largest structure (Table 2). It controls water flow into the main Bantry Canal. Dam No. 18, at the southeast end, controls water flow into nearby Rolling Hills Lake. This lake acts as a balancing reservoir between Lake Newell and the Rolling Hills Canal.

Water flows into Lake Newell from April to November, and out of the lake from May to October. The lake reaches its highest elevation in May and early June, when it is replenished by water from the Bow River via the East Branch Canal and the Bow Slope Canal. The elevation then declines until July or August as water flows out to Bantry Canal and Rolling Hills Lake to meet the peak water demand for irrigation. Between 1985 and 1988, the average inflow from the East Branch and Bow Slope canals was 295 x 10⁶ m³/year (Table 2); 72% of this water arrived via the East Branch Canal and 28% arrived via the Bow Slope Canal. During the same period, outflow averaged 241 x 10⁶ m³/year; 25% of the outflow went to the Rolling Hills Canal and the remainder flowed into the Bantry Canal (East. Irrig. Dist. n.d.).

Table 4. Nutrient, chlorophyll *a* and Secchi depth data for Lake Newell. Average concentrations in μg/L. Composite samples from the euphotic zone collected 14 times from 17 May to 18 Oct. 1983 and 9 times from 02 May to 24 Oct. 1984. S.E. = standard error.

	1983		1984	
	Mean	S.E.	Mean	S.E.
total phosphorus	32	1.5	26	1.7
total Kjeldahl nitrogen	502[a]	48.9	<542	—
NO$_3$ + NO$_2$–nitrogen	<13[b]	—	<9	—
NH$_4$–nitrogen	<19[a]	—	<13	—
iron	<21	—	<17	—
chlorophyll *a*	11.8	2.13	10.2	2.16
Secchi depth (m)	2.4[c]	0.14	2.5	0.18

NOTES: [a]n = 11; [b]n = 13; [c]n = 15
SOURCE: Alta. Envir. n.d.[a], Naquadat stations 05AL05BN9000, 05AL05BN0100

Water levels in Lake Newell have been monitored since 1973 (Fig. 2). Between spring and midsummer, the drop in water level can be quite large. The greatest fluctuation in a single year, 2.76 m, was recorded in 1985. The historic maximum lake elevation (767.79 m) was recorded in May 1985, and the historic minimum (764.63 m) was recorded in August 1974.

Additional water withdrawals from Lake Newell, other than for irrigation, are made by the town of Brooks, Pan Canadian Petroleum and Kinbrook Island Provincial Park (Alta. Envir. n.d.[e]). Brooks was licenced for a withdrawal of 4.93 x 10^6 m^3/year in 1986, and in that year and 1987, the town withdrew an average of 2.68 x 10^6 m^3/year. Pan Canadian Petroleum is licenced for 2.77 x 10^6 m^3/year; in 1987, their withdrawals amounted to 1.31 x 10^6 m^3. The provincial park is licenced for 0.048 x 10^6 m^3/year. In 1986 and 1987, the park withdrew 0.033 x 10^6 m^3/year.

Water Quality

Water quality in Lake Newell was studied by Fish and Wildlife Division during 1981, by Alberta Environment in 1983, and jointly by Alberta Environment and Alberta Recreation and Parks from 1984 to 1986 (Alta. Envir. n.d.[a]; English 1985).

The lake has fresh water that is hard, well-buffered and not very turbid (Table 3). The dominant ions are bicarbonate, sulphate and calcium.

During the open-water season in 1983, the water column was well-mixed (Fig. 3). The maximum surface temperature of 21.7°C was recorded in early August. Concentrations of dissolved oxygen were uniformly high from surface to bottom throughout the open-water period (Fig. 4). In February 1981, dissolved oxygen concentrations decreased gradually with depth, from 13.2 mg/L at the surface to 4.2 mg/L at the bottom.

Lake Newell is mildly eutrophic. In 1983, the average chlorophyll *a* concentration was 11.8 μg/L and the average total phosphorus level was 32 μg/L (Table 4). Maximum values for phosphorus (45 μg/L) and chlorophyll *a* (28 μg/L) were recorded in late July of that year (Fig. 5).

Biological Characteristics

Plants

Phytoplankton species in Lake Newell have not been identified. In a 1981 survey, a Fish and Wildlife Division biologist considered the standing crop of net plankton to be very low (English 1985). There are few data on the macrophytes in the lake. Aquatic vegetation grows along parts of the shoreline, but the density is low because of the large annual water fluctuations.

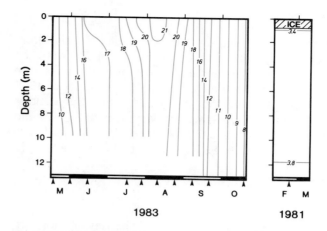

Figure 3. Temperature (°C) of Lake Newell, 1981 and 1983. End of line indicates lake bottom. Arrows indicate sampling dates.
SOURCES: Alta. Envir. n.d.[a]; English 1985.

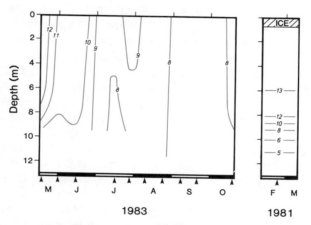

Figure 4. Dissolved oxygen (mg/L) in Lake Newell, 1981 and 1983. End of line indicates lake bottom. Arrows indicate sampling dates.
SOURCES: Alta. Envir. n.d.[a]; English 1985.

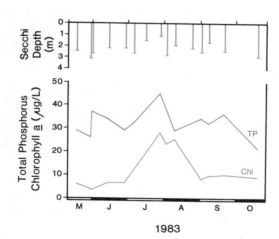

Figure 5. Total phosphorus, chlorophyll *a* and Secchi depth in Lake Newell, 1983.
SOURCE: Alta. Envir. n.d.[a].

Invertebrates

The zooplankton was sampled by Fish and Wildlife Division from May to November in 1981 (English 1985). Copepods were the dominant group. The biomass and abundance of benthos from the deepest area of the lake were measured in May and July of 1981 (English 1985). The average total biomass for the four samples collected on each of the two sampling dates was 4.2 g/m^2, and average total abundance was 3 676 organisms/m^2. Midge larvae (Chironomidae) accounted for 86% of the total biomass and 63% of the total numbers.

Fish

Ten species of fish have been collected in Lake Newell: northern pike, walleye, lake whitefish, yellow perch, white sucker, burbot, rainbow trout, bull trout, brook trout and spottail shiner (English 1985). Lake whitefish eyed-eggs were introduced in 1932, and whitefish quickly became an important part of the commercial harvest. Brook trout were planted in 1938, and cutthroat trout in 1953. The latter apparently have not survived, and other trout species are present only as migrants from the Bow River (English 1985). Attempts to introduce walleye during the 1940s and 1950s also failed. However, several walleye have been caught by the commercial fishery each year from 1983/84 to 1987/88 (Alta. For. Ld. Wild. n.d.).

Lake Newell is managed for recreational and commercial fisheries. The commercial fishery has operated since at least 1942/43, when records were first kept (Alta. For. Ld. Wild. n.d.; Alta. Rec. Parks 1976). Lake whitefish and northern pike are the most important mercial species and burbot, white suckers, and unspecified trout are caught in small numbers. The largest total catch, 208 250 kg, was taken in 1960/61. Between 1968/69 and 1987/88, the average total catch was 41 532 kg/year. Of this, 88% was lake whitefish and 12% was northern pike.

A creel survey was conducted at Lake Newell from May to August 1985 as part of a survey of the Brooks area (English 1986). Lake Newell was second in popularity to Tilley B Reservoir. Although Lake Newell has a reputation for trophy-sized pike in the 10 kg range, none were recorded in the survey. During the 24 days monitored, 159 anglers were interviewed. They fished for a total of 465.5 hours and caught 68 northern pike, which is a catch rate of 0.15 pike/hour. It was estimated that 731 anglers visited the lake and caught 340 pike in 2 232 hours during the total 101–day survey period.

Wildlife

Soon after the reservoir was first filled in 1914, large colonies of water birds began appearing on the new islands at the southern end (Finlay and Finlay 1987). At least 100 species of birds are present in Kinbrook Island Provincial Park, and more than 75 species nest in the immediate area of the park. Lake Newell is the most significant area in the region for nesting California and Ring-billed gulls, and Canada Geese also nest there. Double-crested Cormorants nest on the islands and White Pelicans fish the lake and rest on the islands. A colony of Eared Grebes is present south of Pelican Island (Nordstrom 1977).

Mammals found in the area include coyotes, pronghorn antelope, Richardson's ground squirrels and badgers (Finlay and Finlay 1987).

M.E. Bradford

References

Alberta Environment. n.d.[a]. Envir. Assess. Div., Envir. Qlty. Monit. Br. Unpubl. data, Edmonton.
———. n.d.[b]. Tech. Serv. Div., Hydrol. Br. Unpubl. data, Edmonton.
———. n.d.[c]. Tech. Serv. Div., Surv. Br. Unpubl. data, Edmonton.
———. n.d.[d]. Water Resour. Mgt. Div., Dam Safety Br. Unpubl. data, Edmonton.
———. n.d.[e]. Water Resour. Admin. Div., Sur. Water Rights Br. Unpubl. data, Edmonton.
Alberta Forestry, Lands and Wildlife. n.d. Fish Wild. Div. Unpubl. data, Edmonton.
———. 1988. Boating in Alberta. Fish Wild. Div., Edmonton.
———. 1989. Guide to sportfishing. Fish Wild. Div., Edmonton.
Alberta Recreation and Parks. n.d. Parks Div. Unpubl. data, Edmonton.
Alberta Recreation, Parks and Wildlife. 1976. Commercial fisheries catch statistics for Alberta, 1942–1975. Fish Wild. Div., Fish. Mgt. Rep. No. 22, Edmonton.
Alberta Research Council. 1972. Geological map of Alberta. Nat. Resour. Div., Alta. Geol. Surv., Edmonton.
Clark, D. 1989. East. Irrig. Dist., Brooks. Pers. comm.
Eastern Irrigation District. n.d. Unpubl. data, Brooks.
Energy, Mines and Resources Canada. 1975, 1976. National topographic series 1:50 000 72L/5 (1975), 72L/12 (1975), 82I/8 (1976), 82I/9 (1976). Surv. Map. Br., Ottawa.
English, W.G. 1985. A limnological survey of Newell Reservoir. Alta. En. Nat. Resour., Fish Wild. Div., Edmonton.
———. 1986. A summary of results from the 1985 summer creel survey in the Brooks district (County of Newell). Alta. En. Nat. Resour., Fish Wild. Div. Unpubl. rep., Lethbridge.
Environment Canada. 1982. Canadian climate normals, Vol. 7: Bright sunshine (1951–1980). Prep. by Atm. Envir. Serv. Supply Serv. Can., Ottawa.
Finlay, J. and C. Finlay. 1987. Parks in Alberta: A guide to peaks, ponds, parklands & prairies. Hurtig Publ., Edmonton.
Gross, R. and L. Nicoll Kramer. 1985. Tapping the Bow. East. Irrig. Dist., Brooks.
Kjearsgaard, A.A., T.W. Peters and W.W. Pettapiece. 1983. Soil survey of the County of Newell, Alberta. Alta. Soil Surv. Rep. No. 41, Alta. Inst. Pedol. Rep. No. S–82–41, Ld. Resour. Res. Inst. Contribution No. LRRI 83–48. Agric. Can., Res. Br., Edmonton.
Nordstrom, W. 1977. Colonial waterbirds of Lake Newell. Alta. Rec. Parks, Parks Div. Unpubl. rep., Edmonton.
R.L. & L. Environmental Services Ltd. 1985. A compendium of existing environmental data on Alberta reservoirs. Prep. for Alta. Envir. Res. Trust, Edmonton.
Strong, W.L. and K.R. Leggat. 1981. Ecoregions of Alberta. Alta. En. Nat. Resour., Resour. Eval. Plan. Div., Edmonton.

SPRAY LAKES RESERVOIR

D. Huet

MAP SHEETS: 82J/11, 13, 14, 82O/3

LOCATION: Tp22, 23 R10 W5

LAT/LONG: 50°54'N 115°20'W

Spray Lakes Reservoir is a long, narrow impoundment in a mountain valley perched 400 m above the town of Canmore, which is approximately 100 km west of the city of Calgary on Highway 1. To reach the reservoir from Canmore, cross the bridge over the Bow River then follow the winding road past the Canmore Nordic Center. Continue up a long hill for a total of 20 km to the Three Sisters Dam and the north end of the reservoir (Fig. 1). An alternate route is to start at Peter Lougheed Provincial Park in the Kananaskis Valley and take the Smith-Dorrien/Spray Trail for about 20 km to the southern portion of the reservoir. Spray Lakes Reservoir is located in Kananaskis Country (Improvement District No. 5), an area of mountains and foothills that has been the focus of recreational development since the 1970s.

The name of the reservoir is taken from two tiny lakes, Upper Spray and Lower Spray, which were originally in the valley where the reservoir now lies (Fig. 1, inset). These lakes were on a tributary of the Spray River; Upper Spray Lake drained via Buller Creek to Lower Spray Lake which drained by Woods Creek into the Spray River (Miller and Macdonald 1950). The name Buller Creek now refers to a different creek on the east side of the reservoir. Spray River was named for the spray from the Bow Falls in Banff, which drifts across the mouth of the Spray River where it joins the Bow River (Geog. Bd. Can. 1928).

The history of the Spray area tells of three dynamic and determined men who each etched a colourful chapter in the early days of Alberta. The first white man to visit the Spray Lakes area was James Sinclair. He left Fort Garry (now the city of Winnipeg) in 1841 with 23 families, including a 75–year–old woman, with an aim to settle in the Oregon Territory to reinforce the tenuous British claim to the area. After a brief stop at Fort Edmonton, he was guided by Maskepetoon, the chief of the Wetaskiwin Cree, via Lake Minnewanka to the present site of Canmore and on up the valley where the reservoir now lies. They trekked up the Spray River, then along a tributary, White Man's Creek, and across the Great Divide at White Man's Pass (Fig. 1) (Fraser 1969). The Reverend Robert Rundle was also in the area in 1841. After camping at the confluence of the Bow and Spray rivers, Rundle explored the Spray Valley where it parallels the mountain that now bears his name (Appleby 1975). In 1845, Father Pierre Jean de Smet, a Jesuit priest, came east from Lake Windermere via the Kootenay River and one of its tributaries to the summit of White Man's Pass "where all was wild sublimity". He erected a large cross on the pass, and the river which drains the west side of the pass was henceforth known as the Cross River. From White Man's Pass, de Smet travelled down the Spray River, which was "jewelled with enamelled beads", and on out to the foothills (Fraser 1969).

Canmore, the first divisional point on the Canadian Pacific Railway west of Calgary, was founded in 1884. By 1889, there were 450 residents in the town and the Canmore Mine had been developed to produce coal for the railway (Appleby 1975).

Banff National Park was established in 1885, and in 1902, the boundary was extended to include the Spray and Kananaskis valleys. Mining and lumbering were still permitted, but in 1930, such activities were deemed inappropriate for a national park and the boundary was shifted westward to exclude the Spray and Kananaskis valleys from the park (Appleby 1975).

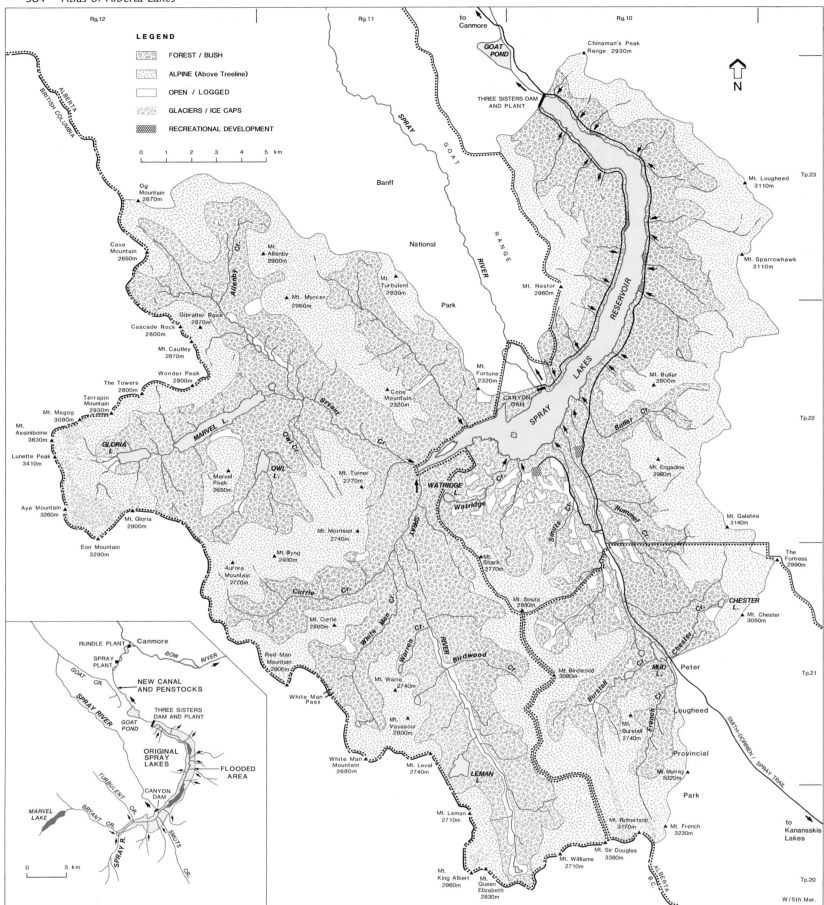

Figure 1. Features of the drainage basin of Spray Lakes Reservoir.
SOURCES: Alta. Envir. n.d.[b]; En. Mines Resour. Can. 1977; 1980. Updated with 1982 aerial photos.

The potential of the Spray Lakes valley for electrical power generation was recognized by 1911. Calgary Power Ltd. (now TransAlta Utilities Corporation) made intensive surveys in 1921 but it was 1948 before permits were acquired. Two dams were built: Canyon Dam across the Spray River and Three Sisters Dam across the valley above Canmore. The reservoir was first filled in 1950, and power generation began the same year (Appleby 1975).

Until Kananaskis Country was established in the 1970s, the only road up to Spray Lakes Reservoir was a narrow, rough track clinging to the side of Mount Rundle. Only a few recreational visitors persevered to visit the valley. The road was improved in the mid–1980s and now provides good access to the reservoir. There is one campground on the reservoir, Spray Lakes West Campground (Fig. 2). It is operated by Alberta Recreation and Parks and provides picnic tables and 20 designated sites for tents and trailers (Alta. Rec. Parks n.d.).

There are five day-use areas near the lake (Fig. 2): Driftwood Day-Use Area is on the east shore near the north end, it provides the

Table 1. Characteristics of Spray Lakes Reservoir drainage basin.

area (excluding lake) (km²)[a, b]	493
soil[c]	Brunisolic and Podzolic Gray Luvisols
bedrock geology[d]	Upper Paleozoic Era: carbonates, shale
	Mesozoic Era: sandstone, siltstone, shale, carbonates
terrain[c]	mountainous
ecoregions[c]	Subalpine and Alpine
dominant vegetation[c]	lodgepole pine, Engelmann spruce, heath
mean annual sunshine (h)[e]	1 970

NOTE: [b]includes drainage area to Mud Lake Diversion Canal
SOURCES: [a]Alta. Envir. n.d.[b]; [c]Strong and Leggat 1981; McGregor 1984; [d]Alta. Res. Counc. 1972; [e]Envir. Can. 1982

only boat launch on the reservoir, as well as picnic tables and firepits. Sparrowhawk and Spray Lakes day-use areas are farther south along the east shore and provide firepits and picnic tables. Buller Mountain Day-Use Area is a centre for cross-country skiing and is open for camping only in the winter; picnic tables and firepits are provided. Mt. Shark Day-Use Area is reached via a 3–km–long access road from the Smith-Dorrien/Spray Trail; it provides parking and picnic tables but no firepits.

Spray Lakes Reservoir is a cold, clear water body with no conspicuous algae. The shores are rocky and kept barren by the fluctuating water level. Recreational use of the lake is low, but fishing for lake trout and mountain whitefish is gaining popularity. Fishing for or with bait fish is not permitted. All tributary streams to the reservoir are closed to fishing for most of the year; in 1989 they were open only from 1 July to 31 October (Alta. For. Ld. Wild. 1989). Some people enjoy power boating on the lake, but boaters should be aware of the risks imposed by very cold water and sudden strong winds. Power boats are restricted to a maximum speed of 12 km/hour in posted areas (Alta. For. Ld. Wild. 1988). Hiking in the southern and western portions of the basin is fairly popular, especially along trails that lead to Mt. Assiniboine Provincial Park in British Columbia. Cross-country skiing is very popular on the network of trails that have been developed around the Buller Mountain and Mt. Shark day-use areas.

Drainage Basin Characteristics

The large drainage basin of the Spray Lakes Reservoir is bounded by the continental divide along the Alberta-British Columbia border and lies in one of the most mountainous areas of Alberta. Within its almost 500 km² area (Table 1), there are 14 mountains with elevations over 3 000 m, including Mt. Assiniboine, one of the highest peaks in Alberta (Fig. 1).

The drainage area lies within the Alpine and Subalpine ecoregions (McGregor 1984). The Alpine Ecoregion is typified by bedrock cliffs and peaks with colluvial slopes. Soil development is negligible and only sparse forbs and grasses exist in cracks and fissures in the rock. Some dwarf shrubs (willow and birch) grow where Cumulic Regosolic soils have developed on the lower slopes. Glaciers cover areas near Mt. Assiniboine in the west and near Mt. Sir Douglas and Mt. French to the south. The lower slopes immediately around the reservoir are a good example of the Subalpine Ecoregion. Brunisolic and Podzolic Gray Luvisols have developed under a closed coniferous forest of lodgepole pine and white and Engelmann spruce, and Humic Gleysols are present in wet depressional areas. Along streams such as Smuts Creek, willows and alder grow on Orthic and Humic Regosols.

The watershed is drained by numerous creeks (Fig. 1): the major ones are Bryant Creek from the Assiniboine area, the Spray River from the southern portion of the drainage basin, and Smuts Creek from the southeast, parallelling the Smith-Dorrien/Spray Trail. The drainage basin was enlarged in 1949 when Calgary Power Ltd. built

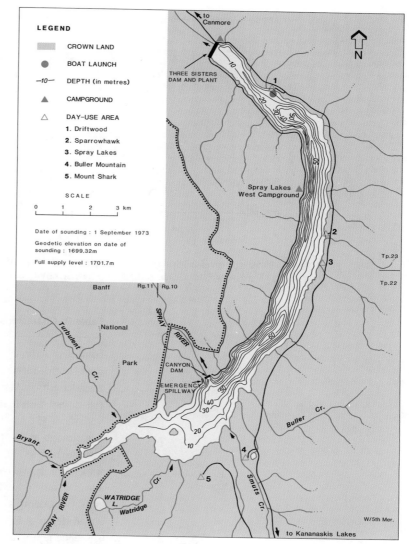

Figure 2. Bathymetry and shoreline features of Spray Lakes Reservoir.
BATHYMETRY SOURCE: Wiebe 1975.

a small dam at the south end of Mud Lake to direct Burstall Creek from the Kananaskis drainage basin into the Spray basin via Smuts Creek. As well, in 1959, a ditch was built at the south end of Mud Lake to divert French Creek from the Kananaskis basin into the Spray basin (TransAlta Util. Corp. n.d.).

The Spray Lakes Reservoir drainage basin is all Crown land; the western half is in Banff National Park, the southeast quarter is in Peter Lougheed Provincial Park and the northeast quarter is in Kananaskis Country. The major land use in the national and provincial parks is preservation and recreation. Some logging occurred in the area south of the reservoir before Kananaskis Country was established. The Mud, Chester and Ranger lakes area was logged from 1954 to 1960 and the Goat Creek area was logged from 1966 to 1969 (Wiebe 1975).

Reservoir Characteristics

The Spray Lakes Reservoir is 21–km long but only 1.6–km wide at its widest point (Table 2). The lake basin slopes steeply along the east and west sides, whereas the slopes at the ends of the reservoir are more gentle. Depths of over 50 m are found along most of the length of the reservoir. The maximum depth found during a brief bathymetric survey in 1973 was 65.4 m (Fig. 2). However, the maximum depth of the original Lower Spray Lake was 29.3 m (Miller and Macdonald 1950) and flooding raised the water level at least 50 m; therefore, it is likely that a small area of the reservoir has a depth close to 80 m. The shore of the reservoir is mostly barren rock and cobble with some muddy areas at the south end.

Two dams, both built by Calgary Power Ltd. in 1949, hold back the water (Fig. 2, Table 2). The Canyon Dam blocks the Spray River but releases a continuous flow of at least 0.43 m³/second under an

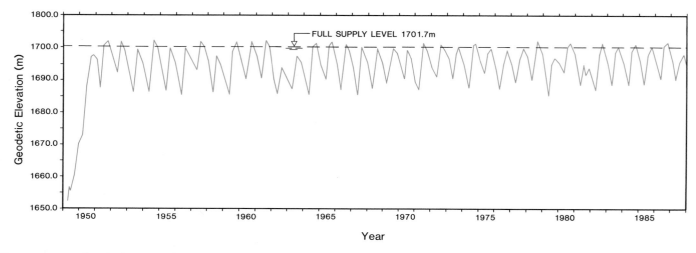

Figure 3. Water level of Spray Lakes Reservoir, 1949 to 1987.
SOURCES: TransAlta Util. Corp. n.d.; 1949–1968; Envir. Can. 1969–1987.

Table 2. Characteristics of Spray Lakes Reservoir.

control structures[a]	Three Sisters Dam; Canyon Dam
dam height (m)[a]	15; 59
crest length (m)[a]	603.5; 195
full supply level (FSL) (m)[a]	1 701.7
volume at FSL (m³)[a]	268.5 x 10⁶
live storage at FSL (m³)[a]	234.5 x 10⁶
surface area at FSL (km²)[a]	19.9
maximum drawdown (m)[b]	16.76
mean annual drawdown (1959–1986) (m)[b]	12.06
maximum depth at FSL (m)[c]	65.4
mean depth at FSL (m)[a]	13.5
shoreline length at FSL (km)[c]	51
maximum lake length at FSL (km)[c]	21
maximum lake width at FSL (km)[c]	1.6
mean annual lake evaporation (mm)[d]	621
mean annual precipitation (mm)[d]	622
mean residence time (yr)[a, e]	0.77
mean annual inflow volume (1977–1986) (m³)[d]	352 x 10⁶
mean annual outflow volume (1979–1986) (m³)[b]	335 x 10⁶ via Three Sisters Dam
mean annual outflow volume (1979–1986) (m³)[f, g]	13 x 10⁶ via Canyon Dam

NOTES: [g]calculated from continuous outflow of 0.42 m³/second; [e]excluding groundwater inflow
SOURCES: [a]TransAlta Util. Corp. n.d.; [b]Envir. Can. 1959–1987; [c]Wiebe 1975; [d]Alta. Envir. n.d.[b]; [f]Hudson 1988

agreement with Parks Canada to maintain fish habitat in the reaches of the Spray River below the dam. The Three Sisters Dam at the north end of the reservoir is operated to release water for electrical power generation (Hudson 1988). The first of three generating stations, the Three Sisters Plant, is at the foot of the dam, approximately 18 m below the full supply level of the reservoir. From there, the water travels via a canal to Goat Pond, then via a 5–km canal and a tunnel to Whiteman's Dam; it then drops 300 m through a penstock to the Spray Plant. Another canal and pond direct the water to a dyke above Canmore; from there the water falls 105 m through another penstock to the Rundle Plant on the bank of the Bow River in Canmore (Fig. 1, inset).

The reservoir is operated to produce electricity when demand is highest, in the early morning and evening. From 1950, when the reservoir was first filled, until the mid–1970s, the reservoir was filled in the spring, then water was stored to maximize power generation in winter when seasonal demand is highest. Since the mid–1970s, water has been released throughout the year, with peak flows from midsummer onward to help meet demand along the Bow River for water for irrigation and other uses (TransAlta Util. Corp. n.d.; Envir. Can. 1969–1987). The water level fluctuates on a regular basis

(Fig. 3). The mean annual drawdown is 12.06 m; the maximum drawdown was 16.76 m in 1956 (Table 2).

Water Quality

The water quality of Spray Lakes Reservoir was studied by Alberta Environment in the summer of 1984 (Alta. Envir. n.d.[a]).

Spray Lakes Reservoir is a freshwater lake. The water is well-buffered and the dominant ions are bicarbonate, calcium and sulphate (Table 3). The reservoir was thermally stratified by 20 June 1984 and a distinct thermocline had developed at a depth of 12 m by 17 July. The water column was well-mixed by 24 September (Fig. 4). Dissolved oxygen concentrations remained close to saturation from surface to bottom throughout the summer (Fig. 4).

Spray Lakes Reservoir is oligotrophic; chlorophyll *a* and total phosphorus levels are low, and the water is clear (Table 4, Fig. 5). The decreased Secchi depth recorded in July 1984 is likely due to suspended silt from runoff.

Table 3. Major ions and related water quality variables for Spray Lakes Reservoir. Average concentrations in mg/L; pH in pH units. Composite samples from the euphotic zone collected 4 times from 20 June to 24 Sep. 1984. S.E. = standard error.

	Mean	S.E.
pH (range)	7.0–8.6	—
total alkalinity (CaCO$_3$)	109	0.8
specific conductivity (μS/cm)	271	10.6
total dissolved solids (calculated)	146	3.6
total hardness (CaCO$_3$)	135	3.1
HCO$_3$	129	5.1
CO$_3$	2	2.1
Mg	9	0.5
Na	<0.6	—
K	<0.2	—
Cl	<0.8	—
SO$_4$	28	3.0
Ca	39	0.4

SOURCE: Alta. Envir. n.d.[a], Naquadat station 05AL05BC1000

Table 4. Nutrient, chlorophyll a and Secchi depth data for Spray Lakes Reservoir. Average concentrations in μg/L. Composite samples from the euphotic zone collected 4 times from 20 June to 24 Sep. 1984. S.E. = standard error.

	Mean	S.E.
total phosphorus	4	0.6
total Kjeldahl nitrogen	353[a]	111.0
NO$_3$ + NO$_2$–nitrogen	9[a]	2.3
NH$_4$–nitrogen	<17[a]	—
iron	<20[a]	—
chlorophyll a	2.1	0.36
Secchi depth (m)	5.9	1.11

NOTE: [a]n = 3
SOURCE: Alta. Envir. n.d.[a], Naquadat station 05AL05BC1000

Biological Characteristics

Plants

There is no information on the algae or aquatic plants in Spray Lakes Reservoir.

Invertebrates

The zooplankton and benthic invertebrates in the reservoir were sampled by Fish and Wildlife Division in September 1973 (Wiebe 1975). *Diacyclops bicuspidatus thomasi* was strongly dominant in the zooplankton and *Daphnia rosea* was secondary in abundance.

Benthic invertebrates were sampled at 10 sites with depths from 7 to 35 m on 9 September 1973. No animals were found at the five sites above the zone of average drawdown. Midge larvae (Chironomidae) were sparse at the other sites and fingernail clams (Sphaeriidae) were found at three sites.

In October 1982, opossum shrimp (*Mysis relicta*) were taken from Upper Kananaskis Lake and stocked in the reservoir to enhance the food supply for young lake trout and cisco. It was hoped that cisco would become the primary prey for adult lake trout (Hughes 1982). The success of the introduction of opossum shrimp had not been monitored as of 1988, but the stomach contents of 51 lake trout caught in 1986 did not include any *Mysis* (Stelfox 1988). This was not surprising, as it took 12 years for the opossum shrimp stocked in the Kananaskis Lakes to become sufficiently established to provide a substantial food source for fish.

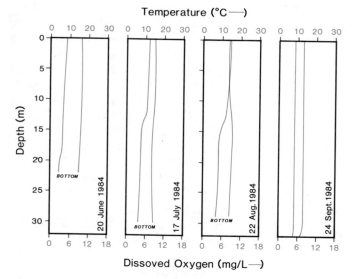

Figure 4. Temperature and dissolved oxygen in Spray Lakes Reservoir, 1984.
SOURCE: Alta. Envir. n.d.[a].

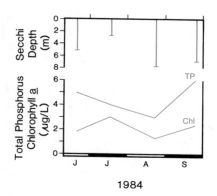

Figure 5. Total phosphorus, chlorophyll a and Secchi depth in Spray Lakes Reservoir, 1984.
SOURCE: Alta. Envir. n.d.[a].

Table 5. Percentage of fish species caught in Spray Lakes Reservoir. Data collected during a creel census in June 1952 and by test netting in Aug. 1962, Sep. 1973, Mar.–Apr. 1981 and Sep. 1986.

	1952[a]	1962[a]	1973[b]	1981[c]	1986[d]
Total Number of Fish	50	135	269	257	226
Percentage Composition:					
cutthroat trout	85	0	<1	0	0
rainbow trout	12	0	0	0	0
bull trout	12	0	0	0	0
lake trout	0	17	11	15	43
cisco	0	59	34	30	24
mountain whitefish	0	12	54	55	33
longnose suckers	0	10	<1	0	0

SOURCES: [a]Alta. For. Ld. Wild. n.d.; [b]Wiebe 1975; [c]Andrew et al. 1981; [d]Stelfox 1988

Fish

The Spray Valley has been renowned for its excellent sport fishery since the Bow Valley was settled. Prior to the filling of the reservoir in 1950, the valley was naturally divided into two zones by Spray Falls, a 12.2–m waterfall on the Spray River upstream of the river's confluence with Smuts Creek (Fig. 1, inset). The lower zone provided an excellent fishery for cutthroat trout and bull trout. Some rainbow trout and mountain whitefish were caught as well. Above Spray Falls, the fishery was for cutthroat and bull trout.

A Fish and Wildlife Division study in 1948 found distinct differences between the populations of cutthroat trout above and below Spray Falls (Miller and Macdonald 1950). The lower population was larger, faster growing (3 times the size of the upper-zone fish at age 4) and had redder flesh. These differences were partially attributed to the better food supply available in the Spray Lakes. It was predicted that the creation of a deep reservoir with large fluctuations in water levels that would inundate the lakes and falls would reduce the cutthroat populations and slow their growth rate. Sampling in the reservoir has traced the decline of the cutthroat population, which fell from 85% of the catch 2 years after reservoir filling (1952), to 0.4% in 1973, to none caught in 1981 or 1986 (Table 5).

To rebuild the sport fishery in the reservoir, Fish and Wildlife Division introduced approximately 400 000 lake trout as eyed-eggs between 1951 and 1954 and 6 million cisco eggs in 1953 (Alta. For. Ld. Wild. n.d.). Lake trout spawn successfully in the reservoir but numbers were still low in the early 1980s. From 1982 to 1986, Fish and Wildlife Division annually stocked 27 000 to 75 000 lake trout averaging 9.0 cm. In 1986, test nets indicated good survival rates of these fish (Stelfox 1988) and anglers reported excellent fishing for lake trout in 1988 (Hudson 1988).

The cisco stocked in 1953 were to have provided a stable food supply for the lake trout. They spawned successfully for a few years, but in 1986, no cisco under 23 years of age were caught, indicating that no succesful spawning has occurred since about 1964 (Stelfox 1988). This species rarely lives over 30 years, so it will likely disappear from the Spray Lakes Reservoir by the end of the 1980s.

Mountain whitefish are abundant in the reservoir and reproduce successfully in the tributaries, but they do not seem to be preyed upon by lake trout. The mountain whitefish population is largely made up of old fish; 50% of those caught in 1986 were over 10 years old. The oldest one caught was 29 years old; it may be the oldest fish of this species ever caught in North America (Stelfox 1988).

The lack of appropriate prey for lake trout in the reservoir has led them to survive almost exclusively on plankton and midge larvae. Only 2% of 51 fish caught in 1986 had fish in their stomachs. The scarcity of fish in the diet of lake trout is likely one reason why the lake trout in Spray Lakes Reservoir die younger and are smaller at all ages than lake trout in lakes with abundant forage fish such as Lake Minnewanka (Stelfox 1988).

Wildlife

The wildlife in the Spray Lakes area is typical of mountain wilderness. Mule deer, elk, moose and black bears are common and grizzly bears are present in the area. Mountain goats and bighorn sheep can be seen on mountain slopes and wolves and cougars are occasionally seen or heard. The Spray Lakes are not used extensively by waterfowl or aquatic mammals because of the scarcity of aquatic vegetation.

J.M. Crosby

References

Alberta Environment. n.d.[a]. Envir. Assess. Div., Envir. Qlty. Monit. Br. Unpubl. data, Edmonton.

———. n.d.[b]. Tech. Serv. Div., Hydrol. Br. Unpubl. data, Edmonton.

Alberta Forestry, Lands and Wildlife. n.d. Fish Wild. Div. Unpubl. data, Edmonton.

———. 1988. Boating in Alberta. Fish Wild. Div., Edmonton.

———. 1989. Guide to sportfishing. Fish Wild. Div., Edmonton.

Alberta Recreation and Parks. n.d. Parks Div. Unpubl. data, Edmonton.

Alberta Research Council. 1972. Geological map of Alberta. Nat. Resour. Div., Alta. Geol. Surv., Edmonton.

Andrew, J.H., J.A. Taylor, A.D. Sekerak and J. Kristensen. 1981. Late winter fisheries studies in the Spray Lakes Reservoir watershed, 1981. Prep. for Alta. En. Nat. Resour., Fish Wild. Div., Edmonton by LGL Ltd. Envir. Res. Assoc., Calgary.

Appleby, E. 1975. Canmore: The story of an era. E. Appleby, Canmore.

Energy, Mines and Resources Canada. 1977, 1980. National topographic series 1:50 000 82J/11 (1977), 82J/13 (1977), 82J/14 (1977), 82O/3 (1980). Surv. Map. Br., Ottawa.

Environment Canada. 1959–1987. Surface water data. Prep. by Inland Waters Directorate. Water Surv. Can., Water Resour. Br., Ottawa.

———. 1982. Canadian climate normals, Vol. 7: Bright sunshine (1951–1980). Prep. by Atm. Envir. Serv. Supply Serv. Can., Ottawa.

Fraser, E. 1969. The Canadian Rockies: Early travels and explorations. M.G. Hurtig Ltd., Edmonton.

Geographic Board of Canada. 1928. Place-names of Alberta. Dept. Interior, Ottawa.

Hudson, B. 1988. TransAlta Util. Corp., Canmore. Pers. comm.

Hughes, G.W. 1982. The introduction of opossum shrimp (*Mysis relicta* Loven) into the Spray Lakes Reservoir. Alta. En. Nat. Resour., Fish Wild. Div., Calgary.

McGregor, C.A. 1984. Kananaskis Country ecological land classification. Alta. En. Nat. Resour., Resour. Eval. Plan. Div., Edmonton.

Miller, R.B. and W.H. Macdonald. 1950. The effect of Spray Lakes development on the sport fishery. Alta. Ld. For., Fish Wild. Div., Edmonton.

Stelfox, J. 1988. Alta. For. Ld. Wild., Fish Wild. Div., Calgary. Pers. comm.

Strong, W.L. and K.R. Leggat. 1981. Ecoregions of Alberta. Alta. En. Nat. Resour., Resour. Eval. Plan. Div., Edmonton.

TransAlta Utilities Corporation. n.d. Unpubl. data, Calgary.

Wiebe, A.P. 1975. A baseline biological inventory of some lakes in the Spray River watershed. Alta. Rec. Parks Wild., Fish Wild. Div., Calgary.

BEAUVAIS LAKE

Alberta Recreation and Parks

MAP SHEET: 82G/8
LOCATION: Tp29 R5 W5
LAT/LONG: 49°25'N 114°06'W

Beauvais Lake is a picturesque lake located about 24 km south-west of the town of Pincher Creek in the Municipal District of Pincher Creek. The view from the lake is of rolling hills covered with a mosaic of spruce, pine, Douglas fir and trembling aspen forests and open grassy slopes. The area is dramatically backed by the snow-capped Rocky Mountains. To reach Beauvais Lake from Pincher Creek, take Secondary Road 507 west for 9 km, then follow Secondary Road 775 south for 8 km to Beauvais Lake Provincial Park (Fig. 1).

Beauvais Lake was named for Remi Beauvais, who arrived from Oregon in 1882 to homestead and raise race horses in the area. His cabin still stands 2.4 km southeast of the park boundary. An anglicized form of the name, "Bovey Lake", appears on maps as recent as 1942 (Pincher Cr. Hist. Soc. 1974; Finlay and Finlay 1987). The land now within the provincial park was homesteaded between 1898 and 1909; the hills were used for grazing cattle and the lake was used for watering stock. Even then, the north shore was a favourite picnic spot. By 1940, a conflict between cattle use and recreational use led to the reservation of 62 ha on the north shore for a provincial park. Between 1940 and 1957, more land was acquired, and in 1957, a 158–ha area officially became Beauvais Lake Provincial Park. In 1959, the lake was added to the park; more land was acquired over the years, and in 1989, the park encompassed 593 ha (Alta. Rec. Parks Wild. 1979). A weir was built on the outlet of Beauvais Lake in 1950 to raise the lake level 1.5 m in order to enhance recreation and to store water for release down Chipman Creek in times of drought (Paetz 1967).

Most of the recreational development in the park is at the north-west end of Beauvais Lake. It includes a boat launch, a pier, a campground with 85 sites plus 10 walk-in tent sites, tap water, public telephones, a children's playground, picnic areas, interpretive programs and a network of hiking trails. A group camping area is located west of the campground and is available by reservation only, and there are day-use areas on the west and north shores (Fig. 2). Approximately 45 private cottages are situated on the north shore. Boat travel is restricted to 12 km/hour on the entire lake (Alta. For. Ld. Wild. 1988).

Beauvais Lake has clear water most of the summer but algae colours the water a murky green by mid-August. Aquatic plants are abundant in the shallow bays by midsummer. Beauvais Lake is actively managed by Fish and Wildlife Division as an excellent summer and winter fishery for rainbow and brown trout. Provincial sport fishing regulations apply to the lake, and the use of bait fish is not permitted (Alta. For. Ld. Wild. 1989). The drainage basin supports a very diverse community of plants, birds and wildlife.

Drainage Basin Characteristics

Beauvais Lake is in the Montane Ecoregion, a small area in the abrupt transition zone from prairie grassland to subalpine forests. The Montane Ecoregion is typified by Douglas fir. North-facing slopes are dominated by spruce interspersed with pine, Douglas fir and trembling aspen. South-facing slopes are open grasslands with pockets of trembling aspen and Douglas fir. Approximately half of the drainage basin is in the provincial park and the rest is leased for grazing (Fig. 1).

The watershed is characterized by rolling foothills. Surface elevations range from 1 368 m along the lakeshore to 1 676 m at the

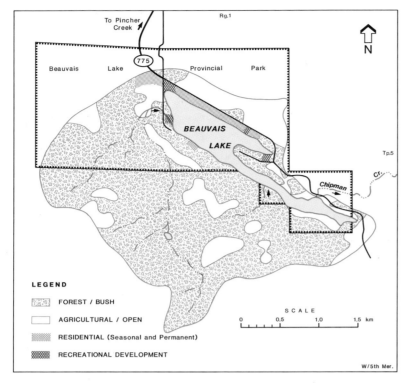

Figure 1. Features of the drainage basin of Beauvais Lake.
SOURCES: Alta. Envir. n.d.[c]; En. Mines Resour. Can. 1977. Updated with 1982 aerial photos.

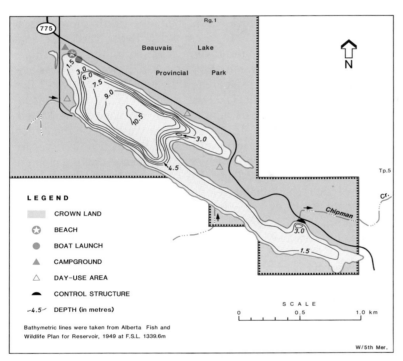

Figure 2. Bathymetry and shoreline features of Beauvais Lake.
BATHYMETRY SOURCE: Alta. For. Ld. Wild. n.d.

Table 1. Characteristics of Beauvais Lake drainage basin.

area (excluding lake) (km²)[a]	7.09
soil[b]	Orthic Dark Gray Chernozemics, Brunisols
bedrock geology[c]	Alberta Group (Upper Cretaceous): shale, sandstone; marine Belly River Formation (Upper Cretaceous): sandstone, siltstone, mudstone, ironstone beds; nonmarine
terrain[d]	rolling foothills
ecoregion[d]	Montane
dominant vegetation[d]	white spruce, trembling aspen, Douglas fir
mean annual inflow (m³)[a, e]	1.02×10^6
mean annual sunshine (h)[f]	2 370

NOTE: [e]excluding groundwater inflow
SOURCES: [a]Alta. Envir. n.d.[c]; [b]Greenlee 1974; [c]Alta. Res. Counc. 1972; [d]Strong and Leggat 1981; [f]Envir. Can. 1982

southwestern corner. Distinctive linear ridges in the watershed were formed by the thrusting of Lower Cretaceous sandstones over Upper Cretaceous shales. Beauvais Lake occupies one of the depressions between two such ridges; its southwestern shore parallels a thrust fault that extends well beyond the park boundary. The crest of the ridge that parallels the northern shore is made of the youngest rocks in the park, Cretaceous-age sandstones of the Belly River Formation (Finlay and Finlay 1987). Soils within the provincial park were mapped in 1974 (Greenlee 1974). The open grasslands and some of the open aspen areas are underlain by Dark Gray Chernozemics, whereas the coniferous forests are underlain by Luvisols and Brunisols.

Lake Basin Characteristics

The Beauvais Lake drainage basin is about 8 times greater in area than the lake (Tables 1, 2). The lake is 3.1–km long and has a maximum width of 0.6 km. The southeastern arm is shallow—the deep part of the lake is at the northwestern end where the basin slopes gradually to the lake's maximum depth of 10.7 m (Fig. 2). A small gravel beach at the northwest end of the lake extends a few metres into the lake. Aquatic macrophytes grow to a depth of 3.5 m (MacNeill 1979); approximately 18% of the lake is less than this depth (Fig. 3).

Beauvais Lake is fed by two small intermittent streams, but most of the inflow is diffuse surficial runoff and precipitation. The outflow is Chipman Creek, which leaves at the southeast end of the lake. The weir built in 1950, which raised the lake level 1.5 m, was rebuilt in 1986 with no change to the full supply level (Table 2). The outflow from the lake flows through a steel culvert with a control gate, but there is no outflow when the lake level is below 1 365.5 m. The water level of the lake is reasonably stable, varying 0.5 m or less in most years (Fig. 4). The water level was dropped in 1981 to facilitate sucker control by Fish and Wildlife Division, and was dropped again in 1985/86 to facilitate rebuilding the weir.

Water Quality

The water quality of Beauvais Lake has been monitored several times a year since 1984 under a joint program between Alberta Environment and Alberta Recreation and Parks (Alta. Envir. n.d.[b]).

Beauvais Lake is a well-buffered, freshwater lake; its dominant ions are calcium and bicarbonate (Table 3). Although the lake is shallow and in a windy area, it becomes weakly thermally stratified in summer. When stratification occurs, as on 14 August 1986 (Fig. 5), anoxic conditions develop near the bottom sediments. In winter, dissolved oxygen falls to zero in the deep areas, but concentrations in the upper layers are sufficient to overwinter trout.

The phosphorus concentration in Beauvais Lake is quite stable through the summer (Fig. 6). Algal growth in August or September

Table 2. Characteristics of Beauvais Lake.

elevation (m)[a, b]	1 367.8
surface area (km²)[a, b]	0.89
volume (m³)[a, b]	3.8 x 10⁶
maximum depth (m)[c]	10.7
mean depth (m)[b, c]	4.3
shoreline length (km)[c]	7.9
mean annual lake evaporation (mm)[d]	715
mean annual precipitation (mm)[d]	602
mean residence time (yr)[d, e]	4.0
control structure[f]	1951, rebuilt 1986; earthfill weir, gated culvert outlet
dam crest elevation (m)[f]	1 368.9
full supply level[f]	1 367.8
minimum controlled drawdown[f]	1 365.5

NOTES: [a]on date of sounding: June 1980; [e]excluding groundwater inflow
SOURCES: [b]Alta. Envir. n.d.[d]; [c]R.L. & L. Envir. Serv. Ltd. 1985; [d]Alta. Envir. n.d.[c];
[f]Alta. Envir. n.d.[a]

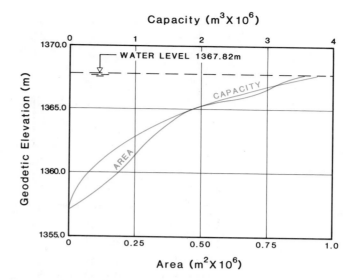

Figure 3. Area/capacity curve for Beauvais Lake.
SOURCE: Alta. Envir. n.d.[d].

Table 3. Major ions and related water quality variables for Beauvais Lake. Average concentrations in mg/L; pH in pH units. Composite samples from the euphotic zone collected 4 times from May to Oct. 1984. S.E. = standard error.

	Mean	S.E.
pH (range)	8.4–8.6	—
total alkalinity (CaCO₃)	148	4.6
specific conductivity (µS/cm)	279	7.7
total dissolved solids (calculated)	148	4.9
total hardness (CaCO₃)	120	5.1
HCO₃	172	6.7
CO₃	<6	—
Mg	13	0.3
Na	11	0.5
K	2	0.1
Cl	<1	—
SO₄	<6	—
Ca	26	2.1

SOURCE: Alta. Envir. n.d.[b], Naquadat station 01AL05AA1000

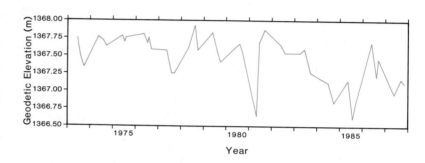

Figure 4. Water level of Beauvais Lake, 1973 to 1987.
SOURCE: Alta. Envir. n.d.[d].

may turn the water a murky green colour (Alta. Envir. n.d.[b]). Beauvais Lake has moderate total phosphorus and chlorophyll *a* concentrations (Table 4). It is classified as a mesotrophic lake.

Biological Characteristics

Plants

Data on the phytoplankton in Beauvais Lake are not available.

Macrophytes were mapped as part of a lake survey by Fish and Wildlife Division in late June 1978 (MacNeill 1979). Five species of emergent plants and nine species of submergent plants were identified (Fig. 7). Macrophytes grew to a depth of 3.5 m. Submergent plants in shallow bays, especially in the southeast arm, become a nuisance to boaters by late summer (Fitch 1988).

Invertebrates

The zooplankton and benthic invertebrates of Beauvais Lake were sampled by Fish and Wildlife Division in late June 1978 (MacNeill 1979). Zooplankton were collected with a No. 40 Wisconsin-style plankton net. The zooplankton community included rotifers, copepods and cladocerans. The density of 300 organisms/L was high compared to that of other pothole lakes in southern Alberta.

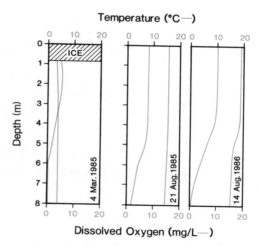

Figure 5. Temperature and dissolved oxygen in Beauvais Lake, 1985 and 1986.
SOURCE: Alta. Envir. n.d.[b].

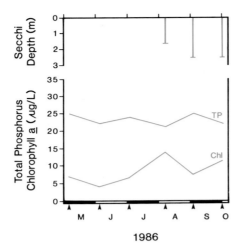

Figure 6. Total phosphorus, chlorophyll *a* and Secchi depth in Beauvais Lake, 1986.
SOURCE: Alta. Envir. n.d.[b].

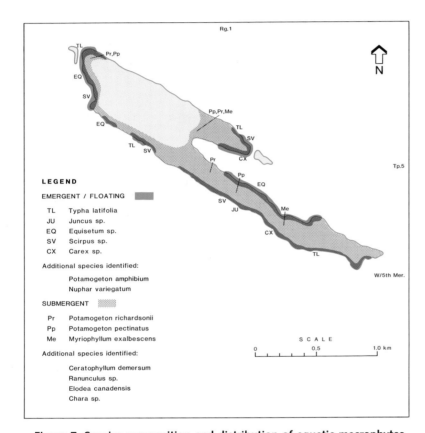

Figure 7. Species composition and distribution of aquatic macrophytes in Beauvais Lake, June 1978.
SOURCE: MacNeill 1979.

The benthic community was sampled by Ekman dredge from a depth of 10.5 m. Aquatic earthworms (Oligochaeta), which were the dominant group, accounted for 92% of the 24 000 organisms/m². The other organisms found were midge larvae (Chironomidae) and phantom midge larvae (Chaoborinae). Shells of clams and snails were also abundant, but no living specimens were found. The total wet weight of organisms was 13.8 g/m².

Fish

Beauvais Lake is actively managed by Fish and Wildlife Division to provide an excellent year-round sport fishery for rainbow trout (Alta. For. Ld. Wild. n.d.; Miller 1957; Paetz 1958; MacNeill 1979; R.L. & L. Envir. Serv. Ltd. 1985). Eight species of fish are native to Beauvais Lake: white sucker, longnose sucker, fathead minnow, brook stickleback, pearl dace, northern redbelly dace, Iowa darter and spoonhead sculpin. Trout are stocked each year; the species introduced since 1947 include rainbow, brown, cutthroat and brook

Table 4. Nutrient, chlorophyll *a* and Secchi depth data for Beauvais Lake. Average concentrations in μg/L. Composite samples from the euphotic zone collected 4 times from May to Oct. 1984 and 6 times from May to Sep. 1986. S.E. = standard error.

	1984		1986	
	Mean	S.E.	Mean	S.E.
total phosphorus	33	2	24	1
iron	93	33	—	—
chlorophyll *a*	13.5	3.3	8.3	2.9
Secchi depth (m)	1.6	0.7	2.1	0.3

SOURCE: Alta. Envir. n.d.[b], Naquadat station 01AL05AA1000

trout. From 1984 to 1987, an average of 58 000 rainbow trout and 43 000 brown trout were stocked each year (Alta. For. Ld. Wild. 1984–1987).

By 1958, fishing in Beauvais Lake required an average of 9.2 hours of angling to catch a trout. Test nets set in the lake in 1958 yielded 86% suckers. Consequently, the lake was treated the same year with three applications of Toxaphene to kill suckers. Until 1973, test netting yielded only 1% suckers, but by 1978 the proportion had risen to 66% (MacNeill 1979). A comparison of size-at-age of rainbow trout showed that fish caught in 1978 were much smaller than similar-aged fish caught from 1960 to 1973 (Alta. For. Ld. Wild. n.d.). For example, the average length of age 1+ fish had declined from 291 mm to 151 mm, the length of age 2+ fish had declined from 390 mm to 246 mm and the length of age 3+ fish had declined from 467 mm to 272 mm.

In 1981, Beauvais Lake was drawn down and treated with rotenone to kill the suckers. The sucker population, although greatly reduced, was not eliminated. The trout population has responded well, with increased survival and growth. The catch rate during a creel census in 1982 was 0.43 trout per hour, the best rate of all of the stocked lakes in the Southern Region (Bishop 1983).

Wildlife

The Beauvais Lake area supports a very diverse community of plants, birds and animals because of its varied habitats and its location in a rapid transition zone between mountains and prairie (Crack and Danielson 1974; Finlay and Finlay 1987). The 316 species of plants recorded include glacier lilies and three species of rare coral-root orchids. More than 110 species of birds have been sighted, including MacGillivray's Warblers and Western Tanagers. The park is situated along the Pacific flyway and is used as a small staging area for waterfowl. The northwest and southeast ends of the lake provide good nesting habitat for waterfowl. Eight species of amphibians and reptiles have been seen in the area, including northern leopard frogs, spotted frogs and garter snakes. Fourteen species of mammals have been recorded; mule deer are common, white-tailed deer are often seen and beaver inhabit the southeast end of the lake.

J.M. Crosby

References

Alberta Environment. n.d.[a]. Devel. Op. Div. Unpubl. data, Edmonton.
———. n.d.[b]. Envir. Assess. Div., Envir. Qlty. Monit. Br. Unpubl. data, Edmonton.
———. n.d.[c]. Tech. Serv. Div., Hydrol. Br. Unpubl. data, Edmonton.
———. n.d.[d]. Tech. Serv. Div., Surv. Br. Unpubl. data, Edmonton.
Alberta Forestry, Lands and Wildlife. n.d. Fish Wild. Div. Unpubl. data, Edmonton.
———. 1984–1987. Fish planting list. Fish Wild. Div., Edmonton.
———. 1988. Boating in Alberta. Fish Wild. Div., Edmonton.
———. 1989. Guide to sportfishing. Fish Wild. Div., Edmonton.
Alberta Recreation, Parks and Wildlife. 1979. Beauvais Lake; Park direction. Alta. Rec. Parks Wild., Lethbridge.
Alberta Research Council. 1972. Geological map of Alberta. Nat. Resour. Div., Alta. Geol. Surv., Edmonton.
Bishop, F.G. 1983. A summary of the 1982 creel survey program: Southern region. Alta. En. Nat. Resour., Fish Wild. Div., Lethbridge.

Crack, S. and B.J. Danielson. 1974. An ecological survey of Beauvais Lake Provincial Park. Prep. for Alta. Ld. For., Prov. Parks Plan., Edmonton.

Energy, Mines and Resources Canada. 1977. National topographic series 1:50 000 82G/8 (1977). Surv. Map. Br., Ottawa.

Environment Canada. 1982. Canadian climate normals, Vol. 7: Bright sunshine (1951–1980). Prep. by Atm. Envir. Serv. Supply Serv. Can., Ottawa.

Finlay, J. and C. Finlay. 1987. Parks in Alberta: A guide to peaks, ponds, parklands & prairies. Hurtig Publ., Edmonton.

Fitch, L. 1988. Alta. For. Ld. Wild., Fish Wild. Div., Lethbridge. Pers. comm.

Greenlee, G.M. 1974. Soil survey of Beauvais Lake Provincial Park and interpretation for recreational use. Alta. Inst. Pedol. Rep. M–74–11. Alta. Res. Counc., Edmonton.

MacNeill, J.W. 1979. Beauvais Lake: Lake survey inventory. Alta. Rec. Parks Wild., Fish Wild. Div. Unpubl. rep., Lethbridge.

Miller, R.B. 1957. Report on a creel census at Beauvais Lake, 1956. Alta. Ld. For., Fish Wild. Div., Edmonton.

Paetz, M.J. 1958. Removal of fish populations by chemical treatment in three Alberta lakes: Beauvais Lake, Michell Lake and Strubel Lake. Alta. Ld. For., Fish Wild. Div. Unpubl. rep., Edmonton.

———. 1967. The relationship of fingerling rainbow trout stocking to the sport fishery of Beauvais Lake, Alberta. Alta. Ld. For., Fish Wild. Div. Unpubl. rep., Edmonton.

Pincher Creek Historical Society. 1974. Prairie grass to mountain pass: History of the pioneers of the Pincher Creek and District. Pincher Cr. Hist. Soc., Pincher Creek.

R.L. & L. Environmental Services Ltd. 1985. A compendium of existing environmental data on Alberta reservoirs. Prep. for Alta. Envir. Res. Trust, Edmonton.

Strong, W.L. and K.R. Leggat. 1981. Ecoregions of Alberta. Alta. En. Nat. Resour., Resour. Eval. Plan. Div., Edmonton.

CHAIN LAKES RESERVOIR

MAP SHEETS: 82J/1, 8
LOCATION: Tp14, 15 R2 W5
LAT/LONG: 50°15′N 112°14′W

Chain Lakes Reservoir is a long, narrow water body set in some of the most beautiful foothills country in Alberta. Located in Improvement District No. 6, between the Porcupine Hills and the front range of the Rocky Mountains, the reservoir is surrounded by natural open grasslands dotted with trembling aspen. In the distance, tree-covered hills and mountain peaks rise as a dramatic backdrop. To reach Chain Lakes, as it is called locally, travel south from the city of Calgary on Highway 2 for 68 km, then continue west from the town of Nanton on Secondary Road 533 for 38 km to Chain Lakes Provincial Park (Fig. 1). One alternate route to the park is to drive south from the town of Black Diamond for 47 km on Highway 22; another alternate route is to drive 95 km north of the town of Pincher Creek on Highway 22.

The reservoir was named for the three Chain Lakes that nearly filled the area now covered by the reservoir. These lakes were fed by numerous springs; in winter, the ice was often so thin that buffalo crossing the lakes would break through and drown (Finlay and Finlay 1987). Cattle grazing has been the major land use since the first ranches were established in the late 1800s. In 1957, the provincial government approached the Prairie Farm Rehabilitation Administration (PFRA) to consider developing storage on Willow Creek to ensure a continuous water supply downstream, mostly to guarantee municipal supply for the towns of Claresholm and Granum (Agric. Can. 1961). In 1966, the PFRA built two dams, the south one across Willow Creek and the north one across Meinsinger Creek. By 1967, the reservoir was full.

Chain Lakes Provincial Park covers 409 ha on the east side of the southern end of the reservoir. Both day-use and camping facilities are provided year-round. The park has a campground with 140 sites, tap water, a telephone, picnic tables and shelters, group camping facilities (by reservation only), a sewage disposal station, a boat launch and a children's fish pond (Alta. Hotel Assoc. 1988). Power boats are allowed on the reservoir, but all vessels are restricted from some posted areas; the speed of power boats is limited to 12 km/hour in other posted areas and boats are not allowed to pull water skiers or surfboards in other posted areas (Alta. For. Ld. Wild. 1988).

The lake is stocked annually with rainbow trout and a moderate sport fishery has developed. The use of bait fish is not permitted in any water in the drainage basin. All streams in the basin are closed to fishing from November through May, no bait of any sort is allowed in streams and no rainbow or cutthroat trout under 25 cm caught in a stream may be kept (Alta. For. Ld. Wild. 1989).

Chain Lakes Reservoir is attractive for recreation. Algae are rarely conspicuous but the water is frequently turbid from silt, which erodes from the east shore. The density of aquatic plants is very low. Popular activities are fishing in winter and summer, boating and hiking. Because the reservoir is located in a zone of rapid transition from grassland to mountain, it provides a variety of habitats for exploring and birdwatching. Underground springs and bedrock outcrops create some unique habitats within the provincial park, where 260 species of vascular plants have been recorded, including Jacob's ladder, scorpion weed and other interesting plants (Crack and Danielson 1974).

Drainage Basin Characteristics

The large drainage basin (209 km^2) of Chain Lakes Reservoir is 67 times the area of the reservoir (Fig. 1, Tables 1, 2). The small portion

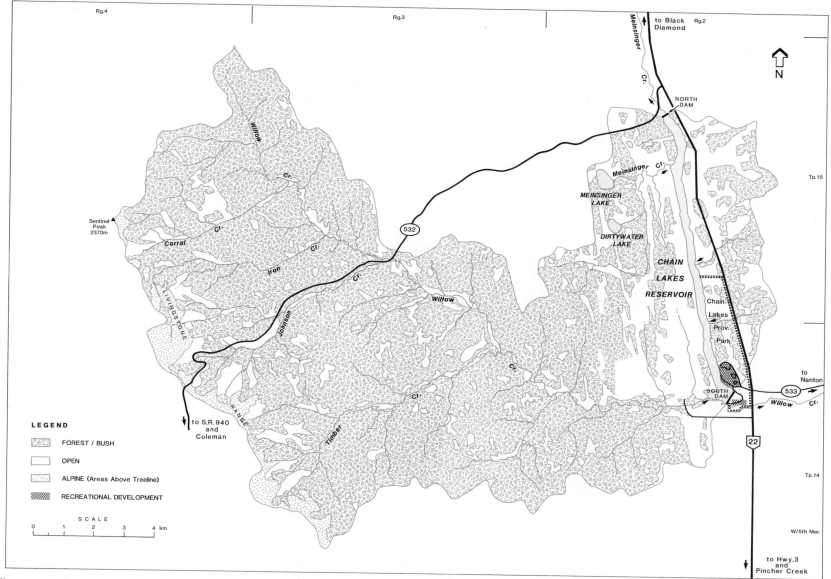

Figure 1. Features of the drainage basin of Chain Lakes Reservoir.
SOURCES: Alta. Envir. n.d.[c]; En. Mines Resour. Can. 1979; 1980. Updated with 1985 aerial photos.

of the drainage basin east of the reservoir extends to a 1600–m–high crest in the Porcupine Hills. This area, in the Aspen Parkland Ecoregion, lies on glacial morainal till with slopes of up to 30%. The vegetation is composed of trembling aspen groves attractively interspersed with open fescue grassland. Soils are Black Chernozemics under the fescue and Eutric Brunisols under the aspen (Strong 1979). Two extensive outcrops of Porcupine Hills sandstone of Tertiary Age occur near the north end of the provincial park (Crack and Danielson 1974; Finlay and Finlay 1987).

The Aspen Parkland Ecoregion surrounds the reservoir and extends westward to the Bow-Crow Forest Reserve Boundary. The reservoir lies in a valley draped with glaciolacustrine sediments. Near the reservoir, the slopes range from 0 to 9% and willow is interspersed with trembling aspen and areas of fescue grass. The reservoir itself is bordered by a narrow area of glaciofluvial eroded channel; willows and grasses underlain by Humic Gleysols predominate. West of the Aspen Parkland is an area of Montane Ecoregion; this is the smallest ecoregion in Alberta and is found in only 0.5% of the province. Here, bedrock outcrops and dry grassy slopes are interspersed with Douglas fir, lodgepole pine and trembling aspen. Slopes range up to 60% and soils are Eutric Brunisols. Up the slope from the Montane Ecoregion is the Subalpine Ecoregion. Slopes are 15 to 45% and are covered with residual materials that support forests of lodgepole pine, Engelmann spruce and alpine fir. The top of the Livingstone Range extends into the Alpine Ecoregion, where altitudes reach up to 2 450 m. Unstable residual slopes of 45 to 60% support little vegetation, and the sparse soils that have developed are Regosols (Strong 1979; Strong and Leggat 1981).

Table 1. Characteristics of Chain Lakes Reservoir drainage basin.

area (excluding lake) (km²)[a]	209
soil[b]	Black Chernozemics, Eutric Brunisols, Regosols
bedrock geology[c]	West: Alberta Group (Cretaceous): shale, sandstone; marine East: Porcupine Hills Formation (Tertiary): sandstone, mudstone; nonmarine
terrain[b]	hilly to mountainous
ecoregion[d]	Groveland Subregion of Aspen Parkland; Montane; Subalpine
dominant vegetation[b]	trembling aspen and fescue; Douglas fir and lodgepole pine; Engelmann spruce and lodgepole pine
mean annual sunshine (h)[e]	1 970

SOURCES: [a]Alta. Envir. n.d.[c]; [b]Strong 1979; [c]Alta. Res. Counc. 1972; [d]Strong and Leggat 1981; [e]Envir. Can. 1982

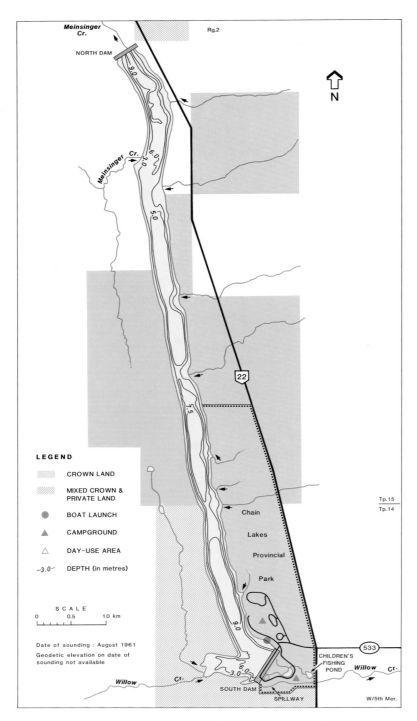

Figure 2. Bathymetry and shoreline features of Chain Lakes Reservoir.
BATHYMETRY SOURCE: Agric. Can. 1961.

There has been almost no cultivation of land in the basin; the open areas shown in Figure 1 are almost all natural grasslands. Most of the land in the basin is Crown land, and much of the area around the reservoir has been leased for grazing. Some of the land bordering the north end of the reservoir is privately owned (Fig. 2). There are no population centres in the basin.

Willow Creek, the major inflow, flows both in and out of the reservoir near the South Dam. Meinsinger Creek, a much smaller creek, enters the reservoir near the north end and flows out of it at the north end. Several small creeks drain the eastern portion of the drainage basin (Fig. 2).

Reservoir Characteristics

Chain Lakes Reservoir is a long (10.7 km), narrow lake; most of it is less than 500 m across (Fig. 2). It fills a steep-sided valley that originally was occupied by three small lakes that drained into Willow Creek and thence to the Oldman River near the town of Fort Macleod. The South Dam, built in 1966 across Willow Creek, backed water up into the Chain Lakes valley. Before the North Dam was

built, also in 1966, Meinsinger Creek drained to the north into Stimson Creek, which empties into the Highwood River, a tributary of the Bow River. Now the North Dam impounds Meinsinger Creek and allows the reservoir level to be raised to higher levels than those that would be possible with only the South Dam.

The residence time of water in the reservoir is estimated to be about half a year (Table 2), but because Willow Creek is "short-circuited" through the south end, the length of time water remains in the central and northern portions may be much longer. The estimated residence time also does not consider groundwater inflow, which is known to be significant although it has not been quantified.

Most of the water leaving the reservoir flows into Willow Creek via a low-level conduit in the South Dam. Riparian flow is released to maintain Willow Creek but the volume of the discharge varies with water supply and demand. When the full supply level (FSL) of the reservoir is exceeded, water flows through the spillway on the west side of the South Dam. Water is also released through the North Dam to maintain Meinsinger and Stimson creeks, but the volume of this release is variable (Alta. Envir. n.d.[a]).

The water level of the reservoir has been monitored since 1977 (Fig. 3). During this time the reservoir has been operated to fill as much as possible in the spring, then to release water slowly through the summer and winter to maintain a stable water supply for Claresholm and Granum and to provide water for other uses, including stockwatering and irrigation. The amount of runoff is variable and has not always been sufficient to bring the reservoir up to FSL. For example, in 1984, the highest level achieved was still 1.5 m below FSL (Fig. 3). The large drawdown in 1985 was the result of a severe drought in southern Alberta in 1983 and 1984. Withdrawals were required to maintain flow to the downstream towns while the volume of inflow was much lower than normal. Drought conditions in 1987 and 1988 led to low water levels in late 1988. The bottom of the reservoir slopes steeply except for the small area where Willow Creek enters so a drawdown of 3 m reduces the lake area by about 15% from the area at full supply level (Fig. 4).

Water Quality

The water quality of Chain Lakes Reservoir was sampled by Alberta Environment twice in August 1972 (Alta. Envir. n.d.[b]). The reservoir has well-buffered, fresh water. The dominant ions are bicarbonate and sodium (Table 3).

Chain Lakes Reservoir probably stratifies intermittently in the summer. The only profile data were taken on 17 May 1978 (Mac-Neill 1978). At that time, the temperature varied from 8.8°C at the surface to 8.2°C at the bottom; the dissolved oxygen concentration was 10.4 mg/L at the surface and decreased to 8.4 mg/L at the bottom. Winter dissolved oxygen concentration has been monitored in late February or early March every year from 1972 to 1980 (Alta. For. Ld. Wild. n.d.) and in most winters until 1988 (Bishop 1989). The concentration of dissolved oxygen at a depth of 1 m has never been less than 9 mg/L. The lowest concentration recorded was 6 mg/L at 4.3 m in 1974. No winterkill of fish has been recorded for Chain Lakes (Bishop 1989).

There are no data on the nutrient status of this water body. The water is usually clear and algae are not conspicuous, but the water is occasionally turbid due to suspended sediment from bank erosion.

Biological Characteristics

Plants

There is no information on algae in Chain Lakes Reservoir. Aquatic plants are scarce; none were collected by grappling in May 1978 (MacNeill 1978).

Invertebrates

The zooplankton was sampled by Fish and Wildlife Division on 17 May 1978 from a depth of 9.5 m to the surface with a No. 40 Wisconsin-style plankton net made of No. 20 silk bolting cloth (Mac-

Table 2. Characteristics of Chain Lakes Reservoir.

control structure[a]	South Dam; North Dam
dam height (m)[a]	South Dam 13.4; North Dam 14.6
crest elevation (m)[a]	South Dam 1 300.1; North Dam 1 300.1
crest length (m)[a]	South Dam 518.2; North Dam 335.3
full supply level (FSL) (m)[a]	1 297.1
volume at FSL (m³)[b]	18.0×10^6
live storage at FSL (m³)[b]	14.6×10^6
surface area at FSL (km²)[b]	3.12
maximum drawdown (m)[c]	4.48
mean annual drawdown (1977–1987) (m)[c]	1.03
maximum depth at FSL (m)[b]	10.4
mean depth at FSL (m)[b]	5.4
shoreline length at FSL (km)[b]	23.1
lake length at FSL (km)[b]	10.7
lake width at FSL (km)[b]	1.3
mean annual lake evaporation (mm)[d]	712
mean annual precipitation (mm)[d]	579
mean residence time (yr)[d, e]	0.54
mean annual inflow volume (1977–1987) (m³)[d, e]	33.6×10^6

NOTE: [e]excluding groundwater inflow
SOURCES: [a]Alta. Envir. n.d.[a]; [b]Agric. Can. 1961; [c]Envir. Can. 1977–1988; [d]Alta. Envir. n.d.[c]

Table 3. Major ions and related water quality variables for Chain Lakes Reservoir. Average concentrations in mg/L; pH in pH units. Samples from the euphotic zone collected on 14 Aug. and 22 Aug. 1972. S.E. = standard error.

	Mean	S.E.
pH (range)	8.2–8.3	—
total alkalinity (CaCO₃)	264	3.5
total dissolved solids (calculated)	297[a, b]	—
turbidity (NTU)	2[c]	—
total hardness (CaCO₃)	140	11.5
HCO₃	321	4.0
CO₃	0	0
Mg	17	1.5
Na	67[c]	—
Cl	4	2.5
SO₄	32	9.5
Ca	28	2.5

NOTES: [a]17 May 1978; [c]n = 1
SOURCES: Alta. Envir. n.d.[b], Naquadat station 01AT05CD2020; [b]Alta. For. Ld. Wild. n.d.

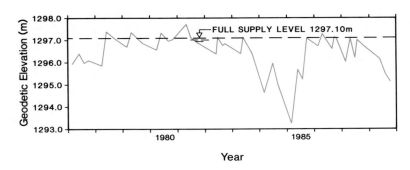

Figure 3. Water level of Chain Lakes Reservoir, 1977 to 1988.
SOURCE: Envir. Can. 1977–1988.

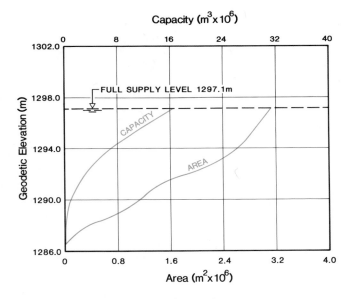

Figure 4. Area/capacity curve for Chain Lakes Reservoir.
SOURCE: Agric. Can. 1961.

Neill 1978). Rotifers were most abundant, with copepods next in abundance. No cladocerans were found.

Benthic samples were taken from a depth of 10 m on 17 May 1978 by Fish and Wildlife Division (MacNeill 1978). Aquatic earthworms (Oligochaeta) were most abundant (3 056/m²), followed by midge (Chironomidae) larvae (538/m²).

Fish

White suckers and rainbow trout are abundant in Chain Lakes Reservoir. Other sport fish that migrate into the reservoir via Willow Creek and which are found occasionally include cutthroat trout, brown trout, brook trout, bull trout and mountain whitefish. Forage fish species include fathead minnow, brook stickleback, longnose dace and lake chub. Longnose sucker also occur (Alta. For. Ld. Wild. n.d.; Walton 1979).

Since 1967, rainbow trout have been stocked annually in the reservoir by Fish and Wildlife Division (Radford 1978; Alta. En. Nat.

Resour. 1979–1985; Alta. For. Ld. Wild. 1986–1988). The trout in the reservoir thrived for the first five or six years when nutrient levels were high after the initial flooding of the valley. Trout growth rates were good and the angler success rate (0.30 trout/hour in 1970) was sufficient to attract numerous anglers. However, by 1970, white suckers became the dominant species in the reservoir and appeared to out-compete the trout for food: 1978 test netting caught 84% suckers (Radford 1978) and 1979 test netting caught 93% suckers (Alta. For. Ld. Wild. n.d.). In May 1978, the growth rate of rainbow trout was slow; age 4+ fish had a mean fork length of 259 mm and a mean weight of 193 g (MacNeill 1978). Angler success had declined to 0.24 trout/hour in 1977, and anglers reported catching up to 10 times as many suckers as trout.

To give the rainbow trout stocked in the reservoir a competitive edge, the fish introduced since 1978 have been approximately 12–cm long rather than fingerlings. However, suckers still dominate the fish community in the reservoir and in 1987 angler success had dropped to 0.17 rainbow trout per hour (based on 301 anglers) (Bishop 1989).

Wildlife

The diverse habitat of the Chain Lakes watershed is home to a wide variety of wildlife, from black and grizzly bears in the mountains to typical prairie animals in the grasslands around the reservoir. The marsh area created by seepage from the South Dam supports a diversity of plants and wildlife in the park, including 57 species of birds. Few waterbirds nest on the reservoir because aquatic vegetation is sparse, but Common Mergansers and Red-necked Grebes remain all summer and Common Loons have been seen nesting. Elk overwinter near the reservoir and moose and deer are present all year. Six colonies of Columbian ground squirrels in the park mark the eastern extent of this species in the area (Finlay and Finlay 1987).

J.M. Crosby

References

Agriculture Canada. 1961. Report on proposed Chain Lakes project. Prairie Farm Rehabilitation Admin. Alta. Reg. Office, Eng. Br., Calgary.

Alberta Energy and Natural Resources. 1979–1985. Fish planting list. Fish Wild. Div., Edmonton.

Alberta Environment. n.d.[a]. Devel. Op. Div., Irrig. Headworks Br. Unpubl. data, Edmonton.

———. n.d.[b]. Envir. Assess. Div., Envir. Qlty. Monit. Br. Unpubl. data, Edmonton.

———. n.d.[c]. Tech. Serv. Div., Hydrol. Br. Unpubl. data, Edmonton.

———. n.d.[d]. Tech. Serv. Div., Surv. Br. Unpubl. data, Edmonton.

Alberta Forestry, Lands and Wildlife. n.d. Fish Wild. Div. Unpubl. data, Edmonton.

———. 1986–1988. Fish planting list. Fish Wild. Div., Edmonton.

———. 1988. Boating in Alberta. Fish Wild. Div., Edmonton.

———. 1989. Guide to sportfishing. Fish Wild. Div., Edmonton.

Alberta Hotel Association. 1988. 1988 Alberta campground guide. Prep. for Travel Alta., Edmonton.

Alberta Research Council. 1972. Geological map of Alberta. Nat. Resour. Div., Alta. Geol. Surv., Edmonton.

Bishop, F. 1989. Alta. For. Ld. Wild., Fish Wild. Div., Lethbridge. Pers. comm.

Crack, S. and B. Danielson. 1974. An ecological survey of Chain Lakes Provincial Park. Alta. Ld. For., Prov. Park Plan. Div., Edmonton.

Energy, Mines and Resources Canada. 1979, 1980. National topographic series 1:50 000 82J/8 (1979), 82J/1 (1980). Surv. Map. Br., Ottawa.

Environment Canada. 1977–1988. Surface water data. Prep. by Inland Waters Directorate. Water Surv. Can., Water Resour. Br., Ottawa.

———. 1982. Canadian climate normals, Vol. 7: Bright sunshine (1951–1980). Prep. by Atm. Envir. Serv. Supply Serv. Can., Ottawa.

Finlay, J. and C. Finlay. 1987. Parks in Alberta: A guide to peaks, ponds, parklands & prairies. Hurtig Publ., Edmonton.

MacNeill, J.W. 1978. Chain Lakes Reservoir: Lake survey inventory. Alta. Rec. Park Wild., Fish Wild. Div., Lethbridge.

Radford, D.S. 1978. Chain Lakes Reservoir: Fishery management plan. Alta. Rec. Park Wild., Fish Wild. Div., Lethbridge.

Strong, W.L. 1979. Ecological land classification and evaluation: Livingstone-Porcupine. Alta. En. Nat. Resour., Resour. Eval. Br., Edmonton.

——— and K.R. Leggat. 1981. Ecoregions of Alberta. Alta. En. Nat. Resour., Resour. Eval. Plan. Div., Edmonton.

Walton, B.D. 1979. The reproductive biology, early life history, and growth of white suckers, *Catastomus commersoni*, and longnose suckers, *C. catostomus*, in the Willow Creek-Chain Lakes system, Alberta. MSc thesis. Univ. Alta., Edmonton.

CROWSNEST LAKE

D. Huet

MAP SHEET: 82 G/10
LOCATION: Tp8 R5 W5
LAT/LONG: 49°38'N 114°38'W

Crowsnest Lake is a deep, blue lake situated in narrow, windswept Crowsnest Pass in southern Alberta, just east of the Alberta-British Columbia boundary. To reach the lake from the city of Lethbridge, follow Highway 3 west for about 135 km to the town of Coleman then continue west for another 10 km to the south side of the lake (Fig. 1). The lake is in the Municipality of Crowsnest Pass.

The origin of the name "Crowsnest" is unclear. It possibly arose following a battle when Blackfoot Indians cornered and defeated a group of Crow Indians, or it may refer to the sighting of a large crow's nest in the area; possibly, the lake was named for a mountain known to the Indians as Crow's Nest Mountain (Cousins 1981). The lake was called Old Man's Lake in the early days of settlement, and the Crowsnest River draining the lake was called the Middle Fork of the Oldman. The first white man through the pass was likely Father Jean de Smet in about 1845. Ten years later, the Palliser Expedition passed through the area.

A dam on the lake and flumes to the river were built in the early 1900s by Peter McLaren (the late Senator McLaren) to release water to float logs to his sawmill in Blairmore (Cousins 1981). This operation closed in 1920 and there is no longer a control structure on the lake. At the eastern end of the lake, the East Kootenay Power company operated a coal-fired power plant from 1927 to the mid–1950s, using locally mined coal. Strip mining for coal was carried out in the Crowsnest Creek drainage area from 1922 to 1929 and on nearby Tent Mountain from 1949 to 1955 and from 1969 to 1980 (Fig. 1). Summit Lime Works extracts lime from quarries along the north shore of Island Lake and along Crowsnest Creek. The limestone is processed at a plant located between Crowsnest and Island lakes. The only residences near Crowsnest Lake are associated with the lime plant and there are almost no other residences in the drainage basin (Fitch 1978). Other developments near Crowsnest Lake include a motel and a church camp on its west shore. The Canadian Pacific Railway hugs the north shore and Highway 3 skirts the south shore.

There is no public campground on Crowsnest Lake; the nearest one is Island Lake Campground, 4 km west on Highway 3. This facility is operated by Alberta Transportation and Utilities and offers 35 campsites, picnic tables and shelters (Alta. Hotel Assoc. 1989). Boat access to Crowsnest Lake is available at a public boat launch at the east end of the lake. There are no boating restrictions for Crowsnest Lake but only battery-powered motors are permitted on adjoining Emerald Lake (Alta. For. Ld. Wild. 1988).

Crowsnest Lake is moderately popular for sport fishing for rainbow trout, mountain whitefish and lake trout. No fishing with bait fish is permitted in the region, including Crowsnest Lake. All flowing water is open to fishing only from 1 June through 31 October. A bait ban is in effect in flowing water except from 15 August to 31 October (Alta. For. Ld. Wild. 1989). The clear water and barren, weed-free shores make Crowsnest Lake attractive for swimming, but the low water temperature deters all but the hardiest swimmers.

Drainage Basin Characteristics

Crowsnest Lake lies in a major mountain pass that cuts through the mountains that form the Continental Divide in southern Alberta. The pass separates two ranges, the northern High Rock Range and the southern Flathead Range (Fig. 1). The highest peaks in the basin are

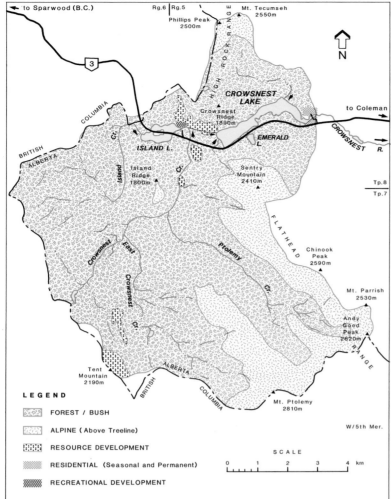

Figure 1. Features of the drainage basin of Crowsnest Lake.
SOURCES: Alta. Envir. n.d.[a]; En. Mines Resour. Can. 1973. Updated with
1985 aerial photos.

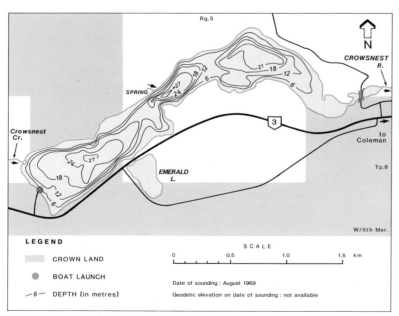

Figure 2. Bathymetry and shoreline features of Crowsnest Lake.
BATHYMETRY SOURCE: Alta. Envir. n.d.[b].

Table 1. Characteristics of Crowsnest Lake drainage basin.

area (excluding lake) (km²)[a]	85.6
soil[b, c]	Eutric Brunisols, Regosols
bedrock geology[d]	Upper Paleozoic Era: carbonates, shale Alberta Group (Upper Cretaceous): shale, sandstone; marine
terrain[b]	mountainous
ecoregion[b]	Montane; Subalpine; Alpine
dominant vegetation[b, c]	Douglas fir, fescue; pine, spruce, trembling aspen; heath, willow
mean annual inflow (m³)[a, e]	27.6 x 10⁶
mean annual sunshine (h)[f]	2 370

NOTE: [e]excluding groundwater inflow
SOURCES: [a]Alta. Envir. n.d.[a]; [b]Strong and Leggat 1981; [c]Boyacioglu and van Waas
1975; [d]Alta. Res. Counc. 1972; [f]Envir. Can. 1982

Mount Tecumseh (2 550 m) to the north and Ptolemy Mountain
(2 815 m) to the south. The drainage basin is bordered on three sides
by the Alberta–British Columbia border. When the British Columbia
border was established in the late nineteenth century, it was to
follow the continental divide—all land in British Columbia was to
drain to the Pacific Ocean and all land east of the border was to drain
to the Atlantic or Arctic oceans. However, recent examination of the
Crowsnest drainage basin shows that the official Alberta–British Columbia boundary strays in some places from the continental divide
(Alta. Envir. n.d.[a]). Therefore, some land in Alberta actually drains
to the Pacific Ocean, whereas some land in southern British Columbia drains to Hudson Bay.

The mountains and ridges surrounding Crowsnest Lake are
formed of erosion-resistant Paleozoic limestone, whereas the lower
ridges are formed of sandstone. The shape of the pass and the
surficial deposits are a result of the last Cordilleran glaciation which
flowed from the divide toward the plains to the east. This ice sheet
deposited a heterogeneous mixture of stony and calcareous glacial
till in lateral moraines along the mountain slopes. These moraines
subsequently eroded and formed alluvial fans throughout the valley;
the area between Island and Crowsnest lakes is an example of such
a fan (Boyacioglu and van Waas 1975).

The Crowsnest Lake basin includes portions of three ecoregions:
Montane, Subalpine and Alpine (Table 1). The Montane Ecoregion
includes the south-facing slopes just north of the lake up to an
elevation of approximately 1 500 m (Boyacioglu and van Waas
1975). On these coarse-textured, dry slopes, Douglas fir groves are
interspersed with areas of grass and low shrubs; the soils are typically
well-drained Eutric Brunisols. The valley floor supports white spruce
and pine, and willow and birch grow in poorly drained areas. The
Subalpine Ecoregion lies above the Montane Ecoregion and extends
up to an elevation of about 2 135 m. Coniferous forests of lodgepole
pine, Engelmann spruce and white spruce are generally present; they
are underlain by Eutric Brunisolic soils. On well-drained south-facing
slopes north of the Crowsnest Valley, areas of trembling aspen and
fescue grasses grow on Chernozemic soils. Above the treeline is the
Alpine Ecoregion (Fig. 1), which supports only sparse vegetation that
consists mostly of forbs, heaths, shrubby willow and dwarf birch,
with patches of krumholz alpine fir and Engelmann spruce. Soils are
Brunisols and Regosols (Strong and Leggat 1981).

A disjunct area that includes most of the shoreline of Crowsnest
Lake, all of Emerald Lake and the south-facing slopes above the
valley has been proposed as a natural area (Alta. For. Ld. Wild.
1987). This area has vegetation typical of the Montane Ecoregion:
Douglas fir, limber pine and grassland. As of 1988, the area had
Protective Notation status.

The major inflow to Crowsnest Lake is Crowsnest Creek, which
flows northward from the slopes of Tent and Ptolemy mountains. It
is joined by the outflow from Island Lake, then enters the west end
of Crowsnest Lake. Emerald Lake, which receives runoff from Sentry
Mountain, also flows into Crowsnest Lake. The only other tributary
of any significance is a stream formed by springs in a cave on the

Table 2. Characteristics of Crowsnest Lake.

elevation (m)[a]	approximately 1 375
surface area (km²)[b, c]	1.19
volume (m³)[b, c]	16.1 x 10⁶
maximum depth (m)[b, c]	27.4
mean depth (m)[b, c]	13.5
shoreline length (km)[b, c]	8.8
mean annual lake evaporation (mm)[d]	615
mean annual precipitation (mm)[d]	569
mean residence time (yr)[d, e]	0.6
control structure	none

NOTES: [b]on date of sounding: Aug. 1969; [e]excluding groundwater inflow
SOURCES: [a]En. Mines Resour. Can. 1973; [c]Alta. Envir. n.d.[b]; [d]Alta. Envir. n.d.[a]

Table 3. Major ions and related water quality variables for Crowsnest Lake. Average concentrations in mg/L; pH in pH units. Samples from the surface collected 6 times from 29 Apr. to 14 Oct. 1976[a]. S.E. = standard error.

	Mean	S.E.
pH (range)	7.9–8.3	—
total dissolved solids (calculated)	214	9.1
turbidity (NTU)	2[b]	0.3
HCO₃	144	4.9
Na	<2	—
K	<1[b]	—
Cl	<2	—
SO₄	23	4.2
Secchi depth (m)	3.0	0.33

NOTES: [a]samples collected by Fish and Wildlife Division, Lethbridge, analysis by Alberta Environment, Edmonton; [b]n = 5
SOURCE: Fitch 1978

north shore; additional groundwater inflow is also likely important in the lake. The outflow from the lake is the Crowsnest River, a major tributary of the Oldman River.

Lake Basin Characteristics

Crowsnest Lake is long (3.9 km) and narrow (maximum width of 0.7 km), with three deep basins connected by slightly shallower shelves (Fig. 2). The lake basin drops steeply on most sides to a maximum depth of 27.4 m (Table 2). Areas shallower than 3 m constitute only 15% of the area of the lake (Fig. 3) and are located mostly at the east end of the lake and in a small area on the north shore.

The shoreline is composed of bedrock outcrops, large boulders and gravel. The substrate is mostly gravel and fractured shale in the littoral zone; deeper areas have a silt substrate. Near the inlet, divers report a whitish-gray deposit, which probably originated from the lime works, and in the western portion of the lake coal particles are common (Fitch 1978). The residence time of water in the lake is estimated to be 0.6 years (Alta. Envir. n.d.[a]). The lake level has not been monitored and there is no information on its fluctuations.

Water Quality

Some components of the water quality of Crowsnest Lake were sampled by Fish and Wildlife Division on six occasions during the open-water season of 1976 (Fitch 1978).

Crowsnest is a freshwater lake (Table 3). In 1976, the temperature and dissolved oxygen concentrations at the top and the bottom of the water column, as well as the Secchi depth, were measured monthly from late April to mid-October (Fitch 1978). Weak thermal stratification was apparent from early July until late August (surface

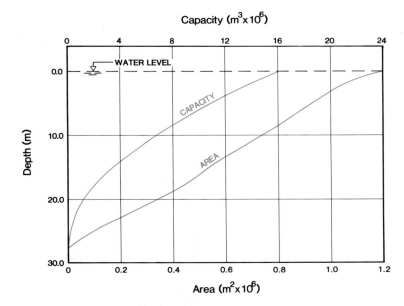

Figure 3. Area/capacity curve for Crowsnest Lake.
SOURCE: Alta. Envir. n.d.[b].

maximum 13.5°C; bottom maximum 10°C). The dissolved oxygen concentration at the surface ranged between 9 and 11 mg/L throughout the summer; in the bottom water, it dropped from 10 mg/L in early June to 7 mg/L in late July. The Secchi depth varied from 1.9 to 4.2 m; turbidity was attributed to silt suspended by wind and to runoff from the lime plant. Under-ice dissolved oxygen concentrations were monitored on 8 January 1981 at a site where the lake was 17–m deep. The concentration of dissolved oxygen dropped from 13 mg/L at the surface to 8 mg/L on the bottom (Alta. For. Ld. Wild. n.d.).

There are no data on nutrients or chlorophyll a concentrations in Crowsnest Lake, so it is difficult to determine the lake's trophic status. The lack of aquatic vegetation, the apparent sparseness of algae, the dominance of diatoms, the high dissolved oxygen concentrations and the low temperatures indicate that the lake is likely oligotrophic.

Biological Characteristics

Plants

The phytoplankton was sampled monthly from April to October in 1976 during a Fish and Wildlife Division study; however, since the net was made of number 20 mesh silk bolting cloth, the small algae were probably missed (Fitch 1978). A total of 25 species were identified. Diatoms (Bacillariophyta) were dominant in every sample; in descending order, the most abundant diatom genera were *Asterionella*, *Melosira*, *Fragilaria*, *Stephanodiscus* and *Tabellaria*. Golden-brown algae (Chrysophyta) were sparse in most samples; *Dinobryon divergens* was the most abundant species. Only one species of green algae (Chlorophyta), *Pediastrum* sp., was found, and then only in early spring and late autumn.

Aquatic macrophytes are very sparse in Crowsnest Lake; the rocky shore and strong wave action inhibit growth along most of the shoreline.

Invertebrates

The zooplankton was sampled monthly from April through October in 1976 with a net of number 20 mesh silk bolting cloth (Fitch 1978). Twelve species were collected. Rotifers, primarily *Keratella cochlearis*, dominated throughout the sampling period and *Polyarthra* (*vulgaris*?), *Asplanchna* (*priodonta*?) and *Synchaeta* (*oblonga*?) were fairly abundant. Copepods, mostly *Diacyclops bicuspidatus thomasi*, were the next most numerous group. Cladocerans formed only a minor component of the zooplankton; *Bosmina longirostris* was the most abundant species.

In 1973, approximately 75 000 opossum shrimp (Mysidacea: *Mysis relicta*) from Kootenay Lake, British Columbia, were released into Crowsnest Lake to augment the food supply for trout (Alta. For. Ld. Wild. n.d.). None were caught in plankton tows in 1976 (Fitch 1978) and none have been seen in the stomach contents of fish caught to date (Fitch 1989).

Benthic invertebrates have not been comprehensively surveyed.

Fish

Six species of fish are known to inhabit the Crowsnest Lake area. Indigenous species include mountain whitefish and longnose suckers; forage species have not been documented (Alta. For. Ld. Wild. n.d.). Rainbow trout are likely indigenous, but they were also stocked in most years from 1926 to 1970 and from 1977 to 1979 in Crowsnest and/or Island lake. Cutthroat trout were planted in either Crowsnest or closely connected Island and Emerald lakes almost annually from 1974 to 1987. As well, an average of 8 500 lake trout were planted annually in Crowsnest Lake from 1977 to 1983 and in 1986 and 1987. Adult brook trout were introduced to Emerald and Island lakes in 1988 (Alta. Ld. For. 1949–1974; Alta. Rec. Parks Wild. 1975–1978; Alta. En. Nat. Resour. 1979–1985; Alta. For. Ld. Wild. 1986–1988).

Despite the intensive fish-stocking program, the sport fishery is poor in Emerald Lake and only sporadically good in Island Lake. Sport fishing for lake trout is moderate in Crowsnest Lake; anglers report catching fish that weigh up to 5 kg (Bishop 1989). Lake trout have also been caught in the Crowsnest River as far downstream as Lundbreck Falls (Fitch 1989). Test netting was carried out in late June and early July in 1986 in Crowsnest, Island and Emerald lakes (Alta. For. Ld. Wild. n.d.). Of the 111 fish caught in Crowsnest Lake, 61% were mountain whitefish, 16% were rainbow trout, 13% were longnose suckers, 7% were lake trout, and 3% were cutthroat trout. In Island Lake, the proportion of longnose suckers caught increased from 5% in 1975 to 30% in 1979 and to 58% in 1986. Of the 1986 catch (total of 103 fish), 22% were mountain whitefish and 20% were cutthroat or brook trout. In Emerald Lake, only three fish were caught—two mountain whitefish and one cutthroat trout. The 1986 test netting indicated that lake trout in Crowsnest Lake grow very slowly to age five, then rapidly after age five. This is likely due to a shift in prey from midge larvae to mountain whitefish.

Wildlife

Crowsnest Lake does not provide good waterfowl habitat because of its rocky, wave-washed shore. Common Mergansers, Canada Geese and Mallards occasionally visit the lake (Fitch 1989).

J.M. Crosby

References

Alberta Energy and Natural Resources. 1979–1985. Fish planting list. Fish Wild. Div., Edmonton.
Alberta Environment. n.d.[a]. Tech. Serv. Div., Hydrol. Br. Unpubl. data, Edmonton.
———. n.d.[b]. Tech. Serv. Div., Surv. Br. Unpubl. data, Edmonton.
Alberta Forestry, Lands and Wildlife. n.d. Fish Wild. Div. Unpubl. data, Edmonton.
———. 1986–1988. Fish planting list. Fish Wild. Div., Edmonton.
———. 1987. A summary of Alberta's natural areas reserved and established. Pub. Ld. Div., Ld. Mgt. Devel. Br. Unpubl. rep., Edmonton.
———. 1988. Boating in Alberta. Fish Wild. Div., Edmonton.
———. 1989. Guide to sportfishing. Fish Wild. Div., Edmonton.
Alberta Hotel Association. 1989. Alberta campground guide 1989. Prep. for Travel Alta., Edmonton.
Alberta Lands and Forests. 1949–1974. Fish planting list. Fish Wild. Div., Edmonton.
Alberta Recreation, Parks and Wildlife. 1975–1978. Fish planting list. Fish Wild. Div., Edmonton.
Alberta Research Council. 1972. Geological map of Alberta. Nat. Resour. Div., Alta. Geol. Surv., Edmonton.
Bishop, F. 1989. Alta. For. Ld. Wild., Fish Wild. Div., Lethbridge. Pers. comm.
Boyacioglu, E. and C. van Waas. 1975. Biophysical analysis and evaluation of capability, Crowsnest Pass. Alta. En. Nat. Resour., Tech. Div., Edmonton.
Cousins, W.J. 1981. A history of Crow's Nest Pass. The Hist. Trails Soc. Alta., Lethbridge.
Energy, Mines and Resources Canada. 1973. National topographic series 1:50 000 82G/10 (1973). Surv. Map. Br., Ottawa.
Environment Canada. 1982. Canadian climate normals, Vol. 7: Bright sunshine (1951–1980). Prep. by Atm. Envir. Serv. Supply Serv. Can., Ottawa.
Fitch, L. 1978. A limnological survey of Crowsnest Lake. Alta. Rec. Parks Wild., Fish Wild. Div., Lethbridge.
———. 1989. Alta. For. Ld. Wild., Fish Wild. Div., Lethbridge. Pers. comm.
Strong, W.L. and K.R. Leggat. 1981. Ecoregions of Alberta. Alta. En. Nat. Resour., Resour. Eval. Plan. Div., Edmonton.

LITTLE BOW LAKE RESERVOIR

MAP SHEET: 82I/2
LOCATION: Tp14 R20 W4
LAT/LONG: 50°12'N 112°40'W

Little Bow Lake Reservoir is a small, off-stream reservoir located in the County of Vulcan, 50 km southeast of the town of Vulcan and 180 km southeast of the city of Calgary. Although the reservoir is in the Oldman River drainage basin, most of its water is diverted to it from the Bow River basin. To reach the reservoir from Calgary, drive south and east on Highway 24 to the village of Champion. Turn east onto Secondary Road 529 and drive for 30 km, then drive south on Secondary Road 845 for about 3.5 km. Turn onto a local road that provides access to a small day-use area at a beach near the main dam (Fig. 1, 2). There are no campgrounds at the reservoir, but the day-use area, which was built in 1978 by Alberta Environment, includes a boat launch and provides the best access to the water. Federal boating regulations and provincial sport fishing regulations apply to Little Bow Lake Reservoir, but there are no additional boating or fishing regulations specific to the reservoir (Alta. For. Ld. Wild. 1988; 1989).

Little Bow Lake Reservoir is situated in a depression surrounded by short grass prairie. For many centuries, members of the Blackfoot, Blood and Peigan tribes traversed the region, following vast herds of buffalo (IEC Beak Consult. Ltd. et al. 1983). Homesteaders settled in the area by 1907, and soon fenced the open range. Grain farming became the primary land use. By 1920, the Canada Land and Irrigation Company had completed construction of both McGregor Lake and Little Bow Lake Reservoir. Large volumes of water were brought by canal from the Bow River near Carseland to McGregor Lake, the water then flowed through 20 km of canal to Little Bow Lake Reservoir, then canals took the water further east to provide water for irrigation. In 1954, Travers Reservoir was built, providing more storage volume and replacing most of the canal between McGregor Lake and Little Bow Lake Reservoir. All three reservoirs and the connecting canals are now owned and operated by Alberta Environment as part of the Carseland-Bow River Headworks System that stores and delivers water for the Bow River Irrigation District to supply water for irrigation and to support multi-purpose water use.

Little Bow Lake Reservoir has very clear water and is locally popular for swimming, sport fishing, power boating and sailing. It also supports a small commercial fishery for lake whitefish. The reservoir has good recreation potential because of its excellent water quality and natural beaches; however, exposure to strong winds and the growth of aquatic plants limit some forms of recreation (Richard Strong Assoc. Ltd. 1983; R.L. & L. Envir. Serv. Ltd. 1985). There are no cottages around the reservoir.

Drainage Basin Characteristics

The natural drainage basin is small, only seven times the reservoir's surface area (Tables 1, 2). The watershed is part of an area with the lowest rainfall and highest evaporation in Canada. The drainage basin has porous soils and produces little natural runoff. The land is part of a flat to gently rolling glacial till plain located in the Short Grass Ecoregion (Strong and Leggat 1981). The natural vegetation, which is typical of short grass prairie, is dominated by grama and spear grasses. Trembling aspen, eastern cottonwood and willows grow along water courses, and buckbrush and wolf willow grow in depressions and coulees. Soils are predominantly Brown Chernozemics (Strong and Leggat 1981; Richard Strong Assoc. Ltd. 1983). There are some oil and gas wells in the drainage basin, but

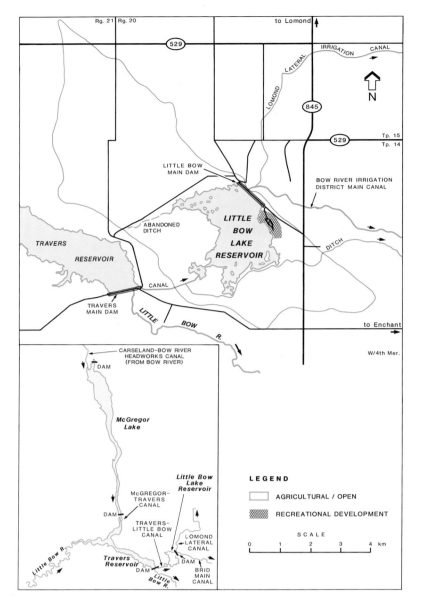

Figure 1. Features of the drainage basin of Little Bow Lake Reservoir.
Inset shows the relationship of the three reservoirs in the Carseland-Bow River Headworks System.
SOURCES: Alta. Envir. n.d.[c]; En. Mines Resour. Can. 1976; 1977. Updated with 1985 aerial photos.

Table 1. Characteristics of Little Bow Lake Reservoir drainage basin.

area (excluding lake) (km^2)[a]	37.6
soil[b]	Brown Chernozemics
bedrock geology[c]	Bearpaw Formation (Upper Cretaceous): shale, thin ironstone and bentonite beds; marine
terrain[b]	flat to gently rolling
ecoregion[b]	Short Grass
dominant vegetation[b]	grama and spear grasses
mean annual sunshine (h)[d]	2 344

SOURCES: [a]Alta. Envir. n.d.[c]; [b]Strong and Leggat 1981; [c]Alta. Res. Counc. 1972; [d]Envir. Can. 1982

Reservoir was built in 1954. Travers Reservoir was built with a full supply level of 856.18 m, which was not sufficiently higher than Little Bow Lake Reservoir to provide ample hydraulic head to move water quickly. Consequently, the operating full supply level of Little Bow Lake Reservoir was dropped almost 2.59 m, to 852.83 m. The canal from Travers Reservoir flows through a concrete chute into the southwest corner of Little Bow Lake Reservoir (Fig. 1). Part of the abandoned 1920 canal, which flowed from McGregor Lake into the northwest corner of Little Bow Lake Reservoir, is still visible. Little Bow Lake Reservoir now acts as a balancing rather than as a storage reservoir; therefore, its level is much more stable than the two upstream storage reservoirs. The details of the main dam are presented in Table 2. There are also four small "saddle dams" at the design full supply level on coulees on the perimeter, but these are now grass-covered and hard to discern.

The only outlet from Little Bow Lake Reservoir is in the main dam, which releases water into a canal that soon branches into the Lomond Lateral Canal and the Bow River Irrigation District Main Canal. All flow, both in and out of the reservoir, occurs between late April and mid-October (Table 2). The reservoir's volume is replaced 16 times per summer, a very high rate of exchange compared to natural lakes and most storage reservoirs.

The shape of Little Bow Lake Reservoir is quite different from that of upstream McGregor Lake and Travers Reservoir, as it fills a gently sloping, rectangular depression rather than a long, narrow, steeply sloping glacial meltwater channel. The bathymetric map (Fig. 2) was drawn for the reservoir's original design full supply level, almost 3 m above current levels. Because 30% of Little Bow Lake Reservoir is less than 2-m deep (Fig. 3), the reservoir is very sensitive to major water level fluctuations. Under present operation, however, a stable level is maintained—from 1975 to 1987, annual fluctuations averaged 0.25 m (Fig. 4).

One consequence of the gently sloping lake bottom and stable water level is that the nearshore areas support extensive weed beds (MacNeill 1978; Richard Strong Assoc. Ltd. 1983). However, strong prevailing westerly winds have created natural sand beaches in some areas, such as by the Alberta Environment day-use area on the east shore.

Water Quality

The water of Little Bow Lake Reservoir was sampled by Alberta Environment biweekly from May until October in 1983 and 1984 (Alta. Envir. n.d.[b]).

The attractive, clear water of the reservoir is a consequence of both its source (primarily the Bow River) and the retention of some suspended material and nutrients in upstream reservoirs (McGregor and Travers). The water chemistry of Little Bow Lake Reservoir is also similar to that of its source; conductivity, alkalinity and total dissolved solids are all low and the dominant ions are bicarbonate, sulphate and calcium (Table 3).

Little Bow Lake Reservoir is well-mixed during the summer because it is exposed to prevailing westerly winds. Consequently, temperatures were uniform throughout the water column from April through October in 1984 (Fig. 5). Dissolved oxygen remained high

no major population centres. The land around the reservoir is all Crown land, and most of it is leased for cattle grazing.

Little Bow Lake Reservoir is the furthest downstream of a series of three reservoirs that store water for the Bow River Irrigation District (Fig. 1, inset). The two others, McGregor Lake and Travers Reservoir, are much larger and provide the major portion of water storage capacity. Although Little Bow Lake Reservoir is considered an off-stream reservoir as it is not on any natural stream, it does have a large volume of water diverted through it from April to October. Except for an insignificant amount of inflow from rain and runoff from the natural drainage basin, all of the water in Little Bow Lake Reservoir comes from Travers Reservoir. In turn, Travers Reservoir receives approximately 90% of its inflow from the Bow River via McGregor Lake (Envir. Can. 1987). The remaining 10% of the water in Travers Reservoir comes from the Little Bow River, which receives about 90% of its inflow from water diverted from the Highwood River near the town of High River. Of the water entering Travers Reservoir, 3% flows over the spillway to maintain flow in the Little Bow River and 97% is diverted to Little Bow Lake Reservoir (Envir. Can. 1987).

Reservoir Characteristics

Little Bow Lake Reservoir was built with a design full supply level of 855.42 m (Table 2) and was operated close to that level until Travers

Table 2. Characteristics of Little Bow Lake Reservoir.

control structure[a]	Little Bow Dam
dam height (m)[a]	12.5
crest length (m)[a]	1 219.2
design full supply level (design FSL) (m)[b]	855.42
operating full supply level (op. FSL) (m)[b]	852.83
volume at op. FSL (m³)[b]	23.6 x 10⁶
volume at design FSL (m³)[b]	39.6 x 10⁶
flooded area at op. FSL (km²)[c]	5.44
maximum drawdown level (m)[c]	845.97
mean annual drawdown (1975–1987) (m)[b]	0.25
maximum depth at op. FSL (m)[b]	11.0
mean depth at op. FSL (m)[b]	4.3
shoreline length at design FSL (km)[d]	28.0
reservoir length at design FSL (km)[d]	4.3
reservoir width at design FSL (km)[d]	4.0
mean annual lake evaporation (mm)[e]	774
mean annual precipitation (mm)[e]	362
mean annual inflow volume (1976–1986) (m³)[f, g]	385.5 x 10⁶
mean annual outflow volume (1976–1986) (m³)[f]	383.7 x 10⁶
mean residence time (1976–1986) (yr)[e]	0.06
outlet capacity (m³/s)[b]	70.75

NOTE: [g]from Travers Reservoir; volume excludes groundwater inflow; natural inflow is insignificant
SOURCES: [a]Alta. Envir. n.d.[e]; [b]Alta. Envir. n.d.[a]; [c]Alta. Envir. n.d.[d]; [d]R.L. & L. Envir. Serv. Ltd. 1985; [e]Alta. Envir. n.d.[c]; [f]Envir. Can. 1987

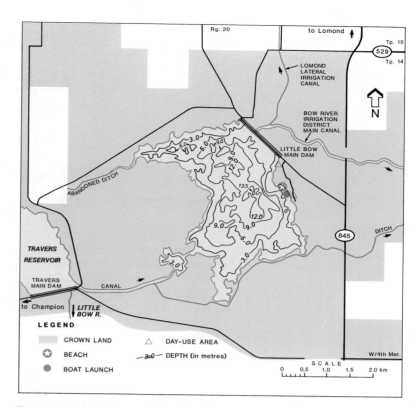

Figure 2. Bathymetry and shoreline features of Little Bow Lake Reservoir. Soundings made when the full supply level (FSL) was 855.42 m. Reservoir now operates at an FSL of 852.83 m.
BATHYMETRY SOURCE: Can. Ld. Irrig. Co. 1914.

Table 3. Major ions and related water quality variables for Little Bow Lake Reservoir. Average concentrations in mg/L; pH in pH units. Composite samples from the euphotic zone collected 9 times from 03 May to 24 Oct. 1984. S.E. = standard error.

	Mean	S.E.
pH (range)	7.1–8.3[a]	—
total alkalinity (CaCO₃)	131	1.8
specific conductivity (μS/cm)	363	6.2
total dissolved solids (calculated)	204	2.7
turbidity (NTU)	2	0.2
total hardness (CaCO₃)	159	2.1
HCO₃	157	2.9
CO₃	0	0
Mg	15	0.2
Na	12	0.4
K	1	0.1
Cl	5	0.1
SO₄	53	1.2
Ca	39	1.0

NOTE: [a]n = 7
SOURCE: Alta. Envir. n.d.[b], Naquadat station 05AL05AC8000

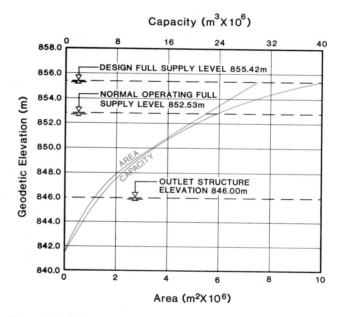

Figure 3. Area/capacity curve for Little Bow Lake Reservoir.
SOURCE: Alta. Envir. n.d.[d].

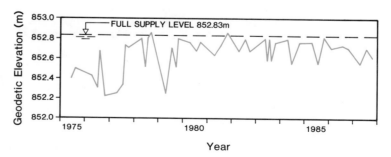

Figure 4. Water level of Little Bow Lake Reservoir, 1975 to 1987.
SOURCE: Alta. Envir. n.d.[a].

from surface to bottom during this period (Fig. 6). No data have been collected in winter, but dissolved oxygen levels must be sufficient for fish, since no winterkills have been reported (Alta. For. Ld. Wild. n.d.).

The mean total phosphorus (14 μg/L) and chlorophyll *a* (2.1 μg L) concentrations during the open-water season (Table 4) are similar to those in Travers Reservoir and are low compared to natural lakes in the area. Chlorophyll *a* concentrations were steady throughout the summer of 1984, with a maximum of 5 μg/L in October (Fig. 7). The fall maximum in Little Bow Lake Reservoir closely followed a September increase to 5.2 μg/L in Travers Reservoir. The trophic status of Little Bow Lake Reservoir is on the border between oligotrophic and mesotrophic.

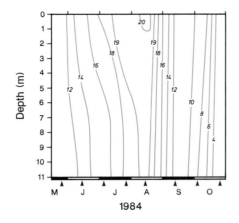

Figure 5. Temperature (°C) of Little Bow Lake Reservoir, 1984. Arrows indicate sampling dates.
SOURCE: Alta. Envir. n.d.[b].

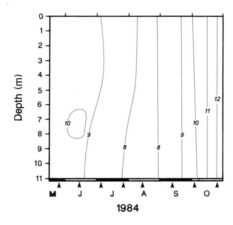

Figure 6. Dissolved oxygen (mg/L) in Little Bow Lake Reservoir. Arrows indicate sampling dates.
SOURCE: Alta. Envir. n.d.[b].

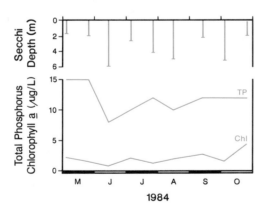

Figure 7. Total phosphorus, chlorophyll *a* and Secchi depths in Little Bow Lake Reservoir, 1984.
SOURCE: Alta. Envir. n.d.[b].

Table 4. Nutrient, chlorophyll *a* and Secchi depth data for Little Bow Lake Reservoir. Average concentrations in μg/L. Composite samples from the euphotic zone collected 13 times from 03 May to 18 Oct. 1983 and 9 times from 03 May to 24 Oct. 1984. S.E. = standard error.

	1983		1984	
	Mean	S.E.	Mean	S.E.
total phosphorus	16[a]	0.9	12	0.8
total Kjeldahl nitrogen	361	32.7	393	93.9
$NO_3 + NO_2$–nitrogen	8	1.6	5	1.0
iron	—	—	17[c]	3.7
chlorophyll *a*	2.2[b]	0.4	2.0	0.4
Secchi depth (m)	3.2	0.3	3.5	0.55

NOTES: [a]n = 12; [b]n = 9; [c]n = 7
SOURCE: Alta. Envir. n.d.[b], Naquadat station 05AL05AC8000

Table 5. Growth rates for lake whitefish captured from Little Bow Lake Reservoir, 1957 to 1978. Samples from commercial harvest and test netting. n = sample size.

Age Class	n	Mean Annual Increase in Length (cm)	Mean Annual Increase in Weight (g)
2	2	14.1	156
3	45	11.3	630
4	150	2.0	160
5	120	3.0	228
6	123	2.6	152
7	62	−0.9	111
8	50	1.8	64
9	34	0.3	56
10	17	2.1	212
11	7	1.2	205
12	1	9.3	1 750

SOURCE: modified from MacNeill 1978

Biological Characteristics

Plants

There are no data on the algae in Little Bow Lake Reservoir, nor are there data on macrophytes except for reports of weedy areas along the shore (MacNeill 1978; Richard Strong Assoc. Ltd. 1983).

Invertebrates

The zooplankton in the reservoir was studied monthly from June until October in 1975 (English 1977). The density of zooplankton was highest in June (2.92 mL/L), when rotifers were dominant, and in July (2.91 mL/L), when copepods were dominant. The density decreased to 0.29 mL/L in August, then increased to 1.15 mL/L in October, when rotifers again were dominant.

The only record of benthic invertebrates is from a 1964 study (MacNeill 1978). Samples were taken from three sites once a month from May to August. Midge larvae (Chironomidae) dominated (by number), except in June, when more clams (Pelecypoda) were found. Scuds (Amphipoda) and aquatic earthworms (Oligochaeta) were also numerous.

Fish

Ten species of fish have been found in Little Bow Lake Reservoir (Alta. For. Ld. Wild. n.d.; MacNeill 1978). Lake whitefish, northern pike, burbot, longnose suckers and white suckers are the most abundant. Rainbow trout are present but, as they cannot spawn in Little Bow Lake Reservoir, the population depends on migration from

Travers Reservoir. Spottail shiners and yellow perch are present, and shorthead redhorse and brown trout are rarely captured. No fish have been stocked in the reservoir. Therefore, those present are either descendants of fish that migrated from McGregor Lake before 1954, or descendants of fish that migrated from Travers Reservoir since 1954. High water velocities through irrigation structures in and out of Little Bow Lake Reservoir prevent fish from moving from Little Bow Lake Reservoir back to Travers Reservoir, or from returning to Little Bow Lake Reservoir once they go through the outlet structure.

Little Bow Lake Reservoir supports a modest sport fishery for northern pike and rainbow trout and a commercial fishery for lake whitefish. There are no catch data for the sport fishery. The commercial fishery has operated since 1948/49; 90% of the catch is lake whitefish. An annual quota of 11 300 kg of whitefish has been in effect since 1968. The annual catch from the 1983/84 season to the 1985/86 season averaged 17 897 kg of lake whitefish, 242 kg of northern pike, 32 kg of suckers, 21 kg of burbot and 15 kg of trout—an average total catch of 18 207 kg/year (Alta. For. Ld. Wild. n.d.; IEC Beak Consult. Ltd. et al. 1983). Table 5 gives the average annual growth rates of lake whitefish in Little Bow Lake Reservoir for the period from 1957 to 1978. Growth rates were more rapid than those in McGregor Lake or Travers Reservoir.

Wildlife

There is little information on the wildlife using Little Bow Lake Reservoir. The reservoir's stable water level, crenate shoreline and many islands provide important nesting areas for geese, gulls and cormorants (Markham 1978; Richard Strong Assoc. Ltd. 1983).

J.M. Crosby

References

Alberta Environment. n.d.[a]. Devel. Op. Div., Irrig. Headworks Br. Unpubl. data, Edmonton.
————. n.d.[b]. Envir. Assess. Div., Envir. Qlty. Monit. Br. Unpubl. data, Edmonton.
————. n.d.[c]. Tech. Serv. Div., Hydrol. Br. Unpubl. data, Edmonton.
————. n.d.[d]. Tech. Serv. Div., Surv. Br. Unpubl. data, Edmonton.
————. n.d.[e]. Water Resour. Mgt. Div., Dam Safety Br. Unpubl. data, Edmonton.
Alberta Forestry, Lands and Wildlife. n.d. Fish Wild. Div. Unpubl. data, Edmonton.
————. 1988. Boating in Alberta. Fish Wild. Div., Edmonton.
————. 1989. Guide to sportfishing. Fish Wild. Div., Edmonton.
Alberta Research Council. 1972. Geological map of Alberta. Nat. Resour. Div., Alta. Geol. Surv., Edmonton.
Canada Land and Irrigation Company. 1914. McGregor Reservoir, Plan. No. 1042. Can. Ld. Irrig. Co., Calgary.
Energy, Mines and Resources Canada. 1976, 1977. National topographic series 1:50 000 82I/7 (1976), 82I/2 (1977). Surv. Map. Br., Ottawa.
English, W.G. 1977. A limnological survey of Little Bow Reservoir. Alta. Rec. Parks Wild., Fish Wild. Div., Lethbridge.
Environment Canada. 1982. Canadian climate normals, Vol. 7: Bright sunshine (1951–1980). Prep. by Atm. Envir. Serv. Supply Serv. Can., Ottawa.
————. 1987. Historical streamflow summary, Alberta. Water Surv. Can., Water Resour. Br., Ottawa.
IEC Beak Consultants Ltd., Techman Engineering Ltd. and Aresco Ltd. 1983. Environmental overview of the Little Bow River basin. Prep. for Alta. Envir., Plan. Div., Edmonton.
MacNeill, J.W. 1978. A review of the history and management of the fishery resource of Little Bow Reservoir. Alta. Rec. Parks Wild., Fish Wild. Div., Edmonton.
Markham, B.J. 1978. Status of the Double-crested Cormorant (*Phalocrocorax auritus*) in Canada. Prep. for Commit. on the Status of Endangered Wild. in Can. by Alta. Rec. Parks Wild., Fish Wild. Div., Edmonton.
Richard Strong Associates Limited. 1983. McGregor, Travers, Little Bow Reservoir vicinity recreation development study. Prep. for Alta. Envir., Plan. Div., Edmonton.
R.L. & L. Environmental Services Ltd. 1985. A compendium of existing environmental data on Alberta reservoirs. Prep. for Alta. Envir. Res. Trust, Edmonton.
Strong, W.L. and K.R. Leggat. 1981. Ecoregions of Alberta. Alta. En. Nat. Resour., Resour. Eval. Plan. Div., Edmonton.

McGREGOR LAKE

MAP SHEET: 82I
LOCATION: Tp17, 18 R21 W4
LAT/LONG: 50°24'N 112°50'W

McGregor Lake is an offstream storage reservoir created in 1920 by the completion of two dams bracketing Snake Lake in Snake Valley. It is situated 30 km east of the town of Vulcan in the County of Vulcan. McGregor Lake, Travers Reservoir and Little Bow Lake Reservoir are all part of the Carseland-Bow River Headworks System that is owned and operated by Alberta Environment and delivers water to the Bow River Irrigation District (BRID) (Fig. 1, inset). McGregor Lake is in the Oldman River drainage basin, but almost all the water in it is derived via diversion from the Bow River near the hamlet of Carseland.

For centuries, the Snake Valley was a major thoroughfare for members of the Blackfoot Confederacy (Milo Dist. Hist. Soc. 1973). By the 1880s, British and European settlers had arrived and ranching was well established; homesteading and cultivation began soon after the turn of the century (IEC Beak Consult. Ltd. et al. 1983). The combination of rich soil and dry climate soon led to an interest in irrigation, and McGregor Lake was one of the first developments to meet this need.

McGregor Lake was created when the British-owned Canada Land and Irrigation Company built the South and North McGregor dams and a canal to bring water from the Bow River near Carseland. The reservoir was named after J.D. McGregor, the company's Canadian manager who became Lieutenant-Governor of Manitoba in 1929 (Holmgren and Holmgren 1976). Construction of the dams started in 1909; the outlet works were completed in 1919 and reservoir filling began in 1920 (Walk and Hurndall 1978[a]; 1978[b]). In 1950, the federal Prairie Farm Rehabilitation Administration assumed control. From 1952 to 1954, the original homogeneous earthfill South Dam was modified to a zoned earthfill dam (Walk and Hurndall 1978[b]). In 1973, McGregor Lake and its control structures were transferred to Alberta Environment.

The population centre closest to the lake is the village of Milo (population 117 in 1986), located about 2 km to the northeast (Fig. 1). The land up to the full supply level of the reservoir is Crown land; the Crown also owns about 30% of the land above the full supply level and most of it is leased for grazing (Fig. 2). There are no cottage developments and very few recreational facilities on the lake. The best access is at McGregor Lake Recreation Area (formerly Milo Campground), an Alberta Environment day-use site at the northwest corner of the lake (Fig. 2). Facilities include a boat launch, a playground, a baseball diamond and two picnic shelters. Small boats can also be launched at Lomond Crossing, where Secondary Road 531 crosses the lake.

McGregor Lake has attractive, clear water. Algal concentrations are usually low and do not interfere with recreational use. Activities enjoyed at the lake include picnicking, swimming, fishing, wind surfing, canoeing, water skiing and power boating. Federal boating regulations apply but there are no restrictions specific to the reservoir (Alta. For. Ld. Wild. 1988). However, boaters should be aware of the strong prevailing winds from the west and southwest that can cause high waves (Richard Strong Assoc. Ltd. 1983). The lake supports a substantial commercial fishery for lake whitefish and a sport fishery for northern pike, lake whitefish and rainbow trout. Provincial sport fishing limits and regulations apply to McGregor Lake. The inflowing canal from the Bow River between Secondary Road 542 and the reservoir is closed to fishing from 1 September to 30 November (Alta. For. Ld. Wild. 1989).

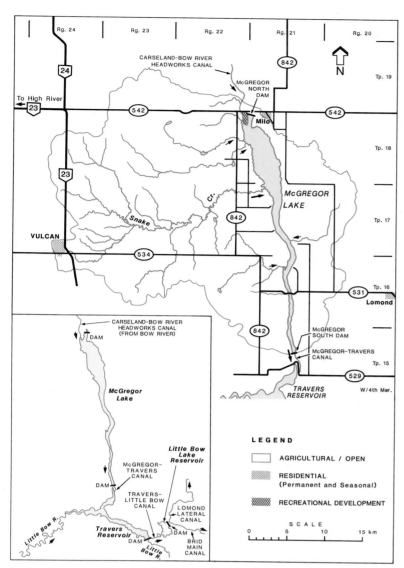

Figure 1. Features of the drainage basin of McGregor Lake. Inset shows the relationship between the three reservoirs in the Carseland-Bow River Headworks System.
SOURCES: Alta. Envir. n.d.[c]; En. Mines Resour. Can. 1977. Updated with 1981 aerial photos.

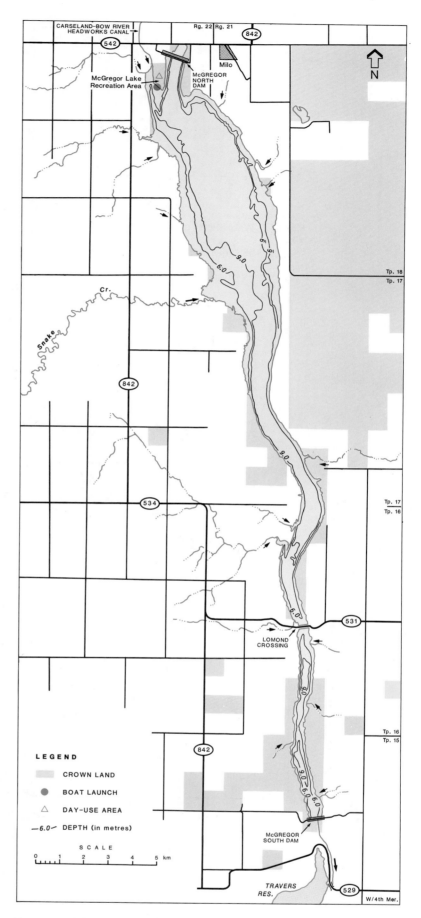

Figure 2. Bathymetry and shoreline features of McGregor Lake.
Surveyed before reservoir was filled.
BATHYMETRY SOURCE: Can. Ld. Irrig. Co. 1914.

Drainage Basin Characteristics

The natural watershed of McGregor Lake is 993 km² (Table 1). The topography of the land varies from generally flat in the north to hummocky and rolling toward the south and southwest (Richard Strong Assoc. Ltd. 1983). The lake is located in a valley that formed as a glacial outwash channel after the last ice-age. The sides of the valley are dissected by coulees.

The basin lies within the Mixed Grass Ecoregion (Strong and Leggat 1981). Natural vegetation in the region consists of short grasses, bunch grasses and long grasses. Woody plants such as trembling aspen, balsam poplar, eastern cottonwood, willow and other shrubs grow in valleys and coulees where more moisture is available than on the arid plain (Richard Strong Assoc. Ltd. 1983). Much of the natural vegetation in the basin has been replaced by cereal crops. Soils are mostly Orthic Dark Brown Chernozemics (Wyatt and Newton 1925; Wyatt et al. 1960; Greenlee 1974).

Cattle grazing and dryland farming of crops such as wheat, barley, hay, canola and rye are the dominant agricultural land uses (IEC Beak Consult. Ltd. et al. 1983). There is a gas processing plant near the south end of the drainage basin, and a large number of cattle and swine feedlots, and several oil, gas and coal fields in the area. The town of Vulcan is located on the western border of the watershed (Fig. 1).

A few small permanent and intermittent streams enter McGregor Lake, but most of the inflow (97%) comes from the Bow River near Carseland via 64 km of canal. This water enters the north end of the

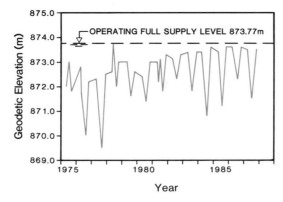

Figure 3. Water level of McGregor Lake, 1975 to 1987.
SOURCE: Alta. Envir. n.d.[a].

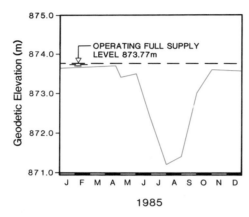

Figure 4. Annual water level fluctuation in McGregor Lake, 1985.
SOURCE: Alta. Envir. n.d.[a].

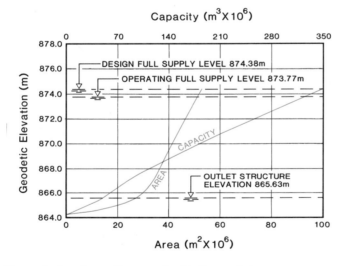

Figure 5. Area/capacity curve for McGregor Lake.
SOURCE: Alta. Envir. n.d.[d].

Table 1. Characteristics of McGregor Lake drainage basin.

area (excluding lake) (km²)[a]	993
soil[b, c]	Orthic Dark Brown Chernozemics
bedrock geology[d]	Bearpaw Formation (Upper Cretaceous): shale, thin ironstone and bentonite beds; marine
	Horseshoe Canyon Formation (Upper Cretaceous): sandstone, mudstone, shale; ironstone, scattered coal and bentonite beds; mainly nonmarine
terrain[b]	level to hilly in north, undulating to hilly in south
ecoregion[e]	Mixed Grass
dominant vegetation[e]	spear, grama, wheat grasses
mean annual sunshine (h)[f]	2 334

SOURCES: [a]Alta. Envir. n.d.[c]; [b]Wyatt and Newton 1925; Wyatt et al. 1960; [c]Greenlee 1974; [d]Alta. Res. Counc. 1972; [e]Strong and Leggat 1981; [f]Envir. Can. 1982

reservoir, flows through four culverts at Lomond Crossing, and leaves through an outlet structure in the dam at the south end. From 1920 to 1954, water flowed out of McGregor Lake through 20 km of canal directly to Little Bow Lake Reservoir. In 1954, Travers Reservoir was built to replace most of this canal; now, water from McGregor Lake flows through the McGregor-Travers Canal to Travers Reservoir, then to Little Bow Lake Reservoir, and then to the Bow River Irrigation District to supply water for irrigation and to support multi-purpose water use.

Reservoir Characteristics

The shore around McGregor Lake varies from hills at the south end, to steep, eroded perpendicular banks in the middle section, to flatlands at the north end (Wyatt and Newton 1925; Wyatt et al. 1960). The bottom sediments range from sandy clay to silt and clay; an artificial beach of sand and gravel has been built at the recreation area at the north end of the lake.

The reservoir was built with a design full supply level of 874.38 m, but the operating full supply level has not exceeded 873.77 m (Alta. Envir. n.d.[a]). The reservoir bottom slopes steeply to a maximum depth of 9.7 m (Table 2, Fig. 2). The mean depth at the operating full supply level is 6.5 m. The reservoir first reached the operating full supply level in 1971. Since then, the surface elevation of the lake during the open-water season has fluctuated between a low of 869.8 m in 1977 and the operating full supply level in 1985 (Fig. 3). Annual fluctuations averaged 2.0 m from 1975 to 1987, but in three years during this period the annual fluctuation exceeded 3.0 m. The lake level stays almost constant from November to May. Typical annual fluctuations are shown in Figure 4; the reservoir is filled in the fall and the level is held steady through the winter, then water is withdrawn throughout the summer to meet demand for water. When the reservoir is drawn down to 2 m below the operating full supply level, the surface area is reduced by 20% (Fig. 5).

The main inflow via the Carseland-Bow River Headworks Canal is usually restricted to the period between late April and early November. The reservoir volume is usually exchanged at least once every summer; virtually no inflow or outflow occurs from November to late April.

Water Quality

McGregor Lake was sampled in 1983 and 1984 by Alberta Environment (Alta. Envir. n.d.[b]). It is a freshwater lake (total dissolved solids average 185 mg/L, Table 3) dominated by bicarbonate, sulphate and calcium ions. The ionic composition of the lake is similar to that of its main source, the Bow River.

In 1984, the central region of McGregor Lake was only very weakly thermally stratified between May and mid-August (Fig. 6).

Table 2. Characteristics of McGregor Lake.

control structures[a]	South McGregor Dam: zoned earthfill North McGregor Dam: homogeneous earthfill
South Dam height (m)[a]	13.1
South Dam crest length (m)[a]	609.6
design full supply level (m)[b]	874.38
operating full supply level (op. FSL) (m)[b]	873.77
live storage at op. FSL (m³)[c]	311 x 10⁶
volume at op. FSL (m³)[c]	333 x 10⁶
flooded area at op. FSL (km²)[b]	51.4
maximum possible drawdown from op. FSL (m)[b]	17.14
mean annual drawdown (1975–1987) (m)[b]	2.90
maximum depth at op. FSL (m)[d]	9.7
mean depth at op. FSL (m)[b, c]	6.5
shoreline length at op. FSL (km)[e]	82.2
lake length at op. FSL (km)[e]	34.3
lake width at op. FSL (km)[e]	3.7
mean annual lake evaporation (mm)[f]	750
mean annual precipitation (mm)[f]	376
mean residence time (yr)[c, g]	0.9
mean annual inflow volume (1976–1986)[g, h]	
—runoff from basin (m³)	15 x 10⁶
—inflow from CBRH Canal (m³)	375 x 10⁶
mean annual outflow volume (1976–1986) (m³)[g]	371.5 x 10⁶
mean May–Oct. discharge (m³/s)[g]	24.0

NOTE: [h]CBRH Canal = Carseland-Bow River Headworks Canal
SOURCES: [a]Alta. Envir. n.d.[e]; [b]Alta. Envir. n.d.[a]; [c]Alta. Envir. n.d.[d]; [d]R.L. & L. Envir. Serv. Ltd. 1985; [e]En. Mines Resour. Can. 1976; 1977; [f]Alta. Envir. n.d.[c]; [g]Envir. Can. 1987

Table 3. Major ions and related water quality variables for McGregor Lake. Average concentrations in mg/L; pH in pH units. Composite samples from the euphotic zone collected 9 times from 03 May to 23 Oct. 1984. S.E. = standard error.

	Mean	S.E.
pH (range)	7.3–8.4[a]	—
total alkalinity ($CaCO_3$)	125	1.9
specific conductivity (μS/cm)	330	7.4
total dissolved solids (calculated)	185	3.1
turbidity (NTU)	3	0.6
total hardness ($CaCO_3$)	153	2.6
HCO_3	152	2.4
CO_3	0	0
Mg	13	0.3
Na	7	0.3
K	1	0.03
Cl	5	0.2
SO_4	41	0.9
Ca	39	0.8

NOTE: [a]n = 7
SOURCE: Alta. Envir. n.d.[b], Naquadat station 05AL05AC7000

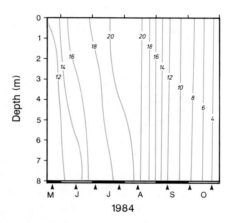

Figure 6. Temperature (°C) in McGregor Lake, 1984. Arrows indicate sampling dates. SOURCE: Alta. Envir. n.d.[b].

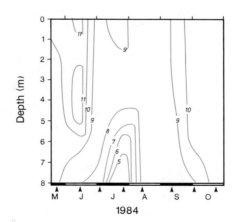

Figure 7. Dissolved oxygen (mg/L) in McGregor Lake, 1984. Arrows indicate sampling dates. SOURCE: Alta. Envir. n.d.[b].

The level of dissolved oxygen at this location declined to less than 5 mg/L near the bottom during late July, but the lake generally remained well-oxygenated throughout the ice-free season (Fig. 7).

Phosphorus levels in the Bow River were reduced after phosphorus removal was initiated at the Calgary sewage treatment plant in the winter of 1982/83 (Charlton and Bayne 1986). Average total phosphorus values in the Bow River at Carseland decreased from 178 μg/L in 1980 to 40 μg/L in 1983. McGregor Lake receives almost all of its inflow from the Bow River, so the reduced phosphorus loading may result in long-term improvement in the reservoir's water quality. Mean total phosphorus levels in the lake declined from 30 μg/L in 1983 to 22 μg/L in 1984 (Table 4). Relatively high nitrite plus nitrate values also originate from the large proportion of water diverted from the Bow River downstream of Calgary. Approximately 50% of nitrogen is removed by sewage treatment.

The peak chlorophyll a value in 1984 (Fig. 8) suggests that, at that time, McGregor Lake was mesotrophic; however, because no recent water quality data are available, the lake's present trophic status cannot be determined.

Biological Characteristics

Plants

There is no detailed information available on the algae in McGregor Lake. During a survey conducted in 1981 (English 1985), the total plankton biomass (settled volume) peaked in July and was dominated at that time by the dinoflagellate (Pyrrhophyta) *Ceratium* sp.

Macrophytes have not been examined, but weedy areas have been reported in the shallow northern end of the lake (Alta. For. Ld. Wild. n.d.).

Table 4. Nutrient, chlorophyll *a* and Secchi depth data for McGregor Lake. Average concentrations in μg/L. Composite samples from the euphotic zone collected 13 times from 11 May to 30 Oct. 1983 and 9 times from 03 May to 23 Oct. 1984. S.E. = standard error.

	1983		1984	
	Mean	S.E.	Mean	S.E.
total phosphorus	30	1.6	22	1.0
total Kjeldahl nitrogen	355	27.4	549	87.8
$NO_3 + NO_2$–nitrogen	42.5[a]	18.6	118	30.3
chlorophyll *a*	9.3	1.2	8.2	0.5
Secchi depth (m)	1.6[a]	0.15	1.9	0.19

NOTE: [a]n = 12
SOURCE: Alta. Envir. n.d.[b], Naquadat station 05AL05AC7000

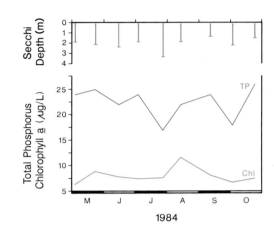

Figure 8. Total phosphorus, chlorophyll *a* and Secchi depths in McGregor Lake, 1984.
SOURCE: Alta. Envir. n.d.[b].

Table 5. Numerical abundance (number/m²) of benthic invertebrates at the north and south ends of McGregor Lake, 1981.

	27 May		23 July	
Organism	North	South	North	South
Diptera				
Chironomidae	3 057	3 283	1 475	1 755
Pelecypoda	22	86	0	22
Annelida				
Tubificidae	11	291	11	140
Nematoda	32	0	32	0
Ephemeroptera	0	11	0	0
TOTAL	3 122	3 661	1 518	1 917

SOURCE: adapted from English 1985

Invertebrates

Zooplankton abundance was measured during a survey in 1981 (English 1985). At the north end of the reservoir, a higher mean density of zooplankton (237/L) and a greater mean settled volume of plankton (0.023 mL/L) was accompanied by a lower transparency (mean Secchi depth of 1.6 m) than at the south end, where mean density was 176/L, mean settled volume was 0.018 mL/L and Secchi depth was 2.3 m. The number of Cladocera in the lake was low and the zooplankton community was dominated by Copepoda and Rotifera; the latter group increased sharply in abundance during September.

The numbers, biomass and composition of benthic invertebrates were also briefly studied in 1981 (Table 5). In May and July, midge larvae (Chironomidae) were dominant at both ends of the reservoir.

Fish

Nine species of fish have been observed in McGregor Lake. Lake whitefish probably were introduced first in 1938 (English 1985). Walleye were introduced as eyed-eggs in 1938, 1949 and 1951 but only a small number are taken each year. Yellow perch likely were introduced between 1938 and 1950, since they were stocked in many Alberta lakes at that time. There are no records of fish having been stocked since 1972 (Alta. For. Ld. Wild. n.d.). Other species that have migrated into the lake via the canal from the Bow River include rainbow trout, northern pike, spottail shiner, longnose sucker, white sucker and burbot. Fish movement is unrestricted throughout the Bow River irrigation system between spring (April or May) and fall (October or November) when the canals are open. During the winter, however, fish are restricted to the reservoirs.

McGregor Lake supports a sport fishery for northern pike, lake whitefish and rainbow trout (Richard Strong Assoc. Ltd. 1983; R.L. & L. Envir. Serv. Ltd. 1985). The lake is heavily fished in summer and in winter. A creel survey was conducted in 1982 at the North Dam

and near the mouth of the inflowing canal (Bishop 1983). At the North Dam between May and August, the catch per unit effort was 0.42 pike/angler-hour; no trout were captured. At the canal mouth between May and October, the catch per unit effort was 0.28 pike/angler-hour and 0.08 trout/angler-hour; lake whitefish were captured during October at this site, as well. Illegal snagging was common.

McGregor Lake has been fished commercially for lake whitefish since about 1948 (Alta. For. Ld. Wild. n.d.). Before 1938, the lake was fished commercially for northern pike. Between the 1980/81 and the 1987/88 seasons, the mean annual commercial catch was 85 230 kg of lake whitefish and 734 kg of northern pike—a total annual average of 85 964 kg of fish. The reservoir was closed to commercial fishing between 1974 and 1978 to allow recovery of the lake whitefish population after an extreme drawdown was followed by a year-class failure in 1972/73. This drawdown resulted from closure of the Carseland-Bow River Headworks Canal when the Bow River diversion structure at Carseland was rebuilt.

In 1978, Fish and Wildlife Division biologists determined the size-at-age and maturity of lake whitefish caught in the McGregor Lake commercial fishery (English 1985). Most of the age four fish were immature, whereas most of the age five fish were mature.

During the late 1950s and early 1960s, there were reports of particularly lean lake whitefish caught by the commercial fishery in McGregor Lake (Alta. For. Ld. Wild. n.d.; Hartman 1957). A 1957 investigation of the invertebrate community on the lake bottom suggested that the north end produced fewer of the prey preferred by lake whitefish than did the south end. The low production at the north end may be due to heavy silt loads deposited by inflowing water during the summer (Hartman 1957). A 1981 study of benthic invertebrates, however, found no difference between the north and south ends of the lake (English 1985).

By 1985, lake whitefish in McGregor Lake were again reported to be lean and continued to be so in 1988. The cause appeared to be a parasite, *Diphyllobothrium dendriticum*, which lives in the intestines of the host lake whitefish. Parasite populations tend to be cyclic and the fish population is expected to be healthier in a few years (Bishop 1988). Even with parasites, the lake whitefish are safe to eat if cleaned and thoroughly cooked.

A 1982 investigation of pesticide and PCB levels in McGregor Lake fish found that concentrations were low and well below safe consumption limits (Alta. Envir. 1982).

Wildlife

McGregor Lake is used as a staging area by waterfowl during migration (IEC Beak Consult. Ltd. et al. 1983; Richard Strong Assoc. Ltd. 1983). The north end of the lake, the slough north of the North Dam, and Snake Creek are important nesting areas for ducks. Gulls use the lake, especially the north end, for resting at night and for staging (Fitch 1988).

J.M. Crosby

References

Alberta Environment. n.d.[a]. Devel. Op. Div., Irrig. Headworks Br. Unpubl. data, Edmonton.
———. n.d.[b]. Envir. Assess. Div., Envir. Qlty. Monit. Br. Unpubl. data, Edmonton.
———. n.d.[c]. Tech. Serv. Div., Hydrol. Br. Unpubl. data, Edmonton.
———. n.d.[d]. Tech. Serv. Div., Surv. Br. Unpubl. data, Edmonton.
———. n.d. [e]. Water Resour. Div., Dam Safety Br. Unpubl. data, Edmonton.
———. 1982. Chemical residues in fish tissues in Alberta: 1. Wabamun Lake, Lake Newell, McGregor Lake, Beaver River, Battle River. Alta. Envir. Centre, Vegreville.
Alberta Forestry, Lands and Wildlife. n.d. Fish Wild. Div. Unpubl. data, Edmonton.
———. 1988. Boating in Alberta. Fish Wild. Div., Edmonton.
———. 1989. Guide to sportfishing. Fish Wild. Div., Edmonton.
Alberta Research Council. 1972. Geological map of Alberta. Nat. Resour. Div., Alta. Geol. Surv., Edmonton.
Bishop, F.G. 1983. A summary of the 1982 creel survey program: Southern region. Alta. En. Nat. Resour., Fish Wild. Div., Lethbridge.
———. 1988. Alta. For. Ld. Wild., Fish Wild. Div., Lethbridge. Pers. comm.

Canada Land and Irrigation Company. 1914. McGregor Reservoir, Plan. No. 1042. Can. Ld. Irrig. Co., Calgary.
Charlton, S.E.D. and D. Bayne. 1986. Phosphorus removal: The impact upon water quality in the Bow River downstream of Calgary, Alberta: Bow River data base 1980–1985. Alta. Envir., Poll. Contr. Div., Edmonton.
Energy, Mines and Resources Canada. 1977. National topographic series 1:250 000 82I (1977). Surv. Map. Br., Ottawa.
English, W.G. 1985. A limnology survey of McGregor Lake Reservoir. Alta. En. Nat. Resour., Fish Wild. Div., Lethbridge.
Environment Canada. 1982. Canadian climate normals, Vol. 7: Bright sunshine (1951–1980). Prep. by Atm. Envir. Serv. Supply Serv. Can., Ottawa.
———. 1987. Historical streamflow summary, Alberta. Water Surv. Can., Water Resour. Br., Ottawa.
Fitch, L. 1988. Alta. For. Ld. Wild., Fish Wild. Div., Lethbridge. Pers. comm.
Greenlee, G.M. 1974. Soil survey adjacent to McGregor Lake, Travers Reservoir, and Little Bow Lake and interpretation for recreational use. Alta. Inst. Pedol. No. M–74–5, Edmonton.
Hartman, G.F. 1957. Investigation of McGregor Lake whitefish. Alta. En. Nat. Resour., Fish Wild. Div., Edmonton.
Holmgren, E.J. and P.M. Holmgren. 1976. Over 2000 place names of Alberta. 3rd ed. West. Producer Prairie Books, Saskatoon.
IEC Beak Consultants Ltd., Techman Engineering Ltd. and Aresco Ltd. 1983. Environmental overview of the Little Bow River Basin. Prep. for Alta. Envir., Plan. Div., Edmonton.
Milo and District Historical Society. 1973. Snake Valley: History of Lake McGregor and area. Milo Dist. Hist. Soc., Milo.
Richard Strong Associates Limited. 1983. McGregor, Travers, Little Bow Reservoir vicinity recreation development study. Prep. for Alta. Envir., Plan. Div., Edmonton.
R.L. & L. Environmental Services Ltd. 1985. A compendium of existing environmental data on Alberta reservoirs. Prep. for Alta. Envir. Res. Trust, Edmonton.
Strong, W.L. and K.R. Leggat. 1981. Ecoregions of Alberta. Alta. En. Nat. Resour., Resour. Eval. Plan. Div., Edmonton.
Walk, H. and B.J. Hurndall. 1978[a]. North McGregor Dam: Summary report. Alta. Envir., Design Const. Div., Dam Safety Br., Edmonton.
———. 1978[b]. South McGregor Dam: Summary report. Alta. Envir., Design Const. Div., Dam Safety Br., Edmonton.
Wyatt, F.A. and J.D. Newton. 1925. Soil survey of the McLeod sheet. Univ. Alta. Bull. No. 11. Univ. Alta., Edmonton.
Wyatt, F.A., T.W. Peters and W.E. Bowser. 1960. Soil survey of Blackfoot and Calgary sheets. Alta. Soil Surv. Rep. No. SS–2, Univ. Alta. Bull. No. 39. Univ. Alta., Edmonton.

PAYNE LAKE

MAP SHEET: 82H/4
LOCATION: Tp2 R28 W4
LAT/LONG: 49°06'N 113°39'W

Payne Lake is an attractive little offstream reservoir nestled in the foothills of southwestern Alberta in the Municipal District of Cardston. The mountains of Waterton National Park that lie 4 km to the southwest provide a dramatic background for the lake. To reach Payne Lake from the town of Cardston, travel 24 km west on Highway 5 to the hamlet of Mountain View, continue west for 2 km on Highway 5, then drive south for about 3 km on the district road that leads to the lake. The road continues across the dam on the east side of the reservoir (Fig. 1).

There are no campgrounds on Payne Lake, but there are two day-use areas operated by Alberta Environment. Both are at the east end of the lake, one on the north shore and one on the south shore (Fig. 2). Both areas provide a boat launch and picnic tables and the area on the south shore has a small pier.

The official spelling of the lake's name has been "Paine" since 1942 (Alta. Cult. Multicult. n.d.). However, requests have been made by local residents since 1972 to change the spelling to "Payne." This was the name of an early settler, Frank Payne, whose name was misspelt in an early surveyor's field book. Signs around the lake say "Payne" but the official version is still "Paine." The lake is also occasionally called Mami Lake.

Before 1942, the area was a shallow slough. That year, the Prairie Farm Rehabilitation Administration of the federal government built an earthfill dam across Mami Creek to create the reservoir. A small earthfill dam was also built across a coulee on the north arm of the lake. Most of the water in the reservoir is diverted from the Belly River about 4 km west of the lake (Fig. 1). Water is released to canals below each of the dams in the Mountview, Leavitt and Aetna irrigation districts, which lie between the lake and Cardston. The reservoir is now owned and operated by Alberta Environment to support multi-purpose water use, including irrigation.

The water in Payne Lake is usually clear but algae may colour the water green at times and there is dense aquatic plant growth in some areas. The lake is stocked with rainbow trout and provides a good local sport fishery. The use of bait fish is not permitted (Alta. For. Ld. Wild. 1989). Boating regulations prohibit the operation of power boats for the purpose of towing people on water skis or surfboards (Alta. For. Ld. Wild. 1988).

Drainage Basin Characteristics

The natural drainage basin of Payne Lake provides only a small amount of runoff to the lake, mostly via Mami Creek (Fig. 1, Tables 1, 2). The drainage basin lies near the edge of the narrow band of foothills east of the Rocky Mountains where the forested hills meet the prairie. Payne Lake lies within an eastward projection of the Groveland Subregion of the Aspen Parkland Ecoregion. The most common habitat type near the lake is fescue grassland, but in low areas and around sloughs there are pockets of trembling aspen, buckbrush, snowberry and rose (Strong and Leggat 1981). The most common land uses are grazing and some cultivation for grain crops. Soils are Black and Dark Brown Chernozemics (Wyatt et al. 1939). The most southwesterly portion of the drainage basin is in Waterton National Park and reaches an altitude of 1 798 m. Here, near the treeline, the vegetation is typical of the Subalpine Ecoregion. Engelmann spruce and lodgepole pine are the dominant trees and soils are Luvisols and Brunisols. At lower elevations, there is an area of Mon-

Table 1. Characteristics of Payne Lake drainage basin.

area (excluding lake) (km²)[a]	24.9
soil[b]	Black and Dark Brown Chernozemics, Luvisols, Brunisols
bedrock geology[c]	Belly River Formation (Upper Cretaceous): sandstone, siltstone, mudstone, ironstone beds; nonmarine
terrain[d]	rolling to hilly
ecoregion[d]	Groveland Subregion of Aspen Parkland; Montane; Subalpine
dominant vegetation[d]	rough fescue, trembling aspen; Douglas fir; Engelmann spruce, lodgepole pine
mean annual sunshine (h)[e]	2 370

SOURCES: [a]Alta. Envir. n.d.[c]; [b]Wyatt et al. 1939; [c]Alta. Res. Counc. 1972; [d]Strong and Leggat 1981; [e]Envir. Can. 1982

Table 2. Characteristics of Payne Lake.

control structures[a]	East: earthfill dam; North: small earthfill dam
full supply level (FSL) (m)[a]	1 343.6
volume at FSL (m³)[a]	9.17×10^6
live storage at FSL (m³)[a]	8.68×10^6
surface area at FSL (km²)[a]	2.28
maximum drawdown (m)[a]	1 337.2
maximum depth at FSL (m)[a]	7.3
mean depth at FSL (m)[a]	3.76
shoreline length at FSL (km)[b]	13.7
lake length at FSL (km)[b]	4.2
lake width at FSL (km)[b]	1.1
mean annual lake evaporation (mm)[c]	729
mean annual precipitation (mm)[c]	687
mean residence time (yr)[c]	0.40
mean (Apr.–Nov.) inflow volume (1974–1985) (m³)[c, d]	21.6×10^6 (via MVID canal) + 2.0×10^6 (natural inflow)

NOTE: [d]excluding groundwater inflow
SOURCES: [a]Alta. Envir. n.d.[d]; [b]English 1981; [c]Alta. Envir. n.d.[c]

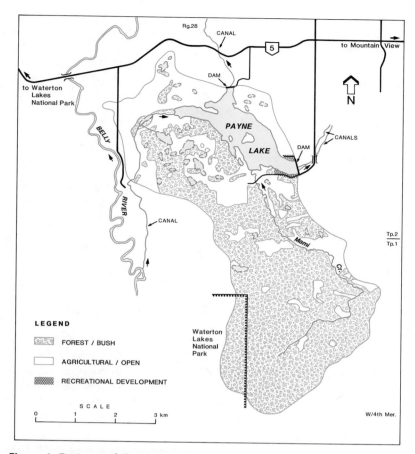

Figure 1. Features of the drainage basin of Payne Lake.
SOURCES: Alta. Envir. n.d.[c]; En. Mines Resour. Can. 1971; English 1981. Updated with 1987 aerial photos.

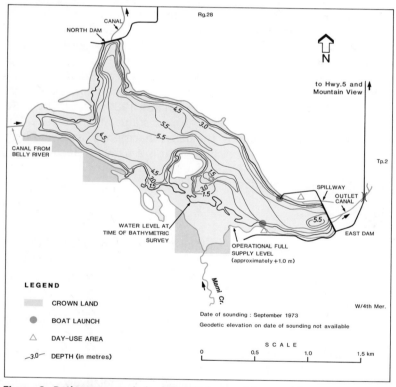

Figure 2. Bathymetry and shoreline features of Payne Lake.
BATHYMETRY SOURCE: Alta. Envir. n.d.[d].

tane Ecoregion, which is typified by Douglas fir. Still lower is the Aspen Parkland Ecoregion, which grades into the Groveland Subregion around Payne Lake.

Most of the water in Payne Lake is diverted from the Belly River, the headwaters of which extend to the alpine regions along the continental divide in Glacier National Park, Montana.

Reservoir Characteristics

Payne Lake is an irregularly shaped, elongate reservoir lying in a shallow coulee. Numerous side coulees along its shore contribute to its relatively long shoreline (13.7 km, Table 2). The deepest area (7.3 m) is near the east dam, but depths over 5 m extend almost the full length of the reservoir (Fig. 2). There are two small islands and one large island in the lake.

Except for a small contribution from Mami Creek, the water that fills Payne Lake is diverted from the Belly River. The amount diverted depends on irrigation demand in the Mountain View, Leavitt and Aetna irrigation districts and the availability of water in the Belly River. Diversion starts slowly in April, usually remains low in May, then increases in June and remains high through September. It then drops in October and stops in late October or early November (English 1981). From 1974 to 1985, the annual volume diverted averaged 21.6×10^6 m³. The volume varies with demand, from a high of 32.9×10^6 m³ in 1977, a dry year, to a low of 8.252×10^6 m³ in 1978, a wet year (Alta. Envir. n.d.[c]). The residence time of the water in the lake over this period ranged from 0.27 years to 1.08 years.

There are no data on water level fluctuations in the reservoir except for a brief period from February to September in 1978, when fluctuations were less than 1 m (English 1981). Water levels can be drawn down to allow maintenance work on the control structures or to facilitate fish management. On these occasions, a small pond is left with a surface area of 0.76 km² and a maximum depth of 1.5 m (English 1981). Water has been drawn down for structure maintenance three times since 1942, the last time in 1979.

Water Quality

Data on the water quality of Payne Lake are sparse. The lake was sampled twice by Alberta Environment in 1983 (Alta. Envir. n.d.[b]) and seven times from February 1978 through March 1979 for selected variables (English 1981). As well, Fish and Wildlife Division samples it for dissolved oxygen concentrations once or twice in most winters (Alta. For. Ld. Wild. n.d.).

Payne Lake has fresh water. The alkalinity is relatively low compared to many prairie lakes, reflecting the input of water from a mountain river. The dominant ions are calcium and bicarbonate (Table 3).

Despite its exposure to the strong westerly winds that sweep down from the mountains, Payne Lake does occasionally become weakly thermally stratified. This was evident in the upper 3 m in 1983 and was noted in June and August 1978. Dissolved oxygen may be slightly depleted in the deeper water in the reservoir. On 7 September 1978, dissolved oxygen concentrations at a depth of 6.5 m were only 1 mg/L.

The reservoir freezes in winter but occasionally becomes ice-free as early as late February. The dissolved oxygen concentration remains high (7 to 12 mg/L) near the surface. Near the bottom, the dissolved oxygen concentration is usually high (over 6 mg/L), even in late winter in many years. In some years, however, the concentration in the bottom stratum drops to 2 mg/L. In the winter of 1979/80, when the water level was severely drawn down to leave a maximum depth of 1.5 m, the dissolved oxygen level remained high enough to maintain trout.

Payne Lake has a moderate phosphorus concentration (Table 4). Chlorophyll *a* concentrations have not been monitored, but algal blooms are common in the summer (English 1981; 1988). There are insufficient data to determine the trophic status of Payne Lake, but the presence of algal blooms, the dense macrophyte beds and high zooplankton biomass all indicate that it is a fairly productive lake.

Biological Characteristics

Plants

There are no data on phytoplankton species in Payne Lake. Aquatic macrophyte beds are extensive in shallow water and are a nuisance to anglers trying to fish from shore. Macrophyte species have not been identified.

Invertebrates

During a Fish and Wildlife Division study in the summer of 1978, the mean wet weight of total zooplankton in Payne Lake was 0.02 mg/L, with 283 zooplankters per litre. This density is relatively high for a small prairie reservoir (English 1981). Benthic invertebrates have not been sampled.

Fish

Ten species of fish have been collected from Payne Lake (English 1981). Nine of these are indigenous to the Belly River watershed. Cutthroat trout, bull trout, mountain whitefish and Arctic grayling occur as migrants; burbot, white sucker, longnose sucker, lake chub and fathead minnows are resident. One species—rainbow trout—has been introduced.

Rainbow trout were introduced to Payne Lake in 1942, the year the reservoir was created. Approximately 300 000 rainbow trout

Table 3. Major ions and related water quality variables for Payne Lake. Average concentrations in mg/L; pH in pH units. Composite samples from the euphotic zone collected twice, on 12 May and 23 Aug. 1983. S.E. = standard error.

	Mean	S.E.
pH (range)	8.1–8.2	—
total alkalinity (CaCO₃)	102	18
specific conductivity (μS/cm)	210	34.5
total dissolved solids (calculated)	103	16.1
turbidity (NTU)	1.0	—
total hardness (calculated)	102	—
HCO₃	124	22.0
CO₃	0	0
Mg	9	0.9
Na	1	0.2
K	0.4	0.04
Cl	0.5	0.20
SO₄	4	0.4
Ca	26	3.6

SOURCE: Alta. Envir. n.d.[b], Naquadat station 05AL05AD1000

Table 4. Nutrient and Secchi depth data for Payne Lake. Average concentrations in μg/L. Composite samples from the euphotic zone collected twice, on 12 May and 23 Aug. 1983. S.E. = standard error.

	Mean	S.E.
total phosphorus	25[a]	—
total Kjeldahl nitrogen	390	70
NO₃ + NO₂–nitrogen	<3	—
NH₄–nitrogen	50	40
Secchi depth (m)	2.5	0.50

NOTE: [a]n = 1, 23 Aug. 1983
SOURCE: Alta. Envir. n.d.[b], Naquadat station 05AL05AD1000

have been stocked annually since 1952; 431 500 were stocked in 1987 (Alta. For. Ld. Wild. n.d.; 1986; 1987; Alta. Ld. For. 1952–1974; Alta. Rec. Parks Wild. 1975–1978; Alta. En. Nat. Resour. 1979–1985). Angling success has been reasonable; in a 1974 creel census over four one-week periods from 23 May to 1 July, the average catch was 0.07 trout/angler-hour (Alta. For. Ld. Wild. n.d.). Growth rates of rainbow trout are similar to those of pothole lakes in southern Alberta; in August 1978, the average age 1+ fish had a fork length of 28.1 cm and a weight of 259 g (Barton 1979). Competition for food by the large sucker population is thought to reduce the potential growth rate. The catch from test nets was 90% suckers and 10% trout (Alta. For. Ld. Wild. n.d.). Elimination or even reduction of the sucker population in Payne Lake is not considered to be feasible because suckers could easily return via the diversion from the Belly River (Fitch 1988).

Wildlife

The area around Payne Lake provides excellent habitat for most of the wildlife species found in the southern foothills of Alberta. Elk, white-tailed deer and mule deer are common, and black bears visit the area, as do coyotes and foxes. The lake provides nesting habitat for dabbling and diving ducks and Canada Geese (Fitch 1988).

J.M. Crosby

References

Alberta Culture and Multiculturalism. n.d. Hist. Resour. Div., Hist. Sites Serv. Unpubl. data, Edmonton.

Alberta Energy and Natural Resources. 1979–1985. Fish planting list. Fish Wild. Div., Edmonton.

Alberta Environment. n.d.[a]. Devel. Op. Div., Headworks Br. Unpubl. data, Edmonton.

———. n.d.[b]. Envir. Assess. Div., Envir. Qlty. Monit. Br. Unpubl. data, Edmonton.

———. n.d.[c]. Tech. Serv. Div., Hydrol. Br. Unpubl. data, Edmonton.

———. n.d.[d]. Tech. Serv. Div., Surv. Br. Unpubl. data, Edmonton.

Alberta Forestry, Lands and Wildlife. n.d. Fish Wild. Div. Unpubl. data, Edmonton.

———. 1986, 1987. Fish planting list. Fish Wild. Div., Edmonton.

———. 1988. Boating in Alberta. Fish Wild. Div., Edmonton.

———. 1989. Guide to sportfishing. Fish Wild. Div., Edmonton.

Alberta Lands and Forests. 1952–1974. Fish planting list. Fish Wild. Div., Edmonton.

Alberta Recreation, Parks and Wildlife. 1975–1978. Fish planting list. Fish Wild. Div., Edmonton.

Alberta Research Council. 1972. Geological map of Alberta. Nat. Resour. Div., Alta. Geol. Surv., Edmonton.

Barton, B.A. 1979. Angler harvest of rainbow trout from two stocking rates in Paine Lake, Alberta. Alta. Rec. Parks Wild., Fish Wild. Div., Calgary.

Energy, Mines and Resources Canada. 1971. National topographic series 1:50 000 82H/4 (1971). Surv. Map. Br., Ottawa.

English, W.G. 1981. A limnological survey of Paine Lake Reservoir. Alta. En. Nat. Resour., Fish Wild. Div., Lethbridge.

———. 1988. Alta. For. Ld. Wild., Fish Wild. Div., Lethbridge. Pers. comm.

Environment Canada. 1982. Canadian climate normals, Vol. 7: Bright sunshine (1951–1980). Prep. by Atm. Envir. Serv. Supply Serv. Can., Ottawa.

Fitch, L. 1988. Alta. For. Ld. Wild., Fish Wild. Div., Lethbridge. Pers. comm.

Strong, W.L. and K.R. Leggat. 1981. Ecoregions of Alberta. Alta. En. Nat. Resour., Resour. Eval. Plan. Div., Edmonton.

Wyatt, F.A., W.E. Bowser and W. Odynsky. 1939. Soil survey of Lethbridge and Pincher Creek sheets. Univ. Alta. Bull. No. 32. Univ. Alta., College Agric., Edmonton.

ST. MARY RESERVOIR

MAP SHEET: 82H
LOCATION: Tp4 R24 W4
LAT/LONG: 49°18'N 113°11'W

St. Mary Reservoir is a large water storage reservoir that fills the valley of the St. Mary River 45 km southwest of the city of Lethbridge in the Municipal District of Cardston. To reach the reservoir from Lethbridge, follow Highway 5 for 53 km southwest to the village of Spring Coulee. Turn west on Secondary Road 505 and drive for 7 km to the dam (Fig. 1), which can be crossed by vehicles. Access to the reservoir is available at two boat launches near the dam, one on the north shore and one on the south shore (Fig. 2). It is not possible to launch a boat at either site when the water level is more than 7 m below the full supply level. All boats are restricted from posted areas in the reservoir (Alta. For. Ld. Wild. 1988). There is a day-use site on the southeast shore just east of an island that shelters the beach from waves; facilities include portable change houses. St. Mary Dam Park (also known as Spring Coulee Park) is located along the river immediately downstream of the dam. This park, operated by Alberta Environment, provides a 32–site campground, a picnic shelter, tables, drinking water and a basketball court (Alta. Envir. n.d.[a]). To provide angling, Fish and Wildlife Division stocks a small pond in the park each year with rainbow and brook trout.

The reservoir was named after the river, which in turn was named after the two St. Mary lakes at its headwaters in Glacier National Park, Montana. These lakes were named by Father Pierre Jean de Smet (1801 to 1873), an early missionary in the west (Holmgren and Holmgren 1976). In about 1750, Blood Indians moved from the Hand Hills near the town of Hanna to the present location of the reservoir. In 1869, a fur trading post, Fort Whoop-up, was built near the confluence of the St. Mary and Oldman rivers. By the 1880s, cattle ranching was a major occupation; the area became the site of large ranches, such as the Cochrane Ranch west of the Belly River and the McIntyre Ranch on Milk River Ridge (Magrath Dist. Hist. Soc. 1974; Cardston Dist. Hist. Soc. 1978). In 1884, the Blood Indians moved onto the Blood Indian Reserve west of the St. Mary River (Cardston Dist. Hist. Soc. 1978).

This area of Alberta receives little rainfall and is almost continuously blown by warm, drying winds that drop from the mountains. The need for irrigation was soon recognized, and members of the Mormon community in Utah, with many years of experience with irrigation, were encouraged to settle in the area. As an incentive, they received cash and land from the Alberta Railway and Irrigation Company (Magrath Dist. Hist. Soc. 1974). By 1890, many small irrigation projects were in place, and in 1900, the "Great Irrigation Canal" was built to divert water from the St. Mary River southeast of the town of Cardston to the Lethbridge area (Cardston Dist. Hist. Soc. 1978).

There were no major storage reservoirs west of Lethbridge until after World War II. In 1946, the Prairie Farm Rehabilitation Administration (PFRA) of the federal government began construction of the St. Mary Dam, then the largest earthfill dam in North America. The reservoir was first filled in 1951 (Magrath Dist. Hist. Soc. 1974). In 1959, a canal was completed to bring additional water from the Belly River to St. Mary Reservoir, and in 1960, another canal was completed to divert water from the Waterton River to the Belly River for diversion to St. Mary Reservoir (Clements 1973). The PFRA operated the reservoir until 1973 when it was turned over to Alberta Environment. More than half of the water leaving the reservoir flows through a system of canals that supplies water for irrigation, domes-

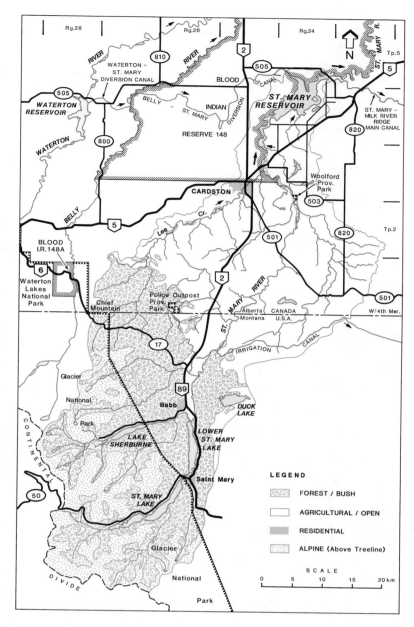

Figure 1. Features of the drainage basin of St. Mary Reservoir.
SOURCES: Alta. Envir. n.d.[c]; En. Mines Resour. Can. 1977 and United States Army 1968. Updated with 1984 aerial photos.

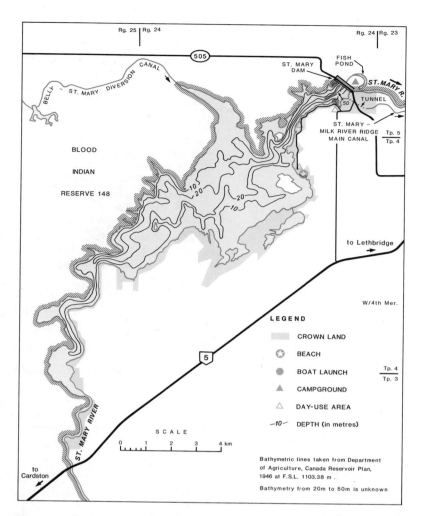

Figure 2. Bathymetry and shoreline features of St. Mary Reservoir.
BATHYMETRY SOURCE: Alta. Envir. n.d.[a].

tic, municipal and industrial uses, and to support wildlife, fisheries and recreational uses as far east as Medicine Hat. In 1988, St. Mary Reservoir provided water to irrigate approximately 190 000 ha in areas that reach as far east as Medicine Hat (Alta. Envir. n.d.[a]). The map in the introduction to the South Saskatchewan and Milk River basins shows the canals and reservoirs along the distribution system for St. Mary Reservoir.

St. Mary Reservoir is used for recreational power boating, water skiing, wind surfing, swimming and sport fishing for northern pike and walleye. Provincial sport fishing regulations apply to the reservoir and angling with bait is not permitted in the trout pond in St. Mary Dam Park (Alta. For. Ld. Wild. 1989). The reservoir also supports a commercial fishery for lake whitefish. The water is clear, relatively algae-free and attractive. However, strong winds and large waves inhibit some recreational uses, and when the reservoir is below full supply level, extensive mud flats detract from its appeal.

Drainage Basin Characteristics

St. Mary Reservoir is an onstream reservoir, and therefore its basin is that of the St. Mary River, which extends south into Montana, U.S.A. and west to the continental divide (Fig. 1). The basin of the St. Mary River includes portions of five ecoregions (Strong and Leggat 1981). Most of the Canadian portion of the basin is in the Fescue Grass Ecoregion. Natural vegetation is dominated by rough

fescue grass with secondary quantities of Parry oat grass; shrubs such as buckbrush and saskatoon grow on north-facing slopes of coulees and in seepage sites. Soils are typically Black Chernozemics, which are excellent for crop production, and much of this ecoregion is cultivated for cereal crops. A small portion of the Aspen Parkland Ecoregion is located along the lower slopes of the foothills along the border between the Aspen Parkland and Fescue Grassland ecoregions. Trembling aspen forms more than 15% of the cover. The balance of vegetation is rough fescue and shrubs such as buckbrush, saskatoon, rose and willow. Soils are Black and Dark Brown Chernozemics. West of the Aspen Parkland is the Montane Ecoregion, where Douglas fir is interspersed with grasslands on south-facing slopes. Soils are Black Chernozemics and Eutric Brunisols. As the basin reaches up into the mountains, the Subalpine Ecoregion is encountered. Vegetation is typically lodgepole pine, white spruce and fir underlain by Eutric Brunisolic soils. South of the Canada-United States border, the drainage basin reaches up to the Alpine Ecoregion, which lies above the treeline. Vegetation is absent from rock peaks that reach an altitude of 3 100 m; lichens, heaths and dryads grow in lower areas, and in sheltered places, stunted alpine fir, Engelmann spruce and alpine larch may grow. Soils are Regosols and Brunisols.

One of the most noticeable aspects of the St. Mary Reservoir area is the wind. It blows down from the mountains to the west almost continuously, and only 2% of the days in a year are calm. Wind speed averages 33 km/hour, but gusts over 170 km/hour have been recorded. The flat topography and scarcity of tree cover allow the wind to sweep the area unimpeded. Dunes have formed in places along the south shore of the reservoir, and when the reservoir is drawn down, fine particles of sand lift off the exposed mud flats to create dust storms (MTB Consult. Ltd. 1977).

The major land use in the Canadian portion of the drainage basin is agricultural—both crop production (cereals and alfalfa) and ranch-

Table 1. Characteristics of St. Mary Reservoir drainage basin.

area (excluding reservoir) (km^2)[a]	2 250
soil[b, c]	Black Chernozemics
bedrock geology[c, d]	St. Mary River Formation (Upper Cretaceous): sandstone, siltstone, mudstone, thin coal beds; nonmarine Willow Creek Formation (Tertiary and Upper Cretaceous): sandstone, mudstone, thin limestone beds; nonmarine
terrain[e]	west—mountainous middle—rolling hills east—gently undulating to flat
ecoregion[e]	Fescue Grass; Aspen Parkland; Montane; Subalpine; Alpine
dominant vegetation[e]	west—heaths, white and Englemann spruce middle—aspen, white spruce, lodgepole pine, Douglas fir east—fescue grass
mean annual sunshine (h)[g]	2 370

NOTE: [c]reservoir area only
SOURCES: [a]Alta. Envir. n.d.[c]; [b]Wyatt et al. 1939; [d]Alta. Res. Counc. 1972; [e]Strong and Leggat 1981; [f]Envir. Can. 1982

Table 2. Characteristics of St. Mary Reservoir.

control structure[a]	St. Mary Dam (zoned earthfill)
dam height (m)[a]	62
crest length (m)[a]	773.0
full supply level (FSL) (m)[a]	1 103.4
volume at FSL (m^3)[a]	396.0 x 10^6
live storage at FSL (m^3)[b]	350 x 10^6
flooded area at FSL (km^2)[b]	37.5
maximum historic drawdown (1954–1988) (m)[c]	24.4
mean annual drawdown (1954–1985) (m)[c]	6.7
maximum depth at FSL (m)[d]	56.4
mean depth at FSL (m)[d]	10.4
shoreline length at FSL (km)[d]	95.1
lake length at FSL (km)[e]	19.2
lake width at FSL (km)[e]	8.0
mean annual lake evaporation (mm)[f]	767
mean annual precipitation (mm)[f]	471
mean residence time (yr)[f]	0.38
mean annual inflow (1980–1986) (m^3)[c, g]	
—from St. Mary River	650 x 10^6
—from Waterton-Belly Diversion	397 x 10^6
mean annual discharge (1980–1986) (m^3)[b]	
—to St. Mary River	326 x 10^6
—to St. Mary-Milk River Ridge Canal	693 x 10^6

NOTE: [g]an additional average of 216 x 10^6 m^3 is diverted out of the basin in the United States (Alta. Envir. n.d.[c]); volume excludes groundwater inflow
SOURCES: [a]Alta. Envir. n.d.[d]; [b]Alta. Envir. n.d.[a]; [c]Envir. Can. 1985; [d]R.L. & L. Envir. Serv. Ltd. 1985; [e]Carlin 1982; [f]Alta. Envir. n.d.[c]

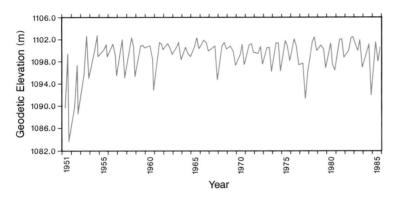

Figure 3. Water level of St. Mary Reservoir, 1951 to 1985.
SOURCE: Envir. Can. 1951–1985.

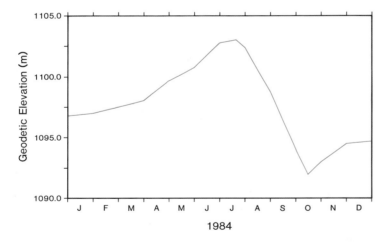

Figure 4. Typical annual water level fluctuation of St. Mary Reservoir, 1984.
SOURCE: Envir. Can. 1951–1985 (1984).

ing. There are two small provincial parks in the basin, Woolford and Police Outpost. About one-half of the American portion of the basin lies within Glacier National Park; the major land use outside of the park is ranching. The population of the basin is low. There is one town, Cardston, in the Canadian portion and two towns, Babb and Saint Mary, in the American portion. The major water use of the St. Mary River in both countries is irrigation. An annual average of 216 x 10^6 m^3 is diverted out of the river on the American side of the border (Table 2).

The only Crown land near the reservoir is the reservoir right-of-way (Fig. 2). Most of this land is leased to local ranchers for grazing or cultivation. The entire north shore, outside the right-of-way, is part of Blood Indian Reserve 148.

Reservoir Characteristics

St. Mary Reservoir has a large surface area relative to the size of its basin (Tables 1, 2). The lake is 19.2–km long and 8.0–km wide at its widest point. The lake bed is that of the St. Mary River, which is deeply incised into the surrounding plain. The lake bottom drops steeply to a maximum depth of 56.4 m near the dam. In the main body of the reservoir the bottom slopes more gently to a maximum depth of 30 m (Fig. 2). When the reservoir level drops by its mean annual drawdown of 6.7 m (Table 2), 46% of the reservoir area is exposed as mudflats (MTB Consult. Ltd. 1977). There are five permanent islands in the reservoir, all near the upstream end. Other islands appear as the water level drops below the full supply level.

The topography of the shore of the reservoir includes areas of flat floodplain near the western end, gradual slopes along much of the southern shore, cliffs up to 7 m high (formed by wave erosion) in areas exposed to the west wind, and areas of slumping along portions of the southwest shore (MTB Consult. Ltd. 1977).

Fifty-nine per cent of the inflow to the reservoir comes from the St. Mary River and 41% comes from the Waterton and Belly rivers via the Belly-St. Mary Canal (Table 2). Tunnels under the dam direct 68% of the outflow to the St. Mary-Milk River Ridge Main Canal;

Table 3. Major ions and related water quality variables for St. Mary Reservoir. Average concentrations in mg/L; pH in pH units. Composite samples from the euphotic zone collected 3 times from 23 May to 13 Aug. 1985. S.E. = standard error.

	Mean	S.E.
pH (range)	7.4–8.0	—
total alkalinity ($CaCO_3$)	98	4.0
specific conductivity (μS/cm)	197	11.5
total dissolved solids (calculated)	108	4.7
total hardness ($CaCO_3$)	96	1.9
dissolved organic carbon	1	0.1
HCO_3	119	4.8
CO_3	<1	—
Mg	8	0
Na	3	0.5
K	1	0.1
Cl	0.3	0.12
SO_4	10	1.3
Ca	25	0.7

SOURCE: Alta. Envir. n.d.[b], Naquadat station 05AL05AE1000

Table 4. Nutrient, chlorophyll *a* and Secchi depth data for St. Mary Reservoir. Average concentrations in μg/L. Composite samples from the euphotic zone collected twice from 22 June to 14 Sep. 1983 and 5 times from 23 May to 13 Aug. 1985. S.E. = standard error.

	1983		1985	
	Mean	S.E.	Mean	S.E.
total Kjeldahl nitrogen	250	90.0	357	125.0
$NO_3 + NO_2$–nitrogen	26	12.5	49	11.5
NH_4–nitrogen	<20	—	<20	—
chlorophyll *a*	—	—	2.9	1.57
Secchi depth (m)	1.2	0.20	1.5	0.20

SOURCE: Alta. Envir. n.d.[b], Naquadat station 05AL05AE1000

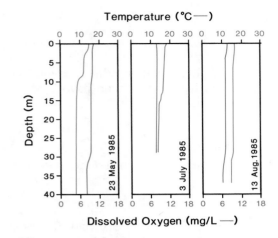

Figure 5. Temperature and dissolved oxygen of St. Mary Reservoir, 1985.
SOURCE: Alta. Envir. n.d.[b].

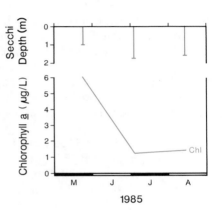

Figure 6. Chlorophyll *a* and Secchi depth in St. Mary Reservoir, 1985.
SOURCE: Alta. Envir. n.d.[b].

the remaining 32% of the outflow forms the downstream portion of the St. Mary River (Alta. Envir. n.d.[a]).

The water level of the reservoir undergoes wide fluctuations. The mean annual drawdown from 1952, the first year of operation, until 1985, was 6.7 m below the full supply level. The lowest level during this period was 12.1 m below the full supply level (Table 2, Fig. 3). In 1987, after 3 very dry years, the water level was drawn down a record 24.4 m below the full supply level (Alta. Envir. n.d.[a]). The reservoir is operated to fill quickly from early April to June; the level is held steady from June to early July, then falls from early July to late October (Fig. 4).

Water Quality

The water quality of St. Mary Reservoir was monitored in 1983 and 1985 by Alberta Environment (Alta. Envir. n.d.[b]; Charlton and Brennan 1986).

St. Mary Reservoir has fresh water (Table 3). The alkalinity is low compared to that of natural prairie lakes. The dominant ions are calcium and bicarbonate. In 1985, the deepest area of the reservoir was weakly thermally stratified from May through August (Fig. 5). The wind and strong current from the inflow likely inhibit stratification in the shallower upstream area. Oxygen depletion occurred with depth but anoxic conditions were not found (Fig. 5).

The reservoir has low chlorophyll *a* concentrations, indicating very low algal biomass (Table 4, Fig. 6). St. Mary Reservoir is likely oligotrophic, but more chlorophyll *a* and phosphorus monitoring is needed to confirm this.

Biological Characteristics

Plants

There are no recent data on the phytoplankton in the reservoir. The extreme annual drawdown and high wave action have kept the reservoir shoreline clear of macrophytes.

Invertebrates

There are no recent data on the invertebrates in St. Mary Reservoir.

Fish

Thirteen species of fish have been found in St. Mary Reservoir (Clements 1973; English 1977; R.L. & L. Envir. Serv. Ltd. 1985). Northern pike are indigenous and provide the bulk of the sport fishery. Walleye were introduced in 1957 and now persist as a small, self-sustaining population that contributes to both the sport and commercial fisheries. Rainbow trout, which are indigenous to the basin and were stocked in the reservoir in the 1950s, are caught occasionally. Burbot and cutthroat trout, which are also native to the system, are caught occasionally as well. Lake whitefish are not native to the system, but were introduced to St. Mary lakes in Montana before 1910; they subsequently migrated downstream to the reservoir and are now the major target of the commercial fishery. Other fish species in the reservoir include white and longnose suckers, and five forage species: trout-perch, spottail shiners, lake chub, fathead minnows and longnose dace.

The commercial fishery has operated since 1962/63. Between the 1968/69 and the 1987/88 seasons, an average of 8 336 kg of fish were caught annually: 88% of the catch was lake whitefish, 10% was pike and 1% was walleye. Lake whitefish are free of the parasite *Triaenophorus crassus* (Alta. For. Ld. Wild. n.d.).

A pond is located in an isolated oxbow immediately below the dam. The continuous flow of water seeping from the dam provides clean, cold water and the pond is stocked annually with yearling rainbow trout that provide an intensive sport fishery. From 1980 to 1987, an average of 2 500 rainbow trout approximately 14—cm long were stocked every spring (Alta. En. Nat. Resour. 1980–1985; Alta. For. Ld. Wild. 1986; 1987). The use of bait fish in this pond is not permitted (Alta. For. Ld. Wild. 1989).

Wildlife

The water level fluctuations of St. Mary Reservoir are too great to provide nesting habitat for most waterfowl, but in 1977, Double-crested Cormorants nested there (Markham 1978) and Canada Geese were seen nesting on one of the islands (MTB Consult. Ltd. 1977).

The area of grassland not disturbed by agriculture is small, and mammals are limited to mule deer, ground squirrels, skunks, long-tailed weasels, mice, voles and an occasional coyote. Upland game birds such as Sharp-tailed Grouse and Hungarian Partridge have been observed in the area (MTB Consult. Ltd. 1977).

J.M. Crosby

References

Alberta Energy and Natural Resources. 1980–1985. Fish planting list. Fish Wild. Div., Edmonton.
Alberta Environment. n.d.[a]. Devel. Op. Div., Headworks Br. Unpubl. data, Lethbridge.
———. n.d.[b]. Envir. Assess. Div., Envir. Qlty. Monit. Br. Unpubl. data, Edmonton.
———. n.d.[c]. Tech. Serv. Div., Hydrol. Br. Unpubl. data, Edmonton.
———. n.d.[d]. Water Resour. Mgt. Div., Dam Safety Br. Unpubl. data, Edmonton.
Alberta Forestry, Lands and Wildlife. n.d. Fish Wild. Div. Unpubl. data, Edmonton.
———. 1986, 1987. Fish planting list. Fish Wild. Div., Edmonton.
———. 1988. Boating in Alberta. Fish Wild. Div., Edmonton.
———. 1989. Guide to sportfishing. Fish Wild. Div., Edmonton.
Alberta Research Council. 1972. Geological map of Alberta. Nat. Resour. Div., Alta. Geol. Surv., Edmonton.
Cardston and District Historical Society. 1978. Chief Mountain Country. Cardston Dist. Hist. Soc., Cardston.
Carlin, G.P. 1982. St. Mary Dam: Safety report, Vol. 1. Alta. Envir., Water Resour. Mgt. Div., Dam Safety Br., Edmonton.
Charlton, S.E.D. and K.A. Brennan. 1986. Water quality among southern Alberta lakes and reservoirs. Alta. Envir., Poll. Contr. Div., Water Qlty. Contr. Br. Unpubl. rep., Calgary.
Clements, S.H. 1973. A review of the history and management of the fishery resource of St. Mary Reservoir. Alta. Ld. For., Fish Wild. Div., Lethbridge.
Energy, Mines and Resources Canada. 1977. National topographic series 1:250 000 82H (1977). Surv. Map. Br., Ottawa.
English, W.G. 1977. A limnological survey of St. Mary Reservoir. Alta. Rec. Parks Wild., Fish Wild. Div., Lethbridge.
Environment Canada. 1951–1985. Surface water data. Prep. by Inland Waters Directorate. Water Surv. Can., Water Resour. Br., Ottawa.
———. 1982. Canadian climate normals, Vol. 7: Bright sunshine (1951–1980). Prep. by Atm. Envir. Serv. Supply Serv. Can., Ottawa.
———. 1985. Historical streamflow summary: Alberta to 1984. Prep. by Inland Waters Directorate. Water Surv. Can., Water Resour. Br., Ottawa.
Holmgren, E.J. and P.M. Holmgren. 1976. Over 2000 place names of Alberta. 3rd ed. West. Producer Prairie Books, Saskatoon.
Magrath and District History Association. 1974. Irrigation builders. Magrath Dist. Hist. Assoc., Magrath.
Markham, B. 1978. Status of the Double-crested Cormorant (*Phalocrocorax auritus*) in Canada. Prep. for Commit. Status Endangered Wild. in Can. by Alta. Rec. Parks Wild., Fish Wild. Div., Edmonton.
MTB Consultants Ltd. 1977. St. Mary Reservoir: Master plan study report—Phase 1: Environmental and recreation assessment. Prep. for Alta. Envir., Plan. Div., Edmonton.
R.L. & L. Environmental Services Ltd. 1985. A compendium of existing environmental data on Alberta reservoirs. Prep. for Alta. Envir. Res. Trust, Edmonton.
Strong, W.L. and K.R. Leggat. 1981. Ecoregions of Alberta. Alta. En. Nat. Resour., Resour. Eval. Plan. Div., Edmonton.
United States Army. 1968. Topographic map 1:250 000 NM 12–10 (1968). Army Map Serv., Corps Eng., Washington, D.C.
Wyatt, F.A., W.E. Bowser and W. Odynsky. 1939. Soil survey of Lethbridge and Pincher Creek sheets. Univ. Alta. Bull. No. 32. Univ. Alta., Edmonton.

TRAVERS RESERVOIR

MAP SHEET: 82I
LOCATION: Tp14, 15 R21 W4
LAT/LONG: 50°13'N 112°51'W

Travers Reservoir was built on the Little Bow River in 1954 to store water for the Bow River Irrigation District and to facilitate the flow of water from McGregor Lake to Little Bow Lake Reservoir. It was named after the hamlet of Travers, which lies 15 km to the east. The reservoir is located between Secondary Highways 522 and 529, east of Carmangay and Champion and about 35 km southeast of the town of Vulcan. It is part of the Oldman River drainage basin but receives most of its water from the Bow River via McGregor Lake and from the Highwood River via a canal to the Little Bow River (Fig. 1).

Tribes of the Blackfoot Confederacy hunted buffalo in this region long before white settlers arrived. During the 1880s, the North West Mounted Police and cattle ranchers arrived in the area, and by 1907 many homesteads were established (Champion Hist. Commit. 1970). Grain farming became important and extended eastward as water was supplied to irrigable land. The success of irrigation after McGregor Lake and Little Bow Lake Reservoir were built, and the drought years of the 1930s prompted nearby communities to request more irrigation projects. At the same time, delivery of water from McGregor Lake to Little Bow Lake Reservoir was difficult due to 20 km of canals connecting the two. In 1951, the Prairie Farm Rehabilitation Administration began construction of Travers Reservoir to replace the canals and to provide additional storage to meet demands for irrigation water. In 1954, the reservoir was filled for the first time.

Access to the reservoir is provided at two locations (Fig. 2). Little Bow Provincial Park, 19 km east and 2 km south of Champion, is a 110–ha area on the north shore of the west arm of the reservoir. Established in 1954, the park's irrigated shrubs and trees create a verdant oasis in the surrounding golden prairie in summer. The park offers a year-round campground with 193 sites, tap water, a public telephone, a boat launch and dock, a sandy beach, picnic tables and shelters, a playground and a concession. Travers Dam Campground, which is operated by the Town of Lomond, is on the north shore of the east arm of the reservoir. It can be reached by driving 30 km east of Champion on Secondary Road 529, then 10 km south on Secondary Road 843. The recreation area is open year-round and offers 100 random campsites, pump water, picnic tables and shelters and a boat launch.

Travers Reservoir is now owned and operated by Alberta Environment as part of the Carseland-Bow River Headworks System. The main purpose of the reservoir is to store water for irrigation and multi-purpose uses. It also serves to minimize flooding of the Little Bow River and to maintain flow in the Little Bow River during low flow periods. Recreation is an important use. The water in Travers Reservoir is very clear and the concentration of algae is very low. Fishing, power boating, wind surfing, sailing and swimming are popular, especially at Little Bow Provincial Park. All boats are prohibited from some posted areas in the reservoir and power boats are restricted to a maximum speed of 12 km/hour in other posted areas (Alta. For. Ld. Wild. 1988). Provincial sport fishing regulations apply to Travers Reservoir, but there are no additional, specific regulations (Alta. For. Ld. Wild. 1989). The reservoir supports a commercial fishery for lake whitefish and northern pike.

Drainage Basin Characteristics

The natural watershed of Travers Reservoir covers an area of 4 230 km² (Table 1) and extends northwest to a minor height of land

623

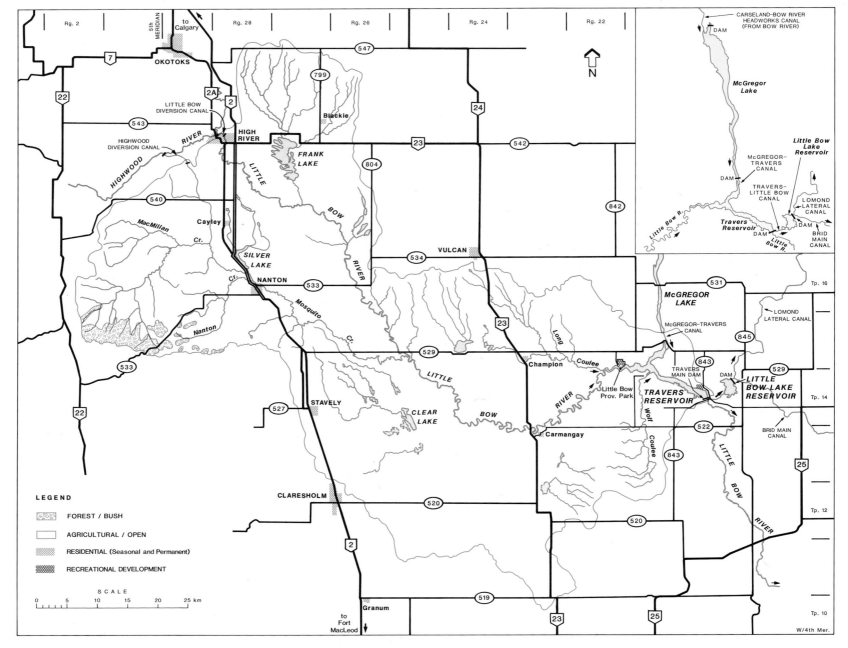

Figure 1. Features of the drainage basin of Travers Reservoir.
SOURCES: Alta. Envir. n.d.[c]; En. Mines Resour. Can. 1977. Updated with 1981 aerial photos.

Table 1. Characteristics of Travers Reservoir drainage basin.

area (excluding lake) (km²)[a]	4 230
soil[b]	Orthic Dark Brown Chernozemics
bedrock geology[c]	Bearpaw Formation (Upper Cretaceous): shale, thin ironstone and bentonite beds; marine Horseshoe Canyon Formation (Upper Cretaceous): sandstone, mudstone, shale; ironstone, scattered coal and bentonite beds; mainly nonmarine
terrain[d]	rolling hills to flat land, dissected by coulees
ecoregions[d]	Mixed Grass in eastern half, Fescue Grass in western half; Aspen Parkland on western border
dominant vegetation[d]	spear, grama, wheat grasses
mean annual sunshine (h)[e]	2 344

SOURCES: [a]Alta. Envir. n.d.[c]; [b]Greenlee 1973; [c]Alta. Res. Counc. 1972; [d]Strong and Leggat 1981; [e]Envir. Can. 1982

separating it from the Highwood River-Bow River drainage system. Mosquito Creek flows eastward from the lower reaches of the foothills and joins the Little Bow River, which flows into Travers Reservoir (Fig. 1). The drainage basin is in a fairly arid region of Alberta so, despite the large size of the drainage area, it provides only about 3% of the water in the reservoir. The balance of water in the reservoir is diverted from the Bow River drainage system (Table 2).

The landscape of the drainage basin varies from rolling hills and hummocky terrain in the west to flat plains in the east (Richard Strong Assoc. Ltd. 1983). The basin includes parts of three ecoregions (Strong and Leggat 1981). The eastern half of the basin, including the area around the reservoir, is in the Mixed Grass Ecoregion. The original vegetation consisted of spear, grama and wheat grasses on the uplands and rose, buckbrush and wolf willow in coulees, where moisture is slightly more available. Eastern cottonwood and willows grow near water courses. Most of the uplands have been cultivated now. Soils are predominantly Orthic Dark Brown Chernozemics, with a few pockets of well-drained Orthic Regosols on steep, eroded slopes and Orthic Gleysols in damp, depressional areas around the reservoir (Greenlee 1973; Strong and Leggat 1981). Much of the land surrounding the reservoir is dissected by coulees; Wolf Coulee on the south shore (Fig. 2) is a spectacular example of a heavily eroded canyon with hoodoos.

Most of the drainage basin west of Clear Lake and Secondary Road 804 is in the Fescue Grass Ecoregion. The natural vegetation

Table 2. Characteristics of Travers Reservoir.

control structure[a]	Travers Dam: earthfill
dam height (m)[a]	42.7
crest length (m)[a]	914.4
full supply level (FSL) (m)[b]	856.18
live storage at FSL (m³)[b]	105 x 10⁶
volume at FSL (m³)[b]	413 x 10⁶
flooded area at FSL (km²)[a]	22.5
maximum possible drawdown (m)[b]	5.18
mean annual drawdown (1975–1987) (m)[b]	2.0
maximum depth (m)[c]	39.6
mean depth (m)[b]	18.3
shoreline length at FSL (km)[d]	99.8
lake length at FSL (km)[e]	19.0
lake width at FSL (km)[e]	2.4
mean annual lake evaporation (mm)[f]	759
mean annual precipitation (mm)[f]	362
mean residence time (1976–1986) (yr)[b, g]	0.82
mean annual inflow volume (1976–1986) (m³)[g]	
—from McGregor Lake	371.5 x 10⁶
—from Little Bow River	32.9 x 10⁶
mean annual outflow volume (1976–1986) (m³)[g]	
—to Little Bow Lake Reservoir	385.5 x 10⁶
—to Little Bow River	10.5 x 10⁶

Sources: [a]Alta. Envir. n.d.[e]; [b]Alta. Envir. n.d.[a]; [c]MacNeill 1978; [d]R.L. & L. Envir. Serv. Ltd. 1985; [e]En. Mines Resour. Can. 1976; 1977; [f]Alta. Envir. n.d.[c]; [g]Envir. Can. 1987

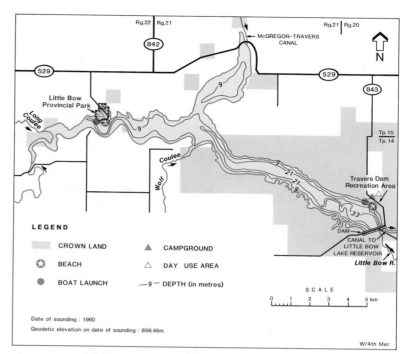

Figure 2. Bathymetry and shoreline features of Travers Reservoir.
BATHYMETRY SOURCE: Alta. Envir. n.d.[d].

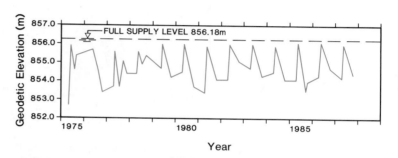

Figure 3. Water level of Travers Reservoir, 1975 to 1988.
SOURCE: Alta. Envir. n.d.[a].

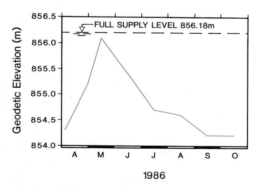

Figure 4. Annual water level regime of Travers Reservoir, 1986.
SOURCE: Alta. Envir. n.d.[a].

is fescue and Parry oatgrass, but most of the area has been cultivated. Soils are Black Chernozemics. On the far western border of the basin, there is a small area of the Groveland Subregion of the Aspen Parkland Ecoregion. Soils are Black Chernozemics, but because the area is damp enough, pockets of trembling aspen are interspersed with the fescue grasslands.

Most of the Crown land around Travers Reservoir (Fig. 2) is leased for crop cultivation and cattle grazing (Richard Strong Assoc. Ltd. 1983). At present, the dominant agricultural activity in the drainage basin is dryland farming of cereals such as wheat and barley, hay, and specialty crops such as canola and rye (IEC Beak Consult. Ltd. et al. 1983). Irrigation farming is carried out along the Little Bow River as far as Travers Reservoir and along Mosquito Creek. Some cattle ranches are located along the southern arm of Travers Reservoir (Richard Strong Assoc. Ltd. 1983). In addition, there are numerous swine and cattle feedlots in the region.

There are no population centres near Travers Reservoir; 1 cottage subdivision, with 13 cottages, is located just east of Little Bow Provincial Park (Alta. Rec. Parks n.d.; Richard Strong Assoc. Ltd. 1983). The villages closest to the reservoir are Champion and Carmangay.

Reservoir Characteristics

Travers Dam was built from 1951 to 1953 by the Prairie Farm Rehabilitation Administration of the federal government, and was officially opened on 13 July 1954. It is now owned and operated by Alberta Environment.

Travers Reservoir lies in an old, eroded glacial meltwater channel; approximately 70% of the lake bottom is very steep, dropping from the valley breaks to depths of 9 m or more (Fig. 2). Thus, large withdrawals of water do not alter the basin morphometry drastically; a water level drop of 2 m below the full supply level results in only an 18% reduction in area (Alta. Envir. n.d.[d]). The deepest part of the reservoir (39.6 m) is located at the eastern end near the dam. Steep sides, the annual water level fluctuations and strong winds result in shoreline erosion and a narrow littoral zone. Around most

of the reservoir, the shoreline is barren gravel (Richard Strong Assoc. Ltd. 1983).

The annual water level fluctuation of Travers Reservoir averaged 2.0 m from 1976 to 1987; the maximum annual fluctuation was 2.5 m (Fig. 3). Typical annual operation of the reservoir includes rapid filling in spring, then fairly steady drawdown through summer (Fig. 4).

Approximately 90% of the water flowing into Travers Reservoir (Table 2) is diverted from the Bow River near Carseland, then through McGregor Lake. The remaining 10% comes from the Little Bow River, which derives most of its flow from two diversions from the Highwood River (Fig. 1), a tributary of the Bow River. Three percent of the water released from Travers Reservoir flows into the

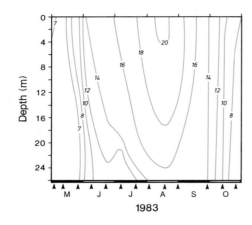

Figure 5. Temperature (°C) of Travers Reservoir, 1983. Arrows indicate sampling dates.
SOURCE: Alta. Envir. n.d.[b].

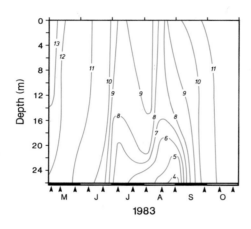

Figure 6. Dissolved oxygen (mg/L) in Travers Reservoir, 1983. Arrows indicate sampling dates.
SOURCE: Alta. Envir. n.d.[b].

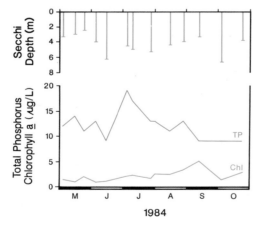

Figure 7. Total phosphorus, chlorophyll *a* and Secchi depth in Travers Reservoir, 1984.
SOURCE: Alta. Envir. n.d.[b].

Table 3. Major ions and related water quality variables for Travers Reservoir. Average concentrations in mg/L; pH in pH units. Composite samples from the euphotic zone collected 12 times from 14 May to 22 Oct. 1984. S.E. = standard error.

	Mean	S.E.
pH (range)	7.2–8.5	—
total alkalinity (CaCO₃)	131	1.6
specific conductivity (μS/cm)	359	5.6
total dissolved solids (calculated)	204	2.8
turbidity (NTU)	1[a]	0.2
total hardness (CaCO₃)	159	2.1
HCO₃	158	2.5
CO₃	<1	—
Mg	15	0.2
Na	12	0.5
K	1	0.03
Cl	5	0.1
SO₄	52	1.2
Ca	39	0.7

NOTE: [a]n = 9
SOURCE: Alta. Envir. n.d.[b], Naquadat station 05AL05AC6000

Table 4. Nutrient, chlorophyll *a* and Secchi depth data for Travers Reservoir. Average concentrations in μg/L. Composite samples from the euphotic zone collected 18 times from 03 May to 25 Oct. 1983 and 14 times from 14 May to 22 Oct. 1984. S.E. = standard error.

	1983		1984	
	Mean	S.E.	Mean	S.E.
total phosphorus	16	1.3	12	0.8
total Kjeldahl nitrogen	345[a]	33.3	385[c]	68.6
chlorophyll *a*	2.2[b]	0.22	2.3[d]	0.28
Secchi depth (m)	3.7	0.28	4.3	0.32

NOTES: [a]n = 13; [b]n = 17; [c]n = 8; [d]n = 15
SOURCE: Alta. Envir. n.d.[b], Naquadat station 05AL05AC6000

Little Bow River and 97% flows via canal to Little Bow Lake Reservoir and subsequently into canals for distribution to the Bow River Irrigation District. The volume of Travers Reservoir is exchanged approximately once a year (Table 2); almost all inflow and outflow occurs between April and October.

Water Quality

Travers Reservoir has been sampled jointly by Alberta Environment and Alberta Recreation and Parks since 1983 (Alta. Envir. n.d.[b]).

The water quality of Travers Reservoir is more like that of the Bow River and intervening McGregor Lake than local natural lakes such as Frank and Clear lakes. The water is well-buffered, and the proportions of the major ions—bicarbonate, sulphate and calcium (Table 3)—are similar to those in the Bow River.

In 1983, the reservoir was weakly stratified from late June to mid-September (Fig. 5). From early July to mid-September, dissolved oxygen slowly decreased in the water near the sediments; the lowest concentration was 4 mg/L (Fig. 6). In February 1975 and 1976, dissolved oxygen concentrations near the main dam were less than 2 mg/L at depths greater than 30 m (English 1977).

The mean open-water chlorophyll *a* and total phosphorus concentrations are low in Travers Reservoir (Table 4) as compared with other prairie lakes. The concentrations of both variables are approximately half those in upstream McGregor Lake. Consequently, the water is clear (Secchi depth averages 4 m) and attractive for recreation. During 1984, the total phosphorus concentration reached a maximum in early July (Fig. 7), possibly because of increased runoff from rain. The maximum chlorophyll *a* concentration was 5 μg/L in

September. Travers Reservoir is classified as oligotrophic. It has the lowest phosphorus and chlorophyll *a* levels of 36 other lakes and reservoirs similarly sampled by Alberta Environment (Alta. Envir. n.d.[b]).

Biological Characteristics

Plants

The only information on algae in Travers Reservoir was collected during a brief fisheries survey in 1955, one year after the reservoir was first filled (Miller 1955). At that time, there was a bloom of *Aphanizomenon* sp. and *Anabaena* sp., starting at the west end of the lake. Algal productivity may have been greater then than it is now, likely as a result of an upsurge in nutrients from newly flooded soils.

There are no data on the macrophytes in the reservoir. Dense aquatic plant growth near the shore of Little Bow Provincial Park has occasionally been a problem for recreational users (Alta. Rec. Parks n.d.).

Invertebrates

When the plankton was sampled in 1955, the year after the reservoir was first filled, only a few invertebrates were found in the eastern end of the reservoir, mostly *Cyclops* sp. and *Diaptomus* sp. The zooplankton was somewhat more abundant in the west end, particularly *Daphnia pulex, D. longispina* and rotifers (Miller 1955). In 1975, the zooplankton was sampled monthly from 16 June to 3 October. The greatest volume of plankton was collected in July (1.32 mL/L); copepods were the dominant group on all dates (English 1977).

The benthic fauna has not been sampled.

Fish

Travers Reservoir supports 14 species of fish. Lake whitefish, northern pike, white suckers, longnose suckers, burbot, walleye and lake chub are abundant (Alta. For. Ld. Wild. n.d.). Other species include rainbow trout, brown trout, trout-perch, shorthead redhorse, spottail shiner, fathead minnow and yellow perch. Lake whitefish are not indigenous to Travers Reservoir or the Little Bow River, but likely migrated from McGregor Lake, where they were stocked in 1943 (MacNeill 1978). They were first noticed in Travers Reservoir in 1955, one year after it was filled (Miller 1955). Walleye, which were introduced as eyed-eggs in 1958, have become established but lake trout, which were stocked in 1959, and kokanee, which were stocked in 1970, did not survive (Alta. For. Ld. Wild. n.d.; MacNeill 1978). Brown trout probably originate from the Bow and Little Bow rivers (MacNeill 1978). The shorthead redhorse is rare in the reservoir (Haugen 1970).

Most fish in the reservoir spawn and overwinter there (IEC Beak Consult. Ltd. et al. 1983). Northern pike, however, spawn upstream in the Little Bow River. Walleye probably spawn in the west end of Travers Reservoir, near the mouth of the Little Bow River (Alta. For. Ld. Wild. n.d.).

Recreational fishing for lake whitefish and northern pike is very popular, both in summer and through the ice in winter. During a creel census conducted on 10 days between February and October in 1982, 276 people were interviewed. They caught 292 pike, with a success rate of 0.46 pike/angler-hour. In the same census, 143 lake whitefish and only 2 trout, 1 burbot and 1 walleye were captured (Alta. For. Ld. Wild. n.d.).

The first commercial harvest from Travers Reservoir was taken in 1956; the catch was mostly northern pike (MacNeill 1978). Since then, lake whitefish have become the most economically important species, followed by northern pike. Between 1980/81 and 1986/87 the mean annual commercial catch was 7 296 kg of lake whitefish,

805 kg of northern pike, 832 kg of suckers, 189 kg of burbot, 18 kg of trout, 8 kg of walleye and 3 kg of yellow perch, a total average catch of 9 151 kg of fish (Alta. For. Ld. Wild. n.d.). Travers Reservoir is estimated to produce a sustainable annual harvest of 13 608 kg of lake whitefish (MacNeill 1978). From 1984/85 to 1986/87 the harvest approached capacity and quotas were set for the 2 main commercial species: 11 350 kg for whitefish and 1 350 kg for pike. In 1987/88, the number of licences issued jumped to 68 from a previous high of 16. That year, a total of 17 823 kg of lake whitefish, 1 723 kg of pike and 204 kg of walleye were harvested (Alta. For. Ld. Wild. n.d.).

The average size of lake whitefish caught in Travers Reservoir in 1958, four years after the reservoir opened, was greater than that of whitefish taken in later samples (Haugen 1970; MacNeill 1978). A study of the age, growth and yield of lake whitefish from Travers and seven other reservoirs in southern Alberta was conducted in 1969 (Haugen 1970). Lake whitefish were found to mature slowly in Travers Reservoir—only 80% of the males and 13% of the females were mature at age 4 compared to 100% maturity at age 4 in most of the other reservoirs studied.

Wildlife

Travers Reservoir has few shallow shoreline areas, and therefore does not support a large population of nesting waterfowl (Richard Strong Assoc. Ltd. 1983). Raptors and geese nest around the reservoir and waterfowl use it for staging during fall migration. Mammals in the area include white-tailed deer, antelope, Richardson's ground squirrels, badgers and coyotes (Finlay and Finlay 1987).

J.M. Crosby

References

Alberta Environment. n.d.[a]. Devel. Op. Div., Headworks Br. Unpubl. data, Edmonton.
———. n.d.[b]. Envir. Assess. Div., Envir. Qlty. Monit. Br. Unpubl. data, Edmonton.
———. n.d.[c]. Tech. Serv. Div., Hydrol. Br. Unpubl. data, Edmonton.
———. n.d.[d]. Tech. Serv. Div., Surv. Br. Unpubl. data, Edmonton.
———. n.d.[e]. Water Resour. Mgt. Div., Dam Safety Br. Unpubl. data, Edmonton.
Alberta Forestry, Lands and Wildlife. n.d. Fish Wild. Div. Unpubl. data, Edmonton.
———. 1988. Boating in Alberta. Fish Wild. Div., Edmonton.
———. 1989. Guide to sportfishing. Fish Wild. Div., Edmonton.
Alberta Recreation and Parks. n.d. Parks Div. Unpubl. data, Edmonton.
Alberta Research Council. 1972. Geological map of Alberta. Nat. Resour. Div., Alta. Geol. Surv., Edmonton.
Champion History Committee. 1970. Cleverville-Champion, 1905–1970: A history of Champion and area. Champion Hist. Commit., Champion.
Energy, Mines and Resources Canada. 1977. National topographic series 1:250 000 82H (1977), 82I (1977), 82J (1977). Surv. Map. Br., Ottawa.
English, W.G. 1977. A limnological survey of Travers Reservoir. Alta. Rec. Parks Wild., Fish Wild. Div., Lethbridge.
Environment Canada. 1982. Canadian climate normals, Vol. 7: Bright sunshine (1951–1980). Prep. by Atm. Envir. Serv. Supply Serv. Can., Ottawa.
———. 1987. Historical streamflow summary, Alberta. Water Surv. Can., Water Resour. Br., Ottawa.
Finlay, J. and C. Finlay. 1987. Parks in Alberta: A guide to peaks, ponds, parklands & prairies. Hurtig Publ., Edmonton.
Greenlee, G.M. 1978. Soil survey of Little Bow Provincial Park and interpretation for recreational use. Alta. Inst. Pedol. Rep. No. M–73–2, Edmonton.
Haugen, G.N. 1970. Age, growth, and yield of lake whitefish *Coregonus clupeaformis* from seven irrigation reservoirs in the South Saskatchewan drainage basin, Alberta. Alta. Ld. For., Fish Wild. Div., Edmonton.
IEC Beak Consultants Ltd., Techman Engineering Ltd. and Aresco Ltd. 1983. Environmental overview of the Little Bow River Basin. Prep. for Alta. Envir., Plan. Div., Edmonton.
MacNeill, J.W. 1978. A review of the history and management of the fishery resource of Travers Reservoir. Alta. Rec. Parks Wild., Fish Wild. Div., Edmonton.
Miller, R.B. 1955. Report on Travers Reservoir. Alta. Ld. For., Fish Wild. Div., Edmonton.
Richard Strong Associates Limited. 1983. McGregor, Travers, Little Bow Reservoir vicinity recreation development study. Prep. for Alta. Envir., Plan. Div., Edmonton.
R.L. & L. Environmental Services Ltd. 1985. A compendium of existing environmental data on Alberta reservoirs. Prep. for Alta. Envir. Res. Trust, Edmonton.
Strong, W.L. and K.R. Leggat. 1981. Ecoregions of Alberta. Alta. En. Nat. Resour., Resour. Eval. Plan. Div., Edmonton.

ELKWATER LAKE

Alberta Recreation and Parks/K. Bocking

MAP SHEET: 72E/9
LOCATION: Tp8 R3 W4
LAT/LONG: 49°39'N 110°18'W

Elkwater Lake is a popular recreational lake located on the northwest corner of Cypress Hills Provincial Park. The closest population centres are the city of Medicine Hat, 65 km northwest, and the town of Irvine, 40 km north. Highway 41 provides easy access to the eastern arm of the lake and to the hamlet of Elkwater on the south shore (Fig. 1).

The lake's name is a translation of the Blackfoot name *Ponokiok-we* (Alta. Cult. Multicult. n.d.). Historically, the lake was a favourite drinking spot for the many ungulates that inhabited the Cypress Hills.

The earliest inhabitants of the Cypress Hills were Plains Indians (Cree, Blood, Assiniboine, Stoney, Peigan, Blackfoot and Gros Ventre), who used the area for hunting, fishing and semipermanent habitation. Anthony Henday, the first European explorer to reach the Cypress Hills, arrived in 1754. The first white settlers arrived at the lake in 1883 and established a lumber mill on the north shore, floating logs across the water. Logging continued until 1912, when most of the timber had been removed (Michael and Johnson 1981). Cattle ranching began in the early 1880s and grazing continues to the present day. The townsite of Elkwater was founded in 1913 when a subdivision was completed on the south shore; by the 1920s, the Elkwater Lake area was a major summer camping spot.

Cypress Hills Provincial Park was originally established in 1929 as Elkwater Resort. It was transferred to the province in 1945, and was designated a provincial park in 1951 (Alta. Rec. Parks n.d.). The present facilities include several launch ramps, boat docks and a marina, which provide boaters with excellent access to the lake (Fig. 2). The launch ramp and dock in the eastern bay are for nonmotorized boats only, and there is a 12 km/hour speed limit in the bay (Alta. For. Ld. Wild. 1988). Power boating and water skiing are allowed in the north and west bays. Children's playgrounds, picnic sites, parking, interpretive trails, overnight camping facilities and a swimming area are also available on, or adjacent to, the south shore.

The water in Elkwater Lake is clear and the sandy beach is clean. The lake supports a year-round sport fishery for northern pike and yellow perch, and is a popular area for swimming and wildlife and waterfowl viewing. Hiking, cross-country skiing and downhill skiing are activities pursued in the surrounding park. There are no sport fishing regulations specific to the lake, but general provincial limits and regulations apply (Alta. For. Ld. Wild. 1989). Users of the marina and boat launches are often concerned about the extensive beds of aquatic plants in the lake, which can foul propellers.

Drainage Basin Characteristics

The watershed of Elkwater Lake (Fig. 1) lies almost entirely within Cypress Hills Provincial Park. The Cypress Hills are a dissected, flat-topped plateau 145–km long and 25–km to 40–km wide that rises approximately 760 m above the surrounding plain. They are the highest point of land in Canada between Labrador and the Rocky Mountains. Elkwater Lake was formed in a depression at the base of the hills. A forested escarpment rises approximately 220 m from the lake's south shore to a plateau in the southern section of the watershed. To the north, the land is flat and reaches an elevation about 8 m higher than the lake. The lake's main inflows are diffuse runoff from the watershed, and numerous underground springs (Alta. En-

Table 1. Characteristics of Elkwater Lake drainage basin.

area (excluding lake) (km²)[a]	25.7
soil[b]	Gray Luvisol, Dark Brown and Black Chernozemics
bedrock geology[c]	Eastend Formation (Upper Cretaceous): sandstone, shale, siltstone, coal beds; shoreline complex
	Whitemud Formation (Upper Cretaceous): sandstone, clay; nonmarine
	Battle Formation (Upper Cretaceous): mudstone, tuff beds; nonmarine
	Ravenscrag Formation (Tertiary): sandstone, clay, mudstone, coal, thin bentonite beds; nonmarine
	Cypress Hills Formation (Oligocene): conglomerate, sandstone; nonmarine
terrain[d]	gently undulating to hilly
ecoregions[b]	Boreal Foothills; Groveland Subregion of Aspen Parkland; Mixed Grass
dominant vegetation[b]	trembling aspen, balsam poplar, lodgepole pine; rough fescue; grama, spear grass
mean annual inflow (m³)[a, e]	1.95 x 10⁶
mean annual sunshine (h)[f]	2 345

NOTE: [e]excluding groundwater inflow
SOURCES: [a]Alta. Envir. n.d.[b]; [b]Strong and Leggat 1981; [c]Alta. Res. Counc. 1972; [d]Lombard North Group 1976; [f]Envir. Can. 1982[b]

Table 2. Characteristics of Elkwater Lake.

elevation (m)[a, b]	1 226.36
surface area (km²)[a, b]	2.31
volume (m³)[a, b]	8.00 x 10⁶
maximum depth (m)[a, b]	8.4
mean depth (m)[a, b]	3.5
shoreline length (km)[c]	10.8
mean annual lake evaporation (mm)[d]	770
mean annual precipitation (mm)[d]	529
mean residence time (yr)[d, e]	6
control structure[f]	weir with drop inlet spillway
weir height (m)[f]	3.65 (from original ground line)
crest length (m)[f]	85
maximum drawdown level (m)[f]	1 224.50
outlet capacity (m³/s)[f]	4.79

NOTES: [a]on date of sounding: Sep. 1976; [e]excluding groundwater inflow
SOURCES: [b]Alta. Envir. n.d.[c]; [c]R.L. & L. Envir. Serv. Ltd. 1985; [d]Alta. Envir. n.d.[b]; [f]WER Eng. 1981

vir. 1982). The outlet, Ross Creek, flows from the northern bay to the South Saskatchewan River.

The bedrock geology beneath the drainage basin is varied (Table 1). The Eastend Formation, which underlies and surrounds the lake, and the Whitemud and Battle formations, which lie to the south of the lake, are groundwater aquifers. The more recent Ravenscrag Formation appears along the upper slopes of the Cypress Hills plateau and the youngest rock, the Cypress Hills Formation, caps the plateau (Alta. Res. Counc. 1972; Lombard North Group 1976). The tops of the hills were not glaciated by any of the great ice sheets that flowed down from the Rocky Mountains or from the Hudson Bay area.

Areas within the Cypress Hills are associated with different microclimates depending on their position relative to the prevailing winds. Low pressure fronts from the northwest encounter the hills and lose their moisture as rain from May through September, mostly on the north-facing slopes. An annual average of 7 cm more rainfall and

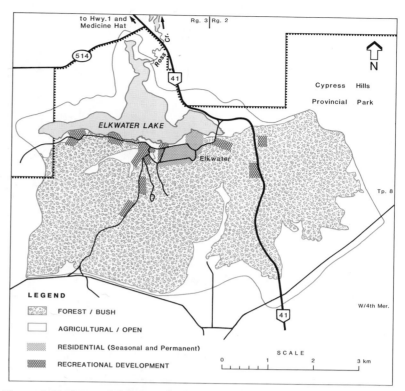

Figure 1. Features of the drainage basin of Elkwater Lake.
SOURCES: Alta. Envir. n.d.[b]; En. Mines Resour. Can. 1978. Updated with 1986 aerial photos.

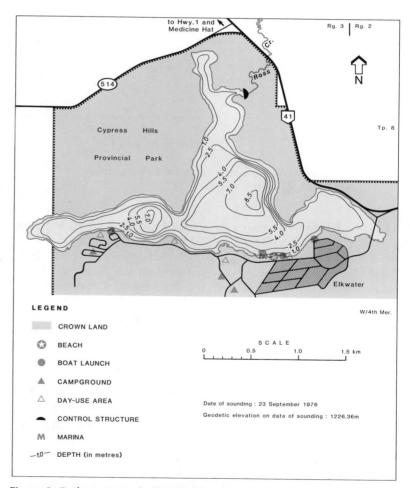

Figure 2. Bathymetry and shoreline features of Elkwater Lake.
BATHYMETRY SOURCE: Alta. Envir. n.d.[c].

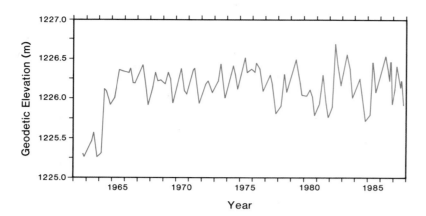

Figure 3. Water level of Elkwater Lake, 1962 to 1987.
SOURCE: Envir. Can. 1962–1987.

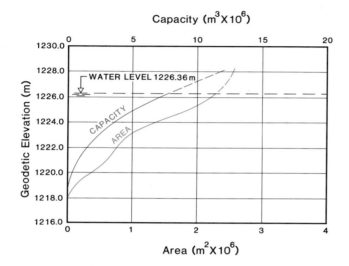

Figure 4. Area/capacity curve for Elkwater Lake.
SOURCE: Alta. Envir. n.d.[c].

Table 3. Major ions and related water quality variables for Elkwater Lake. Average concentrations in mg/L; pH in pH units. Composite samples from the euphotic zone collected 5 times from 16 May to 04 Oct. 1983. S.E. = standard error.

	Mean	S.E.
pH (range)	8.1–8.3[a]	—
total alkalinity ($CaCO_3$)	214	3.6
specific conductivity (µS/cm)	450	10.3
total dissolved solids (calculated)	242[a]	6.5
turbidity (NTU)	4[a]	1.5
total hardness ($CaCO_3$)	207	4.6
HCO_3	252	4.2
CO_3	4	1.7
Mg	30	0.9
Na	14	0.2
K	4	0.1
Cl	9	4.2
SO_4	20	1.3
Ca	35[b]	0.5

NOTES: [a]n = 2; [b]n = 3
SOURCE: Alta. Envir. n.d.[a], Naquadat station 01AL05AH8000

Table 4. Nutrient, chlorophyll *a* and Secchi depth data for Elkwater Lake. Average concentrations in µg/L. Composite samples from the euphotic zone collected 7 times from 16 May to 02 Oct. 1983 and 5 times from 18 June to 02 Oct. 1984. S.E. = standard error.

	1983		1984	
	Mean	S.E.	Mean	S.E.
total phosphorus	38	6.0	48	6.0
total Kjeldahl nitrogen	640[a]	40.0	—	—
chlorophyll *a*	5.0[b]	1.84	6.8	1.78
Secchi depth (m)	2.7[b]	0.82	2.6	0.85

NOTES: [a]n = 2; [b]n = 6
SOURCE: Alta. Envir. n.d.[a], Naquadat station 01AL05AH8000

11 cm more snowfall have been recorded in the Cypress Hills than in nearby Medicine Hat (Envir. Can. 1982[a]).

The Cypress Hills are part of the Boreal Foothills, Aspen Parkland and Mixed Grass ecoregions. Vegetation on the slopes of the hills varies with moisture conditions. For the most part, the south- and west-facing slopes are covered with mixed-grass prairie on Dark Brown Chernozemic soils, whereas north-facing slopes, seepage areas and creek banks support trembling aspen and spruce on Black Chernozemics and Gleysols. At elevations between 1 200 m and 1 300 m, the grasslands are predominantly rough fescue on Black and Dark Brown Chernozemics, and above 1 300 m, the vegetation is trembling aspen, balsam poplar, lodgepole pine and white spruce on Gray Luvisols (Strong and Leggat 1981; Looman and Best 1987). Approximately 80% of the watershed is forested, and about 17% is open grassland, mostly north of the lake and in the southern portion at the basin (Fig. 1). Cattle graze on the park uplands south of the lake and on the lowlands to the northwest. The remaining 3% of the land has been used for residential and recreational development, mainly at Elkwater townsite and along the south shore.

Lake Basin Characteristics

Elkwater Lake has three bays and a shoreline that is almost 11–km long (Fig. 2, Table 2). It is a moderate-sized lake with a maximum length of 3.7 km and a maximum width of 2.3 km. A small, deep area, with a maximum depth of 8.4 m, is located near the centre of the lake.

The lake's outflow has been controlled since 1908 (Alta. Envir. n.d.[e]). In 1907, area landowners complained about unauthorized

deepening of the outlet by the Canadian Pacific Railway, to increase flow to its reservoir at Irvine. The railroad company built a headgate at the outlet in 1907, but only closed the gates in 1908 after repeated requests. The embankments beside the weir washed out in 1917, and repairs were made by the federal government in 1918. In 1948, the timber spillway was rebuilt by the provincial government. In 1978, Alberta Environment replaced the old structure with a drop inlet spillway, which has the capacity to discharge water at a rate of 4.79 m^3/second (WER Eng. 1981). The control structure is operated to meet the needs of downstream water users, users of the lake and the fisheries resource.

The elevation of Elkwater Lake has been monitored since 1962 (Fig. 3). The difference between the minimum elevation (1 225.25 m), recorded in October 1962, and the maximum elevation (1 226.67 m), recorded in June 1982, is 1.42 m. Changes in the lake's surface area and capacity with fluctuating water levels are illustrated in Figure 4. Since the latest control structure was installed in 1978, the maximum range in elevations has been 0.98 m. The target elevation for the lake is 1 226.36 m.

Water Quality

The water quality of Elkwater Lake has been monitored since 1982 by Alberta Environment and Alberta Recreation and Parks (Alta. Envir. n.d.[a]).

The water chemistry of Elkwater Lake is similar to that of many freshwater lakes in southern and central Alberta. The lake is well-buffered, and the dominant ions are calcium and bicarbonate (Table 3). The turbidity is low, and recreational water quality is good, as

Table 5. Aquatic vegetation in Elkwater Lake, 12 August 1982 and 27 July 1983.
Arranged in alphabetical order.

emergent	arrowhead	*Sagittaria* spp.
	bulrush	*Scirpus* spp.
	common cattail	*Typha latifolia*
	horsetail	*Equisetum fluviatile*
	wire rush	*Juncus balticus*
	rush	*J. tenuis*
free-floating	common bladderwort	*Utricularia vulgaris*
	lesser duckweed	*Lemna minor*
	star duckweed	*L. trisulca*
	coontail	*Ceratophyllum demersum*
submergent	large-sheath pondweed	*Potamogeton vaginatus*
	Richardson pondweed	*P. richardsonii*
	Sago pondweed	*P. pectinatus*
	northern watermilfoil	*Myriophyllum exalbescens*
floating-leaved	water smartweed	*Polygonum amphibium*

SOURCE: Alta. Envir. n.d.[d]

indicated by relatively low chlorophyll *a* concentrations and reasonable Secchi depth transparencies (Table 4).

During the open-water period, the entire water column tends to be well-mixed by wind action and therefore well-oxygenated, with a uniform temperature (Fig. 5). Under ice in winter, the water in the deeper portions of the lake can become anoxic, but the surface waters remain well-oxygenated.

Total phosphorus in Elkwater Lake, as in many other shallow lakes in Alberta (Prepas and Trew 1983), increases in late summer and is followed by peak chlorophyll *a* values (Fig. 6). The phosphorus increase is probably due to internal loading from the sediments or phosphorus release from macrophytes (Riley and Prepas 1984). The lake is classified as mesotrophic. The chlorophyll level is less than expected given the total phosphorus values in Table 4; nevertheless, the similar seasonal patterns in chlorophyll, phosphorus and Secchi depth suggest that algal productivity is limited by phosphorus availability.

Biological Characteristics

Plants

Recent information on the phytoplankton community is not available. A single net sample taken from the bottom to the surface in August 1947 indicated low algal biomass (Miller and Macdonald 1950), which is consistent with the low chlorophyll levels reported in Table 4.

Macrophytes were surveyed by Alberta Environment in 1982 and 1983 (Table 5). Of the 15 species identified, Richardson pondweed (*Potamogeton richardsonii*) was dominant at most sites. In 1976, Fish and Wildlife Division reported that a dense band of Canada waterweed (*Elodea canadensis*) encircled the lake between the 1.5–m and 2.5–m contours (MacNeill 1977), but this species was not found in the later surveys. In 1976, rushes (*Juncus* spp.) were mainly concentrated in the northern bay and common cattail (*Typha latifolia*) was present in the eastern and western bays. The free-floating species coontail (*Ceratophyllum demersum*) was found along the south shore at the east and west ends of the lake. Macrophyte problems have been reported near heavily used areas of the lake, particularly at the marina and boat launches. A 1947 study (Miller and Macdonald 1950) noted extensive macrophyte growth, with plants extending to depths of 5 m in some places. Thus, it appears that macrophytes are no more abundant now than they were historically (Reynoldson 1981).

Invertebrates

The zooplankton and benthic communities were sampled in August 1947 (Miller and Macdonald 1950) and on 20 May 1976 (MacNeill 1977). The dominant zooplankton species from the single sample

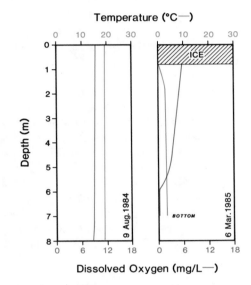

Figure 5. Temperature and dissolved oxygen in Elkwater Lake, 1984 and 1985.
SOURCE: Alta. Envir. n.d.[a].

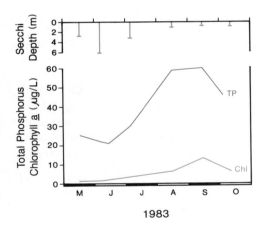

Figure 6. Total phosphorus, chlorophyll *a* and Secchi depth in Elkwater Lake, 1983.
SOURCE: Alta. Envir. n.d.[a].

taken in the earlier study was *Bosmina* sp., a small cladoceran; *Cyclops bicuspidatus*, *Diaptomus* sp. and the rotifer *Anurea* sp. were also present. The later study was less specific.

In the 1947 study, benthic samples (sample size unknown) were taken by a series of dredgings at depths of 0.9, 2.4, 4.9 and 6.4 m. The most abundant animals at the two shallowest depths were scuds (Amphipoda: *Gammarus lacustris*) and phantom midge larvae (Diptera: *Chaoborus* sp.). At the two deeper sites, phantom midge larvae were most numerous. Sphaeriid clams were found at all depths except 2.4 m, and caddis fly larvae (Trichoptera) and leeches (Hirudinea) were found only at the 2.4–m depth. The greatest biomass was measured at the 0.9–m (69 g/m^2) and 2.4–m (56 g/m^2) depths, and the smallest biomass was measured at the 4.9–m (30 g/m^2) and 6.4–m (13 g/m^2) depths.

Fish

Currently, only two sport fish species are present in Elkwater Lake. Northern pike are indigenous to the lake; yellow perch were stocked in 1940 and 1945. Largemouth bass, spottail shiner, walleye and kokanee have also been stocked, but these introductions failed (Fitch 1980). In 1981 and 1982, fathead minnows were planted to provide prey for older northern pike and to buffer the juvenile yellow perch from pike predation. However, no fathead minnows were caught in a 1986 sampling program (Mackay 1988).

A creel survey of Elkwater Lake was conducted by Fish and Wildlife Division in 1979 (Table 6). The recreational fishery was very popular with residents of Medicine Hat and other parts of Alberta in spite of low catch rates. Angler number and effort over the summer decreased as interference from aquatic plants, water skiers and power boats increased. The mean catch rate for northern pike in Elkwater was 0.28 fish/hour, which is substantially lower than the mean catch rate of 0.76 pike/hour averaged for 34 other Alberta lakes. Similarly, the mean catch rate of yellow perch (0.05 fish/hour) was much lower than the mean catch rate averaged in the same study for 19 other Alberta lakes (0.75 perch/hour). These low rates are due to the slow growth rate of pike and the small population of perch (Fitch 1981).

Wildlife

Common Loons and four species of grebes nest on Elkwater Lake, and small numbers of Double-crested Cormorants feed there occasionally. The most frequent nesting sites for Blue-winged Teal, American Widgeons, Pintails and Mallards are grasses and sedges, which are common near the shoreline. Rush and cattail marshes provide cover for Lesser Scaup, and White-winged Scoters nest in the few places where shrubby growth extends to the water's edge (Lombard North Group 1976).

Thirty-seven species of mammals live in Cypress Hills Provincial Park (Finlay and Finlay 1987). Beaver, moose and red squirrels were introduced to the area in the 1940s and 1950s, and elk were reintroduced in 1937. Mule and white-tailed deer are native species and are quite common in the park. Coyotes hunt the area, as do mink, badgers, skunks and bobcats.

M.E. Bradford

References

Alberta Culture and Multiculturalism. n.d. Hist. Sites Serv. Unpubl. data, Edmonton.
Alberta Environment. n.d.[a]. Envir. Assess. Div., Envir. Qlty. Monit. Br. Unpubl. data, Edmonton.
———. n.d.[b]. Tech. Serv. Div., Hydrol. Br. Unpubl. data, Edmonton.
———. n.d.[c]. Tech. Serv. Div., Surv. Br. Unpubl. data, Edmonton.
———. n.d.[d]. Wastes Chemicals Div., Chemicals Pesticides Br. Unpubl. data, Edmonton.

Table 6. Estimated angler numbers, effort and harvest from Elkwater Lake. Estimates based on creel survey data collected from 22 May to 22 Aug. 1979. A total of 41 weekdays and 26 weekend days surveyed; 25 days not included. Information collected at 0900, 1300 and 1700. NP = northern pike; YP = yellow perch.

	NP	YP	Total
number of anglers[a]	—	—	2 500
angler-hours[b]	—	—	3 260
total number fish caught	980	170	1 150
total yield (kg)	458	45	503
mean weight (g)	467	267	—
mean length (mm)	402	263	—
catch/angler-hour[b, c]	0.28	0.05	0.33
catch/angler[a, c]	0.39	0.07	0.46

NOTES: [a]observed no. anglers = 1 873; [b]observed hours = 2 573; [c]observed no. fish caught: NP = 725, YP = 131
SOURCE: Fitch 1981

———. n.d.[e]. Water Resour. Admin. Div., Records Mgt. Sec. Unpubl. data, Edmonton.
———. 1982. Elkwater Lake water balance project, Elkwater Provincial Park. Tech. Serv. Div., Hydrol. Br. Rep. H–05AH–L8, Edmonton.
Alberta Forestry, Lands and Wildlife. 1988. Boating in Alberta. Fish Wild. Div., Edmonton.
———. 1989. Guide to sportfishing. Fish Wild. Div., Edmonton.
Alberta Recreation and Parks. n.d. Parks Div. Unpubl. data, Edmonton.
Alberta Research Council. 1972. Geological map of Alberta. Nat. Resour. Div., Alta. Geol. Surv., Edmonton.
Energy, Mines and Resources Canada. 1978. National topographic series 1:50 000 72E/9 (1978). Surv. Map. Br., Ottawa.
Environment Canada. 1962–1987. Surface water data. Prep. by Inland Waters Directorate. Water Surv. Can., Water Resour. Br., Ottawa.
———. 1982[a]. Canadian climate normals: Temperature and precipitation (1951–1980): Prairie provinces. Prep. by Atm. Envir. Serv. Supply Serv. Can., Ottawa.
———. 1982[b]. Canadian climate normals, Vol. 7: Bright sunshine (1951–1980). Prep. by Atm. Envir. Serv. Supply Serv. Can., Ottawa.
Finlay, J. and C. Finlay. 1987. Parks in Alberta: A guide to peaks, ponds, parklands & prairies. Hurtig Publ., Edmonton.
Fitch, L. 1980. Age, growth and food habits of northern pike (*Esox lucius*) and yellow perch (*Perca flavescens*) in Elkwater Lake, Alberta. Alta. En. Nat. Resour., Fish Wild. Div. Unpubl. rep., Lethbridge.
———. 1981. A creel survey of three lakes in Cypress Hills Provincial Park: Elkwater Lake, Reesor Lake and Spruce Coulee Reservoir. Alta. En. Nat. Resour., Fish Wild. Div. Unpubl. rep., Lethbridge.
Lombard North Group. 1976. Cypress Hills Provincial Park, Alberta, Vol. 1: Resource inventory. Alta. Pub. Works, Alta. Ld. For., Prov. Parks Div., Edmonton.
Looman, J. and K.F. Best. 1987. Budd's flora of the Canadian prairie provinces. Can. Dept. Agric. Res. Br. Publ. 1662 1987. Supply Serv. Can., Hull, Quebec.
Mackay, W.C. 1988. Univ. Alta., Dept. Zool., Edmonton. Pers. comm.
MacNeill, J. 1977. Elkwater Lake: Lake survey inventory. Alta. Rec. Parks Wild., Fish Wild. Div. Unpubl. rep., Lethbridge.
Michael, H. and H. Johnson. 1981. Down the years at Elkwater. Medicine Hat Museum and Art Gallery, Medicine Hat.
Miller, R.B. and W.H. Macdonald. 1950. Preliminary biological surveys of Alberta watersheds, 1947–1949. Alta. Ld. For., Fish Wild. Div., Edmonton.
Prepas, E.E. and D.O. Trew. 1983. Evaluation of the phosphorus-chlorophyll relationship for lakes off the Precambrian Shield in western Canada. Can. J. Fish. Aquat. Sci. 40:27–35.
Reynoldson, T.B. 1981. A preliminary assessment of the trophic state of lakes in the Cypress Hills Provincial Park. Alta. Envir., Poll. Contr. Div., Water Qlty. Contr. Br. Unpubl. rep., Edmonton.
Riley, E.T. and E.E. Prepas. 1984. Role of internal phosphorus loading in two shallow, productive lakes in Alberta, Canada. Can. J. Fish. Aquat. Sci. 41:845–855.
R.L. & L. Environmental Services Ltd. 1985. A compendium of existing environmental data on Alberta reservoirs. Prep. for Alta. Envir. Res. Trust, Edmonton.
Strong, W.L. and K.R. Leggat. 1981. Ecoregions of Alberta. Alta. En. Nat. Resour., Resour. Eval. Plan. Div., Edmonton.
WER Engineering. 1981. South Saskatchewan River Basin structures inventory, Appendix 5 to Vol. 1: Oldman River (2 of 2) and South Saskatchewan River Sub-basins. Prep. for Alta. Envir., Plan. Div., Edmonton.

MILK RIVER RIDGE RESERVOIR

MAP SHEETS: 82H/7, 8
LOCATION: Tp4, 5 R19, 20 W4
LAT/LONG: 49°22'N 112°35'W

Milk River Ridge Reservoir is an attractive offstream reservoir located 8 km south of the town of Raymond in the County of Warner. Its deep, clear water and the pleasant surrounding scenery make it a popular spot for power boating, water skiing and angling. To reach the reservoir, take Highway 5 south from the city of Lethbridge for approximately 27 km, then drive east on Highway 52 for 6 km, south on Secondary Road 844 for about 8 km, and east on Secondary Road 506 for about 12 km. Turn north onto the access road for Ridge Park Municipal Recreation Area, located on the south shore (Fig. 1, 2). This park is operated by the municipal district; it offers 12 campsites, pump water from a cistern, a concrete boat launch, a beach and a playground. As well, an Alberta Environment day-use area with a gravel boat launch is located on the east end of the reservoir (Fig. 2). There are no boating restrictions over most of the reservoir, but in some posted areas all boats are prohibited, and in other posted areas power boats are restricted to a maximum speed of 12 km/hour (Alta. For. Ld. Wild. 1988).

Milk River Ridge Reservoir is named for the gently sloping ridge to the south which provides welcome relief to the flat prairie. The reservoir was built by the federal Prairie Farm Rehabilitation Administration in 1956 as an offstream storage and balancing reservoir for the St. Mary River Irrigation District (SMRID). Alberta Environment has been the owner of the reservoir and all structures since 1974 and operates them in cooperation with the SMRID. As is shown on the map in the introduction to the South Saskatchewan and Milk River basins, Milk River Ridge Reservoir is the third largest of the 12 major reservoirs in the SMRID; only St. Mary and Chin reservoirs are larger. Water enters Milk River Ridge Reservoir via a canal from St. Mary Reservoir. Most of the outflow flows north and east to supply water for irrigation and municipal and domestic use as far east as the city of Medicine Hat; a smaller outflow supplies water to areas just east of the reservoir.

Milk River Ridge Reservoir is a moderately deep, steep-sided reservoir with clear water that is attractive for recreation. Water skiing and power boating are popular on the east end and anglers eagerly seek the reservoir's very large northern pike. In 1974, a pike weighing 17 kg, an Alberta record, was taken (English 1977). There are no regulations specific to the reservoir, but provincial sport fishing regulation and limits apply (Alta. For. Ld. Wild. 1989). A commercial fishery for lake whitefish operates on the reservoir for two weeks in October each year.

The south shore of the reservoir is dissected by many coulees. The natural vegetation in the coulees provides excellent habitat for deer, grouse, pheasants and partridge, and the bays in the lake provide good habitat for waterfowl. The islands at the east end are used by nesting geese and gulls, and pelicans and cormorants can also often be seen there.

Drainage Basin Characteristics

The natural drainage basin of Milk River Ridge Reservoir is about 11 times the area of the lake (Tables 1, 2). The basin is located almost entirely on the north-facing slope of Milk River Ridge (Fig. 1), which rises almost 300 m above the reservoir to an elevation of 1 315 m. Runoff from this area flows through numerous north-draining coulees. Before the dams were built, local runoff filled two sloughs in two large east-west oriented coulees, Kipp Coulee to the west and

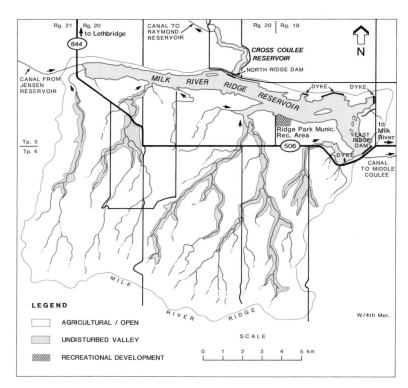

Figure 1. Features of the drainage basin of Milk River Ridge Reservoir. Sources: Alta. Envir. n.d.[d]; En. Mines Resour. Can. 1975. Updated with 1981 aerial photos.

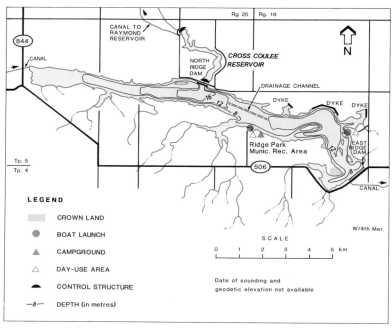

Figure 2. Bathymetry and shoreline features of Milk River Ridge Reservoir. Bathymetry source: Agric. Can. 1957.

Table 1. Characteristics of Milk River Ridge Reservoir drainage basin.

area (excluding lake) (km²)[a, b]	168
soil[c]	Dark Brown Chernozemics
bedrock geology[d]	Oldman Formation (Upper Cretaceous): sandstone, siltstone, mudstone, shale, ironstone beds; nonmarine
terrain[e]	moderately steep north-facing slope
ecoregion[c]	Mixed Grass
dominant vegetation[c]	spear, grama, wheat grasses; rose, silverberry, buckbrush
mean annual sunshine (h)[f]	2 370

NOTE: [b]area of natural basin only (Fig. 1)
SOURCES: [a]Alta. Envir. n.d.[d]; [c]Strong and Leggat 1981; [d]Alta. Res. Counc. 1972; [e]En. Mines Resour. Can. 1975; [f]Envir. Can. 1982

Middle Coulee to the east. Portions of both of these coulees were flooded to form Milk River Ridge Reservoir.

The drainage basin lies in the Mixed Grass Ecoregion (Strong and Leggat 1981). Soils are primarily Dark Brown Chernozemics, which form in moderately to well-drained areas under grasslands. Regosols and Brunisols are present in imperfectly drained and seepage areas. The vegetation was originally dominated by spear, grama and wheat grasses, but now almost all of the natural grassland in the basin has been cultivated to grow wheat and other grains. Natural vegetation remains in the coulees. North-facing coulees, which support shrubs such as wild rose, saskatoon and buckbrush, and trees such as trembling aspen, provide good wildlife habitat. Cottonwood and willow grow along water courses. Most of the basin is privately owned; only a narrow strip around the shore and small area at the east end of the reservoir are Crown land.

Reservoir Basin Characteristics

Milk River Ridge Reservoir was created by the construction of two dams (Fig. 1, Table 2). The North Ridge Dam is in the middle of the north shore and blocks the natural drainage of Kipp Coulee to Cross Coulee. The East Ridge Dam is across Middle Coulee. As well, there are several short dykes and one long dyke along the north shore near the east end. The reservoir is 17.7–km long and has a maximum width of 1.6 km. The reservoir basin drops steeply along the entire shoreline except at the west end where the slope is more gentle. There are two basins: the west one has a maximum depth of 16.5 m and the east one has a maximum depth of 14.0 m. A channel was dug along the bottom of the reservoir to facilitate flow between the basins if the reservoir had to be drawn down to its fullest extent (Fig. 2). The total live storage at the design full supply level is 125 x 10⁶ m³ of water.

Except for a small amount of runoff from the natural drainage basin, the inflow to Milk River Ridge Reservoir enters via a canal at the west end (Table 2). The water in this canal is diverted from the St. Mary, Belly and Waterton rivers to St. Mary Reservoir; it then passes through Jensen Reservoir before making its way to Milk River Ridge Reservoir. Approximately 98% of the water flows out of Milk River Ridge Reservoir via the North Ridge Dam to tiny Cross Coulee Reservoir, which acts as a balancing pond, and then to Raymond Reservoir, which lies parallel to Milk River Ridge Reservoir, about 2 km to the north. The water then snakes its way through canals and a series of reservoirs to supply water for irrigation, municipal, domestic, industrial and recreational uses as far east as Medicine Hat. The remaining 2% of the water flows out of Milk River Ridge Reservoir via the East Ridge Dam to Middle Coulee to supply local irrigation, domestic and municipal needs and to support wildlife and recreational uses.

Large volumes of water pass through Milk River Ridge Reservoir during the period that the canals are flowing, usually from mid-April to mid-October. From 1977 to 1988, the average annual volume was 688.1 x 10⁶ m³ (Alta. Envir. n.d.[b]). The mean residence time

Table 2. Characteristics of Milk River Ridge Reservoir.

control structures[a]	North Ridge Dam across Cross Coulee East Ridge Dam across Middle Coulee dykes on north, east and south shores
dam height (m)[a]	North Ridge Dam: 2.3 m East Ridge Dam: 9.1 m
crest length (m)[a]	North Ridge Dam: 363.6 m East Ridge Dam: 757.6 m
full supply level (FSL) (m)[a, b]	1 033
volume at FSL (m^3)[c]	128.3 x 10^6
live storage at FSL (m^3)[c]	125 x 10^6
surface area at FSL (km^2)[d]	15.32
maximum possible drawdown (m)[c]	13.1
mean annual drawdown (1976–1987) (m)[e, f]	2.43
maximum depth at FSL (m)[c, d]	16.5
mean depth at FSL (m)[g]	8.4
shoreline length at FSL (km)[d]	63.4
lake length at FSL (km)[d]	17.7
lake width at FSL (km)[d]	1.6
mean annual lake evaporation (mm)[g]	798
mean annual lake precipitation (mm)[g]	422
mean residence time (Apr.–Oct.) (yr)[c, h, i]	0.113
mean inflow volume (1977–1988) (m^3)[h, j]	688.6 x 10^6
mean outflow volume (1977–1988) (m^3)[h, k]	649.0 x 10^6 via North Ridge Dam 12.0 x 10^6 via East Ridge Dam

NOTES: [b]original 1956 survey by Prairie Farm Rehabilitation Administration established FSL; [f]1982 to 1983 drawdown of 11.7 m omitted as it was due to repair on structures and is not typical of reservoir operation; [i]excluding groundwater inflow; [j]of this, 8.55 x 10^6 m^3 is from local runoff; balance is via canal from Jensen Reservoir, which flows from mid-April to mid-October only; [k]all flow from mid-April to mid-October
SOURCES: [a]Alta. Envir. n.d.[a]; [c]Butler Krebes Assoc. Ltd. 1978; [d]English 1977; [e]Envir. Can. 1976–1987; [g]Alta. Envir. n.d.[d]; [h]Alta. Envir. n.d.[b]

Table 3. Major ions and related water quality variables for Milk River Ridge Reservoir. Average concentrations in mg/L; pH in pH units. Composite samples from the euphotic zone collected 3 times from 17 June to 07 Oct. 1986. S.E. = standard error.

	Mean	S.E.
total alkalinity ($CaCO_3$)	107	2.0
specific conductivity (μS/cm)	243	13.7
total dissolved solids (calculated)	113[a]	5.5
turbidity (NTU)	3	1.4
total hardness (calculated)	118	—
dissolved organic carbon	2	0.2
HCO_3	130	2.5
CO_3	<1	—
Mg	11	0.5
Na	5	0.9
K	1	0.1
Cl	1	0.2
SO_4	14	2.3
Ca	29	1.7

NOTE: [a]n = 2
SOURCE: Alta. Envir. n.d.[c], Naquadat station 05AL05AF1000

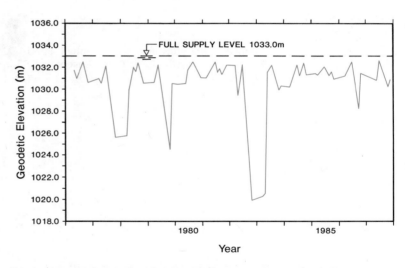

Figure 3. Water level of Milk River Ridge Reservoir, 1976 to 1987.
Source: Envir. Can. 1976–1987.

of water in the reservoir between mid-April and mid-October is only 41.3 days (Table 2). In dry years, such as 1988, the demand for irrigation water is high so the flow-through volume is high and the water residence time is as little as 27 days.

The water level of Milk River Ridge Reservoir is quite variable (Fig. 3). The reservoir is filled each spring when runoff is abundant, then water is released when demand increases in the summer. Usually, the reservoir level drops through the summer until it reaches its winter operating level. If water is available in the fall, the reservoir is filled as much as possible. Drawdown may be less than 1.8 m in some years, but in dry years such as 1977 and 1979, the demand for water is high and drawdown may exceed 6.0 m. In 1982/83, the control structures needed repair and the reservoir was drawn down as far as possible, to 13.1 m below full supply level, leaving only two small, shallow pools. The full supply level is rarely attained; approximately 0.6 m of storage is kept in reserve in case of sudden storms.

Water Quality

The water quality of Milk River Ridge Reservoir was examined by Alberta Environment in 1983, 1985 and 1986 (Alta. Envir. n.d.[c]).

Milk River Ridge Reservoir has well-buffered, fresh water (Table 3). The dominant ions are calcium and bicarbonate. The pH is low compared to that in most other Alberta lakes.

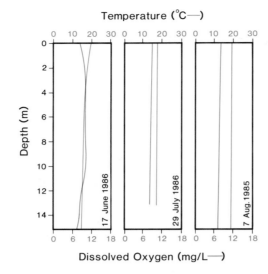

Figure 4. Temperature and dissolved oxygen in Milk River Ridge Reservoir, 1985 and 1986. Source: Alta. Envir. n.d.[c].

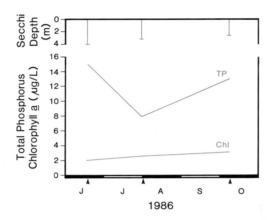

Figure 5. Total phosphorus, chlorophyll *a* and Secchi depth in Milk River Ridge Reservoir, 1986. Source: Alta. Envir. n.d.[c].

Table 4. Nutrient, chlorophyll *a* and Secchi depth data for Milk River Ridge Reservoir. Average concentrations in μg/L. Composite samples from the euphotic zone collected 3 times from 17 June to 07 Oct. 1986. S.E. = standard error.

	Mean	S.E.
total phosphorus	12	2.1
total dissolved phosphorus	<4	—
total Kjeldahl nitrogen	300	11.5
$NO_3 + NO_2$–nitrogen	17	5.2
NH_4–nitrogen	<13	—
iron	60	10.0
chlorophyll *a*	2.6	0.32
Secchi depth (m)	3.2	0.44

SOURCE: Alta. Envir. n.d.[c], Naquadat station 05AL05AF1000

The reservoir is exposed to prevailing west winds, which continuously mix the water and prevent stratification (Fig. 4). Dissolved oxygen concentrations probably remain high from the surface to the bottom throughout the summer (Fig. 4). The dissolved oxygen concentration in winter has been determined only once, on 24 February 1978; the dissolved oxygen concentration was 14 mg/L just under the ice and 1.5 mg/L on the bottom (Alta. For. Ld. Wild. n.d.).

Milk River Ridge Reservoir is a nutrient-poor, oligotrophic reservoir, in contrast to natural lakes in the area. In 1986, phosphorus levels were low and varied only slightly over the summer (Table 4, Fig. 5). Total phosphorus concentrations were highest when the reservoir was being filled in spring and late fall. Chlorophyll *a* concentrations, which were consistently very low, peaked in October at 3.2 μg/L (Fig. 5).

Biological Characteristics

Plants

There are no data on the phytoplankton or macrophytes in Milk River Ridge Reservoir.

Invertebrates

The zooplankton in the reservoir was sampled by Fish and Wildlife Division from June to October in 1975 with a Wisconsin-style plankton net of number 20 mesh silk bolting cloth (English 1977). Densities and volumes were low compared to those in samples taken from other reservoirs in the area during the same period. Copepods were the dominant group throughout the summer; their populations peaked in June. The highest number of rotifers also occurred in June but cladocerans were most abundant in September. There is no information on benthic invertebrates in this reservoir.

Fish

Seven species of fish are known to inhabit Milk River Ridge Reservoir: walleye, northern pike, lake whitefish, longnose sucker, white sucker, burbot and spottail shiner. The sport fishery is aimed primarily at northern pike, which grow to an admirable size. Walleye have migrated naturally to the reservoir but few are caught, possibly because few anglers try for them (Bishop 1988).

Lake whitefish are the target of an annual two-week commercial fishery each October. This species is indigenous to the reservoir, but adult fish were stocked in 1959 and 1960 to hasten development of a commercial fishery, which began in 1968 (Clements 1974). Sixteen licences were issued in the 1987/88 season. The total annual catch averaged 6 251 kg between 1968 and 1987 (excluding the 1983/84 and 1984/85 seasons). The species composition of this catch was 86% lake whitefish, 14% northern pike and less than 1% walleye (Alta. For. Ld. Wild. n.d.). Lake whitefish spawn in shallow water in the fall. The severe drawdown for repairs to the control structures in 1982/83 decimated the entire lake whitefish population. Only one lake whitefish was caught by test netting in 1984 (Alta. For. Ld. Wild. n.d.) and the commercial fishery was poor for several years. Lake whitefish move throughout the irrigation system, however, so re-stocking was not necessary and the commercial fishery had recovered by 1986 (Bishop 1988).

Wildlife

Milk River Ridge Reservoir provides important habitat for waterfowl. The reservoir is a regionally significant nesting area for Canada Geese; most nesting occurs on the islands at the east end (Butler Krebes Assoc. Ltd. 1978). Gulls nest on the islands as well, and pelicans and cormorants rest on the islands during feeding forays. The reservoir is also an important waterfowl staging area for fall migration.

The coulees on the slope south of the reservoir provide prime habitat for mule deer and white-tailed deer, and refuge areas for antelope. Coulees provide excellent habitat for upland game birds such as Hungarian Partridge, Ring-necked Pheasants and Sharp-tailed Grouse.

J.M. Crosby

References

Agriculture Canada. 1957. Topographic plan, Milk River Ridge Reservoir. Prairie Farm Rehabilitation Admin., Eng. Br., Ottawa.

Alberta Environment. n.d.[a]. Devel. Op. Div., Dam Safety Br. Unpubl. data, Edmonton.

———. n.d.[b]. Devel. Op. Div., Irrig. Headworks Br. Unpubl. data, Edmonton.

———. n.d.[c]. Envir. Assess. Div., Envir. Qlty. Monit. Br. Unpubl. data, Edmonton.

———. n.d.[d]. Tech. Serv. Div., Hydrol. Br. Unpubl. data, Edmonton.

Alberta Forestry, Lands and Wildlife. n.d. Fish Wild. Div. Unpubl. data, Edmonton.

———. 1988. Boating in Alberta. Fish Wild. Div., Edmonton.

———. 1989. Guide to sportfishing. Fish Wild. Div., Edmonton.

Alberta Research Council. 1972. Geological map of Alberta. Nat. Resour. Div., Alta. Geol. Surv., Edmonton.

Bishop, F. 1988. Alta. For. Ld. Wild., Fish Wild. Div., Lethbridge. Pers. comm.

Butler Krebes Associates Ltd. 1978. Milk River Ridge Reservoir—Area development plan: Phase I and II, inventory and analysis. Prep. for Alta. Envir., Plan. Div., Edmonton.

Clements, S.M. 1974. The history and management of the fishery resource of Milk River Ridge Reservoir. Alta. Ld. For., Fish Wild. Div., Lethbridge.

Energy, Mines and Resources Canada. 1975. National topographic series 1:50 000 82H/7 (1975), 82H/8 (1975). Surv. Map. Br., Ottawa.

English, W.E. 1977. A limnological survey of Milk River Ridge Reservoir. Alta. Rec. Parks Wild., Fish Wild. Div., Lethbridge.

Environment Canada. 1976–1987. Surface water data. Prep. by Inland Waters Directorate. Water Surv. Can., Water Resour. Br., Ottawa.

———. 1982. Canadian climate normals, Vol. 7: Bright sunshine (1951–1980). Prep. by Atm. Envir. Serv. Supply Serv. Can., Ottawa.

Strong, W.L. and K.R. Leggat. 1981. Ecoregions of Alberta. Alta. En. Nat. Resour., Resour. Eval. Plan. Div., Edmonton.

TYRRELL LAKE

MAP SHEET: 82H/8
LOCATION: Tp5 R17, 18 W4
LAT/LONG: 49°23'N 112°16'W

Tyrrell Lake is an elongate, saline lake lying in a shallow coulee on flat plains. It is located 45 km southeast of the city of Lethbridge in the County of Warner. To reach the lake from Lethbridge, drive southwest on Highway 4 until you are 3 km past the hamlet of New Dayton. Watch for signs and turn east onto a secondary road and drive for 1.5 km to a county-operated day-use site at the northwest end of the lake (Fig. 1, 2). The facilities include a concrete boat launch, a fish cleaning stand, picnic tables and toilets. There is also a day-use site at the south end of the lake; few facilities are provided and the boat launch is quite muddy.

Tyrrell Lake was named for Joseph Burr Tyrrell, a member of the Geological Survey of Canada from 1880 to 1897 (Wrentham Hist. Soc. 1980). The lake is located on the mixed-grass plains, an area that once supported enormous herds of buffalo. The lake was a campsite for Indians when they travelled between the Cardston area and Montana (Warner Old Timers' Assoc. 1962). In the early 1900s, a wave of settlers came to farm the area, and in 1909, the Tyrrell Lake School was built near the southwest shore of the lake (Wrentham Hist. Soc. 1980).

Tyrrell Lake is a natural water body, but historically, the water level has fluctuated greatly. During the dust-bowl years of the 1930s, the lake reputedly became a dry mud flat (Fitch 1980). In the early 1950s, a canal was built from Milk River Ridge Reservoir via Middle Coulee to Tyrrell Lake to help stabilize levels. However, drainage near the lake was still inadequate, so in wet years farmland was flooded; during prolonged droughts the water level of the lake and associated marshes dropped and jeopardized valuable waterfowl habitat. In 1985, the Tyrrell-Rush complex became the first *Wetlands for Tomorrow* project built in Alberta. Joint funding was provided by Alberta Environment, Ducks Unlimited (Canada) and Fish and Wildlife Division. The County of Warner and the St. Mary's River Irrigation District (SMRID) provided enthusiastic cooperation. The canals and structures that were built have allowed water levels to be stabilized in Tyrrell Lake, in nearby Rush Lake and in a large marshland south of Rush Lake to form a major wetland area in a region where waterfowl habitat is scarce and drought is common. Agricultural interests are met because the project included an efficient drainage system to move excess runoff from farmland and direct it into the improved Rush Lake drain, which conveys water to Etzikom Coulee (Fig. 1, inset).

Tyrrell Lake is nutrient rich and supports occasional algal blooms. These blooms and the muddy lake bottom discourage swimming. In posted areas of the lake, power boats are restricted to maximum speeds of 12 km/hour (Alta. For. Ld. Wild. 1988). Because of high salinity, the only native fish species are salt-tolerant minnows. However, the lake is stocked annually with rainbow trout, which exhibit one of the fastest growth rates in North America and provide an excellent sport fishery. Fishing with bait fish is not permitted (Alta. For. Ld. Wild. 1989). The lake is also known for its population of tiger salamanders, although their numbers have been severely reduced since the introduction of trout.

Drainage Basin Characteristics

The drainage basin of Tyrrell Lake is large (122 km², Table 1) and covers an area almost 31 times the size of the lake (3.99 km², Table 2). The watershed is part of the Mixed Grass Ecoregion (Strong and

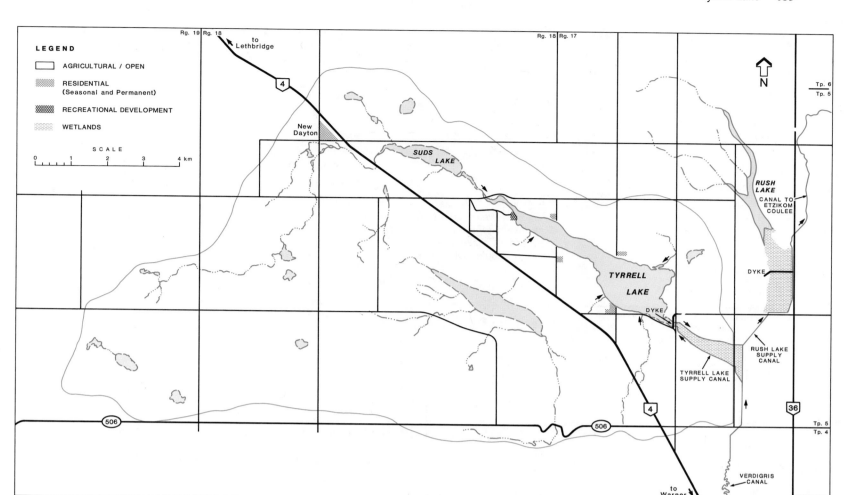

Figure 1. Features of the drainage basin of Tyrrell Lake.
SOURCES: Alta. Envir. n.d.[b]; En. Mines Resour. Can. 1975. Updated with 1981 aerial photos.

Table 1. Characteristics of Tyrrell Lake drainage basin.

area (excluding lake) (km²)[a]	122
soil[b]	Orthic Brown and Dark Brown Chernozemics, strongly alkaline in lake basin
bedrock geology[c]	Foremost Formation (Upper Cretaceous): sandstone, siltstone, mudstone, shale, ironstone beds, thin coal beds; nonmarine
terrain[b]	flat with shallow coulees
ecoregion[d]	Mixed Grass
dominant vegetation[d]	spear, grama, wheat grasses
mean annual inflow (m³)[a, e]	1.06×10^6
mean annual sunshine (h)[f]	2 370

NOTE: [e]natural inflow only; excludes groundwater inflow; in addition, up to 1.85×10^6 m³ of water may be brought in via canal
SOURCES: [a]Alta. Envir. n.d.[b]; [b]Bertrand 1974; [c]Alta. Res. Counc. 1972; [d]Strong and Leggat 1981; [f]Envir. Can. 1982

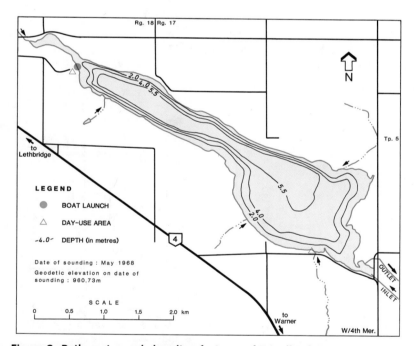

Figure 2. Bathymetry and shoreline features of Tyrrell Lake.
SOURCES: Alta. Ld. For. 1968 (bathymetry); Alta. Envir. 1982; Lindner 1988.

Leggat 1981). The land is flat, but it is dissected by coulees that were formed as glacial outwash channels. Rainfall is scarce (Table 1), the soil is porous, and the evaporation rate is double that of precipitation. Trembling aspen and shrubs such as willow, buckbrush, snowberry and saskatoon can survive only on seepage sites or on the north-facing slopes of coulees or river valleys. The soils are Orthic Brown and Dark Brown Chernozemics (Bertrand 1974). Most of the land has been cultivated for grain and forage crops, but there are some areas of native vegetation around the lake (Wentz 1974).

The hamlet of New Dayton is the only population centre in the drainage basin. Most of the land surrounding the lake is privately owned. There are no cottages near the lake, but there is an intensive livestock operation on the south shore (Fitch 1980).

Table 2. Characteristics of Tyrrell Lake.

elevation (m)[a, b]	959.26
surface area (km²)[c]	3.99
volume (m³)[b]	14.9 x 10⁶
maximum depth (m)[b]	6.1
mean depth (m)[b]	3.8
shoreline length (km)[b]	12.9
mean annual lake evaporation (mm)[d]	775
mean annual precipitation (mm)[d]	375
mean residence time (yr)[d]	not available
control structures[e]	fixed-crest weir; canal from Milk River Ridge Reservoir via Middle Coulee and Verdigris Coulee Diversion
dam height (m)[e]	959.5
full supply level (FSL) (m)[e]	959.2

NOTE: [a]on date of sounding: May 1966
SOURCES: [b]Alta. Ld. For. 1968; [c]En. Mines Resour. Can. 1975; [d]Alta. Envir. n.d.[b];
    [e]Alta. Envir. 1982; Lindner 1988

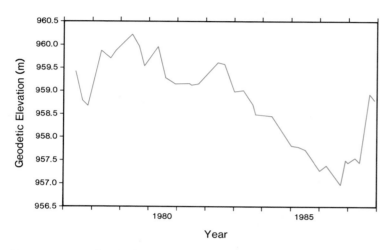

Figure 3. Water level of Tyrrell Lake, 1977 to 1988.
SOURCE: Alta. Envir. n.d.[c].

Table 3. Major ions and related water quality variables for Tyrrell Lake. Average concentrations in mg/L; pH in pH units. Composite samples from the euphotic zone collected on 17 June and 13 Sep. 1983. S.E. = standard error.

	Mean	S.E.
pH (range)	9.0–9.1	—
total alkalinity (CaCO₃)	646	16.0
specific conductivity (μS/cm)	7 745	265.0
total dissolved solids (calculated)	7 062	382.5
turbidity (NTU)	6	4.5
colour (Pt)	25	1.0
total hardness	747	127.8
HCO₃	571	17.5
CO₃	107	18.0
Mg	165	32.5
Na	2 000	10.0
K	50	3.5
Cl	111	9.0
SO₄	4 320	320.0
Ca	28	2.4

SOURCE: Alta. Envir. n.d.[a], Naquadat station 01AL05AF2000

Table 4. Nutrient, chlorophyll *a* and Secchi depth data for Tyrrell Lake. Average concentrations in μg/L. Composite samples from the euphotic zone collected on 17 June and 13 Sep. 1983. S.E. = standard error.

	Mean	S.E.
total phosphorus	150	5
total Kjeldahl nitrogen	2 500	500
NO₃ + NO₂–nitrogen	<8	—
NH₄–nitrogen	85	55
iron	<10	—
chlorophyll *a*	not measured	
Secchi depth (m)	2.2	1.45

SOURCE: Alta. Envir. n.d.[a], Naquadat station 01AL05AF2000

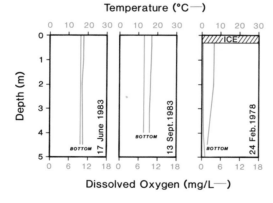

Figure 4. Temperature and dissolved oxygen of Tyrrell Lake, 1978 and 1983.
SOURCE: Alta. Envir. n.d.[a].

Water enters Tyrrell Lake naturally through runoff, either from precipitation or from irrigation return flows. Runoff flows through Suds Lake, an intermittent water body, then into the north end of Tyrrell Lake. Additionally, water is released from Milk River Ridge Reservoir, flows through Middle Coulee and is diverted into the south end of Tyrrell Lake (Fig. 1). Water also leaves Tyrrell Lake from the south end, flows into a wetland, then into Rush Lake (Fig. 1) or north to Etzikom Coulee and east to Pakowki Lake, a large intermittent lake with no outlet.

Lake Basin Characteristics

Tyrrell Lake is fairly long (5 km), narrow (1.2 km at the widest point), and shallow (Table 2). Like other shallow, saline lakes in southern Alberta, the lake basin slopes gently to a flat, central area. The area deeper than 5.5 m occupies approximately one-third of the lake area (Fig. 2). Most of the lake bottom is soft mud.

Prior to the 1950s, the water level of Tyrrell Lake showed extreme fluctuations; the lake was completely dry in the thirties (Fitch 1980). In the 1950s, the provincial government built the Tyrrell Lake Supply Canal to bring water to the lake from Milk River Ridge Reservoir via Middle Coulee. This project helped to stabilize lake levels in dry years, but drainage from the Tyrrell-Rush Lake area in wet years still continued to be inadequate, and over 2 300 acres (931 ha) of farmland were flooded in wet springs. Another concern was that nearby Rush Lake and its associated marshes, which provided the best waterfowl habitat in southern Alberta, were jeopardized during

Table 5. Daily growth rates of age 0+ rainbow trout in Tyrrell Lake, 1974 to 1978.

Date of Stocking	Daily Growth Rate	
	mm/day	g/day
16 May 1974	1.69	2.25
01 May 1975	1.35	2.19
04–06 May 1976	1.10	1.19
14–21 Apr. 1977	1.17	2.03
25 Apr.–02 May 1978	1.17	1.77
MEAN	1.30	1.89

SOURCE: Fitch 1980

droughts (Alta. Envir. 1982). The construction of canals and dykes began in 1983 and was completed in 1986. It is now possible to bring up to 1.85 x 10^6 m^3 of water each year from Milk River Ridge Reservoir to Tyrrell Lake, then to Rush Lake (Fitch 1988). The extremely low water levels in Tyrrell Lake from 1984 to 1986 (Fig. 3) were the result of construction activities and natural drought. Construction was completed in 1987 and diversion to the lake began that year; the lake was still filling in 1988.

Water Quality

The water quality in Tyrrell Lake was monitored in 1977 and 1978 by Fish and Wildlife Division (Fitch 1980) and in 1983 by Alberta Environment (Alta. Envir. n.d.[a]).

Tyrrell Lake has clear, saline water. The dominant ions are sulphate and sodium (Table 3). The concentration of total dissolved solids (a measure of salinity) varies inversely with water level: in 1977, the water level was relatively low (Fig. 3) and the concentration was 6 090 mg/L; in 1978, the water level was higher and the concentration was 4 824 mg/L; and in 1983, the water level was slightly lower than that recorded in 1977, and the concentration of total dissolved solids was 7 062 mg/L.

Tyrrell Lake is exposed to strong winds, which likely keep it well-mixed all summer; the water column was isothermal and well-oxygenated in June and September 1983 (Fig. 4). In 1977, however, dissolved oxygen concentrations in July declined to between 2.5 and 3.5 mg/L throughout the lake. These low concentrations may have resulted from the decay of a blue-green algal bloom. In February 1978, some oxygen depletion occurred toward the bottom, but the dissolved oxygen concentration in the top 2 m was 8 mg/L and sufficient for fish survival (Fig. 4). In some years, winter dissolved oxygen concentrations drop to 4 mg/L at the surface. There are no data for oxygen concentrations at the bottom, but they are likely close to zero.

Tyrrell Lake is nutrient-rich (Table 4). Although the high salinity likely inhibits algal growth (Bierhuizen and Prepas 1985), blooms of blue-green algae occasionally do occur. Algae was reported to form a "coppery-green crust" at the south end of the reservoir in 1960 (Paterson 1960). Chlorophyll a concentrations in Tyrrell Lake have not been monitored. Consequently, it is not possible to categorize the lake's trophic status.

Biological Characteristics

Plants

The algal bloom noted in 1960 was dominated by the blue-green alga *Microcystis*; the green alga *Spirogyra* was also noted (Paterson 1960). Recent information on algae is not available.

Macrophytes form a narrow band around the lake, but despite extensive shallow areas, the abundance of aquatic plants is limited, likely because of high salinity. Salt-tolerant Sago pondweed (*Potamogeton pectinatus*) was the dominant macrophyte observed during studies by Fish and Wildlife Division in 1977 and 1978 (Fitch 1980).

Invertebrates

The zooplankton was sampled by Fish and Wildlife Division in 1977 and 1978 (Fitch 1980). Although species diversity was low, abundance was high. Numerically, the community was dominated by Copepoda (72%), mainly *Diaptomus sicilis*, followed by Cladocera (25%), mainly *Daphnia pulicaria* and Rotifera (3%). Fairy shrimp (*Branchinecta coloradensis*) were recorded in Tyrrell Lake in 1978 (MacNeill 1979). This species is tolerant of saline water but is usually not present with planktivorous fish such as trout.

Benthic invertebrates were sampled by Fish and Wildlife Division in October 1977 (Fitch 1980). The total biomass (60.2 g/m^2 wet weight), which was dominated by midge larvae (Chironomidae), was the third highest of 25 southern Alberta lakes.

Amphibians

In the 1960s, tiger salamanders (*Ambystoma tigrinum*) were very abundant in Tyrrell Lake (Paterson 1960). In October 1962, approximately 250 kg of larval salamanders were captured in one day (Alta. For. Ld. Wild. n.d.). That year, rainbow trout were stocked in the lake and the population of salamanders, a favourite prey of trout, started to decline. Only one salamander was caught in a 1973 test netting and for several years it was assumed that the population had been eliminated. In 1988, however, several salamanders were caught in test nets (Fitch 1988).

Fish

Tyrrell Lake is the most saline lake in Alberta stocked with rainbow trout by Fish and Wildlife Division. The growth rates of the rainbow trout are among the most rapid in North America and the fish of Tyrrell Lake have been the subject of numerous studies (Alta. For. Ld. Wild. n.d.; Haugen 1970; Radford and Clements 1971; MacNeill 1979; Fitch 1980).

Prior to 1950, when Tyrrell Lake was a natural body of water, the only species of fish in it were salt-tolerant species: fathead minnows and brook sticklebacks (Paterson 1960; Fitch 1980). Since 1950, when water diversion to Tyrrell Lake from Milk River Ridge Reservoir began, burbot, white suckers and lake whitefish have been found in small numbers; northern pike, lake chub and longnose suckers have been collected only once (Fitch 1980). Only adults of these species have been found, as they cannot spawn successfully in saline water. In test netting from 1968 to 1978, 95% to 100% of the catch was rainbow trout (Fitch 1980). A creel census in 1982 found that, in 394 angler-hours of angling, 66 trout and 9 suckers were caught (Bishop 1989).

Rainbow trout were first stocked in 1962, then 4 more times until 1973, and annually since 1974 (except in 1981 and 1986). An average of 400 000 fingerlings are introduced each year the lake is stocked (Alta. Ld. For. 1962–1974; Alta. Rec. Parks Wild. 1975–1978; Alta. En. Nat. Resour. 1979–1985; Alta. For. Ld. Wild. 1986–1987). The repeated stockings are necessary due to the low survival rate—less than 1% of the trout survive their first winter (Fitch 1980).

A comparison of the length and weight of rainbow trout stocked in 15 southern Alberta lakes showed that trout in Tyrrell Lake were consistently the longest and heaviest. By autumn, trout age 0+ years from Tyrrell Lake had a fork length of 269 mm and weighed 320 g. This was approximately 4 times heavier than the average trout from 14 other lakes. By age 1+, the average trout weighed 1.5 kg. At ages 1+, 2+ and 3+ the average weight of trout in Tyrrell Lake was 5 times heavier than that from 14 other lakes (Fitch 1980). The growth rate of Tyrrell Lake trout is among the highest in North America and reaches the maximal growth rate for the species (Fitch 1980). Although there is some variability in growth rate from year to year (Table 5), it is consistently exceptional.

The reason for low overwinter survival of trout in Tyrrell Lake is uncertain. One possibility is that, although winter dissolved oxygen concentrations in the lake are usually within the range considered to be sufficiently high for trout survival (over 4 mg/L), very fast-growing fish may require higher dissolved oxygen concentrations. The fast-growing trout in Tyrrell Lake are heavy for their length and have condition factors near 2.0 and therefore have lower gill area to body volume ratios than slower-growing fish with condition factors of 1.3 to 1.5. Thus, higher dissolved oxygen concentrations may be required to maintain even minimal oxygen supply to the tissues (Mac-Neill 1979).

Wildlife

The Tyrrell-Rush Lake complex is an important spring and fall staging area for waterfowl. The Rush Lake area is also important for waterfowl production (2 000 birds per year) and is likely to become even more productive now that water management structures are in place. Ducks Unlimited (Canada) have further improved habitat in the Rush Lake complex by building rock and earth islands for waterfowl and goose nesting, and by managing upland areas for waterfowl and ungulates (Schmidt 1988).

J.M. Crosby

References

Alberta Energy and Natural Resources. 1979–1985. Fish planting list. Fish Wild. Div., Edmonton.

Alberta Environment. n.d.[a]. Envir. Assess. Div., Envir. Qlty. Monit. Br. Unpubl. data, Edmonton.

———. n.d.[b]. Tech. Serv. Div., Hydrol. Br. Unpubl. data, Edmonton.

———. n.d.[c]. Tech. Serv. Div., Surv. Br. Unpubl. data, Edmonton.

———. 1982. Report summary, Tyrrell and Rush lakes flood management project in County of Warner. Envir. Eng. Support Serv., Edmonton.

Alberta Forestry, Lands and Wildlife. n.d. Fish Wild. Div. Unpubl. data, Edmonton.

———. 1986–1987. Fish planting list. Fish Wild. Div., Edmonton.

———. 1988. Boating in Alberta. Fish Wild. Div., Edmonton.

———. 1989. Guide to sportfishing. Fish Wild. Div., Edmonton.

Alberta Lands and Forests. 1962–1974. Fish planting list. Fish Wild. Div., Edmonton.

———. 1968. Hydrographic survey of Tyrrell Lake. Fish Wild. Div., Edmonton.

Alberta Recreation, Parks and Wildlife. 1975–1978. Fish planting list. Fish Wild. Div., Edmonton.

Alberta Research Council. 1972. Geological map of Alberta. Nat. Resour. Div., Alta. Geol. Surv., Edmonton.

Bertrand, R.A. 1974. Soil irrigability of the Tyrrell Lake project. Alta. Agric., Irrig. Div., Tech. Resour. Br., Lethbridge.

Bierhuizen, J.F.H. and E.E. Prepas. 1985. Relationship between nutrients, dominant ions and phytoplankton standing crop on prairie saline lakes. Can. J. Fish. Aquat. Sci. 42:1588–1594.

Bishop, F. 1989. Alta. For. Ld. Wild., Fish Wild. Div., Lethbridge. Pers. comm.

Energy, Mines and Resources Canada. 1975. National topographic series 1:50 000 82H/8 (1975). Surv. Map. Br., Ottawa.

Environment Canada. 1982. Canadian climate normals, Vol. 7: Bright sunshine (1951–1980). Prep. by Atm. Envir. Serv. Supply Serv. Can., Ottawa.

Fitch, L. 1980. A limnological study of Tyrrell Lake. Alta. En. Nat. Resour., Fish Wild. Div., Lethbridge.

———. 1988. Alta. For. Ld. Wild., Fish Wild. Div., Lethbridge. Pers. comm.

Haugen, G.N. 1970. Growth rate and coefficient of condition for rainbow trout, Tyrrell's Lake, Alberta, 1970. Alta. Ld. For., Fish Wild. Div., Lethbridge.

Lindner, D. 1988. Alta. Envir., Design Const. Div., Edmonton. Pers. comm.

MacNeill, J.W. 1979. An evaluation of five years of annual stocking and test netting of Tyrrell Lake (5–17–W4). Alta. Rec. Parks Wild., Fish Wild. Div., Lethbridge.

Paterson, R.J. 1960. Lake survey report—Tyrrell Lake. Alta. Ld. For., Fish Wild. Div., Lethbridge.

Radford, D.S. and S.H. Clements. 1971. A creel survey and population estimate of rainbow trout in Tyrrell Lake, Alberta. Alta. Ld. For., Fish Wild. Div., Lethbridge.

Schmidt, K. 1988. Ducks Unltd. (Can.), Brooks. Pers. comm.

Strong, W.L. and K.R. Leggat. 1981. Ecoregions of Alberta. Alta. En. Nat. Resour., Resour. Eval. Plan. Div., Edmonton.

Warner Old Timers' Association. 1962. Warner pioneers. Lethbridge Herald, Job Dept., Lethbridge.

Wentz, D. 1974. Tyrrell Lake project. Alta. Envir., Irrig. Div., Conserv. Devel. Br., Lethbridge.

Wrentham Historical Society. 1980. Homestead country: Wrentham and area. Friesen Printers, Calgary.

REESOR LAKE

Alberta Recreation and Parks

MAP SHEET: 72E/9
LOCATION: Tp8 R1 W4
LAT/LONG: 49°40′N 110°07′W

Reesor Lake is a small, popular trout-fishing reservoir located within Cypress Hills Provincial Park in the Municipal District of Cypress. It was named after David William Reesor, the son of a Canadian senator, who settled in the area in 1900. The original Reesor ranch house still stands near the shore (Alta. Cult. Multicult. n.d.). Prior to 1960, the lake was two small, separate water bodies, called Twin Lakes. In 1960, a dam was constructed across the southeast end of the valley where the two lakes were located. Water was diverted into the reservoir from Battle Creek, raising the water level and thus creating a single lake (Fig. 1).

Cypress Hills Provincial Park is situated approximately 65 km southeast of Medicine Hat, off Highway 41. Of the 12 campgrounds in the park, two are located near Reesor Lake (Fig. 2). The first of these is Reesor Lake Dock Campground, which is situated on the north shore of the lake off the Reesor Lake Road. It is open year-round and has 24 random campsites, a water pump, a fishing pier and a boat launch. The second campground, Reesor Lake Campground, is located south of the lake on the south side of Battle Creek. It is open from May to September and provides 40 campsites, including 7 walk-in tenting sites, tap water, picnic tables, a picnic shelter, a playground and weekly interpretive programs. A boat launch is located at the western end of the dam. The only boat motors allowed on the lake are electric (Alta. For. Ld. Wild. 1988).

Reesor Lake has one of the more important sport fisheries in southern Alberta and many people visit Cypress Hills Provincial Park only to fish the lake for rainbow trout (Bishop 1989). Fishing regulations prohibit the use of bait fish in the lake (Alta. For. Ld. Wild. 1989). The water is clear during most of the year, but turns green in midsummer. Extensive areas of aquatic macrophytes cover much of the lake bottom and interfere with angling during late summer.

Drainage Basin Characteristics

The Cypress Hills are a remnant of a large depositional plateau that existed about 40 million years ago, but which has eroded since that time. During the Wisconsin Age, the ice sheet that advanced into the region from the north flowed around the plateau and engulfed all but the top 90 m. The plateau is now about 130–km long and 25– to 40–km wide. One-third of it lies in Alberta and the remainder is located in Saskatchewan. The Cypress Hills are the highest point of land in Canada between Labrador and the Rocky Mountains. They form part of the divide that separates streams that flow to Hudson's Bay via the South Saskatchewan River system from streams that flow to the Gulf of Mexico via the Mississippi River system.

Although the natural drainage basin surrounding Reesor Lake is quite small, it is 11 times larger than the lake (Fig. 1, Tables 1, 2). There are no defined natural inlets, and most of the water that enters the lake is brought by a channel and concrete pipe from Battle Creek (Fig. 2).

The bedrock in the drainage basin consists of the Frenchman Formation at lower elevations near the lake and the Ravenscrag Formation along the upper slopes of the plateau (Table 1). Surficial deposits on heavily wooded slopes consist mainly of colluvium, which is composed of sand, silt, clay and bedrock debris that has moved down slope, whereas surficial deposits at the southern end of the lake and along Battle Creek consist mainly of alluvium, which consists of sediments laid down along river beds and floodplains. The

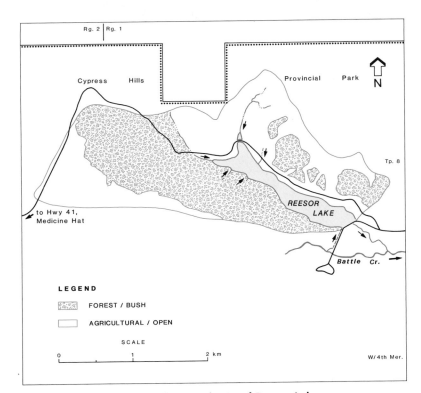

Figure 1. Features of the drainage basin of Reesor Lake.
SOURCES: Alta. Envir. n.d.[b]; En. Mines Resour. Can. 1978. Updated with 1984 aerial photos.

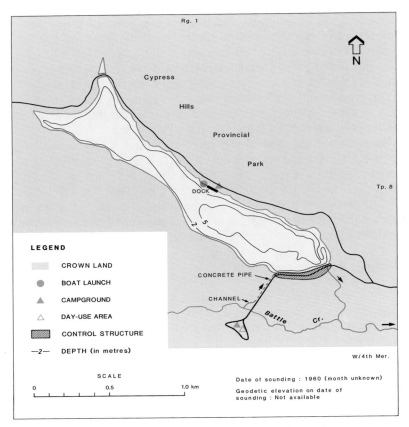

Figure 2. Bathymetry and shoreline features of Reesor Lake.
BATHYMETRY SOURCE: Agric. Can. 1962.

Table 1. Characteristics of Reesor Lake drainage basin.

area (excluding lake) (km²)[a]	5.58
soil[b]	Luvisols, Regosols, Chernozemics
bedrock geology[b, c]	Ravenscrag Formation (Tertiary): sandstone, clay, mudstone, coal, thin bentonite beds; nonmarine Frenchman Formation (Upper Cretaceous): sandstone, shale; nonmarine
terrain[b]	rolling to hilly
ecoregion[d]	Boreal Foothills and Groveland Subregion of Aspen Parkland
dominant vegetation[b, d]	trembling aspen, balsam poplar, lodgepole pine, rough fescue grassland
mean annual inflow (m³)[a, e]	0.424 x 10⁶
mean annual sunshine (h)[f]	2 345

NOTE: [e]excluding groundwater and Battle Creek inflows
SOURCES: [a]Alta. Envir. n.d.[b]; [b]Lombard North Group 1973; [c]Alta. Res. Counc. 1972; [d]Strong and Leggat 1981; [f]Envir. Can. 1982.

alluvial deposits range from gravel and sand to silt and clay (Lombard North Group 1973).

Reesor Lake is situated in a deep, wooded valley. All of the land in the watershed is part of Cypress Hills Provincial Park. The north-facing slopes to the southwest of the lake are forested with white spruce, lodgepole pine and trembling aspen. The latter two species are also the main trees near the lake. The land is more open on the northeast side of the lake, where the vegetation is shrubland, trembling aspen groveland, and fescue and mixed grasslands (Lombard North Group 1973).

Reservoir Characteristics

Reesor Lake is a long, narrow, shallow water body that is oriented in a northwest-southeast direction (Fig. 2). It is a maximum of 2.1-km long and 0.5-km wide, and covers an area of only 0.51 km² at full supply level. The northwestern half of the lake has a flat bottom that reaches a maximum depth between 2 and 5 m. The southeastern half is somewhat deeper: the sides of the basin slope gently to a maximum depth at full supply level of about 5.5 m.

The control structures that created Reesor Lake were built in 1958 by the Prairie Farm Rehabilitation Administration of the federal Department of Agriculture (Agric. Can. 1962). They were upgraded in 1976 by Alberta Environment, which accepted control and maintenance responsibilities in the early 1970s. The 1976 concrete weir and diversion structure in Battle Creek directs water into a short channel that flows into a concrete pipe that enters the lake on the western side of the dam. The amount of water flowing through the pipe is controlled by two gates. The dam is an earthfill structure that has a riparian outlet pipe and gate at its eastern end and two drop-inlet spillways. Outflow is directed into a natural channel which drains back to Battle Creek. Water flows out through the smaller of the two spillways when the lake's elevation reaches the full supply level of 1 226.52 m (Table 2, Fig. 3). The larger spillway is used for emergencies, when the water level rises above 1 226.67 m. Regular releases of water through the outlet gate maintain flow in the stream channel and special releases meet the needs of downstream water users (Didyk 1988).

The elevation of Reesor Lake has been monitored since 1965 (Fig. 4). The historic minimum (1 225.48 m) was recorded in 1980, after the lake level was lowered in late 1979 to facilitate chemical treatment for removal of white suckers. The historic maximum (1 226.57 m) was recorded in May 1986. During the 1960s and 1970s, the lake's elevation was kept near 1 225.91 m, rather than at the design full supply level of 1 226.52 m. Water depths at the lower level were marginal for fish survival (Underwood, McLellan & Assoc. Ltd. 1976) and fish kills occurred in the winters of 1978/79 and 1981/82. However, since 1982, the elevation has been main-

Table 2. Characteristics of Reesor Lake.

control structure[a]	earthfill dam with rock riprap upstream slope, control gate, and two drop-inlet spillways; diversion pipe from Battle Creek
dam crest elevation (m)[b]	1 228.34
crest length (m)[a]	396.24
full supply level (FSL) (m)[b]	1 226.52
volume at FSL (m³)[c]	1.91 x 10⁶
live storage at FSL (m³)[c]	1.68 x 10⁶
surface area at FSL (km²)[c]	0.51
maximum depth at FSL (m)[b]	5.5
mean depth at FSL (m)[c]	3.7
shoreline length (km)[d]	5.5
maximum length (km)[d]	2.1
maximum width (km)[d]	0.5
mean annual lake evaporation (mm)[e]	770
mean annual precipitation (mm)[e]	529
mean residence time (yr)[e, f]	6

NOTE: [f]excluding groundwater and Battle Creek inflows
SOURCES: [a]Underwood, McLellan & Assoc. Ltd. 1976; [b]Agric. Can. 1962; [c]Alta. Envir. n.d.[c]; [d]English 1979; [e]Alta. Envir. n.d.[b]

Table 3. Major ions and related water quality variables for Reesor Lake. Average concentrations in mg/L; pH in pH units. Composite samples from the euphotic zone collected 13 times during the open-water period each year from 1983 to 1987[a]. S.E. = standard error.

	Mean	S.E.
pH (range)	7.5–8.7	—
total alkalinity (CaCO₃)	124	3.6
specific conductivity (μS/cm)	234	5.8
total dissolved solids (calculated)	123	3.5
total hardness (CaCO₃)	112	4.2
HCO₃	148	4.9
CO₃	0.4	0.38
Mg	11	3.6
Na	<3	—
K	2	0.06
Cl	<1	—
SO₄	<5	—
Ca	28	1.4

NOTE: [a]16 May to 13 Sep. 1983 (n = 3); 28 May to 02 Oct. 1984 (n = 3); 03 June to 04 Sep. 1985 (n = 3); 02 June and 11 Aug. 1986; 31 May and 02 July 1987
SOURCE: Alta. Envir. n.d.[a], Naquadat station 05AL11AB4000

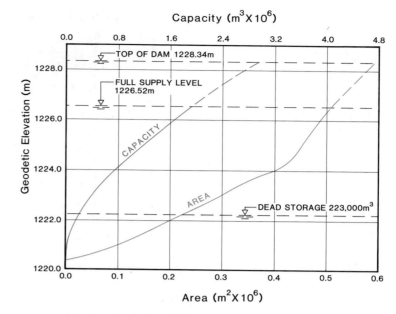

Figure 3. Area/capacity curve for Reesor Lake.
SOURCE: Alta. Envir. n.d.[c].

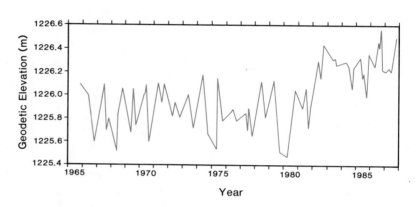

Figure 4. Water level of Reesor Lake, 1965 to 1987.
SOURCE: Envir. Can. 1965–1987.

During winter, dissolved oxygen can become depleted near the bottom, as in March 1985 (Fig. 5). Winterkill is not a major problem, however, because the surface water usually contains sufficient dissolved oxygen for fish survival. Exceptions occurred in the winters of 1978/79 and 1981/82, when dissolved oxygen declined to critical levels.

Reesor Lake is eutrophic. The highest chlorophyll *a* concentration ever recorded in the lake (64 μg/L) occurred in September 1984 (Fig. 6). The long-term average recorded during the open-water season from 1983 to 1987, however, is much lower (14.0 μg/L, Table 4). Chlorophyll *a* concentrations often reach a small peak in May but the highest levels occur in August or September. Total phosphorus is highest in late summer in most years, as well, probably because phosphorus is released from the bottom sediments and then mixed into the overlying water.

Biological Characteristics

Plants

There are no data available for the phytoplankton community in Reesor Lake.

Brief observations of aquatic macrophytes were made by Fish and Wildlife Division on 1 June 1978 (English 1979). Plants grew densely around the entire shoreline to a depth of approximately 4 m, and covered 70 to 80% of the lake bottom. The emergent species identified were common cattail (*Typha latifolia*) and bulrush (*Scirpus* sp.), and the submergent species were Richardson pondweed (*Potamogeton richardsonii*) and coontail (*Ceratophyllum demersum*).

tained closer to the full supply level, and no fish kills have been reported since the winter of 1981/82.

Water Quality

Water quality in Reesor Lake has been monitored since 1982 by Alberta Environment and Alberta Recreation and Parks (Alta. Envir. n.d.[a]). As well, winter dissolved oxygen concentrations have been monitored annually by Fish and Wildlife Division since 1972 (Alta. For. Ld. Wild. n.d.; English 1979).

Reesor Lake has fresh water that is well-buffered and less hard than the water in many Alberta lakes (Table 3). The dominant ions are calcium and bicarbonate. Turbidity is low and the water is quite transparent (Table 4).

The lake is typical of shallow lakes in Alberta: it is easily mixed by wind and, therefore, it rarely stratifies during summer. Levels of dissolved oxygen were uniformly high from top to bottom in August of 1984 (Fig. 5) and 1987, and in September of 1985 and 1986.

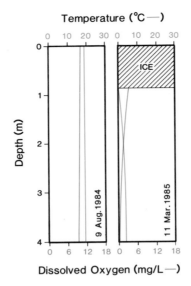

Figure 5. Temperature and dissolved oxygen in Reesor Lake, 1984 and 1985.
SOURCES: Alta. Envir. n.d.[a]; Alta. For. Ld. Wild. n.d.

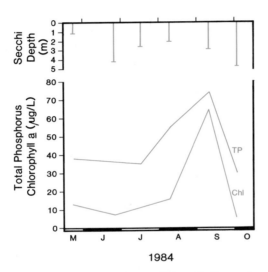

Figure 6. Total phosphorus, chlorophyll *a* and Secchi depth in Reesor Lake, 1984.
SOURCE: Alta. Envir. n.d.[a].

Table 4. Nutrient, chlorophyll *a* and Secchi depth data for Reesor Lake. Average concentrations in µg/L. Composite samples from the euphotic zone collected 24 times during the open-water period each year from 1983 to 1987[a]. S.E. = standard error.

	Mean	S.E.
total phosphorus	36[b]	3.2
chlorophyll *a*	14.0[c]	3.83
Secchi depth (m)	2.9	0.28

NOTES: [a]16 May to 05 Oct. 1983 (n = 6); 28 May to 02 Oct. 1984 (n = 6); 03 June to 04 Sep. 1985 (n = 4); 02 June to 10 Sep. 1986 (n = 4); 31 May to 24 Aug. 1987 (n = 4); [b]n = 19; [c]n = 23
SOURCE: Alta. Envir. n.d.[a], Naquadat station 05AL11AB4000

Invertebrates

The invertebrates in Reesor Lake were sampled by Fish and Wildlife Division on 1 June 1978 (English 1979). Almost 79% of the total number of zooplankton in the sample (138/L) was copepods, 20% was rotifers and less than 2% was cladocerans. The standing crop of zooplankton, particularly Cladocera, was considered to be relatively low. Four samples of benthos were taken with an Ekman dredge from a depth of 6 m. The samples included midges (Chironomidae) and aquatic earthworms (Oligochaeta). Chironomids dominated by weight (6 g/m² wet weight), but oligochaetes were more numerous. Many clam shells (Pelecypoda) were included in the sample, but none contained live animals. The standing crop of benthos (7 g/m² wet weight) was considered to be very low.

Fish

Reesor Lake is managed as a rainbow trout fishery. This species was stocked first in 1960. With the exception of 1979, the lake has been stocked annually since 1967. Between 1981 and 1988, approximately 63 000 trout (1 235 trout/ha) were planted each year (Alta. En. Nat. Resour. 1981–1985; Alta. For. Ld. Wild. 1986–1988). Regular stocking is necessary to maintain the rainbow trout population, since there is no trout spawning habitat available. Brown trout were stocked from 1954 to 1956, before the dam was constructed, but none remain in the lake. Longnose suckers were present prior to 1966, and white suckers migrated into the lake from Battle Creek in 1960, after the water diversion pipe was installed. Suckers compete with trout for food, and are considered detrimental to trout production. In 1966, longnose suckers were successfully removed by chemical rehabilitation, and they have not been caught since. Subsequent to 1966, the white sucker population expanded, and by 1978, test netting indicated that 85% of the fish population was composed of this species. The growth of trout in Reesor Lake in 1978 was comparable to trout growth in lakes with similar sucker populations, such as Chain Lakes Reservoir, but slow compared to trout growth in lakes where there were no suckers, such as Heninger Reservoir (English 1979). White suckers were removed from Reesor Lake by chemical treatment in September 1979. At the same time, a fish barrier was built on the inlet from Battle Creek to prevent reentry of suckers to the lake. Test netting in May 1985 caught rainbow trout only (Bishop 1989), an indication that the sucker removal program and a subsequent winterkill during 1981/82 had eliminated the white sucker population. The status of the forage fish population since the 1979 chemical treatment is unknown, but sticklebacks were identified in rainbow trout stomachs in 1984 (English 1985).

A creel census was conducted by Fish and Wildlife Division between May and August in 1984 (Bishop 1985). The majority of anglers interviewed lived within 80 km of the lake, usually in the Medicine Hat area. The highest catches (0.32 trout/angler-hour) were recorded during May. The success rate improved again in August (0.23 trout/angler-hour), probably because young-of-the-year fish stocked in May had grown to a catchable size. The average catch rate for the survey period was 0.22 trout/angler-hour, and the best catches were usually made near the dock. This catch rate is considerably higher than the 0.05 trout/angler-hour catch rate calculated during a 1979 survey conducted before suckers were removed from the lake (Fitch 1981). The mean length and weight of rainbow trout taken by anglers in 1984 was 27.3 cm and 247 g, respectively (English 1985). Ninety-five percent of these fish were age 1+ years, and had grown at a rate of approximately 1.48 cm/month. This rate is similar to rates recorded in other stocked lakes in the southern region, such as Michelle and Cavan lakes, and is much higher than growth rates in nearby Spruce Coulee Reservoir (0.99 cm/month).

Wildlife

Birds are numerous in the Cypress Hills: more than 200 species have been sighted and about 90 species nest there. Nine species of waterfowl have been observed during summer, but the number of migrants that might use the park lakes for staging purposes is unknown. Mallards, American Widgeons and Lesser Scaup have been sighted on Reesor Lake, and small numbers of Double-crested Cormorants feed there occasionally. Great Blue Herons frequently feed among the cattails, and Belted Kingfishers have also been spotted near the water. Horned Larks are present northeast of the lake in the Cypress Hills area, and Bank Swallows are common near the lakeshore (Lombard North Group 1973). Sixteen Wild Turkeys were introduced into the Cypress Hills in 1962 and a small population has become established. Poor-wills were recorded in 1945 and can still be heard—the Cypress Hills are the only place in Alberta where they are found (Finlay and Finlay 1987).

Elk were brought to the park in 1938 to replace the original population, which had been hunted to extinction by the 1890s. The Cypress Hills area is an important wintering area for elk, mule deer and white-tailed deer. Four moose were introduced to the park in 1956, and a population has become established since that time. Moose are not thought to be native to the park, although there are some reports to the contrary. In the 1980s, the moose herd in the park numbered 60 to 70 (Finlay and Finlay 1987). Moose winter in an area northwest of the lake and in the valley bottom along Battle Creek. Beaver were brought into the park around 1940; in 1973, one beaver lodge and three muskrat houses were sighted at Reesor Lake (Lombard North Group 1973).

M.E. Bradford

References

Agriculture Canada. 1962. General and detail plan, Two Lakes Reservoir, Sec. 20, NE 19, SW 29, SE 30–8–1 W4. Plan. No. 17528. Prairie Farm Rehabilitation Admin., Water Devel. Br., Medicine Hat.

Alberta Culture and Multiculturalism. n.d. Hist. Resour. Div., Hist. Sites Serv. Unpubl. data, Edmonton.

Alberta Energy and Natural Resources. 1981–1985. Fish planting list. Fish Wild. Div., Edmonton.

Alberta Environment. n.d.[a]. Envir. Assess. Div., Envir. Qlty. Monit. Br. Unpubl. data, Edmonton.

———. n.d.[b]. Tech. Serv. Div., Hydrol. Br. Unpubl. data, Edmonton.

———. n.d.[c]. Tech. Serv. Div., Surv. Br. Unpubl. data, Edmonton.

Alberta Forestry, Lands and Wildlife. n.d. Fish Wild. Div. Unpubl. data, Edmonton.

———. 1986–1988. Fish planting list. Fish Wild. Div., Edmonton.

———. 1988. Boating in Alberta. Fish Wild. Div., Edmonton.

———. 1989. Guide to sportfishing. Fish Wild. Div., Edmonton.

Alberta Research Council. 1972. Geological map of Alberta. Nat. Resour. Div., Alta. Geol. Surv., Edmonton.

Bishop, F.G. 1985. Creel census results from six lakes in the Cypress Hills area, southern Alberta. Alta. En. Nat. Resour., Fish Wild. Div. Unpubl. rep., Lethbridge.

———. 1989. Alta. For. Ld. Wild., Fish Wild. Div., Lethbridge. Pers. comm.

Didyk, A. 1988. Alta. Envir., Devel. Op. Div., Lethbridge. Pers. comm.

Energy, Mines and Resources Canada. 1978. National topographic series 1:50 000 72E/9 (1978). Surv. Map. Br., Ottawa.

English, W.G. 1979. Reesor Lake Reservoir: Lake survey inventory. Alta. Rec. Parks Wild., Fish Wild. Div. Unpubl. rep., Lethbridge.

———. 1985. Growth and feeding characteristics of fish creeled by anglers in the Cypress Hills area, southern Alberta. Alta. En. Nat. Resour., Fish Wild. Div. Unpubl. rep., Lethbridge.

Environment Canada. 1965–1987. Surface water data. Prep. by Inland Waters Directorate. Water Surv. Can., Water Resour. Br., Ottawa.

———. 1982. Canadian climate normals, Vol. 7: Bright sunshine (1951–1980). Prep. by Atm. Envir. Serv. Supply Serv. Can., Ottawa.

Finlay, J. and C. Finlay. 1987. Parks in Alberta: A guide to peaks, ponds, parklands & prairies. Hurtig Publ., Edmonton.

Fitch, L. 1981. A creel survey of three lakes in Cypress Hills Provincial Park: Elkwater Lake, Reesor Lake and Spruce Coulee Reservoir. Alta. En. Nat. Resour., Fish Wild. Div., Lethbridge.

Lombard North Group. 1973. Cypress Hills Provincial Park, Alberta, Vol. 1: Resource inventory. Alta. Pub. Works and Alta. Ld. For., Prov. Parks Div., Edmonton.

Strong, W.L. and K.R. Leggat. 1981. Ecoregions of Alberta. Alta. En. Nat. Resour., Resour. Eval. Plan. Div., Edmonton.

Underwood, McLellan & Associates Limited. 1976. Preliminary design: Reesor Lake control works improvements. Prep. for Alta. Envir., Design Const. Div., Edmonton.

Appendix

1. Estimate of depth of the littoral zone in a lake.

In 1986, researchers from the University of Alberta gathered data from 12 Alberta lakes on the maximum depth of rooted plant colonization (MDRPC, m) and the Secchi depth (S, m). The maximum depth of rooted plant colonization is the lower boundary of the littoral zone. Secchi depth provides an indication of light attenuation in lake water. These data were combined with existing information on 32 other low-colour lakes and a model was developed to predict the maximum depth of rooted plant colonization:

$$(MDRPC)^{0.5} = 0.69 \log_{10}(S) + 1.76$$

This model was used to estimate the depth of the littoral zone for many lakes described in the *Atlas*.

Reference: Chambers, P.A. and E.E. Prepas. 1988. Underwater spectral attenuation and its effect on the maximum depth of angiosperm colonization. Can. J. Fish. Aquat. Sci. 45:1010–1017.

2. Conversion Factors for Gram Weight to Equivalence.
(Multiply gram weights by these factors)

Chemical and initial units	to	Conversion factors	
		$\mu EQ/L$	$\mu mol/L$
alkalinity mg/L ($CaCO_3$)		19.98	—
total hardness mg/L ($CaCO_3$)		19.98	—
HCO_3 mg/L		16.39	16.39
CO_3 mg/L		33.32	16.66
Mg mg/L		82.28	41.14
Na mg/L		43.50	43.50
K mg/L		25.58	25.58
Cl mg/L		28.21	28.21
SO_4 mg/L		20.82	10.41
Ca mg/L		49.90	24.95
TP, TDP, SRP μg P/L		N/A	0.03228
N μg N/L (for NO_3, NO_2)		0.0174	0.0174
Kjeldahl N, μg N/L		N/A	0.0174
Fe μg/L (for Ferrous Fe)		0.0358	0.0179
Fe μg/L (for Ferric Fe)		N/A	0.0179

Prepared by: Dr. J. Curtis, Univ. Alta. Dept. Zool.

3. Phosphorus loading coefficients used in the *Atlas of Alberta Lakes*.

For the 24 lakes described in the *Atlas* where Alberta Environment calculated phosphorus loading, information was generated from measurements made at the lake wherever possible. However, often there was insufficient information on the target lakes, and general coefficients, based on data collected in Alberta, had to be used. Similar general coefficients were used by researchers at the University of Alberta when phosphorus budgets were constructed. The same general coefficients were used by both groups, except for precipitation/dustfall as indicated below.

(1) precipitation/dustfall (where m^2 refers to the surface of the lake)
: 22 mg total phosphorus/m^2 per year (Alberta Environment) (Alta. Envir. n.d.)
: 20 mg total phosphorus/m^2 per year (University of Alberta) (Shaw et al. 1989)

(2) watershed (where ha refers to relevant surface area of the drainage basin) (Alta. Envir. n.d.).
: forest/bush — 0.1 kg total phosphorus/ha per year
: agricultural/cleared
—0.2 kg total phosphorus/ha per year for light agriculture,
—0.5 kg total phosphorus/ha per year where intense agricultural practices employed
: residential/cottage — 1 kg total phosphorus/ha per year
: upstream lakes — phosphorus loading to upstream lakes was calculated with loading coefficients applied to the watershed of the upstream lake, and a retention factor for the lake was calculated (Larsen and Mercier 1976). The portion of the phosphorus load not retained by the upstream lake was assumed to enter the lake downstream (for example, Island Lake).

(3) sewage: the amount of sewage actually entering a particular lake was not measured. Instead it was assumed that 4% of the total potential sewage effluent generated by cottages and campgrounds on the lake shore entered the lake. This value was based on an intensive study conducted on Wabamun Lake (Mitchell 1982).

References

Alberta Environment. n.d. Envir. Assess. Div., Envir. Qlty. Monit. Br. Unpubl. data, Edmonton.

Larsen, D.P. and H.T. Mercier. 1976. Phosphorus retention capacity of lakes. J. Fish. Res. Bd. Can. 33:1742–1750.

Mitchell, P.A. 1982. Evaluation of the "septic snooper" on Wabamun and Pigeon lakes. Alta. Envir., Poll. Contr. Div., Water Qlty. Contr. Br., Edmonton.

Shaw, R.D., A.M. Trimbee, A. Minty, H. Fricker and E.E. Prepas. 1989. Atmospheric deposition of phosphorus and nitrogen in central Alberta with emphasis on Narrow Lake. Water, Air, and Soil Poll. 43:119–134.

4. Methods used for analysis of lake water.
Same indicates that a similar approach or method was used in both institutions for the parameter indicated.

Parameter	Methods	
	University of Alberta	*Alberta Environment*
temperature	0.5– to 1–m intervals, resistance thermometer	Hydrolab meter #4041
dissolved oxygen	Winkler[a] within 24 hrs	Hydrolab meter #4041, calibrated to Winkler
pH	Metrohm E588 pH meter immediately after collection or Beckman Expandomatic SS–2 meter in the laboratory	Hydrolab meter #4041, *in situ*
total alkalinity	potentiometric titration[b], within 24 hours	same
specific conductivity	YSI model 31 conductivity bridge at 20°C	conductivity meter at 25°C
total dissolved solids	filter through 0.45–μm membrane filter, evaporate at 103°C	calculated[c]
total hardness	titrate with EDTA[b] can also be calculated from Ca + Mg[d]	automated calmagite colorimetric method[c]
colour	Hellige Aqua Tester model 611A within 7 days	—
turbidity	Hach turbidimeter model 2100A within 7 days	same
total particulate carbon	thermal combustion[b]	same[c]
dissolved organic carbon	thermal combustion[b]	same
HCO_3, CO_3	from alkalinity	same
Mg, Na, K, Ca	atomic absorption spectrophotometer[b]	Mg, Ca-same Na, K—automated flame photometry[c]
SO_4	turbidimetric method[d]	automated methyl-thymol blue colorimetric method[c]
Cl	automated thiocyanate colorimetric method[b]	same[c]
total phosphorus	potassium persulfate[e]	in most cases, same
total dissolved phosphorus	filtered through 0.45–μm HAWP Millipore membrane filter, then as TP	in most cases, same
soluble reactive phosphorus	filtered as TDP[f]	same
total Kjeldahl nitrogen-N	acid indigestion[g] followed by NH_4–N analysis, modified by Prepas and Trew (1983)	semi-automated block digestion, phenate colorimetric method[c]
NO_2 + NO_3–N	autoanalyzer[h]	automated cadmium reduction method[c]
NH_4–N	Solarzano's (1969) phenolhypochlorite method,	automated phenate colorimetric method[c]
total iron	phenanthroline method[d]	atomic absorption[c]
chlorophyll *a*	spectrophotometric technique ethanol extraction[t] (M.L. Ostrofsky described in[i])	fluorometric procedure acetone extraction[k, t]

Note: [t]two techniques give comparable results (Prepas and Trew 1983)
Sources: [a]Carpenter 1965; [b]Envir. Can. 1979; [c]Alta. Envir. Centre 1987; [d]APHA 1980; [e]Riley and Prepas 1984; [f]Murphy and Riley 1962; [g]D'Elia et al. 1977; [h]Stainton et al. 1977; [i]Bergmann and Peters; [k]Yentsch and Menzel 1963. More details on the approaches used can be found in Prepas and Trew (1983) and Alta. Envir. Centre (1987).

References

Alberta Environmental Centre. 1987. Methods manual for chemical analyses of water and wastes. Revised by F.P. Dieken. Publ. No. AECV87–M1. Alta. Envir. Centre, Vegreville, Alta.

American Public Health Association. 1980. Standard methods for the examination of water and wastewater. 15th ed. APHA, AWWA, WPCF. Washington, D.C.

Bergmann, M. and R.H. Peters. 1980. A simple reflectance method for the measurement of particulate pigment in lake water and its application to phosphorus-chlorophyll-seston relationships. Can. J. Fish. Aquat. Sci. 37:111–114.

Carpenter, J.H. 1965. The Chesapeake Bay Institute technique for the Winkler dissolved oxygen method. Limnol. Oceanogr. 10:141–143.

D'Elia, C.F., P.A. Steudler and N. Corwin. 1977. Determination of total nitrogen in aqueous samples using persulfate digestion. Limnol. Oceanogr. 22:760–764.

Environment Canada. 1979. Analytical methods manual. Inland Waters Directorate, Water Qlty. Br., Ottawa.

Murphy, J.A. and J.P. Riley. 1962. A modified single solution method for the determination of inorganic phosphate in natural waters. Anal. Chim. Acta 27:31–36.

Prepas, E.E. and D.O. Trew. 1983. Evaluation of the phosphorus-chlorophyll relationship for lakes off the Precambrian Shield in western Canada. Can. J. Fish. Aquat. Sci. 40:27–35.

Riley, E.T. and E.E. Prepas. 1984. Role of internal phosphorus loading in two shallow, productive lakes in Alberta, Canada. Can. J. Fish. Aquat. Sci. 41:845–855.

Solorzano, L. 1969. Determination of ammonia in natural waters by phenolhypochlorite method. Limnol. Oceanogr. 14:799–801.

Stainton, M.P., M.J. Capel and F.A. Armstrong. 1977. The chemical analysis of freshwater. 2nd ed. Fish. Envir. Can. Miscellaneous Special Publ. 25 (available from the Freshwater Inst., Winnipeg, Manitoba).

Yentsch, C.S. and D.W. Menzel. 1963. A method for the determination of phytoplankton chlorophyll and phaeophytin by fluorescence. Deep-Sea Res. 10:221–231.

Species List

The following lists give the scientific names of all terrestrial plants and vertebrate animals referred to only by common names in the *Atlas*. These lists are not a complete documentation of all the animals or plants that occur in Alberta. The list of animals is in taxonomic order, while terrestrial plants are listed in alphabetical order by common name. The scientific names for aquatic plants, algae and invertebrates are included in the text. The authorities used were:

Mammals: Jones, J.K., Jr., D.C. Carter, H.H. Genoways, R.S. Hoffmann, D.W. Rice and C. Jones. 1986. Revised checklist of North American mammals north of Mexico, 1986. Occasional Paper No. 107, The Museum. Texas Tech. Univ., Texas.
Smith, H.C. 1985. A checklist of the mammals of Alberta. Occasional Paper No. 6. Prov. Museum Alta., Edmonton.

Birds: Godfrey, W.E. 1986. The Birds of Canada. Natl. Museums Can., Ottawa.
Salt, W.R. and A.L. Wilk. Birds of Alberta. 1966. The Queen's Printer, Edmonton.

Reptiles: Cook, F.R. 1984. Introduction to Canadian amphibians and reptiles. Natl. Museum Nat. Sci., Ottawa.

Amphibians: Cook, F.R. 1984. Introduction to Canadian amphibians and reptiles. Natl. Museum Nat. Sci., Ottawa.

Fish: Nelson, J.S. 1990. Univ. Alta., Dept. Zool., Edmonton. Pers. comm.
Paetz, M.J. and J.S. Nelson. 1970. The fishes of Alberta. The Queen's Printer, Edmonton.
Scott, W.B. and E.J. Crossman. 1973. Freshwater fishes of Canada. Fish. Res. Bd. Can. Bull. No. 184, Ottawa.

Plants: Moss, E.H. 1983. Flora of Alberta. 2nd ed. Univ. Toronto Press, Toronto.

MAMMALS

Bats (Order Chiroptera)
Little brown bat	*Myotis lucifugus*
Big brown bat	*Eptesicus fuscus*

Hares and rabbits (Order Lagamorpha)
White-tailed jackrabbit	*Lepus townsendii*
Snowshoe hare; Varying hare	*Lepus americanus*

Rodents (Order Rodentia)
Woodchuck	*Marmota monax*
Hoary marmot	*Marmota caligata*
Richardson's ground squirrel	*Spermophilus richardsonii*
Franklin's ground squirrel	*Spermophilus franklinii*
Columbian ground squirrel	*Spermophilus columbianus*
Least chipmunk	*Eutamias minimus*
Red squirrel	*Tamiasciurus hudsonicus*
Beaver	*Castor canadensis*
Deer mouse	*Peromyscus maniculatus*
Northern bog lemming	*Synaptomys borealis*
Meadow vole	*Microtus pennsylvanicus*
Muskrat	*Ondatra zibethicus*
Porcupine	*Erithizon dorsatum*

Meat-eaters (Order Carnivora)
Coyote	*Canis latrans*
Gray wolf	*Canis lupus*
Red fox	*Vulpes vulpes*

Black bear	Ursus americanus
Grizzly bear	Ursus arctos
Marten	Martes americana
Fisher	Martes pennanti
Ermine	Mustela erminea
Long-tailed weasel	Mustela frenata
Mink	Mustela vison
Least weasel	Mustela nivalis
Wolverine	Gulo gulo
Badger	Taxidea taxus
Striped skunk	Mephitis mephitis
River otter	Lutra canadensis
Cougar	Felis concolor
Lynx	Lynx canadensis
Bobcat	Lynx rufus

Hoofed mammals (Order Artiodactyla)

Wapiti; Elk	Cervus elaphus
Mule deer	Odocoileus hemionus
White-tailed deer	Odocoileus virginianus
Moose	Alces alces
Woodland caribou	Rangifer tarandus
Pronghorn; Antelope	Antilocapra americana
Bison; Buffalo	Bison bison
Mountain goat	Oreamnos americanus
Bighorn sheep	Ovis canadensis

BIRDS

Loons (Order Gaviiformes)

Common Loon	Gavia immer

Grebes (Order Podicipediformes)

Red-necked Grebe	Podiceps grisegena
Horned Grebe	Podiceps auritus
Eared Grebe	Podiceps nigricollis
Western Grebe	Aechmophorus occidentalis

Pelicans (Order Pelecaniformes)

White Pelican	Pelecanus erythrorhynchos
Double-crested Cormorant	Phalacrocorax auritus

Herons (Order Ciconiiformes)

Great Blue Heron	Ardea herodias
Black-crowned Night Heron	Nycticorax nycticorax
American Bittern	Botaurus lentiginosus

Swans, Geese and Ducks (Order Anseriformes)

Whistling Swan	Olor columbianus
Trumpeter Swan	Olor buccinator
Canada Goose	Branta canadensis
White-fronted Goose	Anser albifrons
Snow Goose	Chen hyperborea
Ross's Goose	Chen rossii
Mallard	Anas platyrhynchos
Gadwall	Anas strepera
Northern Pintail	Anas acuta
Green-winged Teal	Anas crecca
Blue-winged Teal	Anas discors
Cinnamon Teal	Anas cyanoptera
American Widgeon	Anas americana
Northern Shoveler	Anas clypeata
Redhead	Aythya americana
Ring-necked Duck	Aythya collaris
Canvasback	Aythya valisineria
Lesser Scaup	Aythya affinis
Common Goldeneye	Bucephala clangula
Barrow's Goldeneye	Bucephala islandica
Bufflehead	Bucephala albeola
Oldsquaw	Clangula hyemalis
White-winger Scoter	Melanitta deglandi
Surf Scoter	Melanitta perspicillata
Ruddy Duck	Oxyura jamaicensis
Hooded Merganser	Lophodytes cucullatus
Common Merganser	Mergus merganser

Hawks (Order Falconiformes)

Turkey Vulture	Cathartes aura
Cooper's Hawk	Accipiter cooperii
Red-tailed Hawk	Buteo jamaicensis
Swainson's Hawk	Buteo swainsoni
Ferruginous Hawk	Buteo regalis
Golden Eagle	Aquila chrysaetos
Bald Eagle	Haliaeetus leucocephalus
Marsh Hawk	Circus cyaneus
Osprey	Pandion haliaetus
Prairie Falcon	Falco mexicanus
Peregrine Falcon	Falco peregrinus
Merlin; Pigeon Hawk	Falco columbarius
American Kestrel; Sparrow Hawk	Falco sparverius

Grouse (Order Galliformes)

Spruce Grouse	Dendragapus canadensis
Ruffed Grouse	Bonasa umbellus
Sharp-tailed Grouse	Tympanuchus phasianellus
Ring-necked Pheasant	Phasianus colchicus
Hungarian Partridge	Perdix perdix
Turkey	Meleagris gallopavo

Cranes and Rails (Order Gruiformes)

Whooping Crane	Grus americana
Sandhill Crane	Grus canadensis
Sora	Porzana carolina
Yellow Rail	Coturnicops noveboracensis
American Coot	Fulica americana

Shorebirds and Gulls (Order Charadriiformes)

Piping Plover	Charadrius melodus
Killdeer	Charadrius vociferus
American Golden Plover	Pluvialis dominica
Black-bellied Plover	Pluvialis squatarola
Common Snipe	Capella gallinago
Long-billed Curlew	Numenius americanus
Spotted Sandpiper	Actitis macularia
Solitary Sandpiper	Tringa solitaria
Greater Yellowlegs	Tringa melanoleucus
Lesser Yellowlegs	Tringa flavipes
Willet	Catoptrophorus semipalmatus
Ruddy Turnstone	Arenaria interpres
Knot	Calidris canutus
Sanderling	Calidris alba
Semipalmated Sandpiper	Calidris pusillus
Least Sandpiper	Calidris minutilla
Pectoral Sandpiper	Calidris melanotos
Baird's Sandpiper	Calidris bairdii
Dunlin	Calidris alpina
Stilt Sandpiper	Micropalama himantopus
Short-billed Dowitcher	Limnodromus griseus
Long-billed Dowitcher	Limnodromus scolopaceus
Buff-breasted Sandpiper	Tryngites subruficollis
Marbled Godwit	Limosa fedoa
Hudsonian Godwit	Limosa haemastica
American Avocet	Recurvirostra americana
Black-necked Stilt	Himantopus mexicanus
Wilson's Phalarope	Phalaropus tricolor
Northern Phalarope	Phalaropus lobatus
Parasitic Jaeger	Stercorarius parasiticus
California Gull	Larus californicus
Ring-billed Gull	Larus delawarensis
Franklin's Gull	Larus pipixcan
Bonaparte's Gull	Larus philadelphia
Sabine's Gull	Xema sabini
Forster's Tern	Sterna forsteri
Common Tern	Sterna hirundo
Black Tern	Chlidonias niger

Pigeons and Doves (Order Columbiformes)

Mourning Dove	Zenaidura macroura

Owls (Order Strigiformes)

Great Horned Owl	Bubo virginianus
Hawk Owl	Surnia ulula

Pygmy Owl	*Glaucidium gnoma*
Barred Owl	*Strix varia*
Great Gray Owl	*Strix nebulosa*
Boreal Owl	*Aegolius funereus*
Saw-whet Owl	*Aegolius acadicus*
Long-eared Owl	*Asio otus*
Short-eared Owl	*Asio flammeus*

Goatsuckers (Order Caprimulgiformes)

Poor-will	*Phalaenoptilus nuttalli*
Common Nighthawk	*Chordeiles minor*

Hummingbirds (Order Apodiformes)

Rufous Hummingbird	*Selasphorus rufus*
Calliope Hummingbird	*Stellula calliope*
Ruby-throated Hummingbird	*Archilocus colubris*

Kingfishers (Order Coraciiformes)

Belted Kingfisher	*Megaceryle alcyon*

Perching Birds (Order Passeriformes)

Horned Lark	*Eremophila alpestris*
Violet-green Swallow	*Tachycineta thalassina*
Tree Swallow	*Iridoprocne bicolor*
Bank Swallow	*Riparia riparia*
Purple Martin	*Progne subis*
Gray Jay	*Perisoreus canadensis*
Black-capped Chickadee	*Parus atricapillus*
Mountain Chickadee	*Parus gambeli*
Boreal Chickadee	*Parus hudsonicus*
Long-billed Marsh Wren	*Telmatodytes palustris*
Sprague's Pipit	*Anthus spragueii*
Black and White Warbler	*Mniotilta varia*
Tennessee Warbler	*Vermivora peregrina*
Orange-crowned Warbler	*Vermivora celata*
Yellow Warbler	*Dendroica petechia*
Magnolia Warbler	*Dendroica magnolia*
Cape May Warbler	*Dendroica tigrina*
Myrtle Warbler	*Dendroica coronata*
Black-throated Green Warbler	*Dendroica virens*
Blackburnian Warbler	*Dendroica fusca*
Chestnut-sided Warbler	*Dendroica pensylvanica*
Bay-breasted Warbler	*Dendroica castanea*
Blackpoll Warbler	*Dendroica striata*
Palm Warbler	*Dendroica palmarum*
Nashville Warbler	*Vermivora ruficapilla*
Mourning Warbler	*Opororonis philadelphia*
Macgillivray's Warbler	*Opororonis tolmiei*
Wilson's Warbler	*Wilsonia pusilla*
Canada Warbler	*Wilsonia canadensis*
American Redstart	*Setophaga ruticilla*
Yellow-headed Blackbird	*Xanthocephalus xanthocephalus*
Redwinged Blackbird	*Agelaius phoeniceus*
Western Tanager	*Piranga ludoviciana*
White-winged Crossbill	*Loxia leucoptera*
Savannah Sparrow	*Passerculus sandwichensis*
Leconte's Sparrow	*Passerherbulus caudacutus*
Vesper Sparrow	*Pooecetes gramineus*
Clay-colored Sparrow	*Spizella pallida*
White-throated Sparrow	*Zonotrichia albicollis*
Swamp Sparrow	*Melospiza georgiana*
Chestnut-collared Longspur	*Calarius ornatus*

REPTILES

Snakes (Order Squamata)

Western garter snake	*Thamnophis elegans*
Plains garter snake	*Thamnophis radix*

AMPHIBIANS

Frogs and toads (Order Anura)

Western toad	*Bufo boreas*
Canadian toad	*Bufo americanus hemiophrys*
Chorus frog	*Pseudacris triseriata*

Northern leopard frog	*Rana pipiens*
Spotted frog	*Rana pretiosa*
Wood frog	*Rana sylvatica*

Salamanders (Order Urodela)

Tiger salamander	*Ambystoma tigrinum*

FISH

Sturgeons (Family Acipenseridae)

Lake sturgeon	*Acipenser fulvescens*

Trout and Whitefish (Family Salmonidae)

Cisco	*Coregonus artedii*
Lake whitefish	*Coregonus clupeaformis*
Shortjaw cisco	*Coregonus zenithicus*
Kokanee	*Oncorhynchus nerka*
Round whitefish	*Prosopium cylindraceum*
Mountain whitefish	*Prosopium williamsoni*
Cutthroat trout	*Salmo clarki* (= *Oncorhynchus clarki*)
Rainbow trout	*Salmo gairdneri* (= *Oncorhynchus mykiss*)
Brown trout	*Salmo trutta*
Brook trout	*Salvelinus fontinalis*
Bull trout	*Salvelinus confluentus*
Lake trout	*Salvelinus namaycush*
Arctic grayling	*Thymallus arcticus*

Mooneye (Family Hiodontidae)

Goldeye	*Hiodon alosoides*

Pike (Family Esocidae)

Northern pike	*Esox lucius*

Minnows (Family Cyprinidae)

Northern redbelly dace	*Phoxinus eos*
Finescale dace	*Phoxinus neogaeus*
Lake chub	*Couesius plumbeus*
Brassy minnow	*Hybognathus hankinsoni*
Emerald shiner	*Notropis atherinoides*
Spottail shiner	*Notropis hudsonius*
Fathead minnow	*Pimephales promelas*
Flathead chub	*Platygobio gracilis*
Longnose dace	*Rhinichthys cataractae*
Pearl dace	*Semotilus margarita*

Suckers (Family Catostomidae)

Quillback	*Carpiodes cyprinus*
Longnose sucker	*Catostomus catostomus*
White sucker	*Catostomus commersoni*
Mountain sucker	*Catostomus platyrhynchus*
Shorthead redhorse	*Moxostoma macrolepidotum*

Cod (Family Gadidae)

Burbot	*Lota lota*

Sticklebacks (Family Gasterosteidae)

Brook stickleback	*Culaea inconstans*
Threespine stickleback	*Gasterosteus aculeatus*
Ninespine stickleback	*Pungitius pungitius*

Trout-perch (Family Percopsidae)

Trout-perch	*Percopsis omiscomaycus*

Perch (Family Percidae)

Yellow perch	*Perca flavescens*
Sauger	*Stizostedion canadense*
Walleye	*Stizostedion vitreum*
Iowa darter	*Etheostoma exile*

Sculpins (Family Cottidae)

Shorthead sculpin	*Cottus confusus*
Slimy sculpin	*Cottus cognatus*
Spoonhead sculpin	*Cottus ricei*
Deepwater sculpin	*Myoxocephalus quadricornis*

TERRESTRIAL PLANTS

Alder	*Alnus* spp.
Aspen, trembling	*Populus tremuloides*
Bearberry, common	*Arctostaphylos uva-ursi*
Birch	*Betula* spp.
Birch, dwarf; Birch, bog	*Betula glandulosa*
Birch, swamp	*Betula pumila*
Birch, white	*Betula papyrifera*
Blueberry	*Vaccinium* spp.
Bluegrass	*Poa* spp.
Buckbrush	*Symphoricarpos occidentalis*
Buffalo-berry	*Shepherdia canadensis*
Bunchberry	*Cornus canadensis*
Cactus, cushion	*Coryphantha vivipara*
Cactus, prickly pear	*Opuntia* spp.
Choke cherry	*Prunus virginiana*
Coral-root orchid, pale	*Corallorhiza trifida*
Coral-root orchid, spotted	*Corallorhiza maculata*
Coral-root orchid, striped	*Corallorhiza striata*
Cottonwood, lance-leaf	*Populus acuminata*
Cottonwood, narrow-leaf	*Populus angustifolia*
Cranberry, low-bush	*Viburnum edule*
Feathermoss	*Pleurozium schreberi*
Feathermoss	*Hylocomium splendens*
Feathermoss	*Ptilium crista-castrensis*
Fescue	*Festuca* spp.
Fescue, rough	*Festuca scabrella*
Fir, alpine	*Abies lasiocarpa*
Fir, balsam	*Abies balsamea*
Fir, Douglas	*Pseudotsuga menziesii*
Fireweed	*Epilobium angustifolium*
Glacier lily	*Erythronium grandiflorum*
Grass, grama	*Bouteloua gracilis*
Grass, june	*Koeleria macrantha*
Grass, oat	*Danthonia* spp.
Grass, Parry oat	*Danthonia parryi*
Grass, reed	*Calamagrostis* spp.
Grass, rye	*Elymus innovatus*
Grass, spear; Needle and thread	*Stipa comata*
Grass, wheat	*Agropyron* spp.
Heath	*Cassiope* spp.
Heath	*Phyllodoce* spp.
Horsetail	*Equisetum* spp.
Jacob's ladder	*Polemonium pulcherrimum*
Indian paint-brush, common red	*Castilleja miniata*
Juniper, creeping	*Juniperus horizontalis*
Labrador tea	*Ledum groenlandicum*
Larch, alpine	*Larix lyallii*
Pine, jack	*Pinus banksiana*
Pine, limber	*Pinus flexilis*
Pine, lodgepole	*Pinus contorta*
Pine, whitebark	*Pinus albicaulis*
Poison ivy	*Rhus radicans*
Poplar, balsam	*Populus balsamifera*
Rose, wild	*Rosa* spp.
Sage	*Artemisia* spp.
Saskatoon	*Amelanchier alnifolia*
Scorpion weed	*Phacelia* spp.
Sedge	*Carex* spp.
Snowberry	*Symphoricarpos albus*
Spruce, black	*Picea mariana*
Spruce, Engelmann	*Picea engelmannii*
Spruce, white	*Picea glauca*
Tamarack	*Larix laricina*
Willow	*Salix* spp.
Wolf willow; Silverberry	*Elaeagnus commutata*

Glossary

acidity: A measure of the capacity of water to neutralize a strong base. In natural water this capacity is usually attributable to the presence of acids such as carbonic, nitric, sulphuric and organic acids or to acid cations like aluminum. *See also* pH. [Lat. *acidus*, sour.]

aeolian deposits: Material, predominantly sand and silt-sized particles, transported and deposited by wind. Sand dunes are examples of aeolian deposits. [Gk. *Aeolus*, god of winds.]

alkalinity: A measure of the capacity of water to neutralize a strong acid. In natural waters this capacity is attributable to basic ions such as bicarbonate, carbonate and hydroxyl ions as well as other ions often present in small concentrations such as silicates and borates. *See also* pH. [Fr. *alcali*, calcined ashes.]

algal bloom: A conspicuous concentration of phytoplankton, often concentrated at or near the surface. It is difficult to quantify what constitutes a "bloom", but a rough estimate places it as a chlorophyll *a* concentration over 30 μg/L. Blue-green algae are the predominant type of algae in most blooms in Alberta.

alluvial deposits: Sediments deposited by water but which may now be dry land. A delta is an example of an alluvial deposit. [Lat. *alluvius*, wash.]

anion: *See* ion.

anoxic: Without oxygen. Anoxic water contains no measurable dissolved oxygen. Anoxic conditions often develop near the bottom of fertile lakes in summer and under ice in winter. [Gk. prefix *a*, without + Fr. *oxygène*.]

arability: A rating indicating the suitability of the soil for the production of crops. [Lat. *arabilis*, plough.]

area/capacity curve: A graph that shows the relationship between the depth, area and capacity (volume) of a lake or reservoir.

bathymetry: The measurements defining the size, depth and shape of a lake. [Gk. *bathys*, deep + *metron*, measure.]

bedrock: Continuous solid rock either exposed at the surface of the earth or overlain by a concealing cover of loose material such as that deposited by glaciers, water or wind.

benthic: Growing or living on or near the bottom of an aquatic system. Benthic invertebrates are small animals without backbones living on the bottom of a lake or river; for example clams and mayfly nymphs. [Gk. *benthos*, depth of the sea.]

benthos: The assemblage of organisms associated with the bottom sediments of aquatic systems. Benthos usually refers to the animals associated with the bottom sediments, but can also include plant and microbial communities. [Gk. *benthos*, depth of the sea.]

biomass: Weight of living matter. [Gk. *bios*, life + Lat. *massa*, a lump.]

blue-green algae: Algae of the Phylum Cyanophyta (also called Cyanobacteria), the most primitive group of algae. Blue-green algae are typified by cells without a true nucleus and with photosensitive pigments dispersed throughout the cell. Some species are capable of using nitrogen gas for metabolism. *See also* algal bloom. [Gk. *cyano*, blue + *phyto*, plant.]

Brunisol: Soils that develop on imperfectly-drained to well-drained sites on various types of parent materials. Brunisols develop under coniferous or deciduous forests.

buffer: A solution of weak acids and their dissolved salts which is able to greatly minimize changes in the hydrogen ion concentration (acidity). Most of the lakes in Alberta are well-buffered by bicarbonate ions and are therefore less susceptible to changes in pH by acid rain than the poorly buffered lakes on the Canadian shield.

buffering capacity: A measure of the resistance to acidification by acids or alkalinization by bases. *See also* buffer.

cation: *See* ion.

Chernozem: A soil group consisting of soils with a thick, nearly black surface horizon that is rich in organic matter from the decomposition of grasses and forbs. The surface horizon is underlain by a lighter-coloured transitional horizon which is above a zone of calcium carbonate accumulation. These soils occur in cool, subhumid to subarid climates under a vegetation of medium to tall grass prairie, and are usually excellent for growing crops.

chlorophyll *a*: One of the green pigments of plants. It is a photo-sensitive pigment that is essential for the conversion of inorganic carbon (for example, carbon dioxide) and water into organic carbon (for example, sugar). The concentration of chlorophyll *a* in water is an indicator of algal concentration. [Gk. *chloros*, green + *phyllon*, leaf.]

cobble: A stone that has been rounded by water, either by flowing water or wave action. Cobbles range in diameter from 7.5 to 25 cm. [W. *cob*, lump.]

colour: In limnology, colour is a measure of the humic material in water. It is measured by comparing filtered lake water to a mixture of platinum (Pt)-cobalt compounds, and is presented as units of Pt.

colluvium: A deposit of rock fragments and soil material that has accumulated at the base of steep slopes.

commercial fishing: The taking of fish to sell for profit. In Alberta, a licence is required for commercial fishing.

conductivity: *See* specific conductivity.

conduit: A pipe, tube or other channel for the conveyance of fluids. There is often a conduit to pass flow under or through major dams. [Lat. *conducere*, *conductum*, to conduct.]

control structure: A structure built to influence the natural flow of water. Dams, weirs and headgates are control structures.

coulee: A secondary valley of a main valley. Most coulees were created by water erosion during a period of high floods but they are now usually dry. Coulees are common in southern Alberta where they were created by meltwater during the retreat of the last glaciation.

creel survey: A census regarding species and numbers of fish caught by anglers over a period of time.

crenate: Indented, scalloped, notched. [Lat. *crenatus*, notched.]

crest: The highest part, as the highest part of a dam. [Lat. *crista*, a crest.]

Crown land: Land owned by the government, either federal (as in National Parks) or provincial.

Cryptophytes: Algae of the Phylum Cryptophyta. A small group of unicellular algae with two flagella emerging from a subapical pit. They usually have two chloroplasts and can be variously pigmented. [Gk. *krupte*, hide + *phyto*, plant.]

dam: A structure built across a waterway or valley to impound water. [Teut. *dam*.]

Denil II fishway: *See* fishway.

density: Mass of a substance in a unit volume, eg. g/cm^3; or numbers per unit area or volume, for example, people per km^2. [Lat. *densitas*, density.]

detritus: Tiny particles of material found in sediments or suspended in water. Organic detritus is derived from the decomposition of organisms; inorganic detritus is derived from the erosion of rocks and other mineral materials. Many text books on limnology restrict the meaning of detritus to include only organic detritus. [Lat. *detritus*, wearing down.]

diatoms: Algae of the Phylum Bacillariophyta. Microscopic unicellular algae occurring singly or grouped in colonies. Diatoms usually have thick, ornate siliceous cell walls. The cell walls form two distinct halves, like the top and bottom of a box, and they are marked with intricate, species-specific patterns. [Lat. *bacillus*, stick + *phyto*, plant.] also [Gk. *diatoms*, alluding to the cells being connected in chains.]

dimictic lake: A lake that undergoes two periods of complete vertical mixing, usually in the spring and in the fall when the water temperature is the same from the surface to the bottom. During the summer, a dimictic lake is thermally stratified. [Gk. *di*, two + *mictic*, mix.]

dinoflagellates: Algae of the Phylum Pyrrhophyta. A diverse group of algae which are single cells with two flagella of different length. One flagellum is located in a transverse furrow which encircles the entire cell, the other is in a longitudinal furrow perpendicular to the first furrow along one half of the cell. Of all the algae, these are the fastest moving. [Gk. *deinos*, terrible + L. *flagellum*, whip.]

dissolved oxygen: Molecular oxygen in solution in a liquid. The amount of oxygen that will stay in solution in water is dependent on temperature, pressure and salinity. More oxygen can be dissolved in cold water than in warm water. For example, at sea level, water at 0°C is saturated with dissolved oxygen when the oxygen concentration is 14.2 mg/L; at 35°C water is saturated when the oxygen concentration is 7.0 mg/L. Saturation is also affected by pressure; as pressure (either atmospheric or hydrostatic) increases, the capacity to hold gases (like oxygen) increases. The capacity of saline water to hold dissolved oxygen is less than that of fresh water.

domestic fishery: The taking of large numbers of fish to form a significant portion of the diet for people or dogs. In Alberta, a licence is required; most licence-holders are native people or Metis on Metis settlement lands.

drainage basin: Defined for the *Atlas* as the land around a water body that contributes surface runoff to that body. *See also* watershed.

drawdown: The lowering of a reservoir or lake by controlled withdrawal.

dyke: A low bank of earth to prevent high water levels from flooding land. [ME. *dik*, dam.]

dystrophic lakes: Brown-water lakes with very low conductivity, low cation content and a very high humus content, often characterized by low plankton production. [Gk. *dys*, badly + *trophein*, to nourish.]

ecoregion: An area characterized by a distinct climate as expressed by vegetation. Ecoregions in Alberta include Short Grass, Mixed Grass, Fescue Grass, Aspen Parkland, Montane, Subalpine, Alpine, Boreal Mixedwood, Boreal Uplands, Boreal Foothills, Boreal Northlands and Boreal Subarctic.

Ekman dredge: A metal traplike device used to sample the soft bottom sediment of a lake or river.

eluviation: The removal of soil material in suspension, or in solution within the soil, by the downward or lateral movement of water.

emergent macrophyte: Large, easily visible plants in which the lower part is submerged in water but the upper part extends above the surface. Bulrushes and cattails are emergent macrophytes.

epilimnion: The uppermost, warmest layer of a lake when a lake becomes thermally stratified in summer. The epilimnion lies above the metalimnion (thermocline). *See also* metalimnion, hypolimnion. [Gk. *epi*, on + *limne*, lake.]

euphotic zone: The upper layer of a water body as defined by light penetration; the upper limit is the water surface, the lower limit is the depth to which sufficient light for photosynthesis can penetrate. The euphotic zone is also called the *trophogenic zone* and occasionally the *photic zone*. The dark region below the euphotic zone is called the *tropholytic zone*. [Gk. *eu*, well + *photo*, light.]

eutrophic lakes: Lakes with a good supply of nutrients and hence a rich organic production of algae and macrophytes. In the *Atlas*, a lake is considered to be eutrophic if the peak chlorophyll *a* concentration exceeds 25 μg/L. [Gk. *eu*, well + *trophein*, to nourish.]

evaporation: The conversion of a liquid into a gas. The movement of molecules from a liquid into the air. [Lat. *evaporo*, *evaporatum*, out.]

fishway: A channel specially designed to facilitate upstream movement of fish in areas where their passage is otherwise blocked by high-velocity flows or vertical jumps. A step-pool fishway is a channel broken into small cascades with intervening resting pools. A Denil II fishway is a sloped channel with interior baffles to retard flow velocities to such a degree that upstream passage of fish is possible.

fluvial deposits: Sediments deposited by flowing water, including glacial meltwater. *See also* glaciofluvial deposits. [Lat. *fluvius*, river.]

freshwater lake: A lake with total dissolved solids concentration below 500 mg/L. *See also* saline lake.

fry: Newly hatched young fish, after the yolk has been used up and active feeding has commenced.

geodetic elevation: Altitude above sea level.

glacial till: Unstratified, poorly sorted material deposited directly by ice, consisting of clay, silt, sand, gravel and boulders intermingled in any proportion.

glaciofluvial deposits: Material moved by glaciers and subsequently sorted and deposited by streams or rivers flowing from the melting ice. The deposits are stratified and may occur in the form of outwash plains, deltas, eskers and kames. [Fr. *glace*, ice + Lat. *fluvius*, river.]

glaciolacustrine deposits: Material moved by glaciers and subsequently deposited in lakes formed by the melting of the ice sheet. [Fr. *glace*, ice + Lat. *lacus*, lake.]

Gleysols: Soils formed under imperfectly to very poorly drained conditions resulting in the reduction of iron and other elements. The soil has a grey mottled appearance with rusty brown iron stains or streaks.

golden-brown algae: Algae of the Phylum Chrysophyta, with dominant pigments chlorophyll *a*, xanthophyll and carotene. Species may be solitary or colonial; some have one or two flagella. [Gk. *khrusos*, gold + *phyto*, plant.]

green algae: Algae of the Phylum Chlorophyta. Pigments are primarily chlorophylls *a* and *b*. Some species have flagella, others are nonflagellate. Some species are solitary, others colonial or filamentous. [Gk. *khloros*, green + *phyto*, plant.]

groundwater: Water naturally flowing below the surface of the land. Surface groundwater is in the upper few metres of land; deep groundwater is below this. Groundwater is commonly a source of water for lakes whose basins are in glacial deposits and extend well below the water table.

hard water: Water containing high concentrations of alkaline earths, such as calcium and magnesium, derived from the drainage of calcareous deposits. Most of the lakes in Alberta are hardwater lakes. *See also* soft water.

hardness: An assessment of water quality based on the content of calcium and magnesium. Different scales are used in England, France, Germany and the United States. In the *Atlas*, hardness is expressed as an equivalent to 1 mg/L $CaCO_3$ following a practice developed by early water-supply engineers who wanted to standardize hardness and alkalinity to the same units.

headworks: The structures built to divert water from a river for irrigation. Most of the headworks in Alberta, such as those on the Bow River at Bassano and on the Highwood River at High River, are operated by the provincial government.

Humic Gleysols: Gleysolic soils which have an enriched layer of organic material that is usually made up of sedges or peat. Humic Gleysols develop in wet sedge meadows and in forested swamps.

hyper-eutrophic lakes: Lakes with very high concentrations of nutrients in the water. Hyper-eutrophic lakes are characterized by abundant plant growth, algal blooms, oxygen depletion and summer and winter fish kills. In the *Atlas*, a lake is considered to be hyper-eutrophic if the peak chlorophyll *a* concentration exceeds 75 μg/L. [Gk. *hyper*, excessive + *eu*, well + *trophein*, to nourish.]

hypolimnion: The deep cold layer of a lake lying below the metalimnion (thermocline) during the time a lake is thermally stratified. *See also* epilimnion, metalimnion. [Gk. *hypo*, under + *limne*, lake.]

ion: An electrically charged particle. Positively charged ions such as the hydrogen ion and metallic ions are called *cations*, negatively charged ions such as the hydroxyl ion and acid ions are called *anions*. [Gk. *ion*, going + *kata*, down + *ana*, up.]

limnology: The study of fresh water, especially the history, geology, biology, physics and chemistry of lakes. [Gk. *limne*, lake + *logia*, discourse.]

littoral zone: The portion of a lake where the bottom is within the euphotic zone and which supports rooted macrophyte growth. Sufficient light for photosynthesis reaches the bottom sediments in the littoral zone. [Lat. *littus*, shore.]

live storage volume: The amount of water in a reservoir that is available for controlled withdrawal. The volume of water in a reservoir between the full supply level and the lowest outlet structure.

Luvisol: A soil developed on a wide range of parent materials under mixed deciduous-coniferous forests in moderately well-drained to imperfectly drained sites.

macrophyte: Large, easily visible plants. Aquatic macrophytes include: emergent macrophytes such as cattails and bulrushes, submergent macrophytes such as pondweeds, floating-leaved macrophytes such as water lilies and free-floating macrophytes such as duckweed. [Gk. *makros*, great + *phyton*, plant.]

mesotrophic lakes: Lakes with moderate concentrations of nutrients in the water and hence support moderate production of algae and macrophytes. In the *Atlas*, a lake is considered to be mesotrophic if the peak chlorophyll *a* concentration is between 5 and 25 μg/L.

metalimnion: The layer of water in a thermally stratified lake between the epilimnion and the hypolimnion. The metalimnion is a narrow zone of rapid temperature change compared to the relatively small temperature changes within either the epilimnion or hypolimnion. *See* thermocline. *See also* epilimnion, hypolimnion. [Gk. *meta*, between + *limne*, lake.]

moraine: A deposit of unsorted, unstratified rock fragments transported by a glacier. Moraines are often hilly or hummocky. [Fr. *moraine*.]

muskeg: Wetland in boreal forest areas, typified by *Sphagnum* moss which accumulates to form peat, and black spruce. Muskeg is widespread in northern Alberta. Various estimates indicate that Canada may have more muskeg (1 300 000 km²) than any other country. [Algonquin *muskeg*, grassy bog.]

neotenic: A condition in which reproductively mature animals retain larvae characteristics. For example mature salamanders which retain external gills are said to be neotenic.

nutrient: A substance which nourishes to promote the growth or repair of organic bodies. The major plant nutrients include carbon, nitrogen, phosphorus and sulphur. [Lat. *nutrire*, nourish.]

offstream reservoir: An impoundment formed by building one or more dams across a relatively dry valley or coulee. Most of the water in the impoundment is brought to it by canal or pipeline from a river. Crawling Valley Reservoir, Milk River Ridge Reservoir and McGregor Lake are all offstream reservoirs.

oligotrophic lakes: Lakes with a low concentration of nutrients in the water and hence a low organic production of algae and plants. In the *Atlas*, a lake is considered to be oligotrophic if the peak chlorophyll *a* concentration is less than 5 μg/L. [Gk. *oligos*, small + *trophein*, to nourish.]

onstream reservoir: An impoundment of water formed by building a dam across a river or large stream which provides most of the water to the impoundment. Gleniffer Lake, Ghost Reservoir and Glenmore Reservoir are onstream reservoirs in Alberta.

Organic soils: Soils in areas of extremely poor drainage and containing a large fraction of plant and animal residues at various stages of decomposition.

peat: Unconsolidated soil material consisting largely of decomposed or partially decomposed organic material accumulated under conditions of excessive moisture. *Sphagnum* moss is often a major component of peat.

pelagial zone: The open water zone of a lake or sea; the zone of a lake or sea far from shore. [Gk. *pelagos*, the high sea.]

penstock: A tube or conduit for conducting water, usually directing flow to electrical generators.

periphyton: Algae growing attached to something. The following communities of periphyton can be differentiated: epipelic algae grow on fine sediments, epilithic algae grow on rocks, epiphytic algae grow on macrophytes, epizooic algae grow on animals, and episammic algae grow on or between grains of sand. [Gk. *peri*, around + *phyto*, plant.]

pH: The negative logarithm of the hydrogen ion activity (approximate concentration) expressed in gram equivalents. On a scale of 1 to 14, solutions with a pH less than 7 are acidic, those with a pH above 7 are basic; a pH of 7 is considered to be neutral.

photic zone: *See* euphotic zone. [Gk. *photo*, light.]

photosynthesis: The process in which light energy in the presence of the chlorophyll pigment, water and adequate nutrients, is used to produce organic carbon or solid plant material from inorganic carbon. [Gk. *photos*, light + *syn*, together + *tithenai*, to place.]

phytobenthos: Algae or rooted plants living on the bottom of a lake or river; the plant component of the benthos. [Gk. *phyto*, plant + *benthos*, depth of the sea.]

phytoplankton: The plant portion of the plankton. *See also* plankton. [Gk. *phyto*, plant + *planktos*, wandering.]

plankton: The free-floating or suspended community of tiny plants (phytoplankton) and animals (zooplankton). [Gk. *planktos*, wandering.]

precipitation of water: Water which falls from the sky as rain, snow, or hail. [Lat. *praecipitium*, falling headlong.]

precipitation in a solution: The formation and settling of minerals or salts from a supersaturated solution.

profundal zone: The deep region of a water body below the limit where light is sufficient for plant growth. [Lat. *profundus*, deep.]

proglacial lake: A lake lying at or near the foot of a glacier. [Lat. *pro*, in front + Fr. *glace*, ice.]

Regosol: Soils that occur where natural disturbance has inhibited the development of soil horizons. These soils are found in well-drained to imperfectly drained sites; they are common near river beds, on colluvium, on steep and active erosional slopes, and on shallow parent material over bedrock in the mountains.

regulated lake: A lake with a surface elevation that is controlled to some extent by a weir or diversion.

residence time: The average length of time that water stays in a reservoir or lake, also called the *hydraulic residence time*. It is usually calculated by dividing the volume of the waterbody by the average annual outflow. In the *Atlas*, the estimate of residence time usually did not consider groundwater inflow or outflow, because they have not been measured in most lakes.

riparian: Pertaining to the bank of a body of water. [Lat. *ripa*, a bank.]

runoff: The water reaching a lake, stream or ocean after flow over land or through the surficial layers of the land. Surface runoff includes streamflow, whereas subsurface runoff moves laterally in the upper soil horizons and groundwater flows laterally deep in the ground.

saline lake: Saline means salty; a saline lake has a higher concentration of salts than a freshwater lake. In the *Atlas*, a freshwater lake is defined as one with a total dissolved solids (TDS) concentration of less than 500 mg/L. A slightly saline lake has a TDS concentration between 500 and 1 000 mg/L, a moderately saline lake has a TDS concentration between 1 000 and 5 000 mg/L, and a highly saline lake has a TDS concentration over 5 000 mg/L. *See also* total dissolved solids. [Lat. *sal*, salt.]

salinity: The ionic composition of water, expressed as mg/L. The concentration of four major cations (calcium, magnesium, sodium, and potassium) and four major anions (bicarbonate, carbonate, sulphate, and chloride) collectively approximate salinity in lakes in the *Atlas*. The relative salinity of lakes is usually determined by comparing their concentration of *total dissolved solids*. [Lat. *sal*, salt.]

salts: A general term for chemical which, when dissolved in water, separate into negatively and positively charged ions.

Secchi depth: The depth in water to which a Secchi disc (a 20-cm diameter disc with alternating black and white quadrants) can be seen from the surface. Secchi depth is an easy measurement of water transparency.

sediment: Material that is too dense to remain suspended and settles to the bottom of a liquid. The sediment usually originates from the remains of phytoplankton, zooplankton and other aquatic organisms, from erosion of surrounding lands, or from chemical precipitation of dissolved minerals. [Lat. *sedimentum*, from *sedeo*, to settle.]

sheet-pile weir: A control structure built of pilings driven into the ground to support sheets of steel to hold back water. Sheet-pile weirs have been built in several Alberta lakes to raise the water level slightly (usually less than 1 m) or to control outflow from the lake.

shore: The land immediately upslope from the surface of a lake or reservoir.

soft water: Water containing low concentrations of calcium and magnesium. Soft water lakes are common on the Precambrian Shield in northern Saskatchewan, Manitoba, Ontario and Quebec; they are not common in Alberta. *See also* hard water.

Solonetzic: An order of moderately well-drained to imperfectly drained soils developed on saline parent material in cool subhumid to subarid climates under grassland vegetation. Solonetzic soils usually occur in association with Chernozemic soils.

specific conductivity: A measure of the ease of passing an electrical current through a liquid from one 1 cm^2 electrode to another 1 cm^2 electrode, 1 cm apart, at 25°C or 20°C. Specific conductivity increases with increased salinity. The units are μS/cm which is equivalent to μmhos/cm (reciprocal of ohms).

spillway: A channel that conducts water past a dam. A spillway routinely passes flow whereas an emergency spillway is used only when the water level of a reservoir exceeds the full supply level.

step-pool fishway: *See* fishway.

stratified: Separated into layers. In stratified lakes, there may be mixing within a layer but little mixing occurs between layers. Layers have different densities, which may be determined either by temperature and/or salinity. *See also* epilimnion, hypolimnion, thermocline, thermally stratified.

sublittoral zone: The zone of the lake bottom that is a transition between the littoral zone and the profundal zone. Light is sufficient in the littoral zone to support abundant rooted plant growth; there is insufficient light in the profundal zone for any plant growth. The sublittoral zone is occupied by scattered plants that may survive a short time and by benthic algae (mostly blue-green) and photosynthetic bacteria. [Lat. *sub*, below + *littus*, shore.]

submergent macrophytes: Large aquatic plants which grow below the surface of the water although the flowers may extend above the surface. Pondweeds and northern water milfoil are submergent macrophytes.

summerkill: An event when large numbers of animals, including fish, die from critically low dissolved oxygen concentrations. When an unusually large population of algae dies, the subsequent decomposition consumes oxygen and summerkill may result. Summerkill of fish also occasionally results from the water temperature rising to near-lethal levels, combined with high concentrations of ammonia released as a consequence of decomposition of plant material.

surficial deposits: Material such as clays and gravels overlying bedrock. Glacial till is a surficial deposit.

thermocline: The depth within the metalimnion of a thermally stratified lake where the temperature gradient is greatest and exceeds a change of 1°C per metre of depth. *See also* metalimnion, thermally stratified. [Gk. *therme*, heat + *kleinen*, to slope.]

thermally stratified: Divided into layers with different density due to temperature differences. In a thermally stratified lake in summer, warmer water in the epilimnion floats above denser, colder water in the hypolimnion; the zone of rapid temperature change is the metalimnion.

topography: The physical features of a landscape, especially its relief and slope. [Gk. *topos*, place + *graphos*, written.]

total dissolved solids: The total inorganic and organic materials dissolved in water. The total dissolved solids in water can be determined after water is filtered through a 0.45 μm filter and evaporated to dryness at 103°C to 105°C, or it can be estimated from concentrations of major ions (calculated).

trophic state: The degree of fertility of a lake. Factors used to assess the trophic state of a lake include chlorophyll *a*, dissolved oxygen and phosphorus concentrations, algal biomass, Secchi depth and macrophyte biomass. *See also* hyper-eutrophic lakes, eutrophic lakes, mesotrophic lakes, oligotrophic lakes, dystrophic lakes. [Gk. *trophe*, nourishment.]

trophogenic zone: *See* euphotic zone. [Gk. *trophe*, nourishment + *gennan*, to produce.]

tropholytic zone: *See* euphotic zone. [Gk. *trophe*, nourishment and *lyo*, to dissolve.]

turbid: Opaque with suspended matter. Water with conspicious amounts of mud, silt or algae suspended in it is said to be turbid. [Lat. *turbidus*, disturbed.]

water column: A vertical segment of a lake that extends from the surface to the bottom.

watershed: The land contributing surface runoff to a stream or lake; a drainage basin.

water table: The upper limit of the soil or underlying rock material that is wholly saturated with water.

weir: A control structure built across a stream or lake outlet to raise the water level a small amount. [OE. *waer*, a fence.]

winterkill: An event when large numbers of animals, including fish, die from critically low oxygen concentrations under the ice. In many shallow Alberta lakes, the decay of algal and plant material under ice consumes so much oxygen that winterkills occur.

zooplankton: The animal portion of the plankton. *See also* plankton. [Gk. *zōon*, animal + *planktos*, wandering.]

Selected References

In citing references, abbreviated titles have been used and are identified by the following:

Admin.	Administration
Aff.	Affairs
Agric.	Agriculture, Agriculturalist
Alta.	Alberta
Ann.	Annual
App.	Applied
Aquat.	Aquatic
Assess.	Assessment
Assoc.	Association, Associates
Atm.	Atmospheric
BC	British Columbia
Bd.	Board
Bibliog.	Bibliography
Biol.	Biology
Bot.	Botany
Br.	Branch
Bull.	Bulletin
ca	circa
Calg.	Calgary
Can.	Canada, Canadian
Chem.	Chemical(s)
Co.	Company, County
Comm.	Communication
Commis.	Commission
Commit.	Committee
Commun.	Community
Conf.	Conference
Conserv.	Conservation
Const.	Construction
Consult.	Consultant(s), Consulting
Contr.	Control
Corp.	Corporation
Counc.	Council
Cr.	Creek
Cult.	Culture
Dept.	Department
Devel.	Development
Dist.	District
E	East
East.	Eastern
Ecol.	Ecology
Econ.	Economic
Ed.	Editor, Edited, Edition
Edm.	Edmonton
EID	Eastern Irrigation District
En.	Energy
Eng.	Engineering
Envir.	Environment(al), Environments
Eval.	Evaluation
Fish.	Fisheries
For.	Forest(ry), Forests
Geog.	Geography, Geographic(al)
Geol.	Geologic(al), Geology
Ges.	Gesamten
Govt.	Government(s)
Hist.	Historic(al), History
Hydrobiol.	Hydrobiologie
Hydrog.	Hydrographic
Hydrol.	Hydrology

ID	Improvement District
Inst.	Institute
Int., Internat.	International(e)
Irrig.	Irrigation
J.	Journal
L.	Lake
Lab.	Laboratory
Ld.	Land(s)
Limnol.	Limnology, Limnologie
Ltd.	Limited
Map.	Mapping
MD	Municipal District
Metro.	Metropolitan
Mineral.	Mineralogist
Mgt.	Management
Monit.	Monitoring
ms	manuscript
MSc	Master of Science
Multicult.	Multiculturalism
Mun.	Municipal
N	North
n.d.	no date
NE	Northeast
NW	Northwest
NWT	Northwest Territories
Nat.	Nature, Natural, Naturalist(s)
Natl.	National
No.	Number
North.	Northern
Ocean.	Oceanography
Ont.	Ontario
Op.	Operations
Pedol.	Pedology
Pers.	Personal
Pest.	Pesticides
PhD	Doctor of Philosophy
Plan.	Planning
Poll.	Pollution
Prelim.	Preliminary
Prep.	Prepared
Proc.	Proceedings
Prog.	Program(s)
Prot.	Protection
Prov.	Province, Provincial
Pub.	Public
Publ.	Publish(ed), Publications, Publishing
Qlty.	Quality
R.	River
Rec.	Recreation
Ref.	Reference
Reg.	Region(al)
Renew.	Renewable
Rep.	Report(s)
Res.	Research
Resour.	Resource(s)
Rev.	Review
S	South
SE	Southeast
SW	Southwest
Sask.	Saskatchewan
Sci.	Science(s), Scientific
Sec.	Section
Secret.	Secretariat
Serv.	Service(s)
Soc.	Society
South.	Southern
Sur.	Surface
Surv.	Survey
SV	Summer Village
Symp.	Symposium
T.	Town
Tech.	Technical
Technol.	Technology
Trans.	Transaction(s)
Transp.	Transportation
Univ.	University
Unltd.	Unlimited
Unpubl.	Unpublished
Util.	Utilities
Verein.	Vereinigung
Verh.	Verhandlungen
Vol.	Volume
W	West
West.	Western
WID	Western Irrigation District
Wild.	Wildlife
Yell.	Yellowhead
YT	Yukon Territory
Zool.	Zoology

Agriculture Canada. 1985–1988. Spring runoff monitoring program: Annual reports. Prairie Farm Rehabilitation Admin., Eng. Serv., Regina, Sask.

Alberta Energy and Natural Resources. 1979–1985. Fish planting list. Fish Wild. Div., Edmonton.

———. 1985. Lakeland sub-regional integrated resource plan. Resour. Eval. Plan. Div., Edmonton.

Alberta Environment. 1977. Cooking Lake area study, Vol. I: Planning report. Plan. Div., Edmonton.

———. 1977. Interim report—Sturgeon River basin study. Plan. Div., Edmonton.

———. 1982. Chemical residues in fish tissues in Alberta: 1. Wabamun Lake, Lake Newell, McGregor Lake, Beaver River, Battle River. Alta. Envir. Centre, Vegreville.

———. 1983. Cold Lake-Beaver River water management study, Vol. 1: Main report. Plan. Div., Edmonton.

———.1985. Cold Lake-Beaver River long term water management plan. Plan. Div., Edmonton.

———. 1989. Algal blooms. Envir. Assess. Div., Envir. Qlty. Monit. Br., Edmonton.

Alberta Forestry, Lands and Wildlife. 1986–1989. Fish planting list. Fish Wild. Div., Edmonton.

———. 1988. Boating in Alberta. Fish Wild. Div., Edmonton.

———. 1988. Guide to sportfishing regulations. Fish Wild. Div., Edmonton.

———. 1989. Guide to game bird hunting. Fish Wild. Div., Edmonton.

———. 1989. Guide to sportfishing. Fish Wild. Div., Edmonton.

Alberta Hotel Association. 1988. 1988 Alberta campground guide. Prep. for Travel Alta., Edmonton.

———. 1989. Alberta campground guide 1989. Prep. for Travel Alta., Edmonton.

Alberta Municipal Affairs. 1978. Cold Lake regional plan, heritage preservation: Heritage resources background paper. Reg. Plan. Sec., Edmonton.

———. 1984. County of Smoky Lake #13 lake planning framework. Plan. Br., Edmonton.

———. 1984. Improvement District No.18 (South) lake planning framework. Plan. Br., Edmonton.

Alberta Native Affairs. 1986. A guide to native communities in Alberta. Native Aff. Secret., Edmonton.

Alberta Recreation and Parks. n.d. Ecological reserves. Now...and forever. Advisory Commit. on Wilderness Areas and Ecol. Reserves, Edmonton.

Alberta Recreation, Parks and Wildlife. 1975–1978. Fish planting list. Fish Wild. Div., Edmonton.

———. 1976. Commercial fisheries catch statistics for Alberta, 1942–1975. Fish Wild. Div., Fish. Mgt. Rep. No. 22, Edmonton.

Alberta Research Council. 1972. Geological map of Alberta. Nat. Resour. Div., Alta. Geol. Surv., Edmonton.

Allan, R.J. and J.D.H. Williams. 1978. Trophic status related to sediment chemistry of Canadian prairie lakes. J. Envir. Qlty. 9:199–206.

Anderson, R.S. 1974. Crustacean plankton communities of 340 lakes and ponds in and near the National Parks of the Canadian Rocky Mountains. J. Fish. Res. Bd. Can. 31:855–869.

Aquatic Environments Limited. 1983. Fisheries studies; main report and detailed data report [Appendices F and G]. In Cold Lake-Beaver River water management study, Vol. 4: Fisheries. Alta. Envir., Plan. Div., Edmonton.

Athabasca Historical Society, D. Gregory and Athabasca University. 1986. Athabasca Landing: An illustrated history. Athabasca Hist. Soc., Athabasca.

Atlas of Alberta. 1969. The Univ. Alta. Press, Edmonton, in assoc. with Univ. Toronto Press, Toronto.

Babin, J. 1984. Winter oxygen depletion in temperate zone lakes. MSc thesis. Univ. Alta., Edmonton.

——— and E.E. Prepas. 1985. Modelling winter oxygen depletion rates in ice-covered temperate zone lakes in Canada. Can. J. Fish. Aquat. Sci. 42:239–249.

Bayrock, L.S. and J.D. Root. 1973. Geology of the Peace-Athabasca River Delta region, Alberta (Section N). *In* The Peace-Athabasca Delta Project, technical appendices, Vol. I: Hydrologic investigations. 1973. Prep. by PADPG for Govt. Can., Alta., Sask. Information Can., Ottawa.

Bell, G., P. Handford and C. Dietz. 1977. Dynamics of an exploited population of lake whitefish (*Coregonus clupeaformis*). J. Fish. Res. Bd. Can. 34:942–953.

Bidgood, B.J. 1972. Divergent growth in lake whitefish populations from two eutrophic Alberta lakes. PhD thesis. Univ. Alta., Edmonton.

Bierhuizen, J.F.H. and E.E. Prepas. 1985. Relationship between nutrients, dominant ions, and phytoplankton standing crop in prairie saline lakes. Can. J. Fish. Aquat. Sci. 42:1588–1594.

Bird, D.F. and J. Kalff. 1984. Empirical relationships between bacterial abundance and chlorophyll concentrations in fresh and marine waters. Can. J. Fish. Aquat. Sci. 41:1015–1023.

Bishop, F.G. 1979. Limnology and fisheries of seven stocked lakes in the Peace River region. Alta. Rec. Parks Wild., Fish Wild. Div., Peace River.

———. 1983. A summary of the 1982 creel survey program: Southern region. Alta. En. Nat. Resour., Fish Wild. Div., Lethbridge.

Borneuf, D. 1973. Hydrology of the Tawatinaw area, Alberta. Alta. Res. Counc., Edmonton.

Bowser, W.E., R.L. Erdman, F.A. Wyatt and J.D. Newton. 1947. Soil survey of Peace Hills sheet. Alta. Soil Surv. Rep. No. 14, Univ. Alta. Bull. No. 48. Univ. Alta., Edmonton.

Bowser, W.E., A.A. Kjearsgaard, T.W. Peters and R.E. Wells. 1962. Soil survey of the Edmonton sheet (83–H). Alta. Soil Surv. Rep. No. 21, Univ. Alta. Bull. No. SS–4. Univ. Alta., Edmonton.

Bowser, W.E., T.W. Peters and J.D. Newton. 1951. Soil survey of Red Deer sheet. Alta. Soil Surv. Rep. No. 16, Univ. Alta. Bull. No. 51. Univ. Alta., Edmonton.

Bradley, G.M. n.d. Preliminary biological survey of six lakes in northern Alberta, 1969. Surv. Rep. No. 15. Alta. Ld. For., Fish Wild. Div., Edmonton.

Brierley, A., W.L. Nikiforuk and L.A. Andriashek. 1988. Soil survey of the County of St. Paul. Interim maps. Alta. Res. Counc., Edmonton.

Burgis, M.J. and P. Morris. 1987. The natural history of lakes. Cambridge Univ. Press, Cambridge, England.

Burland, R.G. 1981. An identification guide to Alberta aquatic plants. Alta. Envir., Poll. Contr. Div., Pest. Chem. Br., Edmonton.

Campbell, C.E. 1986. A study of low chlorophyll levels relative to high phosphorus and nitrogen levels in prairie saline lakes. MSc thesis. Univ. Alta., Edmonton.

——— and E.E. Prepas. 1986. Evaluation of factors related to the unusually low chlorophyll levels in prairie saline lakes. Can. J. Fish. Aquat. Sci. 43:846–854.

Canadian Wildlife Service. 1979. Migratory birds habitat priorities, prairie provinces. Can. Wild. Serv., Edmonton.

Carmichael, W.W. and P.R. Gorham. 1981. The mosaic nature of toxic blooms of Cyanobacteria. *In* W.W. Carmichael [ed.] The water environment: Algal toxins and health. Plenum Press, New York.

Chambers, P.A. and E.E. Prepas. 1988. Underwater spectral attenuation and its effect on the maximum depth of angiosperm colonization. Can. J. Fish. Aquat. Sci. 45:1010–1017.

———. 1990. Competition and coexistence in submerged aquatic plant communities: The paradox revisited. Freshwater Biol. [in press]

Chapman, L.J., W.C. Mackay and C.W. Wilkinson. 1989. Feeding flexibility in northern pike (*Esox lucius*): Fish versus invertebrate prey. Can. J. Fish. Aquat. Sci. 46:666–669.

Chipeniuk, R.C. 1975. Lakes of the Lac La Biche district. R.C. Chipeniuk, Lac La Biche.

Christiansen, D.G. 1978. Preliminary draft of the Battle River basin study: Pigeon Lake, Battle Lake, Samson Lake, Coal Lake, Driedmeat Lake, Forestburg Reservoir. Alta. Rec. Parks Wild., Fish Wild. Div., Edmonton.

Clifford, H.F. n.d. The aquatic invertebrates of Alberta: An illustrated guide. Univ. Alta., Dept. Zool. Unpubl. data, Edmonton.

Cross, P.M. 1979. Limnological and fisheries surveys of the aquatic ecosystems at Esso Resources' Cold Lake base: Data volume. Aquat. Envir. Ltd., Calgary.

Crowe, A.S. 1979. Chemical and hydrological simulation of prairie lake—watershed systems. MSc thesis. Univ. Alta., Edmonton.

Currie, D.V. and N. Zacharko. 1976. Hydrogeology of the Vermilion area. Alta. Res. Counc. Rep. 75–5, Edmonton.

Ducks Unlimited (Canada) and Alberta Energy and Natural Resources. 1986. Waterfowl habitat program. Ducks Unltd. (Can.) Alta. En. Nat. Resour., Fish Wild. Div., Edmonton.

Edmondson, W.T. [ed.] 1959. Fresh-water biology. 2nd. ed. John Wiley & Sons, New York.

Energy, Mines and Resources Canada. National topographic series 1:50 000 and 1:250 000. Surv. Map. Br., Ottawa. Various dates of publication.

Environment Canada. 1982. Canadian climate normals, Vol. 7: Bright sunshine (1951–1980). Prep. by Atm. Envir. Serv. Supply Serv. Can., Ottawa.

———. 1982. Canadian climate normals: Temperature and precipitation (1951–1980): Prairie provinces. Prep. by Atm. Envir. Serv. Supply Serv. Can., Ottawa.

———. 1985. Historical streamflow summary: Alberta to 1984. Prep. by Inland Waters Directorate. Water Surv. Can., Water Resour. Br., Ottawa.

———. 1986. Climate of Alberta. Prep. by Atm. Envir. Serv. Alta. Envir., Edmonton.

———. 1987. Historical streamflow summary: Alberta to 1986. Prep. by Inland Waters Directorate. Water Surv. Can., Water Resour. Br., Ottawa.

———. Surface water data. Prep. by Inland Waters Directorate. Water Surv. Can., Water Resour. Br., Ottawa. Various dates of publication.

Finlay, J. and C. Finlay. 1987. Parks in Alberta: A guide to peaks, ponds, parklands & prairies. Hurtig Publ., Edmonton.

Fraser, E. 1969. The Canadian Rockies: Early travels and explorations. Hurtig Publ., Edmonton.

Gabert, G.M. 1975. Hydrogeology of Red Deer and vicinity, Alberta. Alta. Res. Counc. Bull. No. 31, Edmonton.

Geen, G.H. 1974. Effects of hydroelectric development in western Canada on aquatic ecosytems. J. Fish. Res. Bd. Can. 31:913–927.

Geographic Board of Canada. 1928. Place-names of Alberta. Dept. Interior, Ottawa.

Glendon Historical Society. 1985. So soon forgotten—A history of Glendon and districts. Glendon Hist. Soc., Glendon.

Greenlee, G.M. 1974. Soil survey adjacent to McGregor Lake, Travers Reservoir, and Little Bow Lake and interpretation for recreational use. Alta. Inst. Pedol. No. M–74–5, Edmonton.

Griffiths, D.E. 1987. A survey of wetland wildlife resources, Strathcona County #20, Alberta. Prep. for Co. Strathcona, Sherwood Park.

Griffiths, W.E. and D.B. Ferster. 1974. Preliminary fisheries survey of the Winefred-Pelican area. Alta. Ld. For., Fish Wild. Div., Edmonton.

Gross, R. and L. Nicoll Kramer. 1985. Tapping the Bow. East. Irrig. Dist., Brooks.

Guiltner, J.C. 1972. The Peace River Country and McKenzie Highway—Historical and tourist guide. J.C. Guiltner, Peace River.

Handford, P., G. Bell and T. Reimchen. 1977. A gillnet fishery considered as an experiment in artificial selection. J. Fish. Res. Bd. Can. 34:954–961.

Hanson, J.M. and W.C. Leggett. 1982. Empirical prediction of fish biomass and yield. Can. J. Fish. Aquat. Sci. 39:257–263.

———. 1985. Experimental and field evidence for inter- and intraspecific competition in two freshwater fishes. Can. J. Fish. Aquat. Sci. 42:280–286.

Harvey, R.W. 1987. A fluorochrome-staining technique for counting bacteria in saline, organically enriched, alkaline lakes. Limnol. Oceanogr. 32:993–995.

Haugen, G.N. 1970. Age, growth, and yield of lake whitefish *Coregonus clupeaformis* from seven irrigation reservoirs in the South Saskatchewan drainage basin, Alberta. Alta. Ld. For., Fish Wild. Div., Edmonton.

Heath, D. and D.A. Rolff. 1987. Test of genetic differentiation in growth of stunted and nonstunted populations of yellow perch and pumpkinseed. Trans. Am. Fish. Soc. 116:98–102.

Hickman, M. 1978. Ecological studies on the epipelic algal community in five prairie-parkland lakes in central Alberta. Can. J. Bot. 56:991–1009.

Holmgren, E.J. and P.M. Holmgren. 1976. Over 2000 place names of Alberta. 3rd ed. West. Producer Prairie Books, Saskatoon.

Howitt, R.W. 1988. Soil survey of the County of Beaver. Alta. Soil Surv. Rep. No. 47. Alta. Res. Counc., Terrain Sci. Dept., Edmonton.

Hutchinson, G.E. 1957. A treatise on limnology, Vol. I: Geography, physics and chemistry. John Wiley & Sons, New York.

———. 1967. A treatise on limnology, Vol. II: Introduction to lake biology and the limnoplankton. John Wiley & Sons, New York.

IEC Beak Consultants Ltd., Techman Engineering Ltd. and Aresco Ltd. 1983. Environmental overview of the Little Bow River Basin. Prep. for Alta. Envir., Plan. Div., Edmonton.

Kemper, J.B. 1976. Implications for waterfowl and migratory birds [Appendix 7]. *In* Cooking Lake area study, Vol. IV: Ecology. Alta. Envir., Plan. Div., Edmonton.

Kerekes, J. 1965. A comparative limnological study of five lakes in central Alberta. MSc thesis. Univ. Alta., Edmonton.

——— and J.R. Nursall. 1966. Eutrophication and senescence in a group of prairie-parkland lakes in Alberta, Canada. Verh. Internat. Verein. Limnol. 16:65–73.

Kjearsgaard, A.A. 1972. Reconnaissance soil survey of the Tawatinaw map sheet (83–I). Alta. Inst. Pedol. Rep. No. S–72–29 1972, Univ. Alta. Bull. No. SS–12 1972. Univ. Alta., Edmonton.

———. 1988. Reconnaissance soil survey of the Oyen map sheet–72 M. Alta. Inst. Pedol. Rep No. S–76–36, Ld. Resour. Res. Centre Contribution No. 85–56. Agric. Can. Res. Br., Edmonton.

———, T.W. Peters and W.W. Pettapiece. 1983. Soil survey of the County of Newell, Alberta. Alta. Soil Surv. Rep. No. 41, Alta. Inst. Pedol. Rep. No. S–82–41, Ld. Resour. Res. Inst. Contribution No. LRRI 83–48. Agric. Can., Res. Br., Edmonton.

Kocaoglu, S.S. 1975. Reconnaissance soil survey of the Sand River area (73L). Alta. Soil Surv. Rep. No. 34, Univ. Alta. Rep. No. SS–15, Alta. Inst. Pedol. Rep. No. S–74–34 1975. Univ. Alta., Edmonton.

Larkin, P.A. 1964. Canadian lakes. Verh. Internat. Verein. Limnol. 15:76–90.

Lindsay, J.D., W. Odynsky, J.W. Peters and W.E. Bowser. 1968. Soil survey of the Buck Lake (NE 83B) and Wabamun Lake (E1/2 83G) areas. Alta. Soil Surv. Rep. No. 24, Univ. Alta. Bull. No. SS–7, Alta. Res. Counc. Rep. No. 87. Univ. Alta., Edmonton.

Lombard North Group. 1973. Cypress Hills Provincial Park, Alberta, Vol. 1: Resource inventory. Alta. Pub. Works Alta. Ld. For., Prov. Parks Div., Edmonton.

Longmore, L.A. and C.E. Stenton. 1983. Fish and fisheries; status and utilization [Appendix H]. In Cold Lake-Beaver River water management study, Vol. 5: Fisheries and wildlife. Alta. Envir., Plan. Div., Edmonton.

Looman, J. and K.F. Best. 1987. Budd's flora of the Canadian prairie provinces. Can. Dept. Agric. Res. Br. Publ. 1662 1987. Supply Serv. Can., Hull, Québec.

MacGregor, J.G. 1952. The land of Twelve Foot Davis. Inst. Appl. Art Ltd., Edmonton.

———. 1972. A history of Alberta. Hurtig Publ., Edmonton.

———. 1976. The Battle River valley. West. Producer Prairie Books, Saskatoon, Sask.

MacMillan, R.A. 1987. Soil survey of the Calgary urban perimeter. Alta. Res. Counc., Dept. Terrain Sci., Edmonton.

———, W.L. Nikiforuk and A.T. Rodvang. 1988. Soil survey of the County of Flagstaff. Alta. Soil Surv. Rep. No. 51. Alta. Res. Counc., Edmonton.

Magrath and District History Association. 1974. Irrigation builders. Magrath Dist. Hist. Assoc., Magrath.

Manning, P.G., T.P. Murphy, T. Mayer and E.E. Prepas. 1988. Effect of copper sulfate on pyrite formation in reducing sediments. Can. Mineral. 26:965–972.

Marino, R., R.W. Howarth, J. Shamess and E.E. Prepas. 1990. Molybdenum and sulfate as controls on the abundance of nitrogen-fixing cyanobacteria in Alberta saline lakes. Limnol. Oceanogr. [in press]

Markham, B.J. 1978. Status of the Double-crested Cormorant (Phalocrocorax auritus) in Canada. Prep. for Commit. on the Status of Endangered Wild. in Can. by Alta. Rec. Parks Wild., Fish Wild. Div., Edmonton.

Marshall Macklin Monaghan Western Limited. 1983. Water based recreation [Appendix J]. In Cold Lake-Beaver River water management study, Vol. 6: Recreation. Alta. Envir., Plan. Div., Edmonton.

McCart, P.J., P.M. Cross, R. Green and D.W. Mayhood. 1979. Limnological and fishery surveys of the aquatic ecosystems at Esso Resources' Cold Lake lease. Aquat. Envir. Ltd., Calgary.

McGregor, C.A. 1983. Summary [Appendix K] and Detailed report [Appendix L]. In Cold Lake-Beaver River water management study, Vol. 7: Ecological inventory of lake shorelines. Alta. Envir., Plan. Div., Edmonton.

———. 1984. Ecological land classification and evaluation, Kananaskis Country. Alta. En. Nat. Resour., Resour. Eval. Plan. Div., Edmonton.

Miller, R.B. 1952. A review of the Triaenophorus problem in Canadian lakes. Fish. Res. Bd. Can. Bull. No. 95.

———. 1956. The collapse and recovery of a small whitefish fishery. J. Fish. Res. Bd. Can. 13:135–146.

——— and W.H. Macdonald.1950. Preliminary biological surveys of Alberta watersheds, 1947–1949. Alta. Ld. For., Fish Wild. Div., Edmonton.

Miller, R.B. and M.J. Paetz. 1953. Preliminary biological surveys of Alberta watersheds, Vol. II: 1950–1952. Alta. Ld. For., Fish Wild. Div., Edmonton.

Miller, R.B. and H.B. Watkins. 1946. An experiment in the control of the cestode, Triaenophorus crassus Forel. Can. J. Res. Devel. 24:175–179.

Mitchell, P.A. 1982. Evaluation of the "septic snooper" on Wabamun and Pigeon lakes. Alta. Envir., Poll. Contr. Div., Water Qlty. Contr. Br., Edmonton.

———. 1984. The importance of sediment release in the assessment of a shallow, eutrophic lake for phosphorus control, p. 129–133. In Proceedings of the 3rd annual conference on lake and reservoir management, North American Lake Management Society. USEPA 440/5–84–001. Washington.

Moore, J.W., S. Ramamoorthy and A. Sharma. 1986. Mercury residues in fish from twenty-four lakes and rivers in Alberta. Alta. Envir. Centre, Vegreville.

More, G. 1988. Kananaskis Country computerized bibliography system. Alta. Rec. Parks, Canmore.

Moss, E.H. 1983. Flora of Alberta. 2nd. ed. Univ. Toronto Press, Toronto.

Nanuk Engineering and Hydroqual Consultants Inc. 1986. Battle River basin study phase III, water balance and water quality assessment. Prep. for Alta. Envir., Plan. Div., Edmonton.

National Atlas of Canada, The. 1974. 4th ed. Macmillan Co. Can. Ltd., in assoc. with Dept. En. Mines Resour. and Information Can., Ottawa.

Neill, C.R. and B.J. Evans. 1979. Synthesis of surface water hydrology. Prep. by Northwest Hydraulic Consult. Ltd. for Alta. Envir., Alta. Oil Sands Envir. Res. Project. AOSERP Rep. 60, Edmonton.

Norris, H.J. 1984. A comparison of aging techniques and growth of yellow perch (Perca flavescens) from selected Alberta lakes. MSc thesis. Univ. Alta., Edmonton.

Northcote, T.G. and P.A. Larkin. 1963. Western Canada, p. 463. In F.G. Frey [ed.] Limnology in North America. Univ. Wisconsin Press, Madison, Wisconsin.

Nürnberg, G. and R.H. Peters. 1984. Biological availability of soluble reactive phosphorus in anoxic and oxic freshwaters. Can. J. Fish. Aquat. Sci. 41:757–765.

Nursall, J.R. 1969. Faunal changes in oligotrophic man-made lakes: Experience on the Kananaskis River system, p. 163–175. In Obeng, L.E. [ed.] Man-made lakes: The Accra Symposium. Ghana Univ. Press, Ghana.

Odynsky, W., J.D. Lindsay, S.W. Reeder and A. Wynnyk. 1961. Reconnaissance soil survey of the Beaverlodge and Blueberry Mountain sheets. Alta. Soil Surv. Rep. No. 20, Univ. Alta. Bull. No. SS–3, Res. Counc. Alta. Rep. No. 81. Univ. Alta., Dept. Extension, Edmonton.

Odynsky, W., A. Wynnyk and J.D. Newton. 1952. Reconnaissance soil survey of the High Prairie and McLennan sheets. Alta. Soil Surv. Rep. No. 17, Univ. Alta. Bull. No. 59, Res. Counc. Alta. Rep. No. 63. Univ. Alta., Edmonton.

Oltmann, C.R. 1976. The valley of rumours ... The Kananaskis. Ribbon Cr. Publ. Co., Seebe.

Ozoray, G.F. and A.T. Lytviak. 1980. Hydrogeology of the Sand River area, Alberta. Earth Sci. Rep. 79–1. Alta. Res. Counc., Edmonton.

Paetz, M.J. and J.S. Nelson. 1970. The fishes of Alberta. The Queen's Printer, Edmonton.

Paetz, M.J. and K.A. Zelt. 1974. Studies of northern Alberta lakes and their fish populations. J. Fish. Res. Bd. Can. 31:1007–1020.

Peace-Athabasca Delta Project Group (PADPG). 1972. The Peace-Athabasca Delta, a Canadian resource: Summary report, 1972. Govt. Can., Alta., Sask. Information Can., Ottawa; Queen's Printer, Edmonton; Queen's Printer, Regina.

Pennak, R.W. 1978. Fresh-water invertebrates of the United States. 2nd ed. John Wiley & Sons, Toronto.

Peters, T.W. and W.E. Bowser. 1960. Soil survey of Rocky Mountain House sheet. Alta. Soil Surv. Rep. No. 19, Univ. Alta. Bull. No. SS–1. Univ. Alta., Edmonton.

Pettapiece, W.W. 1986. Physiographic subdivisions of Alberta. Agric. Can., Res. Br., Ld. Resour. Res. Centre, Ottawa.

Prepas, E.E. 1983. The influence of phosphorus and zooplankton on chlorophyll levels in Alberta lakes. Prep. for Alta. Envir., Res. Mgt. Div. Rep. 83/23, Edmonton.

———. 1983. Orthophosphate turnover time in shallow productive lakes. Can. J. Fish. Aquat. Sci. 40:1412–1418.

———. 1983. Total dissolved solids as a predictor of lake biomass and productivity. Can. J. Fish. Aquat. Sci. 40:92–95.

——— and D.O. Trew. 1983. Evaluation of the phosphorus-chlorophyll relationship for lakes off the Precambrian Shield in western Canada. Can. J. Fish. Aquat. Sci. 40:27–35.

Prepas, E.E. and J. Vickery. 1984. Seasonal changes in total phosphorus and the role of internal loading in western Canadian lakes. Verh. Internat. Verein. Limnol. 22:303–308.

———. 1984. The contribution of particulate phosphorus (>250 μm) to the total phosphorus pool in lake water. Can. J. Fish. Aquat. Sci. 41:351–363.

Prepas, E.E., M.E. Dunnigan and A.M. Trimbee. 1988. Comparison of in situ estimates of chlorophyll a obtained with Whatman GF/F and GF/C glass-fiber filters in mesotrophic to hypereutrophic lakes. Can. J. Fish. Aquat. Sci. 45:910–914.

Prepas, E.E. and A.M. Trimbee. 1988. Evaluation of indicators of nitrogen limitation in deep prairie lakes with laboratory bioassays and limnocorrals. Hydrobiologia 159:269–276.

Prepas, E.E., T.P. Murphy, J.M. Crosby, D.T. Walty, J.T. Lim, J. Babin and P.A. Chambers. 1990. The reduction of phosphorus and chlorophyll a concentrations following $CaCO_3$ and $Ca(OH)_2$ additions to hyper-eutrophic Figure Eight Lake, Alberta. Envir. Sci. Tech. [in press]

Prescott, G.W. 1978. How to know the freshwater algae. 3rd. ed. Wm. C. Brown Co. Publ., Dubuque, Iowa.

Randall Conrad & Associates. 1988. Athabasca River basin study: Water based recreation component. Prep. for Alta. Envir., Plan. Div. Unpubl. rep., Edmonton.

Rawson, D.S. 1947. Deterioration of recently established trout populations in lakes of the Canadian Rockies. Can. Fish Culturist 2:14–21.

———. 1947. Fishes of Saskatchewan. In Report of the Royal Commission on the fisheries of Saskatchewan. King's Printer, Ottawa.

———. 1948. Biological investigations on the Bow and Kananaskis rivers in 1947, with special reference to the effects of power development on the availability of game fish in this area. Alta. Ld. Mines, Fish Wild. Div., Edmonton.

———. 1960. A limnological comparison of twelve large lakes in northern Saskatchewan. Limnol. Oceanogr. 5:195–211.

Renewable Resources Consulting Services Ltd. 1971. An ecological study of the wildlife and fisheries in the Pembina and Sturgeon River basins. Prep. for Alta. Envir., Water Resour. Div., Edmonton.

Reynolds, C.S. 1980. Phytoplankton assemblages and their periodicity in stratifying lake systems. Holarctic Ecol. 3:141–159.

Riley, E.T. 1983. Internal phosphorus loading from the sediments and the phosphorus-chlorophyll model in shallow lakes. MSc thesis. Univ. Alta., Edmonton.

——— and E.E. Prepas. 1984. Role of internal phosphorus in two shallow, productive lakes in Alberta, Canada. Can. J. Fish. Aquat. Sci. 41:845–855.

Rippon, B. 1983. Water related wildlife resources [Appendix I]. In Cold Lake-Beaver River water management study, Vol. 5: Fisheries and wildlife. Alta. Envir., Plan. Div., Edmonton.

R.L. & L. Environmental Services Ltd. 1985. A compendium of existing environmental data on Alberta reservoirs. Prep. for Alta. Envir. Res. Trust, Edmonton.

Salt, W.R. and A.L. Wilk. 1972. The Birds of Alberta. Queen's Printer, Edmonton.

SATA Systems Inc. 1983. Profiles of regions and small communities in northern Alberta: Northeast/central. Prep. for North. Alta. Devel. Counc., Peace River.

Scheelar, M.D. and W. Odynsky. 1968. Reconnaissance soil survey of the Grimshaw and Notikewin areas. Univ. Alta. Bull. No. SS–8, Res. Counc. Alta. Rep. No. 88. Univ. Alta., Edmonton.

Scheelar, M.D. and C.F. Veauvy. 1977. Detailed soil survey of Bragg Creek area. Alta. Inst. Pedol. Rep. No. M–77–8. Univ. Alta., Edmonton.

Schwartz, F.W. and D.N. Gallup. 1978. Some factors controlling the major ion chemistry of small lakes: Examples from the prairie parkland of Canada. Hydrobiologia 58:65–81.

Scott, W.B. and E.J. Crossman. 1973. Freshwater fishes of Canada. Fish. Res. Bd. Can. Bull. No. 184, Ottawa.

Shaw, J.F.H. and E.E. Prepas. 1989. Exchange of phosphorus from shallow sediments at nine Alberta lakes. J. Envir. Qlty. [in press]

———. 1989. Relationships between phosphorus in shallow sediments in the trophogenic zone of seven Alberta lakes. Water Res. [in press]

———. 1989. Potential significance of phosphorus release from shallow sediments of deep Alberta lakes. ms submitted to Limnol. Oceanogr.

———. 1989. Temporal and spatial patterns of porewater phosphorus in shallow sediments, and potential transport in Narrow Lake, Alberta. Can. J. Fish. Aquat. Sci. 46:981–988.

Shaw, J.F.H., R.D. Shaw and E.E. Prepas. 1989. Advective transport of phosphorus from lake bottom sediments into lakewater. ms to be submitted.

Shaw, R.D. and E.E. Prepas. 1989. Groundwater-lake interactions: II. Nearshore seepage patterns and the contribution of groundwater to lakes in central Alberta. J. Hydrol. [in press]

———. 1989. Anomalous short-term influx of water into seepage meters. Limnol. Oceanogr. [in press]

Shaw, R.D., J.F.H. Shaw, H. Fricker and E.E. Prepas. 1990. An integrated approach to quantify groundwater transport of phosphorus to Narrow Lake, Alberta. Limnol. Oceanogr. [in press]

Shaw, R.D., A.M. Trimbee, A. Minty, H. Fricker and E.E. Prepas. 1989. Atmospheric deposition of phosphorus and nitrogen in central Alberta with emphasis on Narrow Lake. Water, Air, and Soil Poll. 43:119–134.

Snow, Chief J. 1977. These mountains are our sacred places. Samuel-Stevens Publ., Toronto.

Soper, J.D. 1964. Mammals of Alberta. The Queen's Printer, Edmonton.

Spalding, D.A.E. [ed.] A nature guide to Alberta. Prov. Museum Publ. No. 5. Hurtig Publ., Edmonton.

Stanley Associates Engineering Ltd. 1976. Main report, Data volume and Atlas volume [Appendices 1, 2, 3]. In Cooking Lake area study, Vol. II: Water inventory and demands. Alta. Envir., Plan. Div., Edmonton.

Stolte, W.J. and R. Herrington. 1980. A study of the hydrologic regime of the Battle River Basin. Rep. No. RMD–80/4. Prep. for Alta., Res. Mgt. Div., Edmonton by Dept. Civil Eng., Univ. Sask., Saskatoon.

Stone, D. 1970. The process of rural settlements in the Athabasca area, Alberta. MA thesis. Univ. Alta., Edmonton.

Strathcona County. 1987. Outdoor master plan 1987: Technical report. Rec. Parks Dept., Sherwood Park.

Strong, W.L. 1979. Ecological land classification and evaluation: Livingstone-Porcupine. Alta. En. Nat. Resour., Resour. Eval. Br., Edmonton.

——— and K.R. Leggat. 1981. Ecoregions of Alberta. Alta. En. Nat. Resour., Resour. Eval. Plan. Div., Edmonton.

Thorington, J.M. 1966. A climber's guide to the Rocky Mountains of Canada. American Alpine Club, New York.

Touchings, D. 1976. Heritage resource inventory of the Cooking Lake study area [Appendix 10]. In Cooking Lake area study, Vol. V: Economic base and heritage resources. Alta. Envir., Plan. Div., Edmonton.

Trew, D.O. 1983. Impacts of lake level fluctuations on trophic status [Appendix N]. In Cold Lake-Beaver River water management study, Vol. 8: Water quality. Alta. Envir., Plan. Div., Edmonton.

———, E.I. Yonge and R.P. Kaminski. 1983. Lake trophic assessment [Appendix M]. In Cold Lake-Beaver River water management study, Vol. 8: Water quality. Alta. Envir., Plan. Div., Edmonton.

Trimbee, A.M. and E.E. Prepas. 1987. Evaluation of total phosphorus as a predictor of the relative importance of blue-green algae with emphasis on Alberta lakes. Can. J. Fish. Aquat. Sci. 44:1337–1342.

———. 1988. Dependence of lake oxygen depletion rates on maximum oxygen storage in a partially meromictic lake in Alberta. Can. J. Fish. Aquat. Sci. 45:571–576.

———. 1988. The effect of oxygen depletion on the timing and magnitude of blue-green algal blooms. Verh. Internat. Verein. Limnol. 23:220–226.

Turchenek, L.W. and J.D. Lindsay. 1982. Soils inventory of the Alberta Oil Sands Environmental Research Program study area. Prep. for Alta. Envir., Res. Mgt. Div., AOSERP by Alta. Res. Counc. AOSERP Rep. 122, Edmonton.

Twardy, A.G. and I.G. Corns. 1980. Soil survey and interpretations of the Wapiti map area, Alberta. Alta. Inst. Pedol. Bull. No. 39. Alta. Res. Counc., Edmonton.

Tyrrell, J.B. 1886. Canada geological and natural history survey, annual report: Report on a part of northern Alberta. Dawson Brothers, Montréal.

Vallentyne, J.R. 1974. The algal bowl. Dept. Fish. Oceans, Ottawa.

Wallace, R.R. and P.J. McCart. 1984. The fish and fisheries of the Athabasca River basin: Their status and environmental requirements. Prep. for Alta. Envir., Plan. Div., Edmonton.

WER Engineering. 1981. South Saskatchewan River Basin structures inventory, Appendix 5 to Vol. 1: Oldman River (2 of 2) and South Saskatchewan River sub-basins. Prep. for Alta. Envir., Plan. Div., Edmonton.

Wetzel, R.G. 1983. Limnology. 2nd ed. Saunders College Publ., New York.

Wiseley, A.N. 1979. A review of birds and their habitats in Kananaskis Country. Alta. En. Nat. Resour., Fish Wild. Div., Edmonton.

Woodburn, R.L. 1977. Surplus patterns and water supply alternatives: Cooking Lake moraine. MSc thesis. Univ. Alta., Edmonton.

Wyatt, F.A. and J.D. Newton. 1925. Soil survey of the McLeod sheet. Univ. Alta. Bull. No. 11. Univ. Alta., Edmonton.

Wyatt, F.A., W.E. Bowser and W. Odynsky. 1939. Soil survey of Lethbridge and Pincher Creek sheets. Univ. Alta. Bull. No. 32. Univ. Alta., Edmonton.

Wyatt, F.A., J.D. Newton, W.E. Bowser and W. Odynsky. 1943. Soil survey of Rosebud and Banff sheets. Alta. Soil Surv. Rep. No. 12, Univ. Alta. Bull. No. 40. Univ. Alta., Edmonton.

Wyatt, F.A., T.W. Peters and W.E. Bowser. 1943. Soil survey of Blackfoot and Calgary sheets. Alta. Soil Surv. Rep. No. 39, Univ. Alta. Bull. No. SS–2. Univ. Alta., Edmonton.

Wyatt, F.A., J.D. Newton, W.E. Bowser and W. Odynsky. 1944. Soil survey of Wainwright-Vermilion sheet. Alta. Soil Surv. Rep. No. 13, Univ. Alta. Bull. No. 42. Univ. Alta., Edmonton.

Wynnyk, A., J.D. Lindsay, P.K. Heringa and W. Odynsky. 1963. Exploratory soil survey of Alberta map sheets 83–O, 83–P and 73–M. Res. Counc. Alta. Prelim. Soil Surv. Rep. 64–1. Res. Counc. Alta., Edmonton.

Wynnyk, A., J.D. Lindsay and W. Odynsky. 1969. Soil survey of the Whitecourt and Barrhead area. Alta. Soil Surv. Rep. No. 27, Univ. Alta. Bull. No. SS–10, Res. Counc. Alta. Rep. No. 90. Univ. Alta., Edmonton.

Zelt, K.A. and W.M. Glasgow. 1976. Evaluation of the fish and wildlife resources of the Cooking Lake study area [Appendix 6]. In Cooking Lake area study, Vol. IV: Ecology. Alta. Envir., Plan. Div., Edmonton.

Index